Florida

The Panhandle
p442

Northeast
Florida
p340

Orlando &
Walt Disney
World®
p245

Tampa Bay &
Southwest Florida
p384

The Space
Coast
p322

Southeast
Florida
p203

The
Everglades
p153

Miami
p64

FEB 09 2018

Florida Keys
& Key West
p171

Adam Karlin, Kate Armstrong,
Ashley Harrell, Regis St Louis

Contents

ALEXANDER DEMYANENKO/SHUTTERSTOCK ©

LIFEGUARD HUT, SOUTH
BEACH, MIAMI P65

JUSTIN FOULKES/LONELY PLANET ©

COCKTAILS IN KEY WEST
P198

Contents

HURRICANE IRMA

On September 10, 2017, one of the largest hurricanes ever recorded barrelled over Florida, causing flooding and destruction. Hurricane Irma made landfall in the Florida Keys as a category 4 storm the width of Texas. Homes and businesses in Everglades City were left battered and mud-soaked after an 8-foot storm surge; in the Keys, a FEMA survey reported that 25% of buildings had been destroyed, with another 65% damaged.

This book was researched before the storm hit and sent to print soon after, when Irma's long-term effects were still unknown. Most cities were already announcing intentions to be ready for visitors soon. Still, those traveling to Florida, especially the Keys (www.fla-keys.com) or the Everglades (www.nps.gov/ever), should check official websites for the latest information.

Welcome to Florida

A hundred worlds – from magic kingdoms and Latin American and Caribbean capitals to mangrove islands, wild wetlands and artist colonies – are all contained within this flat peninsula.

Seaside Fantasy

Maybe there's no mystery to what makes the Florida peninsula so intoxicating. Beaches as fine and sweet as powdered sugar, warm waters, rustling mangroves: all conspire to melt our workaday selves. We come to Florida to let go – of worries and winter, of inhibitions and reality. Some desire a beachy getaway of swimming, seafood and sunsets. Others seek the hedonism of South Beach, spring break and Key West. Still more hope to lose themselves within the phantasmagorical realms of Walt Disney World® and Orlando's theme parks.

Sexy Swamps

Within Florida's semitropical wilderness, alligators prowl the waterways, herons strut through ponds, manatees winter in springs and sea turtles nest in summer. Osprey and eagles, dolphins and tarpon, coral-reef forests, oceans of saw grass: despite the best efforts of 21st-century humans, overwhelming portions of Florida remain untamed. In a nation where natural beauty is often measured by topography, flat Florida is underappreciated by outdoors fanatics, but here you can paddle a kayak over the back of a sleeping Jurassic-era alligator, and meet loggerheads and manatees underwater, eye to eye.

Tropical Mosaic

While many know Florida for beaches and theme parks, few understand that this is one of the most populous states in the country, a bellwether for the American experiment. And that experiment – and this state – is more diverse than ever. From rural hunters and trappers in the geographically northern, culturally Southern climes, to Jewish transplants sitting side by side with Latin arrivals from every Spanish-speaking nation in the world, it's hard to beat Florida when it comes to experiencing the human tapestry at its most colorful and vibrant.

Culture By the Coast

Tan, tropical Florida is smarter and more culturally savvy than its appearance suggests. This state, particularly South Florida, has a reputation for attracting eccentrics and idiosyncratic types from across the US, Latin America and Europe. Many of these folks, and their descendants, have gone on to create or provide patronage for the arts, as evidenced by enormous concert spaces in Miami, a glut of museums on the Gulf Coast, and a long, literary tradition – Florida has produced more than its fair share of great American authors.

ROMRODPHOTO/SHUTTERSTOCK ©

Why I Love Florida

By Adam Karlin, Writer

I was raised on wetlands and I'm drawn to wetlands, and I can't think of a state that better combines that favored biome with some of my other great travel loves – good food, ethnic entrepôts, warm weather and nice beaches. What can I say? Give me the ocean on one hand, swamps on the other and some fried conch and iced tea for lunch and I'm happy as a clam (which are great fried at a dockside restaurant, by the way).

For more about our writers, see p544

Above: Everglades National Park (p156)

Florida

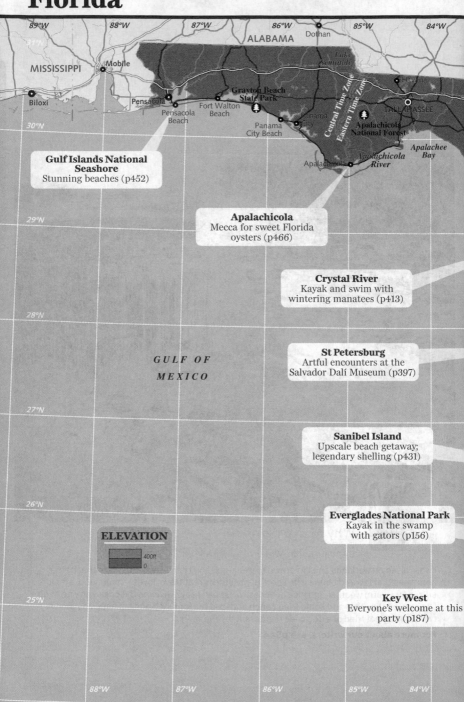

Gulf Islands National Seashore
Stunning beaches (p452)

Apalachicola
Mecca for sweet Florida oysters (p466)

Crystal River
Kayak and swim with wintering manatees (p413)

St Petersburg
Artful encounters at the Salvador Dalí Museum (p397)

Sanibel Island
Upscale beach getaway; legendary shelling (p431)

Everglades National Park
Kayak in the swamp with gators (p156)

Key West
Everyone's welcome at this party (p187)

ELEVATION

400ft
0

GULF OF MEXICO

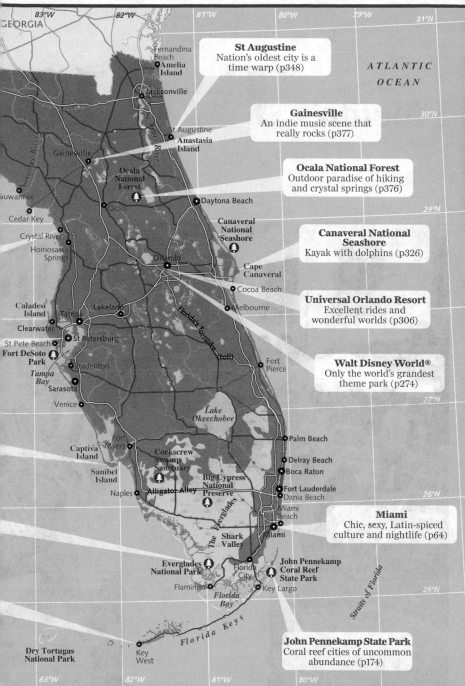

St Augustine
Nation's oldest city is a time warp (p348)

Gainesville
An indie music scene that really rocks (p377)

Ocala National Forest
Outdoor paradise of hiking and crystal springs (p376)

Canaveral National Seashore
Kayak with dolphins (p326)

Universal Orlando Resort
Excellent rides and wonderful worlds (p306)

Walt Disney World®
Only the world's grandest theme park (p274)

Miami
Chic, sexy, Latin-spiced culture and nightlife (p64)

John Pennekamp State Park
Coral reef cities of uncommon abundance (p174)

100 km
50 miles

GEORGIA

ATLANTIC OCEAN

Fernandina Beach
Amelia Island
Jacksonville
St Augustine
Anastasia Island

Gainesville

Suwannee River

St Johns River

Ocala National Forest

uwannee
Cedar Key
Crystal River
Homosassa Springs

Ocala
Daytona Beach

Canaveral National Seashore

Orlando
Cape Canaveral
Cocoa Beach
Melbourne

Florida's Turnpike

Caladesi Island
Tampa
Clearwater
St Petersburg
St Pete Beach
Fort DeSoto Park
Tampa Bay
Bradenton
Sarasota
Venice

Lakeland

(toll)
Fort Pierce

Lake Okeechobee

Fort Myers
Captiva Island
Sanibel Island
Naples

Corkscrew Swamp Sanctuary
Big Cypress National Preserve
Alligator Alley

The Everglades

Palm Beach
Delray Beach
Boca Raton
Fort Lauderdale
Dania Beach
Miami Beach
Miami

Shark Valley

Everglades National Park
Florida City
Flamingo
Florida Bay

John Pennekamp Coral Reef State Park
Key Largo

Straits of Florida

Dry Tortugas National Park
Key West

Florida Keys

Florida's Top 15

Capital of the Americas

1 Many Latin Americans resent it when citizens of the USA call themselves, simply, 'Americans.' 'Are we not citizens of the *Americas* too?' they ask. Yes, and in this vein, Miami (p64) is the capital of America, North and South. No other city blends the Anglo attitude of North America with the Latin energy of South America and the Caribbean. Throw in an African American heritage, gastronomic edge, pounding nightlife, a skyline plucked from a patrician's dream and miles of gorgeous sand, and say hello to the Magic City. Carnaval Miami (p114) celebrations in Calle Ocho

The Magic of Disney

2 Want to set the bar of expectations high? Call yourself 'The Happiest Place on Earth.' Walt Disney World® (p274) does, and then pulls out all the stops to deliver the exhilarating sensation that you are the most important character in the show. Despite all the frantic rides, entertainment and nostalgia, the magic is watching a child swell with belief after they have made Goofy laugh, been curtsied to by Cinderella, guarded the galaxy with Buzz Lightyear and battled Darth Maul like a Jedi knight. Cinderella's Castle, Magic Kingdom (p287), Walt Disney World®

JEFF GREENBERG/GETTY IMAGES ©

STEPHEN SEARLE/ALAMY STOCK PHOTO ©

MARIAKRAYNOVA/SHUTTERSTOCK ©

ROMROPHOTO/SHUTTERSTOCK ©

Kayaking the Everglades

3 The Everglades (p153) are unnerving. They don't reach majestically skyward or fill your heart with the aching beauty of a glacier-carved valley. They ooze, flat and watery; a river of grass mottled by hammocks, cypress domes and mangroves. You can't hike them, not really. To properly explore the Everglades – and meet its prehistoric residents up close – you must leave the safety of land. You must push a canoe or kayak off a muddy bank, tamp down your fear and explore the shallow waterways on the Everglades' own, unforgettable terms.

The Conch Republic

4 Florida has always been a realm of self-imposed exile, but sometimes even the exiles want to be, well, self-exiled. Enter the 'Conchs' (natives) of Key West (p187), a separate island untethered from the nation, the state and even the rest of the island chain, except by a flimsy bridge. A crazy party atmosphere animates Mallory Sq and Duval St nightly, part drunken cabal and part authentic tolerance for the self-expression of every impolite, nonconformist impulse known to humanity. Duval Street (p191), Key West

Canaveral National Seashore

5 If you've been to Florida's Atlantic Coast, you know it's one extremely built-up and crowded stretch of sand. This is partly why the 24 miles of Canaveral National Seashore's (p326) unspoiled barrier island are so special. Here, virtually in the shadow of Kennedy's shuttle launchpad, the dunes, lagoons and white-sand beaches look much as they did 500 years ago when the Spaniards landed. Kayak among the mangroves with dolphins and manatees, observe nesting sea turtles, swim on pristine beaches and camp in solitude.

Coral Reef Symphony

6 Florida's most breathtaking scenery is underwater. The bowl of the peninsula's spoon is edged by more coral reefs than anywhere else in North America, and their quality and diversity rival Hawaii and the Caribbean. The prime protected areas are Biscayne National Park (p169), John Pennekamp Coral Reef State Park (pictured; p174) and Looe Key (p184). See the reefs and their rainbow-hued denizens by glass-bottom boat, snorkeling and diving, or spend the night with the fishes (at John Pennekamp) if you just can't bear to surface.

St Augustine: Fun with History

7 According to legend, the USA's oldest city possesses Ponce de León's elusive fountain of youth. Though apocryphal, this anecdote indicates the breadth of the historic legacy preserved along St Augustine's (p348) streets. Tour Spanish cathedrals and forts, and Henry Flagler's ornate resorts; take ghost tours and join scurvy-dog pirate invasions. Watch reenactors demonstrate blacksmithing, cannon firing, and how to shackle prisoners. Then sip a cup of eternal youth, 'cause you never know.

Culture-Clash St Petersburg

8 It's all too easy to overuse the adjective 'surreal' when discussing Florida. In the case of the Salvador Dalí Museum, surreal is exactly right. Dalí has no connection to Florida whatsoever; this magnificent collection of 96 oil paintings and an overwhelming slew of ephemera landed in St Petersburg (p397) almost by chance. But then, all sorts of cultural offerings are flowering across 'St Pete,' from fine dining to live music to excellent art museums. Here is proof the Gulf Coast can be as cerebral as it is relaxing.

Salvador Dalí Museum (p398)

SEAN PAVONE/SHUTTERSTOCK ©

SEAN PAVONE/SHUTTERSTOCK ©

Sanibel Island: 'Stooping' to Shell

9 Gorgeous Sanibel Island (p431) is famous for the bounty of colorful and exotic shells that wash up along its beaches; the 'Sanibel stoop' is the name for the distinctive profile of avid shellers (who these days save their backs with long-handled scoops). But the dirty little secret is this: like fishing and golf, shelling is just an excuse to do nothing but let the mind wander the paths of its own reckoning. Yet delightfully, when you awake, you're rewarded with a handful of spiral calcium treasures.

Kennedy Space Center

10 Within this 140,000-acre campus, the dreams of some of the greatest scientific minds of the 20th century took flight all the way to the moon and back...and then were defunded and grounded on earth. But the sense of potential that always informed Kennedy Space Center (p324) – indeed, that still pushes NASA to reach out for Mars and beyond – remains palpable in this location, one of the most visited spots in Florida. Learn about the rigors of space exploration training and, of course, try the astronaut ice cream.

Engines of the Saturn V rocket

Gulf Islands National Seashore

11 Near Pensacola, the Panhandle's barrier islands occupy about as much real estate as a string bikini, particularly the sensual stretches that form the Gulf Islands National Seashore (p452). While the region is well known for its activity-fueled beach towns, these are quickly left behind along the park's almost-pure-white quartz-sand beaches, gleaming like new snow. If you really need an activity, tour the moody, crumbling wreckage of historic Fort Pickens or hike the sand-floored woods, but really, isn't this why you came, to nap and tan in paradise?

B CRUZ/SHUTTERSTOCK ©

PETER ETCHELLS/SHUTTERSTOCK ©

Hiking the Ocala National Forest

12 There are moments in the subtropical forests, cypress stands, sinkholes and crystal springs of the Ocala National Forest (p376) and its adjacent state parks that are just otherworldly and strange. You can get lost for weeks along hundreds of miles of forested trails and among countless lakes, while hopping between campgrounds and soaking up Old Florida atmosphere. It's easy enough to dabble, but for dedicated outdoor enthusiasts, draw a big circle around Florida's heart and come here.

Universal Orlando Resort

13 We're not trying to overload you on theme parks, but this is Florida, after all. Universal Orlando Resort (p306) is something else. The theming, the creativity of the rides, the ease of the Express Pass system, the adrenaline rushes, the silly fun – it's the smart and sassy class clown to Disney's teacher's pet. With smart, simple planning you can enjoy attractions like the Wizarding World of Harry Potter (one of the best artificial worlds ever created) without waiting hours to get in or for the rides. Hogwarts Express, Wizarding World of Harry Potter (p312)

CATE_89/SHUTTERSTOCK ©

SEAN PAVONE/SHUTTERSTOCK ©

Apalachicola

14 Apalachicola (p466) is more than a pretty seaside town, although it is a very pretty seaside – well, Gulfside – town. It's an experience and an introduction to the laid-back folkways and crusty exterior of 'Cracker' Florida. No cartoon mice or Latin superstars can be seen; the only thing that blazes across this town are rich orange sunsets and glistening plates of oysters. With its preserved historical core, plentiful shade trees and tourism amenities, 'Apalach' feels welcoming to guests while retaining a distinctive sense of place.

Gainesville

15 If local boy Tom Petty and transplant Bo Diddley are the patron saints of Gainesville's rock-music scene, the University of Florida – the nation's second-largest university – is the engine that keeps it going strong. Gainesville (p377) buzzes with intellectual energy, carefree student attitudes and a general pleasant atmosphere in its well-groomed, shady residential neighborhoods. There are great restaurants and bars to discover in this university town, but they're not as expensive or hectic as spots you'll find elsewhere in Florida.

Need to Know

For more information, see Survival Guide (p517)

Currency
US dollars ($)

Language
English, also Spanish in Tampa, Miami and South Florida and Haitian Creole in South Florida

Visas
Nationals qualifying for the Visa Waiver Program are allowed a 90-day stay without a visa; all others need a visa.

Money
ATMs are widely available everywhere.

Cell Phones
Europe and Asia's GSM 900/1800 standard is incompatible with USA's cell-phone systems. Confirm your phone can be used before arriving.

Time
East of the Apalachicola River, Florida is in the US Eastern Time Zone (GMT/UTC minus five hours). West of the Apalachicola is US Central Time (GMT/UTC minus six hours).

When to Go

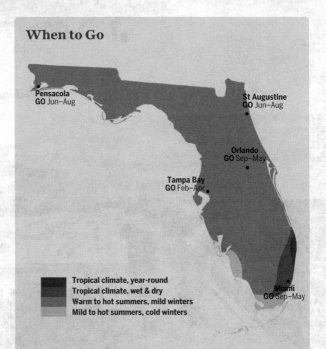

Pensacola
GO Jun–Aug

St Augustine
GO Jun–Aug

Orlando
GO Sep–May

Tampa Bay
GO Feb–Apr

Miami
GO Sep–May

Tropical climate, year-round
Tropical climate, wet & dry
Warm to hot summers, mild winters
Mild to hot summers, cold winters

High Season
(Mar–Aug)

➡ South Florida beaches peak with spring break.

➡ Panhandle and northern beaches peak in summer.

➡ Orlando theme parks are busiest in summer.

➡ Summer wet season is hot and humid (May to September).

Shoulder
(Feb & Sep)

➡ In South Florida, February has ideal dry weather, but no spring-break craziness.

➡ With school in September, northern beaches/theme parks less crowded, still hot.

➡ Prices drop from peak by 20% to 30%.

Low Season
(Oct–Dec)

➡ Beach towns quiet until winter snowbirds arrive.

➡ Hotel prices can drop from peak by 50%.

➡ November-to-April dry season is best time to hike/camp.

➡ Holidays spike with peak rates.

Useful Websites

Visit Florida (www.visitflorida. com) Official state tourism website.

My Florida (www.myflorida.com) Portal to state government.

Miami Herald (www.miami herald.com) Main daily newspaper for metro Miami-Dade.

Tampa Bay Times (www. tampabay.com) News and views for the Gulf Coast.

Florida State Parks (www. floridastateparks.org) Primary resource for state parks.

Lonely Planet (www.lonely planet.com/florida) Destination information, hotel bookings, traveler forum and more.

Important Numbers

Country code	1
International access code	011
Emergency	911
Directory assistance	411

Exchange Rates

Australia	A$1	$0.75
Canada	C$1	$0.74
Euro zone	€1	$1.07
Japan	¥100	$0.91
New Zealand	NZ$1	$0.70
UK	UK£1	$1.28

For current exchange rates see www.xe.com.

Daily Costs

Budget: Less than $140

➡ Dorm beds/camping: $30–50

➡ Supermarket self-catering per day: $20

➡ Beaches: free

➡ Bicycle hire per day: $24–35

Midrange: $140–250

➡ Hotels: $100–200

➡ In-room meals and dining out: $50

➡ Theme park pass: $40–100

➡ Rental car per day: $40–50

Top End: More than $250

➡ High-season beach hotel/ resort: $250–400

➡ Miami gourmet dinner (for two): $150–300

➡ All-inclusive, four- to seven-day theme-park blowout: $1500–4000

Opening Hours

Standard business hours are as follows:

Banks 8:30am to 4:30pm Monday to Thursday, to 5:30pm Friday; sometimes 9am to 12:30pm Saturday.

Bars Most bars 5pm to midnight; to 2am Friday and Saturday.

Businesses 9am to 5pm Monday to Friday.

Post offices 9am to 5pm Monday to Friday; sometimes 9am to noon Saturday.

Restaurants Breakfast 7am to 10:30am Monday to Friday; brunch 9am to 2pm on weekends; lunch 11:30am to 2:30pm Monday to Friday; dinner 5pm to 9:30pm, later on weekends.

Shops 10am to 6pm Monday to Saturday, noon to 5pm Sunday; longer hours in shopping malls.

Arriving in Florida

Miami International Airport (p526) Metrobus ($2.25) runs every 30 minutes, 6am to 11pm, to Miami Beach, 35 minutes. Shuttle vans cost around $22 to South Beach. A taxi to South Beach is $35.

Orlando International Airport (p526) Lynx buses ($2) run from 6am to midnight. Public bus 11 services downtown Orlando (40 minutes), 42 services International Dr (one hour) and 111 services SeaWorld (45 minutes). Complimentary luggage handling and airport transport for guests staying at a Walt Disney World® Resort (Disney's Magical Express). Shuttle vans cost $20 to $30. Taxi costs: Disney area, $65; International Dr and Universal Orlando Resort, $48; downtown Orlando, $42; Winter Park, $50.

Getting Around

Transport in Florida revolves around the car.

Car The most common means of transport. Car-hire offices can be found in almost every town. Drive on the right.

Bus Greyhound and Megabus are cheap, if slow, and serve larger cities.

Train Amtrak's *Silver Service/ Palmetto* runs between Miami and Tampa, and from there connects to a nationwide network. The *Auto Train* runs from the Washington, DC area to Sanford, near Orlando.

Cycling Flat Florida is good for cycling, although hot weather and a lack of highway bike lanes are hindrances.

For much more on **getting around**, see p528

What's New

Volcano Bay Erupts

Universal Studios is adding an entire sun- and slide-soaked water park experience to its slate of attractions: Volcano Bay, the third Universal theme park, will be built around a 200ft tall artificial volcano. If that seems a little over the top – well, welcome to Florida. There will be 18 attractions splayed over this aquatic wonderland, aimed at both families and hard-core thrill seekers. (p311)

Everglades Allure

The admission price for the Everglades National Park has gone up, but there are now loads of free activities organized by the park, including canoe and bike trips, night walks and marshy wetland slogs. (p156)

Legoland

We only need three words to describe this theme park, with its fantastic rides, innovative attractions, Ninjago World and Heartlake City: everything is awesome! (p274)

Panhandle Hiking

Protected areas like Tarkiln Bayou Preserve (p454) and Topsail Hill Preserve State Park (p459) provide a glimpse of the rough wilderness that fronts the Panhandle's Gulf Coast and sprawls across its flat interior.

Microbrews in the Keys

New microbreweries in the Keys are also changing the beer landscape of South Florida. In Islamorada, the excellent, locally owned Florida Keys Brewing Co makes some of the best microbrews in the state. (p180)

Science and High Design

The high-tech Patricia and Phillip Frost Museum of Science opened to much fanfare in 2017 in a breathtaking 250,000-sq-ft space on the waterfront in downtown Miami. (p87)

Walking Mural Tours in St Pete

This fabulous new Saturday morning walking tour introduces visitors to more than 30 vibrant murals that grace the walls of downtown St Pete, rivaling Miami's Wynwood Walls. (p401)

Star Wars: A Galactic Spectacular

However you may feel about Disney purchasing the rights to the *Star Wars* franchise, you knew the company was going to create some enormous spectacle with the brand, and this awesome fireworks show is a good example. (p300)

Brew Bus in Tampa

Craft breweries are everywhere in the Tampa Bay area, and finally someone had the good sense to transport people around to them on a boozy bus. The 'terminal' is also a brewery in Seminole Heights. (p394)

Heroes & Legends and the U.S. Astronaut Hall of Fame at Kennedy Space Center

The newest exhibit at the Kennedy Space Center opened in 2017 to celebrate the pioneers of NASA's early space program and includes a 360-degree film on the lives of astronauts, impressive interactive exhibits and the recently relocated and revamped U.S. Astronauts Hall of Fame. (p324)

For more recommendations and reviews, see lonelyplanet.com/florida

If You Like...

Secluded Islands

The Florida peninsula is ringed with barrier islands and mangrove-fringed keys. Many are accessible by causeways and bridges, but to leave the crowds behind, go by boat. That's the only way to get to these beauties.

Cayo Costa Island Undeveloped and majestic; for real solitude, book a cabin or campsite and spend the night. (p432)

Caladesi Island A 20-minute ferry ride to three miles of sugary, seashell-strewn goodness. (p411)

St Vincent Island Just off the Panhandle coastline, with great hikes, wildlife and beaches. (p466)

Cedar Keys National Wildlife Refuge Cedar Key is like a frontier town, with kayaking among dozens of tiny wildernesses. (p478)

Dry Tortugas Far off Key West in the middle of the sea: camp, stargaze, snorkel coral reefs and barter beers with fishers for lobster. (p201)

Roadside Attractions

Florida boasts mermaids, Hogwarts, Haitian *botanicas* (shops that deal in herbs and charms) and at least three alleged fountains of youth, making the state a roadside-attraction hall of fame. For these, you needn't travel north of I-75.

Coral Castle In Homestead, this monument to unrequited love defies explanation and belief. (p163)

Robert Is Here Also in Homestead, it's just a farm stand with a petting zoo, but feels like...an event. (p166)

Skunk Ape Research Headquarters Apparently, Bigfoot's relatives live in the swamp, and they don't smell too good. (p159)

Ochopee Post Office Not just the tiniest post office in the USA – also the world's most patient postal worker. (p159)

Cycling

Flat, warm and did we mention flat? Florida can be a cyclist's dream, although it may be a bore to mountain bikers (which isn't quite fair, as there are some nice off-road paths out there).

Florida Keys Overseas Heritage Trail Ride alongside the shoulder of the road above the teal horizons of the ocean and Florida Bay. (p176)

Paisley Woods Bicycle Trail Think Florida has nothing for mountain bikers? You'll think again after pounding the scrub on this 22-mile ride through Ocala National Forest. (p376)

West Orange Trail This 24-mile trail passes through about 10 miles of lovely horse country just west of theme-park-studded Orlando. (p258)

Sanibel Island This calm little refuge, with its distinct lack of highway development, is laced with dozens of bicycle paths. (p431)

Legacy Trail Explore the countryside around Sarasota on this lovely 20-mile bike ride, which runs through forests, over bridges and behind backyards. (p418)

Nature Walks

Florida's backyard is an American original – slash pine, clear springs, snowy sands and miles of reptile-rich wetlands bordered by a hairy fringe of spidery mangroves. The following spots get deep in the subtropical mix.

Grayton Beach State Park Traverse a broad mix of biomes, from scrub forest to wetlands to exceedingly rare coastal dune lakes, which can be found nowhere else in the USA. (p459)

Tarkiln Bayou Preserve State Park Boardwalks and trails wind through a Panhandle wilderness of flatwoods and marshlands peppered with carnivorous pitcher plants. (p454)

Egan's Creek Greenway More than 300 acres of grassy paths run by the forests, clear streams and diverse wildlife of Amelia Island. (p366)

Canaveral National Seashore With 24 miles of wilderness beaches, this is the longest stretch of undeveloped coastline on the eastern Florida seaboard. (p326)

Wekiwa Springs State Park Hop on the boardwalk and take in the National Wild and Scenic Rivers–designated Wekiva River. (p260)

Paddling

There are few states that can boast Florida's wealth of kayaking and canoeing opportunities. No matter how developed an area is, a quick paddle will often plunge travelers into other-worldly waterscapes.

The Everglades This expansive wilderness of flooded prairies, swamps and coastal islands cannot truly be explored without a boat. (p10)

Amelia Island This marshy barrier island conceals a wealth of coastal wilderness that is best appreciated from a kayak or canoe. (p366)

Islamorada The mangrove islands of the Florida Keys contains thousands of isolated, watery channels and tributaries. (p179)

Dr Von D. Mizell-Eula Park An old bootlegger's smuggling route is now a magnificent, mangrove-lined kayaking experience. (p207)

Fort Lauderdale The Middle River Loop allows you to kayak into the heart of this burgeoning South Florida metropolis. (p209)

Top: The *mojito* is the unofficial signature drink of Miami

Bottom: Coral Castle (p163), a roadside attraction in Homestead, built and designed by Edward Leedskalnin

Live Music

From gator-swamp rockabilly to sweaty blues to Caribbean street parades, Florida's northern cities flex their Southern roots. The state has a rich, diverse musical heritage, with lots of great venues.

Gainesville Tom Petty's hometown has a first-rate and extensive college-music scene, including some fantastic punk clubs. (p377)

Skipper's Smokehouse Head to Tampa and rock out at this excellent open-air venue while the stars spin above your head. (p395)

Bradfordville Blues Club Tallahassee is known for an energetic blues scene; head for this local legend. (p476)

Naples Philharmonic An unexpected gem of a regional orchestra. (p438)

Ball & Chain Classic Cuban music and contemporary Latin sounds make the rounds at this Miami club. (p144)

Foodie Finds

As Florida's food scene continues to flourish, menus balance between locavore dishes and the international influence of a huge immigrant population. In the meantime, Florida continues to attract accomplished chefs passionate about using products that reflect the Sunshine State's seasonal bounty.

Būccan Small plates take diners on a gastronomic trip around the world down in Palm Beach. (p228)

Havana Cafe If you thought you couldn't find top Floridian cuisine

in the Everglades, come here and have your mind changed. (p162)

Ulele This excellent Tampa eatery serves up top dishes influenced by Floridian Native American culinary traditions. (p391)

27 Restaurant Creative dishes, international influences from far and wide, and a lovely old Miami Beach home. (p130)

Cress Amazing, cutting-edge seasonal cuisine in...DeLand? Damn right. One of the state's culinary gems. (p374)

Baseball

Major League Baseball's spring training – with almost daily exhibition games – is a long-standing Florida tradition drawing hordes of fans. The 'grapefruit league' (www.florida grapefruitleague.com) has 15 pro teams, and two stay when the season starts: the Tampa Bay Rays and Miami Marlins.

St Petersburg The Tampa Bay Rays play the regular season at Tropicana Field. (p405)

Tampa The New York Yankees have spring training at Steinbrenner Field. (p396)

Fort Myers Both the Boston Red Sox and Minnesota Twins hold spring training here. (p426)

Jupiter The St Louis Cardinals have spring training at Roger Dean Stadium, and then the Marlins' minor-league team plays. (p238)

Orlando The Atlanta Braves play within Walt Disney World®, and the Houston Astros hold court in nearby Kissimmee. (p259)

Miami Catch a Miami Marlins game amid the South Florida swelter. (p147)

History

Florida was one of the first places Europeans settled in the continental USA, a state that has been Spanish, English, American, Confederate and American again.

St Augustine The oldest contiguously settled town in the continental United States is centered on an enormous, romantic historical district. (p350)

Key West This former smugglers' port and pirates' den is full of gorgeous historical architecture and elegant homes. (p187)

Mission San Luis This former Spanish mission, located in Tallahassee, takes families on a living history tour of frontier Florida. (p470)

Historic Pensacola Another example of early Florida history coming alive via live, costumed interpreters. (p443)

Gay Nightlife

As much as Manhattan, San Fran and LA, Florida is a destination for gay travelers. It hosts some of the wildest parties and has some of the best-organized gay communities in the country.

Key West The Conch Republic is all about letting your flag fly proud (as long as it's a tolerant one). How established is gay life here? There's even a gay trolley tour. (p187)

Miami In South Beach especially, gay nightlife is almost synonymous with 'nightlife.' Be as out as you like among the fashionistas and celebrities. (p140)

Fort Lauderdale The Lauderdale scene is less snooty than South Beach, and welcomes hordes of sun-seeking gay travelers to its B&Bs and bars. (p207)

MATT MUNRO/LONELY PLANET ©

Dry Tortugas National Park (p201), a secluded island far off Key West

West Palm Beach Palm Beach's hipper sister has a notable and noticeable gay scene. (p230)

Orlando Orlando is gay-friendly year-round, but everyone comes out for Gay Days in early June. (p248)

Pensacola Surprise! Attend Pensacola's Memorial Day party, and you might not recognize the Panhandle. (p443)

Craft Drinks

Florida's drinking profile has increased a fair bit since the early-21st-century heyday of the mighty *mojito*. Be they muddled, shaken, stirred or strained, craft booze is appearing with delicious, inebriating frequency in bars across the state.

Broken Shaker Miami Beach throws its hat in the fancy cocktail ring with this excellent outdoor outpost. (p141)

Stache Craft drinks and beautiful Fort Lauderdale clientele fill this spot. (p213)

Hanson's Shoe Repair Sure, it's a themed flapper-style speakeasy, but this is Orlando. Own the cheesiness and get a good cocktail. (p266)

Vagabond Pool Bar Get your cocktail on in pure Miami style (ie surrounded by beautiful people on floaties) at this hip hotel. (p143)

The Dime Good pours, smart bartenders and a professorial crowd hang at this Gainesville bar. (p381)

Wreck Diving

Skrrriiiitch! What was that sound? Just another oceangoing vessel striking reef and going down off Florida's coast. A few are even shallow enough for snorkelers to access.

Panama City Beach The 'Wreck Capital of the South' boasts over a dozen boats, barges and tugs, plus a WWII Liberty ship and natural reefs. (p462)

Pensacola Dive a 900ft-long aircraft carrier, the *Oriskany*, deliberately sunk in 2006. (p453)

Fort Pierce Snorkel a Spanish galleon, the *Urca de Lima*, under only 10ft to 15ft of water. (p240)

Fort Lauderdale Freighters, steamers, tugs and barges litter the sea floor near Fort Lauderdale. (p207)

Biscayne National Park The Maritime Heritage Trail has six ships, and a two-masted schooner is shallow enough for snorkelers. (p169)

Month by Month

January

☆ College Football Bowl Games

On January 1, Floridians go insane for college football. Major bowls are played in Orlando (Capital One Bowl), Tampa (Outback Bowl) and Jacksonville (Gator Bowl), while Miami's Orange Bowl (January 3) often crowns the collegiate champion (www.ncaa.com).

⚐ Gasparilla Pirate Festival

On the last Saturday of the month, the city of Tampa basically becomes a big pirate party. (p388)

February

Ideal month for less-crowded South Florida beaches; high season ramps up. Still too cool for tourists up north.

☆ Art Wynwood

Contemporary art and hip galleries rule the roost in Miami's bohemian Wynwood district in the middle of the month. (p92)

⚐ Edison Festival of Light

For two weeks, Fort Myers celebrates the great inventor Thomas Edison with a block party, concerts and a huge science fair. February 11, Edison's birthday, culminates in an incredible Parade of Light. (p428)

⚐ Florida State Fair

Over a century old, Tampa's Florida State Fair is classic Americana: two mid-February weeks of livestock shows, greasy food, loud music and old-fashioned carnival rides. (p388)

⚐ Street Painting Festival

You'll never see the streets of Lake Worth quite the same after this festival, which kicks off in late February. The art that is produced isn't just chalk on asphalt; veritable curbside Sistine Chapels blanket Lake Worth's urban landscape. (p222)

✗ South Beach Wine & Food Festival

No paper-plate grub-fest, this late-February event is a Food Network–sponsored culinary celebration of food, drink and celebrity chefs. (p113)

⚐ Mardi Gras

Whether it falls in late February or early March, Fat Tuesday inspires parties statewide. Pensacola Beach, closest to New Orleans, hosts Florida's best (www.pensacolamardi gras.com).

March

Beach resort high season all over, due to spring break. Modest temps and dry weather make for an ideal time to hike and camp. Last hurrah for manatees.

⚐ Spring Break

Throughout March to mid-April, American colleges release students for one-week 'spring breaks.' Coeds pack Florida beaches for debaucherous drunken binges. The biggies? Panama City Beach, Pensacola, Daytona and Fort Lauderdale.

☆ Baseball Spring Training

Through March, Florida hosts Major League Baseball's spring training 'Grapefruit League' (www.floridagrapefruitleague.com): 15 pro teams train and play exhibition games in the Orlando area, the Tampa Bay area and the Southeast.

✦ Carnaval Miami

Miami's premier Latin festival (www.carnavalmiami.com) takes over for nine days in early March: there's a Latin drag-queen show, in-line-skate competition, domino tournament, the immense Calle Ocho street festival, Miss Carnaval Miami and more. (p114)

✦ Captain Robert Searle's Raid

St Augustine re-creates Robert Searle's infamous 1668 pillaging of the town in March (www.visitstaugustine.com). Local pirates dress up again in June for Sir Francis Drake's Raid. Volunteers are welcome!

☆ Winter Music Conference

For five days in late March, DJs, musicians, promoters and music-industry execs converge on Miami to party, strike deals, listen to new dance music and coo over the latest technology. (p114)

April

As spring-break madness fades, prices drop. It's the end of the winter dry season.

☆ Florida Film Festival

Held in Winter Park, near Orlando, this celebration of independent films is fast becoming one of the largest in the southeast. Sometimes held in late March. (p259)

✦ Interstate Mullet Toss

In late April on Perdido Key, near Pensacola, locals are famous for their annual ritual of tossing dead fish over the Florida–Alabama state line. Distance beats style, but some have lots of style. (p454)

✦ Conch Republic Independence Celebration

Honor the (pseudo) independence of the (pseudo) republic of Key West with crazy parties and (pseudo) elections for (pseudo) office. (p194)

May

Summer 'wet' season begins: rain, humidity, bugs all increase with temps. Northern beach season ramps up; southern beaches enter off-season.

✦ Sea Turtle Nesting

Beginning in May and extending through October, sea turtles nest on Florida beaches; after two months (from midsummer through fall), hatchling runs see the kids totter back to sea.

✗ Isle of Eight Flags Shrimp Festival

On May's first weekend, Amelia Island celebrates shrimp, art and pirates, with an invasion and lots of scurvy pirate talk – aaarrrr! (p366)

☆ SunFest

Over five days in early May, West Palm Beach holds South Florida's largest waterfront music and arts festival. (p233)

♟ Memorial Day Circuit Party

For late May's Memorial Day weekend, Pensacola becomes one massive three-day gay party, with lots of DJs, dancing and drinking. (p448)

✗ Palatka Blue Crab Festival

For four late-May days, Palatka celebrates the blue crab and hosts the state championship for chowder and gumbo. That's some serious bragging rights. (p370)

June

Oh my it's getting hot. It's also the start of hurricane season, which peaks in September/October. School's out for summer, so theme parks become insanely crowded.

✦ Gay Days

Starting on the first Saturday of June, and going for a week, upwards of 40,000 members of the LGBT community descend on the Magic Kingdom and other Orlando theme parks, hotels and clubs. Wear red. (p259)

✦ Miami Fashion Week

Miami: so hot right now. Actually, it's hot all the

Top: *A Tribute to The Golden Girls* by Erik Greenawalt and Lori Hughes, Street Painting Festival (p222)

Bottom: Sea turtles nest on Florida beaches from May through October

time, in every sense of the word, but especially so during the city's Fashion Week. (p114)

July

Northern-beach and theme-park high season continues. Swamp trails are unbearably muggy and buggy; stick to crystal springs and coastlines.

✵ Fourth of July

America's Independence Day is cause for parades and fireworks, large and small, across the state. Miami draws the biggest crowd for the best fireworks and laser show.

✗ Steinhatchee Scallop Season

The opening day of scallop season in Steinhatchee can draw a thousand folks, who take to the waters to harvest this delectable bivalve by hand. Anyone can join the following two-month-long treasure hunt (www.steinhatcheescalloping.com).

✵ Goombay Festival

In Miami's Coconut Grove, this massive street party draws well over 300,000 to celebrate the city's Bahamian culture with music, dancing and parades; it's one of America's largest black-culture festivals. (p114)

August

Floridians do nothing but crank the A/C inside while foolish tourists swelter and burn on the beaches –

and run from afternoon thundershowers.

Miami Spice

Miami's restaurants join together in August to offer prix-fixe lunches and dinners in an attempt to draw city residents from their apartments. (p115)

October

Mickey's Not-So-Scary Halloween Party

At Disney World on select evenings over two months (starting in September), kids can trick or treat in the shadow of Cinderella's Castle, with costumed Disney favorites and a Halloween-themed parade. (p290)

Fantasy Fest

Key West pulls out all the stops for this week-long costumed extravaganza culminating in Halloween. Everyone's even crazier than usual, and Key West's own Goombay Festival competes for attention the same week. (p194)

MoonFest

West Palm Beach throws a rockin', riotous block party for Halloween, October 31. Guests are encouraged to come in costume, and dozens of the best local bands play for free (www.moonfest.me).

'Ding' Darling Days

Celebrate Sanibel's favorite wildlife refuge at this week-long festival for nature and conservation. (p433)

Universal's Halloween Horror Nights

Magnificently spooky haunted houses, gory thrills and over-the-top Halloween shows. Watch for goblins, monsters and mummies roaming the streets and creeping up behind you. And remember, this is Universal, not Disney: parents should think carefully before bringing children 13 and under. (p310)

November

Florida's 'dry' winter season begins. Northern 'snowbirds' start flocking to their Florida condos. It's safe to hike again. Thanksgiving holidays spike tourism for a week.

Tampa Cigar Heritage Festival

Tampa's Ybor City has a long history as the cigar-making capital of the US. That heritage, and the cigars themselves, are celebrated in this one-day festival (www.cigarheritagefestival.com).

St Arrrgustine Pirate Gathering

Put on an eye patch and dust off your pirate lingo for this hokey celebration of scurvy dogs and seafaring rascals in St Augustine for three days in November.

White Party

A raucous gay and lesbian celebration (and HIV/AIDS fundraiser), the White Party is actually a series of parties and nightclub events in Miami Beach and Fort Lauderdale over a week in late November. And yes, wear white. (p115)

Frank Brown International Songwriters' Festival

Singer-songwriters play in venues across the Gulf Coast, including Pensacola and Perdido Key. (p455)

December

High season begins for South Florida beaches. Manatees arrive in warm-water springs.

Art Basel Miami Beach

Very simply, early December sees one of the biggest international art shows in the world, with more than 150 art galleries represented and four days of parties. (p115)

Victorian Christmas Stroll

The landmark 1891 Tampa Bay Hotel (now a museum) celebrates Christmas, Victorian-style, for three weeks in December, with folks in period costume acting out fairy tales (www.ut.edu/plantmuseum).

King Mango Strut

Miami's Coconut Grove rings in the New Year with this wacky, freak-alicious, after-Christmas parade, which spoofs current events and local politics. (p115)

Itineraries

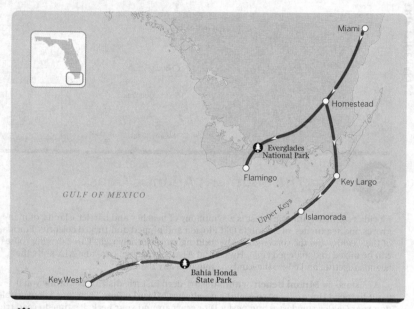

Miami

Homestead

Everglades National Park

Flamingo

Key Largo

GULF OF MEXICO

Upper Keys

Islamorada

Key West

Bahia Honda State Park

7 DAYS Iconic Florida

For sheer iconic box-ticking, you can't do better than spending a week taking in Miami, the Everglades and the Florida Keys.

First off, explore **Miami** for three solid days (more if you can). South Beach's pastel art-deco hotels and hedonistic beach culture? Check. Cuban sandwiches, Haitian *botanicas,* modern art? Check. Charming the velvet ropes, Latin hip-hop, *mojitos*? Hey, we're doing good.

Then take one day and visit the sunning alligators (check) of **Everglades National Park**. On the way, **Homestead** has prime Florida roadside attractions (Coral Castle, Robert Is Here – check and check!), and the **Flamingo visitor center** offers opportunities to kayak among the mangroves (check).

Now spend three days (or more) in the Florida Keys. Stop first in **Key Largo**, for key lime pie, conch fritters and jaw-dropping coral reefs (check x3). Enjoy tarpon fishing in **Islamorada** – check – beach napping at **Bahia Honda State Park** – check – and, finally, hit **Key West** to ogle the Mallory Sq freak show (check) and raise a libation as the tangerine sun drops into an endless ocean – *salut!*

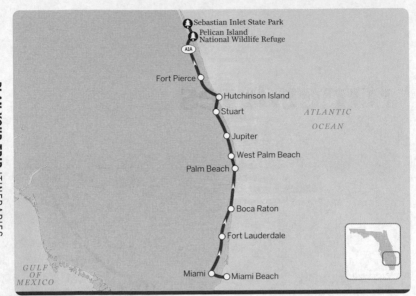

A1A: The Southern Atlantic Coast

Florida's southern Atlantic Coast is a symphony of beaches and barrier islands, of mangroves and sea turtles, of nostalgic Old Florida and nipped-and-tucked celebrity Florida, of the wealthy and the you've-got-to-be-kidding-me obscenely rich. Three driving routes can be mixed and matched (I-95, Hwy 1 and A1A), but scenic, two-lane A1A knits the islands together and edges the sands as much as any road can.

A1A starts in **Miami Beach**, within the art-deco historic district. Naturally you'll want to spend three days or so soaking up all that **Miami** offers. Then rent a convertible, don your Oakley sunglasses and nest a Dior scarf around your neck: it's time to road trip.

There already? First stop is **Fort Lauderdale**. Preen along the promenade among the skating goddesses and be-thonged gay men, ride a romantic gondola in the canals, and enjoy fine art and gourmet cuisine: it's a suite of pleasures the Gold Coast specializes in.

After two or three days, stagger on. Pause for a quiet interlude on the gorgeous beaches of **Boca Raton**, then repeat your Lauderdale experience in **Palm Beach**. Ogle the uberwealthy as they glide between mansion and Bentley and beach, stop by the Flagler Museum to understand how this all got started, and each day decamp to **West Palm Beach**, the hipper, more happening sister city.

After several days, it's time to detox. Heading north, the Treasure Coast is known for unspoiled nature, not condos and cosmopolitans. Stop first in **Jupiter**; among its pretty parks, don't miss the seaside geyser at Blowing Rocks Preserve.

Even better, spend several days in **Stuart**. From here you can kayak the Loxahatchee River, book a fishing charter, snorkel the reefs at St Lucie Inlet, and escape the crowds on nearby **Hutchinson Island** beaches.

If you only have two weeks, then you may have to skip the next offerings. At **Fort Pierce**, admire manatees in winter and snorkel a Spanish galleon. Surfers should pause at **Sebastian Inlet State Park**, and birders detour to the nation's first national wildlife refuge, **Pelican Island**. We've come a long way from Miami, yes?

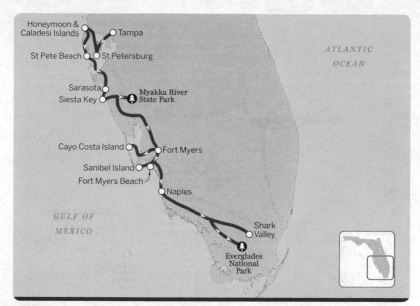

3 WEEKS **Gulf Coast Swing**

Many prefer Florida's Gulf Coast: the beaches aren't as built up, soporifically warm waters lap blindingly white sand, and the sun sets (rather than rises) over the sea. Plus, it's easy to mix urban sophistication with seaside getaways and swampy adventures – just like around Miami, only even more family- (and budget-) friendly.

On this trip, spend your first three to four days in **Tampa** and **St Petersburg**. Stroll the museums and parks along Tampa's sparkling Riverwalk, and spend a day enjoying historic Ybor City's Spanish cuisine, cigars and nightclubs. St Pete offers similar city fun, but above all, don't miss its Salvador Dalí Museum.

Now head west for the barrier islands. Take their full measure by spending one day on unspoiled **Honeymoon and Caladesi Islands**, then enjoy the hyper, activity-fueled atmosphere of **St Pete Beach**.

Next, drive down to **Sarasota** for three days. You'll need that long to take in the magnificent Ringling Museum Complex, the orchid-rich Marie Selby Botanical Gardens, perhaps catch the opera and still allow plenty of time to build sandcastles on the amazing white-sand beaches of **Siesta Key**. If you have extra time, visit **Myakka River State Park** and kayak among the alligators.

Then skip down to **Fort Myers** for two days of regional exploring. Take the ferry to **Cayo Costa Island** for a beach of unforgettable solitude, or go the party route and hit the crowded strands of **Fort Myers Beach**.

You need to save at least two days for **Sanibel Island**. World famous for its shelling, it's also a bike-friendly island stocked with great eats and wildlife-filled bays ripe for kayaking.

Finally end with two to three days in **Naples**, the quintessence of Gulf Coast beach towns: upscale, artistic and welcoming of every age demographic, with perhaps Florida's most pristine city beach. You can eat and shop to your heart's content, and fit in a day trip to the **Everglades**. It's easy – zip along the Tamiami Trail to **Shark Valley**, and take a tram tour or bike ride among the sawgrass plains and sometimes countless alligators.

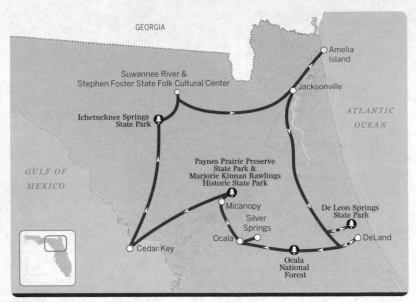

North Florida Backroads

3 WEEKS

North Florida appeals to outdoor-lovers who prefer that days be filled with forests, springs, rivers and fishing, and that evenings be spent reliving these adventures around campfires.

Fly into **Jacksonville**, and spend the first day embracing the Atlantic Ocean on Jax beaches. For a full dose of Florida's Southern personality, have dinner at Southern Charm, then sink a few beers in the Little Five Points neighborhood.

Drive south to small-town **DeLand** and explore **De Leon Springs State Park**, with its crystal-springs kayaking. The big daddy down here is the **Ocala National Forest**, with epic hiking and biking through Florida's fascinating limestone karst terrain. While it may be tough to spot local wildlife, you're in a wilderness that is rife with alligators, foxes, coyotes and black bears: keep your eyes peeled.

Next, scoot over to **Ocala**, a veritable center for Florida agriculture and Old Florida vibe. Here the classic glass-bottom boat tours of **Silver Springs** and high-revving dragster energy of the Don Garlits Museums beckon. Then go north to **Micanopy**, 'the town that time forgot,' for more eerie hikes at **Paynes Prairie Preserve State Park** and a taste of Cracker history at **Marjorie Kinnan Rawlings Historic State Park**, named for the author of *The Yearling,* the classic tale of growing up barefoot and poor in the Depression-era South.

For the next two to four days, string together the following outdoor highlights: drive to **Cedar Key**, where you can kayak among seabirds and unspoiled mangrove-fringed islands; then head further north to **Ichetucknee Springs State Park**, which warrants a half-day of tubing amid its cool blue springs. Save at least a day for a river trip along the **Suwannee River**, a muddy-brown moss-draped meander that's North Florida all over. Reserve ahead for a multiday river-camping trip, and visit the **Stephen Foster State Folk Cultural Center** to learn about the folkways of the 'Cracker' (rural white) cultural roots of the region.

Nothing personal, but it's clean-up time. Drive back to Jacksonville, and spend a final day or three on **Amelia Island**. Spoil yourself with a Victorian B&B and some gourmet seafood, or hit the outdoors again with a paddle around the barrier islands.

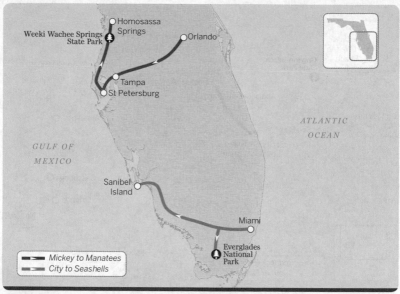

Mickey to Manatees
City to Seashells

1 WEEK Mickey to Manatees

The kids want Disney, but Mom and Dad want beach time, a good meal and some culture. Oh, and you've only got a week.

Presto change-o – here you go! For the first three or four days, stay in **Orlando**. Rather than give in entirely to Walt Disney World®, spend two days there and another day at Universal Orlando Resort, particularly if you've read any of those Harry Potter books.

For the next three or four days, hit Tampa Bay. On one day in **Tampa** choose between its tremendous zoo and aquarium and its fantastic museums, then end in historic Ybor City for Spanish cuisine with a side of flamenco. In **St Petersburg** even kids will find the Salvador Dalí Museum intriguing. Then squeeze in a day trip north for the mermaid shows at **Weeki Wachee Springs State Park** and the manatees of **Homosassa Springs**. Everybody's happy!

1 WEEK City to Seashells

Geez, you really don't want to miss sexy, high-energy Miami, but if you don't get some sandy, leave-me-alone-with-my-novel downtime you'll never make it when you return to work in [insert name of major metropolis here]. Oh, and you've only got a week.

Presto change-o – here you go! Spend the first three days in **Miami** and have a party. Tour the art-deco-district hotels, enjoy the sophisticated art museums, shop for tailored shirts and racy designer dresses, and prance past the velvet ropes to celebrity-spot and dance all night to Latin hip-hop.

Next, spend one day peering at alligators through dark sunglasses in the **Everglades**, just so everyone back home won't be all 'What? You went to Florida and didn't even go?'

For the last three days, chill on **Sanibel Island**. Get a hotel on a private stretch of beach and do nothing but sun, sleep, read and collect handfuls of beautiful seashells as you kick along. Maybe take a bike ride and have a gourmet dinner. But each night, dig your toes in the sand and enjoy the setting sun in romantic solitude.

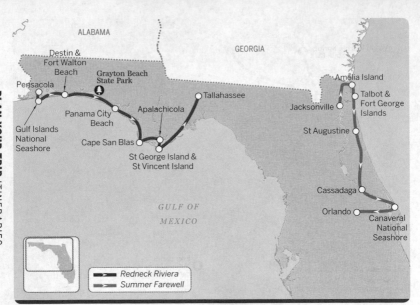

Redneck Riviera
Summer Farewell

10 DAYS Redneck Riviera

Sure, Florida's Panhandle gets rowdy, yet there's family-friendly warmth and unexpected sophistication along with its spectacular bone-white beaches.

Start your tour with a few days in **Pensacola**. Relax on the beaches of the **Gulf Islands National Seashore**, and enjoy Pensacola's historic village and its naval aviation history. The Blue Angels may even put on a show.

Spend another two days in the tourist towns of **Destin** and **Fort Walton Beach**, and don't miss the world-class sand of **Grayton Beach State Park**. If you have kids, a day among the hyperactive boardwalk amusements of **Panama City Beach** is virtually a must.

Afterward shuffle along to the secluded wilderness of **Cape San Blas** and quaint **Apalachicola**, whose romantic historic sweats as heavy as a hot Florida day.

St George and **St Vincent Islands** provide more secluded getaways, but if time is short, spend your last day around **Tallahassee** – admittedly located off the Gulf. Unwind and get a little rowdy in some local live-music joints.

10 DAYS Summer Farewell

Let's say you want the warmest weather but the fewest people. Hello, September! This trip is good anytime, but Florida's north is particularly sweet as school starts and summer fades.

Fly into **Jacksonville**, but go straight to **Amelia Island** for several days of romantic B&Bs, luscious food and pretty sand. The good vibes continue as you kayak and explore the undeveloped beaches of **Talbot** and **Fort George Islands**, just south.

Then spend two to three days in **St Augustine**. America's oldest city preserves its heritage very well, with plenty of pirate tales enlivening the Spanish forts and basilicas.

When you've had enough of fine dining and costumed reenactors, head to **Cassadaga**, a town of spiritualists and New Age wisdom in the middle of the backwoods (because Florida!), and have your fortune told.

At this point, you've filled a week, but a few more days means more kayaking in **Canaveral National Seashore**, and perhaps a day or two in the theme parks of **Orlando**. Where aren't the kids when they are in school? In line.

Kumba roller coaster, Busch Gardens (p390)

Plan Your Trip
Theme Park Trip Planner

Every year Walt Disney World®, Universal Orlando Resort and Legoland draw millions of visitors to Orlando, the theme-park capital of the world, and there are a handful of lesser-known parks beyond their gates. Here's the bottom line on what's what and how to tackle them.

When to Go

Peak Periods

Crowds and prices soar during US school vacations, including summer (June through August), spring break (March through mid-April), Thanksgiving weekend and, especially, the week between Christmas and New Years'. If at all possible, do not visit during these high seasons.

Slow Times

The slowest times are mid-January through February, September through mid-October, the first half of May, and the couple of weeks in between Thanksgiving weekend and mid-December.

Special Events

Some events worth planning for are the Epcot International Food & Wine Festival (late September through early November), Mickey's Very Merry Christmas Party (November to mid-December) and Universal Orlando's Halloween Horror Nights (October).

Florida's Theme Parks

Walt Disney World®

Walt Disney World® (p275) encompasses 40 sq miles and includes four completely separate and distinct theme parks, each with rides and shows: Magic Kingdom (p287), Epcot (p292), Hollywood Studios (p299) and Animal Kingdom (p297). There are also two water parks, Typhoon Lagoon (p301) and Blizzard Beach (p302); more than 20 hotels; almost 140 restaurants; and two shopping and nightlife districts, Disney Springs (p303) and Disney's BoardWalk (p302); as well as four golf courses, two miniature-golf courses, lagoons with water sports, and a spectator-sports complex, all connected by a system of free buses, boats and monorails.

For classic Disney at its best, head to the iconic Magic Kingdom, home to Cinderella's Castle, fairy-tale rides and quintessential Disney parades, shows

and fireworks. Garden-filled Epcot is another favorite: one half is themed around technology and the future, and the other features re-created countries of the world spread along a small lake. Hollywood Studios offers some don't-miss Disney highlights, but they're peppered among filler and fluff and muffled by *Hannah Montana* and *American Idol*–style energy. Africa-inspired Animal Kingdom fuses rides and shows with zoo encounters, animal conservation and, oddly, a dash of dinosaur. This is where you'll find *Finding Nemo: The Musical,* one of Disney's best live performances.

Universal Orlando Resort

In contrast to WDW, Universal Orlando Resort (p306) is a more intimate and walkable complex, with two excellent theme parks, Islands of Adventure (p306) and Universal Studios (p308), and one water park, Volcano Bay (p311), plus four first-rate resorts and a carnival-like restaurant and nightlife district, CityWalk (p306), all connected by garden paths and a quiet wooden boat shuttle.

Universal's theme parks offer shamelessly silly, laugh-out-loud 'wow' for the whole family, with some of Orlando's best thrills, incredibly designed simulated experiences and water rides that leave you soaked.

At Islands of Adventure, each section has its own distinct tone and vibe. Seuss Landing surrounds visitors with the characters and landscapes of the books and the Wizarding World of Harry Potter – Hogsmeade has proven a well-deserved runaway hit.

Universal Studios, just next door, has primarily movie- and TV-themed rides and scheduled shows, emphasizing comic-book superheroes and contemporary favorites like *Despicable Me* and *The Simpsons,* but it also has a sweet Barney Show, an excellent kids' play area, and Diagon Alley, an expansion of the park's enormously successful Potter-themed attractions. Guests with tickets for both theme parks can ride the Hogwarts Express through the 'British' countryside between Hogsmeade and Diagon Alley.

Volcano Bay was just opening at the time of writing. The water park is structured as an artificial Pacific island, centered on its own 200ft high eponymous volcano. Some

18 attractions, ranging from family-friendly lazy rivers to adrenaline-pumping waterslides, beckon visitors to the park.

Legoland

Wonderful Legoland (p274) is as awesome and innovative as your favorite beloved Lego set, except this one is enormous and you can play on it for days.

Tampa Bay Area

Busch Gardens (p390) African-themed wildlife encounters, various shows and musical entertainment, and some of the state's wildest roller coasters.

Adventure Island (p386) Top-notch water park adjacent to and owned by Busch Gardens.

Weeki Wachee Springs (p412) One hour north of Tampa, this Old Florida original is world-famous for its spangly-tailed, long-haired mermaid shows. Plus there's a small spring-fed water park, animal presentations and river canoeing.

KATJA KREDER/GETTY IMAGES ©

Epcot (p292), Walt Disney World®

Staying in the Resorts

Disney and Universal provide great perks for their hotel guests and both offer budget accommodations, so if you'll be spending several days exploring their parks, there's no compelling reason not to stay on site.

If, however, you choose to stay off site, resorts and national chains surround the parks, and many offer theme-park packages. Convenient locations to Disney parks are Lake Buena Vista, Kissimmee and the town of Celebration. International Drive is more convenient for Universal Orlando Resort and SeaWorld. Most hotels offer shuttles to some or all of the theme parks, but be warned that they can be a pain. They leave at prearranged times, make lots of stops, often require advance booking, and, for Disney in particular, you may need to take additional Disney transportation once the hotel shuttle drops you off. Always ask for *precise details* about shuttle logistics.

Disney and Universal hotel rates vary wildly by season and demand, as do hotel rates in Orlando in general, and prices can change dramatically (as in hundreds of dollars) within 24 hours. Stay flexible, be persistent and always ask about packages and specials. Most hotels sleep at least four at no extra charge and several have bunk beds, suites and villas to accommodate larger parties.

Walt Disney World® Resort Hotels

With over two dozen resort hotels, Disney has lodging for every budget, from camping to villas, motel-style complexes to full-service resorts. What you're paying for is convenience, location, recreational amenities and theming; quality-wise, except for the very best deluxe resorts, rooms are no better than good midrange chains

MYMAGIC

MyMagic+ is Disney's system designed to help guests both plan and navigate their Disney vacation. It includes My Disney Experience, FastPass+ and MagicBands (p283).

Fire-spewing dragon at Gringotts Bank, Wizarding World of Harry Potter (p312)

elsewhere, and even the most expensive options pale in comparison to comparably priced luxury resorts elsewhere in Florida.

Guest Perks

Extra Magic Hours Each day, one theme park opens early and closes late for guests at Disney hotels only.

FastPass+ Advanced Reservations Reserve a one-hour window to FastPass+ lines at three attractions per person, per day up to 60 days in advance, thus slashing wait times. Guests staying off site can reserve attractions up to 30 days in advance. This doesn't seem like much, but it makes a difference.

Disney transportation Despite the frustration of tackling Disney buses, boats and monorails, they can be more convenient than off-site hotel shuttles.

Free parking No fee at theme parks or hotels.

Disney's Magical Express Complimentary baggage handling and deluxe bus transport from Orlando International Airport.

Baggage transfer If you change to a different Disney hotel during your stay, you can leave your bags in the morning and they'll be at your new hotel by evening.

Dining plans Only resort guests have access to the meal plans.

Universal Orlando Resort Hotels

Universal has only five resort hotels, but they are top quality, extremely well situated within their more-intimate resort, and highly recommended.

Guest Perks

Early admission to Wizarding World of Harry Potter Theme-park gates open one hour early for access to Harry Potter–themed attractions.

Unlimited Express Pass Up to five guests per room automatically receive unlimited access to Express Pass lines. This is a huge plus, worth hundreds of dollars, but there are two major caveats. One: the major attractions at Wizarding World of Harry Potter do not have Express Pass lines. Two: this perk only applies to guests at Loews Portofino Bay, Hard Rock and Loews Royal Pacific Resort. It does not apply for guests at Loews Sapphire Falls and Cabana Bay Beach Resort.

The Twilight Zone Tower of Terror (p300). Hollywood Studios

sample food and drink from around the world.

Beyond Disney and Universal, the creative twists to dining fade. There's certainly a nod to healthy and interesting, but generally it's the usual overpriced burgers and pizza served cafeteria-style. With the exception of Magic Kingdom, which serves alcohol at only one restaurant (wine and beer only), you'll find plenty of tantalizing cocktails and cold beer throughout the parks.

Disney allows table-service restaurant reservations 180 days in advance, and for a Disney character meal, dinner show or some of the more popular restaurants, you'll need to reserve the moment your 180-day window opens. Seriously. Some of the most coveted seats include Cinderella's Royal Table (p291) inside the castle, the *Beauty and the Beast*–themed Be Our Guest (p291), dinner at California Grill (p281) with fireworks views, and the ultra-chic no-kids-allowed Victoria and Albert's (p281). Always ask about cancellation policies; generally, you can cancel with no penalty up to 24 hours in advance.

Snagging a table at Universal isn't nearly the trouble it is at Disney. Each park has two table-service restaurants that take advance reservations.

Note that restaurants inside theme parks require theme-park admission, but there are plenty of excellent ones, including several that offer character meals, at entertainment

Universal transportation Small boats run between the parks and deluxe resort hotels, and there's complimentary shuttle service to Cabana Bay (an on-site resort), Wet 'n Wild, Aquatica and SeaWorld.

Priority Seating Get first-available seating at select restaurants, but again, only for guests at Loews Portofino Bay, Hard Rock and Loews Royal Pacific Resort.

Dining &
Character Meals

Eating at the theme parks falls into two categories: quick service (a euphemism for 'fast food') and table service. Beyond this, your primary considerations are price, quality and theming fun. Sip on a Flaming Moe or Butterbeer at Universal Orlando Resort, eat under asteroid showers or in a mock drive-in theater at WDW, watch giraffes and ostriches over African fare at Disney's Animal Kingdom Lodge. At Disney's Epcot, it's particularly fun to

---

TICKETS

At Disney and Universal, per-day theme-park admission costs plummet the more days you buy; go to park websites for details on current specials, accommodation packages and dining plans that can save loads.

You do not need admission to enter the resort complexes themselves. Admission tickets are only required to get into the theme and water parks, and there are all kinds of entertainment and activities beyond theme-park gates (especially at WDW).

JOE RAEDLE/GETTY IMAGES ©

CHIP LITHERLAND ©

Top: Roller coaster at Busch Gardens (p390)

Bottom: Legoland (p274), image © 2013 Legoland Florida/ Merlin Entertainments Group, Chip Litherland Photography

districts and resort hotels in both WDW and Universal Orlando Resort.

Essential Theme Park Strategies

In advance

Purchase advance tickets At many parks, tickets cost $10 to $20 less if purchased in advance. Online calendars allow you to peruse prices over several months.

Purchase multiple day-admission tickets and be flexible It's absolutely exhausting tackling the parks at 110% day after day. You'll better enjoy the fun if you allow room for downtime by the pool or beyond.

Reserve Disney dining up to 180 days in advance Select a few don't-miss eating experiences as the backbone of your Disney plans, and be sure to take location into consideration.

Stay at an on-site resort if going to Universal Orlando's Wizarding World of Harry Potter The quality of the accommodations, amenities and service, combined with the time- and stress-saving perks they offer, plus easy access to the parks, makes this a no-brainer if you can swing it. On-site guests can enter Harry Potter–themed attractions one hour earlier than the general public.

Once there

Arrive early Come before park gates open, march straight to popular rides before lines get long, and consider leaving by lunch, when crowds are worst. This probably won't work every day, but a few efficient mornings make a palpable difference.

Pack snacks Something as simple as peanut-butter sandwiches and an apple stuffed in your bag will save time, money and stress.

Factor travel time When planning each day, carefully consider travel to and within the parks. At Disney especially, transportation logistics can waste hours and leave you drained.

Website & Apps

Google 'WDW' and you'll find pages upon pages of websites with detailed menus, crowd calendars, touring plans, images,

Dudley Do-Right's Ripsaw Falls (p307), Islands of Adventure

discounts and more, and there are dozens and dozens of apps to help you navigate the parks in real time. While it's easy to get buried in and stressed by information overload, they can be helpful. Here are some of our favorites – all but two offer both apps and websites:

Walt Disney World® (www.disneyworld.disney.go.com) Official WDW website.

Universal Orlando Resort (www.universalorlando.com) Official Universal website.

My Disney Experience (www.disneyworld.disney.go.com/plan/my-disney-experience) Indispensable Disney app for creating WDW itineraries; reserve FastPass+ and meals.

Orlando Informer (www.orlandoinformer.com) Go-to for all things Universal Orlando, including crowd calendar.

Theme Park Insider (www.themeparkinsider.com) News from theme parks around the world, with painstaking details.

Undercover Tourist (www.undercovertourist.com) Disney, Universal and SeaWorld discounts, car rental, wait times etc.

ESSENTIALS

What to Wear

Floridians can be both laid-back and obsessive about fashion – this is the state where a guy in flip-flop sandals and no shirt hosts a fancy dinner where guests have just arrived from a boutique party. In general, bring beach-y clothes that can double as day outfits (eg a loose button-up). Men and women alike should pack one or two nice outfits in the event of a nice dinner or more expensive clubbing.

What to Take

➡ Sunscreen! That Florida sun will have you burned before you know it.

➡ Bug spray – to be fair, you can buy this in Florida, but buy it fast.

➡ Proof of insurance.

➡ A driver's license issued from your home state or country.

All Ears (www.allears.net) Menus and advice.

WDW Info (www.wdwinfo.com) Go-to source.

MouseSavers (www.mousesavers.com) Money-saving tips.

Our Laughing Place (www.ourlaughingplace.com) WDW Transportation Wizard (TW) plots best routes. Several apps, including planning, TW and dining.

Mom's Panel (https://disneyparksmomspanel.disney.go.com) Perky Disney-sponsored discussion boards run by moms. Website only.

Touring Plans (https://touringplans.com) Tips on best use of FastPass+.

Disney Tourist Blog (www.disneytouristblog.com) Ride guides and more. Website only.

Plan Your Trip
Outdoor Activities

Florida doesn't have mountains, valleys, cliffs or snow. What does it have? Water, and lots of it – freshwater, saltwater, rainwater, spring water, swamp water. Florida's peninsula bends with over 1200 miles of coastline, which include over 660 miles of the best beaches in the US. Plus coral reefs, prehistoric swamps and forests, all teeming with Ice-Age flora and dinosaur-era fauna.

Hiking & Camping

One thing Florida hikers never have to worry about is elevation gain. But the weather more than makes up for it. If your destination is South Florida, it's best to hike and camp from November through March. This is Florida's 'dry season,' when rain, temperatures, humidity and mosquitoes decrease to tolerable levels. In summer, hike before noon to avoid the midday heat and afternoon thundershowers.

One of 11 national scenic trails , the **Florida National Scenic Trail** (www.fs.usda.gov/fnst) and covers 1400 not-yet-contiguous miles. It runs north from the swamps of Big Cypress National Preserve; around Lake Okeechobee; through the Ocala National Forest; and then west to the Gulf Islands National Seashore near Pensacola. All the parks above are filled with great hikes.

Other prime hiking areas include the remote pine wilderness, karst terrain and limestone sinkholes of Apalachicola National Forest and Paynes Prairie Preserve State Park. Wekiwa Springs State Park rewards hikers, paddlers and snorkelers.

South Florida swamps tend to favor 1- to 2-mile boardwalk trails; these are excellent, and almost always wheelchair accessible. But to really explore the wetlands, get in a kayak or canoe. In the Everglades, you can

Life's a Beach

Best Gulf Coast Beaches
Siesta Key (p422)

Fort DeSoto Park (p406)

Honeymoon Island State Park (p411)

Sanibel Island (p431)

Naples Municipal Beach (p436)

Best Atlantic Coast Beaches
Apollo Beach (p327)

Bahia Honda State Park (p185)

Bill Baggs Cape Florida State Park (p104)

Fort Lauderdale (p207)

Lake Worth Beach (p222)

Hutchinson Island (p239)

Best Panhandle Beaches
Grayton Beach State Park (p459)

St George Island State Park (p469)

Pensacola Beach (p452)

Blue Mountain Beach (p459)

also embark on 'wet walks,' which are wading trips deep into the blackwater heart of the swamps. It may seem like folly to tread through the same waters that alligators and crocodiles prowl, but wet walks have been conducted unabated for well over a decade.

Prized camping spots include the shady riverside at Stephen Foster Folk Culture Center State Park; the Ocala National Forest; the Panhandle's St Joseph State Park; Myakka River State Park; the *chickees* (raised platforms) that dot the waterways of the Everglades and the Ten Thousand Islands; and, in the Florida Keys, Bahia Honda State Park.

Just be warned: mosquitoes are an unavoidable reality, especially during the spring and summer months. Sunscreen is a must when hiking, and a good bug repellent (and insect-proof clothes) comes a close second.

For short hikes in national, state or regional parks, free park maps are perfectly adequate. Most outdoor stores and ranger stations sell good topographical (topo) maps.

Resources

Florida Greenways & Trails (www.visitflorida.com/trails) The Florida Department of Environmental Protection has downloadable hiking, biking and kayaking trail descriptions.

Florida Hikes (www.floridahikes.com) A comprehensive, updated, easy-to-search online guide to hikes across the state.

Florida Office of Greenways & Trails (www.dep.state.fl.us/gwt) The state's main database of current and future trails.

Florida State Parks (www.floridastateparks.org) Comprehensive state-park information and all cabin and camping reservations.

AVOIDING HEATSTROKE

One thing Florida hikers never have to worry about is elevation gain. But the weather more than makes up for it. If your destination is South Florida, it's best to hike and camp from November through March. This is Florida's 'dry season,' when rain, temperatures, humidity and mosquitoes decrease to tolerable levels. In summer, hike before noon to avoid the midday heat and afternoon thundershowers.

Florida Trail Association (www.floridatrail.org) Maintains the Florida National Scenic Trail (FNST); a wealth of online advice, descriptions and maps.

Leave No Trace (www.lnt.org) Advice on low-impact hiking and camping.

National Geographic (www.nationalgeographic.com) Custom and GPS maps.

Rails-to-Trails Conservancy (www.railstotrails.org) Converts abandoned railroad corridors into public biking and hiking trails; has a Florida chapter and reviews trails at www.traillink.com.

Recreation.gov (www.recreation.gov) Reserve camping at all national parks and forests, as well as many state parks.

Trails.com (www.trails.com) Create custom, downloadable topo maps.

US Geological Survey (www.store.usgs.gov) Your online one-stop shop for maps and geological surveys of all US states.

Swimming & Springs

Florida's beaches are the best in the continental United States, and incredibly diverse, so let's start with two questions: do you prefer sunrise or sunset? Do you prefer surfing and boogie boarding or sunbathing and sand castles? For sunrise and surfing, hit the bigger, east-facing waves of the Atlantic Coast; for sand castles at sunset, choose the soporific, west-facing waters of the Gulf Coast and the Panhandle.

Would you prefer it if we got a little more nuanced with our sand and surf judgment? Fair enough. There are a few other elements of beachgoing we can certainly address: namely, the 'beach as casual escape' versus 'family destination' versus 'spring-break boozefest' versus 'sexy spot to show off your fashion sense and spot celebrities.' If you're into the last of these, head for Palm Beach, Fort Lauderdale and Miami Beach. These are the spots where you'll see the stars and models decked out in swimwear. Those searching for a casual beach escape or a trip for the family may be better served by the tepid, calm waters of the Gulf; Sanibel Island, off the coast of Fort Myers, may have the most family-friendly beaches in the state. You'll also feel less pressure to look stunning in your skivvies compared to Southeast Florida and Miami. If you're into straight-up partying and a spring-break atmosphere, set your compass to towns like Panama City and Daytona Beach, and kiss your liver goodbye. Fair warning: while the Florida Keys seem like they would possess excellent swaths of sand, they are in fact mangrove islands with few natural beaches to speak of (larger private resorts do tend to create their own artificial beaches).

Beyond that, your main concern is how close to or far from other people you want to be. Even in the most hyper-developed condo canyons of South Florida, it is possible to find state and local parks that provide a relative degree of natural isolation.

With few exceptions, Florida's beaches are safe places to swim; the most dangerous surf will occur just before and after a storm. Also stingrays in summer and occasional jellyfish can trouble swimmers (look for lifeguard-posted warnings).

Don't overlook Florida's lakes, rivers and springs. Taking a dip in one of Florida's 700 freshwater springs – each 72°F (22°C) and, when healthy, clear as glass – is unforgettable. There are too many to list, but good swimming destinations are the Suwannee River, the Ichetucknee River and Ponce de Leon Springs State Park.

Kayaking in Everglades National Park (p156)

Canoeing & Kayaking

To really experience Florida's swamps and rivers, its estuaries and inlets, its lagoons and barrier islands, you need a watercraft, preferably the kind you paddle. The intimate quiet of dipping among mangroves, cruising alligators and startled ibis stirs wonder in the soul.

The winter 'dry' season is best for paddling. That's because 'dry' in Florida is still pretty darn wet. So why come during the dry season? Because evaporation and receding waterlines force wildlife into highly visible concentrations amid the state's waterways and pools. In summer, canoe near cool, freshwater springs and swimming beaches, because you'll be dreaming about them.

In terms of rivers, the 207-mile Suwannee River is quintessential Florida: a meandering, muddy ribbon (ideal for multiday trips) decorated with 60 clear blue springs; it runs from Georgia's Okefenokee Swamp to the Gulf of Mexico. About 170 miles form an official wilderness trail (www.floridahikes.com/suwannee-river-wilderness-trail), and the section near Big

Shoals State Park actually has some Class III rapids – woo-hoo!

Other unforgettable rivers include: the Atlantic Coast's 'Wild and Scenic' Loxahatchee River; Orlando's 'Wild and Scenic' Wekiva River; and the Tampa region's placid Hillsborough River and alligator-packed Myakka River.

You'll tell your grandchildren about kayaking Everglades National Park; Hell's Bay paddling trail is heavenly. The nearby Ten Thousand Islands are just as amazing, and nothing beats sleeping in the Everglades in a *chickee* (a wooden platform raised above the waterline). A truly great Florida adventure – indeed, one of the most unique wilderness experiences in North America – is paddling through the mangrove ecosystem that fringes the entirety of the southern Florida coast.

The remainder of the state's coasts are just as compelling. You'll kick yourself if you don't kayak Miami's Bill Baggs Cape Florida State Park; Tampa Bay's Caladesi Island; Sanibel Island's JN 'Ding' Darling National Wildlife Refuge; and the Big Bend's Cedar Key. There's even an entire 'blueway' – a collection of charted streams, coastline and

CRISTIANL/SHUTTERSTOCK ©

Florida is brimming with fine snorkeling spots

Kayak Online (www.kayakonline.com) A good resource for kayak gear, with links to Florida outfitters.

Paddle Florida (www.paddleflorida.net) First-hand trip reports, maps, photos and detailed guides to dozens of paddling destinations in the state.

Diving & Snorkeling

For diving and snorkeling, most already know about Florida's superlative coral reefs and wreck diving, but northern Florida is also great for cave diving. The peninsula's limestone has more holes than Swiss cheese, and most are burbling goblets of diamond-clear (if chilly) water.

Many diving spots line the Suwannee River: try Peacock Springs State Park (www.floridastateparks.org/peacocksprings), one of the continent's largest underwater cave systems; Troy Springs State Park (www.floridastateparks.org/troyspring); and Manatee Springs State Park. Another fun dive is Blue Spring State Park. Note that you need to be cavern certified to dive a spring (an open-water certification won't do), and solo diving is usually not allowed. Local dive shops can help with both. One place that offers certification courses is Vortex Spring.

Every Florida spring has prime snorkeling. At times the clarity of the water is disconcerting, as if you were floating on air; every creature and school of fish all the way to the bottom feels just out of reach.

If you prefer coral reefs teeming with rainbow-bright tropical fish, you're in luck... Florida has the continent's largest coral-reef system. The two best spots are John Pennekamp Coral Reef State Park in Key Largo, and Biscayne National Park south of Miami, at the tip of the Florida mainland. Biscayne is actually the only national park in the US park service system to exist primarily under the waves – 95% of the park is underwater. If you travel further along the Keys, you won't be disappointed at Bahia Honda State Park or Key West.

Wreck diving in Florida is equally epic, and some are even accessible to snorkelers. So many Spanish galleons sank off the Emerald Coast, near Panama City Beach, that it's dubbed the 'Wreck Capital of the South'. But also check out wreck dives in Pensacola, Sebastian Inlet State Park, Troy Springs, Fort Lauderdale, Biscayne National Park and Key West, a town that historically

rivers – within Lee County in southwest Florida.

On Florida's Atlantic Coast, more mangroves, waterbirds, dolphins and manatees await at Canaveral National Seashore, particularly Mosquito Lagoon, and also seek out Indian River Lagoon. Big and Little Talbot Islands provide more intercoastal magic.

Resources

Water-trail and kayaking information is provided by Florida State Parks (www.floridastateparks.org) and Florida Greenways & Trails (www.dep.state.fl.us/gwt). Here are more resources:

American Canoe Association (www.americancanoe.org) ACA publishes a newsletter, has a water-trails database and organizes courses.

Florida Paddling Trails Association (www.floridapaddlingtrails.com) Divides the state into 15 sections, and provides reports on paddle trails via an interactive map.

Florida Professional Paddlesports Association (www.paddleflausa.com) Provides a list of affiliated member kayak outfitters.

supported itself off the industry of wrecking (salvaging sunken ships and their cargo).

Named for its abundant sea turtles, the Dry Tortugas are well worth the effort to reach them.

Ocean diving in Florida requires an Open Water I certificate, and Florida has plenty of certification programs (with good weather, they take three days). To dive in freshwater springs, you need a separate cave-diving certification, and this is also offered throughout the state.

Resources

Florida Springs Recreation (www.floridasprings. org/visit/recreation) Information on diving in the state's unique spring ecosystems.

National Association for Underwater Instruction (www.naui.org) Information on dive certifications and a list of NAUI-certified Florida dive instructors.

Professional Diving Instructors Corporation (www.pdic-intl.com) Similar to NAUI, with its own list of PDIC-certified Florida dive instructors.

Cycling

Florida is too flat for mountain biking, but there are plenty of off-road opportunities, along with hundreds of miles of paved trails for those who prefer to keep their ride clean. As with hiking, avoid biking in summer, unless you like getting hot and sweaty.

Top off-roading spots include Big Shoals State Park (www.floridastateparks.org/bigshoals), with 25 miles of trails along the Suwannee River, and Paynes Prairie Preserve State Park, with 20 miles of trails through its bizarre landscape. Also recommended are the Ocala National Forest and the Apalachicola National Forest, particularly the sandy Munson Hills Loop.

With so many paved biking trails, it's hard to choose. To dip among the Panhandle's sugar-sand beaches, take the 19-mile Timpoochee Trail, which parallels Hwy 30A. In Tallahassee, the 16-mile Tallahassee-St Marks Historic Railroad State Trail shoots you right to the Gulf. Both paved and off-road trails encircle Lake Okeechobee, which is a great way to take in the surrounding countryside. Two unforgettable paved trails? Palm Beach's Lake Trail, aka the 'Trail of Conspicuous Consumption' for all the mansions and yachts, and the 15-mile Shark Valley Tram Road Trail, which pierces the Everglades' gator-infested saw-grass river.

For more-involved overland adventures, do the Florida Keys Overseas Heritage Trail, which mirrors the Keys Hwy for 70 noncontiguous miles, and the urban-and-coastal Pinellas Trail, which runs 43 miles from St Petersburg to Tarpon Springs.

In Florida's many beach towns, it's easy to find beach-cruiser-style bicycle rentals. These heavy-duty vehicles are made for lazy cycling along flat boardwalks – a perfect casual exercise.

A number of state organizations provide information on biking trails. Florida law requires that all cyclists under 16 wear a helmet (under 18 in national parks).

Resources

Bike Florida (www.bikeflorida.net) A good online resource for local cycling trails.

Florida Bicycle Association (www.floridabicycle. org) Advocacy organization providing tons of advice, a statewide list of cycling clubs, and links to off-road-cycling organizations, racing clubs, a touring calendar and more.

Fishing

The world may contain seven seas, but there's only one Fishing Capital of the World: Florida. No, this isn't typically over-wrought Floridian hype. Fishing here is the best the US offers, and for variety and abundance, few places in the world can compete.

In Florida's abundant rivers and lakes, largemouth bass are the main prize. Prime spots, with good access and facilities, are Lake Manatee State Park (www. floridastateparks.org/lakemanatee), south of St Petersburg; for fly-fishing, Myakka River State Park; and Jacksonville (www. jacksonvillefishing.com), which has charters to the St Johns River and Lake George for freshwater fishing and to the bay for ocean fishing, plus kayak fishing.

Near-shore saltwater fishing means redfish and mighty tarpon, snook, spotted sea trout and much more, up and down both coasts. The jetties at Sebastian Inlet are a mecca for shore anglers on the Atlantic Coast, while on the Gulf, Tampa's Skyway Fishing Pier is dubbed the world's longest fishing pier.

MATT A. CLAIBORNE/SHUTTERSTOCK ©

DAMSEA/SHUTTERSTOCK ©

Top: A *chickee* hut in the Everglades (p153)

Bottom: Crandon Golf Course (p111), Key Biscayne, Miami

In the Keys, Bahia Honda and Old Seven Mile Bridge on Pigeon Key are other shore-fishing highlights.

However, as 'Papa' Hemingway would tell you, the real fishing is offshore, where majestic sailfish leap and thrash. Bluefish and mahimahi are other popular deep-water fish. For offshore charters, head for Stuart, Fort Lauderdale, Lauderdale-by-the-Sea, Destin, Steinhatchee and Miami. The best strategy is to walk the harborside, talking with captains, until you find one who speaks to your experience and interests.

Resources

All nonresidents 16 and over need a fishing license to fish and crab, and Florida offers several short-term options. There are lots of regulations about what and how much you can catch, and where. Locals can give you details, but do the right thing and review the official word on what's OK and what's not: visit the Florida Fish & Wildlife Conservation Commission website.

Florida Fish & Wildlife Conservation Commission (www.myfwc.com) The official source for all fishing regulations and licenses (purchase online or by phone). Also has boating and hunting information.

Florida Fishing Capital of the World (www. visitflorida.com/fishing) State-run all-purpose fishing advice and information.

Florida Sportsman (www.floridasportsman.com) Get the lowdown on sportfishing, tournaments, charters, gear and detailed regional advice.

Sailing

If you like the wind in your sails, Florida is your place. Miami is a sailing sweet spot, with plenty of marinas for renting or berthing your own boat – Key Biscayne is a particular gem. Fort Lauderdale is chock-full of boating options. In Key West, you can sail on a schooner with real cannon, though tour operators are plentiful throughout the Keys. To learn how to sail, check out Pensacola's Lanier Sailing Academy.

Golf

Fun fact: with more than 1250 courses (and counting), Florida has the most golf courses of any US state. Whether or not this is related to Florida's high number of wealthy retirees isn't known, but one thing is certain: if you want to tee up, you won't have to look far.

Towns that are notable for golf include Palm Beach, Naples, Fort Myers, Orlando, Jacksonville, Miami and St Augustine. Near St Augustine is the World Golf Hall of Fame.

For a comprehensive list of Florida courses, see Florida Golf (www.floridagolf. com) and Florida Golfer Guide (www. floridagolferguide.com).

Surfing

Despite its many miles of coastline, Florida is a middle-tier surfing destination. The Gulf Coast is famously placid, and the presence of the Bahamas serves as a barrier to consistent breaks in the southernmost stretches of the Atlantic Coast.

New Smyrna Beach has some of the most consistent waves in the state, while nearby Cocoa Beach is similarly reliable, if a little gentler (and home of Ron Jon Surf Shop). Heading north, St Augustine and Anastasia State Recreation Area both boast popular surf spots, many of which can get crowded. You'll find fewer people in Flagler Beach, which is famous for its winter breaks. Jacksonville area beaches are well regarded, and Atlantic Beach in particular is great for beginners.

While there are some surfing spots in South Beach, we would argue Jupiter Beach is the choice spot in South Florida for solid, consistent breaks. The calm Gulf Coast isn't great for surfing, but you'll occasionally see folks hitting small waves in the area around Pensacola Beach or Destin, especially if the weather is a rough.

Resources

Florida Surfing Association (www.floridasurfing. org) Manages Florida's surf competitions; also runs the surf school at Jacksonville Beach.

Surf Guru (www.surfguru.com) East Coast Florida surf reports.

Surfer (www.surfermag.com) Surfer's travel reports cover Florida and just about every break in the USA.

Eat & Drink Like a Local

The treasures of the ocean, the citrus-scented whiff of farmland and an immigrant population give Florida serious culinary cred. On the flip side, strip malls, an all-too-American emphasis on reliability over adventure and a bad habit of cloning rather than creating trends are all marks against Florida's gastronomic reputation. Where does the truth lie? In the middle. In the meantime, gourmets can genuflect before celebrity chefs, while gourmands hunt Florida's delicacies, like boiled peanuts, frogs legs and gator.

The Basics

Florida has a varied eating scene that jukes from white-tablecloth refinement to roadside fried seafood to themed restaurants in tourist towns and resorts. At higher-end places, especially in big cities like Miami, you need to book seats in advance. At places with lower price points, or in smaller towns, you can usually show up and be seated.

Restaurants

You'll find restaurants in almost every town in Florida, serving any cuisine imaginable.

Bars

Pub grub and bar menus are increasingly popular in Florida night spots.

Theme parks

The food is often overpriced, but the atmosphere is generally delightful.

Destination Dining

Florida has a rich culinary heritage, but the state wasn't known as a place for good restaurants until the 1990s, when a wave of gourmet chefs transformed the Miami dining scene. They dedicated themselves to pleasing sophisticated urban palates by spicing up menus with South Florida's unique combination of Cuban, Caribbean and Latin American influences, which came to be dubbed Floribbean cuisine.

Today Miami remains the epicenter of all things gourmet, and it has the greatest selection of ethnic cuisines. It's a town that is highly susceptible to buzzword-of-the-moment dining trends; at the time of writing, farm-to-table cuisine and an affected focus on rustic simplicity was all the rage.

The ripples of Miami dining have since spread statewide. In big cities and anywhere moneyed tourists and snowbirds land, you will find upscale restaurants and skilled chefs plying their trade, often in contemporary dining rooms framing ocean views.

North of Miami and Miami Beach, Fort Lauderdale, Palm Beach and West Palm

Beach offer the well-heeled foodie oodles of fun. Key West is, as in all things, more laid-back, but its dining scene is notably stocked with creative-fusion cool, and for a town of its size, it possesses a surfeit of excellent dining options.

The southern Gulf Coast is similarly satisfying: Tampa and St Petersburg are riding the cusp of a culinary renaissance, with everything from Old World Iberian to locavore-inspired modern gastronomy. Skip south through the rich beach towns of Sarasota, Sanibel Island and Naples, and a memorable meal is just a reservation away.

As you go north, robust Southern cuisine comes to dominate, and high-end dining favors classic Italian, French and seafood. Though lacking gourmet 'scenes,' great choices are sprinkled through Jacksonville and Tallahassee. Along the Atlantic Coast, Amelia Island and St Augustine are foodie havens, and there's plenty of fresh, upscale seafood in Panhandle resort towns.

In general, Florida offers two kinds of tourism destinations, and in a similar vein, it offers two kinds of eating options. In the more typical beach and tourism towns you'll find family-friendly eateries that emphasize big portions and cheap prices. The more upscale you get, the more rarefied the atmosphere, but with that said, this is always Florida. You'll see people showing up for nice dinners in sandals (almost) everywhere.

Bounty of the Sea

Florida has always fed itself from the sea, which lies within arm's reach of nearly every point of the state. In a country where oysters are served in the rolling plains of Nebraska, there's no excuse not to have seafood in water-bound Florida. If it swims or crawls in the ocean, you can bet some enterprising local has shelled or scaled it, battered it, dropped it in a fryer and put it on a menu next to two plastic cups of tartar and cocktail sauce.

Grouper is far and away the most popular fish. Grouper sandwiches are to Florida what the cheesesteak is to Philadelphia or pizza to Manhattan – a defining, iconic dish, and the standard by which many places are measured. Hunting the perfect

FLORIBBEAN CUISINE

OK, somebody worked hard to come up with 'Floribbean' – a term for Florida's tantalizing gourmet mélange of just-caught seafood, tropical fruits and eye-watering peppers, all dressed up with some combination of Nicaraguan, Salvadoran, Caribbean, Haitian, Cajun, Cuban and even Southern influences. Some call it 'fusion,' 'Nuevo Latino,' 'New World,' 'nouvelle Floridian' or 'palm-tree cuisine,' and it could refer to anything from a ceviche of lime, conch, sweet peppers and scotch bonnets to grilled grouper with mango, adobo and fried plantains.

grilled or fried grouper sandwich is an obsessive Floridian quest (by the way, the issue of fried versus grilled has been known to provoke fights. Well, not really, but it could), as is finding the creamiest bowl of chowder.

Of course, a huge range of other fish is offered. Popular species include snapper (with dozens of varieties), mahimahi (which is sometimes labeled as dolphin, to the hilarious consternation of many a tourist) and catfish.

Florida really shines when it comes to crustaceans: try pink shrimp and rock shrimp, and don't miss soft-shell blue crab – Florida is well known for its blue-crab hatcheries, making them available fresh year-round. Locals will boil their crabs, as is common across the American South, but a plethora of Northeastern transplants means crabs are also steamed. Try them side by side and determine which method you like better.

Winter (October to April) is the season for Florida spiny lobster and stone crab (out of season both will be frozen). Florida lobster is all tail, without the large claws of its Maine cousin, and stone crab is heavenly sweet, served steamed with butter or the ubiquitous mustard sauce.

Finally, the Keys popularized conch (a giant sea snail); now fished out, most conch is from the Bahamas. It has a slightly rubbery texture and a lovely, savory flavor. From July to September, Steinhatchee is the place for fresh scallops, and in fall/winter, Apalachicola

Bay produces 90% of Florida's small but flavorful oysters.

Southern Cooking

The further north you travel in Florida, the more Southern the cooking gets. This is the sort of cuisine that makes up in fat what it may lack in refinement. 'Meat and three' is Southern restaurant lingo for a main meat – like fried chicken, catfish, barbecued ribs, chicken-fried steak or even chitlins (hog's intestines) – and three sides: perhaps some combination of hush puppies, cheese grits (a sort of cornmeal polenta), cornbread, coleslaw, mashed potatoes, black-eyed peas, collard greens or buttery corn. End with pecan pie, and that's living. Po' boys are Southern hoagies, usually filled with fried nuggets of goodness.

These days, Southern food isn't confined to North Florida. Fancy variations on the theme – haute Southern, if you will – are all the rage from Jacksonville to Key West. A new wave of restaurants across the state has upped Southern American cuisine to white-tablecloth heights. Or not – sometimes, the best Southern chefs embrace the modesty of the roots of their culinary genre, and serve award-winning food in places with cafeteria atmosphere.

Barbecue in the American South isn't just something cooked over an open flame. In fact, open flames are anathema to true American barbecue, which refers to a slow cooking process that involves smoke, smoke, more smoke, spices (sometimes), vinegar (maybe), and another dash of smoke.

Southern Floridian cooking is epitomized by writer Marjorie Kinnan Rawlings' famous cookbook *Cross Creek Cookery*. Near Rawlings' former home, the

SUNSHINE STATE FOOD FESTIVALS

Many of Florida's food festivals have the tumultuous air of a county fair, with carnival rides, music, parades, beauty pageants and any number of wacky, only-in-Florida happenings.

Food Fest! by Joan Steinbacher is the definitive guide; her companion website (www.foodfestguide.com) lists festivals for the coming three months.

Everglades Seafood Festival (p161) Everglades City; three-day weekend, early February. Not just seafood, but gator, frogs legs and snakes, oh my!

Swamp Cabbage Festival (www.swampcabbagefestival.org; La Belle; ☺late Feb) LaBelle; three-day weekend, late February. Armadillo races and crowning of the Miss Swamp Cabbage Queen.

Grant Seafood Festival (☎321-723-8687; www.grantseafoodfestival.com; Grant; ☺early Mar) Grant; two-day weekend, early March. This small Space Coast town throws one of Florida's biggest seafood parties.

Florida Strawberry Festival (www.flstrawberryfestival.com; Plant City; ☺early Mar) Plant City; 11 days, early March. Since 1930, over half a million folks come annually to pluck, eat and honor the mighty berry.

Carnaval Miami (p114) Miami; two weeks, early March. Negotiate drag queens and in-line skaters to reach the Cuban Calle Ocho food booths.

Isle of Eight Flags Shrimp Festival (p366) Amelia Island; three-day weekend, early May. Avast, you scurvy dog! Pirates invade for shrimp and a juried art show.

Palatka Blue Crab Festival (p370) Palatka; four-day Memorial Day weekend. Hosts the state championship for chowder and gumbo. Yes, it's that good.

Florida Seafood Festival (p467) Apalachicola; two days, early November. Stand way, way back at its signature oyster-shucking and -eating contests.

Ribfest (p401) St Petersburg; three days, mid-November. Three words: ribs, rock, Harleys.

Top: Stone crabs

Bottom: Bar lined with *mojitos* on Mallory Square (p191)

Yearling Restaurant is a good place to try Southern Floridian (ie North Florida) food.

Iced tea is so ubiquitous it's called the 'wine of the South,' but watch out for 'sweet tea,' which is an almost entirely different Southern drink – tea so sugary your eyes will cross. You may want to specify that your tea come unsweetened if you don't fancy a trip to the dentist.

Cracker cooking is Florida's rough-and-tumble variation on Southern cuisine, but with more reptiles and amphibians. And you'll find a good deal of Cajun and Creole as well, which mix in spicy gumbos and bisques from Louisiana's nearby swamps.

From Farm (& Grove) to Table

Florida has worked long and hard to become an agricultural powerhouse, and it's famous for its citrus. The state is the nation's largest producer of oranges, grapefruits, tangerines and limes, not to mention mangoes and sugarcane. Scads of bananas, strawberries, coconuts, avocados (once called 'alligator pears'), and the gamut of tropical fruits and vegetables are also grown in Florida. The major agricultural region is around Lake Okeechobee, with field upon field and grove upon grove as far as the eye can see.

With the advent of the USA's locavore, farm-to-table movement, Florida started featuring vegetables in its cooking and promoting its freshness on the plate. Florida's regional highlights – its Southern and Latin American cuisines – do not usually emphasize greens or vegetarianism. But today, most restaurants with upscale or gourmet pretensions promote the local sources of their produce and offer appealing choices for vegetarians as well.

That said, old habits die hard. The further you get outside of places such as Miami, Orlando, Sanibel, Fort Lauderdale, St Petersburg and college towns, the fewer the dedicated vegetarian restaurants. In many rural areas and in parts of North Florida, vegetarians can be forced to choose among iceberg-lettuce salads and pastas.

One indigenous local delicacy is heart of palm, or 'swamp cabbage,' which has a delicate, sweet crunch. The heart of the sabal palm, Florida's state tree, it was a mainstay for Florida pioneers. Try it if you can find it served fresh (don't bother if it's canned; it won't be from Florida).

Libations

Is it the heat or the humidity? With the exception of the occasional teetotaling dry town, Florida's embrace of liquor is prodigious, even epic. And as you ponder this legacy – from Prohibition-era rumrunners, spring-break hedonists and drive-through liquor stores to Ernest Hemingway and Jimmy Buffett – it can seem that quantity trumps quality most of the time.

Don't judge local bars too quickly. Surely Anheuser-Busch's Jacksonville brewery will never go out of business, but Tampa also boasts several handcrafted local microbreweries. Daytona's beaches may be littered with gallon-size hurricane glasses, but Miami mixologists hone their reputations with their designer takes on martinis and *mojitos*.

Indeed, Cuban bartenders became celebrities in the 1920s for what they did with all that sugarcane and citrus: the two classics are the Cuba libre (rum, lime and cola) and the *mojito* (rum, sugar, mint, lemon and club soda), traditionally served with *chicharrónes* (deep-fried pork rinds).

As for Hemingway, he favored piña coladas, lots of them. Jimmy Buffett memorialized the margarita – so that now every sweaty beach bar along the peninsula claims to make the 'best.' Welcome, good friends, to Margaritaville.

Cuban & Latin American Cuisine

Cuban food, once considered 'exotic,' is itself a mix of Caribbean, African and Latin American influences, and in Tampa and Miami it's a staple of everyday life. Sidle up to a Cuban *loncheria* (snack bar) and order a *pan cubano*: a buttered, grilled baguette stuffed with ham, roast pork, cheese, mustard and pickles.

Integral to many Cuban dishes are *mojo* (a garlicky vinaigrette, sprinkled on

FLORIDA SPECIALTIES

From north to south, here's a list of dishes strange and sublime, but 100% Florida; try not to leave without tasting them at least once.

Boiled peanuts In rural North Florida, they take green or immature peanuts and boil them until they're nice and mushy, sometimes spicing them up with Cajun or other seasonings. Sure, they feel weird in the mouth, but they're surprisingly addictive.

Tarpon Springs Greek salad We don't know why, but in Tarpon Springs, Greek restaurants started hiding a dollop of potato salad inside a regulation Greek salad – now you can find this odd combination throughout central Florida.

Alligator Alligator tastes like a cross between fish and pork. It's healthier than chicken, with as much protein but half the fat, fewer calories and less cholesterol. The meat comes from the tail, and is usually served as deep-fried nuggets, which overwhelms the delicate flavor and can make it chewy. Try it grilled. Most alligator is legally harvested on farms and it is often sold in grocery stores.

Frogs legs Those who know say the 'best' legs come from the Everglades; definitely ask, since you want to avoid imported ones from India, which are smaller and disparaged as 'flavorless.' Good frogs legs taste, honestly, like chicken, but with a more fishy texture.

Peel-and-eat shrimp A decidedly old-school, Old Florida treat, peel-and-eat shrimp are served boiled and pink in their shells. There's an art to ripping off the legs and stripping down the shells to get to the sweet meat underneath, which is inevitably overwhelmed by a nice dunk in cocktail sauce.

Stone crabs The first recycled crustacean: only one claw is taken from a stone crab – the rest is tossed back into the sea (the claw regrows in 12 to 18 months, and crabs plucked again are called 'retreads'). We know this could be read as a sad metaphor for the futility of our mortal condition, but that claw meat really is good. The claws are so perishable that they're always cooked before selling. October through April is less a 'season' than a stone-crab frenzy. Joe Weiss of Miami Beach is credited with starting it all.

Key lime pie Key limes are yellow, and that's the color of an authentic key lime pie, which is a custard of key lime juice, sweetened condensed milk and egg yolks in a cracker crust, topped with meringue. Avoid any slice that's green or stands ramrod straight.

---

sandwiches), adobo (a meat marinade of garlic, salt, cumin, oregano and sour orange juice) and *sofrito* (a stew-starter mix of garlic, onion and chili peppers). Cuban food may seem foreign and strange, but it's actually quite accessible to even the most conservative palate; this is basically meat-and-starch cuisine, with an emphasis on huge portions. Main-course meats are typically accompanied by rice and beans, and fried plantains.

With its large number of Central and Latin American immigrants, the Miami area offers plenty of authentic ethnic eateries. Seek out Haitian *griot* (marinated fried pork), Jamaican jerk chicken, Brazilian barbecue, Central American *gallo pinto*

(red beans and rice) and Nicaraguan *tres leches* ('three milks' cake).

In the morning, try a Cuban coffee, also known as *café Cubano* or *cortadito*. This hot shot of liquid gold is essentially sweetened espresso, while *café con leche* is just *café au lait* with a different accent: equal parts coffee and hot milk.

Another Cuban treat is *guarapo,* or fresh-squeezed sugarcane juice. Cuban snack bars serve the greenish liquid straight or poured over crushed ice, and it's essential to an authentic *mojito*. It also sometimes finds its way into *batidos,* a milky, refreshing Latin American fruit smoothie.

Plan Your Trip
Travel with Children

The Sunshine State makes it so easy for families to have a good time that many return year after sandy, sunburned year. But with so many beaches, theme parks and kid-perfect destinations and activities, the challenge is deciding exactly where to go and what to do.

Best Regions for Kids

Orlando
A spinning wheel of theme-park fun and oodles of family entertainment beyond the gates.

Tampa Bay & Gulf Coast
Great zoos, aquariums and museums, plus some of Florida's prettiest, most family-friendly beaches and alluring island getaways.

Florida Keys
Snorkeling, diving, fishing, boating and an all-around no-worries vibe.

Space Coast (Hwy A1A)
World-class surfing, nature preserves and sleepy beach towns combine with vintage airplanes and all-things-space to make this 75-mile stretch of barrier islands a favorite.

Emerald Coast
The Panhandle coastline has stunningly white sand beaches, crystal water and pockets of frenetic boardwalk amusements.

Miami
Kid-focused zoos and museums, but also Miami itself, one of the USA's great multicultural cities.

Florida for Kids

Kids love Florida. And what's not to like? Sandcastles and waves, dolphins and alligators, Cinderella and Harry Potter. There are the classics and the don't misses, the obvious and the cliché, but just as memorable – and often far less stressful and less expensive – are the distinctly Floridian under-the-radar discoveries. Roadside attractions, mom-and-pop animal rescues, intimate wildlife expeditions, street festivals and more...and when you've had enough, there's plenty of opportunities to do a whole lot of nothing in the sun.

Theme Parks

The self-contained resort complexes of Walt Disney World® and Universal Orlando Resort offer multiple theme and water parks, on-site hotels and transportation systems, and just beyond their gates you'll find Legoland. The only big-hitter theme park beyond Orlando is Busch Gardens.

Beaches

While the prototypical Florida family beach is fronted by crowded commercial centers, you'll find loads of beaches that echo that quintessential Old Florida feel. Many are protected in state parks, wildlife preserves and island sanctuaries, and there are pockets of road-trip-perfect coastline, with mile upon mile of beautiful emptiness dotted with flip-flop-friendly low-rise towns. There's a distinct difference between Gulf and Atlantic beaches – many find the shallows and gentle surf of the Gulf perfect for kids, but Atlantic beaches often lie on barrier islands that are flanked by calm-water rivers and inlets to the west. Currents can be dangerously strong along both coasts; always pay attention to rip-tide warnings.

Zoos & Museums

Up-close animal encounters have long been a Florida tourist staple. The state has some of the best zoos and aquariums in the country, as well as all kinds of small-scale jewels and Old Florida favorites that offer hands-on interactions and quirky shows. Florida's cities also have top-quality children's museums, and art museums and centers throughout the state almost always offer excellent kids' programs.

Getting into Nature

It's easy to get out into nature in Florida – there are wilderness preserves and state parks up and down the state, and you don't have to drive far, hike long or paddle hard to get away from it all. The best part is, once you get there, you're almost guaranteed to see some pretty cool critters.

Florida is exceedingly flat, so rivers and trails are frequently ideal for short legs and little arms. Placid rivers and intercoastal bays are custom-made for first-time paddlers, and often are so shallow and calm you can just peek over the boat and see all kinds of marine life. Never snorkeled a coral reef or surfed? Florida has gentle places to learn. Book a sea-life cruise, a manatee swim or nesting-sea-turtle watch, or stroll along raised boardwalks through alligator-filled swamps, perfect for pint-size adventurers.

Children's Highlights

Believe it or not, these extensive highlights merely cherry-pick the best of the best.

Family Beach Towns
On the Atlantic

St Augustine (p348) Pirates, forts, jails and reenactors.

Cocoa Beach (p328) Surfing rattle-and-hum energy along the Atlantic with lessons for kids and enjoy easy access to lovely Banana River kayaking.

Vero Beach (p242) Carefully zoned with grassy parks, a pedestrian-friendly downtown and wide, life-guarded beaches.

Indialantic (p337) Flip-flop Old Florida beach life with a boho vibe.

Lauderdale-by-the-Sea (p216) Less snooty than towns just south; great butterfly park.

Stuart (p239) For outdoors-eager families, with getaway beaches and a Smithsonian Marine Station on Hutchinson Island.

Amelia Island (p365) Easygoing and upscale.

On the Gulf

Anna Maria Island (p422) Old Florida, with a low-rise beachfront, independent hotels and a historic fishing pier.

Florida Keys (p171) The whole island chain brims with activities for all ages; be sure to check out the street performances at Key West's Mallory Sq.

Naples (p435) Upscale downtown bustles each evening; easy access to miles of beautiful wide beaches.

Sanibel Island (p431) Bike, kayak and shell the days away; undeveloped beaches but no pedestrian-friendly downtown.

Siesta Key (p422) Crescent of soft white sand, plenty of activities and a lively village scene at night.

Fort Myers Beach (p429) Party atmosphere, lots to do, yet quieter beaches just south (we like Lovers Key State Park).

Gasparilla Island (p439) Intimate, easy and blissfully free of high-rises and chain restaurants and hotels; ditch the car and toot around in a golf cart.

St Pete Beach (p406) Activity-filled social epicenter of Tampa Bay area.

Pensacola Beach (p452) Mix of unspoiled strands and low-key tourist center.

South Walton (p458) Family-perfect Panhandle beauty.

Apalachicola (p466) Tiny historic fishing town on Apalachicola Bay; close to excellent beachside state parks.

Zoos

Lowry Park Zoo (p386) Tampa; fantastic zoo with up-close encounters.

Homosassa Springs Wildlife State Park (p412) Gulf Coast, 70 miles north of Tampa; Old Florida don't-miss staple emphasizing Florida wildlife; underwater manatee observatory.

Zoo Miami (p105) Extensive, with all the big-ticket species.

Monkey Jungle (p107) Miami; the tagline 'Where humans are caged and monkeys run wild' says it all. Unforgettable classic, opened in 1933; don't miss the wild monkey swimming pool.

Jungle Island (p92) Miami; tropical birds and exotic species such as the liger, a tiger-and-lion crossbreed.

Lion Country Safari (p231) West Palm Beach; an enormous drive-through safari park and rehabilitation center.

Brevard Zoo (p335) Melbourne, on the Space Coast; little old-school favorite; feed giraffes and lorikeets.

Nature Centers, Wildlife Preserves & Parks

Everglades National Park (p156) Don't miss the Anhinga Trail, an easy boardwalk past alligators and beautiful birds; for family-friendly kayaking, head to Everglades City and Flamingo centers.

Marjory Stoneman Douglas Biscayne Nature Center (p105) Key Biscayne; kid-friendly intro to subtropical South Florida.

Environmental Learning Center (p242) Vero Beach; Florida ecosystems and touch-tanks.

Loggerhead Marinelife Center (p242) Juno Beach, 18 miles north of West Palm Beach; excellent little turtle rescue and rehabilitation center with children's programs.

McCarthy's Wildlife Sanctuary (p230) West Palm Beach; first-rate animal rescue featuring endangered animals and discarded exotic pets in botanical surrounds and up-close interactions.

Florida Keys Eco-Discovery Center (p191) Key West; entertaining displays pull together Florida Keys ecology.

JN 'Ding' Darling National Wildlife Refuge (p431) Sanibel Island; easy tram tours and the park's education center is tops.

Nancy Forrester's Secret Garden (p191) Key West; intimate labor-of-love parrot rescue and rehab sanctuary in a private garden, with education, bird interaction and storytelling.

Naples Botanical Garden (p435) Designed especially with kids in mind.

Wildlife Encounters on Land

National Key Deer Refuge (p185) Big Pine Key, Florida Keys; kids love spotting these cute-as-Bambi mini deer.

Bill Baggs Cape Florida State Park (p104) Key Biscayne; accessible island-ecology walk.

John D Macarthur State Park (p237) West Palm Beach; ranger-led sea-turtle watches, beautiful beaches, calm-water kayaking.

Corkscrew Swamp Sanctuary (p438) Thirty miles northeast of Naples; maybe the most diverse and rewarding swampy boardwalk trail.

Myakka River State Park (p420) Sarasota; tram and air-boat tours, canoeing, short hikes and hundreds of alligators.

Six Mile Cypress Slough Preserve (p428) Fort Myers; another ideal, shady boardwalk trail often packed with wildlife.

Paynes Prairie Preserve State Park (p381) Gainesville; hiking trails through prairies, woods and wetlands, with alligators, armadillos and more.

Leon Sinks Geological Area (p479) Tallahassee; bizarre sinkhole terrain is bound to make an impression.

St George Island State Park (p469) Apalachicola; loggerhead nesting.

Merritt Island National Wildlife Refuge (p325) Cocoa Beach; Black Point Wildlife Dr and excellent visitors center.

Butterfly World (p217) Coconut Creek, outside Lauderdale-by-the-Sea; sanctuary of butterflies and exotic birds.

Wildlife Encounters by Water

Biscayne National Park (p169) Homestead, 30 miles south of Miami; glass-bottom boat tours, snorkeling over an epic reef.

John Pennekamp Coral Reef State Park (p174) Key Largo, Florida Keys; great coral reefs, by snorkel or glass-bottom boat tour.

Loxahatchee River (p238) Jupiter, 20 miles north of West Palm Beach; one of Florida's two National Wild and Scenic Rivers, this placid 8-mile river is great for kayaking and canoeing.

Canaveral National Seashore (p326) Titusville, 35 miles south of Daytona; easy paddling on the

Top: Anhinga Trail
(p167), Everglades
National Park

Bottom: Zoo Miami
(p105)

Indian River and sea-turtle watches along 24 miles of undeveloped Atlantic Coast beaches.

Crystal River National Wildlife Refuge (p413) 80 miles north of Tampa; legendary manatee spot where you can boat and swim among them.

Ichetucknee Springs State Park (p382) Fort White, 37 miles northwest of Gainesville; inner-tube along crystal-clear slow-moving water with manatees, otters and turtles.

Blue Spring State Park (p375) DeLand, 35 miles north of Orlando; canoe and cruise among manatees.

Suwannee River State Park (p477) 75 miles east of Tallahassee; great muddy river dotted with crystal-clear springs for swimming.

Dolphin Study (p440) Naples; dolphin-spotting ecotours.

Fin Expeditions (p328) Cocoa Beach; kayak through the mangroves with small-group nature tours tailor-made for kids.

Children's Museums

Glazer Children's Museum (p387) Tampa; charming interactive extravaganza.

Museum of Science & Industry (p387) Tampa; huge hands-on science fun, with an IMAX and a planetarium.

Miami Children's Museum (p91) Extensive role-playing environments.

Golisano Children's Museum of Naples (p436) Modern facility geared toward kids under eight.

Planning

If you're a parent, you already know that fortune favors the prepared. In Florida's crazy-crowded, overbooked high-season tourist spots, a little bit of planning can make all the difference. Sort out where to go, where to stay, and a few pillars of plans to hang the trip on in advance – book that manatee cruise, schedule a day at the Kennedy Space Center, reserve a character-meal at Disney, but always check about cancellation policies. Once there, it may turn out that all anyone wants to do is play in the sun and sand.

Resorts & Hotels

The vast majority of Florida hotels stand ready to aid families. They have cribs, roll-away beds and sleeper-sofas, suites and adjoining rooms, refrigerators and micro-waves, and most do not charge extra for kids under 18. Most full-service resorts offer children's programs, including beach walks, art activities and educational workshops exploring Florida sea life, and at theme-park hotels in Orlando you'll find poolside screenings of family-friendly movies.

What to Bring

Pack light rain gear, a snuggly fleece (for air-conditioning and cool nights), water sandals (for beaches, fountains and water parks), mosquito repellent and a simple first-aid kit with band-aids, antibiotic

---

FLORIDA-THEMED BOOKS FOR KIDS

Get kids in a Florida mood with these great books.

➡ *Hoot* (Carl Hiaasen) Zany characters, snappy plot twists and an environmental message.

➡ *Because of Winn-Dixie* (Kate DiCamillo) Heartwarming coming-of-age tale about a 10-year-old girl adjusting to her new life in Florida.

➡ *The Yearling* (Marjorie Kinnan Rawlings) Pulitzer Prize–winning tear-jerking classic about a boy who adopts an orphaned fawn in Florida's backwoods.

➡ *The Treasure of Amelia Island* (MC Finotti) Spanish-ruled Florida through the eyes of an 11-year-old.

➡ *Bad Latitude* (David Ebright) Unabashed pirate adventure.

➡ *Suzanne Tate's Nature Series* More than 30 paperback picture books on south-eastern USA sea animals; there's *Oozey Octopus: A Tale of a Clever Critter*, *Tammy Turtle: A Tale of Saving Sea Turtles*, *Rosie Ray: A Tale of Watery Wings* and more.

cream, tweezers (for splinters), anti-itch cream, children's paracetemol and Vaseline (perfect for little faces after too much sun and wind). If you have infants, a pack-and-play can be helpful, especially if you're road-tripping or sticking to amenity-poor, budget-range motels.

Most importantly, bring and use sunscreen. We've tried them all, from thick white goos that never seem to rub in to fancy stuff from the cosmetic aisle, and our hands-down favorite is the made-in-Florida Sun Bum and their naturally sourced Baby Bum line.

Florida car-seat laws require that children must be in a rear-facing car-seat until they are 20lb and one year old, a separate or integrated child-safety seat until five, and a booster until the seat-belts fit properly (over 4ft 9in and 80lb). Rental-car companies are legally required to provide child seats, but only if you reserve them in advance. Avoid surprises by bringing your own.

Don't sweat it if you forget something. Except for your child's can't-sleep-without stuffed elephant and favorite blanket, you'll be able to find anything you need in Florida.

Hiring Baby Gear

If you prefer to travel light and save the hassle of lugging loads of essentials, several services offer baby-gear rental (cribs, strollers, car seats etc) and infant supplies (diapers, baby food etc), all delivered to your hotel; some deliver to the airport.

Babies Travel Lite (www.babiestravellite.com)

Jet Set Babies (www.jetsetbabies.com)

Traveling Baby Company (www.travelingbabyco.com)

Babysitting & Childcare Centers

Traveling with children doesn't necessarily mean doing *everything* as a family. Several childcare services, including Sunshine Babysitting (www.sunshine babysitting.com), the Babysitting Company (www.thebabysittingcompany.com) and the Disney- and Universal-recommended Kid's Nite Out (p253), offer in-hotel babysitting by certified sitters, and full-service resorts often have childcare centers, organized kids' camps and local sitter recommendations. At Walt Disney World®, you don't need to be a resort guest to reserve a spot at a Disney's Children Activity Center (p253); five centers, located at resort hotels, welcome kids aged three to 12.

Regions at a Glance

Miami

**Museums
Nightlife
Food**

Museums & the Arts

The city og Miami is something of a real-time performance-art piece. There are the major cultural institutions as well as vibrant gallery districts such as Wynwood and architectural masterpieces such as South Beach's deco district.

Miami's Vice

Mix indulgence and a love of beauty, youth and good times, and you get the Miami nightlife cocktail. It's not all glam drag shows and bottle service: authentic Cuban dance halls and grotty dive bars keep things real, while artsy bars and bohemian lounges are peppered throughout.

Ethnic & Gourmet

Miami offers an ideal gastronomic mix of wealth, immigrants and agricultural abundance. Celebrity-chef-driven eateries dot Miami Beach and Coral Gables, and they're balanced out by hole-in-the-wall ethnic eateries that'll leave you wanting more.

p64

The Everglades

**Wildlife-
Watching
Activities
Old Florida**

Find the Fauna

There are 1.5 million alligators in Florida, and in the Everglades, sometimes nearly half of them seem to be within 100 yards. The Everglades can turn anyone into an amateur birder: over 350 species call the swamps home.

Outdoor Adventures

Even a ramble along raised wooden boardwalks can feel like an adventure. Jump into a kayak and be swallowed by watery wilderness for an experience of a lifetime.

Roadside Attractions

Bizarre food, legends of mythical beasts, offbeat roadside stands, monuments to scorned love? Yep, all these and then some pepper the land here, which marches to its own quirky beat.

p153

Florida Keys & Key West

**Activities
Beaches
Nightlife**

Islands & Outdoors

People come to the Keys to do stuff: fish, snorkel, dive, kayak, hike, bike, fish some more, snorkel again, feed tarpon, spot Key deer, hell, let's fish again. North America's best coral reefs provide brag-worthy expeditions.

Mangroves & Sand

Except for Bahia Honda, which often makes 'best beach' lists, Keys beaches aren't as perfect as elsewhere, yet they provide all one needs: a comfortable place to sleep off the night before.

Crazy Key West

No nightlife scene in Florida matches Key West's mix of off-beat craziness, self-conscious performance and gay humor. Hemingway found his perfect bar at the end of the world here; maybe you can too.

p171

Southeast Florida

Beaches
Activities
Entertainment

Buttery Beaches

With monikers such as the Gold Coast and the Treasure Coast, you know where the money's at. Some of these towns are so wealthy it's practically obscene. Do they take care of their beaches? Very well, thank you very much.

Sightseeing

Canal and gondola tours around Fort Lauderdale, river trips on the Loxahatchee, epic wreck diving, snorkeling Spanish galleons, good surfing, sportfishing charters, turtle watches: your menu is full!

Waterfront Fun

Southeast beach towns are just good fun, whether people-watching on Hollywood Broadwalk, partying in Fort Lauderdale, chilling out in Jupiter or gaping at the mansions of Palm Beach.

p203

Orlando & Walt Disney World®

Theme Parks
Entertainment
Activities

Magic Kingdoms

If theme parks are worlds, then Orlando contains a veritable galaxy. Walt Disney World® is a solar system of amusements; Universal Orlando Resort may be smaller but it's equally entertaining.

Family Parties

Start with Disney, which packs evenings with a magical light parade and Cirque du Soleil, or head to Universal, which dishes up a luau and the Blue Man Group. Orlando is rife with bars, movies and music.

Outdoor Exploring

In and around Orlando are plentiful opportunities to bike, golf, kayak, go river tubing and even 'skydive' indoors, not to mention the water play at park resorts.

p245

The Space Coast

Activities
Beaches
History

Surfing & Kayaking

Surfing and kayaking are the Space Coast's unbeatable one-two punch, and when it comes to the former, Cocoa Beach is the scene's epicenter. The wildlife to see among the protected, unspoiled lagoons and intercoastal waterways includes manatees, dolphins and more.

Cosmic Coast

Space Coast beaches are truly swell, with a relaxed and low-key vibe that you'll rarely find to the north or south. Seek out cute Vero Beach and escape on beautiful Apollo Beach.

Kennedy Space Center

The shuttle launches may have ended, but the space center is still a top-notch, immersive experience that throws you into the US space program and the life of an astronaut.

p322

Northeast Florida

Activities
Old Florida
Quirky Sunshine

Outdoor Adventures

Ocala National Forest beckons with a wealth of hikes, crystal springs and tons of camping. The region's interior state parks are all prime, and there's splendid kayaking among northeast waterways.

Old & Oldest Florida

Old Florida is found in places like Cross Creek, where Cracker life is preserved in Marjorie Kinnan Rawlings Historic State Park. 'Oldest' Florida means St Augustine, a splendid time warp back to the days of explorers and real pirates.

Sun & Sand

For a maritime getaway, choose Amelia Island, with its pirate parties and shrimp festivals. Or head to Cassadaga, to have your fortune read in a town full of spiritualists.

p340

Tampa Bay & Southwest Florida

Beaches
Food
Museums

Gulf Breezes

The Gulf Coast from Tampa south enjoys some of Florida's best white-sand beaches. There's too much choice, but Siesta Key, Fort Myers Beach, Honeymoon Island, Naples, Fort DeSoto and Sanibel are all great.

Coastal Cuisine

Tampa has a big-city foodie scene, with several gourmet destinations, and St Petersburg is no slouch. The sophisticated towns of Sarasota, Naples and Sanibel also provide excellent cuisine.

Arts & Culture

The region has two of Florida's best museums – the Salvador Dalí Museum and the Ringling Museum complex – and each are worth seeing. Sophisticated art and cultural institutions are highlights in the region's cities, too.

p384

The Panhandle

Beaches
Activities
Entertainment

Country Coast

The Panhandle, dubbed the 'Redneck Riviera,' could just as easily be called 'pristine snow-white sands lapped by gentle emerald waters.' The beaches are beautiful, and the sometimes-raucous beach towns can be sought out or avoided as you wish.

Springs & Sinkholes

Kayaking around Cedar Key is wonderful, and canoeing the Suwannee River is classic Florida. There's snorkeling and diving in crystal springs, and hiking and biking in the Apalachicola National Forest.

Beaches & Blues

Enjoy the blues clubs of Tallahassee, the boutique beach experience of South Walton and the glass-bottom boat tours of Wakulla Springs State Park.

p442

On the Road

The Panhandle
p442

Northeast
Florida
p340

Orlando &
Walt Disney
World®
p245

Tampa Bay &
Southwest Florida
p384

The Space
Coast
p322

Southeast
Florida
p203

The
Everglades   Miami
p153   p64

Florida Keys
& Key West
p171

Miami

POP 509,000 / 📞 305, 786

Best Places to Eat

➡ Kyu (p134)

➡ 27 Restaurant (p130)

➡ Yardbird (p128)

➡ El Carajo (p136)

Best Places to Sleep

➡ Biltmore Hotel (p125)

➡ Washington Park Hotel (p118)

➡ Langford Hotel (p123)

➡ Betsy Hotel (p119)

➡ Freehand Miami (p122)

➡ EAST, Miami (p123)

Why Go?

Miami has so many different facets to its diverse neighborhoods that it's hard to believe it all fits in one place. By day you can admire incredible photorealistic murals in Wynwood, then spend the evening immersed in Afro Cuban jazz in Little Havana, followed perhaps by rooftop drinks atop the city's latest skyscraper.

Crossing town you can't help feeling like you've passed into another city. Over in Miami Beach, you can wander the streets amid a veritable gallery of deco masterpieces, each one bursting with personality, best followed by late-afternoon strolls along the sands, when the golden light is mesmerizing.

When to Go
Miami

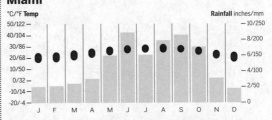

Dec–Mar Warm, dry weather draws in tourists; lots of festivals and events.

Apr–Jun Not as muggy as deep summer, but lusher and greener than winter.

Jul–Oct Prices plummet. When it's not as hot as an oven, there are storms: it's hurricane season.

◉ Sights

◉ South Beach

The most iconic neighborhood in Greater Miami, South Beach is a vertiginous landscape of sparkling beach, beautiful art-deco architecture, high-end boutiques and buzzing bars and restaurants. South Beach has its glamour, but there's more to this district than just velvet ropes and high-priced lodging. You'll find some great down-to-earth bars, good ethnic eating and excellent museums.

★ Wolfsonian-FIU   MUSEUM

(Map p82; ☑ 305-531-1001; www.wolfsonian.org; 1001 Washington Ave; adult/child $10/5, free from 6-9pm Fri; ⊘ 10am-6pm Mon, Tue, Thu & Sat, to 9pm Fri, noon-6pm Sun, closed Wed) Visit this excellent design museum early in your stay to put the aesthetics of Miami Beach into context. It's one thing to see how wealth, leisure and the pursuit of beauty manifests in Miami Beach, but it's another to understand the roots and shadings of local artistic movements. By chronicling the interior evolution of everyday life, the Wolfsonian reveals how these trends were architecturally manifested in SoBe's exterior deco.

Which reminds us of the Wolfsonian's own noteworthy facade. Remember the Gothic-futurist apartment-complex-cum-temple-of-evil in *Ghostbusters*? Well, this imposing structure, with its grandiose 'frozen fountain' and lion-head-studded grand elevator, could serve as a stand-in for that set.

Art Deco Historic District   AREA

(Map p78; Ocean Dr) The world-famous art-deco district of Miami Beach is pure exuberance: an architecture of bold lines, whimsical tropical motifs and a color palette that evokes all the beauty of the Miami landscape. Among the 800 deco buildings listed on the National Register of Historic Buildings, each design is different, and it's hard not to be captivated when strolling among these restored beauties from a bygone era.

One stretch of Ocean Dr has a collection of some of the most striking art-deco buildings in Miami Beach. Between 11th and 14th Sts, you'll see some of the classic deco elements at play in beautifully designed works – each bursting with individual personality. Close to 11th St, the Congress Hotel (p81) shows perfect symmetry in its three-story facade, with window-shading eyebrows and a long marquee down the middle that's reminiscent of the grand movie palaces of the 1930s. About a block north, the **Tides** (Map p78; ☑ 305-250-0784; www.tidessouthbeach.com; 1220 Ocean Dr; r from $340; [P][❄][🛜][🏊]) is one of the finest of the nautical themed hotels, with porthole windows over the entryway, a reception desk of Key limestone (itself imprinted with fossilized sea creatures), and curious arrows on the floor, meant to denote the ebb and flow of the tide. Near 13th St, the Cavalier (p117) plays with the seahorse theme, in stylized depictions of the sea creature and also has palm-tree-like iconography.

Note that it's best to go early in the day when the crowds are thinnest, and the light is best for picture-taking. For deeper insight into the architecture, take a guided walking tour of the area offered daily by the Miami Design Preservation League (p112).

SoundScape Park   PARK

(Map p78; www.nws.edu; 500 17th St) Outside of the New World Center (p68), this park is one of the best places for open-air screenings in Miami Beach. During some New World Symphony performances, the outside wall of the Frank Gehry–designed concert hall features a 7000-sq-ft projection of the concert within.

In addition from October through May, you can watch movies, with weekly film screenings (currently Wednesdays) at 8pm. Bring a picnic and enjoy the free show.

Art Deco Museum   MUSEUM

(Map p82; www.mdpl.org/welcome-center/art-deco-museum; 1001 Ocean Dr; $5; ⊘ 10am-5pm Tue-Sun, to 7pm Thu) This small museum is one of the best places in town for an enlightening overview of the art-deco district. Through videos, photography, models and other displays you'll learn of the pioneering work of Barbara Capitman, who helped save these buildings from certain destruction back in the 1970s, and her collaboration with Leonard Horowitz, the talented artist who designed the pastel color palette that become an integral part of the design visible today.

The museum also touches on other key architectural styles in Miami, including Mediterranean Revival (typefied by the Villa Casa Casuarina; p120) and the post-deco boom of MiMo (Miami Modern), which emerged after World War II, and is particularly prevalent in North Miami Beach.

South Beach   BEACH

(Map p78; Ocean Dr; ⊘ beach 5am-midnight) When most people think of Miami Beach, they're envisioning South Beach, or 'SoBe.' This area is

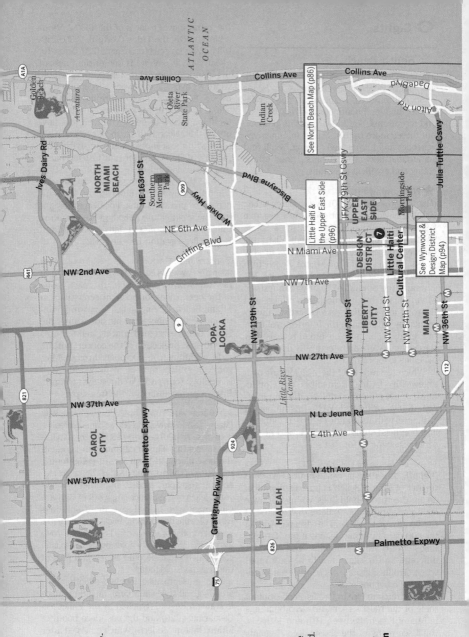

Miami Highlights

1 Art Deco Historic District
(p65) Taking an early-morning stroll along Ocean Dr, seeing South Beach's art-deco beauties.

2 Pérez Art Museum Miami
(p85) Checking out the latest contemporary show and wandering the waterfront sculpture garden.

3 Wynwood Walls
(p92) Checking out the stunning collection of colorful outdoor murals at the epicenter of Wynwood.

4 South Beach
(p65) Sitting on the sands and taking in the colorful blend of peoples and cultures.

5 Vizcaya Museum & Gardens (p98)
Marveling at the collection of art and antiquities, followed

ATLANTIC OCEAN

Golden Beach

Aventura

Collins Ave

Oleta River State Park

Indian Creek

See North Beach Map (p86)

Collins Ave

DadeBlvd

Alton Rd

Ives Dairy Rd

NORTH MIAMI BEACH

NE 163rd St

Southern Memorial Park

909

NE 6th Ave

Griffing Blvd

W Dixie Hwy

Biscayne Blvd

JFK/79th St Cswy

Little Haiti & the Upper East Side (p96)

UPPER EAST SIDE

Morningside Park

Julia Tuttle Cswy

N Miami Ave

DESIGN DISTRICT

Little Haiti Cultural Center

7

See Wynwood & Design District Map (p94)

NW 2nd Ave

NW 7th Ave

NW 79th St

LIBERTY CITY

NW 62nd St

NW 54th St

MIAMI

NW 36th St

OPA-LOCKA

NW 119th St

NW 27th Ave

Little River Canal

N Le Jeune Rd

E 4th Ave

W 4th Ave

Palmetto Expwy

826

112

Palmetto Expwy

821

441

9

924

CAROL CITY

NW 37th Ave

NW 57th Ave

Gratigny Pkwy

75

HIALEAH

A1A

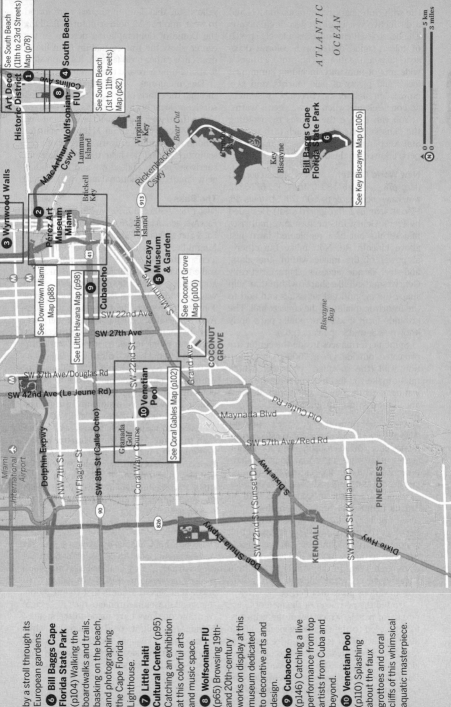

by a stroll through its European gardens.

6 Bill Baggs Cape Florida State Park (p104) Walking the boardwalks and trails, basking on the beach, and photographing the Cape Florida Lighthouse.

7 Little Haiti Cultural Center (p95) Catching an exhibition at this colorful arts and music space.

8 Wolfsonian-FIU (p65) Browsing 19th- and 20th-century works on display at this museum dedicated to decorative arts and design.

9 Cubaocho (p146) Catching a live performance from top artists from Cuba and beyond.

10 Venetian Pool (p110) Splashing about the faux grottoes and coral cliffs of this whimsical aquatic masterpiece.

rife with clubs, bars, restaurants, models and a distinctive veneer of art-deco architecture. The beach itself encompasses a lovely stretch of golden sands, dotted with colorful deco-style lifeguard stations. The shore gathers a wide mix of humanity, including suntanned locals and plenty of pale tourists, and gets crowded in high season (December to March) and on weekends when the weather is warm.

You can escape the masses by avoiding the densest parts of the beach (5th to 15th Sts). Keep in mind that there's no alcohol (or pets) allowed on the beach.

New World Center
NOTABLE BUILDING

(Map p78; ☑305-673-3330, tours 305-673-3331; www.newworldcenter.com; 500 17th St; tours $5; ⊙tours 4pm Tue & Thu, 1pm Fri & Sat) Designed by Frank Gehry, this performance hall rises majestically out of a manicured lawn just above Lincoln Rd. Not unlike the ethereal power of the music within, the glass-and-steel facade encases characteristically Gehry-esque sail-like shapes within that help shape the magnificent acoustics and add to the futuristic quality of the concert hall. The grounds form a 2½-acre public park aptly known as SoundScape Park (p65).

Some performances inside the center are projected outside via a 7000-sq-ft projection wall (the so-called 'Wallcast'), which might make you feel like you're in the classiest open-air theater on the planet. Reserve ahead for a 35-minute guided tour.

Holocaust Memorial
MEMORIAL

(Map p78; www.holocaustmmb.org; cnr Meridian Ave & Dade Blvd; ⊙9:30am-10pm) Even for a Holocaust piece, this memorial is particularly powerful. With over 100 sculptures, its centerpiece is the *Sculpture of Love and Anguish*, an enormous, oxidized bronze arm with an artistic patina that bears an Auschwitz tattooed number – chosen because it was never issued at the camp, in order to represent all prisoners. Terrified families scale the sides of the arm, trying to pass their loved ones, including children, to safety only to see them later massacred, while below lie figures of all ages in various poses of suffering.

Around the perimeter of the memorial are dozens of panels, which detail the grim history that led to the greatest genocide of the 20th century. This is followed by names of many who perished. The memorial doesn't gloss over the past. The light from a Star of David is blotted by the racist label of *Jude* (the German word for 'Jew'); representative of the yellow star that Jews in ghettos were forced to wear, and two Menora sculptures, flanking the Dome of Contemplation descent to the center, show the transformation from life to death in a rather lurid fashion. It's impossible to spend time here and not be moved.

The memorial was completed in 1990 through the efforts of Miami Beach Holocaust survivors, local business leaders and sculptor Kenneth Treister. Download the excellent free app (Holocaust Memorial Miami Beach) for iPhone or Android to learn more about the sculpture as well as hear testimonials from survivors, peruse slideshows and view interactive maps and additional audio and video.

The Bass
MUSEUM

(Map p78; ☑305-673-7530; www.thebass.org; 2121 Park Ave; adult/child $8/6; ⊙noon-5pm Wed & Thu, Sat & Sun, to 9pm Fri) The best art museum in Miami Beach has a playfully futuristic facade, a crisp interplay of lines and a bright, white-walled space – like an Orthodox church on a space-age Greek isle. All designed, by the way, in 1930 by Russell Pancoast (grandson of John A Collins, who lent his name to Collins Ave). The collection isn't shabby either: permanent highlights range from 16th-century European religious works to northern European and Renaissance paintings.

The Bass recently had a $12-million renovation that added 50% more space to its layout. There are three new galleries, a Creativity Center, a new museum store and a cafe. The Bass also rebranded itself – officially adopting the informal name locals always used rather than the more formal 'Bass Museum of Art.' The museum forms one point of the Collins Park Cultural Center triangle, which also includes the three-story Miami City Ballet (p145) and the lovingly inviting Miami Beach Regional Library, which is a great place for free wi-fi.

Jewish Museum of Florida-FIU
MUSEUM

(Map p82; ☑305-672-5044; www.jmof.fiu.edu; 301 Washington Ave; adult/student & senior $6/5, Sat admission free; ⊙10am-5pm Tue-Sun, closed Jewish holidays) Housed in a 1936 Orthodox synagogue that served Miami's first congregation, this small museum chronicles the rather large contribution Jews have made to the state of Florida. After all, it could be said that while Cubans made Miami, Jews made Miami Beach, both physically and culturally. Yet there were times when Jews were barred from

(Continued on p77)

GLOWIMAGES/GETTY IMAGES ©

Art-Deco Miami

South Beach may be known for celebrity spotting, but the area's original cachet owes less to paparazzi and more to preservation. The art-deco design movement, the architectural and aesthetic backbone of SoBe, is powerfully distinctive and finds expression in soft lines, bright pastels and the integration of neon into structural facades.

Contents

Above Detail of a carved art-deco wall, Miami

1. Cardozo Hotel **2.** Lifeguard station on South Beach **3.** Essex House Hotel

Classical Deco South Beach Structures

In the past, South Beach architects distinguished themselves through decorative finials, parapets and neon signage. Miami Beach deco relies on 'stepped-back' facades to disrupt the harsh, flat Florida light. Cantilevered 'eyebrows' jut out above windows to protect interiors from the sun.

Cardozo Hotel (p81)

This lovely building and the Carlyle Hotel were the first buildings rescued by the original Miami Beach preservation league when developers threatened to raze South Beach's deco buildings in the 1980s. With its two hubcap-like emblems on the upper facade and its sleek curves, the Cardozo has been compared to the 1937 Studebaker. Owned by Gloria Estefan.

Essex House Hotel (p121)

Porthole windows lend the feel of a grand cruise ship, while its spire looks like a rocket ship, recalling deco's roots as an aesthetic complement to modernism and industrialism. Beautiful terrazzo floors also cool the lobby.

Deco lifeguard stations on South Beach (p65)

Besides being cubist-inspired exemplars of the classical deco movement, with their sharp, pleasing geometric lines, these stations are painted in dazzling colors. Found all along the beach from 1st to 17th Sts.

Post Office (p77)

This striking building has a round facade and a lighthouse-like cupola. Above the door is the characteristic deco stripe of glass blocks. Step inside for a glimpse of geometrically laid-out post boxes (painted gold) and a fantastical ceiling with an elaborate sunlike deco light fixture orbited by stars.

Deco Elements & Embellishments

As individualized as South Beach's buildings are, they share quirks and construction strategies. Canopy porches provide cool places to sit. To reflect heat, buildings were originally painted white (and later in pastels) with accent colors highlighting smaller elements. Some hotels resemble Mesoamerican temples; others evoke cruise liners.

Room Mate Waldorf Towers (p118)

Deco guru L Murray Dixon designed the tower of this hotel to resemble a lighthouse, surely meant to shine the way home for drunken Ocean Dr revelers.

Colony Hotel (p77)

The oldest deco hotel in Miami Beach; it was the first hotel in Miami, and perhaps America, to incorporate its sign (a zigzaggy neon wonder) as part of its overall design. Inside the lobby are excellent examples of space-age interiors, including Saturn-shaped lamps and Flash Gordon elevators.

1. Cavalier South Beach **2.** Crescent Resort **3.** Room Mate Waldorf Towers

Cavalier South Beach (p117)

This hotel makes clever allusions to nautical themes. The word 'cavalier,' which is a kind of horseman, is actually a play on 'seahorse,' examples of which are depicted in somewhat stylized forms on the facade. The tropical theme continues with palm trees, whose trunks (again as figurative designs) run down both sides of the facade.

Wolfsonian-FIU (p65)

The lobby contains a phenomenally theatrical example of a 'frozen fountain.' The gold-leaf fountain, formerly gracing a movie-theater lobby, shoots vertically up and flows symmetrically downward.

Crescent Resort (p81)

Besides having one of Miami Beach's most recognizable neon facades, the Crescent's signage attracts the eye down into its lobby (the better to pack guests in), rather than up to its roof.

1. Royal Palm 2. White-fronted Delano Hotel 3. Tides

'New' Deco Hotels

Hoteliers such as Ian Schrager combine faith in technology – flat-screen TVs, Lucite 'ghost chairs,' computer-controlled lobby displays – with an air of fantastical glamour. Newer hotels such as the W and Gansevoort South have deco roots, but have expanded the architectural sense of scale, integrating deco style into Miami Modern's (enormous) proportions.

Delano (p121)

The top tower evokes old-school deco rocket-ship fantasies, but the theater-set-on-acid interior is a flight of pure modern fancy. The enormous backyard pool mixes jazz-era elegance with pure Miami muscular opulence.

Carlyle Hotel (p81)

Built in 1941, this was one of the last of the deco hotels built in Miami Beach. Here the eyebrow-like window coverings are semi-circular (rather than rectangular), and its name (borrowed from a hotel in NYC) was meant to evoke wealth and exclusivity. It also has cinematic cachet: *The Birdcage* was filmed here, as was the opening scene from *Miami Vice*.

Tides (p65)

The biggest deco structure of its day was a temple to the deco movement. Today, the lobby feels like Poseidon's audience chamber, while rooms exemplify modern boutique aesthetics.

Royal Palm (p119)

This massive, beautifully restored hotel is an excellent place to feel a sense of seaborne movement. It has a *Titanic*-esque, ocean-liner back lobby. The mezzanine floor has modern dimensions in its enormity, mixed with classic deco styling.

Surfcomber (p119)

One of the best deco renovations on the beach is offset by sleek, transit-lounge lines in the lobby and a lovely series of rounded eyebrows.

Vintage Ford Thunderbird outside the Avalon Hotel

Quirky Deco Delights

Tropical deco is mainly concerned with stimulating the imagination. Painted accents lifted from archaeology sites might make a passer-by think of travel, maybe on a cruise ship. And hey, isn't it funny that the windows resemble portholes? Almost all of the preserved buildings here still inspire this childlike sense of wonder.

Winter Haven Hotel (p121)

Outside, you'll note shade-providing 'eyebrows,' and striking geometry, with an elegant zigzag of windows creating a vertical stripe down the center of the facade. Inside, check out the wild light fixtures that evoke futuristic elements (inspired

perhaps by Fritz Lang's 1927 sci-fi film *Metropolis*).

Avalon Hotel (p118)

The exterior of the Avalon is a fantastic example of classic art-deco architecture – clean lines and old-school signage lit up by tropical-green deco, all fronted by a vintage 1950s Oldsmobile.

11th Street Diner (p127)

It doesn't get much more deco than dining in a classic Pullman train car. Many buildings on Miami Beach evoke planes, trains and automobiles – this diner is actually located in one.

(Continued from p68)

the American Riviera they carved out of the sand, and this museum tells that story, along with some amusing anecdotes (like seashell Purim dresses).

ArtCenter/South Florida GALLERY
(Map p78; ☑305-674-8278; www.artcentersf.org; 924 Lincoln Rd, 2nd fl; ☺11am-7pm Mon-Fri, noon-8pm Sat & Sun) Established in 1984 by a small but forward-thinking group of artists, this compound is the creative heart of South Beach. In addition to some 52 artists' studios (many open to the public), ArtCenter offers an exciting lineup of classes and lectures.

The residences are reserved for artists who do not have major exposure, so this is a good place to spot up-and-coming talent. Monthly rotating exhibitions keep the presentation fresh and pretty avant-garde.

Post Office ARCHITECTURE
(Map p78; 1300 Washington Ave; ☺8am-5pm Mon-Fri, 8:30am-2pm Sat) Make it a point to mail a postcard from this 1937 deco gem of a post office, the very first South Beach renovation project tackled by preservationists in the '70s. This Depression moderne building in the 'stripped classic' style was constructed under President Roosevelt's administration and funded by the Works Progress Administration (WPA) initiative, which supported artists out of work during the Great Depression.

On the exterior, note the bald eagle and the turret with iron railings, and inside, a large wall mural of the Seminole's Florida invasion.

Colony Hotel ARCHITECTURE
(Map p82; 736 Ocean Dr) The Colony is the oldest deco hotel in Miami Beach. It was the first hotel in Miami, and perhaps America, to incorporate its sign (a zigzaggy neon wonder) as part of its overall design. Inside the lobby are excellent examples of space-age interiors, including Saturn-shaped lamps and Flash Gordon elevators.

World Erotic Art Museum MUSEUM
(Map p78; ☑305-532-9336; www.weam.com; 1205 Washington Ave; over 18yr $15; ☺11am-10pm Mon-Thu, to midnight Fri-Sun) In a neighborhood where no behavior is too shocking, the World Erotic Art Museum celebrates its staggering but artful pornography, including pieces by Rembrandt and Picasso. Back in 2005, then 70-year-old Naomi Wilzig turned her 5000-piece private erotica collection into a South Beach attraction.

WEAM takes itself seriously, which is part of the charm of this fascinating collection spanning the ages, from ancient sex manuals to Victorian peep-show photos to an elaborate four-poster (four-phallus rather) Kama Sutra bed, with carvings in wood depicting various ways (138 in fact) to get intimate. Other curiosities include the phallus bone of a whale with hand-carved wolf faces and the oversized sculpted genitals used as a murder weapon in *A Clockwork Orange*.

South Pointe Park PARK
(Map p82; ☑305-673-7779; 1 Washington Ave; ☺sunrise-10pm; 🅟🅱) The very southern tip of Miami Beach has been converted into a lovely park, replete with manicured grass for lounging; a beach; views over a remarkably teal and fresh ocean; a restaurant; a refreshment stand; a tiny waterpark for kids; warm, scrubbed-stone walkways; and lots of folks who want to enjoy the great weather and views sans the South Beach strutting.

Española Way Promenade AREA
(Map p78; btwn 14th & 15th Sts) Española Way is an 'authentic' Spanish promenade...in the Florida theme-park spirit of authenticity. Oh, whatever; it's a lovely, terracotta and cobbled arcade of rose-pink and Spanish-cream architecture, perfect for an alfresco meal with a side of people-watching at one of the many restaurants lining the strip.

Promenade WATERFRONT
(Map p82; Ocean Dr) This beach promenade, a wavy ribbon sandwiched between the beach and Ocean Dr, extends from 5th St to 15th St. A popular location for photo shoots, especially during crowd-free early mornings, it's also a breezy, palm-tree-lined conduit for in-line skaters, cyclists, volleyball players (there's a net at 11th St), dog walkers, yahoos, locals and tourists.

The beach that it edges, Lummus Park, sports six floridly colored lifeguard stands. There's a public bathroom at 11th St; the sinks are a popular place for homeless bathing.

1111 Lincoln Rd ARCHITECTURE
(Map p78; www.1111lincolnroad.com; 🅟) The west side of Lincoln Rd is anchored by a most impressive parking garage: a geometric pastiche of sharp angles, winding corridors and incongruous corners that looks like a lucid fantasy dreamed up by Pythagoras after a long night out.

In fact, the building was designed by Swiss architecture firm Herzog & de Meuron, who

South Beach (11th to 23rd Streets)

N ■ 200 m
0 ■ 0.1 miles

Collins Ave

21
41
36
40 70
74 37
15 31
Collins Park 32 25 38
71 27 30
Liberty Ave 28 35
20th St 68
23
James Ave
21st St
Park Ave 18th St
Miami Beach 19th St
High School 14

Washington Ave

23rd St
21st St

Miami Beach
Convention
Center 73

12
11
New World
Center

Prairie Ave
Convention Center Dr

Dade Blvd 9 Meridian Ct
Miami Beach 18th St Miami
Botanical Beach
Garden 7 19th St City Hall

N Meridian Ave Meridian Ave 17th St

Bayshore
Municipal Jefferson Ave
Golf Course
18th St

Michigan Ave
Collins Canal

Lincoln La N

N Bay Rd Lenox Ave

19th St

Alton Rd
Alton Rd

Dade Blvd

W 24th St
Number 3 West Ave

W 23rd St 18th St
Sunset
Islands
Sunset Dr
Number 4 Bay Rd
W 22nd St Standard
W 21st St (0.25mi)

SUNSET Purdy Ave
HARBOUR 20th St
55 62
76 59 8
52 Maurice Gibb
53 Memorial
20 Park

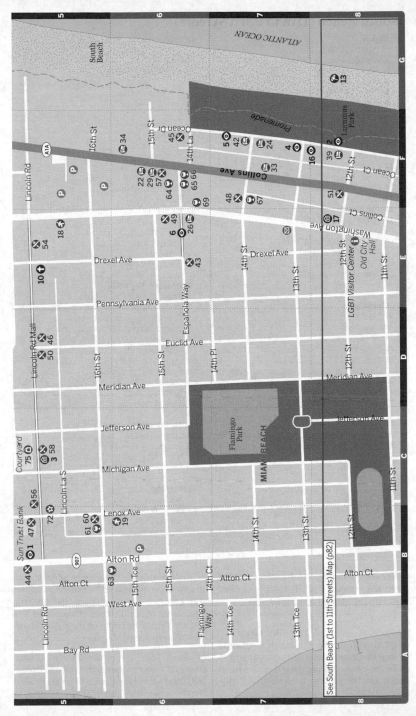

MIAMI

ATLANTIC OCEAN

South Beach

Promenade

Lummus Park

Ocean Dr

Collins Ave

Ocean Ct

Washington Ave

Collins Ct

12th St

LGBT Visitor Center

Old City Hall

11th St

Lincoln Rd

16th St

15th St

14th La

Drexel Ave

Española Way

Euclid Ave

14th Pl

Pennsylvania Ave

Meridian Ave

Jefferson Ave

Michigan Ave

Lenox Ave

Alton Rd

Alton Ct

West Ave

Bay Rd

Lincoln Rd

Lincoln La S

Courtyard

Sun Trust Bank

Lincoln Rd Mall

Flamingo Park

MIAMI BEACH

Meridian Ave

Jefferson Ave

13th St

14th St

12th St

11th St

Alton Ct

Flamingo Way

14th Tce

13th Tce

See South Beach (1st to 11th Streets) Map (p82)

South Beach (11th to 23rd Streets)

describe the structure as 'all muscle without cloth.' Besides parking, 1111 Lincoln is filled with retail shops and residential units.

A1A BRIDGE
'Beachfront Avenue!' The A1A causeway, coupled with the Rickenbacker Causeway in Key Biscayne, is one of the great bridges in America, linking Miami and Miami Beach via the glittering turquoise of Biscayne Bay.

To drive this road in a convertible or with the windows down, with a setting sun behind you, enormous cruise ships to the side, the palms swaying in the ocean breeze, and let's just say 'Royals' by Lorde on the radio, is basically the essence of Miami.

Miami Beach Community Church CHURCH
(Map p78; www.miamibeachcommunitychurch.com; 1620 Drexel Ave; ⊙8am-4pm Tue-Fri, service 10:30am Sun) In rather sharp and refreshing contrast to

all the ubermodern structures muscling their way into the art-deco design of South Beach, this community church puts one in mind of an old Spanish mission – humble, modest and elegantly understated in an area where over-statement is the general philosophy.

Fourteen stained-glass windows line the relatively simple interior, while the exterior is built to resemble coral stone in a Spanish Re-vival style. The congregation is LGBT-friendly and welcomes outside visitors; church service is at 10:30am on Sunday.

Temple Emanu-El SYNAGOGUE
(Map p78; www.tesobe.org; Washington Ave at 17th St) An art-deco temple? Not exactly, but the smooth, bubbly dome and sleek, almost aerodynamic profile of this Conservative synagogue, established in 1938, fits right in on SoBe's deco parade of moderne this and streamline that. Shabbat services are on Fri-day at 7pm and on Saturday at 10am.

Cardozo Hotel ARCHITECTURE
(Map p78; 1300 Ocean Dr; P) The Cardozo and its neighbor, the **Carlyle** (Map p78; 1250 Ocean Dr), were the first deco hotels saved by the Miami Design Preservation League, and in the case of the Cardozo, we think they saved the best first. Its beautiful lines and curves evoke a classic automobile from the 1930s.

Congress Hotel ARCHITECTURE
(Map p82; 1052 Ocean Dr) Close to 11th St, the Congress Hotel is a deco classic, showing perfect symmetry in its three-story facade, with window-shading eyebrows and a long marquee down the middle that's reminis-cent of the grand movie palaces of the 1930s.

Miami Beach Botanical Garden GARDENS
(Map p78; www.mbgarden.org; 2000 Convention Center Dr; suggested donation $2; ☺9am-5pm Tue-Sat) This lush but little-known 2.6 acres of plantings is operated by the Miami Beach Garden Conservancy, and is a veritable secret garden in the midst of the urban jungle – an oasis of palm trees, flowering hibiscus trees and glassy ponds. It's a great spot for a picnic.

Maurice Gibb Memorial Park PARK
(Map p78; 18th St & Purdy Ave, Sunset Harbour) A small bit of green space overlooking the wa-ter, this park has a playground, benches and grassy areas with fine views. There's ample parking here too.

Crescent Resort ARCHITECTURE
(Map p78; 1420 Ocean Dr) Besides having one of Miami Beach's most recognizable neon facades, the Crescent has signage that draws the eye down into its lobby (the better to pack guests in), rather than up to its roof.

◉ North Beach

Aside from the beach, many of the sights in North Beach require some effort to access. You'll need a car for a day's exploring here.

Faena Forum CULTURAL CENTER
(Map p86; www.faena.com; Collins Ave & 33rd St) Part of the ambitious new $1 billion Faena District, this new cultural center has been turning heads ever since its opening in late 2016. The circular Rem Koolhaas–designed building features rooms for performances, exhibitions, lectures and other events. Check the website to see what's coming up.

Oleta River State Park PARK
(☑305-919-1844; www.floridastateparks.org/oletariver; 3400 NE 163rd St; vehicle/pedestrian/bicycle $6/2/2; ☺8am-sunset; P🚲) Tequesta people were boating the Oleta River estuary as early as 500 BC, so you're just following in a long tradition if you canoe or kayak in this park. At almost 1000 acres, this is the largest urban park in the state and one of the best places in Miami to escape the mad-ding crowd. Boat out to the local mangrove island, watch the eagles fly by, or just chill on the pretension-free beach.

On-site BG Oleta River Outdoor Center (p108) rents out kayaks, canoes, stand-up paddleboards, and mountain bikes. It also offers paddling tours, yoga classes on stand-up paddleboards and other activities. The park is off 163rd St NE/FL 826 in Sunny Isles, about 8 miles north of North Miami Beach.

Fontainebleau HISTORIC BUILDING
(Map p86; www.fontainebleau.com; 4441 Collins Ave) As you proceed north on Collins, the condos and apartment buildings grow in grandeur and embellishment until you en-ter an area nicknamed Millionaire's Row. The most fantastic jewel in this glittering crown is the Fontainebleau hotel. The ho-tel – mainly the pool, which has since been renovated – features in Brian de Palma's classic *Scarface*.

This iconic 1954 leviathan is a brainchild of the great Miami Beach architect Morris Lapidus and has undergone many renova-tions; in some ways, it is utterly different from its original form, but it retains that early glamour.

MIAMI

South Beach (1st to 11th Streets)

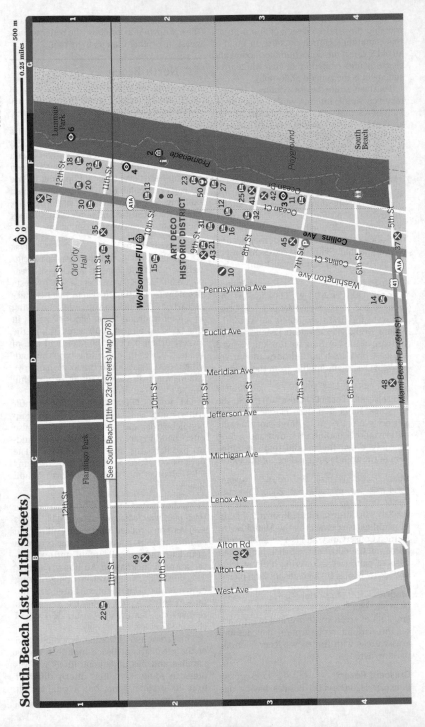

See South Beach (11th to 23rd Streets) Map (p78)

Flamingo Park

Lummus Park

Old City Hall

Wolfsonian-FIU

ART DECO HISTORIC DISTRICT

Promenade

Playground

South Beach

12th St
11th St
10th St
9th St
8th St
7th St
6th St
5th St

Pennsylvania Ave
Euclid Ave
Meridian Ave
Jefferson Ave
Michigan Ave
Lenox Ave
Alton Rd
Alton Ct
West Ave
Washington Ave
Collins Ave
Ocean Dr
Ocean Ct
Collins Ct
Miami Beach Dr (5th St)

0   500 m
0   0.25 miles

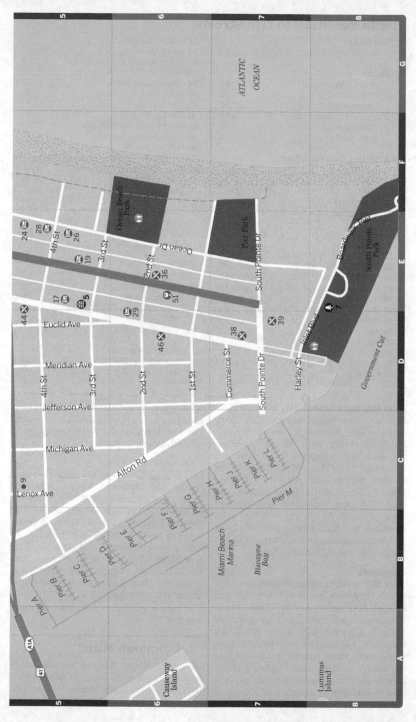

South Beach (1st to 11th Streets)

Eden Roc Renaissance　　HISTORIC BUILDING
(Map p86; www.nobuedenroc.com; 4525 Collins Ave) The Eden Roc was the second ground-breaking resort from Morris Lapidus, and it's a fine example of the architecture known as MiMo (Miami Modern). It was the hangout for the 1960s Rat Pack – Sammy Davis Jr, Dean Martin, Frank Sinatra and crew. Extensive renovation has eclipsed some of Lapidus' style, but with that said, the building is still an iconic piece of Miami Beach architecture, and an exemplar of the brash beauty of Millionaire's Row.

Boardwalk　　BEACH
(Map p86; www.miamibeachboardwalk.com; 21st St-46th St) What's trendy in beachwear this season? Seventeenth-century Polish gabardine coats, apparently. There are plenty of skimpily dressed hotties on the Mid-Beach boardwalk, but there are also Orthodox Jews going about their business in the midst of gay joggers, strolling tourists and sunbathers. Nearby are numerous condo buildings occupied by middle-class Latinos and Jews, who walk their dogs and play with their kids here, giving the entire place a laid-back, real-world vibe that contrasts with the nonstop glamour of South Beach.

Haulover Beach Park　　PARK
(☑ 305-947-3525; www.miamidade.gov/parks/haulover.asp; 10800 Collins Ave; per car Mon-Fri/Sat-Sun $5/7; ☉ sunrise-sunset; ℗) Where are all those tanned men in gold chains and Speedos going? That would be the clothing-optional beach in this 40-acre park hidden from condos, highways and prying eyes by vegetation. There's more to do here than get in the buff, though; most of the beach is 'normal' (there's even a dog park) and is one of the nicer spots for sand in the area. The park is on Collins Ave about 4.5 miles north of 71st St.

◎ Downtown Miami

Downtown Miami, the city's international financial and banking center, is split between tatty indoor shopping arcades on the one hand, and new condos and high-rise luxury hotels in the area known as Brickell on the other. The lazy, gritty Miami River divides Downtown into north and south. Miami is defined by an often frenetic pace of growth, with construction a near constant as new luxury towers arrive with each passing month.

★ **Pérez Art Museum Miami**　　MUSEUM
(PAMM; Map p88; ☑ 305-375-3000; www.pamm. org; 1103 Biscayne Blvd; adult/seniors & students $16/12, 1st Thu & 2nd Sat of month free; ⊙10am-6pm Fri-Tue, to 9pm Thu, closed Wed; P) The Pérez can claim fine rotating exhibits that concentrate on post-WWII international art, but just as impressive are its location and exterior. This art institution inaugurated Museum Park, a patch of land that oversees the broad blue swath of Biscayne Bay. Swiss architects Herzog & de Meuron designed the structure, which integrates tropical foliage, glass and metal – a melding of tropical vitality and fresh modernism that is a nice architectural analogy for Miami itself.

PAMM stages some of the best contemporary exhibitions in Miami. The permanent collection rotates through unique pieces every few months drawing from a treasure trove of work spanning the last 80 years, which is assembled in exhibitions that are always thought-provoking. The temporary shows and retrospectives bring major crowds (past exhibitions have included the works of famed Chinese artist Ai Weiwei and kinetic artist Julio Le Parc). Meanwhile the outdoor space also functions as an open-air sculpture garden.

If you need a little breather amid all this contemporary culture, PAMM has a first-rate cafe, or you can simply hang out in the grassy park or lounge on a deck chair enjoying the views over the water.

★ **HistoryMiami**　　MUSEUM
(Map p88; ☑ 305-375-1492; www.historymiami.org; 101 W Flagler St; adult/child $10/5; ⊙10am-5pm Mon-Sat, from noon Sun; ✦) South Florida – a land of escaped slaves, guerilla Native Americans, gangsters, land grabbers, pirates, tourists, drug dealers and alligators – has a special history, and it takes a special kind of museum to capture that narrative. This highly recommended place, located in the **Miami-Dade Cultural Center**, does just that, weaving together the stories of the region's successive waves of population, from Native Americans to Nicaraguans.

The collection is spread between two buildings. Start off in the permanent collection, which has interactive exhibits showing life among the Seminoles, early Florida industries like sponge diving, and wealth made from 'wreckers' (those who salvaged treasure lost on the reefs). More recent-era exhibits touch on the WWII period (when troops were stationed in Miami Beach), African American history and Cuban refugees (with a rustic homemade boat that managed to survive the treacherous crossing to Florida). Get off the Metromover at the Government Center stop.

★ **Bayfront Park**　　PARK
(Map p88; ☑ 305-358-7550; www.bayfrontpark miami.com; 301 N Biscayne Blvd) Few American parks can claim to front such a lovely stretch of turquoise (Biscayne Bay), but Miamians are lucky like that. Notable park features are two performance venues: the Klipsch Amphitheater (p146), which boasts excellent views over Biscayne Bay and is a good spot for live-music shows, while the smaller 200-seat (lawn seating can accommodate 800 more) **Tina Hills Pavilion** hosts free springtime performances.

Look north for the JFK Torch of Friendship, and a fountain recognizing the accomplishments of longtime US congressman Claude Pepper. There's a huge variety of activities here, including flying trapeze classes and free yoga classes (p110), plus a great playground for the kids.

Noted artist and landscape architect Isamu Noguchi redesigned much of Bayfront Park in the 1980s and dotted the grounds with three sculptures. In the southwest corner is the **Challenger Memorial**, a monument designed for the astronauts killed in the 1986 space-shuttle explosion, built to resemble both the twisting helix of a human DNA chain and the shuttle itself. The **Light**

KEEPING IT KOSHER IN MIAMI BEACH

They're no shtetls, but Arthur Godfrey Rd (41st St) and Harding Ave between 91st and 96th Sts in Surfside are popular thoroughfares for the Jewish population of Miami Beach. Just as the Jewish population have shaped Miami Beach, so has the beach shaped them: you can eat lox y arroz con moros (salmon with rice and beans) and while the Orthodox men don yarmulkes and the women wear headscarves, many have nice tans and drive flashy SUVs.

North Beach

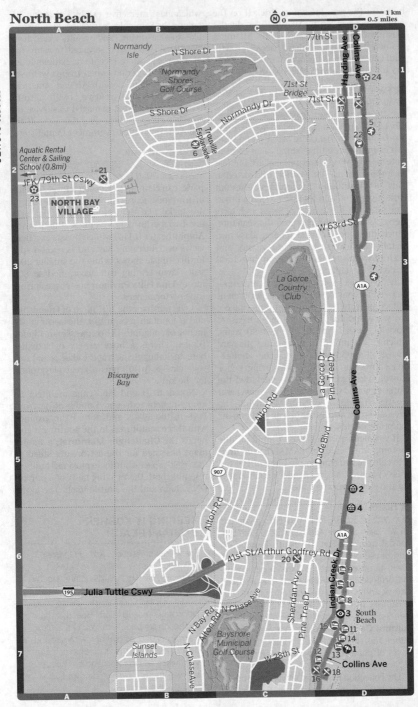

North Beach

MIAMI SIGHTS

Tower is a 40ft, somewhat abstract allusion to Japanese lanterns and moonlight over Miami. Our favorite is the **Slide Mantra**, a twisting spiral of marble that doubles as a playground piece for the kids.

Patricia & Phillip Frost Museum of Science
MUSEUM
(Map p88; ☎305-434-9600; www.frostscience.org; 1101 Biscayne Blvd; adult/child $28/20; ⊗9am-6pm; P⊞) This sprawling new Downtown museum spreads across 250,000 sq ft that includes a three-level aquarium, a 250-seat state-of-the-art planetarium and two distinct wings that delve into the wonders of science and nature. Exhibitions range from weather phenomena to creepy crawlies, feathered dinosaurs and vital-microbe displays, while Florida's fascinating Everglades and biologically rich coral reefs play starring roles.

The new facility, which cost a staggering $305 million to complete, was built with sustainability in mind. It opened in 2017.

Brickell City Centre
AREA
(Map p88; www.brickellcitycentre.com; 701 S Miami Ave; ⊗10am-9:30pm Mon-Sat, noon-7pm Sun) One of the hottest new developments in Miami finally opened its doors in late 2016, after four long years of construction. The massive billion-dollar complex spreads across three city blocks, and it encompasses glittering residential towers, modernist office blocks and a soaring five-star hotel (the EAST, Miami; p123). There's much to entice both Miami residents and visitors to the center, with restaurants, bars, a cinema and loads of high-end retailers (Ted Baker, All Saints, Kendra Scott).

You'll find shops scattered across both sides of S Miami Ave between 7th and 8th Sts, including a massive Saks Fifth Ave. Still in the works was a three-story Italian food emporium, with restaurants, cafes, a bakery, an enoteca and a culinary school. It was slated to open by early 2018.

Miami Riverwalk
WATERFRONT
(Map p88) This pedestrian walkway follows along the northern edge of the river as it bisects Downtown, and offers some peaceful vantage points of bridges and skyscrapers dotting the urban landscape. You can start the walk at the south end of Bayfront Park and follow it under bridges and along the waterline till it ends just west of the SW 2nd Ave Bridge.

The Riverwalk is one small section of the ambitious Miami River Greenway project, which aims to extend a green path along both banks of the river all the way to the river's intersection with the Dolphin Expressway.

Freedom Tower
HISTORIC BUILDING
(Map p88; 600 Biscayne Blvd; ⊗10am-5pm) An iconic slice of Miami's old skyline, the richly ornamented Freedom Tower is one of two surviving towers modeled after the Giralda bell tower in Spain's Cathedral of Seville. As the 'Ellis Island of the South,' it served as an immigration processing center for almost

MIAMI

Downtown Miami

500 m
0.25 miles

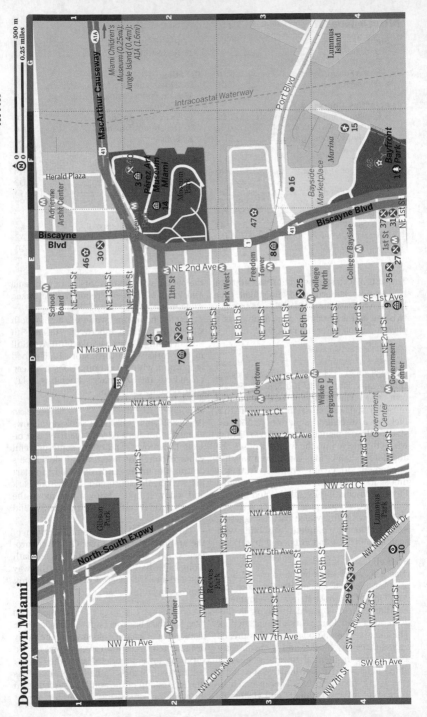

Miami Children's
Museum (0.25mi);
Jungle Island (0.4mi);
A1A (1.6mi)

MacArthur Causeway

Intracoastal Waterway

Port Blvd

Lummus
Island

Herald Plaza

Adrienne
Arsht Center

Pérez Art
Museum
Miami

Museum
Park

Bayside
Marketplace

Marina

Bayfront
Park

15

16

Biscayne
Blvd

46

30

Biscayne Blvd

NE 14th St

NE 13th St

NE 12th St

11th St

NE 2nd Ave

Freedom
Tower

8

1

College /Bayside

1st St

37

NE 1st St

31

27

School
Board

N Miami Ave

26

44

7

NE 10th St

NE 9th St

NE 8th St

NE 7th St

NE 6th St

NE 5th St

NE 4th St

NE 3rd St

Park West

25

College
North

35

SE 1st Ave

9

NE 2nd St

Government
Center

395

NW 1st Ave

NW 1st Ct

Overtown

Wilkie D
Ferguson Jr

NW 1st Ave

4

NW 2nd Ave

NW 3rd St

NW 2nd St

Government
Center

Government
Center

NW 12th St

NW 3rd Ct

Gibson
Park

NW 4th Ave

Lummus
Park

NW 9th St

NW 8th St

NW 5th St

NW 4th St

NW N River Dr

10

Reeves
Park

NW 10th St

NW 5th Ave

NW 6th St

NW 6th Ave

29

32

SW S River Dr

NW 3rd St

NW 2nd St

Culmer

NW 7th Ave

NW 7th St

NW 7th Ave

SW S River Dr

SW 6th Ave

NW 10th Ave

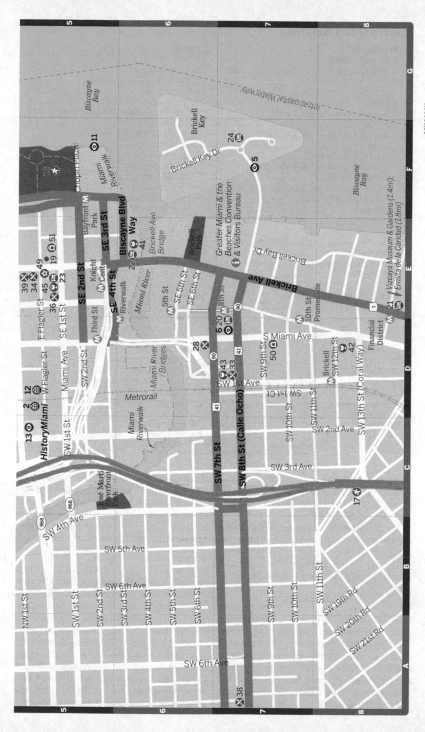

Downtown Miami

half a million Cuban refugees in the 1960s. Placed on the National Register of Historic Places in 1979, it was also home to the *Miami Daily News* for 32 years.

In the beautifully restored lobby, above the elevators and stretching toward the coffered ceiling, you can see reliefs of men at work on the printing presses. The tower also houses the MDC Museum of Art & Design.

Black Archives Historic
Lyric Theater   HISTORIC BUILDING

(Map p88; ☑786-708-4610; www.bahlt.org; 819 NW 2nd Ave; ☺museum 10am-6pm Mon-Sat, noon-5pm Sun) Duke Ellington and Ella Fitzgerald once walked across the stage of the Lyric, a major stop on the 'Chitlin' Circuit' – the black live-entertainment trail of preintegration USA. As years passed both the theater and the neighborhood it served, Overtown, fell into disuse. Then the **Black Archives History & Research Foundation of South Florida** took over the building. Today the theater hosts occasional shows, while the Archives hosts excellent exhibitions exploring African American heritage both in Miami and beyond.

Brickell Avenue Bridge &
Brickell Key   ISLAND

(Map p88) Crossing the Miami River, the lovely Brickell Avenue Bridge between SE 4th St and SE 5th St was made wider and higher several years ago, which was convenient for the speedboat-driving drug runners being chased by Drug Enforcement Administration agents on the day of the bridge's grand reopening! Note the 17ft bronze statue by Cuban-born sculptor Manuel Carbonell of a Tequesta warrior and his family, which sits atop the towering Pillar of History column.

Walking here is the best way to get a sense of the sculptures and will allow you to avoid one of the most confusing traffic patterns in Miami. Brickell Key looks more like a floating porcupine, with glass towers for quills, than an island. To live the life of Miami glitterati, come here, pretend you belong, and head into a patrician hangout like the Mandarin Oriental Miami (p124) hotel, where the lobby and intimate lounges afford sweeping views of Biscayne Bay.

MDC Museum of Art & Design MUSEUM
(Freedom Tower; Map p88; ☑ 305-237-7700; www.mdcmoad.org; 600 Biscayne Blvd) Miami-Dade College operates a small but well-curated art museum in Downtown; the permanent collection includes works by Matisse, Picasso and Chagall and focuses on minimalism, pop art and contemporary Latin American art. The museum's home building is art itself: it's set in the soaring 255ft (78m) Freedom Tower (p87), a masterpiece of Mediterranean Revival, built in 1925.

At research time the collection was inaccessible as the museum was undergoing renovation; check the website for the reopening schedule and other pop-up art programs in the meantime.

Miami City Cemetery CEMETERY
(Map p94; 1800 NE 2nd Ave; ⊙ 7am-3:30pm Mon-Fri, 8am-4:30pm Sat & Sun) This quiet graveyard, the final resting place of some of Miami-Dade's most important citizens, is a sort of narrative of the history of the city cast in bone, dirt and stone. The dichotomy of the past and modernity gets a nice visual representation in the form of looming condos shadowing the last abode of the Magic City's late, great ones.

More than 9000 graves are divided into separate white, black and Jewish sections. Buried here are mayors, veterans (including about 90 Confederate soldiers) and the godmother of South Florida, Julia Tuttle, who purchased the first orange groves that attracted settlers to the area.

Miami Center for Architecture & Design MUSEUM
(Old US Post Office; Map p88; ☑ 305-448-7488; www.miamicad.org; 100 NE 1st Ave; ⊙ 10am-5pm Mon-Fri) FREE It makes sense that the Miami branch of the American Institute of Architects would pick the Old US Post Office as headquarters of their Center for Architecture & Design. Constructed in 1912, this was the first federal building in Miami. It features a low-pitched roof, elaborate doors and carved entryways, and was purchased in 1937 to serve as the country's first savings and loan.

Today it houses lectures and events related to architecture, design and urban planning, and hosts a small but vibrant exhibition on all of the above subjects. Two-hour walking tours on alternate Saturdays depart from here (at 10am), and take in some of the historic buildings of Downtown. Visit the website for upcoming times and reservations.

Miami River RIVER
(Map p88) For a taste of old Florida, take a stroll along the Miami River. A shoreline promenade (p87) leads past a mix of glittering high-rise condos and battered warehouses tinged with graffiti, with a few small tugboats putting along the glassy surface. Fisherfolk float in with their daily catch – en route to places like Casablanca (p131) – while fancy yachts make their way in and out of the bay.

There are some photogenic vantage points over the river from the bridges – particularly the Brickell Ave bridge at dusk, when the city lights glow against the darkening night sky.

Miami Children's Museum MUSEUM
(☑ 305-373-5437; www.miamichildrensmuseum.org; 980 MacArthur Causeway; $20; ⊙ 10am-6pm; ⍟) This museum, located between South Beach and Downtown Miami, isn't exactly a museum. It feels more like an uberplayhouse, with areas for kids to practice all sorts of adult activities – banking and food shopping, caring for pets, and acting as a local cop or firefighter.

Other imaginative areas let kids make music, make wall sketches, go on undersea adventures, explore a little castle made

---

LOCAL KNOWLEDGE

DOWNTOWN MIAMI

Market dining On Mondays, you can join locals in an outdoor setting for a vegetarian feast at Chef Allen's Farm-to-Table Dinner (p131).

Yoga in the park The open-air views of the bay are a perfect backdrop to sun salutations, at free classes by the Tina Hills Pavilion (p110).

Hangouts Linger over excellent coffee and breakfast served at all hours at All Day (p130).

of colored glass or simply play on outdoor playgrounds.

Jungle Island
ZOO

(☑305-400-7000; www.jungleisland.com; 1111 Parrot Jungle Trail, off MacArthur Causeway; adult/child/senior $40/33/38; ☺10am-5pm; P♿) Jungle Island, packed with tropical birds, alligators, orangutans, chimps, lemurs, a (wait for it *Napoleon Dynamite* fans) liger (a cross between a lion and a tiger) and a Noah's Ark of other animals, is a ton of fun. It's one of those places kids (justifiably) beg to go, so just give up and prepare for some bright-feathered, bird-poop-scented fun in this artificial, self-contained jungle.

Cisneros Fontanal Arts Foundation
MUSEUM

(CIFO; Map p88; ☑305-455-3380; www.cifo.org; 1018 N Miami Ave; ☺noon-6pm Thu & Fri, 10am-4pm Sat & Sun) This arts foundation displays the work of contemporary Latin American artists, and has an impressive showroom to boot. Even the exterior blends postindustrial rawness with a lurking, natural ambience, offset by the extensive use of Bisazza tiles to create an overarching tropical motif. The opening hours only apply during exhibition showings, although informal tours can be arranged if you call ahead.

Miami-Dade Public Library
LIBRARY

(Map p88; ☑305-375-2665; www.mdpls.org; 101 W Flagler St; ☺10am-6pm Mon-Sat) To learn more about Florida (especially South Florida), take a browse through the extensive Florida Collection, or ask about the Romer Photograph Collection, an archive of some 17,500 photos and prints that chronicles the history of the city from its early years to 1945. At the library, ask for John Shipley, head of the Florida Collection, for more details.

Miami-Dade County Courthouse
HISTORIC BUILDING

(Map p88; 73 W Flagler St) If you end up on trial here, at least you'll get a free tour of one of the most imposing courthouses in the USA. Built between 1925 and 1929, this a very... appropriate building: if structures were people, the 28-story neoclassical courthouse would definitely be a judge. Some trivia: back in the day, the top nine floors served as a 'secure' prison, from which more than 70 prisoners escaped.

◉ Wynwood & the Design District

Wynwood and the Design District are two of Miami's most creative neighborhoods, and are justly famed for a burgeoning arts scene. Wynwood is packed with galleries, as well as large-format street art covering once industrial spaces. It's also the place for great nightlife, and an emerging restaurant scene. The smaller Design District also has galleries, plus high-end shopping and a mixed bag of bars and eateries.

★ Wynwood Walls
PUBLIC ART

(Map p94; www.thewynwoodwalls.com; NW 2nd Ave btwn 25th & 26th Sts) FREE In the midst of rusted warehouses and concrete blah, there's a pastel-and-graffiti explosion of urban art. Wynwood Walls is a collection of murals and paintings laid out over an open courtyard that invariably bowls people over with its sheer color profile and unexpected location. What's on offer tends to change with the coming and going of major arts events such as Art Basel (p115), but it's always interesting stuff.

If you'd like to get the inside scoop on the latest murals, Wynwood Walls offers private walking tours ($25 per person) led by street artists (book online). If you're in the area on the second Saturday of the month, the Wynwood Art Walk (p113) is an especially great time to see the neighborhood at its most celebratory.

★ Margulies Collection at the Warehouse
GALLERY

(Map p94; ☑305-576-1051; www.marguliesware house.com; 591 NW 27th St; adult/student $10/5; ☺11am-4pm Tue-Sat mid-Oct–Apr) Encompassing some 45,000 sq ft, this vast not-for-profit exhibition space houses one of the best collections in all of Wynwood. Thought-provoking large-format installations are the focus at the Warehouse, and you'll see works by some of the leading 21st-century artists here.

Rotating exhibitions pull from Martin Margulies' awe-inspiring 4000-piece collection, which includes sculptures by Isamu Noguchi, George Segal, Richard Serra and Olafur Eliasson – among many others luminaries in the art world – plus sound installations by Susan Philipsz and jaw-dropping room-sized works by Anselm Kiefer.

Bakehouse Art Complex GALLERY

(BAC; Map p94; ☑ 305-576-2828; www.bacfl.org; 561 NW 32nd St; ⊙noon-5pm; P) FREE One of the pivotal art destinations in Wynwood, the Bakehouse has been an arts incubator since well before the creation of the Wynwood Walls. Today this former bakery houses galleries and some 60 studios, and the range of works you can find here is quite impressive. Check the schedule for upcoming artist talks and other events.

De La Cruz Collection GALLERY

(Map p94; ☑ 305-576-6112; www.delacruz collection.org; 23 NE 41st St; ⊙10am-4pm Tue-Sat) FREE Housing one of Miami's finest private collections, this 30,000-sq-ft gallery has a treasure trove of contemporary works scattered across three floors, which you can roam freely. Rosa and Carlos de la Cruz, who originally hail from Cuba, have particularly strong holdings in postwar German paintings, as well as fascinating works by Jim Hodges, Ana Mendieta and Felix Gonzalez-Torres.

You have to ring the bell to gain admittance – and you might be followed around the gallery by a guard (as we were) – but don't be discouraged: this free gallery is worth the effort to explore.

Fly's Eye Dome SCULPTURE

(Map p94; 140 NE 39th St, Palm Court) Installed during Art Basel in 2014, Buckminster Fuller's striking geodesic dome looks otherworldly as it appears to float in a small reflecting pool surrounded by slender, gently swaying palm trees. The 24ft-tall sculpture was dubbed an 'autonomous dwelling machine' by Fuller when he conceived it back in 1965.

There are some fantastic vantage points for photographers both inside and outside the dome – which also serves as the covered entry/exit point connecting the below-ground parking lot with the plaza.

Palm Court COURTYARD

(Map p94; 140 NE 39th St) At the epicenter of the Design District is this pretty courtyard, which opened just before Art Basel back in 2014. It's set with tall palm trees, two floors of high-end retailers and one eye-catching sculpture, namely the Fly's Eye Dome.

Locust Projects GALLERY

(Map p94; ☑ 305-576-8570; www.locust projects.org; 3852 N Miami Ave; ⊙10am-6pm Tue-Sat) FREE Locust Projects has become a major name for emerging artists in the

WYNWOOD & THE DESIGN DISTRICT

Hangouts The Wynwood Yard (p132) embodies the spirit of this diverse 'hood, with food trucks, a bar (front and center), outdoor dining at picnic tables, and a changing lineup of music.

Beer lore Boxelder (p143) is the go-to spot for brew lovers, and showcases local beers in a friendly, unpretentious setting.

Art revelry On the second Saturday of the month, Wynwood and the Design District hold an Art Walk (p112), where galleries host special exhibitions, plus there's live music, a craft market etc.

contemporary art scene. Run by artists as a nonprofit collective since 1998, LP has exhibited work by more than 250 local, national and international artists. The gallery often hosts site-specific installations by artists willing to take a few more risks than those in more commercial venues.

Art Fusion GALLERY

(Map p94; www.artfusionartists.com; 3550 N Miami Ave; ⊙11am-6pm Mon-Sat) FREE This sprawling gallery in Midtown carries a hugely varied collection, with artists from around the globe. You'll find sculpture, portraiture, landscapes and mixed media spread across two floors of the 8000-sq-ft space.

Living Room PUBLIC ART

(Map p94; cnr NW 40th St & N Miami Ave) Just to remind you that you're entering the Design District is a big, surreal public art installation of, yep, a living room – just the sort of thing you're supposed to shop for while you're here. Actually the *Living Room*, by Argentine husband-and-wife team Roberto Behar and Rosario Marquardt, is an 'urban intervention' meant to be a criticism of the disappearance of public space.

But the piece could just as easily be a metaphor for the Design District as a whole: a contemporary interior plopped into the middle of urban decay.

Bacardi Building ARCHITECTURE

(Map p94; 2100 Biscayne Blvd) FREE You don't need to be a rum-lover to appreciate the former Miami headquarters of the world's largest family-owned spirits company, Bacardi.

Wynwood & Design District

The main event is a beautifully decorated jewelbox-like building built in 1973 that seems to hover over the ground from a central pillar supporting the entire structure. One-inch thick pieces of hammered glass cover the exterior in a wild Meso American–style pattern modeled after a mosaic designed by German artist Johannes M Dietz.

Be sure to walk around the building to see the eye-catching work executed in four different color patterns. Also on site is the older 1963 building, a tower covered with blue-and-white handmade tiles – some 28,000 in fact

– in a striking ceramic pattern designed by Brazilian artist Francisco Brennand.

Rubell Family Art Collection   MUSEUM
(Map p94; ☑ 305-573-6090; www.rfc.museum; 95 NW 29th St; adult/student & under 18yr $10/5; ⏱10am-5:30pm Wed-Sat) The Rubell family – specifically, the niece and nephew of the late Steve, better known as Ian Schrager's Studio 54 partner – operates some top-end hotels in Miami Beach, but they've also amassed an impressive contemporary art collection that spans the last 30 years. The most admirable quality of this collection is its commitment

Wynwood & Design District

to not just displaying one or two of its artists' pieces; the museum's aim is to showcase a contributor's entire career.

Located in Wynwood, the collection will move to a new 100,000-sq-ft location in Allapattah (p105) in late 2018.

Little Haiti & the Upper East Side

Well north of Wynwood and the Design District, these two big neighborhoods see relatively few visitors. Little Haiti still feels derelict in parts, though it has a vibrant Haitian expat community, with much activity revolving around the colorful Little Haiti Cultural Center. Further east, the Upper East Side is best known for its striking modernist buildings lining Biscayne Blvd. It's something of Miami's great new frontier, with new restaurants, hotels and galleries setting up shop here in the last few years.

Little Haiti Cultural Center   GALLERY
(Map p96; ☑305-960-2969; www.littlehaiti culturalcenter.com; 212 NE 59th Tce; ⊙10am-9pm Tue-Fri, 9am-4pm Sat, 11am-7pm Sun) FREE This cultural center hosts an art gallery with often thought-provoking exhibitions from Haitian painters, sculptors and multimedia artists. You can also find dance classes, drama productions and a Caribbean-themed market during special events. The building itself is quite a confection of bold tropical colors, steep A-framed roofs and lacy decorative elements. Don't miss the mural in the palm-filled courtyard.

The best time to visit is for the Sounds of Little Haiti (p113), a music- and food-filled fête.

Miami Ironside   ARTS CENTER
(Map p96; www.miamiironside.com; 7610 NE 4th Ct) ✐ A new hub of creativity in Miami is this urban oasis in an otherwise industrial 'hood known as Little River. Here you'll find art and design studios, showrooms and galleries as

Little Haiti & the Upper East Side

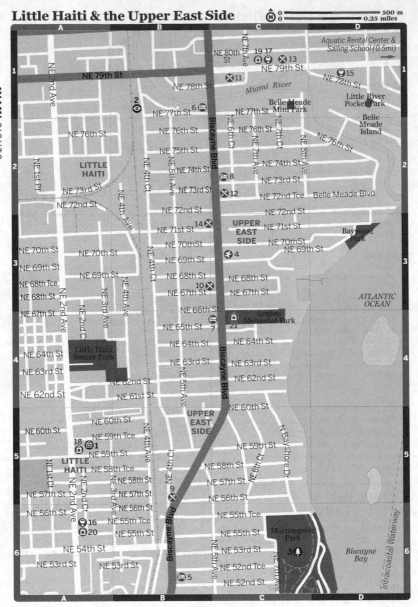

well as a few eating and drinking spaces. It's a lushly landscaped property, with some intriguing public art.

Opening hours vary between the on-site businesses; be sure to check the website for more details.

Morningside Park PARK

(Map p96; 750 NE 55 Tce) On the waterfront, this aptly named park is a great spot to be in the morning, when the golden light is just right for getting a bit of fresh air. There's lots going on in the park, with walking paths,

Little Haiti & the Upper East Side

basketball courts, tennis courts, sports fields, a playground for kids and a swimming pool (admission $3).

If you come on Saturday, you can hire kayaks (from $12 per hour) and stand-up paddleboards (from $20 per hour).

PanAmerican Art Projects   GALLERY
(PAAP; ☑ 305-573-2400; www.panamericanart. com; 6300 NW 2nd Ave; ⊙10am-6pm Tue-Fri, noon-6pm Sat) Despite the name, PanAmerican also showcases work from the occasional European artist. But much of what is on display comes from fine artists representing Latin America, the Caribbean and the USA.

Formerly located in Wynwood, PAAP made the move up to Little Haiti in 2016 – a growing trend as gallerists get priced out of the neighborhood they helped popularize.

◉ Little Havana

Little Havana's main thoroughfare, Calle Ocho (SW 8th St), doesn't just cut through the heart of the neighborhood; it *is* the heart of the neighborhood. In a lot of ways, this is every immigrant enclave in the USA – full of restaurants, mom-and-pop convenience shops and phonecard kiosks. Admittedly the Cubaness of Little Havana is slightly exaggerated for visitors, though it's still an atmospheric place to explore, with the crack of dominoes, the scent of wafting cigars, and Latin jazz spilling out of colorful storefronts.

★**Máximo Gómez Park**   PARK
(Map p98; SW 8th St at SW 15th Ave; ⊙9am-6pm) Little Havana's most evocative reminder of Old Cuba is Máximo Gómez Park, or

'Domino Park,' where the sound of elderly men trash-talking over games of chess is harmonized by the quick clack-clack of slapping dominoes. The jarring backtrack, along with the heavy smell of cigars and a sunrise-bright mural of the 1994 Summit of the Americas, combine to make Máximo Gómez one of the most sensory sites in Miami (although it is admittedly one of the most tourist-heavy ones as well).

Cuban Memorial Park   MONUMENT
(Map p98; SW 13th Ave, btwn 8th & 11th Sts) Stretching along SW 13th Ave just south of Calle Ocho (SW 8th St), Cuban Memorial Park contains a series of monuments to Cuban and Cuban American icons. The memorials include the **Eternal Torch in Honor of the 2506th Brigade**, for the exiles who died during the Bay of Pigs Invasion; a **José Martí memorial**; and a **Madonna statue**, supposedly illuminated by a shaft of holy light every afternoon.

There's also a map of Cuba, with a quote by José Martí. At the center of the map is a massive ceiba tree, still revered by followers of Santeria (a syncretic religion that evolved in Cuba among African slaves in the 18th century).

Bay of Pigs Museum & Library   LIBRARY
(Map p98; ☑ 305-649-4719; 1821 SW 9th St; ⊙9am-4pm Mon-Sat) This small museum is more of a memorial to the 2506th Brigade, otherwise known as the crew of the ill-fated Bay of Pigs invasion. Whatever your thoughts on the late Fidel Castro and Cuban Americans, pay a visit here to flesh out one side of this contentious story. You'll likely see a few

Little Havana

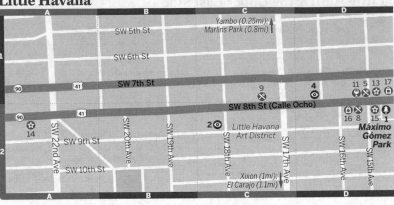

Little Havana

◎ Top Sights
1 Máximo Gómez Park D2

◎ Sights
2 Bay of Pigs Museum & Library C2
3 Cuban Memorial Park E2
4 Little Havana Art District D1

⊗ Eating
5 Azucar D1
6 Doce Provisions F1
7 El Nuevo Siglo E1
8 Exquisito Restaurant D2
9 Lung Yai Thai Tapas C1
10 Viva Mexico F1

⊕ Drinking & Nightlife
11 Ball & Chain D1
12 Los Pinareños Frutería E2

⊕ Entertainment
13 Cubaocho D1
14 Hoy Como Ayer A2
15 Tower Theater D2

⊝ Shopping
16 Cuba Tobacco Cigar Co. D2
17 Guantanamera D1
18 Havana Collection E1

survivors of the Bay of Pigs, who like to hang out here surrounded by pictures of comrades who never made it back to the USA.

Unfortunately the museum's collection is slated to move to a new building way out in Hialeah Gardens, so call before visiting to check where things are at.

Little Havana Art District   AREA
(Map p98; Calle Ocho, btwn SW 15th & 17th Aves) OK, it's not Wynwood. In fact, it's more 'Art Block' than district, with only a few galleries and studios still in business. Regardless, it's still worth a browse. This particular stretch of Little Havana is also the epicenter of the Viernes Culturales (p113) celebration.

◎ Coconut Grove

Coconut Grove was once a hippie colony, but these days its demographic is middle-class,

mall-going Miamians and college students. It's a pleasant place to explore with intriguing shops and cafes, and a walkable village-like vibe. It's particularly appealing in the evenings, when residents fill the outdoor tables of its bars and restaurants. Coconut Grove backs onto the waterfront, with a pretty marina and some pleasant green spaces.

★Vizcaya Museum &
Gardens   HISTORIC BUILDING
(☑305-250-9133; www.vizcayamuseum.org; 3251 S Miami Ave; adult/6-12yr/student & senior $18/6/12; ◎9:30am-4:30pm Wed-Mon; P) They call Miami the Magic City, and if it is, this Italian villa, the housing equivalent of a Fabergé egg, is its most fairy-tale residence. In 1916 industrialist James Deering started a Miami tradition by making a ton of money and building ridiculously grandiose digs. He employed 1000 people (then 10% of the local population) and

stuffed his home with 15th- to 19th-century furniture, tapestries, paintings and decorative arts; today the grounds are used for rotating contemporary-art exhibitions.

The Renaissance-inspired mansion is a classic of Miami's Mediterranean Revival stye. The largest room in the house is the informal living room, sometimes dubbed 'the Renaissance Hall' for its works dating from the 14th to the 17th centuries. The music room is intriguing for its beautiful wall canvases, which come from Northern Italy, while the banquet hall evokes all the grandeur of imperial dining rooms of Europe, with its regal furnishings.

On the south side of the house stretch a series of lovely gardens that are just as impressive as the interior of Vizcaya. Modeled on formal Italian gardens of the 17th and 18th centuries, these manicured spaces form a counterpoint to the wild mangroves beyond. Sculptures, fountains and vine-draped surfaces give an antiquarian look to the grounds, and an elevated terrace (the Garden Mound) provides a fine vantage point over the greenery.

The on-site Vizcaya Cafe has decent light snacks and coffee to keep energy levels up while perusing the lavish collections.

Kampong   GARDENS
(☑ 305-442-7169; www.ntbg.org/tours/kampong; 4013 Douglas Rd; adult/child $15/5; ☉ tours by appointment only 10am-3pm Mon-Sat) David Fairchild, the Indiana Jones of the botanical world and founder of Fairchild Tropical Garden, would rest at the Kampong (Malay/Indonesian for 'village') in between journeys in search of beautiful and economically viable plant life. Today this lush garden is listed on the National Register of Historic Places and the grounds serve as a classroom for the National Tropical Botanical Garden. Self-guided tours (allow at least an hour) are available by appointment, as are $20 one-hour guided tours.

Peacock Park   PARK
(Map p100; 2820 McFarlane Rd) Extending down to the edge of the waterfront, Peacock Park serves as the great open backyard of Coconut Grove. Young families stop by the playground and join the action on the ball fields, while power walkers take in the view on a scenic stroll along the bayfront.

Plymouth Congregational Church   CHURCH
(Map p100; ☑ 305-444-6521; www.plymouth miami.org; 3400 Devon Rd; ☉ hours vary; Ⓟ) This 1917 coral church is striking, from its solid masonry to a hand-carved door from a Pyrenees monastery, which looks like it should be kicked in by Antonio Banderas carrying a guitar case full of explosives and Salma Hayek on his arm. Architecturally this is one of the finest Spanish Mission–style churches in a city that does not lack for examples of the genre.

The church opens rarely, though all are welcome at the organ- and choir-led 10am Sunday service.

Ermita de la Caridad   MONUMENT
(☑ 305-854-2404; www.ermitadelacaridad.org; 3609 S Miami Ave) The Catholic diocese purchased some of the bayfront land from Deering's Villa Vizcaya estate and built a shrine here for its displaced Cuban parishioners. Symbolizing a beacon, it faces the homeland, exactly 290 miles due south. There is also a mural that

---

LOCAL KNOWLEDGE

LITTLE HAVANA

Cuban style Pick up a new outfit at the Havana Collection (p149). *Guayaberas* are the unofficial dress shirts of the neighborhood and you'll fit right in.

Friday fun On the last Friday of the month, Little Havana lets her hair down in a spirited night of live music and special art exhibitions during Viernes Culturales (p113).

Supermarket dining Hidden in the grocery store of the same name, El Nuevo Siglo (p136) is a well-loved local haunt for its delicious reasonably priced cooking.

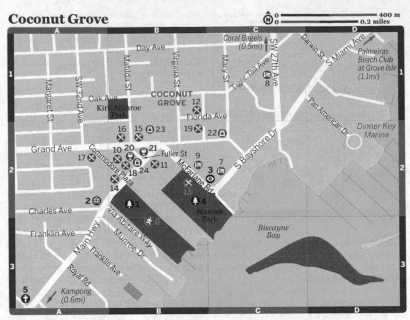

Coconut Grove

depicts Cuban history. Just outside the church is a grassy stretch of waterfront that makes a fine spot for a picnic.

Barnacle Historic State Park STATE PARK
(Map p100; ☎305-442-6866; www.florida stateparks.org/thebarnacle; 3485 Main Hwy; admission $2, house tours adult/child $3/1; ⊙9am-5pm Fri-Mon; ➍) In the center of Coconut Grove village is the 1891, 5-acre pioneer residence of Ralph

Monroe, Miami's first honorable snowbird. The house is open for guided tours (every 90 minutes between 10am and 2:30pm), and the park it's located on is a lovely, shady oasis for strolling. Barnacle hosts frequent (and lovely) moonlight concerts, from jazz to classical.

Eva Munroe's Grave HISTORIC SITE
(Map p100; 2875 McFarlane Rd) Tucked into a small gated area near the Coconut Grove

Library, you'll find the humble headstone of one Ms Eva Amelia Hewitt Munroe. Eva, who was born in New Jersey in 1856 and died in Miami in 1882, lies in the oldest American grave in Miami-Dade County (a sad addendum: local African American settlers died before Eva, but their deaths were never officially recorded).

Coconut Grove Playhouse   HISTORIC BUILDING
(Map p100; 3500 Main Hwy) Built in 1927, this is Miami's oldest theater, which sits in the heart of the Grove. Back in the day this was a grand dame of a building, with a snazzy marquee and a celebrity vibe balanced by a good deal of artsy cred: Samuel Beckett's *Waiting for Godot* had its US premiere here in 1956 (the show was apparently a disaster).

Sadly the theater was shut down during its 50th-anniversary season due to major debt issues and still sits, today, like a sad shell over Main Hwy. As of early 2017, plans were underway to restore the 300-seat playhouse, which will be run by the award-winning theater company GableStage when it opens again (probably 2020 at the earliest). In addition, a second and larger (700-seat) theater will be constructed in the back.

◉ Coral Gables

The lovely city of Coral Gables, filled with Mediterranean-style buildings, feels like a world removed from other parts of Miami. Here you'll find pretty banyan-lined streets, and a walkable village-like center, dotted with shops, cafes and restaurants. The big drawcards are the striking Biltmore Hotel, a lush tropical garden and one of America's loveliest swimming pools.

★ Fairchild Tropical Garden   GARDENS
(☑ 305-667-1651; www.fairchildgarden.org; 10901 Old Cutler Rd; adult/child/senior $25/12/18; ⊙ 9:30am-4:30pm; P ☜) If you need to escape Miami's madness, consider a green day in the country's largest tropical botanical garden. A butterfly grove, tropical plant conservatory and gentle vistas of marsh and keys habitats, plus frequent art installations from artists like Roy Lichtenstein, are all stunning. In addition to easy-to-follow, self-guided walking tours, a free 45-minute tram tours the entire park on the hour from 10am to 3pm (till 4pm weekends).

A favorite among the garden's youngest visitors is the **Wings of the Tropics** exhibition. Inside of an indoor gallery, hundreds of butterflies flutter freely through the air, the sheen of their wings glinting in the light. There are some 40 different species represented, including exotics from Central and South America, like blue morphos and owl butterflies. Visitors can also watch in real time as chrysalises emerge as butterflies at **Vollmer Metamorphosis Lab**.

The lushly lined pathways of the **Tropical Plant Conservatory** and the **Rare Plant House** contain rare philodendrons, orchids, begonias, rare palms, rhododendrons, ferns and moss, while the **Richard H Simons Rainforest**, though small in size, provides a splendid taste of the tropics, with a little stream and waterfalls amid orchids, plus towering trees with lianas (long woody vines) and epiphytes up in the rainforest canopy.

There's a couple of on-site cafes serving simple light fare or you can bring your own picnic and eat on the grounds.

Fairchild Tropical Garden lies about 6 miles south of Coral Gables downtown. It's easiest to get here by car or taxi. Another option is to take metrorail to South Miami, then transfer to bus 57.

★ Biltmore Hotel   HISTORIC BUILDING
(Map p102; ☑ 855-311-6903; www.biltmorehotel.com; 1200 Anastasia Ave; ⊙ tours 1:30 & 2:30pm Sun; P) In the most opulent neighborhood of one of the showiest cities in the world, the Biltmore peers down her nose and says, 'hrmph.' It's one of the greatest of the grand hotels of the American Jazz Age, and if this joint were a fictional character from a novel, it'd be, without question, Jay Gatsby. Al Capone had a speakeasy on site, and the Capone Suite is said to be haunted by the spirit of Fats Walsh, who was murdered here.

Back in the day, imported gondolas transported celebrity guests like Judy Garland and the Vanderbilts around because, of course, there was a private canal system out the back. It's gone now, but the largest hotel pool in the continental USA, which resembles a sultan's water garden from *One Thousand & One Nights*, is still here. If you'd like to side-stroke across it without the price tag of an overnight stay, visitors can use the pool and fitness center by purchasing a $35 day pass.

Lowe Art Museum   MUSEUM
(☑ 305-284-3535; www.miami.edu/lowe; 1301 Stanford Dr; adult/student/child $13/8/free; ⊙ 10am-4pm Tue-Sat, noon-4pm Sun) Your love of the Lowe, on the campus of the University of Miami, depends on your taste in art.

Coral Gables

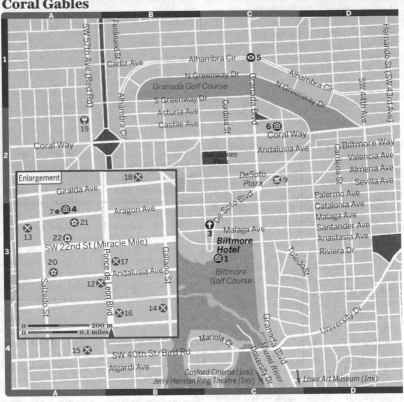

Coral Gables

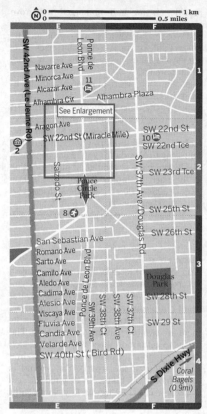

If you're into modern and contemporary works, it's good. If you're into the art and archaeology of cultures from Asia, Africa and the South Pacific, it's great. And if you're into pre-Columbian and Mesoamerican art, it's fantastic.

That isn't to discount the lovely permanent collection of Renaissance and baroque art, Western sculpture from the 18th to 20th centuries, and paintings by Gauguin, Picasso and Monet.

Coral Gables City Hall HISTORIC BUILDING
(Map p102; 405 Biltmore Way; ⏱8am-5pm Mon-Fri) This grand building has housed boring city-commission meetings since it opened in 1928. It's impressive from any angle, certainly befitting its importance as a central government building. Check out Denman Fink's *Four Seasons* ceiling painting in the tower, as well as his framed, untitled painting of the underwater world on the 2nd-floor landing.

There's a small farmers market on site from 8am to 2pm on Saturdays from mid-January to March.

Granada Entrance LANDMARK
(Map p102; cnr Alhambra Circle & Granada Blvd) Coral Gables–designer George Merrick planned a series of elaborate entry gates to the city. The Granada Entrance is among the completed gates worth seeing.

Coral Gables Congregational Church CHURCH
(Map p102; ☎305-448-7421; www.gablesucc.org; 3010 De Soto Blvd; ⏱hours vary) Developer George Merrick's father was a New England Congregational minister, so perhaps that accounts for him donating the land for the city's first church. Built in 1924 as a replica of a church in Costa Rica, the yellow-walled, red-roofed exterior is as far removed from New England as...well, Miami. The interior is graced with a beautiful sanctuary and the grounds are landscaped with stately palms.

It isn't open much, though you can stop in for a look during Sunday services at 9am and 11am.

Merrick House HISTORIC BUILDING
(Map p102; ☎305-460-5361; 907 Coral Way; adult/child/senior $5/1/3) It's fun to imagine this simple homestead, with its little hints of Med-style, as the core of what would eventually become the gaudy Gables. When George Merrick's father purchased this plot, site unseen, for $1100, it was all dirt, rock and guavas. The property is now used for meetings and receptions, and you can tour both the house and its pretty organic garden. The modest family residence looks as it did in 1925, outfitted with family photos, furniture and artwork.

Call ahead for the latest tour times. The house was closed for renovations at research time.

Coral Gables Museum MUSEUM
(Map p102; ☎305-603-8067; www.coralgablesmuseum.org; 285 Aragon Ave; adult/child/student $10/3/8; ⏱noon-6pm Tue-Fri, 11am-5pm Sat, noon-5pm Sun) This museum is a well-plotted introduction to the oddball narrative of the founding and growth of the City Beautiful (Coral Gables). The collection includes historical artifacts and mementos from succeeding generations in this tight-knit, eccentric little village. The main building is the old Gables police and fire station (note the deco-style firemen faces jutting out of the facade), itself

CORAL GABLES

Theater Gables residents have a small but vibrant theater scene, with performances at the **Actors Playhouse** (Map p102; ☎305-444-9293; www.actorsplayhouse.org; Miracle Theater, 280 Miracle Mile; tickets $20-64) and at Gablestage (p147) in the Biltmore.

Markets In front of City Hall (p103), the Coral Gables Farmers Market is the spot to load up on seasonal fruits, fresh breads and other goodies. It happens Saturdays from 8am to 2pm mid-January through March.

Hangouts Threefold (p138) is a neighborhood institution, and a great place to start the day.

a lovely architectural blend of Gables' Mediterranean Revival and a more Miami Beach–esque, muscular Depression-moderne style.

Matheson Hammock Park PARK
(☎305-665-5475; www.miamidade.gov/parks/matheson-hammock.asp; 9610 Old Cutler Rd; per car weekday/weekend $5/7; ☉sunrise-sunset; P⋆) This 630-acre county park is the city's oldest and one of its most scenic. It offers good swimming for children in an enclosed tidal pool, lots of hungry raccoons, dense mangrove swamps and (pretty rare) alligator-spotting. It's just south of Coral Gables.

◉ Key Biscayne

Key Biscayne and neighboring Virginia Key are a quick and easy getaway from Downtown Miami. But once you've passed across those scenic causeways, you'll feel like you've been transported to a far-off tropical realm, with magnificent beaches, lush nature trails in state parks, and aquatic adventures aplenty. The stunning skyline views of Miami alone are worth the trip out.

★Bill Baggs
Cape Florida State Park STATE PARK
(Map p106; ☎305-361-5811; www.floridastateparks.org/capeflorida; 1200 S Crandon Blvd; per car/person $8/2; ☉8am-sunset, lighthouse 9am-5pm; P⋆⋆) ✈ If you don't make it to the Florida Keys, come to this park for a taste of their unique island ecosystems. The 494-acre space is a tangled clot of tropical fauna and dark mangroves – look for the 'snorkel' roots that

provide air for half-submerged mangrove trees – all interconnected by sandy trails and wooden boardwalks, and surrounded by miles of pale ocean. A concession shack rents out kayaks, bikes, in-line skates, beach chairs and umbrellas.

At the state recreation area's southernmost tip, the 1845 brick **Cape Florida Lighthouse** is the oldest structure in Florida (it replaced another lighthouse that was severely damaged in 1836 during the Second Seminole War. Free tours run at 10am and 1pm Thursday to Monday. If you're not packing a picnic, there are several good places to dine in the park, including **Boater's Grill** (Map p106; ☎305-361-0080; mains $14-32, burgers $7-10; ☉9am-8pm Sun-Thu, to 10pm Fri & Sat) and **Lighthouse Cafe** (Map p106; ☎305-361-8487; ☉9am-5:30pm).

**Virginia Key Beach
North Point Park** STATE PARK
(Map p106; 3801 Rickenbacker Causeway, Virginia Key; per vehicle weekday/weekend $6/8; ☉7am-6pm) This lovely green space has several small but pleasing beaches, and some short nature trails. Pretty waterfront views aside, there are two big reasons to come here. The first is to get out on the water by hiring kayaks or stand-up paddleboards at Virginia Key Outdoor Center (p111). The second is to go mountain biking in a gated-off section known as the Virginia Key North Point Trails (p111), with a series of trails ranging from beginner to advanced.

The mountain-bike trails, which are tucked away at the northern tip of the park, are free to use, but you'll need your own bike (and helmet), which you can hire from the nearby Virginia Key Outdoor Center. Coming from Miami, this is the first park entrance (the second leads to the smaller Historic Virginia Key Beach Park).

Historic Virginia Key Park STATE PARK
(Map p106; www.virginiakeybeachpark.net; 4020 Virginia Beach Dr, Virginia Key; vehicle weekday/weekend $5/8, bike & pedestrian free; ☉7am-sunset; ⋆) A short drive (or bike ride) from Downtown Miami, the Historic Virginia Key Park is a fine place for a dose of nature, with a small but pretty beachfront and playgrounds for the kids (as well as a carousel). From time to time there are concerts, ecology-minded family picnics and other events. Coming from Downtown Miami, this is the second park entrance on the left (just past the entrance to the Virginia Key Beach North Point Park).

In the dark days of segregation, this beachfront, initially accessible only by boat, was an official 'colored only' recreation site (African Americans were not allowed on other beaches). Opened in 1945, it remained a major destination for African American communities (as well as Cubans, Haitians and many others from Latin America) seeking to enjoy a bit of the Miami coastline. It was popular until the early 1960s when the city's beaches were finally desegregated.

Marjory Stoneman Douglas Biscayne Nature Center   MUSEUM
(Map p106; ☑305-361-6767; www.biscayne naturecenter.org; 6767 Crandon Blvd, Crandon Park; ☉10am-4pm; P♿) 🏷FREE Marjory Stoneman Douglas was a beloved environmental crusader and worthy namesake of this child-friendly nature center. It's a great introduction to South Florida's unique ecosystems, with hands-on exhibits as well as aquariums in back full of parrot fish, conch, urchins, tulip snails and a fearsome-looking green moray eel. You can also stroll a nature trail through coastal hammock or enjoy the pretty beach in front.

Once a month, the center hosts naturalist-led walks ($14 per person) through seagrass in search of marine life. It's always a big hit with families. Reserve ahead.

Crandon Park   PARK
(Map p106; ☑305-361-5421; www.miamidade.gov/parks/parks/crandon_beach.asp; 6747 Crandon Blvd; per car weekday/weekend $5/7; ☉sunrise-sunset; P♿🐾) This 1200-acre park boasts **Crandon Park Beach**, a glorious stretch of sand that spreads for 2 miles. Much of the park consists of a dense coastal hammock (hardwood forest) and mangrove swamps. The beach here is clean and uncluttered by tourists, faces a lovely sweep of teal goodness and is regularly named one of the best beaches in the USA. Pretty cabanas at the south end of the park can be rented by the day ($40).

Village of Key Biscayne Community Center   PARK
(Map p106; ☑305-365-8900; www.active islander.org; 10 Village Green Way, off Crandon Blvd; daypass adult/child $9/6; ☉community center 6am-10pm Mon-Fri, 10am-8pm Sat & Sun; ♿🐾) 🌿 A top spot for the kids: there's a swimming pool and an activity room with a play set out of a child's happiest fantasies. On the green out front is a huge playground and an African baobab tree that's over a century old and teeming with tropical bird life. For the older set, you can get in a good workout or take a yoga class.

◉ Greater Miami

Deering Estate at Cutler   LANDMARK
(☑305-235-1668; www.deeringestate.org; 16701 SW 72nd Ave; adult/child under 14yr $12/7; ☉10am-5pm; P♿) The Deering estate is sort of 'Vizcaya lite,' which makes sense as it was built by Charles, brother of James Deering (of Vizcaya mansion fame). The 150-acre grounds are awash with tropical growth, an animal-fossil pit of bones dating back 50,000 years and the remains of Native Americans who lived here 2000 years ago. There's a free tour of the grounds at 3pm included in admission, and the estate often hosts jazz evenings under the stars.

Zoo Miami   ZOO
(Metrozoo; ☑305-251-0400; www.zoomiami.org; 12400 SW 152nd St; adult/child $22/18; ☉10am-5pm) Miami's tropical weather makes strolling around the Metrozoo almost feel like a day in the wild. Look for Asian and African elephants, rare and regal Bengal tigers prowling an evocative Hindu temple, pygmy hippos, Andean condors, a pack of hyenas, cute koalas, colobus monkeys, black rhinoceroses and a pair of Komodo dragons from Indonesia. For a quick overview (and because the zoo is so big), hop on the Safari Monorail; it departs every 20 minutes.

Rubell Family Art Collection (Allapattah)   GALLERY
(1100 NW 23rd St) One of the major icons in Miami's art world moves to a new space in Allapattah in late 2018 (in time for Art Basel (p115), which happens in December). The museum will feature a greatly expanded space (some 100,000 sq ft) from its former digs in Wynwood. The 2.5-acre campus will house 40 exhibition galleries, a sculpture garden, research library and a restaurant.

Arch Creek Park   PARK
(☑305-944-6111; www.miamidade.gov/parks/arch-creek.asp; 1855 NE 135th St; ☉9am-5pm Wed-Sun; P♿) This compact and cute park, located near Oleta River, encompasses a cozy habitat of tropical hardwood species that surrounds a pretty, natural limestone bridge. Naturalists can lead you on kid-friendly ecotours of the area, which include a lovely butterfly garden, or visitors can peruse a small but well-stocked museum of Native American

Key Biscayne

N

0 — 1 km
0 — 0.5 miles

SoSUP Key Biscayne (0.2mi);
Miami Catamarans (0.6mi);
Sailboards Miami (1.6mi)

Arthur
Lamb Jr Rd

6

VIRGINIA
KEY

Rickenbacker Cswy

Virginia Key
Outdoor Center (1mi);
Virginia Key
North Point Trails (1.5mi)

3

Bear Cut

Northwest
Point

Biscayne
Bay

Crandon Park
Marina

8

Crandon
Park

2

Crandon
Park Beach

West
Point

KEY
BISCAYNE

15 12

16

Harbor Dr

13

East Dr

10

Village Green
Park
5

E Heather Dr

9

Galen Dr

Harbor
Point

Key
Biscayne

E Wood Dr

ATLANTIC

OCEAN

Southwest
Point

S Mashta Dr

W Mashta Dr

Crandon Blvd

Bill Baggs Cape
Florida State Park 1

Cape Florida Channel

Biscayne
Bay

Cape
Florida

14

Cape Florida
Lighthouse

Key Biscayne

and pioneer artifacts. The excellent Miami EcoAdventures (p111) is based here. The park is just off North Biscayne Blvd, 7 miles north of the Design District.

Ancient Spanish Monastery CHURCH
(☑305-945-1461; www.spanishmonastery.com; 16711 W Dixie Hwy; adult/child $10/5; ⊙10am-4:30pm Mon-Sat, from 11am Sun; P) Finding a fully intact medieval monastery in North Miami Beach is yet another reason why the moniker 'Magic City' seems so fitting. Constructed in 1141 in Segovia, Spain, the Monastery of St Bernard de Clairvaux is a striking early-Gothic and Romanesque building that rather improbably found its way to South Florida. The property – today a church that's part of the Episcopal diocese – gets busy for weddings, so call before making the long trip out here. It's roughly 15 miles north of Downtown Miami.

Pinecrest Gardens PARK
(☑305-669-6990; www.pinecrest-fl.gov/gardens; 11000 SW 57th Ave; adult/senior/child $5/3/5; ⊙10am-6pm Apr-Sep, to 5pm Oct-Mar; P⊕) When Parrot Jungle (now Jungle Island; p92) flew the coop for the big city, the village of Pinecrest purchased the property in order to keep it as a municipal park. It's now a quiet oasis with some of the best tropical gardens this side of the Gulf of Mexico, topped off by a gorgeous centerpiece banyan tree. Outdoor movies and jazz concerts are held here, and all in all this is a total gem that is utterly off the tourism trail.

Monkey Jungle ZOO
(☑305-235-1611; www.monkeyjungle.com; 14805 SW 216th St; adult/child/senior $30/24/28; ⊙9:30am-5pm, last entry 4pm; P⊕) At the Monkey Jungle, the zoo experience gets flipped on its head: visitors step into the cage while monkeys run wild and free. Indeed, you'll be walking through screened-in trails, with primates swinging, screeching and chattering all around you. It's incredibly fun, and just a bit odorous. The big show of the day takes place at feeding time, when crab-eating monkeys and Southeast Asian macaques dive into the pool for fruit and other treats.

Museum of Contemporary Art North Miami MUSEUM
(MoCA; ☑305-893-6211; www.mocanomi.org; 770 NE 125th St; adult/student/child $5/3/free; ⊙11am-5pm Tue-Fri & Sun, 1-9pm Sat; P) The Museum of Contemporary Art has long been a reason to hike up to the far reaches of North Miami. Its galleries feature excellent rotating exhibitions of contemporary art by local, national and international artists.

Gold Coast Railroad Museum MUSEUM
(☑305-253-0063; www.gcrm.org; 12450 SW 152nd St; adult/child 3-11yr $8/6; ⊙10am-4pm Mon-Fri, from 11am Sat & Sun; P) Primarily of interest to train buffs, this museum displays more than 30 antique railway cars, including the Ferdinand Magellan presidential car, where President Harry Truman famously brandished a newspaper with the erroneous headline 'Dewey Defeats Truman.'

The museum offers 25-minute rides on old cabooses ($6) and standard gauge cabs ($12) on weekends. It's advised you call ahead to book rides.

Hialeah Park Casino CASINO
(www.hialeahparkcasino.com; 2200 E 4th Ave; ⊙casino 9am-3am; P) Hialeah is more Havanan than Little Havana (more than 90% of the population speak Spanish as a first language), and the symbol and center of this working-class Cuban community is this grand former racetrack. In 2013 the track was converted into a casino, which also

shows other races (that you can gamble on) via simulcast.

Activities

Miami doesn't lack for ways to keep yourself busy. From sailing the teal waters to hiking through tropical undergrowth, yoga in the parks and (why not?) trapeze artistry above the city's head, the Magic City rewards those who want an active holiday.

South Beach

Fritz's Skate, Bike & Surf
SKATING

(Map p78; ☎305-532-1954; www.fritzsmiami beach.com; 1620 Washington Ave; bike & skate rental per hour/day/5 days $10/24/69; ☺10am-9pm Mon-Sat, to 8pm Sun) Rent your wheels from Fritz's, which offers skateboards, longboards, in-line skates, roller skates, razor scooters and bicycles (cruisers, mountain bikes, kids bikes). Protective gear is included with skate rentals, and bikes come with locks.

Spa at the Setai
SPA

(Map p78; ☎855-923-7908; www.thesetaihotel.com; 101 20th St, Setai Hotel; 1hr massage from $180; ☺9am-9pm) A silky Balinese haven in one of South Beach's most beautiful hotels (p120).

Green Monkey Yoga
YOGA

(Map p78; ☎305-397-8566; www.greenmonkey.net; 1800 Bay Rd; drop-in class $25) This yoga studio has a beautiful setting with huge windows on the top floor of a building in Sunset Harbour. There's a wide range of classes throughout the day, including Vinyasa, power yoga, hip-hop flow and meditation. If you're around for a while ask about the new student special ($69 for one month of unlimited classes).

SoBe Surf
SURFING

(☎786-216-7703; www.sobesurf.com; group/private lesson from $70/120) Offers surf lessons both in Miami Beach and in Coca Beach, where there tends to be better waves. Instruction on Miami Beach usually happens around South Point. All bookings are done by phone or email.

Glow Hot Yoga
YOGA

(Map p78; ☎305-534-2727; www.glowhotyoga miami.com; 1560 Lenox Ave; drop-in class/weekly unlimited rate $27/59) Offers excellent hot yoga classes in a big, inviting studio that's kept sparkling clean. There's also an outdoor patio where you can unwind after an intense Bikram class. It's just south of Lincoln Rd.

North Beach

Russian & Turkish Baths
MASSAGE

(Map p86; ☎305-867-8316; www.russianand turkishbaths.com; 5445 Collins Ave; treatments from $40; ☺noon-midnight) Just because you enjoy a good back rub doesn't mean you need to go to some glitzy spa where they constantly play soft house music on a repetitive loop. Right? Why not head to a favorite 'hot' spot among folks who want a spa experience without the glamour. Enter this little labyrinth of *banyas* (steam rooms) for a plethora of spa choices.

You can be casually beaten with oak-leaf brooms called *venik* in a lava-hot spa (for $40; it's actually really relaxing...well, interesting anyway). There's Dead Sea salt and mud exfoliation ($55), plus the on-site cafe serves delicious borscht, blintzes, dark bread with smoked fish and, of course, beer. The crowd is interesting too: hipsters, older Jews, model types, Europeans and folks from Russia and former Soviet states, some of whom look like, um, entirely legitimate businessmen and we're leaving it at that.

Carillon Miami Wellness Resort
SPA

(Map p86; ☎866-276-2226; www.carillonhotel. com; 6801 Collins Ave, Carillon Hotel; treatments $165-300; ☺8am-9pm) For pure pampering, the Carillon's 70,000-sq-ft spa and wellness center is hard to knock. It has an excellent range of treatments, fitness classes (spinning, power yoga, meditation, core workouts) plus pretty views of the crashing waves.

BG Oleta River Outdoor Center
WATER SPORTS

(☎786-274-7945; www.bgoletariveroutdoor.com; 3400 NE 163rd St; kayak/canoe hire per 90min $25/30; ☺8am-1 hour before sunset; ♿) Located in the Oleta River State Park, this outfitter hires out loads of water-sports gear; for a two-hour rental, options include single/tandem kayaks ($30/60), canoes ($35), stand-up paddleboards ($40) and bikes (from $25).

It also organizes group tours: weekend morning paddles (at 10am, from $45), sunset paddles (on Fridays, from $35), once-a-month full-moon paddles, stand-up paddleboard classes, and stand-up paddleboard yoga classes (Sundays at 9am, $30).

Normandy Isle Park & Pool
SWIMMING

(Map p86; ☎305-673-7750; 7030 Trouville Esplanade; adult/child $10/6; ☺6:30am-8:30pm; ♿) For a fun day out, head to this family-friendly

⚡ Walking Tour
Art-Deco Miami Beach

START ART DECO MUSEUM
END OCEAN'S TEN
LENGTH 1.2 MILES; TWO TO THREE HOURS

Start at the ❶ **Art Deco Museum** (p65), at the corner of Ocean Dr and 10th St (named Barbara Capitman Way here, after the Miami Design Preservation League's founder). Step in for an exhibit on art-deco style, then head north along Ocean Dr; between 12th and 14th Sts you'll see three examples of deco hotels: the ❷ **Leslie**, a boxy shape with eyebrows (cantilevered sunshades) wrapped around the side of the building; the ❸ **Carlyle** (p81), featured in the film *The Birdcage* and boasting modernistic styling; and the graceful ❹ **Cardozo Hotel** (p81), built by Henry Hohauser, owned by Gloria Estefan and featuring sleek, rounded edges. At 14th St peek inside the sun-drenched ❺ **Winter Haven Hotel** (p121) to see its fabulous terrazzo floors, made of stone chips set in mortar that's polished when dry. Turn left and down 14th St to Washington Ave and the ❻ **US Post Office** (p77), at 13th St. It's a curvy block of white deco in the stripped classical style. Step inside to admire the wall mural, domed ceiling and marble stamp tables. Lunch at the ❼ **11th St Diner** (p127), a gleaming aluminum Pullman car that was imported in 1992 from Wilkes-Barre, Pennsylvania. Get a window seat and gaze across to the corner of 10th St and the stunningly restored ❽ **Hotel Astor** (p117), designed in 1936 by T Hunter Henderson. Next, walk half a block east from there to the ❾ **Wolfsonian-FIU** (p65), an excellent design museum. Wealthy snowbirds of the '30s stashed their pricey belongings here before heading back up north. Continue walking Washington Ave, turn left on 7th St and then continue north along Collins Ave to the ❿ **Hotel of South Beach** (p122), featuring an interior and roof deck by Todd Oldham. L Murray Dixon designed the hotel as the Tiffany Hotel, with a deco spire, in 1939. Turn right on 9th St and go two blocks to Ocean Dr, where you'll spy nonstop deco beauties; at 960 Ocean Dr (the middling ⓫ **Ocean's Ten** restaurant) you'll see an exterior designed in 1935 by deco legend Henry Hohauser.

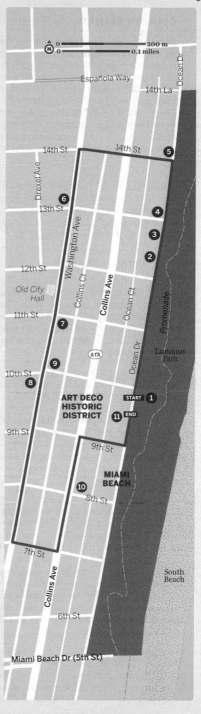

CYCLING IN MIAMI

The Miami-Dade County Parks and Recreation Department maintains a list of traffic-free cycling paths as well as downloadable maps on its website (www.miamidade.gov/parks masterplan/bike-trails-map.asp). For less strenuous rides, try the side roads of South Beach or the shady streets of Coral Gables and Coconut Grove. Some good trails include the **Old Cutler Bike Path**, which starts at the end of Sunset Dr in Coral Gables and leads through Coconut Grove to Matheson Hammock Park and Fairchild Tropical Garden. The **Rickenbacker Causeway** takes you up and over the bridge to Key Biscayne for an excellent workout combined with gorgeous water views. A bit farther out, the **Oleta River State Park** has a challenging dirt trail with hills for off-road adventures. Need to rent a bike? Try the Citi Bike (p151) bike-sharing program.

four-lane pool. It's lap swimming only at various times of day (before 9am and after 7pm), but otherwise it's open to all. There's also an outdoor splash-play area for the kids, with cascades to keep things interesting.

 ## Downtown Miami

Tina Hills Pavilion YOGA
(Map p88; Biscayne Blvd, Bayfront Park) FREE This small open-air pavilion hosts free events, including free 75-minute yoga sessions, suitable for all levels. These take place Mondays and Wednesdays at 6pm, and 9am Saturday morning.

Spa at Mandarin Oriental Miami SPA
(Map p88; ☑305-913-8332; www.mandarin oriental.com/miami/luxury-spa; 500 Brickell Key Dr, Mandarin Oriental Miami; manicures $75, spa treatments $175-425; ☉8:30am-9:30pm) Calling this spa over the top is an understatement. Treatments utilize materials like bamboo and rice paper, and services include Ayurvedic herbal baths, aromatherapy, oiled massages and plenty more decadence.

Miami Yoga YOGA
(Map p88; ☑305-856-1387; www.miamiyoga. com; 301 SW 17th Rd, Brickell; 1-/5-/10-class pass $22/95/180) Yoga fans need not leave their practice behind on a trip to Miami. The style here is a bit eclectic: it's hot power Vinyasa yoga, offering a little bit of everything (strengthening, stretching, meditation) in a studio that's heated but not unbearably so.

Classes run morning, afternoon and evening throughout the week with all skill levels welcome.

Blue Waters II FISHING
(Map p88; ☑305-373-5016; www.fishingmiami. net; 401 Biscayne Blvd, Bayside Marketplace, Pier 5) For an action-filled day out on the water,

book a fishing charter with this top-notch outfit. Captain John Barker has more than 30 years of experience fishing these waters and can take you out on four-, six- or eight-hour private charters around Miami and Key Biscayne.

 ## Little Haiti & the Upper East Side

Kundalini Yoga YOGA
(Map p96; ☑305-603-8540; www.kymiami.com; 6901 Biscayne Blvd; drop-in class $20, mat rental $2; ☉10am-6:30pm Mon-Sat, to 4pm Sun) This yoga studio gets high marks for its classes, which have quite a local following. As with other Kundalini centers, there's very much a spiritual, meditative aspect to the practice here. Classes run 90 minutes.

Coral Gables

★**Venetian Pool** SWIMMING
(Map p102; ☑305-460-5306; www.coralgables venetianpool.com; 2701 De Soto Blvd; adult/child Sep-May $15/10, Jun-Aug $20/15; ☉11am-5:30pm Tue-Fri, 10am-4:30pm Sat & Sun, closed Dec-Feb; ⛲) Just imagine: it's 1923, tons of rock have been quarried for one of the most beautiful neighborhoods in Miami, but now an ugly gash sits in the middle of the village. What to do? How about pump the irregular hole full of water, mosaic and tile up the whole affair, and make it look like a Roman emperor's aquatic playground?

Result: one of the few pools listed on the National Register of Historic Places, a wonderland of coral rock caves, cascading waterfalls, a palm-fringed island and Venetian-style moorings. Take a swim and follow in the footsteps (fin-steps?) of stars like Esther Williams and Johnny 'Tarzan' Weissmuller.

Prana Yoga Center YOGA
(Map p102; ☑305-567-9812; www.pranayoga
miami.com; 247 Malaga Ave; 1-/5-/10-class pass
$20/95/180; ☺8:30am-9pm Mon-Fri, to 4pm Sat
& Sun) In Coral Gables, this is a much-loved
yoga studio with Iyengar and Kundalini
classes as well meditation and relaxation
practices.

🏃 Key Biscayne

★**Virginia Key Outdoor Center** OUTDOORS
(VKOC; www.vkoc.net; 3801 Rickenbacker Causeway,
Virginia Key; kayak or bike hire 1st hour $25, each ad-
ditional hour $10; ☺9am-4:30pm Mon-Fri, from 8am
Sat & Sun) This highly recommended outfitter
will get you out on the water in a hurry with
kayaks and stand-up paddleboards, which
you can put in the water just across from
their office. The small mangrove-lined bay
(known as Lamar Lake) has manatees, and
makes for a great start to the paddle before
you venture further out.

One of the highlights is partaking in one
of VKOC's guided sunset and full moon paddles, which happen several times a month.

You can also hire mountain bikes for the
nearby Virginia Key North Point Trails.

**Virginia Key
North Point Trails** MOUNTAIN BIKING
(3801 Rickenbacker Causeway, Virginia Key Beach
North Point Park) FREE In a wooded section
at the north end of the Virginia Key Beach
North Point Park, you'll find a series of short
mountain-bike trails, color coded for beginner, intermediate and advanced. It's free to
use the trails, though you'll have to pay for
parking at the Virginia Key Beach North
Point Park to get here.

If you are not traveling with a bike, hire
one from the nearby Virginia Key Outdoor
Center.

Miami Catamarans BOATING
(☑305-345-4104; www.facebook.com/miamicata
marans; 3300 Rickenbacker Causeway, Virginia
Key; per hour from $64; ☺11am-6pm Mon-Fri, from
10am Sat & Sun) Head out on the water on a
small Hobie Cat catamaran. If you've never
sailed before, you can take a one-hour lesson
for $120.

Crandon Golf Course GOLF
(Map p106; ☑305-361-9129; www.golfcrandon.
com; 6700 Crandon Blvd; 18-holes $200, after
2pm/3:30pm $70/35) Out on Key Biscayne,
this course has great views over the water. Avid golfers consider it to be one of

the loveliest and most challenging par-72
courses in Florida.

SoSUP Key Biscayne WATER SPORTS
(☑786-301-3557; www.sosupkeybiscayne.com;
3979 Rickenbacker Causeway, Virginia Key;
kayak/stand-up paddleboard per hour $10/20/25;
☺10am-5pm) A good outfitter for all sorts of
outdoor adventures, SoSUP rents out stand-
up paddleboards, kayaks, pedal boats and
bikes from a stall on the beach. Despite the
name, it's located on Virginia Key.

Miami Kiteboarding WATER SPORTS
(Map p106; ☑305-345-9974; www.miamikite
boarding.com; 6747 Crandon Blvd, Crandon Park;
☺10am-6pm Apr-Sep, 9am-5pm Oct-Mar) Offers
a range of private lessons starting from $150
for one hour of one-on-one instruction. Couples get discounted rates.

Sailboards Miami WATER SPORTS
(☑305-892-8992; www.sailboardsmiami.com; 1
Rickenbacker Causeway; windsurf lesson $85, wind-
surf/kayak/SUP hire per hour from $30/20/30;
☺10am-6pm Fri-Tue) A good one-stop spot for
getting out on the water. It offers two-hour
intro windsurfing lessons, or if you already
have the know-how you can simply rent the
gear. You can also hire kayaks and stand-up
paddleboards.

🚣 Courses & Tours

If you're a bona-fide seaworthy sailor,
the **Aquatic Rental Center & Sailing
School** (☑305-751-7514; www.arcmiami.com;
1275 NE 79th St; sailboats per 2hr/3hr/4hr/day
$90/130/160/225; ☺9am-9pm) will rent you a
sailboat. If you're not, it can teach you how

DON'T MISS

MIAMI ECOADVENTURES

The Dade County parks system leads
a variety of tours under the rubric of
Miami EcoAdventures (☑305-666-
5885; www.miamidade.gov/ecoadventures;
bike tours $45, canoeing $30-70), including
excellent bike tours on Key Biscayne and
out in the Everglades. You can also go on
one of six different canoe trips, out on the
Oleta River, on the Matheson Mangrove
trek or paddling to Indian Key down in the
Keys. There's also kayaking, snorkeling
trips, walking tours and birdwatching.
Trips depart from different locations; call
or go online for details

MIAMI COURSES & TOURS

to operate one (sailing courses $450/600 for one/two people).

☞ South Beach

**Miami Design
Preservation League** WALKING

(Map p82; ☑ 305-672-2014; www.mdpl.org; 1001 Ocean Dr; guided tours adult/student $25/20; ⊘ 10:30am daily & 6:30pm Thu) Tells the stories and history behind the art-deco buildings in South Beach, with a lively guide from the Miami Design Preservation League. Tours last 90 minutes. Also offers tours of Jewish Miami Beach, Gay & Lesbian Miami Beach and a once-monthly tour (first Saturday at 9:30am) of the MiMo district in the North Beach area. Check website for details.

Miami Food Tours FOOD & DRINK

(Map p82; ☑ 786-361-0991; www.miamifood tours.com; 429 Lenox Ave; South Beach tour adult/child $58/35, Wynwood tour $75/55; ⊘ tours South Beach 11am & 4:30pm daily, Wynwood 10:30am Mon-Sat) This highly rated tour explores various facets of the city – culture, history, art and of course cuisine – while making stops at restaurants and cafes along the way. It's a walking tour, though distances aren't great, and happens in South Beach and Wynwood.

Bike & Roll CYCLING

(Map p82; ☑ 305-604-0001; www.bikemiami. com; 210 10th St; hire per 2hr/4hr/day from $10/18/24, tours $40; ⊘ 9am-7pm) This well-run outfit offers a good selection of bikes, including single-speed cruisers, geared hybrids and speedy road bikes. Staff move things along

---

YOGA WITH A SIDE OF SALT BREEZE

The beach is definitely not the only place to salute the sun in Miami. There are lovely **Yoga by the Sea** (Map p100; www. thebarnacle.org; class $15; ⊘ 6:30-7:45pm Mon & Wed) lessons offered at the Barnacle Historic State Park (p100) in Coconut Grove. If you don't feel like breaking out your wallet, try the free yoga classes at Bayfront Park (p85), held outdoors at Tina Hills Pavilion, at the south end of the park, three times a week.

Studios offer a large range of classes; bring your own mat (though some places hire out mats as well for around $2 a class).

---

quickly, so you won't have to waste time waiting to get out and riding. Bike tours are also available (daily at 10am).

☞ Downtown Miami

History Miami Tours TOURS

(www.historymiami.org/city-tour; tours $30-60) Historian extraordinaire Dr Paul George leads fascinating walking tours, including culturally rich strolls through Little Haiti, Little Havana, Downtown and Coral Gables at twilight, plus the occasional boat trip to Stiltsville and Key Biscayne. Tours happen once a week or so. Get the full menu and sign up online.

Urban Tour Host WALKING

(Map p88; ☑ 305-416-6868; www.miamicultural tours.com; 25 SE 2nd Ave, Ste 1048; tours from $20) Urban Tour Host runs a program of custom tours that provide face-to-face interaction in all of Miami's neighborhoods. For something different, sign up for a Miami cultural community tour that includes Little Haiti and Little Havana, with opportunities to visit Overtown, Liberty City and Allpattah.

Other tours take in South Beach, Downtown and Coral Gables; Wynwood and the Design District; and the Everglades, among other places.

Island Queen BOATING

(Map p88; ☑ 305-379-5119; www.islandqueen cruises.com; 401 Biscayne Blvd; adult/child from $28/20) This outfit runs 90-minute boat tours that take in Millionaire's Row, the Miami River and Fisher Island. There are frequent daily departures (hourly between 11am and 6pm).

☞ Wynwood & the Design District

Wynwood Art Walk WALKING

(☑ 305-814-9290; www.wynwoodartwalk.com; tours from $29) Not to be confused with the monthly art celebration of the same name, this Wynwood Art Walk is actually a 90-minute guided tour taking you to some of the best gallery shows of the day, plus a look at some of the top street art around the 'hood.

☞ Coral Gables

Coral Gables Tours OUTDOORS

(Map p102; ☑ 305-603-8067; www.coralgables museum.org/tours; 285 Aragon Ave) The Coral

Gables Museum runs tours throughout the month, including downtown walking tours (Saturdays at 11am, $10), exhibition tours at the museum (Sundays at 1pm, free with admission) and bike tours (third Sunday of the month at 10am, $10).

Best of all are the two-hour paddling tours on the Coral Gables Waterway (last Sunday of the month at 9:30am, $40) – a scenic series of constructed canals that provide the chance to take in a bit of nature and history. Call ahead to reserve a spot on a tour.

☞ Key Biscayne

Stiltsville Boat Tour   BOATING
(📞 305-379-5119;   www.islandqueencruises.com/stiltsville.htm; tours $60) Island Queen Cruises, based out of the Bayside Marketplace, offers infrequent trips to Stiltsville (approximately once a month), on three-hour tours narrated by Dr Paul George. Check www.historymiami.org/city-tour for the latest schedule.

✦ Festivals & Events

Viernes Culturales   CULTURAL
(Cultural Fridays; www.viernesculturales.org; ⏰ 7-11pm last Fri of month) No wine-sipping art walk this; Cultural Fridays in Little Havana are like little carnival seasons, with music, old men in *guayaberas* (Cuban dress shirts) crooning to the stars and Little Havana galleries throwing open their doors for special exhibitions.

The Little Havana Arts District may not be Wynwood, but it does constitute an energetic little strip of galleries and studios (concentrated on 8th St between SW 15th Ave & SW 17th Ave), and there's no better time to visit it all than on the last Friday of each month for Viernes Culturales.

Wynwood Art Walk   ART
(www.artcircuits.com; ⏰ 7-10pm 2nd Sat of the month) FREE One of the best ways to take in the burgeoning Miami art scene is to join in the Wynwood Art Walk. Despite the name, these events aren't really about walking, but more about celebration. Many of the galleries around Wynwood host special events and art openings, with ever-flowing drinks (not always free), live music around the 'hood, food trucks and special markets.

It's a fun event – though the crowds are pretty heavy. On the same night, the Design District hosts its own Art Walk. It's less of a party than the Wynwood event, and more about the art.

Sounds of Little Haiti   CULTURAL
(www.rhythmfoundation.com/series/big-night-in-little-haiti; 212 NE 59 Terrace, Little Haiti Cultural Center; ⏰ 6-10pm 3rd Fri of month) FREE For a taste of Caribbean culture, head to this family-friendly fest held on the third Friday of every month. The celebration is rife with music, Caribbean food and kids' activities.

January
Miami Jewish Film Festival   FILM
(www.miamijewishfilmfestival.com; 4200 Biscayne Blvd; ⏰ Jan) A great chance to cinematically *kvetch* with one of the biggest Jewish communities in the USA.

Art Deco Weekend   CULTURAL
(www.artdecoweekend.com; Ocean Dr, btwn 1st St & 23rd St; ⏰ mid-Jan) This weekend fair held in mid-January features guided tours, concerts, classic-auto shows, sidewalk cafes, arts and antiques.

Miami Marathon   SPORTS
(www.themiamimarathon.com; ⏰ late-Jan) The big running event in South Florida is the Miami Marathon, which brings over 25,000 runners racing through the streets along a very scenic course. There's also a half marathon.

February
Original Miami
Beach Antiques Show   FAIR
(www.originalmiamibeachantiqueshow.com; Miami Beach Convention Center; ⏰ Feb) One of the largest events of its kind in the USA, with more than 800 dealers from 20 countries. The action happens over four days.

Art Wynwood   ART
(www.artwynwood.com; ⏰ mid-Feb) The dozens of galleries spread throughout Wynwood strut their artistic stuff during this festival, which showcases the best of Miami's burgeoning arts scene. There's a palpable commercial bent to this artistic event; big wallet buyers are wooed and marketed to. Expect murals and installations to appear throughout the area. Typically held on the third weekend in February.

South Beach Wine &
Food Festival   FOOD & DRINK
(www.sobefest.com; ⏰ late-Feb) A festival of fine dining and sipping to promote South Florida's culinary image. Expect cooking demonstrations, star-studded brunches, dinners and barbecues, plus wine tastings, happy-hour munching and cocktail sipping. Happens over five days in late February.

Coconut Grove Arts Festival   CULTURAL
(www.coconutgroveartsfest.com; Bayshore Dr, Coconut Grove; ☺late-Feb) One of the most prestigious arts festivals in the country, this three-day February fair features works by more than 350 visual artists. There are also concerts, dance and theater troupes, a culinary arts component (with cooking demos) and a global village with vendors selling foods from around the world.

March
Carnaval Miami   CARNIVAL
(Calle Ocho Festival; www.carnavalmiami.com; ☺Mar) One of the biggest events in Little Havana's yearly calendar is this premier Latin festival, which takes over the area for nine days in early March: there's a Latin drag-queen show, inline-skate competition, domino tournament, the immense Calle Ocho street festival, Miss Carnaval Miami and more.

Miami International Film Festival   FILM
(www.miamifilmfestival.com; ☺Mar) This event, sponsored by Miami-Dade College, is an intensive 10-day festival showcasing documentaries and features from all over the world. Over half-a-dozen cinemas participate across the city.

Winter Music Conference   MUSIC
(www.wintermusicconference.com; ☺Mar) Party promoters, DJs, producers and revelers come from around the globe to hear new electronic-music artists, catch up on technology and party the nights away.

Calle Ocho Festival   CULTURAL
(Carnaval Miami; www.carnavalmiami.com; ☺Mar) This massive street party in March is the culmination of Carnaval Miami, a 10-day celebration of Latin culture.

Ultra Music Festival   MUSIC
(www.ultramusicfestival.com; Bayfront Park, 301 N Biscayne Blvd) In late March, huge dance-loving crowds gather at Bayfront Park for three days of revelry. Top DJs

from around the globe jet in to spin electronica on eight different stages scattered about the park. There are light shows, wild costumes and mega-decibel sound systems that spill bass far across the city.

Book tickets early. Over 150,000 attend, and the event always sells out.

April
Miami Beach Gay Pride   PARADE
(www.miamibeachgaypride.com; ☺Apr) In April Miami Beach proudly flies the rainbow flag high in this lively weekend festival that culminates in a colorful street parade along Ocean Dr. Break out the boas, glitter and body paint!

Outshine Film Festival   FILM
(www.mifofilm.com; ☺Apr) Held over 10 days in late April, this annual event screens shorts, feature films and documentaries with a LGBT focus shown at various South Beach theaters. Over 65 films are screened, including many world premieres.

Wynwood Life   MUSIC
(www.wynwoodlife.com; ☺Apr) Held over one weekend in April, this newish festival is a celebration of all things Wynwood, with live music and DJs, a big market of arts and crafts, fashion shows, food trucks, a culinary stage (of cooking demonstrations) and a crew of talented street artists creating live installations throughout the fest.

Billboard Latin Music Awards   MUSIC
(www.billboardevents.com; ☺late-Apr) This prestigious awards show in late April draws top industry execs, star performers and a slew of Latin-music fans.

May, June & July
Miami Museum Month   CULTURAL
(www.miamimuseummonth.com; ☺May) Held through the month of May, this is an an excellent chance to see and hang out in some of the best museums in the city in the midst of happy hours, special exhibitions and lectures.

Miami Fashion Week   CULTURAL
(www.miamifashionweek.com; Miami Beach Convention Center; ☺May or Jun) Models are as abundant as fish in the ocean as designers descend on the city and catwalks become ubiquitous.

Goombay Festival   CULTURAL
(www.goombayfestivalcoconutgrove.com; ☺Jun/Jul) A massive festival, held in June or July, which celebrates Bahamian culture.

MIAMI'S TOP EVENTS

Art Basel Miami, December

Art Deco Weekend (p113), January

Coconut Grove Arts Festival, February

Carnaval Miami, March

Ultra Music Festival, March

LOCAL KNOWLEDGE

MIAMI CRITICAL MASS

If you're in Miami at the beginning of the weekend late in any given month, you may spot hordes of cyclists and, less frequently, some skateboarders, roller-skaters and other self-propelled individuals. So what's it all about?

It's Miami Critical Mass. The event, put on by the Miami Bike Scene (www.themiamibike scene.com) is meant to raise awareness of cycling and indirectly advocate for increased bicycle infrastructure in the city. Anyone is welcome to join; the mass ride gathers at Government Center (by HistoryMiami; p85) at 6:30pm on the last Friday of each month.

The whole shebang departs on the 12-to-18-mile trek at 7:15pm. The average speed of the ride is a not-too-taxing 12mph, and you will be expected to keep up (at the same time, you're not to go faster than the pace setters). All in all, a fun experience, and a good way to meet members of the local cycling community.

Independence Day Celebration   CULTURAL
(Bayfront Park; ⊘ July 4) July 4 is marked with excellent fireworks, a laser show and live music that draw more than 100,000 people to breezy Bayfront Park.

August & September
**Miami Spice
Restaurant Month**   FOOD & DRINK
(www.facebook.com/ilovemiamispice; ⊘ Aug-Sep) Top restaurants around Miami offer three-course lunches and dinners to try to lure folks out during the heat wave. Prices hover around $25 for lunch and $40 for dinner. Reservations essential.

International Ballet Festival   DANCE
(www.internationalballetfestival.org; ⊘ Aug-Sep) Some of the most important dance talent in the world performs at venues across the city. Performances happen over various weekends from August to September.

November
Miami Book Fair International   CULTURAL
(www.miamibookfair.com; 401 NE 2nd Ave; ⊘ Nov) Occurring in mid- to late-November, this is among the most important and well-attended book fairs in the USA. Hundreds of nationally known writers join hundreds of publishers and hundreds of thousands of visitors.

White Party   MUSIC
(www.whiteparty.org; ⊘ Nov) If you're gay and not here, there's a problem. This weeklong extravaganza draws more than 15,000 gay men and women for nonstop partying at clubs and venues all over town.

December
Design Miami   ART
(www.designmiami.com; ⊘ early Dec) Held in conjunction with Art Basel, usually in early December, Design Miami is a high-profile party hosting some of the world's top design professionals and assorted entourages. Design-inspired lectures and showcases center on the Miami Beach Convention Center.

Art Basel Miami Beach   ART
(www.artbasel.com/miami-beach; ⊘ early Dec) One of the most important international art shows in the world, with works from more than 250 galleries and a slew of trendy parties. Even if you're not a billionaire collector, there's much to enjoy at this four-day fest, with open-air art installations around town, special exhibitions at many Miami galleries and outdoor film screenings, among other goings-on.

The main art show happens at the Miami Beach Convention Center (tickets from $50), but there are many other events around town.

King Mango Strut   PARADE
(www.kingmangostrut.org; Main Ave & Grand Ave, Coconut Grove; ⊘ Dec) Held each year just after Christmas since 1982, this quirky Coconut Grove parade is a politically charged, fun freak that began as a spoof on current events and the now-defunct Orange Bowl Parade.

Art Miami   ART
(www.art-miami.com; ⊘ Dec) Held in December, this massive fair displays modern and contemporary works from more than 100 galleries and international artists.

Orange Bowl   SPORTS
(www.orangebowl.org; Hard Rock Stadium, 347 Don Shula Dr, Miami Gardens) Hordes of football fans descend on Miami for the Super Bowl of college football. The game happens either at the end of December (typically

December 30 or 31) or the first few days of January.

🛏 Sleeping

Miami has some alluring lodging options – and for some travelers, it's a big draw to the city. South Beach has all the name recognition with boutique hotels set in lovely art-deco buildings, but there are plenty of other options in Miami – from Downtown high-rises with sweeping views and endless amenities to historic charmers in Coral Gables, Coconut Grove and other less touristy neighborhoods.

🛏 South Beach

SoBe Hostel   HOSTEL $
(Map p82; 🕿 305-534-6669; www.sobe-hostel. com; 235 Washington Ave; dm $22-52; ❄ @ 🛜) On a quiet end of SoFi (the area south of 5th St, South Beach), this massive multilingual hostel has a happening common area and spartan rooms. The staff are friendly and the on-site bar (open to 5am) is a great spot to meet other travelers. Free breakfasts and dinners are included in the rates.

There are loads of activities on offer – from volleyball games to mojito-making nights, screenings of big games and bar crawls.

HI Miami Beach   HOSTEL $
(Map p78; 🕿 305-787-3122; www.hi-miamibeach. com/contact; 1506 Collins Ave; dm $30-50; 🛜) This reliable budget spot from Hostelling International has friendly staff, well-maintained rooms and loads of activities on offer – particularly when it comes to nightlife. There's a kitchen and a terrace, plus some of Miami's best tacos just downstairs. Great location just a short stroll to the beach.

Rock Hostel   HOSTEL $
(Map p78; 🕿 305-763-8146; www.miamirock hostel.com; 1351 Collins Ave; dm $30-50; ❄ 🛜) Party people need only apply at this lively, well-run hostel a few minutes from the beach. Fairly simple six- to 10-bed dorms (including all-female) are enhanced by myriad activities on offer, including nights out to bars and clubs. Located on site, SoCal Cantina doles out tasty tacos and tropical cocktails, plus there's a small front deck overlooking the sidewalk.

The extras include free airport transport, a communal kitchen and a free (but simple) breakfast.

Bed & Drinks   HOSTEL $
(Map p78; 🕿 786-230-1234; http://bedsn drinks.com; 1676 James Ave; dm/d from $29/154) This hostel pretty shamelessly plays to the sex-appeal-seeking crowd – check the name – but hey, it's a few blocks from the beach, so the placement works. The rooms range from average to slightly below average, but the young party-minded crowd (mostly) doesn't mind. Friendly staff, a lively on-site bar and nightlife outings to clubs around town make up for the minuses.

Aqua Hotel   BOUTIQUE HOTEL $
(Map p78; 🕿 305-538-4361; www.aquamiami.com; 1530 Collins Ave; r $110-200; P ❄ 🛜) On the outside this hotel stays true to name and embraces marine-like hues, while the rooms within have a crisp white paint job, with wood floors and a few touches of artwork. Although there's no pool, you can escape the noise of Collins Ave in the small backyard.

Miami Beach International Hostel   HOSTEL $
(Map p82; 🕿 305-534-0268; www.hostelmiami beach.com; 236 9th St; dm/r from $34/150; ❄ @ 🛜) An extensive makeover has turned this reliable old hostel into something like a boutique club with dorm rooms. Bright plaster, marble accents, deco-and-neon decor and hip, clean rooms all make for a good base in South Beach. Wallflowers need not apply: there's a party-friendly social vibe throughout.

Ocean Blue   HOSTEL $
(Map p82; 🕿 305-763-8212; www.oceanblue. miami; 928 Ocean Dr, 2nd fl; dm from $35; P ❄ 🛜) One of the few hostels right on Ocean Dr, this small place has cheerfully painted dorms, some with ocean views. On the downside, the space feels cramped, especially with the three-tiered metal bunks rising to the ceiling, and there's not much of a traveler vibe (no shared kitchen and no common areas aside from the lobby). You can't beat the location though.

Jazz on South Beach   HOSTEL $
(Map p82; 🕿 305-672-2137; www.jazzhostels.com/ jazzlocations/jazz-on-south-beach; 321 Collins Ave; dm $22-40, d from $75; ❄ 🛜) In the quieter southern end of South Beach, this hostel is a fine choice if you're not a socialite – there's no bar, and not much of a traveler vibe, though the lounge is a fine place to kick back. The rooms themselves, which sleep four to 12, are basic to below average, with thin mattresses and noisy air-con. The beach, however, is just around the corner.

Townhouse Hotel
BOUTIQUE HOTEL **$$**

(Map p78; ☑305-534-3800; www.townhouse hotel.com; 150 20th St at Collins Ave; r $200-400; ❋ 🛜) The Townhouse embraces stylish minimalism with a cool white lobby and igloo-like rooms with random scarlet accents. The whole place has a welcoming and somewhat whimsical vibe (who needs mints on pillows when the Townhouse provides beach balls?).

There's a festive rooftop lounge (open 6pm to midnight), a lively ramen and burger bar downstairs (open till 4am) and a pastry and coffee counter (from 7am to 1pm) in the lobby. There's no pool, but guests can swim at the nearby Raleigh Hotel.

Fashion Boutique Hotel
BOUTIQUE HOTEL **$$**

(Map p82; ☑786-398-4408; www.fashion haushotel.com; 534 Washington Ave; r from $179; P ❋ 🛜 🏊) There's a theatrical flair to this budget-friendly hotel in a quieter part of South Beach. The 48 well-equipped rooms have ruby red blankets and throws, light gray walls and thick accordian-like curtains. The signature statement piece though is the massive photo mural over the bed – which depicts a fashion model preening for the camera, and looking somewhat voyeuristic in these quiet rooms. There's also a roof deck.

Catalina Hotel
BOUTIQUE HOTEL **$$**

(Map p78; ☑305-674-1160; www.catalinahotel. com; 1732 Collins Ave; r from $220; P ❋ 🛜 🏊) The Catalina is a lovely example of mid-range deco style. Most appealing, besides the playfully minimalist rooms, is the vibe – the Catalina doesn't take itself too seriously, and staff and guests all seem to be having fun as a result. The back pool, concealed behind the main building's crisp white facade, is particularly attractive and fringed by a whispery grove of bamboo trees.

Clay Hotel
HOTEL **$$**

(Map p78; ☑305-250-0759; www.clayhotel.com; 1438 Washington Ave; r $140-250; ❋ 🛜) Hotels are always nicer when they come packaged in a 100-year-old Spanish-style villa. The Clay has clean and comfortable rooms, not too flashy but hardly spartan, located in a medinalike maze of adjacent buildings. If you're on a budget but don't want dorm-y hostel atmosphere, head here. This is yet another Miami place where Al Capone got some shut-eye.

Chesterfield Hotel
BOUTIQUE HOTEL **$$**

(Map p82; ☑877-762-3477; www.thechesterfield hotel.com; 855 Collins Ave; r from $215; P ❋ 🛜) Hip-hop gets funky with zebra-stripe curtains and cushions in the small lobby, which hosts a chill happy hour at the in-house Safari Bar when the sun goes down. Rooms mix up dark-wood furniture overlaid with bright-white beds and vaguely tropical colors swathed throughout. Be sure to enjoy the view from the roof deck.

Stiles Hotel
BOUTIQUE HOTEL **$$**

(Map p82; ☑844-289-8145; www.thestiles hotel.com; 1120 Collins Ave; r $170-340; P ❋ 🛜 🏊) This Stiles gets positive reviews for its (relatively) fair prices, friendly staff and attractive chambers. Guest rooms are set in sandy earth tones, with natural fiber carpeting, modular bedside lamps and black-out curtains. The courtyard, with three small spa pools, is a fine spot to unwind.

Room Mate Lord Balfour
BOUTIQUE HOTEL **$$**

(Map p82; ☑305-673-0401; www.lordbalfour miami.com; 350 Ocean Dr; r $150-340; P ❋ 🛜) Why not name a hotel for a minor, generally ill-regarded British Prime Minister? Name choice aside, the Lord Balfour features the usual minimalist-plus-pop-art rooms Miami Beach is famous for, along with wood floors, big windows and rain showers – plus a massive mural of a boldly tattooed lass with luxuriant hair behind the bed.

The lobby/bar area is a gem, mixing retro accoutrements with pop art and sweeping lines leading to the terrace out front – a fine spot for taking in this peaceful stretch of Ocean Dr.

Cavalier South Beach
BOUTIQUE HOTEL **$$**

(Map p78; ☑305-673-1199; www.cavaliersouth beach.com; 1320 Ocean Dr; r from $240; P ❋ 🛜) The exterior plays a bit with tropical and marine themes (seahorse-like etchings on the center of the facade, with a palm trunk racing down each side). Inside, a 2015 renovation showcases unique design features uncommon in these parts – namely warm wood hues and exposed-brick walls, plus marble bathrooms, whimsical color-saturated paintings and all the high-tech finishes (including 50-inch-screen smart TVs).

The lobby blends vintage furnishings and modern fixtures with richly painted walls... intriguing results.

Hotel Astor
BOUTIQUE HOTEL **$$**

(Map p82; ☑305-531-8081; www.hotelastor. com; 956 Washington Ave; r/ste from $220/375; P ❋ 🛜 🏊) The Astor aims for retro chic, without being too over-the-top. The lobby is all class, with potted palms, straight lines and geometric marble floors, which flow past a convivial bar and out to the tiny pool, shaded by a single artfully placed palm tree. The pink-toned rooms are relaxing and well appointed.

There are appealing spots for cocktails including a lively downstairs drinking den of throwback 1920s glam, complete with leopard-print loungers.

Kent Hotel
BOUTIQUE HOTEL $$

(Map p82; ☑305-604-5068; www.thekenthotel. com; 1131 Collins Ave; r $120-290; P ❋ ☎) Built in 1936, the Kent has a classic art-deco facade, with striking vertical and horizontal lines that seem to beckon passers to come hither for a closer look. The rooms themselves are small and fairly boxy, with a modern gray-and-white color scheme, and can be noisy on weekend nights.

The terrace restaurant (the Limetree Lounge) is a fine feature, with outdoor seating backed by a small thatch-roof bar.

Hotel St Augustine
BOUTIQUE HOTEL $$

(Map p82; ☑305-532-0570; www.hotelst augustine.com; 347 Washington Ave; r $210-345; P ❋ ☎) Wood that's blonder than Barbie, a soft color palette, and a crisp-and-clean deco theme combine to create one of SoFi's better-value sleeps. The familiar, warm service adds to the value, as do the glass showers that turn into personal steam rooms at the flick of a switch.

On the downside, the hotel is starting to show its age, and some rooms could use an update.

Hotel Shelley
BOUTIQUE HOTEL $$

(Map p82; ☑305-531-3341; www.hotelshelley.com; 844 Collins Ave; r from $170; ❋ ☎) This deco beauty isn't a wallflower. The white and lavender color scheme on the facade screams 'look at me!' and the lively lobby-lounge is pure eye candy with its terracotta tile floors, spider-like chandeliers and distressed walls hung with old photos. The rooms are affordably stylish, but can be on the small side.

Free evening drinks (from 7pm to 8pm) is a nice extra.

Room Mate
Waldorf Towers
BOUTIQUE HOTEL $$

(Map p82; ☑786-439-1600; www.room-mate hotels.com; 860 Ocean Dr; r $190-440; ☎) An immaculate white lobby and stylish rooms comparable to most boutiques on the strip –

light colours, high-design furnishings and sea views (in some rooms) – feature in this place, but the real thing to look for is the streamlined facade and rooftop cupola. Designed by deco godfather L Murray Dixon, it's meant to resemble a lighthouse shining out from its corner on Ocean Dr.

Ocean Five Hotel
BOUTIQUE HOTEL $$

(Map p82; ☑305-532-7093; www.oceanfive.com; 436 Ocean Dr; r/ste from $210/270; P ❋ ☎) This boutique hotel is a cheerfully painted deco building with cozy, quiet rooms that reveal a sleek cabin-like aesthetic. Think whites and light yellows with Italian travertine marble floors and soothing photos of seascapes on the walls. It's not fussy, and overall is good value for South Beach.

Avalon Hotel
HOTEL $$

(Map p82; ☑800-933-3306, 305-538-0133; www. avalonhotel.com; 700 Ocean Dr; r $200-340; ❋ ☎) In a classic, streamlined 1941 building, this hotel is perhaps known more for the white-and-yellow 1955 Lincoln convertible parked out front than for its rooms, which are simple, with puffy white duvets and Ikea-style furniture. Noise on Ocean Dr can be a serious deterrent for many would-be guests, and the whole place could use an update.

★ 1 Hotel
HOTEL $$$

(Map p78; ☑866-615-1111; www.1hotels.com/ south-beach; 2341 Collins Ave; r from $400; ❋ ☎ ❋) 🌱 One of the top hotels in the USA, the 1 Hotel has 400-plus gorgeous rooms that embrace both luxurious and eco-friendly features – including tree-trunk coffee tables/desks, custom hemp-blend mattresses and salvaged driftwood feature walls, plus in-room water filtration (no need for plastic bottles). The common areas are impressive, with four pools, including an adults-only rooftop infinity pool.

The restaurant serves locally sourced farm-to-table fare (under the helm of award-winning chef Tom Colicchio), and the list of amenities is long, with a lavish spa, a 14,000-sq-ft gym (with many classes), watersports activities, a kids club and, of course, direct access to the fine sands of South Beach.

★ Washington
Park Hotel
BOUTIQUE HOTEL $$$

(Map p82; ☑305-421-6265; www.wphsouth beach.com; 1050 Washington Ave; r $250-500; ❋ ☎ ❋) In a great location two blocks from the beach, the Washington Park is spread among five beautifully restored art-deco buildings fronted by a pool and a palm-fringed courtyard. The rooms are all class, with muted color schemes, distressed laminate wood flooring and elegant design touches like bedside globe lamps and wood and cast-iron work desks.

The vibe is welcoming and fun, with bocce in the courtyard, cocktails at Employees Only (a NYC bar that opened on site in 2017) and stylish green Martone bikes for zipping about town.

★**Surfcomber**　　　　HOTEL $$$
(Map p78; ☑305-532-7715; www.surfcomber.com; 1717 Collins Ave; r $250-480; P❄🐾🛜🏊) The Surfcomber has a classic deco exterior with strong lines and shade-providing 'eyebrows' that zigzag across the facade. But it's really the interior that takes most people aback. Rooms have undeniable appeal, with elegant lines in keeping with the deco aesthetic, while bursts of color keep things contemporary.

The lobby and adjoining restaurant are awash with bold colors, decorative wood elements, playful tropical themes and skylights, while a terrace overlooking Collins Ave connects indoor and outdoor spaces. Head around back for a dazzling view: a massive sun-drenched pool, fringed by palm trees and backed by lovely oceanfront, the beach just steps away.

★**Pelican Hotel**　　BOUTIQUE HOTEL $$$
(Map p82; ☑305-673-3373; www.pelicanhotel.com; 826 Ocean Dr; r $260-420; ❄🛜) When the owners of Diesel jeans purchased the Pelican in 1999, they started scouring garage sales for just the right ingredients to fuel a mad experiment: 29 themed rooms that come off like a fantasy-suite hotel dipped in hip.

From the cowboy-hipster chic of 'High Corral, OK Chaparral' to the jungly electric tiger stripes of 'Me Tarzan, You Vain,' all the rooms are completely different, though all set for good times (including quality sound systems and high-end fixtures).

★**Betsy Hotel**　　BOUTIQUE HOTEL $$$
(Map p78; ☑844-862-3157; www.thebetsyhotel.com; 1440 Ocean Dr; r from $310; P❄🛜🏊) One of South Beach's finest hotels, the Betsy has a classy vibe with excellent service and first-rate amenities. The historic gem has two wings, with rooms set in either a colonial style or an art-deco aesthetic – don't miss

HOTEL POOLS
∙∙∙∙∙∙∙∙∙∙∙∙∙∙∙∙∙∙∙∙∙∙∙∙∙∙∙∙∙∙∙∙∙∙∙∙∙
Miami has some of the most beautiful hotel pools around, and they're more about seeing and being seen than swimming. Most of these pools double as bars, lounges or even clubs. Some hotels have a guests-only policy when it comes to hanging out at the pool, but if you buy a drink at the poolside bar you should be fine.

➡ Delano Hotel (p121)
➡ Shore Club (p121)
➡ Kimpton EPIC Hotel (p123)
➡ Biltmore Hotel (p125)
➡ Raleigh Hotel (p121)
➡ Fontainebleau (p123)

the view from the outside of the Dali-esque 'Orb' that joins the two buildings.

Thoughtful touches include orchids in the rooms, a 24-hour fitness center, two swimming pools and rather curious bathroom mirrors with inbuilt LCD TVs.

Gale South Beach　　HOTEL $$$
(Map p78; ☑305-673-0199; www.galehotel.com; 1690 Collins Ave; r $220-410; P❄🛜🏊) The Gale's exterior is an admirable re-creation of classic boxy deco aesthetic expanded to the grand dimensions of a modern SoBe super resort. This blend of classic and haute South Beach carries on indoors, where you'll find bright rooms with a handsome color scheme, sharp lines and a retro chic vibe inspired by the Mid-Century Modern movement.

The elegant rooftop pool is rather narrow but gets sun all day, and the bar and restaurant are a major draw, even for those not staying in the hotel.

Royal Palm　　HOTEL $$$
(Map p78; ☑305-604-5700; www.royalpalmsouthbeach.com; 1545 Collins Ave; r/ste from $260/510; P❄🛜🏊) Even the tropical fish tank with its elegant curves and chrome accents has a touch of deco flair, to say nothing of the streamlined bar with mint-green accents – all of which adds up to South Beach's most striking example of building-as-cruise-liner deco theme. The shipboard theme carries into the plush rooms, which are also offset by bright whites and minty subtle marine-like hues.

As with other big properties anchored between the beach and Collins Ave, the Royal Palm has extensive amenities, including two pools and good drinking and dining spaces, including Byblos, a recommended Greek restaurant.

Standard
BOUTIQUE HOTEL $$$

(☑305-673-1717; www.standardhotels.com/miami; 40 Island Ave; r/ste from $240/510; P✴🔊📶🏊) Look for the upside-down 'Standard' sign on the old Lido building on Belle Island (between South Beach and Downtown Miami) and you'll find the Standard – which is anything but. This boutique blends a bevy of spa services, hipster funk and South Beach sexiness, and the result is a '50s motel gone glam.

There are raised white beds, spa rain showers and gossamer curtains that open onto a courtyard of earthly delights, including a heated *hammam* (Turkish bath).

The Franklin
BOUTIQUE HOTEL $$$

(Map p82; ☑305-432-7061; www.franklinsouthbeach.com; 860 Collins Ave; r $240-490; ✴🔊) A classic from 1934, the Franklin is a beautifully restored art-deco hotel with modern loft-like rooms. Think polished-concrete floors, sleek modular white surfaces, touches of pop art on the walls and good natural light. The rooms are spacious, and the mini kitchen (with coffeemakers) in each is a nice touch.

Friendly service and a great location around the corner from the beach (but not amid the madness of Ocean Dr) add to the value.

Redbury South Beach
BOUTIQUE HOTEL $$$

(Map p78; ☑855-220-1776; www.theredbury.com/southbeach; 1776 Collins Ave; r $250-700; ✴🔊🏊) What sets the Redbury apart is its refusal to toe the line of identikit South Beach minimalist rooms. Rather, the interior here references art across the 20th century, with fun but easygoing comfort in mind (striped carpets, Italian linens and in-room record players – and albums! – available upon request).

A rooftop pool makes for some chilled-out lounging, while the lobby channels East Asian exoticism, plus there's a giant ornamental cage just outside the entrance.

W Hotel
RESORT $$$

(Map p78; ☑305-938-3000; www.wsouthbeach.com; 2201 Collins Ave; r from $440; P✴🔊🏊) There's an astounding variety of rooms available at the South Beach outpost of the W chain, which touts the whole W-brand mix of luxury and style in a big way. The 'spectacular studios' balance long panels of reflective glass with cool tablets of cipollino marble, while the Oasis suite lets in so much light you'd think the sun had risen in your room.

The attendant bars, restaurants, clubs and pool built into this complex are some of the best-regarded on the beach.

Setai
BOUTIQUE HOTEL $$$

(Map p78; ☑305-520-6000; www.thesetaihotel.com; 2001 Collins Ave; r from $745; P✴🔊🏊) Inside a deco building, the Setai has a stunning interior that mixes elements of Southeast Asian temple architecture and contemporary luxury. The spacious rooms are decked out in chocolate teak wood, with clean lines and Chinese and Khmer embellishments. The amenities are exquisite, with a heavenly spa, three palm-fringed swimming pools, a top restaurant and a great beach location.

Sagamore
BOUTIQUE HOTEL $$$

(Map p78; ☑305-535-8088; www.sagamorehotel.com; 1671 Collins Ave; r $270-455; P✴🔊🏊) This hotel-cum-exhibition-hall likes to blur the boundaries between interior decor, art and conventional hotel aesthetics. Almost every space within this hotel, from the lobbies to the rooms, doubles as an art gallery thanks to a talented curator and an impressive roster of contributing artists. Rooms? Soft whites and creams, accented by artsy photography and sleek designer accents.

The Villa Casa Casuarina
RESORT $$$

(Map p82; ☑786-485-2200; www.vmmiamibeach.com; 1116 Ocean Dr; r $750-1400; P✴🔊🏊) Formerly the home of fashion legend Gianni Versace, this jaw-dropping mansion has been turned into one of South Beach's most upscale resorts. You can't help but feel like royalty lodging here. It has a mosaic-lined pool plucked from Ancient Rome, marble-lined corridors and lavishly decorated rooms with antique furnishings and vibrantly painted murals on the walls.

Sense South Beach
BOUTIQUE HOTEL $$$

(Map p82; ☑305-538-5529; www.sensebeachhouse.com; 400 Ocean Dr; r from $280; P✴🔊🏊) The 18-room Sense is fantastically atmospheric – smooth white walls disappearing behind melting blue views of South Beach, wooden paneling arranged around lovely sharp angles that feel inviting rather than imposing, and rooms that contrast two tones (white with either blue-gray or sandy tones). Geometric lamps and slender furnishings round out the MacBook-esque air.

Essex House Hotel
BOUTIQUE HOTEL $$$
(Map p82; ☑305-534-2700; www.clevelander. com; 1001 Collins Ave; r $246-600; ✳✿☎) When you gaze at this lobby, one of the best-preserved interiors in the deco district, you're getting a glimpse of South Beach's gangster heyday. Beyond that the Essex has helpful staff, rooms furnished with subdued colors and a side verandah filled with rattan furnishings that's a particularly pleasant people-watching perch.

Though close to the beach, the Essex is a quieter option than South Beach hotels on the strip. The pool here is small, but guests can take a dip at the larger, livelier Clevelander around the corner door.

Inn at the Fisher Island Club
RESORT $$$
(☑305-535-6000; www.fisherislandclub.com; r $700-4050; P✳✿☎) One of Florida's most exclusive residences, this luxury island resort has beautiful accommodations, which don't quite measure up to the price tag. The amenities, however, are world class: a top-rated spa, plus golf, tennis (clay, grass and hard courts), a fitness center with classes (yoga, crossfit, spinning etc) and half-a-dozen restaurants (from fine dining in a restored 1930s mansion to open-air seaside dining).

And don't forget the lovely beach (with white sand imported from the Bahamas, of course) and a salt-water pool.

National Hotel
HOTEL $$$
(Map p78; ☑305-532-2311; www.nationalhotel. com; 1677 Collins Ave; r $280-490, ste from $600; P✳✿☎) The National is an old-school deco icon, with its bell-tower-like cap and slim yet muscular facade. Inside the hotel itself you'll find elegant rooms with mahogany furnishings offering a timeless look. The lobby and halls are covered in artwork, with the dynamic chords of Rachmaninoff playing overhead, while outside a lovely infinity pool beckons guests.

The decadent cabana suites are exercises in luxury, offering unfettered access to the pool, private terraces and on-site tropical gardens.

Delano
BOUTIQUE HOTEL $$$
(Map p78; ☑305-672-2000; www.delano-hotel. com; 1685 Collins Ave; r from $360; P✳✿☎)

The Delano opened in the 1990s and immediately started ruling the South Beach roost. If there's a quintessential I'm-too-sexy-for-this...South Beach moment, it's when you walk into the Delano's lobby, which has all the excess of an overbudgeted theater set. Rooms are almost painfully white and bright: all long, smooth lines, reflective surfaces and modern, luxurious amenities.

The pool area resembles the courtyard of a Disney princess's palace and includes a giant chess set.

Mondrian South Beach
RESORT $$$
(Map p82; ☑305-514-1500; www.mondrian-miami.com; 1100 West Ave; r/ste from $350/475; P✳✿☎) Morgan Hotel Group hired Dutch design star Marcel Wanders to basically crank it up to 11 at the Mondrian. The theme's inspired by Sleeping Beauty's castle – columns carved like giant table legs, a 'floating' staircase and spectacular bay views from the floor-to-ceiling windows. Upstairs the design whimsy continues with plush rooms sporting Delft tiles with beach scenes instead of windmills, and chandelier-like rainfall showers.

Winter Haven Hotel
BOUTIQUE HOTEL $$$
(Map p78; ☑305-531-5571; www.winterhaven hotelsobe.com; 1400 Ocean Dr; r $265-390; P✳✿☎) Al Capone used to stay here; maybe he liked the deco ceiling lamps in the lobby, with their sharp, retro sci-fi lines and grand-Gothic proportions, and the intriguing Eastern-themed mirrors. The rooms, with their creams, whites and neutral tones coupled with wood accents, have a soothing if fairly conventional aesthetic.

There's a good Italian restaurant, with outdoor seating, on the ground floor.

Raleigh Hotel
BOUTIQUE HOTEL $$$
(Map p78; ☑305-534-6300; www.raleighhotel. com; 1775 Collins Ave; r/ste from $335/520; P✳✿☎) While everyone else was trying to get all modern, the Raleigh painstakingly tried to restore itself to prewar glory. It succeeded in a big way. Celebrity hotelier André Balazs has managed to capture a tobacco-and-dark-wood men's club ambience and old-school elegance while sneaking in modern design and amenities. Have a swim in the stunning pool: Hollywood actress Esther Williams used to.

Shore Club
BOUTIQUE HOTEL $$$
(Map p78; ☑305-695-3100; www.shoreclub.com; 1901 Collins Ave; r from $250; P✳@☎) In

a highly coveted location in South Beach (backing onto lovely beachfront), the Shore Club has airy but rather simply furnished rooms with a few color splashes amid the otherwise white design scheme. There are some appealing areas for amusement, including the **Skybar** (Map p78; ☑305-695-3100; 4pm-2am Mon-Wed, to 3am Thu-Sat), which is a fine garden-like spot for a drink (though located rather surprisingly at ground level).

Hotel Victor
BOUTIQUE HOTEL **$$$**

(Map p82; ☑305-779-8700; www.hotelvictor southbeach.com; 1144 Ocean Dr; r $260-700; 🅿️❄️🛜🏊) Overlooking Ocean Dr, the Hotel Victor has an easygoing style, its lobby full of elegant art-deco fixtures, plus a vintage mural of flamingos and striking ink-on-newsprint portraits of famous faces by Gregory Auerbach. The rooms are comfortable and classically appointed (the best of which have terraces facing the sea), and the pool is a great retreat on hot days.

The Hotel of South Beach
BOUTIQUE HOTEL **$$$**

(Map p82; ☑305-531-2222; www.thehotelof southbeach.com; 801 Collins Ave; r $265-440; 🅿️❄️🛜🏊) This place has style. Which is not surprising since Todd Oldham designed the boldly beautiful rooms. The themed palette of 'sand, sea and sky' adds a dash of eye candy to the furnishings, as do the custom-made mosaic handles and brushed-steel sinks. The Hotel boasts a fine rooftop pool, overshadowed only by a lovely deco spire.

🛏 North Beach

★ Croydon Hotel
BOUTIQUE HOTEL **$$**

(Map p86; ☑305-938-1145; www.hotelcroydon miamibeach.com; 3720 Collins Ave; r from $190; ❄️🛜🏊) The Croydon earns high marks for its bright, classically appointed rooms with dark-wood floors, luxurious beds and modern bathrooms with CO Bigelow products. Head to the ground-floor restaurant with its elaborately patterned ceramic floors for good meals. Fringed by palms, the terrace around the pool has a crisp modern design.

There's also beach service – though the hotel is a block away from the sands.

★ Freehand Miami
BOUTIQUE HOTEL **$$**

(Map p86; ☑305-531-2727; www.thefreehand. com; 2727 Indian Creek Dr; dm $35-55, r $160-250; ❄️🛜🏊) The Freehand is the brilliant re-imagining of the old Indian Creek Hotel, a classic of the Miami Beach scene. The rooms are sunny and attractively designed,

with local artwork and wooden details. The vintage-filled common areas are the reason to stay here though – especially the lovely pool area and backyard that transforms into one of the best bars in town.

Dorms serve the hostel crowd, while private rooms are quite appealing.

Daddy O Hotel
BOUTIQUE HOTEL **$$**

(☑305-868-4141; www.daddyohotel.com; 9660 E Bay Harbor Dr; r $170-290; 🅿️❄️🛜) The Daddy O is a cheerful, hip option that looks, from the outside, like a large B&B that's been fashioned for MTV and Apple employees. This vibe continues in the lobby and the rooms: cool, clean lines offset by bright, bouncy colors, plus a nice list of amenities: flat-screen TVs, in-room Keurig coffeemakers, custom wardrobes, gym access and the rest.

It's about 3 miles north of North Miami Beach.

Circa 39
BOUTIQUE HOTEL **$$**

(Map p86; ☑305-538-4900; www.circa39.com; 3900 Collins Ave; r $180-290; 🅿️❄️🛜🏊) If you love South Beach style but loathe South Beach attitude, Circa has got your back. The lobby has molded furniture and wacky embellishments, and staff go out of their way to make guests feel welcome. Chic (but tiny) rooms, bursting with tropical lime green and subtle earth tones, are attractive enough for the most design-minded visitors.

Red South Beach
BOUTIQUE HOTEL **$$**

(Map p86; ☑305-531-7742; www.redsouth beach.com; 3010 Collins Ave; r $165-400; ❄️🛜🏊) Red is indeed the name of the game, from the cushions on the sleek chairs in the lobby to the flashes dancing around the marble pool to deep, blood-crimson headboards and walls wrapping you in warm sexiness in the small but beautiful guest rooms. Come evening, the pool-bar complex is a great place to unwind and meet fellow guests.

If you score an online deal, Red can be good value for money. Friendly, down-to-earth staff add to the appeal.

Faena Hotel Miami Beach
HOTEL **$$$**

(Map p86; ☑305-534-8800; www.faena.com/ miami-beach; 3201 Collins Ave; r from $525; ❄️🛜🏊) One of Miami Beach's most talked about new hotels, the Faena has lavish, artfully designed spaces both inside and out. The rooms, set with a royal red and teal color scheme, are full of beauty and whimsy: animal-print fabrics, coral and seashell decorative touches, custom-designed carpets and window seats (or terraces) for taking in the views. Each room also has butler service.

Gilded columns and exquisite tropical murals line the lobby, with a pretty pool in back – a few paces away from a fully intact gold-covered woolly mammoth skeleton created by the artist Damien Hirst. Two great restaurants are on hand (and another by the pool), as is a massive spa that takes up one whole floor of the hotel, plus lavish drinking dens and a 150-seat theater inspired by Europe's grand old theaters.

Miami Beach Edition
HOTEL $$$

(Map p86; ☑786-257-4500; www.editionhotels.com/miami-beach; 2901 Collins Ave; d from $420; ❄️❓🏊) Design guru Ian Schrager's latest Miami venture is a gorgeous retooling of a 1950s Mid-Beach classic. The 294-room property (including 28 bungalows) has deep luxury imprint, while its artfully designed lobby and minimalist rooms stay true to mid-century style.

The best features are the pool with its hanging gardens, the plush spa, a top restaurant (Matador by Jean-Georges), a Studio 54–esque nightclub (called Basement Miami) and an indoor skating rink.

Fontainebleau
RESORT $$$

(Map p86; ☑305-535-3283; www.fontainebleau.com; 4441 Collins Ave; r from $360; P❄️❓🏊🐕) The grand Fontainebleau opened in 1954, when it became a celeb-sunning spot. Numerous renovations have added beachside cabanas, a shopping mall, a fabulous swimming pool and one of Miami's best nightclubs. The rooms are surprisingly bright and cheerful – we expected more hard-edged attempts to be cool, but the sunny disposition of these chambers is a welcome surprise.

Eden Roc Renaissance
RESORT $$$

(Map p86; ☑305-531-0000; www.nobuedenroc.com; 4525 Collins Ave; r from $360; P❄️❓🏊🐕) The Roc's immense inner lobby draws inspiration from the Rat Pack glory days of Miami Beach cool, and rooms in the Ocean Tower boast lovely views over the Intracoastal Waterway. All the digs here have smooth, modern embellishments and a beautiful ethereal design. The location backing onto a pristine stretch of Mid-Beach is a big draw.

The amenities are staggering: three swimming pools, two Jacuzzis, an extensive spa, 24-hour fitness center and access to some excellent restaurants.

Casa Faena
HOTEL $$$

(Map p86; ☑305-604-8485; www.faena.com/casa-faena; 3500 Collins Ave; r from $275; ❄️) Part of the growing Faena empire in Mid-Beach, this 1928 Mediterranean-style palace feels like an (Americanized) Tuscan villa, with a honey-stone courtyard, frescoed walls and gleaming stone floors. The sunny rooms have abundant old-world charm, and some rooms have private terraces. Staff are eager to please.

Palms Hotel
HOTEL $$$

(Map p86; ☑305-534-0505; www.thepalmshotel.com; 3025 Collins Ave; r/ste from $270/460; P❄️@❓🏊) The Palms' lobby is imposing and comfortable all at once; the soaring ceiling, cooled by giant, slow-spinning rattan fans, makes for a colonial-villa-on-convention-center-steroids vibe. Upstairs the rooms are perfectly fine, though a touch on the masculine side with tobacco-brown hues and orange-and-brown carpeting. Thoughtful touches include comfy high-end mattresses, iPod docking stations, in-room coffeemakers and Aveda bath products.

🏠 Downtown Miami

Langford Hotel
HERITAGE HOTEL $$

(Map p88; ☑305-250-0782; www.langfordhotelmiami.com; 121 SE 1st St; r from $180; ❄️❓) Set in a beautifully restored 1925 Beaux-Arts high-rise, the Langford opened to much fanfare in 2016. Its 126 rooms blend comfort and nostalgia, with elegant fixtures and vintage details, including white oak flooring and glass-encased rain showers. Thoughtful design touches abound, and there's a rooftop bar and an excellent ground-floor restaurant on site.

EAST, Miami
HOTEL $$$

(Map p88; ☑305-712-7000; www.east-miami.com; 788 Brickell Plaza; r from $260; ❄️❓🏊) Part of the burgeoning Brickell City Centre development, this cosmopolitan hotel has loads of style in its 352 spacious, attractively furnished rooms and suites. Apart from the beach (a 20-minute drive away), you've got everything at your fingertips, with swimming pools, a state-of-the-art fitness center, an excellent Uruguayan-style grillhouse, and a tropically inspired rooftop bar.

Kimpton EPIC Hotel
HOTEL $$$

(Map p88; ☑305-424-5226; www.epichotel.com; 270 Biscayne Blvd Way; r $285-550, ste from $605; P❄️❓🏊) Epic indeed! This massive

MIMO ON BIBO

That cute little phrase means 'Miami Modern on Biscayne Boulevard,' and refers to the architectural style of buildings on North Biscayne Blvd past 55th St. Specifically, there are some great roadside motels here with lovely, Rat Pack–era '50s neon beckoning visitors in. This area was neglected for a long time, and some of these spots are seedy. But north BiBo is also one of Miami's rapidly gentrifying areas, and savvy motel owners are cleaning up their act and looking to attract the hipsters, artists and gay population flocking to the area. There's already exciting food here. Now the lodgings are getting stimulating too. All these hotels provide South Beach comfort at half the price.

➡ Vagabond Hotel (p125)

➡ New Yorker (p124)

➡ Motel Blu (p125)

Kimpton hotel is one of the more attractive options Downtown and it possesses a coolness cred that could match any spot on Miami Beach. Of particular note is the outdoor pool and sun deck, which overlook a gorgeous sweep of Brickell and the surrounding condo canyons.

The rooms are outfitted in designer-chic furnishings and some have similarly beautiful views of greater Miami-Dade. There's a youthful energy throughout that's lacking in other corporate-style Downtown hotels.

Mandarin Oriental Miami HOTEL $$$
(Map p88; ☎ 305-913-8288; www.mandarin oriental.com/miami; 500 Brickell Key Dr; r $400-820, ste from $1100; P❄🛜☒) The Mandarin shimmers on Brickell Key, which is actually annoying – you're a little isolated from the city out here. Not that it matters; there's a luxurious world within a world inside this exclusive compound, from swanky restaurants to a private beach and skyline views that look back at Miami from the far side of Biscayne Bay.

Four Seasons Miami HOTEL $$$
(Map p88; ☎ 305-358-3535; www.fourseasons. com/miami; 1435 Brickell Ave; r/ste from $435/640; P❄🛜☒) The marble common areas double as art galleries, a massive spa caters to corporate types and there

are sweeping, could-have-been-a-panning-shot-from-*Miami-Vice* views over Biscayne Bay in some rooms. The 7th-floor terrace bar, Edge, is pure mojito-laced, Latin-loved swankiness.

🛏 Wynwood & the Design District

Fortuna House APARTMENT $
(Map p94; ☎ 954-232-4705; www.fortunahouse. com; 432 NE 26th St; $90-190; ❄🛜) With sparse lodging options near Wynwood, the Fortuna House is an affordable base for exploring the neighborhood's galleries and bars – though it's still a good 20-minute (1 mile) walk to Wynwood's epicenter. It's set in an attractive but aging three-story building on a quiet street. The accommodations are small and minimally furnished but not a bad option for short stays.

Real Living Residence APARTMENT $$$
(Map p94; ☎ 877-707-0461; www.rlmiami.com; 2700 N Miami Ave, entrance on N 28th St; apt $250-350; P❄🛜☒) A short stroll to the galleries and restaurants of Wynwood, this modern place has 11 studio apartments, with a minimal design of polished-concrete floors, tall ceilings and high-end furnishings. The best (and priciest) studios are rather spacious with a living-room and dining area (though still within the one-room space). All have small kitchen units, washer/dryer, satellite TV and free parking.

🛏 Little Haiti & the Upper East Side

New Yorker HOTEL $
(Map p96; ☎ 305-759-5823; www.hotelnew yorkermiami.com; 6500 Biscayne Blvd; r from $105; P❄🛜☒) Dating back to the 1950s, the New Yorker has an eye-catching design that's right at home in the architecturally rich MiMo district. Renovated in 2009, the New Yorker has comfortable rooms done up with pop art, geometric designs and solid colors; it's not fancy, but the prices are fair.

There's also a small courtyard and a pool. On the downside, the street out front is quite noisy, though thankfully staff provide free earplugs.

Motel Bianco MOTEL $
(Map p96; ☎ 305-751-8696; www.motelbianco. com; 5255 Biscayne Blvd; r from $100; P❄🛜)

The Bianco situates several orange-and-milky-white rooms around a courtyard where coffee is served and guests can get to know each other. Contemporary art designs swirl through the larger rooms, though the whole place is in desperate need of a makeover.

Motel Blu MOTEL $
(Map p96; ☑ 305-757-8451; www.motelblu.com; 7700 Biscayne Blvd; r $85-190; P✻🅰🖭) Situated above Miami's Little River, the Blu may not look like much from the outside, but inside you'll find simple motel rooms with all the modern amenities. Rooms are comfortable and have a pastel-hued interior.

Vagabond Hotel BOUTIQUE HOTEL $$
(Map p96; ☑ 305-400-8420; www.thevagabond hotel.com; 7301 Biscayne Blvd; r $170-275; P✻🅰🖭) An icon in the MiMo district, the Vagabond is a 1953 motel and restaurant where Frank Sinatra and other Rat Packers used to hang out. Today it's been reborn as a boutique hotel, though its lost none of its allure, with plush retro-inspired rooms, a photogenic restaurant (mains $18 to $25) and a lushly landscaped pool, complete with gurgling fountain.

There's also a great bar (p143) fronting the pool – well worth visiting even if you're not lodging here.

🛏 Coconut Grove

Sonesta Hotel & Suites Coconut Grove HOTEL $$
(Map p100; ☑ 305-529-2828; www.sonesta.com/coconutgrove; 2889 McFarlane Rd; r $230-420, ste $305-680; P✻🅰🖭) The Coco Grove outpost of this luxury chain of hotels has decked out its rooms in almost all white with a splash of color (South Beach style). The amenities, from flat-screen TVs to mini-kitchenettes, add a layer of luxury to this surprisingly hip big-box. Make your way to the top of the building to enjoy a wonderful outdoor deck pool.

There's also a fitness center and two squash courts.

Mutiny Hotel HOTEL $$
(Map p100; ☑ 305-441-2100; www.provident resorts.com/mutiny-hotel; 2951 S Bayshore Dr; 1-bedroom ste $170-320, 2-bedroom ste $400-600; P✻🅰🖭) This small, luxury bayfront hotel, with one- and two-bedroom suites featuring balconies, boasts indulgent staff, high-end bedding, gracious appointments,

fine amenities and a small heated pool and Jacuzzi. Although it's on a busy street, you won't hear the traffic once inside. The property has fine views over the water.

Palmeiras Beach Club at Grove Isle RESORT $$$
(☑ 305-858-8300; www.groveisle.com; 4 Grove Isle Dr; r $232-520; P✻🅰🖭) One of those 'I've got my own little island' type places, Grove Isle is off the coast of Coconut Grove. This stunning boutique hotel has colonial elegance, lush tropical gardens, a lovely spa, decadent pool, sunset views over Biscayne Bay, amenities galore and the cachet of staying in your own water-fringed temple of exclusivity.

Ritz-Carlton Coconut Grove RESORT $$$
(Map p100; ☑ 305-644-4680; www.ritzcarlton.com; 3300 SW 27th Ave; r $310-440; P✻🅰🖭🅿) Another member of the Ritz-Carlton organization in Miami, this one overlooks the bay, has immaculate rooms and offers butlers for every need, from shopping to dog-walking. You can while away time beside the heated pool (or swim laps), and find your inner bliss at the massive spa.

🛏 Coral Gables

Extended Stay HOTEL $
(Map p102; ☑ 305-443-7444; www.extended stayamerica.com; 3640 22nd St; r from $125; P✻🅰🖭) Sure it's a chain hotel, but this place has spacious, modern rooms that are decent value for the price, and the good location puts you within walking distance of Coral Gables attractions and eateries.

Rooms get plenty of light and are well equipped with small kitchens.

Hotel St Michel HOTEL $$
(Map p102; ☑ 305-444-1666; www.hotelstmichel.com; 162 Alcazar Ave; r $162-282; P✻🅰) Built in 1926, this building exudes class, with an elegant sense of style that feels more Old Europe than South Florida. Recent renovations have added more light and a refined look to the rooms, while still maintaining the historical charm beneath.

You won't have to go far for a meal. An excellent new Italian restaurant opened on the property in 2017 – though the hotel's location puts you within walking distance of other appealing spots in downtown Coral Gables.

★**Biltmore Hotel** HISTORIC HOTEL $$$
(Map p102; ☑ 855-311-6903; www.biltmorehotel.com; 1200 Anastasia Ave; r/ste from $409/560;

P❋🛜🏊) Though the Biltmore's standard rooms can be small, a stay here is a chance to sleep in one of the great laps of US luxury. The grounds are so palatial it would take a solid week to explore everything the Biltmore has to offer – we highly recommend reading a book in the Romanesque/Arabian Nights opulent lobby, sunning underneath enormous columns and taking a dip in the largest hotel pool in continental USA.

🛏 Key Biscayne

Silver Sands Beach Resort RESORT $$
(Map p106; ☎305-361-5441; www.silversands keybiscayne.net; 301 Ocean Dr; r $169-189, cottages $329-349; P❋🛜🏊) Silver Sands: aren't you cute, with your one-story, stucco tropical tweeness? How this little, Old Florida–style independent resort has survived amid the corporate competition is beyond us, but it's definitely a warm, homey spot for those seeking some intimate, individual attention – to say nothing of the sunny courtyard, garden area and outdoor pool.

Ritz-Carlton Key Biscayne RESORT $$$
(Map p106; ☎305-365-4500; www.ritzcarlton. com; 455 Grand Bay Dr; r/ste from $391/625; P❋🛜🏊) Many Ritz-Carlton outposts feel a little cookie-cutter, but the Key Biscayne outpost of the empire is pretty impressive. There's the magnificent lobby, vaulted by four giant columns lifted from a Cecil B De-Mille set. Tinkling fountains, the view of the bay and the marble grandeur speak less of a chain hotel and more of early-20th-century glamour. Rooms and amenities are predictably excellent.

🍴 Eating

Miami is a major immigrant entrepôt and a sucker for food trends. Thus you get a good mix of cheap ethnic eateries and high-quality top-end cuisine here, alongside some poor-value dross in touristy zones like Miami Beach. The best new areas for dining are in Downtown, Wynwood and the Upper East Side; Coral Gables has great classic options.

🍴 South Beach

Dirt CAFE $
(Map p82; www.dirteatclean.com; 232 5th St; mains $12-15; ⊗9am-9pm) This stylish, sunlit cafe on busy 5th St draws a chatty cross-section of folk, who come for good coffees and deliciously healthy food options. Among the hits: roasted mushroom and raw beet vegan wraps, white bean hummus, and 'bowls' full of sauteed kale, chickpeas and other goodies.

Soups, smashed-avocado toast and craft beer and wine round out the menu. Outdoor dining in front.

Panther Coffee CAFE $
(Map p78; www.panthercoffee.com; 1875 Purdy Ave, Sunset Harbour; coffees $3-6; ⊗7am-9pm) Panther has the best coffee in Miami Beach, though the location is not all that convenient if you're on the beach. It has the same elegant vintage-chic vibe as its Wynwood branch and outdoor seating, though this one serves up pastries from nearby True Loaf.

Taquiza MEXICAN $
(Map p78; ☎305-748-6099; www.taquizamiami. com; 1506 Collins Ave; tacos $3.50-5; ⊗8am-midnight Sun-Thu, to 2am Fri & Sat) Taquiza has acquired a stellar reputation among Miami's street-food lovers. The takeout stand with a few outdoor tables serves up delicious perfection in its steak, pork, shrimp or veggie tacos (but no fish options) served on handmade blue-corn tortillas. They're small, so order a few.

For something a little different, throw in an order of *chapulines* (grasshoppers), and wash it all down with a craft brew.

Tocaya Organica MEXICAN $
(Map p78; ☎305-909-0799; www.tocaya organica.com; 920 Lincoln Rd; mains $11-16; ⊗11am-midnight Mon-Thu, to 2am Fri-Sun; ✒) Next to a gurgling fountain on Lincoln Rd, Tocaya whips up delicious modern Mexican fare with ample healthy and vegetarian options. The menu is a choose-your-own-adventure culinary style: pick from salads, tacos, burritos or veggie-based bowls, top with a protein (like mahimahi, veggie sausage or grilled steak) and cheese of choice, and enjoy.

Creative drink options (like the tequila- and blackberry-based Adios Felisha, served with a popsicle), a good kid's menu and tasty appetizers add to the overall appeal.

True Loaf BAKERY $
(Map p78; ☎786-216-7207; 1894 Bay Rd, Sunset Harbour; pastries $3-5; ⊗7am-6pm Mon-Sat, from 8am Sun) The best bakery in South Beach is True Loaf, a small space where you can pick up heavenly croissants, berry tarts and *kouign amman* (a Breton-style butter cake).

With nowhere to eat these goodies, you'll have to take them around the corner to the waterfront Maurice Gibb Memorial Park (p81) – stopping for Panther Coffee on the way of course.

Pizzarium
PIZZA $

(Map p82; ☑786-452-7261; www.pizzarium.us; 540 Washington Ave; slices around $4; ⊙11am-10pm Sun-Thu, to 11pm Fri & Sat) An excellent place for a quick slice, this Roman-style pizza shop whips up delicious square decadence, piled high with tasty toppings. Grab a seat at a sidewalk table in front and watch the city stroll past.

Paradigm Kitchen
MODERN AMERICAN $

(Map p78; ☑786-453-2488; www.paradigm kitchen.com; 1834 Bay Rd; mains $9-17; ⊙8am-9pm Mon-Thu, to 5pm Fri, 9am-3pm Sat & Sun; ☎) Part of a growing array of restaurants in Sunset Harbour, Paradigm Kitchen has earned a loyal local following for its delectable and nutritious breakfast and lunch offerings – most of which are plant-based. Smashed-avocado toast, roast vegetable dosas, spicy lamb wraps and savory bowls of market greens topped with goodness are among the many hits.

It's a well-designed but laid-back space (order at the counter), and a fine spot to start the day (or end the afternoon).

Moshi Moshi
JAPANESE $

(Map p78; ☑305-531-4674; www.moshimoshi. us; 1448 Washington Ave; mains $10-15, sushi rolls from $4; ⊙noon-5am; ☎) The best-known name in South Beach when it comes to sushi, Moshi Moshi serves up mouthwatering perfection in its tender rolls, daikon salads and steaming noodle soups. Prices are fair and it's open late, meaning you can join the party crowd when yout sushi cravings strike at 3am.

Puerto Sagua
CUBAN $

(Map p82; ☑305-673-1115; 700 Collins Ave; mains $8-18; ⊙7:30am-2am) There's a secret colony of older working-class Cubans and construction workers hidden among South Beach's sex-and-flash, and evidently they eat here. Puerto Sagua challenges the US diner with this reminder: Cubans can greasy-spoon with the best of them. Portions of favorites such as *picadillo* (spiced ground beef with rice, beans and plantains) are enormous.

The Cuban coffee here is not for the faint of heart – strong stuff.

La Sandwicherie
SANDWICHES $

(Map p78; ☑305-532-8934; www.lasandwicherie. com; 229 14th St; mains $6-11; ⊙8am-5am Sun-Thu, to 6am Fri & Sat; ☎) Closed just a few hours each day, this boxcar long eatery does a roaring trade in filling baguette sandwiches sold at rock-bottom prices. Ingredients are fairly classic: roast beef, smoked salmon, avocado or combos like prosciutto with mozzarella, though you can load up with toppings for a deliciously satisfying meal.

Seating is limited to stools lining the restaurant's outside counter, but you can always get it to go and head to the beach.

Pinocchio
CAFE $

(Map p82; ☑305-672-3535; 760 Ocean Dr, entrance on 8th St; mains $7-11; ⊙8am-6pm) A perfectly pulled espresso is surprisingly rare on the oceanfront of South Beach, which makes this tiny, Italian-owned cafe a major draw for those in need of a speedy pick-me-up near the sands. Aside from frothy cappuccinos, you'll also find housemade gelato, crispy bruschetta and design-your-own panini from the deli counter. It's a favorite of Italian expats.

Segafredo L'Originale
CAFE $

(Map p78; ☑305-673-0047; www.sze-originale. com; 1040 Lincoln Rd; mains $8-16; ⊙10am-1am; ☎) Immensely popular with Europeans and South Americans, this chic cafe serves up tasty snacks – pizzas, sandwiches, antipasti plates – and of course, excellent Segafredo coffee. Credited with being the first Lincoln Rd business to open its trade to the outside street.

Paul
BAKERY $

(Map p78; 450 Lincoln Rd; mains $8-18; ⊙8am-10pm; ☎☎) Paul sells itself as a 'Maison de Qualité,' which in other words means you can get some very fine bread here, the sort of crusty-outside and pillow-soft-inside bread you associate with a Parisian boulangerie. Gourmet sandwiches and light pastries make for a refreshing Lincoln Rd lunch stop.

11th St Diner
DINER $

(Map p82; ☑305-534-6373; www.eleventh streetdiner.com; 1065 Washington Ave; mains $10-20; ⊙7am-midnight Sun-Wed, 24hr Thu-Sat) You've seen the art-deco landmarks. Now eat in one: a Pullman-car diner trucked down from Wilkes-Barre, Pennsylvania – as sure a slice of Americana as a *Leave It to Beaver* marathon. The food is as classic as the architecture, with oven-roasted turkey, baby back ribs and mac 'n' cheese among the hits – plus breakfast at all hours.

If there's a diner where you can replicate Edward Hopper's *Nighthawks,* it's here.

A La Folie
FRENCH $

(Map p78; ☎305-538-4484; www.alafolie cafe.com; 516 Española Way; mains $10-17; ⊙9am-midnight; ✍) It's easy to fall for this charming French cafe on the edge of picturesque Española Way. You can enjoy duck confit salad, a decadent onion soup and savory galettes (buckwheat crepes) before satisfying your sweet tooth with dessert crepes – try the Normande (with caramelized apples and Calvados cream sauce).

Vine-trimmed outdoor seating makes for a peaceful setting – and a fine break from the mayhem of Ocean Dr.

Gelateria 4D
ICE CREAM $

(Map p78; ☎305-538-5755; 670 Lincoln Rd; 2-/3-scoops $6/8; ⊙9am-midnight Sun-Thu, to 1:30am Fri & Sat) It's hot. You've been walking all day. You need ice cream, stat. Why hello, 4D! This is an excellent spot for creamy, pillowy waves of European-style frozen goodness, and based on the crowds it's the favorite ice cream on South Beach.

News Cafe
AMERICAN $

(Map p82; www.newscafe.com; 800 Ocean Dr; mains $11-19; ⊙24hr; ☕) News Cafe is an Ocean Dr landmark that attracts thousands of travelers. We find the food to be pretty uninspiring, but the people-watching is good, so take a perch, eat some over-the-average but not-too-special food and enjoy the anthropological study that is South Beach as it skates, salsas and otherwise shambles by.

Pizza Rustica
PIZZA $

(Map p82; ☎305-674-8244; www.pizza-rustica. com; 863 Washington Ave; slices $4-6, mains $9-20; ⊙11am-6am) One of South Beach's favorite pizzerias has several locations to satisfy the demand for crusty Roman-style slices topped with an array of exotic offerings. A slice is a meal unto itself and sure hits the spot after a night of drinking (hence the late hours).

★Yardbird
SOUTHERN US $$

(Map p78; ☎305-538-5220; www.runchicken run.com/miami; 1600 Lenox Ave; mains $18-38; ⊙11am-midnight Mon-Fri, from 8:30am Sat & Sun; ✍) Yardbird has earned a diehard following for its delicious haute Southern comfort food. The kitchen churns out some nice ribs and mac 'n' cheese among the hits – plus shrimp and grits, St Louis–style pork ribs, charred okra, and biscuits with smoked brisket, but it's most famous for its supremely good plate of fried chicken, spiced watermelon and waffles with bourbon maple syrup.

The setting is all charm, with a shabby-chic interior of distressed wood, painted white brick columns, wicker basket-type lamps and big windows for taking in the passing street scene.

★Pubbelly
FUSION $$

(Map p78; ☎305-532-7555; www.pubbellyboys. com/miami/pubbelly; 1418 20th St; sharing plates $11-24, mains $19-30; ⊙6pm-midnight Tue-Thu & Sun, to 1am Fri & Sat; ✍) Pubbelly's dining genre is hard to pinpoint, besides delicious. It skews between Asian, North American and Latin American, gleaning the best from all cuisines. Examples? Try black-truffle risotto, pork-belly dumplings or the mouth watering kimchi fried rice with seafood. Hand-crafted cocktails wash down the dishes a treat.

Lilikoi
CAFE $$

(Map p82; ☎305-763-8692; www.lilikoiorganic living.com; 500 S Pointe Dr; mains $12-20; ⊙8am-7pm Mon-Wed, to 8:30pm Thu-Sun; ✍) Head to the quieter, southern end of South Beach for healthy, mostly organic and veg-friendly dishes at this laid-back indoor-outdoor spot. Start the morning off with big bowls of açaí and granola, bagels with lox (and eggs Benedict on weekends); or linger over kale Caesar salads, mushroom risotto and falafel wraps at lunch.

Rosella's Kitchen
ITALIAN $$

(Map p82; ☎305-397-8852; www.rossellas sobe.com; 110 Washington Ave; mains lunch $12-18, dinner $16-29; ⊙8am-11pm Tue-Fri, from 9am Sat & Sun; ✍) Rosella's well-executed Italian fare served in SoFi ('south of Fifth St') makes this a favorite haunt morning, noon and night. The outdoor tables on the sidewalk feel like the perfect spot for good Italian cooking made with care, including crispy prosciutto and mozzarella panini, crabmeat and feta salads and spaghetti with clams, plus grilled branzino or filet mignon by evening.

Nexxt Cafe
FUSION $$

(Map p78; ☎305-532-6643; www.nexxtcafe.com; 700 Lincoln Rd; mains $14-26; ⊙11:30am-11pm Mon-Fri, from 10am Sat & Sun; ✍) Lincoln Rd has countless open-air eateries offering first-rate people-watching along one of Miami Beach's most fashionable stretches. Nexxt is one of the best of the bunch, with well-placed tables in the heart of Lincoln Rd, and a huge menu that encompasses creative salads, fried calamari, Vietnamese summer rolls, ahi tuna tacos and pasta carbonara.

Big Pink
DINER $$

(Map p82; ☑ 305-532-4700; 157 Collins Ave; mains $13-26; ⊗ 8am-midnight Sun-Wed, to 2am Thu, to 5am Fri & Sat) Big Pink does American comfort food with joie de vivre and a dash of whimsy. The Americana menu is consistently good throughout the day; pulled Carolina pork holds the table next to a nicely done Reuben. The interior is somewhere between a '50s sock hop and a South Beach club; expect to be seated at a long communal table.

Spiga
ITALIAN $$

(Map p82; ☑ 305-534-0079; www.spiga restaurant.com; 1228 Collins Ave; mains $16-32; ⊗ 6pm-midnight) This romantic nook is a perfect place to bring your partner and gaze longingly at one another over candlelight, before you both snap out of it and start digging into excellent traditional Italian such as baby clams over linguine or red snapper with kalamata olives, tomatoes and capers.

Front Porch Cafe
AMERICAN $$

(Map p78; ☑ 305-531-8300; www.frontporch oceandrive.com; 1458 Ocean Dr; mains $10-25; ⊗ 7am-11pm; ☑) An open-sided perch just above the madness of the cruising scene, the Porch has been serving excellent salads, sandwiches and the like since 1990 (eons by South Beach standards). Breakfast is justifiably popular; the challah French toast is delicious, as are fluffy omelets, eggs Benedict and strong coffees.

Tap Tap
HAITIAN $$

(Map p82; ☑ 305-672-2898; www.taptapmiami beach.com; 819 5th St; mains $15-35; ⊗ noon-11pm) In Haiti tap-taps are brightly colored pickup trucks turned public taxis, and their tropi-psychedelic paint schemes inspire the decor at this popular Haitian eatery. Meals are a happy marriage of West African, French and Caribbean: spicy pumpkin soup, snapper in a scotch-bonnet lime sauce, stewed beef and okra, and Turks and Caicos conch.

Macchialina
ITALIAN $$$

(Map p82; ☑ 305-534-2124; www.macchialina. com; 820 Alton Rd; mains $23-32) This buzzing Italian trattoria has all the right ingredients

for a terrific night out; namely great service and beautifully turned out cooking, served in a warm rustic-chic interior of exposed brick and chunky wood tables (plus outdoor tables in front).

Joe's Stone Crab Restaurant
AMERICAN $$$

(Map p82; ☑ 305-673-0365; www.joesstone crab.com; 11 Washington Ave; mains lunch $14-30, dinner $19-60; ⊗ 11:30am-2:30pm Tue-Sat & 5-10pm daily) The wait is long and the prices for iconic dishes can be high. But if those aren't deal-breakers, queue up to don a bib in Miami's most famous restaurant (around since 1913!) and enjoy deliciously fresh stone crab claws.

Juvia
FUSION $$$

(Map p78; ☑ 305-763-8272; www.juviamiami. com; 1111 Lincoln Rd, access via Lenox Ave elevator; mains $27-46; ⊗ 6-11pm daily & noon-3pm Sat & Sun) Juvia blends the trendsetters that have staying power in Miami's culinary world: France, Latin America and Japan. Chilean sea bass comes with maple-glazed eggplant, while sea scallops are dressed with okra and oyster mushrooms. The big, bold, beautiful dining room and open-air terrace, which sit on the high floors of 1111 Lincoln Rd (p77), is quintessential South Beach glam.

Osteria del Teatro
ITALIAN $$$

(Map p78; ☑ 305-538-7850; www.osteriadel teatro.miami; 1200 Collins Ave; mains $28-40; ⊗ 6-11pm Sun-Thu, to midnight Fri & Sat) There are few things to swear by, but the Northern Italian cooking at Osteria, one of the best Italian restaurants in Greater Miami, ought to be one. When you get here, let the gracious Italian waiters seat you, coddle you and guide you along the first-rate menu, with temptations like polenta with wild mushrooms, black squid-ink linguine and locally caught red snapper.

Mr Chow Chinese
FUSION $$$

(Map p78; ☑ 305-695-1695; www.mrchow.com; 2201 Collins Ave, W Hotel; mains $24-51; ⊗ 5:45-11:30pm) Located in the W Hotel (p120), Mr Chow takes Chinese American comfort food to gourmet heights. The setting is almost intimidatingly cool, with dangling moderne-style chandeliers and an enormous bar plucked out of *Sex and the City*, yet service is friendly and the food lovely: prawns with water chestnuts, crispy duck with pancakes and plum sauce, and vermicelli noodles with lobster.

North Beach

Roasters 'n Toasters   DELI $

(Map p86; 305-531-7691; www.roastersn toasters.com; 525 Arthur Godfrey Rd; mains $10-18; 6:30am-3:30pm) Given the crowds and the satisfied smiles of customers, Roasters 'n Toasters meets the demanding standards of Miami Beach's large Jewish demographic, thanks to juicy deli meat, fresh bread, crispy bagels and warm latkes. Sliders (mini-sandwiches) are served on challah bread, an innovation that's as charming as it is tasty.

Josh's Deli   DELI $

(305-397-8494; www.joshsdeli.com; 9517 Harding Ave; sandwiches $14-16; 8:30am-3:30pm) Josh's is simplicity itself. Here in the heart of Jewish Miami, you can nosh on thick cuts of house-cured pastrami sandwiches and matzo ball soup for lunch or challah French toast, eggs and house-cured salmon for breakfast. It's a deliciously authentic slice of Mid-Beach culture.

La Perrada de Edgar   FAST FOOD $

(Map p86; 305-866-4543; www.laperrada deedgar.com; 6976 Collins Ave; hot dogs $5.50-8; noon-midnight) Back in the day, Colombia's most (in)famous export to Miami was cocaine. But seriously, what's powder got on La Perrada and its kookily delicious hot dogs that were devised by some Dr Evil of the frankfurter world? Don't believe us? Try an *especial,* topped with plums, pineapple and whipped cream. How about shrimp and potato sticks?

★27 Restaurant   FUSION $$

(Map p86; 786-476-7020; www.freehand hotels.com/miami/27-restaurant; 2727 Indian Creek Dr; mains $17-28; 6:30pm-2am Mon-Sat, 11am-4pm & 6:30pm-2am Sun;) This new spot sits on the grounds of the very popular Broken Shaker (p141; one of Miami Beach's best-loved cocktail bars). Like the bar, the setting is amazing – akin to dining in an old tropical cottage, with worn wood floorboards, candle-lit tables, and various rooms slung with artwork and curious knickknacks, plus a lovely terrace. The cooking is exceptional, and incorporates flavors from around the globe.

Cafe Prima Pasta   ITALIAN $$

(Map p86; 305-867-0106; www.cafeprima pasta.com; 414 71st St; mains $17-26; 5-11:30pm Mon-Sat, 4-11pm Sun) We're not sure what's better at this Argentine-Italian place: the much-touted pasta, which deserves every one of the accolades heaped on it, or the atmosphere, which captures the dignified sultriness of Buenos Aires. You can't go wrong with the small, well-curated menu, with standouts like gnocchi formaggi, baked branzino, and squid-ink linguine with seafood in a lobster sauce.

Indomania   INDONESIAN $$

(Map p86; 305-535-6332; www.indomania restaurant.com; 131 26th St; mains $18-32; 5:30-10:30pm Mon-Sun & noon-4pm Sat & Sun) There's a lot of watered-down Asian cuisine in Miami; Indomania bucks this trend with an authentic execution of dishes from Southeast Asia's largest nation. Dishes reflect Indonesia's diversity, ranging from braised beef in spicy coconut sauce to gut-busting *rijsttafel,* a sort of buffet of small, tapas-style dishes that reflects the culinary character of particular Indonesian regions.

Shuckers   AMERICAN $$

(Map p86; 305-866-1570; www.shuckers barandgrill.com; 1819 79th St Causeway; mains $12-27; 11am-1am;) With excellent views overlooking the waters from the 79th St Causeway, Shuckers has to be one of the best-positioned restaurants around. The food is pub grub: burgers, fried fish and the like. The chicken wings, basted in several mouthwatering sauces, deep-fried and grilled again, are famous.

Downtown Miami

Manna Life Food   VEGAN $

(Map p88; 786-717-5060; www.mannalife food.com; 80 NE 2nd Ave; mains $8-12; 10am-7pm Mon-Fri, 11am-4pm Sat) This airy, stylish eatery has wowed diners with its plant-based menu loaded with superfoods. Filling 'life bowls,' *arepas* (corn cakes) and noritos (like a burrito but wrapped with seaweed rather than a tortilla) are packed with flavor with ingredients like red quinoa, baked tofu, roasted veggies, coconut brown rice and raw falafel.

All Day   CAFE $

(Map p88; www.alldaymia.com; 1035 N Miami Ave; coffee $3.50, breakfast $10-14; 7am-7pm Mon-Fri, from 9am Sat & Sun;) This is one of the best places Downtown to linger over coffee or breakfast – no matter the hour. Slender Scandinavian-style chairs, wood-and-marble tables and the Françoise Hardy soundtrack lend an easygoing vibe to the place.

Bali Cafe INDONESIAN $

(Map p88; ☏ 305-358-5751; 109 NE 2nd Ave; mains $10-16; ⊙ 11am-4pm Mon-Sun, 6-10pm Mon-Fri; ☕) It's odd to think of the clean flavors of sushi and the bright richness of Indonesian cuisine coming together in harmony, but they're happily married in this tropical hole in the wall. Have some spicy tuna rolls for an appetizer, then follow up with *soto betawi* – beef soup cooked with coconut milk, ginger and shallots.

La Moon COLOMBIAN $

(Map p88; ☏ 305-860-6209; www.lamoon restaurant.com; 97 SW 8th St; mains $7-17; ⊙ 10am-midnight Sun & Tue-Thu, to 6am Fri & Sat) Nothing quite hits the spot after a late night of partying quite like a Colombian hot dog topped with eggs and potato sticks. Or an *arepa* (corn cake) stuffed with steak and cheese. These street-food delicacies are available well into the wee hours on weekend nights, plus La Moon is conveniently located within stumbling distance of bars like Blackbird Ordinary (p142).

180° at DRB BISTRO $

(Map p88; www.gastronomyredefined.com; 501 NE 1st Ave; mains $7-16; ⊙ noon-11pm Mon-Thu, to midnight Fri & Sat, noon-4pm Sun) In the heart of Downtown Miami, this convivial gastropub turns out a satisfying selection of sharing plates and comfort food, including pulled-pork sliders, grilled cheese (made with four cheeses) and swordfish ceviche. The DRB part of the equation stands for Democratic Republic of Beer, and 180° doesn't disappoint, with dozens of microbrews and hard-to-score imports.

Pollos & Jarras PERUVIAN $

(Map p88; www.pollosyjarras.com; 115 NE 3rd Ave; ⊙ noon-10pm Sun-Thu, to 11pm Fri & Sat) The same celebrated team behind CVI.CHE105 (p132) next door also operate this festive spot with outdoor patio. The focus is less on seafood and more on meat: namely outstanding barbecued chicken, though of course signature dishes (including ceviche) are also available.

★ Casablanca SEAFOOD $$

(Map p88; www.casablancaseafood.com; 400 N River Dr; mains $15-34; ⊙ 11am-10pm Sun-Thu, to 11pm Fri & Sat) Perched over the Miami River, Casablanca serves up some of the best seafood in town. The setting is a big draw – with tables on a long wooden deck just above the water, with the odd seagull winging past. But the fresh fish is the real star here.

Chef Allen's
Farm-to-Table Dinner VEGETARIAN $$

(Map p88; ☏ 786-405-1745; 1300 Biscayne Blvd; dinner $25, with wine pairing $40; ⊙ 6:30pm Mon; ☕) On Monday nights, you can feast on a delicious five-course vegetarian meal, served family-style at outdoor tables in front of the Arsht Center. It's an excellent value, with a creative menu inspired by the farmers market held on the same day. Call ahead to reserve a spot.

Verde AMERICAN $$

(Map p88; ☏ 786-345-5697; www.pamm.org/dining; 1103 Biscayne Blvd, Pérez Art Museum Miami; mains $13-19; ⊙ Fri-Tue 11am-5pm, to 9pm Thu, closed Wed; ☕) Inside the Pérez Art Museum Miami (p85), Verde is a local favorite for its tasty market-fresh dishes and great setting – with outdoor seating on a terrace overlooking the bay. Crispy mahimahi tacos, pizza with squash blossoms and goat cheese, and grilled endive salads are among the temptations.

SELF CATERING

If you can tear yourself away from the Cuban sandwiches, celebrity hot spots and farm-to-table gems, Miami has a decent selection of options for self-caterers offering fresh produce and obscure ingredients aplenty.

Epicure Market (Map p78; ☏ 305-672-1861; www.epicuremarket.com; 1656 Alton Rd; mains $8-18; ⊙ 9am-8pm), a gourmet food shop just off Lincoln Rd in South Beach, has a beautiful selection of international cheeses and wines, fresh produce, baked goods and prepared dishes. Many of the more than 25 Publix supermarkets throughout Miami are quite upscale, and the **Whole Foods Market** (Map p82; ☏ 305-938-2800; www.wholefoodsmarket.com; 1020 Alton Rd; ⊙ 8am-11pm) is the biggest high-end grocery store around, with an excellent produce department, pretty good deli and so-so salad bar; its biggest draw is for vegetarians (not so well catered for by markets in these parts) or health nuts who are seeking a particular brand of soy milk or wheat-free pasta.

River Oyster Bar

SEAFOOD $$

(Map p88; ☑ 305-530-1915; www.theriver miami.com; 650 S Miami Ave; mains $16-32; ⊙ noon-10:30pm Mon-Thu, to midnight Fri, 4:30pm-midnight Sat, to 9:30pm Sun) A few paces from the Miami River, this buzzing little spot with a classy vibe whips up excellent plates of seafood. Start off with their fresh showcase oysters and ceviche before moving on to grilled red snapper or yellowfin tuna. For a decadent meal, go for a grand seafood platter ($125), piled high with Neptune's culinary treasures.

NIU Kitchen

SPANISH $$

(Map p88; ☑ 786-542-5070; www.niukitchen. com; 134 NE 2nd Ave; sharing plates $14-25; ⊙ noon-3:30pm & 6-10pm Mon-Fri, 1-4pm & 6-11pm Sat, 6-10pm Sun; ☑) NIU is a stylish living-room-sized restaurant serving up delectable contemporary Spanish cuisine. It's a showcase of culinary pyrotechnics, with complex sharing plates with clipped Catalan names like Ous (poached eggs, truffled potato foam, jamon iberico and black truffle) or Toninya (smoked tuna, green guindillas and pine nuts). Wash it all down with good wine.

PB Station

MODERN AMERICAN $$

(Map p88; ☑ 305-420-2205; http://pbstation. com; 121 SE 1st St, Langford Hotel; mains $20-57; ⊙ 11:30am-3pm & 6-11pm Mon-Sat) The creative team behind the popular Pubbelly (p128) in Sunset Harbour brought their award-winning formula to Downtown in 2016. Set on the ground floor of the Langford Hotel (p123), the dining room channels a classy, old-fashioned elegance with its arched ceilings, globe lights and well-dressed servers. Culinary highlights include bistro classics like grilled bone marrow, French onion soup and grilled octopus.

Garcia's Seafood Grille & Fish Market

SEAFOOD $$

(Map p88; ☑ 305-375-0765; www.garciasmiami. com; 398 NW N River Dr; mains $10-25; ⊙ 11am-10pm Mon-Fri, to 11pm Sat & Sun) Crowds of office workers lunch at Garcia's, which feels more like you're in a smugglers' seafood shack than the financial district. Expect occasionally freshly caught and cooked fish and pleasant views of the Miami River.

CVI.CHE 105

PERUVIAN $$

(Map p88; ☑ 305-577-3454; www.ceviche105. com; 105 NE 3rd Ave; ⊙ noon-10pm Sun-Thu, to 11pm Fri & Sat) White is the design element of choice in Juan Chipoco's ever-popular Peruvian Downtown eatery. Beautifully presented ceviches, *lomo saltado* (marinated steak) and *arroz con mariscos* (seafood rice) are ideal for sharing and go down nicely with a round of Pisco Fuegos (made with jalapeño-infused pisco) and other specialty Peruvian cocktails.

Soya e Pomodoro

ITALIAN $$

(Map p88; ☑ 305-381-9511; www.soyaepomodoro. com; 120 NE 1st St; lunch $11-18, dinner $16-26; ⊙ 11:30am-4:30pm Mon-Fri, 7-11:30pm Wed-Sat) Soya e Pomodoro feels like a bohemian retreat for Italian artists and filmmakers, who can dine on bowls of fresh pasta under vintage posters, rainbow paintings and curious wall-hangings. Adding to the vibe is live Latin jazz (on Thursday nights from 9pm to midnight), plus readings and other arts events that take place here on select evenings.

Bonding

FUSION $$

(Map p88; ☑ 786-409-4796; www.bondingmiami. com; 638 S Miami Ave; mains $16-30; ⊙ noon-11pm Mon-Fri, to midnight Sat, 5pm-midnight Sun; ☑) Multiple Asian cuisines, including Thai, Japanese and Korean, come together into an excellent whole at Bonding. Chicken is expertly tossed with chilies and basil, red curry is deliciously fiery and sushi rolls are given a South Florida splash with ingredients like mango salsa and spicy mayo. The bar here keeps some excellent sake under the counter.

✖ Wynwood & the Design District

Wynwood Yard

FOOD TRUCKS $

(Map p94; www.thewynwoodyard.com; 56 NW 29th St; mains $7-14; ⊙ noon-11pm Tue-Thu, to 1am Fri-Sun; ☑☑) ✔ On a once vacant lot, the Wynwood Yard is something of an urban oasis for those who want to enjoy a bit of casual open-air eating and drinking. Around a dozen different food trucks park here, offering gourmet mac 'n' cheese, cruelty-free salads, meaty schnitzel plates, zesty tacos, desserts and more. There's also a bar, and often live music.

One of the Yard anchors is the **Della Test Kitchen** (Map p94; ☑ 305-351-2961; www.della bowls.com; mains $11-14; ⊙ noon-10pm Tue-Sun; ☑), which serves tasty vegan fare, and even grows some vegetables on site. Live music typically happens on Wednesday to Saturday nights from 9pm, and from 2pm on Sundays. Check the website for other one-off events, including food tastings, pilates and yoga sessions and hands-on art workshops for kids.

Coyo Taco
MEXICAN $

(Map p94; ☑ 305-573-8228; www.coyo-taco.com; 2300 NW 2nd Ave; mains $7-12; ⊙ 11am-2am Mon-Sat, to 11pm Sun; ☑) If you're in Wynwood and craving tacos, this is the place to be. Ever popular, you'll have to contend with lines day or night, but those beautifully turned out tacos are well worth the wait – and come in creative varieties like chargrilled octopus, marinated mushrooms or crispy duck, along with the usual array of steak, grilled fish and roasted pork.

Kush
AMERICAN $

(Map p94; ☑ 305-576-4500; www.kushwynwood. com; 2003 N Miami Ave; mains $13-15; ⊙ noon-11pm Sun-Tue, to midnight Wed-Sat; ☑) Gourmet burgers plus craft brews is the simple but winning formula at this lively eatery and drinking den on the southern fringe of Wynwood. Juicy burgers topped with hot pastrami, Florida avocados and other decadent options go down nicely with drafts from Sixpoint and Funky Buddha. There are great vegetarian options too, including a house-made black-bean burger and vegan jambalaya.

SuViche
FUSION $

(Map p94; ☑ 305-501-5010; www.suviche.com; 2751 N Miami Ave; ceviches $8-14; ⊙ noon-11pm) SuViche is a great place to start off the night, with a buzzing open-sided setting of garrulous couples chatting over swinging chairs, graffiti-esque murals and good beats. The menu is a blend of Peruvian dishes (including half-a-dozen varieties of ceviche) and sushi, which goes down nicely with the creative *macerados* (pisco-infused cocktails).

Salty Donut
DOUGHNUTS $

(Map p94; ☑ 305-925-8126; www.saltydonut.com; 50 NW 23rd St; doughnuts $3-6; ⊙ 8am-6pm Tue-Sun; ☎) Although 'artisanal doughnuts' sounds pretentious, no one can deny the merits of these artfully designed creations featuring seasonal ingredients – probably the best in South Florida. Maple and bacon, guava and cheese, and brown butter and salt are a few classics, joined by changing hits like pistachio and white chocolate or strawberry and lemon cream.

Panther Coffee
CAFE $

(Map p94; ☑ 305-677-3952; www.panthercoffee. com; 2390 NW 2nd Ave; coffees $3-6; ⊙ 7am-9pm

Mon-Sat, from 8am Sun; ☎) Panther – Miami's best independent coffee shop – specializes in single-origin, small-batch roasts, fired up to perfection. Aside from sipping on a zesty brewed-to-order Chemex-made coffee (or a creamy latte), you can enjoy microbrews, wines and sweet treats. The front patio is a great spot for people-watching.

Buena Vista Deli
CAFE $

(Map p94; ☑ 305-576-3945; www.buenavista deli.com; 4590 NE 2nd Ave; mains $8-15; ⊙ 7am-9pm) Never mind the uninspiring name: French-owned Buena Vista Deli is a charming Parisian-style cafe that warrants a visit no matter the time of day. Come in the morning for fresh croissants and other bakery temptations, and later in the day for thick slices of quiche, big salads and hearty sandwiches – plus there's wine, beer and good coffees.

Enriqueta's
LATIN AMERICAN $

(Map p94; ☑ 305-573-4681; 186 NE 29th St; mains $6-9; ⊙ 6am-3:45pm Mon-Fri, to 2pm Sat) Back in the day, Puerto Ricans, not installation artists, ruled Wynwood. Have a taste of those times in this perpetually packed roadhouse, where the Latin-diner ambience is as strong as the steaming shots of *cortadito* (half espresso and half milk) served at the counter. Balance the local gallery fluff with a juicy Cuban sandwich.

Ono Poke
HAWAIIAN $

(Map p94; ☑ 786-618-5366; www.onopokeshop. com; 2320 N Miami Ave; mains $10-16; ⊙ noon-8pm Mon-Sat, to 6pm Sun) This popular little eatery has been all the rage since its 2016 debut. The key to success is all in the execution: diners build their own *poke* bowl, featuring mouth wateringly fresh sushi-grade fish, then place atop greens or rice, and add toppings (ginger, cucumber, scallion), creative extras (wasabi peas), sauce of choice and enjoy – a delicious, nutritious, but refreshingly uncomplicated meal.

Crumb on Parchment
BAKERY $

(Map p94; ☑ 305-572-9444; 3930 NE 2nd Ave; mains $9-15; ⊙ 9am-4pm Mon-Fri; ☎ ☑) When you need a pick-me-up or have a craving for something sweet, there's no better place to be than this outrageously good cafe and bakery in the Design District. Aside from rich chocolate brownies, scones and other baked goods, the charming sun-drenched cafe serves up inventive sandwiches, salads and soups.

Lemoni Café
CAFE $

(Map p94; ☑ 305-571-5080; www.mylemoni cafe.com; 4600 NE 2nd Ave; mains $10-18; ⊙11am-10:30pm Mon-Sat, to 6pm Sun; ⚹) A small, dimly lit cafe, Lemoni has a creative Mediterranean-inspired menu in its panini, salads and appetizers (including hummus, bruschetta and spicy Moroccan eggplant). Weekend brunch (till 2pm Saturday, till 5pm Sunday) features beautifully turned-out French toast and blueberry pancakes. Located in the pretty Buena Vista neighborhood, this is a fine place to grab a sidewalk alfresco lunch or dinner.

Cheese Course
CHEESE $

(Map p94; ☑ 786-220-6681; www.thecheese course.com; 3451 NE 1st Ave; 3-cheese board $18, sandwiches $9-13; ⊙11am-8pm Sun, to 9pm Mon-Wed, to 11pm Thu-Sat; ⚹) We love the idea at this place – pick out a few cheeses with the help of the staff and have them assemble a platter for you with fresh bread, candied walnuts, cornichons or whatever other accoutrement you so desire. There are also sandwiches, spreads and preserves, plus craft beer and wines by the glass – essential pairing for those great cheese options.

★ Kyu
FUSION $$

(Map p94; ☑ 786-577-0150; www.kyumiami.com; 251 NW 25th St; sharing plates $17-38; ⊙noon-11:30pm Mon-Sat, 11am-10:30pm Sun, bar open till 1am Fri & Sat; ⚹) ✿ One of the best new restaurants in Wynwood, Kyu has been dazzling locals and food critics alike with its creative, Asian-inspired dishes, most of which are cooked up over the open flames of a wood-fired grill. The buzzing, industrial space is warmed up via artful lighting and wood accents (tables and chairs, plus shelves of firewood for the grill).

Cake Thai
THAI $$

(Map p94; ☑ 305-573-5082; www.cakethai miami.com; 180 NW 29th St; mains $16-25; ⊙noon-midnight Tue-Sun; ⚹) When cravings for Thai food strike, Wynwooders no longer need to make the trek up to 79th St and Biscayne (Cake Thai's tiny original location). Now they've got expertly prepared Thai cooking right in their backyard, with all of the same culinary wizardry of chef Phuket Thongsodchaveondee (who goes by the name 'Cake').

Michael's Genuine
MODERN AMERICAN $$

(Map p94; ☑ 305-573-5550; www.michaels genuine.com; 130 NE 40th St; mains lunch $16-26, dinner $19-44; ⊙11:30am-11pm Mon-Sat, to 10pm Sun) The liveliest place in the Design District is this long-running upscale tavern that combines excellent service with a well-executed menu of wood-fired dishes, bountiful salads and raw bar temptations (including oysters and stone crabs). Michael's tends to draw a well-dressed crowd, and the place gets packed most days. There's also outdoor dining on the plant-lined pedestrian strip out front.

Zak the Baker
DELI $$

(Map p94; ☑ 786-347-7100; www.zakthebaker.com; 405 NW 26th St; sandwiches $14-18; ⊙8am-5pm Sun-Fri) Miami's best-loved kosher deli is admired by all for its delicious (but pricey) sandwiches: try the braised, handcut corned beef or a satisfying gravlax sandwich. You can also come early for potato latkes and eggs.

The Butcher Shop
AMERICAN $$

(Map p94; ☑ 305-846-9120; www.butcher shopmiami.com/tbs; 165 NW 23rd St; mains $13-34; ⊙11am-11pm Sun-Thu, to 2am Fri & Sat) This Wynwood joint is called the Butcher Shop for a reason, and that's because it's unashamedly aimed at carnivores. From bone-in ribeyes to smoked sausages to full charcuterie, meat lovers have reason to rejoice. Beer lovers too: this butcher's doubles as a beer garden, which gets lively as the sun goes down.

Harry's Pizzeria
PIZZA $$

(Map p94; ☑ 786-275-4963; www.harryspizzeria. com; 3918 N Miami Ave; pizzas $13-17, mains $16-21; ⊙11:30am-10pm Sun-Thu, to midnight Fri & Sat; ⚹) A stripped-down yet sumptuous dining experience awaits (pizza) pie lovers in the Design District. Harry's tiny kitchen and dining room dishes out deceptively simple wood-fired pizzas topped with creative ingredients (like slow-roasted pork or kale and caramelized onion). Add in some not-to-be missed appetizers like polenta fries and you have a great, budget-friendly meal.

There are also non-pizza hits like pan-seared mahimahi and oven-roasted chicken with fennel salad.

Mandolin
GREEK $$

(Map p94; ☑ 305-749-9140; www.mandolin miami.com; 4312 NE 2nd Ave; mains $18-34; ⊙noon-11pm; ⚹) For a quick trip across the Aegean, book a table at Mandolin. The Greek cooking doesn't disappoint, whether you're dining on sea bass grilled in lemon and olive oil, lamb kebabs with spicy yogurt or satisfying mezes such as smoked eggplant and grilled octopus.

★ Alter
MODERN AMERICAN $$$

(Map p94; ☑ 305-573-5996; www.altermiami.com; 223 NW 23rd St; set menu 5/7 courses $69/89; ⊙ 7-11pm Tue-Sun) This new spot, which has garnered much praise from food critics, brings creative high-end cooking to Wynwood courtesy of its award-winning young chef Brad Kilgore. The changing menu showcases Florida's high-quality ingredients from sea and land in seasonally inspired dishes with Asian and European accents. Reserve ahead.

✖ Little Haiti & the Upper East Side

★ Phuc Yea
VIETNAMESE $

(Map p96; ☑ 305-602-3710; www.phucyea.com; 7100 Biscayne Blvd; ⊙ 6pm-midnight Tue-Sat, 11:30am-3:30pm & 6-9pm Sun) Not unlike its cheeky name, Phuc Yea pushes boundaries with its bold and deliciously executed Vietnamese cooking – served up in a hip-hop loving and graffiti-smeared setting. You too can heed the call to get 'Phuc'd up!' (undoubtedly a good thing since 'phuc' means 'blessings and prosperity') by indulging in lobster summer rolls, fish curry, spicy chicken wings and other great sharing plates.

The raw bar in front doles out sushi, fresh oysters and creative cocktails (happy hour runs from 5pm to 7pm). There's also outdoor dining in a paper-lantern-filled garden.

Chef Creole
HAITIAN $

(☑ 305-754-2223; www.chefcreole.com; 200 NW 54th St; mains $7-20; ⊙ 11am-10pm Mon-Sat) When you need Caribbean food on the cheap, head to the edge of Little Haiti and this excellent take-out shack. Order up fried conch, oxtail or fish, ladle rice and beans on the side, and you'll be full for a week. Enjoy the food on nearby picnic benches while Haitian music blasts out of tinny speakers – as island an experience as they come.

Service can be slow: you're on island time at Chef Creole.

Jimmy's East Side Diner
DINER $

(Map p96; ☑ 305-754-3692; 7201 Biscayne Blvd; mains $7-13; ⊙ 6:30am-4pm) Come to Jimmy's, a classic greasy spoon (that happens to be very gay-friendly; note the rainbow flag out front), for big cheap breakfasts of omelets, French toast or pancakes, and turkey clubs and burgers later in the day.

As an aside, the diner played a starring role in the final scene of Barry Jenkins' powerful film *Moonlight*, which won the Oscar for Best Picture in 2017.

Choices
VEGETARIAN $

(Map p96; ☑ 786-408-9122; www.choicescafemiami-ues.com; 646 NE 79th St; mains $10-17; ⊙ 8am-9pm Mon-Fri, 9am-9pm Sat, to 8pm Sun; ☑ ✦) ✔ The description everyone writes when vegan food tastes good is that you're not missing the meat. This trope actually holds true at Choices. With clever ingredient combinations like walnut 'meat' and daiya cheese, this restaurant lives up to its name, offering burgers, tacos and pizza – all 100% vegan, and all delicious.

★ Mina's
MEDITERRANEAN $$

(Map p96; ☑ 786-391-0300; www.minasmiami.com; 749 NE 79th St; mains $16-30, sharing plates $6-16; ⊙ 5-10pm Tue-Thu, to 11pm Fri, noon-11pm Sat, 11am-9pm Sun; ✦) Soaring ceilings, vintage travel posters and a friendly vibe set the stage for a memorable meal at Mina's. The Mediterranean menu is great for sharing, with creamy hummus, refreshing dolmas, spanakopita (spinach-filled pastries) and toothsome fried calamari among the great starters.

Andiamo
PIZZA $$

(Map p96; ☑ 305-762-5751; www.andiamopizzamiami.com; 5600 Biscayne Blvd; pizzas $12-20; ⊙ 11am-11pm Sun-Thu, to midnight Fri & Sat; ✦) In a converted industrial space (once a tire shop), Andiamo fires up some of Miami's best thin-crust pizzas from its brick oven at center stage. With over 30 varieties, Andiamo does not lack for options. It's a lively setting to start off the night, with flickering tiki torches scattered around the outdoor tables and large screens showing sports on big-game nights.

Blue Collar
AMERICAN $$

(Map p96; ☑ 305-756-0366; www.bluecollarmiami.com; 6730 Biscayne Blvd; mains $16-27; ⊙ 11:30am-3:30pm daily, 6-10pm Sun-Thu, to 11pm Fri & Sat; ℙ ☑ ✦) ✔ True to name, Blue Collar tosses pretension aside and fires up American comfort food done to perfection in a classic 1960s coffee-shop-style interior. Start off with shrimp and grits or the fourcheese Mac(aroni) before moving on to seared rainbow trout, a smoky plate of ribs or lip-smacking jambalaya. A well-curated veg board keeps non-carnivores happy.

Little Havana

★ Versailles
CUBAN $

(📞 305-444-0240; www.versaillesrestaurant.com; 3555 SW 8th St; mains $6-21; ⊙ 8am-1am Mon-Thu, to 2:30am Fri & Sat, 9am-1am Sun) Versailles (ver-*sigh*-yay) is an institution – one of the mainstays of Miami's Cuban gastronomic scene. Try the excellent black-bean soup or the fried yucca before moving onto heartier meat and seafood plates. Older Cubans and Miami's Latin political elite still love coming here, so you've got a real chance to rub elbows with Miami's most prominent Latin citizens.

Lung Yai Thai Tapas
THAI $

(Map p98; 📞 786-334-6262; 1731 SW 8th St; mains $10-15; ⊙ noon-3pm & 5pm-midnight) A sure sign of the changing times is this tiny gem in Little Havana, whipping up some truly mouthwatering Thai cooking. Chef Bas performs culinary wizardry with a menu ideal for sharing. You can't go wrong – whether it's perfectly spiced fried chicken wings, tender duck salad or a much-revered Kaho Soi Gai (a rich noodle curry).

El Nuevo Siglo
LATIN AMERICAN $

(Map p98; 1305 SW 8th St; mains $8-12; ⊙ 7am-8pm) Hidden inside a supermarket of the same name, El Nuevo Siglo draws foodie-minded locals who come for delicious cooking at excellent prices – never mind the unfussy ambience. Grab a seat at the shiny black countertop and nibble on roast meats, fried yucca, tangy Cuban sandwiches, grilled snapper with rice, beans and plantains, and other daily specials.

Viva Mexico
MEXICAN $

(Map p98; 📞 786-350-6360; 502 SW 12th Ave; tacos $2; ⊙ 11am-9pm Tue-Thu, to 11pm Fri & Sat, to 6pm Sun) Head up busy 12th Ave for some of the best tacos in Little Havana. From a takeout window, smiling Latin ladies dole out heavenly tacos topped with steak, tripe, sausage and other meats. There are a few outdoor tables – or get it to go.

On the downside, there's nothing here for vegetarians.

Yambo
LATIN AMERICAN $

(1643 SW 1st St; mains $5-12; ⊙ 24hr) If you're a bit drunk in the middle of the night and can find a cab or a friend willing to drive all the way out to Little Havana, direct them to Yambo. At night Yambo does a roaring trade selling trays and take-away boxes about

to burst with juicy slices of *carne asada* (grilled beef), piles of rice and beans, and sweet fried plantains.

San Pocho
COLOMBIAN $

(Map p88; 📞 305-854-5954; www.sanpocho.com; 901 SW 8th St; mains $9-15; ⊙ 7am-8pm Mon-Thu, to 9pm Fri-Sun) For a quick journey to Colombia, head over to friendly, always hopping San Pocho. The meat-centric menu features hearty platters like *bandeja paisa* (with grilled steak, rice, beans, fried plantains, an egg, an *arepa* and fried pork skin). There's also *mondongo* (tripe soup) as well as Colombian-style tamales and requisite sides like *arepas* (corn cakes).

Azucar
ICE CREAM $

(Map p98; 📞 305-381-0369; www.azucaricecream.com; 1503 SW 8th St; ice cream $4-6; ⊙ 11am-9pm Mon-Wed, to 11pm Thu-Sat, to 10pm Sun) One of Little Havana's most recognizable snack spots (thanks to the giant ice-cream cone on the facade) serves delicious ice cream just like *abuela* (grandmother) used to make. Deciding isn't easy with dozens of tempting flavors, including rum raisin, dulce de leche, guava, mango, cinnamon, jackfruit and lemon basil.

Exquisito Restaurant
CUBAN $

(Map p98; 📞 305-643-0227; www.elexquisitomiami.com; 1510 SW 8th St; mains $9-13; ⊙ 7am-11pm) For great Cuban cuisine in the heart of Little Havana, this place is exquisite (ha ha). The roast pork has a tangy citrus kick and the *ropa vieja* (spiced shredded beef) is wonderfully rich and filling. Even standard sides like beans and rice and roasted plantains are executed with a little more care and tastiness. Prices are a steal, too.

★ El Carajo
SPANISH $$

(📞 305-856-2424; www.el-carajo.com; 2465 SW 17th Avenue; tapas $5-15; ⊙ noon-10pm Mon-Wed, to 11pm Thu-Sat, 11am-10pm Sun; 🅿) Pass the Pennzoil please. We know it is cool to tuck restaurants into unassuming spots, but the Citgo station on SW 17th Ave? Really? Really. Walk past the motor oil into a Granadan wine cellar and try not to act too fazed. And now the food, which is absolutely incredible.

Bacon-wrapped stuffed dates are pure decadence on a plate, while fluffy tortillas (thick Spanish omelets) have just the right bite. And don't miss the sardines – cooked with a bit of salt and olive oil till they're dizzyingly delicious.

Doce Provisions

MODERN AMERICAN $$

(Map p98; ✉786-452-0161; www.doceprovisions. com; 541 SW 12th Ave; mains $11-25; ✪noon-3:30pm & 5-10pm Mon-Thu, noon-3:30pm & 5-11pm Fri, noon-11pm Sat, 11am-9pm Sun) If you want a break from old-school Latin eateries, stop in at Doce Provisions, which has more of a Wynwood vibe than a Little Havana one. The stylish industrial interior sets the stage for dining on creative American fare – rock shrimp mac 'n' cheese, fried chicken with sweet plantain waffle, short rib burgers and truffle fries – plus local microbrews.

Brunch is justifiably popular on Sunday (11am to 3pm).

Xixón

SPANISH $$

(✉305-854-9350; www.xixonspanishrestaurant. com; 2101 SW 22nd St; tapas $7-16; ✪11am-10pm Mon-Thu, to 11pm Fri & Sat, noon-5pm Sun; ✍) It takes a lot to stand out in Miami's crowded tapas-spot stakes. Bread that has a crackling crust and a soft center, delicate explosions of *bacalao* (cod) fritters and sizzling shrimp and baby eel cooked in garlic secures Xixón's status as a top tapas contender. The *bocatas* (sandwiches), with lavish Serrano ham and salty Manchego cheese, are great picnic fare.

✖ Coconut Grove

Bianco Gelato

ICE CREAM $

(Map p100; ✉786-717-5315; 3137 Commodore Plaza; ice cream $3.50-7) A much-loved spot in the neighborhood, particularly among Coconut Grove's youngest residents, Bianco whips up amazing gelato. It's made from organic milk and all-natural ingredients. Flavors change regularly, but a few recent hits are guava and cheese, avocado with carmelized nuts, hazelnut, and vegan chocolate.

Last Carrot

VEGETARIAN $

(Map p100; ✉305-445-0805; 3133 Grand Ave; mains $6-8; ✪10:30am-6pm Mon-Sat, 11am-4:30pm Sun; ✍⊞) Going strong since the 1970s, the Last Carrot serves up fresh juices, delicious pita sandwiches, avocado melts, veggie burgers and rather famous spinach pies, all amid old-Grove neighborliness. The Carrot's endurance next to massive CocoWalk is testament to the quality of its good-for-your-body food served in a good-for-your-soul setting.

Coral Bagels

DELI $

(✉305-854-0336; 2750 SW 26th Ave; mains $7-11; ✪6:30am-3pm Mon-Fri, 7am-4pm Sat & Sun; ℗✍) Although it's out of the way (one mile north of Coconut Grove's epicenter), this is a great place to start the day. The buzzing little deli serves proper bagels, rich omelets and decadent potato pancakes with apple sauce and sour cream. You'll be hard pressed to spend double digits, and you'll leave satisfied.

LoKal

AMERICAN $

(Map p100; ✉305-442-3377; 3190 Commodore Plaza; burgers $14-16; ✪noon-10pm Sun-Tue, to 11pm Wed-Sat; ✻✍⊞) ✐ This little Coconut Grove joint does two things very well: burgers and craft beer. The former come in several variations, all utilizing excellent beef (bar the oat bran- and brown-rice-based veggie version). When in doubt, go for the frita, which adds in guava sauce, plus melted gruyere and crispy bacon.

The Spillover

MODERN AMERICAN $$

(Map p100; ✉305-456-5723; www.spillover miami.com; 2911 Grand Ave; mains $13-25; ✪11:30am-10pm Sun-Tue, to 11pm Wed-Sat; ✻✍) Tucked down a pedestrian strip near the CocoWalk, the Spillover serves up locally sourced seafood and creative bistro fare in an enticing vintage setting (cast-iron stools and recycled doors around the bar, suspenders-wearing staff, brassy jazz playing overhead). Come for crab cakes, buffalo shrimp tacos, spear-caught fish and chips, or a melt-in-your-mouth lobster Reuben.

Boho

MEDITERRANEAN $$

(Map p100; ✉305-549-8614; 3433 Main Hwy; mains $19-26, pizzas $12-17; ✪noon-11pm Mon-Fri, from 10am Sat & Sun) This Greek-run charmer is helping to lead the culinary renaissance in Coconut Grove, serving up fantastic Mediterranean dishes, including tender marinated octopus, creamy risotto, thin-crust pizzas drizzled with truffle oil and zesty quinoa and beet salads. The setting invites long, leisurely meals with its jungle-like wallpaper, big picture windows and easygoing vibe.

There's also outdoor tables on the sidewalk in front – a fine spot to take in the passing street scene.

Glass & Vine

MODERN AMERICAN $$

(Map p100; www.glassandvine.com; 2820 McFarlane Rd; mains lunch $9-14, dinner $17-32; ✪11:30am-3:30pm & 5:30-10pm Sun-Thu, to 11pm Fri & Sat) It's hard to beat the open-air setting of this wine-loving eatery on the edge of Peacock Park. Stop by for tabbouleh and shrimp sandwiches at lunch, or charred cauliflower and sea scallops at dinner. All of which go nicely with the extensive wine and cocktail menu. Excellent weekend brunches too.

Bombay Darbar
INDIAN $$

(Map p100; ☑305-444-7272; 2901 Florida Ave; mains $15-23; ⊙noon-3pm Thu-Sun & 6-10pm Wed-Mon, closed Tue; ☑) Indian food is a rarity in Latin-loving Miami and all the more so in Coconut Grove – which makes Bombay Darbar even more of a culinary gem. Run by a couple from Mumbai, this upscale but friendly place hits all the right notes, with its beautifully executed tandooris and tikkas, best accompanied by piping-hot naan and flavor-bursting samosas.

Lulu
MODERN AMERICAN $$

(Map p100; ☑305-447-5858; 3105 Commodore Plaza; mains lunch $12-19, dinner $15-29; ⊙11:30am-10:30pm Sun-Thu, to 11:30pm Fri & Sat; ☑) Lulu is the Grove's exemplar of using local, organic ingredients in its carefully prepared bistro dishes, all of which are best enjoyed at the outdoor tables. You can make a meal of tasty appetizers like roasted dates, Tuscan hummus or Ahi tuna tartare, or go for more filling plates of slow-braised pork tacos and seared diver scallops.

GreenStreet Cafe
AMERICAN $$

(Map p100; ☑305-567-0662; www.greenstreetcafe. net; 3468 Main Hwy; mains $15-29; ⊙7:30am-1am Sun-Tue, to 3am Wed-Sat) Sidewalk spots don't get more popular (and many say more delicious) than GreenStreet, where the Grove's young and gregarious congregate at sunset. The menu of high-end pub fare ranges from roast vegetable and goat cheese lasagna and mesclun endive salad to blackened mahimahi and braised short ribs with polenta.

Jaguar
LATIN AMERICAN $$

(Map p100; ☑305-444-0216; www.jaguarhg.com; 3067 Grand Ave; mains lunch $15, dinner $22-33; ⊙11:30am-11pm Mon-Sat, 11am-10pm Sun) The menu spans the Latin world, but really everyone's here for the ceviche 'spoon bar.' The idea: pick from six styles of ceviche (raw, marinated seafood), ranging from tuna with ginger to corvina in lime juice, and pull a culinary version of DIY. It's novel and fun, and the ceviche varieties are outstanding.

Coral Gables

Threefold
CAFE $$

(Map p102; ☑305-704-8007; 141 Giralda Ave; mains $13-19; ⊙8am-4:30pm; ☑☑) Coral Gables' most talked-about cafe is a buzzing, Aussie-run charmer that serves up perfectly pulled espressos (and a good flat white), along with creative breakfast and lunch fare. Start the morning with waffles and berry compote, smashed avocado toast topped with feta, or a slow-roasted leg of lamb with fried eggs.

Frenchie's Diner
FRENCH $$

(Map p102; ☑305-442-4554; www.frenchiesdiner. com; 2618 Galiano St; mains lunch $14-24, dinner $24-34; ⊙11am-3pm & 6-10pm Tue-Sat) Tucked down a side street, it's easy to miss this place. Inside, Frenchie's channels an old-time American diner vibe, with black-and-white checkered floors, a big chalkboard menu, and a smattering of old prints and mirrors on the wall. The cooking, on the other hand, is a showcase for French bistro classics.

Matsuri
JAPANESE $$

(Map p102; ☑305-663-1615; 5759 Bird Rd; mains $12-19, lunch specials $10; ⊙11:30am-2:30pm Tue-Fri, 5:30-10:30pm Tue-Sat) Matsuri, tucked into a nondescript shopping center, is consistently packed with Japanese customers. They don't want scene; they want a taste of home, although many of the diners are actually South American Japanese who order *unagi* (eel) in Spanish. Spicy *toro* (fatty tuna) and scallions, grilled mackerel with natural salt, and an ocean of raw fish are all *oishii* (delicious).

Bulla Gastrobar
SPANISH $$

(Map p102; ☑305-441-0107; www.bullagastro bar.com; 2500 Ponce de Leon Blvd; small plates $7-19; ⊙noon-10pm Sun-Thu, to midnight Fri & Sat; ☑) With a festive crowd chattering away over delicious bites of tapas, this stylish spot has great ambience that evokes the lively eating and drinking dens of Madrid. *Patatas bravas* (spicy potatoes), *huevos* 'bulla' (eggs, serrano ham and truffle oil) and Iberian ham croquettes keep the crowds coming throughout the night.

Swine
SOUTHERN US $$$

(Map p102; ☑786-360-6433; 2415 Ponce de Leon Blvd; mains $20-38, sharing plates $10-25; ⊙10am-10pm Sun-Thu, to midnight Fri & Sat) Rustic smoked pork and craft cocktails come to Coral Gables at this stylish spot near the Miracle Mile. Amid exposed-brick walls, a cascade of hanging light bulbs and reclaimed wood elements, you'd be forgiven for thinking you took a wrong turn on the way to Brooklyn.

Pascal's on Ponce FRENCH $$$

(Map p102; ☑305-444-2024; www.pascalmiami.
com; 2611 Ponce de Leon Blvd; mains lunch $22-31,
dinner $31-45; ☺11:30am-2:30pm Mon-Fri, 6-10pm
Mon-Thu, to 11pm Fri & Sat) They're fighting the
good fight here: sea scallops with beef short
rib, crispy duck confit with wild mushroom
fricasée and other French fine-dining classics set the stage for a night of high-end
feasting. Pascal's is a favorite among Coral
Gables foodies who appreciate time-tested
standards.

The menu and the atmosphere rarely
change, and frankly that's not a bad thing.
After all, if it ain't broke...

La Palme d'Or FRENCH $$$

(Map p102; ☑305-913-3200; 1200 Anastasia
Ave, Biltmore Hotel; 6-course tasting menu $115;
☺6:30-10:30pm Tue-Sat) The acclaimed Palme
d'Or is the culinary match for the Jazz Age
opulence that ensconces it. With its white-
gloved, old-world class and US attention
to service, unmuddled by pretensions of
hipness, this place captures, in one elegant
stroke, all the refinement a dozen South
Beach restaurants could never grasp.

Caffe Abbracci ITALIAN $$$

(Map p102; ☑305-441-0700; www.caffeabbracci.
com; 318 Aragon Ave; mains $19-45; ☺11:30am-
3:30pm Mon-Fri, 6-11pm daily) Perfect moments
in Coral Gables come easy. Here's a simple
formula: you, a loved one, a muggy Miami
evening, some delicious pasta and a glass of
red at a sidewalk table at Abbracci – one of
the finest Italian restaurants in the Gables.

🍴 Key Biscayne

Oasis CUBAN $

(Map p106; ☑305-361-9009; 19 Harbor Dr; mains
$8-12; ☺8am-9pm) This excellent Cuban cafe
has a customer base that ranges from the
working poor to city players, and the socioec-
onomic barriers come tumbling down fast as
folks sip high-octane Cuban coffee. Come for
decadent, meaty Cuban sandwiches or the
homestyle cooking of platters of pork, rice
and beans and deep-fried plantains, then finish with super-strong coffee.

La Boulangerie Boul'Mich CAFE $

(Map p106; www.laboulangerieusa.com; 328
Crandon Blvd; mains $12-15, pastries $3-6;
☺7:30am-8pm Mon-Sat, 8am-3pm Sun; 🛜✏️)
This delightful French-style bakery whips
up delicious quiches, satisfying veggie- or
meat-filled empanadas, heavenly pastries

and, of course, perfectly buttery croissants.
It's also a fine place for breakfast (fruit
platters, omelets, eggs Benedict) or lunch
(prosciutto and mozzarella sandwiches,
four-cheese gnocchi, quinoa salads).

It's in a shopping complex, but has a classy
vintage vibe, with a few outdoor tables in
front.

Golden Hog Gourmet SUPERMARKET $

(Map p106; 91 Harbor Dr; mains $8-15; ☺8am-
8pm Mon-Sat, to 6:30pm Sun) Tucked into a
small shopping complex, this is the best
place in Key Biscayne to grab picnic fare
before hitting the beach or state parks.
Aside from good cheeses, bakery items,
tasty spreads and fresh fruits, there are
various counters where you can order take-
away sandwiches, soups of the day and
ready-made dishes (oven-roasted salmon,
paella, green beans).

🍴 Greater Miami

Fritanga Montelimar NICARAGUAN $

(☑305-388-8841; 15722 SW 72nd St; mains $8-
14; ☺9am-11pm) A *fritanga* is a Nicaraguan
cafe, and if you've never eaten at one, here's
a warning: Nicaraguans are not scared of
big portions. This beloved spot, located deep
in Kendall, serves up grilled pork, chicken
stew, meltingly soft beef and other goodies
on Styrofoam plates collapsing under the
weight of beans and rice.

Lots of Lox DELI $$

(☑305-252-2010; www.originallotsoflox.com; 14995
S Dixie Hwy; mains breakfast $7-16, lunch $12-16,
dinner $15-19; ☺7am-9pm Mon-Fri, to 4pm Sat &
Sun) In a city with no shortage of delis, especially in mid–Miami Beach, who would have
thought some of the best chopped liver on rye
could be found in this unassuming place all
the way down in Palmetto Bay? It is bustling,
friendly and a great slice of old-school Miami.

Steve's Pizza PIZZA $$

(☑305-891-0202; www.facebook.com/stevespizza
northmiami; 12101 Biscayne Blvd; slices $4, pizzas
$12-23; ☺11am-3am Mon-Thu, to 4am Fri & Sat, to
2am Sun) So many pizza chains compete for
the attention of tourists in South Beach, but
ask a Miami Beach local where to get the
best pizza and they'll tell you about Steve's.
This is New York–style pizza, thin crust and
handmade with care and good ingredients.

New branches of Steve's are opening
elsewhere in Miami, all in decidedly non-
touristy areas, which preserves that feeling

of authenticity. Steve's flagship is in South Miami; the closer North Miami outpost listed here caters to nighthawks, and is about 6 miles (15 minutes' drive) north of the Design District.

Drinking & Nightlife

Too many people assume Miami's nightlife is all about being wealthy and attractive and/or phony. Disavow yourself of this notion, which only describes a small slice of the scene in South Beach. Miami has an intense variety of bars to pick from that range from grotty dives to beautiful – but still laid-back – lounges and nightclubs.

South Beach

★ Sweet Liberty
BAR

(Map p78; www.mysweetliberty.com; 237 20th St; ☺4pm-5am Mon-Sat, from noon Sun) A much-loved local haunt near Collins Park, Sweet Liberty has all the right ingredients for a fun night out: friendly, easygoing bartenders who whip up excellent cocktails (try a mint julep), great happy-hour specials (including 75¢ oysters) and a relaxed, pretension-free crowd. The space is huge, with flickering candles, a long wooden bar and the odd band adding to the cheer.

There's also decent food ($6 to $31) on hand, from crab toast and cauliflower nachos to brisket sandwiches and beet and farro risotto.

★ Bodega
COCKTAIL BAR

(Map p78; ☎305-704-2145; www.bodegasouth beach.com; 1220 16th St; ☺noon-5am) Bodega looks like your average hipster Mexican joint – serving up delicious tacos ($3 to $5) from a converted Airstream trailer to a party-minded crowd. But there's actually a bar hidden behind that blue porta potty door on the right. Head inside (or join the line on weekends) to take in a bit of old-school glam in a sprawling drinking den.

Tarnished mirrors, leather sofas, graffiti-smeared walls, antler chandeliers and curious portraits of famous figures (but with eyepatches) – plus great cocktails and a fun crowd – set the scene for a memorable night out. Go early to avoid the lines.

★ Mango's Tropical Café
BAR

(Map p82; ☎305-673-4422; www.mangostropical cafe.com; 900 Ocean Dr; $10; ☺11:45am-5am) A mix of Latin-loving locals and visitors from far-flung corners of the globe mix things up

at this famous bar on Ocean Dr. Every night feels like a celebration, with a riotously fun vibe, and plenty of entertainment: namely minimally dressed staff dancing on the bar, doing Michael Jackson impersonations, shimmying in feather headdresses or showing off some amazing salsa moves.

It's a kitschy good time, which doesn't even take into consideration the small dance floor and stage in the back, where brassy Latin bands get everyone moving. As with other spots on Ocean Dr, the drinks are ridiculously overpriced (around $10 for a beer and $20 for a cocktail).

Bay Club
COCKTAIL BAR

(Map p78; ☎305-695-4441; 1930 Bay Rd; ☺5pm-2am) A great little nightspot in Sunset Harbour, Bay Club has an enticing low-lit vintage vibe with red banquettes, antique wallpaper, wood paneling and old chandeliers. It's a good date spot with craft cocktails and occasional live music (jazz guitar and other subdued sounds).

Kill Your Idol
BAR

(Map p78; ☎305-672-1852; www.killyouridol. com; 222 Española Way; ☺8pm-5am) Kill Your Idol is a bit of a dive, but it has plenty of appeal, with graffiti and shelves full of retro bric-a-brac covering the walls, drag shows on Monday and DJs spinning danceable old-school grooves. The crowd is a fairly laid-back mix of locals and out-of-towners. The bar is tiny, so prepare for the crowds on weekends.

Rose Bar at the Delano
BAR

(Map p78; ☎305-674-5752; www.delano-hotel. com; 1685 Collins Ave, Delano Hotel; ☺noon-2am) The ultrachic Rose Bar at this elegant Ian Schrager original is a watering hole for beautiful creatures (or at least those with a healthy ego). Get ready to pay up for the privilege – but also prepare to enjoy it.

The pool bar in the back of the Delano (p121) is another winner; wait for staff to set out a wrought-iron table in the shallow end of the pool and you'll start rethinking your definition of opulence.

Campton Yard
BEER GARDEN

(Map p78; 1500 Collins Ave, Hall Hotel; ☺5pm-midnight Mon-Fri, from noon Sat & Sun) Spread beneath a towering banyan tree, this pebble-strewn backyard draws a youthful crowd who come for a night of laid-back merriment beneath the faerie lights. There are games (giant Jenga and Connect 4, ping

SOUTH BEACH SIPPIN'

Greater Miami's coffee scene has improved in leaps and bounds in recent years, though Miami Beach still has limited options (we don't count stand-up Cuban coffee counters, as you can't sit there and read a book or work on your laptop, although if you speak Spanish, they're a good place for hearing local gossip). That said, there are a handful of decent options in Miami Beach.

➡ Panther Coffee (p126) The Wynwood chain has opened a great spot in Sunset Harbour.

➡ Pinocchio (p127) Just off Ocean Dr is this charming Italian spot with excellent espresso. Has just a few seats.

➡ A La Folie (p128) A *tres* French cafe where the waiters have great accents. Why yes, we would like 'zee moka.'

➡ Dirt (p126) The healthy cafe pulls good espressos.

➡ Lilikoi (p128) The best spot in SoFi for a pick-me-up.

pong, beanbag tossing), craft beer, picnic tables and a welcome lack of pretension. Enter through the Hall Hotel, and make your way to the backyard oasis.

Story
CLUB

(Map p82; ☑305-479-4426; www.storymiami.com; 136 Collins Ave; ⊙11pm-5am Thu-Sun) For the big megaclub experience, Story is a top destination. Some of the best DJs (mostly EDM) from around the globe spin at this club, with parties lasting late into the night. It has a fairly roomy dance floor, but gets packed on weekend nights. Be good looking and dress to impress, as getting in can be a pain.

Score
GAY

(Map p78; ☑305-535-1111; www.scorebar.net; 1437 Washington Ave; ⊙10pm-5am Thu-Sun) Muscle boys with mustaches, glistening six-packs gyrating on stage, and a crowd of men who've decided shirts really aren't their thing: do we need to spell out the orientation of Score's customer base? It's still one of the best dedicated – and decadent – gay bars in South Beach.

Lost Weekend
BAR

(Map p78; ☑305-672-1707; www.sub-culture.org/lost-weekend-miami; 218 Española Way; ⊙noon-5am) Lost Weekend is a grimy, sweaty, slovenly dive, filled with pool tables, cheap domestics and – hell yeah – *Golden Tee* and *Big Buck Hunter* arcade games. God bless it. Popular with local waiters, kitchen staff and bartenders.

Abbey Brewery
MICROBREWERY

(Map p78; www.abbeybrewinginc.com; 1115 16th St; ⊙1pm-5am) The oldest brew-pub in South Beach is on the untouristed end of South

Beach (near Alton Rd). It's friendly and packed with folks listening to throwback hits (grunge, '80s new wave) and slinging back some excellent homebrew: give Father Theo's stout or the Immaculate IPA a try.

Mac's Club Deuce Bar
BAR

(Map p78; ☑305-531-6200; www.macsclubdeuce.com; 222 14th St; ⊙8am-5am) The oldest bar in Miami Beach (established in 1926), the Deuce is a real neighborhood bar and hype-free zone. It's just straight-up seediness, which depending on your outlook can be quite refreshing. Plan to see everyone from transgendered ladies to construction workers – some hooking up, some talking rough, all having a good time.

🍸 North Beach

★ Broken Shaker
BAR

(Map p86; ☑305-531-2727; www.freehandhotels.com/miami/broken-shaker; 2727 Indian Creek Dr, Freehand Miami Hotel; ⊙6pm-3am Mon-Fri, 2pm-3am Sat & Sun) Craft cocktails are having their moment in Miami, and if mixology is in the spotlight, you can bet Broken Shaker is sharing the glare. Expert bartenders run this spot, located in the back of the Freehand Miami hotel (p122), which takes up one closet-sized indoor niche and a sprawling plant-filled courtyard of excellent drinks and beautiful people.

Sandbar Lounge
BAR

(Map p86; ☑305-865-1752; 6752 Collins Ave; ⊙4pm-5am) True to its name this dive bar has sand – lots and lots of it covering the floor. Never mind that the beach is a block away, Sandbar's a local institution, and a fine antidote to the high-end drinking spots covering Miami Beach. It has a welcoming vibe, sports on TV, a fun jukebox and great happy-hour specials. Come on in and join the gang.

WunderBar
LOUNGE

(Map p86; ☑ 305-503-1120; www.circa39.com/wunderbar; 3900 Collins Ave, Circa39; ☺ 11am-11pm Sun-Thu, to midnight Fri & Sat) Tucked off to the back of Circa 39's (p122) moody front lobby, this designer dream bar has a warm, welcoming feel to it. Definitely stop in for a drink if you're up this way, before sauntering across the street and checking out the lapping waves on the beach.

☺ Downtown Miami

★ Blackbird Ordinary
BAR

(Map p88; ☑ 305-671-3307; www.blackbirdordinary.com; 729 SW 1st Ave; ☺ 3pm-5am Mon-Fri, 5pm-5am Sat & Sun) Far from ordinary, the Blackbird is an excellent bar, with great cocktails (the London Sparrow, with gin, cayenne, lemon juice and passion fruit, goes down well) and an enormous courtyard. The only thing 'ordinary' about the place is the sense that all are welcome for a fun and pretension-free night out.

You can often catch great bands playing here, and on quiet nights there's always the pool table. Tuesday nights are a wonderful thing for the gals: it's ladies night, and women drink free until 1:30am.

Eleven Miami
CLUB

(E11EVEN; Map p88; ☑ 305-570-4803; www.11miami.com; 29 NE 11th St; ☺ 24hr) Since its opening way back in 2014, Eleven Miami has remained one of the top Downtown clubs. There's much eye candy here (and we're not talking just about the attractive club-goers): go-go dancers, aerialists and racy (striptease-esque) performances, amid a state-of-the-art sound system, laser lights and video walls, with top DJs working the crowd into a frenzy.

Sugar
LOUNGE

(Map p88; 788 Brickell Plaza, EAST, Miami Hotel, 40th fl; ☺ 4pm-1am Mon-Thu, to 3am Fri & Sat, to midnight Sun) One of Miami's hottest bars of the moment sits on the 40th floor of the EAST, Miami Hotel (p123). Calling it a rooftop bar doesn't quite do the place justice. Verdant oasis is more like it, with a spacious open-air deck full of plants and trees –

and sweeping views over the city and Key Biscayne.

Batch Gastropub
BAR

(Map p88; www.batchmiami.com; 30 SW 12th St; ☺ noon-3am Sun-Thu, to 4am Fri & Sat) This gastropub in Brickell draws a fairly straight-laced crowd. But if you don't mind the slacks and the sports on TV, Batch has appeal: namely a first-rate selection of microbrews and fizzes (carbonated cocktails) on tap, plus creative cocktails and lots of great snacks (truffle fries, grouper tacos, brisket burgers, wild-mushroom pizzas).

There are good food and drink deals during happy hour (weekdays 5pm to 8pm).

Area 31
ROOFTOP BAR

(Map p88; www.area31restaurant.com; 270 Biscayne Blvd Way, Kimpton Epic Hotel; ☺ 5-11pm Sun-Thu, to midnight Fri & Sat) On the rooftop of the Kimpton Epic Hotel, this buzzing open-air bar draws in the after-work happy-hour crowd, which morphs into a more party-minded gathering as the evening progresses. The view – overlooking the river and the high-rises of Downtown – is stunning.

Pawnbroker
ROOFTOP BAR

(Map p88; ☑ 305-420-2200; www.pawnbrokermiami.com; 121 SE 1st St, Langford Hotel; ☺ 5pm-midnight Mon-Thu, to 2am Fri & Sat, 4-10pm Sun) Head up to the top (penthouse) floor of the Langford Hotel (p123) for sweeping views of Downtown, first-rate cocktails and a welcoming, snooty-free vibe. It's a lively spot at happy hour (5pm to 7pm weekdays), when you can catch the sunset, though you won't be alone (go early to beat the crowds).

☺ Wynwood & the Design District

★ Lagniappe
BAR

(Map p94; ☑ 305-576-0108; www.lagniappehouse.com; 3425 NE 2nd Ave; ☺ 7pm-2am Sun-Thu, to 3am Fri & Sat) A touch of New Orleans in Miami, Lagniappe has an old-fashioned front room bar, packed with art, faded vintage furnishings and weathered walls. The vibe is just right: with great live music (nightly from 9pm to midnight) and an easygoing crowd, plus there's a sprawling back garden with palm trees and fairy lights.

Bardot
CLUB

(Map p94; ☑ 305-576-5570; www.bardotmiami.com; 3456 N Miami Ave; ☺ 8pm-3am Tue & Wed, to 5am Thu-Sat) You really should aim to see the interior of Bardot before you leave the city. It's all sexy French vintage posters and furniture (plus a pool table) seemingly plucked from a private club that serves millionaires by day, and becomes a scene of decadent excess by night. The entrance looks to be on N Miami Ave, but it's actually in a parking lot behind the building.

Boxelder BAR
(Map p94; ☑305-942-7769; www.bxldr.com; 2817 NW 2nd Ave; ⊙4pm-midnight Mon, 1pm-midnight Tue-Thu, to 2am Fri & Sat, to 10pm Sun) This long, narrow space is a beer-lover's Valhalla, with a brilliantly curated menu of brews from near and far, though its 20 rotating beer taps leave pride of place for South Florida beers. There's also more than 100 different varieties by the bottle. What keeps the place humming is Boxelder's friendly, down-to-earth vibe.

Wynwood Brewing Company MICROBREWERY
(Map p94; ☑305-982-8732; www.wynwood brewing.com; 565 NW 24th St; ⊙noon-10pm Sun & Mon, to midnight Tue-Sat) The beer scene has grown in leaps and bounds in Miami, but this warmly lit spot, which was the first craft brewery in Wynwood, is still the best. The family-owned 15-barrel brewhouse has friendly and knowledgeable staff, excellent year-round brews (including a blonde ale, a robust porter and a top-notch IPA) and seasonal beers, and there's always a food truck parked outside.

Wood Tavern BAR
(Map p94; ☑305-748-2828; www.woodtavern miami.com; 2531 NW 2nd Ave; ⊙5pm-3am Tue-Sat, 3pm-midnight Sun) So many new bars in Miami want to be casual but cool; Wood is one of the few locales achieving this Golden Mean of atmosphere and aesthetic. Food specials are cheap, the beer selection is excellent and the crowd is friendly – this Wood's got the right grain.

Gramps BAR
(Map p94; ☑786-752-6693; www.gramps.com; 176 NW 24th St; ⊙11am-1am Sun-Wed, to 3am Thu-Sat) Friendly and unpretentious (just like some grandpas), Gramps always has something afoot whether it's live music and DJs (Fridays and Saturdays), trivia and bingo nights (Tuesdays and Wednesdays) or straight-up karaoke (Thursdays). The big draw though is really just the sizable backyard that's perfect for alfresco drinking and socializing.

Coyo Taco BAR
(Map p94; www.coyo-taco.com; 2300 NW 2nd Ave; ⊙5pm-midnight Sun-Wed, to 3am Thu-Sat) Secret bars hidden behind taco stands are all the rage in Miami these days. To find this one, head inside Coyo Taco, down the corridor past the bathrooms and enter the unmarked door. Inside you'll find a classy low-lit spot with elaborate ceramic tile floors, a long wooden bar and a DJ booth, with brassy Latin rhythms and Afro Cuban funk filling the space.

Concrete Beach Brewery BREWERY
(Map p94; ☑305-796-2727; www.concrete beachbrewery.com; 325 NW 24th St; ⊙5-11pm Mon-Thu, to 1am Fri, from 1pm Sat & Sun) Concrete Beach is a great little neighborhood brewery, with a gated courtyard where you can linger over hoppy IPAs, wheat beers with a hint of citrus, and easy-drinking pilsners, plus seasonal brews (like a juniper saison called Miami Gras, which typically launches in February). It's not always the liveliest spot, but a fine stop for beer connoisseurs.

🍸 Little Haiti & the Upper East Side

Vagabond Pool Bar BAR
(Map p96; ☑305-400-8420; www.vagabond kitchenandbar.com; 7301 Biscayne Blvd; ⊙5-11pm Sun-Thu, to midnight Fri & Sat) Tucked behind the Vagabond Hotel, this is a great spot to start off the evening, with perfectly mixed

---

ART WALKS: NIGHTLIFE MEETS ART

Ever-flowing (not always free) wine and beer, great art, a fun crowd and no cover charge (or velvet rope): welcome to the wondrous world where art and nightlife collide. The Wynwood and Design District Art Walks are among the best ways to experience an alternative slice of Miami culture. Just be careful, as a lot of galleries in Wynwood are separated by short drives (the Design District is more walkable). Art Walks (p113) take place on the second Saturday of each month, from 7pm to 10pm (some galleries stretch to 11pm); when it's all over, lots of folks repair to Wood Tavern or Bardot. Visit www.artofmiami.com/maps/art-walks for information on participating galleries.

ROOTOP BARS

Miami's high rises are put to fine use in the many rooftop bars you'll find scattered around the city. These are usually located in high-end hotels found in Miami Beach and in Downtown. The view is of course the big reason to come – and it can be sublime, with the sweep of Biscayne Bay or sparkling beachfront in the background. Despite being in hotels, some spots are a draw for locals, and it can be quite a scene, with DJs, a dressy crowd and a discriminating door policy at prime time on weekend nights. If you're here for the view and not the party, come early. Happy hour is fabulous – as you can catch a fine sunset, and getting in is usually not a problem.

cocktails, courtesy of pro bartenders (the kind who will shake your hand and introduce themselves). The outdoor setting overlooking the palm-fringed pool and eclectic crowd pairs nicely with elixirs like the Lost in Smoke (mezcal, amaro, amaretto and orange bitters).

The Anderson
BAR

(Map p96; www.theandersonmiami.com; 709 NE 79th St; ⏰5pm-2am Sun-Thu, to 4am Fri & Sat) The Anderson is a great neighborhood bar with a dimly lit interior sprinkled with red couches, animal-print fabrics, wild wallpaper and a glittering jukebox. Head to the back patio for more of a tropical-themed setting where you can dip your toes in the sand (never mind the absent oceanfront).

Churchill's
BAR

(Map p96; ☎305-757-1807; www.churchillspub.com; 5501 NE 2nd Ave; ⏰3pm-3am Sun-Thu, to 5am Fri & Sat) A Miami icon that's been around since 1979, Churchill's is a Brit-owned pub in the midst of what could be Port-au-Prince. There's a lot of live music here, mainly punk, indie and more punk. Not insipid modern punk either: think the Ramones meets the Sex Pistols.

Boteco
BAR

(Map p96; ☎305-757-7735; www.botecomiami.com; 916 NE 79th St; ⏰noon-midnight) If you're missing the *cidade maravilhosa* (aka Rio de Janeiro), come to Boteco on Friday evening to see the biggest Brazilian expat reunion in Miami. *Cariocas* (Rio natives) and their

countrymen flock here to listen to samba and bossa nova, and chat each other up over the best caipirinhas in town.

Little Havana

Ball & Chain
BAR

(Map p98; www.ballandchainmiami.com; 1513 SW 8th Street; ⏰noon-midnight Mon-Wed, to 3am Thu-Sat, 2-10pm Sun) The Ball & Chain has survived several incarnations over the years. Back in 1935, when 8th St was more Jewish than Latino, it was the sort of jazz joint Billie Holiday would croon in. That iteration closed in 1957, but the new Ball & Chain is still dedicated to music and good times – specifically, Latin music and tropical cocktails.

Los Pinareños Frutería
JUICE BAR

(Map p98; 1334 SW 8th St; snacks & drinks $3-6; ⏰7am-6pm Mon-Sat, to 3pm Sun) Nothing says refreshment on a sultry Miami afternoon like a cool glass of fresh juice (or smoothie) at this popular fruit and veggie stand. Try a combination like the 'abuelo' (sugarcane juice, pineapple and lemon) for something particularly satisfying. The produce is also quite flavorful.

Coconut Grove

Barracuda
BAR

(Map p100; ☎305-918-9013; 3035 Fuller St; ⏰noon-3am Tue-Sun, from 6pm Mon) Coconut Grove has its share of divey, pretension-free bars, and Barracuda is one of the best of the bunch, with a fine jukebox, pool table, darts and sports playing on the various TV screens. It's a fine retreat from CG's shiny shopping surfaces – the inside is decorated with wood salvaged from an old Florida shrimp boat.

Taurus
BAR

(Map p100; ☎305-529-6523; 3540 Main Hwy; ⏰4pm-3am Mon-Fri, from 1pm Sat & Sun) The oldest bar in Coconut Grove is a cool mix of wood-paneling, smoky leather chairs, about 100 beers to choose from and a convivial vibe – as neighborhood bars go in Miami, this is one of the best.

Tavern in the Grove
BAR

(Map p100; ☎305-447-3884; 3416 Main Hwy; ⏰3pm-3am Mon-Sat, from noon Sun) To say this sweatbox is popular with University of Miami students is like saying it rains sometimes in England. More of a neighborhood dive on weekdays.

Coral Gables

Seven Seas   BAR
(Map p102; ☑305-266-6071; 2200 SW 57th Ave; ⊙noon-1am Sun-Wed, to 2am Thu-Sat) Seven Seas is a genuine Miami neighborhood dive, decorated on the inside like a nautical theme park and filled with University of Miami students, Cuban workers, gays, straights, lesbians and folks from around the way. Come for the best karaoke in Miami on Tuesday, Thursday and Saturday, and for trivia on Monday.

Titanic Brewing Company   MICROBREWERY
(☑305-668-1742; www.titanicbrewery.com; 5813 Ponce de Leon Blvd; ⊙11:30am-1am Sun-Thu, to 2am Fri & Sat) By day Titanic is an all-American-type brewpub, but at night it turns into a popular University of Miami watering hole. Titanic's signature brews are quite refreshing – particularly the White Star IPA. Lots of good pub grub on hand, including Sriracha wings, and corn and crawfish fritters.

☆ Entertainment

Miami's artistic merits are obvious, even from a distance. Could there be a better creative base? There's Southern homegrown talent, migratory snowbirds bringing the funding and attention of northeastern galleries, and immigrants from across the Americas. All that adds up to some great live music, theater and dance – with plenty of room for experimentation.

☆ South Beach

New World Symphony   CLASSICAL MUSIC
(NWS; Map p78; ☑305-673-3330; www.nws.edu; 500 17th St) Housed in the New World Center (p68) – a funky explosion of cubist lines and geometric curves, fresh white against the blue Miami sky – the acclaimed New World Symphony holds performances from October to May. The deservedly heralded NWS serves as a three- to four-year preparatory program for talented musicians from prestigious music schools.

Colony Theater   PERFORMING ARTS
(Map p78; ☑305-674-1040, box office 800-211-1414; www.colonymb.org; 1040 Lincoln Rd) The Colony is an absolute art-deco gem, with a classic marquee and Inca-style crenellations, which looks like the sort of place gangsters would go to watch *Hamlet*. This treasure now serves as a major venue for performing arts – from comedy and occasional musicals

to theatrical dramas, off-Broadway productions and ballet – as well as hosting movie screenings and small film festivals.

Miami City Ballet   DANCE
(Map p78; ☑305-929-7000; www.miamicityballet.org; 2200 Liberty Ave) Formed in 1985, this troupe is based out of a lovely three-story headquarters designed by famed local architectural firm Arquitectonica. The facade allows passers-by to watch the dancers rehearsing through big picture windows, which makes you feel like you're in a scene from *Fame,* except the weather is better and people don't spontaneously break into song.

Fillmore Miami Beach   PERFORMING ARTS
(Map p78; ☑305-673-7300; www.fillmoremb.com; 1700 Washington Ave) Built in 1951, South Beach's premier showcase for touring Broadway shows, orchestras and other big musical productions has 2700 seats and excellent acoustics. Jackie Gleason chose to make the theater his home for the long-running 1960s TV show, but now you'll find an eclectic lineup: Catalan pop or indie rock one night, the comedian Bill Maher or an over-the-top vaudeville group the next.

☆ North Beach

North Beach Bandshell   LIVE MUSIC
(Map p86; www.northbeachbandshell.com; 7275 Collins Ave) This outdoor venue features an great lineup of concerts, dance, theater, opera and spoken word throughout the year. Some events are free. It's run by the nonprofit Rhythm Foundation, and the wide-ranging repertoire features sounds from around the globe, with many family-friendly events. Check online to see what's on the roster.

Chopin Foundation of the United States   CLASSICAL MUSIC
(Map p86; ☑305-868-0624; www.chopin.org; 1440 JFK/79th St Causeway) This national organization hosts a treasure trove of performances for Chopin fans – the Chopin Festival, a series of free monthly concerts and the less-frequent National Chopin Piano Competition, an international contest held in Miami every five years.

☆ Downtown Miami

★Adrienne Arsht Center for the Performing Arts   PERFORMING ARTS
(Map p88; ☑305-949-6722; www.arshtcenter.org; 1300 Biscayne Blvd; ⊙box office 10am-6pm

Mon-Fri, and 2 hours before performances) This magnificent venue manages to both humble and enthrall visitors. Today the Arsht is where the biggest cultural acts in Miami come to perform; a show here is a must-see on any Miami trip. There's an Adrienne Arsht Center stop on the Metromover.

This performing-arts center is Miami's beautiful, beloved baby. It is also a major component of Downtown's urban equivalent of a facelift and several regimens of Botox. Designed by César Pelli (the man who brought you Kuala Lumpur's Petronas Towers), the center has two main components, connected by a thin pedestrian bridge.

Inside the theaters there's a sense of ocean and land sculpted by wind; the rounded balconies rise up in spirals that resemble a sliced-open seashell. Hidden behind these impressive structures are highly engineered, state-of-the-art acoustics ensuring that no outside sounds can penetrate, creating the perfect conditions to enjoy one of the 300 performances staged at the center each year.

Klipsch Amphitheater
LIVE MUSIC

(Map p88; www.klipsch.com/klipsch-amphitheater-at-bayfront-park; 301 N Biscayne Blvd, Bayfront Park) In Bayfront Park in Downtown Miami, the Klipsch Amphitheater stages a wide range of concerts throughout the year. The open-air setting beside Biscayne Bay is hard to top.

American Airlines Arena
STADIUM

(Map p88; ☑ 786-777-1000; www.aaarena.com; 601 N Biscayne Blvd) Resembling a massive spaceship that perpetually hovers at the edge of Biscayne Bay, this arena has been the home of the city's NBA franchise, the **Miami Heat**, since 2000. The **Waterfront Theater**, Florida's largest, is housed inside; throughout the year it hosts concerts, Broadway performances and the like.

Olympia Theater
PERFORMING ARTS

(Map p88; ☑ 305-374-2444; www.olympiatheater. org; 174 E Flagler St) This elegantly renovated 1920s movie palace services a huge variety of performing arts including film festivals, symphonies, ballets and touring shows. The acoustics are excellent.

Miami loves modern, but the Olympia Theater at the Gusman Center for the Performing Arts is vintage-classic beautiful. The ceiling, which features 246 twinkling stars and clouds cast over an indigo-deep night, frosted with classical Greek sculpture and

Vienna Opera House–style embellishment, will melt your heart. The theater first opened in 1925.

☆ Wynwood & the Design District

O Cinema Wynwood
CINEMA

(Map p94; ☑ 305-571-9970; www.o-cinema.org; 90 NW 29th St) This much-loved nonprofit cinema in Wynwood screens indie films, foreign films and documentaries. You'll find thought-provoking works you won't see elsewhere.

Light Box at Goldman Warehouse
PERFORMING ARTS

(Map p94; ☑ 305-576-4350; www.miamilight project.com; 404 NW 26th St) The Miami Light Project, a nonprofit cultural foundation, stages a wide range of innovative theater, dance, music and film performances at this intimate theater. It's in Wynwood, and a great place to discover cutting-edge works by artists you might not have heard of. They're particularly supportive of troupes from South Florida.

☆ Little Havana

★ Cubaocho
LIVE PERFORMANCE

(Map p98; ☑ 305-285-5880; www.cubaocho. com; 1465 SW 8th St; ⊙ 11am-10pm Tue-Thu, to 3am Fri & Sat) Jewel of the Little Havana Art District, Cubaocho is renowned for its concerts, with excellent bands from across the Spanish-speaking world. It's also a community center, art gallery and research outpost for all things Cuban. The interior resembles an old Havana cigar bar, yet the walls are decked out in artwork that references both the classical past of Cuban art and its avant-garde future.

Aside from the busy concert schedule, Cubaocho also has film screenings, drama performances, readings and other events.

Tower Theater
CINEMA

(Map p98; ☑ 305-237-2463; www.towertheater miami.com; 1508 SW 8th St) This renovated 1926 landmark theater has a proud deco facade and a handsomely renovated interior, thanks to support from the Miami-Dade Community College. In its heyday, it was the center of Little Havana social life, and via the films it showed served as a bridge between immigrant society and American pop culture. Today it frequently shows independent and Spanish-language films (sometimes both).

Hoy Como Ayer
LIVE MUSIC

(Map p98; ✆305-541-2631; www.hoycomoayer. us; 2212 SW 8th St; ☉8:30pm-4am Thu-Sat) This Cuban hot spot – with authentic music, unstylish wood paneling and a small dance floor – is enhanced by first-rate mojitos and Havana transplants. Stop in nightly for *son* (a salsalike dance that originated in Oriente, Cuba), *boleros* (a Spanish dance in triple meter) and modern Cuban beats.

Marlins Park
BASEBALL

(http://miami.marlins.mlb.com; 501 Marlins Way; tickets from $15) The Miami Marlins' regular season runs from April to September.

☆ Coral Gables

Coral Gables Art Cinema
CINEMA

(Map p102; ✆786-385-9689; www.gablescinema. com; 260 Aragon Ave) In the epicenter of Coral Gables' downtown, you'll find one of Miami's best art-house cinemas. It screens indie and foreign films in a modern 144-seat screening room. Check out cult favorites shown in the original 35mm format at Saturday night midnight screenings (part of the After Hours series).

GableStage
THEATER

(Map p102; ✆305-445-1119; www.gablestage.org; 1200 Anastasia Ave; tickets $48-65) Founded as the Florida Shakespeare Theatre in 1979 and now housed on the property of the Biltmore Hotel in Coral Gables, this company still performs an occasional Shakespeare play, but mostly presents contemporary and classical pieces.

☆ Greater Miami

Miami Symphony Orchestra
CLASSICAL MUSIC

(✆305-275-5666; www.themiso.org; tickets $20-50) Miami's well-loved hometown symphony has many fans. Its yearly series features world-renowned soloists performing at either the Adrienne Arsht Center for the Performing Arts (p145) or the Fillmore Miami Beach (p145). Performances run from November to May.

Ifé-Ilé Afro-Cuban Dance
DANCE

(✆786-704-8609; www.ife-ile.org) Ifé-Ilé is a nonprofit organization that promotes cultural understanding through dance and performs

in a range of styles – traditional Afro Cuban, mambo, rumba, conga, *chancleta, son,* salsa and ritual pieces. Their big event is an Afro Cuban dance festival they headline in August.

Hard Rock Stadium
FOOTBALL

(✆305-943-8000; www.hardrockstadium.com; 347 Don Shula Dr, Miami Gardens; tickets from $35) The newly renovated (and renamed) Hard Rock Stadium (formerly known as Sun Life Stadium) is the home turf of the Miami Dolphins. 'Dol-fans' are respectably crazy about their team, even if a Super Bowl showing has evaded them since 1985. Games are wildly popular and the team is painfully successful, in that they always raise fans' hopes but never quite fulfill them.

University of Miami Hurricanes
SPECTATOR SPORT

(✆800-462-2637; www.hurricanesports.com; tickets $25-70) The Hurricanes were once undisputed titans of university football, but have experienced a slow decline since 2004. Regardless, attending a game surrounded by UM's pack of fanatics is lots of fun. Their season runs from August to December.

Shopping

Temptation comes in many forms in Miami. For shoppers, this means high-end fashion, designer sunglasses, vintage clothing, books, records, Latin American crafts, artwork, gourmet goodies and much more. You'll also find sprawling air-conditioned malls where you can retreat when the weather sours. No matter where you shop, you'll find good restaurant options along the way, as dining is an important part of the whole shopping experience.

☆ South Beach

Taschen
BOOKS

(Map p78; ✆305-538-6185; www.taschen.com; 1111 Lincoln Rd; ☉11am-9pm Mon-Thu, to 10pm Fri & Sat, noon-9pm Sun) An inviting well-stocked collection of art, photography, design and coffee-table books to make your home look that much smarter. A few volumes worth browsing include David Hockney's color-rich art books, the New Erotic Photography (always a great conversation starter) and Sebastião Salgado's lushly photographed human-filled landscapes.

Books & Books
BOOKS

(Map p78; ✆305-532-3222; www.booksand books.com; 927 Lincoln Rd; ☉10am-11pm Sun-Thu, to midnight Fri & Sat) Stop in this fantastic indie bookstore for an excellent selection of new fiction, beautiful art and photography books, award-winning children's titles and more. The layout – a series of elegantly furnished rooms – invites endless browsing, and there's a good restaurant and cafe in front of the store.

Sunset Clothing Co
FASHION & ACCESSORIES

(Map p78; www.facebook.com/SunsetClothing Co; 1895 Purdy Ave; ⊙10am-8pm Mon-Sat, 11am-6pm Sun) A great little men's and women's fashion boutique in Sunset Harbour for stylish gear that won't cost a fortune (though the merchandise isn't cheap either). You'll find well-made long-sleeved shirts, soft cotton T-shirts, lace-up canvas shoes, nicely fitting denim (including vintage Levi's), warm pullover sweaters and other casual gear. Helpful friendly service, too.

Alchemist
FASHION & ACCESSORIES

(Map p78; ☑305-531-4653; 1111 Lincoln Rd; ⊙10am-10pm) Inside one of Lincoln Rd's most striking buildings, this high-end boutique has a wild collection of artful objects, including Warhol-style soup-can candles, heavy gilded corkscrews, Beats headphones by Dr Dre, and mirrored circular sunglasses that are essential for the beach. The clothing here tends to be fairly avant-garde (straight from the runway it seems).

🏠 Downtown Miami

Mary Brickell Village
SHOPPING CENTER

(Map p88; ☑305-381-6130; www.marybrickell village.com; 901 S Miami Ave; ⊙10am-9pm Mon-Sat, noon-6pm Sun) This outdoor shopping and dining complex has helped revitalize the Brickell neighborhood, with a range of boutiques, outdoor restaurants, cafes and bars. It's a magnet for new condo residents in the area, with a central location in the heart of the financial district.

Supply & Advise
CLOTHING

(Map p88; www.supplyandadvise.com; 223 SE 1st St; ⊙11am-7pm Mon-Sat) Supply & Advise brings a heavy dose of men's fashion to Downtown Miami, with rugged, well-made and handsomely tailored clothing plus shoes and accessories, set in a historic 1920s building. Most merchandise here is made in the US. There's also a barbershop, complete with vintage chairs and that impeccable look of bygone days.

🏠 Wynwood & the Design District

Nomad Tribe
CLOTHING

(Map p94; ☑305-364-5193; www.nomadtribe shop.com; 2301 NW 2nd Ave; ⊙noon-8pm) 🥗 This boutique earns high marks for carrying only ethically and sustainably produced merchandise. You'll find cleverly designed jewelry from Miami-based Kathe Cuervo, Osom brand socks (made of upcycled thread), ecologically produced graphic T-shirts from Thinking MU, and THX coffee and candles (which donates 100% of profits to nonprofit organizations) among much else.

Brooklyn Vintage & Vinyl
MUSIC

(Map p94; www.facebook.com/brooklynvintage andvinyl; 3454 NW 7th Ave; ⊙noon-9pm Tue-Sat) Although it opened in late 2016, this record store on the edge of Wynwood has already attracted a following. It's mostly vinyl (plus some cassettes and a few T-shirts), with around 5000 records in the inventory. Staff can give good tips for exploring new music.

Shinola
FASHION & ACCESSORIES

(Map p94; ☑786-374-2994; www.shinola.com; 2399 NW 2nd Ave; ⊙11am-7pm Mon-Sat, noon-6pm Sun; 🛜) This dapper little store by the Detroit-based Shinola proves that American manufacturing is far from dead. Shinola makes beautifully crafted watches, wallets, journals, pens, bicycles and even limited-edition turntables. The prices can be rather staggering, but you can rest assured that the build is of the highest quality.

Art by God
GIFTS & SOUVENIRS

(Map p94; ☑305-573-3011; www.artbygod.com; 60 NE 27th St; ⊙10am-5pm Mon-Fri, 11am-4pm Sat) Take a walk on the wild side at this sprawling warehouse full of relics of days past. Fossils, minerals and semiprecious stones play supporting role to the more eye-catching draws: full-size giraffes, lions, bears and zebras in all their taxidermied glory.

You'll also find rhino heads, dinosaur bones (even a triceratops horn!) and organic parts closer to home – namely skulls with trephination (a primitive surgical practice) from pre-Columbian peoples.

Out of the Closet
THRIFT STORE

(Map p94; ☑305-764-3773; www.outofthecloset. org; 2900 Biscayne Blvd; ⊙10am-7pm Mon-Sat, to 6pm Sun) You'll find all kinds of treasure-trash at this sizable thrift store on busy Biscayne

Blvd: men's and women's clothing, accessories, books, CDs, records, housewares and more. Friendly staff can help guide you on the search.

The store benefits the AIDS Healthcare Foundation and offers free HIV testing.

Malaquita ARTS & CRAFTS
(Map p94; www.malaquitadesign.com; 2613 NW 2nd Ave; ⊙11am-7pm) This artfully designed store has merchandise you won't find elsewhere, including lovely handblown vases, embroidered clothing, Meso-American tapestries, vibrantly painted bowls, handwoven palm baskets and other fair-trade objects – some of which are made by indigenous artisans in Mexico.

Genius Jones TOYS
(Map p94; ✆305-571-2000; www.geniusjones. com; 2800 NE 2nd Ave; ⊙10am-7pm Mon-Sat, noon-6pm Sun) High-end toys, dolls and gear for babies and toddlers and their parents. Fatboy 'beanbag' chairs, ride-on racing cars and Bugaboo strollers: there are loads of covet-worthy gear for the little ones.

Little Haiti & the Upper East Side

Sweat Records MUSIC
(Map p96; ✆786-693-9309; www.sweatrecords miami.com; 5505 NE 2nd Ave; ⊙noon-10pm Mon-Sat, to 5pm Sun) Sweat's almost a stereotypical indie record store – there's funky art and graffiti on the walls, it sells weird Japanese toys, there are tattooed staff with thick glasses arguing over LPs and EPs you've never heard of and, of course, there's coffee and vegan snacks.

Marky's Gourmet FOOD & DRINKS
(Map p96; ✆305-758-9288; www.markys.com; 687 NE 79th St; ⊙9am-7pm Mon-Fri, 10am-6pm Sat, to 5pm Sun) A Miami institution among Russians, Russophiles and those that simply love to explore global cuisine, Marky's has been going strong since 1983. In-the-know foodies from afar flock here to load up on gourmet cheeses, olives, European-style sausages, wines, cakes, teas, jams, chocolates, caviar and much more. As in the good old days of the Soviet Union, service does not come with a smile.

Upper East Side Farmers Market MARKET
(Map p96; Biscayne Blvd at 66th St, Legion Park; ⊙9am-2pm Sat) For a taste of local culture, stop by this small farmers market held each Saturday in the Upper East Side's Legion Park. Here you can meet some of the farmers producing delectable fresh fruits and veggies, plus stock up on breads and crackers, pastries, cheeses, jams, honeys and fresh juices. In short, everything you need for a great picnic. It's open year-round.

Libreri Mapou BOOKS
(Map p96; ✆305-757-9922; www.librerimapou.com; 5919 NE 2nd Ave; ⊙noon-7pm Fri, Sat & Mon-Wed, to 5pm Sun, closed Thu) Haitian bookshop that specializes in English, French and Creole titles and periodicals.

Little Havana

Guantanamera CIGARS
(Map p98; www.guantanameracigars.com; 1465 SW 8th St; ⊙10:30am-8pm Sun-Thu, to midnight Fri & Sat) In a central location in Little Havana, Guantanamera sells high-quality hand-rolled cigars, plus strong Cuban coffee. It's an atmospheric shop, where you can stop for a smoke, a drink (there's a bar here) and some friendly banter. There's also live music here most nights. The rocking chairs in front are a fine perch for people-watching.

Havana Collection CLOTHING
(Map p98; ✆786-717-7474; 1421 SW 8th St; ⊙10am-6pm) One of the best and most striking collections of *guayaberas* (Cuban dress shirts) in Miami can be found in this shop. Prices are high (plan on spending about $85 for shirt), but so is the quality, so you can be assured of a long-lasting product.

Cuba Tobacco Cigar Co CIGARS
(Map p98; www.cubatobaccocigarco.com; 1528 SW 8th St; ⊙10am-5pm) The Bellos family has been making high-quality cigars for over a century. Stop in this tiny welcoming shop to see the handrolling in action, and pick up a few smokable souvenirs for that cigar-loving uncle of yours.

Coconut Grove

Polished Coconut FASHION & ACCESSORIES
(Map p100; 3444 Main Hwy; ⊙11am-6pm Mon-Sat, noon-5pm Sun) 🌿 Colorful textiles from Central and South America are transformed into lovely accessories and home decor at this eye-catching store in the heart of Coconut Grove. You'll find handbags, satchels, belts, sun hats, pillows, bedspreads and table runners made by artisans inspired by traditional indigenous designs.

First Flight Out FASHION & ACCESSORIES
(Map p100; www.thefirstflightout.com; 3015 Grand Ave, CocoWalk; ⊙11am-10pm Mon-Thu, to 11pm Fri-Sun) Inside the CocoWalk shopping gallery, this place sells vintage Pan Am gear – leather satchels, luggage tags, T-shirts and passport covers with that iconic logo from a bygone era of travel. You'll also find swimwear, button-down shirts, summer dresses and other men's and women's clothing, which would pack nicely for today's traveler.

Bookstore in the Grove BOOKS
(Map p100; ☑305-483-2855; www.thebookstore-inthegrove.com; 3390 Mary St; ⊙7am-8pm Mon-Thu, to 9pm Fri & Sat, 8am-8pm Sun) Coconut Grove's independent bookstore is a good spot for all kinds of lit, and has a great cafe (including all-day breakfast and some excellent empanadas), and even happy-hour drink specials.

🔒 Coral Gables

Retro City Collectibles MUSIC
(Map p102; ☑786-879-4407; 277 Miracle Mile, 2nd fl; ⊙5-9pm Mon-Thu, noon-7pm Sat & Sun) This cluttered little upstairs store is a fun place to browse, with all manner of eye-catching and collectible Americana. You'll find comic books, records, baseball cards, Pez dispensers, old film posters and action figures (Star Wars, Star Trek, Dr Who etc).

Books & Books BOOKS
(Map p102; ☑305-442-4408; 265 Aragon Ave; ⊙9am-11pm Sun-Thu, to midnight Fri & Sat) The best indie bookstore in South Florida is a massive emporium of all things literary. B&B hosts frequent readings and is generally just a fantastic place to hang out; there's also a good restaurant, with dining on a Mediterranean-like terrace fronting the shop.

Books & Books has other outposts on Lincoln Rd and at the Bal Harbour shops.

Boy Meets Girl CHILDREN'S CLOTHING
(☑305-445-9668; www.bmgkids.com; 358 San Lorenzo Ave, Village of Merrick Park; ⊙10am-9pm Mon-Sat, noon-7pm Sun) Fantastically upscale and frankly expensive clothing for wee ones – if the kids are getting past puberty, look elsewhere, but otherwise they'll be fashionable far before they realize it.

🔒 Key Biscayne

Metta Boutique GIFTS & SOUVENIRS
(Map p106; ☑305-763-8230; 200 Crandon Blvd; ⊙10am-6pm Mon-Sat) 🍃 A cute store that brings some sustainability to Miami. All of the goodies – clothes, journals, accessories, gifts and tchotchkes – are decidedly green/organic/sustainable/fair trade.

ℹ Information

MEDICAL SERVICES

Mount Sinai Medical Center (☑305-674-2121, emergency room 305-674-2200; www.msmc.com; 4300 Alton Rd; ⊙24hr) The area's best emergency room. Beware that you must eventually pay, and fees are high.

TOURIST INFORMATION

Art Deco Welcome Center (Map p82; ☑305-672-2014; www.mdpl.org; 1001 Ocean Dr, South Beach; ⊙9:30am-5pm Fri-Wed, to 7pm Thu) Run by the Miami Design Preservation League (MDPL), it has tons of art-deco district information and organizes excellent walking tours. There's a museum (p65) attached to the center that provides a great overview of the art-deco district.

Greater Miami & the Beaches Convention & Visitors Bureau (Map p88; ☑305-539-3000; www.miamiandbeaches.com; 701 Brickell Ave, 27th fl; ⊙8:30am-6pm Mon-Fri) Offers loads of info on Miami and keeps up-to-date with the latest events and cultural offerings. Located in an oddly intimidating high-rise building.

LGBT Visitor Center (Map p78; ☑305-397-8914; www.gogaymiami.com; 1130 Washington Ave; ⊙9am-6pm Mon-Fri, 11am-4pm Sat & Sun) An excellent source for all LGBT info on Miami, this friendly welcome center has loads of recommendations on sights, restaurants, nightlife and cultural goings-on. Also has meetings and other events.

Check the website for Pink Flamingo–certified hotels, ie hotels that are most welcoming to the LGBT crowd.

ℹ Getting There & Away

The majority of travelers come to Miami by air, although it's feasible to arrive by car, bus or even train. Miami is a major international airline hub, with flights to many cities across the US, Latin America and Europe. Most flights come into Miami International Airport (MIA), although many are also directed to Fort Lauderdale-Hollywood International Airport (FLL). Figure 3½ hours from New York City, five hours from Los Angeles, and 10 hours from London or Madrid.

Flights, tours and rail tickets can be booked online at www.lonelyplanet.com/bookings.

AIR
Miami International Airport

Located 6 miles west of Downtown, the busy **Miami International Airport** (MIA; ☑ 305-876-7000; www.miami-airport.com; 2100 NW 42nd Ave) has three terminals and serves over 40 million passengers each year. Around 60 airlines fly into Miami. The airport is open 24 hours and is laid out in a horseshoe design. There are left-luggage facilities on two concourses at MIA, between B and C, and on G; prices vary according to bag size.

Fort Lauderdale-Hollywood International Airport

Fort Lauderdale-Hollywood International Airport (www.fll.net), around 26 miles north of Downtown Miami, is a viable gateway airport to the Florida region.

BOAT

Though it's doubtful you'll be catching a steamer to make a trans-Atlantic journey, it is quite possible that you'll arrive in Miami via a cruise ship, as the **Port of Miami** (☑ 305-347-5515; www.miamidade.gov/portmiami), which receives around five million passengers each year, is known as the cruise capital of the world. Arriving in the port will put you on the edge of Downtown Miami; taxis and public buses to other local points are available from nearby Biscayne Blvd.

BUS

For bus trips, **Greyhound** (www.greyhound.com) is the main long-distance operator. **Megabus** (p152) offers service to Tampa and Orlando.

Greyhound's **main bus terminal** (☑ 305-871-1810; 3801 NW 21st) is located near the airport, though additional services also depart from the company's **Cutler Bay terminal** (Cutler Bay; ☑ 305-296-9072; 10801 Caribbean Blvd) and **North Miami terminal** (☑ 305-688-7277; 16000 NW 7th Ave).

If you are traveling very long distances (say, across several states) bargain airfares can sometimes undercut buses. On shorter routes, renting a car can sometimes be cheaper. Nonetheless, discounted (even half-price) long-distance bus trips are often available by purchasing tickets online seven to 14 days in advance.

TRAIN

The main Miami terminal of **Amtrak** (☑ 305-835-1222; www.amtrak.com; 8303 NW 37th Ave, West Little River), about 9 miles northwest of Downtown, connects the city with several other points in Florida (including Orlando and Jacksonville) on the Silver Service line that runs up to New York City. Travel time between New York and Miami is 27 to 31 hours. The Miami Amtrak station is connected by Tri-rail to Downtown Miami and has a left-luggage facility.

Getting Around

TO/FROM THE AIRPORT
Miami International Airport

Airport Express The Miami Beach Airport Express (Bus 150) costs $2.65 and makes stops all along Miami Beach, from 41st to the southern tip. SuperShuttle runs a shared-van service, costing about $22 to South Beach.

Buses Metro buses leave from Miami Airport Station (connected by electric rail to the airport) and run throughout the city; fares are $2.25. The Miami Beach Airport Express (Bus 150) costs $2.65 and makes stops all along Miami Beach, from 41st to the southern tip.

Shared Van You can also take the **SuperShuttle** (☑ 305-871-8210; www.supershuttle.com) shared-van service, which will cost about $22 to South Beach. Be sure to reserve a seat the day before.

Shuttles Some hotels offer free shuttles.

Taxis Taxis charge a flat rate, which varies depending on where you're heading. It's $22 to Downtown, Coconut Grove or Coral Gables; $35 to South Beach; and $44 to Key Biscayne. Count on 40 minutes to South Beach in average traffic, and about 25 minutes to Downtown.

Fort Lauderdale-Hollywood International Airport

GO Airport Shuttle runs shared vans to Miami, with prices around $25 to South Beach. A taxi costs around $75 (metered fare) to South Beach and $65 to Downtown.

BICYCLE

Citi Bike (☑ 305-532-9494; www.citibike miami.com; 30min/1hr/2hr/4hr/1-day rental $4.50/6.50/10/18/24) is a bike-share program where you can borrow a bike from scores of kiosks spread around Miami and Miami Beach. Miami is flat, but traffic can be horrendous (abundant and fast-moving), and there isn't much biking culture (or respect for bikers) just yet. Free paper maps of the bike network are available at some kiosks, or you can find one online. There's also a handy iPhone app that shows you where the nearest stations are.

For longer rides, clunky Citi Bikes are not ideal (no helmet, no lock and only three gears).

Other rental outfits:

Bike & Roll (p112) Also does bike tours.

Brickell Bikes (☏ 305-373-3633; www.brickell bikes.com; 70 SW 12th St; bike hire 4-/8 hours $20/25; ⊘10am-7pm Mon-Fri, to 6pm Sat)

BUS

Miami's local bus system is called **Metrobus** (☏ 305-891-3131; www.miamidade.gov/transit/routes.asp; tickets $2.25) and, though it has an extensive route system, service can be pretty spotty. Each bus route has a different schedule and routes generally run from about 5:30am to 11pm, though some are 24 hours. Rides cost $2.25 and must be paid in exact change (coins or a combination of bills and coins) or with an Easy Card (available for purchase from Metrorail stations and some shops and pharmacies). An easy-to-read route map is available online. Note that if you have to transfer buses, you'll have to pay the fare each time if paying in cash. With an Easy Card, transfers are free.

Megabus (www.us.megabus.com; Miami International Center, 3801 NW 21st St) offers bus service to Orlando and Tampa. Buses depart from a stop near the airport.

MIAMI TROLLEYS

A new free bus service has hit the streets of Miami, Miami Beach, Coconut Grove, Little Havana and Coral Gables, among other locations. The Trolley (www.miamigov.com/trolley) is actually a hybrid-electric bus disguised as an orange and green trolley. There are numerous routes, though they're made for getting around neighborhoods and not *between* them.

The most useful for travelers are the following:

Biscayne Travels along Biscayne Blvd; handy for transport from Brickell to Downtown and up to the edge of Wynwood.

Coral Way Goes from Downtown (near the Freedom Tower) to downtown Coral Gables.

Brickell Connects Brickell area (south of the Miami River in the Downtown area) with the Vizcaya Museum & Gardens.

Wynwood Zigzags through town, from the Adrienne Arsht Center for the Performing Arts up through Wynwood along NW 2nd Ave to 29th St.

MIAMI BEACH TROLLEYS

Miami Beach (www.miamibeachfl.gov/transportation) has four trolleys running along different routes, with arrivals every 10 to 15 minutes from 8am to midnight (from 6am Monday to Saturday on some routes):

Alton-West Loop Runs up (north) Alton Rd and down (south) West Ave between 6th St and Lincoln Rd.

Middle Beach Loop Runs up Collins Ave and down Indian Creek Dr between 20th and 44th Sts (southbound it also zigzags over to Lincoln Rd).

Collins Link Runs along Collins Ave from 37th St to 73rd St. Catch it southbound from Abbott Ave and Indian Creek Dr.

North Beach Loop Runs 65th to 88th St.

TRAIN

The **Metromover** (☏ 305-891-3131; www.miamidade.gov/transit/metromover.asp; ⊘ 5am-midnight Sun-Thu, to 2am Fri & Sat), which is equal parts bus, monorail and train, is helpful for getting around Downtown Miami. It offers visitors a great perspective on the city and a free orientation tour of the area.

Run by Metro-Dade Transit, **Metrorail** (www.miamidade.gov/transit/metrorail.asp; one-way ticket $2.25) is a 21-mile-long heavy-rail system that has one elevated line running from Hialeah through Downtown Miami and south to Kendall/Dadeland. Trains run every five to 15 minutes from 6am to midnight. The one-way fare is $2.25. Pay with either the reloadable Easy Card or single-use Easy Ticket, which are sold from vending machines at Metrorail stations.

The regional **Tri-Rail** (☏ 800-874-7245; www.tri-rail.com) double-decker commuter trains run the 71 miles between Dade, Broward and Palm Beach counties. Fares are calculated on a zone basis; the shortest distance traveled costs $4.40 round-trip; the most you'll ever pay is for the ride between MIA and West Palm Beach ($11.55 round-trip). No tickets are sold on the train, so allow time to make your purchase before boarding. All trains and stations are accessible to riders with disabilities. For a list of stations, log on to the Tri-Rail website.

The Everglades

POP 78,000 / 📞 305, 736, 239

Best Places to Eat

➡ Havana Cafe (p162)

➡ Robert Is Here (p166)

➡ Joannie's Blue Crab Café (p160)

➡ Schnebly Redland's Winery (p163)

➡ Camellia Street Grill (p162)

➡ Oyster House (p163)

Best Places to Sleep

➡ Ivey House Bed & Breakfast (p162)

➡ Everglades International Hostel (p166)

➡ Outdoor Resorts of Chokoloskee (p161)

➡ Flamingo Campground (p169)

➡ Swamp Cottage (p159)

Why Go?

There is no wilderness in America quite like the Everglades. Called the 'River of Grass' by Native American inhabitants, this is not just a wetland, or a swamp, or a lake, or a river, or a prairie, or a grassland – it is all of the above, twisted together into a series of soft horizons, long vistas, sunsets that stretch across your entire field of vision and the toothy grin of a healthy population of dinosaur-era reptiles.

When you watch anhinga flexing their wings before breaking into a corkscrew dive, or the slow, rhythmic flap of a great blue heron gliding over its domain, or the shimmer of sunlight on miles of untrammeled saw grass as it sets behind hunkering cypress domes, you'll get a glimpse of this park's quiet majesty. In a nation where natural beauty is measured by its capacity for drama, the Everglades subtly, contentedly flows on.

When to Go
Everglades City

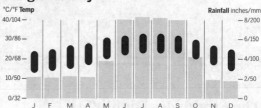

Dec–Mar Dry season: top wildlife viewing along watercourses, but some kayaking will be difficult.

Apr–Jun Although the weather gets pretty hot, there's a good mix of water and wildlife.

Jul–Nov Lots of heat, lots of bugs and (except in October and November) chances of hurricanes.

The Everglades Highlights

1 **Anhinga Trail** (p167) Spotting alligators by day or night, and watching nesting water birds.

2 **Flamingo** (p168) Hiring a canoe or kayak from the marina and paddling through scenic mangrove-lined waterways.

3 **Pa-hay-okee Overlook** (p168) Watching the sun set over the ingress road from the roof of your car.

4 **Slough Slog** (p157) Walking into the muck amid orchids, birds and towering cypress trees.

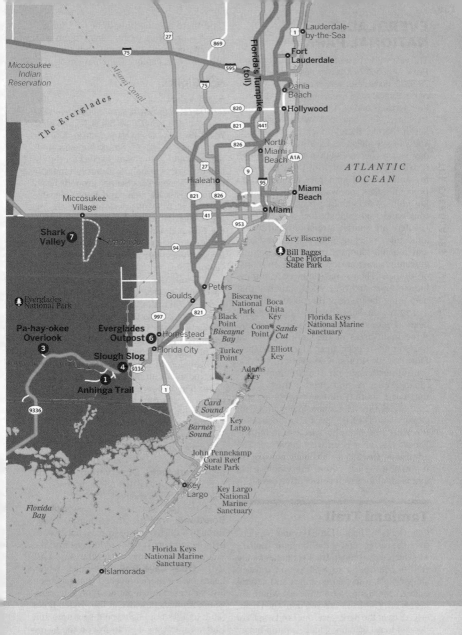

⑤ Museum of the Everglades (p160) Learning about the fascinating human settlement of the Everglades.

⑥ Everglades Outpost (p163) Seeing exotic animal

species – rescued from bad situations.

⑦ Shark Valley (p156) Spying gators and birds on a bike ride or a tram tour.

⑧ 10,000 Islands (p160) Canoeing or kayaking through the scattered islands.

⑨ Loop Road (p158) Taking a drive amid striking wetland scenery.

EVERGLADES NATIONAL PARK

The vast wilderness of **Everglades National Park** (☑ 305-242-7700; www.nps.gov/ever; 40001 SR-9336, Homestead; vehicle pass $25; ☺ visitor center 9am-5pm; ♿), encompassing 1.5 million acres, is one of America's great natural treasures. As a major draw for visitors to South Florida, there's much to see and do. You can spy alligators basking in the noonday sun as herons stalk patiently through nearby waters in search of prey, go kayaking amid tangled mangrove canals and on peaceful lakes, or wade through murky knee-high waters amid cypress domes on a rough-and-ready 'slough slog.'

There are sunrise strolls on boardwalks amid the awakening glimmers of birdsong, and moonlit glimpses of gators swimming gracefully along narrow channels in search of dinner. There's backcountry camping, bicycle tours and ranger-led activities that help bring the magic of this place to life.

The big challenge is deciding where to begin. There are three main entrances and three main areas of the park: one along the southeast edge near Homestead and Florida City (Ernest Coe section); at the central-north side on the Tamiami Trail (Shark Valley section); and a third at the northwest shore (Gulf Coast section), past Everglades City. The Shark Valley and Gulf Coast sections of the park come one after the other in geographic succession, but the Ernest Coe area is entirely separate. The admission fee ($25 for a vehicle pass, or $8 if you're a cyclist) covers the whole park, and is good for seven consecutive days.

Tamiami Trail

Calle Ocho, in Miami's Little Havana, happens to be the eastern end of the Tamiami Trail/US 41, which cuts through the Everglades to the Gulf of Mexico. So go west, young traveler, along US 41, a few dozen miles and several different worlds away from the city where the heat is on. This trip leads you onto the northern edges of the park, past long landscapes of flooded forest, gambling halls, swamp-buggy tours, roadside food shacks and other Old Florida accoutrements.

As you head west you'll see fields and fields of pine forest and billboards advertising swamp tours. Airboat tours are an old-school way of seeing the Everglades

(and there is something to be said for getting a tour from a raging Skynyrd fan with killer tatts and better camo), but there are other ways of exploring the park as well.

◉ Sights

Shark Valley PARK
(☑ 305-221-8776; www.nps.gov/ever/planyourvisit/svdirections.htm; 36000 SW 8th St, N 25°45.27.60, W 80°46.01.01'; car/cyclist/pedestrian $25/8/8; ☺ 9am-5pm; P ♿) ∅ Shark Valley sounds like it should be the headquarters for the villain in a James Bond movie, but it is in fact a slice of National Park Service grounds heavy with informative signs and knowledgeable rangers. Shark Valley is located in the cypress, and hardwood and riverine section of the Everglades, a more traditionally jungly section of the park than the grassy fields and forest domes surrounding the Ernest Coe visitor center.

A 15-mile (24km) **paved trail** takes you past small creeks, tropical forest and 'borrow pits' (human-made holes that are now basking spots for gators, turtles and birdlife). The pancake-flat trail is perfect for bicycles, which can be rented at the entrance for $9 per hour. Bring water with you.

If you don't feel like exerting yourself, the most popular and painless way to immerse yourself in the Everglades is via the two-hour tram tour that runs along Shark Valley's entire 15-mile trail. If you only have time for one Everglades activity, this should be it, as guides are informative and witty, and you'll likely see gators sunning themselves on the road. Halfway along the trail is the 50ft-high **Shark Valley Observation Tower**, an ugly concrete tower that offers dramatically beautiful views of the park.

At the park entrance, the easy **Bobcat Boardwalk Trail** (0.5 miles) makes a loop through a thick copse of tropical hardwoods before emptying you out right back into the Shark Valley parking lot. A little ways past is the **Otter Cave Trail** (0.25 miles) which heads over a limestone shelf that has been Swiss-cheesed into a porous sponge by rainwater. Animals now live in the eroded holes (although it's not likely you'll spot any) and Native Americans used to live on top of the shelf.

Fakahatchee Strand Preserve PARK
(☑ 239-695-4593; www.floridastateparks.org/fakahatcheestrand; 137 Coastline Dr, Copeland; vehicle/pedestrian/bicycle $3/2/2; ☺ 8am-sunset; P ♿) ∅ The Fakahatchee Strand, besides

having a fantastic name, also houses a 20-mile by 5-mile estuarine wetland that could have emerged directly out of the *Jurassic Park* franchise. A 2000ft boardwalk traverses this wet and wild wonderland, where panthers still stalk their prey amid the black waters. While it's unlikely you'll spot any panthers, there's a great chance you will see a large variety blooming orchids, bird life and reptiles ranging in size from tiny skinks to grinning alligators.

Miccosukee Indian Village   MUSEUM
(☎ 305-552-8365; www.miccosukee.com; Mile 70, Hwy 41; adult/child/5yr & under $12/6/free; ⊙ 9am-5pm; [P] [🚗]) Just west of the turnoff to Shark Valley, this 'Indian Village' is an informative open-air museum that showcases the culture of the Miccosukee via guided tours of traditional homes, a crafts gift store, dance and music performances, and an airboat ride (additional $20) into a hammock-cum-village of raised *chickee* (wooden platforms built above the waterline). There's also an alligator 'wrestling' show. Thankfully this is more respectful than it sounds, and is more of a nature demonstration of this iconic reptile.

The art and handmade crafts from the on-site art gallery make good souvenirs. There's a somewhat desultory on-site restaurant if you get hungry.

Miccosukee Resort & Casino   CASINO
(☎ 305-222-4600; www.miccosukee.com; 500 SW 177th Ave) Here the long-storied legacy of the nation's indigenous peoples has culminated in...slots. Lots of slots, and comatose gamblers pouring quarters into them. Still the Miccosukee and Seminole are cashing in on this stuff, so more power to them.

There's also plush rooms (from $139 to $189) if you decide to spend the night.

🕓 Tours

Shark Valley Tram Tour   TOURS
(☎ 305-221-8455; www.sharkvalleytramtours.com; adult/child under 12yr/senior $25/19/12.75; ⊙ departures 9:30am, 11am, 2pm, 4pm May-Dec, 9am-4pm Jan-Apr hourly on the hour) This excellent two-hour tour runs along a 15-mile asphalt trail allowing you to see copious amounts of alligators in the winter months. Tours are narrated by knowledgeable park rangers who give a fascinating overview of the Everglades.

Coopertown   BOATING
(☎ 305-226-6048; www.coopertownairboats.com; 22700 SW 8th St; adult/child $23/11; ⊙ 9am-5pm; [🚗]) One of the first airboat operators you encounter heading west on Hwy 41, Coopertown is still one of the best. Friendly, knowledgeable guides have a knack for spotting wildlife and giving a good overview of this unique environment.

BEST FREE PARK ACTIVITIES

The $25 entrance fee for the Everglades National Park may seem steep, but it's great value if you take advantage of the park's many free ranger-led activities. Reserve popular activities (canoeing, biking) up to one week in advance. Among the highlights:

Slough Slog Escape the crowds and immerse yourself in the wilderness on a fascinating one- to two-mile guided walk/wade through muddy and watery terrain into a cypress dome. Wear long pants, socks and lace-up shoes that can get wet. Meets at Royal Palm Visitor Center.

Starlight Walk Evening walk along the Anhinga Trail (p167) looking for gators and other creatures by nightfall. Bring a flashlight (torch).

Bike Hike A 2½-hour bike ride exploring the Everglades on two wheels. Bikes and helmets provided. Departs from Ernest Coe Visitor Center.

Canoe the Wilderness A three-hour morning paddle through some of the Everglades' most sublime scenery. Meets at Flamingo Visitor Center and at Gulf Coast Visitor Center.

Early Bird Walk Join for a morning hike looking for, and learning about, some of the Everglades' feathered species. Meets at Flamingo Visitor Center.

Glades Glimpse Learn about some of the wonders of the Everglades on a daily talk given by rangers at the Royal Palm Visitor Center and at the Shark Valley Visitor Center (typically from 1:30pm to 2pm).

DETOUR: LOOP ROAD

The 24-mile long Loop Rd, off Tamiami Trail (Hwy 41), offers some unique sites. One: the homes of the **Miccosukee**, some of which have been considerably expanded by gambling revenue. You'll see some traditional *chickee*-style huts and some trailers with massive add-on wings that are bigger than the original trailer – all seem to have shiny new pickup trucks parked out front. Two: great pull-offs for viewing flooded forests, where egrets that look like pterodactyls perch in the trees, and alligators lurk in the depths below. Three: houses with large Confederate flags and 'Stay off my property' signs; these homes are as much a part of the landscape as the swamp. And four: the short, pleasantly jungly **Tree Snail Hammock Nature Trail**. Though unpaved, the graded road is in good shape and fine for 2WD vehicles. True to its name, the road loops right back onto the Tamiami; expect a leisurely jaunt on the Loop to add an hour or two to your trip.

ℹ️ Information

Shark Valley Visitor Center (☎ 305-221-8776; www.nps.gov/ever/planyourvisit/svdirections. htm; national park entry per vehicle/bicycle/ pedestrian $25/8/8; ⊗ 9am-5pm) A good place to pick up information about the Everglades, including trails, wildlife watching and free ranger-led activities.

ℹ️ Getting There & Away

The Tamiami Trail (US 41) can be accessed in Miami. You'll need a car to get out this way and explore. The entrance to Shark Valley is about 40 miles west of downtown Miami.

Big Cypress & Ochopee

The better part of the Tamiami Trail is fronted on either side by long cypress trees overhung with moss. There's endless vistas of soft prairie, which are flooded in the wet season into a boggy River of Grass.

⊙ Sights

Big Cypress National Preserve   PARK
(☎ 239-695-4758; www.nps.gov/bicy; 33000 Tamiami Trail E; ⊗ 24hr; P 🚻) 🅿 FREE The 1139-sq-mile Big Cypress Preserve (named for the size of the park, not its trees) is the result of a compromise between environmentalists, cattle ranchers and oil-and-gas explorers. The area is integral to the Everglades' ecosystem: rains that flood the Preserve's prairies and wetlands slowly filter down through the Glades. About 45% of the cypress swamp (actually mangrove islands, hardwood hammocks, orchid flowers, slash pine, prairies and marshes) is protected.

Great bald cypress trees are nearly gone, thanks to pre-Preserve lumbering, but dwarf pond cypress trees fill the area with their own understated beauty. The helpful Oasis

Visitor Center (p160), about 20 miles west of Shark Valley, has great exhibits for the kids and a water-filled ditch that's popular with alligators.

**Ah-Tah-Thi-Ki Seminole
Indian Museum**   MUSEUM
(☎ 877-902-1113; www.ahtahthiki.com; Big Cypress Seminole Indian Reservation, 34725 West Boundary Rd, Clewiston; adult/child/senior $10/7.50/7.50; ⊗ 9am-5pm) If you want to learn about Florida's Native Americans, come to the Ah-Tah-Thi-Ki Seminole Indian Museum, 17 miles north of I-75. All of the excellent educational exhibits on Seminole life, history and the tribe today were founded on gaming proceeds, which provide most of the tribe's multimillion-dollar operating budget.

The museum is located within a cypress dome cut through with an interpretive boardwalk, so from the start it strikes a balance between environmentalism and education. The permanent exhibit has several dioramas with life-sized figures depicting various scenes out of traditional Seminole life, while temporary exhibits have a bit more academic polish (past ones have included lengthy forays into the economic structure of the Everglades). There's an old-school 'living village' and re-created ceremonial grounds as well. The museum is making an effort to not be a cheesy Native American theme park, and the Seminole tribe has gone to impressive lengths to achieve this.

Kirby Storter Roadside Park   NATURE RESERVE
(www.nps.gov/bicy/planyourvisit/kirby-storter-roadside-park.htm; ⊗ 24hr) FREE Though short in size (1 mile total out and back) this elevated boardwalk leads to a lovely overlook where you can often see a variety of birdlife (ibis and red-shouldered hawks) amid tall cypresses and strangler figs, plus of course alligators.

Big Cypress Gallery
GALLERY

(☎239-695-2428; www.clydebutcher.com; 52388 Tamiami Trail; ⊙10am-5pm; ℗) ⌀ This gallery showcases the work of Clyde Butcher, an American photographer who follows in the great tradition of Ansel Adams. His large-format black-and-white images elevate the swamps to a higher level. Butcher has found a quiet spirituality in the brackish waters. You'll find many gorgeous prints, which make fine mementos from the Everglades experience (though prices aren't cheap).

Private 1½-hour swamp tours tramping through the muck are offered, but the high prices (from $380 for a group of four) keep most would-be swamp-goers away, especially since the national-park service offers free swamp walks out of the Royal Palm Visitor Center.

Skunk Ape Research Headquarters
PARK

(☎239-695-2275; www.skunkape.info; 40904 Tamiami Trail E; adult/child $12/6; ⊙9am-5pm; ℗) This only-in-Florida roadside attraction is dedicated to tracking down southeastern USA's version of Bigfoot, the eponymous Skunk Ape (a large gorilla-man who supposedly stinks to high heaven). We never saw a Skunk Ape, but you can see a corny gift shop and, in the back, a reptile-and-bird zoo run by a true Florida eccentric, the sort of guy who wraps albino pythons around his neck for fun.

The little zoo is good fun for kids, with tiny alligators and (non-venomous) snakes you can hold, and various large birds, including a blushing blue-and-gold macaw named Patches, and a screechy cockatoo named Sassy. There's also a 22ft Burmese python and a few tortoises.

Ochopee
VILLAGE

(38000 Tamiami Trail E, N°25.54.4.64, W°81.17.50.42'; ⊙8-10am & noon-4pm Mon-Fri, 10-11:30am Sat) Drive to the hamlet of Ochopee (population about four)...no...wait...turn around, you missed it! Then pull over and break out the cameras: Ochopee's claim to fame is the country's smallest **post office**. It's housed in a former toolshed and set against big park skies; a friendly postal worker patiently poses for snapshots.

🏃 Activities

Florida National Scenic Trail
HIKING

(☎850-523-8501; www.fs.usda.gov/fnst) There are some 31 miles of the Florida National Scenic Trail within Big Cypress National Preserve.

From the southern terminus, which can be accessed via Loop Rd, the trail runs 8.3 miles north to US 41. The way is flat, but it's hard going: you'll almost certainly be wading through water, and you'll have to pick through a series of solution holes (small sinkholes) and thick hardwood hammocks.

There is often no shelter from the sun, and the bugs are...plentiful. There are three primitive campsites with water wells along the trail; pick up a map and a free hiking permit (required) at the Oasis Visitor Center (p160). Most campsites are free, and you needn't register. Monument Lake has water and toilets.

👉 Tours

Everglades Adventure Tours
TOURS

(EAT; ☎800-504-6554; www.evergladesadventure tours.com; 40904 Tamiami Trail E; 2hr canoe/pole-boat tour per person $89/109) We already like the EAT guys for being based out of the same headquarters as the Skunk Ape people; we like them even more for offering some of the best private Everglades tours. Swamp hikes, 'safaris,' night tours and being poled around in a canoe or skiff by some genuinely funny guys with deep local knowledge of the Grassy Waters; it's an absolute treat.

EAT has set up a campsite at Skunk Ape HQ; it costs $25 to camp here ($30 with electricity), and there's wi-fi throughout the camp.

🛏 Sleeping & Eating

Monument Lake
CAMPGROUND $

(www.recreation.gov; 50215 Tamiami Trail E; tent/RV site per night $24/28; ⊙Aug 15-Apr 15) Reserve months ahead to book one of 10 tent sites (or 26 RV sites) at this appealing campground in the Big Cypress National Preserve. The lake looks quite enticing, but there's no swimming (alligators live here after all).

Swamp Cottage
COTTAGE $$

(☎239-695-2428; www.clydebutcher.com/big-cypress/vacation-rentals; 52388 Tamiami Trail; cottage $250-350; ℗🛜) ⌀ Want to get as close to the swamp as possible without giving up on the amenities? Book a few nights in a bungalow or a two-bedroom cottage, tucked amid lush greenery behind the Big Cypress Gallery. The lodging is comfortably appointed, if not luxurious, and is certainly cozy, though the best feature is having one of America's great wetlands right outside your door.

Joanie's Blue Crab Café
AMERICAN $$

(☏239-695-2682; www.joaniesbluecrabcafe.com; 39395 Tamiami Trail E; mains $12-17; ⊙11am-5pm Thu-Tue; closed seasonally, call to confirm; ☑) This quintessential shack, east of Ochopee, with open rafters, shellacked picnic tables and alligator kitsch, serves filling food of the 'fried everything' variety on paper plates. Crab cakes are the thing to order. There's live music on Saturdays and Sundays from 12:30pm and a rockabilly-loving jukebox at other times.

❶ Information

Big Cypress Swamp Welcome Center
(☏239-695-4758; www.nps.gov/bicy/plan yourvisit/big-cypress-swamp-welcome-center. htm; 33000 Tamiami Trail E; ⊙9am-4:30pm) About 2.5 miles east of the turnoff to Everglades City, this big visitor center is a good one for the kids, with a small nature center where you can listen to recordings of different swamp critters. There's also a viewing platform overlooking a canal where you can sometimes spot manatees. Good spot for information on the reserve.

Oasis Visitor Center
(☏239-695-1201; www. nps.gov/bicy; 52105 Tamiami Trail E; ⊙9am-4:30pm; ◼) This visitor center has hands-on exhibits and info on nearby walks in the Big Cypress National Preserve. A platform overlooking a small water-filled ditch is a great spot to see alligators, particularly in the dry season (December to May).

❶ Getting There & Away

The Oasis Visitor Center is located about 20 miles west of the Shark Valley entrance. All of the above attractions are spaced along the Tamiami Trail (US 41). There is no public transportation out this way.

Everglades City & Chokoloskee Island

On the edge of Chokoloskee Bay, you'll find an old Florida fishing village of raised houses, turquoise water and scattershot emerald-green mangrove islands. 'City' is an ambitious name for Everglades City, but this is a friendly fishing town where you can easily lose yourself for a day or three. You'll find some intriguing vestiges of the past here, including an excellent regional museum, as well as delicious seafood.

Hwy 29 runs south through town onto the small, peaceful residential island of Chokoloskee, which has some pretty views over the watery wilderness of the 10,000 Islands. You can arrange boating excursions from either Everglades City or Chokoloskee to explore this pristine environment.

⦿ Sights

★ Museum of the Everglades
MUSEUM

(☏239-695-0008; www.evergladesmuseum.org; 105 W Broadway, Everglades City; ⊙9am-4pm Mon-Sat; ℙ) 𝗙𝗥𝗘𝗘 For a break from the outdoors, don't miss this small museum run by kind-hearted volunteers, who have a wealth of knowledge on the region's history. Located in the town's formerly laundry house, the collection delves into human settlement in the area from the early pioneers of the 1800s to the boom days of the 1920s and its tragic moments (Hurricane Donna devastated the town in 1960), and subsequent transformation into the quiet backwater of today.

10,000 Islands
ISLAND

One of the best ways to experience the serenity of the Everglades – somehow desolate yet lush, tropical and forbidding – is by paddling the network of waterways that skirt the northwest portion of the park. The 10,000 Islands consist of many (but not really 10,000) tiny islands and a mangrove swamp that hugs the southwestern-most border of Florida.

The **Wilderness Waterway**, a 99-mile route between Everglades City and Flamingo, is the longest canoe trail in the area, but there are shorter trails near Flamingo. Most islands are fringed by narrow beaches with sugar-white sand, but note that the water is brackish, and very shallow most of the time. It's not Tahiti, but it's fascinating. You can camp on your own island for up to a week.

Getting around the 10,000 Islands is pretty straightforward if you're a competent navigator and you religiously adhere to National Oceanic & Atmospheric Administration (NOAA) tide and nautical charts. Going against the tides is the fastest way to make a miserable trip. The Gulf Coast Visitor Center sells nautical charts and gives out free tidal charts. You can also purchase charts prior to your visit – call ☏305-247-1216 and ask for charts 11430, 11432 and 11433.

Smallwood Store
MUSEUM

(☏239-695-2989; www.smallwoodstore.com; 360 Mamie St, Chokoloskee; adult/child $5/free; ⊙10am-5pm Dec-Apr, 11am-5pm May-Nov) Perched on piers overlooking Chokoloskee

AIRBOATS & SWAMP BUGGIES

Airboats are flat-bottomed skiffs that use powerful fans to propel themselves through the water. Their environmental impact has not been determined, but one thing is clear: airboats can't be doing much good, which is why they're not allowed in the park. Swamp buggies are enormous balloon-tired vehicles that can go through wetlands, creating ruts and damaging wildlife.

Airboat and swamp-buggy rides are offered all along US Hwy 41 (Tamiami Trail). Think twice before going on a 'nature' tour. Loud whirring fanboats and marsh jeeps really don't do the quiet serenity of the Glades justice. That said, many tourists in the Everglades are there (obviously) because of their interest in the environment, and they demand environmentally knowledgeable tours. The airboat guys are pretty good at providing these – their livelihood is also caught up in the preservation of the Glades, and they know the backcountry well. We recommend going with the guys at Coopertown (p157), one of the first airboat operators you encounter heading west on 41. Just expect a more touristy experience than the national park grounds.

Bay, this wooden building dates back to 1906, when a pioneer by the name of Ted Smallwood opened his rustic trading post, post office and general store. The wooden shelves are lined with antiques and old artifacts, along with descriptions of events and characters from those rough and tumble days of life on a remote island frontier.

Tours

Everglades Adventures CANOEING
(877-567-0679; www.evergladesadventures.com; 107 Camellia St, Everglades City; 3/4hr tour from $89/99, canoe/kayak rental per day from $35/49) For a real taste of the Everglades, nothing beats getting out on the water. This highly recommended outfitter offers a range of half-day kayak tours, from sunrise paddles to twilight trips through mangroves that return under a sky full of stars.

Smallwood Store Boat Tour BOATING
(239-695-0016; www.smallwoodstoreboattour.com; 360 Mamie St, Chokoloskee; 1hr tour per person $40;) Departing from a dock below the Smallwood Store, this small family-run outfit offers excellent private tours taking you out among the watery wilderness of the 10,000 islands. You'll see loads of birds, and more than likely a few bottlenose dolphins, who enjoy swimming through the boat's wake.

Gulf Coast Visitor Center BOATING
(239-695-2591; www.evergladesnationalparkboattoursgulfcoast.com; 815 Oyster Bar Lane, off Hwy 29; canoe/single kayak/tandem kayak $38/45/55 per day; 9am-4:30pm mid-Apr–mid-Nov, from 8am mid-Nov–mid-Apr;) This is the northwestern-most ranger station for Everglades National Park, and provides access to the 10,000 Islands area. Boat tours, lasting just under two hours, depart from the downstairs marina and go either into the mangrove wilderness (adult/child $48/25) or out among the green islands ($38/20), where if you're lucky you may see dolphins springing up beside your craft.

Keep an eye out for manatees in the marina. It's great fun to go kayaking and canoeing around here; boats can be rented from the marina, but be sure to take a map with you (they're available in the visitor center). Boaters will want to reference NOAA Charts 11430 and 11432.

Festivals & Events

Everglades Seafood Festival FOOD & DRINK
(www.evergladesseafoodfestival.org; Feb) In Everglades City, this three-day festival features plenty of feasting, as well as kiddie rides and live music. The star of the show is of course glorious seafood – stone crab, conch fritters, crab cakes, coconut shrimp, mussels and calamari – though there's also fried gator, frog's legs, pulled-pork barbecue and key lime pie on a stick!

Sleeping

Outdoor Resorts of Chokoloskee MOTEL $
(239-695-2881; www.outdoorresortsofchokoloskee.com; 150 Smallwood Dr, Chokoloskee; r $119;) At the northern end of Chokoloskee Island, this good-value place is a big draw for its extensive facilities, including several swimming pools, hot tubs, tennis and shuffleboard courts, a fitness center and boat rentals. The fairly basic motel-style rooms

have kitchenettes and a back deck overlooking the marina.

Parkway Motel & Marina
MOTEL $

(☑ 239-695-3261; www.parkwaymotelandmarina. com; 1180 Chokoloskee Dr, Chokoloskee; r $110-150; P ❄) A friendly couple runs this veritable testament to the old-school Floridian lodge: cute small rooms and one cozy apartment in a one-story motel building. It's in a peaceful spot on the island of Chokoloskee, and owners Bill and Greci have a wealth of knowledge on the region.

Rod & Gun Club Lodge
LODGE $

(☑ 239-695-2101; www.everglades-rodandgunclub. com; 200 Riverside Dr, Everglades City; r $100-160; P ❄) Built in the 1920s as a hunting lodge by Barron Collier (who needed a place to chill after watching workers dig his Tamiami Trail), this masculine place has simple rooms – the best with views over the water. There's also a restaurant that serves anything that moves in them thar waters. Cash only.

Everglades City Motel
MOTEL $$

(☑ 239-695-4224; www.evergladescitymotel. com; 310 Collier Ave, Everglades City; r $150-250; P ❄ 📶) With large renovated rooms that have all the mod cons (flat-screen TVs, fridge, coffeemaker) and friendly staff that can hook you up with boat tours, this motel provides good value for those looking to spend some time near the 10,000 Islands.

Ivey House Bed & Breakfast
B&B $$

(☑ 877-567-0679; www.iveyhouse.com; 107 Camellia St, Everglades City; inn $100-180, lodge $90-100, cottage $180-230; P ❄ 📶 🏊) This friendly, family-run tropical inn offers a variety of well-appointed accommodations: bright spacious inn rooms overlooking a pretty courtyard, cheaper lodge rooms (with shared bathrooms) and a freestanding two-bedroom cottage with a kitchen and screened-in porch. The pool (covered in winter) is a great year-round option for a swim.

This is a top place to book nature trips (p161), from daytime paddles to six-day packages that including lodging, tours and some meals.

✖ Eating

Sweet Mayberry's
CAFE $

(☑ 239-695-0092; www.sweetmayberryscafe. com; 207 W Broadway Ave, Everglades City; salads & wraps $10-12; ⊙ 9am-4pm Tue-Sat; 📶) The best cafe in town (not that there's much competition), Sweet Mayberry's is an easygoing charmer, with friendly staff whipping up breakfast bagels, tasty homemade wraps, decadent desserts (try the carrot cake) and proper espressos. Have a seat on the front porch and make yourself at home.

Triad Seafood Cafe
SEAFOOD $

(☑ 239-695-0722; www.triadseafoodmarketcafe. com; 401 School Dr, Everglades City; mains $10-17, stone-crab meals $26-44; ⊙ 10:30am-6pm Sun-Thu, to 7pm Fri & Sat) Triad is famous for its stone-crab claws, but they serve up all kinds of coastal seafood that you can enjoy on picnic tables perched over the waterfront. Should you impress the friendly owners with your ability to devour crustaceans (their claws anyway), you get the dubious honor of having your picture hung on the Glutton Board.

★ Havana Cafe
LATIN AMERICAN $$

(☑ 239-695-2214; www.havanacafeoftheeverglades. com; 191 Smallwood Dr, Chokoloskee; mains lunch $10-19, dinner $22-30; ⊙ 7am-3pm Mon-Thu, to 8pm Fri & Sat, closed mid-Apr–mid-Oct) The Havana Cafe is famed far and wide for its deliciously prepared seafood served up with Latin accents. Lunch favorites include stone-crab enchiladas, blackened grouper with rice and beans, and a decadent Cuban sandwich. The outdoor dining amid palm trees and vibrant bougainvillea – not to mention the incredibly friendly service – adds to the appeal.

Reservations are essential on Friday and Saturday nights, when foodies from out of town arrive for stone-crab feasts. Order in advance the astonishingly good seafood paella or seafood pasta – both $50 but serving at least two people.

★ Camellia Street Grill
SEAFOOD $$

(☑ 239-695-2003; 202 Camellia St, Everglades City; mains $13-26; ⊙ noon-9pm; 🐾) In a barn-like setting with fairy lights strung from the rafters and nautical doodads lining the walls, Camellia is an easygoing spot for a down-home seafood feast. Come before sunset to enjoy the pretty views from the waterfront deck. Don't miss the tender stone-crab claws in season.

Other dishes range from fried baskets of catfish, grouper or shrimp to heartier plates of grilled seafood, barbecue ribs or shrimp and grits. There are also crab-cake sandwiches, fish tacos and homemade veggie wraps.

Oyster House   SEAFOOD **$$**
(📞239-695-2073; www.oysterhouserestaurant.
com; 901 Copeland Ave, Everglades City; mains
lunch $12-18, dinner $19-30; ⊙11am-9pm Sun-
Thu, to 10pm Fri & Sat; 🅿🧒) Besides serving
the Everglades staples of excellent seafood
(oysters, crab, grouper, cobia, lobster), this
buzzing, family-run spot serves up alligator
dishes (tacos, jambalaya, fried platters) and
simpler baskets (burgers, fried seafood), plus
not-to-be-missed desserts. The cabin-like in-
terior is decorated with vintage knickknacks
and taxidermy, which might make you feel
like you're in the deep woods.

🛈 Information

Everglades Area Chamber of Commerce
(📞239-695-3941; cnr US Hwy 41 & Hwy 29;
⊙9am-4pm) General information about the
region is available here.

🛈 Getting There & Away

There is no public transit out this way. If driving,
it's a fairly straight 85-mile drive west from Miami.
The trip takes about 1¾ hours in good traffic.

Southern Everglades

Head south of Miami to drive into the
heart of the park and the best horizons
of the Everglades. Plus there are plenty of
side paths and canoe creeks for memorable
detours. You'll see some of the most qui-
etly exhilarating scenery the park has to
offer on this route, and you'll have better
access to an interior network of trails for
those wanting to push off the beaten track
into the buggy, muggy solar plexus of the
wetlands.

Homestead & Florida City

Homestead and neighboring Florida City,
two miles to the south, aren't of obvious ap-
peal upon arrival. Part of the ever-expanding
subdivisions of South Miami, this bustling
corridor can feel like an endless strip of big
box shopping centers, fast-food joints, car
dealerships and gas stations. However, look
beneath the veneer and you'll find much
more than meets the eye: strange curiosi-
ties like a 'castle' built single-handedly by
one lovestruck immigrant, an animal rescue
center for exotic species, a winery showcas-
ing Florida's produce (hint: it's not grapes),
an up-and-coming microbrewery, and one
of the best farm stands in America. Not to

mention that this area makes a great base
for forays into the stunning Everglades Na-
tional Park.

👁 Sights

★Coral Castle   CASTLE
(📞305-248-6345; www.coralcastle.com; 28655 S
Dixie Hwy; adult/senior/child $18/15/8; ⊙8am-
6pm Sun-Thu, to 8pm Fri & Sat) 'You will be
seeing unusual accomplishment,' reads the
inscription on the rough-hewn quarried
wall. That's an understatement. There is no
greater temple to all that is weird and wacky
about South Florida. The legend: a Latvian
gets snubbed at the altar. Comes to the US
and settles in Florida. Handcarves, unseen,
in the dead of night, a monument to unre-
quited love.

This rock-walled compound includes a
'throne room,' a sun dial, a stone stockade
(an intended 'timeout area' for the child
he would never have), a telescope of sorts
trained precisely on Polaris, and a revolving
boulder gate that can be easily opened with
one hand. Even more incredible: all this
was built by one small man – the 5ft-tall,
100-pound Edward Leedskalnin – working
alone without heavy machinery. He accom-
plished all this using pulleys, hand tools
and other improvised devices, and it took
him 28 years to complete his great rock
masterpiece.

Schnebly Redland's Winery   WINERY
(📞305-242-1224; www.schneblywinery.com;
30205 SW 217th Ave; wine tastings/tours $13/8;
⊙10am-5pm Mon-Thu, to 11pm Fri & Sat, noon-5pm
Sun) Tucked along a quiet farm road west of
Homestead, Schnebly has the unusual dis-
tinction of being the southernmost winery
in America. Given the climate, you won't
find malbec, pinot noir or zinfandel here.
The name of the game is fruit. Wines here
are made of mango, passion fruit, lychee,
avocado, coconut and other flavors from the
tropics, and are surprisingly good.

Everglades Outpost   WILDLIFE RESERVE
(📞305-562-8000; www.evergladesoutpost.org;
35601 SW 192nd Ave; adult/child $12/8; ⊙10am-
5:30pm Mon, Tue & Fri-Sun, by appointment Wed &
Thu) The Everglades Outpost houses, feeds
and cares for wild animals that have been
seized from illegal traders, abused, neglect-
ed or donated by people who could not care
for them. Residents of the outpost include a
lemur, wolves, a black bear, a zebra, cobras,
alligators and a pair of majestic tigers (one

THE EVERGLADES: AN OVERVIEW

It's tempting to think of the Everglades as a swamp, but 'prairie' may be a more apt description. The Glades, at the end of the day, are grasslands that happen to be flooded for most of the year: visit during the dry season (winter) and you'd be forgiven for thinking the Everglades was the Everfields.

So where's the water coming from? Look north on a map of Florida, all the way to Lake Okeechobee and the small lakes and rivers that band together around Kissimmee. Florida dips into the Gulf of Mexico at its below-sea-level tip, which happens to be the lowest part of the state geographically and topographically. Run-off water from central Florida flows down the peninsula via streams and rivers, over and through the Glades, and into Florida Bay. The glacial pace of the flood means this seemingly stillest of landscapes is in constant motion. Small wonder the Calusa Indians called the area Pa-hay-okee (grassy water). Beloved conservationist Marjory Stoneman Douglas (1890–1998) called it the River of Grass; in her famous book of the same title, she revealed that Gerard de Brahm, a colonial cartographer, named the region the River Glades, which became Ever Glades on later English maps.

So what happens when nutrient-rich water creeps over a limestone shelf? The ecological equivalent of a sweaty orgy. Beginning at the cellular level, organic material blooms in surprising ways, clumping and forming into algal beds, nutrient blooms and the ubiquitous periphyton, which are basically clusters of algae, bacteria and detritus (ie stuff). Periphyton ain't pretty: in the water they resemble puke streaks and the dried version looks like hippo turds. But you should kiss them when you see them (well, maybe not) because in the great chain of the Everglades, this slop forms the base of a very tall organic totem pole. The smallest tilt in elevation alters the flow of water and hence the content of this nutrient soup, and thus the landscape itself: all those patches of cypress and hardwood hammock (not a bed for backpackers; in this case, hammock is a fancy Floridian way of saying a forest of broadleaf trees, mainly tropical or subtropical) are areas where a few inches of altitude create a world of difference between biosystems.

Fight for the Green Grassy Waters

The Everglades were utter wilderness for thousands of years. Even Native Americans avoided the Glades; the 'native' Seminole and Miccosukee actually settled here as exiles escaping war and displacement from other parts of the country. But following European settlement of Florida, some pioneers saw the potential for economic development of the Grassy Waters.

Cattle ranchers and sugar growers, attracted by mucky waters and Florida's subtropical climate (paradise for sugarcane), successfully pressured the government to make land available to them. In 1905 Florida governor Napoleon Bonaparte Broward personally dug the first shovelful of a diversion that connected the Caloosahatchee River to Lake Okeechobee. Hundreds of canals were cut through the Everglades to the coastline to 'reclaim' the land, and the flow of lake water was restricted by a series of dikes. Farmland began to claim areas previously uninhabited by humans.

Unfortunately the whole 'River of Grass' needs the river to survive. And besides being a pretty place to watch the birds, the Everglades acts as a hurricane barrier and kidney. Kidney? Yup: all those wetlands leached out pollutants from the Florida Aquifer (the state's freshwater supply). But when farmland wasn't diverting the sheet flow, it was adding fertilizer-rich wastewater to it. Result? A very sweaty (and well-attended) biological orgy. Bacteria, and eventually plant life, bloomed at a ridiculous rate (they call it fertilizer for a reason), upsetting the fragile balance of resources vital to the Glades' survival.

Enter Marjory Stoneman Douglas, stage left. Ms Douglas gets the credit for almost single-handedly pushing the now age-old Florida issue of Everglades conservation.

Despite the tireless efforts of Douglas and other environmentalists, today the Florida Aquifer is in serious danger of being contaminated and drying up. The number of wading birds nesting has declined by 90% to 95% since the 1930s. Currently there are over 60 threatened and endangered plant and animal species in the park.

The diversion of water away from the Glades and run-off pollution are the main culprits behind the region's environmental degradation. This delicate ecosystem is the neighbor of one of the fastest-growing urban areas in the US. The current water-drainage system in South Florida was built to handle the needs of two million people; the local population topped six million in 2010. And while Miami can't grow north or south into Fort Lauderdale or Homestead, it can move west, directly into the Everglades. At this stage, scientists estimate the wetlands have been reduced by 50% to 75% of their original size.

Humans are not the only enemy of the Everglades. Nature has done its share of damage as well. During 2005's Hurricane Wilma, for example, six storm water treatment areas (artificial wetlands that cleanse excess nutrients out of the water cycle) were lashed and heavily damaged by powerful winds. Without these natural filtration systems, the Glades are far more susceptible to nutrient blooms and external pollution. Wildfires also leave ever-increasing swaths of devastation across the state each year. In 2016 nearly 4000 acres went up in flames near Long Pine Key.

Restoration of the Everglades

Efforts to save the Everglades began in the late 1920s, but were sidelined by the Great Depression. In 1926 and 1928, two major hurricanes caused Lake Okeechobee to overflow; the resulting floods killed hundreds. The Army Corps of Engineers did a really good job of damming the lake. A bit too good: the Glades were essentially cut off from their source, the Kissimmee watershed.

In the meantime, conservationists began donating land for protection, starting with 1 sq mile of land donated by a garden club. The Everglades was declared a national park in 1947, the same year Marjory Stoneman Douglas' *The Everglades: River of Grass* was published.

By draining the wetlands through the damming of the lake, the Army Corps made huge swaths of inland Florida inhabitable. But the environmental problems created by shifting water's natural flow, plus the area's ever-increasing population, now threaten to make the whole region uninhabitable. The canal system sends, on average, over 1 billion gallons of water into the ocean every day. At the same time, untreated run-off flows unfiltered into natural water supplies. Clean water is disappearing from the water cycle while South Florida's population gets bigger by the day.

Enter the **Comprehensive Everglades Restoration Plan** (CERP; www.everglades restoration.gov). CERP is designed to address the root of all Everglades issues: water – where to get it, how to divert it and ways to keep it clean. The plan is to unblock the Kissimmee, restoring remaining Everglades lands to predevelopment conditions, while maintaining flood protection, providing freshwater for South Florida's populace and protecting earmarked regions against urban sprawl. It sounds great, but political battles have significantly slowed the implementation of CERP. The cost of the project has increased over the years, and a mix of political red tape and maneuvering courtesy of federal and state government has delayed CERP's implementation.

Not to throw another acronym at you, but a major portion of the CERP is the **Central Everglades Planning Project** (CEPP), the rare public works project that is supported by environmentalists and industry alike. The CEPP's aim is to clean polluted water from Florida's agricultural central heartland and redirect it towards the Everglades. The River of Grass would be re-watered, and toxic run-off would no longer flow to the sea. In a bit of good news for the 'Glades, in 2016 the US Congress approved $976 million of funding for CEPP as part of its *Water Infrastructure Improvements for the Nation Act*.

Bringing back the Everglades is one of the biggest, most ambitious environmental restoration projects in US history; one that combines the needs of farmers, fishers, urban residents, local governments and conservationists. The success or failure of the program will be a bellwether for the future of the US environmental movement.

of whom was bought by an exotic dancer who thought she could incorporate it into her act). Your money goes into helping the outpost's mission.

Fruit & Spice Park   PARK

(☑305-247-5727; www.redlandfruitandspice. com; 24801 SW 187th Ave, Homestead; adult/ child/under 6 $8/2/free; ⊙9am-5pm; P) Set just on the edge of the Everglades, this 35-acre public park grows all those great tropical fruits you usually have to contract dysentery to enjoy. The park is divided into 'continents' (Africa, Asia etc) and it makes for a peaceful wander past various species bearing in total around 500 different types of fruits, spices and nuts. Unfortunately you can't pick the fruit, but you are welcome to eat anything that falls to the ground (go early for the best gathering!).

Downtown Homestead   AREA

(☑305-323-6564; www.homesteadmainst.org; Krome Ave) You could pass a mildly entertaining afternoon walking around Homestead's almost quaint main street, which essentially comprises a couple of blocks of Krome Ave extending north and south of the Historic Town Hall. The town hosts one big monthly event from September to April, including concerts, food fests, holiday parades and other events at **Losner Park** (across the street from the Historic Town Hall). It's a good effort at injecting some character into downtown Homestead.

Historic Town Hall   MUSEUM

(☑305-242-4463; www.townhallmuseum.org; 41 N Krome Ave; ⊙1-5pm Tue-Sat) Built in 1917, this stolid white building fulfilled many roles – city council chambers, fire department, police station – in the once tiny township of Homestead. Today it houses a small museum with a collection of old photographs and memorabilia that give a glimpse of 20th-century life in the town. The highlight is a beauty: a 1924 American LaFrance fire truck.

🏃 Activities

Garls Coastal
Kayaking Everglades   KAYAKING

(www.garlscoastalkayaking.com; 19200 SW 344th St; single/double kayak per day $40/55; half-/ full-day tour $125/150) On the property of the Robert Is Here fruit stand, this outfitter leads highly recommended excursions into the Everglades. A full-day outing includes

hiking (more of wet walk/slog into the lush landscape of cypress domes), followed by kayaking in both the mangroves and in Florida Bay, and, time permitting, a night walk.

For a DIY adventure, you can also hire kayaks as well as other gear – including tents, sleeping bags and fishing gear.

🛏 Sleeping

⭐Everglades
International Hostel   HOSTEL $

(☑305-248-1122; www.evergladeshostel.com; 20 SW 2nd Ave, Florida City; camping per person $18, dm $30, d $61-75, ste $125-225; P❋ 🛜 🐾) Located in a cluttered, comfy 1930s boarding house, this friendly hostel has good-value dorms, private rooms and 'semi-privates' (you have an enclosed room within the dorms and share a bathroom with dorm residents). The creatively configured backyard is the best feature.

There's a tree house; a small rock-cut pool with a waterfall; a Bedouin pavilion that doubles as a dance hall; a gazebo; an open-air tented 'bed room'; and an oven built to resemble a tail-molting tadpole. It all needs to be seen to be believed, and best of all you can crash anywhere in the back for $15. Sleep in a tree house! We should add the crowd is made up of free-spirited international types that made you fall in love with traveling in the first place, and the hostel leads excellent tours into the Everglades.

Hotel Redland   HOTEL $

(☑305-246-1904; www.hotelredland.com; 5 S Flagler Ave, Homestead; r $110-150; ❋ 🛜) On the edge of Homestead's quaint downtown, the Hotel Redland is set in a 1904 building that has a warm, cozy vibe thanks to its gracious hosts. The 12 rooms are comfortable, but dated in a charming, grandmotherly way (quilted bedspreads, floral curtains, old photos or framed paintings on the walls).

🍴 Eating

⭐Robert Is Here   MARKET $

(☑305-246-1592; www.robertishere.com; 19200 SW 344th St, Homestead; juices $7-9; ⊙8am-7pm) 🍃 More than a farmers' stand, Robert's is an institution. This is Old Florida at its kitschy best, in love with the Glades and the agriculture that surrounds it. You'll find loads of exotic, Florida-grown fruits you won't elsewhere – including black sapote, carambola (star fruit), dragon fruit, sapodilla, guanabana (soursop), tamarind, sugar apples, longans and passion fruit. The juices are fantastic.

There's also a petting zoo and water-play area for the kids (bring your own towels), live music on weekends and plenty of homemade preserves and sauces. Plus Robert is there every day, working the counter and giving insight into these delectable tropical riches.

Gator Grill
AMERICAN $

(📞 786-243-0620; 36650 SW 192nd Ave; mains $9-16; ⊙ 11am-6:30pm) A handy pit stop before or after visiting the Everglades National Park, the Gator Grill is a white shack with picnic tables, where you can munch on all manner of alligator dishes. There are gator tacos, gator stir fry, gator kebabs and straight-up fried alligator served in a basket.

Rosita's
MEXICAN $

(📞 305-246-3114; www.rositasrestaurantfl.com; 199 W Palm Dr, Florida City; mains $8-12; ⊙ 8:30am-9pm) There's a working-class Mexican crowd here, testament to the sheer awesomeness of the tacos and burritos. Everyone is friendly, and the mariachi music adds a festive vibe to the place.

White Lion Cafe
AMERICAN $$

(📞 305-247-1076; www.whitelioncafe.com; 146 NW 7th St, Homestead; mains $12-27; ⊙ 11am-3pm & 5-10pm Tue-Sat) There's a comfy cabin vibe to this place near downtown Homestead, with indoor and outdoor seating. The menu features American fare along the lines of meatloaf, crab cakes, fried chicken and fresh fruit cobbler.

🍷 Drinking & Nightlife

Miami Brewing Company
BREWERY

(📞 305-242-1224; www.miamibrewing.org; 30205 SW 217th Ave; ⊙ noon-5pm Sun-Thu, to 11pm Fri & Sat) You'll find first-rate craft brews in this enormous warehouse-style tasting room. The brewers here bring more than a hint of Floridian accents in beers like Shark Bait mango wheat ale, Big Rod coconut blond ale and Vice IPA with citrus notes. There's big screens for game days, a pool table, outdoor picnic tables and live music (or DJs) on weekends.

There are also seasonal brews like pumpkin ale, spiced winter ale and a creamy stout with a hint of French vanilla. It's in the same complex (and under the same ownership) as the Schnebly Redland's Winery (p163).

ℹ️ Information

Tropical Everglades Visitor Association (160 N 1st St, Florida City; ⊙ 8am-5pm Mon-Sat, 10am-2pm Sun) Just off the S Dixie Hwy in Florida City, this is the best place in the area for getting info on activities, sites, lodging and dining.

Chamber of Commerce (📞 305-247-2332; www.southdadechamber.org; 455 N Flagler Ave, Homestead; ⊙ 9am-5pm Mon-Fri) Pick up local info on the area here.

ℹ️ Getting There & Away

Homestead runs a free weekend **trolley bus service** (📞 305-224-4457; www.cityof homestead.com; ⊙ Sat & Sun Dec-Apr), which takes visitors from Losner Park (downtown Homestead) out to the **Royal Palm Visitor Center** (p168) in Everglades National Park. It also runs between Losner Park and Biscayne National Park (p169). Call for the latest departure times.

Southern Everglades Highway

As you go past Homestead and Florida City, the farmland loses its uniformity and the flat land becomes more tangled, wild and studded with pine and cypress. In a few miles, you'll reach the entrance post to the southern Everglades. This road is packed with sites, including short nature trails full of great wildlife-watching opportunities, narrow waterways for canoeing, and scenic ponds and lakes. The road ends at Flamingo, where you can arrange boat tours out into Florida Bay, take a coastal walk or simply hang out around the dock looking for manatees and alligators. The 38-mile drive between the park entrance (near Ernest Coe Visitor Center) and Flamingo takes just under an hour, though you could spend many days doing activities (hiking, night walks, canoeing) in this stretch of the national park.

🔘 Sights

★ Anhinga Trail
NATURE RESERVE

(⊙ 24hr) If you do just one walk in the Everglades, make sure it's on the Anhinga Trail. Gators sun on the shoreline, anhinga spear their prey and wading birds stalk haughtily through the reeds. You'll get a close-up view of wildlife on this short (0.8 mile) trail at the Royal Palm Visitor Center. There are various overlooks, where you can sometimes see dozens of alligators piled together in the day.

Come back at night (be sure to bring a flashlight) for a view of the gators swimming along the waterways – sometimes right beside you. The park offers periodic ranger-led walks along the boardwalk at night, though you can always do it yourself. Seeing the glittering eyes of alligators prowling the waterways by flashlight is an unforgettable experience!

Flamingo Visitor Center   VISITOR CENTER
(☑ 239-695-2945; www.nps.gov/ever; State Rd 9336; ☺ 8am-4:30pm mid-Nov–mid-Apr) At the end of State Rd 9336 is the Flamingo Visitor Center, which overlooks a marina and the watery wilderness beyond. The chief draw here is taking either a boat tour or hiring a kayak or canoe – all arranged through the Flamingo Marina, a short stroll from the visitor center. Do spend some time hanging out near the water's edge. This is a great place for seeing manatees, alligators and even the rare American crocodile.

If you prefer to stay on land, you can hike along the **Coastal Prairie Trail** (7.5 miles one way) or the shorter more scenic **Bayshore Loop Trail** (2 miles) – both reached through the campground. You can also look for birds (and gators) along the half-mile trail that circles around nearby Eco Pond.

Royal Palm Visitor Center   PARK
(☑ 305-242-7700; www.nps.gov/ever; State Rd 9336; ☺ 9am-4:15pm) Four miles past Ernest Coe Visitor Center, Royal Palm offers the easiest access to the Glades in these parts. Two trails, the Anhinga and **Gumbo Limbo** (the latter named for the gumbo-limbo tree, also known as the 'tourist tree' because its bark peels like a sunburned Brit), take all of an hour to walk and put you face to face with a panoply of Everglades wildlife.

Ernest Coe Visitor Center   VISITOR CENTER
(☑ 305-242-7700; www.nps.gov/ever; 40001 State Rd 9336; ☺ 9am-5pm mid-Apr–mid-Dec, from 8am mid-Dec–mid-Apr) Near the entrance to the Everglades National Park, this friendly visitor center has some excellent exhibits, including a diorama of 'typical' Floridians (the fisherman looks like he should join ZZ Top).

Pa-hay-okee Overlook   VIEWPOINT
Rte 9336 cuts through the soft heart of the park, past long fields of marsh prairie, white, skeletal forests of bald cypress and dark clumps of mahogany hammock. Further on, the Pa-hay-okee Overlook is a raised platform that peeks over one of the prettiest bends in the River of Grass.

Activities

Flamingo Marina Rentals & Boat Tours   BOATING
(☑ 239-696-3101; www.evergladesnationalpark boattoursflamingo.com; tours per adult/child $38/18, canoe rental 2/4/8hr $20/28/38, kayak rental half-/full day $35/45; ☺ marina 7am-7pm, from 6am Sat & Sun) The most isolated portion of the park is a squat marina where you can go on a backcountry boat tour or rent boats. Due to its isolation, this area is subject to closure during bad weather. You can rent kayaks and canoes here; if you do, you're largely left to explore the channels and islands of Florida Bay on your own.

During rough weather, be cautious, even when on land, as storm surges can turn an attractive spread of beach into a watery stretch of danger fairly quickly.

Hell's Bay Canoe Trail   KAYAKING
Despite the frightening name (and terrible mosquitoes), this can be a magnificent place to kayak. 'Hell to get into and hell to get out of,' was how this sheltered launch was described by old Gladesmen, but once inside you'll find a fairly enchanted world: a capillary network of mangrove creeks, saw-grass islands and shifting mudflats, where the brambles form a green tunnel and all you can smell is sea salt and the dark organic breath of the swamp.

Three *chickee* sites are spaced along the trail. You'll need to pick up a backcountry permit, available at park visitor centers, to camp at one of them. If you're traveling without a boat, you'll be able to hire one in Flamingo.

🛏 Sleeping

National Park Service Campsites   CAMPGROUND $
(NPS; www.nps.gov/ever/planyourvisit/camping. htm; campsite $20) There are campgrounds run by the NPS located throughout the park. Sites are fairly basic, though there are showers and toilets. Depending on the time of year, the cold water can be either bracing or a welcome relief. The NPS information offices provide a map of all campsites, as does the park website.

There are also many backcountry campsites ($2 per night). For these you'll also need a permit ($15) and to reserve ahead (at the visitor center) before disembarking. Sites are free during the off season (May to October). Note that these sites are accessible only by canoe or kayak (excepting one site reachable on foot from Flamingo).

Flamingo Campground   CAMPGROUND $
(☑ 877-444-6777; www.nps.gov/ever/planyour visit/flamcamp.htm; per campsite without/with electricity $20/30) There are over 200 camping sites at the Flamingo Visitor Center, some of which have electrical hookups. Escape the RVs by booking a walk-in site. Be sure to reserve well ahead (via www. reserveamerica.com) for one of the nine waterfront sites.

Long Pine Key Campground   CAMPGROUND $
(☑ 305-242-7700; www.nps.gov/ever/planyour visit/longpinecamp.htm; per campsite $20; ☺ closed Jun–mid-Nov) This is a good bet for car campers, just west of Royal Palm Visitor Center. It has 108 sites, available on a first-come basis (no reservations).

BISCAYNE NATIONAL PARK

Just to the east of the Everglades is **Biscayne National Park** (☑ 305-230-1144, boat tour 786-335-3644; www.nps.gov/bisc; 9700 SW 328th St; boat tour adult/child $35/25; ☺ 7am-5:30pm), or the 5% of it that isn't underwater. In fact, a portion of the world's third-largest reef sits here off the coast of Florida, along with mangrove forests and the northernmost Florida Keys.

A bit shadowed by the Everglades, Biscayne requires a little extra planning, but you get a lot more reward for your effort. The offshore keys, accessible only by boat, offer pristine opportunities for camping. Generally summer and fall are the best times to visit the park; you'll want to snorkel when the water is calm. This is some of the best reef-viewing and snorkeling you'll find in the US, outside Hawaii and nearby Key Largo.

Fortunately this unique 300-sq-mile park is easy to explore independently with a canoe, or via a boat tour.

Biscayne National Park may not be far from Miami, but it feels like a world removed. Encompassing a vibrant swath of biologically rich coral reef, this park is teeming with life – though you'll have to head on a boat tour, or better yet don snorkel and mask – to see it firsthand. Manatees, dolphins and sea turtles are just a few inhabitants of this diverse ecosystem.

There are also over 500 species of reef fish. Meanwhile, above the surface you'll find neotropical water birds and migratory species.

The best introduction to the area is a boat tour, offered by the park, with a ranger giving an overview of the wildlife and history of the area. Three-hour cruises depart once or twice a day on select Thursdays, Fridays and Saturdays from the Dante Fascell Visitor Center (p170). Call to confirm times and book a spot.

🏃 Activities

NEC-FLO Paddlesports   KAYAKING
(☑ 305-390-0393; www.necflo.com; Biscayne National Park, 9700 SW 328th St; ☺ 9am-5pm Wed-Sun) This outfit hires out kayaks from its location in Biscayne National Park. Inquire here about boat tours, too.

Maritime Heritage Trail   DIVING
🐠 The Maritime Heritage Trail takes 'hikers' through one of the only trails of its kind in the USA. If you've ever wanted to explore a sunken ship, this may well be the best opportunity in the country. Six are located within the park grounds; the trail experience involves taking visitors out, by boat, to the site of the wrecks where they can swim and explore among derelict vessels and clouds of fish.

There are even waterproof information site cards placed among the ships. Three of the vessels are suited for scuba divers, but the others – particularly the *Mandalay,* a lovely two-masted schooner that sank in 1966 – can be accessed by snorkelers. Miami outfitters like **South Beach Diver & Surf Center** (Map p82; ☑ 305-531-6110; www.south beachdivers.com; 850 Washington Ave; 2-tank dive trip without/with gear from $90/140, surfboard hire 4hr/all day $30/35; ☺ 9am-7pm Mon-Sat, 10am-6pm Sun) lead excursions here.

🧭 Tours

Biscayne National Park Sailing   BOATING
(☑ 561-281-2689; www.biscaynenationalparksailing. com; 2½/6hr cruise per person $59/149) One of the best ways to experience Biscayne National Park is on this sailing adventure that departs Convoy Point. Full-day sailing trips depart at 10am and cruise along the bay, stopping at Boca Chita or Adams Key, followed by lunch (an extra $25 or you can bring your own), then snorkeling or paddleboarding in

a peaceful spot, and the homeward journey, arriving around 4pm.

Although somewhat pricey, the tour gets rave reviews from those who've made the trip. Two-person minimum, six-people maximum.

Sleeping & Eating

Primitive camping (site per night $25, May-Sep free) is available on Elliott and Boca Chita Keys, though you'll need a boat to get there. No-see-ums (tiny flies) are invasive, and their bites are devastating. Make sure your tent is devoid of minuscule entry points.

No food is available in the park, though nearby you'll find an outdoor restaurant at Homestead's Bayfront Park and Marina. You'll find more dining options (and places to pick up supplies) in Florida City (p166), roughly nine miles west of the park.

ℹ Information

Dante Fascell Visitor Center (☏ 305-230-1144; www.nps.gov/bisc; 9700 SW 328th St; ⊙9am-5pm) Located at Convoy Point, this center shows a great introductory film for an overview of the park, and has maps, information and excellent ranger-led activities. The grounds around the center are a popular picnic spot on weekends and holidays, especially for families from Homestead. Also showcases local artwork. This is the departure point for park-led boat tours.

ℹ Getting There & Away

To get here, you'll have to drive about 9 miles east of Homestead (the way is pretty well signposted) on SW 328th St (North Canal Dr) into a long series of green-and-gold flat fields and marsh.

Florida Keys & Key West

POP 77,482 / ☎ 305. 786

Best Places to Eat

➡ Lazy Days (p180)

➡ Square Grouper (p187)

➡ Keys Fisheries (p183)

➡ Key Largo Conch House (p177)

➡ No Name Pub (p186)

Best Places to Sleep

➡ Kona Kai Resort (p176)

➡ Seascape Motel & Marina (p182)

➡ Bay Harbor Lodge (p176)

➡ Deer Run Bed & Breakfast (p186)

Why Go?

If Florida is a state apart from the USA, the Keys are islands apart from Florida – in other words, it's different down here. This is a place where those who reject everyday life on the mainland escape. What do they find? About 113 mangrove-and-sandbar islands where the white sun melts over tight fists of deep green mangroves; long, gloriously soft mudflats and tidal bars; water as teal as Arizona turquoise; and a bunch of people often like themselves: freaks, geeks and lovable weirdos all.

Key West is still defined by its motto – One Human Family – an ideal that equals a tolerant, accepting ethos where anything goes and life is always a party (or at least a hungover day after). The color scheme: watercolor pastels cooled by breezes on a sunset-kissed Bahamian porch. Welcome to the End of the USA.

When to Go
Key West

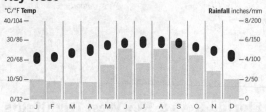

Dec–Mar It's dry, the sun is out, the weather is grand and the lodging is at its most expensive.

Apr–Jun Sea breezes help to keep the summer heat down, and hotel rates drop precipitously.

Jul–Nov There's some rain (and maybe even some hurricanes), but plenty of festivals too.

N

| 0 | | 20 km |
| 0 | | 10 miles |

Gulf of
Mexico

Everglades National Park Boundary

Shark
Point

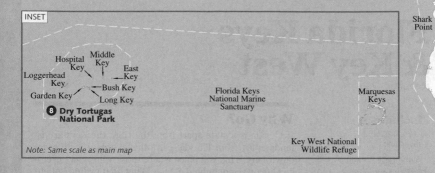

INSET

Hospital
Key

Middle
Key

East
Key

Loggerhead
Key

Bush Key

Garden Key

Long Key

**8 Dry Tortugas
National Park**

Florida Keys
National Marine
Sanctuary

Marquesas
Keys

Key West National
Wildlife Refuge

Note: Same scale as main map

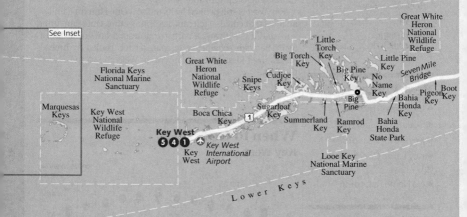

See Inset

Great White
Heron
National
Wildlife
Refuge

Florida Keys
National Marine
Sanctuary

Great White
Heron
National
Wildlife
Refuge

Little
Torch
Key

Big Torch
Key

Little Pine
Key

Snipe
Keys

Cudjoe
Key

Big Pine
Key

No
Name
Key

Seven Mile
Bridge

Boot
Key

Marquesas
Keys

Key West
National
Wildlife
Refuge

Boca Chica
Key

Sugarloaf
Key

Big
Pine

Bahia
Honda
Key

Pigeon
Key

5 4 1 Key West

Key
West

Key West
International
Airport

Summerland
Key

Ramrod
Key

Bahia
Honda
State Park

Looe Key
National Marine
Sanctuary

L o w e r   K e y s

Florida Keys & Key West Highlights

1 Mallory Square (p191)
Watching the sun set over the
ocean as you sit and take in
the raucous show.

2 John Pennekamp Coral

Reef State Park (p174) Diving
around the rainbow reefs.

**3 Indian Key Historic
State Park** (p178) Paddling
out to this eerie, lonely,
beautiful park.

4 Fantasy Fest (p194)
Donning a purple-and-green
crocodile costume and
partying in the streets of Key
West.

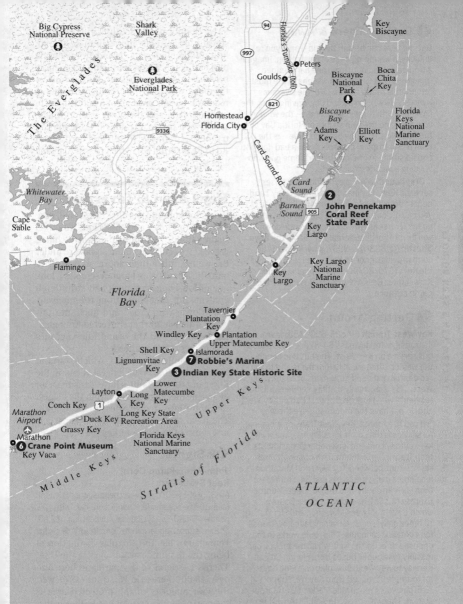

94

Florida's Turnpike (toll)

997

Peters

Goulds

821

Homestead
Florida City

9336

Key
Biscayne

Biscayne
National
Park

Boca
Chita
Key

*Biscayne
Bay*

Florida
Keys
National
Marine
Sanctuary

Adams
Key

Elliott
Key

Big Cypress
National Preserve

Shark
Valley

Everglades
National Park

The Everglades

*Whitewater
Bay*

Cape
Sable

Flamingo

*Florida
Bay*

Card Sound Rd

*Card
Sound*

*Barnes
Sound*

905

2 **John Pennekamp
Coral Reef
State Park**

Key
Largo

Key
Largo

Key Largo
National
Marine
Sanctuary

Tavernier

Plantation
Key

Windley Key

Plantation

Upper Matecumbe Key

Shell Key

Islamorada

Lignumvitae
Key

7 **Robbie's Marina**

3 **Indian Key State Historic Site**

Lower
Matecumbe
Key

Layton

Long
Key

Conch Key

1

Long Key State
Recreation Area

*Marathon
Airport*

Duck Key

Grassy Key

Marathon

6 **Crane Point Museum**

Key Vaca

Florida Keys
National Marine
Sanctuary

Upper Keys

Middle Keys

Straits of Florida

*ATLANTIC
OCEAN*

---

5 **Hemingway House**
(p191) Scratching Papa's six-
toed cats behind their ears.

6 **Crane Point Museum**
(p182) Strolling through the

palm-hammock and pineland
scrub.

7 **Robbie's Marina** (p179)
Feeding the giant tarpon
swimming in circles.

8 **Dry Tortugas National
Park** (p201) Making an island-
hopping day trip and detour.

ⓘ Getting There & Away

Getting here can be half the fun – or, if you're unlucky, a whopping dose of frustration. Imagine a tropical-island hop, from one bar-studded mangrove islet to the next, via one of the most remarkable roads in the world: the Overseas Hwy (US Hwy 1). On a good day, driving along the Overseas Hwy with the windows down – the wind in your face and the twin sisters of Florida Bay and the Atlantic stretching on either side – is the US road trip in tropical perfection. On a bad day, you end up sitting in gridlock behind some guy who is riding a midlife-crisis Harley.

Greyhound (www.greyhound.com) buses serve all Keys destinations along US Hwy 1 and depart from downtown Miami and Key West; you can pick up a bus along the way by standing on the Overseas Hwy and flagging one down. If you fly into Fort Lauderdale or Miami, the **Keys Shuttle** (☑ 888-765-9997; www.keysshuttle.com) provides door-to-door service to most of the Keys ($70/80/90 to the Upper and Middle Keys/Lower Keys/Key West). Reserve at least a day in advance.

ⓘ Getting Around

Key West Transit (☑ 305-600-1455; www.kwtransit.com; day pass $4-8) operates a local bus service on Key West. The bus line connects the western, historical half of the island to the residential units and strip malls of eastern Key West. This is primarily a utility service for island residents who work on the west half of Key West and do not have the means to drive the way.

If you're a tourist, Key West Transit's more useful service is the Lower Keys Shuttle; see www.keywestcity.com and look under Departments, then Transit Department. This commuter bus service runs between Key West and Marathon nine times daily; the fare is just $4. From Marathon you can connect to the 301 Dade-Monroe Express ($2.65), operated by Dade County, which travels between Marathon and Florida City 10 times daily; see www.miamidade.gov/transit for a detailed schedule. This route works in the opposite direction as well, which means you can feasibly take public buses from Florida City all the way to Key West. Just plan on a long day; for example, if you left from Key West at 12:21pm, you'd reach Mile Marker 50 in Marathon at 2pm. Then you'd have to wait till the 301 leaves from Mile Marker 50 at 3:45pm, landing you in Florida City at 6pm.

UPPER KEYS

No, really, you're in the islands!

It is a bit hard to tell when you first arrive, though. The huge, rooty blanket of mangrove forest that forms the South Florida coastline spreads like a woody morass into Key Largo; little differentiates the island from Florida proper. Keep heading south and the scenery becomes more archipelagically pleasant as the mangroves give way to wider stretches of road and ocean, until all of a sudden you're in Islamorada and the water is everywhere. If you want to avoid traffic on US 1, you can try the less trafficked FL 997 and Card Sound Rd to FL 905 (toll $1), which passes Alabama Jack's (p177).

Key Largo & Tavernier

We're not going to lie: Key Largo (both the name of the town and the island it's on) is slightly underwhelming at a glance. 'Under' is the key word, as its main sights are under the water, rather than above. As you drive onto the islands, Key Largo resembles a long line of low-lying hammock and strip development. But that's just from the highway: head down a side road and duck into this warm little bar, or that converted Keys plantation house, and the island idiosyncrasies become more pronounced.

The 33-mile-long Largo, which starts at Mile Marker 106, is the longest island in the Keys, and those 33 miles have attracted a lot of marine life, all accessible from the biggest concentration of dive sites in the islands. The town of Tavernier (Mile Marker 93) is just south of the town of Key Largo.

⊙ Sights

John Pennekamp Coral
Reef State Park   STATE PARK

(☑ 305-451-6300; www.pennekamppark.com; Mile 102.6 oceanside; admission car with 1/2 people $4.50/9, cyclist or pedestrian $2.50; ⊙ 8am-sunset, aquarium to 5pm; P ✚) ⬤ John Pennekamp has the singular distinction of being the first underwater park in the USA. There's 170 acres of dry parkland here and over 48,000 acres (ie 75 sq miles) of wet: the vast majority of the protected area is the ocean. Before you get out in that water, be sure to take in some pleasant beaches and stroll over the nature trails.

The **Mangrove Trail** is a good boardwalk introduction to this oft-maligned, ecologically awesome species (the trees, often submerged in water, breathe via long roots that act as snorkels – neat). Stick around for nightly campfire programs and ranger discussions.

The visitor center is well run and informative and has a small saltwater **aquarium** (8am to 5pm) and nature films that give a glimpse of what's under those waters. To really get beneath the surface, you should take a 2½-hour **glass-bottom boat tour** (adult/child $24/17). You'll be brought out in a safe, modern 38ft catamaran from which you'll get a chance to see filigreed flaps of soft coral, technicolor schools of fish, dangerous-looking barracuda and perhaps massive, yet ballerina-graceful, sea turtles. Besides the swirl of natural coral life, interested divers can catch a glimpse of the *Christ of the Abyss*, an 8.5ft, 4000lb bronze sculpture of Jesus – a copy of a similar sculpture off the coast of Genoa, Italy, in the Mediterranean Sea.

If you want to go even deeper, try straight-up **snorkeling trips** (adult/child $30/25) or **diving excursions** (six-person charter $500, plus equipment rental). DIY-ers may want to take out a canoe ($20 per hour), kayak (per hour/half day from $12/30) or stand-up paddleboard (from $25/40 per hour/half day) to journey through a 3-mile network of trails. Phone for boat-rental information.

To learn more about the reef in this area, go to www.southeastfloridareefs.net.

Caribbean Club Bar FILM LOCATION
(☎ 305-451-4466; www.caribbeanclubkl.com; Mile 104 bayside; ⊙ 7am-4am) Here's one for the movie fans, particularly Bogie buffs: the lively Caribbean Club Bar is, in fact, the only place in Key Largo where *Key Largo*, starring Humphrey Bogart and Lauren Bacall, was filmed (the rest of the island was a Hollywood soundstage). Stop in for drinks, live music (Thursday to Sunday nights) and a dose of old Florida nostalgia – plus great sunsets off the back deck.

If that's not enough, the original *African Queen*, of the same-titled movie, is docked 5 miles south in a channel at the Holiday Inn at Mile Marker 100 – just walk around the back and there she is (assuming the boat's not out for tours; p175).

**Laura Quinn Wild
Bird Sanctuary** WILDLIFE RESERVE
(☎ 305-852-4486; www.keepthemflying.org; 93600 Overseas Hwy, Mile 93.6; donations accepted; ⊙ sunrise-sunset; P 🐾) 🦜 This 7-acre sanctuary serves as a protected refuge for a wide variety of injured birds. A boardwalk leads through various enclosures where you can learn a bit about some of the permanent residents – those unable to be released back in the wild. The species here include masked boobies, great horned owls, green herons, brown pelicans, double-crested cormorants and others. Keep walking along the path to reach a nice vista of Florida Bay and a wading bird pond.

The same organization also runs a bird hospital just south along the main highway. They're the ones to contact if you see injured birds – or have any other bird emergencies – during your travels.

Harry Harris Park PARK
(50 East Beach Rd, Mile 92.6, Tavernier; admission free Mon-Fri, $5 Sat, Sun & holidays; ⊙ 7:30am-sunset; 🐾 🐕) This small park is a good place to take the kids – there's a small playground, picnic tables, grills for barbecuing, basketball courts and ball fields. Rare for the Keys, there's also a good patch of white sand fronting a warm lagoon that's excellent for swimming.

🏃 Activities

**Key Largo Bike and
Adventure Tours** CYCLING
(☎ 305-395-1551; www.keylargobike.com; 2-day tour from $500) This outfit leads a range of bike outings, including two-day tours from Key Largo to Key West. It also hires out bikes for those who want to go it alone (pick up in in Key Largo or Miami and drop off in Key West).

Key Largo Princess BOATING
(☎ 305-451-4655; Key Largo Holiday Inn, 99701 Overseas Hwy; adult/child from $35/20; ⊙ cruises at 10am, 1pm & 4pm; 🐾) Get a glimpse of the Key's undersea beauty on a glass-bottom boat tour. Popular with families, these 75ft, 129-passenger vessels give you the opportunity to see lots of colorful coral, plus sea fans, sharks, tropical fish and the odd sea turtle winging along.

Snacks and drinks available on the boat.

African Queen BOATING
(☎ 305-451-8080; www.africanqueenflkeys.com; Key Largo Holiday Inn, 99701 Overseas Hwy; canal cruise/dinner cruise $49/89) The steamboat used in the 1951 movie starring Humphrey Bogart and Katherine Hepburn has been restored to her former splendor, and you can relive the movie aboard the tiny vessel on a canal or dinner cruise. If you behave better than Hepburn's character, the captain might even let you take the helm for a bit.

FLORIDA KEYS OVERSEAS HERITAGE TRAIL

One of the best ways to see the Keys is by bicycle. The flat elevation and ocean breezes are perfect for cycling, and the **Florida Keys Overseas Heritage Trail** (☎305-853-3571; www.floridastateparks.org/trail/Florida-Keys) gives gorgeous vantage points along the way. This trail still under construction will eventually connect all the islands from Key Largo to Key West. Currently 90 miles of this multi-use trail out of 106 miles are now complete.

If you are keen to ride, it's currently possible to bike through the Keys along portions of this trail (not always easy to follow). In the incomplete parts of the trail, you can ride along the shoulder of the highway if you don't mind traffic whizzing by at 50 mph (crossing the Seven-Mile Bridge is particularly harrowing; taxis in Marathon have bike racks, saving you the stress).

For two-day biking trips between Key Largo and Key West, book a tour with Key Largo Bike and Adventure Tours (p175), which leads a range of bike outings. It also hires out bikes for those who want to go it alone (pick up in in Key Largo or Miami and drop off in Key West).

Jacob's Aquatics Center WATER PARK
(☎305-453-7946; http://jacobsaquaticcenter. org; 320 Laguna Ave, Mile 99.6; adult/child/ student/family weekday \$10/6/8/25, weekend \$12/8/10/30; ⏰10am-7pm May-Sep, to 6pm Oct-Apr; 🚼) Jacob's is a complex of all kinds of aquatic fun. There's an eight-lane pool for lap and open swimming, a therapy pool with handicapped access and water aerobic courses. For the kids there's a small waterpark with waterslides, a playground and, of course, kiddie-sized pools.

👉 Tours

Garl's Coastal Kayaking ECOTOUR
(☎305-393-3223; www.garlscoastalkayaking. com; 4hr tours adult/child \$75/50, kayak hire per day single/double \$40/55) 🌿 Garl's is an excellent ecotour operator that gets customers into the Everglades backcountry and mangrove islets of Florida Bay via kayak and canoe. It also provides reasonable equipment rentals.

🛏 Sleeping

John Pennekamp Coral Reef State Park CAMPGROUND \$
(☎800-326-3521; www.reserveamerica.com; 102601 Overseas Hwy; tent & RV sites \$38.50; P) You don't even have to leave Pennekamp at closing time if you opt for tent or RV camping, but you'll need to make a reservation well in advance, as the 47 sites fill up fast. Well-behaved pets are welcome.

Bay Harbor Lodge MOTEL \$\$
(☎305-852-5695; www.bayharborkeylargo.com; 97702 Overseas Hwy, bayside; r \$150-300; ❄🐾🌐🏊) This 2.5-acre property has its own private beach, a temperature-controlled pool and tropical gardens alive with birdsong. The rooms are clean and comfortable, if somewhat dated, but the service is friendly and the homemade scones (served at breakfast) are all the rage. Excellent value.

Hilton Key Largo Resort HOTEL \$\$
(☎305-852-5553; www.keylargoresort.com; Mile 102 bayside; r/ste from \$200/280; P🐾🌐🏊) This Hilton has a ton of character. Folks just seem to get all laid-back when lounging in clean, designer rooms outfitted in blues and greens with balconies overlooking the water. The grounds are enormous and include an artificial waterfall-fed pool and frontage to a rather large stretch of private white-sand beach. Book online for the best rates.

Kona Kai Resort HOTEL \$\$\$
(☎305-852-7200; www.konakairesort.com; Mile 97.8 bayside; r \$300-440; P🌐🏊) This hideaway is one of the only botanical gardens we can think of that integrates a hotel onto its grounds – or is that the other way around? Either way, this spot, backing onto peaceful waterfront, is lush. The 13 airy rooms and suites (with full kitchens) are all bright and comfortable, with good natural light and an attractive modern design.

Dove Creek Lodge HOTEL \$\$\$
(☎305-852-6200; www.dovecreeklodge.com; 147 Seaside Ave; r \$230-380; P🐾🌐🏊) This mid-sized hotel offers bright rooms decked out in citrus-shaded colors and grounds that front the Atlantic Ocean. It's a family-friendly spot with an old-school resort feel. Can help with booking tours and excursions in the area.

Jules' Undersea Lodge
HOTEL $$$

(☑ 305-451-2353; www.jul.com; 51 Shoreland Dr, Mile 103.2 oceanside; s/d/tr $675/800/1050) There's lots of talk about underwater hotels getting built in Dubai and Fiji, but as of writing, Jules' Undersea Lodge is still the only place in the world outside of a submarine where you and your significant other can join the 'five-fathom club' (we're not elaborating). Once a research station, this module has been converted into a delightfully cheesy Keys motel, but wetter.

In addition to two private guest rooms, there are common rooms, a kitchen-dining room and a wet room with hot showers and gear storage. Telephones and an intercom connect guests with the surface. Guests must be at least 10 years old and you gotta dive to get here – plus, there's no smoking or alcohol. If you just want to visit, you can pop in for a three-hour visit (with pizza!) for $150.

✗ Eating

Harriette's
AMERICAN $

(☑ 305-852-8689; 95710 Overseas Hwy, bayside; mains $7-14; ☻6am-3pm) This sweet, breadbox-sized eatery is famed far and wide for its utterly addictive key lime muffins (so big you'll need a knife and fork to eat them). There's also classic American fare – pancakes, bacon and eggs, and not-to-be-missed fluffy biscuits for breakfast, which is the best time to come. Go early to beat the crowds.

DJ's Diner
AMERICAN $

(☑ 305-451-2999; 99411 Overseas Hwy; mains $8-15; ☻7am-3pm; P 🛜 👪) You're greeted by a mural of Humphrey Bogart, James Dean *and* Marilyn Monroe – that's a lot of Americana. It's all served with a heapin' helpin' of diner faves amid vinyl-boothed ambience. Breakfast is a big draw with fluffy omelets, eggs Benedict and waffles (including a key lime pie version).

Fish House
SEAFOOD $$

(☑ 305-451-4665; www.fishhouse.com; Mile 102.4 oceanside; mains lunch $12-21, dinner $21-30; ☻11:30am-10pm; P 👪) The Fish House delivers on the promise of its title – very good fish, bought whole from local fishermen and prepared fried, broiled, jerked, blackened or chargrilled. Because the Fish House only uses fresh fish, the menu changes daily based on what is available.

Shipwreck's Bar & Grill
AMERICAN $$

(45 Garden Cove Dr, oceanside; mains $13-23; ☻11:30am-10pm) Just off the beaten path, Shipwreck's is a local-loving joint littered with nautical gear and dollar bills stapled to the walls, with a breezy open-air deck. Sit at picnic tables over the water, while noshing on fish sandwiches, peel-and-eat shrimp, conch fritters or an excellent blackened mahimahi. It's a dive, but great value for the money.

Key Largo Conch House
FUSION $$

(☑ 305-453-4844; www.keylargoconchhouse.com; Mile 100.2 oceanside; mains lunch $9-16, dinner $16-30; ☻8am-10pm; P 🛜 🔧 👪) This innovative kitchen likes to sex up local classics (mahimahi cooked in a crust of coconut and crushed macadamia nuts or conch with lobster ceviche). Set in a restored old-school Keys mansion wrapped in a *Gone With the Wind* verandah, it's hard not to love the way the period architecture blends in seamlessly with the local tropical fauna.

Mrs Mac's Kitchen
AMERICAN $$

(☑ 305-451-3722; www.mrsmacskitchen.com; Mile 99.4 bayside; mains breakfast & lunch $9-16, dinner $16-30; ☻7am-9:30pm Mon-Sat; P 👪) When Applebee's stuffs its wall full of license plates, it's tacky. When Mrs Mac's does it, it's homey. Probably because the service is warm and personable, and the breakfasts are delicious. Plus the food packs in the locals, tourists, their dogs and pretty much everyone else on the island (plus, admittedly, a fair few calories, but that's why it tastes good).

🍸 Drinking & Nightlife

Alabama Jack's
BAR

(58000 Card Sound Rd; ☻11am-7pm) Welcome to your first taste of the Keys: zonked-out fishermen, exiles from the mainland and Harley heads getting drunk on a mangrove bay. This is the line where Miami-esque South Florida gives way to the country-fried American South. Wildlife lovers: you may spot the rare mulleted version of *Jacksonvillia Redneckus*!

Everyone raves about the conch fritters; and the fact it has to close because of nightly onslaughts of mosquitoes means this place is as authentically Florida as they come. Country bands take the stage on weekends from 2pm to 5pm. It's just before the tollbooth over the Card Sound Bridge.

ℹ Information

Mariners Hospital (☑ 305-434-3000; www.baptisthealth.net; Mile 91.5 bayside, Tavernier; ☻24hr) The best hospital in the area with a

24-hour emergency room. If you're diving, this is the only place in the Keys that has a hyperbaric chamber.

❶ Getting There & Away

The Greyhound bus stops at Mile Marker 99.6 oceanside. It stops twice a day traveling between Miami and Key West.

Islamorada

📱 305 / POP 6600

Islamorada (eye-luh-murr-*ah*-da) is also known as 'The Village of Islands.' Doesn't that sound pretty? Well, it really is. This little string of pearls (well, keys) – Plantation, Upper and Lower Matecumbe, Shell and Lignumvitae (lignum-*vite*-ee) – shimmers as one of the prettiest stretches of the islands. This is where the scrubby mangrove is replaced by unbroken horizons of ocean and sky, one perfect shade of blue mirroring the other. Islamorada stretches across some 20 miles, from Mile Marker 90 to Mile Marker 74.

◉ Sights

★ Florida Keys History of Diving Museum
MUSEUM

(📱305-664-9737; www.divingmuseum.org; Mile 83; adult/child $12/6; ⊙10am-5pm; P 🖢) You can't miss the diving museum – it's the building with the enormous mural of whale sharks on the side. The journey into the undersea covers 4000 years, with fascinating pieces like the 1797 Klingert's copper kettle, a whimsical room devoted to Jules Verne's Captain Nemo, massive deep diving suits and an exquisite display of diving helmets from around the world. These imaginative galleries reflect the charming quirks of the Keys.

Windley Key Fossil Reef Geological State Site
STATE PARK

(📱305-664-2540; www.floridastateparks.org/windleykey; Mile 85.5 oceanside; admission/tour $2.50/2; ⊙8am-5pm Thu-Mon) To get his railroad built across the islands, Henry Flagler had to quarry out some sizable chunks of the Keys. The best evidence of those efforts can be found at this former quarry-now-state park. Windley has leftover quarry machinery scattered along an 8ft former quarry wall, with fossilized evidence of brain and staghorn coral imbedded right in the rock. The wall offers a cool (and rare) public peek into the stratum of coral that forms the substrate of the Keys.

There are also various short trails through tropical hardwood hammock that make for a pleasant glimpse into the Keys' wilder side. Borrow a free trail guide from the visitor center. From December to April, ranger-led tours are offered at 10am and 2pm Friday to Sunday for $2.50 per person.

Anne's Beach
BEACH

(Mile 73.5 oceanside; 🖢) Anne's is one of the best beaches in these parts. The small ribbon of sand opens upon a sky-bright stretch of tidal flats and a green tunnel of hammock and wetland. Nearby mudflats are a joy to get stuck in, and will be much loved by the kids.

Rain Barrel Sculpture Gallery
ARTS CENTER

(📱305-852-8935; 86700 Overseas Hwy; ⊙9am-5pm) Once you see the giant lobster, you know you've arrived. Welcome to the Rain Barrel, Islamorada's local artists' village, which is packed with souvenir-y tourist tat, island-themed artwork, pottery, glassworks, wood carvings and plenty of other intrigue.

It's a fine place to browse among the various studios and galleries, and if nothing else, be sure to snap a few pics of/with the giant crustacean.

Indian Key Historic State Park
ISLAND

(📱305-664-2540; www.floridastateparks.org/indiankey; Mile 78.5 oceanside; per person $2.50; ⊙8am-sunset) This quiet island was once a thriving city, complete with a warehouse, docks, streets, a hotel and about 40 to 50 permanent residents. There's not much left at the historic site – just the foundation, some cisterns and jungly tangle. Arriving by boat or kayak is the only way to visit. Robbie's hires out kayaks for the paddle out here – around 30 minutes one way in calm conditions.

Lignumvitae Key Botanical State Park
ISLAND

(📱305-664-2540; www.floridastateparks.org/lignumvitaekey; admission/tour $2.50/2; ⊙8am-5pm Thu-Mon, tours 10am & 2pm Fri-Sun Dec-Apr) This key, only accessible by boat, encompasses a 280-acre island of virgin tropical forest and is home to roughly a zillion jillion mosquitoes. The official attraction is the 1919 **Matheson House**, with its windmill and cistern; the real draw is a nice sense of shipwrecked isolation. From December to April, guided walking tours (1¼ hours) are given at 10am and 2pm Friday to Sunday. You'll have to get here via Robbie's Marina; you can hire kayaks from there (it's about an hour's paddle).

Activities

★ Robbie's Marina BOATING

(☎ 305-664-8070; www.robbies.com; Mile 77.5 bayside; kayak & SUP rentals $45-80; ⏰ 9am-8pm; 👪) More than a boat launch, Robbie's is a local flea market, tacky tourist shop, sea pen for tarpons (massive fish) and jump-off point for fishing expeditions, all wrapped into one driftwood-laced compound. Boat-rental and tour options are also available. The best reason to visit is to escape the mayhem and hire a kayak for a peaceful paddle through nearby mangroves, hammocks and lagoons.

You can also book a snorkeling trip ($38), which takes you out on a very smooth-riding Happy Cat vessel for a chance to bob amid coral reefs. If you don't want to get on the water, you can feed the freakishly large tarpons from the dock ($3.40 per bucket, $2 to watch). There's also a 'party boat' (half-day/night trips $40/45), which is less about revelry and more about catching fish.

Sleeping

Conch On Inn MOTEL $

(☎ 305-852-9309; www.conchoninn.com; 103 Caloosa St, Mile 89.5; r $100-180; P 📶) A motel popular with yearly snowbirds, Conch On Inn has simple but cheerfully painted rooms that are clean, comfortable and well equipped. The waterfront deck is a fine spot to unwind – and look for manatees; up to 14 have been spotted off the dock here!

Ragged Edge Resort RESORT $$

(☎ 305-852-5389; www.ragged-edge.com; 243 Treasure Harbor Rd; apt $100-260; P ❄ 📶 🏊) This low-key and popular apartment complex, far from the maddening traffic jams, has 10 quiet units and friendly hosts. The larger studios have screened-in porches, and the entire vibe is happily comatose. There's no beach, but you can swim off the dock and in the heated pool.

Lime Tree Bay Resort Motel MOTEL $$

(☎ 305-664-4740; www.limetreebayresort.com; Mile 68.5 bayside; r $180-360; ❄ 📶 🏊) A plethora of hammocks and lawn chairs provide front-row seats for the spectacular sunsets at this 2.5-acre waterfront hideaway. The rooms are comfortably set, the best with balconies overlooking the water. The extensive facilities include use of tennis courts, bikes, kayaks and stand-up paddleboards.

Casa Morada HOTEL $$$

(☎ 305-664-0044; www.casamorada.com; 136 Madeira Rd, off Mile 82.2; ste incl breakfast $430-680; P ❄ 📶 🏊) Contemporary chic comes to Islamorada, but it's not gentrifying away the village vibe. Rather, the Casa adds a welcome dab of sophistication to Conch chill: a keystone standing circle, freshwater pool, artificial lagoon, plus a *Wallpaper*-magazine-worthy bar that overlooks Florida Bay – all make this boutique hotel worth a reservation. Go to the bar to catch a drink and a sunset.

Ask about yoga on the pier, private sunset sails on a 30ft Skipjack, and kayak or stand-up paddleboard tours.

Eating

Bad Boy Burrito MEXICAN $

(☎ 305-509-7782; www.badboyburrito.com/islamorada; 103 Mastic St, Mile 81.8 bayside; mains $8-15; ⏰ 10am-6pm Mon-Sat; 🌿) Tucked away in a tiny plaza among a gurgling fountain, orchids and swaying palms, Bad Boy Burrito whips up superb fish tacos and its namesake burritos – with quality ingredients (skirt steak, duck confit, zucchini and squash) and all the fixings (shaved cabbage, chipotle mayo, housemade salsa). Top it off with a hibiscus tea and some chips and guacamole.

Midway Cafe CAFE $

(☎ 305-664-2622; www.midwaycafecoffeebar.com; 80499 Overseas Hwy; mains $7-10; ⏰ 7am-3pm Mon-Sat, to 2pm Sun; P 📶 👪) The lovely folks who run this cafe – stuffed with every variety of heart-warming art the coffee-shop trope can muster – roast their own beans, make delectable baked goods and whip up tasty sandwiches, salads, wraps and omelets. You're almost in the Middle Keys: celebrate making it this far with a cup of joe – best enjoyed on the tiny patio beside the cafe.

Bob's Bunz CAFE $

(www.bobsbunz.com; Mile 81.6 bayside; mains $8-15; ⏰ 6am-2pm; P 🌿) The service at this cute cafe is energetic and friendly in an only-in-America kinda way, and the food is fine, filling and cheap. Key lime pie is a classic Keys dish and key lime anything at this bakery is highly regarded, so buy that souvenir pie here.

★ **Lazy Days** SEAFOOD $$
(☎ 305-664-5256; www.lazydaysislamorada.com; 79867 Overseas Hwy, oceanside; mains $18-34; 🅿️ ⬛) One of Islamorada's culinary icons, Lazy Days has a stellar reputation for its fresh seafood plates. Start off with a conch chowder topped with a little sherry (provided), before moving on to a decadent hogfish Poseidon (fish topped with shrimp, scallops and key lime butter) or a straight-up boiled seafood platter (half lobster, shrimp, catch of the day and other delicacies).

Bayside Gourmet AMERICAN $$
(www.baysidegourmet.com; Mile 82.7 bayside; mains breakfast $8-10, lunch & dinner $10-22; ⊙6am-9:30pm Mon-Sat, to 2pm Sun) This stylish, modern, but very friendly deli and restaurant is a family-run affair and feels quite a step up from the average Keys seafood shack. The diverse menu serves up something for all palates, from pancakes and breakfast burritos to grouper sandwiches, lasagna and delicious thin-crust pizzas.

Beach Cafe at Morada Bay AMERICAN $$$
(☎ 305-664-0604; www.moradabay.com/the-beach-cafe; Mile 81.6 bayside; mains lunch $15-22, dinner $22-39; ⊙11:30am-10pm Sun-Thu, to 11pm Fri & Sat; 🅿️) The Beach Cafe has a lot going for it, namely a lovely, laid-back Caribbean vibe, a powder-white sandy beach, nighttime torches, tapas and fresh seafood. It's also a good place to bring the kids, with room to run around, and the adults can come back for a monthly full-moon party, with live music, special cocktails and a beach barbecue.

🍸 Drinking & Nightlife

Florida Keys Brewing Co MICROBREWERY
(☎ 305-916-5206; www.floridakeysbrewingco.com; 200 Morada Way, Mile 81.6; ⊙noon-10pm) Of the two microbreweries in Islamorada, this is the one not to miss. It's locally owned and operated, with excellent beer brewed on site. Come in to the friendly tap room, order a flight and have a chat with one of the brewmasters who's usually on hand.

Morada Bay BAR
(☎ 305-664-0604; www.moradabay.com; Mile 81.6 bayside; ⊙5pm-midnight) In addition to its excellent food, Morada Bay holds monthly full-moon parties that attract the entire party-people population of the Keys. The whole shebang typically starts around 9pm and goes until whenever the last person passes out; check website for dates.

🛍 Shopping

Old Road Gallery ARTS & CRAFTS
(☎ 305-852-8935; Mile 88.8 oceanside; ⊙10am-5pm) Specializing in pottery, painting and sculpture, the Old Road Gallery embodies the Key's most creative side. After browsing the shop, take a stroll through the forested grounds, which are decorated with small, carefully placed works of art. This is one-of-a-kind souvenir shopping.

❶ Getting There & Away
The Greyhound bus stops at the Burger King at Mile Marker 82.5 oceanside. It goes twice daily to both Key West and Miami.

MIDDLE KEYS
On this stretch of the Keys, the bodies of water get wider, and the bridges get more impressive. This is where you'll find the famous Seven Mile Bridge, one of the world's longest causeways and a natural divider between the Middle and Lower Keys. In this stretch of islands you'll cross specks like Conch Key and Duck Key; green, quiet Grassy Key; as well as Key Vaca, where Marathon, the second-largest town and most Key-sy community in the islands, is located.

Grassy Key

⊙ Sights

Curry Hammock State Park STATE PARK
(☎ 305-289-2690; www.floridastateparks.org/curryhammock; Mile 56.2 bayside; car/cyclist $5/2; ⊙8am-sunset; 🅿️ ⬛) 🕊 This park is small but sweet and the rangers are just lovely. Like most parks in the Keys, it's a good spot for preserved tropical hardwood and mangrove habitat – a 1.5-mile hike takes you through both environments. Rent a kayak (single/double for two hours $18/22) or stand-up paddleboard ($22 for two hours). You can also camp at the park for $36 per night – sites have toilets and electric hookups.

🛏 Sleeping

Rainbow Bend HOTEL $$$
(☎ 800-929-1505; www.rainbowbend.com; Mile 58 oceanside; r $220-460; 🅿️ 🛜 🏊) You'll be experiencing intensely charming Keys-kitsch in these big pink cabanas, where the apartments and suites are bright, the tiki huts are

shady and the ocean is right there. Half-day use of the Bend's Boston whalers (motorboats), kayaks and canoes is complimentary. The decor is a bit dated, but the beachfront location is outstanding.

Hawk's Cay Resort
RESORT $$$
(☑ 305-743-7000; www.hawkscay.com; 61 Hawk's Cay Blvd, Duck Key, off Mile 61 oceanside; r $390-700; ⓟ⌔⌖) The Cay is an enormous luxury compound with silky-plush rooms and nicely appointed townhouses, as well as countless island activities. The resort's most concerning feature is the 'Dolphin Connection' program, where guests can interact and swim with captive dolphins. Animal welfare groups claim keeping dolphins inside an enclosed tank is debilitating for the animals, and is made worse by human interaction.

Eating

Grassy Key Outpost
AMERICAN $$
(☑ 305-743-7373; www.grassykeyoutpost.com; 58152 Overseas Hwy; mains $10-29; ⊙8am-9pm, market until 10pm; ⓟ⌔) Equal parts market and restaurant, the Outpost is an interesting spot that skews between fine dining and Keys casualness, both in terms of atmosphere and cuisine. There's a Southern flair to the gastronomy; shrimp and grits comes rich and smoky, while the mac 'n' cheese is laced with decadent slathers of rich lobster.

SS Wreck Galley & Grill
AMERICAN $$
(☑ 305-517-6484; www.wreckgalleygrill.com; Mile 59 bayside; mains $10-26; ⊙11am-9:30pm Tue-Sun; ⓟ) The SS Wreck is a Keys classic, where fisherman types knock back brew and feast on wings. It's definitely a local haunt, where island politicos like to prattle about the issues (fishing). The food is excellent: it grills one of the best burgers in the Keys, and fires up excellent daily specials.

Marathon
☑ 305, 786 / POP 8625

Marathon sits right on the halfway point between Key Largo and Key West, and it's a good place to stop on a road trip across the islands. It's perhaps the most 'developed' key outside Key West (that's really pushing the definition of the word 'developed') in the sense that it has large shopping centers and a population of over 8000. Then again it's still a place where exiles from the mainland fish, booze it up and have a good time, so while Marathon is more family-friendly than Key West, it's hardly G-rated.

⊙ Sights

Florida Keys Aquarium Encounters
AQUARIUM
(☑ 305-407-3262; www.floridakeysaquarium encounters.com; 11710 Overseas Hwy, Mile 53.1 bayside; adult/child $20/15, animal encounters from $30; ⊙9am-5pm; ⌖) A visit to this small, interactive aquarium starts with a free 20-minute guided

---

DOLPHINS IN CAPTIVITY

Aquariums and marine life centers are popular destinations in Florida, particularly those with shows featuring dolphins and other marine mammals. Some even offer one-on-one interaction with dolphins. While swimming across a pool being towed by Flipper may sound like a memorable photo op, such practices raise deep ethical concerns.

The harsh reality of life for dolphins in captivity is hidden from visitors. Dolphins are highly intelligent and complex animals, and an artificial environment prevents them from communicating, hunting, playing and mating as they would in the wild. The stress of living in captivity often leads to a greater incidence of illness, disease and behavioral abnormalities. As a result, dolphins in captivity often live much shorter lives than those in the wild. Those dolphins that remain 'voluntarily' in captivity often do so simply to remain close to food.

As more people become aware of the harm caused to marine mammals kept in captivity, some aquariums in the US are scrapping their dolphin programs. The Baltimore Aquarium, for instance, announced it would remove its dolphins by 2020 and provide a seaside sanctuary for those unable to survive in the wild. For the moment, however, no Florida aquariums have followed suit. You can read more about captive marine life at World Animal Protection (www.worldanimalprotection.us.org), Whale and Dolphin Conservation (www. whales.org/issues/swimming-with-dolphins) and the World Cetacean Alliance (www.world cetaceanalliance.org).

tour of some fascinating marine ecosystems. There are also more immersive experiences, where you snorkel in the coral reef aquarium or the tropical fish–filled lagoon. More controversial are the 'animal encounters' and 'touch tanks' where you can handle shallow water marine species and touch stingrays (the barbs have been removed). The stress of human interaction can be detrimental to the well-being of aquatic creatures (p181).

Some of the ecosystems you will encounter include a mangrove-lined basin full of tarpon, a tidal pool tank with queen conch and horseshoe crabs, and a 200,000-gallon coral reef tank with moray eels, grouper and several different shark species.

You can also observe mesmerizing lionfish, a pig-nosed turtle, juvenile alligators and various fish species from the Everglades, plus snowy egrets and little blue herons that come by for a visit.

Crane Point Museum
MUSEUM

(☑ 305-743-9100; www.cranepoint.net; Mile 50.5 bayside; adult/child $15/10; � 9am-5pm Mon-Sat, from noon Sun; P 🚻 👶) 🥤 This is one of the nicest spots on the island to stop and smell the roses. And the pinelands. And the palm hammock – a sort of palm jungle (imagine walking under giant, organic Japanese fans) that only grows between Mile Markers 47 and 60. There's also the restored Adderly House, a preserved example of a Bahamian immigrant cabin (which must have been *baked* in summer) and 63 acres of green goodness (with 1.75 miles of trails) to stomp through.

Pigeon Key National Historic District
ISLAND

(☑ 305-743-5999; www.pigeonkey.net; Mile 47 oceanside; adult/child $12/9; �is tours 10am, noon & 2pm) For years tiny Pigeon Key, located 2 miles west of Marathon (basically below the Old Seven Mile Bridge), housed the rail workers and maintenance men who built the infrastructure that connected the Keys. Today you can tour the structures of this National Historic District or relax on the beach and get in some snorkeling. Ferries leave from the bright red caboose on Knight's Key (to the left of the Seven Mile Bridge if you're traveling south) to Pigeon.

Call ahead to confirm ferry departure times; the last one returns at 4pm.

Sombrero Beach
BEACH

(Sombrero Beach Rd, off Mile 50 oceanside; � 7:30am-dusk; P 🚻 👶) This is one of the few white-sand, mangrove-free beaches

in the Keys. It's a good spot to lounge on the sand or swim, and there's also a small playground.

Turtle Hospital
WILDLIFE RESERVE

(☑ 305-743-2552; www.theturtlehospital.org; 2396 Overseas Hwy; adult/child $22/11; �is 8:30am-6pm; P 🚻) 🥤 Be it a victim of disease, boat propeller strike, flipper entanglement with fishing lines or any other danger, an injured sea turtle in the Keys will hopefully end up in this motel-cum-sanctuary. We know we shouldn't anthropomorphize animals, but these turtles just seem so sweet. It's sad to see the injured and sick ones, but heartening to see them so well looked after. Ninety-minute tours are educational, fun and offered on the hour from 9am to 4pm.

🏃 Activities

Wheels-2-Go
KAYAKING

(☑ 305-289-4279; http://wheels-2-go.com; 5994 Overseas Hwy; see-through kayaks/bicycles per day $40/15, single/double kayak per day $30/50; �is 9am-5pm) Friendly kayak- and bicycle-rental services. Staff can advise you of the best spots for kayaking, among mangrove tunnels with some great bird-watching opportunities.

Marathon Kayak
KAYAKING

(☑ 305-395-0355; www.marathonkayak.com; 3hr tours $70) Does guided mangrove ecotours, sunset tours and boat rentals. The three-hour paddle through a canopy of red mangroves is highly recommended.

Tilden's Scuba Center
DIVING

(☑ 305-743-7255; www.tildensscubacenter.com; 4650 Overseas Hwy; snorkel/dive trip $60/70, full scuba gear hire $120) This knowledgeable and respected outfit offers snorkeling and diving expeditions through nearby sections of the coral reef. Can also arrange spear-fishing trips.

🛏 Sleeping

Seascape Motel & Marina
MOTEL $$

(☑ 305-743-6212; www.seascapemotelandmarina. com; 1075 75th St Ocean E, btwn Mile 51 & 52; r $250-450; P ❄ 🛜 👶) The classy, understated luxury in this B&B manifests in its 12 rooms, all of which have a different feel – from old-fashioned cottage to sleek boutique. It has a waterfront pool, kayaks and stand-up paddleboards for guests to use, and its secluded setting will make you feel like you've gotten away from it all. Seascape also hosts afternoon wine and snacks (included).

Ranch House Motel
MOTEL **$$**

(305-743-2217; 7251 Overseas Hwy; r $110-200; ❋ 🛜) For the money, this friendly family-run place right off the highway is one of the best-value lodging options in the Keys. The owners go the extra mile to make guests feel at home.

The rooms are clean and well maintained, if somewhat frozen in the 1970s: wood-paneled walls and floral curtains evoke a bit of Keys nostalgia, while good beds, fridges, microwaves, coffeepots and wall-mounted TVs ensure the added features are up to date.

Tropical Cottages
COTTAGE **$$**

(305-743-6048; www.tropicalcottages.net; 243 61st St; cottages $130-200; P ❋ 🛜 ☀) These pretty pastel cottages are a good option, especially if you're traveling in a larger group. The individual cottages aren't particularly plush, but they're cozy, comfortable and offer a nice bit of privacy, along with some Old Florida atmosphere. There's a small tiki bar where you can relax with a refreshing cocktail.

Sea Dell Motel
MOTEL **$$**

(305-743-5161; www.seadellmotel.com; 5000 Overseas Hwy; r $130-210; P ❋ 🛜 ☀) The Sea Dell is a Keys classic: bright, low-slung rooms with a pastel color scheme and floral bedspreads. The rooms are more or less self-sufficient small apartments, and can comfortably accommodate small families. The small pool entices after a day spent exploring.

Tranquility Bay
RESORT **$$$**

(305-289-0667; www.tranquilitybay.com; Mile 48.5 bayside; r $340-700; P ❋ 🛜 ☀) If you're serious about going upscale, you should book in here. Tranquility Bay is a massive condo-hotel resort with plush townhouses, high-thread-count sheets and all-in-white chic. The grounds are enormous and activity filled; they really don't want you to leave.

🍴 Eating

Wooden Spoon
AMERICAN **$**

(7007 Overseas Hwy; mains $5-12; ☺ 5:30am-1:30pm; P) It's the best breakfast around, served by sweet Southern women who know their way around a diner. The biscuits are fluffy, and they drown so well in that thick, delicious sausage gravy, and the grits are the most buttery soft starch you'll ever have the pleasure of seeing beside your eggs.

★ Keys Fisheries
SEAFOOD **$$**

(866-743-4353; www.keysfisheries.com; 3502 Louisa St; mains $12-27; ☺ 11am-9pm; P 🚻) The lobster Reuben is the stuff of legend here. Sweet, chunky, creamy – so good you'll be daydreaming about it afterwards. But you can't go wrong with any of the excellent seafood here, all served with sass. Expect pleasant levels of seagull harassment as you dine on a working waterfront.

Sunset Grille
AMERICAN **$$**

(305-396-7235; www.sunsetgrille7milebridge.com; 7 Knights Key Blvd, Mile 47 oceanside; mains lunch $10-16, dinner $19-30; 🚻) Overlooking the Seven Mile Bridge, this huge, festive spot has an unbeatable location (it's not called Sunset for nothing) and wide-ranging appeal: namely a huge menu of seafood and grilled meat dishes, plus a raw bar, sushi and plenty of kid-friendly options. There's also an appealing swimming pool (heated in winter) that's free and open to all.

Burdines Waterfront
AMERICAN **$$**

(www.burdineswaterfront.com; 1200 Oceanview Ave, end of 15th St, Mile 48 oceanside; mains $10-18; ☺ noon-9pm; 🚻) For a taste of old-school Marathon, head to this barnlike upper-story shack on the waterfront. It's a much-loved local haunt where you can take a seat around the thatch-roof bar or at a picnic table and take in the breezy views while feasting on hearty home cooking: blackened-fish sandwiches, black beans and rice, handcut fries, shrimp baskets and stone crab soup.

🍸 Drinking & Nightlife

★ Hurricane
BAR

(305-743-2200; Mile 49.5 bayside; ☺ 11am-midnight) Locals, tourists, mad fishermen and rednecks saddle up here for endless Jägerbombs before dancing the night away to any number of consistently good live acts. With sassy staff and heart-warming (strong) drinks, this is one of the best bars before Key West, and it deserves a visit.

Island Fish Company
BAR

(305-743-4191; Mile 54 bayside; ☺ 11:30am-10pm) The Island has a friendly staff pouring strong cocktails on a sea-breeze-kissed tiki island overlooking Florida Bay. Chat with your friendly bartender – tip well, and they'll top up your drinks without you realizing it. The laid-back, by-the-water atmosphere is quintessentially Keys. Pretty sunsets and great seafood plates add to the allure.

Brass Monkey BAR
(☑ 305-743-4028; 5561 Overseas Hwy, oceanside; ⏰ 10am-4am) When Colonel Kurtz whispered, 'The horror, the horror,' in *Apocalypse Now* he was probably thinking about the night he got trashed in this scuzziest of dives, the preferred watering hole for off-the-clock bar- and waitstaff in Marathon. Truth be told, there's much fun to be had here, with cheap drinks, a friendly local crowd and live music nightly.

☆ Entertainment

**Marathon Cinema &
Community Theater** CINEMA
(☑ cinema 305-743-0288, theater 305-743-0994; www.marathontheater.org; 5101 Overseas Hwy) A good, old-school, single-stage theater that shows plays and movies in big reclining seats (with even bigger cup holders).

❶ Information

Fishermen's Hospital (☑ 305-743-5533; www.fishermenshospital.org; 3301 Overseas Hwy; ⏰ 24hr) Has a major emergency room, as well as a walk-in clinic for less severe health issues.

❶ Getting There & Away

You can fly into the **Marathon Airport** (☑ 305-289-6060; Mile 50.5 bayside) or go with

Greyhound, which stops at the airport. There's also regular bus service to Key West on **Key West Transit** (p174).

LOWER KEYS

The people of the Lower Keys vary between winter escapees and native Conchs. Some local families have been Keys castaways for generations, and there is somewhat of a more insular feel than other parts of the Overseas Hwy. It's an odd contrast: the islands get at their most isolated, rural and quintessentially 'Keez-y' before opening onto (relatively) cosmopolitan, heterogeneous and free-spirited Key West.

People aside, the big draw in the lower Keys is nature. You'll find the loveliest state park in the Keys here, and one of its rarest species. For paddlers, there is a great mangrove wilderness to explore in a photogenic and pristine environment.

Big Pine Key, Bahia Honda Key & Looe Key

Big Pine is home to endless stretches of quiet roads, Key West employees who found a way around astronomical real-estate rates,

---

NATURAL WONDERS OF THE KEYS

It's easy to think of the Keys, environmentally speaking, as a little boring. The landscape isn't particularly dramatic (with the exception of those sweet sweeps of ocean visible from the Overseas Hwy); it tends toward low brush and...well, more low brush.

Hey, don't judge a book by its cover. The Keys have one of the most remarkable, sensitive environments in the US. The difference between ecosystems here is measured in inches, but once you learn to recognize the contrast between a hammock and a wetland, you'll see the islands in a whole new tropical light. Some of the best introductions to the natural Keys can be found at Crane Point Museum (p182) and the Florida Keys Eco-Discovery Center (p191).

But we want to focus on the mangroves – the coolest, if not most visually arresting, habitat in the islands. They rise from the shallow shelf that surrounds the Keys (which also provides that lovely shade of Florida teal), looking like masses of spidery fingers constantly stroking the waters. Each mangrove traps the sediment that has accrued into the land your tiki bar stool is perched on. That's right, no mangroves = no Jimmy Buffett.

The three different types of mangrove trees are all little miracles of adaptation. Red mangroves, which reside on the water's edge, have aerial roots, called propagules, allowing them to 'breathe' even as they grow into the ocean. Black mangroves, which grow further inland, survive via 'snorkel' roots called pneumatophores. Resembling spongy sticks, these roots grow out from the muddy ground and consume fresh air. White mangroves grow furthest inland and actually sweat out the salt they absorb through air and water to keep healthy.

The other tree worth a mention here isn't a mangrove. The lignum vitae, which is limited to the Keys in the US, is also intriguing. Its sap has long been used to treat syphilis, hence the tree's Latin name, which translates to 'tree of life.'

and packs of wandering Key deer. Bahia Honda has everyone's favorite sandy beach, while the coral-reef system of Looe offers amazing reef-diving opportunities.

◎ Sights

★ Bahia Honda State Park   STATE PARK

(📞 305-872-3210;   www.bahiahondapark.com; Mile 37; car $4-8, cyclist & pedestrian $2.50; ⏰ 8am-sunset; 🖟) 🏊 This park, with its long, white-sand (and at times seaweed-strewn) beach, named Sandspur Beach by locals, is the big attraction in these parts. As Keys beaches go, this one is probably the best natural stretch of sand in the island chain. There's also the novel experience of walking on the **old Bahia Honda Rail Bridge**, which offers nice views of the surrounding islands. Heading out on kayaking adventures (from $12/36 per hour/half day) is another great way to spend a sun-drenched afternoon.

You can also check out the nature trails and science center, where helpful park employees can assist you to identify stone crabs, fireworms, horseshoe crabs and comb jellies. The park concession offers daily 1½-hour snorkeling trips at 9:30am and 1:30pm (adult/child $30/25). Reserve ahead in high season.

No Name Key   ISLAND

Perhaps the best-named island in the Keys, No Name gets few visitors, as it's basically a residential island. It's one of the most reliable spots for Key deer watching. From Overseas Hwy, go on to Watson Blvd, turn right, then left onto Wilder Blvd. Cross Bogie Bridge and you'll be on No Name.

National Key Deer
Refuge Headquarters   WILDLIFE RESERVE

(📞 305-872-0774; www.fws.gov/refuge/National_Key_Deer_Refuge; Big Pine Shopping Center, Mile 30.5 bayside; ⏰ 9am-4pm Mon-Fri, 10am-3pm Sat & Sun; 🖟) What would make Bambi cuter? Mini Bambi. Introducing: the Key deer, an endangered subspecies of white-tailed deer that prance about primarily on Big Pine and No Name Keys. The folks here are an incredibly helpful source of information on the deer and all things Keys. The refuge sprawls over several islands, but the sections open to the public are on Big Pine and No Name.

The headquarters also administers the **Great White Heron National Wildlife Refuge** – 200,000 acres of open water and mangrove islands north of the main Keys that is only accessible by boat. There's no tourism infrastructure in place to get out here, but you can inquire about nautical charts and the heron themselves at the office.

Blue Hole   LAKE

(off Mile 30.5) This little pond (and former quarry) is now the largest freshwater body in the Keys. That's not saying much, but the hole is a pretty little dollop of blue (well, algal green) surrounded by a small path and information signs. The water is home to turtles, fish and wading birds. A quarter-mile further along the same road is **Watson's Nature Trail** (less than 1 mile long) and **Watson's Hammock**, a small Keys forest habitat.

Looe Key National
Marine Sanctuary   PARK

(📞 305-809-4700; www.floridakeys.noaa.gov) Looe (pronounced 'loo') Key, located 5 nautical miles off Big Pine, isn't a key at all but a reef, part of the Florida Keys National Marine Sanctuary. This is an area of some 2800 square nautical miles of 'land' managed by the National Oceanic & Atmospheric Administration. The reef here can only be visited through a specially arranged charter-boat trip, best arranged through any Keys diving outfit, the most natural one being Looe Key Dive Center (p186).

Big Pine Flea Market   MARKET

(www.bigpinefleamarket.com; Mile 30.5 oceanside; ⏰ 8am-2pm Sat & Sun, closed Aug & Sep; 🅿) **FREE** This market, which attracts folks from across the Keys, rivals local churches for weekly attendance. This is an extravaganza of locally made crafts, vintage clothes, handbags, sunglasses, souvenir T-shirts and beach towels, wood carvings, wind chimes and hand tools – plus all the second hand gear you might need for a fishing trip.

🏃 Activities

Serenity Eco Therapy   WATER SPORTS

(📞 305-432-1401;   www.serenityecoguides.com; beach yoga from $12, 2hr paddleboard class $85; 🖟) If you're into yoga and/or stand-up paddle surfing – or just curious about trying something completely new – book a class with Serenity. This outfit runs special yoga-SUP classes on the water, as well as beachfront yoga, meditation and sunset paddles. Most classes are held in Bahia Honda State Park.

Old Wooden Bridge Marina BOATING
(☑ 305-872-2241; 1791 Bogie Dr; 2hr single/double kayak ride $25/35, bike hire half/full day $15/20; ☺ 8am-5pm Sun-Thu, to 6pm Fri & Sat) At the foot of the bridge that takes you over to No Name Key, there's a little wooden shack on the marina where you can hire kayaks and bicycles for the day (plus get staples like beer inside the shop). This is a lovely area to explore either on the water or on two wheels.

Looe Key Dive Center DIVING
(☑ 305-872-2215; www.diveflakeys.com; snorkel/dive from $40/70) Located in a resort of the same name, the Looe Key Dive Center on Ramrod Key runs recommended day trips out to Looe Key departing in morning (at 8am) and afternoon (12:45pm). This two-tank/two-location dive is $70 plus gear for scuba divers, $40 plus gear for snorkelers, and $25 for 'bubblewatchers' who want to come along for the ride.

🛏 Sleeping

★ Bahia Honda State Park Campground CAMPGROUND $
(☑ 800-326-3521; www.reserveamerica.com; Mile 37, Bahia Honda Key; campsites/cabins $40/160; P ☎) ✎ Bahia Honda has the best camping in the Keys. There's nothing quite like waking up to the sky as your ceiling and the ocean as your shower (and: Ow! Sand flies. OK, it's not paradise...). The park has six cabins, each sleeping six people, and 80 campsites a short distance from the beach. Reserve months in advance.

Barnacle Bed & Breakfast B&B $$
(☑ 305-872-3298; www.thebarnacle.net; 1557 Long Beach Dr, Big Pine Key; r $220-290; P ❄ ☎) The Barnacle welcomes you into its atrium with the promise of fresh ocean breezes. Wander around the pond and Jacuzzi, past the swinging hammocks, and into highly individualized rooms that all share a lovingly mad design sense. Tropical knickknacks and big windows that let in lots of Keys sunlight are standard. Meals should be enjoyed on the deck, which overlooks the sea.

★ Deer Run Bed & Breakfast B&B $$$
(☑ 305-872-2015; www.deerrunfloridabb.com; 1997 Long Beach Dr, Big Pine Key, off Mile 33 oceanside; r $300-480; P ❄ ☎ ☷) ✎ This state-certified green lodge and vegetarian B&B is isolated on a lovely stretch of Long Beach Dr. It's a garden of quirky delights, complemented by love-the-earth paraphernalia, street signs

and four simple but cozy rooms. The helpful owners will get you out on a boat or into the heated pool for relaxation while they whip up delicious vegetarian meals.

🍴 Eating

No Name Pub PIZZA $
(☑ 305-872-9115; www.nonamepub.com; N Watson Blvd, Big Pine Key, off Mile 30.5 bayside; mains $10-21; ☺ 11am-10pm; P) The No Name's one of those off-the-track places that everyone seems to know about. Despite the isolated location, folks come from all over to this divey spot to add their dollar bills to the walls, drink locally brewed beer, enjoy a little classic rock playing overhead, and feast on excellent pizzas, burgers and pub grub.

Good Food Conspiracy VEGETARIAN $
(☑ 305-872-3945; Big Pine Key, Mile 30 oceanside; sandwiches $8-14; ☺ 9:30am-7pm Mon-Sat, 11am-5pm Sun; P ✎) ✎ Rejoice health-food lovers: all the greens, sprouts, herbs and tofu you've been dreaming about during that long, fried-food-studded drive down the Overseas Hwy are available at this friendly little macrobiotic organic shop. There is a good sandwich and fresh-juice bar on site, where you can get avocado melts, fresh salads, veggie burgers, homemade soup and fruit smoothies.

🍷 Drinking & Nightlife

Kiki's Sandbar BAR
(☑ 305-872-4500; www.kikissandbar.com; 183 Barry Ave, Mile 28.3 bayside; ☺ 8am-midnight) For drinks with a view, Kiki's is hard to beat. You can have a chat around the bar or retreat for a bit of sunset watching or stargazing from one of the picnic tables on the waterfront lawn – or better yet stroll to the pier, which can be a magical setting when the moon is on the rise.

❶ Getting There & Away

Greyhound (www.greyhound.com) has two buses daily that stop in Big Pine Key on the run between Miami and Key West (one-way from $9).

Key West Transit (p174) runs nine buses daily between Key West and Marathon, stopping in Big Pine Key. The one-way fare is $4.

Sugarloaf Key & Boca Chica Key

This is the final stretch before the holy grail of Key West. There's not much going on – just bridges over lovely swaths of teal and turquoise, a few good eats and a thoroughly batty roadside attraction.

This lowest section of the Keys goes from about Mile Marker 20 to the start of Key West.

⊙ Sights

Sheriff's Animal Farm   ZOO
(Monroe County Sheriff's Office Animal Farm; ✎305-293-7300; 5501 College Rd, Stock Island; ⊙1-3pm 2nd & 4th Sun of the month or by appointment; ⓟⓐ) ⬤ⓕⓡⓔⓔ Just before you hit Key West, you may be tempted to stop at this farm, located near the Monroe County Sheriff's Office and Detention Center (seriously). This shelter for Monroe County animals that have been abandoned or given up is a lovely place to take the kids (call ahead to visit and farmer Jeanne Selander will be happy to show you around).

Sugarloaf Key Bat Tower   LANDMARK
(Sugarloaf Key, Mile17) It resembles an Aztec-inspired fire lookout, but this wooden tower is actually one real-estate developer's vision gone utterly awry. In the 1920s Richter C Perky had the bright idea to transform this area into a vacation resort. There was just one problem: mosquitoes. His solution? Build a 35ft tower and move in a colony of bats (he'd heard they eat mosquitoes). He imported the flying mammals, but they promptly took off, leaving the tower empty.

The tower is in bad shape, and there's no access to the top.

🛏 Sleeping & Eating

Sugarloaf Lodge   MOTEL $$
(✎305-745-3211; www.sugarloaflodge.net; Sugarloaf Key, Mile 17; r $150-240; ⓟ❄🛜🏊) The 55 motel-like rooms are nothing special, though every single one has an excellent bay view from the balcony or patio (1st floor). There is also an on-site restaurant, a tiki bar, a marina and an airstrip, from which you can charter a seaplane tour or go skydiving. Friendly service.

Baby's Coffee   CAFE $
(✎305-744-9866; Mile 15 oceanside; ⊙6:30am-8pm Mon-Sat, 7am-5pm Sun) This very cool coffee counter has an on-site bean-roasting plant and sells bags of the aromatic stuff along with excellent hot and cold java brews – many locals consider this to be some of the best coffee in the islands. Other essentials are sold, from yummy baked goods to fruit smoothies.

Mangrove Mama's   CARIBBEAN $$
(✎305-745-3030; www.mangrovemamas20. com; Mile 20 bayside; lunch $10-15, dinner $15-29; ⊙8am-10pm; ⓟⓐ) This groovy roadside eatery serves Caribbean-inspired seafood – coconut shrimp, plantain-crusted hogfish, cracked conch sandwiches – best enjoyed on the backyard patio and accompanied by a little live music (daily from 5:30pm).

Square Grouper   MODERN AMERICAN $$$
(✎305-745-8880; www.squaregrouperbarandgrill. com/menu; Mile 22.5 oceanside, Cudjoe Key; mains $22-39; ⊙11am-2:30pm & 5-10pm Tue-Sat; ✎) ⬤ One of the most talked-about restaurants in the Keys, Square Grouper hits all the right notes with fresh, locally sourced ingredients, innovative recipes and great service, all dished up in one elegant but unpretentious dining room. Local fish-of-the-day tacos, seared sesame-encrusted tuna loin and a rich seafood stew are among the highlights, though it's worth investigating daily specials.

Reserve ahead. And don't forget to have a pre- or post-dinner drink in the upstairs lounge My New Joint.

🍸 Drinking & Nightlife

★ My New Joint   COCKTAIL BAR
(✎305-745-8880; www.mynewjoint420lounge. com; Mile 22.5, Cudjoe Key; ⊙4:20pm-midnight Mon-Sat) My New Joint brings a serious dash of style to the Lower Keys. This spacious, warmly lit lounge has artfully made cocktails, excellent brews on tap (including local varieties), great tapas plates and platters of oysters, and live music most nights (from 7pm or 8pm). Nibble on house-smoked fish, charred Brussels sprouts, soft-shell crab steamed buns and other gourmet sharing plates.

ⓘ Getting There & Away

Key West Transit (p174) runs nine buses a day between Key Wet and Marathon, stopping in both Boca Chica and Sugarloaf Key. The one-way fare is $4.

KEY WEST

✎305, 786 / POP 26,000

Key West is the far frontier, edgier and more eccentric than the other keys, and also far more captivating. At its heart, this 7-sq-mile island feels like a beautiful tropical oasis, where the moonflowers bloom at night and

Key West

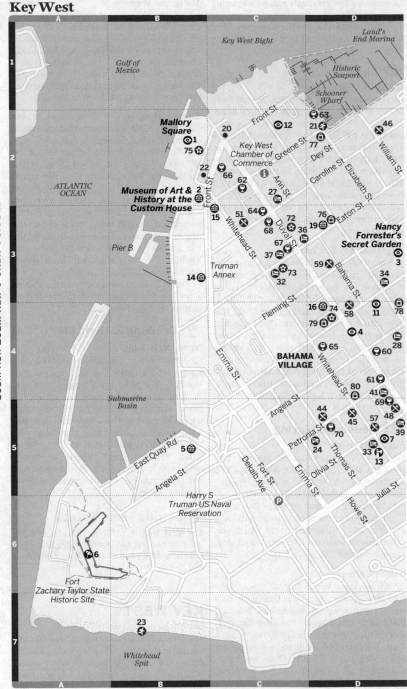

Gulf of Mexico

Key West Bight

Land's End Marina

Historic Seaport

Schooner Wharf

Front St

Mallory Square

20

12

63

21

77

46

William St

1

75

22

66

62

Key West Chamber of Commerce

Greene St

Dey St

Caroline St

Elizabeth St

ATLANTIC OCEAN

Museum of Art & History at the Custom House

2

Ann St

27

Eaton St

Nancy Forrester's Secret Garden

15

51

64

76

19

3

Whitehead St

Duval St

72

68

36

34

Pier B

67

37

59

Bahama St

32

73

Truman Annex

14

Fleming St

16

74

58

11

78

79

BAHAMA VILLAGE

65

4

60

28

Emma St

Whitehead St

80

61

41

69

Submarine Basin

Angela St

44

45

57

48

Petronia St

70

24

Thomas St

33

7

13

39

East Quay Rd

5

Fort St

Dekalb Ave

Emma St

Olivia St

Howe St

Julia St

Angela St

Harry S Truman US Naval Reservation

P

7

6

Fort Zachary Taylor State Historic Site

23

Whitehead Spit

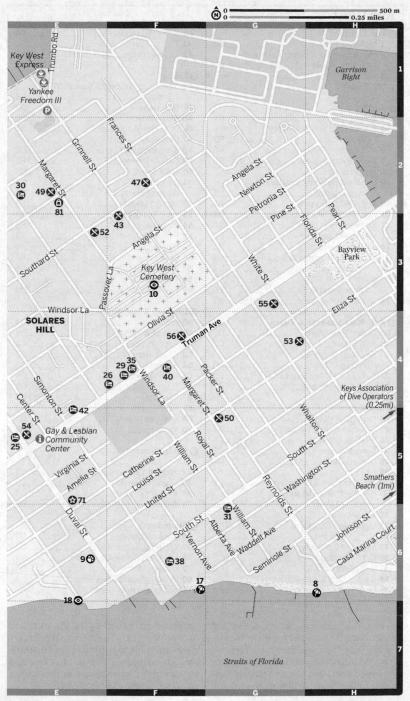

0   500 m
0   0.25 miles

Garrison Bight

Key West Express

Yankee Freedom III

Trumbo Rd

Grinnell St

Frances St

Margaret St

30

49

81

43

52

47

Angela St

Newton St

Petronia St

Pine St

Florida St

Pearl St

Southard St

Passover La

Key West Cemetery

10

White St

Bayview Park

Windsor La

SOLARES HILL

Olivia St

56

Truman Ave

55

Eliza St

53

Simonton St

29 35

26 40

Center St

42

54

25

Gay & Lesbian Community Center

Windsor La

Packer St

Margaret St

Royal St

William St

Catherine St

Louisa St

United St

Virginia St

Amelia St

71

Duval St

9

38

South St

Vernon Ave

Alberta Ave

Waddell Ave

William St

31

Reynolds St

South St

Washington St

Whalton St

Keys Association of Dive Operators (0.25mi)

50

Smathers Beach (1mi)

Seminole St

Johnson St

Casa Marina Court

18

17

8

Straits of Florida

Key West

the classical Caribbean homes are so sad and romantic it's hard not to sigh at them.

While Key West has obvious allure, it's not without its contradictions. On one side of the road, there are literary festivals, Caribbean villas, tropical dining rooms and expensive art galleries. On the other, an S&M fetishist parade, frat boys passing out on the sidewalk and grizzly bars filled with bearded burnouts. With all that in mind, it's easy to find your groove in this setting, no matter where your interests lie.

As in other parts of the Keys, nature plays a starring role here, with some breathtaking sunsets – cause for nightly celebration down on Mallory Sq.

◉ Sights

★ Mallory Square
SQUARE

(www.mallorysquare.com;) Take all those energies, subcultures and oddities of Keys life and focus them into one torchlit, family-friendly (but playfully edgy), sunset-enriched street party. The child of all these raucous forces is Mallory Sq, one of the greatest shows on Earth. It begins in the hours leading up to dusk, the sinking sun a signal to bring on the madness. Watch a dog walk a tightrope, a man swallow fire, and British acrobats tumble and sass each other.

★ Museum of Art & History at the Custom House
MUSEUM

(☑ 305-295-6616; www.kwahs.com; 281 Front St; adult/child $10/5; ⊙ 9:30am-4:30pm) Those wanting to learn a bit about Key West history shouldn't miss this excellent museum at the end of the road. Among the highlights: photographs and archival footage from the building of the ambitious Overseas Hwy (and the hurricane that killed 400 people), a model of the ill-fated USS *Maine* (sunk during the Spanish-American War) and the Navy's role in Key West (once the largest employer), and exhibits on the 'wreckers' of Key West, who made their fortune scavenging sunken treasure ships.

★ Nancy Forrester's Secret Garden
GARDENS

(www.nancyforrester.com; 518 Elizabeth St; adult/child $10/5; ⊙ 10am-3pm;) Nancy, an environmental artist and fixture of the Keys community, invites you into her backyard oasis where chatty rescued parrots and macaws await visitors. Come at 10am when Nancy gives an overview of these marvelously intelligent and rare birds ('Parrot 101' as she calls it). At other times, Nancy is on hand to answer questions and share insight on parrot life. It's a great place for kids, who often leave inspired by the hands-on interactions.

Duval Street
AREA

Key West locals have a love-hate relationship with the most famous road in Key West (if not the Keys). Duval, Old Town Key West's main strip, is a miracle mile of booze, tacky everything and awful behavior. But it's fun.

The 'Duval Crawl' is one of the wildest pub crawls in the country. The mix of neon drink, drag shows, T-shirt kitsch, local theaters, art studios and boutiques is more charming than jarring.

Hemingway House
HOUSE

(☑ 305-294-1136; www.hemingwayhome.com; 907 Whitehead St; adult/child $14/6; ⊙ 9am-5pm) Key West's biggest darling, Ernest Hemingway, lived in this gorgeous Spanish colonial house from 1931 to 1940. Papa moved here in his early 1930s with wife No 2, a *Vogue* fashion editor and (former) friend of wife No 1 (he left the house when he ran off with wife No 3). *The Short Happy Life of Francis Macomber* and *The Green Hills of Africa* were produced here, as well as many six-toed cats, whose descendants basically run the grounds.

Florida Keys Eco-Discovery Center
MUSEUM

(☑ 305-809-4750; http://eco-discovery.com/ecokw.html; 35 East Quay Rd; ⊙ 9am-4pm Tue-Sat; P) 🌊 FREE This 6000-sq-ft center is one of the best places in the Keys to learn about the extraordinary marine environments of South Florida. Start off with the 20-minute film which has some beautiful footage of life among the reefs, hardwood hammocks, seagrass beds and mangroves. Continue to the exhibits of life above the waterline, then look at sea creatures in the small aquarium tanks that make up the 'Living Reef' section.

Studios of Key West
GALLERY

(TSKW; ☑ 305-296-0458; www.tskw.org; 533 Eaton St; ⊙ 10am-4pm Tue-Sat) FREE This nonprofit showcases about a dozen artists' studios in a three-story space, and hosts some of the best art openings in Key West on the first Thursday of the month. Besides its public visual-arts displays, TSKW hosts readings, literary and visual workshops, concerts, lectures and community discussion groups.

Key West Cemetery
CEMETERY

(www.friendsofthekeywestcemetery.com; cnr Margaret & Angela Sts; ⊙ 7am-6pm;) A darkly alluring Gothic labyrinth beckons at the center of this pastel town. Built in 1847, the cemetery crowns Solares Hill, the highest point on the island (with a vertigo-inducing elevation of 16ft). Some of the oldest families in the Keys rest in peace – and close proximity – here. With body space at a premium, mausoleums stand practically shoulder to shoulder.

Island quirkiness penetrates the gloom: seashells and macramé adorn headstones with inscriptions like, 'I told you I was sick.'

Get chaperoned by a guide from the **Historic Florida Keys Foundation** (☑305-292-6718), with guided tours ($15 per person) that usually go at 9:30am on Tuesdays and Thursdays. Call to reserve a spot.

Fort Zachary Taylor State Park   STATE PARK
(☑305-292-6713; www.floridastateparks.org/fort taylor; 601 Howard England Way; per vehicle/pedestrian/bicycle $7/2.50/2.50; ☺park 8am-sunset, fort 8am-5pm) 'America's Southernmost State Park' is home to an impressive fort, built in the mid-1800s that played roles in the American Civil War and in the Spanish-American War. The **beach** here is the best one Key West has to offer – it has white sand to lounge on (but is rocky in parts), water deep enough to swim in and tropical fish under the waves. Learn more about the fort on free guided tours offered at 11am.

The beach is also a great spot to watch the sunset – a fine alternative to the mayhem of Mallory Sq. But you won't be able to stick around and watch the colors light up the sky: all visitors are ushered out right after the sun sinks below the sea. If coming by foot, it's about a half-mile walk (12 minutes) from the entrance to the beach.

Mel Fisher Maritime Museum   MUSEUM
(www.melfisher.org; 200 Greene St; adult/child $15/12; ☺8:30am-5pm Mon-Fri, from 9:30am Sat & Sun) For a fascinating glimpse into Key West's complicated history, pay a visit to this popular museum near the waterfront. It's best known for its collection of gold coins, rare jewels and other treasures scavenged from Spanish galleons by Mel Fisher and crew. More thought-provoking is the exhibition devoted to the slave trade, with artifacts from the wreck of the *Henrietta Marie,* a merchant slave ship that sank in 1700.

Key West First Legal Rum   DISTILLERY
(☑305-294-1441; www.keywestlegalrum.com; 105 Simonton St; ☺10am-8pm Mon-Sat, to 6pm Sun, tours 1pm, 3pm & 5pm Mon-Fri, 1pm & 3pm Sat) Opened in 2013 by a kitesurfing pioneer, this distillery makes some mighty fine rums, which are made with Florida sugarcane and infused with coconut, vanilla and key lime. Try up to eight rums in the shop for $11, which includes a shot glass. You can also take a self-guided audio tour of the small one-room operation, or come for a livelier chef-guided tour held throughout the week.

Key West Distilling   DISTILLERY
(☑305-295-3400; www.kwdistilling.com; 524 Southard St; ☺10am-5pm Mon-Sat) This tiny craft distiller, basically a one-man operation, creates some excellent rums, two types of vodka (including one with horseradish), one gin and one whiskey. The focus is on quality (rather than quantity), and you won't find a better spiced rum in South Florida than its Rambunctious Rum. Stop in for a free tasting and a tour.

**Fort East Martello
Museum & Gardens**   MUSEUM
(☑305-296-3913; www.kwahs.org/museums/fort-east-martello/history; 3501 S Roosevelt Blvd; adult/child $10/5; ☺9:30am-4:30pm) This old fortress was built to resemble an old Italian Martello-style coastal watchtower (hence the name), a design that quickly became obsolete with the advent of the explosive shell. Now the fort serves a new purpose: preserving the old. There's historical memorabilia, artifacts, the folk art of Mario Sanchez and 'junk' sculptor Stanley Papio, who worked with scrap metal plus a genuinely creepy haunted doll.

Perhaps the most haunted thing in Key West, 'Robert the doll' is a terrifying child's toy from the 19th century who reportedly causes much misfortune to those who question his powers. Honest, he looks like something out of a Stephen King novel; see www.robertthedoll.org for more information.

Little White House   HISTORIC BUILDING
(☑305-294-9911; www.trumanlittlewhitehouse. com; 111 Front St; adult/child 5-12yr/senior $16/5/14; ☺9am-4:30pm) This is where President Harry S Truman used to vacation when he wasn't molding post-WWII geopolitics. It's beautifully preserved and open only for guided tours, although you are welcome to visit one small gallery with photographs and historical displays (and a short video) on the ground floor.

Key West Lighthouse   LIGHTHOUSE
(☑305-294-0012; www.kwahs.org/museums/lighthouse-keepers-quarters/history; 938 Whitehead St; adult/child/senior $10/5/9; ☺9:30am-4:30pm) You can climb up 88 spiraling steps to the top of this snowy white lighthouse, built in 1846, for a decent view (perhaps not as enjoyable as it was in the days when a men's clothing-optional resort was next door, but we digress...). Aside from the views, you can also visit the lighthouse keeper's cottage, which has photographs and artifacts with historical tidbits on life for the keepers of the light.

Key West Butterfly & Nature Conservatory
WILDLIFE RESERVE

(✆305-296-2988; www.keywestbutterfly.com; 1316 Duval St; adult/4-12yr $12/8.50; ☺9am-5pm;) This vast domed conservatory lets you stroll through a lush, enchanting garden of flowering plants, tiny waterfalls, colorful birds and up to 1800 fluttering butterflies made up of over 50 different species – all live imports from around the globe.

Southernmost Point
LANDMARK

(cnr South & Whitehead Sts) Although it's the most-photographed spot on the island, this red-and-black buoy isn't even the southernmost point in the USA (that's in the off-limits naval base around the corner). This is the most-overrated attraction in Key West.

🏃 Activities

Nomadic Standup Paddleboard
WATER SPORTS

(✆305-395-9494; www.nomadicsup.com; 3hr paddleboard tour $65) You can't leave the Keys without getting out on the water. This outfit provides one of the best ways to experience the sublime beauty: on a guided paddleboard outing. Cody will pick you up at your hotel and take you and other guests out to some lovely spots where you will paddle peaceful waterways amid the pristine mangroves northeast of Key West.

Yoga on the Beach
YOGA

(✆305-296-7352; www.yogaonbeach.com; Fort Zachary Taylor State Park; class $18; ☺8:15am-9:45am) If you're a yoga fan, you won't want to miss a session on the beach at Fort Zachary Taylor State Park. The daily 90-minute class, held on the sands overlooking gently lapping waves, is simply exhilarating. Class fee includes park admission for the day, and mats are available.

Reelax Charters
KAYAKING

(✆305-304-1392; www.keyskayaking.com; Sugarloaf Key Marina, Mile 17; all-inclusive kayak trips from $240) Get your paddle on and slip silently into the surrounding mangroves and mudflats of the Lower Keys with Andrea Paulson. Based on Sugarloaf Key, about 17 miles northeast of Key West

Keys Association of Dive Operators
DIVING

(www.divekeys.com) The Key West Association of Dive Operators website is a clearing house for information on all of the diving opportunities in the islands; they also work on enhancing local sustainable underwater activities by creating artificial reefs and encouraging safe boating and diving practices.

Jolly Rover
CRUISE

(✆305-304-2235; www.schoonerjollyrover.com; Schooner Wharf, cnr Greene & Elizabeth Sts; day cruise adult/child $45/25, sunset cruise $59/29) This outfit has a gorgeous, tanbark (reddish-brown) 80ft schooner that embarks on daily two-hour cruises under sail. It looks like a pirate ship and has the cannons to back the image up. You can bring your own food and drink (including alcohol) – small coolers only.

👉 Tours

Conch Tour Train
TOURS

(✆888-916-8687; www.conchtourtrain.com; cnr Front & Duval Sts; adult/child under 13yr/senior $32/free/29; ☺tours 9am-4:30pm;) This tour outfit seats you in breezy linked train cars on a 90-minute narrated tour; there are three stops (including one near the Hemingway House), where you can hop off and take a later train. Offers discounted admission to the Hemingway House as well as Ghosts and Graveyards night tours. The best place to board is at the Front St depot.

BEACHES IN KEY WEST

Key West is *not* about beachgoing. In fact, for true sun 'n' surf, locals go to Bahia Honda whenever possible. Still, the three city beaches on the southern side of the island are lovely and narrow, with calm and clear water.

South Beach Tiny beach at the end of Simonton St.

Higgs Beach Located at the end of Reynolds St and Casa Marina Ct, has barbecue grills, picnic tables and a large pier for watching the sunset. **Smathers Beach**, further east on S Roosevelt Blvd, is a longer stretch of sand, though not easily accessible if you're coming on foot.

Fort Zachary Taylor The best local beach. It's worth the admission to enjoy the white sand and relative calm.

Old Town Trolley Tours   TOURS
(☑ 855-623-8289; www.trolleytours.com/key-west; adult/child/senior $32/11/29; ☺ tours 9am-4:30pm; 🔾) These tours are a great introduction to the city. The 90-minute, hop-on, hop-off narrated tram tour starts at Mallory Sq and makes a loop around the whole city, with 12 stops along the way. Trolleys depart every 15 to 30 minutes from 9am to 4:30pm daily. The narration is hokey, but you'll get a good overview of Key West history.

Key West Ghost & Mysteries Tour   TOURS
(☑ 786-530-3122; www.keywestghostandmysteries tour.com; tours depart from Duval & Caroline Sts; adult/child $18/10; ☺ tours 9pm) A playfully creepy ghost tour that's as family-friendly as this sort of thing gets – in other words, no big chills or pop-out screaming.

🎊 Festivals & Events

Key West Literary Seminar   LITERATURE
(www.kwls.org; ☺ Jan) A feast for the literary minded, this four-day yearly event draws top novelists, poets and historians from around the country (although it costs hundreds of dollars to attend). Most book signings and presentations take place in the **San Carlos Institute** (☑ 305-294-3887; www.institutosan carlos.org; 516 Duval St; ☺ noon-5pm Fri-Sun).

Conch Republic
Independence Celebration   CULTURAL
(www.conchrepublic.com; ☺ Apr) A 10-day tribute to Conch Independence; vie for (made-up) public offices and watch a drag queens' footrace.

Hemingway Days Festival   CULTURAL
(www.fla-keys.com/hemingwaymedia/; ☺ late Jul) This long-running fest brings parties, a 5km run, a fishing tournament, arm-wrestling contests, a 'Papa' look-alike contest and the running of the bulls (with mock animals pulled on wheels).

WomenFest   LGBT
(www.womenfest.com; ☺ Sep) One of North America's biggest lesbian celebrations, WomenFest is four days of merrymaking, with pool parties, art shows, roller derby, drag brunches, sunset sails, flag football, and a tattoo and moustache bicycle ride. It's great fun, with thousands descending on Key West from all corners of the US and beyond.

⭐**Fantasy Fest**   CULTURAL
(www.fantasyfest.net; ☺ late Oct) Akin to New Orleans' riotous Mardi Gras revelry, Fantasy Fest is 10 days of burlesque parties, parades, street fairs, concerts and loads of costumed events. Bars and inns get competitive about decorating their properties, and everyone gets decked out in the most outrageous costumes they can cobble together (or get mostly naked with daring body paint).

Goombay Festival   CULTURAL
(www.goombay-keywest.org; ☺ late Oct; 🔾) Held during the same out-of-control week as Fantasy Fest, this is a Bahamian celebration of food, crafts and culture. The family-friendly event runs over two days (typically a Friday and Saturday).

📥 Sleeping

There's a glut of boutique hotels, cozy B&Bs and four-star resorts here at the end of the USA. Unfortunately, the one thing lacking is inexpensive lodging. Aside from sleeping in the town's only hostel, it's not easy finding a place for under $300 a night during the high season. Although some options are more central than others, any hotel in Old Town is within walking distance of all the action.

Casablanca Key West   GUESTHOUSE $$

(📞 305-296-0815; www.keywestcasablanca.com; 900 Duval St; r $180-400; ✳🕏☎) On the quieter end of Duval St, the Casablanca is a friendly eight-room guesthouse with a delightful tropical elegance. The inn, once a private house, was built in 1898 and hosted a few luminaries over the years, including Humphrey Bogart who stayed here in 1937. The rooms are bright with polished wood floors and comfy beds; and some have little balconies.

Old Town Manor   BOUTIQUE HOTEL $$

(📞 305-292-2170; www.oldtownmanor.com; 511 Eaton St; $200-310; ✳☎☏) While it bills itself as a B&B (and breakfast is included), the Old Town feels more like a boutique operation that offers a wide variety of rooms – 14, to be exact, spread amid lush gardens. The digs come in the usual tropically inspired palette (the lime-green walls in some rooms may be too much for some), with quality furnishings.

L'Habitation   GUESTHOUSE $$

(📞 305-293-9203; www.lhabitation.com; 408 Eaton St; r $200-250; ✳☎) A beautiful, classical Keys cottage, L'Habitation has fine rooms kitted out in light tropical shades, with lamps that look like contemporary art pieces and cozy quilts. The friendly bilingual owner welcomes guests in English or French. The front porch, shaded by palms, is a perfect place to stop and engage in Keys people-watching.

Key West Bed & Breakfast   B&B $$

(📞 305-296-7274; www.keywestbandb.com; 415 William St; r $90-280; ✳☎) Sunny, airy and full of artistic touches: hand-painted pottery here, a working loom there – is that a ship's masthead in the corner? There is also a range of rooms to fit every budget.

Key Lime Inn   HOTEL $$

(📞 800-549-4430; www.historickeywestinns.com; 725 Truman Ave; r from $200; P☎☏) These cozy rooms are all scattered around a tropical hardwood backdrop. Inside, the blissfully cool rooms are greener than a jade mine, with tiny flat-screen TVs and artwork on the walls – plus French doors opening onto balconies in some. Start the morning with coffee and breakfast by the pool.

Chelsea House   HOTEL $$

(📞 305-294-5229; www.historickeywestinns.com/the-inns/chelsea-house; 707 Truman Ave; r low season/high season from $200/from $250; P✳@☎☏) This perfect pair of Victorian mansions beckons with big, comfy beds and classy decor. The old-school villa ambience clashes – in a nice way – with the happy vibe of the guests and the folks at reception. Some rooms are quite small and lack windows; make sure you inquire before booking. The tropical gardens make a peaceful setting after a day of exploring.

Caribbean House   GUESTHOUSE $$

(📞 305-296-0999; www.caribbeanhousekw.com; 226 Petronia St; r from $159; P✳☎) This is a cute, dollhouse-like Caribbean cottage in the heart of Bahama Village. The 10 small, brightly colored guest rooms aren't too fancy, but it's a happy, cozy bargain for Key West. The best rooms have small balconies.

Key West Youth Hostel & Seashell Motel   HOSTEL $$

(📞 305-296-5719; www.keywesthostel.com; 718 South St; dm $55, d $120-240; P✳☎) This place isn't winning any design awards, but the staff are kind, and it's one of the only lower-priced choices on the island. The dorms and motel rooms have plain white tile floors, though the cheery paint job in some rooms (yellow or blue and white) somewhat breaks the monotony. The back patio is a fine place to meet other travelers.

⭐ Mermaid & the Alligator   GUESTHOUSE $$$

(📞 305-294-1894; www.kwmermaid.com; 729 Truman Ave; r winter $330-380, summer $230-290; P✳☎☏) It takes a real gem to stand out amid the jewels of Keys hotels, but this place, in a 1904 mansion, more than pulls off the job. Each of the nine rooms is individually designed with a great mix of modern comfort, Keys Colonial ambience and playful laughs.

Tropical Inn   BOUTIQUE HOTEL $$$

(📞 888-611-6510; www.tropicalinn.com; 812 Duval St; r $275-500; ✳☎☏) The Tropical Inn has excellent service and a host of individualized rooms spread out over a historic home property. Each room comes decked out in bright pastels and shades of mango, lime and seafoam. A delicious breakfast is included and can be enjoyed in the jungly courtyard next to a lovely sunken pool.

Gardens Hotel
HOTEL $$$

(☎305-294-2661; www.gardenshotel.com; 526 Angela St; r $400-700; P✴🖂) Would we be stating the obvious if we mentioned this place has really nice gardens? In fact, the rooms are located in the Peggy Mills Botanical Gardens, which is a longish way of saying 'tropical paradise.' Inside, Caribbean accents mesh with antique furniture, polished wood floors, designer linens and marble bathrooms to make for some of Key West's most enticing rooms.

Saint Hotel
BOUTIQUE HOTEL $$$

(☎305-294-3200; www.thesainthotelkeywest.com; 417 Eaton St; r $360-700; ✴🖂) Despite its proximity to Duval St, the Saint feels like a world removed with its plush rooms, chic minimalist lobby, photogenic pool with small cascading waterfall, and artfully designed bar. The best rooms have balconies overlooking the pool.

Seascape Tropical Inn
B&B $$$

(☎305-296-7776; www.seascapetropicalinn.com; 420 Olivia St; r $250-425; ✴🖂) Had this B&B existed back in the day, Hemingway could have stumbled into it after one of his epic drinking binges – it's within hollering distance of his old house. Now you can crash in one of seven rooms, each uniquely designed with floral comforters and artwork on the walls. The best rooms have French doors opening onto private terraces.

Silver Palms Inn
BOUTIQUE HOTEL $$$

(☎305-294-8700; www.silverpalmsinn.com; 830 Truman Ave; r $280-400; P✴🖂) 🏊 Royal blues, sweet teals, bright limes and lemon-yellow color schemes douse the interior of this boutique property, which also boasts bicycle rentals, a saltwater swimming pool and a green certification from the Florida Department of Environmental Protection. Overall the Silver Palms offers more of a modern, large-hotel vibe with a candy-colored dose of Keys tropics attitude.

Lighthouse Court Inn
BOUTIQUE HOTEL $$$

(☎305-294-5229; www.historickeywestinns.com/the-inns/lighthouse-court; 902 Whitehead St; r from $260; ✴🖂) The rooms at the Lighthouse Court are among the most handsomely appointed in town. They're elegant in their simplicity, with the warm earth tones of hardwood floors set off by just the right amount of tropical breeziness and cool colors. Affiliated with Historic Key West Inns.

Mango Tree Inn
B&B $$$

(☎305-293-1177; www.mangotree-inn.com; 603 Southard St; r $235-400; ✴🖂) This down-to-earth B&B offers a courtyard pool and attractive accommodation in a number of airy rooms, each decorated with swaths of tropical-chic accoutrements, from rattan furniture to flowering hibiscus. Rates dip as low as $150 in the low season.

Santa Maria Suites Resort
BOUTIQUE HOTEL $$$

(☎305-296-5678; www.santamariasuites.com; 1401 Simonton St; r from $450; P✴🖂) With its marvelous deco facade, the Santa Maria looks like it took a wrong turn on South Beach, Miami, and ended up in Key West. The suites themselves – all two-bedroom – also show elements of Miami decadence, with spacious sun-drenched interiors, designer kitchens and stylish living rooms that open onto terraces.

Curry Mansion Inn
HOTEL $$$

(☎305-294-5349; www.currymansion.com; 511 Caroline St; r $250-390; P✴🖂) In a city full of stately 19th-century homes, the Curry Mansion is especially handsome. All the elements of an aristocratic American home come together here, from plantation-era Southern colonnades to a New England–style widow's walk and, of course, bright Floridian rooms with canopied beds. Enjoy bougainvillea and breezes on the verandah.

Truman Hotel
HOTEL $$$

(☎305-296-6700; www.trumanhotel.com; 611 Truman Ave; r $320-400; P✴🖂) Close to the main downtown drag, these playful rooms have huge flat-screen TVs, kitchenettes, zebra-print throw rugs and mid-century modern furniture. Try to score an upstairs room overlooking the pool (and away from Truman Ave) for the best light and least noise. The pool, fringed with palm trees, is particularly inviting.

 Eating

BO's Fish Wagon
SEAFOOD $

(www.bosfishwagon.com; 801 Caroline St; mains $12-19, lunch specials $11-17; ⊙11am-9:30pm)

Looking like a battered old fishing boat that smashed onto the shore, BO's is awash with faded buoys, lifesavers and rusting license plates strung from its wooden rafters, and in some spots you needn't step outside to peer up at the moon. Regardless, the seafood is fantastic – with rich conch fritters, softshell crab sandwiches and tender fish tacos.

Date & Thyme
HEALTH FOOD $

(☑305-296-7766; www.helpyourselffoods.com; 829 Fleming St; ☺cafe 8am-4pm, market to 6pm; ☑) ✐ Equal parts market and cafe, Date & Thyme whips up deliciously guilt-free breakfast and lunch plates, plus energizing smoothies and juices. Try the açai bowl with blueberry, granola and coconut milk for breakfast, or lunch favorites like Thai coconut curry with mixed vegetables and quinoa. There's a shaded patio in front, where roaming chickens nibble underfoot (don't feed them).

5 Brothers Grocery & Sandwich Shop
DELI $

(930 Southard St; sandwiches $4-8; ☺6:30am-3pm Mon-Sat) A Key West icon, this tiny grocery store and deli fires up some of the best Cuban-style espresso this side of Miami. Join locals over early-morning *cafe con leche*, guava pastries and bacon and egg rolls, or stop in later for delectable roast pork sandwiches.

Garbo's Grill
FUSION $

(www.garbosgrillkw.com; 409 Caroline St; mains $10-14; ☺11am-10pm Mon-Sat) Just off the beaten path, Garbo's whips up delicious tacos with creative toppings like mango ginger habanero-glazed shrimp, Korean barbecue, and fresh mahimahi with all the fixings, as well as gourmet burgers and hot dogs. It's served out of a sleek Airstream trailer, which faces onto a shaded brick patio dotted with outdoor tables.

Pierogi Polish Market
EASTERN EUROPEAN $

(☑305-292-0464; 1008 White St; mains $5-11; ☺pierogi counter 11am-7pm Mon-Sat, shop 10am-8pm Mon-Sat, noon-6pm Sun; ℗☑) The Keys have an enormous seasonal population of temporary workers largely drawn from Central and Eastern Europe. This is where those workers can revisit the motherland, via pierogies, dumplings, blinis and a great sandwich selection. Although it's called a Polish market, there's food here that caters to Hungarians, Czechs and Russians (among others).

Glazed Donuts
BAKERY $

(☑305-294-9142; 420 Eaton St; doughnuts $2-4; ☺7am-3pm Tue-Sun; ☑⊕) Doughnuts make the world go round, and you'll find some excellent varieties at this cute bakery. The flavors are as eccentric as Key West itself, and reflect the seasons: strawberry shortcake, blood orange marmalade, mango hibiscus and (of course) key lime. Good coffees complete the perfect combo.

★ Thirsty Mermaid
SEAFOOD $$

(☑305-204-4828; www.thirstymermaidkeywest.com; 521 Fleming St; mains $12-28; ☺11am-11:30pm; ☑) Aside from having a great name, the pint-sized Thirsty Mermaid deserves high marks for its outstanding seafood and stylish but easygoing atmosphere. The menu is a celebration of culinary treasures from the sea, with a raw bar of oysters, ceviche, middleneck clams and even caviar. Among the main courses, seared diver scallops or togarashi-spiced tuna with jasmine rice are outstanding.

The Café
VEGETARIAN $$

(☑305-296-5515; www.thecafekw.com; 509 Southard St; mains $12-22; ☺9am-10pm; ☑) The oldest vegetarian spot in Key West is a sunny luncheonette by day that morphs into a buzzing, low-lit eating and drinking spot by night. The cooking is outstanding, with an eclectic range of dishes: Thai curry stir fries, Italian veggie meatball subs, pizza with shaved Brussels sprouts, and a famous veggie burger.

Mangia Mangia
ITALIAN $$

(☑305-294-2469; www.mangia-mangia.com; 900 Southard St; mains $18-29; ☺5:30-10pm) On a peaceful stretch of Southard St, Mangia Mangia cooks up fresh pastas, made in-house from scratch, paired with delicacies such as mixed seafood, lobster and sea scallops (there's also grilled fish and meat dishes). The comfy setting has an old-school vibe, with wood-paneled walls and tropical paintings, though you can also dine in the pleasant side garden.

Six Toed Cat
AMERICAN $$

(☑305-294-3318; 823 Whitehead St; mains $12-21; ☺8:30am-5pm) Simple, fresh and filling breakfast and lunch fare is served just a stone's throw from the Hemingway House (p191) and it is indeed named for the author's six-toed felines. A lobster Benedict with avocado should satisfy the day's protein needs, but if you're here for lunch, don't miss the lovely fried shrimp sandwich.

Point5
FUSION $$
(☏305-296-0669; 915 Duval St; small plates $5-17; ⊘6pm-midnight; 🖋) Point5 is a good deal more sophisticated than the typical Duval St drinkery. It trades in fusion-style tapas with global influence, ranging from marinated octopus salad to Sichuan eggplant and chipotle pork tacos. All go nicely with the wines by the glass and creative cocktail selections.

Blue Macaw
AMERICAN $$
(☏305-440-3196; www.bluemacawkeywest.com; 804 Whitehead St; mains lunch $12-16, dinner $19-34; ⊘9am-10pm; 🖋) Blue Macaw serves nicely executed fish and chips, portabello quesadillas, rack of ribs and sesame-seared tuna, though it's the atmosphere that brings in most people. Its open-air tables are set on a patio trimmed with tropical plants, and there's live music from 11am onward. The other draw: the make-your-own Bloody Marys, a great way to start the day.

Croissants de France
FRENCH $$
(☏305-294-2624; www.croissantsdefrance.com; 816 Duval St; mains $12-19; ⊘7:30am-9pm; 🖋) France comes to the Caribbean at this lovely bistro, with predictably tasty results. Stop by for eggs Benedict, cinnamon brioche French toast or lovely pastries at breakfast, then pop back at lunch for baguette sandwiches, quiche and berry-filled sweet crepes. The setting perfectly seizes Key West's cozy-Caribbean-chic aesthetic.

Mo's Restaurant
CARIBBEAN $$
(☏305-296-8955; 1116 White St; mains $10-21; ⊘11am-10pm Mon-Sat) The words 'Caribbean,' 'home' and 'cooking,' when used in conjunction, are generally always enough to impress. But it's not just the genre of cuisine that wins us over at Mo's – it's the execution.

The dishes are mainly Haitian, and they're delicious – the spicy pickles will inflame your mouth, which can get cooled down with a rich vegetable 'mush' over rice, or try the incredible signature snapper.

El Siboney
CUBAN $$
(☏305-296-4184; www.elsiboneyrestaurant.com; 900 Catherine St; mains $8-19; ⊘11am-9:30pm) This is a rough-and-ready Cuban joint where the portions are big and there's no messing around with high-end embellishment or bells and whistles. It's classic ingredients: rice, beans, grilled grouper, roasted pork,

barbecue chicken, sweet plantains – all cooked with pride to belly-filling satisfaction.

Seven Fish
SEAFOOD $$
(☏305-296-2777; www.7fish.com; 921 Truman Ave; mains $20-34; ⊘6-10pm Wed-Mon) This simply designed spot on busy Truman Ave specializes in the culinary hits from the sea – delectably prepared freshly caught fish and seafood dished up with care. Try the crab and shiitake mushroom pasta, the sea scallops or the straight-up fresh fish of the day. You can't go wrong here.

★ Blue Heaven
AMERICAN $$$
(☏305-296-8666; www.blueheavenkw.com; 729 Thomas St; mains breakfast & lunch $10-17, dinner $22-35; ⊘8am-10:30pm; 🖋) Proof that location is *nearly* everything, this is one of the quirkiest venues on an island of oddities. Customers (and free-roaming fowl) flock to dine in the ramshackle, tropical plant-filled garden where Hemingway once officiated boxing matches. This place gets packed with customers who wolf down delectable breakfasts (blueberry pancakes) and Keys cuisine with French touches (like yellowtail snapper with citrus beurre blanc).

Nine One Five
FUSION $$$
(☏305-296-0669; www.915duval.com; 915 Duval St; mains lunch $14-22, dinner $26-45; ⊘5-11pm Mon & Tue, 11:30am-11pm Wed-Sun; 🖋) Classy Nine One Five certainly stands out from the nearby Duval detritus of alcoholic aggression and tribal-band tattoos. Ignore all that and enter this modern and elegant space, which serves a creative, New American-dips-into-Asia menu. It's all quite rich – imagine a wild salmon with pearl barley, leeks and beurre blanc, or tortelloni with pecorino cream sauce and shaved black truffle.

Café Solé
FRENCH $$$
(☏305-294-0230; www.cafesole.com; 1029 Southard St; mains $25-38; ⊘5-10pm) Conch carpaccio with capers? Lobster bouillabaise? Yes indeed. This locally and critically acclaimed venue is known for its cozy back-porch ambience and innovative menus, cobbled together by a chef trained in southern French techniques who works with island ingredients.

🍷 Drinking & Nightlife

Basically Key West is a floating bar. 'No it's a nuanced, multilayered island with a proud nautical and multicultural histo...' *Bzzzt!* Floating bar. Bars close around 4am. Duval is the famed nightlife strip, which is lined with all manner of drinking dens – from frat boy party hubs to raucous drag-loving cabarets. Live music is a big part of the equation.

★ **Green Parrot**   BAR
(☎305-294-6133; www.greenparrot.com; 601 Whitehead St; ⏰10am-4am) The oldest bar on an island of bars, this rogues' cantina opened in the late 19th century and hasn't closed yet. Its ramshackle interior – complete with local artwork littering the walls and a parachute stretched across the ceiling – only adds to the atmosphere, as does the colorful crowd, obviously out for a good time.

The Green Parrot books some of the best bands – playing funk-laden rock, brassy jazz, juke-joint blues and Latin grooves – that hail from Miami, New Orleans, Atlanta and other places. There's never a cover.

Pilar Bar   BAR
(☎305-294-3200; www.thesainthotelkeywest.com/pilar-bar; 417 Eaton St; ⏰1-11pm) Inside the Saint Hotel, this small, convivial bar deserves special mention for its outstanding Bloody Marys – among the best you'll find in this country. It's also a great setting for a cocktail and high-end pub grub – and feels secreted away from the chaos of nearby Duval St.

About that Bloody Mary… Bartender Paul Murphy, an expat from London, created 'the Almighty,' featuring specially infused Australian vodka and topped with a veritable meal, including Yorkshire pudding, prime rib parcel with horseradish cream, peppered bacon, a blue cheese-stuffed meatball and other ingredients, plus topped with a Key West shrimp.

Porch   BAR
(☎305-517-6358; www.facebook.com/theporchkw; 429 Caroline St; ⏰11am-4am) For a break from the frat-boy bars on the Duval St strip, head to the Porch. Inside a lovely Caribbean-style mansion, this two-part bar serves up craft beer and wine on one side (left entrance) and creative cocktails (right entrance) in a handsomely designed but laid-back setting.

Vinos on Duval   WINE BAR
(☎305-294-7568; www.vinosonduval.com; 810 Duval St; ⏰1pm-1am) On the less rowdy end of Duval St, Vinos pours a good selection of wines from around the globe – Spanish tempranillos, Argentine malbecs, Californian Cabs – in a cozy setting with a touch of Key West eccentricity. Grab a seat at the bar and

have a chat with the knowledgeable staff, or retreat to one of the tables on the porch.

Captain Tony's Saloon   BAR
(☎305-294-1838; www.capttonyssaloon.com; 428 Greene St; ⏰10am-2am) Propagandists would have you believe the nearby megabar complex of Sloppy Joe's was Hemingway's original bar, but the physical place where the old man drank was right here, the original Sloppy Joe's location (before it was moved onto Duval St and into frat-boy hell). Hemingway's third wife (a journalist sent to profile Papa) seduced him in this very bar.

Conch Republic   BAR
(☎305-294-4403; www.conchrepublicseafood.com; 631 Greene St; ⏰noon-midnight) Overlooking the waterfront, this sprawling open-sided eatery and drinking space is a fun place to get you in the Key West spirit. The allure: a festive happy hour, the chatty laid-back crowd, island breezes and live music (nightly from 6pm to 10pm, plus afternoons on Friday and Saturday). The seafood is also quite good (mains $15 to $30).

Vivez Joyeux   WINE BAR
(☎305-517-6799; www.vivez-joyeux.com; 300 Petronia St; ⏰3-10pm) This French-run wine bar is tiny but utterly charming, with velvety red wines by the glass or bottle from an impressive rotation of French and American wine growers. You can pair those wines with first-rate cheese, charcuterie and other snacks.

Bourbon St Pub   GAY & LESBIAN
(☎305-294-9354; www.bourbonstpub.com; 724 Duval St; ⏰10am-4am) A celebratory crowd, great DJs and striking male dancers (who shimmy on top of the bar from 10pm onward) keep the party going at this iconic spot on Duval St. The garden bar in back, with pool and Jacuzzi, is open to men only, and occasionally hosts clothing-optional afternoon parties.

Garden of Eden   BAR
(224 Duval St; ⏰noon-4am) Go to the top of this building and discover Key West's own clothing-optional drinking patio. Lest you get too excited, cameras aren't allowed and most people come clothed. Regardless, the views are great, the mixed crowd is up for a fun time, and it's an obligatory stop when bar-hopping along Duval.

If you go, don't be a voyeuristic wallflower. Get out there and dance!

Aqua
GAY & LESBIAN

(☎305-294-0555; www.aquakeywest.com; 711 Duval St; ⏰3pm-2am) Aqua hosts some of the best drag shows on the island that attracts all types – gay, lesbian, straight, young, old, couples, groups – all wanting to see what the excitement is about. There's also karaoke several nights a week (currently Monday through Wednesday), so if you can sing, get in on the action!

Hog's Breath
BAR

(☎305-296-4222; www.hogsbreath.com; 400 Front St; ⏰10am-2am) A good place to start the infamous Duval Pub Crawl, the Hog's Breath is a rockin' outdoor bar with good live bands and better cold Coronas.

☆ Entertainment

La Te Da
CABARET

(☎305-296-6706; www.lateda.com; 1125 Duval St; ⏰shows 8:30pm) While the outside bar is where locals gather for mellow chats over beer, you can catch high-quality drag acts – big names come here from around the country – upstairs at the fabulous Crystal Room on weekends (admission $26). More low-key cabaret acts grace the downstairs lounge.

The Sunday tea dance – an afternoon dance party (from 4pm to 7pm) by the pool – is a great way to end the weekend.

Virgilio's
LIVE MUSIC

(☎305-296-1075; 524 Duval St; ⏰7pm-3am, to 4am Thu-Sat) This bar-stage is as un-Keys as they come, and frankly, thank God for a little variety. This town needs a dark, candlelit martini lounge where you can chill to blues or jazz and get down with some salsa, which Virgilio's handsomely provides. Enter on Applerouth Lane.

Tropic Cinema
CINEMA

(☎877-761-3456; www.tropiccinema.com; 416 Eaton St) Great art-house movie theater with deco frontage.

Waterfront Playhouse
THEATER

(☎305-294-5015; www.waterfrontplayhouse.org; 310 Wall St, Mallory Sq) Catch high-quality musicals and dramas from the oldest-running theater troupe in Florida. The season runs November through April.

Red Barn Theatre
THEATER

(☎305-296-9911; www.redbarntheatre.com; 319 Duval St; ⏰box office 1-8pm Tue-Fri, 4-8pm Sat & Sun) An occasionally edgy and always fun, cozy little local playhouse.

🛍 Shopping

Salt Island Provisions
GIFTS & SOUVENIRS

(☎305-896-2980; 830 Fleming St; ⏰10am-6pm) This crafty little shop is a fun place to browse for gift ideas. You'll find delicate jewelry made by local artisans, beeswax candles, organic coffee, Florida-related photography books and, of course, salt in its many incarnations: namely salt scrubs and gourmet cooking salts in infusions of merlot, sriracha, curry and white truffle.

Petronia Island Store
ARTS & CRAFTS

(801 Whitehead St; ⏰10am-4pm Thu-Sun) On a shop- and gallery-lined stretch of Whitehead St, this small sunlit store carries a well-curated selection of handmade soaps, jewelry, candles, pretty stationery and organic cotton clothes (with mermaids, mariners and octopi) for the young ones. Run by artists, the hip little outpost carries unique pieces that seem imbued with the creative, crafty ethos of Key West.

Books & Books
BOOKS

(☎305-320-0208; www.booksandbookskw.com; 533 Eaton St; ⏰10am-6pm) Miami's best indie bookshop has a branch in Key West, and it's a magnet for the literary minded. You'll find plenty of titles of local interest (particularly strong on Key West and Cuba), great staff picks and thought-provoking new releases. Regular book signings and author readings take place throughout the year.

Kermit's
FOOD

(www.keylimeshop.com; 200 Elizabeth St; ⏰9am-9:30pm) Satisfy your innermost cravings for all things key lime–related at this long-running institution near the waterfront. You'll find salsa, barbecue sauce, candies, ice cream, dog biscuits and even wine all bearing that distinctive key lime flavor. Purists may prefer to settle for a pie (mini pies available) or perhaps a chocolate-dipped key lime popsicle.

Key West Dream Collection
CLOTHING

(☎305-741-7560; 613 Simonton St; ⏰10am-3pm) This wonderfully eclectic store is a showcase for Key West's creative side with eye-catching vintage apparel, African textiles and glass beads, books and artwork by local writers and artists, and even CDs by homegrown Key West bands.

Leather Master
FASHION & ACCESSORIES

(418 Applerouth Lane; ⏰11am-10pm Mon-Sat, noon-5pm Sun) Besides the gladiator outfits, studded jockstraps and S&M masks, they

do very nice bags and shoes here. Which is what you came for, right?

ℹ Information

Key West Chamber of Commerce (📞305-294-2587; www.keywestchamber.org; 510 Greene St; ⊗9am-6pm) An excellent source of information.

Lower Keys Medical Center (📞305-294-5531; www.lkmc.com; 5900 College Rd, Mile 5, Stock Island) Has a 24-hour emergency room.

Gay & Lesbian Community Center (📞305-292-3223; 513 Truman Ave; ⊗9am-5pm) Serves as a welcome center for LGBT travelers. Loads of great tips on restaurants, bars, lodging and outdoor activities in Key West.

ℹ Getting There & Away

Key West International Airport (EYW; 📞305-809-5200; www.eyw.com; 3491 S Roosevelt Blvd) is off S Roosevelt Blvd on the east side of the island. You can fly into Key West from some major US cities, such as Miami or New York. Flights from Los Angeles and San Francisco usually have to stop in Tampa, Orlando or Miami first. American Airlines (www.aa.com) has several flights a day. From Key West airport, a quick and easy taxi ride into Old Town will cost about $22.

Greyhound (📞305-296-9072; www.greyhound.com; 3535 S Roosevelt Blvd) has two buses daily between Key West and downtown Miami. Buses leave Miami for the 4¼-hour journey at 12:35pm and 6:50pm and Key West at 8:55am and 5:45pm going the other way (from $10 to $40 each way).

You can boat from Miami to the Keys on the **Key West Express** (📞239-463-5733; www.seakeywestexpress.com; 100 Grinnell St; adult/senior/junior/child round-trip $155/145/92/62, one way $95/95/68/31), which departs from Fort Myers beach daily at 8:30am and does a 3½-hour cruise to Key West. Returning boats depart the seaport at 6pm. You'll want to show up 1½ hours before your boat departs. During winter the *Express* also leaves several times a week from Marco Island (the prices and sailing time are identical to Fort Myers departures).

ℹ Getting Around

Once you're in Key West, the best way to get around is by bicycle (rentals from the Duval St area, hotels and hostels cost from $10 a day). For transport within the Duval St area, the free **Duval Loop shuttle** (www.carfreekeywest.com/duval-loop) runs from 6pm to midnight.

Other options include the **Key West Transit** (p174), with color-coded buses running about every 15 minutes; mopeds, which generally cost

from $35 per day ($60 for a two-seater); or the open-sided electric tourist cars, aka 'Conch cruisers,' which travel at 35mph and cost about $140/200 for a four-seater/six-seater per day.

A&M Scooter Rentals (📞305-896-1921; www.amscooterskeywest.com; 523 Truman Ave; bicycle/scooter/electric car per day from $10/35/140; ⊗9am-7pm) rents out scooters and bicycles, as well as open-sided electric cars that can seat from two to six, and offers free delivery

Parking can be tricky in town. There's a free **parking lot** on Fort St off Truman Ave.

DRY TORTUGAS NATIONAL PARK

After all those keys, connected by that convenient road, the nicest islands in the archipelago require a little extra effort.

Dry Tortugas National Park (📞305-242-7700; www.nps.gov/drto) is open for day trips and overnight camping, which provides a rare phenomenon: a quiet Florida beach. A visitor center is located within fascinating Fort Jefferson.

Dry Tortugas National Park is America's most inaccessible national park. Reachable only by boat or seaplane, it rewards you for your effort in getting there with amazing snorkeling amid coral reefs full of marine life. You'll also get to tour a beautifully preserved 19th-century brick fort, one of the largest such fortifications in the US despite its location 70 miles off the coast of Key West.

On paper, the Dry Tortugas covers an extensive area – over 70 sq miles. In reality, only 1% of the park (about 143 acres) consists of dry land, so much of the park's allure lies under the water. The marine life is quite rich here, with the opportunity to see tarpon, sizable groupers and lots of colorful coral and smaller tropical fish, plus the odd sea turtle gliding through the sea.

It was explorer Ponce de León who named this seven-island chain Las Tortugas (The Turtles) for the sea turtles spotted in its waters. Thirsty mariners who passed through and found no water later affixed 'dry' to the name. In subsequent years, the US Navy set an outpost here as a strategic position into the Gulf of Mexico. But by the Civil War, **Fort Jefferson**, the main structure on the islands, had become a prison for Union deserters and at least four other people, among them Dr Samuel Mudd, who had been arrested for complicity in the assassination of Abraham Lincoln. Hence a new nickname: Devil's Island. The name was prophetic: in 1867 a yellow-fever outbreak killed 38 people, and after an 1873 hurricane the fort was abandoned. It opened again in 1886 as a quarantine station for smallpox and cholera victims, was declared a national monument in 1935 by President Franklin D Roosevelt, and was upped to national park status in 1992 by George Bush Sr.

You can come for the day or overnight if you want to camp. Garden Key has 10 campsites ($15 per person, per night), which are given out on a first-come, first-served basis. You'll need to reserve months ahead through the ferry *Yankee Freedom III*, which takes passengers to and from the island. There are toilets, but no freshwater showers or drinking water; bring everything you'll need. You can stay up to four nights. The sparkling waters offer excellent snorkeling and diving opportunities.

In March and April there is stupendous bird-watching, including aerial fighting.

Stargazing is mind-blowing any time of the year.

ℹ️ Getting There & Away

If you have your own boat, the Dry Tortugas are covered under National Ocean Survey chart No 11438. **Key West Seaplanes** (📞 305-293-9300; www.keywestseaplanecharters.com; half-day trip adult/child $330/265, full-day trip $578/462) can take up to 10 passengers (flight time 40 minutes each way). The half-day tour is four hours, allowing 2½ hours on the island. The eight-hour full-day excursion gives you six hours on the island. Again, reserve at least a week in advance. Passengers over age 16 arriving by plane also need to pay an added $10 park admission fee (cash only). Flights depart from **Key West International Airport** (p201).

Yankee Freedom III (📞 800-634-0939; www.drytortugas.com; Key West Ferry Terminal, 100 Grinell St; adult/child/senior $175/125/165) operates a fast ferry departing from the Historic Seaport (at the northern end of Margaret St). Round-trip fares cost $170/125 per adult/child. Reservations are recommended. Continental breakfast, a picnic lunch, snorkeling gear and a 45-minute tour of Fort Jefferson are all included.

Southeast Florida

POP 3,902,740 / ☎ 954, 561, 772

Best Places to Eat

➡ Būccan (p228)

➡ HMF (p228)

➡ Table 26 Degrees (p235)

➡ Burlock Coast (p212)

➡ Paradiso Ristorante (p223)

Best Places to Sleep

➡ Grandview Gardens (p234)

➡ The Breakers (p227)

➡ Costa d'Este (p243)

➡ Parliament Inn (p220)

➡ Brazilian Court (p227)

Why Go?

The endearing collection of beach towns on Florida's southeast coast is a world away from Miami's tanned and diamond-draped clutches. Some towns are classy, others are quirky, but all are unique. From activity-packed, gay- and family-friendly Fort Lauderdale to quiet, exclusive, semi-reclusive Palm Beach, laid-back Lauderdale-by-the-Sea and the rugged coast of Jupiter, you'll find more adventure and nightlife than you can handle. This chunk of coast also includes some of Florida's wealthiest enclaves – enjoy gawking at the castle-like beachfront mansions, but don't rear-end that $350,000 Bentley when parallel parking in front of the Gucci store in Palm Beach!

For those looking for a more down-to-earth setting, the region's numerous natural gems – secluded islands, moss-draped mangrove swamps, wild rivers and empty dunes – will surely satisfy your demands for nonmaterial pleasures.

When to Go
Palm Beach

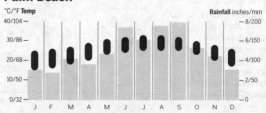

Mar–Apr Spring break hits, packing beaches with party-happy 20-somethings.

Jun–Jul Low-season prices and turtle-nesting season.

Dec–Feb Perfect beach weather and Delray's tennis tournament.

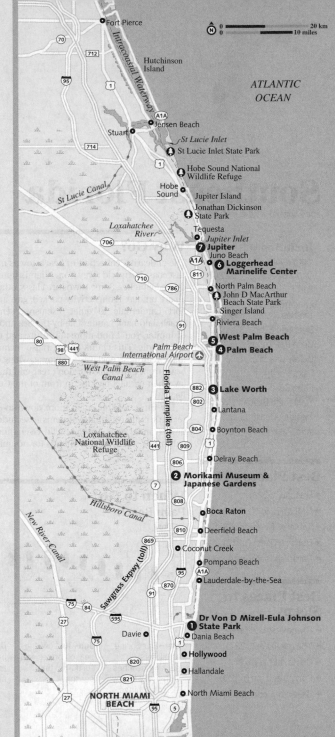

Southeast Florida Highlights

❶ Dr Von D Mizell-Eula Johnson State Park (p207) Gliding through mangroves past undisturbed beaches.

❷ Morikami Museum & Japanese Gardens (p219) Sipping matcha green tea at Delray Beach's serene gardens.

❸ Bamboo Room (p223) Digging Lake Worth's outsized nightlife and music scene.

❹ Palm Beach (p223) Enjoying the high life for free: window-shopping Worth Avenue, strolling the Lake Trail and catching some rays at the local beach.

❺ West Palm Beach (p230) Hitting the funky new restaurants along S Dixie Hwy and surrounds.

❻ Loggerhead Marinelife Center (p242) Getting up close and personal with loggerhead and leatherback turtles as they recuperate.

❼ Jupiter (p237) Kayaking the wild, scenic Loxahatchee River for close-up views of cypress knees, mangrove forests and sunning alligators.

GOLD COAST

Though the 70-or-so miles of sparkling Atlantic shoreline from Hollywood to Jupiter earned its nickname from the gold salvaged from area shipwrecks, it could easily have come from the mix of sapphire skies, cinnamony sands and bejeweled, wealthy residents.

Here the coastline has a split personality. First there's slow-going, ocean-fronting Rte 1, a pleasant drive revealing infinite vistas of unspoiled beaches...though occasionally it feels like driving through a condo canyon. Second there's older Dixie Hwy, running parallel to Rte 1 but further inland, past dive bars and working-class communities. Drive both stretches; each is rich with divergent offerings.

Hollywood

☑ 954 / POP 148,770

Hollywood positions itself as a gateway to Fort Lauderdale. It's divided into two sections: the bustling waterfront section, and small, pleasant historic downtown section, a couple of miles west. Most visitors come for the waterfront, which has earned a sizable wedge of the spring break market since Lauderdale gave revelers the boot. The resulting influx brings with it concerts in the sand, beach-volleyball tourneys and assorted debauchery each March. In recent times, the city has tried to glam up its image with several new South Beach–style developments.

◎ Sights

Anne Kolb Nature Center   PARK

(www.broward.org/parks; 751 Sheridan St; admission $2; ⊘9am-5:30pm) This lovely 1500 acres of coastal mangroves is on one side of West Lake, while opposite is the recreation area (referred to as West Lake Park). The entirely 'wild' section, Anne Kolb Nature Center, is criss-crossed by hiking trails and offers views over West Lake. Such a natural park is a rarity in Broward County. Fortunately environmentalists in the 1970s managed to save it from development, forever preserving its mangroves, wetlands and wildlife.

These days it's one of the most accessible natural places for kayaking, biking and hiking within a largely built-up area. A variable schedule of boat tours departs from the West Lake Marina (adult/under 18 $5/3).

West Lake Park   PARK

(☑954-357-5161; www.broward.org/parks/west lakepark; 1200 Sheridan St; kayak rental per 1/2/4hr $14/24/30; ⊘9am-5pm) Connected to the Anne Kolb Nature Center, this is the more suburban recreation section, with a marina, tennis courts and picnic ground. You can paddle across West Lake and through the mangroves via various locales marked as red, white and green trails.

Hollywood Broadwalk   WATERFRONT

Reminiscent of California's famed Venice Beach, this beach and adjacent promenade teem with scantily clad rollerbladers and fanny-pack-wearing tourists. The Broadwalk itself is a 2.5-mile, six-person-wide path, extending from pretty North Beach Park, where the route is lined with seagrapes, all the way to South Surf Rd. It's regularly clogged with skaters, strollers and entire families pedaling enormous group bikes.

If you feel like rolling along it, a dozen or so Broadwalk vendors rent out bikes ($10/30 per hour/day), in-line skates and other beach gear.

North Beach Park   PARK

(3601 N Ocean Dr; ⊘11am-5pm) **FREE** This is the formal name for the beach, though there is a suburban-style green space behind the boardwalk here, with picnic tables and barbecue grills.

⌡ Sleeping

Hollywood Beach Suites   HOTEL $

(☑954-391-9441; www.hollywoodbeachsuitehotel. com; 320 Arizona St; r from $89; P ❋ @ 🛜) This slick complex comprises a warren of whitewashed, vaguely Moroccan-looking motel units that have been revamped since our visit; it now markets itself as 'boutique.' This is generally a quiet place (versus a party palace), which appeals to families. Surfboards available for use. The reception desk is at the street number cited here.

★Walkabout
Beach Resort   BOUTIQUE HOTEL $$

(☑954-272-6000; www.walkaboutbeachresort. com; 2500 North Surf Rd; d $174-259; ❋ 🛜) If you blink you might miss this classic, baby-pink art-deco hotel that was built in 1947 and sits curvaceously on the Broadwalk. There are just eight rooms, all of which are equipped with kitchenette and dining table. Wooden and terrazzo floors, vintage black-and-white photographs and furnishings, and a miniature on-site tiki bar all combine to create a retro beachside getaway.

Come the 4th July, you even have front-row seats for the fireworks. The suite, located in the gorgeous rounded 'tower' costs a bit more because of its larger size. A small beach bar is at the front of the property.

Sea Downs
APARTMENT $$

(✆954-923-4968; www.seadowns.com; 2900 North Surf Rd; apt $148-169; P❄🐾) This cozy, unpretentious little spot has dated charm, featuring tidy studios and one-bedroom apartments equipped with everything you need to roll out of bed in the morning and stroll along the beach and promenade. Its location is right on the beach, so you can forgive the fact that the decor seems a little old-fashioned.

Seminole Hard Rock Hotel & Casino
HOTEL $$$

(✆866-502-7529; www.seminolehardrockholly wood.com; 1 Seminole Way; r $249-600; ❄🐾♨) This Mediterranean-style monster provides everything you'd ever need under one massive roof. In this case, it's casinos, eateries, theaters, a day spa, 500 swanky guestrooms and some of the most alluring concert bills in the state. It's all very Vegas and, well, Hard Rock-ish. Except for the 4.5-acre lagoon-style pool surrounding a bar – *that's* out of this world.

✕ Eating

Taco Beach Shack
MEXICAN $

(www.tacobeachshack.com; 334 Arizona St; tacos $4-10; ⊙noon-2am) Hipsters and hangers-on lounge around on wicker chaises at this open-air taqueria with a tinge of grunge. The menu has a very of-the-moment mix of ethnic flavors – try the Korean short rib and kimchi tacos. Margarita Mondays have you throwing down these classic cocktails at $2 a pop.

ArtsPark
STREET FOOD $

(Young Circle, off US 1; ⊙5:30pm-10pm Mon) If you're in town on a Monday, head downtown to the ArtsPark, where you'll find a gathering of food trucks.

Pikey
PUB FOOD $$

(✆323-850-5400; www.thepikeyla.com; 7617 W Sunset Blvd, Hollywood; dinner mains $16-32;

11:45am-2am Mon-Fri, from 10:30am Sat & Sun) This tasteful kitchen began life as Coach and Horses, one of Hollywood's favorite dives, before it was reimagined into a place where you can get buffalo burrata with marinated figs, fish crudo with pickled rhubarb and fennel, or fish and chips with romaine and tartar sauce. Produce is organic and local, meats are humanely raised, and the cocktails rock.

Le Comptoir
FRENCH $$

(✆786-718-9441; http://lecomptoir.menubaron. com; 1902 Harrison St; mains $14-26; ⊙5-10pm) It's worth making the trip Downtown for this excellent-value, classic bistro. You'll dine on bowls heaped high with mussels stewed in white wine and Provençal sauces, and dusted with vibrant green parsley. Other signature French dishes include duck with an orange glaze and succulent peppered steak.

Le Tub
AMERICAN $$

(✆954-921-9425; www.theletub.com; 1100 N Ocean Dr; mains $9-20; ⊙11am-1am Mon-Fri, noon-2am Sat & Sun) Decorated exclusively with flotsam collected along Hollywood Beach, this quirky burger joint is routinely named 'Best in America.' Everything is prepared from scratch and in a small kitchen so expect a wait, both for seating and cooking time. It's worth it.

🛍 Shopping

Josh's Organic Garden
FOOD

(cnr Harrison & S Broadwalk; ⊙9am-5:30pm Sun) Beneath tents overlooking the ocean, Josh sells 100% certified organic fruits, veggies, nuts and juices in PLA cups (made from corn and so compostable, like the bags he provides). Buy lots, because it's good for you, but don't worry: whatever remains is donated to a homeless shelter. An adjacent juice stand whips up killer smoothies.

ℹ Getting There & Away

An old-fashioned trolley known as the Sun Trolley travels between downtown Hollywood and the beach. Fares are $1; bright-colored signs mark the stops but don't hold your breath; you could be waiting a long time. (The Sun Trolley's cell phone app might help alleviate waiting times.)

Broward County Transit (BCT; www.broward. org/bct; single fare/day pass $2/5) buses serve Hollywood, connecting to Fort Lauderdale. Fares are $2.

To shoot north to West Palm Beach or south to Miami, head to the **Fort Lauderdale–Hollywood International Airport** (FLL; ✈866-435-9355; www.broward.org/airport; 320 Terminal Dr) on BCT bus 1 and jump on **Tri-Rail** (✈954-783-6030; www.tri-rail.com). Route 4 heads along Hollywood Blvd into the historic downtown

Parking at the beach in Hollywood is hellacious – if you can't find on-street parking (around $2 per hour), try the parking deck at Margaritaville.

Dania Beach

✈954 / POP 29,640

Dania (dane-ya) feels like an extension of the 'burbs of Hollywood; its past vestiges of a mellow little town, with a fledgling antiques district and a breezy fishing pier, are largely disappearing. The main appeal is the Dr Von D Mizell-Eula Johnson State Park on Dania Beach's outskirts.

◉ Sights

Dr Von D Mizell-Eula Johnson State Park   STATE PARK
(✈954-923-2833; www.floridastateparks.org; 6503 N Ocean Dr; vehicle/cyclist $6/2; ⊗8am-sunset) Once an important stop for Prohibition-era bootleggers, lush Whiskey Creek (get it?) is now a kayaking hot spot. The dense mangrove-lined route meanders 1.5 miles through the park, and is shallow and calm. There's also 2.5 miles of undisturbed beach to enjoy. At the northern end is the Port Everglades inlet, where cruise ships and yachts sail past, while at the southern end you'll find the Dania Beach fishing pier. The park also offers some good offshore snorkeling and diving and is an important turtle nesting area.

The **Whiskey Creek Hideout** at the north end of the park provides kayak and canoe rentals ($20 per hour).

✕ Eating

★**Tarks of Dania Beach**   SEAFOOD $
(✈954-925-8275; 1317 S Federal Hwy; mains $6-15; ⊗11am-10pm) This jaunty clam stand has been going strong since 1966 and is now a local landmark. Most of the tiny, very fuggy interior is taken up with the cooking counter, where they broil, fry and steam daily specials. These usually include a combination of steamed, fried and raw clams alongside shrimp, oysters, snow crab and spicy chicken wings.

It can get crazy busy, but food usually vanishes so fast you won't be waiting long.

Jaxson's Ice Cream Parlor   ICE CREAM $
(www.jaxsonsicecream.com; 128 S Federal Hwy; ice cream from $5; ⊗11:30am-11pm Sun-Thu, to midnight Fri, noon-11pm Sun; 🖑) Established in 1956, this place has 80-plus flavors of homemade ice cream.

⊕ Getting There & Away

Broward County Transit (✈954-357-8400; www.broward.org/bct) buses serve Dania, connecting to Fort Lauderdale. Fares are $2.

To shoot north to West Palm Beach or south to Miami, head to the **Fort Lauderdale–Hollywood International Airport** (p207) on BCT bus 1 and jump on Tri-Rail.

Fort Lauderdale

✈954 / POP 165,520

After years of building a reputation as *the* destination for beer-swilling college students on raucous spring breaks, Fort Lauderdale now angles for a slightly more mature and sophisticated crowd. Think martinis rather than tequila shots; jazz concerts instead of wet T-shirt contests. But don't worry, visitors can still enjoy plenty of carrying-on within the confines of area bars and nightclubs.

Few visitors venture far inland – except maybe to dine and shop along Las Olas Blvd; most spend the bulk of their time on the coast. It's understandable. Truly, it's hard to compete with beautiful beaches, a system of Venice-like waterways, an international yachting scene, spiffy new hotels and top-notch restaurants.

The city's Port Everglades is one of the busiest cruise-ship ports in the world, with megaships departing daily for the Caribbean, Mexico and beyond.

◉ Sights

★**Bonnet House**   HISTORIC BUILDING
(Map p208; ✈954-563-5393; www.bonnethouse.org; 900 N Birch Rd; adult/child $20/16, grounds only $10; ⊗9am-4pm Tue-Sun) This pretty plantation-style property was once the home of artists and collectors Frederic and Evelyn Bartlett. It is now open to guided tours that swing through its art-filled rooms and studios. Beyond the house, 35 acres of lush, subtropical gardens protect a pristine

Fort Lauderdale Beach

barrier-island ecosystem, including one of the finest orchid collections in the country.

Fort Lauderdale Beach & Promenade BEACH

(Map p208; P M W) Fort Lauderdale's promenade – a wide, brick, palm-tree-dotted pathway swooping along the beach and the A1A – is a magnet for runners, in-line skaters, walkers and cyclists. The white-sand beach, meanwhile, is one of the nation's cleanest and best. Stretching 7 miles to Lauderdale-by-the-Sea, it has dedicated family-, gay- and dog-friendly sections. Boating, diving, snorkeling and fishing are all extremely popular.

Riverwalk LANDMARK

(Map p212; www.goriverwalk.com) Curving along the New River, the meandering Riverwalk runs from Stranahan House to the Broward Center for the Performing Arts. Host to culinary tastings and other events, the walk connects a number of sights, restaurants and shops.

Las Olas Riverfront WATERFRONT

(Map p212; cnr SW 1st Ave & Las Olas Blvd) A giant alfresco boardwalk area with restaurants,

SOUTHEAST FLORIDA FORT LAUDERDALE

stores and live entertainment nightly; it's also the place to catch many river cruises.

Hugh Taylor Birch State Recreation Area
PARK

(Map p208; ☑954-564-4521; www.florida stateparks.org/park/Hugh-Taylor-Birch; 3109 E Sunrise Blvd; vehicle/bike $6/2; ⊙8am-sunset) This lusciously tropical park contains one of the last significant maritime hammocks in Broward County. There are mangroves and a freshwater lagoon system (great for birding) and several endangered plants and animals (including the golden leather fern and gopher tortoise). You can fish, picnic, stroll the short Coastal Hammock Trail or cycle the 1.9-mile park drive.

Stranahan House
HISTORIC BUILDING

(Map p212; ☑954-524-4736; www.stranahan house.org; 335 SE 6th Ave; adult/student $12/7; ⊙tours 1pm, 2pm & 3pm) Constructed from Dade County pine, grand Stranahan House is a fine example of Florida vernacular design, and one of the state's oldest homes. It served as both home and store for Ohio transplant Frank Stranahan, who built a small empire trading with the Seminoles before committing suicide by jumping into the New River after real-estate and stock-market losses in the late 1920s. The house, with many original furnishings, is open daily for three hour-long tours.

Docents from the house also guide a fun hour-long River Ghost Tour ($25 per person) in conjunction with the water taxi. Tours depart from the house (and include a tour inside) at 7:30pm every Sunday.

NSU Art Museum Fort Lauderdale
MUSEUM

(Map p212; ☑954-525-5500; http://nsuart museum.org; 1 E Las Olas Blvd; adult/student/child $12/free; ⊙11am-5pm Tue-Sat, to 8pm Thu, noon-5pm Sun) A curvaceous Florida standout known for its William Glackens collection (among Glackens fans) and its exhibitions on wide-ranging themes from northern European art to contemporary Cuban art, American pop art and contemporary photography. On Thursday evenings, the museum stays open late and hosts lectures, films and performances, as well as a happy hour in the museum cafe. Day courses and workshops are also available. Check the website for details.

Museum of Discovery & Science
MUSEUM

(Map p212; ☑954-467-6637; www.mods.org; 401 SW 2nd St; adult/child $16/13; ⊙10am-5pm Mon-Sat, noon-6pm Sun; ☒) A 52ft kinetic-energy sculpture greets you here, and fun exhibits include Gizmo City and Runways to Rockets – where it actually *is* rocket science. Plus there's an Everglades exhibit and IMAX theater.

Canine Beach
BEACH

(Map p208; cnr Sunrise Blvd & N Atlantic Blvd; weekend permits $7; ⊙3-7pm winter, 5-9pm summer) This dog-friendly beach is the 100-yard swath running from E Sunrise Blvd to lifeguard station 5.

🏃 Activities

★ Atlantic Coast Kayak Company
KAYAKING

(☑954-781-0073; www.atlanticcoastkayak.com; Richardson Historical Park Boat Dock, 1937 Wilton Dr; per hr/half-day $16/40; ⊙9am-5pm) An excellent alternative to tour-boat cruises is to rent your own kayak in Richardson Park and paddle the 7.5 mile (roughly 2½ to three hours) Middle River loop around the Island City yourself. Day, sunset and moonlight tours, including basic instruction and gourmet sandwiches and soft drinks, are also available on a scheduled calendar. All you need to do is turn up.

Paddleboard instruction and rental is also available.

★ Sea Experience
BOATING, SNORKELING

(Map p208; ☑954-770-3483; www.seaxp.com; 801 Seabreeze Blvd; snorkeling adult/child $40/25; ⊙10:15am & 2:15pm; ☒) Sea Experience takes guests in a 40ft glass-bottom boat along the Intracoastal and into the ocean to snorkel on a natural reef, thriving with marine life, in 10ft to 20ft of water. Tours last 2½ hours. Also offers scuba trips to multiple wreck sites.

Broward BCycle
CYCLING

(☑754-200-5672; https://broward.bcycle.com; first 30min/additional 30min $5/5) Fort Lauderdale is flat and an easy town to traverse via bicycle, or BCycle as the case may be. Broward County–operated bicycle sharing stations can be found throughout town, and they provide easy access to two-wheeled exploration. The maximum daily charge is $50.

Water Taxi
BOATING

(☑954-467-6677; www.watertaxi.com; day pass adult/child $26/12) For the best unofficial tour of the city, hop on the water taxi, whose drivers offer a lively narration as they ply

Fort Lauderdale's canals and waterways from Oakland Park Boulevard to the Riverwalk Arts District. Other routes head down the coast to Hollywood. Check online for locations.

Bahamas Celebration
CRUISE

(☑800-995-3201; www.bahamascelebration.com; trips from $180) Leaves Palm Beach in the afternoon, heads out overnight, then spends two full days in Grand Bahama, before returning overnight on the third night. The boat is furnished with several bars, a casino, four restaurants, a spa and a kids club, and cabins range from barebones to luxe.

Fort Lauderdale Parasail
WATER SPORTS

(Map p208; ☑954-462-7266; www.ftlauderdale parasail.com; 1005 Seabreeze Blvd; per person $85-105) If you're curious how the mansions along Millionaires' Row look from above, sign up for a parasailing trip. You'll soar on a 600ft and 1000ft line (around 300ft to 500ft sailing height) above the waves while strapped securely to an enormous smiley-face parachute.

Fish Lauderdale
FISHING

(Map p208; ☑954-805-3474; www.fishlauderdale.com; 1005 Seabreeze Blvd; up to 6 people per hour from $125; ◎8am-sunset) The waters off Fort Lauderdale are rich with marlin, sailfish, snapper, tarpon, wahoo and more. Naturally there are plenty of fishing charters available – this outfit has four boats to take you trolling for dinner.

👉 Tours

Gondola Man
BOATING

(Map p212; ☑201-919-1999; www.gondolaman.com; SE 1st Ave; tour $175) Explore the 'Venice of America' with a romantic ride in an original Venetian gondola, accompanied by Italian music. The tour lasts roughly 75 minutes and takes you through the canals and past the homes of the rich and famous.

Carrie B
BOATING

(Map p212; ☑954-642-1601; www.carrieb cruises.com; 440 N New River Dr E; tours adult/child $24/13; ◎tours 11am, 1pm & 3pm, closed Tue & Wed May-Sep) Hop aboard this replica 19th-century riverboat for a narrated 90-minute 'lifestyles of the rich and famous' tour of the ginormous mansions along the Intracoastal and New River. Tours leave from Las Olas at SE 5th Ave.

Jungle Queen Riverboat
BOATING

(Map p208; ☑954-462-5596; www.jungle queen.com; 801 Seabreeze Blvd; adult/child $23.50/13; ◎tour hours vary) Jungle Queen Riverboat runs three-hour tours along the waterfront, Millionaires' Row and part of the Everglades on a Mississippi-style paddle-wheeler. In addition to taking daily sightseeing cruises, you can also hop aboard the four-hour evening barbecue cruise at 6pm. It has all-you-can-eat shrimp or ribs, and entertainment (adult/child $43/23).

🛏 Sleeping

★ Island Sands Inn
B&B $$

(☑954-990-6499; www.islandsandsinn.com; 2409 NE 7th Ave, Wilton Manors; r $179-229; P❄🐾🛌) It's hard to say whether it's the beach towels, the luxurious bed and bedding, the thoughtful attention to details (tissues, bath products, mini-bar, microwave) or the utterly unpretentious *ease* of this four-room place that makes Island Sands Inn so comfortable. Certainly your charming hosts, Mike and Jim, unobtrusively ensure that you get the best from your stay.

Tranquilo
MOTEL $$

(Map p208; ☑954-565-5790; www.tranquilofort lauderdale.com; 2909 Vistamar St; r $149-174 Sun-Thu, $189-194 Fri & Sat; P❄🐾🛌) With a successful white-on-white decorative facelift, this retro 1950s motel offers fantastic value for families. Rooms range over three buildings, each with its own pool, and some include newly refurbed kitchens along with access to outdoor grills and laundry services. Complimentary shuttle service to the beach, three blocks away.

B Ocean Resort
HOTEL $$

(Map p208; ☑954-524-5551; www.bhotelsand resorts.com/b-ocean; 1140 Seabreeze Blvd; r from $150; P❄🐾🛌) Defining the southern end of Seabreeze Blvd, this hotel straddles the uberpopular South Beach and offers breezy ocean views from the majority of its airy rooms. Built by M Tony Sherman in 1956, it looks like a giant cruise ship tethered to the sidewalk.

Its 'hull,' the Wreck Bar (p214), is a historic landmark, and offers porthole views on the underwater world of the swimming pool. Come at the weekend and you'll be able to catch the mermaid show at 6:30pm.

Premiere Hotel
HOTEL $$

(Map p208; ☎954-566-7676; www.premiere hotel.com; 625 N Fort Lauderdale Beach Blvd; r from $159, ste fr $249; P ☯ ☲) This recently remodeled, family-run spot is large enough to have good infrastructure – a small bar/ cafe and food menu – but small enough to not feel like you're gobbled up by a re- sort. It's away from the madding crowd, yet opposite the beach, and has simple, white rooms and studio apartments with kitchen- ette. It's a good-value, reliable bet, especially in low season.

Riverside Hotel
HOTEL $$

(Map p212; ☎954-467-0671; www.riverside hotel.com; 620 E Las Olas Blvd; r/ste from $219/479; P ☀ ☯ ☲) This Fort Lauderdale landmark (c 1936) – fabulously located downtown on Las Olas, and with plush floral carpet and an air of grandeur – has two room types: larger, executive rooms in the newer 12-story tower, and those in the historic 1936 building. The classic rooms overlooking Las Olas are the pick of the bunch. Valet parking costs a hefty $27 per night.

★ Lago Mar Resort
RESORT $$$

(☎954-523-6511; www.lagomar.com; 1700 S Ocean Lane; r $300-700; P ☀ ☯ ☲) On the south end of South Beach, this wonderful- ly noncorporate resort has it all: a private beach, over-the-top grand lobby, massive island-style rooms, a full-service spa, on-site eateries, a lagoon-style pool set amid tropi- cal plantings and the personal touch of fam- ily ownership. (And no, not to be confused with President Trump's Mar-a-Lago.) This is unpretentious, but with old-fashioned manners and the feeling of a well-cared-for guesthouse.

★ W Fort Lauderdale
HOTEL $$$

(Map p208; ☎954-414-8200; www.wfortlauder dalehotel.com; 401 N Fort Lauderdale Beach Blvd; r from $284; P ☀ @ ☯ ☲) With an exterior resembling two giant sails and an interior that looks like the backdrop for a J Lo vid- eo, this is where the glitterati stay – bust out your stiletto heels/skinny ties and join them. The massive lobby is built for lei- sure, with a silver-and-aqua lounge area, a moodily lit bar, and a deck lined with wick- er chaises.

Pineapple Point
GUESTHOUSE $$$

(☎888-844-7295; www.pineapplepoint.com; 315 NE 16th Tce; r $329; P ☀ @ ☯ ☲) Tucked away in a quiet residential neighborhood, this guesthouse caters exclusively to a loyal gay male clientele. Suites and apartments are bright and beachy, all clustered around a handful of pools, hot tubs and tree-shaded sitting areas. Daily happy hours ensure mingling, and the super-friendly staff know all the best restaurants and gay bars in town.

✖ Eating

Lester's Diner
DINER $

(☎954-525-5641; www.facebook.com/lesters diner; 250 W State Rd 84; mains $4-17; ☉24hr) Hailed endearingly as a greasy spoon, campy Lester's Diner has been keeping folks happy since the late 1960s. Everyone makes their way here at some point, from business types on cell phones to clubbers and blue-haired ladies with third husbands to travel writers needing pancakes at 4am.

It's the type of place you expect the chef to be flipping pancakes in between a cigarette break. A must-visit for non-Americans.

Tacocraft
MEXICAN $

(Map p212; www.tacocraft.com; 204 SW 2nd St; mains $5-15; ☉11:30am-midnight) One of a stable of funky eateries and bars along this strip, this taqueria and tequila bar serves up a great atmosphere, even better drinks and very good tacos. It attracts both a younger crew and mature hipster crowd who head here for pork belly and ahi tuna fillings. These are chef-inspired (and yep, he's from Mexico).

Tuesday serves up $3 tacos.

Gran Forno Bakery
ITALIAN $

(Map p212; ☎954-467-2244; http://gran-forno. com; 1235 E Las Olas Blvd; mains $6-12; ☉7am- 6pm) This old-school Milanese-style bakery and cafe is a good takeout lunch spot in downtown Fort Lauderdale: warm crusty pastries, bubbling pizzas, and fat golden loaves of ciabatta, sliced and stuffed with ham, roast peppers, pesto and other tasty delicacies.

Louie Bossi's
ITALIAN $$

(www.louiebossi.com; 1032 E Las Olas Blvd; mains $16-30; ☉11am-11pm Mon-Thu, to 1am Fri & Sat, 10am-late Sun) Sit back and enjoy the bossi- ness (managers), the business (servers) and the bolshiness (waiting clients)...this is as Roman an experience as you can ever hope to have in the US. Servers race, crack pepper, sprinkle parmesan cheese. Chatter volume

Fort Lauderdale

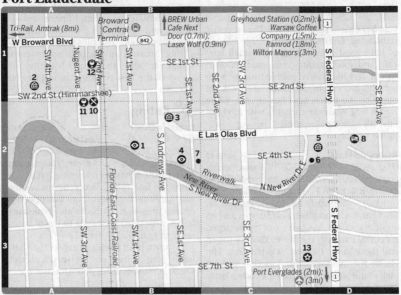

SOUTHEAST FLORIDA FORT LAUDERDALE

is on boom-box blasting levels. Pizzas are churned out of the 900-degree oven every 90 seconds.

Casablanca Cafe　　MEDITERRANEAN **$$**
(Map p208; ☑954-764-3500; www.casablanca cafeonline.com; 3049 Alhambra St; mains $10-34; ☺11:30am-2am) Try to score a seat on the front terrace of this Moroccan-style home where Mediterranean-inspired food and Florida-style ocean views are served. It won't knock your socks off, but it's a classic and it's all about location, location, location. Live music Tuesday to Saturday. Drinkers enjoy its piano bar.

Green Bar & Kitchen　　VEGAN **$$**
(☑954-533-7507; www.greenbarkitchen.com; 1075 SE 17th St; mains $8-12; ☺11am-9pm Mon-Sat, to 3pm Sun; ☑) Discover bright flavors and in-novative dishes at this modern, plant-based eatery located in a strip mall. Instead of pasta-layered lasagna, slivers of zucchini are layered with macadamia ricotta and sundried tomatoes. Almond milk replaces dairy in cold-pressed fruit smoothies, and the delectable cashew cup gives Reese's a run for its money.

It's good, but not worth the trek unless you're dreaming of something refreshingly minus meat or seafood.

★**Burlock Coast**　　INTERNATIONAL **$$$**
(Map p208; ☑954-302-6460; www.burlockcoast. com; Ritz Carlton, 1 N Fort Lauderdale Beach Blvd; mains $14-40; ☺7am-10pm Mon-Fri, noon-5pm Sat & Sun) Situated in the lovely Ritz Carlton Ho-tel, this chic casual spot somehow manages to be all things to all people: a cafe, bar, mar-ket and upmarket restaurant. The menu has been crafted to the mantra: local farmers and vendors. The menu changes seasonally but errs towards modern international, like pork belly with black truffle grits or simple fish and chips.

15th Street Fisheries　　SEAFOOD **$$$**
(☑954-763-2777; www.15streetfisheries.com; 1900 SE 15th St; bar mains $6-16, restaurant mains $26-38; ☑) Tucked away in Lauder-dale Marina with an open-fronted deck of-fering a front-row view of yachts, this place is hard to beat for waterfront dining. The wooden interior is kitted out like an Old Florida boathouse. The fine-dining restau-rant is upstairs and a more informal dock-side bar serves shrimp, crab and grilled mahimahi.

At the weekends there's live music from 6pm to 10pm. You can also reach the Fisher-ies via the water taxi.

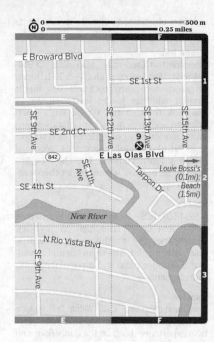

Casa D'Angelo ITALIAN $$$
(☎954-564-1234; http://casa-d-angelo.com; 1201 N Federal Hwy; mains $26-50; ⊙5:30-10:30pm) Chef Angelo Elia presides over an impressive kitchen specializing in Tuscan and southern Italian dishes, many handed down by his mother. Seasonality and quality translate into intense flavors and delightful textures: the sunburst taste of just-ripe tomatoes, peppery arugula, silken sea bass and surprisingly spicy cinnamon gelato. The restaurant stocks one of the finest wine lists in the state.

⟟ Drinking & Nightlife

Fort Lauderdale bars can stay open until 4am on weekends and 2am during the week. A handful of great bars and pubs are found in the Himmarshee Village area on SW 2nd St, while the beach offers plenty of open-air boozing.

★BREW Urban Cafe Next Door CAFE
(☎954-357-3934; www.facebook.com/brewnextdoor; 537 NW 1st Ave; ⊙7am-7pm; 🛜) Despite its unwieldy name, Brew is the coolest thing going in Fort Lauderdale: a kick-ass cafe located in a weird, semi-abandoned studio space filled with bookshelves. It looks like a British lord's library that got lost in an '80s warehouse party. It feels like you're heading to nowhere, but it's worth it for the coffee.

★Stache COCKTAIL BAR
(Map p212; ☎954-449-1044; http://stacheftl.com; 109 SW 2nd Ave; ⊙8am-5pm Mon & Thu, 8am-4am Fri, 8pm-4am Sat) A sexy 1920s drinking den serving crafted cocktails and rocking a crossover classic rock/funk/soul/R&B blend. At weekends there's live music, dancing and burlesque. Dress up; this is where the cool cats come to play. Serves coffee during the day; open late on weekends only.

★Rok:Brgr PUB
(Map p212; ☎754-525-7656; www.rokbrgr.com; 208 SW 2nd St; ⊙11:30am-midnight Mon-Thu, to 2am Fri & Sat, to 11pm Sun) One of several of this strip of hip bars and restaurants, Rok:Brgr shoots for a 1920s Chicago-era gastropub and somehow pulls it off. Edison light bulbs and contemporary industrial creates the ambience, while the cuisine is contemporary gastropub – gourmet burgers using locally sourced ingredients, plus Prohibition-style cocktails.

Warsaw Coffee Company CAFE
(www.warsawcoffee.com; 815 NE 13th St; ⊙7am-10pm Mon-Sat, to 6pm Sun) The coffee spot to

come to if you're serious about your brew. The main features of this industrial space are concrete, Tolix-style designer chairs and floor-to-ceiling windows. Plus fabulous, if pricey, coffee (but yes, a good pour does come at a premium).

Unfortunately the outlook is nothing much – the usual suburban car park – but the rest of the ambience is spot on. Fabulous baked items, too.

The Living Room Lounge
BAR

(Map p208; ☑954-414-8300.; www.wfortlauder dalehotel.com/living-room; The W Hotel, 401 N Fort Lauderdale Beach Blvd; ◐11am Mon-Thu, to 2am Fri & Sat, to midnight Sun) W Fort Lauderdale, the city's poshest digs, is proud of its 'living room' lounge that had a recent makeover. Created to be accessible and casual, it has the air of a relaxed and spacious bar, rather than a nightclub. You can sit at sofas or bar stools and the ambience is a cut above the rest in terms of style and clientele.

Patrons who aren't looking at their cell phones over a classic cocktail are ogling the crowd (and pretending they're not).

Laser Wolf
BAR

(☑954-667-9373; 901 Progresso Dr, Suite 101; ◐6pm-2am Mon-Thu, to 3am Fri, 8pm-3am Sat) We don't want to call Laser Wolf sophisticated, but its extensive booze menu and pop-art styling definitely attracts Fort Lauderdale's cerebral set. But they're an edgy, cerebral set that *loves* to party, so if this wolf is sophisticated, it knows how to let its hair down.

Wreck Bar
BAR

(Sheraton Fort Lauderdale; Map p208; ☑954-524-5551; 1140 Seabreeze Blvd; ◐5:30-11:30pm) After one too many cocktails you might wonder whether you're seeing things as you look through the Wreck Bar's 'portholes' to see three or four mermaids swimming seductively past. Here's our advice: keep drinking and enjoy this piece of priceless Florida kitsch. The show begins at 6:30pm, but you'll want to get there early for a spot.

Rosie's
BAR

(☑954-563-0123; www.rosiesbarandgrill.com; 2449 Wilton Dr; ◐11am-11pm) A low-key, straight-friendly neighborhood watering hole with a solid American menu, a wonderful outdoor patio and a popular Sunday brunch menu.

Ramrod
CLUB

(www.ramrodbar.com; 1508 Wilton Dr; ◐3pm-2am) A leather/bear/cowboy club with plenty to experience (both on the dancefloor and at the regular themed events), Ramrod is hardcore in every sense of the word. If you have to ask, maybe it's not for you.

Georgie's Alibi
CLUB

(www.alibiwiltonmanors.com; 2266 Wilton Dr; ◐11-2am) Georgie's is Wilton Manors' gay landmark, a nightclub featuring a playlist of Top 40s and country blockbusters along with

GAY & LESBIAN FORT LAUDERDALE

Sure, South Beach is a mecca for gay travelers, but Fort Lauderdale nips at the high heels of its southern neighbor. Compared to South Beach, Lauderdale is a little more rainbow-flag-oriented and a little less exclusive. And for the hordes of gay boys who flock here, either to party or to settle down, therein lies the charm.

Fort Lauderdale is home to several dozen gay bars and clubs, as many gay guesthouses, and a couple of way-gay residential areas. **Victoria Park** is the established gay hub just northeast of downtown Fort Lauderdale. A bit further north, **Wilton Manors** is a more recently gay-gentrified area boasting endless nightlife options. Look for Rosie's, a low-key neighborhood watering hole; The Manor, for nationally recognized performers and an epic dance floor; and Georgie's Alibi, best for its Wednesday comedy night with Cashetta, a fabulous female impersonator. There's even a leather/bear/cowboy club, Ramrod.

Gay guesthouses are plentiful; visit www.gayftlauderdale.com. Consult the glossy weekly rag *Hot Spots* (www.hotspotsmagazine.com) to keep updated on gay nightlife. For the most insanely comprehensive list of everything gay, log on to www.jumpon markslist.com.

cheap drinks after 9pm and ever-popular performers (see the website).

The Manor CLUB
(www.themanorcomplex.com; 2345 Wilton Dr; ⊙8pm-4am) This epic nightclub features nationally recognized singers and comedians, a young crowd (18 to 30) and a hot and sweaty dance floor. Saturdays is Latin night.

☆ Entertainment

★ Savor Cinema CINEMA
(Cinema Paradiso; Map p212; ☑954-525-3456; www.fliff.com/Cinema_Paradiso; 503 SE 6th St) This funky church-turned-cinema offers plush velvet seats, film festival entries, independent and European films, and plenty of kid-friendly programs. It's a great rainy-day standby. Events and films are posted on its Facebook page.

Blue Jean Blues JAZZ
(☑954-306-6330; www.bjblive.com; 3320 NE 33rd St; snacks $9-17; ⊙11am-2am Sun-Thu, to 3am Fri & Sat) Get away from the beach for a low-key evening of jazz and blues at this cool little neighborhood bar. There's live music seven nights a week and four afternoons, featuring a who's who of the southern Florida music scene. From East Sunrise Blvd head north for 2.3 miles and then turn left onto NE 33rd Street.

Serves burgers, pizzas and some other snacks, too.

🔒 Shopping

Swap Shop MARKET
(www.floridaswapshop.com; 3291 W Sunrise Blvd; ⊙9am-5pm Mon-Fri, 8am-6:30pm Sat, 7:30-6pm Sun) Perhaps the most fun shopping in town, the state's biggest flea market has acres of stalls selling everything from underwear to antique cookie jars to pink lawn flamingos, and a carnival atmosphere of mariachi music, hot-dog trucks and a 14-screen drive-in movie theater. The flea market is slightly northwest of downtown.

ℹ Getting There & Away

Fort Lauderdale is served by its own international **airport** (p207).

If you're driving here, I-95 and Florida's Turnpike run north–south and provide good access to Fort Lauderdale. I-595, the major east–west artery, intersects I-95, Florida's Turnpike and the Sawgrass Expressway. It also feeds into I-75, which runs to Florida's west coast.

AIR
Fort Lauderdale–Hollywood International Airport (p207) is off I-95 between Lauderdale and Hollywood. The airport has four terminals (following a recent expansion and massive investment) and is served by more than 35 airlines, including many low-cost carriers and nonstop flights from Europe.

From the airport, it's a short 20-minute drive to downtown, or a $25 cab ride.

BOAT
Port Everglades (www.porteverglades.net; 1850 Eller Drive) cruise port is considered one of the busiest ports in the world, accommodating both cruise ships and containers. From the port, walk to SE 17th St and take bus 40 to the beach or to Broward Central Terminal.

If you're heading to Fort Lauderdale in your own boat (not that unlikely here), head for the **Bahia Mar Resort & Yachting Center** (Map p208; ☑954-627-6309; www.bahiamar yachtingcenter.com; 801 Seabreeze Blvd; ⊙7am-6pm).

BUS
The **Greyhound Station** (☑954-764-6551; www.greyhound.com; 515 NE 3rd St) is about four blocks from Broward Central Terminal, the central transfer point for buses in the area.

TRAIN
Tri-Rail (☑954-783-6030; www.tri-rail.com; 6151 N Andrews Ave) runs between Miami and Fort Lauderdale (one way $5, 45 minutes). A feeder system of buses has connections at no charge. You'll find free parking provided at most stations. Provide ample cushion for delays. **Amtrak** (☑800-872-7245; www.amtrak.com; 200 SW 21st Tce) also uses Tri-Rail tracks.

ℹ Getting Around

Sun Trolley (☑954-876-5539; www.suntrolley.com; per ride/day $1/3) runs between Las Olas and the beaches between 9:30am and 6:30pm Friday to Monday. **Broward County Transit** (p206) operates between downtown, the beach and Port Everglades. From **Broward Central Terminal** (Map p212; 101 NW 1st Ave), take bus 11 to upper Fort Lauderdale Beach and Lauderdale-by-the-Sea; bus 4 to Port Everglades; and bus 40 to 17th St and the beaches.

The fun, yellow **water taxi** (p209) travels the canals and waterways between 17th St to the south, Atlantic Blvd/Pompano Beach to the north, the Riverwalk to the west and the Atlantic Ocean to the east. There are also services to Hollywood ($15 per person).

Lauderdale-by-the-Sea

☑ 954 / POP 6390

In the late 1800s southern Florida was a wild frontier, home to a few dozen Seminole families and some hardy settlers. Remnants of this early history can be found in the flow of beachside communities north of Fort Lauderdale along the Intracoastal Waterway. This includes Lauderdale-by-the-Sea, the closest community to Fort Lauderdale. If you enter from the busy highway you'll find it hard to distinguish from Fort Lauderdale's city sprawl. However, turn coastwards for a mile, and you'll find yourself in a pretty town with a laid-back, beach resort feel.

◉ Sights & Activities

Anglin's Pier   LANDMARK

(admission $2; ⊙24hr) This popular fishing pier has a 24-hour tackle shop, night fishing lights and rod rental for $18. The pier itself was built in 1963 after storms destroyed the original, which was constructed in 1942 and had cannons perched on its end in anticipation of attack during WWII.

South Florida Diving Headquarters   DIVING

(☑954-783-2299; www.southfloridadiving.com; 101 N Riverside Dr, Pompano Beach; 2-tank dive/snorkeling $60/30; ⊙trips 8:30am & 1:30pm) Dive natural and artificial reefs, or float along one of the area's famous drift dives with this PADI-certified company. Snorkeling trips will keep nondivers happy.

⏖ Sleeping

★ Blue Seas Courtyard   HOTEL $$

(☑954-772-3336; http://blueseascourtyard.com; 4525 El Mar Dr; r from $139; P ✲ 🛜 ✺) Standing out from the crowd with a hacienda-style roof of clay barrel tiles, Mexican-themed yellow exterior and hand-stenciled decoration, Blue Seas seems to embody the sunny, laid-back disposition of Lauderdale-by-the-Sea. Owners Marc and Cristie have been at the helm since the 1970s, and provide a truly attentive and personalized service that keeps rooms booked up weeks in advance.

★ High Noon Beach Resort   MOTEL $$

(☑954-776-1121; www.highnoonresort.com; 4424 El Mar Dr; r/ste/apt from $188/222/239; ✲ @ 🛜 ✺) Smack bang in the middle of the action, and spilling onto the beach, this ultraclean resort

includes a number of properties in a row. You have a choice of rooms, efficiencies and apartments; these are modern and spotless, thanks to a recent refurb. The friendly owner's parents bought one of the properties in 1961 and it's been family-run ever since.

Seacrest Hotel   HOTEL $$

(☑954-530-8854; www.hotelseacrest.com; 4562 Bougainvillea Dr; r $179-249; P ✲ 🛜 ✺) One of the best-kept secrets in Lauderdale-by-the-Sea, the Seacrest is set back from the beach and offers the polished standards of a hotel within the intimate confines of a converted home. Pad across cool travertine marble floors to enormous beds with plump pillowtops before flicking on your favorite HBO show. There's a generous private pool, and the beach is just five minutes' walk away.

✕ Eating

Pan'e Dolci   CAFE $

(Italian Bakery; ☑954-635-2385; 207 Commercial Blvd; snacks $5-10; ⊙8am-11:30pm Mon-Thu, to midnight Fri-Sun) This smart Italian *dolceria* (cake shop) serves the most expensive cappuccino around ($5), but it's worth it for the authentic and oh-so-delicious Italian cakes. Plus the panini ($10) make a great takeout for the beach. It's handily located on the main drag.

Frenchy's Table   FRENCH $$

(☑954-533-2580; 235 Commercial Blvd; 2-/3-course meal from $28/35; ⊙5pm-late Mon-Sat) The owner, Edith, does the lot here: serves, cooks and chats. So an experience here is neither harried nor hurried, so don't come if you're here to eat and run. It's as French as Limoges (where Edith is from) and the interior is white and chic. It's got a touch of French elegance, and zero snootiness.

Vincent's   ITALIAN $$

(www.facebook.com/vincentsbythesea; 106 E Commercial Blvd; mains $15-39; ⊙noon-midnight) This Italian-American raw bar and pizzeria is the hot new place on the main drag. We had a great experience at the bar over excellent meatballs, but opinions on Vincent's vary. The bar is popular for locals who like to be seen, and the modern, industrial-chic space that opens onto the pavement has a sociable, if very loud, ambience.

Eduardo de San Angel   MEXICAN $$$

(☑954-772-4731; www.eduardodesanangel.com; 2822 E Commercial Blvd; mains $24-34; ⊙5:30pm-10pm Mon-Sat) Dreamy and upscale Mexican-

American fusion cuisine full of romantic ingredients – squash blossoms! Chocolate-chili! Guava syrup! All served in a warmly elegant dining room full of Mexican folk art.

🍸 Drinking & Nightlife

The Village Pump   BAR
(www.villagegrille.com; 4404 El Mar Dr; ⊙9am-2am) Serving sturdy drinks in a nautical wood-paneled room since 1949, the Village Pump simply hums at the daily happy hour where middle-aged regulars spill out onto the streets.

ⓘ Getting There & Away

Tri-Rail (p207) heads north from Fort Lauderdale. If you're driving, try to take A1A (sometimes called Ocean Blvd): the drive is glorious.

   Broward County Transit (p206) buses connect to beaches north of Fort Lauderdale and south to Las Olas in Fort Lauderdale itself. Fares are $2.

Deerfield Beach

☑954 / POP 79,700

Wherever you go along this coastline you'll be spoiled for choice for beaches, but Deerfield Beach is the best of the bunch. Deerfield Beach is a beautifully contained village, with a small core backed (unfortunately, like most of the southeastern coastline) by the US 1 highway. It's super friendly and lacks any pretension or snobbery; so with its lovely stretch of beach and some good eateries, it makes a great base – especially if you don't want to stay in Fort Lauderdale.

⊙ Sights

Deerfield Beach Historical Society   MUSEUM
(☑954-429-0378; www.deerfieldhistory.org; 380 E Hillsboro Rd; ⊙10am-2pm) FREE This organization is volunteer-run and oversees several sites from Deerfield Beach's early days in the 1920s. Back then the community was 1300 people strong and the town consisted of four or five stores, a lodge, a post office and two hotels. The Old Deerfield School, Kester Cottage and the Butler House museum are all open for tours on the first and third Saturday of the month.

Deerfield Beach   BEACH
(www.deerfield-beach.com) Deerfield Beach is an award-winning 'Blue Wave' beach with pristine water, nine lifeguard towers and a designated surfing area north of the pier and south of Tower 7.

Butterfly World   NATURE RESERVE
(www.butterflyworld.com; 3600 W Sample Rd, Coconut Creek; adult/child $30/22; ⊙9am-5pm Mon-Sat, from 11am Sun; 🐾) The first indoor butterfly park in the US is also one of the largest butterfly exhibits anywhere. It features thousands of live, exotic species, such as the bright blue morphos or camouflaged owl butterfly. Various exhibits highlight different creatures – from butterflies to hummingbirds. Butterfly World is an excellent place to spend the better part of a day, especially with wide-eyed children or trigger-happy photography enthusiasts.

🏃 Activities

Ski Rixen   WATER SPORTS
(www.skirixenusa.com; cable pass per hr/half-day $25/40; ⊙noon-8pm Tue-Sun) Deerfield's Quiet Waters Park is home to South Florida's only cable water-ski system. Using an innovative cabling system suspended from towers surrounding a half-mile course, water-skiers (and wake-boarders) are pulled over a wake-free watercourse. Obstacles are available for advanced tricksters; otherwise riders can perfect their water-skiing techniques without the hassle of a boat.

   Skiers under 18 must have a waiver form notarized and signed by their parents.

Island Water Sports   SURFING
(☑954-427-4929; www.islandwatersports.com; 1985 NE 2nd St; rental per hr from $10) The central spot is the kingdom of all things 'hang ten,' from surfboard, bodyboard and stand-up paddleboard rental to surf lessons. To tantalize you, they offer free lessons every Saturday (7am to 9am).

Splash Adventure Park   WATER PARK
(☑955-357-5100; www.broward.org/parks/quiet waterspark; 401 S Powerline Rd, Quiet Waters Park; admission per person/car $1.50/8; ⊙10am-5:20pm; 🐾) Hardly quiet, the 430-acre Quiet Waters Park (open 8am to 6pm) rings with the squeals of children and grown-ups enjoying all kinds of wet 'n' wild fun at its Splash Adventure Park ($5.25 per person). This water playground has a shallow pool and fountains spraying every which way. Be aware that hours may change seasonally.

✗ Eating

★ Tucker Duke's Lunchbox   BURGERS $
(☑ 954-708-2035; http://tuckerdukes.com; 1101 S Powerline Rd; mains $4-11; ⊙ 10:30am-10pm Sun-Wed, to 11pm Thu-Sat) Superior burgers and southern comfort food made from local, seasonal ingredients. The brain behind the brand (yes, it's a chain) is Florida native and *Cutthroat Kitchen* winner chef Brian Cartenuto, who is passionate about getting back to basics in the kitchen.

The Whale's Rib and Raw Bar   SEAFOOD $$
(☑ 954-421-8880; www.whalesrib.com; 2301 NE 2nd St; mains $11-21) If you ask a local where to eat, the Whale's Rib is a frequent suggestion. This seafood joint is renowned for its dolphin fingers and dolphin wrap. And before you report us to animal welfare authorities, they're 'talking mahimahi, not Flipper here,' as we were told. They also serve up tasty and generous helpings of chicken sandwiches and clams over linguine.

❶ Getting There & Away

Broward County Transit (☑ 954-357-8400; www.broward.org/bct) buses serve Deerfield Beach, connecting to Fort Lauderdale. Fares are $2.

Boca Raton

☑ 561 / POP 93,200

The name Boca Raton may mean 'mouth of the rat,' but there's nothing ratty about this proud-to-be-posh coastal town. What began as a sleepy residential community was transformed in the mid-1920s by architect Addison Mizner, who relied on his love of Spanish architecture to build the place into a fancy-pants town. His fingerprints remain on numerous structures throughout the area, though his name is most often invoked when talking about the popular anchor of town – the alfresco mall, Mizner Park. The rest of Boca is a mostly mainstream collection of chain stores and restaurants and, as you near the ocean, some peaceful beaches and parks. Most people don't come to Boca on vacation unless they have family here, as there are almost no beachfront hotels.

⊙ Sights

★ Gumbo Limbo Nature Center   PARK
(☑ 561-544-8605; www.gumbolimbo.org; 1801 N Ocean Blvd; suggested donation $5; ⊙ 9am-4pm Mon-Sat, noon-4pm Sun; ⓐ) Boca's best asset is this stretch of waterfront parkland. It's a preserve of tropical hammock and dunes ecosystems, and a haven for all manner of sea creatures and birds. Dedicated to educating the public about sea turtles and other local fauna, the natural-history displays include saltwater tanks full of critters. The highlight is the sea-turtle rehabilitation center.

Boca Raton Museum of Art   MUSEUM
(☑ 561-392-2500; www.bocamuseum.org; 501 Plaza Real; adult/student $12/free; ⊙ 10am-5pm Tue-Fri, noon-5pm Sat & Sun) In Mizner Park, this elegant museum showcases the minor works of modern masters such as Picasso, Chagall and Modigliani (note: these may rotate). It also has a genuinely worthwhile collection of pieces by 20th- and 21st-century American and European painters, sculptors and photographers. Regular exhibitions to boot.

It's open until 8pm on Thursdays.

Mizner Park   PLAZA
(www.miznerpark.com) Since Boca lacks a cohesive downtown, Mizner Park generally serves as the city's center. At the north end, the Count de Hoernle Amphitheater accommodates more than 4000 people for symphonies, ballet, rock concerts and other cultural events. This Spanish-style outdoor shopping mall, bookended on one side by the Boca Raton Museum of Art, has valet parking and a slew of chichi restaurants and upscale chain stores.

Red Reef Beach   BEACH
(1 N Ocean Blvd; per vehicle Mon-Fri $16, Sat & Sun $18; ⊙ 8am-sunset; ⓐ) Sadly Hurricane Sandy buried most of the artificial reef in 2012, but this beach – one of three in the area – is still tops for water-lovers. There are lifeguards and great shallow pools for beginner snorkelers. Together with neighboring South Beach Park, the beaches encompass some 60 acres of wild shores.

➾ Tours

Loxahatchee Everglades Tours   ECOTOUR
(☑ 800-683-5873; www.evergladesairboattours.com; 15490 Loxahatchee Rd, Parkland; 50min tour adult/child under 12yr $50/25; 70min tour adult/child under 12yr $70/35; ⊙ 9am-3pm) Ten miles west of downtown, Wild Lyle's Loxahatchee Everglades Tours offers 50- and 70-minute ecoexplorations of the

Everglades on one of eight custom airboats (a boat using a fan instead of a propeller to push it over the water). Guests enjoy an adventure ride through swampy marsh, around papyrus and hurricane grass and past long-winged birds and turtles and gators sunning themselves.

🛏 Sleeping & Eating

★ La Boca Casa
APARTMENT $$

(☑ 561-392-0885; www.labocacasa.com; 356 N Ocean Blvd; apt from $189) One of the couple of options in Boca Raton, this surprising find is opposite the beach. The modern self-contained units (19 in total) are housed in a long, white, contemporary building and surrounded by lush, green lawns. It makes a good base for exploring the coast. Minimum two-night stay.

Ben's Kosher Deli
DELI $

(www.bensdeli.net; 9942 Clint Moore Rd; mains $7-15; ⊙11am-9pm) The Florida outpost of a well-loved New York–based deli, Ben's sprawling menu covers all the Jewish classics – corned-beef sandwiches, knishes (potato-stuffed pastries), sweet-and-sour beef tongue and eggs with smoked salmon. The deli is 8 miles northwest of the Mizner Plaza in downtown Boca Raton.

Saquella
CAFE $$

(☑ 561-338-8840; www.saquellacafe.com; Mizner Park; mains $12-30; ⊙7am-9pm Mon-Sat, 7am-3:30pm Sun) The best thing about this place is that it is a 'no fry zone' – they are proud of the fact that nothing on the menu is fried. A shortened version of their self-description is: coffee bar, Italian bistro and restaurant-cum-tapas bar. They are far too sophisticated to say they are a money magnet; it's definitely one of Boca's come-to-be-seen brunch locations.

STaR
AMERICAN $$$

(Six Tables, A Restaurant; ☑ 561-347-6260; www.sixtablesbocaraton.com; Mizner Plaza, 112 NE 2nd St; menu $94; ⊙7-10pm Thu-Sat) Chef Jonathan Fyhrie offers an elegant and romantic dining experience for just six lucky tables. The evening starts with the chef drawing the curtains and locking the door, then a shared glass of bubbles, some cheese puffs and a presentation. Settle in for the evening with a flavorful five-course fixed price menu, which often includes a peerless lobster bisque and chateaubriand.

❶ Getting There & Away

Boca Raton is more or less equidistant (that is, 30 miles) from both **Fort Lauderdale–Hollywood International Airport** (FLL; p207) and **Palm Beach International Airport** (PBI; p236), and sprawls several miles east and west of I-95.

The **Tri-Rail Station** (www.tri-rail.com; 680 Yamato Rd) has shuttle services to both airports. Palm Tran bus 94 connects downtown Boca with the Tri-Rail station.

Palm Tran (http://discover.pbcgov.org/palmtran; per ride $2, day pass $5) serves southeast Florida between Jupiter and Boca Raton. It costs $2 to ride ($5 for a day pass). From the Tri-Rail station, bus 2 takes you to PBI and bus 94 to Florida Atlantic University, where you can transfer to bus 91 to Mizner Park. From Mizner Park, take bus 92 to South Beach Park.

Boca Raton Taxi (☑ 561-600-5051; www.bocaratontaxi.com) serves the area. Cabs to the Fort Lauderdale or Palm Beach airports cost around $58.

Delray Beach

☑ 561 / POP 66,000

Founded by Seminoles, and later settled in the 18th and 19th centuries by African Americans and Japanese agriculturists, who farmed pineapples just east of I-95, this melting pot retooled itself for the tourist trade when the railroads chugged through Delray Beach in 1896. Local hotels and clubs turned a blind eye to Prohibition laws and accommodated everyone. Perhaps this eclectic mix of early residents – from the industrious to the lawless – is the reason Delray so effortlessly juggles a casual seaside vibe and suave urban sophistication.

◎ Sights

★ Morikami Museum & Japanese Gardens
MUSEUM, GARDENS

(☑ 561-495-0233; www.morikami.org; 4000 Morikami Park Rd; adult/child $15/9; ⊙10am-5pm Tue-Sun) Japanese immigrant and pineapple farmer Sukeji 'George' Morikami, a member of the original Yamato settlement of Delray, donated his spectacularly landscaped 200-acre property for the establishment of a museum showcasing Japanese culture. Today you can wander more than a mile of pine-lined nature trails around koi-filled ponds, experiencing different Japanese gardens from bonsai to a 12th-century *shinden* (pleasure) garden modeled on a noble estate. To complement the gardens, the outstanding museum showcases more than 5000 Japanese antiques, objects and works of fine art.

On the third Saturday of the month you can take part in a tea ceremony in the **Seishin-An Teahouse** ($5 with admission to the museum). Classes, cultural and educational events are also offered. Check out the website for details.

The museum's Cornell Cafe serves neo-Japanese cuisine such as sweet-potato tempura, ginger-roasted duck and sushi rolls. It is considered one of the best museum restaurants in the country.

The museum is located 7.5 miles southwest of Old School Square.

Old School Square ARTS CENTER

(☑ 561-243-7922; http://oldschoolsquare.org; 51 N Swinton Ave) Otherwise known as Old School Square, this highly successful preservation project encompasses Delray's 1913 elementary school, 1925 high school and 1926 gymnasium. Now these buildings house the Cornell Art Museum, showcasing rotating exhibitions of local, national and international arts and crafts; the **Crest Theatre**; and a vibrant **School of Creative Arts**, sponsoring a program of classes, events, theater and exhibitions.

Cornell Art Museum MUSEUM

(http://oldschoolsquare.org/about/cornell-museum; Old School Square; suggested donation $5; ⊙ 10am-4:30pm Tue-Sat, from 1pm Sun) Located inside the restored 1913 Delray Elementary building within Old School Square, this charming museum hosts rotating exhibits featuring an eclectic mix of local, national and international fine art, crafts and pop culture.

Public Beach BEACH

(Ocean Blvd) A hip gathering spot for young locals and visitors with excellent surf for swimming and lifeguards. Coin-operated parking meters charge $1.25 per hour.

Atlantic Dunes Park PARK

(www.downtowndelraybeach.com; 1600 Ocean Blvd) Has 7 acres of shorefront, clean restroom facilities, volleyball courts and picnic areas.

🛏 Sleeping

★ Parliament Inn GUESTHOUSE $$

(☑ 561-276-6245; www.florida-info.com; 1236 George Bush Blvd; 2-person ste $99-209, 4-person ste $107-227; Ⓟ❇🤍📶🏊) This lushly planted hideaway is tucked away just off Delray's spectacular 2-mile beach. It's easy to miss given the eight lemon-yellow, single-story units are situated in a gorgeous tropical garden shaded by towering palms. The trees are strung with hammocks from where you can idly contemplate the turquoise pool. Each unit has a kitchen, living space and a private porch.

Wright by the Sea HOTEL $$

(☑ 561-278-3355; www.wbtsea.com; 1901 S Ocean Blvd; studio winter $243-285, summer $147-196; Ⓟ❇🤍📶🏊) With a spiffy green lawn and retro blue shutters, this shipshape little seaside hotel recalls the glory days of 1950s American family travel. The 29 suites are spacious and clean, with pullout couches and private hallways leading from the living room to the bathroom, a boon for those traveling with children. And, yay, there's no minimum stay.

★ Sundy House Inn B&B $$$

(☑ 561-272-5678; www.sundyhouse.com; 106 S Swinton Ave; r Sun-Thu from $299, Fri & Sat from $320; Ⓟ❇🤍📶🏊) Stepping through the front gate at this sumptuous B&B feels like being transported to Bali. Pathways twine through a dense 1-acre garden of trumpet flowers, hibiscus and coconut palms, the vegetation occasionally parting to reveal vintage bird cages or Chinese lion statues. Guestrooms are British-colonial chic, with heavy wood furniture and dark shutters.

Crane's Beach House GUESTHOUSE $$$

(☑ 561-278-1700; www.cranesbeachhouse.com; 82 Gleason St; studio/apt from $349/from $469; Ⓟ❇@🤍📶🏊) This hidden garden guesthouse has some 28 spacious rooms and apartments (with kitchenette), brightly appointed in colorful Key West style with loads of funky local art. Palm-shaded grotto swimming pools and a tiki bar (Thursday to Saturday) and weekend live music add a fun, sociable spirit. The ultrafriendly staff love to chat and help out with tips and restaurant recommendations.

Eating

★ El Camino MEXICAN $

(☑ 561-865-5350; www.elcaminodelray.com; 15 NE 2nd Ave, Pineapple Grove; mains $10-16; ⊙ 11am-2am) It's hard to know what's better: the industrial-chic fitout in this former car garage (complete with original hoists), the new-age interpretation and ambience of a traditional Mexican cantina, or the fabulous array of of tacos and burritos and margaritas. Tuesday Tacos brings a $2 bite of Mexican *paradiso,* though we love the smoked brisket served in an enchilada, quesadilla, whatever...

The New Vegan
VEGAN $

(☑ 561-404-5301; www.thenewvegan.com; 528 NE 2nd St; mains $8-17; ☉10am-3:30pm & 5:30-9:30pm Wed-Sun; ☑) You don't come here for a romantic restaurant meal – it's a light, simple, cafe-style place – but vegans will swoon nonetheless. A rarity in them-these parts, this place practices what it preaches: wholesome burgers, salads, wraps and melts. All 100% vegan.

Cornell Cafe
ASIAN $$

(mains $9-17; ☉11am-3pm Tue-Sun) On the grounds of the gardens of Morikami Museum & Japanese Gardens (p219), Cornell Cafe serves neo-Japanese cuisine such as sweet-potato tempura, ginger-roasted duck and sushi rolls. It is definitely 'up there' when it comes to museum restaurants. It's 7.5 miles southwest of Old School Square.

★ Joseph's Wine Bar
MEDITERRANEAN $$$

(☑ 561-272-6100; www.josephswinebar.com; 200 NE 2nd Ave 107; lunch mains $10-15, dinner mains $22-39; ☉11am-10pm) Hosted by the gregarious Joseph, lunch or dinner at this friendly eatery is an elegant and convivial affair. Everything is made fresh to order so relax, take a wine recommendation from Joseph and await a vibrant selection of dips (including a deliciously smokey baba ghanoush), salads and wraps at lunchtime, and a sophisticated selection of mains in the evening. The baked rack of lamb in an unctuous Chianti sauce is a particular highlight.

J&J Raw Bar
SEAFOOD $$$

(☑ 561-272-3390; www.jjseafooddelray.com; 634 E Atlantic Blvd; mains $21-37; ☉11:30am-10:30pm) Perennially popular raw bar serving up generous platters of little neck clams, Gulf Coast oysters and seasonal stone crab claws. The J&J Seafood Trio appetizer ($16), featuring shrimps, scallops and crab cakes, is big enough for a main. Otherwise opt for the delicious nut-crusted snapper in a sweet lime and rum butter sauce.

Sundy House Restaurant
AMERICAN $$$

(☑ 561-272-5678; 106 S Swinton Ave; mains $28-42, Sunday brunch $58; ☉6-9pm Tue-Sun, brunch 10:30am-2pm Sat & Sun) Nibble on a charcuterie selection and the likes of braised pork shank or seared scallops at Delray's most romantic restaurant, overlooking the primeval Taru Gardens at the Sundy House Inn. The Sunday brunch, featuring made-to-order crepes and a prime rib-carving station, is an extravaganza. (Saturday brunch is à la carte.) Definitely reserve ahead.

🍸 Drinking & Nightlife

★ Dada
BAR

(☑ 561-330-3232; http://sub-culture.org/dada; 52 N Swinton Ave; ☉5pm-2am) Join the cool cats lounging in this 'non-conformist' two-story bungalow to sip cocktails, hear poetry readings or live bands, and nibble on ravioli, salads and hummus. The front porch, outdoor lanterns and boho vibe all add to the romantic charm.

Subculture Coffee
CAFE

(☑ 561-318-5142; http://subculturecoffee.com; 123 E Atlantic Ave; ☉7am-midnight Sun-Thu, 7am–2am Fri & Sat) Calling all coffee snobs. Baristas here sure do know to roast beans, plus how to prepare a macchiato or a flat white (yes, they even know this Australian favorite). A fine spot for a break, though the cafe interiors, despite the amazing espresso machines and hip counter decor, aren't inviting enough to warrant an entire coffee-drinking morning.

☆ Entertainment

★ Arts Garage
ARTS CENTER

(☑ 561-450-6357; www.artsgarage.org; 180 Northeast 1st St; ☉box office 10am-6pm) Delray's community arts center hosts anything from bands and musical performances to radio shows and theater. Patrons can bring their own wine and snacks and, given the intimate size, there isn't a bad seat in the house.

🛍 Shopping

Murder on the Beach Mystery Bookstore
BOOKS

(☑ 561-279-7790; www.murderonthebeach.com; 273 NE 2nd Ave, Pineapple Grove; ☉10am-6pm Mon-Sat, noon-5pm Sun) For those looking for a good beach read, the rather particular Murder on the Beach bookstore specializes in Floridian mystery authors. You can also pick up general interest books on Florida here.

ℹ Getting There & Away

Delray Beach is about 20 miles south of West Palm Beach and 45 miles north of Miami on I-95, US Hwy 1 or Hwy A1A.

The **Greyhound Station** (☑561-272-6447; www.greyhound.com; 1587 SW 4th Ave) is served by **Palm Tran** (p219). Bus 2 takes you to Palm Beach International Airport or Boca Raton; bus 81 services the Tri-Rail station, Amtrak and downtown Delray. Amtrak, half a mile south of Atlantic Ave, shares a station with **Tri-Rail** (☑800-874-7245; www.tri-rail.com; 345 S Congress Ave).

Lake Worth

☑561 / POP 37,000

Billing itself as 'Where the tropics begin,' this bohemian community sits further east than any place in South Florida. Meanwhile, just offshore, the Gulf Stream flows further west than anywhere along the coast. This geographical good fortune means Lake Worth has warm weather year-round. Add to that a distinct artsy vibe, a cool collection of eateries, a robust local music scene and a spectacular sliver of public-access beachfront. It comes as a surprise after its more suburban and suburban-chic neighbors.

◎ Sights & Activities

Lake Worth Beach   BEACH
This stretch of sand is universally agreed to be the finest between Fort Lauderdale and Daytona. Surfers come from miles around to tame the waves; everyone else comes to enjoy the fine white sand.

Snook Islands Natural Area   PARK
(www.lakeworth.org/visitors/parks; Lake Avenue Bridge) Twenty-mile long Lake Worth lagoon is Palm Beach county's largest estuary and an important warm-water refuge for manatees. To reverse some of the damage from years of development, this $18 million natural area was created, stretching 1.2 miles north from Lake Avenue into the lagoon. Restoring miles of mangroves and laying down new oyster beds to encourage the growth of sea grasses, a favorite manatee snack, has enabled a startling number of birds and marine life to return.

Kayak Lake Worth   KAYAKING
(☑561-225-8250; http://kayaklakeworth.com; kayaks 2/4hr $40/50, tours per person $40-60) This mobile kayak and paddleboard operator can kit you up with all the necessary equipment for kayaking, paddleboarding and fishing, mainly in the areas of Snook Islands Natural Area and Bingham Islands. Two- to three-hour eco, sunset and moonlight tours

are also available with knowledgeable local guides Bryce and Emily.

Wet Pleasures   DIVING
(☑561-547-4343; www.wetpleasuresfla.com; 312 W Lantana Rd; ⊙9am-6:30pm Mon & Wed-Sat, to 4pm Sun) Lake Worth enjoys some excellent snorkeling and diving opportunities. Head to this (unfortunately named) dive shop for lessons, equipment and advice. They'll also hook you up with charters to take you diving as far south as the Keys. Prices vary according to the length and type of excursion.

⚑ Festivals & Events

Street Painting Festival   CULTURAL
(www.streetpaintingfestivalinc.org; ⊙Feb) If you're visiting in February, don't miss the fantastic Street Painting Festival, when artists come from far and wide to cover Lake Worth's pedestrianized main streets with more than 200 surreal images of superheroes and Old Masters. Wander the open-air gallery while snacking on barbecue, tacos or cheese sandwiches, then settle down for live music in the park.

🛌 Sleeping & Eating

★**Sabal Palm B&B**   B&B $$
(☑561-582-1090; www.sabalpalmhouse.com; 109 N Golfview Rd; r winter $179-249, summer $109-199; ❄🐱) A classic knickknack-filled B&B, this smart and spotless 1936 house has rooms named after artists. It's frilly, but neatly so; if that's not your thing, opt for the Dali Room that has an art deco, modern vibe. Owners Colleen and John are most helpful. Discount for longer stays.

It's opposite the golf course and the beach is a 10-minute walk over the bridge that spans the Intracoastal Waterway.

Pelican   DINER, INDIAN $
(610 Lake Ave; mains $3-10; ⊙7am-1pm Mon-Fri, to 2pm Sat & Sun; 🍴) This early-risers' place offers hearty portions of perfectly prepared breakfast, plus a carnival of vegetarian-friendly specials with Indian flavors (the owners are Pakistani). It's an old-style diner with dated decor and you can sit at the bar or at inside or outside tables. Don't miss the Nihari beef shank ($17.95).

Downtown Pizza   PIZZA $$
(☑561-586-6448; 608 Lake Ave; pizza $11-22; ⊙11am-11pm) In business for more than 20 years, this sliver of a restaurant serves up delicious pizza with generous toppings (up to 18-inch bases). Meat-lovers should try

the Philly cheese steak pizza with shredded steak tips, peppers and onions.

★ **Paradiso Ristorante**   ITALIAN $$$
(☑ 561-547-2500; www.paradisolakeworth.com; 625 Lucerne Ave; 3-course lunch menu $23, mains $38-56; ⊘ 11:30am-3pm & 5:30-10pm) From the elegant interior to exquisitely presented dishes of homemade pasta, sheep ricotta gnocchi and succulent veal fillet, this is a dining experience to savor. Seasonal delights such as truffles, chestnuts and huckleberries call from the specialty menu. Scheduled wine dinners and theater packages are arranged in conjunction with the Lake Worth Playhouse. Reservations are recommended.

🍷 Drinking & Nightlife

★ **CWS**   BAR
(☑ 561-318-5637; www.cwslw.com; 522 Lucerne Ave; ⊘ 4pm-midnight Mon, 8am-midnight Tue, 8am-1am Wed & Thu, 8am-2am Fri, noon-2am Sat, 11am-midnight Sun) This trendy gastropub has a fabulous speakeasy vibe and whisky den feel. A beer garden attracts the younger crowd for live music but clients of all ages find their own niche and tuck into a choice of beers, classic cocktails and a dram or three of whisky. There are over 400 whiskys (from a collection of over 600).

Oh, and there are fabulous meals (menu changes regularly). The handmade pasta is our fave but go with the specials.

Igot's Martiki Bar   BAR
(☑ 561-582-4468; www.facebook.com/igotsmartiki bar; 702 Lake Ave; ⊘ noon-2am) Get acquainted with Lake Worth's most eccentric locals at this surf-themed watering hole. It's open-sided so you can either sit at the high tops at the bar and watch the ball game or take a pew streetside and watch the sidewalk scene. Drinks are poured strong, and there's live music Thursday through Sunday.

Havana Hideout   BAR
(www.havanahideout.com; 509 Lake Ave; ⊘ 11am-2am) A self-promoted 'dive,' the open-air, palm-fringed Havana has live music most nights, a thoughtful draft-beer selection and an on-site taqueria. Monday is an all-day happy hour.

☆ Entertainment

★ **Lake Worth Playhouse**   THEATER
(☑ 561-586-6410; www.lakeworthplayhouse.org; 713 Lake Ave; tickets $23-35) Housed in a restored 1924 vaudeville venue, this intimate spot stages classic community theater. The attached **Stonzek Studio Theatre** screens independent films (tickets $7 to $9). The Dinner + Theater package with Paradiso Ristorante is an absolute bargain; prices start from $60.

★ **Bamboo Room**   LIVE MUSIC
(☑ 561-585-2583; http://bambooroommusic.com; 25 S J St; ⊘ 7pm-3am Thu-Sat) This favorite spot has an intimate roadhouse feel and features regional and internationally known blues, rockabilly, alt-country and jam bands, drawing music-lovers from miles around.

Lake Worth Drive-In   CINEMA
(☑ 561-965-4518; www.facebook.com/LakeWorth DriveIn; 3438 Lake Worth Rd; tickets adult/child $7/2) When was the last time you went to the drive-in? Screening first-run movies under the stars seven nights a week – drive in, tune in and sit back. Coolers are welcome; dogs are not.

ℹ Getting There & Away

The **Tri-Rail station** (www.tri-rail.com; 1703 Lake Worth Rd) is at the intersection of A St. **Palm Tran** (p219) bus 61 connects the station to downtown.

Palm Beach

🛈 561 / POP 8500

The third-wealthiest city in America, Palm Beach is home to 25 billionaires and looks every inch the playground for the rich and famous. Palatial Greco-Roman mansions line the shore; Bentleys and Porsches cruise the wide avenues of downtown; and streets look clean enough to eat off. Life here revolves around charity balls, designer shopping and cocktail-soaked lunches. Though all the bling may feel a bit intimidating, fear not – much of Palm Beach is within the reach of all travelers. Stroll along the truly gold Gold Coast beach, ogle the massive gated compounds on A1A or window-shop in uber-ritzy Worth Ave – all for free.

These days, Palm Beach is frequently in the news because of US President Donald Trump, whose mansion-cum-private-club, Mar-a-Lago, is here.

Despite all the glitz, the architecture and history is nothing but fascinating, and offers some insight into how it might have been to live during the Gilded Age of the late-19th-century USA.

Palm Beach

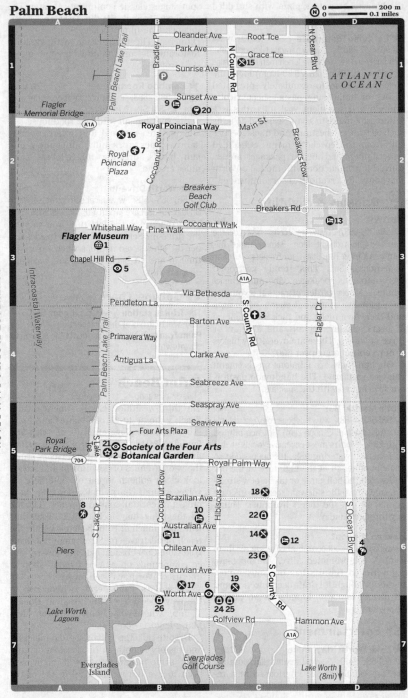

0 200 m
0 0.1 miles

ATLANTIC OCEAN

Oleander Ave
Root Tce
Park Ave
Grace Tce
Sunrise Ave
15
N County Rd
Bradley Pl
N Ocean Blvd

Flagler Memorial Bridge
Palm Beach Lake Trail

Sunset Ave
9
20

A1A

Royal Poinciana Way
Main St
16
Royal Poinciana Plaza
7
Cocoanut Row
Breakers Row

Breakers Beach Golf Club

Breakers Rd
13
Whitehall Way
Pine Walk
Cocoanut Walk
Flagler Museum
1
Chapel Hill Rd
5

Intracoastal Waterway

Via Bethesda
A1A
Pendleton La
Barton Ave
3
S County Rd
Primavera Way
Palm Beach Lake Trail
Antigua La
Clarke Ave
Flagler Dr
Seabreeze Ave
Seaspray Ave
Seaview Ave
Four Arts Plaza
Royal Park Bridge
S Lake Tce
21
Society of the Four Arts
2 **Botanical Garden**
704

Royal Palm Way
Brazilian Ave
18
Cocoanut Row
S Lake Dr
Hibiscus Ave
10
22
8
Australian Ave
14
12
11
Chilean Ave
23
S County Rd
S Ocean Blvd
Piers
Peruvian Ave
4
19
17
6
Worth Ave
26
24 25
Golfview Rd
Hammon Ave
A1A

Lake Worth Lagoon

Everglades Island
Everglades Golf Course
Lake Worth (8mi)

Palm Beach

◉ Sights

★ Flagler Museum
MUSEUM

(☑ 561-655-2833; www.flaglermuseum.us; 1 White-hall Way; adult/child $18/10; ◷ 10am-5pm Tue-Sat, noon-5pm Sun) This museum is housed in the spectacular 1902 mansion built by Henry Flagler as a gift for his bride, Mary Lily Kenan. The Beaux Arts–styled Whitehall was one of the most modern houses of its era and quickly became the focus of the winter season. Designed by John Carrère and Thomas Hastings, both students of the Ecole des Beaux-Arts in Paris and collaborators on other Gilded Age landmarks such as the New York Public Library, the elaborate 75-room house was the first residential home to feature a heating system.

Its modish, pink aluminum-leaf wallpaper was more expensive, at the time, than gold. Downstairs, public rooms such as the 4750-sq-ft Grand Hall, the Library with its painted cast plaster ceiling and the silk- and wood-lined Drawing Room wow visitors with their detailed craftmanship and opulence. Upstairs, intimate bedrooms give an insight into family life. Of particular interest is the **Flagler/Kenan History Room**, which chronicles, through letters, newspaper clippings and photographs, Flagler's personal and professional life and Mary Lily's family history.

If you'd like more than to simply wander around the house, take a look at the website for a whole host of lectures, talks and exhibits, as well as the critically acclaimed **Music Series** that features intimate chamber concerts in the West Room followed by a champagne reception ($70 per person).

Time your visit right and you can segue into a 'Gilded Age Style' lunch in the Café des Beaux-Arts (p229), which is housed in the **Pavilion**, a 19th-century, iron-and-glass railway palace, which also displays Flagler's private railroad car. Here you can dine on finger sandwiches, scones and custom-blended teas while looking out over Lake Worth.

Free, one-hour docent-led tours depart at 11am, 12:30pm and 2pm Tuesday to Saturday or you can pick up a free audioguide. This is a fabulous, not-to-be-missed experience and if there's only one place to visit to immerse yourself in the Gilded Age, this is it.

★ Society of the
Four Arts Botanical Garden
GARDENS

(www.fourarts.org; 2 Four Arts Plaza, via Royal Palm Way; ◷ 10am-5pm) FREE These stunning gardens were originally designed and cultivated by the Garden Club in 1938 as 'demonstration gardens' to showcase tropical plants that suited the South Florida climate. This included a garden suitable for a

Spanish-style house, a moonlight garden of white plants, plus Chinese, rose and jungle gardens, and others with fountains and tropical fruit trees. A landscape architect was employed in the 1950s to bring the elements together, although the 2004 hurricanes destroyed much of the area.

The current club painstakingly reconstructed the gardens, which provide a lovely respite for locals and visitors.

Worth Avenue
AREA

(www.worth-avenue.com) This quarter-mile, palm-tree-lined strip of more than 200 high-end brand shops is like the Rodeo Dr of the east. You can trace its history back to the 1920s when the now-gone Everglades Club staged weekly fashion shows and launched the careers of designers such as Elizabeth Arden. Even if you don't have the slightest urge to sling a swag of glossy bags over your arm, the people-watching is priceless, as is the Spanish Revival architecture.

To learn about the design and fascinating park, don't miss the walking tour.

Sea Gull Cottage
NOTABLE BUILDING

(60 Cocoanut Row) Sea Gull Cottage was constructed in 1886 overlooking what was a freshwater lake (now the Intracoastal Waterway) by RR MCCormick, the Denver railroad and land developer. This was Flagler's first Palm Beach residence after he purchased it in 1893. It is the oldest house on the island, although it used to be located next to the Royal Poinciana Hotel, Flagler's first resort hotel in Palm Beach. It was moved to its current site for preservation in 1984.

Built in the Florida vernacular style, the shingle cottage was famous as the 'showplace along the shores,' so pretty was its stained glass windows, Georgian marble floors and commanding viewing turret. You can't enter the building, but it's worth viewing its exterior in any case.

Bethesda-by-the-Sea
CHURCH

(☑561-655-4554; www.bbts.org; 141 S County Rd; ☺9am-5pm Mon-Sat, 7am-4pm Sun) After visiting Tiffany's windows on Worth Ave, head to Bethesda-by-the-Sea to admire its glorious Tiffany window and grand Gothic architecture. Built in 1926 to replace the first Protestant church of Palm Beach, it has a long community history and has hosted many a celebrity wedding, including those of US President Donald Trump to First Lady Melania Trump, and Michael Jordan.

To the side is a tranquil English-style cloister and the lovely Cluett Memorial Garden.

Phipps Ocean Park
BEACH

South of Southern Blvd on Ocean Blvd, before the Lake Worth Bridge, this is another place to catch rays.

Palm Beach Municipal Beach
BEACH

(Ocean Blvd, btwn Royal Palm Way & Hammon Ave; ☺sunrise-sunset) This is one of Palm Beach's two beautiful public beaches, both of which are kept seaweed-free by the town. Metered beachfront parking costs an absurd $5 per hour – head inland to snag free streetfront parking downtown. This beach can get crowded.

For privacy, head north along S Ocean Blvd and turn left onto Barton Ave. There's free two-hour parking near the church before S County Rd and public access to the beach across from Clarke Ave.

🏃 Activities

★ Palm Beach Lake Trail
WALKING, CYCLING

(Royal Palm Way, at the Intracoastal Waterway) The first 'road' in Palm Beach ran along the Intracoastal Waterway, and provided a 5-mile paved path stretching from Worth Ave (in the south) to Indian Rd (in the north) for Flagler's hotel guests to stretch their legs and scope out the social scene. Nicknamed 'The Trail of Conspicuous Consumption,' it is sandwiched between two amazing views: Lake Worth lagoon to the west, and an unending series of mansions to the east.

To get here from Worth Ave, walk west to S Lake Dr and follow the path north to the Sailfish Club. For an abbreviated version, park in the metered lot off Royal Palm Way (or in the supermarket's lot on Sunset Ave) and head west to pick up the trail. Another nice stretch runs along N County Rd. Park on Sunset Ave and head north on the path running to Palm Beach Country Club. At just under 2 miles, the route is lined with houses and magnificent trees and there are plenty of exotic side streets to explore.

If bike rentals are not available at your hotel, head to Palm Beach Bike Shop. There's a 10 mph speed limit on the trail.

Palm Beach Bike Shop
CYCLING

(☑561-659-4583; www.palmbeachbicycle.com; Royal Poinciana Plaza, Cocoanut Row; ☺9am-5:30pm Mon-Sat, 10am-5pm Sun) This shop rents out all manner of wheeled transportation, including bikes ($39 per day), skates ($39 per day) and scooters ($100 per day). Helmets cost $5 extra.

☞ Tours

★ Island Living Tours   CULTURAL
(✆ 561-868-7944; www.islandlivingpb.com; tours $35-150) Intriguing driving and cycling tours led by local resident Leslie Diver give a hint at some of the personal stories and history behind all the glitz. Her spiel covers the history, architecture and details about famous and infamous residents. Tours vary and can be tailored accordingly, and last between 1½ and 2½ hours or more, depending on the content.

Historical Walking Tour   CULTURAL
(✆ 561-659-6909; www.worth-avenue.com; 256 Worth Ave; $10; ⊙ 11am Wed) If you are here on a Wednesday be sure to head off on a walking tour with local historian and character, Rick Rose. The one-hour tour covers the history of Worth Avenue, giving fabulous context to the Spanish Revival era, the social scene and the fashion behind the town since the Gilded Age.

Tours are popular among middle-aged (mainly) women and groups can get a bit large, but if you are happy with the odd elbow, this is not to be missed. The ticket price is donated to an animal rescue outfit. Meet opposite Tiffany & Co.

🛏 Sleeping

Bradley Park Hotel   HOTEL $$
(✆ 561-832-7050; www.bradleyparkhotel.com; 2080 Sunset Ave; r $229, ste $329-359; P ❋ ☞) The midrange Bradley (built in 1921) offers large, gold-hued rooms, some with original features from the era and characterful furniture. Rooms with kitchens feel like mini-apartments, and it's located just a short walk from the shops and restaurants of Royal Poinciana Way.

Palm Beach Historic Inn   B&B $$
(✆ 561-832-4009; www.palmbeachhistoricinn. com; 365 S County Rd; r $159-239, ste $189-329; ❋ ☞ 🐕) Housed on the 2nd floor of a landmark building brimming with character, this intimate European-style hotel has 13 small, light-filled rooms with hardwood floors and period Palm Beach furnishings. It's more dated and less pretentious than the rest of Palm Beach's offerings, and this is reflected in the price. Stroll a block to the beach, or two to Worth Ave.

★ Brazilian Court   HOTEL $$$
(✆ 561-655-7740; www.thebraziliancourt.com; 301 Australian Ave; r $599-699, ste $799-1200; P ❋ ☞ ☒ 🐕) Built in 1926, this elegant resort is an excellent choice for those who want pampering but not obsequiousness. Trendy but timeless, it's got a lovely Mediterranean style, a romantic courtyard and fashionable suites that effortlessly blend sleek lines and soft comfort. The on-site Frédéric Fekkai salon and renowned (and ultraromantic) French Café Boulud (p228) are major draws, too.

Heading to the beach? Hitch a ride in the hotel's house car – your driver will supply you with chairs, umbrellas, towels, bottled water and magazines. Bliss. Low season rates are significantly lower. Valet parking costs $27 per night.

★ The Breakers   RESORT $$$
(✆ 888-273-2537; www.thebreakers.com; 1 S County Rd; r/ste from $699/from $2000; P ❋ @ ☞ ☒ 🐕) ✆ Originally built by Henry Flagler (in 1904, rooms cost $4 per night, including meals), today this 550-room resort sprawls across 140 acres and boasts a staff of 2000 plus, fluent in 56 languages. Just feet from the county's best snorkeling, this palace has two 18-hole golf courses, a mile of semiprivate beach, four pools and the best brunch around.

For opulence, elegance and old-world charm, there's no other choice; it's one of those once-in-a-lifetime experiences. Green Lodging certified.

Also worth noting is that prices fluctuate enormously and are drastically reduced in low season.

Chesterfield   HOTEL $$$
(✆ 561-659-5800; www.chesterfieldpb.com; 363 Cocoanut Row; r/ste from $310/from $535; P ❋ ☞ ☒ 🐕) From its old-fashioned room keys to the cookie jar in the lobby, this hotel aims for a British-inspired, old-world elegance that's much appreciated by its loyal guests, many of whom have been returning for decades. Room decor varies (each room is unique) from a 'Great White Hunter' feel with plaid wallpaper and murals of monkeys gamboling around the jungle, to padded-fabric walls.

The hotel's Leopard Lounge (p229), with its painted ceilings and tiger-print banquettes, is a perennial favorite for long lunches and evening piano music. You can even have high tea in the small library ($38 per person).

✗ Eating

Green's Pharmacy
DINER $

(☑561-832-0304; 151 N County Rd; mains $4-11; ☺7am-4pm Mon-Fri, to 4pm Sat, to 2pm Sun) Housed inside a working pharmacy, this place hasn't changed since John F Kennedy, looking to slip away from the Secret Service, would stroll across the mint-green linoleum to grab a bite. Choose between a table or a stool at the Formica counter and order from the paper menu just like everyone else, from trust-fund babies to beach-bound college girls.

You'll be largely ignored if you're not a regular, but it's all part of the fun.

Surfside Diner
DINER, BREAKFAST $

(☑561-659-7495; 314 S County Rd; mains $8-12; ☺8am-3pm) This classy remake of a classic diner serves one of the better brunch options in town. Pancakes, chicken breakfast burritos and French toast are all tasty. For lunch there's a healthy offering of grilled cheese and tomato soup, BLTs, PB&Js and sliders.

★ Būccan
MODERN AMERICAN $$

(☑561-833-3450; www.buccanpalmbeach.com; 350 S County Rd; mains $18-45; ☺5pm-midnight Sun-Thu, 5pm-1am Fri & Sat) With its modern American menu and Clay Conley, a James Beard–nominated chef, at the helm, Būccan is the 'it' eatery in Palm Beach. Flavor-hop with a selection of small plates, including snapper ceviche and octopus tabbouleh, and move on to Moroccan chicken. Reservations recommended.

★ HMF
INTERNATIONAL $$

(The Breakers Resort, 1 S County Rd; mains $16-25; ☺5pm-1am) HMF stands for the man himself: Henry Morrison Flagler. This stunning bar-cum-lounge is within the building's North Loggia where you'll definitely feel the ghosts of glitterati past. While the dress codes might differ these days (although most arrive elegantly attired), the party atmosphere – and whispers about the 'who's who, what and where' – is still going strong.

It's chic, sophisticated and a delightful spot for a cocktail and a selection of wines, plus delicious small plates with a very large global influence.

Pizza al Fresco
PIZZA $$

(☑561-832-0032; www.pizzaalfresco.com; 14 Via Mizner; pizzas $15-25, salads $11-22; ☺9am-10pm; 🐾) If Worth Ave shopping is making you feel fatigued, duck into quaint Via Mizner and take the strain off your feet at this alfresco pizza place. Light-spangled palm trees provide evening romance, while efficient wait staff whisk out orders of whole wheat and traditional flat crusts lathered with generous and inventive toppings. A local fave.

It also serves a good selection of salads and sandwiches.

Palm Beach Grill
MODERN AMERICAN $$

(☑561-835-1077; www.hillstone.com; 340 Poinciana Way; mains $19-49; ☺5-10pm Sun-Thu, to 11pm Fri & Sat) This restaurant is a great compromise between Palm Beach chic and casual. During the season it's perpetually packed thanks to good food and a buzzing bar. Securing one of the dining room's leather booths can be nearly impossible at the weekend, so book well ahead.

★ Café Boulud
FRENCH $$$

(☑561-655-6060; www.thebraziliancourt.com; 301 Australian Ave; mains $16-46, fixed-price menu lunch/dinner $32/48; ☺7am-10pm (cafe), to midnight (bar)) Created by renowned New York chef Daniel Boulud, the restaurant at the Brazilian Court is one of the few places in Palm Beach that truly justifies the sky-high prices. The warm dining room and terrace complements a rich menu of classic French and fusion dishes, all displaying Boulud's signature sophistication and subtlety.

Kinder on the purse, the Boulud breakfast is a delicious feast of mini Belgian waffles with caramelized banana and walnut compote; wild mushroom omelets with *mâche* (corn salad) drizzled with truffle vinaigrette; or a classic all-American fry-up.

Happy hour is from 4pm to 6pm in the lounge and there's live jazz post brunch on Sundays

Circle
AMERICAN, EUROPEAN $$$

(☑877-724-3188; www.thebreakers.com; 1 S County Rd, The Breakers Resort; adult/child $110/50; ☺7am-11am Mon-Sat, to 2:30pm Sun) Sure, it's steep, but brunch at the Breakers' storied restaurant will certainly rank among the most amazing you'll ever enjoy. Beneath soaring 30ft frescoed ceilings, surrounded by ocean views and entertained by a roving harpsichordist, guests begin their feast at the breakfast bar, which features homemade doughnuts, tropical fruits and on-demand omelets.

In high season you'll need to reserve weeks in advance.

Café des Beaux-Arts
CAFE $$$

(☑561-655-2833; www.flaglermuseum.us; 1 Whitehall Way, Flagler Museum; cream tea $40; ⊙11:30am-2:30pm Tue-Sat, noon-3pm Sun) Housed in the Pavilion alongside Flagler's private railroad car is this period café, built in the style of a 19th-century, iron-and-glass railway palace. Here you can daintily dine on finger sandwiches, scones and custom-blended teas looking out over Lake Worth. Pinkies out!

Ta-Boo
MODERN AMERICAN $$$

(☑561-835-3500; www.taboorestaurant.com; 221 Worth Ave; mains $22-49; ⊙11am-10pm) If you believe the legend, the Bloody Mary was invented here, mixed to soothe the hangover of Woolworth heiress Barbara Hutton. Today the restaurant boasts the most coveted window seats on Worth Ave. Competition to get in is as stiff as the heiress' drinks. Get past the intricate woodwork and jungle murals, and you'll enjoy a well-executed American bistro meal.

🍷 Drinking & Nightlife

Leopard Lounge
LOUNGE

(www.chesterfieldpb.com/dining/bar; 363 Cocoanut Row; ⊙6:30pm-1am) This swanky gold, black and red place attracts a mature crowd and the occasional celeb (neither photos nor autograph hounds are allowed). Live music – a mix of jazz and classics – nightly.

Cucina Dell'arte
CLUB

(www.cucinadellarte.com; 257 Royal Poinciana Way; ⊙7am-3am) Reminiscent of a Florentine cafe, this high-end eatery overflows with warm colors, art and some of the finest glitterati in Palm Beach. Around 10pm they shove the tables out of the way and blast the music. Pretentious enough to be fun; if you arrive wearing a serious face, you'll be sorry.

☆ Entertainment

Society of the Four Arts
PERFORMING ARTS

(☑561-655-7226; www.fourarts.org; 2 Four Arts Plaza) The concert series here includes cabaret, the Palm Beach Symphony, chamber orchestras, string quartets and piano performances.

🛍 Shopping

Church Mouse
VINTAGE

(☑561-659-2154; www.bbts.org/about-us/churchmouse; 378 S County Rd; ⊙10am-5pm Mon-Sat) Sponsored by Bethesda-by-the-Sea, this little donation-based resale shop has raised more than $4.5 million for Palm Beach charities

in the last 20 years. It stocks 'gently' used castaways, and if you browse carefully you can find Palm Beach classics from Lilly Pulitzer or Chanel.

Il Sandalo
SHOES

(☑561-805-8674; www.ilsandalo.com; via Gucci Courtyard, 240 Worth Ave; ⊙10am-6pm Mon-Sat) Handcrafted leather sandals from Neapolitan brothers Fabio and Pier Paolo Tesorone. Classic styles are embellished with glittering laminates, coral and, in some cases, semi-precious stones. If you can't find anything you like, have a pair made on site to your exact specifications.

C. Orrico
FASHION & ACCESSORIES

(☑561-659-1284; www.corrico.com; 336 S County Rd; ⊙10am-6pm Mon-Sat, from 11am Sun) Lilly Pulitzer, the Palm Beach princess of prints who created a fashion uniform for wealthy socialites, passed away in February 2013, aged 81. Pay homage to this enduring Palm Beach style icon by purchasing one of her lurid print dresses from C. Orrico, and pair it with similarly psychedelic sandals and jewelry.

Daniella Ortiz
FASHION & ACCESSORIES

(☑561-366-0008; www.daniellaortiz.com; 256 Worth Ave; ⊙10:30am-5:30pm Mon-Sat) Shoppers in Daniella Ortiz are like kids in a candy store – they're unable to decide between the rainbow-colored collection of totes, purses, shoulder bags and clutches. Detailed hand-stitching, contrast color linings and jeweled locks and buckles make for a beautiful finish. And the best bit? They retail for around a quarter of the price of the big brands on Worth Ave.

Stubbs & Wootton
SHOES

(☑561-655-6857; www.stubbsandwootton.com; 340 Worth Ave; ⊙10am-6pm Mon-Sat, noon-5pm Sun) If you want to fit in with the no-socks Palm Beach set, head straight to this high-end slippers and sandals shop. Wedges made from woven raffia handcrafted in Spain, hand-embroidered velvet slippers with custom-designed monograms and cool chambray cotton espadrilles are all uniquely Palm Beach.

ℹ Getting There & Away

Palm Tran (p219) bus 41 covers the bulk of the island, from Lantana Rd to Sunrise Ave; transfer to bus 1 at Publix to go north or south along US 1. A single fare costs adult/child $2/1. To get to **Palm Beach International Airport** (p236) in West Palm Beach, take bus 41 to the downtown transfer and hop on bus 44.

West Palm Beach

☑ 561 / POP 108,000

When Henry Flagler decided to develop what is now West Palm Beach, he knew precisely what it would become: a working-class community for the labor force that would support his glittering resort town across the causeway. And so the fraternal twins were born – Palm Beach, considered the fairer of the two, and West Palm Beach, a cooler work-hard-play-hard community. West Palm has a surprisingly diverse collection of restaurants, friendly inhabitants (including a strong gay community) and a gorgeous waterway that always seems to reflect the perfect amount of starlight.

◉ Sights

★ Norton Museum of Art   MUSEUM

(☑ 561-832-5196; www.norton.org; 1451 S Olive Ave; adult/child $12/5; ⊙ noon-5pm Tue-Sun) Undergoing a major renovation at the time of research (the design was done by architect Norman Foster), this is the largest art museum in Florida. It opened in 1941 to display the enormous art collection of industrialist Ralph Hubbard Norton and his wife Elizabeth. The Nortons' permanent collection of more than 5000 pieces (including works by Matisse, Warhol and O'Keeffe) is displayed alongside important Chinese, pre-Columbian Mexican and US Southwestern artifacts, plus some wonderful contemporary photography and regular traveling exhibitions.

To enhance your visit you can join one of the free docent-led tours through the galleries (12:30pm and 2pm Monday to Friday, and 2pm Saturday). Alternatively, drop by on Thursday evenings for the fun 'Art After Dark' series, which includes anything from lectures and live music to conversations with curators and wine tastings.

★ Ann Norton
Sculpture Garden   GARDENS

(☑ 561-832-5328; www.ansg.org; 253 Barcelona Rd; adult/child $15/7; ⊙ 10am-4pm Wed-Sun) This serene collection of sculptures is a real West Palm gem. The historic house, verdant grounds and monumental sculptures are all the work of Ralph Norton's second wife, Ann. After establishing herself as an artist in New York in the mid-1930s, she became the first sculpture teacher at the Norton School of Art in West Palm, and created this luxurious garden as a place of repose.

After poking through Norton's home (the 1st floor has temporary exhibitions), you can wander the grounds and uncover her soaring feats of granite, brick, marble and bronze. Perhaps most awe-inspiring is the 1965 *Cluster*, a collection of seven burka-clad women in pink granite. Before leaving, be sure to peek into Norton's light-filled studio, where dusty tools lie just as she left them.

McCarthy's
Wildlife Sanctuary   WILDLIFE RESERVE

(☑ 561-790-2116; www.mccarthyswildlife.com; 12943 61st St N, Loxahatchee; adult/child $35/25; ⊙ tours 11am, noon, 1pm Tue-Sat) With entry by reservation only, this wildlife sanctuary takes unwanted exotics and treats dozens of native animals that are sick or injured and then releases them back to the wild. On the two-hour guided tour you'll get to see white tigers, panthers and barred owls all from 3ft away. Children under five are not permitted.

The sanctuary is 16 miles northwest of Clematis St, downtown West Palm Beach.

Peanut Island   ISLAND

(http://discover.pbcgov.org; ⊙ 11am-4pm Thu-Sun) Plopped right off the northeastern corner of West Palm, Peanut Island was created in 1918 by dredging projects. Originally named Inlet Island, the spit was renamed for a peanut-oil-shipping operation that failed in 1946. The highlight is, however, the **nuclear fallout bunker** (☑ 561-723-2028; www.pbmm. info; adult/child $17/12; ⊙ 11am-4pm Thu-Sun) that was constructed for John F Kennedy during the days of the Cuban missile crisis. These days, it's run by the Palm Beach Maritime Museum.

It has long been a popular spot for boaters to moor and party by day, and in 2005 the county invested $13 million into island rehabilitation, resulting in **Peanut Island Park**, which includes a pier, an artificial reef and some pretty sweet campsites. There are no roads to the island. Visitors can get there via the shuttle boat that departs every 15 minutes from the Riviera Beach Marina.

Palm Beach County
History Museum   MUSEUM

(☑ 561-832-4164; www.hspbc.org; 300 N Dixie Hwy; ⊙ 10am-2pm Mon, to 5pm Tue-Fri, to 4pm Sat Sep-May) FREE For all the region's activities and museums, it can be hard for outsiders to get an insight into the history and people of the Sunshine State. This small museum, housed in the restored 1916 courthouse and staffed by volunteers, aims to change that. Quirky exhibits – featuring models, photographs and period artifacts – highlight individuals who have contributed to the growth and prosperity of Palm Beach County.

Informative plaques on everyone from Flagler and Mizner to Alligator Joe and the first settlers make the tour a fascinating one. Also has temporary exhibitions that change annually.

Palm Beach Zoo & Conservation Society   ZOO
(☑ 561-547-9453; www.palmbeachzoo.com; 1301 Summit Blvd; adult/child $20/15; ☺ 9am-5pm; ⛴) The highlight of this compact zoo is the Tropics of the Americas exhibit, a 3-acre recreation of a rainforest, stocked with jaguars, monkeys, snakes, macaws and other tropical creatures. The zoo's also home to a few of the last remaining Florida panthers, North America's rarest mammal. Other unusual residents include Komodo dragons (the largest lizard in the world), capybaras (the largest rodent in the world) and one lone red kangaroo.

Like any zoo, the animals are caged, which may be distressful for animal lovers, but the many animal lovers around these parts generously fund the museum to ensure good conditions. The zoo is a brief drive south of downtown.

Lion Country Safari   WILDLIFE RESERVE
(☑ 561-793-1084; www.lioncountrysafari.com; 2003 Lion Country Safari Rd; adult/child $35/26; ☺ 9:30am-5:30pm; ⛴) The first cageless drive-through safari in the country, this incredible animal park puts you in the cage (ie your car) as 900 creatures roam freely, staring at *you*. Equal parts conservation area and safari, the park's 500 acres are home to bison, zebra, white rhinos, chimpanzees and, of course, lions. You tour in your car (unless it's a convertible, in which case short-term rentals are available), driving slowly, hoping the animals approach the vehicle.

The best time to go is when it rains, because the animals are more active when it's cool. The park is 20 miles west of downtown West Palm.

South Florida Science Center & Aquarium   MUSEUM
(☑ 561-832-1988; www.sfsciencecenter.org; 4801 Dreher Trail North; adult/child $16/11.50; ☺ 9am-5pm Mon-Fri, 10am-6pm Sat & Sun) A great little hands-on science center, aquarium and planetarium with weekend programs, traveling exhibits, a science trail, mini-golf and butterfly garden. On the last Friday of the month the museum stays open until 9pm so you can view the night sky from the county's only public observatory (weather permitting). Prices change according to the exhibition.

Ragtops Motorcars Museum   MUSEUM
(www.ragtopsmotorcars.com; 420 Claremore Dr; donations appreciated; ☺ 10am-5pm Wed-Sat) This spot was originally a classic-car dealership with three convertible Mercedes, but Ty Houck's incredible automobile collection quickly grew, compelling area automotive enthusiasts to stop by for a look-see. Today you can test-drive many of the vehicles on display, though it helps to have serious intent to buy. Otherwise you're free to browse the rarities displayed, including an amphibious 1967 Triumph, a regal 1935 Bentley and a 1959 Edsel station wagon.

🏃 Activities

Rapids Water Park   WATER PARK
(☑ 561-842-8756; www.rapidswaterpark.com; 6566 North Military Trail, Riviera Beach; weekday/weekend $43/48; ☺ 10am-5pm) South Florida's largest water park features 30 action-packed acres of wet and wild rides. Don't let the squeals of fear and delight from the Big Thunder funnel put you off. Awesome fun. Parking costs an extra $10.

🚣 Courses & Tours

Palm Beach Water Taxi   BOATING
(☑ 561-683-8294; www.sailfishmarina.com; 98 Lake Dr, Singer Island) Water taxis run between downtown West Palm and Singer Island ($15), as well as to Peanut Island (round-trip $12), leaving from Singer Island. Additionally, the outfit offers guided tours along the Intracoastal, including 90-minute narrated tours of Palm Beach mansions (adult/child $31/15.50).

Diva Duck   BOATING
(☑ 561-844-4188; www.divaduck.com; adult/child $29/15; ⛴) Diva Duck, a hybrid bus-boat, gives quacky 75-minute narrated tours of downtown's historic district, CityPlace (p236), the surrounding waterways and the shores of Peanut Island. Yes, the bus really does float in the water. Tours start at CityPlace.

West Palm Beach

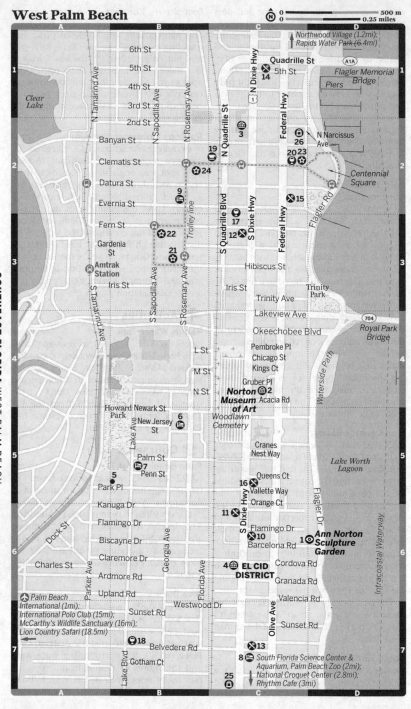

0 500 m
0 0.25 miles

Northwood Village (1.2mi);
Rapids Water Park (6.4mi)

Clear
Lake

Flagler Memorial
Bridge
Piers

Quadrille St
5th St
6th St
5th St
4th St
3rd St
2nd St
Banyan St
Clematis St
Datura St
Evernia St
Fern St
Gardenia St
Iris St

N Tamarind Ave
N Sapodilla Ave
N Rosemary Ave
N Quadrille St
N Dixie Hwy
Federal Hwy

N Narcissus Ave
Centennial Square

Amtrak Station
S Tamarind Ave
S Sapodilla Ave
S Rosemary Ave
Trolley line
S Quadrille Blvd
S Dixie Hwy
Federal Hwy
Flagler Rd

Hibiscus St
Iris St
Trinity Ave
Lakeview Ave
Okeechobee Blvd

Trinity Park

Royal Park Bridge

L St
M St
N St

Pembroke Pl
Chicago St
Kings Ct
Gruber Pl
Acacia Rd

Norton Museum of Art
Woodlawn Cemetery

Cranes Nest Way

Waterside Path

Lake Worth Lagoon

Howard Park
Newark St
New Jersey St
Palm St
Penn St
Park Pl

Lake Ave

Queens Ct
Vallette Way
Orange Ct

Flamingo Dr
Barcelona Rd

S Dixie Hwy

Ann Norton Sculpture Garden

Flagler Dr

Kanuga Dr
Flamingo Dr
Biscayne Dr
Claremore Dr
Charles St
Ardmore Rd
Upland Rd

Georgia Ave
Florida Ave
Parker Ave
Dock St

Cordova Rd
EL CID DISTRICT
Granada Rd
Valencia Rd

Olive Ave

Intracoastal Waterway

Palm Beach International (1mi);
International Polo Club (15mi);
McCarthy's Wildlife Sanctuary (16mi);
Lion Country Safari (18.5mi)

Sunset Rd
Westwood Dr
Sunset Rd

Belvedere Rd
Gotham Ct

Lake Blvd

South Florida Science Center & Aquarium, Palm Beach Zoo (2mi);
National Croquet Center (2.8mi);
Rhythm Cafe (3mi)

West Palm Beach

National Croquet Center SPORTS
(☎561-478-2300; www.nationalcroquetclub.com; 700 Florida Mango Rd; ⏲9am-5pm) FREE Get a real taste of the upper-crust Palm Beach lifestyle at the largest croquet facility in the world. Here genteel sportspeople dressed in crisp whites hit balls through wickets on 12 of the world's biggest, greenest, most manicured lawns. It's members-only, but the public is invited to free lessons on Saturday mornings at 10am.

The pro shop, inside the plantation-style clubhouse, has the latest in mallets and croquet wear. The center is about a 10-minute drive southwest of downtown West Palm.

Armory Art Center ART
(☎561-832-1776; www.armoryart.org; 1700 Parker Ave) FREE With more than a dozen state-of-the-art studios, the center hosts numerous adult and youth courses in ceramics, jewelry, painting, drawing, printmaking, photography and sculpture. Special events, lectures and rotating gallery exhibits also aim to educate and enrich. From June to early August, the Armory hosts a Summer Art Camp for kids between the ages of five and 17.

Festivals & Events

Clematis by Night MUSIC
(☎561-822-1515; http://wpb.org/clematis-by-night; ⏲6-9:30pm Thu) Every Thursday night the city shuts down the eastern terminus of Clematis St, brings in food carts and crafts vendors, and stages a free outdoor music festival under the stars.

Free Outdoor Concerts MUSIC
(www.cityplace.com; ⏲6-10pm Fri & Sat) On Friday and Saturday evenings, CityPlace hosts free outdoor concerts in front of the gorgeous CityPlace Fountain. Bands stick to familiar rock, R&B and occasionally country sounds.

SunFest ART, MUSIC
(www.sunfest.com; ⏲May) Florida's largest waterfront music and art festival, SunFest attracts more than 175,000 visitors for five days in early May.

Sleeping

Peanut Island Camping CAMPGROUND $
(☎561-845-4445; www.pbcgov.com/parks/peanutisland; tent sites $30) This tiny island has 20 developed campsites by reservation only and a host of primitive sites right on the sand on a first-come, first-served basis. There are some restrictions, so call or hit the website.

Hotel Biba MOTEL $
(☎561-832-0094; www.hotelbiba.com; 320 Belvedere Rd; r $149-179; ❄📶🏊) With plain, white, slightly missing-a-small-something rooms, this place lacks a bit of color, but is one of the better (if only) budget options around. It's well located – only a block from the Intracoastal, and perched on the edge of the

El Cid district. Suffice it to say it's clean and fine if you just want a bed.

★Grandview Gardens
B&B $$

(☎561-833-9023; www.grandview-gardens.com; 1608 Lake Ave; r from $229; P❖❄❅) Book a room at this intimate resort and you'll feel like a local in no time. Hidden in a tropical garden on Howard Park, the enormous suites with their wrought-iron and four-poster beds access the pool patio through French doors. They're decorated to reflect the Spanish Mediterranean style that is so popular in these parts.

The house is a period 1925 structure typical of the historic neighborhood and it sits opposite the Armory Art Center, so is perfect for longer stays for the arts-inclined.

Fabulous breakfasts are included. Incredibly, prices are significantly lower outside of high season.

Palm Beach Hibiscus
B&B $$

(☎561-833-8171; www.palmbeachhibiscus.com; 213 S Rosemary Ave; r $199-309; ❖❄) Fabulously located just a block from CityPlace (p236), this pair of 1917 homes has four-poster beds, floral prints, abundant light and a front porch with wooden rockers. Watch the world – including the city trolley, which stops out front – roll by. On the property is a tiki bar lounge that's popular among some locals: sociable, though it dampens the sense of privacy.

Casa Grandview
B&B, COTTAGE $$$

(☎561-313-9695; www.casagrandview.com; 1410 Georgia Ave; r $199-449; P❖❄❅) Hidden behind hedgerows in the historic Grandview Heights neighborhood, this intimate little compound has five B&B rooms, seven cottages and five apartments. B&B rooms are in the main house, which has a charming-if-odd medieval-Spanish feel, with a narrow stone staircase and elf-sized wooden doors in the walls. We love the cozy Library Suite – small but plush.

Luxurious cottages have a stylized 1940s beach chic, with vintage signs and bright tiled kitchens – great for families.

✗ Eating

★Mediterranean Market & Deli
MIDDLE EASTERN $

(☎561-659-7322; www.mediterraneanmarket anddeli.com; 327 5th St; mains $3-12) Don't be put off by the nondescript warehouse exterior – this Middle Eastern deli serves up some of the most flavorful lunches in town. Fresh-baked pita is stuffed with homemade hummus, feta and kefta accompanied by zingy lima bean salad and tabbouleh. You can then order honey-drenched baklava or lady fingers to go.

Johan's Jöe
CAFE $

(Swedish Coffee House & Cafe; www.johansjoe. com; 401 S Dixie Hwy; mains $9-13; ❂7am-6pm) If you can get past the menu's umlaut marks (placed jokingly here on English words), you'll find a delightful array of pastries and cakes. But the sweets are not the only winners; it's hard to go past the likes of pickled herrings and Swedish meatballs and authentic Swedish salads and sandwiches.

Paris Bakery & Cafe
FRENCH $

(www.parisbakerycafe.com; 212 S Olive Ave; mains $9-13; ❂8am-2:30pm Mon & Tue, 8am-2:30pm & 5-9pm Wed-Fri, 9am-2pm & 5-9pm Sat) French owned and operated, this '70s style and very authentic patisserie serves Continental breakfasts of crepes any style, well-priced lunches of smoked salmon and béchamel sauce, and sandwiches stuffed with *paysanne* chicken. On Saturday, lines form down the block for 'Le Frunche.'

Curbside Gourmet
FOOD TRUCK $

(☎561-371-6565; http://curbsidegourmet.com; 2000 S Dixie Hwy) This bright, peppermint truck is Palm Beach's first mobile food truck dedicated to bringing good, seasonal staples to resident gourmets. The short, sweet menu includes a breakfast burrito, BLTs, crab-cake sliders, fresh fish and pork tacos, and a daily panini or frittata. Fries are hand cut; add-ons include heritage tomatoes and Applewood smoked bacon; and dessert is caramelized grapefruit. Yum.

Belle & Maxwell's
INTERNATIONAL $$

(☎561-832-4449; www.belleandmaxwells.com; 3700 S Dixie Hwy; mains $18-32; ❂11am-4pm Mon, to 9pm Tue-Sat) Situated in the middle of Antique Row, this is tea room/cafe is the place to come after some browsing and it's a favorite among the ladies-who-lunch crowd. It looks like the interior of a swap shop, with stained glass pieces, eclectic furniture and lamp shades. Wonderful crab-meat salad ($18) and roast beef and brie sandwich ($14).

Darbster
VEGAN $$

(☎561-586-2622; www.darbster.com; 8020 S Dixie Hwy; mains $14-20; ❂5-10pm Tue-Fri, 10:30am-

3pm & 5pm-10pm Sat, to 9pm Sun) This place is out on a limb in many respects: it's 5 miles south of town in an incongruous location by the S Dixie Hwy on the Palm Beach canal; the menu is 100% vegan; all profits go to a foundation for animal care; and it attracts everyone from Birkenstock-wearing hippies to diamond-wearing Palm Beachers.

Howley's
AMERICAN $$

(4700 S Dixie Hwy; mains $14-25; ⊙11am-2pm Mon-Thu, to 5am Fri & Sat) Open almost all night, this mint-green 1950s diner's tagline is 'cooked in sight, must be right.' The food (shake 'n' bake pork chops, crab hash, tiki-style tuna burgers and banana pancakes) might be described as 'upscale retro' and certainly tastes right – especially at 2am.

Grato
ITALIAN $$

(☑561-404-1334; http://gratowpb.com; 1901 S Dixie Hwy; mains $18-25; ⊙11:30am-10pm; ☑) Service can be a bit hit and miss as it gets so busy at this smart, Italian brasserie-cum-pizzeria, but it's popular for good reason. It spins out great pizzas (including a vegan option), and pasta that is truly *squisito* (delicious!). Throw in two bars for cocktails, a choice of sitting areas, and you've got yourself a relaxing night with the locals.

Sailfish Marina
SEAFOOD $$

(☑561-842-8449; www.sailfishmarina.com; 98 Lake Dr, Singer Island; mains $26-41; ⊙7am-10pm) Located on Singer Island, Sailfish Marina is a good place for a seafood meal, but it's especially fine for Sunday brunch between 8am and 1pm (adults/kids $24/16). Grab a seat close to the water, slowly chew your smoked salmon, tropical fruit or Belgian waffles and watch the resident pelicans paddle around the yachts, searching for their own breakfast.

★ Table 26 Degrees
MODERN AMERICAN $$$

(☑561-855-2660; www.table26palmbeach.com; 1700 S Dixie Hwy; mains $26-41; ⊙11:30am-2pm Mon-Sat, 4:30-10pm Sun-Wed, to 11pm Thu-Sat) Don't be put off by the price of this sophisticated restaurant. It is filled with locals, conversation and the clinking of glasses for good reason. They flock here for the bar (great happy hour 4:30 to 6:30pm daily) plus the share plates and mains that are divided by water, land, field and hands (the latter covers fried chicken and burgers).

★ Rhythm Cafe
FUSION $$$

(☑561-833-3406; www.rhythmcafe.cc; 3800 S Dixie Hwy; mains $21-30; ⊙5:30-10pm Tue-Sat,

to 9pm Sun & Mon) There's no lack of flair at this colorful, upbeat bistro set in a converted drugstore in West Palm's antiques district. It's strung with Christmas lights and hung with bright, bobbing paper lanterns. The menu is equally vibrant, bopping happily from goat's cheese pie to 'the best tuna tartare ever' to the pomegranate-infused catch of the day.

Kitchen
MODERN AMERICAN $$$

(☑561-249-2281; http://kitchenpb.com; 319 Belvedere Road #2; mains $25-42; ⊙6-10pm) Book well ahead if you want to snag a seat at one of the 10 tables in chef Matthew Byrne's contemporary American brasserie. The concept is simple: the freshest ingredients, presented in the simplest, most flavorful manner possible, and *voilà!* Highlights include organic chicken schnitzel dressed in Panko breadcrumbs and topped with charred lemon and a sunny fried egg.

🍷 Drinking & Nightlife

★ Subculture Coffee
CAFE

(☑561-318-5142; http://subculturecoffee.com; 509 Clematis St; ⊙7am-midnight Sun-Thu, to 2am Fri & Sat) Head here to hang out with the hipsters at West Palm's most happening place, located right on Clematis St. First things first: it's got fabulous coffee and baristas know their brews. Apart from that it has a wonderful space with bookshelves and a large bar, and furniture à la 1950s.

The Pawn Shop Lounge
CLUB

(http://pawnshopwpb.com; 219 Clematis St; cover $10; ⊙5pm-3am Tue-Thu, to 4am Fri & Sat) This former Miami dance club and celebrity haunt is situated in the former Dr Feelgood venue. It features the familiar pawn shop trappings along with a life-sized vintage Ferris wheel and a DJ booth designed out of a Mack truck. DJs, dancers and light shows keep the party going until 3am while rivers of alcohol flow from the 175-foot bar.

Blind Monk
WINE BAR

(☑561-833-3605; http://theblindmonk.com; 410 Evernia St #107; ⊙7:30am-11am Mon-Fri, 9:30am-1pm Sat & Sun, 4pm-late daily) With a team of knowledgeable sommeliers behind it, the Blind Monk is arguably the best wine bar in West Palm. It offers an extensive list of wines by the glass, including international labels and local craft beers. Small plates of cheese, salami, grapes, pickles and nuts soak up the vino, while silent old movies play on the wall.

It offers daytime bites as well, including a great brunch.

HG Roosters   GAY

(http://roosterswpb.com; 823 Belvedere Rd; ☺3pm-3am Sun-Thu, to 4am Fri & Sat) A mainstay of West Palm's thriving gay community, this bar has been offering wings, bingo and hot young male dancers since 1984.

☆ Entertainment

Harriet Himmel Theater   THEATER

(☑561-318-7136; www.cityplace.com; 600 S Rosemary Ave) The centerpiece of CityPlace is this theater situated in an attractive Mediterranean plaza. The 11,000-sq-ft historic venue hosts a program of live concerts, art exhibitions, fashion shows and high-school proms. Named after its major benefactor, Harriet Himmel, the 1926 building was previously the Methodist Church. It's regarded as one of the largest Colonial Revival structures of its time.

Palm Beach Dramaworks   THEATER

(☑561-514-4042; www.palmbeachdramaworks. org; 201 Clematis St) 'Theater to Think About' is the tagline of this award-winning resident theater, which is committed to presenting underrated classic and contemporary plays from the likes of Lorca, Steinbeck, Pinter, Hansberry and Stoppard.

CityPlace   CONCERT VENUE

(☑561-366-1000; www.cityplace.com; 700 S Rosemary Ave; ☺10am-10pm Mon-Sat, noon-6pm Sun) This massive entertainment and shopping complex is the crown jewel of West Palm Beach's urban-renewal initiative. At its center is the Harriet Himmel Theater, plus there's a bowling alley, a 20-screen cinema theater, dozens of restaurants and a slew of stores.

Respectable Street   LIVE MUSIC

(www.respectablestreet.com; 518 Clematis St) Respectables has kept South Florida jamming to great bands for two decades; it also organizes October's MoonFest, the city's best block party. Great DJs, strong drinks and a breezy chill-out patio are added bonuses. See if you can find the hole that the Red Hot Chili Peppers' Anthony Kiedis punched in the wall when they played here.

International Polo Club   SPECTATOR SPORT

(☑561-204-5687; www.internationalpoloclub.com; 3667 120th Ave S, Wellington; general admission $10, lawn seating from $30; ☺Sun Jan-Apr) Between January and April the International Polo Club hosts 16 weeks of polo and glamour. As one of the finest polo facilities in the world, it not only attracts the most elite players but also the local and international glitterati who whoop it up in head-turning fashion over champagne brunches (tickets $125). Why not join the fun?

🔒 Shopping

Antique Row   ANTIQUES

(☑561-822-2222; www.westpalmbeachantiques. com; S Dixie Hwy) Just south of town along S Dixie Hwy, between Belvedere Rd and Southern Blvd, this strip of shops over several blocks has more than 30 antiques vendors. You might unearth an incredible find from a Palm Beach estate.

Opening hours vary by shop.

Greenmarket   MARKET

(http://wpb.org/greenmarket; ☺9am-1pm Sat, Oct-Apr) Just north of the plaza at 2nd St and Narcissus Ave (where local schoolkids frolic in the fountains on hot afternoons), this delightful market offers treats ranging from locally grown avocados and orchids to organic coffee and dog treats on Saturday mornings.

❶ Getting There & Away

Palm Beach International Airport (PBI; ☑561-471-7420; www.pbia.org; 1000 James L Turnage Blvd) is served by most major airlines and car-rental companies. It's about a mile west of I-95 on Belvedere Rd. **Palm Tran** (p219) bus 44 runs between the airport, the train station and downtown ($2).

Greyhound (☑561-833-8534; www. greyhound.com; 215 S Tamarind Ave; ☺6am-10:45pm), **Tri-Rail** (☑800-875-7245; www. tri-rail.com; 203 S Tamarind Ave) and **Amtrak** (☑800-872-7245; www.amtrak.com; 209 S Tamarind Ave) share the same building: the historic Seaboard Train Station. Palm Tran serves the station with bus 44 (from the airport).

Once you're settled, driving and parking is a cinch. There's also a cute and convenient (and free!) trolley running between Clematis St and CityPlace starting at 11am.

TREASURE COAST

The Treasure Coast gets its name for being the site of numerous treasure-laden shipwrecks over the years. Today the Treasure Coast is where you'll find Florida's true jewel: unspoiled paradise.

Industrialist billionaire and philanthropist John D MacArthur (1897–1978) once owned almost everything from Palm Beach Gardens to Stuart, and he kept it mostly pristine during his life. Over time he grew concerned that Florida's real-estate bonanza would compromise – or destroy – what he considered paradise. Therefore, in his will, he stated that thousands of acres would be kept wild, and the rest would be deeded out incrementally, in order to save the oceanfront property from Miami's fate. And you know what? His plan worked. Well, almost... In true American style, swaths of highway run north–south along the coast.

Jupiter & Jupiter Island

561 / POP 62,000 & 820

Jupiter is a largely ritzy residential area with one of the wealthiest communities in America. There is no central core to speak of, and for visitors Jupiter is best seen as a jumping-off point for exploring the area's parks, nature preserves and beaches. Unlike those of its southerly neighbors Palm Beach and Boca Raton, the beaches around here are largely untouched by condo development.

Sights

Hobe Sound National Wildlife Refuge
WILDLIFE RESERVE

(772-546-2067; www.fws.gov/hobesound; 13640 SE Federal Hwy; parking $5; sunrise-sunset) A 1091-acre federally protected nature sanctuary, Hobe Sound has two sections: a small slice on the mainland, opposite the Jonathan Dickinson State Park; and the refuge grounds at the northern end of Jupiter Island. The Jupiter Island section has 3.5 miles of beach (it's a favorite sea-turtle nesting ground), while the mainland section is a pine scrub forest. In June and July, nighttime turtle-watching walks take place twice a week (changing days; reservations necessary).

Blowing Rocks Preserve
NATURE RESERVE

(574 S Beach Rd; $2; 9am-4:30pm) This preserve encompasses a mile-long limestone outcrop riddled with holes, cracks and fissures. When the tide is high and there's a strong easterly wind (call for conditions), water spews up as if from a geyser. (At low tide, nothing happens.) When seas are calm you can hike through four coastal biomes: shifting dune, coastal strand, interior mangrove wetlands and tropical coastal hammock.

DON'T MISS

JOHN D MACARTHUR BEACH STATE PARK

While this **state park** (561-624-6950; www.macarthurbeach.org; 10900 Jack Nicklaus Dr; per vehicle/bicycle $5/2; 8am-sunset) is one of the smallest in the region (438 acres), it has some of the best turtle-watching programs around. Loggerhead, green and leatherback turtles nest along the beach between May and August. It's home to aquariums and a spectacular 1600ft boardwalk spanning the mangroves of Lake Worth Cove. The on-site nature center offers kayak rental (unguided; single kayak $12 per hour).

In June and July, lucky visitors might catch a glimpse of hatching baby sea turtles during the ranger-led turtle walks, led nightly at 8:30pm. The park is about 11 miles south of Jupiter.

Jonathan Dickinson State Park STATE PARK

(772-546-2771, activities 561-746-1466; www.floridastateparks.org/jonathandickinson; 16450 SE Federal Hwy; vehicle/bicycle $6/2; 8am-sunset) With almost 11,500 acres to explore, this is an excellent state park between US Hwy 1 and the Loxahatchee River. There's no ocean access in the park, but its attraction lies in its several habitats: pine flatwoods, cypress stands, swamp and increasingly endangered coastal sand-pine scrub. Ranger-led nature walks leave at 2pm on Fridays and Sundays from the Cypress Creek Pavilion, and campfire programs are offered Saturday at dusk next to the Pine Grove campground.

You can rent canoes and kayaks from the concession stand.

Several short-loop hiking and bicycle trails can be explored. Most popular is the Kitching Creek Trail, just north of the boat landing, a short 1.5 miles, but other trails extend from this. Visit www.clubscrub.org for details on cycling options.

Jupiter Inlet Lighthouse LIGHTHOUSE

(www.jupiterlighthouse.org; 500 Capt Armour's Way; adult/child $12/6; 10am-5pm Tue-Sun) Built in 1860, this historic lighthouse hasn't missed a night of work in more than 100 years and is among the oldest lighthouses on the Atlantic coast. Visitors can climb the 105 steps to view the surrounding area and ocean. To visit the lighthouse, you must take a tour; these depart regularly between 10am and 4pm depending on visitor numbers.

There's some interesting Seminole and pioneer Florida memorabilia in the small but smart museum.

🏃 Activities

Canoe Outfitters
CANOEING, KAYAKING

(📞561-746-7053; www.canoeoutfittersofflorida.com; 9060 W Indiantown Rd, Jupiter; double canoes/single kayaks per day $55/45) For a great day exploring the various aquatic preserves, no one beats Riverbend Park's Canoe Outfitters, which provides access to these lush waterways. From the launch, paddle to the right for thick, verdant waterways overhung with fallen branches and a small but thumping rapid; paddle to the left for open vistas and plentiful picnic areas.

Jupiter Outdoor Center
KAYAKING

(📞561-747-0063; www.jupiteroutdoorcenter.com; 1116 Love St; ⊙9am-5pm) The center rents out kayaks and stand-up paddleboards ($35/40 per half day) and organizes themed kayak trips (from $40) in the area, such as languid moonlight excursions and exploratory trips around Jupiter Inlet's mangroves.

Jonathan Dickinson State Park Concession Stand
BOATING

(📞561-746-1466; www.floridaparktours.com; canoes & kayaks single/double $18/24; ⊙9am-5pm) You can rent canoes and kayaks from the concession stand. Guided-tour boat rides of the Loxahatchee River are available throughout the day (adult/child $24/14).

🛏 Sleeping & Eating

Jupiter Waterfront Inn
HOTEL $$

(📞561-747-9085; www.jupiterwaterfrontinn.com; 18903 SE Federal Hwy; r $149-179; 🅿️❄️🛜🏊) As sunny and friendly as can be, this unpretentious, highway-side inn has huge rooms with flat-screen TVs, Intracoastal views and a marina for boaters. Decor is beachy, with Spanish tile floors and cheerful yellow walls. For romance, ask for a room with an in-suite Jacuzzi tub. The inn's own 240ft fishing pier is a big hit with anglers.

It backs onto the major highway, but it's excellent value. Prices include a continental breakfast.

★ Jupiter Donut Factory
BAKERY $

(📞561-741-5290; http://jupiterdonuts.com; 141 Center St; doughnuts from $0.80, dozen $7; ⊙6am-1pm) These fresh-baked doughnuts are what doughnuts dream of being, so get here early so you don't miss out. Doughnuts are usually greedily polished off by mid-morning. If you can't decide between Raspberry Jelly, Banana Coconut, S'mores or Red Velvet, just stick with the most popular order: the Bacon Maple Syrup.

Dune Dog Cafe
AMERICAN $

(📞561-744-6667; http://dunedog.com; 775 A1A Alternate; mains $10-18; ⊙11am-9pm) Smell that oil, baby. It wafts through this indoor-outdoor, ultra-casual, fried food joint on the highway. Its mini palm trees, tasteless decor – pink and blue bar stools, tables made from surf boards and plastic fast food baskets – are part of the fun. Regulars possibly don't even notice. They're here for combo platters of snow crabs and steak or lobster bisque.

★ Little Moir's Food Shack
SEAFOOD $$

(www.littlemoirsfoodshack.com; 103 S US 1; mains $9-24; ⊙11am-9:30pm Mon-Wed, to 10pm Thu-Sat) If you didn't know to look, you'd walk right past this strip-mall hole-in-the-wall. But then you'd miss out on one of Florida's genuine food finds, a neo-Caribbean cafe serving a mouth watering blend of global flavors: sweet-potato crusted fish, Jamaican pepper-pot soup, lobster egg rolls. The seafood is as fresh as you'd expect (but so rarely find) in a seaside town.

Leftovers Cafe
CAFE $$

(📞561-627-6030; www.littlemoirsjupiter.com/leftovers-cafe; 451 University Blvd; mains $8-24; ⊙11am-9:30pm Mon-Wed, to 10pm Thu-Sat) Food guru Mike Moir, who runs Little Moir's Food Shack, also operates the first class Leftovers Cafe, which serves a lighter menu of sandwiches, salads and sweets.

🍸 Drinking & Nightlife

Square Grouper
BAR

(www.squaregrouper.net; 1111 Love St; ⊙11am-midnight Sun-Thu, to 1am Fri & Sat) If this Old Florida dive looks familiar, it's because the video for the Alan Jackson and Jimmy Buffett tune *It's Five O'Clock Somewhere* was shot here. Perched on the water, with an ample (sandy) dance floor, this place is an ultra-casual gem in an otherwise well-heeled town.

☆ Entertainment

Roger Dean Stadium
STADIUM

(📞561-775-1818; www.rogerdeanstadium.com; 4751 Main St; tickets spring training $29-42) It may not be a 'nature' activity, but an afternoon here will get you outdoors. This small but immaculate stadium is home to spring-training action for the Miami Marlins, the St Louis Cardinals and various minor-league baseball teams. Ticket prices vary; call for details.

❶ Getting There & Away

Though I-95 is the quickest way through this area, do yourself a favor and get off the freeway. US Hwy 1 (US 1) runs up the coastline, and Hwy A1A jumps back and forth between the mainland (where it's the same as US 1) and various barrier islands.

Stuart

📞 772 / POP 16,100

Often overlooked in favor of its more famous southern neighbors, Stuart has long been a hush-hush destination for sporty millionaires and their gleaming yachts. Fishing is tops here, which explains Stuart's nickname: 'Sailfish Capital of the World.' It wasn't until the late 1980s, however, that Stuart got its first exit off I-95, which is when the wave of rich folk, leaving places like Boca, started coming in earnest.

Though Stuart's retro, sherbet-colored downtown has some cute restaurants and boutiques, the real draws of the region are the adjacent beach areas of **Jensen Beach** and Hutchinson Island. Jensen Beach, on the mainland facing the Indian River Lagoon, caters to fishers and arty types, with a tiny downtown lined with craft shops and tackle stores. Just across the water by the bridge, narrow Hutchinson Island is where visitors go for sun and fun.

◉ Sights & Activities

Elliott Museum MUSEUM
(📞407-225-1961; www.elliottmuseumfl.org; 825 NE Ocean Blvd, Hutchinson Island; adult/child $14/6; ⊙10am-5pm) The eccentric Elliott collection has a focus on early 20th-century technology, and for good reason – the museum was founded by Harmon Elliott, the son of Sterling Elliott, who invented the kingpin and steering knuckle (which led to steerability for four-wheeled vehicles). Hence the spectacular collection of vintage vehicles, displayed in a $20 million gallery complete with robotic racking system, which ferries cars to the foreground and rotates them for viewing.

Florida Oceanographic Coastal Science Center AQUARIUM
(📞772-225-0505; www.floridaoceanographic.org; 890 NE Ocean Blvd, Hutchinson Island; adult/child $12/6; ⊙10am-5pm Mon-Sat, noon-4pm Sun; ⊞) This center is great for kids who'll be mesmerized by the four 300-gallon tropical-fish aquariums, a worm reef and touch tanks with crabs, sea cucumbers and starfish. There's an excellent menu of guided tours and nature programs, from guided nature walks at 10:15am (except Sundays) to daily stingray feedings to summer sea-turtle-spotting expeditions.

Hutchinson Island BEACH
This long, skinny barrier island, which begins in Stuart and stretches north to Fort Pierce, features a stunning array of unspoiled beaches. All beaches have free access, and are excellent for walking, swimming and even a bit of snorkeling. The beaches get less touristed the further north you go.

Lady Stuart FISHING
(📞772-286-1860; www.ladystuart.com; 555 NE Ocean Blvd, Stuart; adult/child from $45/35) The crew will take you out, bait your hook, and clean and fillet any fish you catch. There make no guarantees of hooking dinner, but know where to sink their lines. Trips depart 8am to 1pm Saturday through Thursday, and 8am to 3pm Friday.

🛏 Sleeping & Eating

★ Old Colorado Inn HOTEL $$
(📞772-215-3437; www.oldcoloradoinn.com; 211 Colorado Ave, Stuart; r & ste $189-399; ⓟ❄🛰) With its pastel-colored Key West vibe and easy charm, the excellent-value 1914 Colorado Inn is a lovely spot. Spacious studio rooms and suites come with gleaming wooden floors and ceilings, tasteful modern furnishings, grand beds and kitchenettes. Hosts Steven and Ashley brim with insightful tips on Stuart and the surrounding beaches.

River Palm Cottages & Fish Camp COTTAGE $$
(📞772-334-0401; www.riverpalmcottages.com; 2325 NE Indian River Dr, Jensen Beach; apt from $119-259; ⓟ❄🛰🐾🌴) Perched on Indian River, this complex has adorable, if simple, cottages with kitchens, some with waterfront views and all sporting cool tiled floors and a breezy, Caribbean style. The peaceful grounds are lush with palm trees, guava and the exotic praying-hands banana tree.

There's a private beach, a ping-pong table and a pier for watching sunrises.

Conchy Joe's　　　　CARIBBEAN, AMERICAN $$
(www.conchyjoes.com; 3945 NE Indian River Dr, Jensen Beach; mains $10-22; ⊘11:30am-10pm) Overlooking St Lucie River, this offers the 'flavor' of old Florida with exotic drinks and pub grub at a palm-tree-filled bar. It's a sure-fire blast when the band's jamming.

11 Maple St　　　　AMERICAN $$$
(☑772-334-7714; www.elevenmaple.com; 3224 NE Maple St, Jensen Beach; mains $25-59; ⊘5:30-10pm Tue-Sat) This romantic spot, a series of rooms inside a historic cottage, has a daily changing menu of eclectic large and small plates, from roasted pompano with saffron essence to grilled elk tenderloin. For special-occasion dinners, this is your best bet short of driving south to Palm Beach.

The Gafford　　　　INTERNATIONAL $$$
(☑772-221-9517; www.thegafford.com; 47 SW Flagler, Stuart; mains $13-38) It's hard to score a seat at Stuart's latest casual-chic, busy and loud eatery (that is, unless you want to eat a full meal at 5:30pm). However, if you do manage to wait it out, it's worth it. You'll be wowed by the likes of Seminole beef fillet mignon, Scottish salmon or a burger (with brisket – heaven).

❶ Getting There & Away

I-95 is the quickest way to and from this area. South of Stuart, US 1 runs up the coastline and then jogs west, into and through town. If you're headed between Stuart and Fort Pierce, the best route is the slow-but-scenic NE Indian River Dr.

Fort Pierce

☑772 / POP 43,600

Fort Pierce has a sleepy feel to it, but includes top sport fishing and some great beaches. Downtown often feels like a ghost town, with lots of vacancies and few people. Orange Ave is the main drag, and is far more vibrant than adjoining blocks.

◉ Sights & Activities

Manatee Observation Center　　　　MUSEUM
(www.manateecenter.com; 480 N Indian River Dr; $1; ⊘10am-5pm Tue-Sat, noon-4pm Sun Oct-Jun, 10am-5pm Thu-Sat Jul-Sep; 🖭) A small center educating the public on the plight of the manatee. Videos and exhibits teach boaters how to avoid hurting the creatures – and

the rest of us how our lifestyle has indirectly eradicated most of the manatee population. Manatee sightings are common-ish in winter in waters along the museum's observation deck.

Fort Pierce Inlet State Park　　　　STATE PARK
(www.floridastateparks.org/fortpierceinlet; 905 Shorewinds Dr; vehicle/bicycle $6/2; ⊘8am-sunset) This 700-acre park has everything you'd want in a waterfront recreation spot: sandy shores, verdant trails, mangrove swamps with a beautiful bird population, and a family-friendly picnic area. You can rent bikes, kayaks and surf boards through the Fort Pierce Outdoor Center.

UDT-SEAL Museum　　　　MUSEUM
(☑772-595-5845; www.navysealmuseum.com; 3300 North Highway A1A; adult/child $10/5; ⊘10am-4pm Tue-Sat, noon-4pm Sun) The world's only museum dedicated to the elite warriors of Naval Special Warfare, this Hutchinson Island exhibit features once-top-secret tools and weapons used by the most elite combat forces of the US.

Urca de Lima　　　　SHIPWRECK
(☑850-245-6444) FREE In 1715 a Spanish flotilla was decimated in a hurricane off the Florida coast. One of the ships, the *Urca de Lima,* went down (relatively) intact. Today, the wooden-hulled ship is partly exposed within snorkeling distance from the beach at Fort Pierce. To get here, exit Ocean Blvd (Hwy A1A) at Pepper Beach Park and walk north along the beach about half a mile from the park boundary.

Fort Pierce Outdoor Center　　　　KAYAKING
(☑772-979-4434; www.fortpierceoutdoorcenter. com; Fort Pierce Inlet State Park; kayak & SUP per hr from $20; ⊘9am-5pm) Located within the Fort Pierce Inlet State Park (and well signed), this outfit can kit you out with everything from kayaks to SUP boards, surfboards and bikes. All of these start at $20 per hour.

⚐ Tours

Dolphin Watch Boat Tours　　　　BOATING
(☑772-464-6673; http://dolphinwatchboattours. com; adult/under 12yr $40/30) Wild dolphins are spotted routinely in the Indian River Lagoon, occasionally from the riverbank. To increase your chances of seeing them, you need to get on the water. Capt Adam Pozniak seems to know instinctively where to find them on these two-hour dolphin-spotting tours on his 25ft pontoon. He's also extremely

knowledgeable about the lagoon and its flora and fauna.

🛌 Sleeping

Savannas Recreation Area CAMPGROUND $
(📞 772-464-7855; www.stlucieco.gov/parks/savannas.htm; 1400 Midway Rd; tent sites $25.25; ⊙ Nov-May) Covering 550 acres and five distinct biological communities – pine flatwoods, wet prairie, marsh, lake and scrub – the Savannas features both primitive and developed campsites.

❶ Getting There & Away

Fort Pierce is reachable via the I-95 or US 1 (a gorgeous drive that's highly recommended as a trip in itself). To get downtown from I-95, take the Orange Ave exit east, crossing US 1 (here called N 4th St).

Sebastian Inlet

📞 772 / POP 22,699

Heading south from Melbourne Beach along Hwy A1A toward Sebastian Inlet, development trickles nearly to a halt. You'll find plenty of access to beaches, and hiking and birding along both the Atlantic Coast and the Indian River here, as well as mile after mile of tidy hedges and bike paths lining the highway.

⊙ Sights

★**Pelican Island**
National Wildlife Refuge WILDLIFE RESERVE
(📞 772-581-5557; www.fws.gov/pelicanisland; Hwy A1A; ⊙ 7:30am-sunset) **FREE** Established in 1903 as a refuge for the endangered brown pelican, Pelican Island was America's first federal bird reservation, the forerunner of today's national wildlife-refuge system. The preserve now encompasses 500 acres along the Indian River Lagoon as well as the 2.2-acre Pelican Island, which can be seen from the observation tower at the end of the **Centennial Trail**. Two trails loop 2.5 miles along the shore and are perfect for bike rides and long hikes.

Pelican Island itself can also be viewed by boat and there are several public boat ramps to access the refuge waters.

Sebastian Inlet State Park STATE PARK
(📞 321-984-4852; www.floridastateparks.org/sebastianinlet; 9700 South State Rd; cyclist/vehicle $2/8; ⊙ 24hr) Stretching along a narrow strip of the barrier island, this busy park, popular with fishers, surfers, boaters and families, is divided into two sections by the inlet bridge. On the north side swimming is safe for children in the calm-water lagoon; on the south you'll find a marina with boat rental.

In June and July you can join ranger-led sea turtle nesting walks (reservations are necessary).

McClarty Treasure Museum MUSEUM
(📞 772-589-2147; Hwy A1A; adult/child under 6yr $2/free; ⊙ 10am-4pm) In 1715 a Spanish ship carrying gold and treasure went down in a hurricane, and survivors built a makeshift camp. This small museum, featuring a 45-minute movie, dioramas and artifacts from the shipwreck, sits on the site of that wreck. Even today, folks looking for a pretty shell stumble upon treasures washed ashore. The museum's 1 mile south of Sebastian Inlet State Park.

🏃 Activities

★**Honest John's Fish Camp** KAYAKING
(📞 321-727-2923; www.honestjohnsfishcamp.com; 750 Mullet Creek Rd; kayaks per hr $12, boats per half/full day $60/90; ⊙ 6am-6pm Wed-Mon) Rent kayaks and motorboats from this 1890s Florida Cracker homestead on the edge of Indian River Lagoon. Set in an old citrus grove on Mullet Creek, it's a prime spot for fishing and spotting manatees. The camp is 10 miles south of Melbourne Beach.

Sebastian Inlet Marina BOATING
(📞 321-724-5424; www.sebastianinlet.com; 9502 South Hwy A1A; ⊙ 8am-5pm Mon-Fri, to 6pm Sat & Sun) On the south side of Sebastian Inlet you'll find a well-equipped marina offering boat ($175 per half day) and kayak rental ($30 per half day), a small fishing museum and an uninspiring campground (from $31 per site).

🛌 Sleeping

★**Seashell Suites** RESORT $$
(📞 321-409-0500; www.seashellsuites.com; 8795 S Hwy A1A; r $225-250; ❄) ⌁ This low-key eco-resort has been designed to blend in with its pristine natural setting. With only eight two-bedroom suites, the atmosphere is intimate and environmental standards are high: there's a saltwater pool and cleaning agents are toxin free. Beach chairs, bikes, umbrellas and bodyboards are all complimentary, and the digital library has a good stock of movies. Rates are reduced for weekly stays.

LOGGERHEAD MARINELIFE CENTER

Juno Beach lies six miles north of John D MacArthur Beach State Park (p237) on the scenic A1A. If you're traveling with a four-legged companion, you can jump out here to enjoy one of the county's only dog-friendly beaches (from Xanadu Lane to Marcinski Rd). But the main reason to visit is for the fascinating **Loggerhead Marinelife Center** (☑ 561-627-8280; www.marinelife.org; 14200 US 1, Juno Beach; suggested donation $5; ⊘ 10am-5pm Mon-Sat, 11am-5pm Sun) FREE, which gives you a close-up-and-personal experience with these beautiful creatures.

View recovering sea turtle patients in specially designed outdoor tanks and watch through the window while surgeons treat the animals. Volunteers stand by turtle tanks with information on their charges: how they sustained their injuries, how they're healing and whether they're good or grumpy patients. It's a privilege to see and learn at such close quarters. All four species – greens, hawksbills, Kemp's ridleys and loggerheads – frequent the local waters.

Around 70 to 80 turtles are treated here and returned to the wild annually. The center runs a host of educational programs, leads ecotours ($35) and a nature tour through the dune system (free), tells 'hatchling tales' to younger kids (10:30am Wednesdays) and offers guided turtle walks (by reservation, $20) from Wednesday to Saturday evenings in June and July.

SOUTHEAST FLORIDA VERO BEACH

❶ Getting There & Away

Sebastian Inlet lies 35 miles south of Cocoa Beach on Hwy A1A, and 15 miles north of Vero Beach. Transport via car makes the most sense, but the **GoLine Bus System** (☑ 772-569-0903; www.golineirt.com; ⊘ 6am-7pm Mon-Fri, 9am-3pm Sat) travels between Vero Beach and Sebastian.

Vero Beach

☑ 772 / POP 15,749

This carefully zoned coastal town, with lovely grassy parks, wide, white beaches and a pedestrian-friendly downtown, has left behind its former nickname 'zero-beach' and re-emerged as 'The Hamptons of Florida.' It's the kind of laid-back, seaside village where people like, say, Gloria Estefan own homes and hotels.

In addition, Vero's unique lack of highrise buildings gives the place a less developed feel, with consistently better sea views than neighboring beach communities. And while many visitors are happy to lose themselves in the lull of beach life, Vero Beach residents (many with sky-high net worth) are committed to supporting both the arts and the environment.

◉ Sights

★ **Vero Beach Museum of Art**   MUSEUM
(☑ 772-231-0707; www.vbmuseum.org; 3001 Riverside Park Dr; adult/under 17yr $10/free; ⊘ 10am-4:30pm Mon-Sat, 1-4:30pm Sun) With changing fine-art exhibitions and regular outdoor jazz concerts, this sleek, white museum in Riverside Park could easily hold its own against any big-city heavy hitter. Look for signs on Hwy A1A.

McKee Botanical Gardens   GARDENS
(☑ 772-794-0601; www.mckeegarden.org; 350 US 1; adult/child 3-12yr $12/8; ⊘ 10am-5pm Mon-Sat, noon-5pm Sun; ▣) In Vero's early-1920s tourist heyday, Waldo Sexton (of the eponymous Waldo's) and Arthur McKee joined forces to open the 80-acre McKee Jungle Gardens, which delighted visitors for decades until Disney stole the show in the 1970s. Much of the land was sold off for development, but passionate locals managed to save 18 acres of tropical garden, which now grows thick with native plants, palms and lily ponds.

Admission prices are subject to seasonal fluctuations.

Environmental Learning Center   NATURE RESERVE
(☑ 772-589-5050; www.discoverelc.org; 255 Live Oak Dr; adult/child under 12yr $5/3; ⊘ 10am-4pm Tue-Fri, 9am-4pm Sat, 1-4pm Sun; ▣) This 64-acre reserve, dedicated to educating folks about the fragile environment of the Indian River estuary, offers hands-on displays and a boardwalk through the mangroves. Check the website for details on **EcoVentures**: guided nature trips including canoe and pontoon boat trips and nature walks.

⚑ Activities

Adventure Kayaking   KAYAKING

(☑772-567-0522; www.paddleflorida.com; adult/child under 12yr $50/25) Vero native Steve Cox runs daily Indian River Lagoon kayak tours to Round and Pelican Islands, Sebastian River and Blue Cypress Lake. Multiday camp-and-kayak tours ($275 to $350 per person per day) are also offered on the lagoon and further afield to the Everglades.

Orchid Island Bikes & Kayaks   CYCLING

(☑772-299-1286; www.orchidislandbikesand kayaks.com; 1175 Commerce Ave; bikes per day/week $24/59, kayaks single/tandem per half-day $79/129, SUP half-day/day/week $45/75/235) Vero Beach is the perfect place to ditch the car for a bike, as even kids can easily pedal to restaurants, hotels and the beach. Alternatively, rent kayaks or paddleboards and tootle around Indian River Lagoon.

☞ Tours

★ Sail Moonraker   BOATING

(☑772-696-2941; www.sailmoonraker.com; Vero Beach Marina, 3611 Rio Vista Blvd; 2-8hr cruises for up to 6 guests $450-975; 🚸) Captain Bruce offers customized dolphin-watching, swimming and sunset cruises in Indian River Lagoon, excellent for children, grandparents and everyone in between, aboard his 40ft catamaran. Cash only.

🛏 Sleeping

Caribbean Court Boutique Hotel   BOUTIQUE HOTEL $$

(☑772-231-7211; www.thecaribbeancourt.com; 1601 S Ocean Dr; r & ste $139-359; 🅿❄🤝🐾) In a quiet residential area a block off South Beach, this lovely spot expertly blends understated elegance with a casual beach vibe. Bougainvillea and palm trees hide a small garden pool, and handsome whitewashed rooms with earthy accents have rattan furnishings, decorative tiled sinks, thick towels and a refrigerator stocked with goodies. Ask about weekday discounts.

★ Costa d'Este Beach Resort & Spa   RESORT $$$

(☑772-562-9919; www.costadeste.com; 3244 Ocean Dr; r $200-300; 🅿❄🤝🐾) Owned by Gloria Estefan and her husband, this chic Miami Beach–style resort drips with style. From the ostentatious entryway fountain to the dazzling sundeck and oceanfront pool (where frozen grapes are always available), every detail reflects the unique and sophisticated taste of the Estefans. A cruise-ship theme dominates throughout shared spaces and the 94 rooms, with porthole-shaped art abounding.

✗ Eating

Barefoot Cafe   CAFE $

(☑772 770-1733; www.thebarefootcafe.com; 2036 14th Ave; sandwiches $5-10; ⊙10am-3pm Mon-Fri) Although it doesn't have a beachside location, this laid-back deli is a surf shack in its soul. Sandwiches, salads and wraps (the most popular of which is the Tuscan wrap) are homemade daily. There's seating inside and out, and the service is super friendly.

★ Riverside Café   SEAFOOD $$

(☑772-234-5550; www.riversidecafe.com; 3341 Bridge Plaza Dr; mains $12-26; ⊙11am-late Mon-Sat, 10am-late Sun) This casual, waterfront eatery and dock sits right on the Indian River Lagoon, with incredible sunset views and tuna nachos so good some folks have considered purchasing second homes nearby. Okay, not really, but man they're good. In the evenings things get a bit rowdy, as the sports fans and salty folks pack the bar.

Waldo's   SEAFOOD $$

(☑772-231-7091; http://waldosvero.com; 3150 Ocean Dr, Driftwood Resort; mains $10-22; ⊙11am-1am Mon-Sat, 10am-9pm Sun; 🅿🚸) Built out of driftwood by pioneering Vero settler Waldo Sexton in 1935, this is a Vero Beach institution for dinner and music for everyone (from 9pm). Eat blackened mahimahi wraps on the deck overlooking the ocean or prop up the rustic bar with the locals.

Tides   MODERN AMERICAN $$$

(☑772-234-3966; 3103 Cardinal Dr; mains $20-38; ⊙5pm-late) This is the hottest fine dining around, with New American and Floridian cuisine spiced up with French, Caribbean, Southern and Latin flair, plus an award-winning wine list with a perfect pair for any dish. The seafood is fresh and local, with top choices including the crab cake appetizer (very meaty) and a tender, flavorful hogfish that's often on special.

If you don't make a reservation far in advance, the hostess will laugh at you.

Maison Martinique   FRENCH $$$

(☑772-231-7299; Caribbean Court Boutique Hotel, 1603 S Ocean Dr; mains $24-42; ⊙5-10pm Tue-Sat) Maison Martinique recently ditched its French roots and began offering American cuisine, while maintaining its first-rate service and intimate surrounds. On warm evenings, eat by the little pool; for something more casual, head to the romantic Havana piano bar upstairs.

Drinking & Nightlife

Kilted Mermaid
PUB

(☏772-569-5533; www.kiltedmermaid.com; 1937 Old Dixie Hwy; ⏰5pm-late Tue-Sun) Do as they say and 'drink outside the box' at this raucous local pub that serves over 80 craft and imported beers. Then order charcuterie or fondue (cheese or chocolate!) to keep the party going. There's an open mike on Wednesday, trivia on Thursday and live music every Friday and Saturday.

Grind + Grape
WINE BAR

(☏772-231-5536; www.facebook.com/grindandgrape; 925 Bougainvillea Lane; ⏰8am-2am Mon-Sat, to 1am Sun) Coffee shop by day, wine bar by night, this place is super cool no matter when you show up. Proving you can never have too many good things under one roof, they've got cold-brew coffee, a vast tequila selection, delicious pastries and handcrafted cocktails. Oh, and there's live music every single evening at 7:30pm on the patio.

ⓘ Getting There & Away

Vero Beach lies 53 miles south of Cocoa Beach on Hwy A1A. The closest international airports are in Orlando, 90 minutes to the northwest; West Palm Beach, 90 minutes to the south; and Melbourne, 30 minutes up the coast. **Vero Beach Airport Shuttle** (☏772-794-8300; www.verobeachairportshuttle.com; Melbourne/Palm Beach/Orlando airport $95/160/160) provides an airport-shuttle service.

Vero Beach Regional Airport (☏772-978-4930; 3400 Cherokee Dr) now offers Elite Airways flights to and from Newark direct.

Orlando &
Walt Disney World®

POP 2.3 MILLION / ☑ 407, 321

Includes ➡

Best Places to Eat

➡ Stubborn Mule (p264)

➡ Jiko (p280)

➡ Rusty Spoon (p264)

➡ Urbain 40 (p264)

➡ DoveCote (p264)

➡ Boma (p281)

Best Places to Sleep

➡ Alfond Inn (p271)

➡ Courtyard at Lake Lucerne (p259)

➡ Disney's Grand Floridian Resort & Spa (p290)

➡ Loews Portofino Bay Hotel (p311)

➡ Disney's Animal Kingdom Lodge (p299)

➡ Floridian Hotel & Suites (p259)

Why Go?

Central Florida is like a *matryoshka*, the Russian doll that encases similar dolls of diminishing size. The region features pretty state parks, gardens and rivers, all ideal for leisurely exploration. One layer down, Central Florida then embraces Kissimmee, Celebration and the vast, sprawling area of Greater Orlando. Greater Orlando's network of multi-lane highways and overpasses leads to a huge number of theme parks, including Walt Disney World®, Universal Orlando Resort, SeaWorld and Legoland. Judging from the crowds, these parks are the reason most people visit.

But at Central Florida's core is a city: pretty, leafy downtown Orlando, whose great field-to-fork eating scene and world-class museums get overlooked by the hype, sparkle and colors of the theme parks. Many visitors never reach this kernel, the final 'doll,' and the city of Orlando tends to lie in the shadow of Cinderella and Hogwarts School of Witchcraft & Wizardry.

When to Go
Orlando

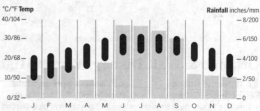

Sep Theme-park crowds thin, accommodation rates drop, summer sizzle fades.

May Lull between spring break and summer vacation peaks; warm, before the rains.

Thanksgiving–mid-Dec Enjoy seasonal festivities (though be aware of soaring prices).

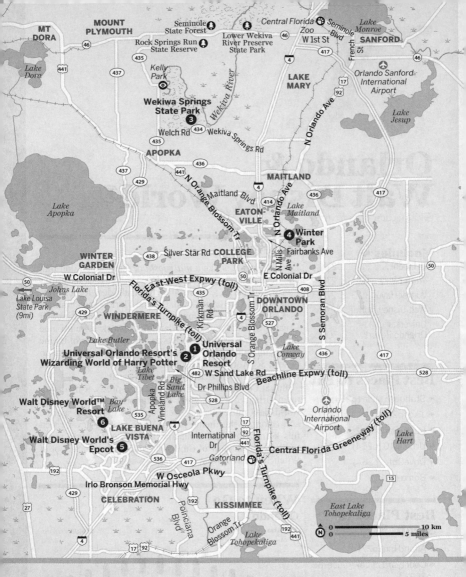

Orlando & Walt Disney World® Highlights

❶ Universal Orlando Resort (p306) Getting your adrenaline to sky-high levels on the hair-raising rides.

❷ Wizarding World of Harry Potter (p316) Wandering Hogsmeade's streets, flying through Hogwarts and passing through Platform 9¾ at Universal Orlando Resort.

❸ Wekiwa Springs State Park (p260) Paddling quietly past alligators and blue herons on the Wekiva River.

❹ Winter Park (p270) Poking through art museums, window-shopping and sampling some of the region's best farm-to-fork dining.

❺ Epcot (p292) Meeting Elsa and Anna from *Frozen* after sipping wine in Italy and watching the Beatles in England at Walt Disney World®.

❻ Walt Disney World® (p275) Stimulating all your senses at four theme parks, two water parks and much, much more on the trip of a lifetime.

ℹ Getting There & Away

AIR

Orlando International Airport (MCO; ☑ 407-825-8463; www.orlandoairports.net; 1 Jeff Fuqua Blvd) Handles more passengers than any other airport in Florida. Serves Walt Disney World®, the Space Coast and the Orlando area.

Orlando Sanford International Airport (☑ 407-585-4000; www.orlandosanfordairport. com; 1200 Red Cleveland Blvd) Small airport 30 minutes north of downtown Orlando and 45 minutes north of Walt Disney World®.

BUS

A Greyhound bus originating in NYC, with stops including Washington, DC, and Daytona Beach, FL, terminates in Orlando (one way from $80 to $200, 24 hours).

CAR

Orlando lies 285 miles from Miami; the fastest and most direct route is a 4½-hour road trip via Florida's Turnpike. From Tampa it is an easy 60 miles along I-4. Both the Beachline Expressway and Hwy 50 will take you east to beaches on the Space Coast in just under an hour.

TRAIN

Amtrak's 97 Silver Meteor and 91 Silver Star from New York to Miami stop at Winter Park, downtown Orlando and Kissimmee. It's about a 22-hour ride from NYC (from $140). The daily Auto Train from Lorton, VA, terminates at Sanford, 30 miles north of downtown Orlando.

ℹ Getting Around

SHUTTLE

Many hotels provide shuttles to Walt Disney World®, Universal Orlando Resort and SeaWorld, to varying timetables. Most hotels just outside Universal Studios and along International Dr provide free shuttle service to Universal Orlando Resort, but many are first-come, first-served. Always ask for details including how often they run and whether or not they take reservations. Call Mears Transportation (☑ 855-463-2776) one day in advance to arrange personalized shuttle service to Disney.

CAR & MOTORCYCLE

Hwy I-4 is the main north–south thoroughfare, though it's labeled east–west: to go north, take the I-4 east (toward Daytona Beach), and to go south, hop on the I-4 west (toward Tampa). Just about every place you'd want to go can be located through an I-4 exit number. From south to north, exits 62 through exit 87, you will find Walt Disney World®, SeaWorld, Aquatica and Discovery Cove, Universal Orlando Resort, downtown Orlando and Thornton Park, Loch Haven Park and Winter Park.

ℹ ADVANCE PLANNING

Three months before Snag a table at Disney character, themed and high-end restaurants.

Two months before Book your hotel, purchase theme-park tickets and reserve Disney FastPass+ attractions (if not staying on-site, reserve 30 days in advance).

Three weeks before Peruse hotel prices and make changes if necessary – cancellation policies are generous and prices fluctuate dramatically. Buy theater tickets.

Both Orlando International and Orlando Sanford International Airports, Walt Disney World® and many hotels have car-rental agencies.

PUBLIC TRANSPORTATION

I-Ride Trolley (☑ 407-354-5656; www.iridetrolley.com; rides adult/child 3-9yr $2/1, passes 1/3/5/7/14 days $5/7/9/12/18; ⊗ 8am-10:30pm) Services International Dr, from south of SeaWorld north to the Universal Orlando Resort area. Buses run at 20- to 30-minute intervals and exact change is required.

Lynx (Map p250; ☑ 407-841-2279, route info 407-841-8240; www.golynx.com; 455 Garland Ave, Downtown; per ride/day/week $2/4.50/16, transfers free; ⊗ call center 8am-8pm Mon-Fri, 8am-6pm Sat & Sun) Orlando's public bus covers greater Orlando, but service is limited after 8pm.

SCOOTER, STROLLER & WHEELCHAIR RENTAL

Tackling Orlando's theme parks requires a huge amount of walking and standing, and can be exhausting for all ages. You can rent at the parks, but they don't all take reservations and you can't use the equipment outside the park. Several companies offer stroller, wheelchair or scooter rentals for the duration of your visit (and will deliver to your hotel).

Kingdom Strollers (☑ 407-271-5301; www.kingdomstrollers.com)

Orlando Stroller Rentals (☑ 800-281-0884; www.orlandostrollerrentals.com)

Walker Mobility (☑ 888-726-6837; https://walkermobility.com)

TAXI

Cabs sit outside the theme parks, Disney Springs, resorts and other tourist centers, but otherwise you'll need to call to arrange a pickup. A ride from the Disney area to downtown Orlando takes 30 minutes and costs about $65; from Universal Orlando Resort to Disney takes

15 minutes and costs $40. Just getting around *within* Walt Disney World® can easily cost $30 in fares.

Casablanca Transportation (🖉 407-927-2773, www.casablancatransportation.com)

Mears Transportation (🖉 855-463-2776)

ORLANDO

AREA 110 SQ MILES (CITY OF ORLANDO); 4012 SQ MILES (GREATER ORLANDO) / 🖉 407

If Orlando were a Disney character, it's fair to say that she's like Dory (of Nemo fame) and lacks a bit of confidence. It's so easy to get caught up in Greater Orlando – in the isolated, constructed worlds of Disney or Universal Orlando (for which, let's face it, you're probably here) – that you forget all about the downtown city of Orlando itself. It has a lot to offer: lovely tree-lined neighborhoods; a rich performing arts and museum scene; several fantastic gardens and nature preserves; fabulous cuisine; and a delightfully slower pace devoid of manic crowds. So, sure, enjoy the theme parks: the sparkles, nostalgia and adrenaline-pumped fantasy, but also take time to 'Find Orlando'. Come down off the coasters for one day to explore the quieter, gentler side of the city. You may be surprised to find that you enjoy the theme parks all that much more as a result.

👁 Sights

👁 Downtown Orlando

Lake Eola Park   PARK
(Map p250; 195 N Rosalind Ave; ⊘6am-midnight; 🚹) Pretty and shaded, this little city park sits between downtown Orlando and Thornton Park. A paved sidewalk circles the water, there's a waterfront playground and you can rent swan paddleboats. On Saturday mornings, the park is home to the Orlando Farmers Market (p268).

Orange County Regional History Center   MUSEUM
(Map p250; 🖉 407-836-8500; www.thehistory center.org; 65 E Central Blvd, Downtown; adult/child 5-12yr $8/6; ⊘10am-5pm Mon-Sat, from noon Sun; 🚹) Orlando before Disney? Permanent exhibits cover prehistoric Florida, European exploration, race relations and citrus production, with a re-created pioneer home and 1927 courtroom.

Wells' Built Museum of African American History & Culture   MUSEUM
(Map p250; 🖉 407-245-7535; http://wellsbuilt museumofafricanamericanhistoryandculture.org; 511 W South St; adult/child $5/2; ⊘9am-5pm Mon-Fri) Dr Wells, one of Orlando's first African American doctors, came to Orlando in 1917. In 1921 he built a hotel for African Americans barred from Florida's segregated hotels, and soon after he built South Street Casino, a venue for African American entertainers. This small museum sits in the original hotel.

Gallery at Avalon Island   GALLERY
(Map p250; www.avalongallery.org; 39 S Magnolia Ave; ⊘11am-6pm Thu-Sat) FREE Contemporary art gallery housed in the oldest commercial building in Orlando (c 1886).

👁 Loch Haven Park

Picturesque Loch Haven Park, with 45 acres of parks, giant shade trees and three lakes, sits a couple of miles north of downtown Orlando.

★ Orlando Museum of Art   MUSEUM
(🖉 407-896-4231; www.omart.org; 2416 N Mills Ave, Loch Haven Park; adult/child $15/5; ⊘10am-4pm Tue-Fri, from noon Sat & Sun; 🚹; 🚌 Lynx 125, 🚉 Florida Hospital Health Village) Founded in 1924, Orlando's grand and blindingly white center for the arts boasts a fantastic collection – both permanent and temporary – and hosts an array of adult and family-friendly art events and classes. The popular First Thursday ($10), from 6pm to 9pm on the first Thursday of the month, celebrates local artists with regional work, live music and food from Orlando restaurants.

★ Mennello Museum of American Art   MUSEUM
(🖉 407-246-4278; www.mennellomuseum.org; 900 E Princeton St, Loch Haven Park, Downtown; adult/child 6-18yr $5/1; ⊘10:30am-4:30pm Tue-Sat, from noon Sun; 🚌 Lynx 125, 🚉 Florida Hospital Health Village) Tiny but excellent lakeside art museum featuring the work of Earl Cunningham, whose brightly colored images, a fusion of pop and folk art, leap off the canvas. Visiting exhibits often feature American folk art. Every four months there's a new exhibition, everything from a Smithsonian collection to a local artist.

★ Harry P Leu Gardens   GARDENS
(🖉 407-246-2620; www.leugardens.org; 1920 N Forest Ave, Audubon Park; adult/child 4-18yr $10/3;

☉9am-5pm, last admission 4:30pm; ☐Lynx 38, 8, 50) Camelias, roses, orange groves and desert plants cover 50 acres, as well as plenty of grassy spots for a lakeside picnic. Pick up supplies at the trendy East End Market (p262), a half-mile east of the entrance gate on Corrine Dr. Tours of **Leu House**, an 18th-century mansion (later owned by the Leu family), run every half-hour from 10am to 3:30pm. See the website for details on outdoor movies, storytelling and live music.

Orlando Science Center   MUSEUM
(☑407-514-2000; www.osc.org; 777 E Princeton St, Loch Haven Park; adult/child $20/14; ☉10am-5pm Thu-Tue; ⚑; ☐Lynx 125, ☐Florida Hospital Health Village) Changing exhibits on dinosaurs, the human body, the solar system and more offer candy-coated science education geared towards children aged five to 12. A giant tree grows through the four-story atrium, at the base of which you'll find alligators and a natural-science discovery room.

Unfortunately, many displays are too complicated to teach anything and too educational to be fun, and the result is a lot of kids just running around punching buttons. Check the website for screenings at the giant **Cinedom Theater**, as well as **Science Live** events including stingray feeding and experiments.

☉ International Drive

I-Drive is Orlando's tourist hub, packed with restaurants, bars, stores, accommodations and Orlando attractions (both tired and new). It parallels I-4 to its east, stretching 17 miles from Orlando Premium Outlets south to World Dr, just east of Walt Disney World®. The section between the convention center and Sand Lake Rd is lined with palm trees, museums and is a relatively pleasant walking district (you'll find the Visitor Center here). From Sand Lake Rd north to the dead end at the outlet mall, it is Orlando tourism at full throttle.

Titanic the Experience   MUSEUM
(Map p254; ☑407-248-1166; www.titanicshipofdreams.com; 7324 International Dr, International Dr; adult/child 6-11yr $22/16; ☉10am-6pm; ⚑; ☐Lynx 8, 42, ☐I-Ride Trolley Red Line Stop 9) Full-scale replicas of the doomed ship's interior and artifacts found at the bottom of the sea. Tour the galleries with guides in period dress or wander through on your own. Kids especially love the dramatic and realistic

interpretation of history – each passenger receives a boarding pass, with the name of a real passenger, and at the end of the experience (once the ship has sunk) you learn your fate.

WonderWorks   MUSEUM
(Map p254; ☑407-351-8800; www.wonderworksonline.com; 9067 International Dr; adult/child 4-12yr $30/24; ☉9am-midnight; ⚑; ☐Lynx 8, 38, 42, ☐I-Ride Trolley Red Line Stop 18 or Green Line Stop 10) Housed in a hard-to-miss, upside-down building, this is yet another bright, loud, frenetic landmark trying to make its mark in Orlando. This one is a cross between a children's museum, a video arcade and an amusement park. Several stories of interactive exhibits offer high-speed, multisensory education. Lie on a bed of nails, sit inside a hurricane simulator and so on...

Younger children may find the pulse disorienting and frightening, but older ones will probably enjoy the cool stuff there is to do. There's also a 36ft indoor ropes course, a 4D theater with changing shows, laser tag and the nightly **Outta Control Magic Show**.

Sea Life   AQUARIUM
(Map p254; ☑866-622-0607; www.visitsealifeorlando; 8449 International Dr, International Dr; adult/child $25/20; ☉10am-9pm) Just when you thought Orlando had every water-themed park and attraction available, along comes Sea Life (one of a chain that operates around the world). Opened in 2016, this is another wildlife showcase of the underwater-world variety. It's divided into many themes; the 360-degree glass tunnel is the highly promoted centerpiece.

It has an educative, sustainable line to its exhibits, including talks and feeding sessions. Online prices are $5 less per person. Combination tickets are available with the Orlando Eye and Madame Tussauds.

SeaWorld   AMUSEMENT PARK
(Map p254; ☑888-800-5447; www.seaworldparks.com; 7007 Sea World Dr; $95, discounts online, prices vary daily; ☉9am-8pm; ⚑; ☐Lynx 8, 38, 50, 111, ☐I-Ride Trolley Red Line Stop 28) One of Orlando's largest theme parks, SeaWorld is an aquatic-themed park filled with marine animal shows, roller coasters and up-close sea-life encounters. However, the park's biggest draw is controversial: live shows featuring trained dolphins, sea lions and killer whales. Since the release of the 2013 documentary *Blackfish*, SeaWorld's treatment

Downtown Orlando

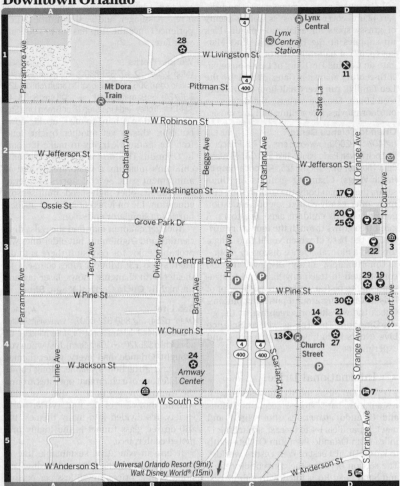

Downtown Orlando

ORLANDO & WALT DISNEY WORLD® ORLANDO

TRAVEL WITH CHILDREN

The challenge for families vacationing in the Theme Park Capital of the World is digging through the overwhelming options and inflated rhetoric to find what best suits your time, budget and family. If time is limited, stick to Disney's iconic Magic Kingdom (p287) and the edgier, less-stressful Universal Orlando Resort, boasting the marvelously themed Wizarding World of Harry Potter (p312).

Though part of the Disney magic is how it magically makes your money disappear, there are plenty of inexpensive highlights in and around Orlando. Tubing at **Kelly Park** (☑ 407-254-1902; www.ocfl.net/cultureparks; 400 E Kelly Park Rd, Apopka; per vehicle $5; ☺ 8am-8pm Mar-Oct, to 6pm Nov-Feb; ♿), canoeing at Wekiwa Springs State Park (p260) and a visit to the lovely Bok Tower Gardens (p260) make perfect day trips. The free outdoor movie at Disney's Chip 'n' Dale Campfire Singalong (p282) is one of the best things at Disney.

Everything in Orlando is an opportunity to attract tourists, and eating is no exception. There are **character meals** both inside the parks and at resort hotels; **dinner shows** at Walt Disney World®, Universal Orlando Resort and venues around town; and **themed restaurants** offering everything from dining under asteroid showers to burgers and milkshakes in a mock drive-in theater.

You may be ready for bed once the sun sets, obsessively checking your watch to see if it's time yet to collapse, but there's more fun to be had. With the exception of Animal Kingdom, all of Disney's theme parks offer **light shows** or **fireworks**; Orlando's performing-arts scene includes excellent **children's theater**, Disney's Cirque du Soleil La Nouba (p305) performs nightly, and Universal's Blue Man Group (p319) is full of silly shenanigans. Disney's Board-Walk, Disney Springs and Universal Orlando Resort's CityWalk all make for a festive evening, with street performers and plenty of eye candy, but if you've had enough adrenaline for one day, kick back in small-town **Celebration** or **Winter Park**. Children appreciate the slow pace, and on a summer evening, after a day slogging through parks, sitting with a glass of wine while the children play in Celebration's lakefront fountain may just be heaven.

Sprinkle in the big-bang, high-energy fun judiciously. Yes, you might ride the Winnie the Pooh seven times in a row, and yes, you may never make it to the Finding Nemo musical in Animal Kingdom. If only we had gotten up earlier, if only we hadn't waited in line for that Mickey ice cream, if only we had scurried out of the park after the fireworks: if only, if only, if only we'd seen this, that and the other thing.

of its captive orcas has come under intense scrutiny and the company has been hit by falling visitor numbers and negative PR.

The film is a damning portrayal of the effects of keeping killer whales in captivity and charts the life of Tilikum, an orca at SeaWorld Orlando that was involved in the deaths of three people, including one of its trainers during a live show. Since its release, many animal welfare groups have come out in support of the film arguing that it is harmful and stressful to keep such sensitive, complex creatures inside an enclosed tank. SeaWorld issued a statement accusing the filmmakers of giving false and misleading information. Since then, much of the controversy has died down but, according to media reports, the company plans to phase out the shows in Orlando by 2019. In their defense, the company does preach a lot about the importance of sustainability through recordings and the like at the entrances of attractions. But, at the time of research, the animal shows were still continuing.

SeaWorld Orlando also features two of Florida's most adrenaline-pumping roller coasters. **Kraken** is a whiplash zip of twists and turns in carriages with no floor so your feet dangle free. In 2016 the ride was retrofitted with virtual-reality headsets for an added thrill. On **Manta** you lie horizontally, face down, several to a row, so that the coaster vaguely resembles a manta ray, and dive and fly through the air in this position, reaching speeds of almost 60mph. There are also many attractions for the under-10s.

Aquatica
AMUSEMENT PARK

(Map p254; ☑ 407-351-3600; www.aquaticaby seaworld.com; 5800 Water Play Way; online advance $50, daily pass $60, with SeaWorld Orlando per day $109; ☺ 9am-6pm; ♿; 🚌 Lynx 8, 38, 50, 111, 🚌 SeaWorld shuttle, 🚌 I-Ride Trolley Red Line Stop 30) This water park filled with tropical

Forget it. There's too much, and you'll never win that game. In the end it's what you do that kids remember, not what you missed.

Baby Basics at the Parks

Hitting Orlando's theme parks with a baby in tow? Children three years and younger do not pay admission. Once in the gates, a few things help navigate your day.

Child Swap (Walt Disney World® and Universal Orlando Resort) Allows caregivers to wait in line together, and then take turns staying behind with a baby or child while the other rides. Perfect for families traveling with multiple-age children or for kids who want a parent to check out the scare-factor before riding. Other parks offer similar options, but can be a bit complicated, so ask the ride attendant.

Disney's Baby Care Centers (Disney theme parks) Toys and Disney cartoons. You can purchase diapers, over-the-counter children's medication and more, and there's a full kitchen.

SeaWorld's Baby Center (SeaWorld) The cute house with rocking chairs on the porch in Shamu's Happy Harbor, with similar facilities to Disney. Women only.

Childcare

Kid's Nite Out (☑ 407-828-0920, freecall 1-800-696-8105; www.kidsniteout.com; 1/2/3/4/5 kids per hr $18//21/24/26/28, 4hr minimum, plus travel fee $10; ⊗ sitters available 24/7) Private in-room childcare or an extra pair of hands at the theme parks for children aged six months to 12 years.

Disney's Children Activity Center (☑ 407-939-3463; www.disneyworld.disney.com.go; select Disney resort hotels; per child per hr $12, 2hr minimum, incl dinner; ⊗ hours vary) Drop-off childcare centers at five Walt Disney World® Resort hotels. Reservations required but you don't need to be a guest at the hotel.

Kids' Camp (☑ Hard Rock 407-503-2200, Loews Portofino Bay 407-503-1200, Loews Royal Pacific 407-503-3200; www.universalorlando.com; Universal Orlando; Portofino Bay, Hard Rock & Royal Pacific Resorts; per child per hr $15; ⊗ 5-11pm Mon-Thu, to midnight Fri & Sat) Drop-off childcare center at Universal Orlando Resort hotels.

greenery offers a sense of Polynesia. You can float about in lazy rivers, splash zones, wave pools and water slides. Aquatica is owned by SeaWorld, and while there are no controversial dolphin or whale shows, the park features a tank of black-and-white Commerson's dolphins that are on show every two hours for feedings. SeaWorld has come under scrutiny for keeping captive marine mammals, and animal welfare organizations make compelling arguments against the practice.

Orlando Eye   AMUSEMENT PARK

(Map p254; www.officialorlandoeye.com; I-Drive 360, 8401 International Dr, International Dr; from $20; ⊗ 10am-10pm Sun-Thu, to midnight Fri & Sat) Orlando has got everything else that goes up and down, so why not round and around? Opened in 2017, the Eye is International Drive's latest landmark. Orlando is flat, but a trip in this, especially at night, affords views of theme parks and the greater area. Check ahead as it sometimes closes for private events.

Combination tickets are available with the Madame Tussauds and Sea Life.

Discovery Cove   AMUSEMENT PARK

(Map p254; ☑ 877-434-7268; www.discoverycove. com; 6000 Discovery Cove Way, International Dr; incl SeaWorld & Aquatica from $179, SeaVenture extra $49-69, prices vary daily; ⊗ 8am-5:30pm; ⊞; ☐ Lynx 8, 38, 50, 111) At Discovery Cove, guests spend the day snorkeling in a fish- and ray-filled reef, floating on a lazy river through an aviary and simply relaxing in an intimate tropical sanctuary of white-sand beaches. For an added price beyond the Resort Only package, you can swim with dolphins and walk along the sea floor.

It may seem like a fun idea, but since the early 1990s, there has been a growing controversy regarding the ethics of dolphin captivity for the purposes of public display

International Drive

Conroy Rd/Conroy Windermere Rd

31

Lake Cane

Wizarding World of Harry Potter – Diagon Alley

Wizarding World of Harry Potter

Vineland Rd

30

Americana Blvd

Lake Marsha

4 5

25

23

Major Blvd

11

33

3

Dr Phillips Blvd

Universal Studios

Islands of Adventure

2

1

18

Universal Orlando Resort

W Oak Ridge Rd

Universal Orlando Water Taxis

Hollywood Way

17

S Kirkman Rd

Florida's Turnpike (toll)

26

27

24

Bay Hill Golf Club
(0.6mi)

19

16

8

International Dr

14

American Way

Sand Lake

Della Dr

29

Spring Lake

13

Canada Ave

Universal Blvd

21

36 32

35

W Sand Lake Rd

W Sand Lake Rd

Little Sand Lake

10

9

Big Sand Lake

28

20

Official Visitor Center –
Visit Orlando

Turkey Lake Rd

International Dr

37

15

39

Beachline Expwy (toll) 528

6

12

Central Florida Pkwy

7

34

22

Palm Pkwy

Lake Willis

International Dr

Vineland Ave

38

International Drive

ORLANDO & WALT DISNEY WORLD® ORLANDO

and human interaction. Both animal-welfare groups and marine scientists have come out against the practice claiming it is debilitating and stressful for these sensitive and complex creatures. Advance reservations are required for the all-day experience.

Madame Tussauds Orlando   MUSEUM
(Map p254; ☑ 866-630-8315; www.madame tussauds.com/orlando; 8387 International Dr; from $20; ☑ I-Ride Trolley Red Line 14, Green Line 8) Kitsch, celebrity-filled and featuring everyone from historic and cultural figures to current film icons. It's part of the Merlin Entertainment section with the Orlando Eye and Sea Life. It's selfie heaven.

Combination tickets are available with the Orlando Eye and Sea Life.

Ripley's Believe It Or Not   MUSEUM
(Map p254; ☑ 407-345-0501; www.ripleys.com/Orlando; 8201 International Dr, International Dr; adult/child 4-12yr $20/13; ⊙ 9:30am-midnight; ♿; ☑ Lynx 8, 38, 42, 50, 58, ☑ I-Ride Trolley Red Line Stop 12) The 1933 World's Fair in Chicago introduced Ripley's collection of 'oddities and unusual people' to the public. It may offend 21st-century politically correct sensibilities, this 'odditorium' offering Ripley's vision with no holds barred. Twenty-first-century additions tend to focus on the creation of odd, such as a dog sculpture made out of clothes pins, rather than the finding of odd.

⦿ Greater Orlando

Audubon Center for
Birds of Prey   WILDLIFE RESERVE
(☑ 407-644-0190; http://fl.audubon.org/audubon-center-birds-prey; 1101 Audubon Way, Maitland; adult/child 3-12yr $8/5; ⊙ 10am-4pm Tue-Sun; ♿) Centered at a cool old house and very much off the beaten track, this little lakeside rehabilitation center for hawks, screech owls and other talon-toed feathered friends offers plenty of opportunities to see the birds up close, just hanging out on the trainers' arms. Look out for Trouble the bald eagle splashing and playing in his bathtub.

Art & History
Museums – Maitland   ARTS CENTER
(☑ 407-539-2181; http://artandhistory.org; 231 W Packwood Ave, Maitland; adult/child $3/2; ⊙ 11am-4pm Tue-Sun) Founded as an art colony in 1937 and listed on the National Register of Historic Places, this lovely little spot provides classes and studio space to area artists,

galleries where they can display their work, and peaceful gardens.

While here, check out the small history museum and telephone museum next door.

Gatorland   ZOO
(☑ 407-855-5496; www.gatorland.com; 14501 S Orange Blossom Trail/Hwy 17, Kissimmee; adult/child $27/19; ⊙ 10am-5pm; ♿; ☑ Lynx 108) With no fancy roller coasters or drenching water rides, this mom-and-pop park harkens back to Old Florida. It's small, it's silly and it's kitschy with, you guessed it, plenty of gators. A splintery wooden boardwalk winds past the hundreds of alligators in the breeding marsh and you can buy hot dogs to feed them. The rather tongue-in-cheek shows are charmingly free of special effects, dramatic music and spectacular light design. But note: they involve animal interaction some might find disturbing.

At the **Jumparoo Show** 10ft-long alligators leap almost entirely out of the water to grab whole chickens from the trainer. **Up-Close Encounters** involves mysterious boxes holding animals the public has sent to the park. The trainers are too scared to open them, so they drag audience members down to help. The **Screamin' Gator Zip Line** (per two hours $70, including park admission) features various ziplines over the park. Note: Lonely Planet does not condone the practice of having your photo sitting on a gator. Parking is free.

Green Meadows Farm   FARM
(☑ 407-846-0770; www.greenmeadowsfarm.com; 1368 S Poinciana Blvd, Kissimmee; adult/child 3-12yr $23/20; ⊙ 9:30am-4:30pm, final tour 2:30pm; ♿) Only 11 miles (30 minutes' drive) from Disney, this little farm makes a pleasant getaway to the countryside and an easy break from the theme-park energy. You can pet the animals, milk a cow and ride a pony, and there's plenty of shade and grass, a picnic area and a playground. Note that you can only see the farm by two-hour tour.

To fully participate in everything offered, arrive by 2:30pm.

Nature Conservancy's Disney
Wilderness Preserve   WILDLIFE RESERVE
(☑ 407-935-0002; www.nature.org/florida; 2700 Scrub Jay Trail, Kissimmee; ⊙ 9am-4:30pm Mon-Fri Apr-Oct, daily Nov-Mar; ♿) FREE Hidden within Orlando's sprawl, this undeveloped and little-visited 11,500-acre preserve is the result of laws that required Walt Disney World® to compensate for the company's impact on

Greater Orlando

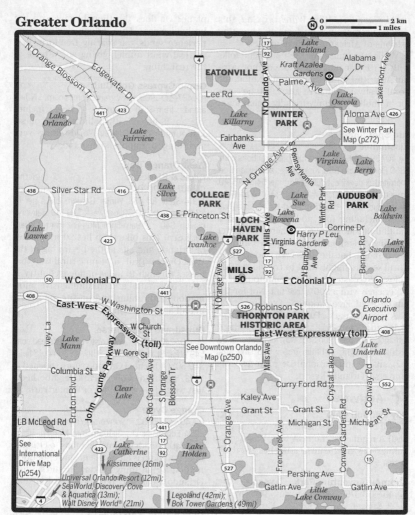

(and devastation of) wetlands and sensitive natural habitats. The park's scrub, fields and woods are home to gopher tortoises, bald eagles, sandhill cranes and hundreds of other wildlife species.

Hike the 1-mile round-trip to Lake Russell, or continue on to the 2.5-mile loop. The park is located just south of Kissimmee, 22 miles from Walt Disney World®.

Central Florida Zoo & Botanic Gardens   ZOO

(☏ 407-323-4450; www.centralfloridazoo.org; 3755 NW Hwy 17-92, Sanford; adult/child 3-12yr

$19.50/13.75, zipline $22-55; ☺9am-5pm; ⓐ) With lush surrounds, this small but satisfying zoo is set apart from the usual intensity of Orlando tourist attractions, with an excellent splash-play area, animal interactions and three zipline courses.

Zora Neale Hurston National Museum of Fine Arts   MUSEUM

(☏ 407-647-3307; 227 E Kennedy Blvd, Eatonville; ☺9am-4pm Mon-Fri, 11am-1pm Sat) FREE Dedicated to Florida writer and anthropologist Zora Neale Hurston (1881–1960), who was born in Eatonville and is famous for her novel *Their Eyes Were Watching God,* this tiny one-room museum features changing exhibits of African American artists.

While the museum itself attracts folks with particular interests in the author, African American studies or a specific exhibit, the Zora! Festival held here attracts thousands for a multiday family-friendly celebration every January.

Fun Spot America – Kissimmee
AMUSEMENT PARK

(☑ 407-397-2509; www.funspotattractions.com; 2850 Florida Plaza Blvd, Kissimmee; admission free, unlimited all-day rides adult/child under 54in $46/40, per ride $3-9; ☺ 10am-midnight; ⚽) Whirling, swinging and twisting old-time carnival rides, including four go-kart tracks and a handful of kiddie options. There's no clever theming or simulated masterpieces and it's pretty dated, but the lines aren't hours long. Thrill-seekers might want to try the 'world's tallest skycoaster', a bungee-jumping-style experience with a 300ft free fall. Not for the fainthearted. Free parking.

A second park, **Fun Spot America – Orlando** (Map p254; ☑ 407-363-3867; http://fun-spot.com; 5700 Fun Spot Way, International Dr; ☺ 10am-midnight; ⚑ I-Ride Trolley Red Line Stop 1, 2), sits on International Dr, minutes from Universal Orlando Resort.

🏃 Activities

Bay Hill Golf Club
GOLF

(☑ 407-876-2429; www.bayhill.com; 9000 Bay Hill Blvd) A regular on the PGA tour, this Arnold Palmer–designed course stretches over 270 acres.

ZoomAir Adventure Park
ADVENTURE SPORTS

(☑ 407-330-0767; www.zoomair.us; 3755 NW Hwy 17-92, Sanford; courses $22-55) Three zipline and high-ropes games courses at the Central Florida Zoo & Botanic Gardens (p257) are geared towards kids aged 10 and older. Stop after the Upland or continue with the higher and more intense Rainforest. The Kids Course is 4ft above ground, and each course takes about an hour.

Come early, as the courses backlog easily and it's frustrating to spend time hanging and waiting on the platforms.

I Fly Orlando
ADVENTURE SPORTS

(Map p254; ☑ 407-903-1150; www.iflyorlando.com; 6805 Visitors Cir, International Dr; adult from $60; ☺ 10:30am-9pm Mon-Fri; ⚽) Think you might like to jump out of a moving plane? Or does the thought give you the heebie-jeebies? This indoor skydiving experience sends you soaring free-form in a vertical wind tunnel, giving you a taste of the real thing.

Grand Cypress Golf Club
GOLF

(☑ 407-239-1909; www.grandcypress.com; 1 N Jacaranda; from $50) Beautiful 45 holes, including an 18-hole Scottish links-style course, just outside Walt Disney World®. Rates vary according to supply and demand.

West Orange Trail Bikes & Blades
CYCLING

(☑ 407-877-0600; www.orlandobikerental.com; 17914 State Rd 438, Winter Garden; bikes per hr $7-11, per day $30-50, per week $99-149, delivery/pickup $40; ☺ 9am-5pm Mon-Fri, from 7:30am Sat & Sun) This bike shop lies 20 miles west of Orlando and sits at the beginning of the West Orange Trail , a 24-mile rural trail that passes through 10 miles of horse country. It offers bike rental and comprehensive information, both online and on-site, on biking in and around Orlando.

Dubsdread Golf Course
GOLF

(☑ 407-246-2551; www.historicaldubsdread.com; 549 W Par St, College Park; 9 holes $30-40, 18 holes $40-60) Old-school Orlando course opened in 1923. Sits in the College Park neighborhood, just west of I-4 and south of Winter Park.

Orange Cycle
CYCLING

(☑ 407-422-5552; www.orangecycleorlando.com; 2204 Edgewater Dr; ☺ 10am-7pm Mon-Fri, 10am-5pm Sat) Provides printable maps to Orlando bike trails and is an excellent source of information for all things biking in and around Orlando. Sells and repairs bikes, but does not rent.

Buena Vista Watersports
WATER SPORTS

(☑ 407-239-6939; www.bvwatersports.com; 13245 Lake Bryan Dr; per hr kayak, canoe or paddleboard $25, jetski $105; ☺ 9am-6:30pm; ⚽) Just outside the Disney gates, with a low-key vibe. Water ski and tube riding include driver/instructor (per hour per boat $165).

🧭 Tours

Central Florida Nature Adventures
KAYAKING

(☑ 352-589-7899; www.kayakcentralflorida.com; 2-3hr per person $64; ⚽) Run by local residents and nature lovers, Jenny and Kenny, these small nature tours make for a relaxing paddle among the alligators, turtles, herons and egrets. They will meet you at different launch sites depending on the tour you choose.

✯ Festivals & Events

Thursday Gallery Hop   CULTURAL
(☑ 407-648-7060; www.orlandoslice.com; ⊙ 6-9pm 3rd Thu of the month) Downtown Orlando art and culture crawl, with live music and monthly themes at various venues on the third Thursday of the month.

Zora! Festival   CULTURAL
(☑ 407-647-3188; www.zorafestival.org; 227 E Kennedy Blvd, Eatonville; ⊙ Jan) Celebrating author Zora Neale Hurston, the festival embraces African American music, art and culture.

Spring Training   SPORTS
(www.springtrainingonline.com; tickets from $3; ⊙ mid-Feb–Apr) Bring a blanket, grab the Cracker Jacks and watch baseball like it was meant to be. The Atlanta Braves play at Walt Disney World's ESPN Center. At the time of research, the Houston Astros were about move to Palm Beach Gardens.

Florida Film Festival   FILM
(☑ 407-629-1088; www.floridafilmfestival.com; 1300 S Orlando Ave, Maitland; films $9-11; ⊙ Apr) Indie and alternative movies organized through the hip Enzian Theater (p267). Multifilm and event packages available from $50.

Orlando International Fringe Festival   CULTURAL
(www.orlandofringe.org; ⊙ May) Fourteen-day festival offering '100% unjuried, 100% uncensored, 100% accessible theater, music, dance and art.'

Gay Days   LGBT
(www.gaydays.com; ⊙ Jun) More than 160,000 folks descend upon the city for a week of events in the theme parks and venues throughout town in the first week of June.

Orlando Film Festival   FILM
(www.orlandofilmfest.com; day pass $20; ⊙ Oct) Indie films screen in downtown Orlando at Cobb Plaza Cinema Cafe. Various packages available.

🛏 Sleeping

Downtown Orlando has some lovely privately owned options, which can be a blessed relief from the resorts.

★ Floridian Hotel & Suites   HOTEL $
(Map p254; ☑ 407-212-3021; www.floridian hotelorlando.com; 7531 Canada Ave, International Dr; r from $75; P ⊜ ✳ ⊗ ☎) A wonderful, privately owned budget hotel with similarities to a chain brand, but oh so much better in other respects: delightful front office staff, spotless rooms with fridges and even a complimentary (if basic) breakfast, plus shuttles to various parks. It's near Restaurant Row and handy to International Dr.

★ Courtyard at Lake Lucerne   B&B $
(☑ 407-648-5188; www.orlandohistoricinn.com; 211 N Lucerne Circle E, Downtown; r incl breakfast from $140; P ✳ ⊗) This lovely option comprises four buildings, all different, from a historic home (1883) to an art-deco gem. The spacious rooms are decorated according to their era. It has enchanting gardens and genteel breakfast. Complimentary cocktails help you forgive its location under two highway overpasses, which were, unfortunately, constructed in the 1970s.

Contrary to the name, it's got nothing to do with the Courtyard Marriott.

★ Hyatt Regency Grand Cypress Resort   RESORT $$
(☑ 800-233-1234, 407-239-1234; www.hyattgrand cypress.com; 1 Grand Cypress Blvd, Lake Buena Vista; r $189-250, resort fee per day $30, self/valet parking $20/29; P @ ⊗ ☎ ☎) Considering the proximity to Disney's Magic Kingdom (7 miles) and Universal Resort Orlando (8 miles), plus the quality of the rooms, service, grounds and amenities, this atrium-style resort is one of the best-value options in Orlando.

There are multiple pools, a waterfall set into a grotto, a splash play area and a winding slide, as well as a beachside lake with hammocks, sailboats and bicycles.

Shuttles go to Disney's Transportation & Ticket Center (from there you must connect with Disney transportation to the other theme parks), to SeaWorld and to Universal Orlando Resort.

★ Hilton Orlando Bonnet Creek   RESORT $$
(☑ 407-597-3600; www.hiltonbonnetcreek.com; 14100 Bonnet Creek Resort Lane, Greater Orlando; r from $210, resort fee per day $30, self/valet parking $22/30; P @ ⊗ ☎) Surrounded by Walt Disney World® and boasting a big pool with a lazy river and a slide, this quintessential full-service resort has a slight corporate feel but makes an excellent alternative to comparable resorts on Disney property. No, you won't enjoy the benefits of staying at a Disney hotel, but the quality more accurately mirrors the price.

WILD ORLANDO

After a few days (or hours, depending on who's asking) in a theme park, the sheer mass of Orlando's artificial environments can get a little overwhelming. If that last sentence made you long for some real fresh air and the smell of dirt, never fear – there are actually a fair few parks and nature preserves in the Greater Orlando area.

Lake Louisa State Park (☑ general 850-245-2157, park 352-394-3969; www.floridastate parks.org/park/Lake-Louisa; 7305 US 27, Clermont; car $5, campsites per person $5, hookups $24, 6-person cabins $120; ⊙ 8am-sundown) Located 30 minutes west of Walt Disney World®, Lake Louisa is an easy getaway. There are several peaceful lakes, lovely beaches and 25 miles of hiking trails through fields, woods and orange groves. For boating on Dixie Lake, you can rent three-person canoes and single-rider kayaks (from $20 to $30) at the ranger station. Twenty cabins, each with two bedrooms (linen included), a fully equipped kitchen and front porch, offer lake views. Camping and cabin reservations can be made up to 11 months in advance.

Wekiwa Springs State Park (☑ 407-884-2009; www.floridastateparks.org/wekiwasprings; 1800 Wekiwa Circle, Apopka; admission $6, campsites per person $5, hookups $24; ⊙ 7am-dusk) Fancy a swim? Head to Wekiwa Springs, located about 20 miles northwest of downtown Orlando, and cool off in the icy spring-fed swimming hole. You can also hike miles of trails and paddle the tranquil, still waters of the Wekiva River. Central Florida Nature Adventures, inside the park, offers 2½-hour guided tours, rents kayaks and canoes (two hours $17, per additional hour $3) and supplies overnight camping supplies. Reserve primitive riverside campsites in advance.

Orlando Wetlands Park (☑ 407-568-1706; www.orlandowetlands.org; 25115 Wheeler Rd, Christmas; ⊙ sunrise-sunset; ☒) Here you'll find woodlands, lakes and marshes flush with migrating birds, alligators, deer and all kinds of other critters. There are 20 miles of hiking trails and dirt roads, as well as restrooms, picnic tables and charcoal grills at the main entrance. Biking is limited to unpaved berm roads. The park, 30 miles east of downtown Orlando, sits about halfway between Orlando and Titusville, home to Canaveral National Seashore and the Kennedy Space Center.

Bok Tower Gardens (☑ 863-676-1408; www.boktowergardens.org; 1151 Tower Blvd, Lake Wales; adult/child $14/5, house tour $6; ⊙ 8am-6pm, last admission 5pm; ☒) While it's not a nature park per se, Bok Tower Gardens is still a breath of clean air from a lovingly designed green lung. Designed by Frederick Law Olmstead Jr and showcasing the meticulously carved, 205ft stone bell tower, this 250-acre National Historic Landmark features beautiful gardens, twice-daily carillon concerts, the Mediterranean-style Pinewood Estates (1930s) and a garden cafe. Kids can pick up special paper at the entry and make a treasure hunt out of looking for the iron rubbing posts, each with a different animal to rub. The gardens hosts outdoor classical-music concerts. The gardens sit an hour south of Orlando, close to Legoland.

The on-site Harvest Bistro serves rather pricey fresh and tasty fare, though children pay half-price for breakfast and are free for dinner.

Aloft Orlando Downtown BUSINESS HOTEL $$ (Map p250; ☑ 497-380-3500; www.aloftorlando downtown.com; 500 S Orange Ave, Downtown; r from $230; ☑ @ ☎ ☒) Open, streamlined and decidedly modern, although the carefully constructed minimalist decor might render the rooms oddly empty for some. The sleek little pool sits unpleasantly on the main road. But it is one of the few hotels within

an easy walk to downtown Orlando's bars and restaurants.

Castle Hotel HOTEL $$ (Map p254; ☑ 407-345-1511, 800-952-2785; www. castlehotelorlando.com; 8629 International Dr; r from $160, parking per day $15; ☑ @ ☎ ☒ ☒; ☒ I-Ride Trolley Red Line Stop 15 or Green Line Stop 69) The story goes that the owner built this for his (then young) daughter who wanted her own Cinderella castle. Indeed, you can't miss the exterior of this International Dr landmark. Inside you'll find gilt, sparkle and antler chandeliers, with rooms decorated with faux lizard and rich browns; outside, a small pool sits next to a modern and airy garden-inspired cafe.

Prices fluctuate enormously.

Hilton Homewood Suites MOTEL $$
(Map p254; ☑ 407-226-0669; http://homewood suites1.hilton.com; 5893 American Way, International Dr; ste $120-299; @ 🖥 🖼 ; 🖵 I-Ride Trolley Red Line Stop 5) Comfy beds and spacious suites, each with a fully equipped kitchen and a low-key feel that is lacking at comparable chain hotels in Orlando. There's a complimentary hot breakfast, a dinner buffet (Monday to Thursday) and a 24-hour snack shop. Great choice, particularly if you're going to Universal Orlando Resort; there's a free shuttle from the hotel.

EO Inn & Spa BOUTIQUE HOTEL $$
(Map p250; ☑ 407-481-8485; www.eoinn.com; 227 N Eola Dr, Thornton Park; r $150-500; P ✳ @ 🖥) Small and understated hotel, and one of the only options on the northeastern shore of Lake Eola, with an easy walk to Thornton Park and downtown Orlando bars and restaurants. The rooms vary dramatically in size. It's got a not-quite-there ambience, but is good value at the lower end of the scale (note: prices fluctuate enormously).

Hilton Garden Inn
International Drive North MOTEL $$
(Map p254; ☑ 407-363-9332, 800-327-1366; www.hiltongardenorlando.com; 5877 American Way, International Dr; r $109-249; P @ 🖥 🖼 ; 🖵 I-Trolley Red Line Stop 5) With an airy garden-style lobby, a poolside tiki bar and an on-site restaurant, this is an excellent midrange option for visiting Universal Orlando. It's less than a mile to the parks and, although it sits on I-4, it's quiet and set apart from the chaos of International Dr.

Omni Orlando Resort at
ChampionsGate RESORT $$
(☑ 800-843-6664, 407-390-6664; www.omnihotels.com; 1500 Masters Blvd, Champions Gate; r from $269, resort fee per day $25, self/valet parking $18/26; @ 🖥 🖼 🖼) Fairly isolated, though buffered from noise and congestion by two golf courses, wetlands and plenty of green space. There's an adult-only pool and a pleasantly landscaped family pool boasting a waterslide and an 850ft lazy river. Villas sleep between six and eight people. The resort lies about 12 miles south of Walt Disney World®, off I-4.

Prices fluctuate enormously depending on whether there's an event on and supply and demand.

Hyatt Regency Orlando
International Airport Hotel HOTEL $$
(☑ 407-825-1234; https://orlandoairport.regency.hyatt.com; 9300 Jeff Fuqua Blvd; r from $219; @ 🖥 🖼) Located inside the main terminal of the Orlando International Airport, it's a useful option for early departures or late arrivals though you might as well go elsewhere if you're hitting the resorts. Has a nice rooftop pool. Prices fluctuate enormously; for cheaper rates book well in advance.

★ Bay Hill Club and Lodge HOTEL $$$
(☑ 407-876-2429, 888-422-9455; www.bayhill.com; 9000 Bay Hill Blvd; r from $300; @ 🖥 🖥) Quiet and genteel Bay Hill feels like a time warp; as though you're walking into a TV set or your grandmother's photo album. It is reassuringly calm and simple. The staff is exceptionally gracious and accommodating, and handsome rooms are spread among a series of two-story buildings bordering the Arnold Palmer–designed golf course. Internet deals are frequent.

Though the lodge seems to attract an older, golfing clientele, and there is nothing trendy or fancy about its pool or amenities, families will find Bay Hill's comforting cocoonlike atmosphere a welcoming oasis after a day tackling Orlando. Theme parks and restaurants are an easy drive. Set in a residential golf community and sporting only a small sign, Bay Hill is difficult to find. Head west from Apopka Vineland Rd on Bay Hill Blvd and look for it 1 mile on the right. There is no daily parking fee or resort fee.

★ Grande Lakes Orlando –
JW Marriott & Ritz-Carlton HOTEL $$$
(Map p254; ☑ JW Marriott 407-206-2300, Ritz-Carlton 407-206-2400; www.grandelakes.com; 4012 Central Florida Pkwy (Ritz Carlton), 4040 Central Park Pkwy (JW Marriott); r from $359, resort fee per day $35, self/valet parking $22/29; P @ 🖥 🖼) Two properties, one a Ritz and the other a Marriott, share facilities. The grounds, peaceful and elegant, with plenty of greenery and the best lazy river pool in Orlando, sit in a sheltered oasis of quiet and luxury. The spa is divine, the service impeccable, the food outstanding and most rooms have balconies overlooking the pool and golf course.

Excellent for honeymooners and families alike, this hotel is the rare Orlando find that seamlessly combines child- and adult-friendly facilities. Rates fluctuate enormously.

Villas of Grand Cypress   RESORT $$$

(☑ 407-239-4700, 887-330-7370; www.grand
cypress.com; 1 N Jacaranda Blvd, Buena Vista; r from $410, 1-/2-/3-/4-bedroom villas from
$460/650/800/1200, resort fee per day $25;
🕸☞) Beautifully appointed rooms and villas, with natural cut stone, deep soaking
tubs and outdoor patios, sit quietly along the
Grand Cypress resort golf course (designed
by Jack Nicklaus). The least expensive option is the 'club suite,' a 650-sq-ft room with
two double beds, a sleeper couch and a small
patio. It's the perfect place if you're over-
stimulated by theme parks.

The spacious villas boast private baths for
each bedroom, living and dining rooms and
fully equipped kitchens. There's a small and
quiet swimming pool, plus complimentary
bikes and helmets for peaceful rides through
the golf course, and an on-demand, door-to-
door shuttle service from your villa to the
Hyatt Grand Cypress across the road. Great
off-peak deals on the prices listed here.

Waldorf Astoria   HOTEL $$$

(☑ 407-597-5500; www.waldorfastoriaorlando.com;
14200 Bonnett Creek Resort Lane, Greater Orlando;
r $200-400, ste $450-560, resort fee per day $30,
valet-only parking $30; ℗@🕸☞) Though this
elegant classic doesn't offer the benefits of
on-site Disney hotels, it's located within the
gates of Walt Disney World® and the quality
of its rooms, amenities and service is impeccable. There's an excellent buffet breakfast, two
grandly styled pools bordering the golf course,
and a spa. Hilton Orlando Bonnet Creek
(p259) shares amenities with the Waldorf.

Bus shuttle to Disney is complimentary but
unreliable if there's traffic – it makes several
stops on the way to/from your destination,
stretching what should be a 15-minute ride
closer to an hour, and so rendering null the
benefit of close proximity to Disney.

Grand Bohemian Hotel   HOTEL $$$

(Map p250; ☑ 407-313-9000; www.grand
bohemianhotel.com; 325 S Orange Ave, Downtown; r
from $389, ste from $489, valet-only parking per day
$26; ℗@🕸☞) Downtown Orlando's most
luxurious and elegant option has marble
floors, a stunning art-deco bar with massive
black pillars, weekend jazz and rich urban
rooms. The small rooftop pool echoes 1950s
Miami Beach. Unfortunately, there's no shuttle to the parks. It's almost not worthwhile
providing prices here; they adhere strictly to
their own, extremely secretive and variable
pricing system.

✖ Eating

★ P Is for Pie   BAKERY $

(☑ 407-745-4743; www.crazyforpies.com; 2806
Corrine Dr, Audubon Park; from $2; ⊙ 7:30am-
4:30pm Mon-Sat; 🖊) Clean-lined with an artisan twist to classic pies (as in sweet tarts
with a biscuit base), offering mini and specialty options. Flavors include key lime and
tiramisu. Sublime.

★ East End Market   MARKET $

(☑ 231-236-3316; www.eastendmkt.com; 3201
Corrine Dr, Audubon Park; ⊙ 10am-7pm Tue-Sat,
11am-6pm Sun; 🖊🖒) ✎ Look for the raised
vegetable beds and picnic tables outside this
little earthy, organic, hip collection of locally
sourced eateries and markets.

Inside there's Lineage, a fabulous coffee
stand (it's worth it for a good brew), Local
Roots Farm Store, specializing in an 'all Florida all year' theme and offering flights of Florida beer and wine at the tiny bar; Gideon's
Bakehouse, with fabulous cakes and cookies;
and the excellent raw-vegan bar Skybird
Juicebar & Experimental Kitchen; and more.

★ Dandelion
Communitea Café   VEGETARIAN $

(☑ 407-362-1864; www.dandelioncommunitea.
com; 618 N Thornton Ave, Thornton Park; mains
$10-14; ⊙ 11am-10pm Mon-Sat, to 5pm Sun; 🖊🖒)
✎ Unabashedly crunchy and definitively
organic, this pillar of the sprouts and tempeh and green-tea dining scene serves up
creative and excellent plant-based fare in a
refurbished old house that invites folks to sit
down and hang out.

There's a drum circle, tables in the yard
and craft and local beers; check the website
for details on art openings, poetry readings
and live music.

Stardust Video & Coffee   CAFE $

(☑ 407-623-3393; www.stardustvideoandcoffee.
wordpress.com; 1842 E Winter Park Rd, Audubon
Park; mains $7-14; ⊙ 7am-midnight Mon-Fri, from
8am Sat & Sun; ℗🕸🖊🖒) 'Don't use the word
hipster to describe this place,' says Tess, the
server. She prefers 'weirdo eclectic.' Whatever you call it, you get the picture. This,
er, hipster-hippie hangout has folks hiding
behind laptops munching on veggie treats
or sipping on freshly squeezed juices by
day. It's an atmospheric craft cocktail and
artisan-beer hot spot by night.

Paper lanterns and twinkly lights dangle
from the ceiling and snapshot-style photographs hang haphazardly from the concrete

walls. Call for information on weekly live music and the Monday evening farmers market.

Pho 88 VIETNAMESE $
(www.pho88orlando.com; 730 N Mills Ave, Mills 50; mains $8-13; ⊙10am-10pm) A flagship in Orlando's thriving Vietnamese district (known as ViMi) just northeast of downtown in an area informally referred to as Mills 50, this authentic, no frills, *pho* (Vietnamese noodle soup) specialist is always packed. Cheap and tasty!

Black Bean Deli CUBAN $
(www.blackbeandeli.com; 1835 E Colonial Dr, Mills 50; mains $7-9; ⊙11am-9pm Mon-Thu, to 10pm Fri & Sat; 🛜) Housed in a fabulous retro-styled building, this former car dealership now wheels and deals exceptionally tasty Cubano specialties.

Blue Bird Bake Shop BAKERY $
(✐407-228-3822; www.bluebirdbakeshop.com; 3122 Corrine Dr, Audubon Park; pastries $2-4; ⊙7am-5pm Mon-Sat, 10am-4pm Sun; 🖩) Tiny retro Blue Bird Bake Shop, named after the favorite bird of the owner's grandma, offers daily baked cupcakes. Flavors range from classic chocolate to quirky vanilla black pepper or sweet potato. Closes early if cupcakes run out. While the coffee is nothing to rave about, it has the best chocolate brownie we've ever tasted. Yes. Ever.

Benjamin French Bakery BAKERY $
(Map p250; ✐407-797-2293; www.benjamin frenchbakery.com; 716 E Washington St, Thornton Park; pastries $4, mains $3-9; ⊙8am-6pm) Bright little French bakery featuring rustic sandwiches, salads and omelets. Your best bet, though, is a pastry and coffee to go. Try the crusty homemade baguette or a croissant of whatever flavor they've made that day.

Bikes, Beans & Bordeaux CAFE $
(✐407-427-1440; www.b3cafe.com; 3022 Corrine Dr, Audubon Park; mains $6-12; ⊙7am-9pm Mon-Fri, from 8am Sat, 8am-5pm Sun; P🛜🍷) Started by keen cyclists for their fellow enthusiasts, the word soon spread. This casual little spot serves up good sandwiches and salads that are much healthier than you'll find elsewhere. The menu is themed along cycling events, sandwiches are named Tour de France and Tour Mediterranean etc. Kids can have 'training wheels' bites, aka smaller meals such as peloton pizzas.

There's weekend live music, couches for lounging and local art.

House of Pizza PIZZA $
(✐407-447-7515; www.orlandohouseofpizza.com; 14650 Gatorland Dr; mains $8-16; ⊙11am-10pm Mon-Sat, noon-9pm Sun; 🖩) It doesn't look like much more than your standard greasy pizza joint, but give it a chance. It's independently owned and has very good pizza, as well as bruschetta, pasta, sandwiches and more. Only useful if you're visiting Gatorland and, after feeding the 'gators, you want to feed yourself.

Havana's Cafe CUBAN $
(✐407-238-5333; www.havanascubancuisine. com; 8544 Palm Pkwy; mains $8-14; ⊙11:30am-10pm Mon-Sat, noon-9pm Sun) This simple and friendly mom-and-pop spot in a suburban mall is a breath of fresh air among the ubiquitous chains, resort dining and high-octane Disney options. Call ahead for take-out. The emphatic 'No strollers!' sign might indicate its smallish size...and clientele.

Eden Bar AMERICAN $
(✐407-629-1088; www.enzian.org; 1300 S Orlando Ave, Maitland; mains $10-16; ⊙11am-11pm Sun-Thu, to 1am Fri & Sat; 🍷) 🍴 Island-vibe outdoor dining under the giant cypress of the ultra-cool Enzian Theater (p267). The delightfully eclectic menu ranges from pear prosciutto pizza and quinoa-stuffed peppers to fried chicken and country fried steak. Try the Mexican *mojito*.

Peach Valley Cafe DINER $
(Map p254; ✐407-522-2601; www.peachvalley restaurants.com; 5072 Dr Phillips Blvd, Restaurant Row; mains $9-13; ⊙7am-2:30pm Mon-Fri, to 3:30pm Sat & Sun; 🖩) Florida chain that offers surprisingly varied and tasty classics, from apple fritters and banana pancakes to chopped Cobb salad and chicken potpie. This is an Aunt-Jemima-and-fried-eggs kind of place – nothing fancy, but solid and reasonably priced.

Keke's Breakfast Cafe CAFE $
(Map p254; ✐407-226-1400; www.kekes.com; 4192 Conroy Rd; mains $8-14; ⊙7am-2:30pm; 🖩) Orlando go-to spot for great breakfasts, including stuffed French toast, eggs Benedict and banana-nut pancakes. Other Orlando locations include one in **Winter Park** (✐407-629-1400; 345 W Fairbanks Ave) and one in **Restaurant Row** (Map p254; ✐407-354-1440; 7512 Dr Phillips Blvd).

Graffiti Junktion
American Burger Bar
BURGERS **$**

(Map p250; ☑407-426-9503; www.graffiti
junktion.com; 700 E Washington St, Thornton Park;
mains $10-14; ⊙11am-2am) This little neon, hap-
penin' hangout, with courtyard dining and
regular drink specials, is all about massive
burgers with attitude. Go with a Brotherly
Love (Angus beef; $11) or veggie option ($7).
It recently moved so lacks the graffiti-covered
walls of its past location.

Dessert Lady Café
BAKERY **$**

(Map p254; ☑407-999-5696; www.dessertlady.
com; 7600 Dr Phillips Blvd, No 78, Restaurant Row;
desserts $9; ⊙10am-6pm Mon-Sat; ⊛) Nation-
ally acclaimed and a local favorite, this is
where the old saying 'desserts to die for'
comes from. Fruit cobbler, bourbon pecan
pie, key lime cake and more. It's mainly takeout but there's a small area should you wish
to eat there.

Greek Corner Restaurant
GREEK **$**

(☑407-228-0303; www.thegreekcorner.net; 1600 N
Orange Ave; mains $10-15; ⊙11am-10pm Mon-Sat,
to 8pm Sun) This little, white-walled cafe with
a small patio sits across from Lake Ivanhoe
(1 mile north of downtown in Ivanhoe). It's
a popular local spot that serves gyros, mous-
saka and other Greek specialties, as well as
pasta and hefty (oh so American) burgers.

★Rusty Spoon
AMERICAN **$$**

(Map p250; ☑407-401-8811; www.therustyspoon.
com; 55 W Church St, Downtown; mains $15-31;
⊙11am-3pm Mon-Fri, 5-10pm Sun-Thu, to 11pm Fri
& Sat; ☑) ☞ Airy, handsome and inviting,
with a brick wall covered in giant photos
of farm animals, a trendy urban vibe and
an emphasis on simply prepared, locally
sourced produce. Kind of pub classics with
delightful (and much more sophisticated)
twists. If it's on the menu, don't bypass the
chocolate 'smores dessert. (We say no more.)

★Urbain 40
AMERICAN **$$**

(Map p254; ☑407-872-2640; http://urbain40.
com/; 8000 Via Dellagio Way, Restaurant Row) Tap
into your inner classy selves and transport
yourself back to the 1940s, where classic
martinis were downed like water by besuit-
ed clients who sat on blue leather bar stools.
This stunning old-style American brasserie
manages to re-create this (without contriv-
ance) and serves up great cuisine as well
as ambience. Do not miss the char-roasted
mussels ($12).

The menu comprises dishes that are all
local, sustainable and farm-to-table (you
get the idea). Sit back and take your time,
plus enjoy the photos of the jazz greats and
actors and artifacts of the era. It's a wonderful respite from the chaotic theme-park
scene.

★Stubborn Mule
MODERN AMERICAN **$$**

(Map p250; www.thestubbornmuleorlando.com;
100 S Eola Drive, Suite 103, Downtown; mains
$19-28; ⊙11am-11pm Tue-Sat, 11am-9pm Sun)
A trendy and very popular gastropub that
serves handcrafted cocktails with flair (yes,
plenty of mules) and good ol' locally sourced,
delicious food that's nothing but contempo-
rary. It serves up the likes of polenta cakes
and smoked Gouda grits and roasted winter
vegetables. It's the new kid on the block and
one definitely worth visiting.

Service can be a bit slow when it's packed,
so go when you have time. Live music on
weekends can make the outdoor seating a
rather noisy affair.

★DoveCote
FRENCH **$$**

(Map p250; http://dovecoteorlando.com/; 390 N
Orange Ave, Ste 110; lunch mains $12-24, dinner
mains $16-30; ⊙11:30am-2:30pm & 5:30-10pm)
One of the hottest tickets in Orlando sits ti-
dily within the city's Bank of America building. It's an all-things-to-all-people kind of
spot with a brasserie and a coffee stop, plus
plenty of cocktails. 'Comfort French' is often
used to describe the cuisine.

Diners love the simplicity of the delectable *croque monsieur* (grilled sandwich of
guyere cheese and ham) and the mussels
and *frites*.

★Slate
AMERICAN **$$**

(Map p254; ☑407-500-7528; www.slateorlando.
com; 8323 W Sand Lake Rd, Restaurant Row; mains
$14-38; ⊙11am-12:30pm & 5-10pm Mon-Fri, 10:30-
3pm & 5-11pm Sat, 10:30-3pm & 5-9pm Sun) One
of Orlando's newest and trendiest places,
it's buzzy, noisy and draws a chatty crowd
after crusty pizza (straight from the large,
copper oven) or contemporary dishes from
brisket to diver scallops. There are several
seating areas, from a communal table to the
wood room, a verandah-style space with a
fireplace.

Yellow Dog Eats
BARBECUE **$$**

(www.yellowdogeats.com; 1236 Hempel Ave, Windermere; mains $8-19; ⊙11am-10pm; ☑⊛) Housed
in what was once a general store, with a tin
roof, courtyard dining, an old school locker

filled with bottled beer, and an eclectic mix of quirky, dog-inspired decor, this laid-back boho Orlando gem serves up excellent barbecue and dishes.

Try the Florida Cracker (pulled pork with Gouda, bacon and fried onions) that, according to the menu, 'Makes you want to slap your Grandma!' Though it feels like a drive into the boondocks to get here, don't be deterred – Yellow Dog is 6 miles northwest of Universal Orlando Resort.

Hamburger Mary's   BURGERS $$

(Map p250; ☑ 321-319-0600; www.hamburger marys.com; 110 W Church St, Downtown; mains $10-16; ☺ 11am-10pm Sun & Mon, 11am-10:30pm Tue-Thu, 11am-11:30pm Fri & Sat) Downtown high-energy diner specializing in over-the-top burgers with sweet-potato fries and serious cocktails. There's a Broadway Brunch with show tunes, drag shows and all kinds of interactive entertainment.

Artisan's Table   AMERICAN $$

(Map p250; ☑ 407-730-7499; www.artisanstable orlando.com; 22 E Pine St, Downtown; mains $12-29; ☺ 7am-10pm Mon-Thu, 7am-midnight Fri, 9am-midnight Sat, 9am-10pm Sun) Chow down on the likes of a breakfast bowl of eggs and grits, or opt for steel-cut oats with agave and an organic smoothie at this under-the-radar locavore favorite offering an ever-changing and eclectic menu. It's extremely accommodating to dietary requirements, too. There's even coffee and cocktails to start and end the day.

If you want both, don't miss the cafe tequila, all fed through a fandangled gravity infusion tower ($7 per shot).

White Wolf Café & Bar   DINER $$

(☑ 407-895-9911; www.whitewolfcafe.com; 1829 N Orange Ave, Ivanhoe Village; mains $14-24; ☺ 8am-3pm Sun-Tue, 8am-9pm Wed & Thu, 8am-10pm Fri & Sat; ☑ Lynx 102) Old-style, neighborhood diner cafe, with Tiffany-styled chandeliers, a massive wooden bar and a mishmash of antiques. Come for the stick-to-your bones breakfasts and a Bloody Mary.

TooJays   DELI $$

(Map p254; ☑ 407-355-0340; www.toojays.com; 7600 Dr Phillips Blvd, Restaurant Row; sandwiches $9-12, mains $13-20; ☺ 7am-9pm Sun-Thu, to 10pm Fri & Sat; ☑) Excellent deli sandwiches to go, but it's a straight up American booth diner experience. If you feel a cold coming on, head here for quintessential homemade chicken noodle or matzo-ball soup.

Dexters of Thornton Park   AMERICAN $$

(Map p250; ☑ 407-648-2777; www.dexters orlando.com; 808 E Washington St, Thornton Park; mains $10-25; ☺ 7am-10pm Mon-Wed, 7am-11pm Thu & Fri, 11am-2am Sat, 10am-10pm Sun) Neighborhood restaurant with outdoor seating and a popular daily brunch that includes interesting twists on breakfast mainstays, including pepper-jack grits. Many diners say they have the best shrimp and grits in town. Sip on a selection of fruity mimosas including peach, mango and pineapple.

There are sister locations in Winter Park (p271) and in Lake Mary (17 miles north of Winter Park, I-4 exit 101).

Shari Sushi   JAPANESE $$

(Map p250; ☑ 407-420-9420; www.sharisushi lounge.com; 621 E Central Blvd, Thornton Park; mains $14-35; ☺ 5-10pm Sun-Wed, to 11pm Thu-Sat) Minimalist decor, huge sidewalk windows and a rather odd variety of tasty sushi, rolls and sashimi, but there's a limited selection of hot dishes. The elaborate drinks menu includes lemongrass *mojitos* and a cilantro-lime sake cocktail. Daily happy hour brings on $4.25 appetizers.

Thai Thani   THAI $$

(Map p254; ☑ 407-239-9733; www.thaithani.net; 11025 International Dr, International Dr; mains $9-22; ☺ 11:30am-11pm; ☑; ☑ I-Ride Trolley Red Line) A friendly, cool and quiet restaurant stuck out on its own in a mall (handy if you're staying near Seaworld), with gilded Thai decor and some tables with traditional floor seating. Good food, but watered-down spice – for a kick, ask for level 5 and above.

Cafe Tu Tu Tango   TAPAS $$

(Map p254; ☑ 407-248-2222; www.cafetutu tango.com; 8625 International Dr, International Dr; share plates $8-14; ☺ 11:30am-midnight Mon-Thu, to 1am Fri & Sat, 10am-11pm Sun) Local artwork, all for sale, crams the adobe-style walls of this bright, fun eatery. It's action packed with music and performers. Or you can relax on the patio with cajun chicken egg rolls and a plate of alligator bites, washed down with a pitcher of sangria. Share plates are 'globally inspired' with Asian and Mediterranean influences. Great for Sunday brunch.

Taverna Opa   GREEK $$

(Map p254; ☑ 407-351-8660; www.opaorlando.com; 9101 International Dr, The Pointe, International Dr; mains $15-40; ☺ noon-midnight Sun-Thu, noon-2am Fri & Sat; ☑; ☑ I-Ride Trolley Red Line) Great spot for Greek classics, including slow-roasted lamb ($14), plenty of vegetarian options and fresh hummus made tableside. Can get loud and crazy late at night, when the belly dancer shimmies and shakes from table to table and it isn't unusual for folks to climb onto the solid tables and kick up their heels. Nightly entertainment from 7pm.

★ K Restaurant   AMERICAN $$$

(🖉407-872-2332; www.krestaurant.net; 1710 Edgewater Dr, College Park; mains $18-40; ☺5-9pm Mon-Thu, 5:30-10pm Fri & Sat, 5:30-8pm Sun; 🅿) 🍴 Chef and owner Kevin Fonzo, one of Orlando's most celebrated and established field-to-fork foodie stars, earns local and national accolades year after year, but this neighborhood favorite remains wonderfully unassuming. There's a wraparound porch, and a lovely little terrace, and herbs and vegetables come from the on-site garden.

Hemingways   SEAFOOD $$$

(🖉407-239-1234; https://grandcypress.hyatt.com; 1 Grand Cypress Blvd, Hyatt Regency Grand Cypress Resort, Buena Vista; mains $29-40; ☺5-10pm) Quiet spot with airy Key West atmosphere. Try the particularly tasty crab cakes, with big chunks of lump crab and very little filler, and ask for a table on the screened-in porch.

🍷 Drinking & Nightlife

Orlando *really* likes to drink, so whether your tastes lean toward a wine flight at a sidewalk cafe, shots of tequila at a pulsing nightclub or a craft cocktail at a stylish bar, you'll be satisfied. International Dr is the center of tourist bars, while neighborhood bars in Winter Park, Thornton Park and Audubon Park offer an appealing neighborhood vibe. Restaurant Row has several good offerings, too.

★ Icebar   BAR

(Map p254; 🖉407-426-7555; www.icebarorlando. com; 8967 International Dr; entry at door/advance online $20/15; ☺5pm-midnight Mon-Wed, to 1am Thu, to 2am Fri-Sun; 🚋I-Trolley Red Line Stop 18 or Green Line Stop 10) More classic Orlando gimmicky fun. Step into the 22°F (-5°C) ice house, sit on the ice seat, admire the ice carvings, sip the icy drinks. Coat and gloves are provided at the door (or upgrade to the photogenic faux fur for $10), and the fire room, bathrooms and other areas of the bar are kept at normal temperature.

Adults over 21 welcome anytime; folks aged between eight and 20 are allowed between 7pm and 9pm only.

Wally's Mills Ave Liquors   BAR

(🖉407-896-6975; www.wallysonmills.com; 1001 N Mills Ave, Thornton Park; ☺7:30am-2am) It's been around since the early '50s, before Orlando became Disney, and while its peeling, naked-women wallpaper could use some updating, it wouldn't be Wally's without it. Nothing flashy, nothing loud, just a tiny, windowless, smoky bar with a jukebox and cheap, strong drinks – as much a dark dive as you'll find anywhere. And yes, it opens at 7:30*am*.

Wednesday night is $3 microbrews, Monday is $2 PBR beer, and the attached package store sells beer, wine and liquor.

Hanson's Shoe Repair   COCKTAIL BAR

(Map p250; 🖉407-476-9446; www.facebook.com/ hansonsshoerepair/; 3rd fl, 27 E Pine St, Downtown; cocktails $12; ☺8pm-2am Tue-Thu & Sat, from 7pm Fri) In a city saturated with over-the-top theming from Beauty and the Beast to Harry Potter, it shouldn't be surprising that you can walk from 21st-century Downtown Orlando into a Prohibition-era speakeasy, complete with historically accurate cocktails and a secret password for entry. To get in, call for the password.

Sure, it leans towards the gimmicky and cocktails are pricey, but this is Orlando, capital of the gimmicky and pricey. There's a dress code – no sloppy gear.

Tin Roof   BAR

(Map p254; 🖉407-270-7926; www.tinrooforlando. com; 8371 International Dr, I-Drive 360, International Dr; ☺11am-2am) The famous live-music joint that encourages performances of all standards. It's part of the I-Drive 360 complex (think the Orlando Eye and more). Serves up reasonable (bordering on very nice) junk food – burgers, mac 'n' cheese – and things that will fuel you until the wee hours.

Bösendorfer Lounge   LOUNGE

(Map p250; 🖉407-313-9000; www.grandbohe mianhotel.com; 325 S Orange Ave, Westin Grand Bohemian; ☺11am-2am) Zebra-fabric chairs, gilded mirrors, massive black pillars and marble floors ooze pomp and elegance. This hotel bar is popular for after-work drinks and the lounge picks up with live jazz at 7pm. The name stems from the lounge's rare Bösendorfer piano.

Courtesy Bar   COCKTAIL BAR

(Map p250; 🖉407-450-2041; www.thecourtesy bar.com; 114 N Orange Ave, Downtown; drinks from $5; ☺7pm-2am Mon & Sat, 5pm-2am Tue-Fri,

3pm-2am Sun) Housed in a historic Orlando space, with brick walls and Jefferson filament bulbs, this old-school cocktail bar serves up high-quality spirits with fresh and quirky artisan twists such as Himalayan pink salt, fresh honeydew juice and dandelion-eucalyptus tincture. We don't even know what all of it means, but what delights! There's also an excellent selection of beer and wine. Keeps odd hours.

Imperial Wine Bar & Beer Garden BAR
(☑ 407-228-4992; www.imperialwinebar.com; 1800 N Orange Ave, Loch Haven Park; snacks $9-16; ☺ 5pm-midnight Mon-Thu, to 2am Fri & Sat; ☐ Lynx 102) With its exposed ceiling pipes, glass mosaic light fixtures and antique furniture, this is a furniture store by day (hence the price tags everywhere) and a neighborhood boho bar by night. Sip on a Cigar City in the quiet nook of a beer garden out back and choose a bite from the limited menu of local fare.

Woods COCKTAIL BAR
(Map p250; ☑ 407-203-1114; www.thewoods orlando.com; 49 N Orange Ave, Downtown; cocktails $12; ☺ 5pm-2am Mon-Fri, from 7pm Sat, 4pm-midnight Sun) Craft cocktails and craft beers hidden in a cozy, smoke-free, 2nd-floor setting (in the historic Rose Building), with exposed brick, a tree-trunk bar and an earthy feel.

Redlight, Redlight BAR
(www.redlightredlightbeerparlour.com; 2810 Corrine Dr, Audubon Park; beers $5-10; ☺ 5pm-2am; ☎) Beer aficionados will love the impressive offerings of craft beers on draft at this local contemporary hangout housed in a former air-conditioner repair shop.

Matador COCKTAIL BAR
(☑ 407-872-0844; 724 Virginia Dr, Mills 50; ☺ 7pm-2am) Deep red walls, a pool table and furniture you'd expect in your grandmother's parlor. Low-key vibe perfect for sipping that Bulleit Rye.

Eola Wine Company WINE BAR
(Map p250; ☑ 407-481-9100; www.eolawinecompany. com; 430 E Central Blvd, Thornton Park; ☺ 4pm-2am Mon-Fri, from noon Sat & Sun) A California-style menu of light foods designed to be paired with wine and quirky independent-label beers. You can also get a flight of beer or wine, and a charcuterie and cheese plate.

Latitudes BAR
(Map p250; ☑ 407-649-4270; www.churchstreet bars.com; 33 W Church St, Downtown; ☺ 4:30pm-2am) An Orlando classic, the island-inspired Latitudes, a rooftop bar with tiki lanterns and city views, is always hopping. You have to walk up past thumping bars on the first two floors to get here, but once up it's a pleasant place to enjoy the Florida night skies.

Independent Bar CLUB
(Map p250; ☑ 407-839-0457; 68 N Orange Ave, Downtown; $10; ☺ 10pm-3am Sun, Wed & Thu, from 9:30pm Fri & Sat) Known to locals as simply the 'I-Bar,' it's hip, crowded and loud, with DJs spinning underground dance and alternative rock unto the wee hours.

Wall Street Plaza BAR
(Map p250; ☑ 407-849-0471; www.wallstplaza.net; 25 Wall St Plaza, Downtown) Eight raucous theme bars, sometimes with live music and always with drink specials, all in one party-palace-style plaza.

☆ Entertainment

★ Mad Cow Theatre THEATER
(Map p250; ☑ 407-297-8788; www.madcow theatre.com; 54 W Church, Downtown; tickets from $26) A model of inspiring regional theater, with classic and modern performances in a downtown Orlando space (located on the 2nd floor).

★ Enzian Theater CINEMA
(☑ 407-629-0054; www.enzian.org; 1300 S Orlando Ave, Maitland; adult/child $10/8; ☺ 5pm-midnight Tue-Fri, noon-midnight Sat & Sun) The envy of any college town, this clapboard-sided theater screens independent and classic films, and has the excellent Eden Bar (p263) restaurant, featuring primarily local and organic fare. Have a veggie burger and a beer on the patio underneath the cypress tree or opt for table service in the theater.

John & Rita Lowndes Shakespeare Center THEATER
(☑ 407-447-1700; www.orlandoshakes.org; 812 E Rollins St, Loch Haven Park; tickets $13-65) Set on the shores of Lake Estelle in grassy Loch Haven Park, this lovely theater includes three intimate stages hosting professional classics such as *Pride and Prejudice* and *Beowulf,* excellent children's theater and up-and-coming playwrights' work.

Beacham & the Social LIVE MUSIC
(Map p250; ☑ 407-246-1419; www.thebeacham. com; 46 N Orange Ave, Downtown; ☺ 9pm-3am) Both the Beacham and the more intimate and recommended Social next door are cornerstones of Orlando's nightclub and

ORLANDO & WALT DISNEY WORLD® ORLANDO

live-music scene. They host bands from punk to reggae on the weekends and hop all week long with music and dancing. Shows are designated 'all ages', '18 plus' or '21 plus'.

Orlando Repertory Theater
THEATER

(☑407-896-7365; www.orlandorep.com; 1001 E Princeton St, Loch Haven Park; tickets $10-25) Performances for families and children run primarily in the afternoons or early evenings. Shows stretch the gamut of styles and content, including *Nancy Drew* and *Curious George*.

Will's Pub
LIVE MUSIC

(☑407-898-5070; www.willspub.org; 1042 N Mills Ave, Thornton Park; tickets $8-16; ⊙4pm-2am Mon-Sat, from 6pm Sun) With $2 Pabst on tap, pinball and vintage pin-ups on the walls, this is Orlando's less-polished music scene, but it enjoys a solid reputation as one of the best spots in town to catch local and nationally touring indie music. Smoke-free; beer and wine only.

Dr Phillips Center for the Performing Arts
ARTS CENTER

(Map p250; ☑844-513-2014; www.drphillipscenter.org; 445 S Magnolia Ave, Downtown; ⊙box office 10am-4pm Mon-Fri, noon-4pm Sat) Covers the full gamut of top-quality entertainment from ballet and opera to jazz and classical music performances.

Tanqueray's Downtown Orlando
LIVE MUSIC

(Map p250; ☑407-649-8540; 100 S Orange Ave, Downtown; ⊙11am-2am Mon-Fri, 6pm-2am Sat & Sun) A former bank vault, this underground smoky dive bar draws folks looking to hang out with friends over a beer. There's Guinness on tap, and you can catch local bands, usually reggae or blues, on the weekend.

SAK Comedy Lab
COMEDY

(Map p250; ☑407-648-0001; www.sakcomedylab.com; 29 S Orange Ave, Downtown; tickets $14, 9pm Tue & Wed $5; ⊙Tue-Sat) Excellent improv comedy in intimate downtown Orlando theater. It's on the 2nd floor of the City Arts Factory.

Orlando Philharmonic Orchestra
PERFORMING ARTS

(☑407-770-0071; https://orlandophil.org) Classics, pop, opera and more, including family-friendly events, performed at venues in and around Orlando, including outdoor performances at Loch Haven Park.

Orlando Ballet
BALLET

(Map p250; ☑407-426-1739; http://orlando ballet.org; from $25) Performs primarily at downtown Orlando's Bob Carr Performing Arts Center (401 W Livingston St).

Amway Center
SPECTATOR SPORT

(Map p250; ☑407-440-7000; www.amwaycenter.com; 400 W Church St, Downtown) The Orlando Magic (National Basketball Association), the Orlando Predators (Arena Football League) and the Orlando Solar Bears (East Coast Hockey League) play here.

🔒 Shopping

Greater Orlando – around the theme parks and lining the highways – is defined by souvenirs, kitschy must-haves, outlet shopping and indoor malls with all the national chains.

Orlando Farmers Market
MARKET

(Map p250; www.orlandofarmersmarket.com; Lake Eola; ⊙10am-4pm Sun) Local produce and a beer and wine garden on the shores of downtown Orlando's Lake Eola.

Orlando Premium Outlets – Vineland Ave
MALL

(Map p254; ☑407-238-7787; www.premium outlets.com/outlet/orlando-vineland; 8200 Vineland Ave; ⊙10am-11pm Mon-Fri, to 9pm Sun; 🚌I-Ride Trolley Red Line 38) Popular outlet mall just outside Walt Disney World® – you'll know you're close when you're stuck in stand-still traffic for upwards of half an hour for no apparent reason.

Eli's Orange World
FOOD

(☑407-396-1306; www.orangeworld192.com; 5395 W Irlo Bronson Memorial Hwy/Hwy 192; ⊙8am-9:45pm) Family-owned, friendly and with plenty of samples of the iconic Florida fruit, as well as jams and kitschy souvenirs. Look for the building shaped like half an orange on the Kissimmee strip.

Pointe Orlando
SHOPPING CENTER

(Map p254; ☑407-248-2838; www.pointeorlando fl.com; 9101 International Dr; ⊙10am-10pm Mon-Sat, 11am-9pm Sun; 🚌I-Ride Trolley Red Line 18, 🚌I-Ride Trolley Green Line 11) Pleasant enough, with brick walkways and a fountain, this small outdoor shopping area features an odd assortment of shops and several good restaurants.

ℹ️ Information

DANGERS & ANNOYANCES

As in any city, take care when walking at night and avoid heading out alone if possible, especially around the secluded lakes and parks. Check with locals as to which areas to avoid. The main dangers relate to the heat. Summer brings a killer humidity. Stay well hydrated if wandering the city's streets and parks.

Central Florida is home to wildlife; alligators and snakes may be found in some waterways and marshes in residential areas and on golf courses and the like.

OPENING HOURS

Bars 4pm to 1am or 2am weekdays, 3am on weekends

Museums 10am to 5:30pm

Nightclubs 9pm to 1am or 2am weekdays, 3am on weekends

Restaurants Breakfast 7am or 8am to 11am; lunch 11am or 11:30am to 2:30pm or 3pm; dinner 5pm or 6pm to 10pm Sunday to Thursday, to 11pm or midnight Friday and Saturday

Shops 10am to 7pm Monday to Saturday, noon to 6pm Sunday

Theme Parks 9am to 6pm, often later and sometimes as late as 1am; check websites for daily hours

POST

Downtown Post Office (Map p250; ☑ 407-425-6464; www.usps.com; 51 E Jefferson St, Downtown; ⊗7am-5pm Mon-Fri)

TOURIST INFORMATION

Official Visitor Center (Map p254; ☑ 407-363-5872; www.visitorlando.com; 8723 International Dr; ⊗8:30am-6pm; 🚌 I-Ride Trolley Red Line 15)

TRAVELERS WITH DISABILITIES

➡ Accommodation in Florida is required by law to offer wheelchair-accessible rooms. For questions about specialty rooms at Walt Disney World® Resort call ☑ 407-939-7807.

➡ Parks allow guests with special needs to avoid waiting in line, but do not offer front-of-the-line access. Disney issues a Disability Access Service card and Universal Orlando Resort issues the Attraction Assistance Pass (AAP). Guests take the card to the attraction they want to experience and they are given a return time based on current wait times. Both are available at Guest Services inside the park.

➡ Wheelchair and electric convenience vehicle (ECV) rental is at Guest Services at Walt Disney World® Resort, Universal Orlando Resort and SeaWorld theme parks.

➡ Go to individual park websites or Guest Services for details on accessibility, services for guests with cognitive disabilities, services for guests who are deaf or have hearing impairments, and services for guests who are

visually impaired. Sign-language interpreting services require advanced reservations.

Resources

➡ Autism at the Parks (www.autismattheparks.com) provides comprehensive information on visiting Orlando theme parks with someone on the autism spectrum.

➡ Download Lonely Planet's free Accessible Travel guide from http://lptravel.to/Accessible Travel.

MEDICAL SERVICES

Arnold Palmer Hospital for Children (☑ 407-649-9111; www.arnoldpalmerhospital.com; 1414 Kuhl Ave; ⊗24hr) Orlando's primary children's hospital. Located just east of I-4 at exit 81.

Centra Care Walk-In Medical (☑ 407-934-2273; www.centracare.org; ⊗8am-midnight Mon-Fri, to 8pm Sat & Sun) Walk-in medical center with more than 20 locations.

Doctors on Call Services (DOCS; ☑ 407-399-3627; www.doctorsoncallservice.com; ⊗24hr) Twenty-four-hour doctors on-call to your hotel, including to Walt Disney World® and Universal Orlando Resort.

Dr P Phillips Hospital (☑ 407-351-8500; www.orlandohealth.com/facilities/dr-p-phillips-hospital; 9400 Turkey Lake Rd; ⊗24hr) Closest hospital to Universal Orlando Resort, SeaWorld and International Dr.

Florida Hospital Celebration Health (☑ 407-303-4000; www.floridahospital.com/celebration-health; 400 Celebration Pl, Kissimmee; ⊗24hr) Closest hospital to Walt Disney World®.

ℹ Getting There & Away

Amtrak (www.amtrak.com; 1400 Sligh Blvd) Offers daily trains south to Miami (from $46) and north to New York City (from $144).

Greyhound (☑ 407-292-3424; www.greyhound.com; 555 N John Young Pkwy) Serves numerous cities from Orlando.

ℹ Getting Around

BUS

Lymmo (www.golynx.com; free; ⊗6am-10pm Mon-Thu, to midnight Fri, 10am-midnight Sat, to 10pm Sun) circles downtown Orlando for free with stops near Lynx Central Station, near SunRail's Church St Station, at Central and Magnolia, Jefferson and Magnolia and outside the Westin Grand Bohemian.

SHUTTLE

Call **Mears Transportation** (☑ 855-463-2776) one day in advance to arrange personalized transport between a long list of hotels and many attractions, including Universal Orlando Resort and SeaWorld. It costs between $21 to $29 per round-trip per person.

Casablanca Transportation (☑407-927-2773, www.casablancatransportation.com) provides good service to the airport and in and around Orlando.

TRAIN

SunRail (www.sunrail.com), Orlando's commuter rail train, runs north–south. It doesn't stop at or near any theme parks.

In addition to the downtown station, **Amtrak** (p269) serves Winter Park, Kissimmee and Winter Haven (home to Legoland).

WINTER PARK

☑407 / POP 30,200

Founded in the mid-19th century and home to the small liberal-arts school Rollins College, the bucolic suburb of Winter Park concentrates some of the area's best-kept secrets – including several of Greater Orlando's most talked about restaurants and field-to-fork favorites – within a few shaded, pedestrian-friendly streets. Shops, wine bars and sidewalk cafes line Park Ave.

⊙ Sights

★Charles Hosmer Morse Museum of American Art   MUSEUM

(☑407-645-5311; www.morsemuseum.org; 445 N Park Ave; adult/child $6/free; ⊙9:30am-4pm Tue-Sat, from 1pm Sun, to 8pm Fri Nov-Apr; ▧) Internationally famous, this stunning and delightful museum houses the world's most comprehensive collection of Louis Comfort Tiffany art. Highlights include the chapel interior designed by the artist for the 1893 World's Columbian Exhibition in Chicago; 10 galleries filled with architectural and art objects from Tiffany's Long Island home, Laurelton Hall; and an installation of the Laurelton's Daffodil Terrace.

Albin Polasek Museum & Sculpture Gardens   MUSEUM

(www.polasek.org; 633 Osceola Ave; adult/child $5/free; ⊙10am-4pm Tue-Sat, from 1pm Sun) Listed on the National Register of Historic Places and perched on the shore of Lake Osceola, this small yellow villa was home to Czech sculptor Albin Polasek. The house serves as a small museum of his life and work, and the gardens house some of his sculptures. Also hosts rotating exhibitions.

Cornell Fine Arts Museum   MUSEUM

(www.rollins.edu/cfam; Rollins College, 1000 Holt Ave; ⊙10am-7pm Tue, 10am-4pm Wed-Fri, noon-5pm Sat & Sun) **FREE** This tiny lakeside museum on the campus of Rollins College houses an eclectic collection of historic and contemporary US, European and Latin American art.

Hannibal Square Heritage Center   MUSEUM

(☑407-539-2860; www.hannibalsquareheritage center.org; 642 W New England Ave; ⊙noon-4pm Tue-Thu, to 5pm Fri, 10am-2pm Sat) **FREE** As far back as 1881, Winter Park's Hannibal Square was home to African Americans employed as carpenters, farmers and household help. The *Heritage Collection: Photographs and Oral Histories of West Winter Park 1900–1980*, on permanent display at this little museum, celebrates and preserves this community's culture and history.

Kraft Azalea Gardens   PARK

(https://cityofwinterpark.org/departments/parks-recreation/parks-playgrounds/parks/kraft-azalea-garden; 1365 Alabama Dr; ⊙8am-dusk) Quiet lakeside park with enormous cypress trees. Particularly stunning January through March, when the azaleas burst into bloom. There's a dock, but no barbecues or picnic tables.

⚜ Festivals & Events

Winter Park Sidewalk Art Festival   CULTURAL

(☑407-644-7207; www.wpsaf.org; Winter Park; ⊙Mar) One of the oldest art festivals in the country where more than 220 artists display work along the sidewalks of small-town Winter Park.

⨆ Sleeping

Park Plaza Hotel   BOUTIQUE HOTEL $$

(☑407-647-1072, 800-228-7220; www.parkplaza hotel.com; 307 S Park Ave; r from $169; ☏) Brick walls, spartan wood furniture, antiques and luscious white cotton bedding create a distinct arts-and-crafts sensibility at this historic two-story hotel. Rooms lining Park Ave share a narrow balcony, each with a private entrance and a few wicker chairs hidden from the street by hanging ferns.

It was built to house the workmen who were building the railway; note: some rooms still receive the blast of the passing warning hoots. It's a wonderful atmosphere, though there are more modern and sparklier options.

★ **Alfond Inn**   BOUTIQUE HOTEL $$$
(☑ 407-998-8090; www.thealfondinn.com; 300 E New England Ave; r from $309; ❉ @ 🛜 ☒ 🐾) Contemporary white-walled elegance, a low-key welcoming vibe, colorful interiors in well-appointed rooms give this Winter Park gem a distinct style. The hotel has a strong commitment to the arts: not only does it house the Alfond Collection of Contemporary Art, but all operating profits fund liberal-arts scholarships at nearby Rollins College.

There's a lovely rooftop pool and an excellent restaurant that serves locally sourced food on courtyard tables. The rate quoted here is for weekends; midweek prices can decrease by around $50.

🍴 Eating

★ **Ethos Vegan Kitchen**   VEGAN $
(☑ 407-228-3898; www.ethosvegankitchen.com; 601b S New York Ave; mains $7-14; ⊙ 11am-11pm Mon-Fri; ☑) ❡ The welcome sign at this meat-free stop says 'get off at Platform One' for a vegan arrival. Ethos Vegan Kitchen offers a range of delights such as pizza with broccoli, banana peppers, zucchini and seitan; meat-free shepherd's pie; pecan-encrusted eggplant; homemade soups and various sandwiches with names such as A Fungus Among Us and Hippie Wrap.

It's a casual spot with a good student vibe, a wide range of craft brews and a selection of New World wines.

The Coop   SOUTHERN US $
(☑ 407-843-2667; www.asouthernaffair.com; 610 W Morse Blvd; mains $10-14; ⊙ 7am-8pm Mon-Thu, to 9pm Fri & Sat) Line up for massive plates of smothered pork chops, fried chicken or chicken potpie, with sides of fried okra, creamed corn, maple-glazed carrots and other Southern classics. Cafeteria-style, with 'make-a-friend' tables or call ahead for sidewalk pick-up.

It's run by the same team as **4 Rivers Smokehouse** (☑ 407-474-8377; https://4rsmokehouse.com; 1600 W Fairbanks Ave; mains $8-18; ⊙ 11am-8pm Mon-Thu, to 9pm Fri & Sat).

Croissant Gourmet   CAFE $
(☑ 407-622-7753; www.facebook.com/thecroissant gourmet; 120 E Morse Blvd; mains $8-12; ⊙ 7am-6pm Sun-Thu, to 8pm Fri & Sat; kitchen closes 6pm daily) Befitting Winter Park's European vibe, start the day with coffee and a pastry at the tiny Paris-perfect Croissant Gourmet. There are classic éclairs, delicious blueberry tarts and massive cinnamon twists, as well as sweet and savory crepes, traditional French breakfasts and lunches, and wine by the glass.

Orchid Thai Cuisine   THAI $
(☑ 407-331-1400; www.orchidthaiwinterpark. com; 305 N Park Ave; mains $8-15; ⊙ 11am-9pm Mon-Wed, 11am-10pm Thu-Sat, noon-9pm Sun; ☑) Contemporary and tasty with pleasant pavement seating. Don't miss the delectable 'Thai Doughnuts': dough balls fried with a sweet condensed-milk dressing and sprinkled with crushed peanuts.

Dexter's of Winter Park   AMERICAN $$
(☑ 407-629-1150; www.dexwine.com; 558 W New England Ave; mains $10-26; ⊙ 11am-10pm Mon-Thu, to midnight Fri & Sat, 10am-10pm Sun) Unpretentious Winter Park go-to spot for creative American fare off the beaten track of Park Ave. There's live music Wednesday through Sunday, primarily of the funk, soul, jazz and blues variety, sidewalk seating and a popular Sunday brunch. Try the pressed duck sandwich, with grilled onions and melted brie ($15).

Briarpatch   CAFE $$
(☑ 407-628-8651; 252 N Park Ave; mains $8-18; ⊙ 7am-5pm Mon-Fri, 8am-5pm Sat & Sun; 🍴) Massive multilayer cakes and hearty breakfasts in white-washed, shabby-chic tearoom environs. A locals' fave for brunches.

Bosphorous Turkish Cuisine   TURKISH $$
(☑ 407-644-8609; www.bosphorousrestaurant.com; 108 S Park Ave; mains $12-22; ⊙ 11am-10pm Sun-Thu, to 11pm Fri & Sat; ☑) An interesting menu and huge helpings of good food make this place stand out along this strip. Try the *lavas* (hollow bread) or the lamb shank ($28).

★ **Ravenous Pig**   AMERICAN $$$
(☑ 407-628-2333; www.theravenouspig.com; 565 W Fairbanks; mains $14-32; ⊙ 11:30am-3pm & 5-10pm Mon-Sat, 10:30am-3pm & 5-9pm Sun) ❡ The cornerstone of Orlando's restaurant trend for locally sourced food, this chef-owned hipster spot moved to its new location in 2016. Here it's all about letting the food do the talking: locavore, omnivore, carnivore – take your pick. Really ravenous pigs can get their teeth into the pork porterhouse or the local seafood (the shrimp and grits is a must; $15). Don't miss.

The menu changes seasonally. Happy Hour (from 3pm to 6pm) in the attached bar, its on-site brewery, offers $3 draft beers, $6 cocktails and cheap pub-fare plates.

Winter Park

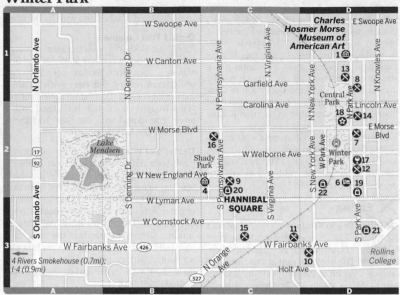

★ Prato

ITALIAN $$$

(☑ 407-262-0050; www.prato-wp.com; 124 N Park Ave; mains $16-33; ⊙ 11:30am-4:30pm Mon & Tues, to 11pm Wed-Sat, to 10pm Sun) A hopping go-to spot with high ceilings, exposed beams and a bar expanding the length of the room. Offers inspired interpretations of classic Italian dishes, house-cured meats and excellent wood-oven pizza ($16).

Luma on Park

AMERICAN $$$

(☑ 407-599-4111; www.lumaonpark.com; 290 S Park Ave; mains $25-30; ⊙ 5:30-10pm Mon-Thu, 5.30-11pm Fri & Sat, 5.30-9pm Sun) 🍴 A must for upscale foodie delights, not to mention people-watching. The menu features rather complicated pairings such as 'red snapper with black and white quinoa, braised watermelon radish, English pea, delta asparagus and citrus olive tapenade.' The recommended $35 prix-fixe menu is offered Sunday, Monday and Tuesday only.

🍷 Drinking & Nightlife

Wine Room

WINE BAR

(☑ 407-696-9463; www.thewineroomonline.com; 270 S Park Ave; tastings from $2.50; ⊙ 2pm-midnight Mon-Wed, from noon Thu, 11:30am-1:30am Fri & Sat, noon-11pm Sun) It's a bit of a gimmick, but you purchase a wine card

and put as much money on it as you'd like. Then simply slide your card into the automated servers for whichever wine looks good, press the button for a taste or a full glass, and enjoy. More than 150 wines, arranged by region and type.

☆ Entertainment

Popcorn Flicks in the Park

CINEMA

(☑ 407-629-1088; www.enzian.org; 251 S Park Ave, Central Park; ⊙ 8pm 2nd Thu of the month; 🚼) Bring a picnic and a blanket, and kick back under the stars for a free outdoor film classic.

🛍 Shopping

Lighten Up Toy Store

TOYS

(☑ 407-644-3528; 348 S Park Ave; ⊙ 10am-5pm Mon-Sat) Small but well-stocked toy store with classics such as marbles and kazoos, outdoor toys including Frisbees, boomerangs and kites, and restaurant-perfect activity and picture books. There's an entire wall of games and puzzles and, for those rainy days stuck in the hotel, 'furniture-friendly bow and arrow rockets.'

Rifle Paper Co

STATIONERY

(☑ 407-622-7679; www.riflepaperco.com; 558 W New England Ave; ⊙ 9am-6pm Mon-Fri, 10am-

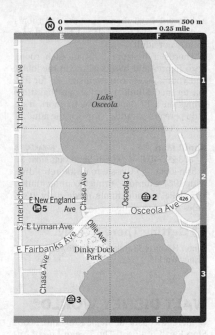

5pm Sat) This tiny retail space, started by a husband and wife team in 2009, sells lovely paper stationery products. It now also ships internationally.

Winter Park Farmers' Market   MARKET
(200 W New England Ave; ◔7am-1pm Sat) Winter Park's historic train station, with its original brick walls and massive vintage wooden sliding doors, houses the Saturday morning Winter Park Farmers' Market. You'll find local cheeses and honey, flowers and herbs, along with several excellent stands selling baked goods, spread out in the station and through the gardens.

It's a small market, but a lovely spot to people-watch over a cup of coffee or an organic Popsicle.

Rocket Fizz   FOOD
(⌕407-645-3499; www.rocketfizz.com; 520 S Park Ave; ◔10:30am-9pm Mon-Thu, 11am-11pm Fri & Sat, 11am-8pm Sun) Satisfy any kind of sweet tooth in this candy emporium, with 1200 different kinds of candy from countries around the world, several hundred varieties of glass-bottled soda and all kinds of gag gifts. Sure, there's classic chocolate and buckets of saltwater taffy, but how about that bacon frosting you've always wanted

to try? Or french-fry lip balm and candy cigarettes?

❶ Getting There & Away

From downtown Orlando, take I-4 to Fairbanks Ave and head east for about 2 miles to Park Ave.

Orlando's **SunRail** (www.sunrail.com) stops at downtown Winter Park.

Lynx 102 bus services Orange Ave from downtown Orlando to Winter Park.

WINTER HAVEN

Legoland is sleepy Winter Haven's main draw (and a lovely one at that), but you'll also find a handful of reasonable restaurants in the small historic downtown. Lovely Bok Tower Gardens (p260) sits 15 miles to the southwest.

◉ Sights

★ Legoland
AMUSEMENT PARK

(☑ 863-318-5346; http://florida.legoland.com; 1 Legoland Way; 1-/2-day tickets adult $93/113, child 3-12yr $86/106; ◷ 10am-5pm; ♿; ☐ Legoland Shuttle) Legoland is a joy. With manageable crowds and lines, and no bells and whistles, this lakeside theme park maintains an old-school vibe – you don't have to plan like a general to enjoy a day here, and it's strikingly stress-free and relaxed. This is about fun (and yes, education) in a colorful and interactive environment. Rides and attractions, including the attached water park, are geared towards children aged two to 12. Opening hours vary seasonally. New things are being added regularly.

Highlights include **Flight School**, a coaster that zips you around with your feet dangling free, **Miniland**, a Lego re-creation of iconic American landmarks and cities, and **Ninjago**, the park's new martial arts–themed section. There are a few remnants from the park's history as the site of Cypress Gardens (circa 1936), including lovely botanical gardens with the giant Banyan Tree and water-ski shows and the classic wooden roller coaster, these days called **Coastercaurus**. The water-ski show centers on a bizarre and rather silly pirate theme, and the Cartoon Network's *Legends of Chima* inspires an entire section.

Don't miss the **Imagination Zone**, a wonderful interactive learning center that's heavily staffed with skilled Lego makers happy to help children of all ages create delights with their blocks.

Legoland Shuttle ($5) runs daily from I-Drive 360 (near the Orlando Eye). Note: you must book this 24 hours before departure. You can park on the bottom floor of the I-Drive 360 parking lot (free). Look for the Legoland-themed bus stop near the back entrance of the Eye on the Universal Boulevard side.

You can rent strollers/wheelchairs/ECVs ($10/12/37) and lockers ($5 to $12). Parking costs $14.

🛏 Sleeping & Eating

★ Legoland Hotel
HOTEL $$$

(1 Legoland Way, Winter Haven; r from $420; ▣ ❄ 🛜) The exterior of this remarkable spot was designed to look like a child built it with Lego bricks. And it succeeds. Bright primary colors and its block-like facade give way to a fun factory. Each floor is based on a different Lego theme and the 152 rooms and suites have peepholes at the level of a child's, not adult's, eyes.

There's a treasure hunt in each room, Lego figures and blocks galore in the lobby, and young guests can even sign up for free master model builder workshops. Nighttime brings on a PJ dance party. In short, it's a little person's paradise. (Info for the adult: it doesn't come cheap.)

Donut Man
BREAKFAST $

(☑ 863-293-4031; 1290 6th St; donuts from $1; ◷ 5am-10pm; ♿) Classic roadside retro dive, with 1967 exterior, Formica-counter dining and delicious doughnuts made daily. It's 5 miles from Legoland.

ℹ Getting There & Away

Winter Haven is 33-mile drive southwest of Walt Disney World®.

WALT DISNEY WORLD®

Cinderella's Castle of Magic Kingdom. Space Ship Earth of Epcot. The Tree of Life of Animal Kingdom. The Chinese Theatre of Hollywood Studios. These are the symbols of magical lands that together make up Walt Disney World®, the world designed by Walt Disney, and opened in 1951, to be the Happiest Place on Earth.

Walt Disney World® itself is like a child. One minute, you think you can't take another looong line. Or cafeteria-style restaurant serving fried food. Or overstuffed shuttle bus. And the next, it does something right – maybe it's the fireworks, maybe it's a particular ride, maybe it's the corny joke of the guy who drives the horse-drawn carriage down Main Street. Or maybe it's seeing the speck of glitter on your kiddies' content faces as they finally fall asleep after a huge day.

All is forgiven. Disney works its magic.

History

When Disneyland opened in southern California, it took off in a huge way, fundamentally transforming the concept of theme parks. Walt Disney, however, was irritated at the hotels and concessions that were springing up in a manner that he felt was entirely parasitic. In 1965, after a secret four-year search, he bought 27,000 acres of swamp, field and woodland in central Florida. His vision was to create a family vacation destination and he wanted to control every aspect – hotels, restaurants, parking and transportation. He would never see the realization of his dreams; in 1966, at age 65, Walt Disney died of lung cancer. His brother Roy took over responsibility for development. Walt Disney World's Magic Kingdom opened in 1971, and three months later Roy died of a brain hemorrhage. Epcot opened in 1982, Hollywood Studios in 1989 and Animal Kingdom in 1998.

◉ Sights

Walt Disney World® (☑407-939-5277; www.disneyworld.disney.go.com; Lake Buena Vista, outside Orlando; daily rates vary, see website for packages & tickets up to 10 days; ▣) is indeed a network: the area covers more than 40 sq miles and includes four separate (walled) theme parks and two water parks (plus some leisure attractions including golf courses), all connected by a complicated system of monorail, boat and bus, and intersected by highways and roads. Attractions, primarily in the form of rides, character interactions, movies and shows, are spread out among the six parks, resort hotels, and, to a far lesser extent, two entertainment districts.

🏃 Activities

Disney offers a dizzying array of recreational activities, most based at Disney hotels and none requiring theme-park admission. Call Walt Disney World® Recreation (☑407-939-7529) for reservations and details on everything from water-skiing lessons to bike rental, tennis to cycling, horse riding to carriage rides; for general information on activities at Walt Disney World®, check www.disneyworld.disney.go.com.

Walt Disney World Bicycle Rental CYCLING (☑407-939-7529; www.disneyworld.disney.go.com; select Walt Disney World® resorts; per hr/day $9/18, surrey bikes per 30min from $25) More than a dozen bike-rental places throughout Walt Disney World® rent on a first-come, first-served basis. A few places, including Disney's BoardWalk, rent two-, four- and six-person surrey bikes, with four wheels, candy-striped tops and bench seats.

Winter Summerland Miniature Golf GOLF (☑407-560-3000; www.disneyworld.disney.go.com; 1548 W Buena Vista, Walt Disney World®; adult/child $14/12; ◷10am-11pm) Two holiday-inspired, season-themed (as in both summer and winter) miniature golf courses next to Blizzard Beach.

Fantasia Gardens and Fairways Miniature Golf GOLF (☑407-560-4870; www.disneyworld.disney.go.com; 1205 Epcot Resorts Blvd, Walt Disney World®; adult/child $14/12; ◷10am-11pm) Two sweet fairyland-themed courses based on the classic animation *Fantasia*.

Disney's Lake Buena Vista Golf Course GOLF (☑407-939-4653; www.golfwdw.com; 2200 Club Lake Dr, Walt Disney World®; per round from $40) A championship golf course, a perfect fit in every way with Disney World. Test out your approach shots – a major feature is its elevated bunkered greens.

PICK YOUR PARK

Magic Kingdom (p287) Low on thrills and high on nostalgia, with Cinderella's Castle and nightly fireworks.

Epcot (p292) A handful of rides on one side, country-based food, shopping and attractions on the other.

Disney's Animal Kingdom (p297) Part zoo and part county fair, with a heavy dusting of Disney-styled Africa.

Hollywood Studios (p299) Movie-based attractions and Pixar characters.

Typhoon Lagoon (p301) Water park particularly excellent for families.

Blizzard Beach (p302) Water park with high-speed twists and turns.

Disney's BoardWalk (p302) Intimate waterfront boardwalk with a handful of shops, restaurants and entertainment; no admission fee.

Disney Springs (p303) Recently revamped area (formerly called 'Downtown Disney'), devoted to shops, bars, live music and entertainment; no admission fee.

Walt Disney World®

Disney's Magnolia Golf Course
GOLF

(☎407-939-4653; www.golfwdw.com; 1950 Magnolia Palm Dr, Disney's Grand Floridian Resort & Spa; per round from $40) The longest of Disney's five golf courses.

Disney's Oak Trail Golf Course
GOLF

(☎407-939-4653; www.golfwdw.com; 1950 Magnolia Pine Dr, Disney's Grand Floridian Resort & Spa; per round from $40) Family-friendly, nine-hole walking course.

Disney's Palm Golf Course
GOLF

(☎407-939-4653; www.golfwdw.com; 1950 W Magnolia Palm Dr, Disney's Grand Floridian Resort & Spa; per round from $40) This Arnold Palmer–designed, 18-hole championship course is one of Disney's most picturesque, with palm trees, lakes and sloping greens.

Fort Wilderness Tri-Circle-D Ranch
HORSEBACK RIDING

(☎407-824-2832; www.disneyworld.disney.go.com; 4510 N Wilderness Trail, Disney's Fort Wilderness Resort & Campground; rides from $8; 🚌Disney, ⛴Disney) Guided trail, pony, wagon, hay and carriage rides.

Disney Boat Rental
BOATING

(☎403-939-7529; www.disneyworld.disney.go.com; select Disney resort hotels; rental per boat per hr from $15) Disney rents canoes, kayaks, Sunfish and catamaran sailboats, pedal boats and motorized boats at several resort hotels, including Disney's Port Orleans, Disney's Caribbean Beach and Disney's Fort Wilderness. Consider reserving a pontoon to watch the fireworks over the Magic Kingdom Castle.

Sammy Duvall's Watersports Centre
WATER SPORTS

(☎407-939-0754; www.sammyduvall.com; 4600 World Dr, Disney's Contemporary Resort; personal watercraft per hr $135, water-skiing, wakeboarding & tubing up to 5 people per hr $165; ⊙10am-5pm; 🚌Disney, ⛴Disney, 🚌Disney) Lessons, rentals and parasailing.

☞ Tours

Disney Tours
TOURS

(☎407-939-8687, VIP tours 407-560-4033; www.disneyworld.disney.go.com; Walt Disney World®; prices vary) Disney offers all kinds of guided tours and specialty experiences, including the **Wild Africa Trek** private safari and backstage Disney tours. For the ultimate in hassle-free touring, with front-of-the-line access to attractions and insider information

ORLANDO & WALT DISNEY WORLD® WALT DISNEY WORLD®

Walt Disney World®

◉ Top Sights

◉ Sights

◉ Activities, Courses & Tours

◉ Sleeping

on the park and its history, consider a **VIP tour** ($400 to $600 per hour per group of up to 10 people).

Note that tours inside theme parks require theme-park admission in addition to the cost of the tour.

✯ Festivals & Events

In November and December, millions of lights and hundreds of Christmas trees, specialty parades and holiday shows celebrate the season throughout Walt Disney World®.

See the individual park coverage later in this chapter for park-specific festivals and events.

🛏 Sleeping

Disney resort hotels are divided according to location: Magic Kingdom (p290), Epcot (p295), Animal Kingdom (p298) and Disney Boardwalk (p302). Prices vary drastically according to season, week and day.

While deluxe resorts are the best Disney has to offer, note that you're paying for Disney theming and location convenience, not luxury. Most offer multiroom suites and villas, upscale restaurants, children's programs and easy access to theme parks.

Disney's Port Orleans French Quarter & Riverside Resorts
RESORT $$
(📞 French Quarter 407-934-5000, Riverside 407-934-6000; www.disneyworld.disney.go.com; 1251 Riverside; r from $225; P ❄ @ 🛜 ⊠; 🚇 Disney, 🚤 Disney) Lush gardens and a jubilant Mardi Gras motif blend in an effort to create a Louisiana feel to these sister resorts. Though the result sometimes falls flat and the simple rooms feel dated, the resort is a mecca

for activities and includes a sea-serpent water slide, boat rental, horse-drawn-carriage rides and evening s'mores.

This is one of the biggest resorts at Disney; a boat connects the two properties, or it's a 15-minute walk.

★ Four Seasons Resort Orlando at Walt Disney World
RESORT $$$
(📞 800-267-3046; www.fourseasons.com; 10100 Dream Tree Blvd; r/ste from $435/430; P ❄ @ 🛜 ⊠) All the luxury, quality and attention to detail you'd expect from a Four Seasons resort. It's one of the few non-Disney resorts

ORLANDO & WALT DISNEY WORLD® WALT DISNEY WORLD®

on the grounds of Walt Disney World® and is marvelously removed from the Disney vortex. A superb experience. Rates fluctuate tremendously; check online.

Disney's Old Key West Resort RESORT $$$

(📞407-827-7700, 407-939-5277; www.disney world.disney.go.com; 1510 N Cove Rd; r from $362; P🏊@🛜🏊; 🚌Disney, ⛴Disney) Victoriana oozes from every gingerbread-accented pastel corner, every palm-tree enclave and from the azure-blue waters. This is an 'all villa' resort. Studios sleep four; one-bedroom villas sleep five, two-bedroom villas sleep eight; and three-bedroom villas sleep 12.

Note: you can try your luck at getting in here but it's a Disney Vacation property (that is, time-share resort). If there's room you might be lucky.

Eating

With the exception of Epcot, expect mediocre fast food, bad coffee and cafeteria cuisine at premium prices. Table-service restaurants accept 'priority seating' reservations up to 180 days in advance. Reserve through Disney Dining (📞407-939-3463), at www.disneyworld.disney.go.com or through the My Disney Experience app. Remember: while restaurants in the theme parks require theme-park admission, resort hotel restaurants do not.

Disney also offers character meals, dinner shows and specialty dining.

Many of the best sit-down dining options at Walt Disney World® are located in the park's resort hotels, as opposed to within the pedestrian areas within the park itself. See later in this chapter for food options within each individual park.

★Sanaa AFRICAN $$

(📞407-939-3463; www.disneyworld.disney. go.com; 3701 Osceola Pkwy, Kidani Village, Disney's Animal Kingdom Lodge; mains $17-26; ⏰11:30am-3pm & 5-9:30pm; 🚗🧒; 🚌Disney) Lovely cafe with Savannah views – giraffes, ostriches and zebras graze outside the window. You almost forget you're in Florida, but, hey, that's Disney. Try slow-cooked and tandoori chicken, ribs, lamb or shrimp; the delicious salad sampler with tasty watermelon, cucumber and fennel salad; and a mango margarita.

★Jiko - The Cooking Place AFRICAN $$$

(📞407-938-4733, 407-939-3463; www.disney world.disney.go.com; 2901 Osceola Pkwy, Disney's Animal Kingdom Lodge; mains $41-55; ⏰5:30-10pm; 🚗🧒; 🚌Disney) Excellent food, with plenty of grains, vegetables and creative twists, a tiny bar and rich African surrounds make this a Disney favorite for both quality and theming. You can relax with a glass of wine on the hotel's back deck, alongside the giraffes and other African beasts.

For a less-expensive option, enjoy an appetizer (the Taste of Africa features various dips and crackers) at the bar. Swing by for

---

DISNEY'S VALUE RESORTS

Five value resorts, the least-expensive Disney properties available (not including camping), have thousands of motel-style rooms and suites; are garishly decorated according to their theme; connect to all the parks by bus only; and cater to families and traveling school groups – expect cheerleader teams practicing in the courtyard or a lobby of teenagers wearing matching jerseys. You will definitely feel the difference because of the lower price: instead of proper restaurants, there are food courts and snack bars, and things are particularly bright, hectic and loud. Some value resorts offer family suites with two bathrooms and a kitchenette.

Disney's Art of Animation Resort (📞407-938-7000, 407-939-5277; www.disneyworld. disney.go.com; 1850 Animation Way; r from $130; P🏊@🛜🏊; 🚌Disney) Inspired by four animated Disney classics (*Finding Nemo, Lion King, Cars* and *Little Mermaid*) and the newest of Disney's Value Resorts (finished in 2012), this dazzlingly bright hotel is the best bet for budget-conscious Disney travel.

Disney's All-Star Resorts Three self-contained hotels, three of Disney's five 'value' accommodation options, let you take your pick between movie, music and sports themes.

Disney's Pop Century Resort (📞407-938-4000, 407-939-5277; www.disneyworld.disney. go.com; 1050 Century Dr; r from $140; P🏊@🛜🏊; 🚌Disney) Each section pays homage to a different decade of the late 20th century, with massive bowling pins that extend beyond the roof and giant Play Doh.

DISNEY DINNER SHOWS

Disney's three dinner shows sell out early, so make your reservation for these up to 180 days in advance; you can cancel up to 48 hours in advance with no penalty. They are each held at a Disney resort, include beer and wine, and do not require theme park admission. They are:

➡ Hoop-Dee-Doo Musical Revue (p282)

➡ Mickey's Backyard Barbecue (p282)

➡ Spirit of Aloha (p282)

dinner, or at least a cocktail, after a day at Animal Kingdom.

★ Boma
BUFFET $$$

(✍407-939-3463, 407-938-4744; www.disney world.disney.go.com; 2901 Osceola Pkwy, Disney's Animal Kingdom Lodge; adult/child breakfast $24.50/13, dinner $40.50/21; ☺7:30-11am & 5-9:30pm; 🛜🚺; 🚍Disney) Several steps above Disney's usual buffet options, this African-inspired eatery offers wood-roasted meats, interesting soups such as coconut curried chicken and plenty of salads. Handsomely furnished with dark woods, decorated with African art and tapestries, and flanked by garden-view windows on one side, Boma offers not only good food but unusually calm and pleasant surrounds.

★ California Grill
AMERICAN $$$

(✍407-939-3463; www.disneyworld.disney.go.com; 4600 World Dr, Disney's Contemporary Resort; mains $36-51; ☺5-10pm; 🚺; 🚍Disney, 🚤Disney, 🚍Disney) Earning consistent oohs and aahs from locals and repeat Disney guests, this rooftop classic boasts magnificent views of Magic Kingdom fireworks and offers everything from quirky sushi to triple-cheese flatbread. Reservations are very difficult to secure, so make them as close to 180 days in advance as possible.

Victoria & Albert's
AMERICAN $$$

(✍407-939-3862; www.victoria-alberts.com; 4401 Floridian Way, Disney's Grand Floridian Resort; prix-fixe from $185, wine pairing from $65; ☺5-9:20pm; 🛜; 🚍Disney, 🚤Disney, 🚍Disney) Indulge yourself in the earthy, cream-colored, Victorian-inspired decor at this elegant restaurant, the crème de la crème of Orlando's dining scene and one of its most coveted reservations. The meal, complete with crystal and live cello music, oozes romance. You must reserve directly (not through Disney World's Dining number).

Dinner at the intimate Chef's Table or Queen Victoria's room includes 13 courses. Children must be aged 10 and over.

Chef Mickey's
AMERICAN $$$

(✍407-939-3463; www.disneyworld.disney.go.com; 4600 World Dr, Disney's Contemporary Resort; adult/child from $41/25; ☺7-11:15am, 11:30am-2:30pm & 5-9:30pm) Nothing says Walt Disney World® Resort more than Mickey Mouse and the monorail, so what better way to start your classic Disney day than a buffet breakfast with Mickey Mouse, Minnie Mouse, Pluto, Donald Duck and Goofy under the roar of the monorail. Head to Chef Mickey's for an early breakfast.

(Reservations required well in advance; prices differ for the various meals). After this, hop on the monorail and get to Magic Kingdom when the gates open.

Todd English's bluezoo
SEAFOOD $$$

(✍407-934-1111; www.swandolphinrestaurants. com; 1500 Epcot Resorts Blvd, Walt Disney World® Dolphin Resort; mains $28-60; ☺5-11pm; 🛜; 🚍Disney, 🚤Disney) Floor-to-ceiling silver threads shimmer in columns at this flashy blue-infused hot spot, evoking a trendy, urban spin on the underwater theme. Excellent seafood makes this one of the few restaurants at Disney where you feel like *maybe* you've gotten your money's worth. A truncated menu in the bar offers less-expensive choices.

Narcoossee's
SEAFOOD $$$

(✍407-939-3463; www.disneyworld.disney.go. com; 4401 Floridian Way, Disney's Grand Floridian Resort; mains $39-67; ☺5-9:30pm; 🚺; 🚍Disney, 🚤Disney, 🚍Disney) Muted waterfront dining on the boat dock at the Grand Floridian makes a convenient, relaxing and lovely respite if you've been at Magic Kingdom for the afternoon and want to return after dinner for the fireworks. Though offering primarily

ORLANDO & WALT DISNEY WORLD® WALT DISNEY WORLD®

seafood, it also serves duck, filet mignon and ahi tuna.

The porch is a good place from which to watch the fireworks in any case.

Cítricos
MEDITERRANEAN **$$$**

(☑ 407-939-3463; www.disneyworld.disney. go.com; 4401 Floridian Way, Disney's Grand Floridian Resort; mains $18-34; ⏱ 5:30-10pm; 🎮; ▢ Disney, 🚢 Disney, ▢ Disney) An extensive wine list and handsome northern California ambience set this low-key brasserie apart from other Disney restaurants; it falls between the hectic family style and self-consciously upscale style, and serves up tasty and fresh eclectic fare, the likes of Key West Shrimp and slow-roasted pork belly.

Artist Point
AMERICAN **$$$**

(☑ 407-939-3463; www.disneyworld.disney.go. com; 901 Timberline Dr, Disney's Wilderness Lodge; mains $30-50; ⏱ 5:30-10pm; 🎮🚸; ▢ Disney, 🚢 Disney) Echoing an American National Park lodge: handsome arts-and-crafts decor with an American West twist and Pacific Northwest fare, including roast venison and salmon, grilled buffalo and berry cobbler. The bar, reminiscent of an old lodge, opens earlier – take your apple martini to the outdoor patio.

🍸 Drinking & Nightlife

Disney Springs and the much smaller Disney's BoardWalk are the designated drinking (and entertainment and shopping) districts at Walt Disney World®, but you'll find bars and sometimes live music at most Disney resorts and within the theme parks. Magic Kingdom sells beer and wine only, available at the more formal, sit-down restaurants. At Epcot, you'll find a tantalizing smorgasbord of spirits and cocktails from around the world.

Tambu Lounge
BAR

(www.disneyworld.disney.go.com; Disney's Polynesian Resort; ▢ Disney, 🚢 Disney) Escape to the islands, Disney-style, with umbrella-topped tropical drinks and Blue Glow-tinis. There's also an excellent selection of bar food, including pulled pork nachos and kebabs, and it's an easy boat or monorail from here to Magic Kingdom.

☆ Entertainment

Go to www.buildabettermousetrip.com/ activity-outdoormovie.php for a schedule of free outdoor screenings of Disney movies at Disney hotels and other locales at Disney's Fort Wilderness.

You'll find fabulous performances in each of the parks. In Disney Springs, Cirque du Soleil La Nouba (p305) fuses gymnastic superfeats with dance, light, music…and Disney.

★ Chip 'n' Dale Campfire Singalong
CINEMA

(☑ 407-939-7529; www.disneyworld.disney.go.com; 4510 N Wilderness Trail, Disney's Fort Wilderness Resort; ⏱ 7pm winter, 8pm summer; ▢ Disney, 🚢 Disney) This intimate and low-key character experience offers singing and dancing with Chip and Dale, campfires for roasting marshmallows, and a free outdoor screening of a Disney film. Every night is a different movie, and Disney doesn't post a schedule on its website – call or search online.

You can buy generously portioned s'mores supplies, and though there are split-log benches, it's better to bring a blanket and pillows to snuggle down on. Cars are not allowed in Fort Wilderness; park at the parking area after the entry gate, or take a Disney bus or boat to the resort, and catch a shuttle the few minutes to the Meadow Recreation Area.

Hoop-Dee-Doo Musical Revue
COMEDY

(☑ 407-939-3463; www.disneyworld.disney.go.com; 4510 N Wilderness Trail, Disney's Fort Wilderness Resort; adult $64-72, child 3-9yr $38-43; ⏱ 4pm, 6:15pm & 8:30pm daily; 🎮; ▢ Disney, 🚢 Disney) Nineteenth-century vaudeville show at Disney's Fort Wilderness Resort, with ribs delivered to your table in metal buckets, corny jokes and the audience singing along to 'Hokey Pokey' and 'My Darling Clementine.' This is one of Disney's longest-running shows and is great fun, once you grab your washboard and get into the spirit of it all.

Spirit of Aloha
DANCE

(☑ 407-939-3463; www.disneyworld.disney.go. com; 1600 Seven Seas Dr, Disney's Polynesian Resort; adult $66-78, child 3-9yr $39-46; ⏱ 5:15pm & 8:15pm; ▢ Disney, 🚢 Disney, ▢ Disney) Hula-clad men and women leap around the stage, dance and play with fire in this South Pacific–style luau at Disney's Polynesian Resort. Pulled pork, barbecue ribs and island-themed specialties like pineapple-coconut bread are served family-style.

Mickey's Backyard Barbecue
COMEDY

(☑ 407-939-3463; www.disneyworld.disney.go. com; 4510 N Fort Wilderness Trail, Disney's Fort Wilderness Resort; adult $62-72, child 3-9yr $37-47;

ORLANDO & WALT DISNEY WORLD® WALT DISNEY WORLD®

⊙hours vary; 🚻; 🛏 Disney, 🍴 Disney) The only dinner theater with Disney characters. Join in on country-and-western singin', ho-down style-stompin' and goofy Mickey antics at this Disney favorite.

ESPN Wide World of Sports SPECTATOR SPORT (☎407-939-4263, visitors center 407-541-5600; www.espnwwos.com; 700 S Victory Way, Walt Disney World®) This 230-acre sports facility at Walt Disney World® hosts Atlanta Braves spring training and hundreds of amateur and professional sporting events.

 Shopping

There are endless stores throughout Walt Disney World®, most of which are thematically oriented. So near the Winnie the Pooh ride you'll find lots of bear stuff; and after the Indiana Jones ride you'll find, well, an Indiana Jones fedora, of course. For a one-stop shop, Disney Springs has the largest Disney character store in the country, with 12 massive rooms chock-a-block with everything you can imagine.

 Information

CHILD CARE

Disney's Children Activity Center (p253) Five Disney resorts offer excellent drop-off children's activity centers for children aged three to 14, with organized activities, toys, art supplies, meals and a Disney movie in the evening. This is particularly handy if you'd like to enjoy

---

MY DISNEY EXPERIENCE: FASTPASS & MAGICBAND

FastPass+ is designed to allow guests to plan their days in advance and reduce time spent waiting in line. Visitors can reserve a specific time for up to three attractions per day through My Disney Experience (www.disneyworld.disney.go.com), accessible online or by downloading the free mobile app. There are also kiosks in each park where you can make reservations.

Resort guests receive a **MagicBand** – a plastic wristband that serves as a room key, park entrance ticket, FastPass+ access and room charge. As soon as you make your room reservation, you can set up your My Disney Experience account and begin planning your day-by-day Disney itinerary. A MagicBand will be sent to you in advance or it will be waiting for you when you check into your hotel. Your itinerary, including any changes you make online or through the mobile app, will automatically be stored in your wristband.

Once at the park, head to your reserved FastPass+ ride or attraction anytime within the preselected one-hour timeframe. Go to the Fastpass+ entrance, scan your MagicBand and zip right onto the attraction with no more than a 15-minute wait. Though it's a simple system, there are some kinks, so a few tips can help you navigate it with optimal benefit.

➡ If you are staying at a Disney Resort, you can access My Disney Experience and start reserving FastPass+ attractions up to 60 days in advance; nonresort guests with purchased theme-park tickets can reserve FastPass+ attractions 30 days in advance.

➡ You can use Fastpass+ selections for rides, character greeting spots (where lines can rival the most popular rides), fireworks, parades and shows.

➡ Some parks use a tiered FastPass+ system – you must choose one attraction from group one and two from group two.

➡ Make reservations for meals and character dining through My Disney Experience.

➡ Change your selections anytime through the website or mobile app. Once you've used the three prebooked FastPass+ attractions, you can add additional FastPass+ at on-site kiosks for free. But note you must use *all three* reserved selections before adding new ones.

➡ Do not waste your limited FastPass+ options on attractions that do not have long lines; carefully consider your day's plan to maximize the benefits of this system. Disney planning websites offer all kinds of tips. At the Magic Kingdom, lines for Seven Dwarf's Mine Train, Peter Pan's Flight, Big Thunder Mountain Railroad, Enchanted Tales with Belle and Space Mountain can be painfully long. Use your FastPass+ for sequential afternoon times at three of these and use the morning, when your patience and energy is stronger and the lines are shorter, for other attractions.

➡ Check the website or call for updated information, as the system is always in flux.

TOP TIPS FOR A SUCCESSFUL FAMILY VACATION TO DISNEY

Disney expectations run high, and the reality of things can be disappointing. Long waits, and getting jostled and tugged through crowds and lines, can leave the kids, and you, exhausted. There are two ways to do this. The first is to plan ahead with scrupulous attention to detail. Make dinner reservations, plan when to go where based on parade and show schedules, decide in advance what attractions to tackle once you're there and reserve FastPass+ selections. The final tip might come as a shock to some (but it worked for us).

Here are some simple tips:

Buy tickets that cover more days than you think you'll need It's less expensive per day, and it gives the freedom to break up time at the theme parks with downtime in the pool or at low-key attractions beyond theme-park gates.

Stay at a Walt Disney World® resort hotel While it's tempting to save money by staying elsewhere, the value of staying at a Walt Disney World® resort lies in the convenience offered. They do vary in standards, however, and are divided by budget, midrange and deluxe.

Download the Disney app 'My Disney Experience' You can make reservations, reserve FastPass+ attractions, view listings and programs as well as your own schedule.

Take advantage of 'My Disney Experience' Reserve your three FastPass+ attractions per day (www.disneyworld.disney.go.com) up to 60 days in advance (30 days for nonresort guests) – this will give you three guaranteed short lines each day. You can redeem additional FastPasses after you use the first three.

Stock up on snacks Even if it's nothing more than some snack packets and some bananas, you'll save the irritation of waiting in line for bad, overpriced food. Or, to avoid the lines, buy a sandwich early on the way in and have a picnic at your leisure.

Arrive at the park at least 30 minutes before gates open Don't window shop or dawdle – just march quickly to the rides and then kick back for the afternoon. If you can only manage this on one day of your trip, make it the day you're going to Magic Kingdom. Factor in the time to get here from the Transportation & Ticket Center (this can take up to an hour).

Speed up, slow down Yes, there's a time to hurry, as 10 minutes of pushing the pedal to the metal could save two hours waiting in line, but allow days to unfold according to the ebbs and flows of your children's moods.

Program 'Disney Dining' into your cell phone While you'll want to make some plans well in advance, once you have a sense of where you'll be at meal time, call ☎ 407-939-3463 to make reservations at table-service restaurants at all four theme parks, Disney resort hotels and at Disney's two shopping districts, Disney Springs and Disney Boardwalk (or go online). Also, check for last-minute cancellations to dinner shows or character meals.

Transport and accommodation When booking accommodation it's worth considering your transport options. All Disney resorts offer bus transportation, but those offering boat and monorail transportation are far more convenient (and, except for camping at Fort Wilderness, more expensive).

Go with the flow This is about managing expectations. If you build up the idea that your child will definitely hug Belle in a so-called 'character meet,' only to see the line is ridiculous, then recalibrate. Suggest initially that you're going to spot, rather than visit, a character. Believe us, you'll end up spotting them in parades or by chance. In addition to your three Fast-Pass+ experiences, you can head to any of the activities listed in the daily schedule/map.

a quiet meal at a Disney resort, as you do not have to be a hotel guest to use the centers. Activity Centers include **Simba's Cubhouse** at Disney's Animal Kingdom Lodge; **Lilo's Playhouse** at Disney's Polynesian Resort; **Sandcastle Club** at Disney's Beach Club Resort;

and **Camp Dolphin** at Walt Disney World® Dolphin Hotel. Reservations, recommended at all locations and required at Camp Dolphin, can be made up to 180 days in advance.

Kid's Nite Out (p253) Walt Disney World® uses Kid's Nite Out for private in-room child care for children aged six months to 12 years. You can also hire a helper if you need an extra pair of hands when you're out and about, but note that you'll have to pay for the caregiver's theme-park ticket. Credit cards only; reservations accepted up to three months in advance.

Stroller Rental

Strollers (single/double per day $15/31, multiday $13/27) are available on a first-come, first-served basis at Disney's four theme parks and Disney Springs, and you can also purchase umbrella strollers.

INTERNET ACCESS

Complimentary wi-fi is available throughout Walt Disney World® parks, entertainment districts, theme parks, water parks and resort hotels. Select Walt Disney World® Resort network, and call ☑ 407-827-2732 if you have technical problems.

KENNELS

With the exception of select campsites at Disney's Fort Wilderness Resort & Campground, pets are not allowed anywhere at Walt Disney World® (service animals excepted, with documentation from Guest Relations).

Best Friends Pet Care at Walt Disney World® Resort (☑ 877-493-9738; www.bestfriends petcare.com/waltdisneyworldresort; 2510 Bonnet Creek Pkwy; per day $18-72, overnight $41-89; ☺1hr before Walt Disney World® parks open to 1hr after closing) Offers overnight boarding and day care for dogs, cats and 'pocket pets.' Rates vary depending on how many walks and extra perks you'd like, and are a bit less for guests staying at a Disney hotel. Reservations and written proof of vaccination (DHLPP, rabies and Bordetella for dogs; FVRCP and rabies for cats) are required.

MAPS

Park maps with listings of the day's scheduled events and activities (including character meets) are available at the park entrances, Guest Services and all retail locations throughout the parks.

MEDICAL SERVICES

Medical facilities are located within each theme park and at both Disney water parks. The closest hospital is **Florida Hospital Celebration Health** (p269). If you need care at your hotel room, **Doctors On Call Service** (p269) provides medical service 24/7.

Lake Buena Vista Centra Care (☑ 407-934-2273, for pickup 407-938-0650; www.centracare.org; 12500 S Apopka Vineland; ☺8am-midnight Mon-Fri, to 8pm Sat & Sun) Nonemergency-care medical facility, offering adult and pediatric care, x-rays, and free

transportation to and from area hotels and attractions.

MONEY

You will find ATMs throughout Walt Disney World®. Guest Services at each park offer limited currency exchange.

OPENING HOURS

Theme-park hours change not only by season, but day to day within any given month. Generally, parks open at 8am or 9am and close sometime between 6pm and 10pm. Every day one of the four theme parks opens one hour early or closes late for guests of Walt Disney World® hotels only – these 'Magic Hours' are a major perk of staying at a Disney resort hotel.

TICKETS

One-day tickets Valid for admission to Magic Kingdom. Separate one-day tickets at slightly lower prices are valid for admission to Epcot, Hollywood Studios or Animal Kingdom.

Multiday tickets Valid for one theme park per day for each day of the ticket (you can leave/re-enter the park but cannot enter another park).

Park Hopper Gives same-day admission to any/all of the four Walt Disney World® parks. Fair warning: hopping between four parks requires a lot of stamina. Two parks a day is more feasible.

Park Hopper Plus The same as Park Hopper, but you can toss in Blizzard Beach, Typhoon Lagoon and Oak Trail Golf Course. The number of places you can visit increases the more days you buy (eg a four-day ticket allows four extra visits; a five-day ticket allows five).

Days	Multiday Prices (age 10+/ age 3-9)	Park Hopper (age 10+/ age 3-9)	Park Hopper Plus (age 10+/ age 3-9)
2	$199/187	$259/247	$274/262
3	$289/271	$349/331	$364/346
4	$350/330	$425/405	$440/420
5	$370/350	$445/425	$460/440
6	$390/370	$465/445	$480/460
7	$410/390	$485/465	$500/480
8	$420/400	$495/475	$510/490
9	$430/410	$505/485	$520/500
10	$440/420	$515/495	$530/510

Disney Dining Offers Complex Disney Dining Plans are available to guests of Disney resort hotels; see www.disneyworld.disney.go.com for prices, and remember – you can add in a dining plan on any day leading up to the time of your reservation.

Buying tickets at the gate This is $20 more expensive than buying online.

TOURIST INFORMATION

For on-site questions and reservations, head to Guest Services, just inside each theme park, or the concierge at any Disney resort hotel.

Important Telephone Numbers

Walt Disney World® (☑ 407-939-5277) Central number for all things Disney, including packages, tickets, room and dining reservations, and general questions about hours and scheduled events. They'll connect you to anything you need.

Walt Disney World® 'Disney Dining' (☑ 407-939-3463) Book priority dining reservations up to 180 days in advance, including character meals, dinner shows and specialty dining. You can also book online, by phone or through your My Disney Experience app (www.disneyworld.disney.go.com).

Walt Disney World® 'Enchanting Extras Collection' (Recreation) (☑ 407-939-7529) Horseback riding, boating and more.

Walt Disney World® 'Enchanting Extras Collection' (Tours) (☑ 407-939-8687) Tours at all of Disney's four theme parks. One of these gives a 'behind the scenes' look; excellent for return visitors.

Walt Disney World® 'Theme Parks Lost & Found' (☑ 407-824-4245) Items are sent to this central location at the end of each day; also see Guest Services at individual parks.

❶ Getting There & Away

TO & FROM AIRPORT

Disney's Magical Express (☑ 866-599-0951; www.disneyworld.disney.go.com) If you're staying at a Walt Disney World® hotel and are arriving at the Orlando International Airport (as opposed to Sanford), arrange in advance for complimentary luggage handling and deluxe bus transportation. They will send you baggage labels in advance, collect your luggage at the airport, and if during your stay you transfer from one Disney hotel to another, the resort will transfer your luggage while you're off for the day.

BUS

Orlando's **Lynx** (p247) bus 50 connects the downtown central station to Disney's Transportation & Ticket Center and Disney Springs, but it's an hour ride. Bus 56 runs along Hwy 192, between Kissimmee and Disney's Transportation & Ticket Center. From there, you can connect to any theme park or hotel.

CAR & MOTORCYCLE

Disney lies 25 minutes' drive south of downtown Orlando. Take I-4 to well-signed exits 64, 65 or 67.

Alamos and National car rental is available inside the Walt Disney World® Dolphin Resort.

Car Care Center (☑ 407-824-0976; 1000 W Car Care Dr, Walt Disney World®; ◷7am-7pm Mon-Fri, 7am-4pm Sat, 8am-3pm Sun) is a full-service garage, providing services (roadside assistance including towing, flat tire and battery jump starts) on Disney property only.

Parking

If you're staying at a Disney resort, parking at all the theme parks and hotels is free; otherwise, it costs $20 per day. Note: It's not made clear, but parking tickets bought at one park are good all day for all Disney parks.

Parking lots sit directly outside the gates of all the parks, except for Magic Kingdom; if you're driving to Magic Kingdom, you have to park at the Transportation & Ticket Center and take a monorail or ferry to the park. Parking at Disney Springs, the water parks, ESPN Wide World of Sports and all the golf courses is free, but there is no transportation from these attractions to any of the four theme parks. Valet parking at deluxe hotels costs around $25 per day.

Transportation & Ticket Center (TTC) (www.disneyworld.disney.go.com; Walt Disney World®; Magic Kingdom parking $20) is Disney's transportation epicenter. From here, one monorail goes to Magic Kingdom, Disney's Polynesian Resort, Disney's Contemporary Resort and Disney's Grand Floridian Resort; a second monorail connects directly to Epcot; a third monorail connects directly to Magic Kingdom; ferries go to Magic Kingdom; and buses service attractions and hotels throughout Walt Disney World®.

TAXI

Taxis can be found at hotels, theme parks, the Transportation & Ticket Center and Disney Springs.

❶ Getting Around

The Disney transportation system utilizes boat, bus and a monorail to shuttle visitors to hotels, theme parks and other attractions within Walt Disney World®. The Transportation & Ticket Center operates as the main hub of this system. Note that it can take an hour to get from point A to point B using the Disney transportation system, and there is not always a direct route.

BOAT

Disney World Water Transportation (https://disneyworld.disney.go.com/guest-services/water-transportation/; Walt Disney World®) runs complimentary Disney boats that connect Magic Kingdom to Magic Kingdom resorts and the Transportation & Ticket Center; and Epcot resorts to Hollywood Studios, Disney's Boardwalk and Epcot.

Water launches (water taxis) circulate directly between Magic Kingdom and Disney's Grand Floridian Resort and Disney's Polynesian Resort; a second route connects Magic Kingdom to Disney's Contemporary Resort, Disney's Fort Wilderness Resort & Campground and Disney's Wilderness Lodge; and a third route, utilizing 600-passenger ferries, connects Magic Kingdom to the Transportation & Ticket Center.

Boats also loop between Epcot, Hollywood Studios, Disney's BoardWalk, Disney's Yacht & Beach Club Resorts, and Walt Disney World® Swan & Dolphin Resorts.

Finally, boats connect Disney Springs to Disney Springs resort hotels.

BUS

Everything at Disney World is accessible by a free bus, but not all destinations are directly connected. Buses from Disney Springs, for example, do not connect directly to any theme parks. To this end, some routes may involve a combination of bus, monorail or boat. So-called 'cast members' (that is, staff) are willing to assist.

MONORAIL

Three separate monorail routes service select locations within Walt Disney World®. The Resort Monorail loops between the Transportation & Ticket Center, Disney's Polynesian Resort, Disney's Grand Floridian Resort, Magic Kingdom and Disney's Contemporary Resort. A second monorail route connects the Transportation & Ticket Center directly to Magic Kingdom; and a third route connects the Transportation & Ticket Center directly to Epcot.

Magic Kingdom

When most people think of Walt Disney World®, they're thinking of one of the four theme parks – the **Magic Kingdom** (☎407-939-5277; www.disneyworld.disney.go.com; 1180 Seven Seas Dr, Walt Disney World®; $100-119, prices vary daily; ☺9am-11pm, hours vary; ☑Disney, ☑Disney, ☑Disney). This is the Disney of commercials, of princesses and pirates, of dreams come true; this is quintessential old-school Disney with classic rides such as It's a Small World and Space Mountain.

At its core is Cinderella's Castle, the iconic image (this over-used phrase is used correctly here) of the television show. Remember when Tinkerbell dashed across the screen as fireworks burst across the castle turrets?

You'll see it as soon as you enter the park and emerge onto Main Street, USA. A horse-drawn carriage and an old-fashioned car run for the first hour from the park entrance to

AROUND WALT DISNEY WORLD®

If you don't stay in a Walt Disney World® resort, countless other hotels, motels and resorts in Lake Buena Vista, Kissimmee and Celebration lie within a few miles of Walt Disney World®. There's an excellent selection of chain motels along grassy Palm Pkwy just outside Disney's gates and a cluster of seven upscale chain hotels (www.downtowndisneyhotels.com) across from Disney Springs.

the castle (though most people walk), and from there paths lead to the four 'lands' – Fantasyland, Tomorrowland, Adventureland and Frontierland, as well as two other areas: Liberty Square and Main Street, USA.

◉ Sights

Fantasyland   AREA
(www.disneyworld.disney.go.com; Magic Kingdom; theme-park admission required; ☺9am-9pm, hours vary; ➡; ☑Disney, ☑Disney, ☑Lynx 50, 56) Quintessential Disney, Fantasyland is the highlight of any Disney trip for both the eight-and-under crowd and grown-ups looking for a nostalgic taste of classic Disney. Littlies, especially, love the character-focused experiences and attractions, while tweens too cool for fairy tales and teens looking for thrills may turn up their noses.

The Beast's castle houses Disney's **Be Our Guest,** Disney's hottest themed restaurant and **Cinderella's Royal Table**, where you can dine inside the castle with a rotating cast of the classic Disney princesses. (Reserve ahead for both; reservations can be made up to 180 days before your visit.)

Without a doubt the best 3D show in Disney, **Mickey's PhilharMagic** takes Donald Duck on a whimsical adventure through classic Disney movies. Ride with him through the streets of Morocco on Aladdin's carpet and feel the champagne on your face when it pops open during *Beauty and the Beast*'s 'Be Our Guest.' Fun, silly and light-hearted, this is Disney at its best.

It's A Small World, a sweet boat trip around the globe, has captivated children since the song and ride debuted at the 1964 New York World's Fair. Small boats gently glide through country after country, each decked out from floor to ceiling with elaborate and charmingly dated sets inhabited by hundreds of automated animals and children. Yes, it's so well known how the song sticks irritatingly in your head for weeks, that it's become a Disney cliché. But there's something poignantly endearing, almost melancholy, in this simple ride. Little ones love it though we're not suggesting it's worth a long wait so be discerning.

Race your way through a diamond mine in the **Seven Dwarfs Mine Train**, a family roller coaster (but it still zips along). Board a pirate ship and fly through fog and stars over London to Never Never Land on **Peter Pan's Flight**; take a sweet journey through the Hundred Acre Wood on the **Many Adventures of Winnie the Pooh** and ride through the *Little Mermaid* on **Under the Sea: Journey of the Little Mermaid**. At **Dumbo the Flying Elephant** toddlers love jumping on a Dumbo and riding slowly around and around, up and down, and thrill at the chance to control how high they go. Lines here can be unbelievably long and slow, and the ride is incredibly short – hit this when the park gates open. The **Mad Tea Party** is a basic spinning ride, and you and others in the teacup decide just how much you'll be twirling.

Fantasyland offers all kinds of excellent character-interaction opportunities. Watch a Princess tale at the little stone grotto of **Fairytale Garden**; listen to Belle tell a story at **Enchanted Tales with Belle**; meet Ariel at **Ariel's Grotto** and Gaston by **Gaston's Tavern**; or hop in line and catch a handful of princesses in **Fairytale Hall**. And of course, always keep an eye out for Cinderella, Alice in Wonderland and other favorites hanging out throughout Fantasyland. (Note: Mary Poppins is, er, a 'floater'; she appears at different lands at different times. Ask a staff member (known as 'cast character') where she might be appearing.)

Adventureland
AREA

(www.disneyworld.disney.go.com; Magic Kingdom; theme-park admission required; ⊙9am-9pm, hours vary; ♿; ♿ Disney, ⛴ Disney, ⛴ Lynx 50, 56) Adventure Disney-style means pirates and jungles, magic carpets and tree houses, and whimsical and silly representations of the exotic locales from storybooks and imagination. Don't miss **Pirates of the Caribbean** – the slow-moving boat through the dark and shadowy world of pirates remains one of the most popular attractions at Disney.

Drunken pirates sing pirate songs, sleep among the pigs and sneer over their empty whiskey bottles, but unless you're scared of the dark or growling pirates, it's a giggle not a scream. And Jack Sparrow looks so incredibly lifelike that you'll swear it's Johnny Depp himself. The silliness continues at **Jungle Cruise** (Fast-Pass+), but this time the captain takes you past fake crocodiles, elephants and monkeys, all the while throwing out the cheesiest jokes in all of Disney World.

Kids love flying around on **Magic Carpets of Aladdin**, but skip the slow train of folks climbing 116 steps at **Swiss Family Treehouse**, a replica tree house of the shipwrecked family from the book and movie *The Swiss Family Robinson*. Animatronic birds sing and dance Hawaiian-style at the **Enchanted Tiki Room**, a silly and rather bizarre two-bit attraction that opened in 1963 and continues to enjoy a curious cult following. You won't find lines, and it makes for a perfect spot to relax out of the heat for a bit.

Frontierland
AREA

(www.disneyworld.disney.go.com; Magic Kingdom; theme-park admission required; ⊙9am-9pm, hours vary; ♿; ♿ Disney, ⛴ Disney, ⛴ Lynx 50, 56) Wild West Disney-style. **Splash Mountain** depicts the misadventures of Brer Rabbit, Brer Bear and Brer Fox, complete with chatty frogs, singing ducks and other critters. The 40mph drop into the river makes for one of the biggest thrills in the park, and you will get very wet! With no steep drops or loop-dee-loops, mild **Big Thunder Mountain Railroad** coaster is a great choice for little ones.

The 'wildest ride in the wilderness' takes you through the desert mountain and a cave of bats, past cacti and hot-spring geysers. The line can feel never-ending, winding

---

TOP TIPS: MAGIC KINGDOM

➡ Best attractions to use as your three FastPass+ selections are Peter Pan's Flight, Big Thunder Mountain Railroad, Splash Mountain, Space Mountain, Seven Dwarf's Mine Train, Princess Fairytale Hall and Enchanted Tales with Belle; alternatively, hit them when the park gates open.

➡ It's a Small World, Mickey's PhilharMagic, and Monsters, Inc. Laugh Floor are air-conditioned attractions with short waits.

and winding more than you think, so this is a good attraction to reserve as one of your three FastPass+ choices.

Dubbed by many as a peaceful escape, **Tom Sawyer Island** may be a disappointment to some, lovely to others. This was originally designed for California's Disneyland in 1955, and in its day, when Disney was smaller and children's expectations were lower, it was a place for adventure. Today, some people mill about, not sure what to do and wondering why they waited so long in line to take a boat out here.

In the odd and strangely dated **Country Bear Jamboree**, stuffed bears emerge from the stage and sing corny country songs.

Tomorrowland

AREA

(www.disneyworld.disney.go.com; Magic Kingdom; theme-park admission required; ⊙9am-9pm, hours vary; ♿; ⬜ Disney, ⬛ Disney, ⬜ Lynx 50, 56) Though the theming as a Jetsons-inspired peek into the future falls flat, Tomorrowland holds a few wildly popular Disney highlights. Come first thing or use a FastPass+ for **Space Mountain**, an indoor coaster into the star-studded galaxies of outer space, and **Buzz Lightyear's Space Ranger Spin**, a cross between a ride and a video game.

At the interactive comedy show **Monsters, Inc Laugh Floor**, monsters from the film must harness human laughter rather than screams. A screen projects characters from the movie, each doing a stand-up comedy routine that surprises audience members by unexpectedly incorporating them. It's pretty funny, and every show is different. Kids can put the pedal to the metal on grand-prix-style cars at **Indy Speedway**, but the cars are fixed to the track and you don't control the steering. Note that kids must be 52in tall to 'drive' on their own, which pretty much eliminates this ride's target audience.

Liberty Square

AREA

(www.disneyworld.disney.go.com; Magic Kingdom; theme-park admission required; ⊙9am-9pm, hours vary; ⬜ Disney, ⬛ Disney, ⬜ Lynx 50, 56) The ramblin' 19th-century mansion houses **Haunted Mansion**, another classic favorite piece of low-on-thrill and high-on-silly fun, and the only real ride in Liberty Square. Cruise slowly past the haunted dining room, where apparitions dance across the stony floor, but beware of those hitchhiking ghosts – don't be surprised if they jump into your car uninvited. While mostly it's lighthearted ghosty goofiness, kids may be frightened by spooky preride dramatics.

All sorts of presidential memorabilia decorates the waiting area of the **Hall of Presidents**, where people are herded into a theater to watch a superpatriotic flick on US history, ending with every US president standing before you on stage.

Main Street, USA

AREA

(www.disneyworld.disney.go.com; Magic Kingdom; theme-park admission required; ⊙9am-9pm, hours vary; ♿; ⬜ Disney, ⬛ Disney, ⬜ Lynx 50, 56) Fashioned after Walt Disney's hometown of Marceline, MO, Main Street, USA, is best experienced with an aimless meander. Peruse the miniature dioramas of Peter Pan and Snow White in the street windows; pop in to catch the black-and-white movie reels of old Disney cartoons, and browse the hundreds of thousands of must-have Disney souvenirs.

☞ Tours

Keys to the Kingdom

WALKING

(☎407-939-8687; www.disneyworld.disney.go; Magic Kingdom; tours $99, theme-park admission required; ⊙8am, 8:30am, 9am & 9:30am) Quintessential Disney, this popular five-hour tour peeks into the Magic Kingdom's underground tunnels and backstage secrets – no children allowed, so as not to destroy the magic!

✦ Festivals & Events

★ Festival of Fantasy

PARADE

(www.disneyworld.disney.go.com; Magic Kingdom; theme-park admission required; ⊙morning & afternoon daily, hours vary; ⬜ Disney, ⬛ Disney, ⬜ Lynx 50, 56) Introduced in 2014, with elaborate floats and dancing characters, including the Disney princesses, Rapunzel, Merida, Peter Pan and Sleeping Beauty. Plus Maleficent, the fire-breathing dragon.

★ Wishes Nighttime Spectacular

FIREWORKS

(www.disneyworld.disney.go.com; Magic Kingdom; theme-park admission required; ⊙8pm, hours vary; ⬜ Disney, ⬛ Disney, ⬜ Lynx 50, 56) At the time of research, this was about to be replaced with another no-doubt sparkly, light extravaganza, called **Happily Ever After**.

Once Upon a Time

LIGHT SHOW

(www.disneyworld.disney.go.com; Magic Kingdom; theme-park admission required; ⊙nightly, hours vary; ⬜ Disney, ⬛ Disney, ⬜ Lynx 50, 56) Seasonally changing light-and-music show that's projected onto Cinderella's Castle. It highlights Disney movies and characters. It takes place before or after the Nighttime Spectacular.

Mickey's Not-So-Scary Halloween Party
CARNIVAL

(☑ 407-939-5277; www.disneyworld.disney.go.com; Magic Kingdom; adult/child $65/60, theme-park admission required; ⊙ select nights Sep & Oct; ▣ Disney, ▣ Disney, ▣ Lynx 50, 56) Characters decked out in costumes, trick-or-treating and Halloween-inspired fireworks, parade and events. Discounted tickets available if purchased in advance online.

Mickey's Very Merry Christmas Party
CHRISTMAS

(☑ 407-939-5277; www.disneyworld.disney.go.com; Magic Kingdom; prices vary; ⊙ select nights 7pm-midnight Nov-Dec; ▣ Disney, ▣ Disney, ▣ Lynx 50 & 56, ▣ Disney) Christmas songs, decorations and festivities Disney-style saturate Disney's Magic Kingdom park, including a Christmas parade, snowfall on Main Street and seasonal shows. Prices change annually and are posted nearer the event.

🛏 Sleeping

There are a number of resorts in the area that offer easy access to the theme parks. Staying at one of the resorts on Bay Lake has the advantage of allowing you to get to or from Magic Kingdom with no need for a transfer.

★ Disney's Fort Wilderness Resort
CAMPGROUND, CABIN $

(☑ 407-939-5277, 407-824-2900; www.disneyworld. disney.go.com; 4510 N Fort Wilderness Trail; tent sites $76, RV sites $97-122, 6-person cabins $359; ✳@🛜☀; ▣ Disney, ▣ Disney) Located in a huge shaded natural preserve, Fort Wilderness caters to kids and families with its hay rides, fishing and nightly campfire sing-alongs. Cabins sleep up to six and are hardly rustic, with cable TV and full kitchens, and while cars aren't allowed within the gates, you can rent a golf cart to toot around in.

Staff keep a strict eye on after-hours noise; the grounds are meticulously maintained; and there's a wonderfully casual and friendly state-park-like tone to the entire resort.

★ Disney's Grand Floridian Resort & Spa
RESORT $$$

(☑ 407-939-5277, 407-824-3000; www.disneyworld. disney.go.com; 4401 Floridian Way; r from $616; ▣✳@🛜☀; ▣ Disney, ▣ Disney, ▣ Disney) One easy monorail stop from Magic Kingdom, the Grand Floridian rides on its reputation as the grandest, most elegant property in Disney World, and it does indeed exude a welcome calm and charm. The four-story lobby, with a live orchestra playing jazz (and yes, Disney classics), oozes all the accoutrements of Old Florida class and style.

At its heart, though, this is Disney. Sparkling princesses ballroom-dance across the oriental rugs; exhausted children sit entranced by classic Disney cartoons; and babies cry. In contrast to the massive ferries from the Transportation & Ticket Center, small wooden boats shuttle folks back and forth to Magic Kingdom.

★ Disney's Wilderness Lodge
RESORT $$$

(☑ 407-939-5277, 407-824-3200; www.disney world.disney.go.com; 901 Timberline Dr, Walt Disney World®; r from $359; ▣✳🛜☀; ▣ Disney, ▣ Disney) The handsome lobby's low-lit tepee chandeliers, hand-carved totem pole and dramatic 80ft fireplace echo national-park lodges of America's old West. Though it's meant to feel as if you're in John Muir country, with its wooded surrounds and hidden lagoonside location, the fake geyser and singing waiters in the lobby restaurant dispel the illusion mighty quick.

Disney's Polynesian Resort
RESORT $$$

(☑ 407-824-2000, 407-939-5277; www.disney world.disney.go.com; 1600 Seven Seas Dr; r from $479; ▣✳@🛜☀; ▣ Disney, ▣ Disney, ▣ Disney) With faux-bamboo decor, a jungle motif in the lobby, and coconut-shell cups and shell necklaces in the store, you just may think you're in the South Pacific. The rounded lagoonside pool features a slide, a zero entrance perfect for little ones and an excellent view of Cinderella's Castle.

Disney's Contemporary Resort
RESORT $$$

(☑ 407-939-5277, 407-824-1000; www.disneyworld. disney.go.com; 4600 N World Dr; r from $388; ▣✳@🛜☀; ▣ Disney, ▣ Disney, ▣ Disney) The granddaddy of Disney resorts, the Contemporary's futuristic A-frame opened Walt Disney World® in 1971 but feels uninspired and disappointing by today's standards. Yes, it's cool to see the monorail zip silently through the lobby, and its withering grandeur evokes melancholy sentimental attachment, but the years have faded this iconic hotel's sparkle.

On the upside, you can't beat the location. Balcony rooms front Magic Kingdom;

an excellent top-floor restaurant lures folks with its drop-dead views of Disney's fireworks; and renovated streamlined suites in Bay Lake Towers sleep five and are some of the most handsome digs at Disney.

✗ Eating

Eating at Magic Kingdom is less about great food than theming, festive environs and character dining opportunities. There are snacks, fast-food eateries and table-service restaurants at every turn, but there's little here worth seeking out. For sit-down meals, make a reservation at one of Disney's Magic Kingdom Resorts – Disney's Polynesian, Disney's Contemporary, Disney's Grand Floridian – they're any easy hop monorail or boat from Magic Kingdom.

Gaston's Tavern   AMERICAN $
(www.disneyworld.disney.go.com; Magic Kingdom; mains $6-16, theme-park admission required; ⊙9am-park closing; 🛜🚹; 🚻Disney, 🚻Disney, 🚻Lynx 50, 56) Homage to that superego Gaston, with giant cinnamon rolls and hummus. It's an odd mix of quick-service options, but the re-created tavern with the giant portrait of Gaston is well done. Try Le Fou's Brew, Disney's counter to Universal's runaway hit Butterbeer.

Main Street Bakery   BAKERY $
(www.disneyworld.disney.go.com; Magic Kingdom; items $5-10, theme-park admission required; ⊙9am-park closing; 🚻Disney, 🚻Disney, 🚻Lynx 50, 56) Few places require good strong java more than Walt Disney World®, and few places are as notorious for bad coffee as the Happiest Place on Earth. The Main Street Bakery has Starbucks. It might (or might not be) the answer to your prayer.

Columbia Harbour House   AMERICAN $
(www.disneyworld.disney.go.com; Magic Kingdom; mains $10-15, theme-park admission required; ⊙11am-park closing; 🛜🚹; 🚻Disney, 🚻Disney, 🚻Lynx 50, 56) Decent vegetarian chili, unusually tasty clam chowder, chicken potpie and salmon. The interior is charming as you're inside an old boat that has 'docked' in the US, having come from the UK. (Use your imagination: this is Walt Disney World® after all).

Sleepy Hollow   AMERICAN $
(www.disneyworld.disney.go.com; Magic Kingdom; snacks $6-9, theme-park admission required; ⊙9am-park closing; 🚻Disney, 🚻Disney, 🚻Lynx 50, 56) This small walk-up 'window' produces a yummy ice-cream sandwich with oozing vanilla ice cream squished between warm, fresh-baked chocolate-chip cookies. Look for the brick house in Liberty Square, just across the bridge from Cinderella's Castle.

★ Jungle Navigation Co. Ltd Skipper Canteen   INTERNATIONAL $$
(www.disneyworld.disney.go.com; Magic Kingdom; mains $17-30; ⊙11:30am-9pm) This adventure-themed spot harks back to days of boat exploration. It has three delightful areas based around boat skippers' tropical headquarters. Enjoy a meal in the Secret society of Adventurer's Room, the Jungle Room or the Mess. It's the most atmospheric of options in the park and the meals are large, but by far the healthiest.

The menu features 'sustainable fish' and Skip's Beefy Bakes pasta.

Cinderella's Royal Table   AMERICAN $$$
(📞407-934-2927; www.disneyworld.disney.go.com; Cinderella's Castle, Magic Kingdom; adult/child from $60/35; ⊙8-10:15am, 11:30am-2:50pm & 4-10:20pm (hours vary); 🛜🚹; 🚻Disney, 🚻Disney, 🚻Lynx 50, 56) Cinderella greets guests and sits for a formal portrait (included in the price), and a sit-down meal with princesses is served upstairs. This is the only opportunity to eat inside the iconic castle – make reservations six months in advance.

Be Our Guest   AMERICAN $$$
(📞407-939-3463; www.disneyworld.disney.go.com; Magic Kingdom; mains breakfast $24, lunch $13-17, dinner $26-35; ⊙8am-10:30am, 11am-2.30pm & 4-10pm, hours vary; 🛜🚹; 🚻Disney, 🚻Disney, 🚻Lynx 50, 56) Set inside the Beast's marvelously detailed castle, this experience is a must for *Beauty and the Beast* fans. Options include braised pork, carved turkey and the most talked about dessert at Disney, the Master's Cupcake. But it's the attention to theming that is the real draw.

Come for quick-service lunch when the door opens or expect upwards of two hours' wait; reservations are accepted for dinner only, but you'll need to make them as close to six months in advance as you can. The Beast makes regular appearances and after your meal you can explore his castle and have your picture taken with him in his study.

Crystal Palace   AMERICAN $$$
(📞407-939-3463; www.disneyworld.disney.go.com; Magic Kingdom; buffet $35-60, theme-park admission required; ⊙8-10:45am, 11:30am-2:45pm

& 3:15-9:15pm – hours vary) The buffet at this character meal inside Magic Kingdom is surprisingly tasty. At lunch, there's a wide selection of salads, glazed carrots, mashed potatoes and green beans, as well as a carving station with ham and steak. The real draw, though, is the glass-enclosed garden atmosphere and Winnie-the-Pooh and friends mingling around the tables.

🛍 Shopping

Bibbidi Bobbidi Boutique   COSMETICS
(📞 407-939-7895; www.disneyworld.disney.go.com; Magic Kingdom; hair & makeup from $60; ⊙ 10am-8pm, hours vary) Inside Cinderella's Castle, fairy godmothers finalize your kid's transformation from shorts and T-shirt to bedazzling princess with fanciful hairstyling and makeup.

Girls aged from three to 12 can choose from the Coach (hair and makeup from $55), the Crown (add nails, from $60), the Courtyard (add T-shirt and tutu, from $95) or the Castle (hair, makeup, nails, full costume and photograph, from $190). For boys, there's the Knight Package (hair, a sword and a shield, $15). It's a more expensive and elaborate version of the spiky green hair or a pink updo and Disney sequins ($10 to $20) at the Harmony Barber Shop on Magic Kingdom's Main Street. There's a second Bibbidee Bobbidee Boutique in Disney Springs.

ℹ Getting There & Away

The only direct way to get to Magic Kingdom is by water taxi or monorail from Disney's Contemporary Resort, Disney's Grand Floridian or Disney's Polynesian Resort; by water taxi from Disney's Fort Wilderness Resort and Disney's Wilderness Lodge; by passenger ferry or monorail from the Transportation & Ticket Center, or by bus from any Disney resort hotel or Transportation & Ticket Center.

If you drive, you *must* park at the Transportation & Ticket Center and then take the monorail, bus or the ferry to the park. With its massive parking lot and endless lines for bus shuttles, the Transportation & Ticket Center, however, can be unbearable, with tempers on edge and impatient people.

Consider hopping the monorail or water launch to a Magic Kingdom resort and then taking a cab to your hotel. If you coordinate reserved breakfast or dinner at one of these resorts, and many offer character meals, this works particularly nicely, and you can park at resort hotels free of charge if you have restaurant reservations. Note

that you can get to Magic Kingdom via monorail from Epcot, but you must switch trains at the Transportation & Ticket Center.

For the first hour after opening, a horse-drawn carriage or old-fashioned car carries folk back and forth down Main Street, USA, from the entrance gate to Cinderella's Castle. The open-air Walt Disney World® Railroad follows the perimeter of the park and stops at Main Street, USA, Fantasyland and Frontierland.

Epcot

With no roller coasters screeching overhead, no parades, no water rides and plenty of water, things here run a bit slower in **Epcot** (📞 407-939-5277; www.disneyworld.disney.go.com; 200 Epcot Center Dr, Walt Disney World®; $100-119, prices vary daily; ⊙ 11am-9pm, hours vary; 🚇 Disney, 🚤 Disney) than in the rest of Walt Disney World®. Slow down and enjoy. Smell the incense in Morocco, listen to the Beatles in the UK and sip miso in Japan.

The park is divided into two sections situated around a lake. **Future World** has Epcot's only two thrill rides plus several pavilions with attractions, restaurants and character greeting spots. **World Showcase** comprises 11 re-created nations featuring country-specific food, shopping and entertainment.

There are two entrances (though only one is shown on the official map). The main entrance, next to the bus and monorail stations, sits at the landmark geodesic dome of Spaceship Earth in Future World. The back entrance ('International Gateway') is for those catching a boat from Disney's BoardWalk, Hollywood Studios and Disney Epcot resort hotels.

⊙ Sights

★ World Showcase   AREA
(www.disneyworld.disney.go.com; Epcot; theme-park admission required; ⊙ 9am-6pm, hours vary; 🚇 Disney, 🚤 Disney, 🚇 Disney) Who needs the hassle of a passport and jet lag when you can travel the world right here at Walt Disney World®? World Showcase, one of two themed sections of Epcot, comprises 11 countries arranged around a lagoon. Watch belly dancing in Morocco, eat pizza in Italy and buy personally engraved bottles of perfume in France, before settling down to watch fireworks about world peace and harmony. Disney was right. It truly is a small world after all.

MEETING DISNEY CHARACTERS

Folks of all ages pay a lot of money and spend hours in line to get their photo taken with Winnie the Pooh, Donald Duck, Elsa and other Disney favorites. If this is what makes you swoon (versus just spotting them from a short distance, which can also be fun), see www.disneyworld.disney.go.com. There is a plethora of opportunities to sidle up next to a princess, villain or furry friend.

Note that character experiences in the resort hotels do not require theme-park tickets.

Disney Character Dining (☎ 407-939-3463; https://disneyworld.disney.go.com/dining/#/character-dining; Walt Disney World® theme parks & resort hotels; prices vary) Make reservations up to six months (yes, six!) for any of the 20 or so character-dining meals at Walt Disney World®. They're hardly relaxing and are rather loud and chaotic. Characters stop at each table to pose for a photograph and interact briefly. Disney's Grand Floridian Resort (p290) has a buffet breakfast featuring Winnie the Pooh, Mary Poppins and Alice in Wonderland, plus it holds the the **Perfectly Princess Tea Party**. There's a jam-packed breakfast and dinner with Goofy, Donald Duck and pals at **Chef Mickey's** in **Disney's** Contemporary Resort (p290); princesses mingle in Epcot's Norway at the **Akershus Royal Banquet**; and the 100 Acre Wood folk come to Magic Kingdom's **Crystal Palace** for three meals a day.

Character Spots Each Walt Disney World® theme park has specific spots where Disney characters hang out, and you can simply hop in line (and wait and wait) to meet them and have your photo taken. A few character spots, such as **Enchanted Tales with Belle**, include a short performance. In addition, check your map and Times Guide for times and locations of scheduled character greetings, and always keep your eyes open – you never know who you'll see!

Cinderella's Royal Table (p291) Cinderella greets guests and sits for a formal portrait (included in the price), and a sit-down meal with princesses is served upstairs. This is the only opportunity to eat inside the iconic castle – make reservations six months in advance. Hours vary.

Chip 'n' Dale Campfire Singalong (p282) A campfire singalong at Disney's Fort Wilderness Resort.

Sure, this is quite a sanitized stereotypical vision of the world, but so what? This is, after all, a theme park. And who knows, an afternoon here might just inspire you to hop a plane and check out the real thing, and it certainly is a fun way to show kids a little something about the world.

The best way to experience the World Showcase is to simply wander as the mood moves you, poking through stores and restaurants, and catching what amounts to Bureau of Tourism promotional films and gentle rides through some of the countries. Donald Duck and his comrades take you through Mexico in **Gran Fiesta Tour Starring the Three Caballeros**; Norway's rather odd boat ride **Maelstrom** meanders past Vikings, trolls and waterfalls; and the **American Adventure** show features audio-animatonic figures presenting a simplified interpretation of US history. The featured countries from left to right around the water are Mexico, Norway, China, Germany, Italy, USA ('The American Adventure'), Japan, Morocco, France, the UK and Canada.

★ **Soarin' Around the World**   RIDE (www.disneyworld.disney.go.com; Future World, Epcot; theme-park admission required; ⊙ 9am-6pm, hours vary; 🖵 Disney, 🚊 Disney, 🖵 Disney) Soar up and down, hover and accelerate as the giant screen in front of you takes you over and around the globe. We don't want to give too much away. Suffice to say that it's an extraordinarily visceral experience as aroma effects blast the smells of the earth at you as you ride (such as the elephants and grasses of Africa). Ask for a front-row seat; feet dangling in front of you can ruin the effect.

While not at all scary in terms of speed or special effects, people with agoraphobia or motion sickness may feel a bit uneasy. Reserve a FastPass+ or hit this first thing in the morning, as it's one of the best rides at Disney.

Seas with Nemo & Friends Pavilion
RIDE, SHOW

(www.disneyworld.disney.go.com; Future World, Epcot; theme park admission required; ⊙9am-6pm, hours vary; 🖳Disney, 🖳Disney, 🖳Disney) Kids under 10 won't want to miss the two *Nemo*-themed attractions at Epcot's Future World. Ride a clamshell through the ocean with Nemo on **Seas with Nemo & Friends** and talk face-to-face with Crush in the interactive **Turtle Talk with Crush**, a Disney highlight.

A small blue room with a large movie screen holds about 10 rows of benches with sitting room for kids in front. Crush talks to the children staring up at him, taking questions from the 'dude in the dark-blue shell' and cracking jokes about how sea grass gives him the bubbles. Dory shows up and gets squished against the screen by the whale, and there's plenty of silliness and giggling.

Frozen Ever After
RIDE

(https://disneyworld.disney.go.com/attractions/epcot/frozen-ever-after/; Norway, Epcot; ⊙9am-6pm, hours vary) One of Disney's current 'hot' rides, Frozen Ever After takes you on an ancient Norwegian vessel as you sail off into the wintery world of *Frozen*, set to your favorite *Frozen* tunes, of course. *Frozen* friends make appearances and there's plenty of special effects. Not too much detail: we don't want to thaw your expectations here.

Mission Space
RIDE

(www.disneyworld.disney.go.com; Future World, Epcot; theme-park admission required; ⊙9am-6pm, hours vary; 🖳Disney, 🖳Disney) One of two thrill rides at Future World, Epcot, Mission Space straps you into a tiny four-person spaceship cockpit and launches you into, you guessed it, space. While this is a simulated experience and not a high-speed ride, the special effects can be nauseating and the dire warnings are enough to scare away even the most steel-bellied folk. There are two options, one with less intensity than the other.

Test Track
RIDE

(www.disneyworld.disney.go.com; Future World, Epcot; theme-park admission required; ⊙9am-6pm, hours vary; 🖳Disney, 🖳Disney) Board a car and ride through heat, cold, speed, braking and crash tests. At one point a huge semi with blinding lights heads right for you, its horn blaring. When testing the acceleration, the car speeds up to 60mph within a very short distance, but there are few turns and no ups and downs like a roller coaster.

At the ride's entrance you can virtually design your own car, and at the exit you'll find all kinds of car-themed games and simulators.

Ellen's Energy Adventure
RIDE

(☎407-939-5277; www.disneyworld.disney.go.com; Future World, Epcot; theme-park admission required; ⊙9am-6pm, hours vary; 🖳Disney, 🖳Disney, 🖳Disney) This 45-minute multimedia ride is the oddest attraction in Orlando, perhaps in the entire state of Florida. It begins with a movie during which Ellen DeGeneres dreams that she is playing Jeopardy! with Jamie Lee Curtis. Determined to outsmart her know-it-all opponent, Ellen joins Bill Nye the Science Guy on a trip through history to learn about energy sources. At this point, you board a 96-passenger vehicle and lurch slowly through the darkness into the Cretaceous period.

Giant dinosaurs stomp about menacingly and, in one particularly surreal display, a mannequin Ellen battles a ferocious one. After this jaunt through dinosaur land, the movie preaches wind energy, hydro-energy and other alternative fuel sources, and concludes with Ellen's Jeopardy! victory. The whole thing is just very bizarre.

Spaceship Earth
RIDE

(www.disneyworld.disney.go.com; Future World, Epcot; theme-park admission required; ⊙9am-6pm, hours vary; 🖳Disney, 🖳Disney) Inside what people joke is a giant golf ball landmark at the front entrance, Spaceship Earth is a bizarre, kitschy, slow-moving ride past animatronic scenes depicting the history of communication from cave painting to computers. Yes, it sounds boring, and yes, it sounds weird. But it's surprisingly funny and a cult favorite.

In recent years they've tried to modernize it with an interactive questionnaire about your travel interests, but we like the retro aspects better.

🎆 Festivals & Events

IllumiNations: Reflections of Earth
LIGHT SHOW

(www.disneyworld.disney.go.com; Epcot; theme-park admission required; ⊙nightly, hours vary; 🖳Disney, 🖳Disney, 🖳Lynx 50, 56) Epcot's night show incorporates fireworks, elaborate light theatrics and dramatic music to create a fiery narrative of the Earth's history, beginning with 'the Earth is born.' It centers around a massive globe illuminated with LED lights in the middle of World Showcase Lagoon – find a spot at least an hour early.

Epcot International
Flower & Garden Festival
FAIR

(☑ 407-939-5277; www.disneyworld.disney.go.com; Epcot; theme-park admission required; ☉ Mar-May; ▣ Disney) Spectacular Disney-themed topiary and garden displays, and all the countries in the World Pavilion celebrate spring with seasonal delicacies.

Epcot International Food &
Wine Festival
FOOD & DRINK

(☑ 407-939-5277; www.disneyworld.disney.go.com; Epcot; theme-park admission required; ☉ Aug-early Nov (changing dates); ▣ Disney) Disney-fied food and drink from around the world. You need to pay park admission, and then pay anywhere from $3 to $10 for food samples of varying quality. This is a very popular event – come early, expect crowds, and allow at least half a day.

🛏 Sleeping

One of the best parts about this cluster of hotels on the shore of Crescent Lake is their easy access to restaurants and entertainment in Epcot, Hollywood Studios and Disney's BoardWalk. The area is pedestrian-friendly and it's a pleasant walk or an easy boat ride to Epcot and to Hollywood Studios.

★ Walt Disney World
Swan & Dolphin Hotels
RESORT $$

(☑ Dolphin 407-934-4000, Swan 407-934-3000; www.swandolphin.com; 1200 & 1500 Epcot Resorts Blvd; r $160-380; P ✳ @ ☞ ✖; ▣ Disney, ☝ Disney) These two Michael Graves–designed, high-rise luxury hotels, which face each other on Disney property and share facilities, offer a distinctly toned-down Disney feel but all the Disney perks, including Disney transportation and Magic Hours (where a theme park opens early and closes late for guests at Disney hotels only).

Perched along the bay between Epcot and Hollywood Studios, these are the only non-Disney hotels next to a theme park. On-line and last-minute deals can save literally hundreds of dollars.

Disney's Caribbean
Beach Resort
RESORT $$

(☑ 407-934-7639, 407-939-5277; www.disney world.disney.go.com; 900 Cayman Way, Walt Disney World®; r from $192; ✳ ☞ ✖; ▣ Disney) A Disney taste of the islands means painted beds, pastel rooms, a food court that looks like a street festival during Carnival and a pool with a vague resemblance to ancient temple ruins. This hotel sits along 45-acre Barefoot Bay, and does not have convenient boat transportation to Epcot and Hollywood Studios.

Rooms, some pirate-themed, spread out among two-story, motel-like buildings.

Disney's Yacht Club Resort and
Disney's Beach Club Resort
RESORT $$$

(☑ Beach Club 407-934-8000, Walt Disney World® 407-939-5277, Yacht Club 407-934-7000; www. disneyworld.disney.go.com; 1700 & 1800 Epcot Resorts Blvd, Walt Disney World®; r from $410; ✳ ☞ ✖; ▣ Disney, ☝ Disney) These handsome sister resorts, pleasantly located along the water and a five-minute walk from Epcot, strive for old New England beachside charm. The pools, boasting sandy shores and a slide off a ship's mast, earn rave reviews. At the time of research they were ever-so-slightly tired, but by the time you read this all rooms should have been refurbished.

🍴 Eating

Eating at Epcot is as much about the experience as the food, and many of the restaurants go overboard to create an atmosphere characteristic of their country. Cuisine here is a cut above that at other theme parks.

La Cantina de San Angel
MEXICAN $

(www.disneyworld.disney.go.com; Mexico, Epcot; mains $11-13, theme park admission required; ☉ 11am-park closing; ☞ ⚡; ▣ Disney, ☝ Disney) One of the best fast-food places in the park. Try the tacos, served with surprisingly tasty *pico de gallo* (fresh salsa of tomatoes, onion and jalapeños) and fresh avocado. Great guacamole, too.

Les Halles
Boulangerie Patisserie
FRENCH $

(www.disneyworld.disney.go.com; France, Epcot; snacks $5-12, theme-park admission required; ☉ 9am-park closing; ▣ Disney, ☝ Disney) Most folks come for cakes, éclairs and cookies, but it also sells French-bread pizza, quiche and those baguette sandwiches that are ubiquitous in France, as well as wine and champagne.

Yorkshire County Fish Shop
BRITISH $

(www.disneyworld.disney.go.com; UK, Epcot; fish & chips $11, theme-park admission required; ☉ 11:30am-park closing; ☞ ♿; ▣ Disney, ☝ Disney)

Crispy fish with vinegar and Bass Ale at the walk-up window outside the pub in UK.

★ Tutto Gusto ITALIAN $$

(☎ 407-939-3463; https://disneyworld.disney.go.com/dining/epcot/tutto-gusto-wine-cellar/; Italy, Epcot; mains $12-18; ⊙ 11:30am-9pm; ⊛ 🐾 🖤) Full marks for this authentic Italian brasserie and wine bar. It oozes style and serves up excellent small plates, including meats and cheeses. Definitely the place to come for an excellent glass of Italian wine and homemade pasta served at the bar, high bar tables or while you are nestled cozily in a sofa. Recommended for dinner before the night spectaculars at Epcot.

Rose & Crown BRITISH $$

(☎ 407-939-3463; www.disneyworld.disney.com; UK, Epcot; mains $13-21, theme-park admission required; ⊙ 11:30am-park closing; 🐾 🖤; 🖤 Disney, 🐾 Disney, 🖤 Disney) Housed in a British pub, this little spot smells of fish and serves up shepherd's (cottage) pie, scotch eggs and bangers and chips. Wash it down with Bass on tap and head across the path for a garden concert with the Fab Four or settle on the patio for the nightly light show illuminations.

It's the least appealing of the options, but it has a well-placed terrace over the water.

San Angel Inn MEXICAN $$

(☎ 407-939-3463; www.disneyworld.disney.com; Mexico, Epcot; mains $20-26, theme-park admission required; ⊙ 11am-park closing; 🐾 🖤 🖤; 🖤 Disney, 🐾 Disney, 🖤 Disney) Set inside an Aztec pyramid and surrounded by a re-created Mexican market, with perpetual night skies twinkling with Disney stars. Solid Mexican fare. Ask about vegetarian options as there's a separate menu available.

Teppan Edo JAPANESE $$$

(☎ 407-939-3463; www.disneyworld.disney.com; Japan, Epcot; mains $30-36, theme-park admission required; ⊙ 11am-park closing; 🖤) Chefs toss the chicken, fling the chopsticks and frenetically slice and dice the veggies in this standard cook-in-front-of-you eatery next to Japan's gardens. It's housed in a stunning Japanese building, decked out in a black-and-red color theme and with contemporary flair.

Restaurant Marrakesh MEDITERRANEAN $$$

(☎ 407-939-3463; www.disneyworld.disney.com; Morocco, Epcot; mains $19-30, theme-park admission required; ⊙ 11:30am-park closing; 🐾 🖤 🖤;

🖤 Disney, 🐾 Disney, 🖤 Disney) Sparkling belly dancers shimmy and shake past the massive pillars and around the tables of the Sultan's Palace, magnificently decorated with mosaic tiles, rich velvets and sparkling gold. While the beef kebabs, vegetable couscous and other dishes are okay, the windowless elegance is a fun escape from the searing sun and kids love to join in the dancing.

Akershus Royal Banquet Hall NORWEGIAN $$$

(☎ 407-939-3463; www.disneyworld.disney.go.com; Norway, Epcot; buffet $35-60, theme-park admission required; ⊙ 8-11am, noon-3:30pm & 5-8:30pm; 🖤 Disney, 🖤 Disney) Join Disney princesses (a selection of Snow White, Cinderella, Belle, Aurora or Ariel) for a Norwegian-inspired feast in medieval surrounds – Disney-style, of course, so you'll find pizza and Minute Maid lemonade with a glowing Ariel alongside Norwegian meatballs with lingonberries. It's one of the better character meals, both in terms of ambience and food.

La Hacienda de San Angel MEXICAN $$$

(☎ 407-939-3463; www.disneyworld.disney.com; Mexico, Epcot; mains $23-30, theme-park admission required; ⊙ 4pm-park closing; 🖤; 🖤 Disney, 🐾 Disney, 🖤 Disney) Authentic Mexican rather than Tex Mex, this lagoonside eatery is tops for location and features excellent specials from chicken to seared-meat specialties. Why not make a day of it with on-the-rocks margaritas, ranging from avocado-infused to a classic with cactus lemongrass salt on the rim?

Via Napoli PIZZA $$$

(☎ 407-939-3463; www.disneyworld.disney.com; Italy, Epcot; pizzas $22-37, theme-park admission required; ⊙ 11:30am-park closing; 🐾 🖤; 🖤 Disney, 🐾 Disney, 🖤 Disney) It's more tasteful than your standard clichéd Giussepe-style pizza joint. Here, you sit at massive communal tables and the air is steamy with the aroma of thin-crust pizza cooked in a wood-burning stove. The toppings take things beyond run-of-the-mill pepperoni.

Le Cellier Steakhouse STEAK $$$

(☎ 407-939-3463; www.disneyworld.disney.com; Canada, Epcot; mains $29-54, theme-park admission required; ⊙ 12:30pm-park closing; 🐾 🖤; 🖤 Disney, 🐾 Disney, 🖤 Disney) If you love meat, this place is for you. Try the buffalo. Dark and cavernous, with stone walls and lanterns, it makes a good spot to escape the heat, but the dense sauces and decadent desserts might not be the best fuel to get you through the day.

Chefs de France   FRENCH $$$

(☑ 407-939-3463; www.disneyworld.disney.com; France, Epcot; mains $26-36, 3-course $40, theme-park admission required; ⊘ 4pm-park closing; 📶; 🖥 Disney, 🍴 Disney, 🚻 Disney) Bright yellow and with lovely big windows, this bustling French brasserie features *boeuf bourguignon*, lobster bisque and other bistro classics. The likes of macaroni and cheese sound a lot better in French *(gratin de macaroni)*; it's one of a small selection of rather plain vegetarian options.

Biergarten   GERMAN $$$

(☑ 407-939-3463; www.disneyworld.disney.go.com; Germany, Epcot; buffet lunch adult/child $20/11, buffet dinner $40/22, theme-park admission required; ⊘ noon-9pm; 📶 📶; 🖥 Disney, 🍴 Disney, 🚻 Disney) Satisfy a hearty appetite with traditional German foods (don't miss the pretzel bread) and a massive stein of brew. The restaurant interior is made to look like an old German village, with cobblestones, trees and a Bavarian oompah band in the evening.

🍸 Drinking & Nightlife

★ La Cava del Tequila   BAR

(☑ 407-939-3463; www.disneyworld.disney.go.com; Mexico, Epcot; theme-park admission required; ⊘ 11am-park closing; 🖥 Disney, 🍴 Disney, 🚻 Disney) Pop in for a cucumber, passion fruit or blood-orange margarita. Can't decide? Try a flight of margaritas or shots. The menu features more than 220 types of tequila, and it's a cozy, dark spot, with tiled floors, Mexican-styled murals and a beamed ceiling.

La Cava is connected to San Angel Inn, a full-service, sit-down restaurant, but it does not take reservations.

ℹ Getting There & Away

A pleasant, well-lit, paved waterfront path or water taxi connects Epcot to Hollywood Studios, Disney's BoardWalk and Epcot resorts. The monorail runs a direct line between Epcot and the Transportation & Ticket Center; from there, catch a monorail, ferry or bus (slower) to Magic Kingdom. Disney buses depart from Epcot's main gate to Disney resorts, Hollywood Studios and Animal Kingdom.

ℹ Getting Around

Within the park, a ferry shuttles folks to and from International Gateway from two boat docks just outside Future World.

Animal Kingdom

Set apart from the rest of Disney both in miles and in tone, **Animal Kingdom** (☑ 407-939-5277; www.disneyworld.disney.go.com; 2101 Osceola Pkwy, Walt Disney World®; $100-119, prices vary daily; ⊘ 9am-7pm, hours vary; 🖥 Disney) attempts to blend theme park and zoo, carnival and African safari, with a healthy dose of Disney characters, storytelling and transformative magic.

Short trails around Animal Kingdom's Discovery Island lead to quiet spots along the water, where a handful of benches make a great place to relax with a snack. Keep an eye out for animals such as tortoises and monkeys.

At the time of research, Animal Kingdom was about to open another area: the much-awaited **Pandora – The World of Avatar**. Its highlights will be Flight of Passage, where you get to soar on backs of the Mountain Banshees; the Na'vi River Journey, a boat ride through the bioluminescent rain forest; and Valley of Mo'ara, a walk-through extravaganza comprising floating mountains, Na'vi totems and a drum circle.

◉ Sights

Africa   AREA

(www.disneyworld.disney.go.com; Animal Kingdom; theme-park admission required; ⊘ 9am-6pm, hours vary; 🖥 Disney) Board a jeep and ride through the African Savannah on **Kilimanjaro Safaris**, pausing to look at zebras, lions, giraffes and more, all seemingly roaming free. This is one of the Animal Kingdom's most popular attractions, so come early or use your FastPass+.

The **Festival of the Lion King**, a Lion King–themed song and dance performance, earns rave reviews, but we were somewhat underwhelmed.

The **Gorilla Falls Exploration Trail** passes gorillas, hippos, a great bat display and a hive of naked mole rats – nothing more than you'd find in any zoo, but those mole rats sure are cute.

Asia   AREA

(www.disneyworld.disney.go.com; Animal Kingdom; theme-park admission required; ⊘ 9am-6pm, hours vary; 🖥 Disney) Home to two of Animal Kingdom's three most popular rides: **Expedition Everest**, a great roller coaster with a yeti twist, and **Kali River Rapids**, a water ride. Owls, peregrine falcons and many

INTERACTIVE DISNEY

Disney parks offer self-paced, treasure-hunt-styled experiences that attract fans of all ages.

Sorcerers of the Magic Kingdom (Magic Kingdom) Join Merlin in his efforts to find and defeat Disney villains. Key cards activate hidden game portals throughout Magic Kingdom and the spell cards work magic. Stop by the firehouse by the main gate on Main Street to sign up.

Pirates Adventure – Treasure of the Seven Seas (Magic Kingdom) Pick up a talisman at the Crow's Nest (Adventureland) and help Captain Jack collect the pirate gold.

Agent P's World Showcase Adventure (Epcot) Phineas and Ferb–themed game. Make the beer steins in Germany sing, see the soldiers dance and activate surprises from China to the UK.

Wilderness Explorers (Animal Kingdom) Pick up a Wilderness Explorers Handbook and follow the adventures of Russell and Dug the dog (from the movie *Up!*) through jungles, forests and woods while completing self-guided activities. Collect a badge as a reward. Grab the guide from Wilderness Explorer stops or from 'headquarters,' on the bridge between Discovery Island and the Oasis.

other birds dazzle audiences at **Flights of Wonder**. It's got some cheesy dialogue, but the animals are spectacular as they zoom around over your head on cue.

Maharajah Jungle Trek is a self-guided path past Bengal tigers, huge fruit bats and Komodo dragons.

Discovery Island AREA
(www.disneyworld.disney.go.com; Animal Kingdom; theme-park admission required; ☉9am-6pm, hours vary; 🖵Disney) The only attraction here is the *Bugs' Life*–themed **It's Tough to Be a Bug!**, a 4D movie that includes periods of darkness, dry ice and flashing lights. Though it's a lot of fun and very cute, it can terrify little ones – you will definitely hear children crying by the end.

Dinoland AREA
(www.disneyworld.disney.go.com; Animal Kingdom; theme-park admission required; ☉9am-6pm, hours vary; 🖵Disney) This bizarre dinosaur-themed section seems more like a tired carnival than Disney Magic, with garish plastic dinosaurs, midway games and 'Trilo-Bite' snacks. But little ones will like the kids' coaster **Primeval Whirl**, and **DINOSAUR** is a really fun jeep ride with a *Jurassic Park* twist.

Rafiki's Planet Watch ZOO
(www.disneyworld.disney.go.com; Animal Kingdom; theme-park admission required; ☉9am-6pm, hours vary; 🖫; 🖵Disney) Veterinarians care for sick and injured animals at **Conservation Station**. You can check out pet sheep and goats at **Affection Section**. On the **Habitat Habit!** trail check out the

adorable, fist-sized tamarin monkeys. But ultimately, the **Wildlife Express Train** you take to get here might just be the best part of this Disney enigma.

Oasis ZOO
(www.disneyworld.disney.go.com; Animal Kingdom; theme-park admission required; ☉9am-6pm, hours vary; 🖫; 🖵Disney) Oasis is the first themed section of Animal Kingdom. It has cool critters, including a giant anteater, but it's best to move along to other attractions and pause to enjoy the animals on your way out.

🛏 Sleeping

Along with Disney's value resorts, the hotels here are the most inconveniently located of all Disney hotels. They are the furthest from all the parks except Animal Kingdom and the only Disney transportation is by bus.

Disney's Coronado Springs Resort RESORT $$
(☏407-939-5277, 407-939-1000; www.disneyworld. disney.go.com; 1000 W Buena Vista Dr; r from $210; 🅿❄@🛜🏊; 🖵Disney) The Southwestern theme, evidenced in the warm pink-and-yellow guest rooms, the lights strung across the Pepper Market and the adobe-colored buildings, creates a low-key tone that sets this resort apart from other Disney hotels. Several pleasantly landscaped two-story buildings, some with their own private and quiet pools, sit along a central lake.

There's plenty of grass, and little beaches with hammocks. At the central pool, an open-air slide zooms down a Maya pyramid.

Suites and casitas sleep up to five, and the hotel is popular for conventions.

Disney's Animal Kingdom Lodge
RESORT $$$

(☎407-938-3000, 407-939-5277; www.disney world.disney.go.com; 2901 Osceola Blvd; r from $319; P ✳ @ 🛜 🛝; ☐ Disney) With an abutting 33-acre savannah parading a who's who of Noah's Ark past hotel windows and balconies, park rangers standing ready to answer questions about the wildlife, and African-inspired food being served at the recommended restaurants, this resort offers particularly fun and quirky theming.

Ask about storytelling and singing around the fire. If you want to see giraffes and ostriches out your room window, you'll have to reserve the more expensive savannah-view rooms, but anyone can enjoy the animals from the observation decks. Even if you're not staying here, swing by for a drink after an afternoon at Animal Kingdom.

✗ Eating

Plenty of quick counter-service joints disguised behind African names and offering nods to a somewhat tribal feel define eating options at Animal Kingdom.

Yak and Yeti
ASIAN $$

(☎407-939-3463, 407-824-9384; www.disney world.disney.go.com; Animal Kingdom; mains $15-29, theme-park admission required; ⊙11am-park closing; 🛜 ✏ 🛝; ☐ Disney) Sharing the name of Kathmandu's exclusive digs in the real Nepal, decorated with a vaguely Nepalese-infused decor, and serving pan-fried noodles, pot stickers, tempura, and icy Tsingtao, this recommended getaway at the base of Mt Everest transports you from Disney to the Himalayas. The food is surprisingly good and is one of the best bets for eating inside the park.

Flame Tree Barbecue
BARBECUE $$

(www.disneyworld.disney.go.com; Animal Kingdom; mains $11-20, theme-park admission required; ⊙11am-6pm; 🛜 🛝; ☐ Disney) Counter-service barbecue ribs and chicken, a favorite with in-the-know Disney fans.

🍺 Drinking & Nightlife

Dawa Bar
BAR

(www.disneyworld.disney.go.com; Animal Kingdom; theme-park admission required; ⊙11am-park closing; 🛜 🛝; ☐ Disney) The best place in Animal Kingdom for a cocktail. Sidle up to the flat-roofed bar, kind of like an African 'shebeen', and order a sugarcane mojito and rest those Disney-weary bones.

☆ Entertainment

★ Finding Nemo: the Musical
PERFORMING ARTS

(www.disneyworld.disney.go.com; Animal Kingdom; theme-park admission required; ⊙ several shows daily; 🛝; ☐ Disney) Arguably the best show at Walt Disney World® and a favorite of both kids and adults, this sophisticated musical theater performance features massive and elaborate puppets on stage and down the aisles, incredible set design and fantastic acting.

The music was composed by Robert Lopez and Kirsten Anderson-Lopez, who also wrote *Frozen*'s Academy Award–winning 'Let It Go', and the spectacular puppets were created by Michael Curry, the creative and artistic force behind the the puppets in Broadway's *The Lion King*.

Rivers of Light
SHOW

(www.disneyworld.disney.go.com; Animal Kingdom; ⊙7:15pm, 8:30pm, times vary) This sound-and-light show over water focuses on the theme of nature. It presents stunning effects, from fireflies flitting across the lake to 'spirit forms' of the world's animals, and is a fitting end to this little, tropical, ever so controlled and very animal sanitized 'paradise'. Reserve ahead with your Fastpass+.

ⓘ Getting There & Away

Disney buses stop at Animal Kingdom, but be warned that the ride here can be up to 45 minutes, maybe longer. There is parking just outside the park gates.

Hollywood Studios

The least charming of the Walt Disney World® theme parks, **Hollywood Studios** (☎407-939-5277; www.disneyworld.disney. go.com; 351 S Studio Dr, Walt Disney World®; $100-119, prices vary daily; ⊙9am-10pm, hours vary; ☐ Disney, 🛝 Disney) offers none of the nostalgic charm of Magic Kingdom, sophisticated delights of Epcot or kitschy fun of Animal Kingdom. It's meant to conjure the heydays of Hollywood, with a replica of Graumann's Chinese Theatre (the main focal icon) and Hollywood Brown Derby, but most of the attractions reflect unabashed 21st-century energy. Young future Jedi line up to prepare for *Star Wars* Jedi

ORLANDO & WALT DISNEY WORLD® WALT DISNEY WORLD®

Training and souvenirs from *Frozen* line store shelves.

Make a right onto Sunset Blvd to hit the roller coasters, *Beauty and the Beast* show and Fantasmic (a nighttime spectacular).

You might not need a whole day here – come first thing in the morning, linger for lunch then take off to relax by the pool or, if you have a Park Hopper ticket, stroll or catch a boat over to Epcot's World Showcase for the afternoon.

◉ Sights

Jedi Training: Trials of the Temple
MARTIAL ARTS

(www.disneyworld.disney.go.com; Hollywood Studios; theme-park admission required; ☺ from 9am, up to 15 times a day) A group of children don brown robes, pledge the sacred Jedi oath and grab a light saber for on-stage training by a Jedi Master. But it's first-come, first-served, so get to Hollywood Studios when gates open and line up at the Indiana Adventure Outpost, near the 50's Prime Time Café, to sign up for one of the many classes held throughout the day. For children aged four to 12.

Sunset Boulevard
AREA

(www.disneyworld.disney.go.com; Hollywood Studios; theme-park admission required; ☺ Hollywood Studios hours; 📶; 📺 Disney, 🎬 Disney) The simple and sweet outdoor theater performance of **Beauty and the Beast – Live on Stage** follows the storyline, incorporates the classic songs, and doesn't fall back on any special effects or crazy shenanigans. It's a rock-solid classic hit with the Disney-princess-loving crowd. For thrills and chills rather than frills, two of Disney's most talked about rides are in Sunset Blvd: The **Twilight Zone Tower of Terror** and **Rock 'n Roller Coaster Starring Aerosmith**.

Hollywood Boulevard & Echo Lake
AREA

(www.disneyworld.disney.go.com; Hollywood Studios; theme-park admission required; ☺ Hollywood Studios hours; 📶; 📺 Disney, 🎬 Disney) This is where you'll find the *Star Wars*–themed Star Tours (FastPass+), one of Disney's best 3D-simulated experiences, the over-the-top stunt show **Indiana Jones Epic Stunt Spectacular** (Fastpass+), held in a huge outdoor theater, and **Frozen's For the First Time in Forever Sing-Along**.

Star Tours: The Adventure Continues
RIDE

(www.disneyworld.disney.go.com; Hollywood Studios; theme-park admission required; ☺ Hollywood Studios hours; 📶; 📺 Disney, 🎬 Disney) Board a Star Speeder 1000 and blast into the galaxy at this 3D *Star Wars*–themed simulation ride.

Pixar Place & Mickey Avenue
AREA

(www.disneyworld.disney.go.com; Hollywood Studios; theme-park admission required; ☺ Hollywood Studios hours; 📶; 📺 Disney, 🎬 Disney) Lines are always long at **Toy Story Mania!** (FastPass+), where folks don 3D glasses and shoot their way through games trying to score points.

🎆 Festivals & Events

Star Wars: A Galactic Spectacular
FIREWORKS

(https://disneyworld.disney.go.com/entertainment/hollywood-studios/star-wars-galactic-spectacular/; Hollywood Studios; ☺ nightly, hours vary) Absolutely zapping and bursting with pyrotechnics, special effects and more lasers than a *Star Wars* movie set, this display emulates a space battle in the stars, with the, you guessed it, *Star Wars* musical soundtrack. Of course, you wouldn't feel the Force without the Jedi, Ewoks, Jawas and other characters.

Fantasmic
LIGHT SHOW

(☎ 407-939-5277; www.disneyworld.disney.go.com; Hollywood Studios; theme-park admission required; ☺ nightly; 📶; 📺 Disney, 🎬 Disney) Dramatic and overhyped water, music and light show centers on a vague, rather disconnected and confusing plot in which Mickey Mouse proves victorious over a cast of Disney villains. All the characters sail by on Steamboat Willie (in case the little ones didn't get a chance to see their favorite character).

Seating for the 25-minute show begins 90 minutes in advance, and even though the outdoor amphitheater seats more than 6000 people, it's always crowded.

🍴 Eating

Hollywood Studios offers some of the most novel eating experiences. From a meal at a drive-in in your very own car, to enjoying hospitality in a 1950s kitchen, there's much themed fun to be had as you chomp down everything from a burger to upscale tapas.

★ Sci-Fi Dine-In Theater
AMERICAN $$

(☑ 407-939-3463; www.disneyworld.disney.go.
com; Hollywood Studios; mains $15-24, theme-park
admission required; ☉ 11am-8:30pm; 🛜 ♿; 🚊 Dis-
ney, 🚢 Disney) Burgers, ribs and glow-in-the-
dark drinks served drive-in style. Climb into
your convertible Cadillac, order from the car
hop, sip on a Lunar Landing and sit back
for animations, a silly horror movie or sci-fi
flick (on loop for 47 minutes). This is Disney
theming at its best.

There are a handful of normal tables on
the side, so if you want your table in a car,
request one up to six months in advance.

★ 50's Prime Time Café
AMERICAN $$

(☑ 407-939-3463; www.disneyworld.disney.go.
com; Hollywood Studios; mains $17-23, theme-park
admission required; ☉ 11am-park closing; 🛜 ♿;
🚊 Disney, 🚢 Disney) Step into a quintessential 1950s home with TVs, linoleum floors,
some of the funkiest of funky retro furniture
around and, of course, home-cooked meals,
including Grandma's Chicken-Pot-Pie, Aunt
Liz's Golden Fried Chicken and Mom's
Old-Fashioned Pot Roast, served up on a
Formica tabletop.

Waitresses in pink plaid and white aprons
banter playfully and admonish those diners
who don't finish their meals, putting their
elbows on the table with a sassy 'shame,
shame, shame.' Such, such fun.

Hollywood Brown Derby Lounge
TAPAS $$

(☑ 407-939-3463; www.disneyworld.disney.go.
com; Hollywood Studios; tapas $8-18; ☉ 11am-
park closing; 🛜 ♿; 🚊 Disney, 🚢 Disney) Upscale,
small-bite menu with lump-crab cocktail,
mussels and beef sliders, and an excellent
selection of cocktails. It's generally pret-
ty easy to snag a table at the bistro-style
sidewalk patio, a great place to relax and
people-watch over a flight of scotch, cham-
pagne, martinis or margaritas, or order a
drink to go. Not exactly fast food, but reser-
vations are not accepted.

Hollywood Brown Derby
AMERICAN $$$

(☑ 407-939-3463; www.disneyworld.disney.go.
com; Hollywood Studios; mains $19-49, theme-park
admission required; ☉ 11:30am-park closing; 🛜 ♿;
🚊 Disney, 🚢 Disney) Semi-upscale surround-
ings modeled after the LA original, with an
odd selection of gourmet eats ranging from
a vegetarian pho (noodle soup) to charred
fillet of beef and, of course, that Derby classic, the Cobb salad. This is heavy fare, not
the place for a quick light lunch.

❶ Getting There & Away

A paved waterfront walkway and a boat shuttle
connect Hollywood Studios, Disney's Board-
Walk, Disney Epcot resorts (BoardWalk Inn,
Yacht & Beach Clubs, Swan & Dolphin) and
Epcot. It is about a 25-minute walk from Epcot
to Hollywood Studios and the path is pleasant.
Look for the sign near Jellyrolls and the Atlantic
Dance Hall.

Disney buses provide transportation to other
parks, hotels and the Transportation & Ticket
Center, sometimes requiring a transfer.

You cannot take the monorail to Epcot and
then walk or take a boat to Hollywood Studios
unless you have a Park Hopper ticket. The
monorail is at Epcot's front entrance, and access to Hollywood Studios is from Epcot's back
entrance.

Typhoon Lagoon & Blizzard Beach

In addition to the four theme parks, Disney
boasts two distinctly themed water parks.
Of the two, Blizzard Beach boasts the better
thrills and speed, but Typhoon Lagoon has
the far superior wave pool, a fantastic lazy
river and tots' play area and plenty of room
to splash on the beach.

Be prepared to spend upwards of 30 minutes in line for a ride that's over in less than
a minute, and take those wait times seriously – if it says the wait is 60 minutes, it's 60
minutes. Yes, 60 minutes for *one* slide. Both
parks have fast-food restaurants and an outdoor pool bar.

Disney's water-park hours vary seasonally
and by the day, but are generally open from
10am to 5pm and from 9am to 10pm in the
summer. From late October through March
one water park is closed for refurbishment.

◉ Sights

Typhoon Lagoon
AMUSEMENT PARK

(☑ 407-939-5277, 407-560-4120; www.disney
world.disney.go.com; 1145 Buena Vista Dr, Walt Disney World®; adult/child $53/45, prices vary daily;
☉ hours vary; 🚊 Disney) An abundance of palm
trees, a zero-entry pool with a white sandy
beach, high-speed slides and the best wave
pool in Orlando make this one of the most
beautiful water parks in Florida. Little ones
will love floating along **Castaway Creek**
and splashing at **Ketchakiddee Creek**.

Included in admission is snorkeling equipment for small group swims with the tropical
fish, stingrays, and leopard and bonnethead

sharks in the 68°F (20°C) waters of **Shark Reef**.

Blizzard Beach
AMUSEMENT PARK

(☑ 407-939-5277, 407-560-3400; www.disney world.disney.go.com; 1534 Blizzard Beach Dr, Walt Disney World®; adult/child $53/45, incl in Water Park Fun & More with Magic Your Way theme park ticket; ◷ hours vary; ◙ Disney) The newer of Disney's two water parks, themed as a melted Swiss ski resort complete with a ski lift, Blizzard Beach is the 1980s Vegas Strip hotel to Typhoon Lagoon's Bellagio. At its center sits **Mt Gushmore**, from which water slides burst forth.

🎓 Courses

Typhoon Lagoon Surf Lessons
SURFING

(☑ 407-939-7529; www.disneyworld.disney.go. com; 1145 Buena Vista Dr, Typhoon Lagoon; $165; ◷ times vary; ◙ Disney) No, Orlando is not on the ocean, but that doesn't stop Disney. Typhoon Lagoon gives surf lessons before the water park opens to the public. Price includes 30 minutes on land and two hours in the water, and nonpaying family and friends are welcome to come and watch. If you stick around after the park opens, you must purchase admission tickets.

ℹ️ Information

Swimsuits with buckles or metal parts aren't allowed on most of the rides. Hours vary by day and by season; call the individual parks for current hours. From October through March, only one Disney water park is open at a time. You can buy individual park tickets; Park Hopper Plus tickets include entrance to both the water parks.

ℹ️ Getting There & Away

Disney buses stop at both Typhoon Lagoon and Blizzard Beach, and there is complimentary self-parking at both parks.

Disney's BoardWalk

Far less harried and crowded than Disney Springs, the very small **Disney's BoardWalk** (☑ 407-939-5277; www.disneyworld.disney.go.com; 2101 Epcot Resorts Blvd, Walt Disney World®; ◙ Disney, ◙ Disney) area across from Epcot and along Crescent Lake echoes waterfront boardwalks of turn-of-the-century New England seaside resorts. On Thursday to Saturday evenings magicians, jugglers and musicians give a festive vibe, and there are a handful of good restaurants and bars. Pick up a doughnut or cute li'l Mickey Mouse cakes at the bakery, and toot around on a surrey-with-the-fringe-on-top bike.

🛏️ Sleeping & Eating

★ Disney's BoardWalk Inn
RESORT $$$

(☑ 407-939-5277, 407-939-6200; www.disney world.disney.go.com; 2101 Epcot Resorts Blvd; r from $400; P ✱ @ 🛜 🏊; ◙ Disney, ◙ Disney) This resort embodies the seaside charm of the 1930s Atlantic City Boardwalk in its heyday, with a waterfront the color of saltwater taffy, tandem bicycles with candy-striped awnings, and a splintery boardwalk. The lovely lobby features sea-green walls, hardwood floors and vintage seating areas. Elegant rooms have a terrace or balcony.

The resort is divided into two sections, the Inn and the Villas; the Inn, with cute picket-fenced suites, quiet pools and plenty of grass, is far nicer and subdued. Accommodations range from rooms sleeping up to five to two-bedroom cottages.

Flying Fish
SEAFOOD $$$

(☑ 407-939-2359, 407-939-3463; www.disney world.disney.go.com; Disney's BoardWalk; mains $37-59; ◷ 5-9:30pm; 🅿️ 🚲; ◙ Disney) Flying Fish, specializing in complicated and innovative seafood dishes, consistently ranks as one of the best upscale dining spots at Disney. It's a contemporary, slick spot with a modern ocean theme (note the bubble chandeliers). Be sure to reserve ahead. Kids' meals are significantly cheaper (from $13 to $17).

New Zealand salmon ($39) and plancha-seared Hokkaido scallops ($43) are two of the most popular dishes.

🍸 Drinking & Nightlife

★ Belle Vue Room
BAR

(☑ 407-939-6200; www.disneyworld.disney.go. com; 2101 Epcot Resorts Blvd, Disney's Board-Walk Inn; ◷ 6:30-11am & 5pm-midnight; ◙ Disney, ◙ Disney) On the 2nd floor of Disney's BoardWalk Inn, this is an excellent place for a quiet drink. It's more like a sitting room: you can relax and play a board game, listen to classic radio shows such as *Lone Ranger,* or simply take your drink to a rocking chair on the balcony and watch the comings and goings along Disney's Boardwalk.

Atlantic Dance Hall
CLUB

(www.disneyworld.disney.go.com; Disney's Board-Walk; ◷ 9pm-2am, over 21yr only) Blaring Top

40 tunes, dancing and a massive screen with music videos by request. If you really want to shake your booty, this is your only Disney option, though pick your time as it can be relatively empty.

Big River Grille & Brewing Works BREWERY
(✓407-560-0253; www.disneyworld.disney.go.com; Disney's BoardWalk; ⊙11am-11pm) Open-air microbrewery with unique brews sold only on location, plus soups and pastas. Lovely outdoor seating along the water.

Jellyrolls BAR
(✓407-560-8770; www.disneyworld.disney.go.com; Disney's BoardWalk; cover $12; ⊙7pm-2am) Comedians on dueling pianos encourage the audience to partake in all kinds of musical silliness and singalongs.

ESPN Club SPORTS BAR
(✓407-939-5100; www.disneyworld.disney.go.com; Disney's BoardWalk; ⊙11am-midnight) So many TVs screening the hottest games that even in the bathroom you won't miss a single play.

ⓘ Information

Public areas at Disney's BoardWalk are open from 6:30am to 2am.

ⓘ Getting There & Away

A well-lit paved walking path (unsigned) and small boats connect Disney's BoardWalk to Epcot and Hollywood Studios, as well as to Disney Epcot resorts (BoardWalk Inn, Yacht & Beach Clubs and Swan & Dolphin). Disney buses stop at the BoardWalk Resort (at the entrance to the BoardWalk) and there's also parking here – be sure to say you're visiting the BoardWalk and you won't be charged.

Disney Springs

Stretching along the shore of Lake Buena Vista, the **Disney Springs** (✓407-939-6244; www.disneyworld.disney.go.com; 1490 E Buena Vista Dr, Walt Disney World®; ⊙8:30am-2am; 🚌Disney, 🚤Disney, 🚌Lynx 50) smart, outdoor pedestrian mall lures tourists with a huge number of restaurants, bars, music venues and shops. This is also where you'll find the stage show Cirque du Soleil La Nouba (p305), and the largest Disney store in the world. There's a Disney-styled party atmosphere, particularly on the weekends, with street performers dancing on stilts, parents pushing strollers loaded with Disney shopping bags and hundreds upon hundreds of

---

ⓘ STAYING ON BAY LAKE

The number-one advantage to staying at one of the resorts on Bay Lake is that they are one easy monorail or boat ride from Magic Kingdom – they're the only hotels at Walt Disney World® where you can get to classic Disney with no need for transfers. This may not sound like much, but when you're slogging home with three exhausted children or are desperate for a quick afternoon dip in the pool, it makes a world of difference. You can also take the monorail to Epcot, though you have to transfer at the Transportation & Ticket Center, and there are nonstop buses to Animal Kingdom and Hollywood Studios.

---

people enjoying the waterside drinking and excellent cuisine. Since the area's revamp a couple of years ago, it's booming and has lured some of Orlando's best eateries to join the scene, some of which are headed by well-known chefs.

Not yet opened at the time of research (but also worth looking out for) are **Polite Pig** (run by the same couple who run Ravenous Pig (p271) in Winter Park) and **Wine Bar George**.

◉ Sights

DisneyQuest Indoor Interactive Theme Park AMUSEMENT PARK
(✓407-828-3800; www.disneyworld.disney.go.com; 1620 East Buena Vista Dr, Disney Springs; ⊙noon-9pm; 👪; 🚌Disney, 🚤Disney, 🚌Lynx 50) With five dizzying floors of exhibits designed to indulge video-game addicts, this 'interactive theme park' makes the perfect place to while away a rainy or hot afternoon. Virtual-reality attractions include a trip on Aladdin's magic carpet over Agrabah and a float down a river into the Mesozoic Age. You can design and 'ride' your own roller coaster, or simply lose yourself for hours in old-school video games and pinball machines.

Amphicar Tours BOATING
(✓407-939-2628; www.theboathouseorlando.com; 1620 East Buena Vista Dr, Disney Springs; up to 3 people 25min $125; ⊙10am-10pm; 🚌Disney, 🚤Disney, 🚌Lynx 50) Go for a spin in these extraordinary, genuine German vintage amphicars. They drive on land and then enter the water

for a tour of waterside Disney Springs. Pricey, but definitely a once-in-a-lifetime experience. The mooring is next to the Boathouse.

Characters in Flight   RIDE

(☑ 407-939-7529; www.disneyworld.disney.go.com; 1620 East Buena Vista Dr, Disney Springs; adult/child $18/15; ⊘ 8:30am-midnight; ▭ Disney, ▣ Disney, ▣ Lynx 50) Guests climb onboard the basket of this massive tethered gas balloon and ascend 400ft into the air for 360-degree views. Between 8:30am and 10am they offer a special for $10 per person.

🛏 Sleeping & Eating

Disney Springs is becoming a magnet for some well-known chefs-about-town so the quality of nosh is high and refreshingly unthemed. The setting, over the lake and canals, is pretty in the contrived Disney kind of way. There's also plenty of casual options and takeouts to appeal to the entire range of consumer.

There are no hotels at Disney Springs, though several are within a few miles.

Earl of Sandwich   SANDWICHES $

(www.disneyworld.disney.go.com; 1620 East Buena Vista Dr, Disney Springs; sandwiches $5-8; ⊘ 8:30am-11pm; P 🛜 🛗; ▭ Disney, ▣ Disney, ▣ Lynx 50) Surprisingly good toasted sandwiches ranging from basic to exotic. One of

the most satisfying lunches at Disney, with plenty of bang for your buck; but in the end, it's a fast-food sandwich chain.

Ghiradelli Soda Fountain & Chocolate Shop   ICE CREAM $

(www.disneyworld.disney.go.com; 1620 East Buena Vista Dr, Disney Springs; ice cream $3-8; ⊘ 9:30am-11:30pm Sun-Thu, 9:30am-midnight Fri & Sat; P 🛜 🛗; ▭ Disney, ▣ Disney, ▣ Lynx 50) Decadent ice-cream concoctions involving entire chocolate bars blended into milkshakes.

★ Frontera Cocina   MEXICAN $$

(☑ 407-560-9197; www.fronteracocina.com; 1620 East Buena Vista Dr, Disney Springs; mains $22-34; ⊘ 11am-10pm Sun-Wed, 11am-10.45pm Thu-Mon; ▭ Disney, ▣ Disney, ▣ Lynx 50) A smart, trendy version of modern Mexico where, thanks to Chef Rick Bayless, corn, chili and salsa are whipped up into contemporary tastes in a delightfully light, bright and bustling environment. A pleasant change from some southern flavors. Fun margarita-filled happy hours, too.

Paradiso 37   SOUTH AMERICAN $$

(☑ 407-934-3700; www.paradiso37.com; 1620 East Buena Vista Dr, Disney Springs; mains $17-34; ⊘ 11am-11pm Sun-Thu, 11am-midnight Fri & Sat; P 🛜 🛗; ▭ Disney, ▣ Disney, ▣ Lynx 50) With an impressive cocktail list and a menu representing 37 countries of North, South and

---

DISNEY PARADES, FIREWORKS & LIGHT SHOWS

It takes a little bit of planning to coordinate your schedule to hit Disney's parades and nighttime spectaculars. Note that times vary according to day and season. In addition to the following cornerstones, check www.disneyworld.disney.go.com for holiday celebrations and specialty parties.

Festival of Fantasy (p289) Elaborate floats and dancing characters, including Dumbo, Peter Pan and Sleeping Beauty.

IllumiNations: Reflections of Earth (p294) This fiery narrative, with a light show and fireworks, centers around a massive globe illuminated with LED lights in the center of Epcot's World Showcase Lagoon.

Happily Ever After This fireworks and light-show extravaganza (often promoted as the 'Nighttime Spectacular') was about to be launched with a bang at the time of research.

Fantasmic (p300) Dramatic and overhyped water, music and light show centers on a vague, rather disconnected and confusing plot in which Mickey Mouse proves victorious over a cast of Disney villains. Seating for the 25-minute show begins 90 minutes in advance, and even though the outdoor amphitheater seats more than 6000 people, it's always crowded.

Star Wars: A Galactic Spectacular A firework and light show topped off with projected clips of the Star Wars on the Chinese Theatre.

Rivers of Light Animal Kingdom's recently introduced light show that features its beautiful baobab tree, the 'tree of life'.

Central America (or so they claim), this contemporary waterfront spot is one of Disney Spring's best bets.

Though Paradiso 37 is family-friendly, with an excellent 'little tykes' menu, the mood becomes decidedly barlike as the night progresses, and there's live music. Call directly for reservations – it often has more flexibility and openings than Disney Dining, and try for a seat on the back patio.

Chef Art Smith's Homecoming
AMERICAN $$

(☑407-560-0100; www.disneyworld.disney.go.com; Disney Springs; mains $22-31; ⊙11am-11pm; ☐Disney, ☀Disney, ☐Lynx 50) Chef Art Smith is a local celebrity chef, so local fans love his Floridian farm-to-fork, old-style-meets-modern flavors. We're talkin' fried chicken, shrimp and grits, and pork barbecue.

T-Rex Cafe
AMERICAN $$

(☑407-828-8739; www.disneyworld.disney.go.com; 1620 East Buena Vista Dr, Disney Springs; mains $12-26; ⊙11am-11pm Sun-Thu, to midnight Fri & Sat; P☎♿; ☐Disney, ☀Disney, ☐Lynx 50) Over-the-top multisensory overload, with massive autotronic dinosaurs, volcanoes erupting, light shows and meteor showers every 15 minutes. The menu features Woolly Mammoth Chicken, Caveman Punch and Chocolate Extinction – you get the idea. Kids will love it and the food is better than you might expect.

★Paddlefish
INTERNATIONAL $$$

(www.disneyworld.disney.go.com; 1620 East Buena Vista Dr, Disney Springs; ⊙11:30am-11pm; ☐Disney, ☀Disney, ☐Lynx 50) This paddle steamer has had an entire revamp and reopened in February 2016. It's smart, contemporary and chic. Its lovely dining areas are ingeniously incorporated into different parts of the boat, so you have a choice of ambience: over water, at the stern or snuggled in elsewhere. It's the place to go for a leisurely and sophisticated meal.

Seafood is on the menu here; on Sundays they do an excellent brunch (mains $16 to $23). Worth reserving ahead.

🍸 Drinking & Nightlife

★ Jock Lindsay's
BAR

(www.disneyworld.disney.go.com; 1620 East Buena Vista Dr, Disney Springs; ⊙11:30-midnight; ☐Disney, ☀Disney, ☐Lynx 50) According to, er...'old' Disney folklore, Jock (the pilot in *Raiders of the Lost Ark*) 'arrived here in 1938 while chasing down a mythology-based tip in central

Florida.' He liked the natural springs and lush terrain, and so bought some land. His hangar (his home base) became popular for world travelers and locals...and here you now are.

Yes, it's heavily themed and that's the idea. But the alcohol and fun is very real.

Boathouse
BAR

(☑407-939-2628; www.theboathouseorlando.com; 1620 East Buena Vista Dr, Disney Springs; ⊙11-1.30am) A series of three bars are spread over this smart waterfront place, with classic craft cocktails and a good wine list (that showcases American wines). Nightly music entertains you well into the morning. After a drink or three, head off for a spin and a float in a genuine amphicar (p303).

Raglan Road
PUB

(☑407-938-0300; www.raglanroad.com; 1620 East Buena Vista Dr, Disney Springs; ⊙10-2am; ☎♿; ☐Disney, ☀Disney) Traditional Irish ditties, Irish dancing, solid tasty fare, cozy pub decor and beer flights with Guinness, Harp, Smithwicks and Kilkenny complete the leprechaun mood.

☆ Entertainment

★Cirque du Soleil La Nouba
PERFORMING ARTS

(☑407-939-7328, 407-939-7600; www.cirquedusoleil.com; 1478 Buena Vista Dr, Disney Springs; adult $59-139, child $48-115; ⊙6pm & 9pm Tue-Sat; ☐Disney, ☀Disney, ☐Lynx 50) Disney's best live show features mind-boggling acrobatic feats expertly fused to light, stage and costume design to create a cohesive artistic vision. And of course, there's a silly Disney twist involving a princess and a frog. This is a small horseshoe theater, with roughly 20 rows from the stage to the top, and no balcony.

Disney built the theater specifically to house La Nouba – there are no bad seats. See website for black-out dates.

AMC Downtown Disney 24 – Dine-In Theatres
CINEMA

(☑888-262-4386; www.amctheatres.com/dinein; 1500 E Buena Vista Dr, Disney Springs; tickets $7-16; ♿) Several screens offer Fork and Screen Theater, where you can order meals and have them delivered to your seat, and the bar sells beer, wine and cocktails to take into the flick.

House of Blues
LIVE MUSIC

(☑407-934-2583; www.houseofblues.com; 1490 Buena Vista Dr, Disney Springs; ⊙10am-11pm

Mon-Thu, to midnight Fri & Sat, 10:30am-11pm Sun; 🔊 ♿; 🚇 Disney, 🚌 Disney, 🚌 Lynx 50) Top acts visit this national chain serving Southern cooking and blues. It's particularly popular for the Sunday Gospel Brunch buffet.

🛍 Shopping

Lego Imagination Center   TOYS
(📞 407-828-0065; www.disneyworld.disney. go.com; 1672 Buena Vista Dr, Disney Springs; ⊙ 9am-11pm; 🚇 Disney, 🚌 Disney, 🚌 Lynx 50) Life-size Lego creations, tables to create your own masterpieces and a wall of individually priced Lego pieces.

Once Upon a Toy   TOYS
(📞 407-824-4321; www.disneyworld.disney.go.com; 1375 Buena Vista Dr, Disney Springs; ⊙ 10am-11:30pm; 🚇 Disney, 🚌 Disney, 🚌 Lynx 50) Design a personalized My Little Pony, build your own light saber and create your own tiara at one of the best toy stores anywhere. You'll find old-school classics such as Mr Potato Head and Lincoln Logs, board games, action figures, stuffed animals and more.

World of Disney   GIFTS & SOUVENIRS
(📞 407-939-6224; www.disneyworld.disney.go.com; Disney Springs; ⊙ 9am-11pm; 🚇 Disney, 🚌 Disney, 🚌 Lynx 50) Room after room of Disney everything at this Disney mega-super-duper store (the country's largest).

ℹ Information

Public areas at Disney Springs are open from 10am to midnight.

ℹ Getting There & Away

Disney Springs is accessible by water taxi from Disney Springs resorts and by bus from everywhere else. There is complimentary self parking, but no direct Disney transportation to any of the theme parks. Lynx bus 50 services Disney Springs from downtown Orlando and SeaWorld.

ℹ Getting Around

You can walk from one end of Disney Springs to the other or catch a boat shuttle.

UNIVERSAL ORLANDO RESORT

Pedestrian-friendly **Universal Orlando Resort** (Map p254; 📞 407-363-8000; www. universalorlando.com; 1000 Universal Studios Plaza; single park adult 1/2 days $105/185, child $100/175, both parks adult/child $155/150; ⊙ daily, hours vary; 🚌 Lynx 21, 37 & 40, 🚌 Universal) has got spunk, spirit and attitude. With fantastic rides, excellent children's attractions and entertaining shows, it's comparable to Walt Disney World®. But Universal does everything just a bit smarter, funnier, and more smoothly, as well as being smaller and easier to navigate. Universal offers pure, unabashed, adrenaline-pumped, full-speed-ahead fun for the entire family.

The Universal Orlando Resort consists of two (three by the time you read this) theme parks – Islands of Adventure, with the bulk of the thrill rides, and Universal Studios, with movie-based attractions and shows (including the Wizarding World of Harry Potter). Volcano Bay opened in 2017 as a water park of thrills and splashes and state-of-the-art rides through a 200ft volcano.

Universal's dining/entertainment district is **CityWalk** (Map p254; 📞 407-363-8000; www. citywalk.com; 6000 Universal Studios Blvd, Universal Orlando Resort; ⊙ 7am-2am, hours vary; 🚌 Lynx 21, 37 or 40, 🚌 Universal) and it has five resort hotels (a sixth, Universal's Aventura Hotel, will open in 2018). Water taxis and pleasant walking paths connect the entire resort.

◉ Sights

◉ Islands of Adventure

Islands of Adventure (Map p254; 📞 407-363-8000; www.universalorlando.com; 6000 Universal Blvd, Universal Orlando Resort; adult 1/2 days $105/185, child $100/175; ⊙ from 9am (closing hours vary); 🚌 Lynx 21, 37 or 40, 🚌 Universal) is just plain fun. Scream-it-from-the-rooftops, no-holds-barred, laugh-out-loud kind of fun. Superheroes zoom by on motorcycles, roller coasters whiz overhead and plenty of rides will get you soaked. The park is divided into distinct areas, including the dinosaur-themed Jurassic Park and cartoon-heavy Toon Island, each with rides, play areas and dining. Harry Potter fans please note: Harry Potter attractions are split between Wizarding World of Harry Potter – Hogsmeade (p312), at Islands of Adventure, and Wizarding World of Harry Potter – Diagon Alley (p312), at Universal Studios. The Hogwart's Express train links the two parks.

Skull Island Reign of Kong   RIDE
(Map p254; www.universalorlando.com; Islands of Adventure; theme-park admission required;

9am-6pm, hours vary) Head off on one of the park's newest rides – on a 3D simulated, 1930s-style, volunteer expedition on 'off-road' terrain. Witness natives and prehistoric predators and fight to survive. Enter Kong, the colossal ape. Friend or foe? (We won't spoil this one.) Suffice to say, not for littlies.

Seuss Landing
RIDE

(Map p254; www.universalorlando.com; Islands of Adventure; theme-park admission required; 9am-6pm, hours vary; ; Lynx 21, 37 or 40) Anyone who has fallen asleep to the reading of *Green Eggs and Ham* or learned to read with Sam I Am knows the world of Dr Seuss: the fanciful creatures, the lyrical names, the rhyming stories. Here, realized in magnificently designed three-dimensional form, is Dr Seuss' imagination. The Lorax guards his truffula trees; Thing One and Thing Two make trouble; and creatures from all kinds of Seuss favorites adorn the shops and the rides.

Drink moose juice or goose juice; eat green eggs and ham; and peruse shelves of Dr Seuss books before riding through The Cat in the Hat or around and around on an elephant-bird from *Horton Hears a Who*. Seuss Landing is one of the best places for little ones in all of Orlando's theme parks, bringing the spirit and energy of Dr Seuss' vision to life. So come on in, walk into his world and take a spin on a fish.

Jurassic Park
RIDE

(Map p254; www.universalorlando.com; Islands of Adventure; theme-park admission required; 9am-6pm, hours vary; ; Lynx 21, 37 or 40) Oddly quiet, with no screams or loud music and no neon colors or hawking vendors, this oasis of palm trees, greenery and ferns offers a handful of attractions with a prehistoric twist. **Jurassic Park River Adventure** (Express Pass) floats you past friendly vegetarian dinosaurs, and all seems well and good until...things go wrong and those grass-munchin' cuties are replaced with the stuff of nightmares.

To escape the looming teeth of the giant T Rex, you plunge 85ft to the water below. Little children might be terrified by the creatures, the dark and the plunge, but if yours are tough as nails they'll love it. At **Pterandoon Flyers**, kids fly over the lush landscape and robotic dinosaurs of Jurassic Park. Note that you must be between 36in and 56in tall to fly, and adults can't fly

without a kid (note: it sways quite severely; you don't just 'float' along). Waits can be upwards of an hour for the 80-second ride and there's no Express Pass.

Lost Continent
AREA

(Map p254; www.universalorlando.com; Islands of Adventure; theme-park admission required; 9am-6pm, hours vary; ; Lynx 21, 37 or 40) Magic and myth from across the seas and the pages of fantasy books inspire this mystical corner of the park. Here you'll find dragons and unicorns, psychic readings and fortune-tellers. And don't be startled if that fountain talks to you as you walk past. The **Mystic Fountain** banters sassily, soaking children with its waterspouts when they least expect it and engaging them in silly conversation.

At the swashbuckling **Eighth Voyage of Sinbad Stunt Show** (Express Pass), Sinbad and his sidekick Kabob must rescue Princess Amoura from the terrible Miseria and, of course, Sinbad has to tumble and jump around to do it. Or head into the ancient Temple of Poseidon in **Poseidon's Fury**, with an archaeologist who leads you deep into the temple... until you're 'trapped' in a massive battle. Think lasers, water, fireballs.

Toon Lagoon
RIDE

(Map p254; www.universalorlando.com; Islands of Adventure; theme-park admission required; 9am-6pm, hours vary; ; Lynx 21, 37 or 40) Island of Adventure's sparkly, lighthearted cartoon-themed Toon Lagoon transports visitors to the days when lazy weekends included nothing more than mornings watching Popeye and afternoons playing in the sprinkler. This is where you'll find most of Universal's water attractions, including **Popeye and Bluto's Bilge-Rat Barges** (Express Pass), a favorite that's short on thrills but high on silly soaking fun; and **Dudley Do-Right's Ripsaw Falls** (Express Pass), a classic with a short but steep fall.

Be warned that you will get drenched, so protect phones and cameras, wear water-friendly shoes, and bring a change of clothes. If you forget, there are of course plenty of shops that sell towels, flip-flops and clothes.

Marvel Super Hero Island
RIDE

(Map p254; www.universalorlando.com; Islands of Adventure; theme-park admission required; 9am-6pm, hours vary; ; Lynx 21, 37 or 40) Bright, loud and fast moving, Marvel Super Hero Island is sensory overload and a thrill-lover's paradise. Don't miss the

BEST OF UNIVERSAL ORLANDO RESORT

Universal and its top-notch ride engineers have designed some of the most incredible simulated rides you'll see anywhere. They are constantly updating and rethinking its attractions, pushing the limits of ride engineering and incorporating new movies and shows into its repertoire.

On top of that, Universal's Express Pass system almost eliminates line anxiety on all but a few rides, and, if you're OK riding without your friends and family, many rides offer single-rider lines that are usually much shorter than the standard line – always ask.

Universal Studios

➜ The Simpsons Ride (p310)

➜ Hollywood Rip Ride Rockit

➜ Revenge of the Mummy

➜ Men in Black Alien Attack

➜ Harry Potter and the Escape from Gringotts (p312)

➜ Despicable Me: Minion Mayhem

➜ Transformers: The Ride 3-D

Islands of Adventure

➜ Harry Potter and the Forbidden Journey (p312)

➜ Incredible Hulk Coaster (p307)

➜ Amazing Adventures of Spider-Man (p307)

➜ Dragon Challenge (p312)

➜ Dudley Do-Right's Ripsaw Falls (p307)

motion simulator **Amazing Adventures of Spider-Man** (Express Pass recommended), where super-villains rendered in incredible 3D are on the loose, jumping on your car and chasing you around the streets of New York City, and the wild and crazy **Incredible Hulk Coaster** (Express Pass).

At **Dr Doom's Fearfall** (Express Pass), you rocket 150ft up in the air and free-fall down. Comic-book characters patrol this area, so keep an eye out for your favorites and check your map for scheduled meet-and-greet times.

⊙ Universal Studios

Divided geographically by film-inspired and region-specific architecture and ambience, and themed as a Hollywood backlot, **Universal Studios** (Map p254; ☑ 407-363-8000; www. universalorlando.com; 1000 Universal Studios Plaza, Universal Orlando Resort; adult 1/2 days $105/185, child $100/175; ⊙ from 9am (closing hours vary); ⊡ Lynx 21, 37 or 40, ⊠ Universal) has shows and magnificently designed, simulation-heavy rides dedicated to silver-screen and TV icons. Drink Duff beer, a Homer favorite, in

Springville; ride the Hogwarts Express into Diagon Alley; and challenge the host of *The Tonight Show* to a scavenger hunt. And if you're looking for thrills, Hollywood Rip Ride Rockit and Revenge of the Mummy are two of Orlando's best coasters.

For some downtime, a fenced-in grassy area with shade trees, flowers and views across the lagoon sits just across from the entrance to Woody Woodpecker's KidZone. Spread out a blanket and enjoy a snack or simply chill out. It makes an excellent meeting spot.

E.T. Adventure　　　　　　　RIDE
(Map p254; www.universalorlando.com; Universal Studios; theme-park admission required; ⊙ from 9am; ⊡ Lynx 21, 37 or 40) This is one of Universal's classic rides and one for the nostalgia seekers. For some people, *E.T.* is Universal. Jump aboard the flying bicycle and assist E.T. to save the planet. Dodge the baddies while soaring into the stars and into E.T.'s magical world. Sure it might be dated compared to some hi-tech 'competitors,' but it's sweet. And after all, who can resist a little, shriveled alien.

Production Central AREA

(Map p254; www.universalorlando.com; Universal Studios; theme-park admission required; ⊙ from 9am; ♿; 🖳 Lynx 21, 37 or 40) Home to two of Universal's most talked-about rides, the incredible 3D simulation **Transformers: The Ride 3-D** (Express Pass) and the high-thrill coaster **Hollywood Rip Ride Rockit** (Express Pass). This roller coaster is not for the faint of heart – you *Rip* up to 65mph, *Ride* 17 stories above the theme park and down a crazy-steep drop, and *Rockit* to customized music.

At **Shrek 4-D** (Express Pass), Shrek and Donkey try to save Princess Fiona from a dragon. And that dragon is indeed fierce, probably too fierce for tiny tots – it pops out at you with red eyes, spitting fire into your face. Unfortunately, the nonsensical pre-show spiel goes on too long.

San Francisco AREA

(Map p254; www.universalorlando.com; Universal Studios; theme-park admission required; ⊙ from 9am; ♿; 🖳 Lynx 21, 37 or 40) San Francisco, themed heavily around the city as the site of the massive 1906 earthquake and the inspiration behind the 1974 film *Earthquake*, is home to Chez Alcatraz (p318), a tiny and pleasant outdoor bar in Fisherman's Wharf; Lombard's (p314), one of the park's two restaurants that accept reservations; and a couple of outdoor shows.

A fast-talking Hollywood casting agent casting a disaster movie chooses a handful of audience members and gives them directions ('Give me terror like Britney Spears is your babysitter'), and then each volunteer is filmed for a second or so. Everyone then heads to the 'set' and boards a subway train in the incredibly authentic replica of a San Francisco BART (Bay Area Rapid Transit) station. Suddenly, the big one hits: tracks buckle, the place crumbles and general mayhem ensues. Hint: 65,000 gallons of water are released and recycled every six minutes, but you don't get wet. And yes, you do see the footage of those volunteers.

New York AREA

(Map p254; www.universalorlando.com; Universal Studios; theme-park admission required; ⊙ from 9am; ♿; 🖳 Lynx 21, 37 or 40) **Revenge of the Mummy** (Express Pass) combines roller-coaster speed and twists with in-your-face special effects. Head deep into ancient Egyptian catacombs in near pitch black, but don't anger Imhotep the mummy – in

his wrath he flings you past fire, water and more.

A radio announces a severe storm warning and slowly you see and feel the change in weather. The sign rattles above the old gas station, and tumbleweed blows across the set. You see a tornado developing, far off in the distant sky, and it's coming, closer and closer, louder and louder. Anyone who has felt the fear of living through a real tornado, or children who already wake up scared of them thanks to sirens, hours in the basement and the eerie blanket of tornado-breeding green skies, should think twice before going to this attraction.

Despicable Me: Minion Mayhem RIDE

(Map p254; www.universalorlando.com; Universal Studios; theme-park admission required; ⊙ from 9am; 🖳 Lynx 21, 37 or 40) Fans of *Despicable Me* won't want to miss the chance to become one of Gru's minions in this 3D simulated ride, one of Universal's best 3D experiences. There's lots of silliness, in the best of Minion traditions, and there's nothing particularly scary. Note that even ExpressPass+ lines can soar upwards from 30 minutes, so come first thing.

Hollywood AREA

(Map p254; www.universalorlando.com; Universal Studios; theme-park admission required; ⊙ from 9am; 🖳 Lynx 21, 37 or 40) With glorious 3D film footage, live action stunts and 4D special effects, **Terminator 2: 3-D** (Express Pass) is complete sensory overload – delicious fun for some, overwhelming and scary for others.

If you're really into horror makeup, **Universal Horror Make-Up Show** (Express Pass) may be a little too short and thin on substance. It's humorous and full of silly antics, but optical illusions could freak out kids if they're not really clear from the get-go that it's not real.

World Expo AREA

(Map p254; www.universalorlando.com; Universal Studios; theme-park admission required; ⊙ from 9am; 🖳 Lynx 21, 37 or 40) The main attraction here is **Men in Black Alien Attack** (Express Pass), a 3D interactive video game that is a lot of fun but not at all scary. Your car swings and spins through a danger-laden downtown Manhattan, with all kinds of silly-looking aliens all over the place, and you aim your lasers and shoot away to rack up points. Oddly, Universal is adamant that you put all bags in the complimentary locker before boarding.

ORLANDO & WALT DISNEY WORLD® UNIVERSAL ORLANDO RESORT

Woody Woodpecker's KidZone AREA

(Map p254; www.universalorlando.com; Universal Studios; theme-park admission required; ☺ from 9am; ☐ Lynx 21, 37 or 40) Kid-friendly shows and rides, a fantastic water-play area and supercool foam-ball cannons – it rivals Islands of Adventure's Seuss Landing (p307) as a Universal favorite of the eight-and-under crowd.

Springfield AREA

(Map p254; www.universalorlando.com; Universal Studios; theme-park admission required; ☺ from 9am; ⊞; ☐ Lynx 21, 37 or 40) In 2013 Universal opened *Simpsons*-themed Springfield, home to that iconic American TV family. Hang at Moe's Tavern, grab doughnuts at Lard Lad, and meet Krusty the Clown, Sideshow Bob and the Simpson family themselves. The child-friendly **Kang & Kodos' Twirl & Hurl** offers an interactive twist to whirling, and don't miss **The Simpsons Ride** (Express Pass).

It's one of the best simulated experiences at Universal, a highlight even if you're not a *Simpsons* fan. Kids will want to try Springfield's signature drink, a bubbling and steaming **Flaming Moe** that rivals the theming fun of Harry Potter's Butterbeer and tastes surprisingly good! Sure, it's just an orange soda, but it's a pretty cool orange soda, the cup makes a good souvenir, and in the eyes of an eight-year-old, it's worth every penny of that seven bucks.

◉ CityWalk

Across the canal from the three theme parks is CityWalk, Universal's entertainment district comprising a pedestrian mall with restaurants, clubs, bars, a multiplex movie theater, miniature golf and shops. Live music and *mucho* alcohol sums up the entertainment options here. Although nights can be packed with partying 20-somethings, bachelorette parties and general drunken mayhem, there's a distinct family-friendly vibe and several bars have reasonable food. Oh, and although it feels like a partying theme park in it's own right, you can come here even if you're not visiting the Universal theme parks.

🎊 Festivals & Events

Universal's Superstar Parade PARADE

(www.universalorlando.com; Universal Studios; theme park admission required; ☺ daily; ⊞; ☐ Lynx 21, 37 or 40) Elaborate floats and lights featuring the likes of Dora and Diego, *Despicable Me* characters, SpongeBob and whichever trend has taken the young ones' worlds by storm. Check the schedules as they change regularly.

Mardi Gras CARNIVAL

(www.universalorlando.com; Universal Studios; theme-park admission required; ☺ nightly Feb-Mar; ☐ Lynx 21, 37 or 40) Parades, live music and Cajun food mimic the iconic New Orleans street festival, Universal-style.

★ Halloween Horror Nights CARNIVAL

(www.halloweenhorrornights.com/orlando; Universal Studios; $70-81, plus theme-park admission; ☺ select nights Sep & Oct; ☐ Lynx 21, 37, or 40) Magnificently spooky haunted houses, gory thrills and over-the-top Halloween shows – watch for goblins, monsters and mummies roaming the streets, creeping up behind you, and remember, this is Universal, not Disney. It isn't Mickey-coated scares, and parents should think carefully before bringing children 13 and under.

This is a very popular event and tickets are limited; advanced purchase recommended.

Grinchmas CARNIVAL

(www.universalorlando.com; Islands of Adventure; theme-park admission required; ☺ Dec; ⊞; ☐ Lynx 21, 37, or 40) A whimsical holiday spectacular at Seuss Landing pays homage to that classic Christmas story. At the center is a musical production of *How the Grinch Stole Christmas*.

Macy's Holiday Parade PARADE

(www.universalorlando.com; Universal Studios; theme-park admission required; ☺ select nights Dec; ☐ Lynx 21, 37, or 40) Echoes the real thing in New York City, with giant balloons, Santa Claus, Christmas music and a tree-lighting ceremony. Dates can change slightly.

🛏 Sleeping

Universal Orlando Resort boasts five excellent resort hotels. Staying at a resort eliminates many logistical hassles: it's a pleasant gardened walk or a quiet boat ride to the parks; most offer Unlimited Express Pass access to park attractions and priority dining; several popular rides, such as Wizarding World of Harry Potter, opens one hour early for all guests; and the Loews Loves Pets program welcomes Fido as a VIP.

Cabana Bay Beach Resort RESORT $$

(Map p254; ☎ 407-503-4000; www.universalorlando.com; 6550 Adventure Way, Universal Orlando

Resort; r $149-172, parking $12; [P][✳][🔊][🖵]; [🖵Uni-versal) Evoking the spirit of road trips c 1957, Cabana Bay Beach Resort has a beautifully themed, hip, retro-Florida vintage vibe. It offers moderate and good-value accommodation. Family suites have kitchenettes and sleep six; and there are two pools, a bowling alley, a food court and a lazy river.

While guests can enjoy early admission to the Wizarding World of Harry Potter (a huge plus), they do not benefit from perks afforded to guests at the other Universal Resorts, including Unlimited Express Pass, priority dining status and boat transportation to the parks. You must either walk the 20 minutes or take a Universal bus to the theme parks.

★**Loews Portofino Bay Hotel**   RESORT $$$
(Map p254; ☎407-503-1000; www.loewshotels.com/portofino-bay-hotel; 5601 Universal Blvd, Universal Orlando Resort; r & ste $325-$390, self/valet parking per day $22/30; [P][✳][@][🔊][🖵][🏊]; [🏊Universal) Sumptuous and elegant, with beautiful rooms, cobblestone streets and sidewalk cafes around a central lagoon, this resort evokes the relaxing charm of seaside Italy. There's a sandy zero-entrance family pool, the secluded Hillside pool and the elegant Villa pool, as well as the Mandara Spa, evening waterside minstrel music and the excellent Mama Della's Ristorante (p317). Rates include one-hour early entrance to the Wizarding World of Harry Potter and an Unlimited Express Pass.

Loews Royal Pacific Resort   RESORT $$$
(Map p254; ☎407-503-3000; www.loewshotels.com/royal-pacific-resort; 6300 Hollywood Way, Universal Orlando Resort; r & ste $272-$341, self-/valet parking per day $22/30; [P][✳][@][🔊][🖵][🏊]; [🏊Universal) The glass-enclosed Orchid Court, with its reflecting pool, Balinese fountains and carved stone elephants, sits at the center of the airy lobby at this friendly South Pacific-inspired resort. The grounds are gorgeous with lush tropical plantings, flowers and palm trees. Excellent on-site restaurants. Rates include one-hour early entrance to the Wizarding World of Harry Potter and an Unlimited Express Pass.

Kids will love the family-friendly pool, with real sand, and the 6pm 'dive-in movie' where they can swim while watching a poolside screen showing the likes of Harry Potter and Universal favorites. Note that the rooms here tend to be smaller than those at other Universal hotels. Rates are significantly lower outside peak season.

VOLCANO BAY

Universal Resort's third theme park – **Volcano Bay** (Map p254; www.universalorlando.com; 6000 Universal Blvd, Universal Resort; ⊙ from 9am – closing hours vary) water park – launched in 2017. Representing a Pacific island, the tropical oasis' main feature is a colossal volcano through and down which, you guessed it, will run watery thrills and spills. There's winding rivers with family raft rides to convoluted body slides that somehow launch riders above the spray and wave pools.

It's located alongside Islands of Adventure and Universal.

Loews Sapphire Falls Resort   HOTEL $$$
(Map p254; ☎1-888-273-1311; www.universalorlando.com/sapphirefalls; 6601 Adventure Way; r $192-$225, self-/valet parking per day $22/30; [P][✳][🔊][🖵]) Opened in July 2016, this is the latest in the Universal Resort hotels. Inspired by the Caribbean, it has a tropical vibe and a mélange of eras, from colonial to the 1950s. The property's water features include lovely rivers and waterfalls. Rooms have a weird mix of Caribbean colors and patterned decor, but as with everything park-Orlandesque, it's all about the theming.

Some of the best eateries and bars are located within the resort, including the fabulous bar Strong Water Tavern (p318).

Hard Rock Hotel   RESORT $$$
(Map p254; ☎407-503-2000; www.hardrockhotels.com/orlando; 5800 Universal Blvd, Universal Orlando Resort; r & ste $329 to $393, self-/valet parking per day $22/30; [P][✳][@][🔊][🖵][🏊]; [🏊Universal) From the grand lawn with the massive guitar fountain at its entrance to the pumped-in, underwater music at the pool, the modern and stylized Hard Rock embodies the pure essence and energy of rock 'n' roll cool. Rates include one-hour early entrance to the Wizarding World of Harry Potter and an Unlimited Express Pass.

There's a huge zero-entry pool with a waterslide and families mingle harmoniously alongside a young party crowd, but the loud live band that sometimes plays in the lobby and the rockin' vibe may be overkill for folk looking for a peaceful getaway. If you're looking for something more subdued, head to Portofino Bay.

WIZARDING WORLD OF HARRY POTTER

The hottest thing to hit Orlando since Disney's Cinderella's Castle, and further expanded in 2014, the magnificently whimsical **Wizarding World of Harry Potter** invites muggles into JK Rowling's imagination. Alan Gilmore and Stuart Craig, art director and production designer for the films, collaborated closely with the Universal Orlando Resort engineers to create what is without exception the most fantastically realized themed experience in Florida. The detail and authenticity tickle the fancy at every turn, from the screeches of the mandrakes in the shop windows to the groans of Moaning Myrtle in the bathroom; keep your eyes peeled for magical happenings.

The Wizarding World of Harry Potter is divided into two sections, each with rides, attractions and over-the-top detailed theming: **Hogsmeade** sits in Islands of Adventure and **Diagon Alley** is in Universal Studios. If you have a park-to-park ticket, you can ride the Hogwarts Express from one section to the other.

Hogsmeade (Islands of Adventure)

Poke around among the cobbled streets and impossibly crooked buildings of Hogsmeade at the **Wizarding World of Harry Potter – Hogsmeade** (Map p254; ☎407-363-8000; www.universalorlando.com; Islands of Adventure; theme-park admission required; ⏲9am-6pm, hours vary; 🚌Lynx 21, 37 or 40); munch on Cauldron Cakes; and mail a card via Owl Post – all in the shadow of Hogwarts Castle. Two of Orlando's best rides are here – **Harry Potter and the Forbidden Journey** and **Dragon Challenge**. Come first thing when the park gates open, before the lines get too long and the crowds become unbearable. Guests staying at Universal Orlando Resort hotels get one hour early admission.

Harry Potter and the Forbidden Journey Wind through the corridors of Hogwarts, past talking portraits, Dumbledore's office and other well-known locations, to one of the best rides in Orlando. You'll feel the cold chill of Dementors, escape a dragon attack, join a Quidditch match and soar over the castle with Harry, Hermione and Ron. Though it's not a fast-moving thrill ride, this is scary stuff. Little ones can enjoy the castle but sit out the ride with a parent in the Child Swap waiting room. There's a single rider line as well, but it's tricky to find – ask at the Hogwarts entrance.

Dragon Challenge Gut-churning roller coasters twist and loop, narrowly avoiding each other; inspired by the first task of the Triwizard Tournament in *Harry Potter & the Goblet of Fire*.

Ollivander's Wand Shop Floor-to-ceiling shelves crammed with dusty wand boxes and a winding staircase set the scene for a 10-minute show that brings to life the iconic scene in which the wand chooses the wizard. Come first thing, as the line quickly extends upwards of an hour.

Flight of the Hippogriff (Express Pass) Family-friendly coaster passes over Hagrid's Hut; listen for Fang's barks and don't forget to bow to Buckbeak!

Honeydukes Sweet Shop Bertie Botts Every Flavor Beans, Chocolate Frogs, Rock Cakes and other Harry Potter–inspired goodies.

Owl Post & Owlery Buy Wizarding World stamps and send a card officially postmarked Hogsmeade.

Filch's Emporium of Confiscated Goods Souvenir shop with the Marauders Map on display.

Three Broomsticks & Hog's Head Tavern Surprisingly good shepherd's pie, pumpkin juice and Hog's Head Brew.

Dervish & Banges Magical supplies and Hogwarts robes for sale.

Diagon Alley (Universal Studios)

The **Wizarding World of Harry Potter – Diagon Alley** (Map p254; www.universalorlando.com; Universal Studios; theme-park admission required; ⏲from 9am; 🚌Lynx 21, 37 or 40), lined with magical shops selling robes, Quidditch supplies, wands, brooms and more, leads to the massive Gringotts Bank, home to one of Universal Studio's multi-sensory thrill rides, **Harry Potter and the Escape from Gringotts**. To get here, you must walk through Muggles' London at Universal Studios or, if you have a park-to-park ticket, ride the Hogswarts Express from Islands of Adventure's Hogsmeade to King's Cross Station.

Grab some bangers and mash at the **Leaky Cauldron**, a scoop of quirky wizarding-themed ice cream at **Florean Fortescue's Ice-Cream Parlor** and wander down the 'darkest of dark places,' Knockturn Alley, to pick up tools of the Dark Arts at **Borgin and Burkes**.

Given the creative spirit and success of Islands of Adventure's Hogsmeade, Diagon Alley is theme-park magic at its best. Lines and crowds are insane – stay at a Universal Orlando Resort so you can enter Diagon Alley one hour before the park opens to the general public.

Interactive Wands

Wands at Universal Orlando's Wizarding World of Harry Potter come in two varieties, interactive ($48) and noninteractive ($40). Interactive wands, including Hermione's and Harry's, can be used in both Diagon Alley and Hogsmeade to activate magical windows and displays. Make it rain down on an umbrella, illuminate lanterns, watch the marionettes dance. They can be a bit touchy to get used to – use small, gentle movements, and if you have trouble, ask a nearby wizard for help.

Gold medallions on the ground indicate spots where you can cast your spells, and how to move your wand to cast the spell, and each wand comes with a map. Some secret spell locations, however, aren't marked at all, either on the map or by a gold medallion, but we're not telling where they are. Hint: secret spells respond to a triangle swoop.

Top Tips for Visiting Harry Potter's Hogsmeade & Diagon Alley

You haven't seen crowds and lines until you've seen Universal's Wizarding World of Harry Potter during high season. It can be upwards of five hours *just to enter* the Harry Potter–themed section, and then there's the lines for rides, restaurants and shops once you get in. It can be a nightmare. But don't be deterred: with a little bit of smart planning, a visit to Hogsmeade and Diagon Alley can be magnificently joyful, easy and stress-free.

Stay at a Universal Orlando Resort Hotel Harry Potter attractions open one hour early for guests at four (of the five) on-site hotels. Arrive at least 30 minutes before the gates open to the general public, and do not dawdle.

Strategize Head to Islands of Adventure's Hogsmeade on one morning – hit Harry Potter and the Forbidden Journey, Dragon Challenge, Flight of the Hippogriff, and finally shops and restaurants (in that order). The other morning, zip straight to Universal Studio's Diagon Alley, hop on Escape from Gringotts, and then explore at leisure. There is an Ollivander's Wand Shop in both parks – on one of the two days, make this your first stop.

Buy a park-to-park ticket This allows you to ride the Hogwarts Express between Diagon Alley and Hogsmeade.

Visit during low season It's best not to go Christmas through early January, March and summertime.

Take advantage of Universal's 'return time' tickets If the Wizarding World of Harry Potter *does* reach capacity during your visit (usually after 10:30am), it only allows new guests to enter once others have left – this electronic ticket allows you to enjoy other attractions and return for entry into the Wizarding World within a specific window of time. Look for the blue banner directing you to the easy-to-use kiosks.

✗ Eating

The only restaurants in the theme parks that take advance reservations are Finnegan's Bar & Grill and Lombard's Seafood Grille in Universal Studios, and Mythos Restaurant and Confisco Grille in Islands of Adventure.

Each Universal resort has high-quality bars and restaurants that you can enjoy even if you're not a guest. For kids, some even offer 'character dining' options where Universal characters visit one of the resort hotel restaurants.

✗ Islands of Adventure

All the usual fast-food suspects are sold throughout the park, but with a commitment to theme that you don't see elsewhere. Sip a Predator Rocks in the lush foliage of the Cretaceous period in Jurassic Park or grab a Hog's Head Brew in Hogsmeade.

★ Three Broomsticks   BRITISH $

(Map p254; www.universalorlando.com; Islands of Adventure; mains $12-17, theme-park admission required; ⏰ 9am-park closing; 🏷; 🚍 Lynx 21, 37 or 40) Fast-food-styled British fare inspired by Harry Potter, with cottage (shepherd's) pie and Cornish pasties, and rustic wooden bench seating. There's plenty of outdoor seating out back, too, by the river.

Confisco Grille &
Backwater Bar   AMERICAN $

(Map p254; ☎ 407-224-4012; www.universalorlando.com; Islands of Adventure; mains $6-22, theme-park admission required; ⏰ 11am-4pm; 🏷🏷; 🚍 Lynx 21, 37 or 40) Under-the-radar and often overlooked, the recommended Confisco Grille has outdoor seating, freshly made hummus, tasty wood-oven pizzas and a full bar.

Mythos Restaurant   MEDITERRANEAN $$

(Map p254; ☎ 407-224-4012, 407-224-4534; www.universalorlando.com; Islands of Adventure; mains $14-23, theme-park admission required; ⏰ 11am-3pm; 🏷; 🚍 Lynx 21, 37 or 40) Housed in an ornate underwater grotto with giant windows and running water and overlooking a lake, this is a more upmarket experience and the best of the selection. Menu changes seasonally but you can chomp on anything from pad thai noodles to risotto.

✗ Universal Studios

There's both usual suspects and some fun themed eateries at Universal, including lots of burgers and ice-cream offerings. But for something different, head to Duff Brewery (p318) in Springfield (p310) for a Flaming Moe, a nonalcoholic orange-flavored concoction that gurgles like a volcano, or an icy mug of Homer Simpson's favorite brew.

Leaky Cauldron   BRITISH $

(Map p254; www.universalorlando.com; Universal Studios; mains $8-15, theme-park admission required; ⏰ 8am-park closing; 🚍 Lynx 21, 37 or 40) Wizard servers in marvelous Harry Potter surrounds with classic English breakfasts, shepherd's pie, Guinness beef stew and sticky toffee pudding. You order fast-food style and the food is brought to your table – refectory of course, à la Potteresque boarding-school experience).

The only drinks are Potter-themed delights, including nonalcoholic Peachtree Fizzing Tea and Fishy Green Ale, as well dark ale Wizards Brew and the malty Dragon Scale.

Florean Fortescue's
Ice-Cream Parlour   ICE CREAM $

(Map p254; www.universalorlandoresort.com; Diagon Alley, Universal Studios; ice cream $4-8, theme-park admission required; ⏰ park opening 1hr before park closing; 🚍 Lynx 21, 37 or 40) In *Harry Potter and the Prisoner of Azkaban,* young Harry spends several weeks living at the Leaky Cauldron and Florean Fortescue gives him free ice cream whenever he pops into the store. His bright and charming shop, just across from the fire-spewing dragon on top of Gringotts Bank, is now open to muggles – bizarre and delectable flavors include Butterbeer, sticky toffee pudding and clotted cream, as well as pumpkin juice.

Mel's Drive-In   BURGERS $

(Map p254; www.universalorlando.com; Universal Studios; mains $10-14, theme-park admission required; ⏰ 11am-park closing; 🏷; 🚍 Lynx 21, 37 or 40, 🚊 Universal) Based on the movie *American Grafitti,* this rockin' rollin' joint features classic cars and performing bands outside, '50s-diner style inside. This is a fast-food eatery, not much different really than your standard well-known burger joint, but it's a lot more fun!

Lombard's Seafood Grille   SEAFOOD $$

(Map p254; ☎ 407-224-3613, 407-224-6401; www.universalorlando.com; Universal Studios; mains $15-28, theme-park admission required; ⏰ 11am-park closing; 📶🏷; 🚍 Lynx 21, 37 or 40) A more upmarket experience (and good for older folk). Features oriental rugs, a huge fish tank and a solid seafood menu. It's a calming respite from Universal Orlando's energy.

Finnegan's Bar & Grill PUB FOOD $$

(Map p254; ☑ 407-224-3613; www.universal orlando.com; Universal Studios; mains $10-23, theme-park admission required; ⊙ 11am-park closing; 🛜 👪; 🚌 Lynx 21, 37 or 40) An Irish pub with live acoustic music plopped into the streets of New York. Serves Cornish pasties and Scotch eggs, as well as Harp, Bass and Guinness on tap. Annoyingly (as with many establishments, it seems), the prices are not shown on the outside menu.

Superstar
Character Breakfast AMERICAN $$$

(Map p254; ☑ 407-224-7554; www.universal orlando.com; Cafe La Bamba, Universal Studios; adult/child $35/21, theme-park admission required; ⊙ 9-11am; 🚌 Lynx 21, 37 or 40) Breakfast with the likes of Gru and his minions, SpongeBob Squarepants and others from the Universal Superstar Parade at Universal Studio's Cafe La Bamba. Note that once you make and pay for online reservations, you must still call to confirm it.

🗡 CityWalk

The entrance hub to the theme parks, CityWalk is lined with some great eateries and bars. Many of these shift to become live-music venues at night that charge covers after 9pm. To avoid the individual cover charges, you can purchase a CityWalk Party Pass ($12; free with multiday theme-park admission) for unlimited all-night club and bar access; add a movie (extra $3) or dinner and movie (extra $10).

★ Toothsome Chocolate Emporium
& Savory Feast Kitchen INTERNATIONAL $

(Map p254; http://stayinguniversal.com/menus/ toothsome-chocolate-emporium-menu/; City Walk; ⊙ 11am-11pm Sun-Thu, 11am-11:30pm Fri & Sat) A delightfully quirky steampunk-meets-Willy-Wonka experience. Oh, and did we mention chocolate? If this description doesn't make sense, it isn't meant to, for that would spoil the surprise. Follow your nose here – head behind the smokestacks and into a world of chocolatey wonder with gadgets, gizmos and the 'creator', Prof Dr Penelope Tibeaux-Tinker Toothsome.

Seafood and steak dishes. Chocolate bread. Chocolate chicken wings. Chocolate gnocchi. If the savory cuisine is wonderful, the chocolate desserts are wickedly sublime. And it's all thanks to Prof Toothsome who, upon returning to London after traveling globally in the 19th century, wanted to share her newfound skills: fascinating methods of infusing chocolate. Thus she opened the Toothsome Chocolate Emporium & Savory Feast Kitchen. Penelope makes an appearance and will check on what you are (or are not) eating. A fun start or end to the park experience.

Cowfish AMERICAN $$

(Map p254; ☑ 407-224-3663; www.universal orlando.com; CityWalk, Universal Resort; mains $15-23; ⊙ 10:30am-11pm Sun-Thu, to midnight Fri & Sat) 'Burgushi'...this is something you'd only find in the US. Surely. Yes, a fusion between a burger and sushi. In reality, it's more sushi with a burger component rather than fusion cuisine. But it's good. Cowfish (getting the idea, here?) is a mighty popular spot with a fabulous bar.

Throw in a sake or three or a craft beer and you've got yourself a fun CityWalk experience.

Hard Rock Café AMERICAN $$

(Map p254; ☑ 407-351-7625; www.hardrock. com/cafes/orlando; CityWalk; mains $13-27; ⊙ 8:30am-midnight; 👪; 🚌 Lynx 21, 37 or 40, 🚢 Universal) Excellent burgers and a rock 'n' roll theme make this a fan favorite. Plus it's open for breakfast – handy for a prepark carbo-fill. Reservations not accepted, but you can ring ahead for 'priority seating,' meaning that if there's a wait, you can queue-jump (but are not guaranteed a seat).

Bob Marley – A Tribute to
Freedom JAMAICAN $$

(Map p254; ☑ 407-224-3663; www.universal orlando.com; CityWalk; mains $15-18; ⊙ 4pm-2am; 🚌 Lynx 21, 37 or 40, 🚢 Universal) Jerk-spiced chicken, monk stew and veggie patties with yucca fries served in a replica of the reggae master's Jamaican home. There's live reggae in the courtyard every evening, and after 9pm you must be 21 to enter.

NBC Sports Grill & Brew AMERICAN $$

(Map p254; www.universalorlando.com; City Walk, Universal Orlando Resort; mains $14-40; ⊙ 11am-1.30am) In their own PR terms 'a game changer'. This massive sports grill and brew brings on all the sporting analogies. Not only is there a 120ft-wide screen (playing the greatest moments in NBC sports history), but another 100 smaller screens showing live coverage of all types of games, plus

UNIVERSAL FOR CHILDREN

The word on the street says that Universal Orlando Resort is great for teens and adults but doesn't offer much for kids under seven. This is simply not true. No, it doesn't have as much as Walt Disney World® and you won't find Disney's nostalgic charm, but Universal Orlando Resort is a master at blending attractions for all ages into one easily digestible and navigable package of fun. Dr Seuss' Grinch, superheroes and all kinds of Universal favorites make appearances at theme parks, and characters from *Despicable Me* and other kid-friendly shows swing by hotel restaurants. CityWalk is very family-friendly, despite its many bars and live music, with a sci-fi-themed miniature golf course and a splash fountain, and the Wantilan Luau at Loews Portofino Bay Hotel gives folks of all ages a taste of the islands.

Most of the kid-friendly attractions cluster at Universal Studios Woody Woodpecker's KidZone (p310), and Islands of Adventure's Seuss Landing (p307) and Toon Lagoon (p307), and the **Wizarding World of Harry Potter** (Map p254; ☑ 407-363-8000; www.universalorlando.com; Islands of Adventure & Universal Studios; theme park admission required; ☻from 9am (closing hours vary); ☐ Lynx 21, 37 or 40). Bring a change of clothes, as both parks have attractions designed to get kids wet!

Best for Kids: Islands of Adventure

One Fish, Two Fish, Red Fish, Blue Fish Ride a Seussian fish around, slowly up and down, with just enough spin to thrill.

Caro-Seuss-al Hop on a fanciful Seuss character.

The Cat in the Hat Classic ride through a storybook.

The High in the Sky Seuss Trolley Train Ride Soar gently over the park.

If I Ran the Zoo Colorful interactive play area with water-spurting triggers.

Me Ship, the Olive Kids crawl, climb and squirt on Popeye's playground ship and zoom down tunnel waterslides.

Popeye & Bluto's Bilge-Rat Barges Float, twist, bump and giggle along on a circular raft – no sharp falls but you will get drenched!

Hogwarts Little (and big) ones too young for the scary Harry Potter and the Forbidden Journey ride can simply walk through the magical charms of the most famous school of witchcraft and wizardry. The separate line for this isn't marked, so ask the accommodating Universal folks. Other kid-friendly highlights in the Wizarding World of Harry Potter (p312) are Ollivander's Wand Shop (10-minute show) and family coaster the Flight of the Hippogriff.

Best for Kids: Universal Studios

A Day in the Park with Barney Delightfully gentle theater-in-the-round live performance and sing-along.

Animal Actors on Location! Big stage show that highlights exploits of animal actors.

Curious George Goes to Town Best tiny-tot water-play area in any of the theme parks, and a giant room of nerf balls to throw and shoot from cannons.

E.T. Adventure (p308) Board a bike and ride through the woods, the police in hot pursuit, before rising safely into the sky through outer space to E.T.'s fanciful home planet. There are a few spooky spots – prepare kids for darkness, loud noises and steam – but there are no spins, speeds or plummets.

Fievel's Playground Imagine you've been shrunk to the size of a mouse...and let loose. Kids have a ball.

Woody Woodpecker's Nuthouse Coaster Gentle coaster for kids three and up.

more than 100 beers, from craft to regional brews.

If all that (lack of) exercise makes you hungry, there's food, too. The expansive menu has everything from chicken wings to a seven-layer Big Banana Cake. It's a full-on, testosterone, boisterous (and, oh so fun) experience.

Jimmy Buffett's Margaritaville
CARIBBEAN $$

(Map p254; ☑ 407-224-2155; www.margarita villeorlando.com; CityWalk; mains $10-18; ⏲ 11:30am-2am; 👪; 🚌 Lynx 21, 37 or 40, 🚇 Universal) Island-inspired festivity, with three bars, patio dining and live music Jimmy Buffett-style after 10pm. Try the tantalizing and colorful margarita flight – four minidrinks, frozen or on-the-rocks.

Check out the Lone Palm tiki bar on the water across from Margaritaville – just look for the plane (from Jimmy Buffett's own collection) parked outside. It's a nice spot for a drink.

🍴 Resort Hotels

Emack & Bolio's Marketplace
ICE CREAM $

(Map p254; ☑ 407-503-2000; www.emackand bolios.com; 5800 Universal Blvd, Hard Rock Hotel; ice cream $3-8; ⏲ 6am-10pm Sun-Thu, to 11pm Fri & Sat; 🛜👪; 🚇 Universal) Originally from Boston, Emack and Bolio's ice cream beats other national chains hands down. And of course, only at this bastion of rock 'n' roll will you find a flavor called Deep Purple.

★ Mama Della's Ristorante
ITALIAN $$

(Map p254; ☑ 407-503-3463; www.universal orlando.com; 5601 Universal Blvd, Loews Portofino Bay Hotel; mains $10-22; ⏲ 5:30-11pm; 🍴👪; 🚇 Universal) Charming, cozy and friendly, with vintage wallpaper, dark wood and several rooms with romantic nooks. You really do feel like you're a welcomed guest at a private home nestled in Italy. Strolling musicians entertain tableside and the simple Italian fare is both fresh and excellent; the service is efficient but relaxed.

Good wine, old-fashioned soda in a bottle and a bowl of pasta at Mama Della's makes a very nice ending to a day at the parks, for both kids and adults.

Orchid Court Sushi Bar
JAPANESE $$

(Map p254; ☑ 407-503-3000; www.universal orlando.com; 6300 Hollywood Way, Loews Royal Pacific Resort; sushi $5-16, mains $13-20; ⏲ 6-11am & 5-11pm; 👪; 🚇 Universal) This small, informal sushi bar oozes calm inside the light-and-airy, glass-enclosed lobby of the Royal Pacific Resort, and is decked out with cushioned couches and chairs. Try the moonstone lychetini (or whatever 'tini' they have going; $15). It's also open for breakfast.

Emeril's Tchoup Chop
SEAFOOD $$$

(Map p254; ☑ 407-503-2467; www.emerils restaurants.com; 6300 Hollywood Way, Loews Royal Pacific Resort; mains $24-36; ⏲ 11:30am-2:30pm & 5-10pm; 🚇 Universal) Island-inspired food, including plenty of seafood and Asian accents, prepared with the freshest ingredients. With stunning decor (massive orange and yellow lighting) and a more mellow ambience, this is one of the best sit-down meals at the Universal Orlando Resort.

Kitchen
AMERICAN $$$

(Map p254; ☑ 407-503-2430; www.loewshotels. com/hard-rock-hotel/dining/restaurant; 5800 Universal Blvd, Hard Rock Hotel; mains $15-40; ⏲ 7am-10pm Sun-Thu, to 11pm Fri & Sat; 👪; 🚇 Universal) Music paraphernalia and patio poolside dining. Come for flatbreads, steak and comfort food such as chicken potpie and roast chicken. Children can head to the Kids' Crib, which has bean-bag chairs, cartoons and toys, while parents dine in the big-people restaurant. Every night two characters visit tables.

Palm Restaurant
STEAK $$$

(Map p254; ☑ 407-503-7256; www.thepalm.com; 5800 Universal Studios Blvd, Hard Rock Hotel; mains $38-59; ⏲ 5-10pm; 🚇 Universal) The original Palm opened in New York City in 1926 and, though there are now more than 30 locations, it remains a family-owned bedrock American steakhouse, albeit up there in the price stakes, too. Classic cocktails, a steady din and big plates of steak, lobster and Italian fare.

🍷 Drinking & Nightlife

🍺 Islands of Adventure

Hog's Head Pub
PUB

(Map p254; www.universalorlando.com; Islands of Adventure, Universal Studios; drinks $4-8, theme-park admission required; ⏲ 11am-park closing; 🚌 Lynx 21, 37 or 40) Butterbeer, frozen or frothy, real beer on tap, pumpkin cider and more. Keep an eye on that hog over the bar – he's more real than you think! If the lines at the Butterbeer carts outside are too long, head inside. Same thing, same price.

♀ Universal Studios

★ Moe's Tavern
BAR

(Map p254; www.universalorlando.com; Springfield, Universal Studios; drinks $3-9, theme-park admission required; ⊙11am-park closing; ☏; 🚌Lynx 21, 37 or 40) Brilliantly themed *Simpsons* bar with Isotopes memorabilia, the Love Tester and Bart Simpson crank-calling the red rotary phone; it's as if you walked straight into your TV to find yourself at Homer's favorite neighborhood joint. Buy a Krusty Burger from the neighboring food court and sidle up for a Duff Beer, Duff Lite or Duff Dry.

Duff Brewery
BAR

(Map p254; www.universalorlando.com; Springfield, Universal Studios; snacks $5-12, theme-park admission required; ⊙11am-park closing; ☏; 🚌Lynx 21, 37 or 40) Outdoor lagoonside bar serving Homer Simpson's beer of choice, on tap or by the bottle, and Springfield's signature Flaming Moe. Look for the topiary Seven Duffs out front.

Chez Alcatraz
BAR

(Map p254; www.universalorlando.com; San Francisco, Universal Studios; theme-park admission required; ⊙11am-park closing; ☏; 🚌Lynx 21, 37 or 40) Frozen mojitos, flatbread and homemade potato chips on the waterfront at Fisherman's Wharf. With the sound of the boats jingling at the docks, views over the water to the *Simpsons*-themed Springfield, and Bruce the infamous shark from *Jaws* dangling as a photo-op, this little outdoor bar makes a pleasant spot to kick back and relax.

♀ CityWalk

Red Coconut Club
CLUB

(Map p254; ☎407-224-4233; www.universalorlando.com; CityWalk; after 10pm $7; ⊙8pm-2am Sun-Thu, from 6pm Fri & Sat; 🚌Lynx 21, 37 or 40, 🚇Universal) This place is meant to tap into a '50s Cuba, retro Polynesian and contemporary feel. It may be a mélange, but it has hip vibe, plus live bands, a martini bar and rooftop balcony.

Pat O'Brien's
BAR

(Map p254; ☎407-224-2106; www.universalorlando.com; CityWalk; after 10pm $7; ⊙4pm-2am, piano bar from 5pm; 🚌Lynx 21, 37 or 40, 🚇Universal) A replica of a bar of the same name in New Orleans, this has Cajun food (mains $8 to $17), dueling pianos and a pleasant outdoor patio.

Groove
CLUB

(Map p254; ☎407-224-2165; www.universalorlando.com; CityWalk; ⊙9pm-2am; 🚌Lynx 21, 37 or 40, 🚇Universal) Dance club with sleek blue neon walls, multiple bars, three themed lounges and blaring music.

♀ Resort Hotels

★ Strong Water Tavern
BAR

(Map p254; www.loewshotels.com/sapphire-falls-resort/dining/lounges; Loews Sapphire Falls Resort, Universal Orlando Resort; ☏) This sophisticated rum and tapas bar will transport you to the Caribbean. Rum barrel lids are suspended overhead, and other wood accents transform this hotel bar into an atmospheric, stylish place. You can take a journey through different types of rum (there are more than 60 to try) and a rum counsel is on hand to advise.

Jake's American Bar
BAR

(Map p254; www.universalorlando.com; Loews Royal Pacific Resort, Universal Orlando Resort; ⊙11am-1:30am) Glide into this South Seas island experience where 'Jake', imaginary pilot of an island-hopper aircraft, runs this pleasant place. We don't want to overstress the theming here, and we're not talking *Gilligan's Island* though the 'pilot log book' menu (mains $13 to $17) is kind of fun. It is a stylish locale, worthy of the Royal Pacific.

Serves everything from beer flights to great snacks. Try the killer crab-cake sandwich ($16).

☆ Entertainment

CityWalk, Universal Orlando's entertainment district (free access to the public) throbs with live music and clubs.

Wantilan Luau
LUAU

(Map p254; ☎407-503-3463; www.universalorlando.com; 6300 Hollywood Way, Loews Royal Pacific Resort; adult $70-76, child 3-9yr $35-40; ⊙6pm Sat; 🚇Universal) Pacific Island fire dancers shimmy and shake on stage while guests enjoy a tasty buffet of roast suckling pig, guava-barbecued short ribs and other Polynesian-influenced fare. The atmosphere is wonderfully casual and, like everything at Universal Orlando, this is simple unabashed silliness and fun. Unlimited mai tais, beer and wine are included in the price.

The Maori warriors' roar can be rather scary and the fire a bit close for comfort in the eyes of little ones, but there's a pleasant grassy area next to the open-air dining theater where kids can muck about. Reservations accepted up to 60 days in advance.

Blue Man Group
PERFORMING ARTS

(Map p254; ♫ 407-258-3626; www.universal orlando.com; CityWalk; adult/child from $60/30; ☺ times vary; ☒ Lynx 21, 37 or 40, ☻ Universal) Originally an off-Broadway phenomenon in 1991, this high-energy, comedy theatrical troupe at Universal Orlando Resort features all kinds of multisensory craziness – percussion 'instruments,' paintballs, marshmallows, modern dancing and general mayhem.

Universal's Cinematic Spectacular
CINEMA

(Map p254; ♫ dining reservations 407-224-7554; www.universalorlando.com; Universal Studios; theme-park admission required; ☺ evenings, times vary; ☒ Lynx 21, 37 or 40) This dramatic film tribute narrated by Morgan Freeman combines fireworks, a water and light show, and clips from movie classics projected on a massive screen over the lagoon.

Universal offers waterfront-view reserved seating for the show with Universal's Cinematic Spectacular Dining Experience (adult/child $45/17). It includes dinner at Lombard's Seafood Grille (p314) and a dessert buffet on the deck. After reserving and paying, you must still call to confirm.

CityWalk's Rising Star
KARAOKE

(Map p254; ♫ 407-224-4233; www.universal orlando.com; CityWalk; cover $7; ☺ 8pm-2am; ☒ Lynx 21, 37 or 40, ☻ Universal) Karaoke to live music and with backup singers or join a talent contest. It has heaps of cocktails to give you courage.

Hard Rock Live
LIVE MUSIC

(Map p254; ♫ 407-351-5483; www.hardrock.com; CityWalk; tickets $20-40; ☺ box office 10am-9pm; ☒ Lynx 21, 37 or 40, ☻ Universal) This 3000-person-capacity landmark draws some fairly big rock 'n' roll names and comedy acts. Full bar.

Dive-In Movies
CINEMA

(☺ dusk; ☻ Universal) Free family-friendly movies screened poolside at Universal Orlando's deluxe resort hotels: Loews Portofino Bay, Hard Rock and Loews Royal Pacific Resort. Details vary seasonally and sometimes films are screened several nights a week.

AMC Universal Cineplex 20
CINEMA

(Map p254; ♫ 407-354-3374; www.amctheatres. com; adult/child from $11/8; ☒ Lynx 21, 37 or 40,

DELANCY STREET PREVIEW CENTER

Some Universal Orlando visitors could be pulled from the crowds and asked to go to the **Delancy Street Preview Center** (in the New York section of Universal Studios) to watch clips from a TV pilot or movie and to give their opinions. It's a way of testing potential new shows – and the best part is participants are compensated for their time. As in money. They're looking for a particular demographic based on the material, and it's not always open, but if you stop by and ask you just may be what they want.

☻ Universal) On-site bar and restaurant. Parking costs $16/3 before/after 6pm.

ℹ Information

CHILD CARE

Kids' Camp (p253) Every week one deluxe Universal Orlando Resort hotel offers a drop-off child-care center, with DVDs, arts and crafts, organized activities and games, for children aged four through 14. Reservations recommended but not required; you must be a guest at one of the five Universal Orlando Resort hotels. Optional dinner for an extra $15.

INTERNET ACCESS

Complimentary wi-fi is available throughout Universal Studios, at the Starbucks inside Islands of Adventure and at CityWalk, as well as at Universal Orlando Resort hotels (guests only, though ask about public access in hotel lobbies and pools).

KENNELS

Universal Orlando Resort Kennel (♫ 407-224-9509; www.universalorlando.com; Universal Orlando Resort; per pet per day $15; ☺ 7am-3am) Day boarding for dogs and cats, but you must return to walk your pet. Located on the left side of the RV/camper parking area at Universal Orlando Resort parking lot. Note that pets are welcome at all on-site hotels except Cabana Bay.

LOCKERS

Available inside both Islands of Adventure and Universal Studios parks from $10 per day. Several rides require that all loose items, including backpacks and small purses, be secured in complimentary short-term lockers. If you are carrying something too big for the locker, you

MEETING CHARACTERS AT UNIVERSAL ORLANDO RESORT

Characters roaming Universal Studios and Islands of Adventure may include anyone/anything from the likes of Curious George and SpongeBob Square Pants to Marilyn Monroe, as well as the cast of characters from *The Simpsons, Shrek,* and Dr Seuss books. Some favorites have scheduled meet-and-greets, so be sure to check your park map for times and places. In addition, Universal offers several character dining options.

can take advantage of the Bag Swap option – wait in line together, one person rides while the other holds the bag, and then swap.

MAPS

Pick up a free map at each park entrance (and dotted around at stands within the park). They also list the attractions, with a schedule outlining events, shows and locations of free character interactions. The monthly *Times & Info Guide* lists larger parades and events, too.

MEDICAL SERVICES

Each theme park has medical facilities. A handy hospital from all parks is **Dr P Phillips Hospital** (p269), 5.5 miles south on Turkey Lake Rd.

OPENING HOURS

Theme-park hours change seasonally and daily. Generally, parks open at 8am or 9am and close sometime between 6pm and 10pm. Guests at any of the five on-site hotels can enter the parks one hour before official opening times.

TICKETS

Tickets for adults to one or both Universal Orlando Resort Parks (Islands of Adventure and Universal Studios) cost the following:

No of Days	One Park ($) adult/child	Two Parks ($) adult/child
1	105/100	155/150
2	185/175	235/225
3	204/195	260/245
4	215/205	265/255

➡ Tickets are good anytime within 14 consecutive days, and multiple-day tickets include admission to paid venues in CityWalk. Universal Orlando Resort participates in the Orlando Flex Ticket available online or in person at the Orlando **Official Visitor Center** (p269).

➡ Avoid lines at designated Islands of Adventure and Universal Studios rides by flashing your Express Pass at the separate Express Pass line. The standard one-day pass (for one park $50 to $60; for two parks from $65) allows one-time Express Pass access to each attraction. Alternatively, purchase the bundled two-day Park-to-Park Ticket Plus Unlimited Express (from $220), which includes admission to both parks and unlimited access to Express Pass rides. With this, you can go to any ride, any time you like, as often as you like. If you are staying at one of Universal Orlando's deluxe resort hotels – Universal Orlando's Loews Portofino Bay, Hard Rock or Loews Royal Pacific Resort – up to five guests in each room automatically receive an Unlimited Express Pass. A limited number of passes per day are available online or at the park gates. Check www.universalorlando.com for a calendar of prices and black-out dates. Note that Unlimited Express Passes are sold bundled to park admission online, but, if they're available, you can add them to an existing ticket at the park.

➡ Once Volcano Bay has opened, a three-day, three-park ticket (two to five days duration) will cost from $245/235 per adult/child.

TOURIST INFORMATION

Guest Services inside each park and at CityWalk can help with anything you need, and there are concierge desks at the five on-site hotels. Furthermore, the front desk of just about any Orlando area hotel provides Universal Orlando Resort tourist information.

Important Telephone Numbers

Dining CityWalk & Theme Parks (📞 407-224-9255) Advanced priority seating for CityWalk, Islands of Adventure and Universal Studios.
Dining Resort Hotels (📞 407-503-3463) Advanced priority seating for Loews Portofino Bay, Hard Rock and Loews Royal Pacific Resorts.
Guest Services (📞 407-224-6350, 📞 407-244-4233)
Resort Hotel Reservations (📞 888-273-1311, for vacation packages 📞 888-343-3636) Accommodation at Universal's five on-site resort hotels.
Universal Orlando Resort (📞 407-363-8000, toll-free 📞 800-232-7827) Central number for all things Universal (although infuriatingly automated).
Universal Orlando Resort Lost & Found (📞 407-224-4233) Located inside Guest Services.

Websites

Orlando Informer (www.orlandoinformer.com) Excellent and detailed information on all things

Universal, including park changes, money-saving tips, menus and a crowd calendar.

Universal Orlando Resort (www.universal orlando.com) Official site for information, accommodation and tickets.

TRAVELERS WITH DISABILITIES

➡ The *Universal Orlando Rider's Guide,* available online at www.universalorlando.com and at Guest Services, includes ride requirements and attraction accessibility details for travelers with disabilities. There are also sign-language-interpreting, closed-captioning and assistive-listening devices available at some attractions, and large-print and Braille maps. TDD-equipped (Telecommunications Device for the Deaf) telephones are located throughout the park.

➡ Wheelchairs and Electric Convenience Vehicles (ECV) can be rented from the entrance to each park; ECVs are best reserved in advance (☑ 407-224-4233).

❶ Getting There & Away

BOAT

Universal Orlando Water Taxis (Map p254; www.universalorlando.com; Universal Orlando Resort; ☺7am-2am) Water taxis, which leave each point roughly every 15 minutes, shuttle regularly and directly between four of the five deluxe Universal hotels (Cabana Bar excepted) and CityWalk. From here, it's a five-minute walk across the canal to the theme parks.

BUS

Lynx buses 21, 37 and 40 service the Universal Orlando Resort parking garage (40 runs directly from the downtown Orlando Amtrak station). International Dr's **I-Ride Trolley** (p247) stops at Universal Blvd, a 0.6-mile walk away.

CAR

From the I-4, take exit 74B or 75A and follow the signs. From International Dr, follow the signs west onto Universal Blvd.

Parking

Parking for both theme parks and CityWalk is available inside a giant garage structure (self-/valet parking $20/30). Hotels charge per day for self-parking (from $22) or valet (from $29).

❶ Getting Around

Universal Orlando Resort – that is, Universal Orlando's resort hotels, Islands of Adventure and Universal Studios theme parks and City-Walk – are linked by pedestrian walkways. It's a 10- to 15-minute walk from the theme parks and CityWalk to the deluxe resort hotels. Cabana Bay Beach Resort is about a 25-minute walk. Several hotels outside the park are within a 20-minute walk, but it's not a very pleasant journey.

Rent strollers, wheelchairs and Electric Convenience Vehicles (ECVs) at the entrance to each park and manual wheelchairs at the Rotunda section of the parking lot.

The Space Coast

POP 186,510 / ☎ 321

Includes ➡

Best Places to Eat

➡ Dixie Crossroads (p338)

➡ Green Room Cafe (p330)

➡ Fat Snook (p330)

➡ Ocean 302 (p336)

➡ Chef Larry's (p338)

➡ Crush Eleven (p334)

Best Places to Sleep

➡ Solrisa Inn (p334)

➡ Beach Place Guesthouses (p330)

➡ Port d'Hiver (p335)

➡ Crane Creek Inn (p335)

➡ Casa Coquina del Mar (p338)

Why Go?

More than 40 miles of barrier-island Atlantic Coast stretch from Canaveral National Seashore south to Melbourne Beach, encompassing undeveloped stretches of endless white sand, an entrenched surf culture and pockets of Old Florida.

The Kennedy Space Center and several small museums dedicated to the history, heroes and science of the United States' space program give the Space Coast its name, and the region's tourist hub of Cocoa Beach is just south of Cape Canaveral's launching point for massive cruise ships. But beyond the 3-D space movies, tiki-hut bars and surf shops, the Space Coast offers quintessential Florida wildlife for everyone from grandmas to toddlers. Kayak with manatees, camp on a private island or simply stroll along miles and miles of sandy white beaches – it's easy to find a quiet spot.

When to Go
Cocoa Beach

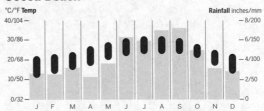

Jul Crowds diminish; prices drop; loggerhead sea turtles nest along miles of sandy coastline.

Apr More sunny days than any other month, and most spring-breakers have come and gone.

Fall Peak migratory-bird season and drier weather make for prime wildlife-spotting.

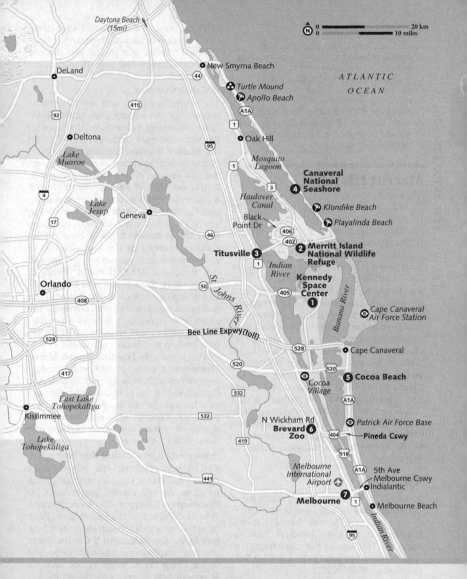

The Space Coast Highlights

❶ Kennedy Space Center (p324) Letting America's space program and the passion of its astronauts fill you with awe and wonder.

❷ Merritt Island National Wildlife Refuge (p325) Kayaking with manatees and dolphins.

❸ Titusville (p337) Watching a rocket launch from Space View Park or grabbing a beer in the historic downtown.

❹ Canaveral National Seashore (p326) Spotting nesting turtles and diving pelicans.

❺ Cocoa Beach Pier (p328) Surfing Florida's hottest waves or simply soaking up the scene.

❻ Brevard Zoo (p335) Learning about conservation while kayaking past giraffes and zip-lining over alligator pits.

❼ Melbourne (p334) Catching community theater and symphony in the historic downtown.

ⓘ Getting Around

Space Coast Area Transit (http://321transit.com) operates a local bus service including routes from Titusville down the coast, from Cape Canaveral to Cocoa Beach and from Cocoa Beach to Cocoa Village. There are also buses circling through Titusville, Merritt Island, Cocoa Village and Melbourne. Surfboards and bikes are allowed on the bus, space permitting. Greyhound (www.greyhound.com) buses stop along the mainland.

Merritt Island

📁 321 / POP 34,743

In 1958, in the aftermath of WWII, the US government selected the east coast of Florida as the base of its newly formed National Aeronautics and Space Administration (NASA). From here new-age captains would launch rockets, telescopes and shuttles into the orbiting circle of the Earth to discover new worlds and galaxies. Thousands of acres of scrubland were commandeered at the northern end of Merritt Island; a third of it was cleared to form the new NASA base, while the remainder was given over to the US Fish and Wildlife Service to operate as the Merritt Island National Wildlife Refuge and the Canaveral National Seashore. The refuge and seashore provide the military with a secure and impenetrable buffer zone while also offering some 500 species of wildlife a pristine coastal habitat of saltwater marshes, hardwood hammocks, pine flatwoods and scrub.

⊙ Sights

Merritt Island is home to a triumvirate of the Space Coast's main attractions: Kennedy Space Center, Merritt Island National Wildlife Refuge and Canaveral National Seashore. This one of the most important turtle-nesting beaches in the US, with 7470 recorded nestings in 2015.

★ **Kennedy Space Center**   MUSEUM
(📞 866-737-5235;   www.kennedyspacecenter.com; NASA Pkwy, Merritt Island; adult/child 3-11yr $50/40; ⊙9am-6pm) Whether you're mildly interested in space or a die-hard sci-fi fan, a visit to the Space Center is awe inspiring. To get a good overview, start at the Early Space Exploration exhibit, progress to the 90-minute bus tour to the Apollo/Saturn V Center (where you'll find the best on-site

cafe) and finish at the awesome *Atlantis* exhibit, where you can walk beneath the heat-scorched fuselage of a shuttle that traveled more than 126,000,000 miles through space on 33 missions.

➡ **Visitor Complex**

The Visitor Complex, with several exhibits showcasing the history and future of US space travel and research, is the heart of the Kennedy Space Center. Here you'll find the **Rocket Garden**, featuring replicas of classic rockets towering over the complex; the new **Heroes & Legends and the U.S. Astronaut Hall of Fame**, with films and multimedia exhibits honoring astronauts; and the hour-long **Astronaut Encounter**, where a real, live astronaut fields questions from the audience. A NASA Now exhibit includes **Journey to Mars**, a collection of related shows and interactive exhibits, and two delightful **IMAX films**: *A Beautiful Planet* offers footage of Earth from space and an optimistic look at the future of the planet (narrated by Jennifer Lawrence), and *Journey to Space 3-D* features interviews with astronauts and an overview of NASA's past, present and future endeavors.

The stunningly beautiful **Space Mirror Memorial**, a shiny granite wall standing four stories high, reflects both literally and figuratively on the personal and tragic stories behind the theme-park energy that permeates the center. Several stone panels display the photos and names of those who died in shuttle disasters.

➡ **Kennedy Space Center Bus Tour**

This 90-minute bus tour is the only way to see beyond the Visitor Complex without paying for an add-on tour. The first stop is the **LC 39 Observation Gantry**, a 60ft observation tower with views of the twin launch pads. From here, the bus winds through the launch facilities to the **Apollo/Saturn V Center**, where you don't want to miss the multimedia show in the Firing Room. Video footage on three screens depicts America's first lunar mission, the 1968 launch of *Apollo VIII*, before you're ushered through to an enormous hangar displaying the real *Apollo 14* Command Module and the 363ft *Saturn V* moon rocket. This 6.5 million pound marvel of engineering boosted into space on November 9, 1967.

Tours depart every 15 minutes from 10am to 3:30pm. Look for the coach buses and long lines to the right when you enter the Visitor Complex.

Space Shuttle Atlantis

Blasted by rocket fuel and streaked with space dust, space shuttle *Atlantis,* the final orbiter among NASA's fleet, is the most impressive exhibit in the complex. Suspended in a specially designed, $100-million space, it hangs just a few feet out of reach, nose down, payload doors open, as if it's still orbiting the earth. It's a creative and dramatic display, preceded by a chest-swelling film that tells the story of the shuttle program from its inception in the 1960s to *Atlantis'* final mission in 2011. Around the shuttle, interactive consoles invite visitors to try to land it or dock it at the International Space Station, touchscreens offer details of missions and crews, and there's a full-size replica of the Hubble Space Telescope and a not-very-scary 'shuttle launch experience.' Docents, many of whom worked on the shuttle program, are stationed around the exhibits to answer questions and tell tall space tales.

Heroes & Legends and the U.S. Astronaut Hall of Fame

Next to the Rocket Garden, the newest exhibit at the center celebrates pioneers of NASA's early space programs, inspiring a new generation to keep their intergalactic dreams alive. It starts with a 360-degree film on the lives of astronauts, then guides visitors through displays of a Redstone rocket, space shuttles and astronauts' personal belongings, along with stations organized under character traits of astronauts, such as 'passionate,' 'tenacious' and 'disciplined.' The exhibit also features the Mercury Mission Control room and the 4-D movie *Through the Eyes of a Hero*, about the lives of the 93 Hall of Fame inductees. Finally, inside the recently relocated and revamped U.S. Astronauts Hall of Fame, visitors are welcomed by a statue of Alan Shepard, along with interactive video displays of the astronauts and their missions.

Add-on Experiences

Extended tours offer the opportunity to visit the **Vehicle Assembly Building**, **Cape Canaveral Air Force Station** and Mercury and Gemini launch sites, and the **Launch Control Center**, where engineers perform system checks. Great for kids, **Lunch with an Astronaut** offers a chance to hang out with a real astronaut, while the **Cosmic Quest** is an action-oriented game-play experience featuring real NASA missions

---

---

involving a rocket launch, redirection of an asteroid and building a martian habitat.

❶ Getting There & Away

Bus Gray Line offers round-trip transportation from Orlando locations ($59).

Car The Space Center is east across the NASA Pkwy on SR 405. Parking costs $10.

Merritt Island National Wildlife Refuge

Sharing a boundary with the Kennedy Space Center, the **Merritt Island National Wildlife Refuge** (321-861-5601; www.fws.gov/merrittisland; Black Point Wildlife Dr, off FL-406; vehicle $10; ☉dawn-dusk) FREE is one of the most diverse natural habitats in America. The unspoiled 140,000-acre wilderness ranges from saltwater marshes and estuaries to hardwood hammocks, pine flatwoods, scrub and coastal dunes that support more than 1500 species of plants and animals, 15 of which are listed as threatened or endangered – than at any other site in the continental US. Between October and May the refuge is also filled with migrating and wintering birds; the best viewing is on Black Point Wildlife Drive (p326) during the early morning and after 4pm.

🏃 Activities

Hiking along one of the refuge's seven **trails** is best during fall, winter and early spring. The shortest hike is 0.25 miles along a raised boardwalk behind the visitor center, while the longest is the 5-mile **Cruickshank Trail**, which forms a loop around Black Point Marsh, making it an excellent place to view wading birds.

A Day Away Kayak Tours   KAYAKING
(✅ 321-268-2655; www.adayawaykayaktours.com; adult/child day tours $36/24, night tours $34/26) Launching off from Haulover Canal, these kayak tours offer the opportunity to glide alongside manatees and dolphins. On night tours the dark waters sparkle as comb jellyfish and bioluminescence illuminate cleaving paddle blades.

Mosquito Lagoon   KAYAKING
Hugging the western side of the barrier-island strip, Mosquito Lagoon is an incredibly peaceful waterway connected to the ocean by the Ponce de León Inlet. At barely 4ft deep, it's a great place to paddle between island hammocks and dense mangroves observing the birds, manatees and dolphins.

A **manatee observation deck** can be found on the northeastern side of the **Haulover Canal**, which connects the lagoon to the Indian River Lagoon. This also makes a great launch point for kayaks. Boat launches (requiring a Refuge Day Pass, $5) are available at Bairs Cove, Beacon 42 and the Bio Lab.

The lagoon is aptly named, so bring bug repellent.

👉 Tours

Black Point Wildlife Drive   DRIVING
(off FL-406; per vehicle $10) One of the best places to see wildlife is on this self-guided, 7-mile drive through salt- and freshwater marshes. A trail brochure detailing 12 stops and the habitats and wildlife found there is available at the entry point.

In season you'll see plenty of waterfowl, wading birds and raptors, including luridly colored roseate spoonbills. Alligators, otters, bobcats and various species of reptile may also be visible in the early morning and at sunset. The drive takes approximately 40 minutes.

🛏 Sleeping & Eating

There are no accommodations or restaurants in the refuge. Nearby, Titusville, Cape Canaveral and Cocoa Beach offer a variety of options.

ℹ Tourist Information

This helpful **Visitor Information Center** (✅ 321-861-0669; www.fws.gov/merrittisland; off FL 402; ⊙ 8am-4pm) offers displays on the refuge's habitats and wildlife, information on conservation programs and hiking trail maps. You can also check out the schedule of bird tours (usually at 9am and 1pm) and sign up for seasonal **turtle-nesting tours** (p327) along the Canaveral National Seashore in June and July.

ℹ Getting There & Away

You'll need a car, and can access the refuge via the A. Max Brewer Memorial Pkwy from Titusville.

Canaveral National Seashore
✅ 321

Part of America's national-park system, spectacular Canaveral National Seashore includes enormous stretches of undeveloped white-sand beach. Two roads squeeze along a skinny bridge of barrier island, one heading 6 miles south from the small beach town of New Smyrna Beach and another 6 miles north from Merritt Island National Wildlife Refuge. Each road dead-ends, leaving about 16 miles of wild beach between them.

The best time to visit the park is between October and April, when migrating birds flock to the beaches. During the drier months wildlife-viewing opportunities are also better and there are fewer mosquitoes. Turtle-nesting tours run in June and July.

👁 Sights

**Canaveral
National Seashore**   NATIONAL PARK
(✅ 386-428-3384; www.nps.gov/cana; car/bike $10/1; ⊙ 6am-8pm) The 24 miles of pristine, windswept beaches here comprise the longest stretch of undeveloped beach on Florida's east coast. They include family-friendly **Apollo Beach** on the north end with its gentle surf, untrammeled **Klondike Beach** in the middle – a favorite of nature lovers – and **Playalinda Beach** to the south, which is surfer central and includes a nudist section near lot 13.

Mosquito Lagoon, with islands and mangroves teeming with wildlife, hugs the west side of the barrier island. Rangers offer two-hour pontoon boat tours (per person $20) from the visitor information center on Friday, Saturday and Sunday. In June and July, rangers lead groups on nightly turtle-nesting tours (adult/child eight to 16 years $14/free; 8pm to midnight); reservations required.

★ Klondike Beach
BEACH

The stretch between Apollo and Playalinda is as pristine as it gets: there are no roads and it's accessible only on foot or by bike (if you can ride on the beach). You need to obtain a back-country permit ($2 per person per day) from the entrance station before setting off.

Turtle Mound
ARCHAEOLOGICAL SITE

Located at the northern end of Mosquito Lagoon, Turtle Mound is one of the largest shell middens on the Florida coast. It stands around 35ft high and consists of 1.5 million bushels (53 million liters) of oyster shells, the remains of an ancient civilization that existed on these shores for five centuries prior to European contact. It can be reached via hiking trails from Apollo Beach and offers panoramic views over the park and ocean.

Apollo Beach
BEACH

This 6-mile beach, at the northern end of the park and immediately south of New Smyrna, attracts families. It has boardwalk access (wheelchair accessible), and a longer stretch of road along the dunes with fewer parking lots than at Playalinda. There are several hiking trails nearby, including the **Eldora Trail**. It feels more isolated and is perfect for cycling or turtle-watching in June and July.

Playalinda Beach
BEACH

At the southern end of Mosquito Lagoon, Playalinda is popular with surfers. Boardwalks provide beach access, but only 2 miles of park road parallel the dunes and there are more parking lots than at Apollo, with fewer opportunities to access the lagoon. Note that the remote areas north of parking lot 13 are often populated by nudists.

Eldora State House Museum
HISTORIC BUILDING

(⊙noon-4pm Tue-Sun) Eldora was a small waterfront community of around 100 citrus farmers and fishers, many of them veterans of the Civil War, who settled here between 1877 and 1900. Eldora depended on the waterway for supplies, tourists and transport. It was fairly prosperous – at least prosperous enough for the construction of the colonial-revival Eldora House, which has now been renovated as a small house museum detailing the life of the settler community via photos, videos and artifacts.

To reach the house, take the Eldora Trail at parking area 8 in the North District. The trail winds through a coastal hammock to the shoreline of Mosquito Lagoon, where you'll find the house.

☞ Tours

★ Sea-Turtle Nesting Tours
ECOTOUR

(☑386-428-3384; adult/child 8-16yr $14/free; ⊙8pm-midnight Jun & Jul) In the summer, rangers lead groups of up to 30 people on these nightly tours, with about a 75% chance of spotting the little guys. Reservations are required (beginning May 15 for June trips, June 15 for July trips); children under eight are not allowed.

Pontoon Boat Tours
BOATING

(☑386-428-3384; per person $20) Two-hour ranger-led tours leave from the Visitor Information Center on Friday, Saturday and Sunday.

🛌 Sleeping & Eating

Required permits for tent camping, the only option for staying here, are available up to seven days in advance. Be sure to bring plenty of water.

At the gate there's a vending machine that sells water and other beverages. But once inside, there are no designated picnic areas, food, phones or drinking water. Come prepared.

Island Camping
CAMPGROUND $

(www.recreation.gov; tent sites $20) Fourteen primitive campsites scattered throughout the islands in Mosquito Lagoon are available year-round.

ℹ️ Information

Canaveral National Seashore Visitor Information Center (☑386-428-3384; www.nps.gov/cana; 7611 S Atlantic Ave, New Smyrna; ⊙8am-6pm Oct-Mar, to 8pm Apr-Sep) is located just south of the North District entrance gate. Alternatively, the visitors center at **Merritt Island National Wildlife Refuge** (p325) can also provide information.

There is a fee station at both the North and South District entrances. There is a toilet at most beach parking areas.

Note that the park can experience temporary closures around launch time. For information on launch closures, call ☑ 321-867-4077.

❶ Getting There & Away

To get to the North District take I-95 to SR 44 (exit 249), head east to New Smyrna Beach, and then south on A1A, 7 miles to the entrance gate.

Access to the South District is 12 miles east of Titusville, through Merritt Island National Wildlife Refuge (I-95 exit 220 to SR 406).

There is no public transportation to or within the park and there's also no road access to Klondike Beach.

Cocoa Beach

☑ 321 / POP 11,325

As America raced to the moon in the wake of WWII, Cocoa Beach hustled to keep up with growth, building dozens of motels and gaining a reputation as a party town. That vibe has remained largely intact, and the area seems eternally populated with beer-wielding, scantily clad youth.

Cocoa Beach's other claim to fame is surfing. Eleven-time surfing world champion Kelly Slater, born and raised here, learned his moves in Cocoa Beach and thus established it as one of Florida's best surf towns.

◉ Sights

Cocoa Beach Pier PIER
(☑ fishing info 321-783-7549; www.cocoabeachpier.com; 401 Meade Ave; parking $10; ⊗ 7-10pm) Souvenir shops, restaurants and bars stretch along this 800ft pier built as a family attraction in 1962. It remains the focus of annual events such as the Easter Surf Festival. Fishing rods are available to rent for $20, and there's a $7 fee to fish on the pier with your own equipment.

Lori Wilson Park PARK
(1500 N Atlantic Ave) A 32-acre, coastal park with a mellow vibe and facilities including wheelchair access, a playground, picnic tables and grills and a small dog-play area. Parking is free and plentiful. The sand is soft and the water is shallow, with small, consistent waves that are great for anyone learning to surf.

Sidney Fischer Park BEACH
(Hwy A1A; parking $5) The closest beach to downtown Cocoa Beach, Fischer Park is crowded with surfers and cruise-ship visitors.

🏃 Activities

Cocoa Beach Aerial Adventures OUTDOORS
(☑ 321-613-0047; http://cocoabeachadventure park.com; 6419 N Atlantic Ave; adult/child 7-15yr/child 5-6yr $45/35/25; ⊗ 10am-5pm Sun-Thu, to 6pm Fri & Sat) Constructed among century-old oaks, this aerial adventure park is like a playground in the air, complete with ziplines and seven different rope courses featuring more than 50 obstacles. The most challenging tasks take place at 40ft in the air, and once each is complete, a zipline back to the main tower is the ultimate reward.

Ron Jon Surf Shop WATER SPORTS
(☑ 321-799-8888; www.ronjonsurfshop.com; 4151 N Atlantic Ave; ⊗ 24hr) Rents just about anything water related, from fat-tired beach bikes ($15 daily) to surfboards ($30 daily). You can also sign up here for surf school.

With live music, classic cars and a warehouse jammed with everything you could possibly need for a day at the beach, the massive 52,000-sq-ft Ron Jon is more than a store. And should you find yourself needing surf wax at 4am, no worries – it's open 24 hours a day.

Ron Jon Surf School SURFING
(☑ 321-868-1980; www.cocoabeachsurfingschool.com; 150 E Columbia Ln; 1hr surf lesson semiprivate/private $50/65, introductory kiteboarding course $225; ⊗ 9am-5pm) The long-running Ron Jon Surf School offers lessons for everyone from groms (that's surf talk for beginners) to experts. Kiteboarding classes are also offered.

🐦 Courses & Tours

Surf Art Camps SURFING
(☑ 321-799-3432; www.marymoonarts.com; per child $295; ⊗ 9am-3pm Jun-Aug) For children aged five to 17, Beach Place Guesthouses hosts weeklong Surf Art Camps.

Fin Expeditions KAYAKING
(☑ 321-698-7233; www.finexpeditions.com; 599 Ramp Rd; per person $40; 🖝) The calm waters, stable kayaks and attentive and enthusiastic guides make this an excellent tour company for families. You'll likely see a few mangrove species, cormorants, horseshoe crabs and

Cocoa Beach

even a dolphin or a manatee at the right time of year. Reservations required; cash only.

🎉 Festivals & Events

Easter Surf Festival   SURFING
(☏321-799-0493; www.eastersurffest.com; Cocoa Beach Pier; ☉Easter) Hosted by Ron Jon Surf School, this Easter weekend surfing festival has been a tradition since 1964 and now draws crowds of more than 100,000 fans to watch some of the best surfers in the world.

🛏 Sleeping

Sea Aire Motel   MOTEL $$
(☏321-783-2461; 181 N Atlantic Ave; r $90-120; ▣❄🛜) This retro mom-and-pop motel has been around since the 1950s. The place is affordable and right on the beach, with comfortable units containing kitchenettes and homey wood paneling.

Surf Studio   MOTEL $$
(☏321-783-7100; http://surf-studio.com; 1801 S Atlantic Ave; r & ste $135-180; ▣❄🛜🐾🐕) This old-school, single-story, family-owned motel sits on the ocean and offers basic doubles

and apartments surrounded by grass and palms. One-bedroom apartments sleeping six cost $205 to $215; there's no charge for children under 10.

Fawlty Towers
MOTEL $$

(☑321-784-3870; www.fawltytowersresort.com; 100 E Cocoa Beach Causeway; r $112-238; [P][✳][🌐][🏊]) After flirtations with being a nudist resort went limp, this motel returned to its gloriously garish and extremely pink roots: straightforward rooms with an unbeatable beachside location, a quiet pool and a BYOB tiki hut.

★ Beach Place Guesthouses
APARTMENT $$$

(☑321-783-4045; www.beachplaceguesthouses. com; 1445 S Atlantic Ave; ste $199-399; [P][🌐]) A slice of heavenly relaxation in Cocoa Beach's partying beach scene, this laid-back two-story guesthouse has roomy suites with hammocks and a lovely deck, all just steps from the dunes and beach. Colorful art and greenery abound on the property.

✕ Eating

★ Green Room Cafe
VEGETARIAN $

(☑321-868-0203; http://greenroomcafecocoa beach.com; 222 N 1st St; mains $6-12; ⊙10:30am-9pm Mon-Sat; ✍) Focusing all its energies on the 'goodness within', this super cafe delights the health-conscious with fruit-combo açai bowls, wheat- and gluten-free sandwiches, real fruit smoothies and homemade soups and wraps. If the 'Tower of Power' smoothie (açai, peach, strawberry, honey and apple juice) fails to lift you, the vibrant decor and friendly company will.

Simply Delicious
CAFE $

(☑321-783-2012; 125 N Orlando Ave; mains $7-15; ⊙8am-3pm Tue-Sat, to 2pm Sun) In a darling little yellow house on the southbound stretch of A1A, this homey establishment packs in locals for a scrumptious menu with unusually delicious delights including fresh strawberry crepes and malted waffles.

Slow and Low Barbecue
BARBECUE $$

(www.slowandlowbarbeque.com; 306 N Orlando Ave; mains $7-20; ⊙11am-10pm) After a day on the beach, nothing satisfies better than a plate overflowing with barbecue ribs, fried okra, turnip greens and sweet fried potatoes. There's a daily happy hour and live music Thursday through Sunday. A second location

opened recently on Stadium Pkwy in Rockledge, south of Cocoa Village.

Squid Lips Overwater Bar & Grill
SEAFOOD $$

(☑321-783-1350; www.squidlipsgrill.com; 2200 S Orlando Av; mains $15-26; ⊙11am-10pm Wed-Sun) With its outdoor seating, the newest member of the three-restaurant franchise pretty much rules. You cross a moat filled with koi to enter, and the views out over the Banana River are stunning. The Cajun bacon-wrapped scallops and stuffed flounder are excellent.

★ Fat Snook
SEAFOOD $$$

(☑321-784-1190; www.thefatsnook.com; 2464 S Atlantic Ave; mains $22-33; ⊙5:30-10pm) Hidden inside an uninspired building, tiny Fat Snook stands out as an oasis of fine cooking. Under the direction of Mona and John Foy, gourmet seafood is expertly prepared with unexpected herbs and spices influenced by Caribbean flavors. Reservations strongly recommended.

The new sister restaurant in Cocoa Village, Crush Eleven (p334), also gets top marks for its modern-American menu and crafted cocktails. Brunch on Sunday is the real highlight, with inventive dishes such as cilantro-lime crab cakes Benedict and carrot-cake pancakes.

🍷 Drinking & Nightlife

Rikki Tiki Tavern
BAR

(www.cocoabeachpier.com; Cocoa Beach Pier; ⊙11am-10pm) Kick back at this bar at the very tip of Cocoa Beach Pier and soak up the surfing-town mood.

Coconuts on the Beach
BAR

(☑321-784-1422; www.coconutsonthebeach.com; 2 Minutemen Causeway; mains $8-18; ⊙11am-midnight Mon-Thu, to 1am Fri & Sat, 9am-midnight Sun) Coconut isn't just a name; it's a favored ingredient. The oceanfront 'party deck' hosts regular live music and gets packed with revelers, especially during the high season and on spring break.

☆ Entertainment

Beach Shack
LIVE MUSIC

(☑321-783-2250; www.facebook.com/beachshack cocoabeach; 1 Minutemen Causeway; ⊙10am-1am Mon-Thu, to 2am Fri-Sun) A classic locals' bar with two pool tables, a beachfront patio, and blues Thursday to Sunday.

WHAT'S AILING THE INDIAN RIVER LAGOON?

The Indian River Lagoon is the largest marine nursery in the US and the most biologically diverse estuary in North America. Straddling temperate and subtropical zones, the lagoon (actually an ecosystem of three separate estuaries) stretches 156 miles from New Smyrna to Jupiter Inlet and is washed by tidal waters through six inlet channels. The resulting warm, shallow, soupy water is a dynamic environment for 4300 species of animal, plant and bird and exploring it is one of the true highlights of this coastline.

But all is not well in this natural paradise. In March 2016, the lagoon experienced its worst fish kill in history after an algal bloom, seemingly caused by pollution from septic tanks, fertilizers and/or storm-water runoff, stripped the lagoon of oxygen. Thousands of fish carcasses washed up on shore from Melbourne to Titusville, appalling residents and visitors and raising health concerns.

The poor state of the lagoon is nothing new. For years, unprecedented runoff from Lake Okeechobee has lowered the salinity of the lagoon, flushed it with silt and created high levels of nitrogen and phosphorus from industrial agriculture and domestic fertilizer. The result has been a 60% decline in sea-grass beds along with poisonous algal blooms. In 2013 scientists reported that these issues caused the deaths of 84 dolphins and more than 120 manatees.

In early 2017 Governor Rick Scott finally included the Indian River Lagoon in the state budget proposal. He asked for $60 million to help residents switch from septic tanks to sewer systems in affected areas, and to improve water quality by adding storage areas for polluted water to the north, east and west of Lake Okeechobee. With an annual economic impact of $4 billion and thousands of livelihoods at stake, figuring out exactly what's ailing the lagoon (and fixing it) remains the biggest environmental and economic challenge facing the Sunshine State.

THE SPACE COAST CAPE CANAVERAL

Shopping

Sunseed Food Co-op   FOOD & DRINKS
(321-784-0930; www.sunseedfoodcoop.com; 6615 N Atlantic Ave; 9:30am-7pm Mon-Fri, 10am-6pm Sat & Sun) Swing by this healthy oasis for locally grown fruit, veggies, microbrew beers, wines and after-sun lotions.

Getting There & Away

Three causeways – Hwy 528, Hwy 520 and Hwy 404 – cross Indian River Lagoon, Merritt Island and Banana River to connect Cocoa Beach to the mainland. At Ron Jon's, Hwy 528 (also Minutemen Causeway) cuts south and becomes Hwy A1A (also Atlantic Ave), a north–south strip with chain hotels and restaurants, tourist shops and condos. Hwy A1A divides into two one-way roads (southbound Orlando Ave and northbound Atlantic Ave) for a couple of miles, reconnects and continues south along the barrier-island coast 53 miles to Vero Beach and beyond.

Cocoa Beach is also served by **SCAT** (321-633-1878; http://321transit.com; per ride $1.50, 10-ride/30-day pass $6/21; schedule varies) buses. Rte 9 connects the town with Cape Canaveral, and Rte 26 connects it with

the beaches to the south, all the way down to Indialantic.

Cape Canaveral
321 / POP 9988

In 1951 the US Army Corps of Engineers carved out an inlet to facilitate the shipping of goods to the Space Center. In the process it laid the foundations for Port Canaveral, now the second-busiest cruise port in the United States.

To the north of the port, Cape Canaveral Air Force Station remains the primary launch head of the nation's Eastern Range. To the south, Cape Canaveral has evolved into a quiet, residential community for space workers and their families, though several chain hotels and restaurants here cater to cruise-ship passengers and space tourists.

Sights

Jetty Park   PARK
(321-783-7111; www.jettyparkbeachandcampground.com; 9035 Campground Circle; nonresident/resident per vehicle $15/5) Facing the

SPACE MISSIONS THEN & NOW

Early Space Exploration

In 1949 President Harry S Truman established the Joint Long Range Proving Grounds at Cape Canaveral for missile testing. The first rocket was launched on July 24, 1950, and in 1958 the National Aeronautics and Space Administration (NASA) was born to 'carry out the peaceful exploration and use of space.'

Though Soviet cosmonaut Yuri Gagarin took the honor of the first man in space on April 12, 1961, Alan Shepard became the first American just one month later. In February 1962 John Glenn launched from Cape Canaveral, circled the Earth three times in the world's first orbital flight, and landed four hours later in the Atlantic Ocean off Bermuda.

Project Apollo & Space Shuttle Program

John Glenn's seminal voyage fueled support for the space program, and President Kennedy vowed to land a man on the moon by the end of the decade. On July 16, 1969, a *Saturn V* rocket shot out from Kennedy Space Center. Four days later Neil Armstrong spoke the immortal phrase: 'That's one small step for man, one giant leap for mankind.' Between 1969 and 1972, six more Apollo missions were launched to explore the moon.

In 1976 NASA introduced the space shuttle, a reusable occupied space vehicle designed to rocket into space with a booster (which is later shed), orbit the earth, and glide back safely to solid ground. Five years later, in 1981, NASA's successful launch of the *STS-1*, piloted by John Young and Robert Crippen, opened a new era of American space exploration. Tragedy struck, however, with the January 28, 1986 *Challenger* explosion. Seven astronauts were killed, as was schoolteacher Christa McAuliffe, who was to be the first ordinary citizen to go into space. NASA stopped all launches until that of shuttle *Discovery* in 1988. Throughout the 1990s, shuttles allowed American astronauts to maintain the Hubble Space Telescope and help construct the International Space Station.

On February 1, 2003, *Columbia* exploded upon re-entry, again killing all seven astronauts on board, and NASA again stopped the shuttle program. Missions resumed in 2005, but closed indefinitely in 2011.

Future Space Exploration

NASA is currently developing the most advanced rocket ever created, the *Orion* spacecraft, and has plans to send astronauts beyond the moon, eventually reaching destinations including Mars, sometime in the 2030s. A shorter-term NASA endeavor, the Asteroid Redirect Mission, involves the first-ever attempt to capture an asteroid, and, if all goes according to plan, redirect the asteroid to orbit the moon, where astronauts will explore it and bring back samples. This is penciled in for 2020.

Meanwhile, Elon Musk has claimed his commercial venture SpaceX will send astronauts to Mars as soon as 2025. Although Musk is known for ambitious scheduling, his company recently leased the Kennedy Space Center's Launch Complex 39A, and in February 2017 conducted the first launch from the pad since NASA's shuttle program ended in 2011. SpaceX's *Dragon* spacecraft lifted off toward the International Space Station to deliver cargo and supplies, and the company continues to launch satellites and rockets a couple of times a month.

distant Cape Canaveral Lighthouse, this 35-acre coastal park is a prime spot for sunbathing, fishing and watching cruise ships set sail. Chairs, umbrellas, kayaks and paddleboards can all be rented at the beach, which is patrolled by lifeguards. There are also grills, a playground and a couple of food concessions.

Sleeping & Eating

There are quite a few chain hotels here, largely catering to families visiting Kennedy Space

Center and cruise-ship passengers coming and going. Jetty Park is a good option for camping.

Jetty Park CAMPGROUND **$**
(321-783-7111; www.jettyparkbeachandcampground.com; 400 Jetty Rd; campsites $27-49, cabins $84; P 🐾 📶 🐕) Jetty Park offers cabins, fire pits for RV sites, a playground, two pavilions, 93 barbecue grills, beach access and a fishing pier.

Residence Inn Cape Canaveral HOTEL **$$**
(321-323-1100; www.marriott.com; 8959 Astronaut Blvd; r from $140; P ❄ 📶 🐕) If you want to get away from the Cocoa Beach party scene, book into this comfortable Marriott hotel. Rooms may be corporate, but they offer acres of space, comfortable beds and kitchenettes. Staff are also extremely accommodating and there's a pretty pool area. Popular with the precruise crowd.

★ Seafood Atlantic SEAFOOD **$$**
(321-784-1963; www.seafoodatlantic.org; 520 Glen Cheek Dr, Port Canaveral; mains $8-19; ⊙11am-7pm Wed-Sun, seafood market from 10am) With deep roots in Canaveral's fishing industry, this restaurant (with outdoor deck) is one of the few places to serve locally sourced shrimp, crabs, mussels, clams, oysters and fish. If they're in, order a bucket of Florida's deep-sea golden crab, which has a deliciously moist and creamy texture. Also, bring a bag and stock up at the market next door.

☗ Drinking & Nightlife

Preacher Bar BAR
(321-613-4629; http://preacherbar.com; 8699 Astronaut Blvd; ⊙11am-late) This bizarre and colorful watering hole is decked out in Day of the Dead portraits, animal skulls and stained-glass windows. Seating is communal and the bartenders are clad in plaid skirts. Try a homemade Moscow mule with ginger-infused vodka.

ⓘ Getting There & Away

There are two ways to arrive in Cape Canaveral: traveling north on A1A from Cocoa Beach, or west on A1A across the Banana River via Merritt Island.

Cape Canaveral is served by **SCAT** (p331) buses. Rte 9 connects it with Cocoa Beach and Rte 4 connects it with Cocoa Village.

Cocoa Village
321 / POP 5937

Originally a trading post along the Indian River Lagoon, Cocoa Village started serving tourists in the late 19th century when steamboat travelers disembarked along Riverfront Park to stretch their legs. Now the historic downtown offers a pleasant alternative to Cocoa Beach. Its main drag, Delannoy Ave, is lined with historic structures such as the SF Travis Building, which houses a hardware store (the village's oldest existing business).

◉ Sights

EFSC Planetarium & Observatory OBSERVATORY
(321-433-7373; www.easternflorida.edu/community-resources/planetarium; Bldg 19, 1519 Clearlake Rd; shows adult/child under 12yr $8/5; ⊙shows 2pm Wed, 7pm & 8:15pm Fri & Sat, observatory dusk-10pm Fri & Sat) Discover new galaxies and constellations in this 70ft domed planetarium that projects the night skies in startling detail, enhanced with laser effects and accompanied by soaring soundtracks from Pink Floyd, Jimi Hendrix and the Beatles. On Friday and Saturday nights, volunteers help visitors navigate the real night sky through one of the largest telescopes in Florida, powerful enough to bring the rings of Saturn into focus and highlight lunar craters.

The planetarium is located on the campus of Brevard Community College, 10 minutes north of Cocoa Village off Clearlake Rd.

⌖ Tours

Indian River Queen BOATING
(321-454-7414; www.indianriverqueen.com; Cocoa Village Marina, 90 Delannoy Ave; cruises $35-60) Take a trip back in time on this romantic paddleboat. The history-themed tour includes a narrated presentation on 19th-century Cocoa Village, when paddleboats were the norm and homesteaders hung a white cloth at the end of their pier to flag them down. Dinner and sunset booze cruises are also available. Check the website for the schedule.

Grasshopper Airboat Eco Tours ECOTOUR
(321-631-2990; www.airboatecotours.com; 5665 Lake Poinsett Rd; adult/child 7-12yr $45/40) Often referred to as the Central Florida

Everglades, the marshy shallows of the St Johns River are packed with alligators and migrating birds. Hop on board with US Coast Guard Master Captain Rick for thrilling ecotours through the marshy shallows. Afternoon tours see the best alligator sunbathing.

🛏 Sleeping & Eating

★ Solrisa Inn
B&B $$

(☑321-917-3487; http://solrisainn.com; 241 Indian River Dr; r $200-250; P ❋ 🐾 🐕) Solrisa sits on the banks of the Indian River Lagoon and comes complete with a dock where guests sip sundowners and push off their paddleboats. Inside, the turn-of-the-century house unfolds in sunny Caribbean colors, and period floorboards gleam beneath Persian rugs. Accommodation is in three meticulously decorated rooms, and each room comes with its own deck and rocking chair.

Ossorio
CAFE $

(☑321-639-2423; 316 Brevard Ave; mains $7-9; ☺8am-8:30pm Mon-Sat, 9am-6pm Sun) Fuel up pre- or postbeach at this sunny cafe serving sandwiches, flatbread pizza, ice cream and coffee.

Cocoa Village Farmers Market
MARKET $

(http://cocoamainstreet.com/projects/farmers market; Myrt Tharpe Sq; ☺10am-3pm Thu) Weekly farmers market with fresh, organic produce, local honey and more.

Lone Cabbage Fish Camp
SEAFOOD $$

(☑321-632-4199; www.twisterairboatrides.com; 8199 Hwy 520; mains $8-15; ☺10am-9pm Sun-Thu, to 10pm Fri & Sat) Come to this redneck fish camp for cold beers, fried gator tail and sunset views over the Indian River. If you want, you can even scoot around the lagoon on its airboats (adult/child $24/16). You'll find it west of Cocoa Village on Hwy 520.

★ Crush Eleven
MODERN AMERICAN $$$

(☑321-634-1100; www.crusheleven.com; 11 Riverside Dr; mains $18-49; ☺5-9pm daily, 11am-3pm brunch Sun) Sister restaurant to the Fat Snook (p330), Crush Eleven gets top marks for its modern American menu and crafted cocktails. Don't miss the bacon-infused Old Fashioned cocktail.

Café Margaux
MEDITERRANEAN $$$

(☑321-639-8343; http://margaux.com; 220 Brevard Ave; mains $15-45; ☺11:30am-2pm & 5-9pm Mon-Sat) A longtime favorite of Cocoa Village regulars is this creative Mediterranean restaurant.

Dine on the patio or in one of the themed dining rooms on chili-seared red snapper or Syrah-braised short ribs. To accompany your meal choose from a wine list that runs to 4000 labels.

☆ Entertainment

There are a couple of decent pubs in the area, and the best spot for craft cocktails is Crush Eleven.

Cocoa Village Playhouse
PERFORMING ARTS

(☑321-636-5050; www.cocoavillageplayhouse. com; 300 Brevard Ave) Stages locally produced plays on the site of the ornate Historic Cocoa Village Playhouse, built in 1924.

🔒 Shopping

Village Outfitters
SPORTS & OUTDOORS

(☑321-633-7245; www.villageoutfitters.com; 229 Forrest Ave; ☺10am-5pm Mon-Fri, 8:30am-4pm Sat) Outdoor and camping gear, as well as kayak rental.

ℹ Information

Space Coast Office of Tourism (☑321-433-4470; www.visitspacecoast.com; 430 Brevard Ave; ☺9am-5pm Mon-Fri) Inside the Bank of America, one block south of the Village Playhouse.

ℹ Getting There & Away

Cocoa Village stretches west from S Cocoa Blvd to the Indian River Lagoon and south from King St about five blocks. Having a car is most convenient, but Rte 1 **SCAT** (p331) buses pass through Cocoa Village on a north–south route, as does the Rte 4 SCAT bus, which connects to Merritt Island and Cocoa Beach.

ℹ Getting Around

Cocoa Village is best explored on foot, as it's only about five city blocks long and wide.

Melbourne

☑321 / POP 77,508

Historic Melbourne was established in the 1870s by freed slaves and pineapple farmers who built homesteads on a small peninsula between the Indian River Lagoon and Crane Creek. A fire destroyed the burgeoning town in 1919, but the newly reconstructed downtown along New Haven Ave remains much as it was in the 1920s, offering a small-town feel with several good restaurants, coffee shops and bars.

Across the lagoon, Melbourne Beach has a more chill vibe and a variety of beachfront accommodations.

◉ Sights

★ Brevard Zoo   ZOO
(☑ 321-254-9453; www.brevardzoo.org; 8225 N Wickham Rd; adult/child 2-12yr $20/15, Tree Top Trek adult/small child $40/15; ⊙9am-3:30pm) For more than 22 years this community-built zoo has set standards for imaginative design, immersive wildlife experiences, education and conservation. Since hammer-holding locals came out in force in March 1994 to start construction, the zoo's landscape has evolved via winding boardwalks through hardwood hammocks into distinct geographical zones featuring wildlife from Florida, South America, Africa and Australia. Specially designed enclosures merging with the undergrowth and free-flight aviaries give a real sense of wandering through a wilderness.

The zoo's best experiences are the **kayak tours** past gangling giraffes down the Nyami Nyami river and the **Tree Top Trek**, an aerial adventure course incorporating ziplines over wetland ponds and alligator pools.

Once you've got over the enjoyment of wandering around the zoo's unique environment, you'll begin to notice its dedication to the serious work of conservation and wildlife education. The **Paws On** children's area invites kids to build, explore and splash around on a real sand beach, engage in hookless fishing and pet the resident pygmy goats and alpacas. Volunteers work tirelessly to create oyster mats for the oyster-reef-regeneration project in Indian River, and the **Wildlife Detective Training Academy** encourages curiosity and inquiry in older kids through self-guided mystery tours designed around the zoo.

In addition, there are night hikes, a Junior Zoo Keeper's Club, animal-adoption programs, summer camps and well-attended community events, including the popular **Boo at the Zoo** Halloween celebration. For kids and animal lovers this may well outshine the Space Center.

Melbourne Beach   BEACH
(Ocean Park, Atlantic St) Backed by **Ocean Park** with its boardwalk, gazebo and showers, Melbourne Beach, along with its neighbor, Indialantic Beach (to the north), offers miles and miles of white, sandy shoreline

unspoiled by high-rise condos and commercialism. Pick up picnic essentials at the Melbourne Beach Market (p336).

Ryckman Park   PARK
(cnr Ocean Ave & Riverside Dr, Melbourne Beach) Located in Melbourne's historic district, this family-friendly park features a large playground, bocce and basketball courts and the nationally registered **Melbourne Beach Pier** (1889). The latter extends into the fish-rich Indian River Lagoon, making it a fantastic fishing spot.

🛏 Sleeping

There aren't many good options in the downtown area, with the exception of Crane Creek Inn. Head over to Melbourne Beach for oceanfront stays with lots of local character.

Crane Creek Inn Waterfront
Bed & Breakfast   B&B $$
(☑ 321-768-6416; www.cranecreekinn.com; 907 E Melbourne Ave; r $175; P❋🐾❋) Two blocks from downtown Melbourne, this attractive 1925 home sits directly on Crane Creek, where manatees, dolphins and waterbirds can be seen. The five rooms are furnished in period style with lazy ceiling fans, and there is a two-person hammock beside the river.

Sea View Motel   MOTEL $$
(☑ 321-723-0566; www.seaviewmelbourne.com; 4215 S Hwy A1A, Melbourne Beach; r & ste from $180; ❋🐾❋) Located directly on the beach, this renovated 1950s motel has eight simple rooms with quilts, wood floors and fully equipped kitchens.

★ Port d'Hiver   BOUTIQUE HOTEL $$$
(☑ 321-722-2727; www.portdhiver.com; 201 Ocean Ave, Melbourne Beach; r $279-329, ste $479-519; P❋🐾❋) Constructed in 1916, this cypress-built, colonial-style beach house sits amid tall palms, hidden behind flowering bougainvillea and bright pink allamanda. Brick-paved courtyards connect the main house with seven cabana rooms and the carriage-house suite, and views of the Atlantic are complemented by artful interior decor incorporating French printed fabrics, candelabra chandeliers, antique dressers and four-poster beds.

✕ Eating

Seafood is top-notch both downtown and out at the beach, and the talk of the town is the new dock-to-table establishment Ocean 302.

Ichabods Dockside
AMERICAN $

([☑]321-952-9532; www.ichabodsbarandgrille-florida. com; 2210 Front St; mains $8-12; ⊘11am-11pm) Eddy Fisher's laid-back bar is a local favorite for its easygoing barside banter and top-quality burgers, jerked grouper wraps and mind-blowingly good buffalo wings.

El Ambia Cubano
CUBAN $

(www.elambiacubano.com; 950 E Melbourne Ave; mains $8-15; ⊘11am-2:30pm & 5-9pm Mon-Thu, 11am-10pm Fri, noon-10pm Sat) Conga stools, weekend salsa, jazz and acoustic guitar, and tasty family cooking in a tiny spot across from Crane Creek.

Melbourne Beach Market
MARKET $

([☑]321-676-5225; 302 Ocean Ave; ⊘8am-8pm Mon-Sat, to 7pm Sun) Pick up picnic essentials here, including ready-to-eat Greek and Italian meals.

Matt's Casbah
SUSHI $$

([☑]321-574-1099; www.mattscasbah.com; 801 E New Haven Ave; mains $10-15; ⊘11am-midnight Mon-Thu, to 2am Fri & Sat, to 10pm Sun) In the heart of downtown, this popular eatery features a delicious sushi bar, exotic options such as fried whole fish and desserts that arrive flaming in 151 rum. Check the website for nightly specials, live music and other event announcements.

★Ocean 302
SEAFOOD $$$

([☑]321-802-5728; http://ocean302.com; 302 Ocean Ave; charcuterie small/large $17/30, mains $21-34; ⊘4-10pm Mon-Thu, 10am-10pm Sat & Sun) Melbourne Beach has gone fancy with this new, dock- and farm-to-table establishment ensconced in an otherwise unimpressive shopping plaza. With adventurous offerings such as octopus confit and Seminole pride grass-fed-beef bone marrow, this place will soon be luring foodies from up and down the Space Coast. Make reservations just in case.

🍷 Drinking & Nightlife

On Friday and Saturday nights, East New Haven Ave in downtown Melbourne is transformed into an urban block party.

Meg O'Malley's
IRISH PUB

([☑]321-952-5510; www.megomalleys.com; 812 E New Haven Ave; ⊘10:30am-10pm Mon & Tue, to 11pm Wed, to midnight Thu, to 1:30am Fri & Sat, to midnight Sun) This authentic, ever-hoppin' Irish pub serves up 18¢ bowls of Parliament soup and Guinness with live music.

Foo Bar & Lotus Gallery
LOUNGE

([☑]321-728-7179; 816 E New Haven Ave; ⊘5pm-2am Mon-Fri, 3pm-2am Sat & Sun) Draws an older crowd with an Asian-themed menu, craft cocktails and an exquisite interior gallery. Cabaret shows and '80s nights occur frequently.

Sand on the Beach
BAR

([☑]321-327-8951; http://sandonthebeach.com; 1005 Atlantic St; ⊘8am-late) The only place where you can keep the sand between your toes and a margarita in your hand. And with bars on three levels, you've also got sea views for miles in either direction.

Main Street Pub
PUB

([☑]321-723-7811; http://mainstreetpub.cc; 705 E New Haven Ave; ⊘11:30am-late Tue-Fri, 4pm-late Mon & Sat) Offers a good selection of beers and a nice deck.

☆ Entertainment

While Cocoa Beach pays homage to the gods of commercialism, Melbourne prefers to pay its dues to those of culture with a thriving community arts, music and theater scene.

★Melbourne Civic Theatre
THEATER

([☑]321-723-6935; www.mymct.org; 817 E Strawbridge Ave; tickets $31; ⊘box office 11am-3pm Tue-Fri, 2pm-6pm Sat) The Space Coast's oldest community theater stages early Broadway productions and popular contemporary pieces in a tiny spot in the shopping plaza La Galerie. They're a talented bunch and with only 90 seats in the auditorium it's an exciting space in which to experience live performances.

Brevard Symphony Orchestra
CLASSICAL MUSIC

([☑]321-242-2219; https://brevardsymphony.com; King Center, 3865 N Wickham Rd) This 65-strong, not-for-profit orchestra has been bringing music to Melbourne residents for more than 60 years and is one of the finest in the country. For the July 4 celebrations the symphony plays at the Cocoa Riverfront Park beneath a spectacular fireworks display.

Henegar Center
ARTS CENTER

([☑]321-723-8698; www.henegar.org; 625 E New Haven Ave) Melbourne's one-time high school now houses a community arts center and a

500-seat proscenium-style theater that stages musicals and comedies.

ℹ Getting There & Away

Driving to and from Melbourne is the most sensible option, although several **SCAT** (p331) routes do connect Melbourne to most neighboring destinations and loop through several areas of the city.

The **Orlando Melbourne International Airport** (☑ 321-723-6227; www.mlbair.com; 1 Air Terminal Pkwy) is located to the northeast of the city and works with a limited number of commercial airlines.

Indialantic

☑ 321 / POP 2755

Indialantic, a blink-and-you-miss-it beach town 16 miles south of Cocoa Beach, isn't expansive, but it sure feels homey. You'll find a pizza place and a handful of other businesses, and the same surf and white sand, but it's worlds away from the Cocoa Beach rattle and hum.

✳ Activities

Longboard House   SURFING
(☑ 321-951-8001; www.longboardhouse.com; 101 5th Av; per day surfboard/bodyboard $29/10; ☺8:30am-9pm Mon-Sat, to 6pm Sun) A long-standing surf shop, with an impressive selection of surfboards for rent and purchase.

Paddleboard House   WATER SPORTS
(☑ 321-676-9773; www.facebook.com/pbhdave/; 110 S Miramar Av; 3hr/day $30/50; ☺8:30am-6:30pm Mon-Sat, to 6pm Sun) This place rents paddleboards at reasonable rates.

Bob's Bicycle Shop   CYCLING
(☑ 321-725-2500; http://bobsbicycles.com; 113 5th Ave; road bike per day/week $65/180; ☺9:30am-6pm Mon-Fri, 10am-6pm Sat, 11am-3pm Sun) Rents road bikes and cruisers, and sells fat bikes, which are especially fun to ride in the sand.

🛏 Sleeping & Eating

There are a few scattered cottages along the coastline in Indialantic, but head north to Cocoa Beach or south to Melbourne Beach for a larger variety of options.

Beachside Cafe   CAFE $
(☑ 321-953-8444; www.thebeachsidecafe.com; 109 5th Ave; mains $6-12; ☺7am-2pm; 🖰) It's worth the wait to grab a booth at this family-owned, friendly downtown breakfast cafe, where servers regularly top up coffee as locals scarf plates of stuffed French toast, griddled Belgian waffles and pastrami omelets.

Bizarro Famous NY Pizza   PIZZA $$
(☑ 321-724-4799; www.theoriginalbizzarro.com; 4 Wave Crest Ave; pizza $11-36; ☺10am-10pm Mon-Sat, noon-9pm Sun) This NY-style pizza joint sits in a majestic spot beside the beach in Indialantic. Service is brusque – think 'the soup Nazi' but for pizza. But the spinach slice is divine with extra marinara sauce.

Scott's on Fifth   MEDITERRANEAN $$$
(☑ 321-729-9779; www.scottsonfifth.com; 141 5th Ave; mains $26-39; ☺5:30-9pm Tue-Sun) This elegant restaurant on 5th Ave serves up European classics as part of a seasonally appropriate menu that changes daily, with highlights often including grouper specials, escargot and stuffed shrimp. It's easy to miss as it's tucked behind a tiny storefront, and as there are only 12 tables you'll need to reserve in advance.

🍷 Drinking & Nightlife

Copperhead Tavern   CRAFT BEER
(☑ 321-802-4700; www.copperheadtavern.com; 205 5th Av; ☺11am-2am Mon-Sat, to midnight Sun) The best (and only) bar in town, Copperhead Tavern offers craft beer, juicy burgers (served til close) and a fire pit in the outdoor beer garden.

Titusville

☑ 321 / POP 44,206

Essentially NASA's bedroom community, the small but quaint town of Titusville is just across the Indian River Lagoon from the Kennedy Space Center, and its prosperity is inextricably tied to that of the space program. When humans goes to Mars, Titusville will boom.

In the meantime, the historic downtown has shown signs of life, with the addition of a hip craft brewery and plans for a bicycle trail segment that will eventually extend across Florida all the way to St Petersburg. A quirky B&B, a couple of good restaurants and a great park for watching spacecraft launches round out the offerings.

👁 Sights

Valiant Air Command Warbird Museum   MUSEUM
(☑ 321-268-1941; www.valiantaircommand.com; 6600 Tico Rd; adult/military/child $20/18/5;

⊘9am-5pm; 📶) What started off as a hobby for 12 combat veterans has grown into a 1500-member-strong club and fascinating museum, which celebrates the region's aviation heritage with an impressive stock of more than 45 classic planes. A memorabilia hall kicks off the tour, then you're free to roam through three hangars, one a restoration workshop and the other two housing vintage aircraft from WWII, the Vietnam War and the Korean War.

The VAC's flagship, the *Tico Belle,* a 1942 C-47A that dropped paratroopers at the D-Day landings, sits combat ready next to a restored *Top Gun*–style Grumman Wildcat that took more than 30,000 hours to restore.

In March or April the museum hosts a family-friendly air show when combat veterans put on a three-hour aerial display and offer the next generation of ace pilots a chance to fly in a unique piece of history. Alternatively, drop by on the second Saturday of the month to enjoy a fly-in breakfast ($12; available 8am till 10:30am) and ask about 'champagne flights,' which fly the coast in a WWII C-47 about once a month ($250 per person).

Space View Park   PARK

(17 Orange St) Directly across the Indian River Lagoon from Kennedy Space Center, this park is one of the best spots on the coast from which to observe launches. Its 2-plus acres also contain the U.S. Space Walk of Fame, a collection of monuments, exhibits and plaques commemorating space missions.

🛏 Sleeping & Eating

★Casa Coquina del Mar   B&B $$

(☎321-268-4663; www.casacoquina.com; 4010 Coquina Av; $105-174; 🅿❄🤍) This quirky, family-owned B&B is set in a 1927 mansion with eight rooms, each uniquely furnished and named for gemstones (most impressive is the Black Pearl, spacious and beautifully adorned with antiques from the Orient). There's a huge replica of a knight riding a horse in the downstairs living room, and a hot tub in the gazebo out back.

In the morning, the owners serve up an impressive buffet breakfast including freshly baked bread, an egg dish, baked ham, fresh fruit, coffee, tea and juice.

Wild Ocean Seafood   MARKET $

(www.wildoceanmarket.com; 688 S Park Ave; mains $9-12; ⊘11am-6pm Mon-Thu, 10am-6pm Fri & Sat,

11am-4pm Sun) With more than 80 species of harvestable Florida seafood, Wild Ocean Seafood market believes in diversifying consumers' palates and therefore carries low trophic level fish as well as predatory species. They serve prepared seafood right in the store, including a mouthwatering Asian tuna burger and a 'not-from-a-can' tuna melt, and hold tastings and attend food festivals to educate the public. There's a second location in Cape Canaveral.

★Dixie Crossroads   SEAFOOD $$

(☎321-268-5000; http://dixiecrossroads.com; 1475 Garden St; mains $8-46; ⊘11am-9pm Sun-Thu, to 10pm Fri & Sat; 📶) Rodney Thompson developed the rock-shrimp fishery off Canaveral's coast in the early 1970s and in 1983 his daughter, Laurilee, opened the Dixie Crossroads Seafood Restaurant. The aim: to put local shrimp back on the Canaveral's tables. Today this local landmark continues to serve up seasonal shrimp, including sweet, blush-colored royal reds, succulent white shrimp and melt-in-your-mouth, broiled rock shrimp.

Rock shrimp are ordered by the dozen, and arrive sliced open by a wondrous machine invented by the Thompsons and accompanied by sweet potato, coleslaw and grits. Other menu highlights include fresh Indian River Lagoon red mullet, oysters and juicy prime rib. Despite the generous seating in the funky wooden chalet, there's often a queue at peak times, so order a drink in the gazebo bar.

★Chef Larry's   MODERN AMERICAN $$

(☎321-368-9123; www.cheflarrysspice.com; 1111 S Washington Ave; lunch mains $7-10, dinner mains $12-15; ⊘11am-1:30pm Tue-Fri, 5-7pm Fri & Sat) The best meal in Titusville is procured in a historic pink home filled with old Americana and run by a Hollywood chef who 'retired' to Titusville. He runs a tight, somewhat odd ship, opening for just a couple of hours on particular days (definitely reserve ahead) and serving just a few dishes, most notably teriyaki bourbon barbecue baby back ribs.

Cash only.

🍷 Drinking & Nightlife

Playalinda
Brewing Company   MICROBREWERY

(☎321-225-8978; www.playalindabrewingcompany. com; 305 S Washington Ave; ⊘4-11pm Mon-Thu, 3pm-midnight Fri, noon-midnight Sat, noon-9pm

Sun) In historic downtown Titusville, this microbrewery is set in a 100-year-old former hardware store and features a great selection of local and national craft beer, including a few really tasty stouts and porters. The brewery also serves delicious food, including the Ploughman's Platter (charcuterie with cheese, fruits and veggies) and a pretzel-bowl, beer-cheese soup.

A newer, sister restaurant called Brix Project is located down the road and offers a larger space and menu.

Bar IX BAR
(☎ 321-567-7604; http://barixfl.com; 317 S Washington Ave; ⊘ 11am-midnight Mon-Thu, to 2am Fri & Sat, to 11am Sun) Good local watering hole with a selection of tap and bottled craft beer and frequent live music.

❶ Getting There & Away

A car is the best way to go in Titusville, which is accessible via Hwy 1 from the north and south. On the northern end of town, the A. Max Brewer Memorial Pkwy extends east over the Indian River Lagoon to Merritt Island National Wildlife Refuge. To the south, NASA Pkwy stretches east over the lagoon to the Kennedy Space Center Visitor Complex.

SCAT (p331) bus Rte 1 connects Titusville with the cities to the south (including Cocoa Village) and Rte 2 loops around Titusville.

Northeast Florida

POP 1.18 MILLION

Best Places to Eat

➜ Southern Charm Kitchen (p380)

➜ Present Moment Cafe (p355)

➜ Dragonfly (p380)

➜ Bearded Pig BBQ (p359)

➜ Cress (p374)

Best Places to Sleep

➜ Addison (p367)

➜ At Journey's End (p354)

➜ Hotel Palms (p364)

➜ Grady House Bed & Breakfast (p382)

➜ Jaybird's Inn (p354)

Why Go?

The northeast corner of Florida is a jumble of farmland, forests and pasture, urban sprawl and college towns, built-up beaches and bucolic sea islands. You'll find spots like Amelia Island – a natural escape for the country-club crowd – a mere hour's drive north from Jacksonville, one of the most spread out, sprawling cities in the country. Hit the road for a little more and you're in Gainesville, peppered with fair-trade coffee shops and craft cocktail bars (and, to be fair, a raucous fraternity-friendly party scene).

St Augustine, the oldest continuously occupied city in the US, has something for everyone – history, architecture, culture, a gamut of excellent dining and plenty of kid-friendly tourist schmaltz. Further south, you'll find odd-duck antique-laden small towns and (hey, it's Florida) more miles of soft, sandy beach.

When to Go
Daytona Beach

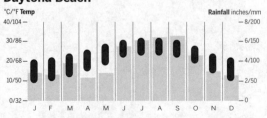

Nov–Feb Discounted hotel rates in St Augustine, Amelia Island and the Jacksonville area beaches.

Mar & Apr Spring break brings college students, who become a noticeably loud presence in area beaches.

Jun–Aug Summer can be sweltering, but it's much quieter in Gainesville, as many students leave campus.

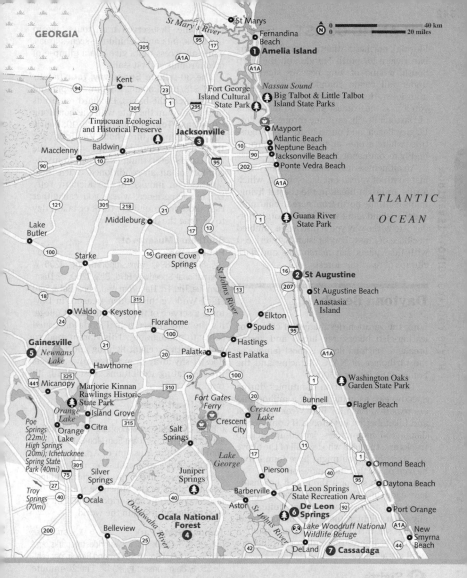

Northeast Florida Highlights

❶ Amelia Island (p365)
Kayaking into the waterways that surround this pretty barrier island.

❷ St Augustine (p348)
Exploring Spanish-colonial architecture, fascinating museums and centuries of history in America's oldest city.

❸ Jacksonville (p358)
Discovering more culture and quirkiness than you may expect in Florida's biggest city.

❹ Ocala National Forest (p376) Hiking, canoeing and camping your way through this pristine, wildlife-dense forest.

❺ Gainesville (p377)
Rocking out in the home of

Florida's largest university; cheap eats and cool bars.

❻ De Leon Springs State Park (p373) Marveling at the cool azure waters.

❼ Cassadaga (p371) Having your fortune read and your life's purpose re-aligned in this spiritualist camp-cum-small town.

ATLANTIC COAST

Florida's northern Atlantic Coast is an exurban riviera for north Florida and the Deep South, a land of long beaches shadowed under tall condo complexes and seaside mansions. Heading from south to north, you'll pass the exhaust pipes and biker bars of Daytona Beach, continue through mellow Flagler Beach, and on to historic St Augustine, where a one- or two-night sojourn is highly recommended.

An affluent series of beaches can be found just south of spread-out Jacksonville, which forms an urban break in the coastal living; many continue north from here to charming Amelia Island and the Florida–Georgia border. Along the way you'll discover a jumbled necklace of grassy barrier islands, interlaced with tidal inlets, salt marsh flats and dark clumps of maritime forest.

Daytona Beach

📞 386 / POP 62,316

Long the vacation destination of choice for leather-clad bikers, rev heads and spring breakers, Daytona Beach is most famous as the birthplace of NASCAR racing and the home of the Daytona 500.

The area's population quintuples during Speedweeks; as many as half a million bikers roar into town for Bike Week in March and Biketoberfest in October. If Confederate flags, loud motorcycles, jacked-up pick-up trucks and the folks who love all of the above are your thing, you might have found your heaven on earth. If not, move on.

If you can see past the garish beachside barricade of '70s high-rise blocks, nightclubs and tourist traps (if not quite literally), you might witness the phenomena of nesting sea turtles (in season) or explore a handful of interesting and worthwhile cultural attractions.

👁 Sights

★ Daytona International Speedway   STADIUM

(📞 800-748-7467; www.daytonainternationalspeedway.com; 1801 W International Speedway Blvd; tours from $18; ⏱ tours 9:30am-3:30pm) The Holy Grail of raceways has a diverse race schedule. Ticket prices skyrocket for good seats at big races, headlined by the **Daytona 500** in February. It's worth wandering the massive stands for free on non-race days.

First-come, first-served tram tours take in the track, pits and behind-the-scenes areas, while all-access tours give you a glimpse of media rooms and pit stalls.

The 30-minute **Speedway Tour** (adult/child $18/12; 11:30am, 1:30pm, 3:30pm and 4pm) covers the basics. Die-hard rev heads may wish to up the ante with the hour-long **All Access Tour** (adult/child $25/19; hourly 10am to 3pm) or three-hour **VIP Tour** ($52 1pm Tuesday, Thursday and Saturday); the last covers everything NASCAR from the comfort of an air-conditioned coach. Real fanatics can indulge in the Richard Petty Driving Experience, where you can either ride shotgun around the track or take a day to become the driver.

Southeast Museum of Photography   MUSEUM

(📞 386-506-3894; www.smponline.org; 1200 W International Speedway Blvd, Bldg 1200; ⏱ 11am-5pm Tue, Thu, Fri, 11am-7pm Wed, 1-5pm Sat & Sun) **FREE** We love this hidden treasure in Daytona, a service of the Daytona State College: it's the only museum in Florida dedicated solely to photography. This vibrant modern gallery with excellent lighting and facilities doesn't shy away from provocative subjects in its rotating exhibitions. Best of all, it's free!

Cici & Hyatt Brown Museum of Art   MUSEUM

(📞 386-255-0285; www.moas.org; 352 S Nova Rd; adult/child $11/5; ⏱ 10am-5pm Mon-Sat, from 11am Sun) Part of the Museum of Arts & Sciences complex, this striking must-see museum, designed to look like a rural Floridian house, tells the story of the Sunshine State via the largest collection of Florida-themed oil and watercolor paintings in the world.

Tomoka State Park   STATE PARK

(📞 386-676-4050; www.floridastateparks.org/tomoka; 2099 N Beach St, Ormond Beach; per vehicle $5; ⏱ 8am-sunset; 🅿 🚻) 🐾 The 20-minute drive here from downtown Daytona Beach is almost as pleasant as the park itself, a bird-watchers' heaven of former indigo fields turned hardwood forests. A canopy of trees overhangs the two-lane road like a green tunnel, letting in only the stray dapple of sunlight.

Daytona Beach Drive-In Church   CHURCH

(📞 386-767-8761; www.driveinchurch.net; 3140 S Atlantic Ave; ⏱ services 8:30am & 10am Sun; 🅿) At Daytona Beach Drive-In Church you can get your daily dose of (Protestant) religion from the comfort of your car. Pull in to the former drive-in movie theater, hook up a speaker or tune your radio to 680AM or 88.5FM and behold the word of...the Reverend. He and the choir hold services on a balcony overlooking the sea of cars. There's free coffee and doughnuts between services. That's right...free doughnuts – What are you waiting for? Only in Daytona.

The church dates back to 1954. When the old Neptune Drive-In Theater closed, this car-obsessed town devised a novel solution for increasing church attendance: getting the good news while sitting in your vehicle. Again: only in Daytona.

Marine Science Center   AQUARIUM
(📋 386-304-5545; www.marinesciencecenter.com; 100 Lighthouse Dr, Ponce Inlet; adult/child $5/2; ⊙10am-4pm Tue-Sat, noon-4pm Sun; 🖤) 🍃 We were impressed by this center's rescue, rehab and release programs for sea turtles and seabirds that nest on Daytona's beaches. It's a fun and environmentally conscious place where adults and kids can enjoy learning about our underwater friends. Exhibits include a 5000-gallon reef aquarium, a stingray touch pool and a bird-observation tower. Open until 5pm during summer.

Museum of Arts & Sciences   MUSEUM
(MOAS; 📋 386-255-0285; www.moas.org; 352 S Nova Rd; adult/child $12.95/6.95; ⊙10am-5pm Tue-Sat, from 11am Sun; 🖤) This self-guided museum has a healthy dose of brain food for a fast and furious little town like Daytona. There's a delightful mishmash of everything from Cuban art to Coca-Cola memorabilia, train cars to teddy bears, a 13ft skeleton of a giant sloth, and a planetarium. Admission is free on the first Tuesday of the month.

Jackie Robinson
Ballpark & Museum   STADIUM
(📋 386-257-3172; www.daytonacubs.com; 105 E Orange Ave; ⊙9am-5pm; 🖤) FREE 'The Jack' made history when, in 1946, the Montreal Royals, Jackie Robinson's team, were in Florida to play an exhibition against their parent club, the Brooklyn Dodgers: other Florida cities refused to let the game proceed due to segregation laws, but Daytona Beach cried, 'Play ball!' Robinson went on to be the first African American baseball player in the majors. The ballpark here was renamed in his honor in 1990. A small open-air museum tells the story.

Gamble Place   MUSEUM
(📋 386-304-0778; www.moas.org/gamble.place. html; 1819 Taylor Rd, Port Orange; adult/child $3/ free; ⊙8am-5pm Wed-Sun; 🅿) Twenty minutes south of Daytona but a million miles away, the winter estate of the Gamble family (of Procter & Gamble fortune) lies in a sun-dappled glade. The Cracker-style house and several whimsically-named cottages (including a replica Snow White and the Seven Dwarfs house) are closed to the public unless you're on a guided tour (10-person minimum), but you can walk the grounds of the estate.

Daytona Beach   BEACH
(per car $10; ⊙beach driving 8am-7pm May-Oct, sunrise-sunset Nov-Apr) This perfectly planar stretch of sand was once the city's raceway. Sections of the beach still welcome drivers to the sands at a strictly enforced top speed of 10mph. Beachside rentals for ATVs, fat-tired cruisers, recumbent trikes and all manner of water sports are ubiquitous. Of course you're free to frolic anywhere on the beach, off the roadway, assuming you don't like to mix your sand with oil fumes and engines.

🚐 Tours

Richard Petty
Driving Experience   DRIVING
(📋 800-237-3889; www.drivepetty.com; from $109; ⊙dates vary) If merely watching NASCAR drivers streak around the track isn't adrenaline-pumping enough for you, get in the car yourself via the Richard Petty Driving Experience. Choose from several levels of death-defying action, from the three-lap passenger-seat Race Ride (from $109) to the intensive Racing Experience ($3200), which puts you behind the wheel for 50 white-knuckle laps. Dates vary; check the website.

Angell & Phelps
Chocolate Factory   TOURS
(📋 386-252-6531; www.angellandphelps.com; 154 S Beach St; ⊙tours 10am, 11am, 1pm, 2pm 3pm, 4pm Mon-Sat) FREE Get your cacao fix at Angell & Phelps Chocolate Factory, a downtown Daytona tradition since 1925. Free 20-minute tours of the production area include a sweet taste of the goods. While you're here, snag a bag of chocolate-covered potato chips, chocolate gators or the factory's signature creation: a caramel, cashew and chocolate confection known as the Honeybee.

Daytona Beach

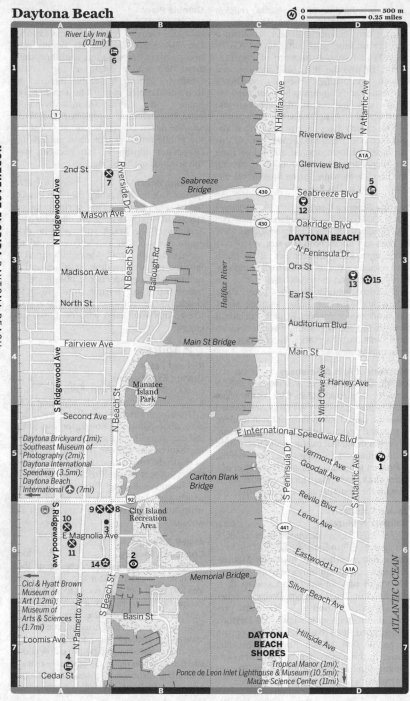

0   500 m
0   0.25 miles

River Lily Inn
(0.1mi)

6

2nd St

7

Riverside Dr

Mason Ave

N Ridgewood Ave

Seabreeze
Bridge

430

N Halifax Ave

Riverview Blvd

Glenview Blvd

N Atlantic Ave

A1A

Seabreeze Blvd

5

12

430

Oakridge Blvd

DAYTONA BEACH

Madison Ave

North St

S Beach St

Ballough Rd

Halifax River

N Peninsula Dr

Ora St

Earl St

13   15

Fairview Ave

Main St Bridge

Main St

Auditorium Blvd

Manatee
Island
Park

Second Ave

N Beach St

Daytona Brickyard (1mi);
Southeast Museum of
Photography (2mi);
Daytona International
Speedway (3.5mi);
Daytona Beach
International ✈ (7mi)

S Ridgewood Ave

Harvey Ave

S Wild Olive Ave

E International Speedway Blvd

Vermont Ave

Goodall Ave

S Peninsula Dr

Revilo Blvd

Lenox Ave

S Atlantic Ave

1

7

92

9 8

10

3

E Magnolia Ave

11

14

2

City Island
Recreation
Area

Carlton Blank
Bridge

441

Eastwood Ln

A1A

Memorial Bridge

Silver Beach Ave

ATLANTIC OCEAN

Cici & Hyatt Brown
Museum of
Art (1.2mi);
Museum of
Arts & Sciences
(1.7mi)

Loomis Ave

N Palmetto Ave

S Beach St

Basin St

**DAYTONA
BEACH
SHORES**

Hillside Ave

4

Cedar St

Tropical Manor (1mi);
Ponce de Leon Inlet Lighthouse & Museum (10.5mi);
Marine Science Center (11mi)

S Ridgewood Ave

1

Daytona Beach

✪ Festivals & Events

Budweiser Speedweeks   SPORTS
(www.daytonainternationalspeedway.com; ⊙ Feb)
Over a week in February a bunch of races
lead up to the big event, the Daytona 500.
At the same time, 200,000 rowdy folks do a
lot of partying.

Bike Week   CULTURAL
(www.officialbikeweek.com; ⊙ Mar) For 10 days
in March, 500,000 bikers drool over each
other's hogs and party around the clock.

Coke Zero 400   SPORTS
(www.daytonainternationalspeedway.com; ⊙ 4 Jul
weekend) NASCAR fans fly the checkered flag
at this 400-lap race.

Biketoberfest   CULTURAL
(www.officialbikeweek.com; ⊙ mid-Oct) Lots of
drinking, loud bikes, burly blokes and all the
rest. It generally begins the weekend following Columbus Day.

🛏 Sleeping

Tropical Manor   RESORT $
(☑ 386-252-4920; www.tropicalmanor.com; 2237
S Atlantic Ave, Daytona Beach Shores; r $88-135;

P� 🛜 🏊) This immaculate, family-friendly
beachfront property is like a playful pastel
vision of Candy Land (which admittedly
might be a bit too much for some). A variety of configurations from motel rooms to
suites and cottages are available; many have
kitchen facilities and no two rooms are the
same.

River Lily Inn   B&B $$
(☑ 386-253-5002; www.riverlilyinnbedandbreak
fast.com; 558 Riverside Dr; r $129-235; P 🛜 🏊)
There's a grand piano in the living room,
Belgian waffles for breakfast and, oh yes,
a heart-shaped pool in the backyard. What
more could you want in a B&B? Add to that
a quiet location on an oak-shaded property
overlooking the river, elegant rooms with
high ceilings (some with private balconies),
and friendly-as-can-be owners, and you've
got the recipe for a perfect getaway.

Plaza Resort & Spa   RESORT $$
(☑ 844-248-2685; www.plazaresortandspa.com;
600 N Atlantic Ave; r from $109; P 🛜 🏊) Built
in 1908, Daytona's most historic resort has
undergone extensive renovations in its time,
but still maintains its old-world charm. If
only the walls could talk... From the miles
of honey-colored marble lining the lobby to
the 42in plasma TVs and cloud-soft beds in
the rooms, to the 15,000-sq-ft spa, this resort
coos luxury.

A variety of room types are available – not
all face the ocean.

Coquina Inn B&B   B&B $$
(☑ 386-254-4969; www.coquinainn.com; 544 S
Palmetto Ave; r $110-150; P 🛜) Shaded by an
ancient oak, this sweet yellow-and-stone
cottage smells of homemade cookies and
looks like your grandma's house – in a good
way (painted flowers on the wall, snowy
white quilts, holiday decorations). It's locat-
ed in a quiet residential neighborhood near
downtown.

**Hyatt Place Daytona
Beach Oceanfront**   HOTEL $$
(☑ 386-944-2010; www.daytonabeach.place.
hyatt.com; 3161 S Atlantic Ave, Daytona Beach
Shores; r from $114; P @ 🛜 🏊) Some of Day-
tona's freshest, funkiest and most functional
rooms can be found here. All rooms feature
balconies, plush bedding, separate living
and sleeping areas and a nifty panel to easily connect your laptop or iPod to the 42in
panel TV.

✗ Eating

Cracked Egg Diner
BREAKFAST $

(☑ 386-788-6772; www.thecrackedeggdiner.com; 3280 S Atlantic Ave, Daytona Beach Shores; breakfast items $4-11; ☺ 7am-3pm; ℗ ♿) Best for breakfast, this cheery joint in Daytona Beach Shores became so popular they annexed the building next door. Brainchild of brothers Chris and Kevin, one of whom will usually greet you at the door with a smile, their mission is to deliver breakfast egg-cellence. (Sorry. It had to happen.) We think they do a pretty fine job.

Dancing Avocado Kitchen
CAFE $

(☑ 386-947-2022; www.dancingavocadokitchen.com; 110 S Beach St; mains $8-14; ☺ 8am-4pm Tue-Sat; ☑ ♿) Gluten-free and predominantly vegetarian-friendly items feature at this colorful kitchen serving breakfasts, lunches and light meals, although you'll still find a spicy jerk chicken wrap and the obligatory mahi sandwich basket among the tofu, hummus and liberal servings of fresh avocado. Healthy and delicious!

Chucherias Hondureñas
LATIN AMERICAN $$

(☑ 386-239-0548; www.chucheriashondurenas.com; 101 2nd St; mains $10-18; ☺ 11am-3pm & 5-9pm Wed-Sun; ℗) One of the brightest stars in the local culinary firmament, Chucherias' cuisine is a blend of bold, rich Latin American and Caribbean flavors – shellfish are dressed with *chimol* (a Central American salsa), while pork is roasted with citrus and garlic. A colorful interior and friendly management make this one a don't-miss.

Ronin Sushi and Sake Bar
SUSHI $$

(☑ 386-252-6320; www.roninsushiandbar.com; 111 W International Speedway Blvd; sushi rolls from $8; ☺ 5-10pm Sun-Thu, to 11pm Fri & Sat; ℗) Daytona may be a racing town, but it's also a seaside spot where fresh-from-the-boat seafood is in plentiful supply. So: good sushi. This popular, atmospheric joint does American-style sushi rolls well, has a full bar with plenty of sake choices, and delicious small plates like baked mussels and Kobe-beef sliders from the kitchen.

Zen Bistro
THAI $$

(☑ 386-248-0453; www.zenbistrodaytona.com; 223 Magnolia Ave; lunch $8-11, dinner $12-20; ☺ 11am-3pm, 5-9pm Mon-Fri, to 10pm Fri, 5-10pm Sat; ℗☑) With alfresco dining, a fire pit and a bar, this is not your everyday Thai restaurant. Add in solid curries, noodle and rice dishes cooked to your preferred degree of spiciness, and finish it off with attentive, polite staff and you've found a wonderful alternative to Daytona's many fast-food outlets.

Aunt Catfish's on the River
SOUTHERN US $$

(☑ 386-767-4768; www.auntcatfishontheriver.com; 4009 Halifax Dr, Port Orange; mains $8-28; ☺ 11:30am-9pm Mon-Sat, from 9am Sun; ℗♿) Fresh-from-the-boat grouper and mahimahi lolling in butter or deeply and deliciously fried, as well as Southern-style Cajun-spiced catfish make this riverside seafood establishment insanely popular with tourists: table waits can be expected. It's just outside Daytona Beach in Port Orange.

Rose Villa Southern Table and Bar
MODERN AMERICAN $$$

(☑ 386-615-7673; www.rosevillarestaurant.com; 43 West Granada Blvd, Ormond Beach; mains $19-34; ☺ 11am-3pm & 5-10pm Tue-Sat; ℗) Intimate and delightful, this under-the-radar fine-dining bistro occupies a charming Victorian house and garden a few miles north of Daytona. The eclectic menu skews toward haute Southern, and does it well – wild sea scallops and grits are a treat, as are fancy chicken and waffles. Highly recommended.

The Cellar
ITALIAN $$$

(☑ 386-258-0011; www.thecellarrestaurant.com; 220 Magnolia Ave; mains $23-46; ☺ 5-10pm Tue-Sat, to 9pm Sun; ℗) Now you can tell your friends that you've dined in the summer mansion of 29th US President Warren G Harding. While Harding is consistently ranked as one of the worst presidents in history, the restaurant rates much better; its classic, upscale Italian fare and elegant ambience have made it Daytona's go-to spot for special-occasion dinners.

🍸 Drinking & Nightlife

Daytona Taproom
BEER HALL

(☑ 386- 872-3298; 310 Seabreeze Blvd; burgers $4-13; ☺ noon-3am Mon-Sat, to 2am Sun; 🛜) A bright spot among the biker and beach bum status quo, this 'burger joint with a drinking problem' has 50 taps of regional and national microbrews and pretty damn fine burgers to boot. May close earlier in slow season.

Mai Tai Bar
BAR

(☑ 386-947-2493; www.maitaibar.com; 250 N Atlantic Ave; ☺ 2pm-2am Mon-Fri, from 11am Sat & Sun) A party-happy crowd downs crayon-colored rum drinks at this Hawaiian-themed bar overlooking the Atlantic Ocean. The late-night happy hours (9pm to 1am Monday to

Saturday, 4pm to midnight Sunday) are hard to argue with.

☆ Entertainment

★ Cinematique of Daytona   CINEMA
(☑ 386-252-3778; www.cinematique.org; 242 S Beach St) Home to the Daytona Beach Film Festival, Daytona's only art-house cinema screens independent and foreign films and serves booze and snacks to your table/high-boy/sofa in its intimate screening room.

Daytona Beach Bandshell
(☑ 386-671-8250; www.daytonabandshell.com; 70 Boardwalk) Constructed in 1937 from coquina shell, this landmark venue with a killer beachfront location stages a free summer concert series and summer outdoor movies. Worth a look.

🔒 Shopping

J&P Cycles Destination
Daytona Superstore   SPORTS & OUTDOORS
(☑ 386-615-0950; www.jpcycles.com/pages/daytona; 253 Destination Daytona Ln, Ormond Beach; ⊙ 9am-6pm Mon-Sat, 10am-5pm Sun) Just north of Daytona Beach at the Junction of I-95 and US 1, this is the place to go to gear up for Bike Week: you're bound to find something to make you look and feel the part among the 15,000 sq ft of aftermarket motorcycle accessories and clothing. Stays open an hour later during summer months.

Daytona Flea & Farmers Market   MARKET
(☑ 386-253-3330; www.daytonafleamarket.com; 1425 Tomoka Farms Rd; ⊙ 9am-5pm Fri-Sun) With more than 1000 booths and 600 vendors, this gargantuan market is one of the world's largest. Fans of garage and car-boot sales will not want to miss this: allocate plenty of time. It's at the corner of US 92 at I-95, 1 mile west of the Speedway.

ℹ Getting There & Away

Daytona Beach is close to the intersection of two major interstates, I-95 and I-4. The I-95 is the quickest way to Jacksonville (about 90 miles) and Miami (260 miles), though Hwy A1A and US Hwy 1 are more scenic. Beville Rd, an east–west thoroughfare south of Daytona proper, becomes I-4 after crossing I-95; it's the fastest route to Orlando (55 miles).

Daytona Beach International Airport (☑ 386-248-8030; www.flydaytonafirst.com; 700 Catalina Dr) Just east of the Speedway; is served by Delta and US Airways, and all major car-rental companies.

Greyhound (☑ 386-255-7076; www.greyhound.com; 138 S Ridgewood Ave) Has connections to most major cities in Florida, and beyond.

Flagler Beach
☑ 386 / POP 4655

Just 21 miles north of Daytona, isolated Flagler Beach is far removed from the towering hotels, dizzying lights and tire-tracked sands of its rowdy neighbor. On a 6-mile stretch of beach, this string of modest residences and smattering of shops has a three-story cap on buildings to preserve its spectacular sunrises and an end-of-the-earth feel.

◉ Sights

Washington Oaks Gardens
State Park   STATE PARK
(☑ 386-446-6780; www.floridastateparks.org/washingtonoaks; 6400 N Oceanshore Blvd; per vehicle/bicycle $5/4; ⊙ 8am-sunset; P) 🅿 The landscaped grounds of the property once owned by Owen and Louise Young has been converted into a small, gorgeous park that is a lovely spot for a picnic. Or you could just wander; it's easy to lose a few hours strolling amid the resplendent camellia and bird-of-paradise-filled gardens.

Flagler Beach Fishing Pier   LANDMARK
(☑ 386-517-2436; www.cityofflaglerbeach.com/thepier; 105 S 2nd St; entry $1.50, fishing pole & permit $6; ⊙ 6am-midnight) Rent a pole and some bait to try your luck against the deep blue sea by fishing off this historic landmark, or just walk the pier at a leisurely pace: it's breathtaking at sunrise.

🛏 Sleeping

You might wish to spend a night or two at sleepy Flagler Beach as an alternative to garish Daytona – you'll have miles of sandy shores largely to yourself.

Gamble Rogers Memorial
State Recreation Area   CAMPGROUND $
(☑ 386-517-2086; www.floridastateparks.org/gamblerogers; 3100 S Ocean Shore Blvd; per vehicle $5, tent & RV sites $28; ⊙ 8am-sunset; P) 🅿 Nature lovers can camp beachside at Gamble Rogers Memorial State Recreation Area, which straddles the A1A. Kayaks, canoes and bicycles are available for rent at the ranger station.

Flagler Beach Motel   MOTEL $
(☑ 386-517-6700; www.flaglerbeachmoteland vacationrentals.com; 1820 S Oceanshore Blvd;

studio from $85, 2-bed unit from $130; ⓢ⌇) Of several inexpensive motels, the standout is the Flagler Beach Motel. Its spotless studio and one- and two-bedroom motel-style units – many with full kitchen facilities and views of the Atlantic – feature artwork by local artists. Located across the road from the beach, this is a wonderful place to disappear for a while.

Island Cottage Oceanfront Inn & Spa INN $$$

(☑386-439-0092; www.islandcottagevillas.com; 2316 S Oceanshore Blvd; r $200-370; Ⓟⓢ) If romance is on the agenda, head to the Island Cottage Oceanfront Inn & Spa for a little pampering and indulgence. The over-the-top decor won't be to everyone's taste, but the level of attentive service offered is otherwise hard to come by and the included luxuries such as plush four-poster beds and double Jacuzzis aren't difficult to enjoy!

✕ Eating

Vessel Sandwich Company SANDWICHES $

(☑386- 693-5085; www.vesselsandwichco.com; 213 South 2nd St; sandwiches $7-9; ⊙11am-4pm Mon-Sat, to 9pm Fri; Ⓟ☑⛄) After a long swim in the ocean, a sandwich is kind of perfect, right? It's even more perfect if it's served at this excellent joint, which slings a good *banh mi*, a brisket Sloppy Joe, aged cheddar and apple grilled cheese, and chicken sandwiches slathered in Alabama white barbecue sauce.

High Tides at Snack Jack SEAFOOD $$

(☑386-439-3344; www.snackjacks.com; 2805 Hwy A1A; mains $11-22; ⊙11am-9pm; Ⓟⓢ⛄) The valet parking adds to the fun of this wonderfully laid-back, open-to-the-elements beachfront bar and diner, loved by locals and visitors alike for its location, vibe and flavor. Food runs along the line of cheeseburgers, coconut shrimp and decadent fried seafood platters.

The original Jack's has been providing local surfers with beer and nourishment since 1947, but you'd only know that by reading the menu: today it's as modern, clean and quirky as they come. Did we mention the view? Because, man, the view!

ⓘ Getting There & Away

Flagler Beach is located about 21 miles north of Daytona Beach, and 35 miles south of St Augustine. You'll find beach-y rentals stretching along the A1A in each direction.

St Augustine

☑904 / POP 13,700

The oldest continuously occupied European settlement in the US, St Augustine was founded by the Spanish in 1565. Today, its 144-block National Historic Landmark District is a major tourist destination. For the most part, St Augustine exudes charm and maintains its integrity, although there's no denying the presence of some tacky tourist traps: miniature theme-parks, tour operators at almost every turn and horse-drawn carriages clip-clopping past townsfolk dressed in period costume.

What makes St Augustine so genuinely endearing is the accessibility of its rich history via countless top-notch museums and the authenticity of its centuries-old architecture, monuments and narrow cobbled lanes. Unlike Florida's numerous historical theme parks, St Augustine is the real deal.

You'll find a diverse array of wonderful B&Bs, cozy cafes and lamp-lit pubs, and while fine dining might not be the first thing that comes to mind at Florida's mention, it is certainly synonymous with St Augustine.

⊙ Sights

All of St Augustine's historic district feels like a museum; there are literally dozens of attractions to choose from. Narrow little **Aviles St**, the oldest European-settled street in the country, and long, pedestrian-only **St George St** are both lined with galleries, cafes, museums and pubs, and are attractions in themselves.

★ Lightner Museum MUSEUM

(☑904-824-2874; www.lightnermuseum.org; 75 King St; adult/child $10/5; ⊙9am-5pm) Henry Flagler's former Hotel Alcazar is home to this wonderful museum, with a little bit of everything, from ornate Gilded Age furnishings to collections of marbles and cigar-box labels. The dramatic and imposing building itself is a must-see, dating back to 1887 and designed in the Spanish Renaissance–revival style by New York City architects Carrère & Hastings.

Villa Zorayda Museum MUSEUM

(☑904-829-9887; www.villazorayda.com; 83 King St; adult/child $10/4; ⊙10am-5pm Mon-Sat, 11am-4pm Sun; Ⓟ) Looking like a faux Spanish castle from a medieval theme park, this gray edifice was built out of a mix of concrete and

THERE BE PIRATES

Notorious throughout the Caribbean and the Americas, pirates routinely ransacked St Augustine, given its vulnerable seaside location. Laying in wait along the coast, pirates would pounce on silver- and gold-laden fleets returning to Europe from Mexico and South America. When ships weren't around, they'd simply raid the town (which was home to the Spanish Royal Treasurer for Florida, no less).

Among the many brutal attacks on St Augustine was Sir Francis Drake's raid in June 1586, when he and his cohort pillaged the township before burning it down. Perhaps even more violent was Jamaican pirate Robert Searle's attack in 1668. After capturing a Spanish ship, Searle and his crew went on a plundering and killing spree. No one was safe: one of Searle's victims was a five-year-old girl, whose ghost, it is said, haunted him to madness and ultimately suicide.

Both events are meticulously reenacted every year in St Augustine. Participants must conform to rigid requirements, including no skull-and-crossbones emblems (they weren't used regularly by pirates until the early 1700s); no polyester or modern items of any kind, including eyeglasses and wristwatches; and no 'silly plumes.' If you're interested in participating, get thee to St Augustine in March (to reenact Searle's raid) or June (for Drake's). For more information, log on to www.searlesbucs.com.

Other local pirate activities include September's 'Talk Like a Pirate Day' (www.talklikeapirate.com), a global event that is particularly popular in this place, and October/November's St Augustine Pirate Gathering (www.thepirategathering.com). These events feel a bit more like a scene culled from the *Pirates of the Caribbean* cutting room floor. On that note, for all the shiver-me-timbers branding you'll find in this part of Florida, it's worth remembering piracy was incredibly brutal – basically, it was *Game of Thrones* on a boat – and ultimately inflicted heinous amounts of violence on civilian populations.

local coquina shells in 1883. The structure was the fantasy (and maybe fever dream) of an eccentric millionaire who was obsessed with Spain's 12th-century Alhambra Palace. Today, it's an odd but engaging museum. The Moorish-style atrium and rooms contain quirky antiques, archaeological pieces and other artifacts: highlights being a 2400-year-old mummy's foot and an Egyptian 'Sacred Cat Rug.'

Castillo de San Marcos
National Monument   FORT
(☑ 904-829-6506; www.nps.gov/casa; 1 S Castillo Dr; adult/child under 15 $10/free; ⊗ 8:45am-5pm; ⓟ ⬧) ⬧ This photogenic fort is an atmospheric monument to longevity: it's the country's oldest masonry fort, completed by the Spanish in 1695. In its time, the fort has been besieged twice and changed hands between nations *six* times – from Spain to Britain to Spain Part II to the USA to the Confederate States of America to the USA again. Park rangers lead programs hourly and shoot off cannons most weekends.

There is a parking lot on site, but blink your eye and it will be filled up.

Ximenez-Fatio House   MUSEUM
(☑ 904-829-3575; www.ximenezfatiohouse.org; 20 Aviles St; adult/student $7/5; ⊗ 11am-4pm Tue-Sat) Dating to 1798, this fascinating museum complex includes the main house building, the area's only detached kitchen building and a reconstructed washhouse. All are set on immaculately manicured grounds, dating to St Augustine's original town plan of 1572. Magnificently restored and chock-a-block full of artifacts and relics, the museum focuses primarily on the property's role as a boarding house/inn during the period from 1826 to 1875.

Hotel Ponce de León   HISTORIC BUILDING
(☑ 904-823-3378; http://legacy.flagler.edu/pages/tours; 74 King St; tours adult/child $10/1; ⊗ tours hourly 10am-3pm summer, 10am & 2pm during school year) This striking former luxury hotel, built in the 1880s, is now the world's most gorgeous dormitory, belonging to Flagler College, who purchased and saved it in 1967. Guided tours are recommended to get a sense of the detail and history of this magnificent Spanish Renaissance building. At the very least, take a peek inside the lobby for free.

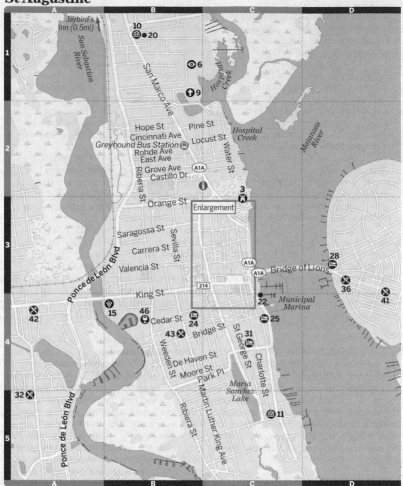

Tours are occasionally cancelled for college functions; check the website for details.

Colonial Quarter
MUSEUM

(☏ 904-342-2857; www.colonialquarter.com; 33 St George St; adult/child $13/7; ⊙ 10am-5pm) See how they did things back in the 18th century at this re-creation of Spanish-colonial St Augustine, complete with craftspeople demonstrating blacksmithing, leather working, musket shooting and sorts of historical stuff.

Discounted combination tickets including admission to the Pirate & Treasure Museum (p352) and the First Colony exhibit at Government House are available (adult/child $28/16).

Plaza de la Constitution
SQUARE

In the heart of downtown, this grassy square, the oldest public park in the US and a former marketplace for food (and slaves), has an attractive gazebo, some cannons, the remains of the town well and a monument to Confederate veterans.

Spanish Military Hospital Museum
MUSEUM

(☏ 904-342-7730; www.spanishmilitaryhospital. com; 3 Aviles St; adult/child $10/5; ⊙ 10am-6pm)

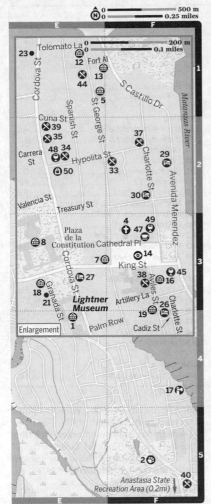

tourist hordes at this terrific park, which is a beautiful quilt of estuarine marsh, maritime forest, boardwalk paths and sandy beach. There's also a **campground** (campsites $28) and rentals for all kinds of water sports.

Alligator Farm Zoological Park ZOO
(☑904-824-3337; www.alligatorfarm.com; 999 Anastasia Blvd; adult/child $23/12; ☺9am-5pm, to 6pm summer; ⊕) Herpetophobes should run in the other direction of this facility – the only one on the planet with every species of crocodilian in residence. Nature lovers, on the other hand, will love it. Look for albino alligators, gorgeous gharials and seven different species of endangered monkey, including the world's smallest, the pygmy marmoset. There are talks and shows throughout the day; catch hungry alligators snapping their jaws at feeding times (noon and 3pm).

The park is a five-minute drive from downtown St Augustine along Anastasia Blvd.

St Augustine Beach BEACH
(350 A1A Beach Blvd; ☺sunrise-sunset) This white-sand beach almost gets lost in the historical mix, but hey, it's Florida, so a visit wouldn't be complete without a little bit of sun and surf. There's a visitor information booth at the foot of **St Johns Pier**, where you can rent a rod and reel (two hours for $3, plus $1 for each additional hour). About three blocks south of the pier, the end of A St has – as Florida goes – some fine waves.

Cathedral Basilica of St Augustine CHURCH
(☑904-824-2806; www.thefirstparish.org; 38 Cathedral Pl; ☺mass 7am) **FREE** With its magnificent bell tower lording it over the Plaza de la Constitution, this Spanish-mission-style cathedral is likely the country's first Catholic house of worship. Masses are held daily; check the website for services past the daily 7am service.

Government House HISTORIC BUILDING
(☑904-825-5034; www.staugustine.ufl.edu/gov House.html; 48 King St; ☺10am-5pm) **FREE** A government building has stood on this site since 1598 and served as a residence, courthouse, administrative headquarters and post office. Today, it is maintained by the University of Florida as a public museum and exhibition space showcasing temporary exhibitions on Florida history.

Not for the faint of heart, guided tours of this museum discuss Colonial-era medical techniques in all their gory glory: amputations, leeching, the whole shebang. Housed in a reconstruction of the original hospital, the museum will make you glad you're not a patient in 1791. Discounted tickets can be reserved online.

Anastasia State Recreation Area BEACH
(☑904-461-2033; www.floridastateparks.org/anastasia; 300 Anastasia Park Rd; car/bike $8/2; ☺8am-sunset) Locals come to escape the

St Augustine

Discounted combination tickets including admission to Government House's First Colony Exhibit as well as Colonial Quarter (p350) and the Pirate & Treasure Museum are available (adult/child $28/16).

Mission of Nombre de Dios CHURCH
(☑ 904-824-2809; www.missionandshrine.org; 27 Ocean Ave; ⊙ museum 9am-5pm Mon-Sat, noon-4pm Sun; ℗) FREE Just north of downtown on the A1A, the mission dates back to the earliest days of Spanish settlement. Today, the peaceful memorial gardens feature a replica of the original altar, a tiny ivy-shrouded chapel and a small museum.

Pirate & Treasure Museum MUSEUM
(☑ 877-467-5863; www.thepiratemuseum.com; 12 S Castillo Dr; adult/child $14/7; ⊙ 10am-7pm; ♠) Little kids and big kids alike will enjoy this mash-up of theme park and museum: a celebration of all things pirate. As well as genuine historical treasures (including real gold) there's plenty of animatronic pirates, blasting cannons and a kid-friendly treasure

hunt. The historical worth is dubious – pirate life is pretty romanticized.

Discounted combination tickets including admission to the Colonial Quarter (p350) and the First Colony exhibit at Government House are available (adult/child $28/16).

Oldest House MUSEUM
(☑ 904-824-2872; www.saintaugustinehistorical society.org; 14 St Francis St; adult/student $8/7; ⊙ 10am-5pm; ℗) ∅ Also known as the González-Alvarez House, this is the oldest surviving Spanish-era home in Florida, dating to the early 1700s and sitting on a site occupied since the 1600s. The house is part of a complex that also contains two small historical museums and a lovely ornamental garden.

San Sebastian Winery WINERY
(☑ 904-826-1594; www.sansebastianwinery.com; 157 King St; ⊙ 10am-6pm Mon-Sat, 11am-6pm Sun) FREE Free hour-long tours at this winery are capped with wine tastings and a video about Florida wine-making since the 1600s; if you're

around in August, join the squishy fun during the annual grape-stomping competitions.

Old Jail
HISTORIC BUILDING

(🔌 904-829-3800; 167 San Marco Ave; adult/child $9/5; 🕙 tours every 20min 9am-4:30pm) Built in 1891, this is the former prison and residence of the town's first sheriff, Charles Joseph 'the terror' Perry (towering menacingly at 6ft 6in tall and weighing 300lb). Today, costumed 'deputies' escort visitors through cellblocks and detail the site's arresting history.

Oldest Wooden School House
HISTORIC BUILDING

(🔌 888-653-7245; www.oldestwoodenschoolhouse. com; 14 St George St; adult/child $3/2; 🕙 9am-6pm) Built from red cedar and cypress, the 200-year-old building contains animatronic teachers and students, and provides a glimpse into 18th-century life and education. Naughty kids may be frightened into civility when they see the dungeon.

St Augustine Lighthouse
LIGHTHOUSE

(🔌 904-829-0745; www.staugustinelighthouse. com; 81 Lighthouse Ave; adult/child $13/1; 🕙 9am-6pm) The light produced by this 1870s striped lighthouse beams all the way downtown. A great place to bring kids over six and more than 44in tall (since all climbers must be able to ascend and descend the tower under their own power). A variety of special themed tours, such as the spooky 'Dark of the Moon' paranormal tour and the 'Lost Ships' archaeology tour, are held on a regular basis. Consult the website for what's on when.

Fountain of Youth
HISTORIC SITE

(🔌 904-829-3168; www.fountainofyouthflorida. com; 11 Magnolia Ave; adult/child $15/9; 🕙 9am-6pm; 👶) Insert tongue firmly in cheek and step right up for an acrid cup of eternal youth at this kitschy 'archaeological park.' As the story goes, Spanish explorer Juan Ponce de León came ashore here in 1513, considered this freshwater stream the possible legendary Fountain of Youth, and promptly charged folks 15 bucks to take a gander. We may be kidding about that last part. At the least, there is some kid-friendly living history reenactment going on at this spot.

🏃 Activities

Pit Surfshop
SURFING

(🔌 904-471-4700; www.thepitsurfshop.com; 18 A St; lesson $75; 🕙 9am-7pm) Stop in here on St Augustine Beach for late-breaking surf conditions, to rent or buy a board, or to sink into the comfy couch in the screening room for a free, inspirational surf film. Lessons and surf camps are available.

👉 Tours

★ St Augustine Gold Tours
TOURS

(🔌 904-325-0547; www.staugustinegoldtours.com; 6 Cordova St; adult/child $25/15) This outfit, the brainchild of a retired British couple, is a standout in the crowded St Augustine tour scene. You're assured a fascinating and articulate insight into St Augustine's history. Private and small-group tours are conducted in a quiet electric vehicle that gets into places where the other tours can't.

★ St Augustine Eco Tours
KAYAKING

(🔌 904-377-7245; www.staugustineecotours. com; 111 Avenida Menendez; adult/child $45/35; 🕙 mid-morning & dusk) 🌊 This eco-outfitter has certified naturalists who take kayakers on 3-mile ecology trips. It also runs 1½-hour boat tours which explore the estuary and use hydrophones to search for bottlenose dolphins. A portion of profits goes to environmental organizations.

Ripple Effect Ecotours
KAYAKING

(🔌 904-347-1565; www.rippleeffectecotours.com; 101 Tolstoy Lane; kayak tours adult/child from $55/45) 🌊 Explore the hundreds of channels and backwaters that lace through northeast Florida with this outfit, which works with the University of Florida's Whitney Laboratory for Marine Bioscience. They also offer a tour on a boat powered by vegetable oil culled from nearby restaurants (adult/child $50/40). Can also arrange kayak rentals (half day from $40).

St Augustine City Walks
WALKING

(🔌 904-825-0087; www.staugcitywalks.com; 4 Granada St; tours $15-60; 🕙 9am-8:30pm) Extremely fun walking tours of all kinds, from silly to serious, including history, culinary and pub walks. A variety of free tours are also available.

Old Town Trolley Tours
TOURS

(🔌 844-388-6452; www.trolleytours.com; 167 San Marco Ave; adult/child $25/10; 👶) These hop-on, hop-off narrated trolley tours are family-friendly and underwhelming, but if you want a historical introduction to the town and don't like walking, this is an option. Tickets are valid for three consecutive days.

WORTH A TRIP

FORT MATANZAS NATIONAL MONUMENT

The tiny, 1742-built **Fort Matanzas National Monument** (☑ 904-471-0116; www.nps.gov/foma; 8635 Hwy A1A, Rattlesnake Island; ☉ 9am-5:30pm; ℗) 🏁 **FREE** is located on Rattlesnake Island, near where Menéndez de Avilés executed hundreds of shipwrecked French soldiers and colonists when rations at St Augustine ran low. Today it makes a terrific excursion via a free 10-minute ferry that launches every hour (at half-past) from 9:30am to 4:30pm, weather permitting. Once there, the ranger provides an overview and lets you wander.

Rattlesnake Island is located about 15 miles south of downtown St Augustine, and can be reached via Florida A1A. To catch the 35-person ferry to the monument, go through the visitor center and out to the pier.

🛏 Sleeping

For convenience and atmosphere, stay in the historic downtown area where there's a plenitude of classic B&Bs; check out the selection on www.staugustineinns.com. For larger rooms and cheaper prices, there are many chain motels on San Marco Ave and Ponce de Leon Blvd. Otherwise, head to the beach. St Augustine is a popular weekend escape for Floridians – prices go up by about 30% on weekends and a minimum two-night stay is often required.

Pirate Haus Inn   HOSTEL $

(☑ 904-808-1999; www.piratehaus.com; 32 Treasury St; dm $25, r from $119; ℗ ☎) A-har me hearties! Although far from St Augustine's fanciest digs, this family-friendly European-style guesthouse/hostel may well be the cheapest and most cheerful. Kids love it – themed private rooms and dorms are squeaky clean, the location is hard to beat, and who doesn't love fresh 'pirate pancakes' for breakfast? Staff speak a variety of languages.

They've also banned bachelor/bachelorette parties, which is a pro move, as far as we're concerned.

★ At Journey's End   B&B $$

(☑ 904-829-0076; www.atjourneysend.com; 89 Cedar St; r $166-289; ℗ ☎ ☀) Free from the granny-ish decor that haunts many St Augustine B&Bs, this pet-friendly, kid-friendly and gay-friendly spot is outfitted in a chic mix of antiques and modern furniture and is run by friendly, knowledgeable hosts. Mouthwatering breakfasts and complimentary wi-fi, concierge services, and beer, wine and soda throughout your stay are some of the inclusions that set At Journey's End apart.

Jaybird's Inn   MOTEL $$

(☑ 904-342-7938; www.jaybirdsinn.com; 2700 N Ponce de Leon Blvd; r $110-150; ☎ ☀) This older motel has been revamped to the highest of standards and modernity, with fresh and funky decor in an aquamarine color scheme that works. Beds are big and comfy, continental breakfast is included and free bikes will get you whizzing around in no time. There's an on-site restaurant as well.

Casa de Solana   B&B $$

(☑ 904-824-3555; www.casadesolana.com; 21 Aviles St; r $109-300; ℗ ☎) Just off pedestrian-only Aviles St in the oldest part of town, this utterly charming little inn remains faithful to its early-1800s period decor. Rooms aren't the largest in town, but the location is killer. Rumors of a resident ghost might sway some potential guests in (or drive them off).

Edgewater Inn   MOTEL $$

(☑ 904-825-2697; www.stayatedgewater.com; 2 St Augustine Blvd; r from $140; ℗ ☎) For something a little different, try this charming waterfront motel across the bridge, overlooking St Augustine's historic downtown. Rooms are on the smaller side, but are pleasantly decorated. The waterfront rooms' sitting areas are unique in town, if a little close together: great for the social traveler, not so great for the reclusive.

Beachfront B&B   B&B $$

(☑ 904-461-8727; www.beachfrontbandb.com; 1 F St, St Augustine Beach; r from $180; ☎ ☀) If you're looking to stay by the beach to avoid the tourist crowds, look no further. This sun-drenched oceanfront beach house features canopy beds, rich pine floors and has a private heated pool. Most rooms feature private entrances and fireplaces for romantic wintry nights.

Casa Monica   HISTORIC HOTEL $$$

(☑ 904-827-1888; www.casamonica.com; 95 Cordova St; r $200-280, ste from $440; ℗ ☎ ☀) 🏁 Built in 1888, this is *the* luxe hotel in town, with turrets and fountains adding to the Spanish-Moorish castle atmosphere. Rooms are appropriately richly appointed, with wrought-iron triple-sheeted beds and Bose sound systems in every room. Some suites have decadent Jacuzzis, and the location can't be beaten.

St Francis Inn
INN $$$

(☑ 800-824-6062, 904-824-6068; www.stfrancis inn.com; 79 St George St; r $150-340; ❈ 🕸) St Augustine's oldest inn has been in continuous operation since 1791. Crushed-coquina-shell and ancient wood-beam architecture create a period ambience, abetted by open fireplaces, a maze of antique-filled nooks and crannies, beds with handmade quilts and a lush walled courtyard. Sumptuous buffet breakfasts, free local wine and complimentary evening desserts round out the picture.

Guests also have day access to a beach-front cottage, perfect for a day away from the crowds. Rates vary greatly by season.

Hilton St Augustine Historic Bayfront
HOTEL $$$

(☑ 904-829-2277; www.hilton.com; 32 Avenida Menendez; r from $200; 🅿 🕸 🏊) This Hilton is a fair cut above its corporate brethren. Rooms are a tasteful blend of hardwood dark hues and fluffy pale linen bedding, while the hotel itself has the whole lemon-colored Spanish villa vibe down pat. Relax by the pool, or under the eaves of the lobby, which resembles a Mediterranean palazzo.

Bayfront Marin House
INN $$$

(☑ 904-824-4301; www.bayfrontmarinhouse. com; 142 Avenida Menendez; r from $220; 🕸 🏊) Created by joining three old houses, this buttercup-yellow waterfront inn is dominated by a bi-level wraparound porch with a commanding view of Matanzas Bay. Rooms are sumptuously decorated with four-poster beds and lots of rich brocades – for character, choose a room in the 1700s-era wing with cool crushed-coquina-shell walls, or inquire about the private Vilano Beach cottage.

🍴 Eating

★ Present Moment Cafe
VEGAN $

(☑ 904-827-4499; www.thepresentmomentcafe. com; 224 W King St; mains $8-16; ⊘ 11am-9pm Mon-Thu, to 9:30pm Fri, 10am-9:30pm Sat; 🍴) Dishing up 'Kind Cuisine,' this folksy restaurant serves only vegan and raw food. To the delight (and surprise) of many patrons, the healthy, organic dishes created by this soulful cafe are bursting with flavor. If you need something a little bit naughty with your nice, try the gluten-free chocolate marble torte with drunken banana – one to turn even the most die-hard carnivores.

Nalu's Tropical Take Out
HAWAIIAN $

(☑ 904-501-9592; www.nalusstaugustine.com; 1020 Anastasia Blvd; ⊘ 11am-sunset Wed-Mon; 🅿) St Augustine may not be Hawaii, but the weather sometimes does a fair approximation, and that's when we like to hit up this takeout stand (which, to be fair, is wonderful whatever the weather). Cop a seat on a bench and order some sashimi, fish tacos or shrimp quesadillas, and leave room for *poke* (marinated raw fish salad).

Bunnery Bakery & Café
BAKERY $

(☑ 904-829-6166; www.bunnerybakeryandcafe. com; 121 St George St; items $4-12; ⊘ 8am-4pm Mon-Fri, to 5pm Sat & Sun) The friendly staff at this family-owned bakery pour frosting on your cinnamon rolls to your individual specifications. Strudels, panini and fat, wedge-shaped scones are all hits, as are the noteworthy hot breakfasts. Expect major lines at noon, although it's always busy.

Back 40 Urban Cafe
CAFE $

(☑ 905-824-0227; www.back40cafe.com; 40 S Dixie Hwy; items $7-12; ⊘ 11am-9pm) Flavored with the spices of Mexico and the Southwest, this cozy, unpretentious joint is favored by locals for its cheap and tasty tacos, burgers and comfort foods. We couldn't go past the chili mac bowl. There's a good selection of cold beer too.

Hyppo
DESSERTS $

(☑ 904-217-7853; www.thehyppo.com; 48 Charlotte St; popsicles $4; ⊘ 11am-9pm Sun-Thu, to 10pm Fri & Sat; 🍴) On steamy St Augustine afternoons, seek out the Hyppo, a slip of a popsicle shop with an ever-changing whiteboard menu of outrageous flavors – pineapple-cilantro, rice pudding and Kick (an energizing blend of espresso, green tea *and* chocolate). Keep your eyes open for anything containing datil pepper, a high-octane local chili beloved by Spanish settlers – it goes great with strawberry.

Spanish Bakery & Cafe
BAKERY $

(☑ 904-342-7859; www.spanishbakerycafe.com; 42½ St George St; mains $4-6.50; ⊘ 10am-5pm Sun-Thu, to 8pm Fri & Sat) This diminutive stucco bakeshop serves empanadas, sausage rolls and other conquistador-era favorites. Don't hesitate; it sells out quick.

Gas Full Service
MODERN AMERICAN $$

(📞904-217-0326; 9 Anastasia Blvd; mains $9-28; ⊙11am-9pm Tue-Thu, to 10pm Fri & Sat) You'll likely be vying for a table at this fantastic retro gas-station-esque cafe. The buzz is about the burgers: freshly baked buns, local beef, fried green tomatoes and crispy bacon all feature. How about the 'burger Benedict,' smothered in hollandaise? And did we mention waffle fries, Reuben egg rolls and the lobster corn dog?

Maple Street Biscuit Company
AMERICAN $$

(📞904-217-7814; www.maplestreetbiscuits.com; 39 Cordova St; mains $6-10; ⊙7am-2pm Mon-Thu, to 3pm Fri & Sat; 🚸) The name of this place delivers on its promise: they do biscuits (the Southern flaky kind, not British cookies), and they do them *right*. There's plenty of variations; we love the Sticky Maple, which comes with fried chicken, maple syrup and bacon, because damn that diet anyways.

Floridian
MODERN AMERICAN $$

(📞904-829-0655; www.thefloridianstaug.com; 39 Cordova St; mains $14-25; ⊙11am-3pm Wed-Mon, 5-9pm Mon-Thu, to 10pm Fri & Sat) Oozing hipster-locavore earnestness, this farm-to-table restaurant serves whimsical neo-Southern creations in an oh-so-cool dining room. Although the service and general vibe might be a little too cool for school, it's hard to fault the food: fried green tomato bruschetta and seafood zucchini linguini pair perfectly. No reservations means long waits.

O'Steen's
SEAFOOD $$

(📞904-829-6974; www.osteensrestaurant.com; 205 Anastasia Blvd; mains $13-23; ⊙11am-8:30pm Tue-Sat) Locals claim this seafood shack has the best shrimp on the East Coast, and having eaten our weight in shrimp, we think they're close to the mark. If you're allergic to shellfish, don't despair: the tilapia and catfish (broiled or fried) are pretty good too. O'Steen's ain't no secret, so prepare to wait for a table or plan to take out and picnic.

La Herencia Café
CUBAN $$

(📞904-829-9487; www.laherenciacafe.com; 4 Aviles St; mains $12-25; ⊙8:30am-8pm Mon-Fri, to 10pm Sat & Sun) On St Aug's oldest street, this brightly painted Cuban cafe serves all-day breakfasts and killer Cuban sandwiches – it's one of the better lunch deals downtown.

★Collage
INTERNATIONAL $$$

(📞904-829-0055; www.collagestaug.com; 60 Hypolita St; mains $28-45; ⊙5:30-9pm) This upscale restaurant is renowned for its impeccable service, intimate atmosphere and the consistency of its cuisine: the menu makes the most of St Augustine's seaside locale and nearby local farms. It's all here: artisan salads, chicken, lamb, veal and pork, lobster, scallops and grouper. A subtle mélange of global flavors enhance the natural goodness of the freshest produce.

Preserved
AMERICAN $$$

(📞904-679-4940; www.preservedrestaurant.com; 102 Bridge St; mains $24-30; ⊙4-10pm Tue-Fri, 10am-3pm & 4-11pm Sat, 10am-3pm & 4-9pm Sun; 📷) If you're looking to do a date night in St Augustine, it's hard to beat Preserved. They take the locally sourced Southern genre to delicious heights in the airy, historic-chic dining room; shrimp and grits come with creamed corn and bacon lardons, while roasted chicken comes with glistening black-eyed peas and cornflour dumplings. Make reservations.

🍸 Drinking & Nightlife

Kookaburra
CAFE

(📞904-209-9391; www.kookaburrashop.com; 24 Cathedral Pl; coffee $2.40-5; ⊙7:30am-9pm Mon-Thu, to 10pm Fri & Sat, 8am-8pm Sun; 📶) 🌿 Ethically sourced Australian-American coffeehouse serving real Aussie meat pies and the best barista coffee in the historic quarter.

Ice Plant
BAR

(📞904-829-6553; www.iceplantbar.com; 110 Riberia St; ⊙11:30am-2am Tue-Fri, 10am-2am Sat, 10am-midnight Sun, 11:30am-midnight Mon; 📶) The hottest spot in St. Augustine – with nary a Spanish colonial morsel in sight – flaunts exposed concrete, raw brickwork and soaring windows surrounding a vintage, dual-facing centerpiece bar all carved out of a former ice factory. Here coolsters imbibe some of Florida's finest cocktails, mixed by overall-clad bartenders, and snack on farm-to-table bites.

TradeWinds Lounge
LOUNGE

(📞904-826-1590; www.tradewindslounge.com; 124 Charlotte St; ⊙11am-2am) Tiny bathrooms and big hairdos rule this nautical-themed dive. Smelling sweetly of stale beer, this classic dive bar has survived two locations and six decades. Crowds tumble out the door during happy hour, and there's live music – mostly

Southern rock or '80s – nightly. Smoky (for the moment), fun and old school.

Cellar Upstairs — WINE BAR

(☑ 904-826-1594; www.sansebastianwinery.com; 157 King St; ⊙ 11:30am-11pm Fri & Sat, to 6pm Sun) On the grounds of the San Sebastian Winery (p352); head on up to this pretty rooftop patio for alfresco tasting plates ($6 to $14), sandwiches, local wines by the glass ($5 to $7) and free live jazz.

Scarlett O'Hara's — PUB

(☑ 904-824-6535; www.scarlettoharas.net; 70 Hypolita St; ⊙ 11am-1am Mon-Thu & Sun, to 2am Fri & Sat; 🛜) Good luck grabbing a rocking chair: the porch of this pine building is packed all day, every day. Built in 1879, today Scarlett's serves regulation pub grub, but it's got the magic ingredients – hopping happy hour, live entertainment nightly, hardworking staff, funky bar – that draw folks like spirits to a séance.

A1A Ale Works — PUB

(☑ 904-829-2977; www.a1aaleworks.com; 1 King St; ⊙ 11am-11:30pm Sun-Thu, to 1am Fri & Sat; 🛜) This waterfront brewery has a bit of a cheesy vibe, but it's on the water, and there's good, fine-crafted beer, so we're not complaining.

☆ Entertainment

Café Eleven — LIVE MUSIC

(☑ 904-460-9311; www.originalcafe11.com; 501 A1A Beach Blvd, St Augustine Beach; ⊙ 7am-9pm) In the evening as it closes it at 9pm, the tables of this slick beach cafe get shoved aside and the place transmogrifies into a theater for indie rock acts and the like.

🛍 Shopping

Second Read Books — BOOKS

(☑ 904-829-0334; 51 Cordova St; ⊙ 10am-8pm Mon-Sat, to 7pm Sun) Used bookstores are always a great thing, and this shop is no exception. The cobbles and stucco of the old town somehow amplify the attractive mustiness of the stacks – old books just seem to come more alive in an old neighborhood.

ⓘ Information

Visitor Information Center (☑ 904-825-1000; www.FloridasHistoricCoast.com; 10 W Castillo Dr; ⊙ 8:30am-5:30pm) Helpful, period-dressed staff sell tour tickets and can advise you on everything St Augustinian. The nearby parking garage is your best bet if you can't find parking elsewhere in town.

ⓘ Getting There & Away

Driving from the north, take I-95 exit 318 and head east past US Hwy 1 to San Marcos Ave; turn right and you'll end up at the Old City Gate, just past the fort. Alternatively, you can take Hwy A1A along the beach, which intersects with San Marco Ave, or US Hwy 1 south from Jacksonville. From the south, take exit 298, merge onto US 1 and follow it into town.

Cars are a nightmare downtown, with one-way and pedestrian-only streets and severely limited parking; outside the city center, you'll need wheels. There's a big parking lot at the Visitor Information Center. Use it.

NORTHEAST FLORIDA ST AUGUSTINE

WORLD GOLF VILLAGE

The ultimate monument to a good walk spoiled, the **World Golf Village** (☑ 888-868-1728; www.worldgolfvillage.com; 1 World Golf Pl) is a massive golf resort, golf-course complex, golf museum and all-around golf-themed attraction.

Fans of the sport flock here to the **World Golf Hall of Fame** (☑ 904-940-4133; www.worldgolfhalloffame.org; 1 World Golf Pl; adult/child $20/5; ⊙ 10am-6pm Mon-Sat, noon-6pm Sun), an 18-exhibit museum: the front nine cover the history of the sport and the back nine examine modern professional golf. Separating them is the Hall of Fame itself, with multimedia exhibits on inductees. Admission includes nine holes on a real grass putting green designed to PGA specifications, and an IMAX film.

Two legendary on-site courses, **King & Bear** and **Slammer & Squire**, are open for public tee times. If you're keen to improve your swing, try the two- to five-day PGA Tour Golf Academy (www.touracademy.com) packages starting from $800 (without accommodation); more expensive packages include accommodation at one of four on-site resorts. Private lessons start at $125 per hour.

World Golf Village is just off I-95 via exit 323, about halfway between St Augustine and Jacksonville.

Northeast Florida Regional Airport (📞 904-209-0090; www.flynf.com; 4900 US Hwy 1), 5 miles north of town, receives limited commercial flights. **Airport Express** (📞 904-824-9400; www.airportexpresspickup.com) charges $65 to drop you downtown in a shuttle. For an additional $20, it'll take you to your hotel. Reservations required. Private services are also available.

The **Greyhound bus station** (📞 904-829-6401; www.greyhound.com; 52 San Marcos Ave) is just a few blocks north of the visitor center

❶ Getting Around

The **Sunshine Bus Company** (📞 904-209-3716; www.sunshinebus.net; $1) runs from approximately 7am to 6pm and serves downtown, the beaches and the outlet malls, as well as many points in between.

Solano Cycle (📞 904-825-6766; www.solanocycle.com; 32 San Marco Ave; 2hr/5hr/24hr $8/11/18; ⊙10am-6pm) rents bicycles – great for exploring flat St Augustine.

Jacksonville

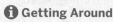

📞 904 / POP 842,580

At a whopping 840 sq miles, Jacksonville is the largest city by area in the contiguous United States and the most populous in Florida. The city *sprawls* along three meandering rivers, with sweeping bridges and twinkling city lights reflected in the water. A glut of high-rises, corporate HQs and chain hotels can make 'Jax' feel a little soulless, but patient exploration yields some interesting streets, curious characters and a Southern-fried, friendly heart.

The city's museums and restored historic districts are worth a wander if you have the time, and the Five Points and San Marco neighborhoods are charming, walkable areas lined with bistros, boutiques and bars.

The Jacksonville area beaches – a world unto themselves – are 30 to 50 minutes' drive from the city, depending on traffic and where you're coming from.

◉ Sights

★ Cummer Museum of Art & Gardens
MUSEUM

(www.cummer.org; 829 Riverside Ave; adult/student $10/6; ⊙10am-9pm Tue, to 4pm Wed-Sat, noon-4pm Sun) This handsome museum, Jacksonville's premier cultural space, has a genuinely excellent collection of American and European paintings, Asian decorative art and antiquities. An outdoor area showcases classical English and Italian gardens, and is one of the loveliest alfresco spaces in the city.

★ Museum of Contemporary Art Jacksonville
MUSEUM

(MOCA; 📞 904-366-6911; www.mocajacksonville.org; 333 N Laura St; adult/child $8/2.50; ⊙11am-5pm Tue-Sat, to 9pm Thu, noon-5pm Sun) The focus of this ultramodern space extends beyond painting: get lost among contemporary sculpture, prints, photography and film. Check out jacksonvilleartwalk.com for details of the free MOCA-run Art Walk, held on the first Wednesday of every month from 5pm to 9pm: it has over 56 stops and is a great way to see the city.

Jacksonville Zoological Gardens
ZOO

(📞 904-757-4463; www.jacksonvillezoo.org; 370 Zoo Pkwy; adult/child $18/13; ⊙9am-5pm Mon-Fri, to 6pm Sat & Sun; 🅿️🚻) Northeast Florida's only major zoo opened in 1914 with one deer; today it's home to over 1800 exotic animals and hectares of beautiful gardens. Favored fauna from around the world include elephants, jaguars, rare Florida panthers, gators, kangaroos and komodo dragons. There's an elevated viewing platform that brings you face to nose with giraffes. The zoo is 15 minutes north of downtown off I-95.

Value tickets (adult/child $25/18) include general admission as well as entry to Butterfly Hollow, Stingray Bay and unlimited train and carousel rides.

Treaty Oak
LANDMARK

(1123 Prudential Dr, Jesse Ball duPont Park) At first glance, it looks like a small forest is growing in the middle of the concrete on Jacksonville's south side. But upon closer inspection you'll see that the 'forest' is really one single enormous tree, with a trunk circumference of 25ft and a shade diameter of nearly 200ft. According to local lore, the live oak tree is the oldest thing in Jacksonville – its age is estimated to be 250 years.

Southbank Riverwalk
WATERFRONT

This 1.2-mile boardwalk, on the south side of the St Johns River, opposite downtown and Jacksonville Landing, has excellent views of the city's expansive skyline. Most nights yield scenes that'll up your likes on social media, but firework displays are a real blast. The Southbank Riverwalk connects the museums flanking Museum Circle and makes a pleasant promenade.

Museum of Science & History   MUSEUM

(MOSH; ☎ 904-396-6674; www.themosh.org; 1025 Museum Circle; adult/child $12.50/10; ⊘ 10am-5pm Mon-Thu, to 8pm Fri, to 6pm Sat, noon-5pm Sun; ⊕) Traveling with kids? This awesomely named museum (MOSH) offers dinosaurs, all things science and exhibits on Jacksonville's cultural and natural history. Be sure to check out the Bryan Gooding Planetarium, one of the largest single-lens planetariums in the country. Shows and their times vary, so check www.moshplanetarium.org for details.

☞ Tours

Anheuser-Busch
Budweiser Brewery   TOURS

(☎ 904-751-8117; www.budweisertours.com; 111 Busch Dr; ⊘ 10am-4pm Thu-Tue, to 5pm Jun-Aug) FREE Enjoy a free tour of the iconic brewery (and free beer if you're over 21).

🛏 Sleeping

Jacksonville suffers a serious dearth of interesting private hotels, but there's a plethora of chain options dotted throughout the city and around highway interchanges: the cheapest rooms are along I-95 and I-10.

As most hotels here are big-box affairs, you can get big discounts booking online and in advance.

Riverdale Inn   B&B $$

(☎ 904-354-5080; www.riverdaleinn.com; 1521 Riverside Ave; r $155-185, ste $225-285; P 🛜) In the early 1900s this was one of 50 or so mansions lining Riverside. Now there are only two left, and you're invited to enjoy the Riverdale's tastefully decorated rooms, within walking distance of the Five Points, with full breakfast.

Hotel Indigo Jacksonville   HOTEL $$

(☎ 877-846-3446; www.hoteldeerwoodpark. com; 9840 Tapestry Park Circle; r from $150; P 🛜 ❄ 🐾) Lush blue color accents and airy, design-conscious rooms with hardwood floors, fluffy king beads, flat-screen TVs and a general sense of stylish yet accessible luxury define the experience at this excellent branch of the Indigo chain. Located about 11 miles south of downtown Jacksonville.

Homewood Suites by
Hilton Downtown   HOTEL $$

(☎ 904-396-6888; www.homewoodsuites.com; 1201 Kings Ave; r from $149; P @ 🛜) These tasteful, modern suites in the central San

Marco neighborhood feature full kitchens and business traveler–style rooms that are efficient and comfy, if not terribly exciting.

Omni Jacksonville Hotel   HOTEL $$

(☎ 904-355-6664; www.omnihotels.com; 245 Water St; r from $170; P 🛜 ❄ 🐾) Within sight of Jacksonville Landing, this stylish 354-room hotel has lavish, amenity-laden rooms, acres of marble, a heated rooftop pool and free wi-fi.

🍴 Eating

The Five Points neighborhood, southwest of downtown, and the San Marco neighborhood, across the river from downtown, are where you'll find the most trendy cafes and bars with outdoor seating. The city's suit-and-tie financial industry means lots of steakhouses and upscale bistros.

Bearded Pig BBQ   BARBECUE $

(☎ 904-619-2247; www.thebeardedpigbbq.com; 1224 Kings Ave; mains $8-17; ⊘ 11am-10pm Mon-Sat, to 9pm Sun; P ⊕) At this San Marco spot, barbecue and a beer garden meet in perfect marriage and have delicious pork rib and craft beer babies, all of which we devour, with pleasure. Look: it's got perfectly smoked sausage, brisket and ribs, and cold draft beer on tap. Why are you still reading?

Southern Charm   AMERICAN $

(☎ 904-517-3637; www.artscrackercooking. moonfruit.com; 3566 St Augine Rd; mains $8-17; ⊘ 11:30am-2:30pm Tue-Fri, 6:30-8:30pm Tue-Sat, 11:30am-3pm Sun) Yes, this is Southern Charm: the place that looks like an automotive garage on a torn-up stretch of sidewalk. The restaurant, run by beloved Jacksonville chef and all-round character Art Jennette, serves enormous, cardiac-straining portions of

Downtown Jacksonville

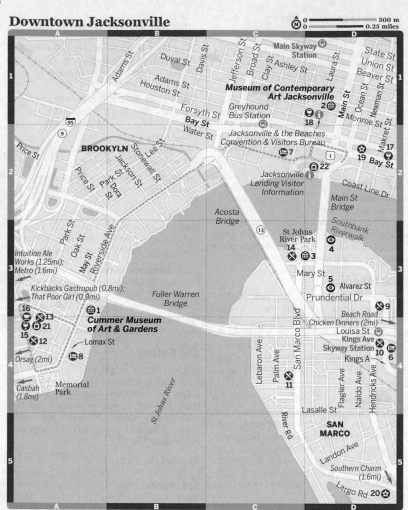

Southern and soul food: pork chops, fried fish, collard greens and fried green tomatoes. Atmosphere of the moon, but food of the gods, people.

Note that hours may be dependent on how busy the place is – and when food runs out, it's out.

French Pantry
FRENCH $

(☑904-730-8696; 6301 Powers Ave; items $6-14; ⏱11am-2pm Mon-Fri) The secret is well and truly out about this inconveniently located but thoroughly hopping weekday lunch-only joint, serving fresh-filled French rolls

and panini, soups, salads and incredible pastries and desserts. Another downside is that folks line up to get in and the service can get frustrating. If you're not fussy, grab your grub and devour it in your car.

Hawkers Asian Street Fare
ASIAN $

(www.eathawkers.com; 1001 Park St; mains $5-10; ☑) This small local chain tries to re-create an Asian food hawker court à la Singapore. There are no plastic stools to squat on, but the food is varied and good: curry duck noodles, *laksa* (noodle soup), *roti canai* (flaky flat bread with dipping sauce), grilled skewers

Downtown Jacksonville

and summer rolls are just a sampling of an intimidatingly large menu.

This is the sort of place you'll want to order a bunch of dishes and share.

Beach Road Chicken Dinners SOUTHERN US $
(☎904-398-7980; www.beachroadchickendinners. com; 4132 Atlantic Blvd; items $5-12; ☺11am-8:30pm Tue-Sat, to 6pm Sun) You know a place does it right if their signature meal predates the Cold War, and this deliciously retro joint has been frying chicken since 1939. Tear off a chunk of tender thigh meat and wrap it up in a fluffy biscuit, and you'll understand why people line up every day at this much-loved shack.

★**Black Sheep Restaurant** MODERN AMERICAN $$
(☎904-380-3091; www.blacksheep5points.com; 1534 Oak St; lunch/dinner mains from $9/14; ☺10:30am-10pm Mon-Thu, to 11pm Fri & Sat, 9:30am-3pm Sun; ⊕) ✐ A commitment to good, local ingredients, delicious food, plus a rooftop bar and a craft cocktail menu? Sign us up! Try miso-glazed duck confit, citrus-marinated tofu, pastrami sandwiches made from in-house deli meat, or crispy skinned steelhead fish cooked in brown butter; it's all good. The cardamom pancakes and salmon on bagels served for Sunday brunch are pretty fine, too.

On Fridays and Saturdays, the Sheep serves a limited bar menu from 11pm until midnight.

bb's FUSION $$
(☎904-306-0100; www.bbsrestaurant.com; 1019 Hendricks Ave; lunch/dinner mains from $11/24; ☺11am-10:30pm Mon-Thu, to midnight Fri & Sat)

This groovy establishment, with its molded-concrete bar, clean, modern lines and daily cheese selection champions fresh local produce that is crafted into arty, flavorful dishes from scratch: a gourmand's delight. Suggested wine pairings keep things simple. Connoisseurs of dessert needn't look elsewhere – the chocolate ganache cake alone is worth the trip.

Casbah MIDDLE EASTERN $$
(☎904-981-9966; www.thecasbahcafe.com; 3628 St Johns Ave; mains $8-15; ☺11am-2am) All the swords, camels and Moorish lanterns lining the walls could be a little much, but they ultimately add to the lively atmosphere at this divey local favorite, which features authentic Middle Eastern dishes, beer, music and belly dancing. For the scent-sensitive, note that the cafe doubles as a hookah lounge with dozens of flavorful tobacco concoctions.

Clark's Fish Camp SOUTHERN US $$
(☎904-268-3474; www.clarksfishcamp.com; 12903 Hood Landing Rd; mains $10-23; ☺4:30-9:30pm Mon-Thu, to 10pm Fri, 11:30am-10pm Sat, 11:30am-9pm Sun; P) Sample Florida's Southern 'Cracker' cuisine surrounded by the surreal animal menagerie of America's largest private taxidermy collection, which resembles the freakish love child of Tim Burton and Mr Kurtz from *Heart of Darkness*. This swamp shack is unforgettable: gator, smoked eel, fried snake and frogs legs all make menu appearances amid more prosaic offerings such as catfish and steak.

If the grotesque taxidermy menagerie – monkeys prowl the ceiling, while leopards glare glassily from the corners – puts you off, you can always sit outside by the murky water. But a word to the wise: don't feed the gators. It's far south of downtown Jacksonville.

River City Brewing Company   SEAFOOD $$
(☑ 904-398-2299; www.rivercitybrew.com; 835 Museum Circle; mains $9-23; ⊙ 11am-3pm & 4-9:30pm Mon-Sat, 10:30am-2:30pm Sun; 🐾) Jax's premier riverfront restaurant is a good place to quaff a microbrew and enjoy some upscale seafood overlooking the water. Prices are reasonable for the location and quality of the food.

Orsay   FRENCH, SOUTHERN $$$
(☑ 904-381-0909; www.restaurantorsay.com; 3630 Park St; mains $16-39; ⊙ 4-10pm Wed-Sun, to midnight Thu-Sat, 11:30am-3:30pm Sat & Sun; 🐾) This minimalist bistro in Riverside merges traditional French fare with Southern intuition, leading to a menu chock-full of rich and vibrant dishes, most of which are locally sourced. We may or may not have delighted ourselves silly sopping up our incredible bouillabaisse gravy with black truffle mac 'n' cheese, chased with a few of the creative and boozy cocktails.

The cassoulet, Berkshire pork chop, beef stroganoff and Carolina trout are all standout dishes as well – but you can't go wrong.

Bistro Aix   FRENCH, MEDITERRANEAN $$$
(☑ 904-398-1949; www.bistrox.com; 1440 San Marco Blvd; mains $14-37; ⊙ 11am-10pm Mon-Thu, to 11pm Fri, 5-11pm Sat, 5-9pm Sun) Dine with the fashionable food mavens on fusion-y Mediterranean dishes at Aix, whose menu bursts with global flavors, from wine-braised chicken to duck cassoulet. There are over 250 wines by the bottle, and 50 by the glass. Reservations recommended.

🍷 Drinking & Nightlife

★ Birdies   BAR
(☑ 904-356-4444; www.birdiesfivepoints.com; 1044 Park St; ⊙ 4pm-2am) There's funky local art on the walls, old-school video games in the back, a mix of old timers and tatted hipsters, retro neon vibe, indie rock on the radio, DJs on the weekends and general good vibes throughout at this excellent watering hole.

★ Intuition Ale Works   BREWERY
(☑ 904-683-7720; www.intuitionaleworks.com; 720 King St; ⊙ 3-10pm Tue-Thu, to 11pm Fri, 11am-11pm

Sat, 11am-8pm Sun) Stop by for a pint or three in the taproom of this funky local brewery serving, you guessed it – beer only! Feel free to order pizza from the neighborhood when you get peckish. With 14 homemade brews on tap, this is a must for beer fans.

Wall Street Deli   BAR
(☑ 904-355-6969; 1050 Park St; ⊙ 2pm-2am Mon-Fri, noon-2am Sat & Sun) We guess they serve sandwiches here, but not to suited-up brokers coming off the trading floor. This place is a dive, straight up – you can still smoke inside. It's full of a cross-section of Jacksonville, and they're all getting tipsy (or more) on strong drinks served with little embellishment, besides maybe an extra finger of booze.

Volstead   BAR
(☑ 904-414-3171; www.thevolsteadjax.com; 115 W Adams St; ⊙ 4pm-2am Mon-Sat, 7pm-2am Sun) Jacksonville's contribution to the speakeasy genre is this sexy mash-up of dark wood furniture, early-20th-century aesthetic and modern takes on brown liquor – whiskey, bourbon and the like – plus classic cocktails. An alluring mix of old-school and contemporary class, this is a local standout.

Kickbacks Gastropub   BAR
(☑ 904-388-9551; www.kickbacksjacksonville.com; 910 King St; ⊙ 7am-3am; 🐾) This sprawling copper-toned, penny-lined low-brow gastropub in Riverside has 204 craft beers on tap, including several of Jacksonville's finest. It's divided between the old bar and the new bar; the latter is an industrial hodgepodge of massive ceiling fans and Edison-era light bulbs.

BREW Five Points   CAFE
(☑ 904-374-5789; www.brewfivepoints.com; 1024 Park St; ⊙ 7:30am-10pm Tue & Wed, to midnight Thu & Fri, 9am-midnight Sat, 9am-9pm Sun, 7:30am-2pm Mon) BREW sits at an odd juncture: it's a hybrid craft beer bar and espresso cafe, for those days when you need a pick-me-up *and* a sedative, we guess. Jokes aside, the coffee is excellent, the beer list is extensive and the vibe is modern and friendly, so we're all on board.

Metro   GAY
(☑ 904-388-8719; www.metrojax.com; 849 Willow Branch Ave; ⊙ 2pm-2am Sun-Thu, to 2:30am Fri & Sat) Metro, Jacksonville's top gay entertainment complex, has a disco, a cruise bar, a piano bar, a games room with pinball machines,

a smoke-free chill-out loft, a leathery boiler room and a show bar.

Mark's
BAR

(☎904-355-5099; www.marksjax.com; 315 E Bay St; ☉4pm-2am Tue-Fri, from 8pm Sat, to 10pm Mon) Dress to impress at this upscale cocktail bar and nightclub. Midweek it's chatty and social, but Friday and Saturday nights are *unsa-unsa* dance parties.

☆ Entertainment

★ Florida Theatre
THEATER

(☎904-355-5661; www.floridatheatre.com; 128 E Forsyth St) Home to Elvis' first indoor concert in 1956, which a local judge endured to ensure Presley was not overly suggestive, this opulent 1927 venue is an intimate place to catch big-name musicians, musicals and movies.

San Marco Theatre
CINEMA

(☎904-396-4845; www.sanmarcotheatre.com; 1996 San Marco Blvd) A landmark 1938 art-deco movie theater where you can order beer, wine, pizza and sandwiches while watching a flick.

🛍 Shopping

That Poor Girl
JEWELLERY

(☎904-525-0490; www.thatpoorgirl.com; 1504 King St; ☉3-6pm Tue-Fri, noon-6pm Sat) Get your bargain on in this excellent vintage shop with a clever name (doubly so; the owner's name is Tori Poor). Need some weird gifts or accessories, like pink lawn flamingos or random coffee mugs? They have those too!

Bead Here Now
GIFTS & SOUVENIRS

(☎904-475-0004; www.beadherenow.org; 1051 Park St; ☉11am-6pm Mon-Sat, noon-4pm Sun) Yes, there are beads – more beads than you may know what to do with – but this cozy little shop also has cute local art and gifts.

Jacksonville Landing
SHOPPING CENTER

(☎904-353-1188; www.jacksonvillelanding.com; 2 W Independent Dr; ☉10am-8pm Mon-Thu, to 9pm Fri & Sat, noon-5:30pm Sun) At the foot of highrise downtown, this prominent shopping and entertainment district has about 40 mostly touristy shops surrounding a food court with outdoor tables and regular, free live entertainment.

ℹ Orientation

As big as it is, Jacksonville can be a bit tricky to navigate. A few things to know:

➨ Jacksonville is trisected by a very rough T formed by the St Johns River. Downtown Jacksonville is on the west side of the St Johns.

➨ I-95 comes in straight from the north to a junction just south of downtown with I-10. Follow I-10 east into downtown, where a maze of state highways offers access to surrounding areas.

➨ Three bridges cross the river and will take you to San Marco: Fuller Warren (I-10), Acosta (Hwy 13) and Main St Bridge.

➨ I-295 breaks off from I-95, forming a circle around the city.

➨ Though the city is enormous, most sites of interest are concentrated along the St Johns River's narrowest point: downtown; Five Points, just south of downtown along the river; and the elegant San Marco Historical District along the southern shore.

ℹ Information

Jacksonville & the Beaches Convention & Visitors Bureau (☎800-733-2668; www.visitjacksonville.com; 208 N Laura St, Suite 102; ☉9am-5pm Mon-Fri) Has all there is to know about Jax and surrounds. There's also a branch at **Jacksonville Landing** (☎904-791-4305; 2 Independent Dr; ☉11am-3pm Mon-Thu, 10am-7pm Fri & Sat, noon-5pm Sun) and the airport.

ℹ Getting There & Away

Jacksonville International Airport (JAX; ☎904-741-4902; www.flyjax.com; 2400 Yankee Clipper Dr; 🛜), about 18 miles north of downtown on I-95, is served by major and regional airlines and car-rental companies. A cab downtown costs around $35. Otherwise, follow the signs for shuttle services: there are numerous licensed providers and reservations aren't necessary.

The **Greyhound bus station** (☎904-356-9976; www.greyhound.com; 10 Pearl St) is at the west end of downtown. The **Amtrak station** (☎904-766-5110; www.amtrak.com; 3570 Clifford Ln) is five miles northwest of downtown.

ℹ Getting Around

The Jacksonville Transportation Authority (www.jtafla.com) runs buses and trolleys around town and the beaches (fare $1.50), as well as a free, scenic (and underused) river-crossing Skyway (monorail).

Jacksonville Area Beaches

Jacksonville's beaches are its prime tourism draw, and with good reason: besides the usual appeal of sun, sand and salt water, there's a nice, chilled vibe here. Locals are mellow compared to the folks in south Florida, or even the rest of north Florida, for that matter.

Moving from south to north, **Ponte Vedra Beach** is the posh home of the ATP and PGA golf tours: golf courses, resorts and mansions are here. Urban **Jacksonville Beach** is where to eat, drink and party, while cozy **Neptune Beach** is more subdued, as is **Atlantic Beach**.

◉ Sights & Activities

Kathryn Abbey Hanna Park   PARK
(📋904-249-4700; www.coj.net; 500 Wonderwood Dr, Atlantic Beach; vehicle/bicycle entry $5/3; ☺6am-8pm Mon-Fri; P ♠) ✦ If you want a beach that's away from any crowds – and a slice of Atlantic coast natural beauty – come to this 450-acre park, which boasts 2.5 miles of undeveloped shoreline, dune ecosystems and maritime forest dripping with Spanish moss.

Rent Beach Stuff   CYCLING
(📋904-305-6472; www.rentbeachstuff.com; 11 1st St N, Jacksonville Beach; ☺9:30am-5pm) The roads are flat and the towns are small: why not rent a bike? In addition to a bunch of other beach and water-sports equipment, these guys will deliver a 26in beach cruiser to your hotel for $30 per day.

⊨ Sleeping

With a mix of B&Bs and spiffy resorts, Jacksonville's beaches offer more lodging variety than you'll find downtown.

Kathryn Abbey Hanna Park   CAMPGROUND $
(📋904-249-4700; www.coj.net; 500 Wonderwood Dr, Atlantic Beach; tent/RV sites $22/34, cabins $34; P) This pleasant park and shaded campground is a stone's throw from Atlantic Beach and has its own freshwater lake. Basic cabins require two-night minimum stays.

★Hotel Palms   HOTEL $$
(📋904-241-7776; www.thehotelpalms.com; 28 Sherry Dr, Atlantic Beach; r $140-180, ste from $200; ♠) An old-school courtyard motel turned into a chic little property with reclaimed headboards, concrete floors and open, airy design? We'll take it. Treat yourself to an outdoor shower, free beach-cruiser bicycles, an outdoor fireplace and some gorgeous rooms pulled straight off some fancy interior decorator's Instagram.

Courtyard by Marriott Jacksonville Beach Oceanfront   HOTEL $$
(📋904-435-0300; www.marriott.com; 1617 1st St N, Jacksonville Beach; r from $199; P ♠) Of the smattering of chain hotels in Jax Beach, we love this waterfront property for its practical, pleasant rooms and friendly, attentive staff. It's right on the beach and has everything you need to drop in and chill out.

Sea Horse Oceanfront Inn   MOTEL $$
(📋904-246-2175, 800-881-2330; www.jacksonvilleoceanfronthotel.com; 120 Atlantic Blvd, Neptune Beach; r $130-180, ste $200-240; ♠ ▧) Each room in this flamingo-colored hotel has a view of both the kidney-shaped pool and the ocean. This is definitely a cut above the average beach motel, with big flat-screen TVs and friendly management. Regulars return year after year.

One Ocean   HOTEL $$
(📋904-249-7402; www.oneoceanresort.com; 1 Ocean Blvd, Atlantic Beach; r from $185; ♠ ▧) This stylish resort hotel has been favored by A-list celebs for its low-key oceanfront locale. The grand lobby is modern and elegant: white marble, rippling iridescent walls and suited staff. Rooms follow suit with clean, contemporary lines, touches of silver, pewter and sea green – most have views. Complete your indulgence with a treatment in the day spa.

Lodge at Ponte Vedra   RESORT $$$
(📋888-774-1477; www.pontevedra.com; 100 Ponte Vedra Blvd, Ponte Vedra Beach; r from $319; P ♠ ▧) Well-heeled families love this opulent Mediterranean-style resort – a historic landmark – where kids play by the pool while the grown-ups enjoy a much-needed beachfront massage. Rooms and suites are plush and airy, with tasteful sage-and-sand decor and super-luxe granite-and-marble bathrooms.

✗ Eating

European Street   CAFE $
(📋904-249-3001; www.europeanstreet.com; 992 Beach Blvd, Jacksonville Beach; items $6-13; ☺10am-10pm; P) Assemble the perfect picnic (or just get a great sandwich) at this excellent combination chocolatier, deli, bar (boasting 150 imported beers) and gourmet market, with a huge menu of salads, sandwiches and German fare.

Colonel Mustard's Phatburger   BURGERS $
(📋904-247-5747; www.jaxbestburgers.com; 1722 3rd St N, Jacksonville Beach; burgers from

$6; ⊘8am-10pm; 🎵) Even the children get involved at this no-frills, friendly, family-owned-and-operated burger joint a few blocks back from the beach. It's cheap and cheery and guaranteed to please, although vegetarians will be disappointed. Breakfasts are as good as the burgers and the well-done fries and hash browns will sate even the most hard-ass *connoisseur du frites*.

Beach Hut Café — SOUTHERN US $

(☎904-249-3516; 1281 3rd St S, Jacksonville Beach; items $4-10; ⊘6am-2:30pm) Don't let its strip-mall location deceive you: the food here is finger-lickin' good. Famous for its big, all-day Southern breakfasts, it draws *huge* lines – especially on weekends.

Metro Diner — DINER $$

(☎904-853-6817; www.metrodiner.com; 1534 N 3rd St, Jacksonville Beach; mains $9-16; ⊘6:30am-2:30pm; P🎵) An excellent breakfast/brunch spot in Jacksonville Beach, this tried-and-true diner has been in business since 1938. These days it's usually packed, especially on weekends. Benedicts for brunch, meatloaf, big fish sandwiches and chicken pot pie all feature.

Eleven South — MODERN AMERICAN $$$

(☎904-241-1112; www.elevensouth.com; 216 11th Avenue S, Jacksonville Beach; mains $26-32; ⊘11am-11pm Tue-Fri, 5-11pm Sat-Mon) For an updated bit of fine contemporary global dining that's still within spitting distance of the beach, head to Eleven South, where the date-night atmosphere is thick and the rack of lamb is as delectable as the lobster paella. Reservations are recommended, especially on weekends. Try to score a seat on the patio.

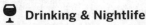 Drinking & Nightlife

Surfer the Bar — BAR

(☎904-372-9756; www.surferthebar.com; 200 1st St N, Jacksonville Beach; ⊘11am-2am) This enormous spot is what happens when you blend a beach bar with a contemporary interiors magazine; if you're wondering about the design sense (and name), this is a brick-and-mortar bar operated by *Surfer* magazine. There's two levels, an indoor Airstream trailer selling food, live music on some nights and, generally, big crowds looking to get a little crazy by the water

Casa Marina — BAR

(☎904-270-0025; www.casamarinahotel.com; 691 N 1st St, Jacksonville Beach; ⊘3pm-midnight Mon-Thu, to 2am Fri, 1pm-2am Sat, noon-midnight Sun; 🛜) Atop the restored 1925 Casa Marina hotel you'll find a compact yet happening beach-front bar with killer views and ambient tunes from its ample rooftop deck. There's a live DJ Thursday to Saturday nights.

ⓘ Getting There & Away

Traveling by car from Jacksonville, follow I-10 to Atlantic Beach, and Hwy 90 (Beach Blvd) directly to Jacksonville Beach. Coming from St Augustine, you follow Hwy A1A due north.

Jacksonville Transportation Authority (www.jtafla.com) operates buses from Jacksonville to the beaches ($1.50).

Amelia Island

Located just 13 miles from the Georgia border, Amelia Island is a moss-draped, sun-and sand-soaked blend of the Deep South and Florida coast. It is believed the island's original inhabitants, the Timucuan tribespeople, arrived as early as 4000 years ago. Since that time, eight flags have flown here, starting with the French in 1562, followed by the Spanish, the English, the Spanish again, the Patriots, the Green Cross of Florida, the Mexican Rebels, the US, the Confederates, then the US again.

Vacationers have flocked to Amelia since the 1890s, when Henry Flagler converted a coast of salt marsh and unspoiled beaches into a vacation spot for the wealthy. The legacy of that era is evident in the central town of Fernandina Beach, 50 blocks of historic buildings, Victorian B&Bs and restaurants housed in converted fishing cottages. Dotting the rest of the island are lush parks, green fairways and miles of shoreline.

⊙ Sights

Fort Clinch State Park — STATE PARK

(☎904-277-7274; www.floridastateparks.org/fort clinch; 2601 Atlantic Ave, Fernandina Beach; car/pedestrian $6/2; ⊘park 8am-sunset, fort 9am-5pm; P) ✦ Although construction commenced in 1847, rapid technological advancements rendered Fort Clinch's masonry walls obsolete by as early as 1861, when the fort was taken easily by Confederate militia in the Civil War and later evacuated. Federal troops again occupied the fort during WWII. Today, the park offers a variety of activities, a half-mile-long fishing pier, serene beaches for shelling (of the non-military kind) and 6 miles of peaceful, unpaved trails for hiking and cycling.

On the first weekend of the month, authentically outfitted troops perform a re-enactment of the Confederate evacuation that extends to cooking in the old kitchen's massive iron cauldron and sleeping on straw mats in the soldiers' barracks. Candlelight tours ($3; May to September) are a treat.

Amelia Island
Museum of History
MUSEUM

(☑ 904-261-7378; www.ameliamuseum.org; 233 S 3rd St, Fernandina Beach; adult/student $8/5; ⊙ 10am-4pm Mon-Sat, 1-4pm Sun) Housed in the former city jail (1879–1975), this oral-history museum has tiny but informative exhibits exploring Native American history, the Spanish Mission period, the Civil War and historic preservation. A variety of tours are available, including the eight-flags tour (11am and 2pm Monday to Saturday and 2pm Sunday), providing lively interpretations of the island's fascinating history, and architecture tours, pub crawls and cell-phone walking tours.

American Beach Museum
MUSEUM

(☑ 904-510-7036; www.americanbeachmuseum. org; 1600 Julia St, American Beach; ⊙ 10am-2pm Fri & Sat, 2-5pm Sun; P) This small museum offers a vibrant overview of life in American Beach, one of the few seaside resort communities built for African Americans in the segregated South. Call ahead for potential tours by appointment.

Maritime Museum of
Amelia Island
MUSEUM

(☑ 904-432-7086; www.fbmaritimemuseum.org; 115 2nd St, Fernandina Beach; ⊙ 9:30am-6pm Tue-Sat) This small museum on the harborfront has an entertaining collection of maritime bric-a-brac presented with a kid-friendly lashing of pirate-y flair.

🏃 Activities

There are myriad ways of exploring Amelia Island, but we prefer doing so from the back (or interior) of a boat with some oars.

Egan's Creek Greenway
WALKING

(☑ 904-310-3363; 2500 Atlantic Ave, Fernandina Beach) 🏃 FREE A network of grassy trails covering over 300 acres, the Egan's Creek Greenway is the perfect place to spot alligators, snakes, bobcats and countless species of birds. Interpretive displays line the trails. Well soled, covered footwear is recommended.

🧭 Tours

★ Kayak Amelia
KAYAKING

(☑ 904-261-5702, 904-251-0016; www.kayak amelia.com; 4 N 2nd St, Fernandina Beach; tours adult/child from $65/55; rental half day/day from $37/49) The charms of Amelia Island are best appreciated through a quiet day on the water, with the sun glinting off the estuaries and cordgrass. That's the experience offered by Kayak Amelia, which leads paddling excursions into the watery ecosystem that ensconces the Atlantic barrier island. They also offer stand-up paddleboarding (SUP) classes and SUP yoga (both $30).

You can also book SUP ecotours (from $55) or rent kayaks and stand-up paddleboards. For four weeks in spring, Kayak Amelia offers a dusk firefly tour into local maritime forests that is especially magical.

Amelia River Cruises
BOATING

(☑ 904-261-9972; www.ameliarivercruises. com; 1 N Front St, Fernandina Beach; tours from $22; 🖐) Explore Amelia and nearby Cumberland Island, GA, stopping to marvel at plantation ruins and dense tracts of Spanish-moss-covered forest. In summers (June to August), this outfit runs a cool **shrimping ecotour** (adult/child $27/17) where guests learn to operate an Otter Trawl shrimp net. The boat then traverses backwaters and creeks, before the caught shrimp are released back into the water.

Old Towne Carriage Company
TOURS

(☑ 904-277-1555; www.ameliacarriagetours.com; 115 Beech St, Fernandina Beach; half-hour adult/child $15/7) Horse carriages clip-clop through the historical downtown, offering half-hour or hour-long rides.

🎊 Festivals & Events

Isle of Eight Flags
Shrimp Festival
FOOD & DRINK

(www.shrimpfestival.com) Pirates (the fake, fun kind, not the real, scary version) invade Amelia Island for shrimp and a juried art show in late April or early May.

🛏 Sleeping

Fort Clinch State Park
CAMPGROUND $

(☑ 904-277-7274; www.floridastateparks.org/ fortclinch; 2601 Atlantic Ave; tent & RV sites $26; P) 🏃 Take your pick (if you're lucky) of riverside or oceanfront sites in this lovely and extremely popular park. The oak-and-moss-protected Amelia River sites

WORTH A TRIP

CUMBERLAND ISLAND NATIONAL SEASHORE

The largest wilderness island in the US, **Cumberland Island** (☑912-882-4336; www.nps. gov/cuis; $7) 🖉 lies just over the Georgia state line. At 17.5 miles long and 3 miles wide, almost half of its 36,415 acres is marshland, mudflats and tidal creeks. Only 300 visitors at any given time are allowed on the island, which is accessible by a 45-minute ferry ride.

Ashore, rangers lead free one-hour tours concluding at the ruins of Thomas and Lucy Carnegie's 1884 mansion, Dungeness. Along the way rangers interpret the rich bird and animal life – including sandpipers, ospreys, painted buntings, nesting loggerhead turtles, armadillos and deer – and detail 4000 years of human history that spans Timucuans, British colonists and Spanish missionaries.

After the Civil War, freed slaves purchased parcels of land at the island's northern end and founded the First African Baptist Church in 1893. The tiny, 11-pew, white-painted wooden church was rebuilt in the 1930s, and the late John Kennedy Jr and Carolyn Bessette were married in it in 1996. It's open to the public, but it's a hefty 15-mile hike from the ferry drop through moss-draped thickets.

The historic village of **St Marys** (www.stmaryswelcome.com) is the island's charming gateway: there are no shops on the island. Bring food, insect repellent and your camera! Accommodation options on the island range from an opulent mansion to rugged camping. Check the St Marys website for details.

Ferries (☑877-860-6787; www.nps.gov/cuis; round-trip adult/senior/child $28/26/16) depart at 9am and 11:45am, returning at 10:15am and 4:45pm (an additional ferry runs at 2:45pm Wednesday to Saturday from March to November; no ferries run on Tuesday or Wednesday from December to February). Reservations are recommended.

From northern Florida, take I-95 north to St Marys Rd exit 1. Turn right onto GA-40/St Marys Rd E and follow it to the end.

NORTHEAST FLORIDA AMELIA ISLAND

are more private than the exposed beach sites. Be sure to make reservations well in advance.

Fairbanks House
B&B **$$**

(☑904-277-0500; www.fairbankshouse.com; 227 S 7th St, Fernandina Beach; r/ste/cottage from $195/240/240; P🛇🖳) You could imagine Indiana Jones retiring to a place like this grand Gothic Victorian property; it's stuffed to the gills with silk carpets, heavy leather-bound books and global knickknacks. Oversized guestrooms are individually styled to suit the period of the house. If you're not sleeping, make use of the small pool and butterfly garden in the backyard.

Hampton Inn & Suites
HOTEL **$$**

(☑904-491-4911; www.hamptoninn.com; 19 S 2nd St, Fernandina Beach; r/ste from $139/259; 🛇🖳) Location can sometimes be everything: walk to all that downtown Fernandina Beach has to offer from this hotel, located in the heart of the historic downtown, just steps from the harborfront. Offering excellent value in an expensive destination, guestrooms and suites feature comfy bedding, neutral furnishings and good showers. Optional kitchens add bang for the buck.

Florida House Inn
HISTORIC HOTEL **$$**

(☑904-491-3322; www.floridahouseinn.com; 22 S 3rd St, Fernandina Beach; r $172-200; P🛇) Florida's oldest hotel features an atmospheric structure dating to 1857 that is battling real estate with an ever-expanding 400-year-old oak tree. Past that, you've got your choice of 17 rooms, most of which are heavy on the lace-curtain-and-quilt vibe.

★ Addison
B&B **$$$**

(☑904-277-1604; www.addisononamelia.com; 614 Ash St, Fernandina Beach; r $215-315; P🛇) 🖉 Built in 1876, the Addison has modern upgrades (whirlpool tubs, deluge showers, Turkish-cotton towels and wi-fi) that'll trick you into thinking it was finished last week. The Addison's white, aqua and sage color scheme is bright and totally un-stuffy. Enjoy daily happy hours overlooking a delightful courtyard with some of the friendliest (and funniest) innkeepers on Amelia.

Eco-conscious guests take note: the inn's water- and energy-saving efforts have earned it a Green Lodging certification from the state.

Elizabeth Pointe Lodge
B&B **$$$**

(☑904-277-4851; www.elizabethpointelodge.com; 98 S Fletcher Ave, Fernandina Beach; r/ste from

$299/380; P �In) Atmosphere oozes from this eccentric yet stylish 1890s Nantucket-shingle-style maritime inn, perched on the ocean, 2 miles from downtown. Rocking-chair-laden porches offer the best seats on the island for beholding a sunrise. Classic, elegant rooms have plush, chunky beds and oversized tubs (some are jetted).

Ritz Carlton
HOTEL $$$

(☑ 904-277-1100; www.ritzcarlton.com/en/Properties/AmeliaIsland; 4750 Amelia Island Pkwy, Fernandina Beach; r from $299; P In 꾜) The height of luxury, decadence and impeccable service awaits at this unexpectedly located Ritz Carlton. Set on 13 miles of pristine beaches, with its own private 18-hole golf course and lavish rooms and suites furnished with casual elegance, this is a property for those with fat wallets, accustomed to the best in life, or for that very special vacation experience.

Hoyt House
B&B $$$

(☑ 904-277-4300; www.hoythouse.com; 804 Atlantic Ave, Fernandina Beach; r from $212; P In 꾜) This stately, award-winning Victorian B&B perched on the edge of downtown boasts an enchanting gazebo that begs idle time with a cool drink. Each of the 10 rooms have their own stylish mix of antiques and found treasures. Room service is available.

Omni Amelia Island Plantation Resort
RESORT $$$

(☑ 904-261-6161; www.omnihotels.com/Amelia Island; 39 Beach Lagoon, Fernandina Beach; r/ste from $296/431; P In 꾜) This solid beachfront resort, located about 9 miles south of Fernandina Beach, has a wide variety of dining options and an array of stylish, check-in and tune-out guestrooms and villas. It's perfect for those who prefer seclusion and amenities to the intimacy of Fernandina's homely B&Bs.

✕ Eating

T-Ray's Burger Station
BURGERS $

(☑ 904-261-6310; www.traysburgerstation.com; 202 S 8th St, Fernandina Beach; mains $6-9; ⊙ 7am-2:30pm Mon-Fri, 8am-1pm Sat) Inside an Exxon gas station, this high-carb, high-fat, low-pretense diner and takeout joint is worth the cholesterol spike. Revered by locals, the big breakfasts are just that, and daily specials sell out fast. Juicy burgers, chunky fries, fried shrimp and tender crab cakes all make the mouth water. Believe the hype: the line's there for a reason.

Hola Cuban Cafe
CUBAN $

(☑ 904-206-1985; www.holacubancafe.com; 117 Centre St, Fernandina Beach; mains $7-8; ⊙ 9am-4pm Thu-Sat & Mon, 10:30am-4pm Sun; P ✿) This may be as far north as you can get good Cuban food in Florida (yes, yes, we realize there's still Cuban food in the rest of the country). Have a hot Café Cubano, then down a classic Cuban sandwich hot off the *plancha* (sandwich press). Or just snack on some sweet *maduros* (fried plantains). It's all good.

This is a breakfast and lunch counter, so you'll have to find big Cuban dinners like *ropa vieja* (pulled braised brisket) elsewhere (we recommend Tampa or Miami). There's a dog-friendly patio if you and Fido want to dine alfresco.

29 South
SOUTHERN US $$

(☑ 904-277-7919; www.29southrestaurant.com; 29 S 3rd St, Fernandina Beach; mains $16-28; ⊙ 11:30am-2pm Wed-Sun, 5:30-9:30pm daily; P) Lobster corn dogs, sweet-tea-brined pork chops, homemade doughnut-bread pudding and coffee ice cream – we're in business. Tucked into a pale-purple cottage, this neo-Southern bistro takes culinary risks and executes them well. It's casual yet classy and full of flavor.

Gilbert's Underground Kitchen
MODERN AMERICAN $$

(☑ 904-310–6374; www.undergroundkitchen. co; 510 S 8th St, Fernandina Beach; mains $13-23; ⊙ 11am-9pm Mon-Sat) Celebrity *Top Chef* Kenny Gilbert's Underground Kitchen has sleepy Amelia Island abuzz with culinary glee. Feast on inventive Southern-soul hybrid dishes such as alligator barbecue ribs, noodles with collard green pesto or fried chicken with datil pepper hot sauce.

Café Karibo & Karibrew
FUSION $$

(☑ 904-277-5269; www.cafekaribo.com; 27 N 3rd St, Fernandina Beach; mains $8-26; ⊙ 11am-3pm Mon, to 9pm Tue-Sat, 10:30am-3pm Sun; In) This funky side-street favorite serves a large and eclectic menu of sandwiches, soups, salads and healthy treats in a sprawling two-story space with a shady patio hung with twinkling Christmas lights. Have a crab-cake sandwich, or down a Sloppy Skip's Stout at the adjacent Karibrew brewpub, which has its own menu of global pub grub.

Burlingame Restaurant
MODERN AMERICAN $$$

(☑ 904-432-7671; www.burlingamerestaurant.com; 20 South 5th St, Fernandina Beach; ⊙ 5-10:30pm

Tue-Sat, 10am-2pm daily; P 💺) 🌿 Amelia – a marsh and forest island in a brackish estuary that feeds into the Atlantic – has an incredible wealth of fish, game and produce, and this bounty is treated with love at Burlingame, which serves up seasonally inspired regional cuisine of the highest order. Shrimp and grits and rabbit cassoulet are two of our favorites. Reservations recommended.

Le Clos FRENCH $$$
(✆904-261-8100; www.leclos.com; 20 S 2nd St, Fernandina Beach; mains $19-32; ⊙5:30-9:30pm Mon-Sat) Dine on classic French dishes with a light Florida twist – fish with citrus glazes, tender *steak frites,* shatteringly crisp *crème brûlée* – at this almost-too-cute-for-words but almost-too-busy-to-be-romantic patio bistro. Its reputation for ambience, quality meals and service excellence precedes it.

🍸 Drinking & Nightlife

★**Palace Saloon** BAR
(www.thepalacesaloon.com; 113-117 Centre St, Fernandina Beach; ⊙noon-2am) Push through the swinging doors at the oldest continuously operated bar in Florida (since 1878), and the first thing you'll notice is the 40ft gas-lamp-lit bar. Knock back the saloon's rum-laced Pirate's Punch in dark, velvet-draped surroundings, curiously appealing to both bikers and Shakespeare buffs. At the time of writing, patrons could still smoke inside. Nostalgic!

Green Turtle Tavern BAR
(✆904-321-2324; www.greenturtletavern.com; 14 S 3rd St, Fernandina Beach; ⊙3pm-1am) You can't get much more laid-back or friendly than this colorful, peaced-out bar in a crooked little cottage with a wraparound porch. It serves cocktails, bourbon of all sorts and plenty of cold beer.

🛍 Shopping

Eight Flags Antiques Market ANTIQUES
(✆904-277-8550; 602 Centre St, Fernandina Beach; ⊙10am-6pm Mon-Sat, from noon Sun) Three dozen antique dealers sprawl across one large indoor space. Bargains on the 'treasures' of a hundred Southern attics await to be discovered.

ℹ Information

Shrimping Museum & Welcome Center
(✆904-261-7378; 17 Front St, Fernandina Beach; ⊙10am-4pm Mon-Sat, 1-4pm Sun)

Friendly welcome center with maps, pamphlets and exhibitions on the local shrimping industry.
Historic Downtown Visitor Center (✆904-277-0717; www.ameliaisland.com; 102 Centre St, Fernandina Beach; ⊙10am-4pm) Reams of useful information and maps in the old railroad depot. A fun stop in itself.

ℹ Getting There & Away

Hwy A1A splits in two directions on Amelia Island, one heading west toward I-95 and the other following the coast; both are well marked.

To get to Amelia, the fastest route from the mainland is to take I-95 north to exit 373 and head east about 15 miles straight to the island.

Want a prettier route? Heading from Jacksonville Beach to the town of Mayport, catch the **St Johns River Ferry** (✆904-241-9969; www.stjohnsriverferry.com; per car $5; ⊙from Maryport every 30min 6am-7pm Mon-Fri, 7am-8:30pm Sat & Sun; from George Island every 30min 6:15am-7:15pm Mon-Fri, 7:15am-8:45pm Sat & Sun), which runs around every 30 minutes.

Palatka

✆386 / POP 10,485
In its heyday, the village of Palatka (pronounced puhl-*at*-kuh), almost midway between St Augustine and Gainesville, was the furthest south you could travel by steamship, and boasted more than 7000 hotel rooms for wealthy snowbirds. Today, visitors are trickling back to this sweet, sleepy-verging-on-comatose town for fishing, Memorial weekend's **Blue Crab Festival**, and simply to get away from the coastal crowds.

◉ Sights

Ravine Gardens State Park GARDENS
(✆386-329-3721; www.floridastateparks.org/ravinegardens; 1600 Twigg St; per car/cyclist/pedestrian $5/2/2; ⊙8am-sunset; P) 🌿 A pleasant 2-mile walkable road loops the inner boundary of this 182-acre state park. A ravine, created millions of years ago by the St Johns River, slices through the center of this pristine picnic spot. Some of the best views of this shallow gorge are from the swinging suspension footbridge. It's at its most spectacular between late February and early March when a riot of pink and red azaleas weave skeins through the deep-green foliage.

Bronson-Mulholland House HISTORIC BUILDING
(✆904-329-2704; www.bronsonmulhollandhouse.com; 100 Madison St; ⊙by appointment; P) FREE

NORTHEAST FLORIDA PALATKA

AFRICAN AMERICAN HERITAGE ON AMERICAN BEACH

Insurance magnate AL Lewis, Florida's first black millionaire, founded American Beach in 1935, creating the first black beach community on Florida's segregated shores. In its heyday American Beach catered to throngs of African Americans who arrived by the busload to enjoy the beaches and African American–owned motels, restaurants and nightclubs, where shows with Ray Charles, Louis Armstrong and others made for some of the biggest bills in Florida. In 1964, however, Hurricane Dora destroyed many homes and businesses; shortly thereafter desegregation allowed African Americans to stroll the beaches closer to their homes. Golf courses and gated communities have encroached upon what's left of American Beach, though beach access is possible via Lewis St, off Hwy A1A, on the south end of Amelia Island.

Once here, you'll find a quiet, pleasant stretch of shoreline dotted with some information boards that give insight into the area's history. Although it's only open during limited hours, you can also check out the American Beach Museum (p366) for some insight into the history of one of the few dedicated vacation spots for African Americans in the segregated South.

The former home of Judge Isaac Bronson, the green-shuttered 1854 Bronson-Mulholland House now serves as a historic museum; the on-site manager conducts 30-minute tours by appointment (call well in advance). Note the full-length glass doors opening onto the verandah: when the property was built, homes were taxed according to the number of windows, so many installed French-style doors instead.

✯ Festivals & Events

Palatka Blue Crab Festival   FOOD & DRINK
(www.bluecrabfestival.com; ☺Memorial Day weekend) Hosts the state championship for chowder and gumbo. Yes, it's that good. There's also music, food stalls and lots of outdoor entertainment.

✕ Eating

Angel's Dining Car   AMERICAN $
(☎386-325-3927; 209 Reid St; mains $3-8; ☺6am-9pm; ℙ⑪) Looking like the spawn of a soda can and a subway car, Angel's offers curbside service and sit-in dining. Honk your horn or slide into a vinyl booth for iconic menu items like Monnie (mini) burgers, black-bottom eggs (scrambled with hamburger meat) and Pusalow (pronounced 'puss-uh-loh'): chocolate milk with vanilla syrup and crushed ice. Opened in 1932, this is Florida's oldest diner.

ⓘ Getting There & Away

Palatka is located about 60 miles south of Jacksonville (via US 17 or I-95), and 30 miles west of St Augustine (via SR 207).

Talbot Island & Fort George Island

In between Amelia Island and Jacksonville, you'll find a pair of fantastic green diversions that hold high appeal for history and nature lovers. Amid the shorelines and breezy woods of Fort George and Talbot Islands, you'll discover exceptional kayaking, distinctive state parks, and riverbank and beachside camping galore. It's a wonderful day trip, and an invigorating breath of fresh air after passing the developments that clog the Atlantic Coast.

⊙ Sights

Little Talbot Island State Park   STATE PARK
(☎904-251-2320; www.floridastateparks.org/park/Little-Talbot-Island; 12157 Heckscher Dr; per vehicle/cyclist $5/2; ☺8am-sunset; ℙ) ⊘ This pristine island (which despite the name is almost the same size as Big Talbot Island) has 5 miles of unspoiled beaches, river otters, marsh rabbits, bobcats and grand tidal fishing for mullet and sheepshead.

Camping (p371) available.

Big Talbot Island State Park   STATE PARK
(☎904-251-2320; www.floridastateparks.org/bigtalbotisland; State Rd A1A N; per vehicle $3; ☺8am-sunset; ℙ) ⊘ Deposit your fee in the blue envelope and pull into the lone parking lot at this stark but lovely park. Take your camera on the short trail to Boneyard Beach, where salt-washed skeletons of live oak and cedar trees litter the white sand, framed by a 20ft bluff of eroded coastline. Magical.

Fort George Island
Cultural State Park STATE PARK
(☑ 904-251-2320; www.floridastateparks.org/fort georgeisland; 11241 Fort George Rd; ☺8am-sunset; ℗) FREE Although the exact location of the fort erected by the British in 1736 remains uncertain, the island still bears its name. In pre-WWII glory days, flappers flocked here to the ritzy Ribault Club, built in 1928, for lavish Gatsby-esque bashes. Now housing the visitor center (9am to 5pm Wednesday to Sunday), the meticulously restored mansion flaunts grand archways and three dozen French doors. It's the starting point of the 4.4-mile Saturiwa loop trail, which you can walk, bike or drive.

Enormous shell middens date the island's habitation by the Timucuan tribespeople to over 4000 years ago.

Kingsley Plantation HISTORIC BUILDING
(☑ 904-251-3537; www.nps.gov/timu; 11676 Palmetto Ave, Fort George Island; ☺9am-5pm; ℗) ✐FREE Tour portions of the oldest standing plantation house in Florida as well as the remains of 23 tabby-construction slave cabins at this former cotton and citrus plantation. The main house is under near-constant restoration due to termites and humidity, but the sprawling shaded grounds and mangroves make a unique spot for a picnic. Weekend tours leave on a limited basis from 11am to 3pm; call ahead to determine availability.

Purchased by Zephaniah Kingsley in 1814, the plantation was managed with his wife, Anna Jai, whom he had purchased as a slave and later married in a traditional African ceremony, subsequently freeing both her and their children.

🛏 Sleeping & Eating

Little Talbot Island Camping CAMPGROUND $
(☑ 800-326-3521; http://floridastateparks. reserveamerica.com; tent & RV sites $24; ℗) There are few more beautiful ways of waking up in Florida than doing so on one of her last undeveloped barrier islands. Campsites have electricity, and are nestled amid rolling dunes and shady spreads of marine hammock forest.

Sandollar SEAFOOD $$
(☑ 904-251-2449; www.sandollarrestaurantjax.com; 9716 Heckscher Drive, Fort George Island; mains $12-20; ☺11am-9pm Sun-Thu, to 10pm Fri & Sat; ℗🐾) This classic waterfront spot does tasty seafood with a view out to the breeze-kissed water.

Enjoy a drink and some blackened Mahi or a basket of shrimp, and heave a good sigh of relaxation. Located about 5 miles south of Little Talbot Island. There's live music on the deck Friday through Sunday.

ℹ Information

Ribault Club (☑ 904-251-2802; www.nps.gov/timu; 11241 Fort George Rd, Fort George Island; ☺9am-5pm Wed-Sun) The Fort George Island Visitor Center is located within the Ribault Club, built in 1928 as a venue for millionaires who needed a warmer spot to perfect their *Great Gatsby* parties.

ℹ Getting There & Away

Talbot Island is about 11 miles south of Amelia Island; you can arrive here via State Road A1A. If you're coming from Jacksonville, you can either take Fl 105 to the A1A, or head north from the beaches along A1A and jump on the **St Johns River Ferry** (p369) in Mayport, which heads to Fort George (connected by road to Talbot Island).

NORTH CENTRAL FLORIDA

In one of the least visited parts of the state, you'll discover crystal-clear springs, meandering back roads and small Victorian gingerbread towns reminiscent of a time before the tourism explosion. North Central Florida is more 'Southern' than Florida's South; you may well come across more Confederate flags here than you'd find in states like Alabama or Mississippi.

The horse town of Ocala is as agriculturally focused as Florida gets, while Gainesville, home of the University of Florida, is a charming college town worth a day's diversion. If anything else, don't forget to have your fortune read in the spiritualist camp of Cassadaga. Otherwise, soak up the region's bucolic beauty; you'll find more rolling countryside here than you'd ever expect in a state like Florida.

Cassadaga
☑ 386 / POP 100

In 1894, 27-year-old New Yorker George Colby was suffering from tuberculosis. Seneca, Colby's Native American spirit guide, told him to head south to a lake and establish a spiritualist community, where he'd be healed. Colby did it, and Cassadaga (pronounced kassuh-*day*-guh) was born.

Today, Colby's camp – a collection of mainly 1920s Cracker cottages – is a registered historic district, the oldest active religious community in the US, and home to the Southern Cassadaga Spiritualist Camp Meeting Association, who believe in infinite intelligence, prophecy, healing and communicating with the dead. Some say the area is part of an energy vortex where the spirit and earthly planes are exceptionally close, creating a portal between the two. As you might gather, there's a distinct New Age vibe in this tiny town. Tiny Cassadaga doesn't have an ATM or gas station.

◉ Sights

There are 30-some spiritual practitioners in 'town' who offer a variety of psychic readings, starting at around $20 for a quick question-and-answer session, or $50 for a good half-hour deep-dive into your consciousness. Many psychics practice out of the second floor of the Cassadaga Hotel.

Cassadaga Camp Bookstore HISTORIC SITE
(☑386-228-2880; www.cassadaga.org; 1112 Stevens St, Lake Helen; ⊙10am-6pm Mon-Sat, 11.30am-5pm Sun; **P**) **FREE** Cassadaga's heart is the Cassadaga Camp Bookstore, which sells New Age books, crystals and incense, and serves as the visitor center for the town. Attached is an old spiritualist camp meeting hall, adorned with signs and photos from the camp's early days circa the late 19th and early 20th centuries.

The whiteboard in the back room connects you with which psychics are working that day. The store also organizes historical tours of the village (1pm and 3pm Saturday, $15) and orb tours (8pm Saturday, $25), where photographers shoot glowing balls of light – reportedly spirits from another world. A $1 donation gets you a camp directory, allowing you to take a pretty good self-guided tour. Mandatory stop: Spirit Lake, where residents scatter the ashes of the departed.

⌲ Tours

Cassadaga Historical Tours WALKING
(☑386-228-2880; www.cassadaga.org; adult/child/under 6 $15/7.50/free; ⊙Thu, Fri & Sat 2pm) These walking tours of 'downtown' Cassadaga provide a fairly on-brand message about local history, the importance of spirituality,

expanded consciousness, and all that good stuff. The tours are as enjoyably eccentric as Cassadaga itself. Nighttime tours that seek out spirit-energy hot spots are held at 7:30 on Saturdays (adult $25, child $15). Book all tours ahead via the bookstore.

🛏 Sleeping & Eating

Cassadaga Hotel HOTEL **$**
(☑386-228-2323; www.cassadagahotel.net; 355 Cassadaga Rd; r from $65; **✳ 🛜**) The original Cassadaga Hotel burned down in 1926. Today, ghosts reportedly lurk in the shadows of the rebuilt hotel (sniff for Jack's cigar smoke and listen for two girls terrorizing the upstairs halls). Past all that, the hotel has a charming Old Florida vibe, and there are psychics on hand to provide readings (starting at $20); that's concierge service.

Sinatra's Ristorante ITALIAN **$$**
(☑386-218-3806; www.sinatras.us; 355 Cassadaga Rd; $13-25; ⊙11am-8pm Mon & Tue, til 9pm Wed & Thu, til 10pm Fri & Sat, til 4pm Sun) Look, we like old-school, red-sauce Italian cuisine as much as the next traveler, and the chicken stewed in tomato sauce and Tuscan seafood stew here are great. But it's even better because you can have a glass of wine and a tarot reading at the same time, seeing as Sinatra's is located in the Cassadaga Hotel.

This place also hosts dueling piano nights, because nothing adds to the surreal vibe of an Italian meal in a psychic colony like competing takes on Gaga's 'Bad Romance.'

ℹ Getting There & Away

You wouldn't find Cassadaga if you weren't looking for it. The easiest way here is via I-4; take exit 116 onto Orange Camp Rd to get here. If you're using a GPS, enter the address of the Cassadaga Camp Bookstore: 1112 Stevens St, Lake Helen, FL.

DeLand

☑386 / POP 28,200

While much of Florida seems frantic to cover itself in neon and high-rises, stoic DeLand shrugs that off as nonsense. The quaint, walkable Woodland Blvd, bisecting the east side of town from the west, is home to independent shops and restaurants – modern yet thoroughly small town. Ancient oaks lean in to hug each other over city streets, Spanish moss dribbles from their branches, and picture-perfect Stetson University forms the town's heart. The whole scene screams Old Florida, although ironically, DeLand was the first town in the state to enjoy electricity.

Despite this tradition of, well, tradition, risk-taking flows through DeLand's blood. In the 1870s New York baking-soda magnate Henry DeLand traveled down the St Johns River with a vision of founding the 'Athens of Florida.' That moniker has stuck, but these days DeLand is most famous for skydiving – the tandem jump was invented here.

◉ Sights & Activities

Several historic buildings are open for tours. Check out the West Volusia Historical Society for info (www.delandhouse.com).

De Leon Springs State Park STATE PARK
(☑386-985-4212; www.floridastateparks.org/deleonsprings; 601 Ponce de Leon Blvd, De Leon Springs; car/bike $6/2; ⊗8am-sunset; ℗♿) ∥ Fifteen minutes north of town, these natural springs flow into the 18,000-acre Lake Woodruff National Wildlife Refuge and were used by Native Americans 6000 years ago. Today they're a popular developed swimming area that's great for kids. Water-equipment rentals and boat tours are available: inquire at the park office. Experienced hikers can attack the robust, blue-blaze 4.2-mile Wild Persimmon Trail, meandering through oak hammocks, floodplains and open fields.

Museum of Art – DeLand MUSEUM
(☑386-734-4371; www.moartdeland.org; 600 N Woodland Blvd; adult/child $5/free; ⊗10am-4pm Tue-Sat, from 1pm Sun; ℗♿) A slate of innovative temporary exhibitions traipses across the gallery space and attractive atrium of this energetic local museum, which has been bringing art to the region for six decades. There is a satellite modern gallery space and museum store located at 100 N Woodland Blvd.

DeLand House Museum MUSEUM
(☑386-740-5800; www.delandhouse.com/hospital; 137 W Michigan Ave; adult/child $5/3; ⊗noon-4pm Tue-Sat; ℗) **FREE** This historical home, built in 1886, now serves as the headquarters of the West Volusia Historical Society and a museum for the county. You'll find lots of memorabilia and artifacts and earnest tour guides – it's like peaking into grandma's attic, if grandma was a Central Florida county.

Skydive DeLand SKYDIVING
(☑386-738-3539; www.skydivedeland.com; 1600 Flightline Blvd; tandem jumps $189) If plummeting toward earth at speeds of 120mph sounds like a whiz-bang time, you're in the right place. A short briefing and a seasoned professional strapped to your back is all it takes to experience the least-boring two minutes of your life above some glorious countryside with Skydive DeLand. Experienced skydivers can jump solo or advance their skills at this first-rate facility.

⎚ Sleeping

Artisan Downtown HOTEL $$
(☑386-873-4675; www.delandartisaninn.com; 215 S Woodland Blvd; r $189-219; ⊜) This centrally located boutique hotel was fully renovated in 2013 and features the trendiest rooms in DeLand, with whirlpool baths and cozy sitting areas. The on-site bar and restaurant is a nice bonus, from which noise doesn't appear to be an issue.

DeLand Country Inn B&B $$
(☑386-736-4244; www.delandcountryinn.com; 228 W Howrie Ave; r $99-119, cottage $149; ℗⊜) Popular with skydivers, this sweet B&B is run by a lovely English couple, who'd possibly like to redefine the acronym to read 'Best & British.' Six cozy rooms in the 1883 guesthouse feature comforting, antique-y echoes of Mother England. Of course, a full English breakfast is fried up daily.

✗ Eating

Cook's AMERICAN $
(☑386-734-4399; www.cooksbuffetdeland.com; 704 N Woodland Blvd; mains $7-9, buffet $11; ⊗11am-8:30pm Sun-Thu, to 9pm Fri & Sat; ♿) It's hard not to enjoy a buffet when it is done well, with plenty of selections kept clean, fresh and warm. Cook's does just that: roast meats, veggies, soups and salads, plus a modest selection of à la carte deli sandwiches on freshly baked breads. Cheap and cheerful. Grandma will love it!

Buttercup Bakery BAKERY $
(☑386-736-4043; www.buttercupbakeryfl.com; 197 E Church St; snacks $3.25-8; ⊗8am-5pm Mon-Thu, from 9am Fri, 10am-3pm Sat; ℗) Inside this sunny yellow cottage the pastry cases are stacked high with luscious sweets: lemon-curd bars, white chocolate and apricot bars, chocolate-chip bread pudding and more. It also serves organic coffee, tea and salad.

Doug & Lil's Potato Patch DINER $

(☑386-734-8181; 635 S Woodland Blvd; mains $5-11; ☺7am-2pm Tue-Sun; P) Country breakfasts and country vibes are the name of the game here – the menu serves up stick-to-your-ribs fare like biscuits and gravy, country fried steak, pancakes and omelettes (the crab omelette goes down a treat, FYI).

★**Cress** AMERICAN $$$

(☑386-734-3740; www.cressrestaurant.com; 103 W Indiana Ave; mains $19-34; ☺from 5:30pm Tue-Sat) Citified foodies have been known to trek to sleepy DeLand just to eat at this cutting-edge bistro, whose menu might offer such delights as local seafood *mofongo* (a classic Caribbean dish), Indonesian shrimp curry, and a salad of delicate pea tendrils with passion-fruit emulsion. Three-course fixed menus ($40, with wine pairing $58) are excellent.

This is a can't-miss restaurant if you're in the area. Look for lots of fiery Indian flavors – chef Pulapaka was born in Mumbai, and ditched a career as a math professor to follow his passion for food.

Drinking & Nightlife

Abbey Bar BAR

(☑386-734-4545; 117 N Woodland Blvd; ☺11:30am-1am Mon-Thu, to 2am Fri, 12:30pm-2am Sat, 1pm-midnight Sun) This is a genuinely funky, fun drinking option in the heart of town. The bar has some great brews on tap, board games in the corner, a house selection of mead (why not?) and a quirky, neighborhood-pub feel that is immediately warm and enjoyable.

☆ Entertainment

Athens Theatre THEATER

(☑386-736-1500; www.athensdeland.com; 124 N Florida Ave) Dating back to 1922, this historic theater, designed in a gorgeous Italian Renaissance style, is a good spot for live music and drama performances courtesy of an in-house theater company.

❶ Getting There & Away

DeLand sits off of I-4 and is bisected by Hwy 17. It's located roughly 50 miles north of Orlando, 25 miles west of Daytona Beach, and 60 miles east of Ocala. There is no Greyhound out here, and while **Votran** (☑386-756-7496; www.votran.org; per trip $1.75) offers limited bus service around town, you really need a car to explore the area.

Ocala

☑352 / POP 57,500

Blanketed by velvety paddocks where sleek-limbed horses neigh in the misty morning air, the outskirts of Greater Ocala look like the US Dept of Agriculture–certified 'Horse Capital of the World' *should* look. There are about 1200 horse farms in Marion County, with more than 45 breeds represented.

Downtown Ocala, however, ain't so grand – there's a reason locals call it 'Slo-cala.' ('Strip-Mall-Cala' would also be accurate, if not as clever with the wordplay.) But it's not the downtown you're here for – this rural city is surrounded by beautiful clear springs and the best backyard in Florida: Ocala National Forest.

◉ Sights & Activities

Silver Springs State Park STATE PARK

(☑352-236-7148; www.floridastateparks.org/silversprings; 1425 NE 58th Ave; car/pedestrian $8/2; ☺10am-5pm; P) ✦ This state park was once an amusement park – glass-bottomed boats were invented here in 1878 to show visitors the natural springs and stunningly clear waters of the Silver River. Although the amusement side of things closed in 2013, the natural beauty and the boat tours (adult/child $11/10) over Mammoth Spring remain. The spring is the world's largest artesian limestone spring, gushing 550 million gallons of 99.8%-pure spring water per day.

Don Garlits Museums MUSEUM

(☑352-245-8661; www.garlits.com; 13700 SW 16th Ave; adult/child $20/10; ☺9am-5pm; P) Local drag racer Don 'Big Daddy' Garlits won 144 national events and 17 World Championship titles, shattering numerous records in hand-built breakneck speedsters along the way. In his **Museum of Drag Racing**, you'll find engine collections and an impressive lineup of dragsters, including Garlits' custom-designed 'swamp rats.' The adjacent Antique Building, also known as the **Museum of Classic Cars** (10am to 4pm daily), houses Don's impressive attic of automobiles, including the two-toned 1950 Mercury driven by the Fonz in *Happy Days*.

Cactus Jack's Trail Rides HORSEBACK RIDING

(☑352-266-9326; www.cactusjackstrailrides.com; 11008 S Hwy 475A; from $50) You're in the horse capital of America, so saddle up and let Cactus Jack's take you trotting through shady forests and clover-green fields on the

BLUE SPRING STATE PARK

The largest spring on the St Johns River, Blue Spring maintains a constant 72°F. Between November and March it becomes the winter refuge for up to 200 West Indian manatees. The best time to see them is before 11am; there's a wheelchair-accessible path to the viewing platform. There's a tranquil **state park** (☎386-775-3663; www.floridastateparks.org/bluespring; 2100 W French Ave, Orange City; car/bike $6/2; ☉8am-sunset; P) 🛈 located about 10 miles south of DeLand that is a revitalizing spot to swim (prohibited when manatees are present), snorkel or canoe. Campsites ($24), basic cabins ($95) and gear rentals are available.

You can also spend two hours cruising the peaceful waters with **St Johns River Cruises** (☎386-917-0724; www.sjrivercruises.com; 2100 West French Ave, Orange City; adult/child $25/18; ☉tours 10am & 1pm) 🛈, whose nature tours offer a thoughtful insight into this fragile ecosystem.

backs of their handsome quarter horses and thoroughbreds.

🕮 Tours

Farm Tours Ocala
OUTDOORS

(☎352-895-9302; www.farmtoursofocala.com; 801 SW 60th Ave; $45) Ocala is one of the most important agricultural towns in Florida. On this tour, you'll get an unvarnished, informative peek into life on a working horse farm, and learn some of the ins and outs of raising, breeding and training thoroughbred horses. Tours run for just over three hours, starting at 8:45am and concluding at noon.

🛏 Sleeping

Silver River State Park
CAMPGROUND $

(☎352-236-7148; www.floridastateparks.org/silversprings; 1425 NE 58th Ave; campsites $24, cabins $110; 🐾) Pets are welcome at any of the 59 campsites nestled among the woods at this 5000-acre park. If you want something more sumptuous (but canine-free), try the park's fully equipped cabins, which sleep up to six – they have two-night minimums on weekends and holidays.

Hilton Ocala
HOTEL $$

(☎352-854-1400; www.hiltonocala.com; 3600 SW 36th Ave; r $130-180; 🛜🏊) Ocala's paddock-side Hilton has its own Clydesdale horse, Buddy (and free horse cookies for you to feed him), who waits patiently to take guests on free carriage rides. There's a jogging trail, too. Cookie-cutter rooms.

Shamrock Thistle & Crown
B&B $$

(☎800-425-2763; www.shamrockbb.com; 12971 SE Hwy 42, Weirsdale; r $99-170; P) If you're not a fan of *intensely* colorful accommodations, you may want to pass on this friendly B&B. If you don't mind a truly idiosyncratic property with rooms that, yes, have some strong color combinations, plus warm management, stop on in – you'll be treated like family. Rates go up on weekends.

🍴 Eating

⭐ Big Lee's
BARBECUE $

(☎352-817-7914; www.mybigleesbbq.com; 3925 SE 45th Ct; mains $10-14; ☉11:30am-6pm Fri, to 5.30pm Sat; P) It's only open Friday and Saturdays, the hours are fungible – if they run out of food, they'll close, so arrive early – it's a little ways out of town, and there's not even a restaurant to sit in, just a food truck and some picnic tables. So why come? Because this is some damn fine barbecue.

The char on the skin is crunchy, the brisket glistens like a jewel, and the enormous beef ribs ($25) taste like smoky heaven.

Brooklyn's Backyard
AMERICAN $

(☎352-304-6292; www.brooklynbackyard.com; 2019 E Silver Springs Blvd; mains $10-15; ☉11am-9pm Mon-Wed, to 11pm Thu-Sat, to 8pm Sun; P🛈) Craft beers and pub grub-y mains – mussels sauteed in hot sauce, brie cheese burgers, full pizzas and shrimp macaroni and cheese – set the tone at this restaurant, which has a bit of a backyard vibe (despite its location in a strip mall). The main bar area stays open later on busy weekend nights.

🛈 Getting There & Away

Greyhound (☎352-732-2677; www.greyhound.com; 4032 Hwy 326 W) is in the Central Transfer Station, at the corner of NE 5th St, just a few blocks from downtown. The transfer station for **Amtrak** (☎352-629-9863; www.amtrak.com; 531 NE 1st Ave) is here.

WORTH A TRIP

MARJORIE KINNAN RAWLINGS HISTORIC STATE PARK

Marjorie Kinnan Rawlings (1896–1953) was the author of the Pulitzer Prize-winning novel *The Yearling*, a coming-of-age story set in what's now Ocala National Forest. Her former Cracker-style **home** (☏352-466-3672; www.floridastateparks.org/MarjorieKinnanRawlings; 18700 S CR 325, Cross Creek; per vehicle $3; ⊙9am-5pm; P) is open for tours (adult/child $3/2) on the hour (except noon). You can stroll the orange groves, farmhouse and barn on your own – pick up a self-guided walking brochure from the car park. The estate is 23 miles north of Ocala in the small town of Cross Creek, off Hwy 325 between Island Grove and Micanopy.

Hungry? Cross Creek's cedar-shingled **Yearling Restaurant** (☏352-466-3999; www.yearlingrestaurant.net; 14531 Hwy 325, Hawthorne; mains $6-15; ⊙noon-8pm Thu-Sun, to 9pm Fri & Sat; P🚗) serves 'Cracker cuisine' like gator tail, frog legs, hush puppies and catfish in an atmospheric wood-paneled dining room decorated with historical photos and paintings. It's worth a stop just to try its famous sour orange pie. Live music performances kick off on a pretty regular basis.

Rawlings' career flourished only after Max Perkins, Rawlings' (and also Ernest Hemingway's and F Scott Fitzgerald's) editor, told her that her letters about her friends and neighbors were more interesting than her Gothic fiction, inspiring her to write Cross Creek, a book about her life in old Cracker Florida.

Ocala National Forest

The oldest national forest east of the Mississippi River and the southernmost national forest in the continental US, the 400,000-acre Ocala National Forest is one of Florida's most important natural treasures. An incredible ecological web, the park is a tangle of springs, biomes (sand-pine scrub, palmetto wilderness, subtropical forest) and endangered flora and fauna.

With 18 developed campgrounds and 24 primitive ones, 219 miles of trails and 600 lakes (30 for boating), there are enormous opportunities for swimming, hiking, cycling, horseback riding, canoeing, bird- and wildlife-watching – or just meditating on how great it is that the government got here before the theme parks did.

Two highways cross the region: Hwy 19 runs north–south and Hwy 40 runs east–west.

◎ Sights

Ocala National Forest　　　　FOREST
(☏352-669-7495; www.fs.usda.gov/main/ocala; off FL 40; P🐾) 🅵🆁🅴🅴 The second-largest nationally protected forest in the state of Florida, Ocala National Forest is a treasure to be savored. Hidden within 607 square miles of pristine wilderness, you'll find longleaf pine, sand-pine scrub and coastal oak copses, as well some 600 springs, rivers and lakes. Miles of hiking, biking and horse-riding trails cut through Ocala's green, woodsy heart, which also contains a staggeringly diverse range of local wildlife.

🏃 Activities

Also referred to as the Ocala Trail, roughly 61 miles of the Florida National Scenic Trail spears the center of the forest north–south. Marked with orange blazes, pick-up points include Juniper Springs, Alexander Springs and Clearwater Lake recreation areas. Outside hunting season, hikers can camp anywhere 200ft from the trail, but if you prefer to commune with others you'll find spur trails to developed campgrounds every 10 to 12 miles.

The 8.5-mile St Francis Trail (blue blazes) winds through riverine and bayhead swamp to the abandoned 1880s pioneer town of St Francis on the St Johns River. No buildings remain, but you'll see the old logging railroad bed and levee built for rice growing.

Paisley Woods Bicycle Trail　　CYCLING
(www.pwbt.weebly.com) Passing through prairies and live-oak domes, the popular backwoods Paisley Woods Bicycle Trail rolls 22 miles from Alexander Springs to the north and Clearwater Lake to the south (it's shaped like a figure eight so you can do either half as a loop). Bring a bike that can handle off-road conditions, and plenty of water (there is none available along the trail).

Juniper Springs
Recreation Area   OUTDOORS
(☑ 352-625-3147; www.juniper-springs.com; 26701 Hwy 40, Silver Springs; $5; ⊙8am-8pm) ⚡ Ocala National Forest's flagship recreation area was developed in the mid-1930s as part of the work of the Civilian Conservation Corps. Swimming is sublime at Juniper Springs: the water is a crisp 72°F (22°C) year-round. Concessions sell groceries and firewood, and rent kayaks and canoes ($33.50 per day) for making the 7-mile, palmetto- and cypress-lined run down Juniper Creek. Also has campsites ($21).

There's a pick-up and return shuttle at the end of the creek ($6 per person and $6 per boat).

Alexander Springs
Recreation Area   OUTDOORS
(☑ 352-625-2520; www.fs.usda.gov/ocala; 49525 County Rd 445, Altoona; $5.50; ⊙8am-8pm) ⚡ This picturesque recreation area has one of the last untouched subtropical forests left in Florida. The stunning sapphire-blue freshwater spring attracts wildlife, swimmers, scuba divers (an extra $6.50 fee) and sunbathers. Canoe rental (two hours/daily $16/38) includes a welcome re-haul at the end of the 7-mile paddle. Has campsites ($22), too.

Salt Springs Recreation Area   OUTDOORS
(☑ 352-685-2048; www.floridasprings.org/visit/map/salt-springs; 13851 N Hwy 19, Salt Springs; $6; ⊙8am-8pm) ⚡ Enriched by mineral deposits that include potassium, magnesium and sodium salts (hence the name), and rumored to have curative powers, Salt Springs is a favorite with RV owners for its lovely shady areas (sites with/without hookups $29/20.50). There's lovely swimming available, and local canoeing is supremely relaxing.

⌂ Sleeping & Eating

There are dozens of different camping options in the national forest. Campsites are available from $21 and there are cabins available that sleep up to 10 people (weekend/week $420/800). Visit the National Forest website (www.fs.usda.gov/recarea/ocala) for a full breakdown on all campsites; book through www.recreation.gov.

Stock up on food in Ocala or DeLand before arriving. Be careful how you store food – the forest boasts Florida's largest population of wild black bears.

ⓘ Getting There & Away

Several different entrances can be used to access Ocala National Forest. From Orlando take Hwy 441 north to the Eustis turnoff and continue north on Hwy 19 (about 40 miles); from Daytona take Hwy 92 west to DeLand, then head north on Hwy 17 to Barberville and west on SR 40 (about 30 miles); from Ocala take Silver Springs Blvd due west about 6 miles to the forest's main entry.

Gainesville
☑ 352 / POP 130,000

The state's premier college town is an energetic change of pace from rural, conservative north Florida. While Gainesville is hardly hippie central, you'll find graffiti murals, fair-trade coffee, funky music and similar amenities that feel a little incongruous after miles of countryside. With that in mind, it's worth remembering said countryside gives way to pristine nature, itself a major attraction for the outdoors-loving residents of Gainesville.

Originally a whistle-stop along the Florida Railroad Company's line, today this town is home to the nation's second-largest university, the sprawling University of Florida (UF). The campus itself is 2 miles from downtown, but the student vibe infuses the entire city, which is part of the reason Gainesville has such a thriving music scene. The most notable band to hail from here is Tom Petty and the Heartbreakers, but there's also an old-school, vibrant punk rock scene.

◉ Sights

★ Florida Museum of
Natural History   MUSEUM
(☑ 352-846-2000; www.flmnh.ufl.edu; 3215 Hull Rd; ⊙10am-5pm Mon-Sat, 1-5pm Sun; ᴘ⛟) FREE The highlight of this excellent natural-history museum is the expansive Butterfly Rainforest (adult/child $13/6). Hundreds of butterflies from 55 to 65 species flutter freely in the soaring, screened vivarium. As you stroll among waterfalls and tropical foliage, peek at scientists preparing specimens in the rearing lab of this, the world's largest butterfly research facility. Other exhibits include displays on fossils and Floridian ecosystems.

Bat House & Bat Barn   LANDMARK
(www.flmnh.ufl.edu/bats; Museum Rd; ᴘ) FREE Across from Gainesville's little Lake Alice, adjacent to a student garden, stands what

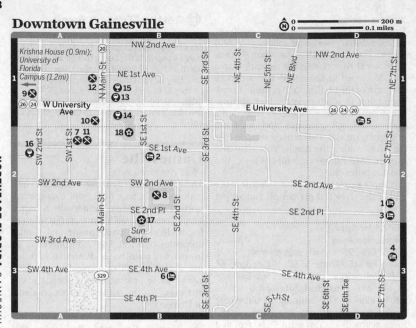

Downtown Gainesville

N 0 / 0   200 m / 0.1 miles

Downtown Gainesville

🛏 Sleeping
1 Camellia Rose... D2
2 Hampton Inn & Suites – Gainesville
   Downtown... B2
3 Laurel Oak Inn....................................... D2
4 Magnolia Plantation............................. D3
5 Sweetwater Branch Inn D1
6 Zen Hostel... B3

✖ Eating
7 Crane Ramen.. A2
8 Dragonfly B2
9 Flaco's Cuban Bakery............................ A1
10 Manuel's Vintage Room........................ A1

11 Paramount Grill A2
12 The Top.. A1

🍸 Drinking & Nightlife
13 Arcade Bar B1
14 Dime.. B1
15 University Club B1
16 Whiskey House A2

🎭 Entertainment
   Bull...(see 7)
17 Hippodrome..B2
18 Lillian's Music Store..............................B2

appears to be two oversized birdhouses. However, these stilted gray-roofed structures are actually home to a family of Brazilian free-tailed bats. Built in 1991 after the flying mammals' poop began stinking up the campus, the population has since exploded to more than 300,000. Each night just after sundown, the bats drop from their roost – at the amazing rate of 100 bats per second – and fly off to feed.

Samuel P Harn Museum of Art　GALLERY
(☑ 352-392-9826; www.harn.ufl.edu; 3259 Hull Rd; ⊙ 11am-5pm Tue-Fri, 10am-5pm Sat, 1-5pm Sun; ℗) **FREE** Peer in at ancient Native American sculptures and contemporary paintings at this excellent art gallery on the University of Florida campus. Also open on the second Thursday of the month (6pm to 9pm).

Kanapaha Botanical Gardens　GARDENS
(☑ 352-372-4981; www.kanapaha.org; 4700 SW 58th Dr; adult/child $8/4; ⊙ 9am-5pm Fri-Wed; ℗ 🐾) ✿ Central Florida's lush native plants – azaleas, rare double-crowned cabbage palms, southern magnolias – are on proud display at this highly rated 62-acre garden, with hiking paths, a labyrinth, a children's koi pond and special herb and

ginger gardens. Especially cool is the dense bamboo garden, whose dark groves look like fairy homes. Dogs are welcome!

Devil's Millhopper State Geological Site
PARK

(☑ 352-955-2008; www.floridastateparks.org/devilsmillhopper; 4732 Millhopper Rd; car/pedestrian $4/2; ⊙9am-5pm Wed-Sun; P) ✐ As the name indicates, this is not your average park. The site centers on a 120ft-deep, 500ft-wide funnel-shaped rainforest which you enter by descending a 232-step wooden staircase. Water trickles down the slopes from the surrounding springs; some of it flows into a natural drain and ultimately to the Gulf of Mexico. The park is about 20 minutes northwest of downtown by car.

University of Florida
UNIVERSITY

(UF; ☑ 352-392-3261; www.ufl.edu; Welcome Center, cnr Museum Rd & Reitz Union Dr) The city is dominated by the UF campus, the second largest in the country. Pop in to the Welcome Center for tips on where best to wander around to check out the student vibe.

⌖ Tours

Gainesville has a unique citywide cell-phone audio tour – when you spot a placard, dial the number listed for information about historical and cultural sites.

⌂ Sleeping

Zen Hostel
HOSTEL $

(☑ 352-336-3613; www.zenhostel.com; 404 SE 2nd St; dm $25, r $35-90; 🛜) Look for the Tibetan prayer flags decorating the porch of this rambling yellow house, which feels like an old-school 1970s commune: chickens in the yard, barefoot children, kombucha tea fermenting in the shared kitchen. Popular among visiting students from nearby massage and acupuncture schools, it's got creaky-floored dorms and rooms decorated with thrift-store furniture and relatively clean shared facilities.

Hampton Inn & Suites – Gainesville Downtown
HOTEL $$

(☑ 352-240-9300; www.hamptoninnandsuitesgainesville.com; 101 SE 1st Ave; d from $140; P🛜) Located in the heart of downtown Gainesville, you couldn't ask for a better location from which to explore this quaint district. The attractive facade of this new hotel is echoed in the stylish interior. Guestrooms are furnished to a high standard. Free wi-fi

and a light hot breakfast is provided, and there's plenty to eat, drink and enjoy nearby.

Magnolia Plantation
B&B $$

(☑ 352-375-6653; www.magnoliabnb.com; 309 SE 7th St; r/cottages from $160/200; P🛜) Lovingly restored, this French Second Empire–style mansion was unique to Gainesville when constructed by a woodworker in 1885. It's still unique today. The main house boasts five rooms, 10 fireplaces (check the detailing in those mantels) and snacks around the clock. Outside, a tangled hidden garden has a pond and chairs for relaxing.

Sweetwater Branch Inn
B&B $$

(☑ 352-373-6760, 800-595-7760; www.sweetwaterinn.com; 625 E University Ave; r $144-174; @✉) In this wedding cake mansion, you'll find 20 rooms – no two exactly alike – decorated in an Old Florida aesthetic, with hardwoods, classic furniture and artwork that recalls the state's natural beauty and history. An on-site pool and mod-cons like cable TV and noise diffusers add the right touch of contemporary comfort.

Camellia Rose
B&B $$

(☑ 352-395-7673; www.camelliaroseinn.com; 205 SE 7th St; r $145-225; P🛜) Modern upgrades (like Jacuzzi tubs) integrate seamlessly with antique furniture in this fabulously restored 1903 Victorian building featuring a wide, relaxing front porch.

Laurel Oak Inn
B&B $$

(☑ 352-373-4535; www.laureloakinn.com; 221 SE 7th St; r $135-180; P🛜) The 1885 Lassiter House has been splendidly redone as a handsome yellow B&B, with high ceilings, velvet fainting couches and fresh flowers everywhere.

✗ Eating

Satchel's Pizza
PIZZA $

(☑ 352-335-7272; www.satchelspizza.com; 1800 NE 23rd Ave; menu items $3-15; ⊙11am-10pm Tue-Sat; P) Satchel's makes a strong claim to the best pizza on Florida's east coast, a reputation buttressed by enormous crowds of happy patrons. Grab a seat at a mosaic courtyard table or in the back of a gutted 1965 Ford Falcon. Most nights there's live music in the Back 40 Bar, with its head-scratchingly eccentric collection of trash and treasure.

There's always a wait, so just kick back, down a beer and watch the peeps.

Dave's New York Deli
DELI **$**

(☑ 352-333-0291; www.davesnydeli.com; mains $7-12; ☺ 9am-8pm Mon-Sat, 11am-3pm Sun) The NYC-transplant force is strong at Dave's, where the pastrami and corned beef is stacked precariously high on rye, and if you order anything else, you're kind of a *schmuck*. Just kidding! There are plenty of good choices here, from potato knish to delicious, oversized salads.

Crane Ramen
JAPANESE **$**

(☑ 352-727-7422; www.craneramen.com; 16 SW 1st Ave; mains $9-13; ☺ 11am-4pm & 5-11pm, Tue-Sun) College students are famous for living on ramen, but those packaged noodles are roughly a thousand steps below the quality of the soup served at this elegant, playful eatery. Seven variations on ramen broth can be accessorized into whatever soup your heart desires, and chased with plenty of sake off an extensive drinks menu to boot.

Flaco's Cuban Bakery
CUBAN **$**

(☑ 352-371-2000; 200 W University Ave; mains $4-6; ☺ 11:30am-2:30am Tue-Fri, noon-2:30am Sat) It's funny, because 'Flaco' is Spanish for 'skinny,' and if you eat at Flaco's, you will be anything but. That's OK – we still love coming here, especially late at night (because not much else is open, food-wise), for hot pressed sandwiches, *arepas* (corn cakes), empanadas, *ropa vieja* (pulled braised brisket) and other Latin American favorites.

Krishna House
VEGETARIAN **$**

(☑ 352-222-2886; www.krishnalunch.com; 214 NW 14th St; by donation; ☺ noon-3pm Mon-Fri; ☕) For tasty vegetarian soul food on a budget during school sessions, head to Krishna House on the UF campus, make a small donation and fill your belly. Who said there's no such thing as a (karma) free lunch?

★ Southern Charm Kitchen
AMERICAN **$**

(☑ 352-505-5553; www.southerncharmkitchen.com; 1714 SE Hawthorne Rd; mains $10-16; ☺ 7am-10pm; P ☕ ♿) There's plenty of fancy gastronomy in Gainesville, and cozy, unpretentious, friendly Southern Charm Kitchen gives them all a run for their money. This is food like your mom made, if your mom was an amazing cook who made sorghum ribs, barbecue goat, spicy corn waffles and shrimp, and decadent fried chicken.

There are plenty of veggie options too, including pickled watermelon tofu, roasted beets and sherry tomatoes, and a gorgeous take on Hoppin' John (black-eyed peas and tempeh).

Civilization
INTERNATIONAL **$**

(☑ 352-380-0544; www.welcometocivilization.com; 1511 NW 2nd St; mains $12-16; ☺ 11am-2pm Tue-Fri, 5:30-9pm Tue-Thu, 5:30-9:30pm Fri & Sat, 10am-2pm Sat & Sun; ☕) Restaurants with extensive vegan offerings are a relative rarity in north central Florida, which makes this spot a veritable outpost of civilization for non-carnivores (see what we did there?). That's not to say there isn't meat on offer – you can find excellent shrimp and grits and moussaka, for example. But don't pass on falafel burgers or masala dosa either.

The Top
FUSION **$$**

(☑ 352-376-1188; www.chompmenus.com/the-top-gainesville; 30 N Main St; mains $11-25; ☺ 5pm-2am Tue-Sat, 11am-11pm Sun; ☕) Combining 1950s kitsch, hunter-lodge decor and giant owl art, this place is both hip and comfortable. Vegetarians will thrill at the options here and everyone will appreciate the working photo booth in the back ($2). Carnivores can rejoice as well – the burgers are awesome. Just as popular for the nightlife as it is for food.

Dragonfly
JAPANESE **$$**

(☑ 352-371-3359; www.dragonflyrestaurants.com; 201 SE 2nd Ave; small plates $4-14; ☺ 11:30am-2pm Thu & Fri, 5-10pm Sun-Thu, to 11:30pm Fri & Sat; ☕) Head to Dragonfly for excellent sushi, sake and small plates done Japanese style. Grilled tiger shrimp is fire-kissed and savory, miso black cod is a revelation and ginger salad is a delight. The enormous dining space is colorful, bustling and great for a big group of friends.

Manuel's Vintage Room
ITALIAN **$$**

(☑ 352-375-7372; www.manuelsvintageroom.com; 6 S Main St; mains $16-24; ☺ 5-10pm Tue-Sun) Warm, intimate and friendly, Manuel's is the perfect spot for a romantic dinner in the heart of downtown. Pasta aplenty and dishes such as veal porcini and pork Milanese cooked to your liking are sure to satisfy.

Paramount Grill
MODERN AMERICAN **$$$**

(☑ 352-378-3398; www.paramountgrill.com; 12 SW 1st Ave; mains $15-37; ☺ 5-9:30pm Mon, 11am-2pm & 5-9:30pm Tue-Sat, Sun from 10am) Very Scandinavian chic, with minimalist wood tables and apple-green walls decorated with vintage sailor photos, this is the top spot for innovative upscale-casual eats in Gainesville.

PAYNES PRAIRIE PRESERVE STATE PARK

Wild horses and bison roam the 20 biological communities that constitute 21,000-acre **Paynes Prairie Preserve State Park** (☑ 352-466-3397; www.floridastateparks.org/Paynesprairie; 100 Savannah Blvd; per vehicle/bicycle $6/2; ⊙ 8am-sunset; P) ✐. This slightly eerie preserve's wet prairie, swamp, hammock and pine flatwoods are crisscrossed by multiple trails which can easily eat up a day of wandering. The 3-mile La Chua Trail takes in the Alachua Sink and Alachua Lake, offering opportunities to spot alligators and sandhill cranes.

Just north of the visitor center, climb the 50ft observation tower for panoramas. Campsites cost $18, and include water and electricity.

The park is located about 11 miles south of downtown Gainesville, off of US 441-S.

A globally influenced menu spans crab cakes, duck dishes and homemade ravioli.

🍸 Drinking & Nightlife

★ Dime   COCKTAIL BAR
(☑ 352-692-0068; 4 E University Ave; ⊙ 4pm-2am) A small bar, some dim lighting, talented bartenders and strong, delicious cocktails – that's what you get at The Dime, a gin joint that feels like it made a wrong turn in 1930s Manhattan and ended up in central Florida.

Whiskey House   BAR
(☑ 352-519-5534; 60 SW 2nd St; ⊙ 5:30pm-2am Wed-Sat, from 7pm Sun-Tue) There's a very contemporary vibe going on at the swish Whiskey House, which draws in an attractive crowd that loves to mingle on the big outdoor patio. Anyways, that's all well and good, but there's something like 300 whiskeys behind the bar, so goodbye reader, because we're moving here.

Arcade Bar   BAR
(www.arcadebargainesville.com; 6 E University Ave; ⊙ 5pm-2am Mon-Sat, to midnight Sun) Three floors of old-school arcade goodness are the order of the day at Arcade Bar, which is filled with coin-operated games, pinball machines and plenty of other diversions that – we know, we know – you're *really* good at, unless you've had a bunch of beers, which is inevitably what ends up happening if you stick around for awhile.

Curia On the Drag   CAFE
(☑ 352-792-6444; www.curiaonthedrag.com; 2029 NW 6th St; ⊙ 7am-midnight Mon-Fri, from 9am Sat & Sun) There's plenty of good coffee in this college town, but we love Curia, both for its not super-milky coffee and its young, smart, accommodating staff. Yes, it's a mural-chic, bohemian kinda coffee spot – it's just executing that genre very well.

University Club   GAY & LESBIAN
(☑ 352-378-6814; www.ucnightclub.com; 18 E University Ave; ⊙ 5pm-2am Sun-Fri, from 9pm Sat) Predominantly gay, but straight-friendly, this place is the hub of the local gay and lesbian scene and is famous for its drag shows. The entrance is around back. DJs spin most nights, and there are more than a few evenings when this place gets to-the-gills crowded.

☆ Entertainment

Live music is to Gainesville what mouse ears are to Orlando, and many bars double as music venues. For an up-to-the-minute overview of local music, check out www.gainesvillebands.com. The downtown drinking scene is pretty diverse, and while you'll find student bars, there's more variety afoot as well.

Hippodrome   THEATER
(☑ 352-375-4477; www.thehipp.org; 25 SE 2nd Pl) In an imposing historic edifice (1911), the Hippodrome is the city's main cultural center, with a diverse theater and independent-cinema program.

Bull   LIVE MUSIC
(☑ 352-672-6266; 18 SW 1st Ave; ⊙ 4pm-2am Mon-Sat) There's never a cover and almost always some music happening at The Bull, and if music isn't going down, there's art on the walls, craft beer on tap, strong coffee brewing and a mellow atmosphere that attracts a lot of local artists and musicians.

Lillian's Music Store   LIVE MUSIC
(☑ 352-372-1010; 112 SE 1st St; ⊙ 2pm-2am Mon-Sat, to midnight Sun) The crowd's a little older than in the clubs along University, so they

WORTH A TRIP

ICHETUCKNEE SPRINGS STATE PARK

Relax in a giant inner tube and float through gin-clear waters at this popular **park** (☑ 386-497-4690; www.floridastateparks.org/ichetuckneesprings; 12087 SW US 27, Fort White; car/person $6/5; ☉ 8am-sunset; P) ✎, plopped on the lazy, spring-fed Ichetucknee River.

Various water sports are available here, but tubing is certainly the most popular. Floats last from 45 minutes to 3½ hours, with scattered launch points along the river. The park runs regular trams bringing tubers to the river and also a free shuttle service (May to September) between the north and south entrances.

To minimize environmental impact, the number of tubers is limited to 750 a day; arrive early as capacity is often reached mid-morning. Use the south entrance: the shuttle service takes you to the launch points, allowing you to raft back down to your car.

You'll see farmers advertising tube rental as you approach the park along Hwy 238 and 47 (the park itself does not rent tubes). Tubes are $5 and one- or two-person rafts cost $10 to $15. At the end of the day, leave your gear at the tube drop at the southern end of the park; it'll be returned. The park is located about 16 miles northwest of High Springs.

appreciate that elegant stained-glass partition and the 3ft-tall gorilla at the entrance. Monday night jam sessions really pack 'em in.

ℹ️ Information

Pride Community Center (☑ 352-377-8915; www.gainesvillepride.org; 3131 NW 13th St; ☉ 3-7pm Mon-Fri, noon-4pm Sat) Resource center for LGBT information in north central Florida.

ℹ️ Getting There & Away

Located about 70 miles from both Jacksonville and St Augustine, Gainesville sits smack in the north central portion of north central Florida. How's that for a geographic hall of mirrors?

Gainesville Regional Airport (☑ 352-373-0249; www.gra-gnv.com; 3880 NE 39th Ave) is located 10 miles northeast of downtown and is served by a handful of domestic carriers. The **Greyhound bus station** (☑ 352-376-5252; www.greyhound.com; 101 NE 23rd Ave) is a mile or so north of downtown.

High Springs

☑ 386 / POP 5530

Quaint and quiet High Springs is a hub for antiquers, bikers and locals seeking a getaway. Main St, dotted with shops, galleries and restaurants, is the major north–south divider, and feels lifted out of a *Leave it to Beaver* episode (albeit, a hot and humid *Leave it to Beaver* episode).

With that said, we find that we don't spend much time in the town of High Springs itself. Instead, we come here for its namesake: local crystal-clear springs that constitute one of Florida's unique natural treasures.

⊙ Sights

Poe Springs   SPRING

(☑ 352-548-1210; 28800 NW 182nd Ave; ☉ 9am-6pm Thu-Sun; P) **FREE** Shallow Poe Springs, which has steps leading all the way down to the bright blue water, is perfect for small children. It's one of the least crowded springs in the area – depending on the time of year, you could find yourself in blissful isolation. From High Springs, follow CR-340 west for 2 miles to reach the park.

Ginnie Springs   SPRING

(☑ 386-454-7188; www.ginniespringsoutdoors. com; 7300 NE Ginnie Springs Rd; adult/child $14/3.70; ☉ 8am-7pm Mon-Thu, to 10pm Fri & Sat, to 8pm Sun) Of the two springs in High Springs, Ginnie Springs is a little older and more developed than Poe Springs, with a handful of campsites ($22) on hand and scuba divers plying its clear waters. Closes a couple of hours earlier in winter.

🛏️ Sleeping & Eating

Grady House Bed & Breakfast   B&B $$

(☑ 386-454-2206; www.gradyhouse.com; 420 NW 1st Ave; r $140-170, cottage $280; P 🛜) Characterful B&B offering warm-hearted accommodations across five rooms, all themed according to color. The Red Room has more than 350 classic nudes gracing the walls; the Navy Room is styled nautically.

Great Outdoors Restaurant   AMERICAN $$

(☑ 386-454-1288; www.greatoutdoorsdining. com; 65 N Main St; mains $10-29; ☉ 11am-9pm Tue-Thu & Sun, to 10pm Fri & Sat; 🍴) This woodsy, lantern-lit steakhouse and saloon, located in the former downtown Opera

House, has an inviting patio area for alfresco dining. The menu is old-school Florida, if a little elevated: low country boils, ribs, big burgers and deep-fried seafood.

ⓘ Getting There & Away

Located about 22 miles north of Gainesville, High Springs is located off of US 441 and US 41. There is no bus service here.

Barberville

☑ 386

All of north central Florida is, in some ways, a call back to the state's not so distant frontier past, but Barberville takes this embrace of rural heritage to the next level. Amid this tiny town's palm- and oak-shaded country lanes, you'll find a re-created pioneer settlement that speaks to the people who hacked a place to live out of the nearby vine-clad woods and backwater swamps.

⦿ Sights

Barberville
Pioneer Settlement   HISTORIC SITE
(☑386-749-2959; www.pioneersettlement.org; 1776 Lightfoot Lane, Pierson; adult/child $8/4; ⊙9am-4pm Tue-Sat year-round, also noon-4pm Sun Nov-May; P⊡) ✐ Try to set aside at least an hour to fully explore old Barberville, a re-created pioneer settlement carved out of the central Florida woods. Costumed interpreters will give kid-friendly lessons on Old Florida life in front of blacksmith forges and in rebuilt schoolhouses. Check the website to take advantage of a regular calendar of events, from monthly music workshops to harvest festivals.

✪ Festivals & Events

Barberville Jamboree   MUSIC
(www.pioneersettlement.org; Barberville; ⊙Nov; ⊡) On the first weekend of November, the Pioneer Settlement for the Creative Arts hosts Florida's best pioneer-heritage festival, with folk music and demonstrations of Cracker (rural Floridian) life.

🔒 Shopping

Barberville Roadside
Yard Art & Produce   MARKET
(☑386-749-3562; www.barbervilleroadside.com; 140 West State Rd 40; ⊙9am-6pm) On Rte 40, plunked halfway between Ocala and Daytona and roughly one-third the way between DeLand and Palatka, nestled cozily beneath a Spanish-moss canopy, sits the king of roadside stands, Barberville Roadside Yard Art & Produce. Offering more than fruits, veggies and honey, this open-air market fills 3 acres with wrought-iron furniture, gazing balls, ceramic drop-in sinks and old-fashioned peanut brittle.

There's even an 8ft-tall aluminum rooster. Who doesn't need one of those?

ⓘ Getting There & Away

Little Barberville sits at the intersection of US 17 and Fl 40 – where those roads meet, you'll find Barberville, although if you blink, you'll miss it. DeLand is located about 15 miles south on US 17.

Tampa Bay & Southwest Florida

POP 3.1 MILLION / ☏ 813, 863, 727, 352, 941, 239

Best Places to Eat

➡ Bha! Bha! Persian Bistro (p438)

➡ Ulele (p391)

➡ Owen's Fish Camp (p420)

➡ Brick & Mortar (p402)

➡ D (p431)ixie Fish Company (p431)

Best Places to Sleep

➡ Harrington House (p423)

➡ Gasparilla Inn (p439)

➡ Hollander Hotel (p401)

➡ Mango Street Inn (p430)

➡ 'Tween Waters Inn (p434)

Why Go?

To drive southwest Florida's Gulf Coast is to enter an impressionistic watercolor painting: first, there's the dazzling white quartz sand of its barrier-island beaches, whose turquoise waters darken to silver-mantled indigo as the fiery sun lowers. Later, seen from the causeways, those same islands become a phosphorescent smear beneath the inky black night sky.

The Gulf Coast's beauty is its main attraction, but variety is a close second: from Tampa to St Petersburg to Sarasota to Naples, there's urban sophistication and exquisite cuisine. There are secluded islands, family-friendly resorts and spring break–style parties.

Here Salvador Dalí's melting canvases, Ringling's Venetian Gothic palace and Chihuly's tentacled glass sculptures fit perfectly – all are bright, bold, surreal entertainments to match wintering manatees, roseate spoonbills, open-mouthed alligators and the peacock-colored, sequined costumes of twirling trapeze artists.

When to Go
Tampa Bay

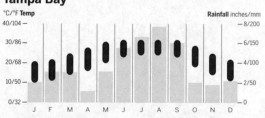

°C/°F **Temp**　　　　　　　　　　　　　　　　**Rainfall** inches/mm

Mid-Feb–mid-Apr	**Jun-Sep** Hot and	**Nov-Dec** Snow-
Peak season, ideal	rainy. Low season	birds arrive.
weather, high	means beach	Weather cools
prices. Best for	bargains; some	and dries; decent
camping, hiking,	places close.	off-season prices.
manatees.		

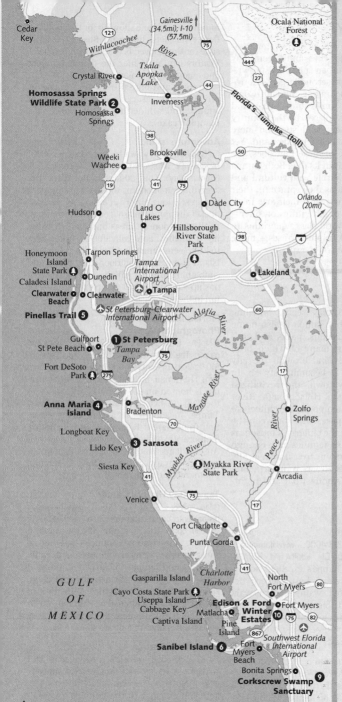

Tampa Bay & Southwest Florida Highlights

❶ St Petersburg (p397) Sampling craft beer and wandering through Salvador Dalí's dreams in virtual reality.

❷ Homosassa Springs Wildlife State Park (p412) Paddling the waterways beside slow-moving manatees.

❸ Ringling Museum Complex (p416) Juggling art and circus.

❹ Anna Maria Island (p422) Finding Old Florida and nibbling on edible gardens.

❺ Pinellas Trail (p400) Freewheeling from St Pete all the way to Tarpon Springs, and rewarding yourself with baklava cheesecake.

❻ Sanibel Island (p431) Hunting for shells with the kiddos.

❼ Marco Island (p439) Cruising by mangrove islands and dolphin-spotting.

❽ Naples (p435) Window shopping on Third Street South and attending the symphony.

❾ Corkscrew Swamp Sanctuary (p438) Admiring bald cypress and wood storks.

❿ Edison & Ford Winter Estates (p428) Studying bright ideas from the region's most famous residents.

TAMPA BAY

Surrounding the gorgeous deep-water Tampa Bay are two major cities and a seemingly endless expanse of urban-suburban sprawl – forming the state's second-largest metropolitan area – which along the Gulf Coast is edged by some 35 miles of barrier-island beaches. Not many places in the country offer as much big-city sophistication mere minutes from so much dazzling sand. Yet since Miami is one of those that does, the bay area is rarely given its due. Both Tampa and St Petersburg burble with cultural and culinary excitement as they spruce up their historic districts and polish their arts institutions. The range of adventures on offer – from fine arts to world-class aquariums to hot nightclubs and dolphin cruises – make this a compelling region to explore.

Tampa

📋 813 / POP 352,957

On first glance it may seem sprawling and businesslike, but Tampa is also home to a bunch of museums, parks and ambitious restaurants, many of which have popped up recently and brought the city dangerously close to becoming stylish. In the heart of downtown, the revitalized Riverwalk along the Hillsborough River glitters with contemporary architecture and scenic green spaces. Plus, between the zoo, the aquarium, the children's museums and the theme parks, families have enough top-shelf entertainment to last a week. By evening Ybor City's streets transform into southwest Florida's hottest bar and nightclub scene.

⊙ Sights

★ Florida Aquarium   AQUARIUM
(Map p388; 📋 813-273-4000; www.flaquarium. org; 701 Channelside Dr; adult/child $25/20; ⊙9:30am-5pm; 🚼) Tampa's excellent aquarium is among the state's best. Cleverly designed, the re-created swamp lets you walk among herons and ibis as they prowl the mangroves. Programs let you swim with the fishes (and the sharks) or take a catamaran ecotour in Tampa Bay.

Wat Mongkolratanaram   BUDDHIST TEMPLE
(📋 813-621-1669; 5306 Palm River Rd; ⊙8:30am-2:30pm Sun) Why is there a Buddhist Thai temple in the middle of Tampa? Who cares, the noodle soup is amazing. On Sundays hundreds of people show up for the food and flower markets, lining up Busch Gardens–style for the beloved beef soup with fish balls. Visitors can also enter the temple barefoot and enjoy traditional music.

Orchids and bonsai trees are for sale, as are Thai iced teas, egg rolls and a variety of strange and wonderful desserts (go for the pumpkin cake).

Adventure Island   AMUSEMENT PARK
(📋888-800-5447; www.adventureisland.com; 10001 McKinley Dr; adult/child 3-9yr $55/50, parking $15; ⊙hours vary) This 30-acre water park has everything a modern, top-flight water park requires: a long lazy river, a huge wave pool, bucket-dumping splash zones, a swimming pool, sandy lounge areas and enough twisting, plunging, adrenaline-fueled waterslides to keep teens lining up till closing. Adventure Island also features outdoor cafes, picnic and sunbathing areas, a gift shop and a championship sand volleyball complex for hours of fun in the sun.

Florida Museum of
Photographic Arts   MUSEUM
(FMoPA; Map p388; 📋813-221-2222; www.fmopa.org; The Cube, 400 N Ashley Dr; adult/student $10/8; ⊙11am-6pm Mon-Thu, to 7pm Fri, noon-5pm Sun) This small, intimate photography museum is housed on the 2nd and 3rd stories of the Cube, a five-story atrium in downtown Tampa. In addition to a permanent collection from Harold Edgerton and Len Prince, temporary exhibits have included the work of Ansel Adams, Andy Warhol and contemporary photographers such as Jerry Uelsmann. Photography courses are also offered.

Tampa Bay History Center   MUSEUM
(Map p388; 📋813-228-0097; www.tampabayhistorycenter.org; 801 Old Water St; adult/child $13/8; ⊙10am-5pm) This first-rate history museum presents the region's Seminole and Miccosukee people, Cracker pioneers and cattle breeders, and Tampa's Cuban community and cigar industry. The cartography collection, spanning six centuries, dazzles. At the time of research, the museum had just announced an $11-million expansion involving pirate history and a 60ft replica of a pirate ship.

Lowry Park Zoo   ZOO
(📋813-935-8552; www.lowryparkzoo.com; 1101 W Sligh Ave; adult/child $33/25; ⊙9:30am-5pm; 🅿🚼) North of downtown, Tampa's zoo gets you as close to the animals as possible, with several free-flight aviaries, giraffe

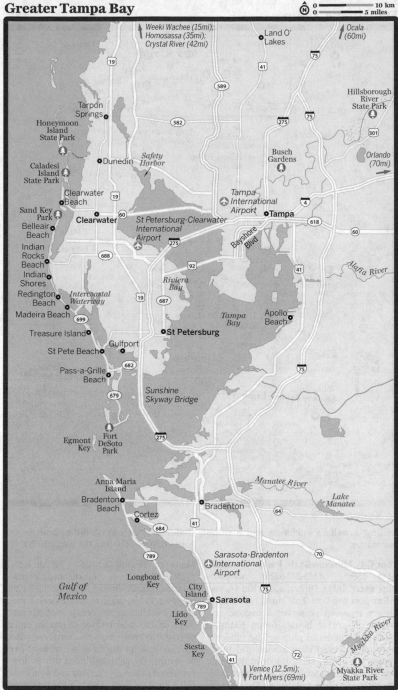

Downtown Tampa

feeding, a wallaby enclosure and a rhino 'encounter.'

Ybor City Museum State Park MUSEUM

(Map p388; ☑ 813-247-6323; www.ybor museum.org; 1818 E 9th Ave; adult/child $4/free; ⏱ 9am-5pm Wed-Sun) This dusty, old-school history museum preserves a bygone era, with cigar-worker houses (open 10am to 3pm) and wonderful photos. The museum store offers expert cigar advice and information on a free, self-guided, multimedia tour of Ybor City, which is accessible with any internet-connected device. The tour in-

cludes 21 stops and narration from prominent characters within the community.

Manatee Viewing Center WILDLIFE RESERVE

(☑ 813-228-4289; www.tampaelectric.com/ manatee; 6990 Dickman Rd, Apollo Beach; ⏱ 10am-5pm 1 Nov-15 Apr) FREE One of Florida's more surreal wildlife encounters is spotting manatees in the warm-water discharge canals of coal-fired power plants. Yet these placid mammals show up here so reliably from November through April that this is now a protected sanctuary. Tarpon and sharks can be spotted as well, and a new interactive

Downtown Tampa

stingray exhibit in a 10,000-gallon tank allows up-close interaction.

A snack bar, bathrooms and picnic tables round out the sight. It's half an hour from downtown Tampa; take I-75 south to exit 246 and follow signs.

Tampa Museum of Art   MUSEUM

(Map p388; ☏ 813-274-8130; www.tampamuseum.org; 120 W Gasparilla Plaza; adult/student $15/5; ⊙ 11am-7pm Mon-Thu, to 10pm Fri, to 5pm Sat & Sun) Architect Stanley Saitowitz's dramatically cantilevered museum building appears to float above Curtis Hixon Park overlooking the Hillsborough River. Inside its sculptural shell six galleries house a permanent collection of Greek and Roman antiquities beside contemporary exhibitions of photography and new media. The museum's Sono Café (p390), by the creative team behind Mise en Place (p394), is a great place for brunch or cocktails overlooking the river. Access the cafe through an admission-free entrance.

Henry B Plant Museum   MUSEUM

(Map p388; ☏ 813-254-1891; www.plantmuseum.com; 401 W Kennedy Blvd; adult/child $10/5; ⊙ 10am-5pm Tue-Sat, noon-5pm Sun) The silver minarets of Henry B Plant's 1891 Tampa Bay Hotel glint majestically, testimony to the vaunting ambitions of its creator who first brought the railroad to the city – and then extended it so guests could disembark straight into the lobby of his 511-room hotel. Never-before-seen-luxuries such as private baths, telephones and electricity became the talk of the town, as did the hotel's European decor of Venetian mirrors, French porcelain and exotic furnishings.

Now part of the University of Tampa, one section re-creates the original hotel's gilded late-Victorian world.

Tampa Riverwalk   WATERFRONT

(www.thetampariverwalk.com) Downtown, the attractive Tampa Riverwalk connects most sights. Located along the Hillsborough River, this undulating green space, with playgrounds and restrooms, makes a pretty walk from the museums edging Curtis Hixon Park, past the Convention Center, to the aquarium at the far end.

Glazer Children's Museum   MUSEUM

(Map p388; ☏ 813-443-3861; www.glazermuseum.org; 110 W Gasparilla Plaza; adult/child $15/9.50; ⊙ 10am-5pm Mon-Fri, to 6pm Sat, 1-6pm Sun; ⊕) This crayon-bright, interactive museum provides a creative play space for kids under 10. The staff are delightful and the adjacent Curtis Hixon Park is picnic- and playground-friendly.

Museum of Science & Industry   MUSEUM

(MOSI; ☏ 813-987-6000; www.mosi.org; 4801 E Fowler Ave; adult/child $27/21, parking $5; ⊙ 9am-5pm Mon-Fri, to 6pm Sat & Sun; ⊕ ⊕)

TAMPA BAY & SOUTHWEST FLORIDA TAMPA

BUSCH GARDENS

Orlando doesn't hold a monopoly on the Florida theme park experience. In Tampa, **Busch Gardens** (☏888-800-5447; www.buschgardenstampabay.com; 10165 McKinley Dr; 3yr & up $95; ☉10am-6pm, hours vary) presents visitors with 10 loosely named African zones, which flow together without much fuss and happen to contain some of the best roller coasters in the country. The entire park – located about 9 miles north of downtown Tampa – is walkable. Admission includes three types of fun: epic roller coasters and rides, animal encounters, and various shows, performances and entertainment. All are spread throughout the park, so successful days require some planning: check show schedules before arriving and plan what rides and animals to visit around the shows. Coaster lines only get longer as the day goes on. Parking costs $20.

Egypt Home to the park's newest attraction, a unique spin coaster called Cobra's Curse featuring a 70ft vertical lift and an encounter with an 80ft snake. There's also Montu, one of the tallest and longest inverted roller coasters in the world.

Pantopia The newly reimagined Pantopia drips with elaborate jewels and features animal- and travel-themed restaurants, entertainment, shopping, a recently renovated indoor theater and rides, of course. At its center is Falcon's Fury, a 335ft-high freestanding drop tower (America's tallest) that plunges riders earthward at 60mph.

Serengeti Plain This 65-acre habitat mimics the African plains, with hundreds of free-roaming animals including reticulated giraffes, rhinos and wildebeests. You can view it from the Serengeti Railway train ride, a Skyride gondola, various walkways or the Serengeti Safari Tour (from $29 to $44 per person), which lets you out of the truck to feed giraffes.

Edge of Africa A newer region offering a walking safari with sightings of hippopotamuses, lions, lemurs, meerkats and crocodiles in an apparently abandoned African fishing village. Also here is the ride Cheetah Hunt, a low-to-the-ground scream-fest meant to mimic a cheetah's acceleration, and a seasonal night tour that focuses on the nocturnal behavior of hippos and lions ($75 per person).

There's something intriguing for all ages at this interactive science museum. Younger children go straight to Kids in Charge, where a wealth of hands-on activities hides science beneath unadorned play. The frank human body exhibit – with 3-D printed fetuses and cautionary looks at pregnancy and health – is best for older kids. Don't miss the IMAX movie; it's included with admission.

👉 Tours

Ybor City Historic Walking Tours   WALKING
(☏813-505-6779; www.yborwalkingtours.com; adult/child $20/10) For a guided, 90-minute walking tour, reserve ahead with Ybor City Historic Walking Tours; they typically run twice daily, at 11am and 2pm.

✯ Festivals & Events

Gasparilla Pirate Festival   CULTURAL
(www.gasparillapiratefest.com; ☉Jan) On the last Saturday in January, pirates invade and parade in Tampa's version of Mardi Gras.

Outback Bowl   SPORTS
(☏813-874-2695; www.outbackbowl.com; tickets $80; ☉1 Jan) If you've never seen a US college football game, definitely don't miss the Outback Bowl, an NCAA (National College Athletic Association) football game on New Year's Day.

Florida State Fair   CULTURAL
(www.floridastatefair.com; 4800 US Hwy 301; weekday/weekend $11/13, weekday/weekend rides armband $25/35; ☉Feb) Classic Americana for more than 100 years; enjoy rides, food and livestock for two weeks in February.

Ybor City Heritage & Cigar Festival   CULTURAL
(☉early Dec) Music and cigars in Centennial Park in early December.

🛏 Sleeping

Gram's Place Hostel   HOSTEL $
(☏813-221-0596; www.grams-inn-tampa.com; 3109 N Ola Ave, Seminole Heights; dm $28, r $55-65; ✻@🛜) As charismatic as an aging rock star, Gram's is a small, welcoming hostel for

Morocco You'll find Gwazi, a huge but traditional wooden coaster, along with monkey and ape encounters and the Moroccan Palace Theater, which puts on Iceploration, the park's most impressive ice show, combining world-class skaters, larger-than-life puppets, original music and animal stars. It's close to the other main animal exhibits in Egypt and Nairobi.

Nairobi Devoted mostly to animals, Nairobi features an elephant interaction area and a flamingo petting station at Animal Connections. It's also the location of the Animal Care Center, which offers educational behind-the-scenes tours of vets at work with some of the park's 12,000 animals.

Congo The Kumba roller coaster is a long-standing favorite. It features three gulp-inducing loops and a 360-degree spiral. Recover on the Congo River Rapids, a water ride.

Jungala Designed for younger kids, Jungala has a fantastic climbing structure, a splash area and a zip-line ride, as well as encounters with tigers and orangutans.

Stanleyville Another all-star coaster, SheiKra is North America's first dive coaster, which plunges straight down and even goes underground.

Safari of Fun & Bird Gardens The Sesame Street–themed Safari of Fun has awesome fenced-in play and climbing structures and splash zones that will keep kids busy for hours. Don't miss the Elmo and Friends show; reserve ahead to dine with costumed characters. Adjacent Bird Gardens (the seed of the modern park) has the quintessential flock of flamingos and a walk-in aviary.

Near Busch Gardens, at the corner of Busch Blvd and 30th St, you'll find several mid-range chain hotels. While they may advertise being 'walkable' to the park, it is an *extremely* long walk that isn't recommended (especially with young kids). Just north of Busch Gardens, and across from University of South Florida, Fowler Ave also is home to a string of dependable midrange chains.

international travelers who prefer personality over perfect linens. Dig the in-ground hot tub and Saturday night jams. Breakfast is not included, but there are two fully serviced kitchens. Gram's Place is in Tampa Heights, 2 miles north of the Museum of Art.

★**Epicurean Hotel** BOUTIQUE HOTEL **$$**
(☎813-999-8700; www.epicureanhotel.com; 1207 S Howard Ave, South Tampa; r $180-499; P❋@☎≋) Foodies rejoice! Tampa's coolest hotel, which opened in 2014, is a food-and-drink-themed boutique Eden steeped in detailed design: vertical hydroponic lettuce and herb walls, a zinc bar, reclaimed woods from an 1820s railway station, oversize whiskers as test-kitchen door handles – everywhere you look, a story, usually involving Bern's Steak House (p394), who are partners.

Warm-toned rooms, Sunday pool parties and one of Tampa's only rooftop bars round out the craft-curated experience.

Tahitian Inn HOTEL **$$**
(☎813-877-6721; www.tahitianinn.com; 601 S Dale Mabry Hwy, South Tampa; r from $155;

P❋@☎≋❋) The name is reminiscent of a tiki-themed motel, but this family-owned, full-service hotel offers fresh, boutique stylings on the cheap. Nice pool, and the quaint cafe offers outdoor seating by a waterfall and koi pond. Also pets are welcome, and airport/cruise terminal transportation is included.

Hilton Garden Inn Ybor City HOTEL **$$**
(Map p388; ☎813-769-9267; www.hiltongarden inn.com; 1700 E 9th Ave, Ybor City; r $160-300; P❋☎≋) This attractive, efficient and friendly branch of the Hilton Garden chain is just a few blocks from 7th Ave. Rooms are vast and comfortable, there's a nice, private pool area, and the breakfast is generous and cooked to order. An on-call free shuttle is also available for those who want to head downtown.

Hampton Inn & Suites Ybor City HOTEL **$$**
(Map p388; ☎813-247-6700; www.hamptoninn. hilton.com; 1301 E 7th Ave, Ybor City; r $130-300; P❋☎≋) The red-brick Hampton Inn offers a good level of comfort, a free shuttle

downtown and a tiny pool. Its location on 7th Ave means rooms at the front can be noisy.

Le Meridien Tampa
HISTORIC HOTEL $$$
(Map p388; ☑813-221-9555; www.lemeridien tampa.com; 601 North Florida Ave; r $265-309; P✳︎☜☂) If you've longed to see the bowels of a federal courthouse but are hesitant to commit crimes, here's your chance. Le Meridien painstakingly restored this century-old courthouse, where judges' chambers and courtrooms now serve as guest rooms and a witness stand has become the front desk for the restaurant, Bizou Brasserie. Also preserved are the crown molding, terrazzo marble and judges' benches.

✗ Eating

Tampa has an excellent restaurant scene, though precious little is downtown. Ybor City is jam-packed with restaurants, particularly Spanish and Italian, while the Seminole Heights neighborhood (along Florida Ave) is an up-and-coming hipster hangout. Other good spots include gentrified Hyde Park Village, south of downtown, and design-savvy Palma Ceia. SoHo (South Howard Ave) in South Tampa has been dubbed 'restaurant row'; the stretch between Kennedy and Bayshore Blvds is prime.

Wright's Gourmet House
SANDWICHES $
(www.wrightsgourmet.com; 1200 S Dale Mabry Hwy, South Tampa; sandwiches & salads $6.75-11; ☉7am-6pm Mon-Fri, 8am-4pm Sat) From the outside this place looks like it could be a paint store. The inside isn't much better; green vinyl tablecloths and bare white walls. But the red velvet cake, pecan pie and monster sandwiches (try the beef martini with roast beef, wine-marinated mushrooms and bacon), well, these explain what all the fuss is about.

Tre Amici @ the Bunker
CAFE $
(Map p388; ☑813-247-6964; www.bunkery bor.com; 1907 19th St N, Ybor City; items $3-8; ☉8am-8pm Mon-Sat, 10am-4pm Sun) Ybor City's hipster contingent wake up at this relaxed community coffeehouse, which offers a range of breakfast burritos, soups and sandwiches all day. Come evening, it hosts open mikes, poetry slams and 'noise nights,' which are exactly what they sound like.

Sono Café
CAFE $
(Map p388; ☑813-421-8384; 120 W Gasparilla Plaza; mains $5-14; ☉11am-5pm Mon-Thu, Sat &

Sun, to 8pm Fri) Marty Blitz and Maryann Ferenc, the creative duo behind Mise en Place (p394), are also authors of the Sono Café at the Museum of Art (p387). It's a great place for brunch or cocktails with views over the Hillsborough River. The cafe is accessible through an admission-free entrance.

La Segunda Bakery
BAKERY $
(www.lasegundabakery.com; 2512 N 15th St, Ybor City; items $1-8; ☉6:30am-5pm Mon-Fri, 7am-3pm Sat) At 15th Ave and 15th St, just outside Ybor's main drag, this authentic Spanish bakery cranks out delicious breads and pastries, rich Cuban coffee and maybe Tampa's best Cuban sandwich. Here since 1915, it bustles every morning with a cross section of Tampa society.

★ Ulele
AMERICAN $$
(Map p388; ☑813-999-4952; www.ulele.com; 1810 N Highland Ave; mains $10-36; ☉11am-10pm Sun-Thu, to 11pm Fri & Sat; ☜) Located in a pleasant Riverwalk setting, this former water-pumping station has been transformed into an enchanting restaurant and brewery whose menu harkens back to native Floridan staples made over for modern times. That means liberal use of datil peppers, sides like alligator beans and okra 'fries' (amazing!), mains like local pompano fish and desserts like guava pie.

Refinery
MODERN AMERICAN $$
(☑813-237-2000; www.thetamparefinery.com; 5137 N Florida Ave, Seminole Heights; mains $9-25; ☉5-10pm Mon-Thu, to 11pm Fri, 11am-2:30pm & 5-11pm Sat, 11am-2:30pm & 5-10pm Sun; ☝) This blue-collar gourmet joint promises chipped plates and no pretensions, just playful, delicious hyper-local cuisine that cleverly mixes a sustainability ethic with a punk attitude. Owners Michelle and Greg Baker are among a tiny number of Florida restaurateurs who are known outside the area, thanks no doubt to Greg's three James Beard nominations.

Rooster & the Till
FUSION $$
(☑813-374-8940; www.roosterandthetill.com; 6500 N Florida Ave, Seminole Heights; plates $8-19; ☉4-10pm Mon-Thu, to 11 Fri & Sat) With an impressive culinary pedigree – and a recent Best Chef South nomination from the James Beard Foundation – Ferrell Alvarez and Ty Rodriguez are behind Seminole Heights' most ambitious farm-to-table restaurant. The recently expanded restaurant specializes in shared and small plates bursting with

flavor, most notably a gnocchi with short ribs, smoked ricotta, San Marzano tomatoes and pickled peperonata.

Other dishes rotate based on seasonal and local availability, and there's a wallet-friendly four-tier wine list with bottles at $35, $55, $75 and $90. Happy hour runs 4pm to 6pm.

Ichicoro
RAMEN $$

(☑ 813-517-9989; http://ichicoro.com; 5229 N Florida Ave, Seminole Heights; ramen $12-16; ☺ noon-11pm Mon-Wed, to 1am Thu & Fri, 11am-1am Sat, 11am-11pm Sun) This chic space in Tampa's Seminole Heights neighborhood dishes out some of the best craft ramen (yes, ramen can be craft, too) south of New York City. And that's actually where the recipes for these fancy noodle bowls were conceived. We'd tell you the ingredients but all you really need to know is, it's delicious.

Go for the shoyu and pair it with an *ochu sangreezy* (that's a cocktail with elderflower liquor).

Fodder & Shine
SOUTHERN US $$

(☑ 813-234-3710; www.fodderandshine.com; 5910 N Florida Ave, Seminole Heights; mains $13-19; ☺ 5pm-midnight Mon-Thu, 11:30am-2am Fri & Sat, to 10pm Sun) Billing itself as a Southern public house, this sister restaurant to Refinery (p391) serves up Old Cracker cuisine, with its roots in Scottish, Irish, African and Spanish cultures. 'Suppers' include hand-pounded country fried steak and hardwood smoked mullet, and everything's made from scratch, down to the chicken pot pie crust. The other draw is craft cocktails, made with freshly squeezed juice.

Ella's Americana Folk Art Cafe
AMERICAN $$

(☑ 813-234-1000; www.ellasfolkartcafe.com; 5119 N Nebraska Ave, Seminole Heights; mains $11-22; ☺ 5-11pm Tue-Thu, to midnight Fri & Sat, 11am-8pm Sun) After one too many Boozy Suzys the visionary outsider art on Ella's walls starts to make a lot of sense. But it's not just the eccentric art and cocktails that keep locals loyal; it's also the cozy vibe, the heartwarming soul food and the weekly roster of events from live music to craft beer and cocktail tastings.

Oxford Exchange
AMERICAN $$

(Map p388; ☑ 813-253-0222; www.oxford exchange.com; 420 W Kennedy Blvd; mains $17-32; ☺ 7:30am-5pm Mon-Wed & Fri, to 9pm Thu, 9am-5pm Sat, 9am-8pm Sun) Built in 1891 as a stable for the Plant hotel (p387), the reima-gined Oxford Exchange takes its inspiration from the venerable Wolseley in London. The American menu is served beneath sculptural palm fronds in a greenhouse atrium, and there's also a wood-paneled bookstore, a Buddy Brew coffee stand and TeBella bar. Beer, wine, craft cocktails and cold-pressed juices are all on offer.

Special events like afternoon teas and panel discussions with famous writers (recently they managed to land George Saunders!) are not uncommon.

Piquant
FRENCH $$

(☑ 813-251-1777; 1633 W Snow Ave, South Tampa; mains $9-18; ☺ 8am-8pm Sun-Wed, to 9pm Thu-Sat; ☑) Hot-to-trot French pastries, French-inspired salads and sandwiches dominate the menu at this bakery in Hyde Park Village. The 'Power Salad' comes heaped with avocado, spinach, feta, chickpeas, shredded chicken and roasted red peppers atop a base of brown rice. Gluten-free and vegetarian options are also available.

L'Eden Cafe & Bar
FRENCH $$

(Map p388; ☑ 813-221-4795; www.edencafebar. com; 500 N Tampa St; mains $9-22; ☺ 11am-8pm Mon-Thu, to 11pm Fri, 9am-3pm Sat) The sunny, southern Mediterranean menu at L'Eden reflects chef Gerard Jamgotchian's Marseillais roots. Flaky-crust quiches cradle a velvety mix of ham and cheese; crepes come drizzled with cheese or chocolate; and the show-stealing Nicoise salad is dressed in crunchy green beans and a signature vinaigrette. Breakfast is also good.

★ Columbia Restaurant
SPANISH $$$

(Map p388; ☑ 813-248-4961; www.columbia restaurant.com; 2117 E 7th Ave, Ybor City; mains lunch $11-26, dinner $20-31; ☺ 11am-10pm Mon-Thu, to 11pm Fri & Sat, noon-9pm Sun) Celebrating its centennial in 2015, this Spanish Cuban restaurant is the oldest in Florida. Occupying an entire block, it consists of 15 elegant dining rooms and romantic, fountain-centered courtyards. A number of the gloved waiters have been here a lifetime, and the owner Richard Gonzmart is zealous about authentic Spanish and Cuban cuisine.

Reserve ahead for twice-nightly flamenco Monday to Saturday, and look out for one helluva good birthday party.

★ Restaurant BT
FUSION $$$

(☑ 813-258-1916; www.restaurantbt.com; 2507 S MacDill Ave, South Tampa; mains $23-32; ☺ 5-10pm Tue-Thu, to 11pm Fri & Sat) ☑ Chef

Trina Nguyan-Batley has combined her high-fashion background and Vietnamese upbringing to create this ultra-chic temple to sustainable, locavore gastronomy. More recently she opened the equally delicious BT To Go down the street, serving lunch and takeout meals from 11am to 7:30pm Monday to Saturday.

Mise en Place
MODERN AMERICAN $$$

(Map p388; ☑ 813-254-5373; www.miseonline.com; 442 W Kennedy Blvd; lunch mains $10-15, mains $20-35; ☺ 11:30am-2:30pm & 5:30-10pm Tue-Fri, 5:30-11pm Sat) This landmark Tampa restaurant has been a destination for romantic, sophisticated dining for more than 30 years. The menu emphasizes contemporary American cuisine with Floribbean accents, and constantly evolves with nods to culinary fashions without ever feeling pretentious or 'trendy.' Go all out with the great-value 'Get Blitzed' tasting menu ($55) with wine pairings (an additional $35).

Haven
MEDITERRANEAN $$$

(☑ 813-258-2233; http://haventampa.com; 2208 W Morrison Ave, South Tampa; tapas $8-14, butcher's plates $42, cheese monger plates $47; ☺ 5-10pm Mon-Thu, to 11pm Fri & Sat) In 2015 this ambitious Mediterranean venture opened under the same ownership as its famous neighbor, Bern's Steak House, with a new small-plates and charcuterie-centric concept. It feels refined but casual, and excels in house-aged cocktails, wines preserved with the Coravin program and more than 300 different types of whiskey. The cheese monger plate comes with 18 delicious samples and is worth every penny.

Bern's Steak House
STEAK $$$

(☑ 813-251-2421; www.bernssteakhouse.com; 1208 S Howard Ave, South Tampa; steaks for 1-2 people $32-105; ☺ 5-10pm Sun-Thu, to 11pm Fri & Sat) This legendary, nationally renowned steakhouse is an event as much as a meal. Dress up, order caviar and on-premises dry-aged beef, ask to tour the wine cellar and kitchens, and *don't* skip dessert in the specially designed Harry Waugh Dessert Room.

 ## Drinking & Nightlife

Restaurants with great bars include Mise en Place and the Sono Café (p390) in the Museum of Art. For nightlife, Ybor City is party central; SoHo and Seminole Heights have a more grown-up vibe. Most clubs are open from 10pm to 3am Thursday to Saturday and charge a cover of between $10 and $30. Tampa Bay's alternative weekly is Creative Loafing (www.cltampa.com), with event and bar listings.

Independent Bar
BAR

(☑ 813-341-4883[]; www.independenttampa. com; 5016 N Florida Ave, Seminole Heights; ☺ 9am-midnight Sun-Wed, to 1am Thu-Sat) If you appreciate craft brews, roll into this converted gas station, now a low-key hip bar in Seminole Heights. You can count on one or more local Cigar City Brews, and it serves some mean pub grub.

Cigar City Brewing
BREWERY

(☑ 813-348-6363; www.cigarcitybrewing.com; 3924 W Spruce St, North Tampa; ☺ 11am-11pm Sun-Thu, to 1am Fri & Sat) This is Tampa's premier craft brewery, although the original owners were bought out in 2016. It has dozens of crafted brews on tap, some exclusive to the brewery. There are food trucks in the parking lot in the evenings and all day Saturday, and you can take tours of the brewery for $8 (with tastes of beer included).

You'll find it west of downtown, north off I-275.

Brew Bus Terminal & Brewery
CRAFT BEER

(☑ 888-945-2739; www.brewbususa.com; 4101 N Florida Ave, Seminole Heights; tours $11-56; ☺ 4-10pm Mon-Thu, noon-midnight Fri, 11am-midnight Sat, 11am-8pm Sun) Tampa Bay's craft-beer scene is booming, so it was only a matter of time before somebody thought to put people on a bus with the beer and drive them around. Brew Bus also has its own 'terminal' (a brewery), and offers public and private tours a few times a week, getting people drunk all over the Tampa Bay area.

The most popular option, dubbed 'the full pour,' departs from the terminal on Saturdays at noon, bringing craft-beer enthusiasts to three rotating breweries. They get a pint at each stop, a tour at one place, and two Brew Bus beers while in transit. It's $58 per person.

Angry Chair Brewing
MICROBREWERY

(☑ 813-238-1122; http://angrychairbrewing.com; 6401 N Florida Ave, Seminole Heights; ☺ 4pm-late Tue-Wed, 3-11pm Thu, noon-midnight Fri & Sat, noon-9pm Sun) A bunch of dudes trying to escape 'the monotony, the rat race and the white-collar world' got together and made some beer that thankfully wound up less cliched than their reasons for existing. In the convivial tasting room, they serve up

HILLSBOROUGH RIVER STATE PARK

When Tampa residents need a woodsy escape, they head to this fantastic 3400-acre **state park** (☑ 813-987-6771; www.floridastateparks.org/hillsboroughriver; 15402 US 301 N; cyclist/car $2/6; ⊘ 8am-sunset; ⓐ), just 20 miles (30 minutes) northeast of Tampa. For visiting families, it provides easy, kid-friendly encounters with Florida's wilderness, and you'll find the region's best (nonbeach) camping. The best thing to do is get out on the water (canoes two hours/full day $25/50; kayaks $15 per hour), gliding beneath Spanish moss on the look out for raptors, deer, foxes and alligators. Morning is best for spotting wildlife.

The flat, winding park roads also make for scenic cycling (bike rental $10/25 per hour/day), and there are more than 10 miles of equally easy hiking trails through pine flatwoods and cypress swamps. In summer the biggest draw is the giant half-acre swimming pool ($4 per person). On weekends arrive by 8:30am or it might already be full (then you can't enter till someone leaves).

The pretty 114-site campground (sites $27) has good facilities and solar-heated hot water, but not a lot of privacy. Spots along the river are prime, and camping is best (and busiest) during the October to March dry season (book up to a year in advance). Midweek is always less busy.

hoppy, fruity pale ales and creamy porters like Two Pump Chump Porter w/Hazelnut, among other tasty brews.

Cigar City Cider & Mead   MICROBREWERY
(Map p388; ☑ 813-242-6600; www.cigarcitycider. com; 1812 N 15th St; tours $10; ⊘ 3-9pm Wed, to 11pm Thu, noon-midnight Fri & Sat, to 8pm Sun) In historic Ybor City, this tasting room offers a good selection of honey and apple-based booze, all brewed with local, natural ingredients. On Saturdays, tours begin at 5pm and come with a 12oz pour of hard cider, along with samples of other ciders and mead.

Anise Global Gastrobar   COCKTAIL BAR
(Map p388; ☑ 813-225-4272; 777 N Ashley Dr; ⊘ 11am-1am Mon-Thu & Sun, to 2am Fri & Sat; ⓐ) Located at the base of the soaring SkyPoint building, Anise has a long sleek bar and a short, smart cocktail list. Even mixers are taken seriously here, from Fever Tree Tonic to Mexican Coke (sweetened with sugarcane, not high-fructose corn syrup). There's also a globetrotting wine list and an Asian-inspired tapas menu (from $8 to $18).

Club Prana   CLUB
(Map p388; www.clubprana.com; 1619 E 7th Ave, Ybor City; ⊘ 9pm-3am Thu-Sat) Many nightclubs come and go, but Club Prana, rising five floors from its lounge to the rooftop Sky Bar, has stood the test of time.

Four Green Fields   IRISH PUB
(Map p388; ☑ 813-254-4444; www.fourgreen fields.com/tampa; 205 W Platt St, South Tampa;

⊘ 11am-late) This thatched-roof, plaster-sided bit o' blarney in Hyde Park looks like a traditional Irish cottage, and the gregarious Irish staff, football shirts, draft Guinness and Irish menu (items from $11 to $13) will have you affecting your own Irish brogue.

☆ Entertainment

★**Skipper's Smokehouse**   LIVE MUSIC
(☑ 813-971-0666; www.skipperssmokehouse.com; 910 Skipper Rd, Village of Tampa; cover $5-25; ⊘ 11am-10pm Tue & Wed, to 10:30pm Thu, to 11pm Fri, noon-11pm Sat, 1pm-9:30pm Sun) Like it blew in from the Keys, Skipper's is a beloved, unpretentious open-air venue for blues, folk, reggae and gator-swamp rockabilly. It's 9 miles directly north of downtown on N Nebraska Ave.

★**Tampa Theatre**   CINEMA
(Map p388; ☑ 813-274-8981, box office 813-274-8286; www.tampatheatre.org; 711 N Franklin St; tickets $11) This historic 1926 theater in downtown is a gorgeous venue in which to see an independent film. The mighty Wurlitzer organ plays before most movies. Too bad showtimes are so limited, with only one or two films playing on any given day. Look for special events.

Straz Center for the Performing Arts   PERFORMING ARTS
(Map p388; ☑ 813-229-7827; www.strazcenter. org; 1010 MacInnes Pl) This enormous, multi-venue complex draws the gamut of fine-arts performances: touring Broadway

shows, pop concerts, opera, ballet, drama and more.

Cinebistro
CINEMA

(☑813-514-8300; www.cinebistro.com; 1609 W Swann Ave, Hyde Park Village; matinee/evening $13.50/16) Cross a trendy South Beach nightclub with a plush art-house cinema, and you get this: a snazzy lobby cocktail bar and upscale munchies (mains from $10 to $23) so you can nosh at your seat while you watch. It's movie-going with style.

Improv Comedy Theater
COMEDY

(Map p388; ☑813-864-4000; www.improvtampa. com; 1600 E 8th Ave, Centro Ybor; tickets $10-30) This 21-plus comedy club in Ybor City brings the funny five nights a week with local and national acts.

Amalie Arena
HOCKEY

(Map p388; ☑813-301-6500; www.amaliearena. com; 401 Channelside Dr) The NHL's Tampa Bay Lightning play hockey at the newly re-named Amalie Arena (formerly it was the Tampa Bay Times Forum) from October to April. The arena also hosts basketball games, wrestling, football, concerts and ice shows.

Steinbrenner Field
BASEBALL

(☑813-875-7753; www.steinbrennerfield.com; 1 Steinbrenner Dr) The New York Yankees play spring-training baseball games in March at Steinbrenner Field, the 10,000-seat stadium modeled after the 'House that Ruth Built' (ie Yankee Stadium in New York).

USF Sun Dome
STADIUM

(www.sundomearena.com; 4202 E Fowler Ave) On the USF campus, the Sun Dome hosts rock, jazz, pop and other concerts – from Jimmy Buffet to Ludacris, from Luciano Pavarotti to the World Wrestling Federation (now there's some 'performing arts' for you!).

Raymond James Stadium
FOOTBALL

(☑813-350-6500; http://raymondjamesstadium. com; 4201 N Dale Mabry Hwy) The NFL's Tampa Bay Buccaneers play at Raymond James Stadium from August (preseason) to December, but single-game tickets are hard to come by; most games sell out.

🛍 Shopping

Dysfunctional Grace Art Co.
ART

(Map p388; ☑813-842-0830; www.facebook.com/ DysfunctionalGrace; 1903 E 7th Ave, Ybor City; ⊙10am-6pm Mon-Thu, to 8pm Fri & Sat) This creepy but awesome art shop contains cu-rios such as a taxidermic giraffe wearing a monocle, a live albino pacman frog and a diaphonized zebra moray eel suspended in glycerine. Everything's pricey, but probably worth it? And looking is free.

Inkwood Books
BOOKS

(☑813-253-2638; www.inkwoodbooks.com; 216 S Armenia Ave; ⊙11am-5pm Sun & Mon, 10am-5pm Tue-Sat) In a small house close to Hyde Park, Tampa's best independent bookstore has a fantastic selection of new Florida titles, both nonfiction and mystery, and wonderful chil-dren's books. It also hosts a whole roster of readings and signing events.

Metropolitan Cigars
CIGARS

(Map p388; ☑813-248-2304; 2014 E 7th Ave, Ybor City; ⊙10am-8pm Mon-Sat, to 4pm Sun) The store itself is actually a humidor; perhaps the best cigar shop in Tampa Bay.

Ybor City Saturday Market
MARKET

(Map p388; www.ybormarket.com; Centennial Park, 8th Ave & 18th St, Ybor City; ⊙9am-3pm Sat) An outdoor market emphasizing arts, crafts and local food products.

Hyde Park Village
MALL

(www.hydeparkvillage.com; South Tampa; ⊙10am-7pm) Tampa has its share of malls, but for upscale trends and fashion, seek out this outdoor complex, in the lovely Old Hyde Park neighborhood in South Tampa. You'll find it between Swann and Morrison Aves.

King Corona Cigar Factory
CIGARS

(Map p388; www.kingcoronacigars.com; 1523 E 7th Ave, Ybor City; ⊙8am-midnight Mon-Wed, to 1am Thu, to 2am Fri, 10am-2am Sat, noon-midnight Sun) The city's largest cigar emporium, complete with an old-fashioned cigar bar.

La France
VINTAGE

(Map p388; ☑813-248-1381; 1612 E 7th Ave, Ybor City; ⊙11am-8pm Mon-Thu, to 10pm Fri & Sat, noon-7pm Sun) Thanks to an influx of wealthy snowbirds, Tampa has a thriving vintage scene. With four street-front windows rotat-ing displays of flapper dresses, ornamental umbrellas, feathered hats and men's leisure suits, La France is like a living museum with-out a cover charge. Inside you can browse racks of 1930s maxi-dresses, sparkling 1940s swing dresses and mod suits from the '60s.

Some items are newly made from period designs, while others come from estate sales and private sellers.

ℹ Information

TOURIST INFORMATION

Tampa Bay Convention & Visitors Bureau
(Map p388; ☑ 813-226-0293; www.visittam-pabay.com; 615 Channelside Dr; ⊙10am-5:30pm Mon-Sat, 11am-5pm Sun) The visitor center has good free maps and lots of information. Book hotels directly through the website.

Ybor City Visitor Center (Map p388; ☑ 813-241-8838; www.ybor.org; 1600 E 8th Ave; ⊙10am-5pm Mon-Sat, noon-5pm Sun) Provides an excellent introduction with walking-tour maps and info.

DANGERS & ANNOYANCES

Tampa has big-city problems with homelessness, panhandlers and crime. Both downtown and Ybor City are safe in themselves, but they are bordered by tough neighborhoods; don't wander aimlessly. Panhandlers tend to gather on the median at traffic lights and approach drivers; to end a solicitation, simply shake your head.

MEDIA

The Tampa Bay area has two major daily newspapers: the **Tampa Bay Times** (www.tampabay.com) and **Tampa Tribune** (www.tbo.com).

MEDICAL SERVICES

Tampa General Hospital (☑ 813-844-7000; www.tgh.org; 1 Tampa General Circle, Davis Island; ⊙24hr) South of downtown on Davis Island.

ℹ Getting There & Away

AIR

➤ **Tampa International Airport** (TPA; Map p392; ☑ 813-870-8700; www.tampaairport.com; 4100 George J Bean Pkwy) is the region's third busiest hub. It's 6 miles west of downtown, off Hwy 589.

➤ HART bus 30 ($2, 25 minutes, every 30 minutes) picks up and drops off at the Red Arrival Desk on the lower level of the airport; exact change is required.

➤ All major car agencies have desks at the airport. By car, take the I-275 to N Ashley Dr, turn right and you're in downtown.

BOAT

Cruise passengers often start or end Caribbean explorations at **Port Tampa Bay** (www.tampaport.com).

BUS

Greyhound (Map p388; ☑ 813-229-2174; www.greyhound.com; 610 E Polk St) Serves the region and connects Tampa with Miami, Orlando, Sarasota and Gainesville.

CAR & MOTORCYCLE

➤ Between Tampa and Orlando, take the I-4.

➤ The fastest route to Miami is via I-75 south, which turns east at Naples and meets I-95 south at Fort Lauderdale. Another option, with Everglades detours, is to pick up US 41 (Tamiami Trail) at Naples, and follow this directly to Miami.

TRAIN

Amtrak (www.amtrak.com) operates several daily shuttles between Tampa and Orlando ($12 to $26, two hours) from **Tampa Union Station** (☑ 800-872-7245; www.amtrak.com; 601 N Nebraska Ave).

ℹ Getting Around

HART In-Towner (⊙6am-8:30am & 3:30-6pm Mon-Fri, 11am-7pm Sat) Within downtown, HART's inexpensive trolley runs up and down Florida Ave, Tampa St and Franklin St every 15 minutes.

Hillsborough Area Regional Transit (HART; Map p388; ☑ 813-254-4278; www.gohart.org; 1211 N Marion St; fares/day passes $2/4) HART buses converge at the Marion Transit Center. Routes service the zoo, Busch Gardens, the Henry Plant Museum and Ybor City.

TECO Line Streetcars (☑ 813-254-4278; www.tecolinestreetcar.org; adult/child $2.50/1.25; ⊙7am-10pm Mon-Thu, to 1:30am Fri, 11am-1:30am Sat, noon-8pm Sun) HART's old-fashioned electric streetcars connect downtown's Marion Transit Center with a number of attractions downtown, along with Ybor City, running every 20 to 30 minutes.

St Petersburg

☑ 727 / POP 257,083

Long known as little more than a bawdy spring-break party town and a retirement capital, St Petersburg is now forging a new name for itself as a culturally savvy southern city. Spurred on by awe-inspiring downtown murals, a revitalized historic district and the stunning Dalí Museum, the downtown energy is creeping up Central Ave, spawning sophisticated restaurants, craft breweries, farmers markets and artsy galleries, all of which are attracting a younger professional crowd and a new wave of culturally curious travelers.

⊙ Sights

When taking in the sights, visitors can confine themselves to a walkable, T-shaped route: along Central Ave, mainly from 8th

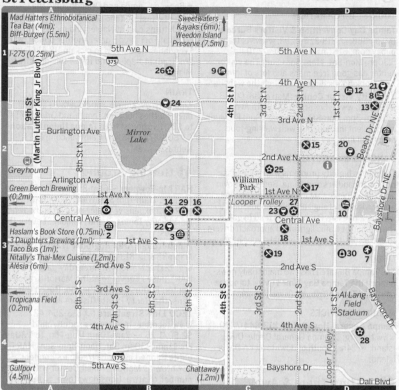

St to Bayshore Dr, and along Bayshore Dr from the Dalí Museum to the bayfront parks in the Old Northeast neighborhood. From here the **pier** juts out to sea. While the pier itself is open to walkers, the iconic, inverted pyramid amusement complex at its end remains closed for redevelopment.

★ Salvador Dalí Museum   MUSEUM
(☎ 727-823-3767; www.thedali.org; 1 Dali Blvd; adult/child 6-12yr $24/10, after 5pm Thu $10; ⏱ 10am-5:30pm Fri-Wed, to 8pm Thu) The theatrical exterior of the Salvador Dalí Museum augurs great things: out of a wound in the towering white shoe box oozes a 75ft geodesic glass atrium. Even better, what unfolds inside is like a blueprint of what a modern art museum, or at least one devoted to the life, art and impact of Salvador Dalí, should be. Even those who dismiss his dripping clocks and curlicue mustache will be awed by the

museum and its grand works, especially the *Hallucinogenic Toreador.*

The Dalí Museum's 20,000 sq ft of gallery space was designed to display all 96 oil paintings in the collection, along with key works of each era and medium: drawings, prints, sculptures, photos, manuscripts, movies and even a virtual reality exhibit in which guests enter Dalí's dreams. Everything is arranged chronologically and explained in context. The garden out back is also a delight, with a wish tree, a melting clock bench and a giant steel mustache sculpture.

Excellent, free docent tours occur hourly (on the half hour); these are highly recommended to help crack open the rich symbolism in Dalí's monumental works. Audioguides are also free, and contain secret, deeply hilarious narration from a voice claiming to be Dalí's mustache. To top everything off,

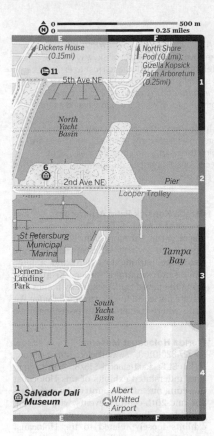

TAMPA BAY & SOUTHWEST FLORIDA ST PETERSBURG

there's a Catalan-inspired cafe and a first-rate gift store. Up to 5000 people have been known to visit in a day, so get here early or wait for everything.

★ Weedon Island Preserve NATURE RESERVE
(☏727-453-6500; www.weedonislandpreserve.org; 1800 Weedon Dr NE; ⊙7am-sunset) Like a patchwork quilt of variegated greens tossed out over Tampa Bay, this 3700-acre preserve protects a diverse aquatic and wetland ecosystem. At the heart of the preserve is the excellent Cultural and Natural History Center (open from 11am to 4pm Thursday to Saturday) where you can browse exhibits about the natural environment and the early Weedon Island people. Sign-up also for interpretive hikes over miles of boardwalk or go it alone with the online map.

Morean Arts Center ARTS CENTER
(☏727-822-7872; www.moreanartscenter.org; 719 Central Ave; ⊙10am-5pm Mon-Sat, noon-

5pm Sun) FREE This lively community arts center hosts interesting rotating exhibits in all media. If you love glass, don't miss Morean's attached Hot Shop (p401) where full-blast glassmaking demonstrations occur every hour from 11am to 4pm Monday to Saturday and 1pm to 4pm Sunday. Reserve ahead for a one-on-one 'hot glass

SUNSHINE SKYWAY BRIDGE

Supported by canary-yellow cables, the impressive, 4-mile Sunshine Skyway Bridge ($1.25 toll) spans Tampa Bay south of St Petersburg. It's worth the toll just to experience this dramatic arc over the bay. This bridge is actually a replacement for the original span, which was destroyed in 1980 when a boat, *Summit Venture*, rammed into its base. Bits of the old bridge now bookend the modern one and form what is proudly hailed as the 'world's largest fishing pier.'

At about 2 miles, the **South Skyway Fishing Pier** is the longest stretch. Both north and south piers offer dramatic bay-and-bridge views, especially at sunset, and there are bait shops with rentals for the anglers crowding the railings. To enter the piers, sight-seeing costs $4 per car; fishing costs $4 per car plus $4 per person. Just want a quick peek? Free public parks are situated at each pier's base.

experience' ($75) and take home your own creation.

St Petersburg
Museum of Fine Arts
MUSEUM

(☑727-896-2667; http://mfastpete.org; 255 Beach Dr NE; adult/child 7-18yr $17/10; ⊙10am-5pm Mon-Sat, to 8pm Thu, noon-5pm Sun) The Museum of Fine Arts' collection is as broad as the Dalí Museum's is deep, traversing the world's antiquities and following art's progression through nearly every era.

Chihuly Collection
GALLERY

(☑727-896-4527; www.moreanartscenter.org; 720 Central Ave; $19.95; ⊙10am-5pm Mon-Sat, noon-5pm Sun) Dale Chihuly's glass works are displayed at the Metropolitan Museum of Art in New York, the Victoria and Albert Museum (V&A) in London and the Louvre in Paris. But his permanent collection resides here in St Petersburg, at a new location on Central Ave housing his principal exhibits, *Ruby Red Icicle Chandelier* and the multi-colored *Persians* ceiling.

The new space also contains a meditation garden and a theater that screens a rotation of documentary films. Tickets for the gallery include a glass-blowing demonstration across the street at the affiliated Morean Arts Center (p399).

St Petersburg
Museum of History
MUSEUM

(☑727-894-1052; www.spmoh.org; 335 2nd Ave NE; adult/child 6-17yr $15/9; ⊙10am-5pm Mon-Sat, noon-5pm Sun) As city history museums go, St Pete's is intriguingly oddball: a real 3000-year-old mummy, a two-headed calf and a life-size replica of a Benoist plane, plus exhibits on the bay's ecology and the Tampa Bay Rays, and the world's largest collection of autographed baseballs.

Gizella Kopsick Palm Arboretum
PARK

(⊙sunrise-sunset) FREE This is an open 2-acre garden of more than 800 palms, all signed and lovingly landscaped. There are also large parking lots here and a long, white-sand swimming beach. Keep going along the paved trail, past pretty homes and private docks, all the way to small Coffee Pot Park, where manatees can occasionally be spotted.

Florida Holocaust Museum
MUSEUM

(☑727-820-0100; www.flholocaustmuseum.org; 55 5th St S; adult/student $16/8; ⊙10am-5pm) The understated exhibits of this Holocaust museum, one of the country's largest, present mid-20th-century events with moving directness. Temporary, contemporary art exhibits loosely related to the Holocaust and other human rights issues are also displayed. Note: if your car is left in the parking lot a minute past 5pm, it will likely be towed.

🏃 Activities

⭐ Pinellas Trail
CYCLING

(www.pinellascounty.org/trailgd) This 47-mile county-maintained trail along an abandoned railroad corridor calls to dedicated urban cyclists and runners. The paved path starts along 1st Ave S and Bayshore Dr in St Petersburg and continues, through town, country and suburb, north to Tarpon Springs. Download trail maps and route details online.

Sweetwater Kayaks
KAYAKING

(☑727-570-4844; www.sweetwaterkayaks.word press.com; 1800 Weedon Dr NE; kayaks per 1/4hr $17/40; ⊙10am-6pm Mon-Tue & Thu & Fri, 9am-6pm Sat, 9am-3pm Sun) This local outfitter has the largest selection of seawater kayaks in the area. Knowledgeable staff also lead lessons in foundation skills, sea kayaking and paddleboard yoga, and head up tours ($25/55 with/without kayak rental) off Weedon Island Preserve and other nearby St Pete waterways.

Boyd Hill Nature Park   HIKING
(📞727-893-7326; 1101 Country Club Way S; adult/child $3/1.50; ⊙9am-7pm Tue & Wed & Sun, to 6pm Thu & Fri, 7am-6pm Sat) A low-key, hidden oasis, Boyd Hill has more than 6.5 miles of nature trails and boardwalks amid its 390 acres of pine flatwoods and swampy woodlands. Alligators, snowy egrets and bald eagles are among the wildlife you might see. The property also contains a rescue center for raptors and hosts regular events and guided hikes.

From downtown, follow Martin Luther King Jr Blvd (9th St) south to 50th Ave and follow the signs.

North Shore Pool   SWIMMING
(📞727-893-7441; 901 N Shore Dr NE; adult/child $5/4.50; ⊙9am-4pm Mon-Fri, 10am-4pm Sat, 1-4pm Sun) Has three gorgeous swimming pools, including a kids' pool with waterslide. Rents out paddleboards by the hour.

🐢 Courses & Tours

Hot Shop   ART
(📞727-822-7872; $19.95; ⊙11am-4pm Mon-Sat, 1-4pm Sun) If you love glass, don't miss Morean's (p399) attached Hot Shop where full-blast glassmaking demonstrations occur every hour. Reserve ahead for a one-on-one 'hot glass experience' ($75) and take home your own creation.

★Walking Mural Tours   CULTURAL
(📞727-821-7391; http://stpetemuraltour.com; adult/child $19/11; ⊙10-11:30am Sat) This excellent walking tour introduces visitors to St Pete's vibrant mural scene, which got its start when artists were given cheap gallery space downtown after the economy crashed in 2008. Now upward of 30 highly creative and one-of-a-kind murals, many with nods to the city's history and culture, grace its buildings and rival Miami's Wynwood Walls.

The tour begins at the Florida CraftArt (p405), which partnered up with StPete MuralTour.com to begin offering the walks. Proceeds go toward commissioning more murals.

St Pete Preservation
Walking Tours   WALKING
(📞727-824-7802; www.stpetepreservation.org; $10; ⊙10am Sat Oct-Apr) Join these two-hour tours run by knowledgeable docents from the Preservation Society. Tours take in historic downtown architecture and well-preserved suburbs such as Old Northeast, Bahama Shores and Kenwood.

★☆ Festivals & Events

Art Walk   ART
(https://stpeteartsalliance.org/artwalk; ⊙5-9pm 2nd Sat of the month) This monthly art event takes place on the second Saturday of each month and involves all the major downtown galleries. You can easily walk the route or you can hop aboard the free trolley service.

Mainsail Arts Festival   CULTURAL
(www.mainsailart.org; Vinoy Park; ⊙Apr) Live music, food and kids' activities sit alongside 200 art-and-craft exhibitors at this two-day art extravaganza.

Tampa Bay Blues Festival   MUSIC
(www.tampabaybluesfest.com; Vinoy Park; ⊙Apr) Three days of first-rate blues in early April.

International Folk Fair   CULTURAL
(www.spiffs.org; Vinoy Park; ⊙Oct) A four-day fair in late October showcasing different cultures through traditional foods, crafts and folk dancing.

Ribfest   FOOD & DRINK
(www.ribfest.org; Vinoy Park; ⊙mid-Nov) St Petersburg; three days, mid-November. Three words: ribs, rock, Harleys.

🛏 Sleeping

With its impressive stock of period homes and newly minted waterfront hotels, St Petersburg has an excellent selection of accommodations. That said, many of the old, locally owned favorites are struggling and even going out of business because they can't compete with the rise of home-sharing services.

★Hollander Hotel   BOUTIQUE HOTEL $$
(📞727-873-7900; www.hollanderhotel.com; 421 4th Ave N; $98-140; 🅿❄🤖🛜🏊) The Hollander can do no wrong with its art-deco flavor, 130ft porch, convivial Tap Room, full-service spa and Common Grounds coffee shop. Shared spaces feature gorgeous period detailing and rooms retain a hint of 1930s romance with their polished wooden floors, lazy ceiling fans

and cane furniture. The new pool and bar out back becomes a party scene on weekends.

★ Dickens House
B&B $$

(☑ 727-822-8622; www.dickenshouse.com; 335 8th Ave NE; r $139-243; P ✳ @ 🛜) Five lushly designed rooms await in this passionately restored arts-and-crafts-style home. The gregarious, gay-friendly owner whips up a gourmet breakfast often involving egg-white frittata.

Ponce de Leon
BOUTIQUE HOTEL $$

(☑ 727-550-9300; www.poncedeleonhotel.com; 95 Central Ave; r from $111; ✳ @ 🛜) A boutique hotel with Spanish flair in the heart of downtown. Splashy murals and designer-cool decor are highlights; off-site parking is a bummer.

Birchwood Inn
BOUTIQUE HOTEL $$$

(☑ 727-896-1080; www.thebirchwood.com; 340 Beach Dr NE; r incl breakfast from $275; P ✳ 🛜) Rooms are simply gorgeous at this boutique gem: spacious, with claw-foot baths and king canopy beds, and oozing vintage bordello elegance sexed up with a little South Beach sauciness. Canopy (p404), the rooftop bar, is the hottest spot in town for cocktails.

Watergarden Inn at the Bay
INN $$$

(☑ 727-822-1700; www.innatthebay.com; 126 4th Ave N; r $165-290, ste $290; P ✳ 🛜 🎦) This fabulous 1910 inn carved from two old neighborhood houses offers 14 rooms and suites in a mature, half-acre garden. Outside a bright tropical palette and palm-fringed pool give the complex a beachy Key West vibe, while inside four-poster beds, two-person Jacuzzis and fluffy robes conjure romance. The couple that owns the place are sociable and kind.

Renaissance Vinoy Resort
HOTEL $$$

(☑ 727-894-1000; www.vinoyrenaissanceresort.com; 501 5th Ave NE; r $189-349; P ✳ @ 🛜 🎦) St Pete's coral-pink grande dame, the lavishly renovated 1925 Vinoy, is a sumptuous concoction of period style and 21st-century comforts, including an 18-hole golf course, a private marina, tennis courts, five restaurants and a 5000-sq-ft fitness center. Take note of off-season and online deals. It's worth it just for the gorgeous pool.

✕ Eating

St Pete's restaurant scene has exploded in recent years, rivaling its more refined northwestern neighbor (that's Tampa, for those who forgot) with innovative new concepts and rampant openings. Beach Dr remains a well-heeled scene lined with attractive waterfront restaurants, while Central Ave has become a haven for more experimental and ambitious culinary projects.

Nitally's Thai-Mex Cuisine
FUSION $

(☑ 727-321-8424; info@nitallys.com; 2462 Central Ave N; mains $7-19; ⏱ 11am-1:30pm & 5:30-9:30pm Tue-Fri, 11am-2pm & 5:30-9pm Sat) Owned by a Thai-Mexican couple, this delicious fusion concept worked its way up from a food truck to a brick-and-mortar establishment. Items like Thai peanut chicken tortillas and Penang mole burritos were always going to be winners, but the inferno soup challenge, which dares guests to consume a hospital-trip spicy pepper broth, put this place on the map.

Taco Bus
MEXICAN $

(☑ 727-322-5000; www.taco-bus.com; 2324 Central Ave; mains $6-13; ⏱ 11am-10pm Sun-Thu, to 4am Fri & Sat; 🛜) When this taco- and burrito-slinging food truck needed a brick-and-mortar location, they just rolled right up next to a good-time patio and didn't skip a beat. *Cochinita pibil,* carnitas and *pollo chipotle* are highlights. A Tampa Bay institution, with $2 taco Tuesdays.

Meze 119
VEGETARIAN $

(☑ 727-498-8627; www.meze119.com; 119 2nd St N; mains $7-14; ⏱ 11am-9pm Sun-Thu, to 10pm Fri & Sat; 🍴) Using Middle Eastern spices to create rich, complex flavors, this vegetarian restaurant satisfies even demanding omnivores with its Scotch egg and falafel, panko fried with tahini sauce, and couscous and raisin-stuffed acorn squash. Other popular standards include the multiflavor hummus plate and sautéed eggplant on open-faced pita bread. Wash it all down with the delightful house 'meze-naide.'

★ Brick & Mortar
MODERN AMERICAN $$

(☑ 727-822-6540; www.facebook.com/brickand mortarkitchen; 539 Central Ave; mains $14-25; ⏱ 5pm-9pm Tue, to 10pm Wed & Thu; 4:30pm-11pm Fri & Sat) A husband-and-wife catering team launched this, well, brick-and-mortar establishment in 2015, and despite the fact that St Pete has been overrun with great restaurants, this New American experiment dominated. Best thing in the menu? A divine house carpaccio with leek, some goat's cheese mousse, a touch of truffle oil and a single ravioli stuffed with deliciously runny egg yolk.

★ Annata Wine Bar
ITALIAN $$

(☎727-851-9582; www.annatawine.com; 300 Beach Dr NE; charcuterie 3/5 selections $14/20; ⊙4-10pm Sun-Thu, to 11pm Fri & Sat) This swanky wine bar is an anchor of the Beach Dr restaurant scene and also of St Pete's charcuterie obsession, with a range of meats and cheeses and fine Italian wine pairings that will astonish and delight. Service is friendly and the atmosphere is surprisingly chilled – outside, dogs can be served a board of special treats cleverly dubbed 'paw-cuterie.'

Locale Market
MARKET $$

(☎727-523-6300; www.localegourmetmarket.com; 179 2nd Ave N; ⊙8am-9pm Sun-Thu, to 10pm Fri & Sat) Within the Sundial shopping center, this culinary marketplace features fresh, local products handpicked by prominent chefs Michael Mina and Don Pintabona. There are cheese and charcuterie counters, a sushi bar, heaps of fresh produce, racks of salami, bountiful desserts stands and more. On the first Friday of every month, Locale offers chef-curated tastings throughout the market (6:30pm to 8:30pm, $19.99).

Iberian Rooster
PORTUGUESE $$

(☎727-258-8753; www.iberianrooster.com; 475 Central Ave N; mains $13-32; ⊙11am-3am Mon-Sat, 10am-3am Sun; 🍷) Billing itself as 'colonial Portuguese fusion,' this newer place on Central Ave blends complex flavors from the streets of Mozambique, Macau, Brazil and Goa, and serves them up on tapas plates. For example, the chimichurri Moroccan beef comes with potato purée, charred okra and chorizo palm oil. Vegan, vegetarian and gluten-free options abound.

Alésia
FRENCH, VIETNAMESE $$

(☎727-345-9701; http://alesiarestaurant.com; 7204 Central Ave; mains $7.50-18; ⊙11:30am-2:30pm & 5:30-9pm Tue-Fri, 10am-2:30pm & 5:30-9pm Sat) Lovely Alésia, with its big windows, laid-back soundtrack and umbrella-clad courtyard, is the brainchild of Sandra Ly-Flores, Erika Ly and Paul Hsu, who wanted to re-create the French Vietnamese cafes of their Parisian youth. Here you'll agonize over the tiered pastry selection, breakfast on crepes or *croque monsieur,* and linger over bowls of spicy pho and crunchy summer rolls.

Red Mesa Cantina & Lucha Bar
MEXICAN $$

(☎727-896-8226; www.redmesacantina.com; 128 3rd St S; mains $10-17; ⊙11am-10pm Sun-Thu, to 11pm Fri & Sat) Rounding out St Pete's plethora of contemporary ethnic cuisine, Red Mesa dishes up tasty, updated Mexican mains, plus a range of interesting ceviches and tacos. The Oaxacan chef does triple duty at an older, sister restaurant to the north, Red Mesa, and a newer fast-food restaurant and market, Red Mesa Mercado, which opened at the end of 2014. All are worthwhile.

Mazzaro's Italian Market
SUPERMARKET $$

(☎727-321-2400; www.mazzarosmarket.com; 2909 22nd Ave N; ⊙9am-6pm Mon-Fri, to 2:30pm Sat) The charcuterie craze in St Pete started here, at this specialty Italian grocery store in a nondescript suburb northwest of downtown. Mazzaro's fresh bread, sliced meat and delicious cheese has customers lined up at every counter, salivating and staring at the wall's painted scenes of Italy. Around Christmastime, don't even think about it.

Chattaway
AMERICAN $$

(☎727-823-1594; 358 22nd Ave S; mains $9-20; ⊙11am-9:30pm Sun-Thu, to 10pm Fri & Sat) A true slice of Old St Pete, this quirky establishment a bit south of downtown draws regulars back time and again with high tea, tasty burgers and oversized chicken wings. The relaxed outdoor seating area hosts live music regularly, and the service couldn't be friendlier. Dogs welcome. Cash only.

Moon Under Water
INDIAN $$

(☎727-896-6160; www.themoonunderwater.com; 332 Beach Dr NE; mains $9-17; ⊙11am-10pm Sun-Thu, to 11pm Fri & Sat) Sporting an upbeat, 19th-century British-colonial atmosphere, Moon Under Water serves admirably flavorful Indian curries; ask for a capsicum 'enhancer' to adjust the heat to your palate. The British side of the menu specializes in fish and chips, shepherd's pie and bangers and mash. Both imported British and local Cigar City brews are on tap.

Mill
MODERN AMERICAN $$$

(☎727-317-3930; http://themilldtsp.com; 200 Central Ave; charcuterie 3 for $18, mains $15-29; ⊙11am-11pm Tue-Thu, to midnight Fri, 10am-midnight Sat, 10am-10pm Sun) After opening in 2015, the Mill and its barnyard-chic interior design quickly became St Pete's it restaurant, particularly at brunch. The walls are adorned in farm equipment repurposed as abstract art, with rusty gears, a pitchfork and a saddle all polished and arranged to seem devastatingly hip. Menu items are no less of a production, as has always been the case when serial restaurateur and chef Ted Dorsey gets involved.

Farmtable Kitchen MODERN AMERICAN $$$
([icon]727-566-6555; www.localegourmetmarket.com/farmtable-kitchen; 179 2nd Av N; mains $17-38; [clock]11am-10pm Mon-Thu, to 11pm Fri & Sat, 5-9pm Sun) The affiliated, upstairs neighbor of Locale Market (p403) makes use of the gourmet products below on it's farm-and-Gulf-to-table menu, a collaboration of chefs Michael Mina and Don Pintabona (who contribute their respective Californian and Italian influences). The elegant establishment is renowned for its fresh, seasonal salads, dry-aged beef burgers and wood-fired grilled steaks, along with its eight-course tasting menu available Thursday to Saturday.

🍷 Drinking & Nightlife

★ St Petersburg

Shuffleboard Club SPORTS BAR
([icon]727-822-2083; http://stpeteshuffle.com; 559 Mirror Lake Dr N; [clock]6-9pm Tue & Thu, 7-11pm Fri) **FREE** Previously a sport reserved for retirees, shuffleboard first transitioned into an all-ages affair on these very courts, which also happen to be the world's oldest and most numerous. Friday nights come alive when families, hipsters, young people, old people and everybody else shows up (toting

their own alcohol in many cases) to slide discs back and forth until someone wins.

Mandarin Hide COCKTAIL BAR
(www.mandarinhide.com; 231 Central Ave N; [clock]4:30pm-3am Tue-Thu, noon-3am Fri & Sat) This dimly lit cocktail bar is totally hipstered out, with craft libations, retro chandeliers and a giant, fake, mounted buffalo head. The pours are heavy and the ingredients fresh, with offerings like Port of Envy, which contains Angel's Envy bourbon, St Germain elderflower liqueur, tawny port and black walnut bitters, along with a splash of ginger beer for effervescence.

Canopy COCKTAIL BAR
([icon]727-896-1080; www.thebirchwood.com; 340 Beach Dr NE, Birchwood Inn; [clock]4pm-2am) The 5th-floor rooftop bar of the Birchwood Inn (p402) is currently the hottest ticket in town for late-night drinking thanks to its sexy ambience and panoramic views of Beach Dr. Couples loiter in the hope of snagging one of the private cabanas, while party-lovers lounge on long sofas warmed by the glow of fire pits.

Mad Hatters Ethnobotanical Tea Bar GAY
([icon]727-521-9514; www.madhattersteabar.com; 4685 28th St N; [clock]24hr) Headed up by two of St Pete's best-known bartenders gone sober,

---

ST PETE'S CRAFT BEER CRAZE

Since the opening of Dunedin Brewery across the bay in 1996, there's been a growing enthusiasm for locally produced craft beers in the Tampa Bay area. Tourism officials even started marketing a craft-beer trail from Tarpon Springs to Gulfport. Here are five of St Pete's best downtown breweries:

Brewers Tasting Room ([icon]727-873-3900; www.brewerstastingroom.com; 11270 4th St N; [clock]11am-11pm Sun-Thu, to midnight Fri & Sat) Experimental brewpub with a rotating lineup of beers made by home brewers, accompanied by Cajun food and live music. Located 10 miles north of the Museum of Art.

3 Daughters Brewing ([icon]727-495-6002; www.3dbrewing.com; 222 22nd St S; [clock]2-9pm Mon-Tue, to 10pm Wed-Thu, to midnight Fri, noon-midnight Sat, 1-8pm Sun) A 30-barrel brewhouse with a range of styles from light sessions to barrel-aged stouts.

Green Bench Brewing ([icon]727-800-9836; http://greenbenchbrewing.com; 1133 Baum Ave N; [clock]noon-10pm Tue-Thu & Sun, to midnight Fri & Sat) A red-brick garage now does duty as a 15-barrel brewhouse with a family-friendly beer garden.

Cycle Brewing (534 Central Ave; [clock]3pm-midnight Mon-Thu, to 1am Fri, noon-1am Sat, noon-10pm Sun) Hipster brewhouse with sidewalk seating serving 24 rotating taps of world-class beer. No website but it's on social media.

Ale & the Witch ([icon]727-821-2533; www.thealeandthewitch.com; 111 2nd Ave NE; [clock]hours vary) The 'Burg's favorite tap house, serving more than 32 craft beers and a $7 'witch flight', consisting of four 4oz sample servings.

Judah and Levi Love, this trippy tea bar now serves up exotic nonalcoholic concoctions like kava, made from the dried root of a South Pacific plant, and kratom, from the leaves of a Southeast Asian tree containing opioid compounds. Bar games and spooky *Alice in Wonderland* murals abound; service is super-friendly.

☆ Entertainment

★ Jannus Live   CONCERT VENUE
(☑727-565-0550; www.jannuslive.com; 16 2nd St N) Well-loved outdoor concert venue inside an intimate courtyard; national and local bands reverberate downtown.

American Stage   THEATER
(☑727-823-7529; www.americanstage.org; 163 3rd St N; tickets $29-59) One of the Tampa Bay area's most highly regarded regional theater companies presents American classics and recent Tony winners, along with improv comedy.

Florida Orchestra   CLASSICAL MUSIC
(☑727-892-3331; www.floridaorchestra.com; 244 2nd Ave N, suite 420; tickets $15-75) The Florida Orchestra's office is in St Petersburg; it plays at Tampa's Straz Center (p396) as often as at Mahaffey downtown.

Mahaffey Theater   PERFORMING ARTS
(☑727-892-5767; www.mahaffeytheater.com; 400 1st St S; tickets $15-70) The gorgeous, 2031-seat Mahaffey Theater hosts a wide range of performing arts, from touring comedy acts to Broadway, dance, orchestras and more.

Coliseum Ballroom   DANCE
(☑727-892-5202; www.stpete.org/coliseum; 535 4th Ave N; tea dances $7-10) This old-fashioned 1924 ballroom hosts occasional events and has regular tea dances on the first and third Wednesday of each month from October through May.

Tropicana Field   STADIUM
(www.raysbaseball.com; cnr 1st Ave S & 16th St S; tickets $9-85; ☉9am-5pm) Home to the major-league Tampa Bay Rays, who play baseball from April to September. There's a 360-degree walkway around the ballpark from which fans can observe the action. Huge parking lots line 10th St S near 1st Ave S.

🛍 Shopping

Saturday Morning Market   MARKET
(www.saturdaymorningmarket.com; Al Lang Field, cnr 1st St & 1st Ave S; ☉9am-2pm Oct-May) For a slice of local life, head down to the Al Lang Field parking lot on Saturday mornings when more than 200 vendors gather for the local farmers market. In summer (from June to August) it moves to the shadier location of Williams Park, and goes from 9am to 1pm.

Florida CraftArt   ARTS & CRAFTS
(☑727-821-7391; www.floridacraftart.org; 501 Central Ave; ☉10am-5:30pm Mon-Sat, to 5pm Sun) A nonprofit association runs this gallery-store dedicated to Florida craftspeople. Find unusual, unique, high-quality ceramics, jewelry, glass, clothing and art.

Haslam's Book Store   BOOKS
(☑727-822-8616; www.haslams.com; 2025 Central Ave; ☉10am-6:30pm Mon-Sat, noon-5pm Sun) A half-block long, with a tremendous selection of new and used books and a fantastic Florida section, Haslam's claims to be the largest independent bookstore in the US southeast.

❶ Information

St Petersburg Area Chamber of Commerce (☑727-821-4069; www.stpete.com; 100 2nd Ave N; ☉9am-5pm Mon-Fri) This helpful, staffed chamber office has good maps and a driving guide.

Bayfront Medical Center (☑727-823-1234; www.bayfront.org; 701 6th St S; ☉24hr) A convenient option downtown.

John's Hopkins All Children's Hospital (☑727-898-7451; www.allkids.org; 501 6th St S; ☉24hr) The area's largest hospital.

❶ Getting There & Away

AIR
Albert Whitted Airport (107 8th Ave SE) Service to Ft Lauderdale and the Bahamas.

St Petersburg-Clearwater International Airport (Map p392; ☑727-453-7800; www.fly2pie.com; Roosevelt Blvd & Hwy 686, Clearwater) Mainly regional flights; international services to Toronto, Ottawa, and Halifax, Nova Scotia.

BUS
Greyhound (☑727-898-1496; www.greyhound.com; 180 Dr Martin Luther King Jr St N) Buses connect to Miami, Orlando and Tampa.

Pinellas Suncoast Transit Authority (PSTA; www.psta.net; adult/student $2.20/1.10) St Petersburg buses serve the barrier-island beaches and Clearwater; unlimited-ride Go Cards cost $5 per day.

CAR

➜ From Tampa, take I-275 south over the Howard Frankland Bridge. Reach downtown via either I-375 or I-175.

➜ To Sarasota, continue on I-275 south over the Sunshine Skyway Bridge, which connects with I-75 and US 41 (Tamiami Trail).

➜ To St Pete Beach, take I-275 to exit 17, and follow US 682/Pinellas Bayway. Or take Central Ave due west to Treasure Island Causeway; or turn south on 66th St to the Corey Causeway.

➜ To Clearwater Beach, go north on US 19 (34th St in St Petersburg) to Gulf to Bay Blvd; turn west and follow signs.

❶ Getting Around

Downtown Looper (www.loopertrolley.com; fare 50¢; ⏲10am-5pm Sun-Thu, to midnight Fri & Sat) Old-fashioned trolley cars run a downtown circuit every 15 to 20 minutes; great for sightseeing.

St Pete Beach & Barrier Island Beaches

Just 20 minutes from downtown St Petersburg, the legendary barrier-island beaches are the sandy soul of the peninsula. This 30-mile-long stretch of sun-faded towns and sun-kissed azure waters is the perfect antidote to city life and the primary destination of most vacationers. Winter and spring are the high seasons, particularly January through March. During these months, readiness is all: book rooms far in advance, and get up early to beat the traffic and to snag sometimes-elusive parking spaces.

While St Pete Beach is the biggest town, the string of beach communities each has something unique to offer.

◉ Sights

Barrier-island beaches are almost uniformly excellent in terms of their quality. Rather, they are distinguished by how amenable they are to day-trippers: some have much more public parking and better access, commerce and hotels, while others are largely residential. From south to north this stretch of beach passes through the sun-faded towns of Pass-a-Grille, St Pete Beach, Treasure Island, Madeira, Redington, Indian Shores, Indian Rocks and Belleair. Limited public parking at Belleair keeps out the day-trippers, who are better served just north at Sand Key and Clearwater.

Parking meters cost $1.25 per hour; some lots have pay-and-display kiosks.

★ **Fort DeSoto Park** BEACH
(☎727-552-1862; www.pinellascounty.org/park; 3500 Pinellas Bayway S; ⏲sunrise-sunset) FREE
With 1136 acres of unspoiled wilderness, Fort DeSoto is one of Florida's premier beach parks. It includes 7 miles of beaches (including a dog beach), two fishing piers and an extensive nature trail hopping over five interconnected islands. Of its two swimming areas, the long, silky stretch of North Beach is the best, with grassy picnic areas, a cafe and a gift store (open 10am to 4pm Monday to Friday, to 5pm Saturday and Sunday). The cafe organizes hourly bike ($10) and kayak ($23) rentals.

East Beach, meanwhile, is smaller and coarser, and consequently less crowded. The fort after which the park is named, and which dates from the 1898 Spanish-American War, is in the southwest corner of Mullet Key, which was once inhabited by Tocobaga Native Americans. Union troops were later stationed here and on uninhabited Egmont Key during the Civil War. You can visit Egmont's ruined Fort Dade by **ferry** (☎727-398-6577; www.hubbardsmarina.com/egmont; adult/child 11 & under $20/10) from the park. Once there you can explore the fort and abandoned houses, say hello to the protected gopher tortoises, and go shelling and snorkeling (equipment hire $5) off the beach.

Fort DeSoto Park is signed off US 682/Pinellas Bayway (exit 17 off I-275). Parking costs $5.

★ **Pass-a-Grille Beach** BEACH
(www.pass-a-grillebeach.com; Gulf Way) The epic sliver of sand that is Pass-a-Grille Beach is the most idyllic barrier-island beach, backed only by beach houses and a long stretch of metered public parking. Here you can watch boats coming through Pass-a-Grille Channel, hop aboard the **Shell Key Shuttle** (☎727-360-1348; www.shellkeyshuttle.com; Merry Pier, Pass-a-Grille; adult/child $25/12.50; ⏲shuttles 10am, noon & 2pm) to unspoiled **Shell Key,** and retire for eats and ice cream in the laid-back village center.

Egmont Key State Park STATE PARK
(www.fws.gov/egmontkey; ⏲8am-sunset) Union troops were stationed on uninhabited Egmont Key during the Civil War, and you can visit Egmont's ruined Fort Dade by ferry (p406) from Fort DeSoto Park. Once here

you can explore the ruined fort and abandoned houses, say hello to the protected gopher tortoises and go shelling and snorkeling (equipment hire $5) off the beach.

Seaside Seabird Sanctuary
WILDLIFE RESERVE

(☑727-392-4291; www.seabirdsanctuary.com; 18328 Gulf Blvd, Indian Shores; admission by donation; ☉8am-4pm) The largest wild-bird hospital in North America, this sanctuary has more than 100 sea and land birds for public viewing, including a resident population of permanently injured pelicans, owls, gulls and falcons, and an elderly red-tailed hawk named Isis. A couple thousand birds are treated and released back to the wild annually. Unsurprisingly, the place smells a little fishy.

St Pete Beach
BEACH

(www.stpetebeach.org; Gulf Blvd) Anchored by the huge, historic Moorish Mediterranean Don CeSar Hotel, St Pete Beach is a long, double-wide strand with parasail booths and chair rentals seemingly every 50ft. It's crowded with families and spring breakers, who appreciate the big public parking lots, restaurants, bars and motels just steps away.

Treasure Island
BEACH

(Gulf Blvd) Even wider than St Pete Beach and more jam-packed with fun-seekers, concessions and motels. Very built up, with lots of public access, volleyball courts and beach-side tiki bars, many of which are connected by the Treasure Island Beach Trail – a mile-long, concrete walkway that was revamped in 2013.

Indian Rocks Beach
BEACH

(www.indian-rocks-beach.com; Gulf Blvd) This quieter, family-oriented beach appeals to day-trippers looking for their own stretch of sand. Most of the action is clustered around 17th Ave, where there are public restrooms and several popular seafood restaurants and bars. Headed south there's a beloved nature preserve, and folks can park boats (from 7am to 9pm) at the only free public dock on the Intracoastal Waterway.

🛏 Sleeping

If you don't want a beach-based vacation, Fort DeSoto, Pass-a-Grille and St Pete Beach are an easy day trip from St Petersburg. If, against all advice, you show up without a reservation, cruise Gulf Blvd in St Pete Beach and Treasure Island: the main drag is packed shoulder-to-shoulder with motels, hotels and condos. Low season means deep discounts.

★Fort DeSoto Park Campground
CAMPGROUND $

(☑727-582-2100; www.pinellascounty.org/park; 3500 Pinellas Bayway S; tent sites $34-36, RV sites $40-42; ☉office 9am-6pm Sat-Thu, to 9pm Fri; P🐾) The Gulf Coast hardly offers better camping than the 200-plus sites here. Well shaded by thick-growing palms, many face the water, and there are good facilities, hot showers, a grassy field and small camp store, in addition to other park concessions. Online reservations can be made three months in advance, but a few first-come, first-served sites are available every Friday.

Postcard Inn
MOTEL $$

(☑727-367-2711; www.postcardinn.com; 6300 Gulf Blvd, St Pete Beach; r from $230; P❄@❤️) For its vintage 1950s hang-ten style alone, the Postcard Inn leads the pack in St Pete Beach. The long, double-armed shell of a 1957 Colonial Gateway has been transformed into a designer-chic surf shack with rooms sporting murals of wave riders in the curl. Some have hammocks; all surround the sizable pool. Plus there's Ping-Pong, a tiki bar and beach access.

The recently renamed and revamped hotel restaurant next door, Boathouse, has a smoker and knows how to use it (say yes to the smoked brisket melt).

Bon-Aire Resort Motel
RESORT $$

(☑727-360-5596; www.bonaireresort.com; 4350 Gulf Blvd, St Pete Beach; r from $170; P❄🛜❤️) Family-owned and operated for more than 60 years, the Bon-Aire is one of St Pete's best-kept secrets. Looking pretty much as it did when it was built in 1953, it sits on a wide beach with a variety of rooms, efficiencies and apartments dotted around mature, blooming gardens. Two pools, shuffleboard courts and the locally popular tiki bar, **Sandbar Bill's** (☑727-360-5596; 4350 Gulf Blvd, St Pete Beach; mains $5-10; ☉11am-8pm), keep loyal customers returning. Book ahead.

Don CeSar Hotel
RESORT $$$

(☑727-363-5079; www.loewshotels.com/don cesar; 3400 Gulf Blvd, St Pete Beach; r $250-400; P❄@🛜❤️) The magnificent, coral-pink Don CeSar shimmers like a mirage as you approach St Pete Beach from the causeway.

Built in 1928 it's the sort of elegant seaside palace you imagine F Scott Fitzgerald spilling cocktails in, with chandelier-dominated hallways and white cabanas by the glittering pool. You'd never guess that in the '40s it served as a military hospital.

Rooms are more relaxed roosts, and the full-service, four-diamond property has all you need: fine dining, a European-style spa, kids programs and, most of all, its own sultry beach. The latest addition is an open-air, beachfront sports bar with fire pits.

Inn on the Beach   MOTEL $$$
(☑ 727-360-8844; www.innonbeach.com; 1401 Gulf Way, Pass-a-Grille; r $195-450; P❋⌚) For a quiet, relaxing seaside getaway, these 12 rooms and four cottages are unqualified gems. With bright coral and teal accents, functional kitchenettes and lovely tiled bathrooms, these quarters are a pleasure to return to in the evening; a couple of 2nd-floor rooms have stunning Gulf views and the top-floor Ibis honeymoon suite is swoonworthy.

Coconut Inn   INN $$$
(☑ 727-367-3030; www.pagbeachinns.com; 113 11th Ave, Pass-a-Grille; r $290-395; P❋@⌚) Keeping with the village's low-level, Old Florida vibe, this two-story clapboard house offers 11 homey studios with kitchenettes, some with lounge seating, others with balconies offering garden or Gulf views. They're set around a courtyard pool, although with complimentary beach chairs and bikes you won't have much time for swimming.

Thunderbird Beach Resort   MOTEL $$$
(☑ 727-367-1961; www.thunderbirdflorida.com; 10700 Gulf Blvd, Treasure Island; r & apt from $247; P❋⌚) The art-deco sign has beckoned travelers since 1958, and the Thunderbird remains a reliable choice in the thick of the Treasure Island commercial corridor. Clean, standard decor eschews seaside kitsch for sage and coppery hues. The real amenities, though, are the pool, tiki bar and beach.

✕ Eating

★ Walt'z Fish Shak   SEAFOOD $
(☑ 727-395-0732; www.waltzfishshak.com; 224 Boardwalk Pl E, Madeira Beach; mains $4-12; ⊙5-8:30pm Tue-Fri, noon-3pm & 5pm-8:30pm Sat, noon-3pm Sun) The MO at Walter Gerbase's fish shack is simple: the day's domestic-only catch (often featuring grouper, cobia and amberjack) is chalked on the board;

you choose one grilled, fried or blackened and served with coleslaw, salad or raw veg. When they run out, that's it for the night. Get there early to grab a table and the best of the day's selection.

Paradise Grille   SEAFOOD $
(☑ 727-367-1495; 900 Gulf Way, Passe-a-Grille; items $6-10; ⊙8am-sunset) With a deck right over the beach, cold beer and the best pound of shrimp on the beach, this is indeed a little slice of paradise. It also does a mean breakfast, and there's a craft market and live music on Fridays, Saturdays and Sundays.

Guppy's   SEAFOOD $$
(☑ 727-593-2032; www.3bestchefs.com; 1701 Gulf Blvd, Indian Rocks; lunch mains $9-14, mains $13-25; ⊙11:30am-10pm, to 10:30pm Fri & Sat) For variety, quality and price, it's hard to beat Guppy's, which packs diners in nightly. Preparations are diverse, skillfully spanning styles (and budgets), from ocean-raised, garlicky cobia to Kona-coffee-dusted deep-sea scallops. Guppy's doesn't take reservations for parties of five or fewer, but its 'call-ahead seating' gets your name on the wait list an hour before arrival.

Ted Peter's Famous Smoked Fish   SEAFOOD $$
(☑ 727-381-7931; www.tedpetersfish.com; 1350 Pasadena Ave, St Pete Beach; mains $6.50-19; ⊙11:30am-7:30pm Wed-Mon) Since the 1950s, Ted Peter's has been smoking fresh salmon, mackerel, mahimahi and mullet in the little smokehouse here, then dishing it up whole or in sandwich spreads. You eat at outdoor picnic tables; nothing fancy. Cash only. And if you bring your own catch, they'll smoke it for you for $2 a pound.

★ Fetishes   FRENCH $$$
(☑ 727-363-3700; www.fetishesrestaurant.com; 6305 Gulf Blvd, St Pete Beach; mains $19-60; ⊙5-10pm Tue-Sat) Under Bruce Caplan's eagle eye sumptuous classics such as steak Diane, coquilles St Jacques and sole meunière are sautéed, brandied and flambéed tableside for tongue-tingling flavor. Go the whole hog and splash out on a spicy, black-cherry-flavored Silver Oak Alexander Valley Cabernet from the glassed-in wine cellar.

Salt Rock Grill   SEAFOOD $$$
(☑ 727-593-7625; www.saltrockgrill.com; 19325 Gulf Blvd, Indian Shores; mains $15-40; ⊙4-10pm Mon-Thu, to 11pm Fri & Sat, noon-10pm Sun) This contemporary, upscale harborside eatery

puts everything on display: the basement wine cellar through a floor cutaway, the waterfront from sweeping windows and the outdoor deck, and the open kitchen's wood-fired grill, where seafood and steaks sizzle at a promised 1200°F (650ºC).

 Drinking & Nightlife

Hurricane BAR

(☑ 727-360-9558; www.thehurricane.com; 807 Gulf Way, Pass-a-Grille; ⊙ 7am-10pm Mon-Thu & Sun, to 11pm Fri & Sat) Skip the mediocre restaurants and head straight to the rooftop bar for 360-degree views and the best sundowner spot on the beach. The Bloody Marys are famous here, and well paired with the fresh grouper sandwich.

Undertow Bar BAR

(www.undertowbeachbar.com; 3850 Gulf Blvd, St Pete Beach; ⊙ 11am-3am) Locals, bikers and coeds all mingle along the three flag-stone-topped bars to booze it up and flirt, day or night, on the edge of the sand. When live reggae or DJs aren't playing, country music dominates the jukebox.

ⓘ Getting There & Away

These islands can be reached from the mainland via the following roads (starting from the southernmost): the Pinellas Bayway, Pasadena Ave S, the Treasure Island Causeway, 150th Av, Park Blvd N, Walsingham Rd and W Bay Dr. Gulf Blvd also connects the northernmost barrier island to Clearwater Beach.

ⓘ Getting Around

Suncoast Beach Trolleys (☑ 727-540-1900; www.psta.net; fares/day passes $2.25/5; ⊙ 5:05am-10:10pm Mon-Thu & Sun, to midnight Fri & Sat) ply the entirety of Gulf Blvd, every 20 to 30 minutes, from St Pete Beach north to Clearwater, and connect with other peninsula trolley and bus services.

Tampa Bay Taxi (☑ 727-398-6577; www.tampabayferry.com; one way/passes $10/19.50; ⊙ 10am-7:45pm), a new water taxi, transports passengers up and down the barrier islands.

Clearwater & Clearwater Beach

☑ 727 / POP 113,003

Clearwater Beach is an upscale if somewhat bland wisp of a barrier island, while its neighbor to the east is one wacky and decidedly low-class municipality. While Clearwater Beach might make for a better

vacation, Clearwater makes for more lively dinner conversation, as the indefatigable Hooters restaurant chain was invented here in 1983, and its burgers-and-babes dining concept encapsulates the spring break party scene.

While Clearwater Beach offers idyllic beaches and parks, Clearwater has a stuck-in-amber, gray-suited, 1950s-era downtown that's dominated by the international spiritual headquarters of the Church of Scientology. The Clearwater Church, known as Flag Land Base, has occupied the historic Fort Harrison Hotel since the late 1970s, and has upward of 60 more properties in the city. None of this is open to the public, and Clearwater itself remains deeply ambivalent about being home to the largest concentration of Scientologists outside of Los Angeles.

☉ Sights

Clearwater Marine Aquarium AQUARIUM

(☑ 727-447-1790; www.seewinter.com; 249 Windward Passage, Clearwater; adult/child 3-12yr $22/17; ⊙ 9am-6pm) The home of Winter the dolphin, this nonprofit aquarium rescues and rehabilitates injured sea animals, such as dolphins, sea otters, fish, rays, and loggerhead and Kemp's ridley sea turtles. It also allows visitors to interact with the animals, many of which are resident due to injuries that prevent their return to the wild. Regardless, interaction with humans can be stressful for dolphins and sharks, and animal welfare experts recommend that they be kept in sea pens rather than put on display for paying visitors.

Sand Key Park & Beach BEACH

(1060 Gulf Blvd, Sand Key; ⊙ 7am-sunset) If you'd like a less-crowded beach day, free of commercial folderol, head to this 65-acre, family-friendly beach park. It's at the northern tip of the barrier island to the south, just over the Clearwater Pass Bridge. The sand isn't nearly as fine as at Clearwater Beach, but it's a wide strand with decent shelling that's popular with local families. It has restrooms and outdoor showers, but bring lunch. Clearwater's Jolley Trolley stops here. Daily parking costs $5.

Pier 60 BEACH

(☑ 727-449-1036; www.sunsetsatpier60.com; 1 Causeway Blvd, Clearwater Beach) In high season, Clearwater's long stretch of smooth, white sand becomes a scrum of sun-baked coeds and extended families. Hotels, resorts and raucous beach bars line the sand, particularly near Pier 60, where sunset is 'celebrated' each night with a festive menagerie of musicians, magicians, performers and trinket stands hawking their wares. On Coronado Dr across from the pier, activity booths offer parasailing, fishing, cruises and so on.

🛏 Sleeping & Eating

Parker Manor Resort   MOTEL $$
(☑727-446-6562; www.parkermanor.com; 115 Brightwater Dr, Clearwater Beach; r $100-130, 2-bed apt $170-185; P ❄ 🤖 ≋) On the harbor, but a walkable distance to the beach, this small, well-kept complex attracts an older crowd who enjoy playing billiards in the covered courtyard and lounging by the small pool. Suites are fully loaded for cooking and extended stays.

Opal Sands Resort   RESORT $$$
(☑727-450-0380; www.opalsands.com; 430 S Gulfview Blvd, Clearwater Beach; from $375; P ❄ 🤖) The glistening-white, semicircular facade of Opal Sands Resort is the talk of Clearwater Beach, where the resort is the latest addition to the luxurious Opal Collection. Rooms are comfy and spacious, featuring balconies and expansive views of the Gulf, while the zero-entry pool mimics the experience of walking into the ocean. The oddly named Italian restaurant Sea-Guini is hip and delicious.

SandPearl Resort   RESORT $$$
(☑727-441-2425; www.sandpearl.com; 500 Mandalay Ave, Clearwater Beach; r $500-600; P ❄ 🤖 ≋) Clearwater's Sandpearl is an LEED Silver-certified beach resort within walking distance of Pier 60 and Clearwater's restaurant row. Following all the most fashionable trends, it touts an eco-conscious spa, boat slips, 253 sandy-hued rooms and suites with dark-wood furniture and Gulf-gazing balconies.

Frenchy's Original Cafe   SEAFOOD $
(☑727-446-3607; www.frenchysonline.com; 41 Baymont St, Clearwater; mains $8-15; ⏱11am-11pm) This beach-bum-casual hole-in-the-wall serves grouper sandwiches you'll dream about months later. These crusty beauties on an onion roll go perfectly with its light-and-sweet pineapple coleslaw. Well-loved Frenchy's has four Clearwater locations.

☆ Entertainment

Shephard's Beach Resort   LIVE MUSIC
(☑727-442-5107; www.shephards.com; 619 S Gulfview Blvd, Clearwater Beach) Nine times out of 10 the biggest party in Clearwater Beach is at Shephard's, where three bars and a raucous nightclub brim with revelers. The Tiki Beach Bar often showcases local bands on its stage and (all too frequently) line dancing on its dance floor, while the two-level Wave nightclub and its state-of-the-art light and sound systems feature well-known DJs.

ⓘ Getting There & Away

Driving from the peninsula, take Hwy 19 to Hwy 60/Gulf to Bay Blvd, and follow it west to Memorial Causeway and the beach. Be warned: beach traffic is a nightmare. If you're coming for sun and fun, ditch the car as soon as you can and walk.

Suncoast Beach Trolley (☑727-540-1900; www.psta.net; adult/reduced $2/1; ⏱5:15am-10:50pm Sun-Thu, to 12:20am Fri & Sat) PSTA's Suncoast Beach Trolley connects downtown Clearwater, Clearwater Beach and the barrier-island beaches south to Pass-a-Grille.

ⓘ Getting Around

Jolley Trolley (☑727-445-1200; www.clearwaterjolleytrolley.com; adult/reduced $2.25/1.10, day passes $5; ⏱10am-10pm Sun-Thu, to 11:30pm Fri & Sat) Tootles around Clearwater Beach and south to Sand Key.

Gulfport

☑727 / POP 12,164

Don't tell anyone, but Gulfport is the cutest, quirkiest little beach town that's not on the barrier island beaches. Nestled at peninsula's end within Boca Ciega Bay, this LGBT-friendly artist community exudes that elusive, easygoing, fun-loving attitude that Florida made famous. The hard-to-resist spell is in full effect on sultry evenings when the trees along Beach Blvd glow with lights and the outdoor restaurants burble with laughter.

It doesn't compare to the barrier islands, of course, but Gulfport does have a beach with a playground and a shady picnic area.

✲ Festivals & Events

Gulfport Art Walk   ART
(3007 Beach Blvd; ⏱6-10pm 1st Fri & 3rd Sat of each month) Experience the full dose of

Gulfport's wry local sensibilities during the twice-monthly art walk, essentially a low-key street party.

Gulfport Fresh Market FOOD & DRINK
(www.facebook.com/gulfportfreshmarket; ⊘9am-2pm Tue May-Sep, to 3pm Oct-Apr) The Tuesday fresh morning market lines Bayshore Dr and is a fun local shindig.

Sleeping

Peninsula Inn INN $$
(☑727-346-9800; www.historicpeninsulainn.com; 2937 Beach Blvd; r $155-243; ❋@☎) If you're tempted to spend the night in Gulfport, the historic Peninsula Inn has been renovated into a pretty, romantic choice. It also has a recommended restaurant, Isabelle's, which serves classic Southern cuisine and live music performances, often involving piano and a Sinatra singer.

Drinking & Nightlife

Manatees on the Bay BAR
(☑727-592-2842; 3128 Beach Blvd S; ⊘10am-2pm) This lively new place offers sweeping views of the beach, pier and bobbing boats from its open-air, 2nd-story bar, along with $2 domestic beers during the longest happy hour in all the land, from 11am to 7pm. Bonuses include a piano with a manatee painted on the top and foosball and pool tables.

Getting There & Away

➜ To get there from St Petersburg, take I-275 exit 19 onto 22nd Ave S/Gulfport Blvd, and turn left onto Beach Blvd into town.
➜ From St Pete Beach, the Corey Causeway connects to Gulfport Blvd.

Honeymoon Island & Caladesi Island

Two of the best beaches in the US are just north of Clearwater: Honeymoon Island, which you can drive to (west on Curlew Rd/Hwy 586 from Dunedin), and the ferry-only Caladesi Island. In fact, the two islands were once part of a single barrier island, split in half during the hurricane of 1921. Together, they offer nearly a thousand acres of coastal wilderness not much changed since Spanish explorers first surveyed this coast in the mid-1500s.

Sights & Activities

★**Caladesi Island State Park** STATE PARK
(Map p392; ☑727-469-5918; www.floridastateparks.org/caladesiisland; boat/kayak $6/2; ⊘8am-sunset) FREE Directly to the south of Honeymoon, this park is accessible only by boat and is virtually as nature made it: unspoiled and pristine. Consequently, it often tops national beach polls, and its 3 palm-lined miles of sugar-sand beaches should make the top of your list, too. Secluded and uncrowded it nevertheless boasts a 110-slip marina, kayak rentals, a tiny cafe, restrooms and showers.

Honeymoon Island State Park STATE PARK
(Map p392; ☑727-469-5942; www.floridastateparks.org/honeymoonisland; 1 Dunedin Causeway; car/cyclist $8/2; ⊘8am-sunset; ⛵) This park, so named in the 1940s when marketeers pitched the island as the perfect getaway for newlyweds, is graced with the Gulf Coast's legendary white sand, a dog-friendly beach and warm aquamarine water.

Sail Honeymoon Inc. KAYAKING
(☑727-734-0392; http://sailhoneymoon.com; 61 Causeway Blvd; single/double kayak 2hr $30/40; ⊘8am-7pm) Rents kayaks, stand-up paddleboards and trimaran sailboats, which can be used to travel to Caladesi Island.

Eating

South Beach Pavilion Cafe CAFE $
(www.romantichoneymoonisland.com; Honeymoon Island; mains $3-13; ⊘11am-6pm Mon-Thu, 10am-6pm Fri, 8am-6pm Sat & Sun) Next to the pet beach, this cafe offers basically the same stuff as the Island Cafe up the beach, with a special fish fry at 4pm on Fridays, and pancake breakfasts on Saturday and Sunday from 8am to 11am.

Island Cafe CAFE $
(☑727-260-5503; Honeymoon Island; mains $5-9; ⊘9am-5pm) On the beach, the Island Cafe serves sandwiches, snacks and beer, and offers bicycle ($20 per hour), kayak ($10 to $20 per hour) and umbrella ($25 per day) rentals.

Getting There & Away

Caladesi Connection Ferry (☑727-734-5263; www.caladesiferry.org; adult/child round-trip $14/7; ⊘10am-4pm) runs half-hourly ferries from Honeymoon Island beginning at 10am and ending around 4pm. Capacity is 62 people, and ferries often fill up. Also, officially you must catch a return ferry within four hours. If you're late, passengers with the correct return times board first.

You can also get to Caladesi Island via kayak, stand-up paddleboard or trimaran sailboat from **Sail Honeymoon Inc.** (p411) on Causeway Blvd. It's an easy 15-minute journey to the island.

NATURE COAST

Florida's Nature Coast tracks south from the Panhandle through a largely rural landscape of parkland, preserves and estuaries. As such, it retains more of that oft-promised but hard-to-find Old Florida atmosphere, with its moss-draped rivers, warm-water springs and quiet creeks and bays filled with scallops and tarpon. It's highly recommended to travel here with a boat or kayak, as its one thing to see these amazing rivers and creeks, but quite another to get out on their crystal-clear waters.

Weeki Wachee Springs

🌐 352 / POP 12

Were the 'City of Mermaids' ever to close up shop, a bit of Florida's soul would be lost forever. The 'city' of Weeki Wachee is almost entirely constituted by Weeki Wachee Springs State Park and is dedicated to its underwater mermaid show that has entertained families since 1947.

◉ Sights & Activities

**Weeki Wachee
Springs State Park**   STATE PARK

(🌐352-592-5656; www.weekiwachee.com; 6131 Commercial Way, Spring Hill; adult/child 6-12yr $13/8; ⊙9am-5:30pm) Since 1947 tourists have been lured by the siren song of Weeki Wachee Springs, one of Florida's original roadside attractions. Esther Williams, Danny Thomas and Elvis Presley have all sat in the glass-paneled underwater theater and watched as pink-tailed mermaids perform pirouettes while turtles and fish swim past. The three daily half-hour shows (at 11am, 1:30pm and 3pm) remain gleeful celebrations of nostalgic kitsch, particularly the mainstay, *The Little Mermaid*.

While there's no mystery to the trick – the mermaids hold air hoses as they swim and gulp air as needed – there's an undeniable theatrical magic to their effortless performances.

The park also offers a sedate riverboat cruise and a modest, weekend-only water park, plus picnic areas. It's quite perfect for an afternoon's entertainment.

Prices are reduced in the off-season when the water park is closed.

★ **Boating in Florida**   KAYAKING

(🌐352-597-8484; 6131 Commercial Way, Spring Hill; single/double kayaks $34.61/39.94, stand-up paddleboard $34.61; ⊙8am-noon) Kayaking and stand-up paddleboarding the Weeki Wachee River are perhaps the region's best adventures. Weeki Wachee's spring – a 100ft hole that pumps about 170 million gallons of water daily – is actually the headwater of the crystal-clear river. The 5.5-mile route includes beaches with good swimming and rope swings, plus you'll see fish and even manatees in winter and spring.

🛈 Getting There & Away

➡ The springs are about 45 miles north of Clearwater via US 19.

➡ It's about an hour from Tampa; take I-75 north to Hwy 50 then head west.

Homosassa Springs

🌐 352 / POP 13,791

As any fly-fisher will tell you, the Homosassa River is a popular feeding ground for the Silver King of the sea world, Atlantic tarpon. Every summer, the river is dotted with 20 to 30 flat boats as anglers sit in hushed concentration hoping to see one roll. The tarpon begin to run in May and fade out in July, usually about when the area's other main draw returns – scallop season. Although the timing varies, for three months midyear hundreds of people descend on Homosassa to comb the sea-grass beds and fill their 2-gallon-per-day scallop quota. Outlets offer half- and full-day trips for fishing and scalloping, along with shore lunches.

The warm waters of the river are also a favorite hangout for slow-moving West Indian manatees between October and March. To view them, visit the Homosassa Springs Wildlife State Park, which is quieter than Crystal River.

◉ Sights & Activities

**Homosassa Springs
Wildlife State Park**   STATE PARK

(🌐352-628-5343; www.floridastateparks.org/ homosassasprings; 4150 S Suncoast Blvd; adult/

child 6-12yr $13/5; ⊘9am-5:30pm) This state park is essentially an old-school outdoor Florida animal encounter that features Florida's wealth of headliner species: American alligators, black bears, whooping cranes, Florida panthers, tiny Key deer and – especially – manatees. Homosassa's highlight is an underwater observatory directly over the springs, where through glass windows you can eyeball enormous schools of some 10,000 fish and ponderous manatees nibbling lettuce.

Various animal presentations happen daily, but time your visit for the manatee program (11:30am, 1:30pm and 3:30pm). The park itself is a short, narrated boat ride from the visitor center.

Homosassa Inshore Fishing FISHING
(☑352-422-4141; www.homosassainshorefishing. com; half-/full-day $350/400) Captain William Toney is a fourth-generation Homosassa fisherman specializing in red fish, trout fishing and scalloping, along with cooking up inshore lunches. You can't get a better guide.

🛏 Sleeping & Eating

MacRae's MOTEL $$
(☑352-628-2602; www.macraesofhomosassa. com; 5300 S Cherokee Way; r from $100; ❄🐾) MacRae's is a good sleeping option 3 miles from the Homosassa Springs park off W Yulee Rd. It's a fisher's paradise of pseudo log cabins and has 22 rooms (some with kitchens) complete with front-porch rockers. MacRae's also operates the riverfront tiki bar called The Shed, which is perfectly perched for exceptional afternoon drinks.

Greenhouse Bistro & Market BISTRO $$
(☑352-503-7276; www.greenhousebistromarket. com; 2420 S Suncoast Blvd; mains $12-33; ⊘11am-8pm Wed & Thu, to 9pm Fri & Sat, 10am-2pm Sun) This cute, shamrock-green bistro, with it's gluten-free attitude and from-scratch ethos, is a welcome addition to the otherwise unsophisticated dining scene of Homosassa. The menu isn't particularly adventurous, but does feature an excellent cheese platter, some healthy salads, and plenty of local favorites, like pan-seared Gulf grouper, free-range chicken and grass-fed beef.

❶ Getting There & Away

To reach the center of Homosassa, leave US 19 along Hwy 490/W Yulee Rd (just south of the park) and enter an Old Florida time warp, where live oaks dripping in Spanish moss curtain a roadway dotted with local eateries and funky galleries.

Crystal River
☑352 / POP 3062

Florida has some 700 freshwater springs, 33 of which are categorized as first magnitude, meaning they discharge at least 100 cubic feet of water per second. The Nature Coast boasts several of these high volume springs, the largest of which are the 30-odd springs that feed Kings Bay, near the town of Crystal River. Maintaining an average temperature of 72°F (22.5°C), the water attracts upwards of 800 manatees (and many more tourists) during the winter months between October and March. Were it not for the manatees, Crystal River, like Homosassa and Cedar Key, would be a low-key fishing community.

◉ Sights

**Crystal River National
Wildlife Refuge** WILDLIFE RESERVE
(☑352-563-2088; www.fws.gov/crystalriver; 1502 SE Kings Bay Dr; ⊘8am-5:30pm Mon-Fri) The winter home of nearly 20% of Florida's West Indian manatee population, this wildlife refuge protects almost the whole of Kings Bay. Up to 800 of these gentle, endangered sea creatures have been counted in a single January day, and like any wildlife spectacle, this draws crowds of onlookers, as well as swimmers and snorkelers. Many of these seem intent on getting as close as possible to the animals, which some may find uncomfortable. Note that conservationists advise against swimming with or touching manatees, arguing that this causes the animals undue stress.

Nearly 50 commercial operators offer rentals and guided tours, via every type of nautical conveyance, and the chance to swim with wild manatees. In season, the corralled manatees and crowded bay are a far cry from any natural wildlife interaction, which is better gained by taking one of the area's top-notch paddle tours. One place to begin is the refuge headquarters (open 8am to 4pm), though at the time of research it had been flooded and was closed indefinitely. Another is the park's Three Sisters trail. Note that although manatees live in Kings Bay year-round, the population dwindles to a few dozen between April and September.

Three Sisters Springs SPRING

(☎352-586-1170; www.threesistersspringsvisitor.org; 123 NW US 19; adult/child $15/7.50; ⏰8am-5pm) One of the newer attractions in the Crystal River National Wildlife Refuge (p413) is Three Sisters Springs, which contains 57 acres of wildlife flanked by a boardwalk for strolling through it all. The area features underwater vents, sand boils and manatee-filled crystal-clear spring water that feed Kings Bay, the headwaters of the Crystal River. There's no on-site parking, but you can take the trolley to the boardwalk.

Activities

The largest draws to Crystal River are swimming with manatees and scalloping. The best time to go for manatees is November to April, when hundreds come from the ocean into the relatively warm water in the springs to feed on sea grass. The timing varies for scalloping, but it takes place over three months midyear, when hundreds of people show up to comb the sea-grass beds and fill a 2-gallon-per-day scallop quota.

★ Aardvark's Florida Kayak Company KAYAKING

(☎352-795-5650; www.floridakayakcompany.com; 707 N Citrus Ave; tours $50-100) Rents kayaks and stand-up paddleboards (SUP), as well as guiding excellent ecotours to Kings Bay, Chassahowitzka, Ozello backcountry and Rainbow River. Guided tours are led by knowledgeable wildlife biologists, naturalists and a former park ranger.

Florida Circumnavigational Saltwater Paddling Trail KAYAKING, CANOEING

(www.floridapaddlingtrails.com) This 1515-mile kayaking trail (the longest in Florida) contains a 20-mile stretch within the rich estuarine ecosystem of the Nature Coast. It begins on the Salt River off Crystal River, then meanders east on the Homosassa River, finally cutting south to the mouth of the Chassahowitzka River.

As part of the Great Florida Birding Trail, the early stages of the route are rich with birdlife and you'll likely spot pelicans, gulls, hawks, bald eagles, cormorants, storks and other wading birds. Particularly good is the 5.3-mile Ozello Trail, which passes through the St Martins Aquatic Preserve. Beware, this is not a beginners trail and much of the paddle is remote, so come prepared with a GPS and file a float plan. Otherwise, hire a guide.

To reach Ozello and the aquatic preserve, follow Hwy 494W through Crystal River National Wildlife Refuge.

Scalloping with Captain Nick Warhurst FISHING

(☎352-812-2528; $75) Captain Nick Warhurst, aka Scallop Man, has been taking guests on mollusk hunts in Crystal River and Homosassa for more than three decades. He picks guests up at their hotels and boats them through scenic backwaters and out into the Gulf, where scallopers float over grass flats in 4-6ft of water, trying to spot blue scallop 'eyes.'

Bird's Underwater Dive Center OUTDOORS

(☎352-563-2763; www.birdsunderwater.com; 320 NW Hwy 19; ⏰9am-5pm) This recommended outdoors company offers snorkeling with manatees, scalloping trips, kayak rentals and scuba courses. Guidelines regulating the manatee snorkeling are important for the safety of the animals and should be followed at all times: essentially, it's looky don't touchy. The manatee trips leave at 6am and 11pm daily.

Sleeping & Eating

Kings Bay Lodge LODGE $$

(☎352-795-2850; www.kingsbaylodgefla.com; 506 NW 1st Av; r weekday/weekend $129/139; P❄📶) Built in 1957 and entirely redone in 2016 after Hurricane Hermine flooded it, Kings Bay Lodge is one of the few independently owned hotels in Crystal River. Its 18 rooms surround a large oak tree and are quaint and well kept. The property also features a spring-fed, crystal-clear, natural pool with living plants, fish and the occasional crab.

Charlie's Fish House SEAFOOD $$

(☎352-795-3949; www.charliesfishhouse.com; 224 US 19; mains $13-20; ⏰11am-9pm) A long-time local favorite, this waterfront establishment offers fantastic views of Kings Bay, along with reliably good seafood dishes like stone crab claws and crab-meat-stuffed flounder. Charlie's also doubles as a fish market from Monday to Saturday, 8am to 5:30pm, offering oysters and stone crab seasonally, along with grouper, mullet and red snapper.

ℹ️ Getting There & Away

Crystal River is 73 miles north of Clearwater via US 19. It's about an hour and a half from Tampa; take I-75 north to Hwy 50 then head west.

Tarpon Springs

📞 727 / POP 23,871

Welcome to America's Greek-est city. Tarpon Springs began to earn this distinction back in the late 1800s, after somebody realized there were abundant sea sponges in the Gulf, and a bunch of Greek divers came with wet suits and diving helmets to build the industry. In the 1900s scuba gear only got more advanced, allowing the divers to go deeper and stay down longer. The sponge industry boomed, and Tarpon Springs became known as the 'Sponge Capital of the World.'

The industry faltered in the 1940s when sponges were tougher to come by, but was revived in the 1980s, and today Tarpon Springs remains a leader in the natural sponge market. All aspects of the unique industry are on display for visitors, from sponge docks to sponge museums to the town's heavy Greek influence, which is most apparent in the delicious restaurants and at the lively festivals.

◉ Sights

St Nicholas Greek Orthodox Cathedral
CATHEDRAL

(📞727-937-3540; www.stnicholastarpon.org; 17 E Tarpon Ave; ⊙office 9am-5pm Mon-Thu) Erected in 1907, this historic cathedral doubles as a Greek American community center and host for the yearly Epiphany celebration. With a stately dome, ornate relics and stained-glass windows, the Neo-Byzantine structure was modeled after the Saint Sophia Cathedral in Istanbul, and its 60-ton marble altar, a gift from Greece, took part in the first New York World's Fair.

There are services in English at 10:45am Sunday.

Historic Sponge Docks
HISTORIC SITE

(https://spongedocks.net; Dodecanese Blvd) A walk along the docks on Dodecanese Blvd takes visitors past working sponging boats loaded up with giant specimens, along with numerous (and fairly tacky) souvenir shops, Greek restaurants and advertisements for local boating excursions. Signage tells the history of the sponge business, which got its start in the late 1800s.

✨ Festivals & Events

Epiphany
CULTURAL

(⊙Jan 6) Each January 6 for the last hundred years plus, the masses have gathered in Tarpon Springs to watch men dive into the water and compete to find a submerged wooden cross. There is also a celebration with Greek food, traditional dancing and a ceremony to honor the cross retriever.

🛏️ Sleeping & Eating

⭐1910 Inn
B&B $$

(📞727-424-4091; www.the1910inn.com; 32 W Tarpon Ave; r $170-198) Distinguished for its Queen Anne architecture and listing in the Historic Registry of Tarpon Springs, this c 1910 home now serves as a B&B and event space. Guests adore the light blue-green facade, expansive wraparound porch and rounded tower, and the six units inside feature sky-high ceilings and glistening wood floors. Great location downtown, near St Nicholas Greek Orthodox Cathedral.

⭐Dimitri's on the Water
GREEK $$

(📞727-945-9400; http://dimitrisonthewater.com; 690 Dodecanese Blvd; mains $12-28; ⊙11am-10pm) Tarpon Springs' most ambitious Greek restaurant is set on the Anclote River, with a pleasant outdoor deck and idyllic sunset views. The food is the real draw, though, particularly the oversize lamb wraps, fresh Greek salads and mouthwatering moussaka (a baked, layered eggplant dish with seasoned ground beef and a creamy béchamel).

Hellas Restaurant and Bakery
GREEK $$

(📞727-943-2400; www.hellasbakery.com; 785 Dodecanese Blvd; mains $8-18; ⊙11am-10pm Sun-Thu, to 11pm Fri & Sat) A long-standing favorite for its baklava cheesecake and fall-off-the-bone lamb shank, this Greek restaurant has been killing it since 1970. The place is decked out in a blue-and-white color scheme and plenty of Greek paraphernalia, including a mini-Parthenon and scenic paintings of Greece. The service is prompt and upbeat. The bakery opens at 9am daily.

Rusty Bellies Waterfront Grill
SEAFOOD $$

(📞727-934-4047; www.rustybellies.com; 937 Dodecanese Blvd; mains $13-28; ⊙11am-9pm Sun-Thu, to 10pm Fri & Sat) This indoor-outdoor restaurant and tiki bar at the end of Dodecanese is named after the large, male gag grouper with the same nickname, and accordingly, the place is all about seafood. Fishers bring their fresh catch to the dock here daily, and that often includes grouper, mahimahi and mullet. There's live music at the tiki bar all weekend long.

 Drinking & Nightlife

Cliché Piano Bar and Pool Lounge LOUNGE
(☑727-935-6309; 121 E Tarpon Ave; ⊘8pm-2am Wed-Sat; 🖥) An upscale and lavishly adorned new martini bar in Tarpon Spring's historic downtown, defined by inlaid brick, velvet couches and ostentatious chandeliers.

 Shopping

Spongeorama Sponge Factory GIFTS & SOUVENIRS
(☑727-943-2164; https://spongeorama.com; 510 Dodecanese Blvd; ⊘10:30am-5pm) Here you'll find the world's largest collection of natural sea sponges, along with souvenirs of all kinds – art, jewelry, loofahs, paintings, Greek stuff, Florida stuff, you get the point. In back is the Spongeorama Museum, which tells the story of Tarpon Springs' sponge industry through exhibits and a short film.

The museum was damaged in Hurricane Hermine and was closed during our visit, but was likely to reopen in summer 2018.

Tarpon Springs House of Jerky FOOD
(☑727-940-8432; https://houseofjerky.net; 840 Dodecanese Blvd; python/alligator/wild-boar jerky $21/22.50/30; ⊘12:30-6pm) A wildly expensive but fun shop selling exotic jerkies, from alligator to python to wild boar.

🛈 **Getting There & Away**

➜ Arriving by car is best, and the city is best accessed from the north or south via N Pinellas Ave, which bisects it.

➜ Intrepid travelers may choose to arrive or depart via bicycle on the **Pinellas Trail** (p400), a 37-mile bike path that stretches all the way from Tarpon Springs to St Pete.

➜ The closest airport is the **St Petersburg-Clearwater International Airport** (p405), 17 miles away.

SOUTHWEST GULF COAST

People who prefer Florida's Gulf side over its Atlantic one generally fall in love with this stretch of sun-kissed coastline from Sarasota to Naples. These two affluent, cultured towns set the tone for the whole region, where visits sway between soporific beach days and art-museum meanders, fine dining and designer cocktails. With their rowdy bars and casual fun, Siesta Key and Fort Myers Beach are slight exceptions, but even they don't reach the same pitch of spring break hysteria just north. No, in this region you'll remember hunting prehistoric shark's teeth in Venice and jewel-like tulip shells in Sanibel, a night at the circus in Sarasota and buying art in Matlacha.

Sarasota
☑941 / POP 53,326
Vacations today can be spent soaking up the sights and beaches of sophisticated Sarasota, but this city took its time becoming the culturally rich place it is today. After marauding Spanish explorers expelled the Calusa people in the 15th century, this land lay virtually empty until the Seminole Wars inspired the Armed Occupation Act (1842), which deeded 160 acres and six months' provisions to anyone who would settle here and protect their farms. Sailing boats and steamships were the only connection to the outside world, until the Tampa railroad came in 1902. Sarasota then grew popular as a winter resort for the affluent, and the city's arts institutions followed. Finally circus magnate John Ringling decided to relocate his circus here, building a winter residence, art museum and college, and setting the struggling town on course to become the welcoming, well-to-do bastion of the arts it is today.

⊙ **Sights**

★**Ringling Museum Complex** MUSEUM
(☑941-359-5700; www.ringling.org; 5401 Bay Shore Rd; adult/child 6-17yr $25/5; ⊘10am-5pm Fri-Wed, to 8pm Thu; 🚼) The 66-acre winter estate of railroad, real-estate and circus baron John Ringling and his wife, Mable, is one of the Gulf Coast's premier attractions and incorporates their personal collection of artworks in what is now Florida's state art museum. Nearby, Ringling's Circus Museum documents his theatrical successes, while their lavish Venetian Gothic home, Cà d'Zan, reveals the impresario's extravagant tastes. Don't miss the PBS-produced film on Ringling's life, which is screened in the Circus Museum.

Sarasota

Sarasota

◉ Sights
1 Art Center Sarasota	A2
2 Island Park	B4
3 Marie Selby Botanical Gardens	C5
4 Marina Jack	B4

⌂ Sleeping
5 Hotel Indigo	B2
6 Hotel Ranola	C3

✖ Eating
7 Farmers Market	C3
8 Indigenous	D4
9 Main Bar Sandwich Shop	D3

Marina Jack's Restaurant	(see 4)
10 Owen's Fish Camp	C4

◐ Drinking & Nightlife
11 Jack Dusty	A3

✪ Entertainment
12 Burns Court Cinema	C4
13 McCurdy's Comedy Theatre	D3
14 Players Theatre	B2
15 Westcoast Black Theater Troupe	C1

⌂ Shopping
16 Towles Court Artist Colony	D4

➡ John & Mable Ringling Museum of Art

The Ringlings aspired to become serious art connoisseurs, and they amassed an impressive collection of 14th- to 18th-century European tapestries and paintings. Housed in a grand Mediterranean-style palazzo, the museum covers 21 galleries showcasing many Spanish and baroque works, and includes a world-renowned collection of Rubens canvases, including the *Triumph of the Eucharist* cycle. One wing presents some rotating exhibits and one permanent collection of contemporary art, and the Searing Wing offers *Joseph's Coat*, a stunning 3000-sq-ft James Turrell–designed 'Sky Space.' Opened in 2016, the newest wing contains historical and contemporary Asian art. Free on Mondays.

➡ Cà d'Zan

Ringling's winter home, Cà d'Zan (House of John; 1924–26), displays an unmistakable theatrical flair evocative of his two favorite Venetian hotels, the Danieli and the Bauer Grunwald. Ceilings are painted masterpieces, especially Willy Pogany's *Dancers of Nations* in the ballroom, and even the patio's zigzag marble fronting Sarasota Bay dazzles. Self-guided tours ($10) include the 1st floor's kitchens, taproom and opulent public spaces, while guided tours ($20) add the 2nd floor's stupendous bedrooms and bathrooms.

➡ Circus Museum

This is actually several museums in one, and they are as delightful as the circus itself. One building preserves the hand-carved animal wagons, calliopes and artifacts from Ringling Bros' original traveling show. Other exhibits trace the evolution of the circus from sideshow to Cirque du Soleil. Yet in the center ring, so to speak, is the miniature Howard Bros Circus: a truly epic re-creation at 1/12th scale of the entire Ringling Bros and Barnum & Bailey Circus in action. This intricately detailed work occupies its own building, and exists thanks to the 60-year labor of love of one man, Howard Tibbels.

Island Park   PARK

Sarasota's marina is notable for Island Park, an attractive green space poking into the harbor: it has a great playground and play fountain, restrooms, tree-shaded benches, a restaurant and tiki bar; and kayak, WaveRunner and boat rentals.

Marietta Museum of Art & Whimsy   MUSEUM

(☑ 941-364-3399; www.whimsymuseum.org; 2121 N Tamiami Trail; suggested donation $5; ☉ 1-4pm Wed-Sat) Dedicated to all things whimsical, this bright pink museum and its adjacent outdoor sculpture garden do not fail to inspire. Although exhibits rotate regularly, expect an abundance of hidden surprises, animal sculptures, trippy paintings, eclectic textiles and swing chairs to relax in.

Marie Selby Botanical Gardens   GARDENS

(☑ 941-366-5731; www.selby.org; 811 S Palm Ave; adult/child 4-11yr $20/10; ☉ 10am-5pm) If you visit just one botanical garden in Florida, choose Selby, which has the world's largest scientific collection of orchids and bromeliads – more than 20,000 species. Selby's genteel outdoor gardens are exceptionally well landscaped and relaxing, with 80-year-old banyan trees, koi ponds and splendid bay views. Art exhibits, a cafe and an enticing plant shop complete the experience.

Marina Jack   MARINA

(☑ 941-955-9488; www.marinajacks.com; 2 Marina Plaza) Sarasota's plush deep-water marina is within walking distance of downtown and is well served with alfresco and fine-dining restaurants, numerous sightseeing cruises and private charters. Head here for boat rentals, water sports, sailing and fishing charters.

St Armands Circle   SQUARE

(www.starmandscircleassoc.com) Conceived by John Ringling in the 1920s, St Armands Circle is an upscale outdoor mall surrounded by posh residences on St Armands Key. More so even than the downtown, this traffic circle is Sarasota's social center, where everyone strolls in the early evening, window shopping while enjoying a Kilwin's waffle cone. Numerous restaurants, from diners to fine dining, serve all day.

Art Center Sarasota   GALLERY

(☑ 941-365-2032; www.artsarasota.org; 707 N Tamiami Trail; donation $3; ☉ 10am-4pm Tue-Sat) This community-oriented nonprofit gallery has four exhibition spaces that mix local and out-of-town artists. Hosts frequent events, including a lecture series featuring local artists talking about what informs their artistic practice.

Activities

The pleasant, flat Legacy Trail is a 15-mile paved bike path that connects Sarasota to

Venice via the old railroad line that once transported the tents and animals of the Ringling Bros. and Barnum & Bailey Circus.

Myakka Outpost KAYAKING
(☑941-923-1120; www.myakkaoutpost.com; 13208 SR 72; canoes/bikes per hour $20/15; ⊙9:30am-5:30pm Sun-Fri, 8:30am-5:30pm Sat) A camp store and cafe, from where you can also organize tours and kayak, canoe and bike rentals for Myakka River State Park.

☞ Tours

★Siesta Key Rum DISTILLERY
(Drum Circle Distilling; ☑941-702-8143; www.drumcircledistilling.com; 2212 Industrial Blvd; ⊙noon-5pm Tue-Sat) FREE The oldest rum distillery in Florida offers an educational and intoxicating tour in its facility within an industrial park a bit outside of town. You'll learn the entire rum-making process from the company founder Troy, who is a gifted and hilarious public speaker. Delicious free samples at the end will likely result in purchases.

✲ Festivals & Events

★Forks & Corks FOOD & DRINK
(☑941-365-2800; info@dineoriginal.com; ⊙Jan) A multiday epicurean event held in venues throughout Sarasota, including the courtyard of the Ringling Museum of Art (p416). Includes food and wine tastings, vintner events, seminars, samples from local restaurants and entertainment.

Art & Craft Festivals ART
(www.artfestival.com; ⊙Mar) For two days in late March, an explosion of art and craft stalls dominates downtown Sarasota. The same happens in Siesta Village in late April.

Sarasota Film Festival FILM
(www.sarasotafilmfestival.com; ⊙Mar-Apr) If you enjoy seeing serious independent films and wearing your flip-flops to free outdoor screenings at the beach, then head to Sarasota's 10-day film festival.

Sailor Circus PERFORMING ARTS
(☑941-355-9805; http://circusarts.org; 2075 Bahia Vista St; adult/child $20/15; ⊙Apr; ⊡) One of the living circuses in Sarasota is performed by kids, and it's incredible. The Sailor Circus, founded in 1949, is a unique extracurricular activity for Sarasota County students, who gear up for one big show over

six days in April. They call it 'The Greatest Little Show on Earth,' but don't be fooled: there's nothing little about it.

It includes high wire and trapeze, hand balancing and unicycles, and innumerable midair ballets while dangling from tissues, rings and bars. If you miss the show, consider arranging a tour; customized individually, they include the big tent, costume shop, museum and – hopefully – attending practice. Bring your own kids; just know they will nurture, forever after, dreams of running away to the circus.

⌑ Sleeping

★Hotel Ranola BOUTIQUE HOTEL $$
(☑941-951-0111; www.hotelranola.com; 118 Indian Pl; r $109-179, ste $239-269; ⓟ❋⏽) The nine rooms feel like a designer's brownstone apartment: free-spirited and effortlessly artful, but with real working kitchens. It's urban funk, walkable to downtown Sarasota.

Hotel Indigo HOTEL $$$
(☑941-487-3800; www.srqhotel.com; 1223 Blvd of the Arts; r $300-420; ⓟ❋@⏽☲☷) A boutique-style chain that's reliable and attractive, as well as being close to downtown. Rooms are modern and comfortable, with murals depicting wildlife from Marie Selby Botanical Gardens. Good off-season discounts.

✗ Eating

★Jim's Small Batch Bakery BAKERY $
(☑941-922-2253; 2336 Gulf Gate Dr; items $1-10; ⊙8am-6pm Mon, to 4pm Tue-Thu, 9am-4pm Fri & Sat) Real small-batch, scratch baking makes Jim's a delicious stop for breakfast and lunch. All-butter hand-laminated croissants, candied bacon BLTs, creamy quiches, and cups of soup for $3.50.

Farmers Market MARKET $
(☑941-225-9256; www.sarasotafarmersmarket.org; 1420 State St; ⊙7am-1pm Sat) This farmers market is one of the best in the state.

Main Bar Sandwich Shop SANDWICHES $
(☑941-955-8733; www.themainbar.com; 1944 Main St; sandwiches from $7; ⊙10am-4pm Mon-Sat; ⊡) The Main Bar is a Sarasota classic: an old-school, booth-filled, diner-style deli founded by retired circus performers whose photos blanket the walls. It offers a ton of sandwiches, but – no kidding – order the 'famous' Italian, which instantly transports you to 1958 Brooklyn.

WORTH A TRIP

MYAKKA RIVER STATE PARK

Florida's oldest resident – the 200-million-year-old American alligator – is the star of this 39,000-acre **wildlife preserve** (☑941-361-6511; www.floridastateparks.org/park/Myakka-River; 13208 State Rd 72; car/bike $6/2; ☺8am-sunset). Between 500 and 1000 alligators make their home in Myakka's slow-moving river and its shallow, lily-filled lakes. You can get up close and personal via canoe, kayak and pontoon-style airboat. During mating season in April and May, the guttural love songs of the males ring out across the waters.

The extensive park offers much more besides: its hammocks, marshes, pine flat-woods and prairies are home to a great variety of birds and wildlife, and 38 miles of trails crisscross the terrain. In winter, airboat trips (adult/child $15/7.50) depart at 10am, 11:30am, 1pm and 2:30pm; call for summer times. Winter-only wildlife trams run at 11:30am, 1pm and 2:30pm and cost the same.

Camping (sites $27.12) is prime during dry season, from January to April; avoid rainy, buggy summer. The five cabins ($70 per night) have kitchens, air-con and linens. Book through www.reserveamerica.com.

To reach the park from Sarasota, take US 41 south to Hwy 72/Clark Rd and head east for about 14 miles; the park is about 9 miles east of I-75.

★ **Indigenous** MODERN AMERICAN $$
(☑941-706-4740; www.indigenoussarasota.com; 239 S Links Ave; mains $14-26; ☺5:30-8:30pm Tue-Sat) Focusing on the popular farm-to-table and hook-to-fork movements, chef Steve Phelps whips up innovative American creations such as Parmesan beignets with honey, pears and thyme, and an ever-popular wild mushroom bisque. Indigenous is housed in a funky, Old Florida bungalow with a broad deck and an intimate 'wine cottage' serving biodynamic and small-production wine labels.

★ **Owen's Fish Camp** SOUTHERN US $$
(☑941-951-6936; www.owensfishcamp.com; 516 Burns Lane; mains $10-28; ☺4pm-9:30pm Sun-Thu, to 10:30pm Fri & Sat) The wait rarely dips below an hour at this hip, Old Florida swamp shack downtown. The menu consists of upscale Southern cuisine with an emphasis on seafood, including whatever's fresh, and solid regular dishes like scallops with braised pork, succotash and grits. Those willing to eat in the courtyard order at the bar, which also serves wine and craft beer.

Monk's Steamer Bar SEAFOOD $$
(☑941-927-3388; www.monkssteamerbar.com; 6690 Superior Ave; mains $7-30; ☺4pm-1am Mon-Fri, noon-1am Sat & Sun) Order a spicy oyster shooter (a Bloody Mary with an oyster in it) or oyster 'Monkafellas' (baked with signature toppings) and watch bar staff expertly shuck the gnarly shells in front of you. Or guzzle 2lb of sweet, steamed mussels or

Cajun crawdads (crayfish) before lining up for a game of pool at this ever-popular local sports bar.

Madison Avenue Cafe & Deli CAFE $$
(☑941-388-3354; www.madisoncafesarasota.com; 28 Blvd of the Presidents, St Armands Circle; items $10-12; ☺8am-5pm; 🔊☑) One of the most popular places on the Circle, this upscale cafe has outdoor seating and a generous menu of sandwiches, wraps and salads. Everything is made fresh to order, and sandwiches come bursting with deli meats, crunchy veg and thick slabs of cheese.

Antoine's Restaurant EUROPEAN $$$
(☑941-331-1400; www.antoinessarasota.com; 1100 N Tuttle Ave; mains $19-33; ☺5-9pm Thu-Tue) Newly relocated to an otherwise un-exciting strip mall, Antoine's is a French bistro serving elegant dishes such as scallop risotto with a candied, tangerine sauce. But this isn't faddish fusion food: the owners hail from Belgium and the restaurant reflects a classic European style. Save room for the Belgian chocolate desserts; you won't regret it.

Marina Jack's Restaurant SEAFOOD $$$
(☑941-365-4232; www.marinajacks.com; 2 Marina Plaza; sandwiches $9-13, mains $25-34; ☺11:15am-10pm) Anchoring the marina is this well-loved multilevel, multivenue eatery that offers something for everyone, but most especially that quintessential harbor-at-sunset ambience. Be serenaded by steel drums in the relaxed downstairs cafe and

lounge, with expansive outdoor seating, tropical cocktails and an easy-on-the-wallet menu. The Bayfront dining room upstairs positions formal tables before curving, two-story windows and serves surf 'n' turf; make reservations.

Drinking & Nightlife

Perq COFFEE
(www.perqcoffeebar.com; 1821 Hillview St; ⊙7am-5pm Mon-Fri, 8am-5pm Sat & Sun) Sophisticated brewing methods and sourcing of single-origin beans make Perq the best third-wave coffee bar in Sarasota.

Green Bean Coffee House COFFEE
(☑941-355-0205; www.thegreenbeancoffeehousecafe.com; 3521 Bradenton Rd; ⊙9am-4pm Mon-Sat; 🛜) In north Sarasota, this environmentally conscious coffee shop (lunch $5 to $10) serves up tasty coffee wraps, salads and breakfasts filled with vegetables from the nearby community garden and poultry products from their own backyard chickens. With wood floors and lots of local art on the walls, the place feels super homey – likely because the owners built the business within their own home.

Jack Dusty BAR
(Ritz-Carlton; ☑941-309-2266; http://jackdusty.com; 1111 Ritz-Carlton Dr; ⊙7am-11pm) The Ritz-Carlton's gold-trimmed restaurant features one of the sexiest drinking dens in town, with a marble bar, delicious Mote Marina oysters and terrace seating with Gulf views. The bar is headed up by mixologist Candice Marie, who devises sought-after cocktails such as the smoking jacket, with Four Roses single-barrel bourbon, Angostura bitters, burnt sugar syrup and a smoked glass.

☆ Entertainment

Circus Arts Conservatory CIRCUS
(☑941-355-9335, box office 941-355-9805; http://circusarts.org; 2075 Bahia Vista St; ⊙9am-5pm Mon-Fri) In addition to putting on the ever-popular Sailor Circus (p419) each year, this circus center offers professional performances along with circus training and summer camp. The performances are usually held in a one-ring European-style big top, and feature Circus Sarasota, a traditional troupe, and Cirque des Voix, which combines singing and orchestral performance with circus arts.

Tickets for performances run between $15 and $55, and most of the revenue goes toward community outreach efforts; for example, a humor therapy program.

Westcoast Black Theater Troupe THEATER
(☑941-366-1505; www.wbttsrq.org; 1646 10th Way; tickets $20-40) One of only two African American theater ventures in Florida, WBTT has a reputation for high-quality musicals and thought-provoking dramas. Through the company's mentorship numerous national and international careers have been launched.

Asolo Repertory Theatre THEATER
(☑941-351-8000; www.asolorep.org; 5555 N Tamiami Trail; tickets $20-50; ⊙Nov-Jul) This lauded regional theater company is also an acting conservatory (in partnership with Florida State University). It presents a mix of commissioned works, classics and current Tony-winning dramas on two main stages. The Sarasota Ballet (www.sarasotaballet.org) also performs here.

McCurdy's Comedy Theatre COMEDY
(☑941-925-3869; www.mccurdyscomedy.com; 1923 Ringling Blvd; tickets $20) Within the walls of this recently remodeled, bright-purple venue in the heart of historic downtown Sarasota, a rotating cast of stand-up comedians put on intimate and highly entertaining shows. The theater also houses a bar, the Green Room, and the Humor Institute, which helps aspiring comedians develop stand-up and performance skills and routines.

Burns Court Cinema CINEMA
(☑941-955-3456; 506 Burns Lane) This wee theater in an alleyway off Pineapple Ave presents independent and foreign films. It's run by the Sarasota Film Society (SFS; www.filmsociety.org), which screens more than 40 of the year's best international films in November during the annual 10-day CINE-World Film Festival.

Players Theatre THEATER
(☑941-365-2494; www.theplayers.org; 838 N Tamiami Trail; tickets from $20) This highly regarded nonprofit community theater stages popular Broadway musicals, new plays and collaborations.

🛍 Shopping

Towles Court Artist Colony ARTS & CRAFTS
(www.towlescourt.com; 1938 Adams Lane; ⊙11am-4pm Tue-Sat) A dozen or so hip galleries occupy quirky, parrot-colored bungalows in this artists colony. The most lively time to

be here is during the art walk on the third Friday of each month (6pm to 9pm). Outside of this, individual gallery hours can be whimsical.

🛈 Getting There & Away

Sarasota is roughly 60 miles south of Tampa and about 75 miles north of Fort Myers. The main roads into town are Tamiami Trail/US 41 and I-75.

Greyhound (☑ 941-342-1720; www.greyhound. com; 5951 Porter Way; ⊙ 8:30am-10am & 1:30pm-6pm) Connects Sarasota with Miami, Fort Myers and Tampa.

Sarasota-Bradenton International Airport (SRQ; Map p392; ☑ 941-359-2770; www. srq-airport.com; 6000 Airport Circle) Served by many major airlines. Go north on Hwy 41, and right on University Ave.

🛈 Getting Around

Sarasota isn't that big, but sights are spread out and not well served by public transportation. You'll also want your own car to explore Sarasota's Keys; while Lido and St Armands are really just extensions of downtown, Anna Maria Island is 16 miles north.

Sarasota County Area Transit (SCAT; ☑ 941-861-5000; www.scgov.net/SCAT; cnr 1st St & Lemon Ave; fares $1.25; ⊙ 6am-6:30pm Mon-Sat) Buses have no transfers or Sunday service. Bus 4 connects Ringling Blvd with St Armands Circle and Lido Key Beach; bus 11 heads to Siesta Key.

Sarasota Keys

For sun-worshippers and salty dogs alike, Sarasota's Keys offer an irresistible combination of fabulous beaches, laid-back living and endless watery pursuits. Geographically the Keys are a series of barrier islands that stretch 35 miles from south of Sarasota north to Anna Maria Island, across the causeway from Bradenton. Each has its own distinct identity, but all offer access to miles of glorious beach.

◉ Sights

★ Anna Maria Island   ISLAND

The perfect antidote to party-loving Siesta Key, Anna Maria Island appears beached in a 1950s time warp, with sun-faded clapboard houses, teenagers hanging outside ice-cream stores and a clutch of good seafood restaurants. The island is made up of three beach towns: at the southern end is Bradenton Beach, midisland is Holmes Beach, which is

considered the hub, and at the northern tip is Anna Maria village.

The best beaches are to the south and north. Southern **Coquina Beach** has plenty of pavilions, lifeguards and restrooms, and is backed by a stand of Australian pines through which the **Coquina Bay Walk** meanders. To the north, **Anna Maria Bayfront Park** sits on Tampa Bay, offering views of the Sunshine Skyway Bridge, plus a playground and restrooms. The latter is within walking distance of the **City Pier** and the center of Anna Maria. The northernmost, lesser-visited and thoroughly gorgeous beach is **Bean Point.**

Siesta Key   BEACH

At 8 miles long, Siesta Key is most popular beach hangout in the area, with a family-friendly village and a public beach of pure quartz sand so fine it's like confectioners' sugar. The enormous parking lot (at the corner of Beach Rd and Beach Way) has an information booth dispensing info on all types of activities and water sports (parasailing, Jet Ski rental, kayaks, bikes and more), plus nice facilities, a snack bar and covered eating areas.

Mote Marine Laboratory   AQUARIUM

(☑ 941-388-4441; www.mote.org; 1600 Ken Thompson Pkwy, City Island; adult/child $20/15; ⊙ 10am-5pm) The Mote bills itself as a research facility and aquarium, and has a large department dedicated to the study of sharks. Exhibits include a preserved giant squid (37ft long when caught) and a shark tank where you can watch training sessions in action. In a separate building the aquarium organizes encounters with sea turtles, manatees, otters and alligators. It may seem like a lovely idea, but studies show that interaction with sea creatures held in captivity creates stress for them.

Lido Key   ISLAND

Just a hop, skip and jump across from St Armands Circle, Lido Key is barely 15-minutes' drive from downtown Sarasota. Lido Beach is an excellent, wide stretch of white sand backed by a number of nature trails. Street and lot parking is free, so expect crowds. A pavilion at the parking lot has food, restrooms and even a small lap **swimming pool** (☑ 941-954-4182; 400 Benjamin Franklin Dr; adult/child 4-11yr $4/2; ⊙ 10am-4:45pm Tue-Sun). About a mile south is South Lido Beach, whose grills and grassy lawns are extremely popular with picnicking families; strong currents here discourage swimming.

Pine Avenue
GARDENS

(http://pineavenueinfo.com; Pine Ave; ⏰24hr) **FREE** Headed up by former Florida governor Lawton Chiles' son Ed, the restoration of Anna Maria's 'historic boutique business district' has the island abuzz. The renovated, brightly colored homes, boutiques, restaurants and galleries are delightful enough, but tourists will flip for the edible teaching garden out front, with 30 planter boxes filled with stuff like Ethopian kale and Chinese spinach. Delicious.

👉 Tours

Sarasota Bay Explorers
BOATING

(☏941-388-4200; www.sarasotabayexplorers.com; 1600 Ken Thompson Pkwy, Mote Marine Laboratory) Under the supervision of marine biologists, boat cruises trawl a net and then examine the sponges, sea horses and various fish caught. The marine safari (adult/child $45/40) heads out to Lido Key and nearby sandbars where participants get out into the grass flats to commune with crabs, sea horses and sea stars under the guidance of a marine biologist.

It also offers guided kayak tours (adult/child $55/45). To get to Mote Marine Laboratory, head to St Armands Circle in Sarasota, then take John Ringling Blvd north to Ken Thompson Pkwy; follow to end.

🛏 Sleeping

Turtle Beach Campground
CAMPGROUND $

(☏941-861-2267; 8862 Midnight Pass Rd, Siesta Key; campsites $32-60; P🐾) This county-operated campground is small, caters to RVs, has little privacy and doesn't allow campfires. But it's well worth camping here to be mere steps from Turtle Beach and a quick drive from Sarasota. Max vehicle length is 38ft.

Hayley's Motel
MOTEL $$

(☏941-778-5405; www.haleysmotel.com; 8102 Gulf Dr, Anna Maria Island; r from $199; P🌺🐾) Owner-operated Hayley's offers motel rooms, one-bedroom suites and buckets of 1950s charm. Super-quaint and competitively priced for Anna Maria. You'll find it about a block back from Holmes Beach. There's a $50 fee for pets, though they aren't allowed in high season (February to April) and the beaches on Anna Maria don't allow dogs.

★Harrington House
B&B $$$

(☏941-778-5444; www.harringtonhouse.com; 5626 Gulf Dr, Anna Maria Island; ste/bungalows from $220/254; P🌺🐾) Sneak away to this beachside B&B and fantasize about your own little seaside paradise. Made up of three former beach houses, the B&B's guest suites and bungalows have sun porches overlooking an idyllic beach. Common rooms ooze Old Florida charm with their wing-back armchairs, mahogany sideboards and candelabra lights. Children under 12 are discouraged.

Siesta Key Inn
APARTMENT $$$

(☏941-349-4999; www.siestakeyinn.com; 1017 Point of Rocks Rd, Siesta Key; r Feb-Apr $269-329, May-Jan $179-249; P🌺🐾) These beachy suites sit within a tropical garden a few steps from the shore and the Crescent Beach shops. And when they say these suites are fully equipped, they mean it. Aside from the usual beach chairs and towels, you'll find beach coolers, beach toys, car seats, snorkeling equipment and even in-line skates.

🍴 Eating

Lélu Coffee Lounge
CAFE $

(☏941-346-5358; www.lelucoffee.com; 5251 Ocean Blvd, Siesta Key; items $5.50-13; ⏰7am-7:30pm Sun-Wed & Fri, to 10pm Thu & Sat) Look no further than this retro coffee lounge for laid-back lounging over your early-morning espresso or honey latte. Surfboards dangle from the ceiling; comfortable sofas beckon; and there's a short menu of fruit smoothies, plenty of vegan options and smashed omelets stuffed with local produce. Come nightfall there's a martini bar, open mike and jazz events.

Ginny's & Jane E's
CAFE $

(☏941-778-3170; www.ginnysandjanees.com; 9807 Gulf Dr, Anna Maria Island; items $2-12; ⏰7:30am-4pm; 🐾) Housed in an old village grocery, this unique cafe, coffee-and-ice-cream bar and vintage shop sells furniture, flip-flops, and outsider art and trinkets. The sandwiches are divine, as is the giant hunk of Connie Wolgast's pecan pie. Plop down on the sofa next to other beachcombers; this place is made for socializing.

Sandbar
SEAFOOD $$

(☏941-778-0444; http://sandbar.groupersandwich.com; 100 Spring Ave; mains $15-28; ⏰11am-9pm Sun-Thu, to 10pm Fri & Sat) 🍴 A long-standing favorite haunt, the Sandbar offers casual dining with toes in the sand, local food on the plate, and a heaping side of innovation. For instance, the caramelized pork slider contains 'local wild hog,' which is part of an effort to control feral pig populations. Although some of the seafood is a bit mediocre, the setting is unbeatable.

Dry Dock
SEAFOOD $$
(🖉 941-383-0102; www.drydockwaterfrontgrill. com; 412 Gulf of Mexico Dr, Longboat Key; mains $7-19; ⊙ 11am-9pm Sun-Thu, to 10pm Fri & Sat) With a deck overhanging the water and panoramic views from its upstairs dining room impeded only by shady palm fronds, it's hard to beat Dry Dock for waterside dining. Match that with excellent blackened or grilled grouper sandwiches, a half-pound chargrilled burger and Caribbean shrimp tacos and you'll see why the wait time is usually around 40 minutes.

★ Beach Bistro
MODERN AMERICAN $$$
(🖉 941-778-6444; www.beachbistro.com; 6600 Gulf Dr, Anna Maria Island; mains $20-60; ⊙ 5-10pm) Sean Murphy's Beach Bistro is Anna Maria's best date night. Perfectly executed Floridian dishes showcase the best locally and nationally sourced farm products, including fresh line-caught seafood, Hudson Valley foie gras and prime USA beef tenderloin. The Bistro Bouillabaisse is legendary, stacked with lobster tail, jumbo shrimp, shellfish and calamari, and stewed in a fresh tomato, saffron and anise flavored broth.

Cottage
FUSION $$$
(🖉 941-312-9300; www.cottagesiestakey.com; 153 Avenida Messina, Siesta Key; tapas $9-15, mains $20-30; ⊙ 11am-10pm Sun-Thu, to 11pm Fri & Sat) Siesta Key's hottest restaurant has a recently revamped menu with innovative items like guava slaw, slow-braised Korean short ribs and Hawaiian escolar, which comes with corn and edamame succotash and bathed in a lobster and crab velouté sauce. Pair with a frozen *mojito*. The result is perfection.

🍸 Drinking & Nightlife

Doctor's Office
COCKTAIL BAR
(🖉 941-213-9926; https://doctorsofficeami.com; 5312 Holmes Blvd, Anna Maria Island; ⊙ 5-11:45pm) With an eye chart, old filing cabinets and a 'doctor's in' sign on the door, this new craft cocktail establishment makes certain customers are aware that yes, this was once an actual doctor's office! There's no need

for such um, cleverness, as the cocktails are fresh and delicious, and the atmosphere lively and elegant.

Gilligan's Island Bar & Grill
BAR
(🖉 941-346-8122; www.gilligansislandbar.net; 5253 Ocean Blvd, Siesta Village; ⊙ 11am-2am) Classic Florida thatched-roof tiki-bar vibe, with VW bus, outdoor courtyard and strong cocktails. Live music.

Beach Club
BAR
(🖉 941-349-6311; www.beachclubsiestakey.com; 5151 Ocean Blvd, Siesta Village; ⊙ 11am-2am) Cavernous bar with pool tables, a stage, a great white shark and giant Connect Four. Live music often; ladies' night every Wednesday.

❶ Getting There & Away

➜ Anna Maria Island can be accessed via Manatee Ave and Cortes Rd, and it's possible to drive south from there to Longboat Key (which is also accessible from Lido Key to the south).

➜ John Ringling Blvd will take you to Lido Key from the mainland.

➜ Siesta Key can be reached via Siesta Dr and Stickney Point Rd.

➜ A car keeps things simple, but there are also MCAT (🖉 941-749-7116; www.ridemcat.org/bus-routes; ⊙ 5:30am-8pm Mon-Sat) trolleys and buses between Anna Maria Island and Longboat Key, and SCAT (🖉 941-861-5000; rides/7-day passes $1.25/20; ⊙ 5:20am-8:40pm Mon-Sat) buses that run between Sarasota and Lido and Siesta Keys.

Venice
🖉 941 / POP 21,253
About the only resemblance Venice has to its Italian namesake is that it's an island in the sea. Venice has scenic, tan-sand beaches but is otherwise a quiet seaside town that's most popular with retirees and families with young kids, who enjoy hunting for sharks' teeth. It also appeals to budget-minded travelers looking for a low-key getaway – far from the condos and hard-drinking beach bars elsewhere. Here entertainment pretty much begins and ends with saluting the tangerine sun's nightly descent into the shimmering ocean.

⊙ Sights

Nokomis Beach
BEACH
(www.nokomisbeachflorida.com; 100 Casey Key Rd, Nokomis) North of Venice on Casey Key,

HISTORIC SPANISH POINT

Explore layers of history at this environmental and archaeological site, which covers a 30-acre peninsula jutting out into Little Sarasota Bay. Covered in shell middens, small pioneer cottages, a chapel and a citrus packing house, the peninsula was bought in 1910 by wealthy widow Bertha Potter Palmer, one of Sarasota's most dynamic entrepreneurs. A museum on the property tells her story beside a unique excavated shell midden and several pioneer homesteads and outbuildings.

Oddly, there were never any Spaniards at **Historic Spanish Point** (☎941-966-5214; www.historicspanishpoint.org; 337 N Tamiami Trail, Osprey; adult/child 5-12yr $12/5; ◷9am-5pm Mon-Sat, noon-5pm Sun). Instead the name derives from a friendly Spanish trader who tipped off early settlers John and Eliza Webb about the idyllic location when they were searching for land to farm in 1867. The narrow peninsula stretches out into Little Sarasota Bay, with an undulating landscape of prehistoric middens covered in tropical foliage. Eventually the Webbs accumulated the entire peninsula, which they planted with citrus they shipped to market in Cedar Key and Key West. Wander the 1-mile trail (tours via electric cart are also available) around the site and you can see the wooden packing house, Mary's Chapel, the Webb-family cemetery and Frank Guptill's beautiful wooden homestead, which he built for their daughter Lizzie.

The Webbs farmed here for more than 40 years before selling the land to Bertha Palmer in 1910. The prominent Chicago real-estate developer and cofounder of Marshall Field and Company treasured the beauty of the place when she selected it as the anchor of her 350-acre winter estate. She left intact the shell middens as well as the Webb homestead, outbuildings and chapel while developing her gardens in keeping with the tropical landscape. Now pergolas, classic Greek columns, lawns and flower gardens punctuate the wild foliage.

To cap it all, between 1959 and 1962 the Smithsonian Institution partially excavated one of the shell middens. You can enter the mound and see what the layers of shell deposits and prehistoric paraphernalia look like from the inside. It's the only such site in Florida and is quite fascinating. Viewed altogether, the Point offers a unique narrative of Florida's prehistoric and pioneering history.

Nokomis is yet another attractive, low-key beach. Its 'minimalist'-style beach pavilion is an intriguing architectural bauble; it has nice facilities but no kiosks (so bring lunch). Also, an hour before sundown on Wednesday and Saturday nights things get groovy: the **Nokomis Beach Drum Circle** gathers and its rhythm draws upward of several hundred folks. To get to Nokomis Beach take US 41 N to Albee Rd W.

Caspersen Beach   BEACH
One-and-a-half miles south of Venice Pier along Harbor Dr, Caspersen is famous for the fossilized prehistoric sharks' teeth that wash up. Most teeth are the size of a fingernail, but occasionally finger-long specimens are found. Its attractive, palmetto-backed sand, playground and paved bike path also make Caspersen popular; there are facilities but no kiosks.

Venice Train Depot   HISTORIC BUILDING
(☎941-412-0151; www.veniceareahistoricalsociety. org; 303 E Venice Ave) Built in 1927 the historic Venice Train Depot was the last stop on the line for the Seaboard Air Line Railway that extended south from Tampa to Sarasota. Passenger trains stopped coming in 1971 and freighters in 1997, but Sarasota County restored the depot to its original condition and opened it to the public in 2003. There are free, docent-led tours offered by the Venice Area Historical Society.

Venice Beach   BEACH
Where W Venice Ave dead-ends you'll find a covered beach pavilion with restrooms and a snack bar. There's free yoga on the sand daily at 8am and 9am (and also at 5pm on Monday, Thursday and Saturday), and free acoustic music from Saturday to Wednesday from around 5pm to 8pm. Sea turtles nest on Venice Beach from May to October.

🏃 Activities

Warm Mineral Springs   SPA
(☎941-426-1692; www.scgov.net/warmmineral springs; 12200 San Servando Ave; adult/child

$20/15; ⊙9am-5pm) Was this warm mineral spring the actual fountain of youth Ponce de León was hunting? So they say. And it's an appropriate fable for this Old Florida throwback. The spring's 84–87°F (28.8–30.5°C) waters, which have the highest mineral content of any in the US, have long been a favored health tonic for elderly Eastern Europeans.

🛏 Sleeping

Banyan House
RENTAL HOUSE $$

(☑941-484-1385; www.banyanhouse.com; 519 S Harbor Dr; weekly $550-750; P ❋ 🛜 🐾) Suites and apartments within one of Venice's grand old homes are available for weekly rental. They all share a heated pool, a lemon-yellow sunroom, a billiards room and a hammock beneath the namesake banyan tree.

★ Inn at the Beach
RESORT $$$

(☑941-484-8471; www.innatthebeach.com; 725 W Venice Ave; r $225-350, ste $353-515; ❋ @ 🛜 🐾) Right across from the beach and a perfect choice for an extended stay, this well-managed hotel-style resort worries about the details so you don't have to. Each room's attractive palette of cream yellow, burnt umber and sage avoids seaside cliches, and the fully functional kitchenettes are a pleasure to cook in.

🍴 Eating & Drinking

Robbi's Reef
SEAFOOD $

(☑941-485-9196; www.robbisreef.com; 775 Hwy 41 By-Pass S; mains $8-15; ⊙11am-9pm Tue-Thu & Sun, to 10pm Fri & Sat) This perfect simulacrum of a harbor seafood shack is incongruously sited in a strip mall a half mile south of Venice Ave. From the walls crammed with fishing photos to the flagstone bar to the unpretentious, delicious cooking, you'd swear you were at the docks. Fish tacos and Bayou Willy's pasta get high marks.

★ Crow's Nest
Marina Restaurant
SEAFOOD $$

(☑941-484-9551; www.crowsnest-venice.com; 1968 Tarpon Center Dr; mains lunch $10-15, dinner $20-41; ⊙11:30am-10pm Mon-Wed & Sun, to 11pm Thu, to 12:30am Fri & Sat,) With Venice Inlet and marina views from an elegant 2nd-floor dining room within a restored Victorian, this is a longtime surf 'n' turf favorite. Popular dishes include the filet mignon and the Key Largo grouper, and do save space for the key lime pie. Downstairs offers a more tavern-y

vibe, and a charming gazebo and stained-glass windows throughout add style points.

Outside, kayaks and electric boats are available for rent.

Ristorante San Marco
ITALIAN $$

(☑941-254-6565; http://sanmarcovenice.com; 305 W Venice Ave; mains lunch $13-17, dinner $19-26; ⊙11am-2:45pm & 5-9:30pm Mon-Sat, 5-9:30pm Sun) Superlative southern Italian cuisine served in a romantic art-filled dining room. All breads and pastas are made on site and daily specials showcase seasonal ingredients. Reservations advised.

Fins at Sharky's
FUSION $$$

(☑941-786-3068; www.finsatsharkys.com; 1600 Harbor Dr S; sushi $8-16, mains $26-36; ⊙noon-2:30pm & 4-10pm) Head upstairs from Sharky's (p426) for well-executed sushi, prime cuts of mesquite-charcoal-grilled meat and sophisticated seafood dishes such as pan-seared, orange-glazed golden tilefish. The floor-to-ceiling window in the dining room offers excellent views of the Venice Pier and shoreline.

Sharky's on the Pier
BAR

(☑941-488-1456; www.sharkysonthepier.com; 1600 Harbor Dr S; ⊙11:30am-10pm Sun-Thu, to midnight Fri & Sat) With the prime sunset spot at **Venice Pier**, Sharky's doesn't have to try too hard. It's a typical, middle-of-the-road seafood restaurant (mains $10 to $27) featuring good grouper sandwiches, frozen drinks and a tiki bar perfectly positioned for evening's magic moment.

ℹ Getting There & Away

From US 41/Tamiami Trail, Venice Ave heads west directly to Venice Beach. About five blocks east of the beach, the main downtown commercial district lies along W Venice Ave between US 41 and Harbor Dr.

Fort Myers

☑239 / POP 68,190

Nestled inland along the Caloosahatchee River, and separated from Fort Myers Beach by several miles of urban sprawl, the city of Fort Myers is often defined by what it's not: it's not an upscale, arty beach town like Sarasota or Naples, and it's not as urbanely sophisticated as Tampa or St Petersburg. While it isn't a city to base a trip around, it's worth a trip to browse its brick-lined main street and visit Thomas Edison's winter home and laboratory.

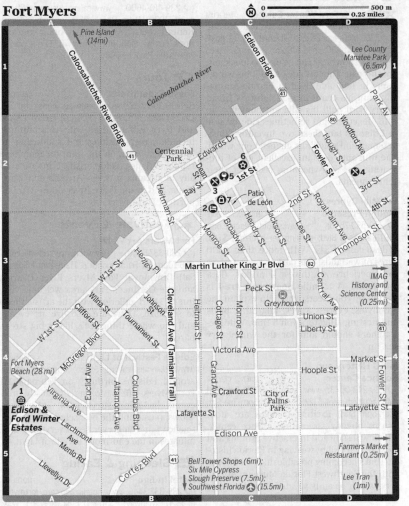

Fort Myers

0 — 500 m
0 — 0.25 miles

Fort Myers

◎ Top Sights
1 Edison & Ford Winter
  Estates A4

🛏 Sleeping
2 Hotel Indigo C2

🍴 Eating
3 City Tavern C2
  Twisted Vine Bistro .... (see 3)

4 Wisteria Tea Room D2

🍷 Drinking & Nightlife
5 Firestone Sky Bar C2

✪ Entertainment
6 Arcade Theatre C2

🛍 Shopping
7 Franklin Shops C2

◉ Sights & Activities

★ Edison & Ford Winter Estates   MUSEUM

(☑ 239-334-7419; www.edisonfordwinterestates. org; 2350 McGregor Blvd; adult/child $20/12, guided tours adult $30, child $18-25; ⊙ 9am-5:30pm) Florida's snowbirds can be easy to mock, but not this pair. Thomas Edison built his winter home in 1885 and lived in Florida seasonally until his death in 1931. Edison's friend Henry Ford built his adjacent bungalow in 1916. Together, and sometimes side by side in **Edison's lab**, these two inventors, businessmen and neighbors changed our world. The **museum** does an excellent job of presenting the overwhelming scope of their achievements.

Six Mile Cypress Slough Preserve   NATURE RESERVE

(☑ 239-533-7550; www.sloughpreserve.org; 7791 Penzance Blvd; parking per hour/day $1/5; ⊙ dawn-dusk) **FREE** With more than 3500 acres of wetlands, this park is a great place to experience southwest Florida's flora and fauna. A 1.2-mile **boardwalk trail** is staffed by volunteers who help explain the epiphytes, cypress knees, migrating birds and nesting alligators you'll find. Wildlifewatchers should aim for the winter dry season.

IMAG History and Science Center   SCIENCE CENTER

(☑ 239-243-0043; www.i-sci.org; 2000 Cranford Ave; adult/student $12/8; ⊙ 10am-5pm Tue-Sat, noon-5pm Sun) Exciting changes are afoot at this already fascinating science center, which will soon add interactive exhibits and even virtual reality, weaving in Florida history. That's becoming possible due to a merger with the Southwest Florida Museum of History, which recently vacated its old historic railroad depot and began moving various objects into IMAG, including a diorama of the military fort for which Fort Myers is named.

Lee County Manatee Park   WILDLIFE RESERVE

(☑ 239-690-5030; www.leeparks.org; 10901 State Rd 80; parking per hour/day $2/5; ⊙ sunrisesunset daily) **FREE** December through March, manatees flock up the Orange River to this warm-water discharge canal from the nearby power plant. The waterway is now a protected sanctuary, with a landscaped park and playground in addition to viewing platforms at water's edge, where manatees swim almost at arm's reach.

Calusa Blueway Outfitters   KAYAKING

(☑ 239-481-4600; www.calusabluewayoutfitters. com; 10901 Palm Beach Blvd; ⊙ 9am-3:30pm) Rents kayaks (from $15 per hour) and canoes (from $20 per hour) at Lee County Manatee Park (p428).

⌲ Tours

Fossil Expeditions   BOATING

(☑ 239-368-3252; www.fossilexpeditions.com; 213 Lincoln Ave; ⊙ hours vary) Small-group kayak and river-walking trips with this outfitter include screen-washing and snorkeling in knee-deep water, on the hunt for mammal, reptile and megalodon fossils. Trips are usually in streams between Arcadia and Wauchula, and in the Peace River, 45 to 70 miles north of Fort Myers.

✻ Festivals & Events

Fort Myers Art Walk   ART

(☑ 239-337-5050; www.fortmyersartwalk.com; ⊙ 6-10pm 1st Fri of month & 11am-4pm following Sat) Downtown Fort Myers River District and the Gardner's Park area welcome visitors to 14 art galleries, with the artists there to socialize. There are also live art events and the whole thing feels like a big street party.

Edison Festival of Light   CULTURAL

(www.edisonfestival.org; ⊙ Feb) For two weeks around Edison's birthday on February 11, Fort Myers offers dozens of mostly free events including street fairs, antique-car shows, music and the best school-sponsored science fair you'll ever see. Everything culminates in the enormous Parade of Light.

🛏 Sleeping & Eating

Hotel Indigo   HOTEL $$

(☑ 239-337-3446; www.hotelindigo.com/fortmyers fl; 1520 Broadway; r $109-419; ✳ @ 🕈 🌊) Now anchoring the downtown historic district, this boutique chain makes an attractive, reliable stay. The 67 rooms have powder-blue comforters, wall murals, a mix of wood floors and carpets, and snazzy glass-door showers. The kicker is the small rooftop pool and bar, with panoramic views of the scenic riverfront. Valet parking costs $18.

Wisteria Tea Room   CAFE $

(☑ 239-689-4436; http://wisteriatearoom.com; 2512 2nd St; lunch items $5-12, afternoon tea $9-24; ⊙ 11am-3pm Mon-Sat) Housed in a remodeled Florida bungalow, this quaint tearoom is a favorite ladies lunch spot. Beat them to it, as the thick slabs of quiche, homemade sweet-and-spicy turkey sandwiches and fragrant asparagus soup are excellent. And that's to say nothing of the outstanding savory teas, which come with tiers of apricot scones and dollops of Devonshire cream.

Farmers Market Restaurant　　SOUTHERN US $$
(📞239-334-1687; http://farmersmarketrestaurant.com; 2736 Edison Ave; mains $12-14; ⊙6am-8pm Mon-Sat, 7am-7pm Sun) Pleasing diners with its simple Southern comfort food since the 1950s, this modest place has a loyal local following. It's nothing fancy, but if you're hankering after some fried chicken and mustard greens or whitefish and grits, this is the place for you. It's a five-minute drive southwest of downtown.

City Tavern　　AMERICAN $$
(📞239-226-1133; www.mycitytavern.com; 2206 Bay St; mains $8-16; ⊙11am-2am) This former dive bar may have retained the TVs, dartboards and pool table, but TV chef Brian Duffy has revamped its tired menu and brew list to include packed *muffuletta* and Cuban sandwiches, and craft brews.

★**Twisted Vine Bistro**　　AMERICAN $$$
(📞239-226-1687; www.twistedvinebistro.com; 2214 Bay St; mains $22-36; ⊙11am-10pm Mon-Thu, to 11pm Fri & Sat, 10am-9pm Sun) Two words: truffle fries. OK, a few more words. This cozy American restaurant and boutique wine bar specializes in surf 'n' turf, offering certified Angus beef and mouthwatering seafood, along with fantastic salads, soups, artisanal cheeses, and herbs and spices straight from the courtyard garden. On weekends, there's also live entertainment. But seriously, did we mention the truffle fries?

🍷 **Drinking & Nightlife**

Firestone Sky Bar　　ROOFTOP BAR
(📞239-334-3473; www.firestonefl.com; 2224 Bay St; ⊙4pm-late) Want to feel like you're above it all in Fort Myers? Firestone Sky Bar is the only rooftop, waterfront drinking establishment in the downtown area, so you're gonna want to get your VIP bottle service here. On weekends, those that feel like shakin' it can head downstairs to the martini bar, where there's a dance floor and neon purple lighting.

☆ **Entertainment**

★**Arcade Theatre**　　THEATER
(📞239-332-4488; www.floridarep.org; 2267 1st St; tickets $25-52; ⊙Oct-May) The 1908 Arcade

Theatre is home to the **Florida Repertory Theatre**, one of the best regional theaters in the state. It produces popular comedies, musicals and recent Tony winners, such as *The Seafarer*.

JetBlue Park　　STADIUM
(📞239-334-4700; http://boston.redsox.mlb.com/bos/ballpark/jetblue_park.jsp; 11500 Fenway S Dr) March in Fort Myers means major-league baseball's spring training. Boston Red Sox (www.redsox.com) fans literally camp out for tickets to JetBlue Park on Hwy 876.

🔒 **Shopping**

Franklin Shops　　ARTS & CRAFTS
(📞239-333-3130; www.thefranklinshops.com; 2200 1st St; ⊙10am-8pm Mon-Sat, 11am-6pm Sun) Riding Fort Myers' upsurge in artsy cool, this gift store and gallery represents more than 60 local artists and businesses, which rotate often. Great for only-in-southwest-Florida gifts.

ℹ️ **Getting There & Away**

A car is essential. US 41/S Cleveland Ave is the main north–south artery. From downtown, both Summerlin Rd/Hwy 869 and McGregor Blvd/Hwy 867 eventually merge and lead to Sanibel Island; they also connect with San Carlos Blvd/Hwy 865 to Fort Myers Beach.

Greyhound (📞239-334-1011; www.greyhound.com; 2250 Widman Way) Connects Fort Myers to Miami, Orlando and Tampa.

LeeTran (📞239-533-8726; www.rideleetran.com; 3401 Metro Pkwy; rides $1.50) Routes run to Fort Myers Beach and Pine Island, but not to Sanibel or Captiva Islands.

Southwest Florida International Airport (RSW; 📞239-590-4800; http://flylcpa.com; 11000 Terminal Access Rd) Take I-75 from Fort Myers and exit 131/Daniels Pkwy.

Fort Myers Beach

📞239 / POP 6676

Like Clearwater Beach and St Pete Beach, Fort Myers Beach foments a party atmosphere year-round, and spring unfolds like one long-running street festival-slash-fraternity bash. And yet, situated on the 7-mile-long Estero Island, Fort Myers Beach has sand and space enough to accommodate all needs and ages. In the north, the so-called Times Sq area is a walkable concentration that verily epitomizes 'sun-bleached seaside party town.' Head south and the beachfront becomes more residential, less crowded and much quieter.

⊙ Sights

Bowditch Point Park
PARK

(☏239-765-6794; www.leegov.com/parks; 50 Estero Blvd; ☺7am-sunset) At the island's northernmost tip, Bowditch is a favorite with families and picnickers. The small parking lot ($2 per hour) fills up fast, so come early. There's a good snack bar, free boat dockage, and kayak and paddleboard rentals. You'll also find a butterfly garden, picnic areas and a replenished beach that narrows around the tip. It's a good place to view dolphins fishing in the Matanzas Pass and there's a paddle launch onto the Great Calusa Blueway paddling trail (www.calusablueway.com).

Lovers Key State Park
STATE PARK

(☏239-463-4588; www.floridastateparks.org/loverskey; 8700 Estero Blvd; car/bike $8/2; ☺8am-sunset) In the mood for a good hike, bike or kayak, with a chance to spot manatees in spring and summer? Come to Lovers Key, just south (and over a bridge) from Estero Island. Canals and 2.6 miles of trails around inner islands provide head-clearing quietude and bird-watching. The long, narrow beach is excellent for shelling, but erosion can make it too slim to lay a towel at high tide.

Fort Myers Beach
BEACH

Fort Myers Beach is long, long, long. The southern end is dominated by condos, with very little public access. The low-key middle has a large number of end-of-road access points with metered lots. The northern Times Sq area, right where the causeway dumps visitors, has large paid lots ($5 to $10 per day) and raucous beach bars.

🎉 Festivals & Events

Fort Myers Beach Shrimp Festival
FOOD & DRINK

(www.fortmyersbeachshrimpfestival.com; ☺Mar) For two weekends in early March, Fort Myers celebrates the glorious Gulf pink shrimp with parades, beauty queens, craft fairs and lots of cooking.

American Sandsculpting Championship
CULTURAL

(www.fmbsandsculpting.com; ☺Nov) Four-day national sand-sculpting event, with amateur and pro divisions, usually held in early November.

🛏 Sleeping

Dolphin Inn
MOTEL $

(☏239-463-6049; www.dolphininn.net; 6555 Estero Blvd; r $80-140; ❄@🛜🏊) This vintage Old Florida motel is best if you get one of the newly renovated rooms. However, all rooms sport no-fuss furniture and have full kitchens; the best are bayside, overlooking a scenic residential harbor where manatees play. Amenities include a sizable L-shaped pool, communal grills, loaner kayaks, a DVD library and cheap bike rental.

★ Mango Street Inn
B&B $$

(☏239-233-8542; www.mangostreetinn.com; 126 Mango St; ste incl breakfast $120-182; ❄🛜🏊) Mango St's affable husband-and-wife owners Dan and Tree have created a winning seaside B&B: its idiosyncratic decor is funky and memorable but relaxed enough to feel homey. The six rooms with full kitchens hug an interior courtyard that has a wood deck and pretty pergola. It's a short walk to the beach, and the B&B offers bikes and beach gear.

Manatee Bay Inn
INN $$

(☏239-463-6906; www.manateebayinn.com; 932 Third St; r $135-255; P❄🛜🏊) Situated a block back from Times Sq with views over a sleepy inlet, Manatee Bay offers the best of both worlds. By day you can position yourself on one of the sun loungers on the deck overhanging the water, and by night stroll down to Times Sq for cocktails, eats and fun.

Sea Gypsy Inn
INN $$

(☏239-765-0707; www.theseagypsyinn.com; 1698 Estero Blvd; r $99-300; P❄🛜) A couple of miles down the beach from Times Sq, this is a cute and reasonably priced collection of apartments and suites, which each feature comfy beds and full kitchens. The cheery yellow reception and gift shop was formerly the first public library in Lee County, holding 1500 books.

Edison Beach House
HOTEL $$$

(☏239-463-1530; www.edisonbeachhouse.com; 830 Estero Blvd; ste $140-430; ❄🛜🏊) This 24-suite hotel was designed smartly from the ground up and proudly maintains impeccable standards. Attractive decor and rattan furniture are pleasing and all suites frame perfect ocean views from nice balconies. The more sizable rooms are comfortable for longer stays. Fully equipped kitchens feature good-quality appliances; each room has a washer-dryer and newly renovated bathroom.

🍴 Eating

Heavenly Biscuit
BREAKFAST $

(110 Mango St; items $3-8; ☺7:30am-1pm Tue-Sun) This unassuming shack offers two

genuine delights: sumptuous fresh-baked buttermilk biscuits – overflowing with eggs, cheese and bacon – and delectable cinnamon rolls. Eat directly off the waxed paper on the tiny porch or get it to go; you can build a bigger breakfast with grits and home fries. It's nothing fancy or highbrow: just a simple thing done right.

★ **Dixie Fish Company**   SEAFOOD $$
(☑ 239-233-8837; www.dixiefishfmb.com; 714 Fishermans Wharf; mains $10-22; ⊙ 11am-10pm) Next to Doc Ford's and under the same ownership, this fish house recently opened in a 1937 wooden structure that originally contained a fish market. The catch comes straight off the local crab and shrimping boats, which can be viewed from the open-air seating area. Dressings are made in house, and the whole fried fish with garlic butter kills it.

Doc Ford's   SEAFOOD $$
(☑ 239-765-9660; www.docfords.com; 708 Fishermans Wharf; mains $10-22; ⊙ 11am-10pm) Part-owner Randy Wayne White once lived on the marina here, and he named this scenic wharf eatery, which has two sister restaurants in Sanibel and Capitva, after his beloved mystery-novel protagonist, marine biologist Doc Ford. The wood-sided building with spacious decks, big windows and multiple bars (open till late) emphasizes Floribbean flavors and a Latin American spice rack.

Fresh Catch Bistro   SEAFOOD $$$
(☑ 239-463-2600; www.freshcatchbistro.com; 3040 Estero Blvd; mains $14-50; ⊙ 5-10pm Sun-Thu, to 9pm Fri & Sat) This nautically themed bistro is a cut above other seafood restaurants on the beach. Inside, a wall of windows frames stunning sunsets or lightning streaks across the waves, and a vaulted wooden roof arcs over linen-dressed tables. Here diners tuck in to Pine Islands clams on ice, Point Judith calamari fried with mild cherry peppers and delicious lobster mac 'n' cheese.

🍸 Drinking & Nightlife

Smokin' Oyster Brewery   BAR
(☑ 239-463-3474; www.smokinoyster.com; 340 Old San Carlos Blvd; ⊙ 11am-11pm Sun-Thu, to 11:30pm Fri & Sat) You can rock up in your bathing suit and flip-flops at this open-air beach bar just steps from Fort Myers Beach. Order a platter of oysters or a bucket of steamed shrimp, corn and red potatoes (mains $6 to $14).

Caught your own? Bring it along and they'll cook it up. Every evening there's live music, and happy hour runs from 3pm to 6pm.

ℹ️ Getting There & Around

The main drag, Estero Blvd, runs the island's length, from Bowditch Point Park in the north to Lover's Key State Park.

Key West Express (☑ 239-463-5733; www.seakeywestexpress.com; 1200 Main St; single fare adult/child $95/31) Offers daily sailings to the Keys, departing at 8:30am from a dock on the mainland (take a left just before the causeway). The trip takes 3½ hours, so you may want to consider an overnight stay.

LeeTran Trolley (☑ 239-533-8726; www.rideleetran.com; adult/reduced $0.75/0.35; ⊙ 7:05am-8:45pm) Plies the island's length daily, and connects to Fort Myers buses at Summerlin Sq on the mainland.

Sanibel Island

☑ 239 / POP 6913

By preference and by design, island life on Sanibel is informal and egalitarian, and riches are rarely flaunted. Development on Sanibel has been carefully managed: the northern half is almost entirely protected within the JN 'Ding' Darling National Wildlife Refuge. While there are hotels aplenty, the beachfront is free of commercial-and-condo blight. Plus public beach access is limited to a handful of spread-out parking lots, so there is no crush of day-trippers in one place.

👁️ Sights

The quality of shelling on Sanibel is so high that dedicated hunters are identified by their hunchbacked 'Sanibel stoop.' If you're serious, buy a scoop net, get a shell guide from the visitor center and peruse the blog www.iloveshelling.com.

Fourteen miles of largely public-access beaches give you lots of room to choose from. Most beaches except Blind Pass have restrooms; none of the beaches have concessions or snack bars. Parking is $2 per hour.

JN 'Ding' Darling National Wildlife Refuge   WILDLIFE RESERVE
(☑ 239-472-1100; www.fws.gov/dingdarling; 1 Wildlife Dr; car/cyclist/pedestrian $5/1/1; ⊙ 7am-sunset) Named for cartoonist Jay Norwood 'Ding' Darling, an environmentalist who helped establish more than 300 sanctuaries across the USA, this 6300-acre refuge is home to an

WORTH A TRIP

CAYO COSTA STATE PARK

Slim as a supermodel and as lovely, Cayo Costa Island is almost entirely preserved as a 2500-acre **state park** (941-964-0375; www.floridastateparks.org/cayocosta; $2; 8am-sunset). While its pale, ash-colored sand may not be as fine as that of other beaches, its idyllic solitude and bathtub-warm waters are without peer. Bring a snorkel mask to help scour sandbars for shells and conchs – delightfully, many still house colorful occupants (who, by law, must be left there). Cycle dirt roads to more-distant beaches, hike interior island trails and kayak mangroves.

The ranger station near the dock sells water and firewood, and rents bikes and kayaks, but otherwise bring everything you need. The 30-site campground ($22 per tent) is exposed and hot, with fire-pit grills, restrooms and showers, but sleeping on this beach is its own reward. Twelve plain cabins ($40 per night) have bunk beds with vinyl-covered mattresses. January to April is best; by May, the heat and no-see-ums (biting midges) become unpleasant.

The only access is by boat, which doubles as a scenic nature-and-dolphin cruise. Captiva Cruises offers ferry service to the park from locations in Punta Gorda, Pine Island, Fort Myers, Sanibel Island and Captiva Island.

abundance of seabirds and wildlife, including alligators, night herons, red-shouldered hawks, spotted sandpipers, roseate spoonbills, pelicans and anhingas. The refuges 5-mile **Wildlife Drive** provides easy access, but bring binoculars; flocks sometimes sit at expansive distances. Only a few very short walks lead into the mangroves.

Don't miss the free **visitors center** (open 9am to 4pm), which has excellent exhibits on refuge life and Darling himself. Naturalist-narrated Wildlife Drive tram tours depart from the visitor-center parking lot, usually on the hour from 10am to 4pm. For the best, most intimate experience, canoe or kayak Tarpon Bay.

Bowman's Beach
BEACH

(1700 Bowman's Beach Rd) Bowman's Beach is the quintessential Sanibel beach, a bright dollop of coast with soft white sand, supplied with a playground and excellent facilities. It's remote in the sense that it rarely feels crowded, except perhaps at the height of tourist season. Alphabet cones, angel wings, lightning whelks and horse conch shells all glitter on the powder. Excellent views to the west make for truly magical sunsets.

Sanibel Historical Village
HISTORIC SITE

(239-472-4648; www.sanibelmuseum.org; 950 Dunlop Rd; adult/child $10/free; 10am-4pm Tue-Sat) Well polished by the enthusiasm of local volunteers, this museum and collection of nine historic buildings preserves Sanibel's pioneer past. It gives a piquant taste of settler

life, with a general store, post office, cottage and more.

Bailey-Matthews National Shell Museum
MUSEUM

(239-395-2233; www.shellmuseum.org; 3075 Sanibel-Captiva Rd; adult/child 5-12yr/child 12-17yr $15/7/9; 10am-5pm) Like a mermaid's jewelry box, this museum is dedicated to shells, yet it's much more than a covetous display of treasures. It's a crisply presented natural history of the sea, detailing the life and times of the bivalves, mollusks and other creatures who reside inside their calcium homes. It also shows the role of these animals and shells in human culture, medicine and cuisine. Fascinating videos show living creatures. It's nearly a must after a day spent combing the beaches.

Lighthouse Beach
BEACH

(112 Periwinkle Way) The most photogenic of the beaches, Lighthouse Beach sports Sanibel's historic metal lighthouse (1884) on the eastern tip of the island. There's also a T-dock, off which pelicans dive-bomb, and a short boardwalk around the point. Park in the lot and walk over a bridge to the narrow beach.

 Activities

Tarpon Bay Explorers
KAYAKING

(239-472-8900; www.tarponbayexplorers.com; 900 Tarpon Bay Rd; 8am-5pm) Within the Darling refuge, this outfitter rents canoes and kayaks ($25 for two hours) for easy, self-guided paddles in Tarpon Bay, a perfect place for young paddlers. Guided kayak trips (adult from $30 to $40, child from $20 to $25) are also excellent, and there's a range of other trips and deck talks. Reserve ahead or come early, as trips book up.

Billy's Rentals
CYCLING

(☏239-472-5248; www.billysrentals.com; 1470 Periwinkle Way; bikes per 2hr/day $5/15; ◷8:30am-5pm) Billy's rents every type of wheeled contrivance, including joggers, tandems, surreys, scooters and more. From Monday to Saturday, by reservation, it also offers three Segway tours (per person $65) at 9am, 11:30am and 2pm.

☆ Festivals & Events

Sanibel Music Festival
MUSIC

(www.sanibelmusicfestival.org; ◷Mar) A classical- and chamber-music festival that draws international musicians for a month-long concert series every Tuesday and Saturday in March.

'Ding' Darling Days
CULTURAL

(www.dingdarlingsociety.org/articles/ding-darling-days; ◷Oct) A week-long celebration of the wildlife refuge (p431), with birding tours, workshops and guest speakers.

Sanibel Luminary Fest
CULTURAL

(◷Dec) Sanibel's signature street fair occurs the first weekend of December, when paper luminaries line the island's bike paths.

🛏 Sleeping

Sandpiper Inn
INN $$

(☏239-472-1606; www.palmviewsanibel.com; 720 Donax St; r $149-229; P❄🛜) Set a block back from the water and in close proximity to the shops and restaurants on Periwinkle Way, this Old Florida inn offers good value for Sanibel. Each of the one-bedroom units has a functional (if dated) kitchen and a spacious sitting area decked out in tropical colors.

Tarpon Tale Inn
COTTAGE $$

(☏239-472-0939; www.tarpontale.com; 367 Periwinkle Way; r $230-290; ❄@🛜) The charming, tile-floored rooms evoke a bright, seaside mood and are well located for Sanibel's Old Town; each has a shady porch, tree-strung hammock and super-comfy bed (or two), and some offer full kitchens. With the outdoor lounge, library and loaner bikes, this feels like a B&B without the breakfast, although there is a coffee bar with homemade treats.

West Wind Inn
INN $$$

(☏239-472-1541; http://westwindinn.com; 3345 West Gulf Dr; r $200-335; P🛜❄) An older inn tucked away from the action and just steps from the beach, this place excels for its friendly service and low-key, homey vibe. Decor is a bit dated, but the attractive grounds, heated pool and shuffleboard courts more than compensate.

✗ Eating

Sanibel Bean
CAFE $

(☏239-395-1919; www.sanibelbean.com; 2240 Periwinkle Way; mains $5-9; ◷7am-9pm; 🛜❄) Popular local hangout with an extensive cafe menu of quick, cheap eats that are surprisingly tasty and prepared with love. The staff are as friendly as they come.

Over Easy Cafe
CAFE $

(☏239-472-2625; www.overeasycafesanibel.com; 630 Tarpon Bay Rd; breakfast $4-12; ◷7am-3pm; 🛜❄) Despite the Provençal decor, the menu offers strictly top-quality diner fare, including eggs every which way. Add fluffy pancakes, good coffee and friendly, efficient service, and this becomes Sanibel's go-to morning choice – so expect a wait. In summer it also opens for dinner from Tuesday to Saturday.

Gramma Dot's
SEAFOOD $$

(☏239-472-8138; www.sanibelmarina.com; N Yachtsman Dr, Sanibel Marina; lunch $11-15, dinner $19-25; ◷11:15am-8pm) Pull up a bar stool next to the charter-boat captains at this long-time Sanibel Marina favorite. Enjoy a no-fuss fried-oyster sandwich, mesquite-grilled grouper or the coconut shrimp. A great lunch stop.

Island Cow
SOUTHERN US $$

(☏239-472-0606; www.sanibelislandcow.com; 2163 Periwinkle Way; mains $8-19; ◷7am-10pm) This colorful island cafe goes heavy on the cow puns, offering a cheery 'at-moo-sphere' and tons of options, from 'cowabunga' breakfast to 'udderly great' sandwiches and wraps. A new tropical cocktail menu and frequent live music make it an easy choice any time of day.

★ Mad Hatter Restaurant
AMERICAN $$$

(☏239-472-0033; www.madhatterrestaurant.com; 6467 Sanibel-Captiva Rd; mains $29-45; ◷5:30-9pm) 🍃 Vacationing Manhattan urbanites flock to what is widely regarded as Sanibel's best locavore restaurant. Contemporary seafood is the focus, with tempting appetizers such as oysters and a seafood martini, while mains include black-truffle sea scallops, bigeye tuna and a rack of lamb. As the name suggests, it's not stuffy but is for culinary mavens seeking quality regardless of price.

★ Sweet Melissa's Cafe AMERICAN $$$
(☑239-472-1956; http://sweetmelissascafe.com; 1625 Periwinkle Way; tapas $9-16, mains $26-34; ⊙11:30am-2:30pm & 5pm-close Mon-Fri, 5pm-close Sat) From menu to mood, Sweet Melissa's offers well-balanced, relaxed refinement. Dishes, including things like farro fettuccine, escargot with marrow and whole crispy fish, are creative without trying too hard. Lots of small-plate options encourage experimenting. Service is attentive and the atmosphere upbeat.

ⓘ Getting There & Away

Driving is the only way to come and go. The Sanibel Causeway (Hwy 867) charges an entrance toll (cars/motorcycles $6/2). Sanibel is 12 miles long, but low speed limits and traffic makes it seem longer. The main drag is Periwinkle Way, which becomes Sanibel-Captiva Rd.

Captiva Island
☑239 / POP 379

The pirate José Gaspar, who called himself Gasparilla, once roamed the Gulf Coast plundering treasure and seizing beautiful women, whom he held captive on the aptly named Captiva Island. Today the tiny village is confined to a single street, Andy Rosse Lane, and there are still no traffic lights. The preferred mode of transport is the family-friendly bike, and life here is informal and egalitarian, with island riches rarely being flaunted. Captiva's mansions are hidden behind thick foliage and sport playful names such as 'Seas the Day.'

⊙ Sights & Activities

Captiva Beach BEACH
(14790 Captiva Dr) Besides looking directly out onto heart-melting Gulf sunsets, Captiva Beach has lovely sand and is close to several romantic restaurants. Arrive early if you want to park in the small lot or come by bike.

Captiva Cruises CRUISE
(☑239-472-5300; www.captivacruises.com; 11400 Andy Rosse Lane) Departing from **McCarthy's Marina** (☑239-472-5200; www.mccarthysmarina.

com; 11401 Andy Rosse Lane), Captiva Cruises offers everything from dolphin and sunset cruises (from $27.50) to various island excursions, such as Cayo Costa ($40), Cabbage Key ($40) and Boca Grande ($50) on Gasparilla Island.

🛏 Sleeping

★'Tween Waters Inn RESORT $$$
(☑239-472-5161; www.tween-waters.com; 15951 Captiva Dr; r $185-285, ste $270-410, cottages $265-460; ✳ ❄ ⓦ ✹ ☎) For great resort value on Captiva, choose 'Tween Waters Inn. Rooms are attractive roosts with rattan furnishings, granite counters, rainfall showerheads and Tommy Bahama–style decor. All have balconies and those directly facing the Gulf are splendid. The tidy little cottages are romantic. Families make good use of the big pool, tennis courts, full-service marina and spa. Multinight discounts are attractive.

South Seas Island Resort RESORT $$$
(☑239-472-5111; www.southseas.com; 5400 Plantation Rd; r from $299) Captiva's poshest resort complex expands over 330 acres with a wildlife preserve, cottages and condos galore, three pools (including waterslides and a tiki bar), six restaurants and 2.5 miles of white-sand beach. Guests spend their days at the spa, shelling on the beach or playing with water toys like WaveRunners, stand-up paddleboards and chartered boats.

✕ Eating & Drinking

Bubble Room DESSERTS $$
(☑239-472-5558; www.bubbleroomrestaurant.com; 15001 Captiva Dr; cakes $8-9, mains $14-30; ⊙11:30am-3pm & 4:30-9pm) This Captiva institution is oddly festooned in kitsch, pastels and Christmas decor year-round, with trains running on three floors and a special 'elf room.' Dishes are named for old-time legends like Mae West and Louis Armstrong, but the truly famous items here are the desserts. The buttercrunch pie has ice cream blended with Butterfinger candy bars and an Oreo crust.

Doc Ford's SEAFOOD $$$
(☑239-312-4275; www.docfords.com/captiva-island; 5400 S Seas Plantation Rd; mains $20-28; ⊙11am-10pm) The newest location in the Doc Ford's chain is attached to South Seas Island Resort (p434) and accordingly upscale, but nonguests are welcome. The menu is full of delightful 'Floribbean' fare, with lots of fresh

local seafood, a raw bar and a large selection of rum. There's pleasant outdoor seating and live music on weekends.

Mucky Duck
PUB

(☑239-472-3434; www.muckyduck.com; 11546 Andy Rosse Lane; ⊙11:30am-3pm & 5-9:30pm) The unpretentious, shingle-roofed Mucky Duck is perfectly positioned for Captiva sunsets, and devoted locals jockey for beach chairs and picnic tables each evening. The extended menu offers more than just pub grub, with pasta, steak, chicken and seafood (mains $10 to $25). Really, though, it's the friendly bar and toes-in-the-sand Gulf views that keep 'em coming.

❶ Getting There & Around

Driving is the only way to come and go. The Sanibel Causeway (Hwy 867) charges an entrance toll (cars/motorcycles $6/2).

Captiva is 5 miles long, but low speed limits and traffic make it seem longer. The main drag is Sanibel-Captiva Rd.

Naples

☑239 / POP 20,573

For upscale romance and the prettiest, most serene city beach in southwest Florida, come to Naples, the Gulf Coast's answer to Palm Beach. Development along the shoreline has been kept residential. The soft white sand is backed only by narrow dunes and half-hidden mansions. More than that, though, Naples is a cultured, sophisticated town, unabashedly stylish and privileged but also welcoming and fun-loving. Families, teens, couture-wearing matrons, middle-aged executives and smartly dressed young couples all mix and mingle as they stroll downtown's 5th Ave on a balmy evening. Travelers sometimes complain that Naples is expensive, but you can spend just as much elsewhere on a less impressive vacation.

❂ Sights

Downtown Naples is laid out on a grid. There are two primary retail corridors: the main one is 5th Ave between 9th St S/US 41 and W Lake Dr. The other retail district runs along 3rd St S between Broad Ave S and 14th St S; this area, called **Third St South**, forms the heart of Old Naples. Throughout the area there's a mix of Mediterranean Revival and board-and-batten Cracker cottages. From spring to fall the Old Naples district hosts a range of events: music,

DETOUR: THE EVERGLADES

If you've traveled as far south as Naples, you really owe it to yourself to visit the Everglades. Heading west on the Tamiami Trail/Hwy 41, you can be in Everglades City in half an hour, Big Cypress in 45 minutes and Shark Valley in 75 minutes.

art and a Saturday-morning farmers market. See the online calendar at www.thirdstreet south.com.

Naples also features 9 miles of idyllic white-sand beaches, and all downtown parking (off-beach) is free.

★ Baker Museum
MUSEUM

(☑239-597-1900; www.artisnaples.org; 5833 Pelican Bay Blvd; adult/child $10/free; ⊙10am-4pm Tue-Thu & Sat, to 8pm Fri, noon-4pm Sun) The pride of Naples, this engaging, sophisticated art museum is part of the Artis–Naples campus, which includes the fabulous Philharmonic Center next door. Devoted to 20th-century modern and contemporary art, the museum's 15 galleries and glass dome conservatory host an exciting round of temporary and permanent shows, ranging from postmodern works to photography and paper craft to glass sculpture, including a stunning Chihuly exhibition.

★ Naples Botanical Gardens
GARDENS

(☑239-643-7275; www.naplesgarden.org; 4820 Bayshore Dr; adult/child 4-14 $15/10; ⊙9am-5pm) This outstanding botanical garden styles itself as 'a place of bliss, a region of supreme delight.' And after spending some time wandering its 2.5-mile trail through nine cultivated gardens you'll rapidly find your inner Zen. Children will dig the thatched-roof tree house, butterfly house and interactive fountain, while adults get dreamy-eyed contemplating landscape architect Raymond Jungles' recently redesigned Scott Florida garden, filled with cascades, 12ft-tall oolite rocks and legacy tree species like date palms, sycamore leaf figs and lemon ficus.

Rookery Bay National Estuariane Research Reserve
NATURE RESERVE

(☑239-530-5940; https://rookerybay.org; $5; ⊙learning center 9am-4pm Mon-Fri, plus Sat in high season) This reserve protects 110,000 acres of coastal lands and marine estuaries at the northern end of the Ten Thousand Islands, just south of Naples and north of Marco Island. A two-story learning center features an auditorium where guests watch an excellent video, along with a marine touch tank and 2300-gallon aquarium with a climb-in bubble. From there, popular activities include kayak and boating tours, a nature walk and birding excursions.

Golisano Children's Museum of Naples
MUSEUM

(C'mon; ☑ 239-514-0084; www.cmon.org; 15080 Livingston Rd; $10; ☉10am-5pm Mon & Tue & Thu-Sat, 11am-4pm Sun; ♿) Designed by kids (and child psychologists) for kids, this interactive children's museum is devoted to learning through play. A trolley takes kids to various exhibits, including a virtual pond, where they can observe fish and growing water plants, and a produce market, where fruit and veggies are sorted and sold to other kid 'customers.' Best of all is the Journey Through the Everglades with its boardwalk winding up into a two-story banyan tree overlooking a mangrove maze.

Naples Municipal Beach
BEACH

(12th Ave S & Gulf Shore Blvd) Naples city beach is a long, dreamy white strand that succeeds in feeling lively but rarely overcrowded. At the end of 12th Ave S, the 1000ft pier is a symbol of civic pride, having been constructed in 1888, destroyed a few times by fire and hurricane, and reconstructed each time. Parking is spread out in small lots between 7th Ave N and 17th Ave S, each with 10 to 15 spots of mixed resident and metered parking ($1.50 per hour).

Naples Nature Center
NATURE RESERVE

(☑ 239-262-0304; www.conservancy.org/naturecenter; 1450 Merrihue Dr; adult/child 3-12yr $13/9; ☉9:30am-4:30pm Mon-Sat, plus Sun Nov-Apr) One of Florida's premier nature-conservancy and advocacy nonprofits, the Conservancy of Southwest Florida is a must-visit destination for anyone interested in Florida's environment and its preservation. While the new Discovery Center immerses visitors in southwest Florida environments, with informative films, displays and a rare peek into an avian, reptile and mammal nursery, the 21-acre preserve offers a half-mile trail and naturalist boat rides.

Palm Cottage
HISTORIC BUILDING

(☑ 239-261-8164; www.napleshistoricalsociety.org/palm-cottage; 137 12th Ave S; adult/child under 10yr $13/free; ☉1-4pm Tue-Sat) The oldest home in Naples and last remaining tabby-mortar cottage in Collier County, this quaint abode was built in 1895 for Henry Watterson, the editor of the *Louisville Courier Journal*. It then offered overflow accommodations for the Old Naples Hotel, hosting movie stars such as Hedy Lamarr. After more recent renovations it now houses the Naples Historical Society, which offers engaging guided tours of the house, in addition to talks by local authors and artists in the adjacent Norris Gardens.

Naples Zoo at Caribbean Gardens
ZOO

(☑ 239-262-5409; www.napleszoo.com; 1590 Goodlette-Frank Rd; adult/child 3-12yr $23/15; ☉9am-5pm) Caribbean Gardens is an Old Florida attraction that's been updated into a modest zoo. It has narrated boat rides in a lake to visit free-roaming, island-bound monkeys, giraffe and alligator feeding attractions, and some unique species such as honey badgers and the Madagascan fossa, which looks something like a cougar crossed with a mongoose. All presentations are included in admission; last tickets sold at 4pm.

Delnor-Wiggins Pass State Park
STATE PARK

(☑ 239-597-6196; www.floridastateparks.org/delnorwiggins; 11135 Gulf Shore Dr; car/bike $6/2; ☉8am-sunset) This lovely state park and beach extends for a mile from the mouth of the Cocohatchee River. It boasts gorgeous white sands, which are protected during turtle-nesting season (from May to October). There's an **observation tower** at the north end, but swimming is best south of the pass' fast-moving waters. The beach is supplied with food concessions (at parking lot four) and showers, and has every item you might need for a day in the sun for hire.

Clam Pass County Park
BEACH

(☑ 239-252-4000; ☉8am-sunset) This county park covers 35 acres of coastal habitat, including a 0.75-mile boardwalk through a mangrove forest that leads out to a powdery white-sand beach. It's next to Naples Grand Beach Resort, which runs both the water-sports rentals and the free tram that travels between the large parking lot and the well-groomed beach. It's a favorite with families and young adults. The snack bar serves beer and cocktails.

✨ Festivals & Events

Naples Winter Wine Festival FOOD & DRINK
(www.napleswinefestival.com; ⊘ Jan) This multi-day event features celebrity wine tastings, chef-hosted dinners and a high-yielding auction – the proceeds of which go to benefit 20 children's charities in Collier County.

🛏 Sleeping

Gondolier INN $$
(☏ 239-262-4858; www.gondolierinnnaples.com; 407 8th Ave S; r $90-198; P❄🖥) This classic 1950s Googie-style bungalow with sharp angles, overhanging roof and kitsch Gondolier signage is well located on a quiet street in Old Naples. Rooms are of a similar vintage and have hand-hewn kitchens and period furniture. Better still, it's just a few blocks' walk to the beach. Deep discounts for extended stays.

Lemon Tree Inn MOTEL $$
(☏ 239-262-1414; www.lemontreeinn.com; 250 9th St S; r incl breakfast $134-213; P❄@🖥🐾) Value for money is high at the Lemon Tree, where 34 clean and brightly decorated rooms (some with passable kitchenettes) form a U around pretty, private gardens. Screened porches, free lemonade and continental breakfasts are nice, but most of all you'll treasure being walking distance to the 5th Ave corridor.

★ Escalante BOUTIQUE HOTEL $$$
(☏ 239-659-3466; www.hotelescalante.com; 290 5th Ave S; r $200-700) Hidden in plain sight at 5th Ave and 3rd St, the wonderful Escalante is a boutique hotel crafted in the fashion of a Tuscan villa. Rooms and suites are nestled behind luxuriant foliage and flowering pergolas, and feature plantation-style furniture, European linens and designer bath products.

Inn on 5th HOTEL $$$
(☏ 239-403-8777; www.innonfifth.com; 699 5th Ave S; r $399, ste incl breakfast $599-999; P❄@🖥🐾) This well-polished, Mediterranean-style luxury hotel provides an unbeatable location on either side of 5th Ave. Stylish rooms are a bit more corporate-perfect than historic-romantic, but who complains about pillowtop mattresses and glass-walled showers? Full-service amenities include a 2nd-floor heated pool, business and fitness centers, and an indulgent spa. Free valet parking.

🍴 Eating

Food & Thought MARKET, CAFE $
(☏ 239-213-2222; www.foodandthought.com; 2132 Tamiami Trail N; mains $3-10; ⊘ 7am-8pm Mon-Sat; 🐾) You won't find anything that isn't 100% organic on the shelves of this market or in its ever-busy cafe. Vegetarians will delight in the artfully layered raw lasagna.

The Café CAFE $$
(☏ 239-430-6555; www.thecafeon5th.com; 821 5th Ave S; mains breakfast $8-14, lunch $11-17; ⊘ 7:30am-3pm; 🐾) You could easily walk past this unassuming cafe, but then you'd be missing out on a superlative breakfast of fluffy, organic eggs, grilled Canadian bacon and perfectly toasted artisan bread. And that's just the standard; Ironman oatmeal topped with flax seeds, almonds, raisins and apples; açai bowls; crepes; and lox bagels topped with pale-pink salmon satisfy healthier cravings.

IM Tapas SPANISH $$
(☏ 239-403-8272; www.imtapas.com; 965 4th Ave N; tapas $5.50-18; ⊘ from 5:30pm Mon-Sat) Off the beaten path in a strip mall, this simply decorated, romantic Spanish restaurant serves Madrid-worthy tapas. The mother-daughter team presents contemporary interpretations of classics such as Serrano ham, *angula* (baby eels) and shrimp with garlic. Also on offer: innovative and adventurous plates such as venison tenderloin carpaccio.

The Local MODERN AMERICAN $$
(☏ 239-596-3276; www.thelocalnaples.com; 5323 Airport Pulling Rd N; mains $12-29; ⊘ 11am-9pm Sun-Thu, to 9:30pm Fri & Sat; 🖥) 🐾 The irony of driving 6 miles from downtown to eat local aside, this strip-mall farm-to-table bistro is worth the carbon footprint for fab sustainable fare, from the Mediterranean watermelon salad to the grass-fed beef. Escape tourists. Eat local.

Campiello ITALIAN $$
(☏ 239-435-1166; www.campiello.damico.com; 1177 3rd St S; lunch $14-22, dinner $18-40; ⊘ 11:30am-3pm & 5-10pm Sun-Thu, to 10:30pm Fri & Sat) Campiello hits you with the perfect one-two combo: an attractive, umbrella-shaded patio for stylish alfresco dining along the 3rd St shopping corridor, and Italian cuisine priced for midrange budgets. Go light with a wood-fired pizza or a housemade pasta, or tuck into rich versions of beef tenderloin or grilled Gulf cobia. Frequent live jazz and delicious craft cocktails. Reservations recommended.

WORTH A TRIP

CORKSCREW SWAMP SANCTUARY

The crown jewel in the National Audubon Society's sanctuary collection, the **Corkscrew Swamp Sanctuary** (☎ 239-348-9151; www.corkscrew.audubon.org; 375 Sanctuary Rd W; adult/child 6-18yr $14/4; ⊙ 7am-5:30pm, 4:30 last entry) provides an intimate exploration of six pristine native habitats, including saw grass, slash pine and marsh, along a shady 2.25-mile boardwalk trail. The centerpiece is North America's oldest virgin bald-cypress forest, with majestic specimens more than 600 years old and 130ft tall.

Abundant wildlife includes nesting alligators, night herons, endangered wood storks and trees full of ibis. However, two rare species, when spotted, make the news: the famed ghost orchid and the elusive Florida panther. Volunteers help point out wildlife, and signage is excellent; the visitor center rents out binoculars ($3). Corkscrew is as good as the Everglades.

The preserve is southeast of Fort Myers and northeast of Naples; take I-75 exit 111 and head east on Hwy 846/Imokalee Rd to Sanctuary Rd; follow the signs. Bring repellent for deer flies in late spring.

★ **Bha! Bha! Persian Bistro** IRANIAN $$$
(☎ 239-594-5557; http://bhabhabistro.com; 865 5th Ave S; mains $26-38; ⊙ 5-9pm Sun-Thu, to 10pm Fri & Sat) This experimental, high-end establishment takes its name from the Farsi phrase for 'yum, yum,' and that turns out to be a serious understatement. Wash down the pistachio lamb meatballs with a saffron lemongrass martini, then continue on to a kebab marinated in exotic spices or the duck fesenjune, slow braised with pomegranate and walnut sauce.

★ **USS Nemo** SEAFOOD $$$
(☎ 239-261-6366; https://ussnemorestaurant.com; 3745 Tamiami Trail N; mains $19-33; ⊙ 11am-2pm & 4:30-9:30pm Mon-Thu, 11am-2pm & 4:30-10pm Fri, 4:30-10pm Sat, 4:30-9:30pm Sun) In a nondescript strip mall in north Naples, this wildly popular seafood establishment is festooned in porthole art and known for insanely delicious miso-glazed sea bass and mouthwatering truffle lobster risotto. The wine list is extensive and the cocktails are impressive; try the mango bravo with tequila, triple sec, mango and jalapeño. The place fills up very quickly. Make reservations.

Turtle Club SEAFOOD, AMERICAN $$$
(☎ 239-592-6557; www.theturtleclubrestaurant.com; Vanderbilt Beach Resort, 9225 Gulf Shore Dr; mains $9-42; ⊙ 11am-2:30pm & 5-9pm) How do you compete with the showstopping sunsets on the Gulf of Mexico? The Turtle Club at the Vanderbilt Resort tries hard with kick-ass cocktails and a short, sharp seafood menu rocking Pine Island lump crab, shrimp and crab Napoleon with mango and jicama, and mouthwatering 'oysters

turtlefeller.' Get there *early* to snag a place on the sand.

Drinking & Nightlife

HobNob Kitchen + Bar COCKTAIL BAR
(☎ 239-580-0070; http://hobnobnaples.com; 720 5th Ave S; ⊙ 3:30-9:30pm Mon-Wed, to 10pm Thu-Sat, to 9pm Sun) This place is about as hipster-chic as Naples gets, with opulent modern decor and 'nobtails' like the strawberry-watermelon fresca, made with pearl cucumber vodka. Don't miss the innovative, New American appetizers, particularly the stuffed sweet peppers with chorizo, Italian sausage and crab. The crowd is lively and the bartenders have big personalities.

Entertainment

★ **Naples Philharmonic** CLASSICAL MUSIC
(☎ 239-597-1900; www.artisnaples.org; 5833 Pelican Bay Blvd) Naples' 85-piece Philharmonic Orchestra is increasingly recognized as one of the country's best young orchestras. Andrey Boreyko was named as music director in 2013. The season runs from September to June, but the Artis complex within which it lives runs a year-round schedule of concerts and performances, including events for children.

Sugden Community Theatre THEATER
(☎ 239-263-7990; www.naplesplayers.org; 701 5th Ave; tickets $30-40; ⊙ box office 10am-4pm Mon-Fri, to 1pm Sat, noon-2pm Sun) Home of the Naples Players, the Sugden boasts two state-of-the-art stages, on the boards of which are enacted seven main-stage performances and four studio productions each year, including four

KidzAct performances. It's well attended so book ahead.

ℹ Getting There & Away

A car is essential; ample and free downtown parking makes things easy. Naples is about 40 miles southwest of Fort Myers via I-75.

Greyhound (✆239-774-5660; www.greyhound. com; 2669 Davis Blvd) Connects Naples to Miami, Orlando and Tampa.

Southwest Florida International Airport (p429) This is the main airport for Naples. It's about a 45-minute drive north, along I-75.

Gasparilla Island

✆ 239 / POP 1230

Out of all the treasure-plundering, rum-smuggling pirates to have set foot in southwest Florida, José Gaspar, better known as Gasparilla, is the most notorious. He set up his headquarters at Boca Grande on Gasparilla Island, so the story goes, where he built a palmetto palace and furnished it with the treasures he swiped from his high-seas adventures. Serious historians may doubt his existence, but Boca Grande continues to woo the great and the good who come to chase the glint of silver scales on the monstrous Atlantic tarpon that swim in its passes.

Despite its popularity as a blue-blooded bolt-hole, Boca Grande has a quaint fishing-village feel and is a great destination for families. It has miles of undeveloped white-sand beaches encompassed within the Gasparilla Island State Park.

◉ Sights

Gasparilla Island State Park   STATE PARK
(✆941-964-0375; www.floridastateparks.org/ gasparillaisland; 880 Belcher Rd; car/pedestrian $3/2; ☉8am-sunset) This parks centers on the restored, historic Boca Grande lighthouse, which was a beacon to mariners since 1890. The interior has been converted into a museum featuring old photographs, bones, fossils, shells and exhibits dedicated to the area's first inhabitants (open 10am to 4pm Monday to Saturday, from noon Sunday). Apart from touring the lighthouse, guests often swim, snorkel, fish or shell hunt on the park's virtually deserted beaches.

🛏 Sleeping

Anchor Inn   INN $$
(✆941-964-5600; www.anchorinnbocagrande. com; 450 4th St E; r $175-240; P❋🗢☒) This

historic 1925 home passes for the budget option in Boca Grande. With only four suites, book far, far in advance.

★**Gasparilla Inn**   HISTORIC HOTEL $$$
(✆941-964-4500; www.gasparillainn.com; 500 Palm Ave; r $235-480; P❋🗢☒) Retire beneath the pillared Georgian entrance of this historic 1913 hotel and you'll be transported to a more genteel age. Bellhops and butlers are on hand to attend to your every need and rooms offer splendidly unpretentious coral-and-pistachio-accented comfort. Your days will no doubt drift by in a blur of golf, tennis, fishing and seaplane tours.

Marco Island

✆ 239 / POP 16,413

The largest and northernmost of the Ten Thousand Islands, Marco Island also offers the highest point of elevation – 58ft above sea level – in all of southwestern Florida. It was the Calusa Indians who long ago made this vantage point possible with the construction of an enormous shell mound over hundreds of years, which now stands in a residential neighborhood dubbed Indian Hill.

Modern development of the island only began in the 1960s, and draws today include miles upon miles of white-sand beach, boating and fishing among the mangroves islands and a more relaxed, natural vibe than many of the coastal communities to the north. Shelling is also a big thing, with the best specimens often turning up at Tigertail Beach or on the nearby shores of Keewaydin Island, which remains largely pristine and inaccessible by car.

◉ Sights & Activities

Tigertail Beach   BEACH
(✆239-389-8414; 400 Hernando Dr; nonresident parking $8) This white-sand, family-friendly beach is ideal for shelling, tide-pool exploration and hanging out at the playground. It also happens to be a fantastic birding site, with abundant shorebirds, gulls and raptors, and plenty of other species flitting among the nearby mangroves and lagoon. Facilities include restrooms, a boardwalk, a picnic area and a concession stand that rents out water toys.

Hemingway Water Shuttle   BOATING
(✆239-315-1136; www.hemingwaywatershuttle. com; 951 Bald Eagle Dr; adult/child $44/22; ☉departures for Keewaydin at 8:30am, 10:30am,

12:30pm & 2:30pm) A family-owned boating company that departs from **Rose Marina** (☑239-394-2502; http://rosemarina.com; ☺7am-6pm) out to Keewaydin Island and for an occasional sunset cruise in Marco Island's bay. Kids and adults will love spotting dolphins, manatees and birds (baby ospreys are common) on the way. A friendly labradoodle named Riley often comes for the ride and has become known as 'the dolphin whisperer.'

☞ Tours

Dolphin Study ` `
ECOTOUR

(☑239-642-6899; www.dolphin-study.com; 951 Bald Eagle Dr; $59) One of the best ways to explore the marine ecosystem around Marco Island is with the Dolphin Study, a long-term scientific study of the behavior and movements of southwestern Florida's bottlenose dolphins. Using photo ID of dorsal fins, tour participants have the opportunity to get involved in sighting, counting and confirming individual sightings, data which is then shared with the Mote Marine Laboratory (p422) in Sarasota.

Passing around a heavy photo album of dorsal fins, naturalist Kent Morse points out bite marks and tears that will help you tell the difference between Ripples, Nibbles and Flag. While close enough to ID the different dolphins, the catamaran always keeps a respectful distance. Sometimes whole pods are sighted nosing around the mangroves or playing in family groups. If you spot a dolphin not already catalogued, you may even get to name it. Along the way, you'll stop at some of the most remote and beautiful, unbridged barrier islands such as shell-tastic **Keewaydin**.

Tours last three hours and depart from Rose Marina.

🛏 Sleeping & Eating

Boat House Motel
MOTEL $$

(☑239-642-2400; www.theboathousemotel.com; 1180 Edington Pl; r $110-150; P✳🛜🏊) The most reasonable accommodations on the island, this 'boatel' in historic Old San Marco is family-owned and quaint, with just 20 rooms adorned in turquoise trim and in some cases featuring views of the Marco River. Those who arrive by boat can tie up at the private dock; there's a charcoal grill to cook your catch.

Marco Beach Ocean Resort
CONDO $$$

(☑239-393-1400; www.marcoresort.com; 480 S Collier Blvd; r $260-360; P✳🛜🏊) This condo resort perches on a 5-mile stretch of white-sand beach and is consistently ranked among the top luxury stays in Marco Island. The 98 suites offer full kitchens and private balconies or patios, many with excellent sunset views. There's also a sumptuous spa, a beachfront southern Italian restaurant and nearby golf and tennis facilities.

★ Doreen's Cup of Joe
CAFE $

(☑239-394-2600; www.doreenscupofjoe.com; 257 N Collier Blvd; breakfast $7-15; ☺7:30am-2pm) This charming, recently revamped breakfast-all-day spot is the perfect place to grab coffee, some freshly squeezed orange juice and a stack of famous key lime pancakes before a morning boat excursion.

Snook Inn
SEAFOOD $$

(☑239-394-3313; www.snookinn.com; 1215 Bald Eagle Dr; mains $13-25; ☺11am-10pm) Right by the docks and with stunning views of Marco Bay, this long-standing restaurant and bar is the social hub of the island. The kitchen serves up excellent grouper sandwiches and will also fry up your catch. The Chickee Bar offers tasty frozen cocktails and live music every day.

ℹ Getting There & Away

Having a car is optimal and pretty much essential. From the junction of Collier Blvd and the Tamiami Trail, go south on Collier Blvd to reach Marco Island. Or by all means, come by boat.

Pine Island

☑239 / POP 9000

The 17-mile-long Pine Island, the region's largest, is a mangrove island with no sandy beaches to call its own, but offers relaxing, quiet lodgings for anglers, kayakers and romantics fleeing the tourist hordes. It encompasses several communities: Matlacha, the island's center, with a small amount of commerce and funky Old Florida art galleries; the northern communities of Pineland and Bokeelia, where you can find boat and fishing charters; and the largely residential St James City at the southern tip. Pine Island is a great jumping-off point for all-day adventures among the region's tarpon-rich waterways and gorgeous barrier islands.

⊙ Sights

The tiny fishing village of **Matlacha** (pronounced mat-la-shay) straddles the drawbridge to Pine Island and provides a quirky window into local life. In addition to its un-pretentious fresh-seafood markets and restaurants, a collection of old fishing huts have been transformed into gift shops that sit like a clutch of chattering Day-Glo-painted tropical birds.

 Activities

Tropic Star   BOATING
(☑239-283-0015; www.cayocostaferry.com; Jug Creek Marina, Bokeelia; ☺daily ferry at 9:30am) Cruises and ferries to Cayo Costa depart from Jug Creek Marina. Ferries (adult/child $35/25) take an hour; other options include stops at Cabbage Key for lunch (adult/child $35/25). It also offers private water taxis ($150 per hour), which are much faster and offer island-hopping to Useppa and Gasparilla Islands. Parking per half-day/full day/overnight is $6/8/10.

Gulf Coast Kayak   KAYAKING
(☑239-283-1125; www.gulfcoastkayak.com; 4120 Pine Island Rd NW; ☺9am-5pm Nov-May) In Matlacha, just past the drawbridge, Gulf Coast offers several kayak tours ($55/35 per adult/child) in the wildlife-rich Matlacha Pass Aquatic Preserve. You can also rent a canoe or kayak (half/full day $35/50) and paddle yourself. Want to kayak to Cayo Costa? Talk to them.

Matlacha Bridge   FISHING
They call this causeway between Cape Coral and Matlacha the 'fishingest bridge in the US,' sitting as it does at the center of several dynamic tidal flows. Anglers are here literally 24/7, especially during tarpon season.

Sleeping & Eating

Tarpon Lodge   INN $$
(☑239-283-3999; www.tarponlodge.com; 13771 Waterfront Dr, Pineland; r $125-190; P✳☎) The atmosphere at this genteel 1926 fishing inn seems barely to have changed since the door opened. Rooms have a comfortable, retro feel while the dining room has a clubby vibe thanks to its gleaming wooden interior and black-and-white portraits of previous angling patrons. The family also manages the rental cottages on Cabbage Key Island.

Cabbage Key Inn   INN $$
(☑239-283-2278; www.cabbagekey.com; Cabbage Key; r $100-150, cottages $195-525; ☺7:30-9am, 11:30am-3pm & 6-8:30pm) Stay in one of the inn's six rooms or eight cottages, all of which are Old Florida atmospheric with pretty touches (Rinehart and Dollhouse are favorites), though they aren't resort-plush: no TVs, no pool and wi-fi only in the restaurant. But you're not exactly marooned: the inn serves powerful cocktails and full dinner nightly (from $16 to $29, and they'll cook your catch), but make reservations.

★**Perfect Cup**   BREAKFAST $
(☑239-283-4447; 4548 Pine Island Rd, Matlacha; mains $5-10; ☺6am-4pm Mon-Sat, 6am-3pm Sun) A genuine local gathering place, Perfect Cup offers just that: a bottomless mug of flavorful house-roasted coffee ($2) to go with its top-quality diner-style fare – creative omelets, French toast and pancakes.

Shopping

★**Lovegrove Gallery**   ARTS & CRAFTS
(☑238-938-5655; www.leomalovegrove.com; 4637 Pine Island Rd, Matlacha; ☺11am-6pm Mon-Sat) If Matlacha is unexpectedly groovy for such a sun-faded fishing village, you can thank artist Leoma Lovegrove. Her gallery has transformed a fishing shack into a whimsical vision of tile mosaics and paintings, with a loopy 'Tropical Waterways Garden' in back. Now the whole block is a bona fide slice of roadside Americana, with unusual gift and craft shops.

Getting There & Away

Pine Island is due west of North Fort Myers and is not accessible by public transportation. By car, take US 41 to Pine Island Rd (Hwy 78), and head west. Boat charters and water taxis are available at Pineland and Matlacha Marinas.

The Panhandle

POP 1.5 MILLION / ☎ 850, 386

Best Places to Eat

➡ Up the Creek Raw Bar (p468)

➡ Iron (p451)

➡ George's at Alys Beach (p461)

➡ Kool Beanz Café (p475)

➡ Tin Cow (p450)

Best Places to Sleep

➡ Hibiscus Coffee & Guesthouse (p460)

➡ Wisteria Inn (p463)

➡ Aunt Martha's Bed & Breakfast (p456)

➡ Pearl (p461)

➡ Hotel Duval (p475)

Why Go?

The most geographically northern end of Florida is by far its most culturally Southern side.The Panhandle – that spit of land embedded in the left shoulder of the Florida peninsula – is hemmed in by Alabama and Georgia, and in many ways the region's beaches are effectively coastal extensions of those states.

What beaches they are, though! All powdered white-sand and teal- to jade-green waters, this is a coast of primal, wind-blown beauty in many places, particularly the undeveloped stretches of salt marsh and slash pine that spill east and west of Apalachee Bay. In other areas, the seashore is given to rental houses and high-rise condos.

Inland, you'll find a tangle of palmetto fans and thin pine woods interspersed with crystal springs, lazy rivers and military testing ranges – this area has one of the highest concentrations of defense facilities in the country.

When to Go
Pensacola

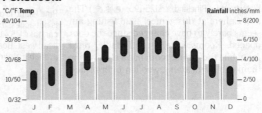

Mar–Apr Destin and Panama Beach are full of spring breakers, and best avoided unless you want to party.

May & Oct Enjoy the most temperate weather in South Walton.

Nov–Feb Usually too cold for sitting on the beach or swimming, but rates at local lodgings drop.

GULF COAST

The Panhandle's Gulf Coast has a very specific draw: beach. Its shimmering, curving miles of vanilla-white shoreline were formed from a glut of silicate quartz that has been crushed by geologic eons into sugary powder.

It's not all sun and sand, though. From Naval Air Station Pensacola in the west to Tyndall Air Force Base in the east, one can find a seemingly unbroken stretch of defense installations and military bases, and the towns here reflect that reality – between the resorts and vacation rentals, you'll find a glut of federal contracting offices and cigar bars servicing active duty and ex-service members.

Thanks to clouds of green forest, long acres of coastal marsh and a few remaining stretches of stunning sand dune hills, there is a gentle, breeze-blown prettiness to the Gulf Coast. Be on the lookout for decent dining and nightlife in Pensacola and larger base towns such as Destin.

Pensacola

✆850 / POPULATION 52,700

The Alabama border is just a few miles down the road, which helps explain the vibe of Pensacola, a city that jumbles laid-back Southern syrup with Florida brashness. With lively beaches, a Spanish-style downtown, and a thrumming military culture, this is by far the most interesting city in the Panhandle.

While urban-chic trends (locavore food, craft cocktails, etc) are taking root, visitors still primarily come to Pensacola for an all-American, blue-collar vacation experience: white-sand beaches, fried seafood and bars serving cheap domestics. During March and April, things reach fever pitch when droves of students descend for the weeklong bacchanalia of spring break. Beware.

Downtown, centered on Palafox St, lies north of the waterfront. Across the Pensacola Bay Bridge from here is the mostly residential peninsula of Gulf Breeze. Cross one more bridge, the Bob Sikes (toll $1), to reach pretty Pensacola Beach, the ultimate destination for most visitors.

◎ Sights

A combo ticket (adult $8, child $4) gets you seven days access to Historic Pensacola Village, the Pensacola Children's Museum, the TT Wentworth Jr Florida State Museum and Voices of Pensacola. The combo ticket can be purchased at any of the included museums.

★**National Naval
Aviation Museum**   MUSEUM
(Map p446; ✆800-327-5002; www.navalaviation museum.org; 1750 Radford Blvd; ◎9am-5pm; ♿)
FREE A visit to Pensacola is not complete without a trip to this enormous collection of military aircraft muscle and artifacts. Adults and children alike will be fascinated by the range of planes on display: more than 150! That's before we even get to the high-tech stuff like flight simulators and an IMAX theater. You can watch the Blue Angels (p448) practice their death-defying air show at 8:30am most Tuesdays and Wednesdays between March and November.

**Fort Barrancas &
Advanced Redoubt**   FORT
(Map p446; ✆850-934-2600; www.nps.gov/guis/planyourvisit/fort-barrancas; 3182 Taylor Rd; $7; ◎8:30am-4:30pm; ℗) ✎ On a dramatic bluff overlooking Pensacola Bay, 19th-century Fort Barrancas was built by slaves atop an abandoned 18th-century Spanish fort. The fort, now part of the National Park Service, has endless dark passageways to explore but not much in the way of displays. A half-mile away via a walking trail lie the ruins of Advanced Redoubt, a Civil War–era fort. Call ahead to ask about scheduled tours.

Historic Pensacola Village   MUSEUM
(Map p450; ✆850-595-5985; www.historic pensacola.org; Tarragona & Church St; adult/child $8/4; ◎10am-4pm Tue-Sat; ℗♿) ✎ Pensacola's rich colonial history spans more than 450 years. This fascinating and attractive village is a self-contained enclave of photogenic historic homes turned into museums: it's the perfect starting point for familiarizing yourself with the city. Admission is good for one week and includes a guided tour and entrance to each building.

Voices of Pensacola   MUSEUM
(Map p450; ✆850-595-5985; www.historic pensacola.org; 117 E Government St; adult/child $8/4; ◎10am-4pm Tue-Sat) ✎ Part oral history archive, part interpretive center, this museum highlights, via videos and audio recordings, the different cultural groups that have contributed to the demographic soup that is Pensacola.

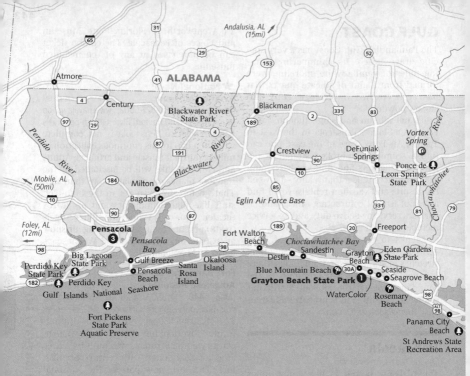

Andalusia, AL
(15mi)

ALABAMA

Atmore

Century

Blackwater River
State Park

Blackman

Crestview

DeFuniak
Springs

Vortex
Spring

Ponce de
Leon Springs
State Park

Perdido River

*Mobile, AL
(50mi)*

Milton

Bagdad

Blackwater River

Eglin Air Force Base

Freeport

*Foley, AL
(12mi)*

Pensacola ❸

*Pensacola
Bay*

Gulf Breeze

Pensacola
Beach

Santa
Rosa
Island

Okaloosa
Island

Fort Walton
Beach

Destin

Choctawhatchee Bay

Sandestin

Grayton
Beach

Eden Gardens
State Park

Seaside

Seagrove Beach

Blue Mountain Beach ❼ 30A

Grayton Beach State Park ❶

WaterColor

Rosemary
Beach

Panama City
Beach ❹

St Andrews State
Recreation Area

Big Lagoon
State Park

Perdido Key
State Park

Perdido Key

Gulf Islands National Seashore

Fort Pickens
State Park
Aquatic Preserve

GULF OF MEXICO

Ⓝ

0 ———————————— 100 km
0 ———————————— 50 miles

The Panhandle Highlights

❶ **Grayton Beach State
Park** (p459) Gaze at the gulf
waters, home to the country's
most beautiful beaches.

❷ **Apalachicola** (p466)
Embracing your inner

romantic in the gulf's most
charming town.

❸ **National Naval Aviation
Museum** (p443) Marveling at
the Blue Angels' death-defying
maneuvers and then getting

hands-on with the amazing
exhibits.

❹ **St George Island State
Park** (p469) Windswept
dunes, salt-marsh trails and
clean, pristine beaches.

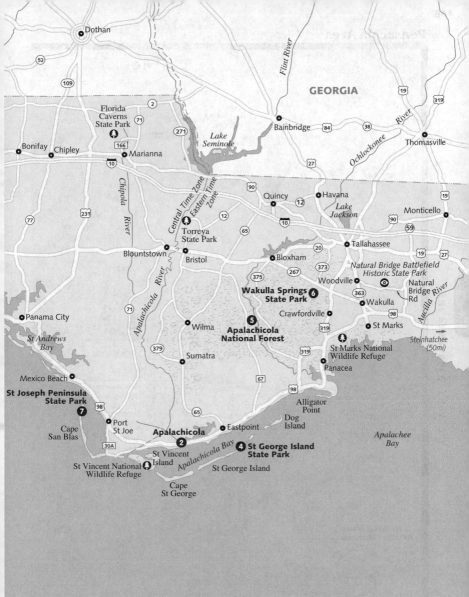

5 **Apalachicola National Forest** (p479) Seeking out coyotes, panthers and black bears, if you dare, in the wilderness of Florida's largest forest.

6 **Wakulla Springs State Park** (p481) Picking your jaw up off the floor of this park, where mossy cypress and mangroves mingle with manatees, alligators and birds.

7 **St Joseph Peninsula State Park** (p465) Marveling at the dune, forest and salt marsh quilt of the best Panhandle wilderness.

Pensacola Area

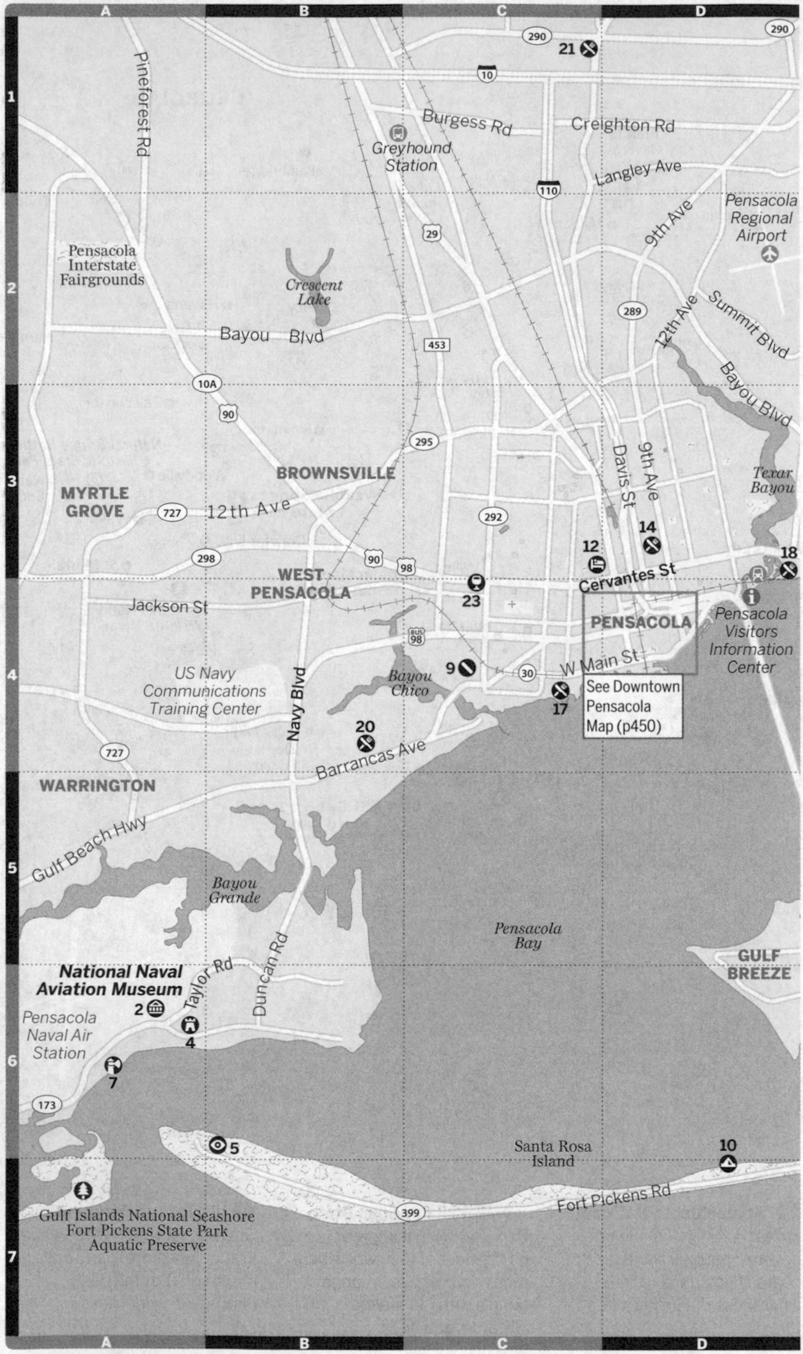

A
B
C
D
1
2
3
4
5
6
7
290
21
10
Pineforest Rd
Burgess Rd
Creighton Rd
Greyhound Station
Langley Ave
110
Pensacola Regional Airport
9th Ave
29
Pensacola Interstate Fairgrounds
Crescent Lake
289
12th Ave
Summit Blvd
Bayou Blvd
453
Bayou Blvd
10A
90
295
Davis St
9th Ave
Texar Bayou
BROWNSVILLE
MYRTLE GROVE
727
12th Ave
292
14
12
18
298
90
98
WEST PENSACOLA
23
Cervantes St
Jackson St
PENSACOLA
Pensacola Visitors Information Center
BUS 98
9
30
W Main St
US Navy Communications Training Center
Navy Blvd
Bayou Chico
17
See Downtown Pensacola Map (p450)
20
Barrancas Ave
727
WARRINGTON
Gulf Beach Hwy
Bayou Grande
Pensacola Bay
GULF BREEZE
National Naval Aviation Museum
Taylor Rd
Duncan Rd
2
4
Pensacola Naval Air Station
7
173
5
Santa Rosa Island
10
Fort Pickens Rd
399
Gulf Islands National Seashore Fort Pickens State Park Aquatic Preserve

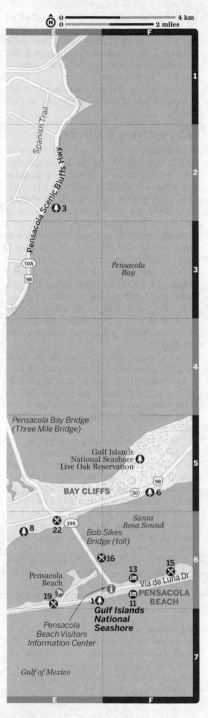

Pensacola Area

◎ Top Sights

◎ Sights

◎ Activities, Courses & Tours

◎ Sleeping

◎ Eating

◎ Drinking & Nightlife

THE PANHANDLE PENSACOLA

Pensacola Museum of Art   MUSEUM
(Map p450; ☏850-432-6247; www.pensacola museum.org; 407 S Jefferson St; adult/student $7/4; ◷10am-5pm Tue-Fri, 11am-4pm Sat; P) In the city's old jail (1908), this lovely art museum features an impressive, growing collection of major 20th- and 21st-century artists, spanning cubism, realism, pop art and folk art.

Bay Bluffs Park   PARK
(Map p446; www.pensacolascenicbluffs.org; 3400 Scenic Hwy; ◷sunrise-sunset; P) ⊘ FREE Off Pensacola Scenic Bluffs Hwy, this 32-acre park has wooden boardwalks that lead you along the side of the steep bluffs, through clutches of live oaks, pines, Florida rosemary and holly down to the empty beach below. With all of that said, persistent litter can be an issue.

WORTH A TRIP

PENSACOLA SCENIC BLUFFS HIGHWAY

This 11-mile stretch of road, which winds around the precipice of the highest point along the Gulf Coast, makes for a peaceful drive or slightly challenging bike ride. You'll see stunning views of Escambia Bay and pass a notable crumbling brick chimney – part of the steam-power plant for the Hyer-Knowles lumber mill in the 1850s – the only remnant of what was the first major industrial belt in the area.

TT Wentworth Jr Florida State Museum   MUSEUM

(Map p450; www.historicpensacola.org; 330 S Jefferson St; adult/child $8/4; ⊙10am-4pm Tue & Wed, to 7pm Thu-Sat, noon-4pm Sun; P) Housed in an enormous historic mansion, this state museum showcases two floors of Florida and Pensacola history, and one floor of Wentworth's collection of oddities, including his famous (and disgusting) petrified cat.

Pensacola Children's Museum   MUSEUM

(Map p450; ☑850-595-1559; 115 E Zaragoza St; adult/child $8/4; ⊙10am-4pm Tue-Sat; P♿) Learn about more than 450 years of local history and have some fun along the way in this compact museum occupying two floors of the historic (and allegedly haunted) Arbona building. The first hands-on level is aimed at youngsters up to nine years old, while the 2nd floor has a little more to offer older kids, including dress-ups.

Pensacola Lighthouse   LIGHTHOUSE

(Map p446; ☑850-393-1561; www.pensacolalighthouse.org; 2081 Radford Blvd; adult/child $7/4; ⊙10am-5:30pm Mon-Sat, from noon Sun; P) Be on the lookout for ghosts of past lighthouse keepers as you climb the 177 steps of this 160ft, 1859 lighthouse, rumored to be haunted. The views are quite stunning, as you might expect. If you're afraid of heights, you can hang back and take a look at the adjacent museum.

🏃 Activities

Garcon Point Trail   HIKING

(FL 281; ♿) 🅿 FREE The Panhandle's interior hides some large swaths of Florida wilderness. One example: the long fields of wire grass, longleaf pine and oak hammocks that blanket the land cut through by the Garcon Point Trail, about 16 miles east of Pensacola. An easy 1.7-mile loop circles through a flat, vibrantly green plain where the sky touches down to the palmettos.

Look for the trailhead just north of the toll plaza that precedes the bridge to Gulf Breeze.

🎊 Festivals & Events

Blue Angels   AIR SHOW

(☑850-452-3806; www.naspensacolaairshow.com; 390 San Carlos Rd, Suite A; ⊙8:30am Tue & Wed Mar-Nov) FREE To maintain its profile after WWII, and to reinforce its recruitment drive, the US Navy gathered some of its elite pilots to form the Blue Angels, a flight-demonstration squadron traveling to air shows around the country. The squadron's practice sessions can be observed here at their home base twice a week (weather permitting) from spring through autumn. Bleachers are available for the first 1000 spectators, so arrive early; BYO coffee and lawn chairs. There are also big performances early July and around Veteran's Day (Nov 11).

The viewing area is behind the National Naval Aviation Museum (p443) parking lot.

The name 'Blue Angels' caught on during the original team's trip to New York in 1946, when one of the pilots saw the name of the city's Blue Angel nightclub in the New Yorker.

These days, performing for about 15 million people a year, 'the Blues' (never 'the Angels'), their C130 Hercules support aircraft named *Fat Albert* and their all-Marine support crew visit about 35 show sites a year. Six jets execute precision maneuvers, including death-defying rolls and loops, and two F/A-18s undertake solo flights; the show culminates in all six planes flying in trademark delta formation.

Each of the Blues does a two-year tour of duty. In addition to the six pilots (which always include one Marine) is a narrator, who'll then move up through the ranks, and an events coordinator.

Gay Memorial Day   LGBT

(⊙late May) A three-day fiesta (across the Memorial Day weekend) of DJ soirees, all-night beach parties, drag shows and general fun and frivolity: crowds reach as many as 50,000, so book ahead!

🛏 Sleeping

Solé Inn
MOTEL $

(Map p450; ☎850-470-9298; www.soleinnand suites.com; 200 N Palafox St; r $79-199; 🛜🌀) Just north of downtown, this renovated motel goes for a 1960s mod look, with a black-and-white color scheme, animal-print accents and acrylic bubble lamps. Rooms aren't huge, but price, location and originality make up for the lack of space. There's complimentary continental breakfast.

Lee House
BOUTIQUE HOTEL $$

(Map p450; ☎850-912-8770; www.leehouse pensacola.com; 400 Bayfront Pkwy; ste $165-255; 🛜) Waterfront location and historical architectural charm come together at the Lee House, which boasts nine individually appointed, attractively decorated suites. The exterior feels plucked from old time, Gulf South central casting; the rooms have a modern, Ikea-ish vibe.

New World Inn
BOUTIQUE HOTEL $$

(Map p450; ☎850-432-4111; www.newworld landing.com; 600 S Palafox St; r from $170; 🅿🛜) Peek under the lid of this former box factory and you'll find surprisingly lovely rooms with luxe bedding and attractive hardwood flooring. They've got the location game down pat – the attractions of Historic Pensacola are just a few blocks away.

Noble Manor
B&B $$

(Map p446; ☎850-434-9544; www.noblemanor. com; 110 W Strong St; r $170, ste $195; 🅿🛜🌀) This pretty, Tudor-style 1905 mansion in the historic North Hill district is all kinds of charming. Innkeeper Bonnie runs a one-woman show, from shining up those spick-and-span hardwood floors to whipping up praline French toast for breakfast. Attractive rooms are basically business casual in style – neither too historic nor overtly contemporary.

Pensacola Victorian B&B
B&B $$

(Map p450; ☎850-434-2818; www.pensacola victorian.com; 203 W Gregory St; r $95-150; 🅿🛜) This stately 1892 Queen Anne building offers four lovingly maintained guest rooms. The standout is Suzanne's Room, with its hardwood floors, blue toile prints and clawfoot tub. It's about a mile north of downtown Pensacola.

Crowne Plaza Pensacola Grand
HOTEL $$

(Map p450; ☎850-433-3336; www.pensacola grandhotel.com; 200 East Gregory St; d from $130) The most attractive element of this hotel is the setting: the historic 1912 L&N Rail passenger terminal, which now serves as the hotel lobby, complete with period antique furnishing. The problem is, trains still arrive near here, and the walls are thin, so while rooms are fine, your sleep quality may not be.

✗ Eating

Taqueria El Asador
MEXICAN $

(Map p446; ☎850-696-3232; 7955 N Davis Hwy; tacos $2, burritos $8; ⏱10am-8:30pm Mon-Sat) There's a certain kind of insufferable American food snob who will tell you at every opportunity: 'You can't get good Mexican outside of [insert border state here].' We like to take these people to El Asador, which boasts a simple setting, a smoking grill and a menu of basic Mexican staples (tacos, burritos, tostadas) that are executed to near perfection.

Blue Dot
BURGERS $

(Map p450; ☎850-432-0644; 310 N De Villiers St; burgers $7; ⏱11:30am-3pm Tue-Fri, noon-3pm Sat) The line swells with locals in the know before 11am for these burgers – a simple, greasy and perfectly seasoned affair – and nobody is here to dance. Know what you want before you get to the counter (No cheese! No fries!) and dress appropriately (No wife beaters! No tanktops!). You're familiar with *Seinfeld*'s Soup Nazi? Meet the Burger Nazi.

Get here early – they always run out before closing. Cash only.

Pensacola Cooks Kitchen
INTERNATIONAL $

(Map p446; www.pensacolacooks.rezclick.com; 3670 Barrancas Ave; mains $10-13; ⏱10am-2pm Mon-Fri; 🍴♿) This cooking and catering outfit also offers one of the best lunch services in town. Enjoy fresh, creative takes on old-school classics such as spaghetti and meatballs, pork schnitzel and chicken salad sandwiches. Both your wallet and mouth will be grateful.

Al Fresco
FOOD TRUCK $

(Map p450; www.eatalfresco.com; 501 S Palafox; mains $8-13; ⏱hours vary) For cheap eats, check out Al Fresco, a collection of five Airstream trailer food trucks on the corner of Palafax and Main Streets. In general, the food trucks are there from 11am until 8pm or 9pm, but they'll close earlier if they run out of food.

Downtown Pensacola

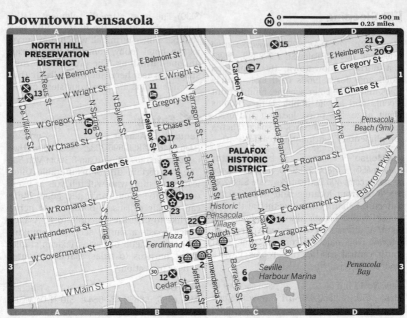

Downtown Pensacola

End of the Line Cafe   VEGAN **$**

(Map p450; ☎850-429-0336; www.eotlcafe.com; 610 E Wright St; items $7-11; ⊙8am-10pm Tue-Sat, 11am-2pm Sun; ⊕⊘) A funky, fair-trade cafe with velour and vinyl lounges, this is the place for such casual vegan fare as tempeh reubens and tofu BLTs, as well as cooking classes and cultural events, including big open-mic night on the second Friday of the month. There's also free wi-fi.

Joe Patti   SEAFOOD **$**

(Map p446; ☎850-432-3315; www.joepattis.com; 534 South B St, at Main St; items from $2.50; ⊙7:30am-6pm) At this beloved seafood emporium, get dock-fresh fish and seafood, prepared picnic food and sushi.

★Tin Cow   MODERN AMERICAN **$$**

(Map p450; ☎850-466-2103; www.thetincow. com; 102 S Palafox Pl; burgers $6-17; ⊙11am-midnight Sun-Tue, to 2am Wed-Sat; ⊕) Burger fans can't leave town without sampling the oozy, mountainous delight that is the Tin Cow burger: choose from signature suggestions or enjoy the freedom of building your own. With a tasty and original starter menu – blue balls (yes), truffle Parmesan fries and fried pickle spears – a stocked fridge of craft beers and sweet shakes, this joint is a solid bet.

Dharma Blue INTERNATIONAL $$
(Map p450; ☑850-433-1275; www.dharmablue. com; 300 S Alcaniz St; mains $15-30; ☺10am-2pm & 5-9:30pm Sat & Sun, 5-9:30pm Mon-Fri;) The eclectic menu of this compact local favorite ranges from semolina-dusted calamari and grilled duck to mouthwatering sushi, the latter being the most popular. A casual, welcoming vibe extends from the charming, cozy, chandelier-adorned interior to the sunny patio out front.

Five Sisters Blues Cafe CAFE $$
(Map p450; ☑850-912-4856; www.fivesisters bluescafe.com; 421 W Belmont St; mains $7-18; ☺11am-9pm Tue-Thu, to 10pm Fri & Sat, 10am-4pm Sun) Come get your weekly dose of soulful blues (Thursday to Sunday) and good ole Southern cuisine (crab cakes, fried green tomatoes, seafood gumbo) at this smart, classic diner in the heart of Pensacola. Even more fun – if you can get a table – are the Sunday jazz brunches: chicken and Belgian waffles, shrimp over grits and crab-cake Benedicts.

My Favorite Things CAFE $$
(Map p446; ☑850-346-1707; www.myfavorite thingstoo.com; 2183 E Cervantes S; mains $8-23; ☺10am-3pm Tue & Wed, to 9pm Thu & Fri, 9am-9pm Sat, 9am-3pm Sun) This rustic cafe on the edge of town serves equally delightful soups, sandwiches, salads and a small selection of simple seafood mains including grilled shrimp and pan-seared scallops. Best, however, are the breakfasts: fluffy omelets, decadent French toast and eggs Benedict with Canadian bacon: as it should be.

Bonnelli's Cafe Italia ITALIAN $$
(Map p446; ☑850-466-3002; www.bonellis cafeitalia.com; 1217 N 9th Ave; mains $11-25; ☺5-10pm Tue-Sat;) When you've got the Italian urge, Bonnelli's delivers, though not literally. All your favorites are represented: chunky meatballs, cheesy pizzas, creamy pastas, baked ziti and stuffed eggplant. Meals are hearty and well priced.

★**Iron** MODERN AMERICAN $$$
(Map p450; ☑850-476-7776; www.restaurant iron.com; 22 N Palafox St; mains $26-46; ☺4:30-10pm Tue-Thu, to 1am Fri & Sat;) Armed with New Orleans experience, chef Alex McPhail works his ever-changing menu magic at downtown's Iron, the best of Pensacola's new line of vibrant, locally sourced, high-end culinary hotbeds. Extremely friendly mixologists know their craft; and McPhail's food – from beer-braised pork belly to Creole-seasoned catch of the day – punches above the Emerald Coast's weight class.

 Drinking & Nightlife

In season, the beachside bars have more of a spring-break vibe (tequila and sozzled new drinkers); downtown offerings tend to be slightly more sophisticated. Many restaurants have their own bars. Check out www.pnj.com/entertainment for music listings.

Cabaret GAY
(Map p450; ☑850-607-2020; 101 S Jefferson St; ☺3pm-3am) A funky interior and a vibe that ranges from trivia nights to drag shows is the defining experience at this friendly 'gay-borhood' bar, a Pensacola gem that's open to all sexualities.

Roundup GAY
(Map p450; ☑850-433-8482; www.theroundup. net; 560 E Heinberg St; ☺2pm-3am) For those who like their men manly, check out this niche-y, neighborhood hangout with a killer furry-friendly patio. Ladies are welcome, but cowboys, tradies and bikers are always flavor of the month. There's a Facebook page for event listings.

Elbow Room PUB
(Map p446; ☑850-434-0300; 2213 W Cervantes St; ☺4pm-2am Tue-Sat) Although it doesn't have much external visual appeal, this funky, dark, retro dive bar in suburban Pensacola houses a whole world of fun and a mellow vibe.

McGuire's Irish Pub PUB
(Map p450; ☑850-433-6789; www.mcguires irishpub.com; 600 E Gregory St; ☺11am-2am) This ginormous Irish theme park of a pub gets rowdy around 9pm and is super-popular at dinner time: the pub grub is top notch. Remember, don't try to pay for your drinks with one of the thousands of dollar bills hanging from the ceiling – a local recently found himself in the slammer that way!

Seville Quarter CLUB

(Map p450; ☑850-434-6211; www.sevillequarter.com; 130 E Government St; cover $3-10; ☺7am-3am Mon-Sat, from 11am Sun) Taking up an entire city block, this monster of an entertainment complex contains seven separate eating, drinking and music venues, along with HG Wells-ian 1890s decor. For all of the different venues, the crowd is pretty consistent: locals getting off work, or getting their weekend on, and getting drunk.

☆ Entertainment

Saenger Theatre THEATER

(Map p450; ☑850-595-3880; www.pensacolasaenger.com; 118 S Palafox Pl) This Spanish baroque beauty was reconstructed in 1925 using bricks from the Pensacola Opera House, which was destroyed in a 1916 hurricane. It now hosts popular musicals and top-billing music acts and is home to the Pensacola Symphony Orchestra and the Pensacola Opera.

Vinyl Music Hall LIVE MUSIC

(Map p450; ☑877-435-9849; www.vinylmusichall.com; 2 S Palafox Pl; box office noon-5pm Mon-Fri) This is a solid venue for live music, booking acts that run from mainstream headliners to indie. Check the website for listings.

ⓘ Information

Pensacola Visitors Information Center (Map p446; ☑800-874-1234; www.visitpensacola.com; 1401 E Gregory St; ☺8am-5pm Mon-Fri, 9am-4pm Sat, 10am-4pm Sun) Come to the foot of the Pensacola Bay Bridge for a bounty of tourist information, knowledgeable staff and a free internet kiosk.

ⓘ Getting There & Away

Pensacola Regional Airport (Map p446; ☑850-436-5000; www.flypensacola.com; 2430 Airport Blvd) is served by most major US airlines. Primary direct connections outside Florida include Atlanta, Charlotte, Dallas and Houston. It's 4 miles northeast of downtown off 9th Ave on Airport Blvd. A taxi costs about $20 to downtown and $35 to the beach. Try **Yellow Cab** (☑850-433-3333; www.yellowcabpensacola.com).

The **Greyhound station** (Map p446; ☑850-476-4800; www.greyhound.com; 505 W Burgess Rd) is located north of the downtown area. **Escambia County Transit** (ECAT; ☑850-595-3228; www.goecat.com; rides $1.75) has a free trolley service connecting downtown Pensacola and the beach between Memorial Day weekend and the end of September.

I-10 is the major east–west thoroughfare used by buses, and many pass down Palafox St.

Pensacola Beach

☑850 / POP 8065

Distinctly separate from Pensacola itself, Pensacola Beach is a pretty stretch of powdery white sand, gentle, warm waters and a string of mellow beachfront hotels. The beach occupies nearly 8 miles of the 40-mile-long Santa Rosa barrier island, surrounded by the Santa Rosa Sound and the Gulf of Mexico to the north and south, and by the federally protected Gulf Islands National Seashore on either side. Though determined residents have protected much of the barrier island from development, several high-rise condos have created a bit of a Gulf Coast skyline.

The area is a major hub for local entertainment and special events, including Mardi Gras celebrations, a triathlon, wine tastings, a summer music series and parades.

⊙ Sights & Activities

★**Gulf Islands National Seashore** PARK

(Map p446; ☑850-934-2600; www.nps.gov/guis; vehicle $15; ☺sunrise-sunset; ⊞) ⌀ The highlight of the Florida Panhandle, this 150-mile stretch of mostly undeveloped white-sand beach is a prime example of what the Gulf Coast looked like before human settlement (which, to be fair, can often be seen in the form of high rises in the distance). The National Seashore is not contiguous, but you'll find portions all along the coast: long swaths of sugar white dunes crowned with sea oats, a perfect example of pristine flatland beach.

Naval Live Oaks Reservation PARK

(Map p446; ☑850-934-2600; US 98; ☺8:30am-4:30pm Mon-Fri; ℗) ⌀ FREE This section of Gulf Islands National Seashore doesn't actually contain (much) seashore – instead, it consists of groves of local maritime hammock (forest) cut through by 7.5 miles of hiking trails. What's in a name? Local live oaks, prized for their toughness and durability, were used as timber for early American warships.

Fort Pickens HISTORIC SITE

(Map p446; ☑850-934-2600; www.nps.gov/guis/learn/historyculture/fort-pickens; 1400 Fort Pickens Rd; 7-day pass pedestrian & cyclist/car $7/15; ☺sunrise-sunset; ℗⊞) ⌀ Part of the Gulf Islands National Seashore, this 1834 historic fort perched at the western extent of the Santa Rosa barrier island has survived wars and scores of hurricanes to remain a fascinating and scenic excursion. Pick up a self-guided-tour map from the visitor center.

Shoreline Park UFO Spotting PARK
(Map p446; 700 Shoreline Dr, Gulf Breeze; P) Maybe it's activity from the nearby Pensacola Naval Air Station, but this stretch of the gulf has apparently had hundreds of UFO sightings in the past few decades, with reports right along the coast. Local skywatchers (including members of the Mutual UFO Network) gather at this park with binoculars and lawn chairs in the hope of a close encounter: as good a reason as any to spread out a beach blanket and gaze at the stars.

MBT Divers DIVING
(Map p446; 850-455-7702; www.mbtdivers. com; 3920 Barrancas Ave; courses from $239; 8am-6pm Mon-Sat, to 3pm Sun) The *Oriskany* CV/CVA-34 aircraft carrier, at approximately 900ft long and 150ft tall, was the largest vessel ever sunk as an artificial reef when it was submerged in 2007 off Pensacola Beach. This professional outfitter will gear up and help experienced divers plan their dive. A variety of dive courses are also available, including an exclusive *Oriskany* class.

🤿 Courses

Lanier Sailing Academy BOATING
(Map p450; 850-432-3199; www.laniersail. com/a1/pensacola-3; 997 S Palafox St; sailboat rental from $245; 9am-5pm Tue-Sun) Conditions at Pensacola Bay are perfect for sailing, and this award-winning school offers a variety of courses, including a basic three-day introduction to sailing ($550). Those in the know can rent a Capri 22 from $245 daily.

🛏 Sleeping

Fort Pickens Campground CAMPGROUND $
(Map p446; 850-934-2600; www.recreation. gov; Fort Pickens entrance, Gulf Islands National Seashore; tent & RV sites $26; P) 🍴 Amid the windblown trees across from the beach, these two pleasant campgrounds are popular with RV-ers, though you'll see the odd tent or two. There are fire pits, a bathhouse and a small camp store. Park entrance fees

to Gulf Islands National Seashore must be paid separately.

Holiday Inn Resort HOTEL $$
(Map p446; 850-203-0635; www.holidayinn resortpensacolabeach.com; 14 Via de Luna Dr; r from $210; ⊛) This beachfront hotel has cool, inviting rooms with ultra-comfy beds, flat-screen TVs and great showers. Oceanfront rooms have spacious balconies overhanging the soft, white sands and the cool turquoise waters below. Suites and kids' suites are available, and the pool is killer. Friendly, obliging staff help seal the deal. Excellent value.

Paradise Inn MOTEL $$
(Map p446; 850-932-2319; www.paradiseinn-pb. com; 21 Via de Luna Dr; r $99-140; P ⊛ 🛜 ⊛) Across from the beach, this sherbet-colored motel is a lively, cheery place thanks to its popular bar and grill (ask for a quiet room near the parking lot). Compact quarters are spick and span with tiled floors and brightly painted walls. Online specials offer even better value.

Margaritaville Beach Hotel HOTEL $$$
(Map p446; 850-916-9755; www.margarita villehotel.com; 165 Fort Pickens Rd; r from $230; ⊛ 🛜 ⊛) Jimmy Buffett, of Vegas' Margaritaville fame, isn't known for his good taste; however, this beachfront hotel challenges that reputation. Spacious rooms are styled in crisp whites and aquas, with arty murals and huge flat-screen TVs. Downstairs, a grown-up crowd swans around the lobby and sips cocktails by the pool.

🍴 Eating

Native Café BREAKFAST $
(Map p446; www.thenativecafe.com; 45a Via de Luna Dr; mains $5-13; 7:30am-3pm; 🛜 🍴) This funky breakfast and lunch spot, 'owned and operated by friendly natives,' is a welcome addition to the fried-fish stretch. Try a shrimp po' boy, grilled chicken sandwich, fish tacos, rice and beans or seafood gumbo – or, for a cheap morning jump-start, eggs Benedict or pancakes.

Wild Roots HEALTH FOOD $
(Map p446; 850-816-8870; www.wildroots organicfoods.com; 820 Gulf Breeze Pkwy, Gulf Breeze; mains $8-17; 10am-7pm; P 🍴) 🍴 There's not a ton of health-food stores in Panhandle, but Wild Roots kind of makes up for the lack. Self-cater with vegan wraps, enormous salads, pizzas and sandwiches –

and for what it's worth, there's meat options too, if that's how you like your protein.

Dog House Deli
DINER $

(Map p446; ☑ 850-916-4993; www.doghousedeli. com; 35 Via de Luna Dr; items from $3; ⊗ 8:30am-3:30pm; ⊕) For cheap and easy beachfront eats, try this local favorite, in business for more than 35 years, serving a range of signature or build-your-own dogs as well as a tasty breakfast menu.

Peg Leg Pete's
SEAFOOD $$

(Map p446; ☑ 850-932-4139; www.peglegpetes. com; 1010 Fort Pickens Rd; mains $9-25; ⊗ 11am-10pm; ⊕) Ah-har, me hearties, walk ye olde plank, blah blah pirate stuff...you get the idea, this place has a theme going. Anyways, pop into Pete's for almost-beachfront oysters, fat grouper sandwiches, crab legs and jumbo sea scallops. There's nothing fancy about the woodsy, somewhat grungy sea-shanty decor, but the service is swift and smiley, despite how busy it gets.

Grand Marlin
SEAFOOD $$$

(Map p446; ☑ 850-677-9153; www.thegrandmarlin. com; 400 Pensacola Beach Rd; mains $14-38; ⊗ 11am-10pm Mon-Thu, to 11pm Fri & Sat, 10am-10pm Sun) This versatile seafood restaurant and oyster bar gives you the best of both worlds: enjoy a casual alfresco atmosphere on the best-for-sunset patio, or treat yourself to formal fine dining indoors. Either way, expect excellent service and oceanic delights such as blue crab, lobster mac 'n' cheese (yum!) and fresh-from-the-boat seafood cooked any way you like.

ℹ Information

Pensacola Beach Visitors Information
Center (Map p446; ☑ 850-932-1500; www. visitpensacolabeach.com; 735 Pensacola Beach Blvd; ⊗ 9am-5pm) On the right as soon as you enter Pensacola Beach; this is a small place with some useful maps and brochures about goings-on, road closures (due to storms) and anything else beach-oriented.

Perdido Key

☑ 850 / POP 29,395

About 12 miles southwest of Pensacola, off Hwy 292 (which becomes Hwy 182), the easternmost Florida section of the Gulf Islands National Seashore spans Perdido Key's crystalline waters. These powdery dunes are home to the endangered Perdido Key beach mouse, which blends in well with the white-quartz sands here. There are two coastal state parks in the area: Perdido Key State Park and, on the northern side of the lagoon, between Perdido Key and the mainland, Big Lagoon State Park, with great crabbing in the lagoon's shallows. You'll find several free beach areas along the stretch of Perdido Key town – an otherwise unseemly blot of high-rise condos and share houses.

◉ Sights

Perdido Key State Park
STATE PARK

(☑ 850-492-1595; www.floridastateparks.org/perdidokey; 15301 Perdido Key Drive; vehicle $3; ⊗ 8am-sunset; P) ✅ This alluring coastal state park protects the 247-acre barrier island of the same name, a windblown, sand-strewn landscape of rolling dunes, tufts of beach grass and the soft bending sea oats that give the region such an unmistakable allure.

Tarkiln Bayou Preserve State Park
PARK

(☑ 850-492-1595; www.floridastateparks.org/park/Tarkiln-Bayou; 2401 Bauer Rd; vehicle/cyclist $3/2; ⊗ 8am-sunset; P) ✅ This fascinating park preserves ecosystems that run from wet prairie to sandy shoreline to the eponymous Tarkiln Bayou, an eerie, alluring spill of dark water, brightly flowering plants and thin trees. Peppered throughout are trails, boardwalks, and four species of the endangered pitcher plant, a carnivorous plant that lures insects to death in its digestive, petal-crowned gullet.

The park is located about 8 miles north of Perdido Key, and 15 miles west of Pensacola.

Big Lagoon State Park
STATE PARK

(☑ 850-492-1595; www.floridastateparks.org/biglagoon; 12301 Gulf Beach Hwy; vehicle $6; ⊗ 8am-sunset; P) ✅ Get a taste of the wilds on the Panhandle at Big Lagoon, a quilt of salt marshes, pine forest, bays, ponds and beaches, all interconnected by boardwalks and easy walking trails. Bird-watchers will be in heaven, which goes for anyone who wants a little peace and quiet.

✤ Festivals & Events

Interstate Mullet Toss
CULTURAL

(⊗ Apr) On the last full weekend in April, locals gather on both sides of the Florida–Alabama state line for a time-honored tradition: the mullet toss. The idea – apart from a very fine excuse for a party – is to see who can throw their (dead) mullet (an abundant local fish) the furthest across the border from Florida into Alabama.

People have developed their own techniques: tail first, head first, or breaking its spine and bending it in half for better aerodynamics. The mullet toss is organized by Perdido Key's Flora-Bama Lounge, Package and Oyster Bar, a legendary bar and roadhouse just east of the state line.

Frank Brown International Songwriters' Festival
MUSIC
(www.frankbrownsongwriters.com; ⊗Nov) This 10-day concert series features hundreds of singer-songwriters performing around the Gulf Coast region, including Perdido Key and Pensacola.

🛏 Sleeping

Big Lagoon State Park Camping
CAMPGROUND $
(📞800-326-3521; www.reserveamerica.com; 12301 Gulf Beach Hwy; campsite $20; P) ⊘ There are 75 bucolic campsites in this state park peppered among the pine woods. Electric hookups and drinkable water.

🍷 Drinking & Nightlife

Flora-Bama Lounge, Package and Oyster Bar
BAR
(📞850-492-0611; www.florabama.com; 17401 Perdido Key Dr; ⊗11am-3am) This legendary bar and roadhouse just east of the state line hosts the annual mullet toss and Polar Bear Dip (a New Year's dip in the cold sea – comes with a free drink). Flora-Bama has tried to get mullet tossing into the *Guinness Book of World Records*, but its time hasn't come, yet.

ℹ Getting There & Away

Perdido Key runs right to the state line. From here, you can follow Hwy 182 straight into Alabama and take Hwy 59/US 90 north to connect with I-10.

If you're arriving in Perdido Key on Hwy 182 from the west, welcome to Florida.

Fort Walton Beach
📞850 / POP 20,600
Stretching along US 98 – maybe a little euphemistically relabeled the Miracle Strip in these parts – Fort Walton Beach is a jumble of strip malls, beachfront mansions, seaside restaurants and neon; there's

a pretty downtown-ish strip that rambles from Perry Ave to Florida Place. 'FWB' isn't as tourism-minded as towns like nearby Destin, and the place pretty much feels like a base town that happens to be perched near the Gulf Coast.

Between Fort Walton Beach and Destin, which bend around Choctawhatchee Bay like two crab claws, lies pristine beachfront owned by the US Air Force, whose largest base, Eglin, is here.

◉ Sights
The most attractive element of Fort Walton Beach lies just outside of its borders: the **Okaloosa Day Use Area** section of Gulf Islands National Seashore (p452), located just east of town. This long stretch of quiet, windblown dunes and sea oats is jarringly wild when contrasted to the neon strips of beachside development that bracket it. The parking area leads to a beach access point and picnic tables.

Indian Temple Mound & Museum
ARCHAEOLOGICAL SITE
(📞850-833-9595; www.fwb.org/museums/indian-temple-mound-museum; 139 Miracle Strip Pkwy SE; adult/child $5/3; ⊗8am-4:30pm Mon-Sat; P) ⊘ One of the most sacred sites for local Native American culture to this day, the 17ft-tall, 223ft-wide ceremonial and political temple mound, built with 500,000 basket-loads of earth and representing what is probably the largest prehistoric earthwork on the Gulf Coast, dates back to somewhere between AD 800 and 1500. On top of the mound you'll find a re-created temple, which houses a small exhibition center.

The museum offers an extensive overview of 12,000 years of Native American history, and houses flutes, ceramics and artifacts fashioned from stone, bone and shells, as well as a comprehensive research library.

US Air Force Armament Museum
MUSEUM
(📞850-882-4062; www.afarmamentmuseum.com; 100 Museum Dr, Eglin Air Force Base; ⊗9:30am-4:30pm Mon-Sat; P) FREE One for military buffs. The exterior of this hangar-style museum, flanked by fighter planes, appears small, but inside are extensive weapons displays – including an F-105 Thunderchief missile and a Warthog simulator – as well as a detailed history of Eglin base, the largest in the US. Expect an un-apologetically pro-American spin on US military history. The museum is about 9 miles northeast of Fort Walton Beach.

Okaloosa Island Pier & Boardwalk   PIER

(1030 Miracle Strip Pkwy E; access $2, fishing adult/child $7.50/4.50; ⏰24hr Apr-Oct, 5am-9pm Nov-Mar; P) Stretching out almost a quarter of a mile into the Atlantic, this popular recreational-fishing pier is open 24 hours in the summer and is illuminated for night fishing. Rental gear is available (from $7) and there are no fishing-license requirements. Otherwise, the pier and adjacent boardwalk are good for a leisurely stroll, and the adjacent beach is simply a damn fine stretch of sand.

🛏 Sleeping

★ Aunt Martha's
Bed & Breakfast   B&B $$

(✆850-243-6702;   www.auntmarthasbedand breakfast.com; 315 Shell Ave SE; r $105-115; ❊🕸) A short walk from downtown, this charming inn overlooks the Intracoastal. Elegant, unfussy rooms with big brass beds look out into the leafy branches of live oak trees. The common area has a baby grand piano, a well-stocked library and French doors that open onto a breezy verandah.

Martha's Southern breakfasts – crawfish quiche, ham and cheese grits, stuffed French toast, you name it – are a veritable feast.

Henderson Park Inn   INN $$

(✆888-836-1105;   www.hendersonparkinn.com; 2700 Hwy 98; r from $199; ❊🕸🏊🐾) This classy shingled inn has 35 tastefully decorated rooms with high-end Egyptian cotton linens, and thoughtful touches such as chocolates on your pillow. Breakfast, lunch, drinks and snacks are all included, making this a popular spot with honeymooners.

🍴 Eating

Lanie's Kitchen II   FILIPINO $

(✆850-243-6780;   www.lanieskitchen.com;   202 Ferry Rd SE; lunch buffet $10; ⏰11am-3pm Mon-Sat; P🐾) If you find an American base town, you usually don't have to look far to find an excellent Filipino restaurant, thanks to a traditionally large American military presence in the Philippines. Lanie's is the cream of the Panhandle crop, serving up amazing value buffets of pork and chicken adobo (in a vinegar, soy and garlic sauce), pancit (thin-rice) noodles and spicy bicol express (a kind of pork stew).

Stewby's Seafood Shanty   SEAFOOD $

(✆850-586-7001; www.stewbys.com; 427 Race-track Rd NW; items $5-18; ⏰10am-9pm; P🐾)

Off the main drag, en route to Eglin base, this unpretentious, predominantly takeout restaurant is famed for its signature sandwiches, fried seafood platters and excellent value for money. Go for the soft-shell crab if it's in season.

Bay Café   FRENCH $$

(✆850-344-7822;   www.baycafewaterfront.com; 233 Alconese Ave; mains $16-28; ⏰11am-3pm & 5-10pm; P) Foie gras, pan-seared scallops and filet mignon all feature on the menu at this *très-jolie* French cafe on the waterfront beneath the shadow of the Brooks Bridge. Loved by locals for more than 30 years, the cafe has an indoor-outdoor patio with wonderful views of the bay, and an extensive wine list.

🍷 Drinking & Nightlife

Props Craft Brewery   BREWERY

(✆850-586-7117;   www.propsbrewery.com;   255 Miracle Strip Pkwy SE; ⏰11am-11pm) A friendly, unassuming spot to down a cold, locally brewed craft beer, and check out some sport on the big screen or hang in the beer garden to mingle with locals.

❶ Getting There & Away

Fort Walton Beach is about 55 miles west of Panama City Beach and about 41 miles east of Pensacola, along Hwy 98.

Destin–Fort Walton Beach Airport (Northwest Florida Regional Airport; VPS; ✆850-651-7160; www.flyvps.com; 1701 State Road 85 N) serves the Destin–Fort Walton area. In addition, the **Emerald Coast Rider** (✆850-833-9168; www.ecrider.org; $1.50; ⏰8am-7pm Mon-Fri) runs a shuttle service between Fort Walton Beach and Destin.

Destin

✆850 / POP 13,260

Destin has the odd claim of appealing to retirees, families and spring breakers. The skin of this town is admittedly not too appealing – from the road, Destin looks like an endless chain of strip malls, high-rise condos and mini amusement parks. But local beaches are a veritable balm for the soul, and are quite beautiful besides.

Deep-sea fishing is an entrenched part of the area's tradition, with an offshore shelf dropping to depths of 100ft about 10 miles off Destin's east pass. Locals call their town the 'world's luckiest fishing village' – not that it looks much like a village anymore.

◉ Sights

Destin boasts more than 24 miles of beach, which are by far the main draw for visitors. On sunny days, the sand truly is almost uncannily white – ironically, these sea-level beaches derive their pale hue from crushed quartz that washed down from the ancient Appalachian mountains. There are 13 public access points to local beaches. Check www.cityofdestin.com for a full breakdown. Parking around access points is often limited.

Henderson Beach State Park   BEACH
(📞850-837-7550; www.floridastateparks.org/park/Henderson-Beach; 17000 Emerald Coast Pkwy; vehicle $6; ⊗8am-sunset; P🐾) 🐾 Our favorite beach area in Destin is this state park, which includes a 0.8-mile nature trail. There are also some excellent beachside campsites ($30), which include running water and electric hookups.

Seascape Beach   BEACH
(www.cityofdestin.com; 2966 Hwy 98; ⊗sunrise-sunset; P🐾) FREE Although all of Destin's beaches are family-friendly, this beach is maybe a little *more* family-friendly, given the presence of restrooms, a picnic area and shaded pavilions.

Destin Boardwalk & HarborWalk Village   WATERFRONT
(📞850-687-1237; www.destinboardwalk.com; 102 Harbor Blvd; P🐾) This tourist mecca of timeshare condos, boutiques, restaurants, nightclubs and a marina is worth a stroll, especially if you have kids. Most of the area's tour operators (including private fishing charters) have kiosks here and there are plenty of activities to enjoy, albeit at tourist prices.

🏃 Activities

Just Chute Me   WATER SPORTS
(📞850-213-1971; www.parasaildestin.com; 500 Harbor Blvd; per person from $50; ⊗8am-sunset Feb-Oct) Calm waters and stunning vistas make the gulf a great place for parasailing. This professional operator takes beginners into the great blue yonder above to gaze at the great blue wonder below.

ScubaTech   DIVING
(📞850-837-2822; www.scubatechnwfl.com; Harbor Blvd & Marler St; snorkeling from $30, scuba diving from $90; ⊗9am-5pm Mon-Sat, to 4pm Sun) Take advantage of the region's great diving with this competent outfitter.

A four-hour, two-tank, 58ft to 90ft dive is $90; a complete gear package, including fins, mask and snorkel, costs $65. Two-hour snorkeling trips including gear and wetsuit cost $30.

⛵ Tours

Southern Star Dolphin Cruises   CRUISE
(📞850-837-7741; www.dolphin-sstar.com; 100 Harbor Blvd, Suite A; adult/child $29/16) This environmentally conscious operator has been sailing for more than 20 years, observing the bottlenose dolphins that live in these temperate waters. Two-hour cruises operate year-round from an 80ft glass-bottom boat. Check the website for schedules.

🛏 Sleeping

Many visitors opt to stay in vacation rentals, which are listed on a variety of websites, including www.destinvacation.com and www.destinflrentals.com.

Henderson Beach State Park   CAMPGROUND $
(📞850-837-7550; www.floridastateparks.reserveamerica.com; 17000 Emerald Coast Pkwy; tent & RV sites $30, day use $6; P) This coastal paradise has 54 very private sites and good restrooms amid twisted scrub pines, with a 0.75-mile nature walk through the dune system. It's better suited to RVs than tents.

Candlewood Suites Destin-Sandestin   HOTEL $$
(📞850-337-3770; www.candlewooddestin.com; 11396 Hwy 98; d from $118; P🐾) Smart, practical rooms and extra-courteous staff make this modern highway hotel at the eastern extent of town a good-value offering. All rooms have kitchen facilities, comfy bedding and free wi-fi.

🍴 Eating

Donut Hole Café & Bakery   BAKERY $
(📞850-837-8824; 635 Harbor Blvd; items from $4; ⊗6am-10pm; 🐾) This simple bakery-diner is a local favorite, serving sit-down breakfasts, fluffy takeout buttermilk doughnuts and bakery items, including generous wedges of decadent key lime pie.

Boathouse Oyster Bar   SEAFOOD $
(📞850-837-3645; www.boathouseoysterbar.com; 288 Harbor Blvd; items $4-18; ⊗11am-11pm; P) What looks like a waterfront shed is...well, a waterfront shed, but a shed where live music, raw oysters, boiled crawfish, fried seafood,

buckets of cold beer and waterfront vibes are ubiquitous. Closing times are a little fungible, depending on what band is playing.

McGuire's
STEAK $$

(www.mcguiresirishpub.com; 33 E Hwy 98; mains $12-33; ⊙11am-2am; P ⚡) This enormous Irish-pub-microbrewery-steakhouse complex is a Panhandle institution; despite it's size, it always seems to be packed to the gills. There's a reason for that; this may be a mall-sized complex with kitschy stuff on the walls (which would usually raise our warning lights), but the food is great, especially the steaks and burgers. House-brewed beers round out the experience.

This spot is extremely popular with local military families; a good chunk of the US Navy and Air Force has had a steak or two (and a beer or four) at this spot. Closing time varies, but McGuire's usually closes around 2am.

Zesty Baguette Bistro
VIETNAMESE $$

(✐850-460-8797; www.zestybaguettebistro.com; 4418 Commons Dr E; mains $14-25; ⊙11am-9pm; P ✐⚡) A genuinely creative menu mixes up Vietnamese, French and even Southern influences in this unexpected gem. Pillow-y jasmine rice cradles grilled shrimp, while scallops come with creamy mashed potatoes and a tart ginger sauce. Located within the enormous Destin Commons mall complex.

Craft Bar
AMERICAN $$

(✐850-460-7907; www.thecraftbarfl.com/destin; 4424 Commons Dr E; mains $15-27; ⊙11am-11pm Mon-Thu, to midnight Sat, to 10pm Sun; P) As much restaurant as bar, Craft Bar brings a bit of 21st-century foodie fanaticism and craft-beer obsession to Destin (and a few other spots in North Florida; this is a local chain). Billing itself as 'a Florida gastropub,' the airy, modern interior is attached to a kitchen that serves pecan-crusted fish, tuna burgers and bison burgers.

The attached liquor and beer store has a fantastic selection of booze.

Dewey Destin's
SEAFOOD $$

(✐850-837-7525; www.destinseafood.com; 202 Harbor Blvd; mains $12-30; ⊙11am-9pm; P ⚡) Refreshingly human-scale compared to some of the corporate-behemoth restaurants on Destin's main strip, this longtime local favorite serves up simple fried and steamed seafood platters and cool rum drinks in a crowded old beach shack decorated with vintage Florida photos.

Louisiana Lagniappe
SEAFOOD $$$

(✐850-837-0881; www.thelouisianalagniappe.com/destin; 775 Gulf Shore Dr; mains $18-39; ⊙5-9pm Mon-Fri, to 10pm Sat & Sun; P ⚡) Decent New Orleans–style cooking can be found right here in Destin, and there's a gorgeous view overlooking the water to boot. Ocean-fresh seafood includes grouper stuffed with soft-shell crab, redfish stuffed with – hey, why not? – more crab, and blackened shrimp with a pineapple rum sauce. Did we mention the views?

Drinking & Nightlife

HarborWalk Village (just off US 98, on the very western edge of Destin, before the bridge to Okaloosa Island) and the boardwalk on Okaloosa Island (p456), about 6 miles west of Destin proper, have plenty of nightlife – mainly busy, tourist-oriented pubs and restaurants overlooking the water. The bars here tend to attract a mix of older tourists and military folks. While the atmosphere can feel a little casual earlier in the evening, the party can get pretty raucous later in the night.

Shopping

Destin Commons
MALL

(✐850-337-8700; www.destincommons.com; 4100 Legendary Dr; ⊙10am-9pm Mon-Sat, 11am-7pm Sun) Yes, this is an enormous mall complex, but as outdoor mall complexes go, it's quite attractive, and an easy place to take the family if they need to lose themselves amid dozens of shops and a gigantic movie theater.

Getting There & Away

Destin is about 45 miles west of Panama City Beach and about 47 miles east of Pensacola, along Hwy 98. **Destin–Fort Walton Beach Airport** (p456), sometimes still referred to as Northwest Florida Regional Airport, serves the Destin–Fort Walton area, with direct services to many US cities, including Chicago and Tampa.

South Walton & 30A Beaches

✐850 / POP 12,446

Sandwiched between Destin and Panama City along **Scenic Hwy 30A** are 16 unincorporated communities collectively known as South Walton (or The Beaches of South Walton, if you love chamber of commerce branding, but we draw the line at 'SoWal'). Each town has its own identity, and most are master-planned resort towns with architecture following set themes. If you're wondering what happens when you bake New Urbanism in the Florida sun, here's the answer.

If you only make two stops, we recommend delightful **Grayton Beach**, which feels as though it was settled by old-school hippies who came into money (stay a night here if you can) and the meticulously manicured village of **Seaside**, which is so well planned they filmed *The Truman Show* here. Other points of interest include the whimsically named community of Water-Color, Moroccan-themed Alys Beach and the Dutch-inspired hamlet of Rosemary Beach. For more information, check out www.discover30a.com.

⊙ Sights

There are more than 50 public access points to the South Walton beaches with varying degrees of accessibility; a complete list can be found at www.visitsouthwalton.com. Parking lots can fill fast, especially on the weekends, so it's best to arrive early.

★ Grayton Beach State Park   STATE PARK
(☑850-267-8300; www.floridastateparks.org/graytonbeach; 357 Main Park Rd, Grayton Beach; vehicle $5; ☺8am-sunset; ℗) ⌀ An 1133-acre stretch of marble-colored dunes rolling down to the water's edge, this state park's beauty is genuinely mind-blowing. The park sits nestled against the wealthy but down-to-earth community of Grayton Beach, home to the famed Red Bar and to the quirky **Dog Wall** – a mural on which residents paint portraits of their dogs.

Locals flock here for nightly sunsets and to wakeboard on the unique coastal dune lakes that shimmer across the sand from the gulf. The park also contains the Grayton Beach Nature Trail (start your self-guided tour at the gate), which runs from the eastern side of the parking lot through the dunes, magnolias and pine flatwoods and onto a boardwalk to a return trail along the beach.

Topsail Hill Preserve
State Park   STATE PARK
(www.floridastateparks.org/park/Topsail-Hill; 7525 W Scenic Hwy 30A, Santa Rosa; vehicle/pedestrian $6/2; ☺8am-sunset; ℗) ⌀ There's some 1640 acres of natural beauty to discover at Topsail, including quiet white-sand

WORTH A TRIP

PONCE DE LEON SPRINGS STATE PARK
Located about 50 miles north of South Walton, **Ponce de Leon Springs State Park** (☑850-836-4281; www.floridastateparks.org/poncedeleonsprings; 2860 Ponce de Leon Springs Rd, Ponce de Leon; vehicle $4; ☺8am-sunset; ℗) ⌀ features one of Florida's loveliest and least touristed springs. The spring has clear, almost luminescent waters, like something from a fairy tale, and is studded with knobby trees and surrounded by ladders for easy swimming access. Two short trails skirt the bank of nearby Blackwater Creek. The water temperature remains a constant 68°F.

beaches, sun-battered wetlands, sand pine scrub forest, a 2.5-mile nature trail, and three rare coastal dune lakes – inland bodies of water located less than 2 miles from the coast, connected to the Gulf via outfall channels that run through the dunes.

Accommodation options (p460) available.

Deer Lake State Park   STATE PARK
(☑850-267-8300; 6350 E County Rd 30-A, Santa Rosa Beach; car/bicycle/pedestrian $3/2/2; ☺8am-sunset; ℗) ⌀ Named for its eponymous coastal dune lake – a body of water that sits inland from the Gulf, but is connected to it – this park is rich in scrub oaks, magnolia trees, palmetto copses and wildflowers. A boardwalk path makes for a delightful means of observing all of the above.

Blue Mountain Beach   BEACH
(2365 S Scenic Highway 83; ☺sunrise-sunset; ℗ 🚻) **FREE** Towering a cloud-kissing (if by cloud-kissing we mean fog) 64ft-high, 'Blue Mountain' is supposedly the highest point on the pancake-flat Gulf Coast. Be on the lookout for blue lupine flowers, which supposedly gave this alpine peak it's name. Relax on the exquisite beach in the shadow of this mighty massif. (Note: 'mountain' does not actually provide a ton of shade.)

Eden Gardens State Park   STATE PARK
(☑850-267-8320; www.floridastateparks.org/edengardens; 181 Eden Gardens Rd, Santa Rosa Beach; $4, tours adult/child $4/2; ☺8am-sunset, tours 10am-3pm Thu-Mon; ℗) ⌀ Inland from 30A on a peninsula jutting into Choctawhatchee Bay, manicured gardens and lawns front the

1800s estate home of the Wesleys, a wealthy Florida timber family. The white-columned house was purchased and renovated in 1963 by Lois Maxon, who turned it into a showcase for Louis XVI furniture and many other heirlooms and antiques. Visitors can relax in the oak-lined grounds or the lovely picnic area by the water.

Inlet Beach

BEACH

(S Orange St & W Park Place Ave; ☉ sunrise-sunset; P 🅟 🚹) FREE This is one of the larger beach access points in South Walton. Inlet Beach itself is hugged by high dunes and old-school A-frame houses, both of which you will walk by as you stroll from the parking lot to a wide sweep of sand.

Dune Allen Beach

BEACH

(Hwy 30A & Fort Panic Rd; ☉ sunrise-sunset; P 🅟) FREE Simply one of the more pleasant beaches along South Walton, Dune Allen is a family-friendly slice of sand that's great for the kids, or adults who just want a view of the water and sand between their toes.

🏃 Activities

The area is ideally suited for cyclists. You can follow the 19-mile paved Timpoochee trail, which parallels Scenic Hwy 30A; the 8-mile Longleaf Pine Greenway hiking and cycling trail, paralleling Hwy 30A inland from just east of SR 395 to just before SR 393; and the Eastern Lake trail, which starts in Deer Lake State Park and links up with the western end of the Longleaf Pine Greenway.

If you prefer four wheels to two, allow at least two hours to drive the short stretch of the 30A between Destin and Panama City Beach, even if you're not planning to stop: speed limits are low, kids and cars are plentiful and the beaches are mesmerizing. Visit www.waltonoutdoors.com for more information.

30A Bike Rentals

CYCLING

(☎ 850-865-7433; www.30Abikerentals.net; 5399 E County Hwy 30A, Santa Rosa Beach; ☉ rental per day from $20) The flat Florida coast is perfect for casual two-wheeled exploration, and this is a good spot for a bicycle rental, including free delivery and pickup to most locations on the highway. Also rents regular ($20) and beach ($50) wheelchairs by the day.

Big Daddy's

CYCLING

(☎ 850-622-1165; www.bigdaddysbikes.com; 2217 W County Hwy 30A, Santa Rosa Beach; rentals from $45; ☉ 9am-5pm Mon-Sat) 'Dangerously

Optimistic since 1998,' Big Daddy will get you wheelin' down this picturesque coastal road, or on the beach itself, in no time at all. A plethora of two-wheeled rentals include helmet, lock and free delivery to and pickup from most locations on Hwy 30A.

🏳 Tours

Choctawhatchee Basin Alliance

ECOTOUR

(☎ 850-200-4171; www.basinalliance.org; 109 Greenway Trail, Santa Rosa Beach) ✈ The Basin Alliance is an important non-profit in the region working to improve environmental awareness and protect the Panhandle's unique ecosystem, including rare coastal dune lakes. The Alliance runs a series of tours during the summer, ranging from nature walks (from $15) to kayaking tours ($35); call them for more information, including tour times.

🛏 Sleeping

For rentals, try www.graytoncoastrentals.com, www.30avacationrentals.com or www.cottagerentalagency.com.

Grayton Beach State Park

CAMPGROUND $

(☎ 850-267-8300; www.floridastateparks.org/graytonbeach; 357 Main Park Rd, Grayton Beach; tent & RV sites from $24, cabins $110-130; P 🅟) ✈ It might be tricky to make spending the rest of your life here in paradise a reality, but it doesn't mean you can't afford to stay here for a short time. Cheap-as-chips camping and compact, cozy cabins make a taste of Grayton Beach living – albeit in the rough – a possibility for everybody. Newer tent sites have electric hookups ($30 per night).

Topsail Hill Preserve State Park

CAMPGROUND $

(☎ 800-326-3521; www.reserveamerica.com; 7525 W Scenic Hwy 30A, Santa Rosa; tents/bungalows/cabins $24/120/145; P 🅟 ❄) ✈ Topsail Hill (p459) includes tent sites, comfortable bungalows with cable TVs and full furnishing, and quite dapper cabins that come with kitchens and living rooms, and can sleep up to six guests. Rates for cabins and bungalows drop by around $15 from August to January. Cabins require a two-night minimum stay on weekends.

★ Hibiscus Coffee & Guesthouse

GUESTHOUSE $$

(☎ 850-231-2733; www.hibiscusflorida.com; 85 Defuniak St, Grayton Beach; r $135-175, apt $245-285; P 🅟 ❄) Tucked into a tree-studded corner of the area's oldest township, you'll find this delightfully chilled-out garden guesthouse. A variety of self-contained rooms and apartments are done up with tropical prints and funky folk paintings, like an arty friend's beach house.

Pearl
HOTEL $$$

(📞 877-935-6114; www.thepearlrb.com; 63 Main St, Rosemary Beach; r/ste from $300/430) It's hard to miss the Pearl – this Victorian-style building dominates the architectural landscape, which is saying something in New Urbanist Rosemary Beach, where the hotel is located. Inside, you'll find rooms that mush pseudo-historical vibe with integrated guest-service apps that will book your dinner reservations, as well intelligent lighting and temperature control.

Rosemary Beach Inn
BOUTIQUE HOTEL $$$

(📞 866-348-8952; www.rosemarybeach.com/the-rosemary-beach-inn; 78 Main St, Rosemary Beach; r from $199; P 🛜) This sunset-red, delightfully renovated hotel in downtown Rosemary Beach is styled like a European inn. There's no lobby, and the 11 guest rooms are quiet and individually decorated, with mod cons including flat-screen TVs and Keurig coffeemakers. Guests receive complimentary access to the local racquet club and fitness center.

WaterColor Inn & Resort
RESORT $$$

(📞 888-991-8878; www.watercolorresort.com; 34 Goldenrod Circle, Santa Rosa Beach; r from $450; P @ 🛜 ≋) This lauded, full-service luxury resort designed by architect David Rockwell occupies almost 500 acres of beachfront land. Contemporary rooms feature soft linens in seaside tones, large windows and balconies. Many have ocean views or are steps from the beach. No fewer than six gorgeous pools are there to distract you from the stunning waters of the gulf.

✖ Eating

Meltdown on 30A
FAST FOOD $

(📞 850-231-0952; 2235 E County Hwy 30A, Seaside; items from $5; ⏱ 11am-7pm Mon-Thu, 10am-9pm Fri, 8am-9pm Sat, 8am-7pm Sun; P) Unless you're gluten- and dairy-intolerant, we dare you to go past this excellent food truck, a vendor of oozy grilled-cheese deliciousness (we couldn't resist the avocado-and-bacon-jam creation). It also serves cheese-tastic breakfast biscuits and grits till 11am. Eat in the shade or on the beach – cheap, cheery and...did we mention the cheese?

Cafe Hibiscus
BREAKFAST $

(📞 850-231-1734; www.hibiscusflorida.com/cafe; 85 Defuniak St, Santa Rosa Beach; mains $4-9; ⏱ 8am-11am; P ✖) Located on the grounds of the Hibiscus Guesthouse (p460), this cafe serves great coffee, tasty granola, fluffy waffles and biscuits smothered in a vegan-sausage gravy. A gorgeous spot for breakfast and caffeine.

Red Bar
PUB FOOD $$

(📞 850-231-1008; www.theredbar.com; 70 Hotz Ave, Grayton Beach; dinner mains $14-25; ⏱ 11am-3pm & 5-10pm, bar open to 11pm Sun-Thu, to midnight Fri & Sat; P) There's live music most nights at this hippy, homely, funky local fave, housed in an old general store stuffed with knick-knacks and general weirdness. It draws friendly mobs who hunker down for beers, goss and good tunes, or to tuck into a small selection of well-prepared dishes, such as crab cakes, shrimp-stuffed eggplant and manicotti.

Roux 30A
INTERNATIONAL $$$

(📞 850-213-0899; www.roux30a.com; 114 Logan Lane, Santa Rosa; themed prix-fixe dinner $65, Sun brunch mains $11-22; ⏱ 11am-3pm Fri, 11am-2pm Sun, select nights for dinner; P) This odd-duck gem has a strong commitment to working closely with local farmers and fishermen – and producing an eclectic menu that jukes from New American brunch to Friday Indian lunch (veg/nonveg curries $12/15) to dinner menus themed around world cuisines such as Cuba and Chile, only available a few evenings of the month (check website or call for details).

George's at Alys Beach
AMERICAN $$$

(📞 850-641-0017; www.georgesatalysbeach.net; 30 Castle Harbour Dr, Alys Beach; mains $20-45; ⏱ 11am-3pm & 5-9pm; P 🍴) 🏄 We give this playful Southern-style coastal seafood spot credit for their menu divisions – 'behave,' which includes locally sourced, organic fare like jerk-roasted snapper, and 'misbehave,' fried oyster plates, steals and the like.

Cafe Thirty-A
AMERICAN $$$

(📞 850-231-2166; www.cafethirtya.com; 3899 E Scenic Hwy 30A, Seagrove Beach; mains $14-39; ⏱ 5-9pm; P) Set in a modern, Frank Lloyd Wright–esque townhouse, this smart-casual fine-dining establishment feels good from the moment you walk through the door. Seafood delights include Maine lobster in paradise and wood oven–roasted grouper, but you can enjoy a filet mignon cooked to perfection or pan-roasted chicken if you just gotta have some turf with your surf.

Fish Out of Water
SEAFOOD **$$$**

(☑ 850-534-5050; 34 Goldenrod Circle; mains $23-44; �)8-11am daily, 5:30-9pm Tue-Sat; P) With a menu focusing on local bounty – roasted black grouper, steamed red snapper, fresh Apalachicola oysters – a dining room oozing understated good taste and alfresco dining on the breathtaking sunset deck, this is a destination restaurant. For the experience minus the sunset (and the dent in the wallet), come for breakfast.

Bud & Alley's
AMERICAN **$$$**

(☑ 850-231-5900; www.budandalleys.com; 2236 East County Rd 30A, Seaside; mains $30-39; ☉8am-9:30pm; P) This landmark seafood restaurant, with dining room and rooftop tables overlooking the gulf, is a happening place to be – especially at sunset, when locals and visitors gather to cheer on the sky while enjoying cold beers and dishes such as seared halibut and grilled shrimp and grits. The view is great, but isn't matched by the food.

☆ Entertainment

Bayou Arts Center
ARTS CENTER

(☑ 850-622-5970; www.culturalartsalliance.com; 105 Hogtown Bayou Ln, Santa Rosa Beach; ☉8am-4pm) ✐ Home of the South Walton Cultural Arts Alliance, the Bayou Arts Center serves as a multipurpose space, frequently playing the part of art gallery, performance venue and lecture space, among other roles. Check the website for details on upcoming shows and exhibitions.

🔒 Shopping

Sundog Books
BOOKS

(☑ 850-231-5481; www.sundogbooks.com; 89 Central Sq; ☉9am-9pm) Need a beach read? Or just a book in general? Sure you do. Head to this hip, indie book and music shop, which carries great literature, coffee-table pieces and uber-cool tracks.

Blue Giraffe
ART

(☑ 850-231-5112; www.bluegiraffe30a.com; 1777 E County Hwy 30A, Watercolor; ☉10am-6pm) Part gift shop of quirky handmade goods, part gallery of local artists, part showcase of Gulf Coast authors, the Blue Giraffe is a good spot to search for a South Walton souvenir. The shop supports plenty of local

charitable causes and creative initiatives, and the owners are connected to the local arts scene.

Justin Gaffrey Gallery
ART

(☑ 850-267-2022; www.justinmadebyhand.com; 21 Blue Gulf Drive, Santa Rosa Beach; ☉10am-5pm Mon-Sat) Self-taught artist Justin Gaffrey is a Walton county treasure. His work mixes media and textures, and constantly challenges expectations. Catch his gallery of paintings and sculpture.

ℹ Information

Beaches of South Walton Tourist Center

(☑ 800-822-6877; www.beachesofsouth walton.com; cnr Hwys 331 & 98; ☉8am-4:30pm) The tourist center is inland, between SR 283 and SR 83. There's also a bulletin board with tourist brochures on the eastern end of Seaside Town Sq.

ℹ Getting There & Away

The South Walton beaches stretch in a thin line along the 30A coast road, starting with Dune Allen (about 15 miles east of Destin) to Carillon Beach (about 13 miles west of Panama City Beach).

Panama City Beach

☑ 850 / POP 12,064

Don't expect mellow Old Florida vibes in Panama City Beach, an overdeveloped Gulf-front pocket about 10 miles west of unremarkable Panama City. 'PCB' has embraced a transformation from 1970s resort town to over-commercialized condo hot spot. Families come here for cheap vacays, retirees move here to live out their days, and youngsters flock to get smashed in the sunshine.

Architecturally dire high-rises spring up from the beachfront and block both sunlight and vistas for those on the streets below, which are lined with more strip malls, chain hotels, amusement arcades, uninspiring restaurants and dive bars than good taste allows. From March to May the place goes bonkers as a spring-break destination, when students from 150 colleges east of the Mississippi roar into town to drink and party till they puke.

That said, PCB's beaches are objectively lovely, with dozens of natural, historic and artificial reefs attracting spectacular marine life.

◉ Sights

★ Shell Island   PARK
(☏ 850-233-0504; www.shellislandshuttle.com; 4607 State Park Lane; round-trip adult/child $19/10) ⌖ Offshore from St Andrews State Park (p463), this sandy 'desert' island is fantastic for sunbathing, swimming and snorkeling. There are neither facilities nor shade: wear a hat and plenty of sunscreen. To get here, buy tickets for the Shell Island Shuttle (p465) at Pier Marketplace in the park; there's a trolley service to the boat. Snorkeling packages ($27) and kayak rental (single/tandem $55/65 per day) are available – the price includes your shuttle trip to the island. Check website for details and schedules.

St Andrews State Park   STATE PARK
(☏ 850-233-5140; www.floridastateparks.org/standrews; 4607 State Park Lane; vehicle/pedestrian $8/2; ◷ 8am-sunset; ℗) ⌖ This peaceful 1260-acre park is graced with nature trails, swimming beaches and wildlife, including foxes, coyotes, snakes, seabirds and alligators (fear not: gators live in freshwater, and the swimming areas – including the kiddie pool's 4ft-deep water, near the jetties – are in the ocean). You can still see the circular cannon platforms from when this area was used as a military reservation during WWII; look for them on the beach near the jetties.

Excellent waterfront campsites are available year-round for $28.

Man in the Sea Museum   MUSEUM
(☏ 850-235-4101; www.maninthesea.org; 17314 Panama City Beach Pkwy; adult/child $5/free; ◷ 10am-4pm Tue-Sat; ℗ ♿) Owned by the Institute of Diving, this museum takes a close look at the sport. Interactive exhibits let you crank up a Siebe pump, climb into a Beaver Mark IV submersible, check out models of underwater laboratory Sealab III and find out how diving bells really work. There's also a cool collection of old diving suits and a sea life–filled aquarium.

WonderWorks   MUSEUM
(☏ 850-249-7000; www.wonderworksonline.com/panama-city-beach; 9910 Front Beach Rd; adult/child $28/22; ◷ 10am-8pm Sun-Thu, to 10pm Fri & Sat; ♿) Designed to look like an upside-down building (complete with an upside-down lawn and palm trees), this wacky interactive museum and fun center is impossible to miss (even if you want to).

While hands-on exhibits like a spinning g-force bike, an obstacle climbing course and virtual-reality soccer may give some grown-ups a migraine, kids will have a blast: literally, in the case of the laser-tag maze (extra $7).

⫯ Activities

Divers are in luck: more than a dozen boats are rusting underwater offshore, including a 441ft WWII Liberty ship and numerous tugs, earning the place its nickname Wreck Capital of the South. There are more than 50 artificial reefs made from bridge spans, barges and a host of other sunken structures, as well as natural coral reefs. Visibility varies from 10ft to 80ft, averaging around 40ft. In winter, the average water temperature is 60°F, rising to 87°F in summer.

Dive Locker   DIVING
(☏ 850-230-8006; www.divelocker.net; 106 Thomas Dr; discover dive/open-water course $95/325; ◷ 8am-6pm Mon-Fri, from 7am Sat & Sun) This well-respected outfitter and dive school knows all the local dive sites, including artificial reefs based around sunken naval ships and oil supply ships, as well as local inland springs – a unique, only-in-Florida diving experience.

⫿ Sleeping

The code words 'family-friendly' or 'families only' mean you'll avoid spring breakers.

Wisteria Inn   MOTEL $$
(☏ 850-234-0557; www.wisteria-inn.com; 20404 Front Beach Rd; d from $119; ℗ ♨ ❅) This sweet little 15-room motel has a variety of tastefully themed rooms from South Beach to the Far East, as well as poolside mimosa hours and an 'adults only' policy that discourages spring breakers. It's also very pet-friendly, so feel free to bring Fido. Rates drop like a rock in winter.

Sheraton Bay Point Resort   HOTEL $$
(☏ 850-236-6000; www.sheratonbaypoint.com; 4114 Jan Cooley Dr; r from $140; ❅ ❄ ♨ ❅) One of the more comfortable bases in PCB is this pleasantly appointed resort, featuring views of St Andrews Bay, two golf courses, water-sports rentals, a lovely pool, three on-site restaurants and a full-service spa. Rooms are cozy, modern and airy.

Holiday Inn Resort   HOTEL $$
(☏ 850-230-4080, 800-633-0266; www.hipcbeach.com; 11127 Front Beach Rd; r from $150;

SEACREST WOLF PRESERVE

Located about 40 miles north of Panama City Beach, **Seacrest Wolf Preserve** (📞 850-773-2897; www.seacrestwolfpreserve.org; 3449 Bonnett Pond Rd, Chipley; $25; ⊙ tours 1-4:30pm Sat; 🅿) 🦮, the only one of its kind in Florida, should fascinate wildlife lovers. Visitors will see and have (limited) interaction with four on-site wolf packs, as well as a slate of wolf puppies, but only after extensive educational lectures. Fair warning: Saturday tours can get crowded, and you may find yourself waiting for long periods with limited views of the animals. That said, if you love wolves, it's worth it. No children under 10. Reservations essential.

There's a decent-sized checklist of clothing you can and can't wear, and other rules to follow; check the website for more information. More expensive VIP tours for one to 10 people are also available at other times ($400 for two people, $75 for each additional participant).

🅿 🛜 🎮) This half-moon-shaped beachfront mega-hotel has large, refurbished rooms, although it's impossible to fully shake its '70s *Boogie Nights* vibe. It's got something for everyone, from party-hearty spring breakers to holidaying families and lonely solos looking for love. The sheer hulking size of the place means good deals can usually be found.

🍴 Eating

Andy's Flour Power Bakery
BAKERY $

(📞 850-230-0014; www.andysflourpower.com; 3123 Thomas Dr; mains from $4; ⊙7am-2pm Mon-Sat, from 8am Sun; 🐾) Come for hands-down the best breakfasts in town: fluffy rolled omelets cooked to perfection, cheesy grits, breakfast frittata, Belgian waffles and, of course, bacon and eggs, any way you like 'em. Locals are known to start the day with breakfast here and come back for lunch: tasty New York deli–style sandwiches galore on freshly baked breads. Highly recommended.

Dee's Hangout
CREOLE $$

(www.deeshangout.com; 529 Richard Jackson Blvd; mains $10-28; ⊙11am-9pm Mon-Sat; 🐾) This popular eatery gets points for classic American favorites (burgers and such), family-friendly atmosphere, and some tasty Louisiana-inspired goodness, including New Orleans–style barbecue shrimp cooked in a rich butter sauce, po' boys (New Orleans–style sandwiches) served on Leidenheimer bread straight outta the Crescent City, and red beans and rice.

★ Firefly
MODERN AMERICAN $$$

(📞 850-249-3359; www.fireflypcb.com; 535 Richard Jackson Blvd; mains $25-43, sushi $6-16; ⊙5-10pm) This uber-atmospheric, casual fine-dining establishment glistens with hundreds of fairy lights and beckons with seafood dishes including sesame tempura shrimp, andouille crusted snapper and a wide variety of sushi and sashimi. It was good enough for a former US president – Obama dined here, and the regulars won't let you forget it.

🍷 Drinking & Nightlife

During spring break, most PCB bars are basically filling stations for getting as much alcohol down your throat as quickly as possible. Outside of spring break...well, imagine those bars in slow season. They're kind of sad. Still, a few worthwhile options are available.

Craft Bar
BAR

(www.thecraftbarfl.com; 15600 Panama City Beach Pkwy, Pier Park North; ⊙11am-11pm Mon-Thu, to midnight Fri & Sat, to 10pm Sun) Head to this anti-PCB choice to trade pirate-themed camp and beach blanket anarchy for 30 thoughtfully sourced microbrews on tap, craft cocktails and excellent, elevated pub grub (mains $12 to $35) – shares a menu with the sister location in Destin (p458).

Tootsie's Orchid Lounge
LOUNGE

(📞 850-236-3459; www.tootsies.net; 700 S Pier Park Dr; ⊙11am-3am) It lacks the dusty character of the Nashville original, but the nonstop live country music is still plenty boot-stompin' for y'all. Closes about a half-hour earlier during the winter.

ℹ Getting There & Away

The **Northwest Florida Beaches International Airport** (PFN; 📞 850-763-6751; www.ifly beaches.com; 6300 W Bay Pkwy) is served by Delta and Southwest, with daily nonstop flights to Atlanta, Baltimore, Houston, Nashville and St Louis.

For bus services connecting throughout the continental USA, head to the **Greyhound** (☑850-785-6111; www.greyhound.com; 917 Harrison Ave, Panama City) bus station, although it's not the most inviting of places for visitors to arrive or depart!

Panama City Beach is almost halfway between Tallahassee (about 130 miles) and Pensacola (95 miles). By car, coming along the coast, Hwy 98 takes you into town; from I-10 take either Hwy 231 or Hwy 79 south.

❶ Getting Around

The Bay Town Trolley (www.baytowntrolley. org) runs in Panama City Beach. The service continues to add stops and routes to its coverage, but its schedule is still limited to Monday to Saturday between 6am and 7pm. The fare is $1.50.

Classic Rentals (☑850-235-1519; www. classicrentalsinc.com; 13226 Front Beach Rd; scooter/motorcycle half day rental $25/85; ☺8am-5pm) rents scooters (half-/full day $25/45) and old-school Harleys (half-/full day $85/135).

Shell Island Shuttle (☑850-233-0504; www. shellislandshuttle.com; 4607 State Park Ln; adult/child $19/10; ☺9am-5pm) takes visitors between Shell Island and St Andrews State Park.

Cape San Blas & Port St Joe

☑850 / POP 3450

Delicate Cape San Blas curls around St Joseph Bay at the southwestern end of the bulge in the Panhandle, starting on the mainland at Port St Joe and ending at its undeveloped, 10-mile-long tip with gorgeous St Joseph Peninsula State Park.

Across the bay, which has gentle rip- and current-free swimming, the town of **Port St Joe** was once known as 'sin city' for the casinos and bordellos that greeted seafarers. Note the switch in time zones from Central to Eastern here: even though Port St Joe is west of some Central Time communities, it goes by Eastern Time.

The Florida Constitution was originally drafted here in 1838, but scarlet fever and hurricanes combined to stymie its progression as one of Florida's boom towns. These days it's anchored by a small historic district that can occupy a visitor for an hour or so.

◉ Sights

★**TH Stone Memorial St Joseph Peninsula State Park**   STATE PARK
(St Joseph Peninsula State Park; ☑850-227-1327; www.floridastateparks.org/stjoseph; 8899 Cape San Blas Rd; vehicle $6; ☺8am-sunset) This lovely park, a quilt of beach and pine forest, brackish bays and fuzzy salt marsh, is a fine slice of increasingly rare Gulf Coast wilderness. Visitors can wander amid sugar-sand beaches that stretch for 2516 acres along grassy, undulating dunes, edging wilderness trails. Cyclists, walkers and bladers can set out on the Loggerhead Run Bike Path, named for the turtles that inhabit the island, which runs about 9 miles to **Salinas Park** (280 Cape San Blas Rd; ☺sunrise-sunset; P🅰) 🆓FREE.

🛏 Sleeping

TH Stone Memorial St Joseph Peninsula State Park Campgrounds   CAMPGROUND $
(☑850-227-1327; http://floridastateparks.reserve america.com; 8899 Cape San Blas Rd; tent site/ cabin $24/100; P) 🅰 This state park is one of the most prized camping spots along the Gulf Coast, home to 114 sites in two separate developed grounds. You can stay in loft-style timber cabins with queen beds and walkways leading from your back door to the water, or opt for primitive camping. You'll need to bring everything, including water and a camp stove. Note that cabins are booked out months in advance.

Port Inn   INN $
(☑850-229-7678; www.portinnfl.com; 501 Monument Ave/Hwy 98, Port St Joe; r $99-140, ste from $160; 🅰🅰🅰🅰) A really pleasant Panhandle overnight stop is the Port Inn, with front-row seats for the sunsets over the bay. A timber porch with rocking chairs runs the full length of this lovely inn, which has bay-view rooms with sisal carpet, wicker furniture and sparkling bathrooms. Its Thirsty Goat lounge bar is a nice, mellow spot to wind up your evening with a cold brew.

🍴 Eating

★**Sand Dollar Cafe**   AMERICAN $
(☑850-227-4865; www.sanddollarcafepsj.com; 301 Monument Avenue, Port St Joe; breakfast & lunch plates $10-12; ☺7am-3pm Wed-Mon; 🅰🅰) What happens when a pair of award-winning chefs from Georgia move out to a little town in the Panhandle and open a restaurant? A perfect storm of playful kitsch, warm hospitality, reasonable pricing and innovative Southern

home cooking, from meatloaf and tomato chutney to four-cheese mac 'n' cheese with bacon.

Indian Pass Raw Bar SEAFOOD $$
(☑850-227-1670; www.indianpassrawbar.com; 8391 Indian Pass Rd; mains $10-17; ⊙noon-9pm Tue-Sun, Wed-Sat only Jan; P) On a rural stretch of 30A outside Port St Joe, this old wooden building might look like an abandoned general store, but in fact it's Indian Pass Raw Bar, a rickety outpost of old Gulf culture. The menu, posted above the bar, is simple: oysters three ways (raw, steamed or baked with Parmesan cheese), crab legs and a handful of shrimp dishes.

Inside, grab a beer from the cooler (on the honor system) and take a seat at a share table, if you can find a spot. And, of course, you should get the oysters – even if you think you don't like the salty bivalves, you'll be surprised at the sweetness of these guys, drawn just this morning from the waters of nearby Apalachicola. Stay for a slice of key lime pie and impromptu line dancing on the porch. If you're lucky, Jimmy will be firing up the drum grill out front with his specialty drunken chicken.

❶ Getting There & Away

Port St Joe is about 24 miles west of Apalachicola and 70 miles east of Panama City Beach – either way in, you'll be arriving on US 98. State Road 30A is a scenic route that partly hugs the water and extends south of Port St Joe to the state park; you can also take this route to Apalachicola, which we recommend doing.

Apalachicola

☑850 / POP 2260

Slow, mellow, shaded by live oaks and flush with historically preserved buildings sweating in the soft Gulf Coast sun, Apalachicola is one of the gulf's most appealing villages. It's the kind of town that has been discovered by exiles who have fixed up homes and built nice restaurants, bars and bookstores, all threaded together by an attractive grid of walkable streets. 'Apalach' is hugely popular as a romantic weekend getaway – stroll through the historic district at sunset and you'll understand why.

While best known for its oysters (which are increasingly hard to find), the fact is this town caters more to tourists than the fishermen who attract said tourists. That doesn't mean the local seafood isn't still fresh and

delicious – just take the persistent nautical aesthetics with a grain of sea salt.

◉ Sights

The main sights are well marked on a historic walking-tour guide and map, available free from the Chamber of Commerce (p468) and most B&Bs. Apalachicola's main drag is Ave E, and the entire historic district is easily walked and is lined with interesting shops and restaurants.

St Vincent Island WILDLIFE RESERVE
(☑850-653-8808; www.fws.gov/saintvincent) ⬦ Just a few minutes from Apalachicola, but accessible only by boat, lies this pristine island. Its pearly dunes reveal 5000-year-old geological records, while its pine forests and wetlands teem with endangered species such as red wolves, sea turtles, bald eagles and peregrine falcons. Fishing's permitted on lakes except when bald eagles are nesting (generally in winter). For those sick of the high-rises and bikini-clad crowds of the gulf beaches, it's the perfect getaway for a day of hiking and solitude.

The island is home to a family of red wolves, one of the last wild populations in the world. These rust-colored wolves once populated the forests and marshes of Eastern North America, but were driven to the point of extinction by human expansion and hunting. You probably won't see them – the wolves are notoriously elusive, and reserve managers do what they can to keep them from becoming too comfortable around people – but you may well spot their tracks on the beach.

To get here, hop aboard the St Vincent Island Shuttle (p469), which can also take your bike ($20), or rent you one of its own ($25, including boat trip). Phone for schedules and reservations; they require a certain number of passengers to depart.

The St Vincent National Wildlife Refuge Visitors Center (p468) is located a few minutes walk from downtown Apalachicola, in the historic Fry-Conter house.

Apalachicola Maritime Museum MUSEUM
(☑850-653-2500; www.ammfl.org; 103 Water St; ⊙10am-5pm Mon-Sat; P) ⬦ FREE The small Apalachicola Maritime Museum, which rests on the banks of the Apalachicola River, gives a breakdown on the history of oystering, fishing and boat building in Apalachicola; as regards the last trade, a workshop where traditional boat-building

skills are taught and practiced is attached. The museum also conducts tours of the river and estuary.

Trinity Episcopal Church CHURCH

(☑850-653-9550; www.trinityapalachicola.org; 79 6th St) This handsome church was built in New York state and cut into sections, which were shipped down the Atlantic Coast and around the Keys before making their way to this spot where the church was reassembled in 1836.

John Gorrie State Museum MUSEUM

(☑850-653-9347; www.floridastateparks.org/johngorriemuseum; 46 6th St; $2; ⊙9am-5pm Thu-Mon; ℗) Dr John Gorrie (1803–55), one of Apalachicola's most famous sons, developed an ice-making machine to keep yellow-fever patients cool during an epidemic. He died poor and unknown, unaware of how his invention laid the groundwork for modern refrigeration and air-conditioning. This tiny museum commemorates the man and his life, and is located on one of the town's most attractive squares.

☞ Tours

Maritime Museum Tours ECOTOUR

(www.ammfl.org/tours-trips-classes; 103 Water St; tours $15-50) ⊘ The Apalachicola Maritime Museum (p466) runs a series of lovely tours, including eco-tours of the estuary ($40) and cruises around Apalachicola's historic waterfront ($15). Call the museum in advance, as tour times (and availability) can change throughout the year.

Backwater Guide Service BOATING

(☑850-899-0063; www.backwaterguideservice.com; tours $200-350; ⊙by appointment) ⊘ Offers private wildlife-spotting boat tours, where alligators, wading birds and willowy trees are the main attractions, and fishing charters with the promise of snagging your own red fish or speckled trout for grilling.

✹ Festivals & Events

Florida Seafood Festival FOOD & DRINK

(☑850-653-4720; www.floridaseafoodfestival.com; ⊙early Nov) Stand way, way back at the signature two-day oyster-shucking and -eating contests.

⌨ Sleeping

Water Street Hotel HOTEL $$

(☑850-653-3700; www.waterstreethotel.com; 329 Water St; r from $169; ☎) Attractive, modern yet classically styled one- and two-bedroom suites with full kitchens, four-poster beds and awesome, broad, covered porches overlooking the Apalachicola River await at this delightful boutique hotel and marina located a short walk from downtown.

Riverwood Suites INN $$

(☑850-653-3848; www.riverwoodsuites.com; 29 Ave F; r $139-169; ℗☎) The four spacious rooms inside this formerly abandoned tin warehouse – the 'Baltimore Building' – have hardwood floors, artsy headboards, modern fixin's and tuck-your-self-away romance. As local hotels go, this one strikes a good balance between historic skin and an interior stuffed with contemporary amenities.

Apalachicola River Inn INN $$

(☑850-653-8139; www.apalachicolariverinn.com; 123 Water St; r from $179; ☎) Strung with Christmas lights that twinkle across Apalachicola Bay, this waterfront inn has tasteful, old-fashioned rooms in pastel shades, many with water views. The on-site restaurant, Caroline's River Dining, is one of the best places in town for breakfast (it's open to the general public, but breakfast is included for guests).

Coombs House Inn B&B $$

(☑888-244-8320, 850-653-9199; www.coombshouseinn.com; 80 6th St; r $99-159; ☎) This stunning yellow Victorian inn was built in 1905 and features black-cypress wall paneling, nine fireplaces, a carved oak staircase, leaded glass windows and beadboard ceilings. Settle into one of the fabulous rooms and be sure to join the other guests for nightly wine socials in the dining room, where a lavish breakfast is also served each morning.

Gibson Inn INN $$

(☑850-653-2191; www.gibsoninn.com; 51 Ave C; r $140-185; ☎) This grand 1907 cracker-style inn has 30 somewhat creaky rooms with bright colors and high antique beds. Ask for a 2nd-floor room that opens onto the sprawling verandah – or, if you're game, request reputedly haunted room 309.

✻ Eating

Bite Me Deli SANDWICHES $

(☑850-653-3354; 146 Ave E; sandwiches $6-9; ⊙11am-3:30pm Mon-Fri; ℗⊘⟟) While there are a lot of restaurants in Apalachicola, the town was in serious need of a simple sandwich spot. Enter: Bite Me Deli, with its fish tacos, lamb wraps, burgers and various takes on the theme of 'tasty things between bread,' plus a good list of soups and salads.

★ **Up the Creek Raw Bar** SEAFOOD $$
(☑ 850-653-2525; www.upthecreekrawbar.com; 313 Water St; mains $7-20; ☉ noon-9pm; 🖬) You came to Apalachicola to eat oysters. You'd best have a few here. There's a variety of toppers, but we loved the 'classic': lightly cooked with Colby-Jack cheese, chopped jalapeños and bacon – a great way to introduce oyster virgins to the bivalve. The views out to the estuary and salt marsh are incredible.

Order at the counter and pull up a pew in the shade house or on the deck. A bunch of tasty burgers and salads are available. You just can't beat the combination of the food, the view and a cold beer.

Owl Cafe & Tap Room MODERN AMERICAN $$
(☑ 850-653-9888; www.owlcafeflorida.com; 15 Ave D; mains $10-28; ☉ 11am-3pm & 5:30-10pm Mon-Sat, 10:30am-3pm Sun; 🍴) Everyone is catered to in this local favorite, with casual fine dining in the upstairs cafe, and wine room and craft beers and tap-room-only offerings below. The eclectic menu both includes and deviates from the seafood theme: vegetarian pastas, pork tenderloin, chicken marsala and jumbo gulf shrimp all make appearances. Brunches here are wonderful.

Tamara's Café Floridita SOUTH AMERICAN $$$
(☑ 850-653-4111; www.tamarascafe.com; 17 Ave E; mains $16-34; ☉ 8:30am-10pm Tue-Sun) In the heart of town, Tamara's popular cuisine is influenced by the spices of her native Venezuela, in dishes like grilled, herbed pork chop with shrimp and scallops in a creamy tomato-tarragon sauce, and margarita chicken sautéed in honey, tequila and lime glaze with scallops.

🍸 Drinking & Nightlife

Bowery Station BAR
(☑ 850-653-2211; www.bowerystation.us; 131 Commerce St; ☉ 2-9pm Wed-Sun) Bowery Station looks like the epitome of a Florida fisherman's bar: dusty shelves, mariners supply accoutrements, guys who look like ZZ Top stumbling in wearing 'Salt Life' gear and wraparound sunglasses.They've got live music come evening and cold beer whenever you ask for it.

Oyster City Brewing Company MICROBREWERY
(☑ 850-653-2739; www.oystercitybrewingco.com; 17 Avenue D; ☉ tasting room noon-7pm Mon-Thu, to 8pm Fri, to 5pm Sun) Take a little tour of this energetic microbrewery, sip on their three excellent beers, and then slurp down some of those raw oysters the place is named for. Life is good.

🛍 Shopping

Richard Bickel Photography ART
(☑ 850-653-2828; www.richardbickelphotography.com; 81 Market St; ☉ 11am-4pm Tue-Sat; 🎟) Bickel is a renowned photographer with credits in the *The New York Times*, *Newsweek*, *Die Zeit* and *The Times* (London) among others. He is particularly attracted to water and waterscapes – hence his settling in Appalachicola, where he maintains a gallery of his excellent work.

Downtown Books & Purl BOOKS
(☑ 850-653-1290; www.downtownbooksandpurl.com; 67 Commerce St; ☉ 10am-5:30pm Mon-Sat, to 4pm Sun) Need books? How about yarn? How about *both*? Well, you've found the right shop: an adorable, independent bookstore that happens to also include an entire knitting accessory shop. The bookstore contains some excellent small trade books written by local authors, including compilations of Panhandle folklore and quirky guidebooks (not that you need another guidebook).

Tin Shed ANTIQUES
(☑ 850-653-3635; www.thetinshednautical.com; 170 Water St; ☉ 10am-5pm) The Tin Shed really is that – a big shack with a corrugated roof, decorated with brightly painted nautical buoys and flags. Once inside, you will find – seriously – every damn maritime souvenir under the sun, or the sea, as the case may be.

ℹ Information

Apalachicola Bay Chamber of Commerce (☑ 850-653-9419; www.apalachicolabay.org; 122 Commerce St; ☉ 9am-5pm Mon-Fri) Offers loads of tourist information, oyster facts, downtown, more oyster facts, walking maps, helpful advice and oyster facts.

St Vincent National Wildlife Refuge Visitors Center (☑ 850-653-8808; www.fws.gov/saintvincent; 96 5th St; ☉ 10am-3:30pm Mon-Thu) The information center for visitors headed to St Vincent National Wildlife Refuge is located in the historic Fry-Conter house.

ⓘ Getting There & Away

Hwy 98 (which becomes Market St) brings you into town from either direction. It's easy (and delightful) to wander around downtown, but you'll need a car to explore the greater area.

To get to St Vincent Island, hop aboard the **St Vincent Island Shuttle** (☑ 850-229-1065; www.stvincentisland.com; 690 Indian Pass Rd, Port St Joe; adult/child $10/7) in Port St Joe, which can also take your bike ($20), or rent you one of theirs ($25, including boat trip). Phone for schedules and reservations.

St George Island

☑ 850 / POP 300

This 28-mile-long barrier island is home to white-sand beaches, bay forests, salt marshes and an inoffensive mix of summer homes and condos. It's a fine spot for shelling, kayaking, sailing, swimming, or just generally zoning out in waterfront bliss. At the end of every street on the island you'll find public beach access and, generally, plentiful parking.

For all that, the highlight of the island is St George Island State Park, which preserves a breathtaking slice of coastal wilderness. The primal, yet gentle beauty of the dunes and marshes is a world removed from the rental houses mere miles away.

◉ Sights & Activities

★**St George Island State Park**   STATE PARK
(☑ 850-927-2111; www.floridastateparks.org/stgeorgeisland; 1900 E Gulf Beach Drive; vehicle $6; ☺ 8am-dusk; ℗ ♿) ✦ St George island at its undeveloped best is found here, in the 9 miles of glorious beach and sand dunes that make up this pristine park. A 2.5-mile nature trail offers exceptional birding opportunities, and throughout the park boardwalks lead to shell-sprinkled beaches, with shallow waters perfect for canoeing, kayaking, and fishing for flounder and whiting. See loggerhead sea turtles from May, when they come ashore to dig nests and lay their eggs, yielding hatchlings that race into the gulf.

Camping ($24) is permitted at one of the 60 campsites with hookups, or at the Gap Point primitive campsites, accessible by boat or a 2.5-mile hike.

Apalachicola National Estuarine Research Reserve   WILDLIFE RESERVE
(☑ 850-670-7700; www.dep.state.fl.us/coastal/sites/apalachicola; 108 Island Dr, Eastpoint; ☺ 9am-4pm Tue-Sat) ✦ Just over the bridge from Apalachicola, in Eastpoint, this reserve provides a great overview of its research site, which encompasses more than 246,000 acres in Apalachicola Bay, with giant aquariums simulating different habitats. A half-mile boardwalk leads down to the river, where you'll find a free telescope on a turret.

St George Lighthouse   LIGHTHOUSE
(☑ 850-927-7745; www.stgeorgelight.org; 2B East Gulf Beach Dr; adult/child $5/3; ☺ 10am-5pm Mon-Wed, Fri & Sat, noon-5pm Sun; ℗) Originally built in 1858, this little lighthouse was painstakingly reconstructed in 2008 after collapsing into the sea in 2005 due to erosion. Today you can climb the 92 steps to the top for good water views.

Island Adventures   CYCLING
(☑ 850-927-3655; www.sgislandadventures.com; 105 E Gulf Beach Dr; bicycle per day from $15; ☺ 10am-5pm) This convenient emporium rents out bicycles, beach wheelchairs, foldout chairs and other types of beach gear.

⌖ Tours

Journeys   BOATING
(☑ 850-927-3259; www.sgislandjourneys.com; 240 E 3rd St; kayak/boat tour from $40/250; ☺ 9am-5pm Mon-Sat) This outfitter leads boat and kayak tours, and rents kayaks (from $50 per day), pontoon boats and catamarans (both $300 per day). All are ideal ways to make the voyage to Cape St George.

🛏 Sleeping

Sleeping options are surprisingly limited. Most visitors to the island rent cottages, which can be anything from a humble beach shack to a multistory mansion: try www.resortvacationproperties.com.

St George Inn   INN $
(☑ 850-927-2903; www.stgeorgeinn.com; 135 Franklin Blvd; r from $115-245; 🛜 ❄) One of the few historic structures on an island lined with new condo developments, this rambling clapboard inn has comfy, if creaky, rooms and numerous cozy sitting areas filled with dog-eared books. The more expensive rooms may have Jacuzzis and

kitchens, but we wouldn't say this justifies their price.

Buccaneer Inn
MOTEL $

(☑800-847-2091; www.buccinn.com; 160 W Gorrie Dr; r $60-140; P� 🗢🕿) Right on the gulf, rooms here are like those of a basic, design-challenged motel – dated green carpet, painted cinder-block walls. But all are clean, bright and surprisingly spacious, and some have kitchenettes.

✖ Eating

Blue Parrot Oceanfront Café
SEAFOOD $$

(☑850-927-2987; www.blueparrotcafe.net; 68 W Gorrie Dr; mains $9-26; ⊙11am-9pm; 🖬 🕾) Out the back of this relaxed and breezy gulf-front cafe-bar, locals sip rum runners and down oversized po' boys, fish sandwiches and burgers.

❶ Getting There & Away

From the dock-lined town of Eastpoint on Hwy 98, 7 miles east of Apalachicola, follow the 4-mile-long causeway onto the island until you reach Gulf Beach Dr, also known as Front Beach Dr, at the end. Turning left brings you to the state park; a right turn takes you toward Government Cut, which separates Little St George Island.

BIG BEND

The crook of Florida's upside down 'L' is home to its state capital and an otherwise little visited region known as Big Bend. The area is characterized by ragged pine woods and freshwater springs of the greater Panhandle mixed with long stretches of salt marsh and thin beachfront. Fishing villages and biker bars perforate the small towns scattered around the region, offset by low-lying Gulf islands and the edges of the Apalachicola National Forest.

Tallahassee

☑850 / POP 187,000

Florida's capital, cradled between gently rising hills and nestled beneath tree-canopied roadways, is geographically closer to Atlanta than it is to Miami. Culturally, it's far closer to the Deep South than the majority of the state it governs.

Despite its status as a government center, and the presence of two major universities

(Florida State and Florida Agricultural & Mechanical University), the pace here is slower than syrup. That said, there are a handful of interesting museums and outlying attractions that will appeal to history and nature buffs and could easily detain a visitor for a day or two.

◉ Sights

★Tallahassee Museum of History & Natural Science
MUSEUM

(Map p471; ☑850-575-8684; www.tallahasseemuseum.org; 3945 Museum Rd; adult/child $11.50/8.50; ⊙9am-5pm Mon-Sat, from 11am Sun; P🖬) ✔ Occupying 52 acres of pristine manicured gardens and wilderness on the outskirts of Tallahassee, near the airport, this wonderful natural-history museum features living exhibits of Floridian flora and fauna – including the incredibly rare Floridan panther and red wolf – and has delighted visitors for more than 50 years. Be sure to check out the otters in their new home, or try ziplining above the canopy in the Tree to Tree Adventures – a variety of scenarios are available, from $25.

Museum of Fine Arts
MUSEUM

(Map p473; ☑850-644-6836; http://mofa.fsu.edu; 530 W Call Street; ⊙9am-4pm Mon-Fri year-round, 1-4pm Sat & Sun Sep-Apr; P) **FREE** Florida State University boasts its own Museum of Fine Arts, which features temporary exhibitions that range from internationally renowned artists to graduating FSU arts students.

Mission San Luis
HISTORIC SITE

(Map p471; ☑850-245-6406; www.missionsanluis.org; 2100 W Tennessee St; adult/child $5/2; ⊙10am-4pm Tue-Sun; P🖬) ✔ This 60-acre site is home to a 17th-century mission that housed Spanish colonists and Apalachee tribespeople. The compound has been nicely reconstructed, especially the soaring Council House. Tours (included with admission) provide a fascinating taste of life 300 years ago. Costumed interpreters are on-site, and kids who are into history will have a blast.

Meek-Eaton Black Archives
MUSEUM

(Southeastern Regional Black Archives Research Center & Museum; Map p471; ☑850-599-3020; www.famu.edu/BlackArchives; 445 Gamble St; ⊙9am-5pm Mon-Fri; P) ✔**FREE** The Southeastern Regional Black Archives Research Center & Museum was a forerunner

Tallahassee

Tallahassee

◎ Top Sights
1 Tallahassee Museum of History &
   Natural Science A4

◎ Sights
2 Florida State University B3
3 Meek-Eaton Black Archives C4
4 Mission San Luis B3

✦ Activities, Courses & Tours
5 Great Bicycle Shop C2
6 Munson Hills Loop C5

⌂ Sleeping
7 Little English Guesthouse C1

✕ Eating
8 Bella Bella C2
9 Kool Beanz Café C2
10 Mr B's Real Grill BBQ C4
11 Paisley Cafe C2
12 Reangthai D1

♨ Drinking & Nightlife
13 Madison Social B3
14 Waterworks C2

⌂ Shopping
15 Railroad Square Art Park C3

in research on African American influence on US history and culture. Now known as the Meek-Eaton Black Archives, the center and museum holds one of the country's largest collections of African American and African artifacts, as well as a huge collection of papers, photographs, paintings and documents pertaining to black American life. The complex is located within the Florida Agricultural & Mechanical University, usually shortened to FAMU (fam-you).

FAMU was founded in 1887 as the State Normal College for Colored Students, with 15 students and two instructors. Today it's home to about 10,000 students of all races.

Tallahassee Automobile & Collectibles Museum   MUSEUM
(☑850-942-0137; www.tacm.com; 6800 Mahan Dr; adult/student/child under 10yr $16/12/8; ☺8am-5pm Mon-Fri, from 10am Sat, from noon Sun; ℗) If you like motor vehicles, welcome to heaven! This museum houses a pristine collection of more than 130 unique and historical automobiles from around the world. Top that with collections of boats, motorcycles, books, pianos and sports memorabilia and you've got a full day on your hands. It is about 8 miles northeast of downtown, off I-10.

Florida State University   UNIVERSITY
(FSU; Map p471; ☑850-644-2882; www.fsu.edu; Hendry St; ℗) FREE A liberal-arts school of more than 35,000 undergraduate and graduate students, Florida State University specializes in sciences, computing and performing arts (and football). From September to April, free campus tours depart from **Visitor Services** (☑850-644-3246; 100 S Woodward Ave) Monday to Friday. Call for a schedule.

Museum of Florida History   MUSEUM
(Map p473; ☑850-245-6400; www.museumof floridahistory.com; 500 S Bronough St; ☺9am-4:30pm Mon-Fri, from 10am Sat, from noon Sun; ♿) FREE Florida's history is splayed out in fun, crisp exhibits, from mastodon skeletons to Florida's Paleo-Indians and Spanish shipwrecks, the Civil War to 'tin-can tourism'.

Florida Historic Capitol Museum   MUSEUM
(Map p473; ☑850-487-1902; www.flhistoric capitol.gov; 400 S Monroe St; ☺9am-4:30pm Mon-Fri, from 10am Sat, from noon Sun) FREE Adorned with candy-striped awnings and topped with a reproduction of its original

glass dome, the 1902 Florida capitol building now houses an interesting political museum, including a restored House of Representatives chamber and governor's reception area, numerous portraits, and exhibits on immigration, state development and the infamous 2000 US presidential election.

Florida State Capitol   NOTABLE BUILDING
(Map p473; www.floridacapitol.myflorida.com; 400 South Monroe St; ☺8am-5pm Mon-Fri) FREE The stark and imposing 22-story Florida State Capitol's top-floor observation deck affords 360-degree views of the city. In session the capitol is a hive of activity, with politicians, staffers and lobby groups buzzing in and around its honeycombed corridors. There are few states that have as diverse a legislature as Florida's – in one hall, you may hear Cuban Americans from Miami brokering deals with good old boys from the Panhandle. America!

Knott House Museum   HISTORIC BUILDING
(Map p473; ☑850-922-2459; www.museumofflor idahistory.com; 301 E Park Ave; ☺1-3pm Wed-Fri, 10am-3pm Sat; ℗) FREE This stately, white, columned 1843 house, affiliated with the history museum, is a quirky attraction. Occupied during the Civil War by Confederate and then Union troops before the Emancipation Proclamation was read here in 1865, it's otherwise known as 'the house that rhymes'. That's because in 1928 it was bought by politico William V Knott, whose poet wife, Luella, attached verses on the evils of drink to many of the furnishings. Free tours offered on the hour.

Florida Caverns State Park   STATE PARK
(☑850-482-1228; www.floridastateparks.org/ floridacaverns; 3345 Caverns Rd, Marianna; vehicle $5; ☺8am-sunset; ♿) ✆ Just over an hour from Tallahassee or Panama City, on Hwy 166, the 1300-acre Florida Caverns State Park on the Chipola River has fascinating caves unique to Florida. Eerie stalactites, stalagmites and flowstone (formed by water flowing over rock) fill the lighted caves, along with calcified shapes created over centuries as calcite has bubbled through the stone. Visitors can take a 45-minute guided tour (adult/child $8/5; 9am to 4pm) with a volunteer. There are also campsites here ($20).

They've come up with some quirky names to describe the various rock formations in

Downtown Tallahassee

Downtown Tallahassee

◉ Sights

1 Florida Historic Capitol Museum	C4
2 Florida State Capitol	C4
3 Knott House Museum	D3
4 Museum of Fine Arts	A2
5 Museum of Florida History	B4

🛏 Sleeping

6 aloft Tallahassee Downtown	C2
7 Four Points Tallahassee Downtown	B1

8 Governor's Inn	C3
9 Hotel Duval	D1

✖ Eating

10 Andrew's	C3
11 China Delight	C1
12 Cypress	D1

🍷 Drinking & Nightlife

13 Fermentation Lounge	B5

WORTH A TRIP

ST MARKS NATIONAL WILDLIFE REFUGE

About 25 miles southeast of Tallahassee you'll find the **St Marks National Wildlife Refuge** (☑ 850-925-6121; www.fws.gov/refuge/St_Marks; 1255 Lighthouse Rd, St Marks; ⊙ 8am-sunset; P) 🖈 FREE, established in 1931 to provide a winter habitat for migratory birds. It spans a whopping 70,000 acres and has approximately 43 miles of gulf shore-line along its coastal boundary. Within the park's protected marshes, rivers, estuaries and islands, a diverse range of flora and fauna thrives. It's a wildlife photographer's dream, with beautiful contrasts between land, sea and sky.

Be sure to start your visit with a trip to the visitor center for information on the park's numerous walking and hiking trails and the lowdown on just how many species of critter live here. If you only have time for a short visit, follow Lighthouse Rd all the way to the coast to enjoy Florida's most photographed lighthouse, completed in 1842 and still a functioning beacon today.

the cave, from 'wedding cake' to 'bacon'. Outside, the Blue Hole swimming area makes for a fun – if freezing – dip.

🏃 Activities

Tallahassee's famed oak- and moss-shrouded canopy roads make for lovely afternoon drives and rides. Roads to visit include Old St Augustine Rd, Centerville Rd, Meridian Rd, Miccosukee Rd and Old Bainbridge Rd. Check the Leon County Canopy Roads website (www.leoncountyfl.gov/pubworks/oper/canopy) for info and a map.

Tallahassee-St Marks Historic
Railroad State Trail   CYCLING
(☑ 850-519-6594; www.floridastateparks.org/tallahasseestmarks; 1358 Old Woodville Rd, Crawfordville; ⊙ 8am-sunset) 🖈 FREE The ultimate treat for runners, skaters and cyclists, this trail has 16 miles of smooth pavement shooting due south to the gulf-port town of St Marks and not a car or traffic light in sight. It's easy and flat for all riders, sitting on a coastal plain and shaded at many points by canopies of gracious live oaks.

More experienced riders may opt for forest trails, such as the rugged 7.5-mile Munson Hills Loop trail (p480), which navigates sand dunes and a towering pine forest.

Great Bicycle Shop   CYCLING
(Map p471; ☑ 850-224-7461; www.greatbicycle.com; 1909 Thomasville Rd; ⊙ 10am-6pm Mon-Fri, to 5pm Sat, noon-4pm Sun) This professional outfitter will rent you a bike to cruise around Tallahassee's many excellent bike paths. Rentals start at $35 per day.

🛏 Sleeping

With just a couple of charming exceptions, you'll find that Tallahassee's hotels are mostly midrange chains, clumped at exits along I-10 and along Monroe St between I-10 and downtown. Be sure to book well ahead during the legislative session and football games, when prices peak.

Little English Guesthouse   B&B $$
(Map p471; ☑ 850-907-9777; www.littleenglishguesthouse.com; 737 Timberlane Rd; r from $99; ❋❄) In a peaceful residential neighborhood 20 minutes from downtown Tallahassee, London-bred Tracey has turned her suburban house into a homey little English-themed B&B, complete with a friendly golden retriever.

aloft Tallahassee Downtown   HOTEL $$
(Map p473; ☑ 850-513-0313; www.alofttallahassee.com; 200 N Monroe St; r $115-230; P❄) This branch of the popular aloft chain boasts a prime downtown location and funky, functional rooms. Bathrooms feature counter-to-ceiling mirrors and lots of space for all the makeup in the world. Beds are uber-comfy, and free high-speed internet is included.

Four Points
Tallahassee Downtown   HOTEL $$
(Map p473; ☑ 850-422-0071; www.fourpointstallahasseedowntown.com; 316 W Tennessee St; d from $161; P❄❅) Discounted prepaid rates are available online for this comfortable, central hotel that looks a little like a massive blue cigar. With an emphasis on service and style, guest rooms feature floor-to-ceiling windows and most have great neighborhood

views. The pool area is a nice place to while away an afternoon.

Hotel Duval HOTEL $$$
(Map p473; ☎850-224-6000; www.hotelduval.com; 415 N Monroe St; r $184-309; P 📶) Slick, sleek and ultra modern, this centrally located 117-room hotel has all the mod cons, and a hip interior that is actually more stylish than pretentious – rare with spots that are so overtly design-conscious. The rooftop bar and lounge is open until 2am most nights.

Governor's Inn HOTEL $$$
(Map p473; ☎850-681-6855; www.thegovinn.com; 209 S Adams St; r $240-309; P ❄ 📶) In a stellar downtown location, this inviting inn has everything from single rooms to two-level loft suites, plus a daily cocktail hour. The interior lobby and common area is attractive in a historical chic kind of way, but rooms feel a little fusty.

Eating

Mr B's Real Grill BBQ BARBECUE $
(Map p471; ☎850-541-4474; 312 E Orange Ave; ⏰11am-8pm Thu-Sat; P) A little orange shack in South Tallahassee serves up delicious smoked barbecue – ribs, chopped pork, and all the fixin's – to customers who either take their 'cue to go, or eat at a picnic table.

Paisley Cafe CAFE $
(Map p471; ☎850-385-7268; www.thepaisleycafe.com; 1123 Thomasville Rd; mains $12-18; ⏰11am-2:30pm Mon-Thu, to 3pm Fri, 10am-3pm Sat & Sun; 📶) A wonderful midtown cafe with delectable pressed sandwiches, salads and insane desserts (the slutty brownie will have you forgiving its ridiculous name in no time).

Kool Beanz Café FUSION $$
(Map p471; ☎850-224-2466; www.koolbeanz-cafe.com; 921 Thomasville Rd; mains $17-24; ⏰11am-10pm Mon-Fri, 5:30-10pm Sat, 10:30am-2pm Sun; P 🌿 👪) It's got a corny name but a wonderfully eclectic and homey vibe – plus great, creative fare. The menu changes daily, but you can count on finding anything from hummus plates to jerk-spiced scallops to duck in blueberry-ginger sauce.

Reangthai THAI $$
(Map p471; ☎850-386-7898; www.reangthai.com; 2740 Capital Circle NE; mains $13-25; ⏰5-10pm Mon, noon-2pm & 5-10pm Tue-Sat, noon-2pm & 5-8pm Sun; P 🌿) The real deal, and elegant despite its suburban strip-mall setting, Reangthai serves the kind of spicy, fish saucy, explode-in-your-mouth cuisine so many American Thai restaurants shy away from. Worth the drive.

Andrew's AMERICAN $$
(Map p473; ☎850-222-3444; www.andrewsdowntown.com; 228 S Adams St; mains downstairs $12-25, upstairs $18-44; ⏰downstairs 11:30am-10pm, upstairs 6-10pm Mon-Sat) Downtown's see-and-be-seen political hot spot. At this split-level place, the downstairs (Andrew's Capital Grill and Bar) serves casual burgers and beer. It's somewhere between a family-friendly joint and a bro-kegger, but fun for what it is. Upstairs is Andrew's 228, which offers a more upscale atmosphere and serves Tuscan-Southern fusion cuisine such as pecan-pesto pasta.

Bella Bella ITALIAN $$
(Map p471; ☎850-412-1114; www.thebellabella.com; 123 E 5th Ave; mains $14-19; ⏰11am-10pm Mon-Fri, 4-10pm Sat; P) Come for authentic Italian cuisine in a modern setting. Try the bruschetta and stuffed mushrooms, then move on to creamy pastas or shrimp scampi or chicken Parmesan.

China Delight CHINESE $$
(Map p473; ☎850-222-8898; www.chinadelighttallahassee.com; 220 W Tennessee St; dishes $7-26; ⏰11am-9:30pm Mon-Sat; P) If you've had more Southern cooking and seafood than you can handle, you might find this no-frills downtown Chinese joint a welcome relief. Prices are reasonable, servings are generous and all the usual suspects are represented: the best Peking duck in town, beef with broccoli, chunky egg rolls and *ma po* tofu.

Cypress MODERN AMERICAN $$$
(Map p473; ☎850-513-1100; www.cypressrestaurant.com; 320 E Tennessee St; mains $21-36; ⏰5-10pm Mon-Sat; P 🌿) This unassuming spot is the domain of local chef David Gwynn, whose regional Southern outshines expectations. Start with the roasted Brussels-sprout salad with poached egg and move on to souped-up classics such as pork belly with pecan-fried quail, or shrimp and grits with bourbon-orange-thyme jus. .

Drinking & Nightlife

Most of the frat bars (and there are many) are in and around Tennessee St between Copeland St and Dewey St. There are a few good options around town, too. For a comprehensive guide to cultural events in town, such as lectures and art exhibits, be sure to visit the handy online calendar at www.morethanyouthought.com.

Waterworks
BAR

(Map p471; ☑850-224-1887; 1133 Thomasville Rd; ⊙11:30am-2am Tue-Fri, from 2pm Sat, from 7pm Sun, from 5pm Mon) This popular, gay-friendly place in midtown has a Polynesian tiki-bar theme, and packs 'em in with nights of live jazz and Latin salsa as well as rotating DJs.

Madison Social
PUB

(Map p471; ☑850-894-6276; www.madisonsocial.com; 705 South Woodward Ave; mains $9-20; ⊙11:30am-2am Sun-Thu, from 10am Fri & Sat; ☜) Never mind the trend of flipping former transmission shops into hipster locales, this trendy hot spot was built to look that way from go. It swarms with a bold and beautiful mix of locals and FSU students, downing drinks at the stellar bar or aluminum picnic tables as the sun sets over Doak Campbell football stadium, the largest continuous brick structure in the USA.

Fermentation Lounge
BAR

(Map p473; ☑850-727-4033; www.fermentationlounge.com; 113 All Saints St; ⊙5pm-1am) Sandwiched between the universities, this cool little bar packs a punch: with a chilled vibe attracting an unusual mix of punters from all walks of life and, more importantly, an ever-changing selection of most excellent craft beers and tasty bar snacks.

☆ Entertainment

Bradfordville Blues Club
LIVE MUSIC

(☑850-906-0766; www.bradfordvilleblues.com; 7152 Moses Lane, off Bradfordville Rd; tickets $15-35; ⊙10pm Fri & Sat) Down the end of a dirt road lit by tiki torches, you'll find a bonfire raging under the live oaks at this hidden-away juke joint that hosts excellent national blues acts. Also open some Thursdays from 8:30pm; check online.

🛍 Shopping

Railroad Square Art Park
ARTS & CRAFTS

(Map p471; ☑850-224-1308; www.railroadsquare.com; 567 Industrial Dr; ⊙hours vary) This collection of studios, shops, cafes and independent art galleries hosts a festive First Fridays gallery hop monthly. Hours vary by business.

ℹ Information

Florida Welcome Center (Map p473; ☑850-488-6167; www.visitflorida.com; cnr Pensacola St & Duval St; ⊙8am-5pm Mon-Fri) In the Florida State Capitol, this is a fantastic resource.

Leon County Welcome Center (Map p473; ☑850-606-2305; www.visittallahassee.com; 106 E Jefferson St; ⊙8am-5pm Mon-Fri) Runs the excellent visitor information center, with brochures on walking and driving tours.

ℹ Getting There & Away

Tallahassee is 98 miles from Panama City Beach, 135 miles from Jacksonville, 192 miles from Pensacola, 120 miles from Gainesville and 470 miles from Miami. The main access road is I-10; to reach the Gulf Coast, follow Hwy 319 south to Hwy 98.

The tiny **Tallahassee International Airport** (Map p471; ☑850-891-7802; www.talgov.com/airport; 3300 Capital Circle SW) is served by American and Delta for US domestic and international connections, and Silver Airways for direct flights to Tampa and Orlando. It's about 5 miles southwest of downtown, off Hwy 263. There's no public transportation. Some hotels have shuttles, but otherwise a taxi to downtown costs around $20: try **Yellow Cab** (☑850-999-9999; www.tallahasseeyellowcab.com).

The **Greyhound bus station** (Map p473; ☑850-222-4249; www.greyhound.com; 112 W Tennessee St) is at the corner of Duval, opposite the downtown **StarMetro** (Map p473; ☑850-891-5200; www.talgov.com/starmetro; per trip/day $1.25/3) transfer center.

ℹ Getting Around

Tallahassee is a spread out city, and it helps to have wheels to get around. For public transport, **StarMetro** (p476), the local bus service for the greater Tallahassee area, has its main transfer point downtown on Tennessee St at Adams St.

Steinhatchee
☑352 / POP 1047

While the name looks like a mash-up of a Jewish family and a Florida Native American tribe, Steinhatchee (that's *steen*-hatch-ee) is an under-the-radar fishing haven that sits in a secret crevice of the Big Bend. The town rests beneath towering pines, mossy oaks and pink, juicy sunsets. It's claim to fame is its scallop season, which runs from July to early September and brings up to 1000 boats

UPON THE SUWANNEE RIVER

Flowing 207 miles, the Suwannee River was immortalized by Stephen Foster in Florida's state song, 'Old Folks at Home'. Foster himself never set eyes on the river but thought 'Suwannee' (or 'Swannee', as his map apparently stated, hence his corruption of the spelling) sounded suitably Southern. As it happened he was right; the river winds through wild Spanish moss–draped countryside from the far north of the state to the Gulf of Mexico in the curve of the Big Bend. See it for yourself along the **Suwannee River Wilderness Trail** (www.suwanneeriver.com), which covers 169 miles of the river to the gulf, with nine 'hubs' – cabins – spaced one day's paddle apart. They book up fast, so reserve as early as possible. River camps along the banks of the trail are also in the pipeline.

The trail starts at the **Stephen Foster State Folk Cultural Center** (☎386-397-2733; www.floridastateparks.org/stephenfoster; Hwy 41 N, White Springs; vehicle $5; ⊙park 8am-sunset, museum 9am-5pm; P) , north of White Springs. With lush green hills and monolithic live oak trees, the park has a museum of Florida history that you'd swear is a 19th-century plantation. The three-day Florida Folk Festival, a celebration of traditional Floridian music, crafts, food and culture, takes place here every Memorial Day weekend. Next door to the park, canoe rentals are available from **American Canoe Adventures** (☎386-397-1309; www.aca1.com; 10610 Bridge St, White Springs; ⊙9am-6pm Wed-Mon), which offers day trips ($35 to $60, depending on mileage and terrain) where you're transported upstream and then paddle down. Overnight canoe rentals are $25.

The **Suwannee River State Park** (☎386-362-2746; www.floridastateparks.org/suwanneeriver; 3631 201st Path, Live Oak; vehicle $5; ⊙8am-sunset; P) , at the confluence of the Withlacoochee and Suwannee Rivers, has Civil War fortifications. Camping is available, as well as basic cabins that sleep up to six people. The park is 13 miles west of Live Oak, just off US 90 – follow the signs.

on its opening day to the otherwise peaceful waters of Dead Man's Bay. The season is kind of like a twisted Easter egg hunt, with locals and visitors taking a mesh bag, donning a snorkel and mask, and snatching up their own seafood as they swim. Locals will often clean your catch in exchange for half the meat.

🏃 Activities

Fishing and scalloping is where it's at: depending on the season, cobia, sea trout, mackerel, tarpon and the famous scallops are plentiful.

Reel Song Charters   FISHING
(☎352-895-7544; www.reelsongcharters.com; 13 Fourth Street SE; trips from $400) For a guided fishing charter with locals who know the waters, Reel Song Charters specialize in near-shore and flats fishing for trout, red fish and scallops.

River Haven Marina   BOATING
(☎352-498-0709; www.riverhavenmarinaand motel.com; 1110 Riverside Dr; ⊙9am-5pm) Rent a variety of fishing boats (from $60 per half-day) and kayaks including pick-up and

drop-off ($30/40 per half-day single/tandem): great for exploring the local maze of waterways.

🍴 Sleeping & Eating

Steinhatchee River Inn Motel   MOTEL $
(☎352-498-4049; www.steinhatcheeriverinn.net; 1111 Riverside Dr; r from $90; ❄🛜🐾) This classic motel-style inn has decent-size rooms and is close to the marina. Some rooms have kitchens, and all have TVs, coffeemakers, wi-fi and refrigerators.

Steinhatchee Landing   RESORT $$
(☎352-498-0696; www.steinhatcheelanding.com; 315 Hwy 51 NE; cottages $150-300; ❄🐾🐾) This riverside resort community has one-through four-bedroom self-catering cottages clustered around a loop road, with a pool, country store, spa, and lusciously manicured grounds bursting with hibiscus and palms. A two-night minimum stay is often required.

Roy's   SEAFOOD $$
(☎352-498-5000; www.roys-restaurant.com; 100 1st Ave; mains $15-25; ⊙11am-9pm; P🐾) Since 1969, Roy's, which sits overlooking the gulf,

has been a favorite for seafood – fresh, local caught and cooked to order, nestled up to sides that include heaping portions of grits, fries, baked potatoes and hush puppies.

🛈 Getting There & Away

Coming from either the north or south, take Hwy 19 (also called Hwy 19/27 and Hwy 19/98), then drive west on Hwy 51 to the end, about 12 miles.

Cedar Key

📞 352 / POP 700

Jutting 3 miles into the Gulf of Mexico, this windswept, isolated island feels like a frontier outpost mushed with a tacky seaside resort. The ramshackle downtown is stuffed with historic buildings and Harley motorcycles; we prefer the uninhabited bayou, meadows and bay on the outskirts. The otherworldly landscape sings with marshes that reflect candy-colored sunsets, and tiny hills offering sweeping island views. Cedar Key is just one of 100 islands (13 of which are part of the Cedar Keys National Wildlife Refuge) that make up this coastal community, which is gloriously abundant with wildlife.

As the western terminus of the trans-Florida railroad in the late 1800s, Cedar Key was one of Florida's largest towns, second only to St Augustine. Its primary industry was wood (for Faber pencils), which eventually deforested the islands; an 1896 hurricane destroyed what was left. Consequently, the trees here are less than 100 years old.

⊙ Sights & Activities

Cedar Keys National Wildlife Refuge   WILDLIFE RESERVE

(📞352-493-0238; www.fws.gov/cedarkeys; ⊙8am-sunset; P) 🚸 Home to 250 species of bird (including ibises, pelicans, egrets, herons and double-crested cormorants), 10 species of reptile and one romantic lighthouse, the 13 islands in this refuge can only be reached by boat. The islands' interiors are generally closed to the public, but during daylight hours you can access most of the white-sand beaches, which provide great opportunities for both fishing and manatee viewing.

Cedar Key Museum State Park   MUSEUM

(📞352-543-5350; www.floridastateparks.org/cedarkeymuseum; 12231 SW 166th St; $2; ⊙10am-5pm Thu-Mon) 🚸 This eclectic museum features the historic house, remodeled to its 1902 state, of St Clair Whitman. A main player in both the pencil factory and the local fiber mill, he arrived in the area in 1882 and started collecting everything he saw: insects, butterflies, glass, sea grass, bottles and infinite varieties of seashell. After your visit, enjoy a bucolic walk on the surrounding nature trails.

Cedar Key Historical Society Museum   MUSEUM

(📞352-543-5549; www.cedarkeyhistoricalmuseum.org; 609 2nd St; adult/child $1/50¢; ⊙1-4pm Sun-Fri, 11am-5pm Sat) 🚸 This small museum packs a punch with its exhibits of Native American, Civil War and seafood-industry artifacts, and especially for its extensive collection of Cedar Key historic photographs.

WORTH A TRIP

MANATEE SPRINGS STATE PARK

Manatee Springs (📞352-493-6072; www.floridastateparks.org/manateesprings; 11650 NW 115th St, Chiefland; vehicle $6; ⊙8am-sundown; P ♿) 🚸 is worth a stop for a dip into the 72°F crystalline waters of the beautiful eponymous spring. On dry land – a spongy combo of sand and limestone shaded by tupelo, cypress and pine – there's the 8.5-mile-long North End hiking/cycling trail. You can also scuba dive (bring your own gear and register at the office) at the springhead, which gushes 117 million gallons of water per day, or canoe or kayak along the spring run (kayak/canoe $16/20 per hour).

Camping ($20 per night) is also available at 94 shady spots with picnic tables and ground grills. A highlight here is the wheelchair-accessible raised timber boardwalk that traces the narrow spring down to the Suwannee River as it flows to the gulf and out to sea. Ranger programs include guided canoe journeys, moonlight hikes, nature walks and occasional covered-wagon rides. Contact the park office for details.

Kayak Cedar Keys
KAYAKING

(📋352-543-9447; www.kayakcedarkeys.com; 6027 A St; kayaks per 3hr from $25; ◷10am-4pm) ✐ The waterways and estuaries in and around Cedar Key make for superb kayaking, which you can access via map-guided tours. This outfitter also will rent you gear and can arrange to take you to offshore clam beds.

☞ Tours

Tidewater Tours
BOATING

(📋352-543-9523; www.tidewatertours.com; 4 Dock St) ✐ Tidewater Tours runs two-hour nature tours of the islands of the national wildlife refuge ($26), trips along the Suwannee River ($45) and trips into the wild marshy coastline ($35).

🛏 Sleeping

★Island Hotel
HOTEL $$

(📋352-543-5111; www.islandhotel-cedarkey.com; 224 2nd St, at B St; r $100-155; ❈🛜) A night in this old-fashioned, 1859 tabby shell and oak building will relax you for sure. Listed on the National Register of Historic Places, it has 10 simple and romantic rooms with original hand-cut wooden walls, a wraparound balcony with rocking chairs, a history of notable guests – including John Muir and President Grover Cleveland – and, by all reports, as many as 13 resident ghosts.

Faraway Inn
MOTEL $$

(📋352-543-5330; www.farawayinn.com; 847 3rd St; r from $90, cottages from $150; ❈🛜🐾🎮) Overlooking a silent, glassy stretch of bay, this funky little motel complex has rooms and cottages decorated in driftwood art and brightly colored prints. Guests chill on waterfront porch swings to watch mind-blowing sunsets.

✕ Eating

AdaBlue Cafe
AMERICAN $

(📋352-543-9300; www.cedarkeyrv.com/adablue; 11846 SR 24; mains $6-10; ◷7:30am-2:30pm Fri-Wed; 🅿) Ada's is a little blue shack plopped in front of an RV resort that serves up tons of home-cooked barbecue, sides of smothered potatoes and coleslaw, and (why not?) trays of fudge.

Tony's
SEAFOOD $$

(📋352-543-0022; www.tonyschowder.com; 597 2nd St; mains $8-28; ◷11am-8pm Mon-Thu, to 9pm Fri-Sun) Creamy, whole-clam-studded clam chowder – Tony's claim to fame – is truly superlative, and a reason to visit this otherwise mediocre seafood restaurant in a downtown storefront.

❶ Getting There & Away

There's no public transportation to Cedar Key, but driving is easy: take Hwy 19/98 or I-75 to Hwy 24 and follow it southwest to the end.

❶ Getting Around

You'll see locals zipping around in golf ('gulf') carts, which are perfect for traversing the little island; try **Cedar Key Gulf Kart Company** (📋352-543-5090; www.gulfkartcompany. com; 8030 A St; carts per 2hr/day from $25/55).

Apalachicola National Forest

The largest of Florida's three national forests, the **Apalachicola National Forest** (📋850-523-8500, 850-643-2282; www.fs.usda. gov/main/apalachicola; entrance off FL-13, FL-67, & other locations; day-use fee $3; ◷8am-sunset; 🐾) ✐ occupies almost 938 sq miles – more than half a million acres – of the Panhandle from just west of Tallahassee to the Apalachicola River. It's made up of lowlands, pines, cypress hammocks and oaks, and dozens of species call the area home, including mink, gray and red foxes, coyotes, six bat species, beavers, woodpeckers, alligators, Florida black bears and the elusive Florida panther. Numerous lakes and miles of trails make this one of the most diverse outdoor recreation areas in the state.

◉ Sights

Leon Sinks Geological Area
PARK

(off US 319; vehicle $3; ◷8am-sunset; 🅿) ✐ FREE More than 6 miles of trails and boardwalks marked with interpretive signs wind past sinks and swamps in this fascinating place. Be sure to stay on the trails, as the karst is still evolving, and new sinkholes could appear any time. At **Big Dismal Sink** you'll see ferns, dogwoods and dozens of other lush plants descending its steep walls.

The sinks are at the eastern end of Apalachicola National Forest, just west of US 319, about 10 miles south of Tallahassee.

Silver Lake
LAKE

(📋850-643-2282; www.fs.usda.gov/apalachicola; off FL 20; vehicle $3; ◷8am-sunset; 🅿🐾) ✐ FREE You can sunbathe on the white-sand shores or swim in the waters of this gorgeous lake, surrounded by cypress groves, palmetto fronds, hardwood hammock and pine woods. Be on the lookout for soaring bald eagles and creeping gators. Located about 8 miles west of Tallahassee on state highway FL 20.

Fort Gadsen Historic Site   HISTORIC SITE
(Prospect Bluff; Fort Gadsen Rd; ⊗ Thu-Sun 8am-6pm; P) FREE This is the former location of an 1814 British fort manned by African American and Native American soldiers armed and trained by the British to defend against Spain's hold on Florida. The fort was blown to pieces two years later, killing more than 200 people, but its rebuilt fortification would later be used by Confederate troops. These days it's a green, serene picnic area, with an interpretive trail detailing its history.

From Hwy 65, turn west on Forest Rd 129, then south on Forest Rd 129B.

Wright Lake   LAKE
(☑ 850-643-2282;   www.fs.usda.gov/apalachicola; Wright Lake Rd; vehicle $3; ⊗ 8am-sunset; P 🐾) ⚑ This quiet, scenic lake is hemmed by a pleasant white-sand beach; it's great for a picnic or a stroll. It's located just off of FL65, about 35 miles north of Apalachicola.

Camel Lake   LAKE
(☑ 850-643-2282;   www.fs.usda.gov/apalachicola; National Forest Rd 105; vehicle $3; ⊗ 8am-sunset; P) ⚑ FREE This attractive lake, which is close to a fascinating pitcher-plant bog system (pitcher plants are carnivorous plants), is a focal point for local camping, fishing, boating and recreation.

🏃 Activities

There are plentiful opportunities for canoeing along the forest's rivers and waterways. Information on canoeing in the area and canoe rental is available from the ranger stations and on the excellent website for Florida Greenways & Trails (www.dep.state. fl.us/gwt), which have updated lists of outfitters in the surrounding towns. Canoe rentals cost around $25 to $35 per day.

Powerboats are allowed on the rivers but not on the glassy lakes.

The **Florida National Scenic Trail** (www. fs.usda.gov/fnst) cuts a northwest-southeast swath through the Apalachicola National Forest. Prepare to get soaked if you opt for the **Bradwell Bay Wilderness** section,

which involves some waist-deep swamp tramping. You can pick up the trail at the southeastern gateway, just east of Forest Rd 356 on Hwy 319, or at the northwestern corner on Hwy 12.

Munson Hills Loop   CYCLING
(Map p471) ⚑ On the eastern side of the Apalachicola National Forest is the 7.5-mile Munson Hills Loop bicycle trail, which spurs to the Tallahassee-St Marks Historic Railroad State Trail. Experienced off-road cyclists can tackle this area made up of hammock, dunes, hills and brush, though its soft sand can make this a challenging route. If you run out of steam halfway through, take the Tall Pine Shortcut out of the trail, roughly at the halfway point, for a total distance of 4.5 miles.

🛏 Sleeping

Camel Lake Campground   CAMPGROUND $
(☑ 877-444-6777; www.recreation.gov; Forest Rd 105; tent sites with/without hookup $10/15; P) ⚑ The Camel Lake campground includes electric hookups, flush toilets and a bathhouse.

Wright Lake Camping   CAMPGROUND $
(☑ 877-444-6777; www.recreation.gov; Wright Lake Rd; campsites $10; P 🐾) This quiet campground sits on the shores of Wright Lake, and includes flush toilets and showers, but no hookups.

Hickory Landing   CAMPGROUND $
(☑ 850-643-2282; www.fs.usda.gov; off Hickory Landing Rd; $3; P) There's drinking water and 10 campsites here, but not much else, other than a bucolic forest setting.

🍴 Eating

There are small towns with convenience stores dotted around the National Forest, but it's a good idea to bring your own foodstuffs. Always dispose of your food responsibly – the forest is home to a population of black bears.

❶ Information

Apalachicola Ranger Station (☑ 850-643-2282; www.fs.usda.gov/apalachicola; 11152 NW SR-20, Bristol) The western half of the forest is controlled by the Apalachicola Ranger Station, northwest of the forest near the intersection of Hwys 12 and 20, just south of Bristol.

Wakulla Ranger Station (☑ 850-926-3561; www.fs.usda.gov/apalachicola; 57 Taff Dr,

WORTH A TRIP

WAKULLA SPRINGS STATE PARK

Glowing an otherworldly aqua and overhung with Spanish moss, the natural spring at the center of 6000-acre **Wakulla Springs** (☑850-561-7276; www.floridastateparks.org/ wakullasprings; 465 Wakulla Park Dr, Wakulla Springs; vehicle/pedestrian $6/2; ☺8am-sunset; P ⊞) ✎ feels like something from the set of an exotic adventure movie, and indeed parts of *Tarzan's Secret Treasure* and *The Creature from the Black Lagoon* were filmed here. Gushing 1.2 billion gallons of water daily, the spring is deep and ancient: the remains of at least 10 ice-age mammals have been found. Fair warning – this spot can get crowded.

Don't miss the chance to take a 40-minute guided boat tour (adult/child $8/5), which glides under moss-draped bald cypress trees and past an array of creatures, including precious manatees (in season), alligators, tribes of red-bellied turtles and graceful wading birds. Tours depart between 11am and 3pm. You can also crash here: **the Lodge at Wakulla Springs** (☑850-421-2000; www.wakullaspringslodge.com; 550 Wakulla Park Dr; r from $130; P) is an early-20th-century classic.

You can swim in the deep, gin-clear waters or dive off the elevated platform.

Crawfordville) The eastern half of the forest is managed by the Wakulla Ranger Station, just off Hwy 319 behind the Winn Dixie in Crawfordville.

❶ Getting There & Away

You'll need wheels to explore the forest, either a bicycle for the exceedingly fit, or a car for the rest of us. Given that the woods cover such an enormous area, there are multiple entry points, including along SR 65 (easier if you're coming from Apalachicola) and SR 20 (good for those coming from Tallahassee).

Quincy

☑850 / POP 7965

The bucolic village of Quincy makes a nice day trip from Tallahassee. Once nicknamed 'Cola-Cola Town', Quincy struck it rich in the early 20th century by investing, en masse, in Coke stock. The town struck fizzy black gold, and became the wealthiest per capita in the state. There's an original 1905 Coca-Cola mural on E Jefferson St, and 36 blocks of pretty historic buildings built on the dividends of America's favorite soft drink. Thanks to that prosperity, Quincy feels significantly more alive and energetic than many Panhandle towns of a similar size.

Historical side note: Quincy was also a flash point during the Civil Rights movement. The African American population of surrounding Gadsden County was well organized and unafraid of armed resistance against the violent militias that sought to suppress civil rights in other parts of the South.

◉ Sights

Quincy Historic District   HISTORIC SITE

FREE The little town of Quincy boasts one of the densest concentrations of historic buildings in the state. The area bounded by Sharon, Clark, Stewart and Corry Sts contains 145 historic buildings, including a few wedding-cake mansions. Most historic homes are marked by a plaque, but remain private residences.

Gadsden Arts Center   ARTS CENTER

(☑850-875-4866; www.gadsdenarts.org; 13 North Madison St; suggested donation $5; ☺10am-5pm Tue-Sat; ⊞) The Gadsen is a treasure of a museum for a small town like Quincy. The permanent exhibition includes works of Southern vernacular art (ie art made by local, untrained artists) and the space hosts exhibitions that often display regional artwork. Located in the 1912 Bell & Bates hardware store.

🛏 Sleeping & Eating

Allison House Inn   B&B $$

(☑888-904-2511; www.allisonhouseinn.com; 215 North Madison St; r $95-140; P 🛜 🐾) The former 1843 home of soldier and lawyer General AK Allison (who traveled to Washington to secure Florida's status as a state and was jailed for six months on charges of treason on his return) has peaceful, antique-y rooms with brass or four-poster beds, and no shortage of flowered bedspreads. There are continental breakfasts daily, with full breakfasts on weekends.

McFarlin House Bed & Breakfast
B&B $$

(☑ 850-524-0640; www.mcfarlinhouse.com; 305 E King St; r $110-249; 🅿) The turreted 1895 Queen Anne home of tobacco planter John Lee McFarlin, who helped develop the shade tobacco process, offers nine museum-piece (if fussy) rooms. The King's View room is a gem; it is inside the turret and has a two-person spa.

El Tamaulipeco
MEXICAN $

(☑ 850-627-1003; 40 Pavillion Dr; mains $7-13; ☺ Tue-Thu & Sun 9:30am-7:30pm, to 10pm Fri & 11:30pm Sat; 🅿) You wouldn't expect to find a Mexican gem in a little town like Quincy, but along comes El Tamaulipeco, with a solid menu of steaks, *barbacoa* (barbecue) and *chicharron* (fried pork). Impressive, especially given how bare-bones the venue is. Located west of the town center.

☆ Entertainment

Quincy Music Theatre
THEATER

(☑ 850-875-9444; www.quincymusictheatre.com; 118 E Washington St; 🎭) Located in the historic Leaf Theater building, this is an energetic local performing arts center that puts on a busy schedule of live theater.

ℹ Getting There & Away

Quincy isn't served by public transport. The town is 25 miles west of Tallahassee, spaced along US 90W.

Understand Florida

Florida Today

Florida is undergoing seismic shifts in demographics, state identity, and – if the environment doesn't improve – state topography, thanks to immigration, economic recession and resurgence, and climate change. These developments, and how the state adapts and responds to them, will shape life in the Sunshine State for the foreseeable future. In the meantime, the state is constantly re-evaluating and evolving its tourism infrastructure to accommodate an ever-increasing number of visitors.

Best on Film

Scarface (1983) Al Pacino finds the American Dream. Sort of.
The Birdcage (1996) Robin Williams and Nathan Lane as gay lovers.
There's Something about Mary (1998) A Miami-set comedy of errors.
Key Largo (1948) A classic of Sunshine State noir.

Best in Print

Pilgrim in the Land of Alligators (Jeff Klinkenberg; 2008) Profiles of wacky Floridians.
Salvaging the Real Florida (Bill Belleville; 2011) Moving nature essays on a fragile landscape.
Paradise Screwed (Carl Hiaasen; 2001) *Miami Herald* columns of biting sarcasm and outrage.
Weird Florida (Charlie Carlson; 2005) Too easy. Like shooting two-headed fish in a barrel.

Preserving the Peninsula

One of Florida's deepest cultural fault lines runs across the debate over development versus conservation. For years, development held sway in the state, which has long had one of the most robust housing markets in the country, and not coincidentally, one of the fastest growing populations – said population is projected to double in the period from 2006 to 2060. As of writing, Florida is just behind New York as the third-most populous state in the country.

All of those people need places to live, and in Florida, the need for housing and businesses has traditionally taken precedence over preservation. But a new check on growth has emerged that even some of the most gung-ho developers are noting. In the environmental controversies of the 21st century, low-lying Florida is on the ecological front lines of both the climate-change and water-table debates.

Florida is a peninsula largely below sea level, and the ocean is rising even as the peninsula is crumbling. The culprits behind the crumble are artificial canals and waterways dredged in the early 20th century. Those public works directed water away from the Everglades and the South Florida aquifer, eroding the wetlands and depleting freshwater reserves. In the meantime, interior freshwater sources are increasingly under pressure from runaway development, which has led to high levels of nutrients – and subsequent blooms of toxic algae – in lakes including Lake Okeechobee.

While the interior of the state is trying to clean its water sources, coastal areas are trying to ward water away. Rising sea levels can be traced to climate change; rains in Miami that would have been an afterthought a decade ago are now flooding main thoroughfares. Local governments are moving forward with climate-change plans to deter the worst fallout of a potential ecological disaster.

A House Divided

The long, vicious 2016 election cycle ended with Florida reasserting its identity as the swing state to end all swing states. While rust-belt states including Wisconsin and Michigan may have ultimately put the nail in Hillary Clinton's electoral coffin, Florida – which went for Barack Obama twice, but voted for Donald Trump in 2016 – provided a solid base of the electoral votes needed for the final Republican victory.

In many ways, the Sunshine State is the true base of President Trump – more so even than his native New York. His Mar-a-Lago compound has become not only his retreat, but, in some ways, his base of operations, a new, de facto Camp David, where matters of state are debated and decided upon. The fact that members of the club, who pay six figures in annual dues, have unprecedented access to the president, speaks to a decidedly Palm Beach approach to politics: money talks. This is the old Florida frontier mentality, which fueled the settlement of the state.

Of course, that's not the only face of Florida. In truth, there's no one identity in a state that is home to so many foreign-born and domestic transplants, gun lovers and hippie communes, art lovers and theme-park engineers, Cuban refugees and Cracker country boys, Northeast Jews and South American intellectuals, college students and gator trappers. Florida, at the end of the day, lets people be what they want to *be*, even when those different roles end up clashing. The many identities that incubate in this state mean it's a tough place to predict – again, see the 2016 elections – but it always keeps observers, and more importantly, residents, guessing at what will come next.

POPULATION: **19.89 MILLION**

AREA: **65,755 SQ MILES**

UNEMPLOYMENT: **5%**

if Florida were 100 people

55 would be Caucasian
24 would be Hispanic
17 would be black
3 would be Asian
1 would be other

belief systems
(% of population)

 46
Protestant

 21
Roman Catholic

 17
nonreligious

3
Jewish

 13
other

population per sq mile

FLORIDA

ORLANDO

MIAMI

= 385 people

History

Florida has the oldest recorded history of any US state, and it might qualify as the most bizarre too. Something about this swampy peninsula invites exaggeration and inflames desire, then gleefully bedevils those who pursue their visions. Spanish explorers chased rumors of golden cities, yet only a fun-house mirror separates them from Disney and its promised Magic Kingdom. The constant in this state is wild-eyed speculation, great tides of immigration, and inevitably, a crash. It certainly makes for great storytelling.

First Inhabitants & Seminoles

Florida's original inhabitants never organized into large, cohesive tribes. For some 11,500 years, they remained split into numerous small chiefdoms or villages, becoming more settled and agricultural in the north and remaining more nomadic and warlike in the south.

The Apalachee in Florida's Panhandle developed the most complex agriculture-based society. Other tribes included the Timucua in northern Florida, the Tequesta along the central Atlantic Coast and the fierce Calusa in southern Florida. Legends say it was a poison-tipped Calusa arrow that killed Ponce de León.

The most striking evidence of these early cultures is shell mounds (middens). Florida's ancestral peoples ate well, and their discarded shells reached 30ft high and themselves became the foundations of villages, as at Mound Key.

When the Spanish arrived in the 1500s, the indigenous population numbered perhaps 250,000. Over the next 200 years, European diseases killed 80% of them. The rest were killed by war or sold into slavery, so that by the mid-1700s, virtually none of Florida's original inhabitants were left.

However, as the 18th century unfolded, Creeks and other tribes from the north migrated into Florida, driven by or enlisted in the partisan European feuds for New World territory. These tribes intermingled and intermarried, and in the late 1700s they were joined by numerous runaway black slaves, whom they welcomed into their society.

Seminole & Indian Resources

Ah-Tah-Thi-Ki Museum (www. ahtahthiki.com)

The Museum (www.flamuseum. com)

Seminole Tribe of Florida (www. semtribe.com)

TIMELINE	10,000 BC	AD 500	1513
	After crossing the Bering Strait from Siberia some 50,000 years earlier, humans arrive in Florida, hunting mastodon and saber-toothed tigers, at the end of the last ice age.	Indigenous peoples settle in year-round villages and begin farming, cultivating the 'three sisters' of corn, beans and squash, plus pumpkins, lemons and sunflowers.	Ponce de León lands in Florida, south of Cape Canaveral, believing it an island. Since it's around Easter, he names it La Florida, 'The Flowery Land' or 'Feast of Flowers.'

At some point, these uncooperative, fugitive, mixed peoples occupying Florida's interior were dubbed 'Seminoles,' a corruption of the Spanish word *cimarrones,* meaning 'free people' or 'wild ones.' Defying European rule and ethnic category, they were soon considered too free for the newly independent United States, who brought war to them.

Five Flags: Florida Gets Passed Around

All Floridian schoolchildren are taught that Florida has been ruled by five flags: those of Spain, France, Britain, the US and the Confederacy.

Spain claimed Florida in 1513 – when explorer Ponce de León arrived. Five more Spanish expeditions followed (and one French, raising its flag on the St Johns River), but nothing bore fruit until 1565, when St

THE UNCONQUERED SEMINOLES

The US waged war on Florida's Seminoles three times. The First Seminole War, from 1817 to 1818, was instigated by Andrew Jackson, who ruthlessly attacked the Seminoles as punishment for sheltering runaway slaves and attacking US settlers.

Trouble was, Florida was controlled by Spain. After Jackson took over Pensacola, Spain protested this foreign military incursion, forcing Jackson to halt.

In 1830, 'Old Hickory,' now President Andrew Jackson, passed the Indian Removal Act, which aimed to move all Native Americans to reservations west of the Mississippi River. Some Seminoles agreed to give up their lands and move to reservations, but not all. In 1835 US troops arrived to enforce agreements, and Osceola, a Seminole leader, attacked an army detachment, triggering the Second Seminole War.

The war was fought guerrilla style by 2000 or so Seminoles in swamps and hammocks, and it's considered one of the most deadly and costly Indian wars in US history. In October 1837 Osceola was captured under a flag of truce and later died in captivity, but the Seminoles kept fighting. In 1842 the US finally called off its army, having spent $20 million and seen the deaths of 1500 US soldiers.

Thousands of Seminoles had been killed or marched to reservations, but hundreds survived and took refuge in the Everglades. In 1855 a US army survey team went looking for them, but the Seminoles killed them first. The resulting backlash turned into the Third Seminole War, which ended after Chief Billy Bowlegs was paid to go west in 1858.

But 200 to 300 Seminoles refused to sign a peace treaty and slipped away again into the Everglades. Technically, these Seminoles never surrendered and remain the only 'unconquered' Native American tribe.

In the 1910s, brutally impoverished, the Seminoles discovered that tourists would pay to watch them in their temporary camps, and soon 'Seminole villages' were a mainstay of Florida tourist attractions, often featuring alligator wrestling and Seminole 'weddings.'

In 1957 the US officially recognized the Seminole Tribe (www.semtribe.com), and in 1962 the Miccosukee Tribe (www.miccosukee.com).

1539	1565	1702	1776
Hernando de Soto arrives in Florida with 800 men, seeking rumored cities of gold. He fights Native Americans, camps near Tallahassee, but, finding no precious metals, keeps marching west.	Pedro Menéndez de Avilés founds St Augustine, which becomes the first permanent European settlement in the New World and is the oldest city in the continental US.	In their ongoing struggle with Spain and France over New World colonies, the British burn St Augustine to the ground; two years later they destroy 13 Spanish missions in Florida.	The American Revolution begins, but Florida's two colonies don't rebel. They remain loyal to the British crown, and soon English Tories flood south into Florida to escape the fighting.

Augustine was settled. A malarial, easily pillaged outpost that produced little income, St Augustine truly succeeded at only one thing: spreading the Catholic religion. Spanish missionaries founded 31 missions across Florida, converting and educating Native Americans, occasionally with notable civility.

In 1698 Spain established a permanent military fort at Pensacola, which was thence variously captured and recaptured by the Spanish, French, English and North Americans for a century.

Spain found itself on the losing side of the 1754–63 French and Indian War, having backed France in its fight with England. Afterward, Spain bartered with the English, giving them Florida in return for the captured Havana. Almost immediately, the 3000 or so Spaniards in Florida gratefully boarded boats for Cuba.

The British held Florida for 20 years and did marginally well, producing indigo, rice, oranges and timber. But in 1783, as Britain and the US were tidying up accounts after the close of the American Revolution, Britain handed Florida back to Spain – which this time had supported the winning side, the US.

The second Spanish period, from 1783 to 1819, was marked by one colossal misjudgment. Spain needed settlers, and quickly, so it vigorously promoted immigration to Florida, but this backfired when, by 1810, those immigrants (mainly North American settlers) started demanding 'independence' from Spain. Within a decade, Spain threw up its hands. It gave Florida back to the US for cash in a treaty formalized in 1822. In 1845 Florida became the 27th state of the US, but in 16 short years, it would reconsider that relationship and raise its fifth flag.

From Civil War to Civil Rights

In 1838 the Florida territory was home to about 48,000 people, of whom 21,000 were black slaves. By 1860, 15 years after statehood, Florida's population was 140,000, of whom 40% were slaves, most of them working on highly profitable cotton plantations.

Thus, unsurprisingly, when Abraham Lincoln was elected president on an antislavery platform, Florida joined the Confederacy of southern states that seceded from the Union in 1861. During the ensuing Civil War, which lasted until 1865, only moderate fighting occurred in Florida.

Afterward, from 1865 to 1877, the US government imposed 'Reconstruction' on all ex-Confederate states. Reconstruction protected the rights of freed African Americans, and led to 19 African Americans becoming elected to Florida's state congress. This radical social and political upheaval led to a furious backlash.

When federal troops finally left, Florida 'unreconstructed' in a hurry, adopting a series of Jim Crow laws that segregated and disenfranchised

---

Best Florida Histories

The New History of Florida, Michael Gannon

The Everglades: River of Grass, Marjory Stoneman Douglas

Dreamers, Schemers and Scalawags, Stuart B McIver

The Enduring Seminoles, Patsy West

Miami Babylon, Gerald Posner

Alleged Fountains of Youth

Fountain of Youth (p353), St Augustine

De Leon Springs State Park (p373), DeLand

Warm Mineral Springs (p425), Venice

1816–58	1823	1835	1845
The three Seminole Wars pit the United States against the Seminole nation and allies, including escaped slaves. Although most Seminoles are exiled, small bands remain in the Everglades.	Tallahassee is established as Florida's territorial capital because it's halfway between Pensacola and St Augustine. Later attempts to move the state capital fail.	In attacks coordinated by Seminole leader Osceola, Seminoles destroy five sugar plantations on Christmas Day and soon after kill 100 US soldiers marching near Tampa, launching the Second Seminole War.	Florida is admitted to the Union as the 27th state. Since it is a slave state, its admission is balanced by that of Iowa, a free state.

African Americans in every sphere of life – in restaurants and parks, on beaches and buses – while a poll tax kept African Americans and the poor from voting. From then until the 1950s, African American field hands in turpentine camps and cane fields worked under a forced-labor 'peonage' system, in which they couldn't leave till their wages paid off their debts, which of course never happened.

The Ku Klux Klan thrived, its popularity peaking in the 1920s, when Florida led the country in lynchings. Racial hysteria and violence were commonplace; most infamously, a white mob razed the entire town of Rosewood in 1923.

In 1954 the US Supreme Court ended legal segregation in the US with Brown v Board of Education, but in 1957 Florida's Supreme Court rejected

BLACK MARKET FLORIDA

In 1919, when the US passed the 18th Amendment – making liquor illegal and inaugurating Prohibition – bootleggers discovered something that previous generations of black slaves and Seminoles knew well: Florida is a good place to hide.

Almost immediately Florida became, as the saying went, 'wet as a frog,' and soon fleets of ships and airplanes were bringing in Cuban and Jamaican rum, to be hidden in coves and dispersed nationwide.

Interestingly, Florida rum-running was conducted mostly by local 'mom-and-pop' operations, not the mob, despite the occasional vacationing mobster like Al Capone. In this way, Prohibition really drove home the benefits of a thriving black market. When times were good, as in the 1920s, all that (illicit) money got launder-...um...pumped into real estate, making the good times unbelievably great. When hard times hit in the 1930s, out-of-work farmers could still make bathtub gin and pay the bills. Because of this often-explicit understanding, Miami bars served drinks with impunity throughout the 1920s, and local police simply kept walking.

In the 1960s and '70s the story was repeated with marijuana. Down-on-their-luck commercial fishers made a mint smuggling plastic-wrapped bails of pot, and suddenly Florida was asking, 'Recession? What recession?' West Florida experienced a condo boom.

In the 1980s cocaine became the drug of choice. But this time the smugglers were Colombian cartels, and they did business with a gun, not a handshake. Bloody shootouts on Miami streets shocked Floridians (and inspired the *Miami Vice* TV show), but they didn't slow the estimated $10-billion drug business – and did you notice Miami's new skyline? In the 1980s so much cash choked Miami banks that smuggling currency itself became an industry – along with smuggling out guns to Latin America and smuggling in rare birds, flowers and Cuban cigars.

By the 1990s the cartels were finished and banking laws were stricter, but some still believed that smuggling remained Florida's number-one industry.

1861	1889	1894–95	1912
Voting 62 to seven, Florida secedes from the US, raising its fifth flag, that of the Confederacy. Florida's farms and cattle provide vital Confederate supplies during the ensuing Civil War.	Key West becomes the largest, most populous city in Florida largely due to the wrecking industry – salvaging cargo from ships that sink in the treacherous surrounding waters.	The Great Freeze ruins citrus crops across the agricultural belt in Central Florida. Settlers begin moving to South Florida seeking warmer climes and longer growing seasons.	'Flagler's Folly,' Henry Flagler's 128-mile overseas railroad connecting the Florida Keys, reaches Key West. It's hailed as the 'Eighth Wonder of the World' but is destroyed by a 1935 hurricane.

this decision, declaring it 'null and void.' This sparked protests but little change until 1964, when a series of demonstrations, some led by Martin Luther King, Jr, and race riots rocked St Augustine and helped spur passage of the national Civil Rights Act of 1964.

More race riots blazed across Florida cities in 1967 and 1968, after which racial conflict eased as Florida belatedly and begrudgingly desegregated itself. Florida's racial wounds healed equally slowly – as evidenced by more race riots in the early 1980s. Today, despite much progress and the fact that Florida is one of the nation's most ethnically diverse states, these wounds still haven't completely healed.

Draining Swamps & Laying Rail

By the middle of the 19th century, the top half of Florida was reasonably well settled, but South Florida was still an oozing, mosquito-plagued swamp. So, in the 1870s, Florida inaugurated its first building boom by adopting laissez-faire economic policies centered on three things: unrestricted private development, minimal taxes and land grants for railroads.

In 10 years, from 1881 to 1891, Florida's railroad miles quintupled, from 550 to 2566. Most of this track crisscrossed northern and central Florida, where the people were, but one rail line went south to nowhere. In 1886 railroad magnate Henry Flagler started building a railroad down the coast on the spectacular gamble that once he built it, people would come.

In 1896 Flagler's line stopped at the squalid village of Fort Dallas, which incorporated as the city of Miami that same year. Then, people came, and kept coming, and Flagler is largely credited with founding every town from West Palm Beach to Miami.

It's hard to do justice to what happened next, but it was madness, pure and simple – far crazier than Ponce's dream of eternal waters. Why, all South Florida needed was to get rid of that pesky *swamp*, and then it really *would* be paradise: a land of eternal sunshine and profit.

In 1900 Governor Napoleon Bonaparte Broward, envisioning an 'Empire of the Everglades,' set in motion a frenzy of canal building. Over the next 70 years, some 1800 miles of canals and levees were etched across Florida's porous limestone. These earthworks drained about half the Everglades (about 1.5 million acres) below Lake Okeechobee, replacing it with farms, cattle ranches, orange groves, sugarcane and suburbs.

From 1920 to 1925 the South Florida land boom swept the nation. In 1915 Miami Beach was a sand bar; by 1925 it had 56 hotels, 178 apartment buildings and three golf courses. In 1920 Miami had one skyscraper; by 1925, 30 were under construction. In 1925 alone, 2.5 million people moved to Florida. Real-estate speculators sold undeveloped

The Florida State Archives website (www.florida memory.com) presents a fascinating collection of historical documents (a 1586 map of St Augustine, Civil War letters), plus oodles of great photos, both historic and modern.

1923	1926	1933–40	1935
The African American town of Rosewood, in Levy County, is wiped off the map by a white lynch mob; former residents are scattered and resettle elsewhere.	A major hurricane flattens and floods South Florida. Nearly 400 people die, most drowning when Lake Okeechobee bursts its dike. Two years later, another hurricane kills 2000 people.	New Deal public-works projects employ 40,000 Floridians and help save Florida from the Great Depression. The most notable construction project is the Overseas Hwy through the Keys, replacing Flagler's railroad.	'Swami of the Swamp' Dick Pope opens Cypress Gardens, the USA's first theme park, with water-ski stunts, topiary and Southern belles. Allegedly, this inspires Walt Disney to create California's Disneyland.

land, undredged land, and then just the airy paper promises of land. Everything went like hotcakes.

Then, two hurricanes struck, in 1926 and 1928, and the party ended. The coup de grâce was the October 1929 stock-market crash, which took everyone's money. Like the rest of the nation, Florida plunged into the Great Depression, though the state rode it out better than most due to New Deal public works, tourism and a highly profitable foray into rum-running.

Tin-Can Tourists, Retirees & a Big-Eared Mouse

For the record, tourism is Florida's number-one industry, and this doesn't count retirees – the tourists who never leave.

Tourism didn't become a force in Florida until the 1890s, when Flagler built his coastal railroad and his exclusive Miami Beach resorts. In the 1920s, middle-class 'tin-can tourists' arrived via the new Dixie Hwy – driving Model Ts, sleeping in campers and cooking their own food.

In the 1930s, to get those tourists spending, savvy promoters created the first 'theme parks': Cypress Gardens and Silver Springs. But it wasn't until after WWII that Florida tourism exploded. During the war, Miami was a major military training ground, and afterward, many of those GIs returned with their families to enjoy Florida's sandy beaches at leisure.

In addition, after the war, social security kicked in, and the nation's aging middle class migrated south to enjoy their first taste of retirement. As old folks will, they came slowly but steadily, at a rate of a thousand a week, till they numbered in the hundreds of thousands and then millions. Many came from the East Coast, and quite a few were Jewish: by 1960, Miami Beach was 80% Jewish, creating a famous ethnic enclave.

Then one day in 1963, so the story goes, Walt Disney flew over central Florida, spotted the intersection of I-4 and the Florida Turnpike, and said, 'That's it.' In secret, he bought 43 sq miles of Orlando-area wetlands. Afterward, like an expert alligator wrestler, Disney successfully negotiated with the state of Florida and was granted unprecedented and unique municipal powers to build his tourist mecca.

Exempt from a host of state laws and building codes, largely self-governing, Disney World opened in 1971. How big did it become? In 1950 Florida received 4.5 million tourists, not quite twice its population. By the 1980s, Walt Disney World® alone was drawing 40 million visitors a year, or four times the state population.

After WWII the advent of effective bug spray and affordable air-conditioning did more for Florida tourism than anything else. With these two technological advancements, Florida's subtropical climate was finally safe for delicate Yankee skin.

1941–45	1942	1946	1946
The US enters WWII. Two million men and women receive basic training in South Florida. At one point, the army commandeers 85% of Miami Beach's hotels to house personnel.	From January to August, German U-boats sink more than two dozen tankers and ships off Florida's coast. By war's end, Florida holds nearly 3000 German POWs in 15 labor camps.	The development of modern air-conditioning, coupled with a postwar economic boom, opens the door to thousands of transplants settling in the state.	Frozen concentrated orange juice is invented. As the nation's top orange producer, this event leads to Florida's orange boom, giving birth to the orange millionaires of the '50s and '60s.

Disney had the Midas touch. In the shadow of the Magic Kingdom, Florida's old-school attractions – Weeki Wachee, Seminole Village, Busch Gardens; all the places made famous through billboards and postcards – seemed hokey, small-time. The rules of tourism had changed forever.

Viva Cuba Libre!

South Florida has often had a more intimate relationship with Cuba than with the rest of the US. Spain originally ruled Florida from Havana, and in the 20th century so many Cuban exiles sought refuge in Miami, they dubbed it the 'Exile Capital.' Later, as immigration expanded, Miami simply became the 'Capital of Latin America.'

From 1868 to 1902, during Cuba's long struggle for independence from Spain, Cuban exiles settled in Key West and Tampa, giving birth to Ybor City and its cigar-rolling industry. After independence, many Cubans returned home, but the economic ties they'd forged remained. Then, in 1959, Fidel Castro's revolution (plotted partly in Miami hotels) overthrew the Batista dictatorship. This triggered a several-year exodus of more than 600,000 Cubans to Miami, most of them white, wealthy, educated professionals.

In April 1961 Castro declared Cuba a communist nation, setting the future course for US–Cuban relations. The next day, President Kennedy approved the ill-fated Bay of Pigs invasion, which failed to overthrow Castro, and in October 1962, Kennedy blockaded Cuba to protest the presence of Russian nuclear missiles. Khrushchev famously 'blinked' and removed the missiles, but not before the US secretly agreed never to invade Cuba again.

None of this sat well with Miami's Cuban exiles, who agitated for the USA to free Cuba (chanting 'Viva Cuba libre': long live free Cuba). Between 1960 and 1980, a million Cubans emigrated – 10% of the island's population; by 1980, 60% of Miami was Cuban. Meanwhile, the USA and Cuba wielded immigration policies like cudgels to kneecap each other.

Unlike most immigrant groups, Cuban exiles disparaged assimilation (and sometimes the US), because the dream of return animated their lives. Miami became two parallel cities, Cuban and North American, that rarely spoke each other's language.

In the 1980s and 1990s, poorer immigrants flooded Miami from all over the Latin world – particularly El Salvador, Nicaragua, Mexico, Colombia, Venezuela, the Dominican Republic and Haiti. These groups did not always mix easily or embrace each other, but they found success in a city that already conducted business in Spanish. By the mid-1990s, South Florida was exporting $25 billion in goods to Latin America, and Miami's Cubans were more economically powerful than Cuba itself.

At the height of the industry in the 1940s, Florida's sugarcane fields produced one of every five teaspoons of sugar consumed in the US.

1947	1961	1969	1971
Everglades National Park is established, successfully culminating a 19-year effort, led by Ernest Coe and Marjory Stoneman Douglas, to protect the Everglades from the harm done by dredging and draining.	Brigade 2506, a 1300-strong volunteer army, invades Cuba's Bay of Pigs on April 16. President Kennedy withholds air support, leading to Brigade 2506's immediate defeat and capture by Fidel Castro.	*Apollo 11* lifts off from Cape Canaveral, landing on the moon on July 20, winning the space race with the Russians. Five more lunar-bound rockets take off through 1972.	Walt Disney World® opens in Orlando and around 10,000 people arrive on the first day. The park attracts 10 million visitors during its first year.

Today, Miami's Cubans are firmly entrenched, and those of its younger generation no longer consider themselves exiles.

Hurricanes, Elections & the Everglades

Florida has a habit of selling itself too well. The precarious foundation of its paradise was driven home in 1992, when Hurricane Andrew ripped across South Florida, leaving a wake of destruction that stunned the state and the nation. Plus, mounting evidence of rampant pollution – fish kills, dying mangroves, murky bays – appeared like the bill for a century of unchecked sprawl, population growth and industrial nonchalance.

Newcomers were trampling what they were coming for. From 1930 to 1980, Florida's population growth rate was 564%. Florida had gone from the least-populated to the fourth-most-populated state, and its infrastructure was woefully inadequate, with too few police, overcrowded prisons, traffic jams, ugly strip malls and some of the nation's worst schools.

In particular, saving the Everglades became more than another environmental crusade. It was a moral test: would Florida really squander one of the Earth's wonders over subdivisions and a quick buck? Remarkably, legislation was passed: the Florida Forever Act and the Comprehensive Everglades Restoration Plan were both signed into law in 2000. Meanwhile, the actual implementation of Everglades restoration has been delayed and held up by bureaucracy and politicking at the federal, state and local levels.

Yet 2000 became even more emblematic of Florida's deeply divided self. That year's tight presidential election between Republican George W Bush and Democrat Al Gore hung on Florida's result. However, Florida's breathtakingly narrow vote in favor of Bush unraveled into a fiasco of 'irregularities,' including defective ballots, wrongly purged voter rolls and mysterious election-day roadblocks. After months of legal challenges and partial recounts, Florida's vote was finally approved, but its reputation had been tarnished.

As the 21st century dawned, Florida's historic tensions – between its mantra of growth and development and the unsustainable demands that placed on society and nature – seemed as entrenched and intractable as ever.

Southernmost Schisms

The beginning of this century was a politically polarizing time across much of the United States, and Florida, being in many ways a microcosm of the nation as a whole, was not immune to the trend. If anything,

It's all too easy to mock Florida for its bumbling 2000 presidential vote, but the HBO movie *Recount* (2008) doesn't. Instead, it cogently shows what happened and unearths the political grudges that shadowed an honest recount.

May 1980	1980	1984	1992
In the McDuffie trial, white cops are acquitted of wrongdoing in the death of an African American man, igniting racial tensions and Miami's Liberty City riots, killing 18 people.	Castro declares the Cuban port of Mariel 'open.' The USA's ensuing Mariel Boatlift rescues 125,000 Marielitos, who face intense discrimination in Miami.	TV show *Miami Vice* debuts, combining music-video sensibilities, pastel fashions, blighted South Beach locations and cynical undercover cops battling gun-wielding Miami cocaine cartels.	On August 24, Hurricane Andrew devastates Dade County, leaving 41 people dead and more than 200,000 homeless, and causing $15.5 billion in damage.

Florida's ideological divisions were exacerbated by deep boundaries that run along its geographic and ethnic lines.

While the governorship has remained securely in Republican hands since 1999, the state itself is a toss-up in every presidential election (it narrowly broke for George W Bush twice and Barack Obama twice). This is largely due to redistricting practices, widely seen as gerrymandering (ie drawing voting districts to bolster a political party's performance), which have driven a deep rift between the state's political camps. With that said, past governors such as Jeb Bush (George W

TRAYVON MARTIN & STAND YOUR GROUND

One of the most divisive racial and political incidents of the early 21st century began in Florida.

On the night of February 26, 2012, 17-year old African American Trayvon Martin walked to his temporary home in the Central Florida town of Sanford. Martin, clad in a hoodie, was carrying a pack of Skittles and some Arizona Iced Tea. To get home quickly, he cut across yards in a gated community. Following him was George Zimmerman, a 28-year-old mixed-race Hispanic and neighborhood watch coordinator. Against the advice of police, Zimmerman confronted Martin, leading to an altercation. In the subsequent fight, Zimmerman received head and facial injuries, and shot and killed the unarmed Martin.

Zimmerman was taken into police custody and released; under Florida's recently passed Stand Your Ground law, police did not believe he had committed a crime. Under the Stand Your Ground statue, in a self-defense incident a victim does not have to exercise the traditional Duty to Retreat, common across American legal code, which states someone who kills in self-defense must have exhausted their opportunities to avoid conflict.

Media attention and a subsequent national outcry led to Zimmerman being rearrested on a charge of second-degree (ie nonpremeditated) murder on April 11, 2012. A trial in the summer of 2013 found Zimmerman not guilty. The decision outraged many, who felt Zimmerman had (literally) gotten away with the murder of an unarmed teenager. On the flip side, gun-rights advocates believed Zimmerman had exercised his rights to self-defense during the course of an assault.

The role of Stand Your Ground was invoked and discussed by pundits and commentators, even though Zimmerman's legal team did not utilize Stand Your Ground in their defensive arguments. Nonetheless, there were calls for boycotts of Florida tourism over the law. To date, these boycotts have not had much impact on travel in the state.

Since the Trayvon Martin incident, Florida has become a petri dish for Stand Your Ground legislation. While the *Journal of the American Medical Association* (JAMA) published a 2016 investigation linking the law to increased homicide rates in the state, as of this writing, the state senate had passed a bill that relaxed the requirements needed by a defendant to invoke the law's protections.

1999	2000	2000–10	2004
On Thanksgiving, five-year-old Elián Gonzalez is rescued at sea, his Cuban mother having died en route. Despite wild protests by Miami's Cuban exiles, the US returns Elián to his father in Cuba.	Before the presidential election, Florida mistakenly purges thousands of legitimate voters from rolls. George W Bush then narrowly defeats Al Gore by 537 votes in Florida to win the presidency.	High-rise architecture sweeps Miami; during this period, 20 of the city's 25 tallest buildings are erected, a trend some call the 'Manhattanization' of Miami.	Florida records its worst hurricane season ever, when four storms – Charley, Frances, Ivan and Jeanne – strike the state over two months, causing 130 deaths and $22 billion in damage.

Bush's younger brother; 1999–2007) and Charlie Crist (2007–11) toed the centrist line within the Republican policy universe, generally skewing towards conservative economics and lenient policies regarding immigration.

Indeed, Crist, who supports same-sex marriage but is also pro-gun ownership, made the relatively rare American political move of defection, joining the Democratic Party in 2012. That he did so a month after Barack Obama's re-election did not help his reputation as a political opportunist, although defenders say he is merely flexible and open to changing his position on past issues. His ouster and political conversion came amid the 2008 financial crisis, which particularly devastated the Florida housing market.

Rick Scott settled into the gubernatorial office in Tallahassee in 2011 and has been instrumental in setting the state's political compass since. An unabashedly antiregulation businessman (prior to election, Scott had been a CEO and venture capitalist with a net worth of $218 million), he has also been sympathetic to Everglades protection policies, which speaks to the very delicate balancing act Scott maintains on a daily basis. He must constantly both diffuse and harness the tension between the white, conservative northern end of the state, the more liberal and Latin American south, and the mishmash of identities and interests that lies in between. Stand Your Ground, Everglades restoration, climate-change denial and climate-change preparation are the policies of today's Florida, in all its contradictions.

HISTORY SOUTHERNMOST SCHISMS

2008	2010	2014	2017
Wanting greater influence in the Democratic presidential nomination, Florida moves its primary up to January. The Democratic Party strips Florida of its delegates, so its votes don't count.	In the Gulf, *Deepwater Horizon*'s offshore oil spill becomes the worst in US history. Oil only affects Panhandle beaches, but Florida tourism plummets, with losses estimated at $3 billion.	The 0.75-mile Port of Miami Tunnel, which connects the MacArthur Causeway on Watson Island with the Port of Miami on Dodge Island, opens to the public.	Outgoing president Barack Obama ends 'wet foot, dry foot', a policy that allows Cubans who make it to the USA without a visa to become permanent residents.

People & Culture

Florida's people and culture are a compelling mix of accents and rhythms, of pastel hues and Caribbean spices, of rebel yells and Latin hip-hop, of Jewish retirees and Miami Beach millionaires. Florida is, in a word, diverse. Like the prehistoric swamp at its heart, it is both fascinatingly complex and too watery to pin down, making for a very intriguing place to explore. Is there tension? Absolutely. But that tension drives a social dynamic that is undoubtedly one of the most fascinating in the country.

Portait of a Peninsula

Pessimists contend that the state is so socially and culturally fractured that it will never have a coherent identity. Optimists, strangely enough, say nearly the same thing. Florida is almost too popular for its own good, and it can never quite decide if the continual influx of newcomers and immigrants is its saving grace or what will eventually strain society to breaking point.

In terms of geography, Florida is a Southern state. Yet culturally, only Florida's northern half is truly of the South. The Panhandle, Jacksonville and the rural north welcome those who speak with that distinctive Southern drawl, serve sweet tea as a matter of course and still remember the Civil War. Here, the stereotype of the NASCAR-loving redneck with a Confederate-flag bumper sticker on a mud-splattered pickup truck remains the occasional reality.

But central Florida and the Tampa Bay area were a favored destination for Midwesterners, and here you often find a plain-spoken, Protestant worker-bee sobriety. East Coast Yankees, once mocked as willing dupes for any old piece of swamp, have carved a definable presence in South Florida – such as in the Atlantic Coast's Jewish retirement communities, in calloused, urban Miami, and in the sophisticated towns of the southern Gulf Coast.

Rural Florida, meanwhile, whether north or south, can still evoke America's western frontier. In the 19th century, after the West was won, Florida became one of the last places where pioneers could simply plant stakes and make a life. These pioneers became Florida's 'Crackers,' the poor rural farmers, cowhands and outlaws who traded life's comforts for independence on their terms. Sometimes any Florida pioneer is called a Cracker, but that's not quite right: the original Crackers scratched out a living in the backwoods (in the Keys, Crackers became Conchs). They were migrant field hands, not plantation owners, and with their lawless squatting, make-do creativity, vagrancy and carousing, they weren't regarded kindly by respectable townsfolk. But today, all native Floridians like to feel they too share that same streak of fierce, undomesticated self-reliance.

And yet, stand in parts of Miami and even Tampa, and you won't feel like you're in the US at all, but tropical Latin America. The air is filled with Spanish, the majority of people are Roman Catholic, and the politics of Cuba, Haiti or Colombia animate conversations.

'Crackers' got the name most likely for the cracking of the whips during cattle drives, though some say it was for the cracking of corn to make cornmeal, grits or moonshine. For a witty, affectionate look at what makes a Cracker, pick up *Cracker: The Cracker Culture in Florida History* by Dana Ste Claire.

Ultimately, Florida satisfies and defies expectations all at once, and is a study in contrasts. From Cuban lawyers to itinerant construction works, from fixed-income retirees to gay South Beach restaurateurs, it's one of the USA's more bizarre dinner parties come to life.

However, most residents do have something in common: in Florida, nearly everybody is from someplace else. Nearly everyone is a newcomer and, one and all, they wholeheartedly agree on two things: today's newcomers are going to ruin Florida, and wasn't it great to beat them here?

Immigrants & the Capital of Latin America

Like Texas and California, modern Florida has been largely redefined by successive waves of Hispanic immigrants from Latin America. What sets Florida apart is the teeming diversity of its Latinos and their self-sufficient, economically powerful, politicized, Spanish-speaking presence.

How pervasive is Spanish? One in four Floridians speak a language other than English at home, and three-quarters of these speak Spanish. Further, nearly half of these Spanish-speakers admit they don't speak English very well – because they don't need to. This is a sore point with some Anglo Floridians, perhaps because they see it as evidence that Florida's Latinos are enjoying America's capitalism without necessarily having to adopt its culture or language.

Florida's Cuban exile community (concentrated in Little Havana and Hialeah Park), who began arriving in Miami in the 1960s following Castro's Cuban revolution, created this from the start. Educated and wealthy, these Cubans ran their own businesses, published their own newspapers and developed a Spanish-speaking city within a city. Their success aggravated some members of Florida's African American population, who, at the moment the civil rights movement was opening the doors to economic opportunity, found themselves outmaneuvered for jobs by Hispanic newcomers.

Then Latinos kept arriving, nonstop, ranging from the very poorest to the wealthiest, and evincing the entire ethnic palette. In Miami they found a Spanish-speaking infrastructure to help them, while sometimes being shunned by the insular Cuban exiles who preceded them.

Today, every Latin American country is represented in South Florida. Nicaraguans arrived in the 1980s, fleeing war in their country, and now number more than 100,000. Miami's Little Haiti is home to more than 70,000 Haitians, the largest community in the US. There are 80,000 Brazilians, and large communities of Mexicans, Venezuelans, Colombians, Peruvians, Salvadorans, Jamaicans, Bahamians and more. This has led to

In *Dream State*, bawdy, gimlet-eyed journalist Diane Roberts weaves her family's biography with Florida's history to create a compelling, unique, hilarious masterpiece: Roberts is like the trouble-making cousin at Florida's family reunion, dishing the dirt everyone else is too polite to discuss.

IMMIGRATION BY THE NUMBERS

For the past 70 years, the story of Florida has been population growth, which has been driven mostly by immigration. Before WWII, Florida was the least populated state (with less than two million), and today it is the fourth most populated, with 20.6 million in 2016.

Florida's growth rate has been astonishing – it was 44% for the 1970s. While it's been steadily declining since, it was still over 17% for the 21st century's first decade, twice the national average.

Florida ranks fourth in the nation for the largest minority population (7.9 million), as well as for the largest number and percentage of foreign-born residents (four million people, who make up 20%). In Miami, the foreign-born population exceeds 50%, which is easily tops among large US cities. Some 850,000 Floridians are undocumented immigrants, many of whom are Cubans who no longer benefit from the recently dropped wet-foot, dry-foot policy that granted Cubans automatic lawful residence if they reached American soil.

significant in-migration around South Florida, as groups displace each other and shift to more fertile ground.

The children of Cuban exiles are now called YUCAs, 'young urban Cuban Americans,' while the next generation of Latinos has been dubbed Generation Ñ (pronounced 'en-yey'), embodying a hybrid culture. For instance, the traditional Cuban *quinceañera*, or *quince*, celebrating a girl's coming of age at 15, is still celebrated in Miami, but instead of a community-wide party, kids now plan trips. With each other, young Latinos slip seamlessly between English and Spanish, typically within the same sentence, reverting to English in front of Anglos and to Spanish or old-school Cuban in front of relatives.

It's worth noting that there are a lot of expats in Florida from Spain, which means some of the state's Spanish-speaking population is not technically Latino (ie Latin American).

Florida has also welcomed smaller waves of Asian immigrants from China, Indonesia, Thailand and Vietnam. And, of course, South Florida is famous for its Jewish immigrants, not all of whom are over 65 or even from the US. There is a distinctly Latin flavor to South Florida Judaism, as Cuban and Latin American Jews have joined those from the US East Coast, Europe and Russia. Overall, Florida is home to 850,000 Jews, with two-thirds in the Greater Miami area.

Life in Florida

Let's get this out of the way first: Florida is indeed the nation's oldest state. It has the highest percentage of people over 65 (more than 19%) – that demographic includes over *half* of the population of Sumter County (near Orlando). In fact, ever since WWII, South Florida has been 'God's waiting room' – the land of the retiree.

But the truth is, most immigrants to the state (whether from within the US or abroad) are aged 20 to 30, and they don't come for the early-bird buffet. They come because of Florida's historically low cost of living and its usually robust job and real-estate markets.

When times are good, what they find is that there are plenty of low- to midwage construction, tourist and service-sector jobs, and if they can buy one of those new-built condos or tract homes, they're money ahead, as Florida home values usually outpace the nation's. But in bad times when real estate falters – and in Florida, no matter how many warnings people get, the real-estate market does eventually falter – home values plummet, construction jobs dry up and service-sector wages can't keep up with the bills. Thus, those 20- to 30-year-olds also leave the state in the highest numbers.

In recent years, the growing wealth gap in America has made it increasingly difficult for middle-income earners to afford rent (let alone a mortgage) in Florida's growing urban areas. While businesses have always been able to fall back on cheap migrant labor from Latin America, the Caribbean and Eastern Europe, there has also usually been an accompanying nucleus of lifer service-industry professionals. Said professionals are increasingly finding Florida unaffordable, though, which bears the question: how can a state that is supported by tourism survive if folks can't afford to live on what the tourism industry pays?

Florida's urban and rural divides are extreme. Urban sprawl, particularly around Miami, Orlando and Tampa, is universally loathed – because who likes traffic jams and cookie-cutter sameness? Well, some folks like the sameness; Florida wouldn't be famous for its suburbs and shopping malls if people didn't occupy them. In addition new immigrants tend to gravitate to the suburbs – the green-lawns predictability rejected by so many Americans seeking a new urbanism are seen as signs of a high

When former *David Letterman* writer Rodney Rothman burned out, he decided to test-drive 'retirement' in Boca Raton – at age 28. A good Jewish boy, Rothman crafts a very personal anthropological study of the unsentimental world of Florida retirees in *Early Bird: A Memoir of Premature Retirement*.

Florida real estate is a continual Ponzi scheme. For a heartfelt look at the human cost of the Florida real-estate market collapse in 2007, read *Exiles in Eden* by Paul Reyes, a reporter who joined the family business of 'trashing out' foreclosed homes.

CELEBRATING FLORIDA HERITAGE & CULTURE

Florida's diversity really comes alive in its many cultural festivals. Here are a handful worth planning a trip around.

Zora Neale Hurston Festival of the Arts and Humanities (p259) For 20 years, Zora Neale Hurston's hometown has honored her with this African American cultural festival, culminating in a lively three-day street fair. Runs for one week in late January or early February.

Carnaval Miami (p114) The Calle Ocho festival in Little Havana, which runs for 10 days in early March, is the USA's biggest Hispanic street fair. There are domino tournaments, cooking contests, Latin-music concerts and more.

Florida Folk Festival (☏877-635-3655; www.floridastateparks.org/folkfest; 11016 Lillian Saunders Drive, White Springs; adult/child weekend pass $50/5; ☉Memorial Day weekend) ✦ Since 1953 the Stephen Foster State Folk Cultural Center has held this enormous heritage festival, with hundreds of Florida musicians – from gospel singers to banjo pickers – plus storytellers and Seminole craft demonstrations. Held on Memorial Day weekend.

Goombay Festival (p114) One of the nation's largest black-culture festivals celebrates Miami's Bahamian immigrants with tons of Caribbean music, dancing and food. Held over four days in early June.

Barberville Jamboree (p383) On the first weekend of November, the Pioneer Settlement for the Creative Arts hosts Florida's best pioneer-heritage festival, with folk music and authentic demonstrations of Cracker life.

---

quality of life for émigrés from Haiti and Cuba. In any case, almost everyone really does have a tan. It's nearly unavoidable: 80% of Floridians live within 10 miles of the coast because that's why everyone came – the beach.

So, along the peninsula's urbanized edges, everyone rubs up against each other: racial, ethnic and class tensions are a constant fact of life, but they have also calmed tremendously in recent decades. In general, tolerance (if not acceptance) of diversity is the norm, while tolerance of visitors is the rule. After all, they pay the bills.

But wilderness and rural life define much of interior and northern Florida: here, small working-class towns can be as white, old-fashioned and conservative as Miami is ethnic, gaudy and permissive. This is one reason why it's so hard to predict Florida elections, and why sometimes they turn on a handful of votes.

A large military presence in the Florida Panhandle makes for an area that is generally quite conservative in its politics, but thanks to overseas rotations, a bit more cosmopolitan than the deep piney villages of the North Florida interior.

Floridians at Play

Floridians are passionate about sports. If you let them, they'll fervently talk baseball, football, basketball and NASCAR through dinner, dessert and drinks on the porch.

For the majority of Floridians, college football is the true religion. Florida has three of the country's best collegiate teams – the University of Miami Hurricanes, the University of Florida Gators (in Gainesville) and the Florida State University Seminoles (in Tallahassee). Between them, these teams have won nine national championships, and if anything, they are even more competitive with each other. It's hardly an exaggeration to say that beating an in-state rival is – at least for fans, who take deep pleasure in *hating* their rivals – almost more important than winning

Profiles of Peoples

Voices of the Apalachicola by Faith Eidse

Jews of South Florida by Andrea Greenbaum

Cuban Miami by Robert M Levine and Moisés Asís

all the other games. If you want to cause a scene in Florida, tell an FSU student how much you love the Gators, or mention to a UF student how great the 'Noles are.

Florida also boasts three pro football teams: the Miami Dolphins, Tampa Bay Buccaneers and Jacksonville Jaguars. There's a reason college football is so popular in Florida: in recent years all three professional teams have (sorry, it must be said) royally sucked. The Jaguars in particular seem to have made it a point of pride to be consistently the worst team in the NFL.

Florida has two pro basketball teams, the Orlando Magic and Miami Heat. The Heat, who won back-to-back NBA championships in 2012 and 2013 (and have since kind of cooled their heels) are loved in Miami and pretty much loathed everywhere else.

The Stanley Cup–winning Tampa Bay Lightning is one of several pro and semipro ice-hockey teams in the state, including the Miami-based Florida Panthers.

Major-league baseball's spring training creates a frenzy of excitement from February each year, when 15 pro teams practice across southern Florida. The stadiums then host minor-league teams, while two pro teams are based here: the Miami Marlins and the Tampa Bay Rays (in St Petersburg). The Minnesota Twins and Boston Red Sox both have their training facilities in Fort Myers.

NASCAR originated among liquor bootleggers who needed fast cars to escape the law – and who later raced against each other. Fast outgrowing its Southern redneck roots to become popular across the US, NASCAR is near and dear to Floridians and hosts regular events in Daytona.

Imported sports also flourish in South Florida. One is the dangerous Basque game of jai alai, which is popular with Miami's cigar-smoking wagering types. Another is cricket, thanks to the Miami region's large Jamaican and West Indian population.

Religion

Florida is not just another notch in the South's evangelical Bible belt. It's actually considerably more diverse religiously than its neighboring states.

In Florida, religious affiliations split less along urban/rural lines than along northern/southern ones. About 40% of Florida is Protestant, and about 25% of Protestants are Evangelicals, who tend to be supporters of the religious right. However, these conservative Protestants are much more concentrated in northern Florida, nearer their Southern neighbors.

The majority of the state's Roman Catholics (who make up 21%) and Jews (3%) live in South Florida. In South Florida, Jews make up 12% of the population, the second-highest percentage after the New York metro area. The high Catholic population reflects South Florida's wealth of Latin American immigrants.

South Florida also has a growing Muslim population, and it has a noticeable number of adherents of Santeria, a mix of West African and Catholic beliefs, and *vodou* (voodoo), mainly practiced by Haitians.

Further, about 17% of Floridians say that they have no religious affiliation. That doesn't mean they lack spiritual beliefs; it just means their beliefs don't fit census categories. For instance, one of Florida's most famous religious communities is Cassadaga (www.cassadaga.org), a home for spiritualists for more than 100 years.

The Arts

Florida has a well-earned reputation as a welcoming port for all manner of kitsch and low-brow entertainment. It invented the theme park, spring break, *Miami Vice* and its own absurdist, black-comic semitropical crime noir. But there's so much more. Should we dismiss Florida's contributions to high culture just because the colors are always sunshine bright? At their best, Florida traditions are simultaneously homegrown and cosmopolitan, and vibrate with the surreal, mercurial truths of everyday life in this alligator-infested, hurricane-troubled peninsula.

Literature

Beginning in the 1930s, Florida cleared its throat and developed its own bona fide literary voice, courtesy mainly of three writers. The most famous was Ernest Hemingway, who settled in Key West in 1928 to write, fish and drink, not necessarily in that order. 'Papa' wrote *For Whom the Bell Tolls* and *A Farewell to Arms* here, but he only set one novel in Florida, *To Have and Have Not* (1937), thus making his life more Floridian than his writing.

The honor of 'most Floridian writer' is generally bestowed on Marjorie Kinnan Rawlings, who lived in Cross Creek between Gainesville and Ocala. She turned her sympathetic, keen eye on Florida's pioneers – the Crackers who populated 'the invisible Florida' – and on the elemental beauty of the state's swampy wilderness. Her novel *The Yearling* (1938) won the Pulitzer Prize, and *Cross Creek* (1942) is a much-lauded autobiographical novel. Her original homestead is now a museum.

Rounding out the trio is Zora Neale Hurston, an African American writer who was born in all-black Eatonville, near Orlando. Hurston became a major figure in New York's Harlem renaissance of the 1930s, and her most famous novel, *Their Eyes Were Watching God* (1937), evokes the suffering of Florida's rural blacks, particularly women. In *Seraph on the Suwanee* (1948), Hurston portrays the marriage of two white Florida Crackers. Controversial in her time, Hurston died in obscurity and poverty.

Another famous window on Florida's pioneers is Patrick Smith's *A Land Remembered* (1984), a sprawling, multigenerational saga that highlights the Civil War. Meanwhile Peter Matthiessen's *Shadow Country* (2008) is an epic literary masterpiece. A trilogy revised into a single work, *Shadow Country* fictionalizes the true story of EJ Watson, a turn-of-the-century Everglades plume hunter who murdered his employees, and who in turn was murdered by the townsfolk.

Florida writing is perhaps most famous for its eccentric take on hard-boiled noir crime fiction. Carl Hiaasen almost single-handedly defines the genre; his stories are hilarious bubbling gumbos of misfits and murderers, who collide in plots of thinly disguised environmentalism, in which the bad guys are developers and their true crimes are against nature. Some other popular names are Randy Wayne White, John D MacDonald, James Hall and Tim Dorsey.

Naked Came the Manatee (1998) is a collaborative mystery novel by a constellation of famous Florida writers: Carl Hiaasen, Dave Barry, Elmore Leonard, James Hall, Edna Buchanan and more. It's like nibbling a delectable box of cyanide-laced chocolates.

FLORIDA PULP

Florida mystery writers love to tickle the swampy underbelly of the Sunshine State. This list focuses on early novels of famous series. Grab one and hit the beach for another murderous day in paradise.

➡ *Rum Punch* (Elmore Leonard, 1992) Leonard is the undisputed master of intricate plots, crackling dialogue and terrific bad guys. Set in Miami, *Rum Punch* inspired Tarantino's movie *Jackie Brown*.

➡ *Double Whammy* (Carl Hiaasen, 1987) Hiaasen perfected his absurdist, black-comic rage in his second novel; you'll laugh till you cry. *Skinny Dip* and *Hoot* are also Hiaasen gems.

➡ *The Girl in the Plain Brown Wrapper* (John D MacDonald, 1968) The godfather of Florida crime fiction introduces us to Travis McGee, who saves a girl from suicide and gets trouble as thanks.

➡ *Sanibel Flats* (Randy Wayne White, 1990) With crisp prose and tight plotting, White introduces his much-beloved 'retired' NSA agent/marine biologist Doc Ford.

➡ *Miami Blues* (Charles Willeford, 1984) Willeford first made it big with this addictive novel about a denture-wearing detective's chase after a quirky criminal.

➡ *Cold Case Squad* (Edna Buchanan, 2001) Miami police sergeant Craig Burch leads the cold-case squad in this novel, written by a Pulitzer Prize–winning former crime reporter for the *Miami Herald*.

➡ *Torpedo Juice* (Tim Dorsey, 2005) Zany Serge A Storms only kills people who really deserve it – people who disrespect Florida – as he searches for love in the Keys.

➡ *Tropical Depression* (Laurence Shames, 1996) Shames is off-the-wall silly. Here, an inept Jersey bra magnate seeks to find himself in Key West. Yeah, right.

Florida's modern novelists tend to favor supernatural, even monstrously absurd Southern Gothic styles, none more so than Harry Crews; try *All We Need of Hell* (1987) and *Celebration* (1999). Two more cult favorites are *Ninety-two in the Shade* (1973) by Thomas McGuane and *Mile Zero* (1990) by Thomas Sanchez, both writerly, dreamlike Key West fantasies. Also don't miss Russell Banks' *Continental Drift* (1985), about the tragic intersection of a burned-out New Hampshire man and a Haitian woman in unforgiving Miami. Karen Russell's *Swamplandia!* (2011), about the travails of a family of alligator wrestlers, marries Hiaasen-style characters with swamp-drenched magical realism.

You can count among Florida's snowbirds over the years some of the USA's best writers, such as Robert Frost, Stephen King, Isaac Bashevis Singer and Annie Dillard, and every January the US literati holds court at the annual Key West Literary Seminar.

Cinema & Television

Get this: Jacksonville almost became Hollywood. In the 1910s Jacksonville had 30 production companies – far more than Hollywood – who used its palm-tree-lined beaches as 'exotic' backdrops for 120 silent films. Yet, even as Laurel and Hardy were becoming famous in one-reeler slapstick comedies, religiously conservative Jacksonville decided to run those wild movie types out of town. Then Florida's 1926 real-estate bust (and the talkies) killed what Florida moviemaking remained.

Still, it was a close call, and you can see why: Florida, like California, has always fostered dreams and fantasies. Only in Florida, they come to life as theme parks.

Actually, Hollywood has returned to Florida time and again to film both TV shows and movies, and Florida courts both. Some of the more notable popular films include the Marx Bros farce *Cocoanuts*, *Creature from the Black Lagoon* (filmed at Wakulla Springs), *The Truman Show* (filmed at Seaside), *Ulee's Gold, Donnie Brasco, Get Shorty, Hoot* and *Miami Blues.*

Florida, as setting, has been a main character in a number of TV shows. In the 1960s the most famous were *Flipper*, about a boy and his dolphin, and *I Dream of Jeannie*. Set in Cocoa Beach, *Jeannie* was Florida all over: an astronaut discovers a pinup-gorgeous female genie in a bottle, only she never quite fulfills his wishes like he wants.

In the 1980s, Miami was never the same after *Miami Vice* hit the air, a groundbreaking cop drama that made it OK to wear sport coats over T-shirts and which helped inspire the renovation of South Beach's then-dilapidated historic district. The popular *CSI: Miami* owed a debt to actor Don Johnson and *Miami Vice* that it could never repay.

What's fascinating about modern Miami cinematic media is its willingness to peer past the pastel and deco. Of course, shows such as *Miami Vice* were always comfortable with Miami's seedy side, but recent forays into film and television are looking at the savagery and darkness that seem to lurk side by side with the glittery celebrity facade. Shows such as *Dexter* have dipped past Miami's glamor directly into its bucket of weirdness. The Netflix series *Bloodline* also continues the long tradition of Florida's 'sunshine noir' genre, following the dark history and dealings of a family in the Florida Keys. The 2016 film *Moonlight*, which won best picture at the Academy Awards, is largely set in Miami, and explores themes of homosexuality, racism and crime.

It's also worth noting that Miami is one of the centers of American Spanish-language media, especially film and television. The first Spanish-language presidential debate in the United States was hosted at the University of Miami on Univision, while Spanish-language network Telemundo is based in Hialeah, a suburb of Miami.

Music

Florida's musical heritage is as rich and satisfyingly diverse as its cuisine. Folk and blues are deep-running currents in Florida music, and pioneers Ray Charles and Cannonball Adderley both hailed from the state. For folk, visit the Spirit of the Suwannee Music Park (www.musicliveshere.com), near Suwannee River State Park, while Tallahassee has a notable blues scene.

Florida's state song, 'Old Folks at Home,' was written by Stephen Foster in 1851. Best known for the refrain 'Waaaay down upon the Suwanee River...,' it is a lament of an exile for his home, on the one hand – but also, quite explicitly, a nostalgic missive by a slave who longs for his old plantation. In recent decades, Florida has sought to modernize the lyrics so that the song's sentimental paean to Old Florida is sanitized of its inherent racism, but some argue it should be retired nonetheless.

Florida definitely knows how to rock. Bo Diddley, after helping define rock and roll, settled near Gainesville for the second half of his life. North Florida is one of the wombs of that particularly American subgenre of the musical catalog, Southern rock. The style is characterized by roots-laden references to old-school honky tonk overlaid with sometimes folksy, sometimes rowdy lyrics. Tom Petty, Lynyrd Skynyrd and the Allman Brothers form Florida's holy Southern rock trio.

In more recent years, bands including Matchbox Twenty, Dashboard Confessional, Radical Face and Iron & Wine have gotten their start in Florida. Indie-rock sounds are strong across the state, from the expected college towns such as Gainesville to the perhaps unexpected Latin streetscape of Miami.

Two of the best film festivals in the US are the Miami International Film Festival (p114), a showcase for Latin cinema, and the up-and-coming Florida Film Festival (p259) in Orlando.

The 1960 movie of Glendon Swarthout's novel *Where the Boys Are* is largely responsible for spring break as we know it today. It's a bawdy, cautionary coming-of-age tale about four Midwest coeds visiting Fort Lauderdale for sun, sand and sex.

THE ARTS MUSIC

PERFORMING ARTS

Iconic American playwright Tennessee Williams called Key West home on and off for more than 30 years, but Florida doesn't have much of a homegrown theater or dance tradition. However, several South Florida cities offer top-drawer performing arts and some spectacular stages.

Naturally, Miami leads the way. The Miami City Ballet, a Balanchine company, is one of the nation's largest. The statewide Florida Dance Association (www.floridadanceassociation.org) promotes dance performances and education. Miami's showstopper is the Adrienne Arsht Center for the Performing Arts, but also don't miss the New World Center. Tampa and St Petersburg also have large, lauded performing-arts centers.

For good regional theater, head for Miami, Sarasota, Orlando and even Fort Myers.

The popular musician who most often defines Florida is Jimmy Buffett, whose heart lives in Key West, wherever his band may roam. His fans, known as Parrotheads, are a particularly faithful (some might say obsessed) bunch. If you've never heard Buffet's music, it's basically crowd-pleasing beach tunes with a gentle, anti-authoritarian bent – anarchy via sandals and piña coladas, if you will. In a state where musical tastes tend to divide along sharp cultural fault lines, Buffet's easygoing guitar riffs are a bridge between camps. The more conservative side of the state appreciates his yacht-y swagger, while liberals like his gentle advocacy for environmentalism.

Orlando (by way of Lou Pearlman, who died in 2016) bestowed upon the world a special genre of music: the boy bands of 'N Sync and Backstreet Boys. In fact, in many ways Orlando via Disney is responsible for shaping the soundscape of much of the world's teen- and tween-focused pop music; Miley Cyrus and Britney Spears may not be from Florida, but they perfected the art of mass marketability via trained Disney handlers and tastemakers. While the aim of pop is to create a universal sound that cuts across borders, Florida's native beat works its way into the most globally marketed Orlando albums, from Hollywood native Victoria Justice's mall-rat anthems to Boca Raton–born Ariana Grande's Latin-spiced dance numbers.

Rap and hip-hop have flourished in Tampa and Miami, from old-school 2 Live Crew to Trick Daddy, Rick Ross, DJ Khaled and Pitbull, the most visible link between North American hip-hop and Latin American reggaeton. The latter has its roots in Panama and Puerto Rico, and blends rap with Jamaican dancehall, Trinidadian soca, salsa and electronica.

Miami, of course, is a tasty mélange of Cuban salsa, Jamaican reggae, Dominican merengue and Spanish flamenco, plus mambo, rumba, cha-cha, calypso and more. Gloria Estefan & the Miami Sound Machine launched a revival of Cuban music in the 1970s, when they mixed Latin beats with disco with 'Conga.' While disco has thankfully waned, Latin music has not; for a taste of hip-hop Miami-style, check out Los Primeros. The best times to see ensemble Cuban bands – often with up to 20 musicians and singers – is during celebrations such as Carnaval Miami.

Electric music is ubiquitous across South Florida, especially in Miami, which celebrates the genre with two of its biggest festivals: the Ultra Music Festival and the Winter Music Conference, both of which kick off in March (the two festivals essentially piggyback off one another).

The Florida Division of Cultural Affairs (http://dos.myflorida.com/cultural) is a great resource for statewide arts organizations and agencies. It's Florida Artists Hall of Fame memorializes the Sunshine State's creative legacy.

Architecture

Like its literature, Florida's architecture has some distinctive homegrown strains. These run from the old – the Spanish-Colonial and revival styles of St Augustine – to the aggressively modern, as in Miami and particularly South Beach.

At the turn of the century, Henry Flagler was instrumental in promoting a particularly Floridian Spanish-Moorish fantasia, which blended Italian villas with North African courtyards and open spaces. Prime examples are the monumental Hotel Ponce de León in St Augustine (now Flagler College), Whitehall Mansion in Palm Beach (now Flagler Museum) and Miami's awesome, George Merrick–designed Coral Gables.

Miami Beach got swept up in the art-deco movement in the 1920s and '30s (which Florida transformed into 'tropical deco'), and today it has the largest collection of art-deco buildings in the US. These languished until the mid-1980s, when their rounded corners and glass bricks were dusted off and spruced up with new coats of pastel-pink and aquamarine paint.

Florida's vernacular architecture is the oft-maligned 'Cracker house.' However, these pioneer homesteads were cleverly designed to maximize comfort, before air-conditioning, in a subtropical climate. Raised off the ground, with windows and doors positioned for cross-ventilation, they had extra-wide gables and porches for shade, and metal roofs reflecting the sun. They weren't pretty, but they worked. A great example is Marjorie Kinnan Rawlings' home in Cross Creek.

Painting & Visual Arts

Florida has an affinity for modern art, and modern artists find Florida allows them to indulge their inner pink. In 1983 Bulgarian artist Christo 'wrapped' 11 islands in Biscayne Bay in flamingo-colored fabric, so that they floated in the water like giant discarded flowers, dwarfing the urban skyline.

Everyone loved it; it was so Miami.

But then so was Spencer Tunick when he posed 140 naked women on hot-pink rafts in the Sagamore hotel pool in 2007, and Roberto Behar and Rosario Marquardt when they plunked salmon-colored *The Living Room* in the Design District. Whatever the reasons, cartoon-hued silly-happy grandeur and exhibitionism seem Miami's calling cards. That certainly applies to Brazilian-born Romero Britto, whose art graces several buildings, such as the Miami Children's Museum. Miami's prominence in the contemporary-art world was cemented in 2002, when the Art Basel festival

Folk Art & Florida Funkiness

Mennello Museum of American Art (p248), Orlando

Richard Bickel Photography (p468), Apalachicola

Lovegrove Gallery (p441), Matlacha

Fort East Martello Museum & Gardens (p192), Key West

Big Cypress Gallery (p159), Everglades National Park

THE ARTS PAINTING & VISUAL ARTS

THE FLORIDA HIGHWAYMEN

Beginning in the 1950s, about two dozen largely self-taught African American painters made a modest living selling vivid, impressionistic 'Florida-scapes' on wood and Masonite for about $20 a pop. They sold these romantic visions of raw swamps and technicolor sunsets from the trunks of their cars along I-95 and A1A, a practice that eventually gave them their name.

The Highwaymen were mentored and encouraged by AE 'Beanie' Backus, a white artist and teacher in Fort Pierce. Considered the 'dean' of Florida landscape art, Beanie was also largely self-taught, often preferring the rough strokes of a palette knife over a brush. Backus and his contemporaries from the '50s and '60s are also referred to as the Indian River School, a reference to the famous Hudson River School of naturalist landscape painters.

Today, this outsider art is highly revered and collected. To learn more, pick up Gary Monroe's excellent book *The Highwaymen;* visit the Highwaymen website (www.florida-highwaymenpaintings.com); and visit the AE Backus Museum & Gallery (www.backus-gallery.com) in Fort Pierce.

arrived, and without question, Miami's gallery scene is unmatched outside of LA and Manhattan.

Some say Florida's affinity for bright colors started with the Florida Highwaymen (p505) and their vernacular, supersaturated Florida landscapes. Another famous self-taught folk artist was Earl Cunningham, sometimes nicknamed 'Grandpa Moses' for his naive portraits of a bygone Florida world.

And Florida does not lack for high-quality art museums. In addition to Miami, other notable cities are Fort Lauderdale, West Palm Beach, St Petersburg, Tampa, Sarasota, Naples and even Orlando.

Landscape & Wildlife

The shapely Floridian peninsula represents one of the most ecologically diverse regions in the world. Eons ago, a limestone landmass settled just north of the Tropic of Cancer. A confluence of porous rock and climate gave rise to a watery world of uncommon abundance – one that could be undone by humanity in a geological eye blink.

The Land

Florida is many things, but elevated it is decidedly not. This state is as flat as a pancake, or as naturalist Marjory Stoneman Douglas once said, like a spoon of freshwater resting delicately in a bowl of saltwater – a spongy brick of limestone hugged by the Atlantic Ocean and the Gulf of Mexico. The highest point, the Panhandle's Britton Hill, has to stretch to reach 350ft, which isn't half as tall as the buildings of downtown Miami. This makes Florida officially the nation's flattest state, despite being 22nd in total area with 58,560 sq miles.

However, more than 4000 of those square miles are water; lakes and springs pepper the map like bullet holes in a road sign. That shotgun-sized hole in the south is Lake Okeechobee, the second-largest freshwater lake in North America. Sounds impressive, but the bottom of the lake is only a few feet above sea level, and it's so shallow you can practically wade across.

Every year, Lake Okeechobee ever so gently floods the southern tip of the peninsula. Or it wants to – canals divert much of the flow to either irrigation fields or Florida's bracketing major bodies of water: the Gulf of Mexico and the Atlantic Ocean. But were the water to follow the natural lay of the land, it would flow down: from its center, the state of Florida inclines about 6in every 6 miles until finally, the peninsula can't keep its head above water anymore. What was an unelevated plane peters out into the 10,000 Islands and the Florida Keys, which end with a flourish in the Gulf of Mexico. Key West, the last in the chain, is the southernmost point in the continental United States.

Incidentally, when the waters of Okeechobee *do* flood the South Florida plain, they interact with the local grasslands and limestone to create a wilderness unlike any other: the Everglades. They also fill up the freshwater aquifers that are required for maintaining human existence in the ever-urbanizing Miami area. Today numerous plans, which seem to fall prey to private interest and bureaucratic roadblocks, are being discussed for restoring the original flow of water from Central to South Florida, an act that would revitalize the 'Glades and, to some degree, address the water supply needs of Greater Miami.

What really sets Florida apart, though, is that it occupies a subtropical transition zone between northern temperate and southern tropical climates. This is key to the coast's florid coral-reef system, the largest in North America, and the key to Florida's attention-getting collection of surreal swamps, botanical oddities and monstrous critters. The Everglades gets the most press, and as an International Biosphere, World Heritage Site and National Park, this 'river of grass' deserves it.

Great Nature Guides

The Living Gulf Coast (2011), Charles Sobczak

Priceless Florida (2004), Ellie Whitney, D Bruce Means & Anne Rudloe

Seashore Plants of South Florida & the Caribbean (1994), David W Nellis

But while the Glades are gorgeous, there is far more waiting to be discovered. The Keys are dollops of intensely beautiful mangrove forest biomes. The white-sand beaches of the Gulf Coast have been gently lapped over geological millennia into wide ribbons of sugar studded with prehistoric shells. The Panhandle's Apalachicola River basin has been called a 'Garden of Eden,' in which ice-age plants survive in lost ravines, and where more species of amphibians and reptiles hop and slither than anywhere else in the US. The Indian River Lagoon estuary, stretching 156 miles along the Atlantic Coast, is the most diverse on the continent. And across North Florida, the pockmarked and honeycombed limestone (called karst terrain) holds the Florida Aquifer, which is fed solely by rain and bubbles up like liquid diamonds in more than 700 freshwater springs.

Animals

With swamps full of gators, rivers full of snakes, manatees in mangroves, sea turtles on beaches, and giant flocks of seabirds taking wing at once, how is it, again, that a squeaky-voiced mouse became Florida's headliner?

Birds

Nearly 500 avian species have been documented in the state, including some of the world's most magnificent migratory waterbirds: ibis, egrets, great blue herons, white pelicans and whooping cranes. This makes Florida the ultimate bird-watcher's paradise.

A KINDER, GENTLER WILDERNESS ENCOUNTER

While yesterday's glass-bottom boats and alligator wrestling have evolved into today's swamp-buggy rides and manatee encounters, the question remains: just because you can do something, does that mean you should? In Florida, everyone can be involved in protecting nature just by considering the best ways to experience it without harming it in the process.

For most activities, there isn't a single right answer; specific impacts are often debated. However, here are a few guidelines:

Airboats and swamp buggies While airboats have a much lighter 'footprint' than big-wheeled buggies, both are motorized (and loud) and have far larger impacts than canoes when exploring wetlands. As a rule, nonmotorized activities are least damaging.

Dolphin encounters Captive dolphins are, for better or worse, usually already acclimated to humans. However, when encountering wild dolphins in the ocean, it is illegal by federal law to feed, pursue or touch them. Keep in mind that habituating any wild animal to humans can lead to the animal's death, since approaching humans often results in conflict and accidents (as with boats).

Manatee swims When swimming near manatees, a federally protected endangered species, look but don't touch. 'Passive observation' is the standard. Harassment is a rampant problem that may lead to stricter 'no touch' legislation.

Feeding wild animals In a word, don't. Friendly animals such as deer and manatees may come to rely on human food (to their detriment), while feeding bears and alligators just encourages them to...hunt you.

Sea-turtle nesting sites It's a federal crime to approach nesting sea turtles or hatchling runs. Most nesting beaches have warning signs and a nighttime 'lights out' policy. If you do encounter turtles on the beach, keep your distance and don't take flash photos.

Coral-reef etiquette Coral polyps are living organisms and touching or breaking coral creates openings for infection and disease. To prevent reef damage, never touch the coral. It's that simple.

Nearly 350 species spend time in the Everglades, the prime bird-watching spot in Florida. But you don't have to brave the swamp. Completed in 2006, the Great Florida Birding Trail (www.floridabirding trail.com) runs 2000 miles and includes nearly 500 bird-watching sites. Nine of these are 'gateway' sites, with staffed visitor centers and free 'loan' binoculars; see the website for downloadable guides and look for brown road signs when driving.

Among the largest birds, white pelicans arrive in winter (October to April), while brown pelicans, the only pelican to dive for its food, live here year-round. To see the striking pale-pink roseate spoonbill, a member of the ibis family, visit JN 'Ding' Darling National Wildlife Refuge, the wintering site for a third of the US roseate spoonbill population.

About 5000 nonmigratory sandhill cranes are joined by 25,000 migratory cousins each winter. White whooping cranes, at up to 5ft the tallest bird in North America, are nearly extinct; about 100 winter on Florida's Gulf Coast near Homosassa.

Songbirds and raptors fill Florida skies, too. The state has more than 1000 mated pairs of bald eagles, the most in the southern US, and peregrine falcons, which can dive up to 150mph, migrate through in spring and fall.

Back in the day, birds were both legally hunted and poached for their gorgeous feathers, which were molded, shaped and accessorized into fashion accoutrements. Miami-based journalist and Everglades advocate Marjory Stoneman Douglas wrote about this practice and the subsequent loss of avian life, a move that laid the foundation for both wilderness protection and wildlife conservation in the state.

Land Mammals

Florida's most endangered mammal is the Florida panther. Before European contact, perhaps 1500 roamed the state. The first panther bounty ($5 a scalp) was passed in 1832, and over the next 130 years they were hunted relentlessly. Though hunting was stopped in 1958, it was too late for panthers to survive on their own. Without a captive breeding program, begun in 1991, the Florida panther would now be extinct and with only around 120 known to exist, they're not out of the swamp yet. The biggest killers of panthers are motor vehicles. Every year, a handful – sometimes more – of panthers are killed on roads; pay particular attention to speed limits posted in areas such as the Tamiami Trail, which cuts through Everglades National Park and the Big Cypress Preserve.

You're not likely to see a panther, but black bears have recovered to a population of around 3000; as their forests diminish, bears are occasionally seen traipsing through suburbs in Northern Florida.

Easy to find, white-tailed deer are a common species that troubles landscaping. Endemic to the Keys are Key deer, a Honey-I-Shrunk-the-Ungulate subspecies: less than 3ft tall and lighter than a 10-year-old boy, they live mostly on Big Pine Key.

Although they are ostensibly native to the American West, the adaptable coyote has been spotted across Florida, appearing as far south as the Florida Keys. Hopefully they won't swim too much further or else they'll end up on Big Pine Key, home of the aforementioned Key deer.

The critically endangered red wolf once roamed the bottomlands, marshes and flooded forests of the American Eastern seaboard, particularly the southeast. Due to hunting and habitat loss, the red wolf was almost wiped out, but a breeding population has been established at the St Vincent National Wildlife Refuge, located off the coast of the Panhandle.

LANDSCAPE & WILDLIFE ANIMALS

Naturalist Doug Alderson helped create the Big Bend Paddling Trail, and in his book *Waters Less Traveled* (2005) he describes his adventures: dodging pygmy rattlesnakes, meeting Shitty Bill, discussing Kemp's ridley turtles and pondering manatee farts.

The Florida chapter of the Nature Conservancy (www. nature.org) has been instrumental in the Florida Forever legislation. Check the web for updates and conservation issues.

Marine Mammals

Florida's coastal waters are home to 21 species of dolphins and whales. By far the most common is the bottlenose dolphin, which is highly social, extremely intelligent and frequently encountered around the entire peninsula. Bottlenose dolphins are the species most often seen in captivity.

The North Atlantic population of about 300 right whales comes to winter calving grounds off the Atlantic Coast near Jacksonville. These giant animals can be more than 50ft long, and are the most endangered species of whale.

Winter is also the season for manatees, which seek out Florida's warm-water springs and power-plant discharge canals, beginning in November. These lovable, lumbering creatures are another iconic Florida species whose conservation both galvanizes and divides state residents.

Reptiles & Amphibians

Boasting an estimated 184 species, Florida has the nation's largest collection of reptiles and amphibians, and unfortunately, it's growing. No, we're not antireptile, but invasive scaly species are wreaking havoc on Florida's native, delicate ecosystem. Uninvited guests add to the total regularly, many establishing themselves after being released by pet owners. Some of the more dangerous, problematic and invasive species include Burmese pythons, black and green iguanas and Nile monitor lizards.

The American alligator is Florida's poster species, and they are ubiquitous in Central and South Florida. They don't pose much of a threat to humans unless you do something irredeemably stupid, like feed or provoke them. With that said, you may want to keep small children and pets away from unfamiliar inland bodies of water. South Florida is also home to the only North American population of American crocodile. Florida's crocs number around 1500; they prefer saltwater, and to distinguish them from gators, check their smile – a croc's snout is more tapered and its teeth stick out.

Audubon of Florida (http://fl.audubon.org) is perhaps Florida's leading conservation organization. It has tons of birding and ecological information, and it publishes *Florida Naturalist* magazine.

FLORIDA'S MANATEES

It's hard to believe Florida's West Indian manatees were ever mistaken for mermaids, but it's easy to see their attraction: these gentle, curious, colossal mammals are as sweetly lovable as 10ft, 1000lb teddy bears. Solitary and playful, they have been known to 'surf' waves, and every winter, from November to March, they migrate into the warmer waters of Florida's freshwater estuaries, rivers and springs. Like humans, manatees will die if trapped in 62°F (17°C) water for 24 hours, and in winter Florida's eternally 72°F (22°C) springs are balmy spas.

Florida residents for more than 45 million years, these shy herbivores have absolutely no defenses except their size (they can reach 13ft and 3000lb), and they don't do much, spending most of each day resting and eating 10% of their body weight. Rarely moving faster than a languid saunter, manatees even reproduce slowly; females birth one calf every two to five years. The exception to their docility? Mating. Males are notorious for their aggressive sex drive.

Florida's manatees have been under some form of protection since 1893, and they were included in the first federal endangered species list in 1967. Manatees were once hunted for their meat, but today collisions with boats are a leading cause of manatee death, accounting for over 20% annually. Propeller scars are so ubiquitous among the living, they are the chief identifying tool of scientists.

Population counts are notoriously difficult and unreliable. In 2013 a bloom of red tide algae in southwest Florida and illness caused the death of 16% of the total population of these gentle giants. At the time of writing there were roughly 6000 manatees left in the state.

Turtles, frogs and snakes love Florida, and nothing is cuter than watching bright skinks, lizards and anoles skittering over porches and sidewalks. Cute doesn't always describe the state's 44 species of snakes – though Floridian promoters emphasize that only six species are poisonous, and only four of those are common. Feel better? Of the baddies, three are rattlesnakes (diamondback, pygmy, canebrake), plus copperheads, cottonmouths and coral snakes. The diamondback is the biggest (up to 7ft), most aggressive and most dangerous. But rest assured, while cottonmouths live in and around water, most Florida water snakes are not cottonmouths. Whew!

Sea Turtles

Most sea-turtle nesting in the continental US occurs in Florida. Predominantly three species create more than 80,000 nests annually, mostly on southern Atlantic Coast beaches but extending to all Gulf Coast beaches. Most are loggerhead, then far fewer green and leatherback, and historically hawksbill and Kemp's ridley as well; all five species are endangered or threatened. The leatherback is the largest, attaining 10ft and 2000lb in size.

During the May-to-October nesting season, sea turtles deposit from 80 to 120 eggs in each nest. The eggs incubate for about two months, and then the hatchlings emerge all at once and make for the ocean. Contrary to myth, hatchlings don't need the moon to find their way to the sea. However, they can become hopelessly confused by artificial lights and noisy human audiences. For the best, least-disruptive experience, join a sanctioned turtle watch; for a list, visit www.myfwc.com/seaturtle, then click on 'Educational Information' and 'Where to View Sea Turtles.'

Plants

The diversity of the peninsula's flora, including more than 4000 species of plants, is unmatched in the continental US. Florida contains the southern extent of temperate ecosystems and the northern extent of tropical ones, which blend and merge in a bewildering, fluid taxonomy of environments. Interestingly, most of the world at this latitude is a desert, which Florida definitely is not.

Wetlands & Swamps

It takes special kinds of plants to thrive in the humid, waterlogged, sometimes-salty marshes, sloughs, swales, seeps, basins, marl prairies and swamps of Florida, and several hundred specialized native plants evolved to do so. Much of the Everglades is dominated by vast expanses of saw grass, which is actually a sedge with fine toothlike edges that can reach 10ft high. South Florida is a symphony of sedges, grasses and rushes. These hardy water-tolerant species provide abundant seeds to feed birds and animals, protect fish in shallow water, and pad wetlands for birds and alligators.

The strangest plants are the submerged and immersed species that grow in, under and out of the water. Free-floating species include bladderwort and coontail, a species that lives, flowers and is pollinated entirely underwater. Florida's swamps are abundant with rooted plants with floating leaves, including the pretty American lotus, water lilies and spatterdock (if you love quaint names, you'll love Florida botany!). Another common immersed plant, bur marigolds, can paint whole prairies yellow.

Across Florida, whenever land rises just enough to create drier islands, tracts, hills and hillocks, dense tree-filled hammocks occur; ecological zones can shift as dramatically in 1ft in Florida as they do in a 1000ft elsewhere. These hammocks go by many names depending on

Great Conservation Reads

The Swamp (2006), Michael Grunwald

Losing It All to Sprawl (2006), Bill Belleville

Zoo Story (2010), Thomas French

Green Empire (2004), Kathryn Ziewitz & June Wiaz

Manatee Insanity (2010), Craig Pittman

location and type. Tropical hammocks typically mix tropical hardwoods and palms with semideciduous and evergreen trees such as live oak.

Another dramatic, beautiful tree in Florida's swamps is the bald cypress, the most flood-tolerant tree. It can grow 150ft tall, with buttressed, wide trunks and roots with 'knees' that poke above the drenched soil. Cypress domes are a particular type of swamp, which arise when a watery depression occurs in a pine flatwood.

Forests, Scrubs & Flatwoods

In Florida, even the plants bite: the Panhandle has the most species of carnivorous plants in the US – a result of its nutrient-poor sandy soil.

Florida's northern forests, particularly in the Panhandle, are an epicenter of plant and animal biodiversity, just as much as its southern swamps. Here, the continent's temperate forests of hickory, elm, ash, maple, magnolia and locust trees combine with the various pine, gum and oak trees that are common throughout Florida along with the saw grass, cypress and cabbage palms of southern Florida. The wet but temperate Apalachicola forest supports 40 kinds of trees and more insect species than scientists can count.

Central and northern Florida were once covered in longleaf and slash-pine forests, both prized for timber and pine gum. Today, due to logging, only 2% of old-growth longleaf forests remain. Faster-growing slash pine has now largely replaced longleaf pine in Florida's second-growth forests.

Scrubs are found throughout Florida; they are typically old dunes with well-drained sandy soil. In central Florida (along the Lake Wales Ridge), scrubs are the oldest plant communities, with the highest number of endemic and rare species. Sand pines, scrub oak, rosemary and lichens predominate.

Scrubs often blend into sandy pine flatwoods, which typically have a sparse longleaf or slash-pine overstory and an understory of grasses and/or saw palmetto. Saw palmetto is a vital Florida plant: its fruit is an

KEEPERS OF THE EVERGLADES
....

Anyone who has dipped a paddle among the saw-grass and hardwood hammocks of Everglades National Park wouldn't quibble with the American alligator's Florida sobriquet, 'Keepers of the Everglades.' With their snouts, eyeballs and pebbled backs so still they hardly ripple the water's surface, alligators have watched over the Glades for more than 200 million years.

It's impossible to count Florida's wild alligators, but estimates are that 1.5 million lumber among the state's lakes, rivers and golf courses. No longer officially endangered, they remain protected because they resemble the still-endangered American crocodile. Alligator served in restaurants typically comes from licensed alligator farms, though since 1988, Florida has conducted an annual alligator harvest, open to nonresidents, that allows two alligators per person.

Alligators are alpha predators that keep the rest of the food chain in check, and their 'gator holes' become vital water cups in the dry season and during droughts, aiding the entire wetlands ecosystem. Alligators, which live for about 30 years, can grow up to 14ft long and weigh 1000lb.

A vocal courtship begins in April, and mating takes place in May and June. By late June, females begin laying nests of 30 to 45 eggs, which incubate for two months before hatching. On average, only four alligators per nest survive to adulthood.

Alligators hunt in water, often close to shore; typically, they run on land to flee, not to chase. In Florida an estimated 15 to 20 nonfatal attacks on humans occur each year, and there have been 26 fatal attacks since 1973.

Some estimate an alligator's top short-distance land speed at 30mph, but it's a myth that you must zigzag to avoid them. The best advice is to run in a straight line as fast as your little legs can go.

Manatee, Crystal River (p413)

important food for bears and deer (and an herbal medicine that some believe helps prevent cancer), it provides shelter for panthers and snakes, and its flower is an important source of honey. It's named for its sharp saw-toothed leaf stems.

Mangroves & Coastal Dunes

Where not shaved smooth by sand, Southern Florida's coastline is often covered with a three-day stubble of mangroves. Mangroves are not a single species; the name refers to all tropical trees and shrubs that have adapted to loose wet soil, saltwater, and periodic root submergence. Mangroves have also developed 'live birth,' germinating their seeds while they're still attached to the parent tree. Of more than 50 species of mangroves worldwide, only three predominate in Florida: red, black and white.

Mangroves play a vital role on the peninsula, and their destruction usually sets off a domino effect of ecological damage. Mangroves 'stabilize' coastal land, trapping sand, silt and sediment. As this builds up, new land is created, which ironically strangles the mangroves themselves. Mangroves mitigate the storm surge and damaging winds of hurricanes, and they anchor tidal and estuary communities, providing vital wildlife habitats.

Coastal dunes are typically home to grasses and shrubs, saw palmettos and occasionally pines and cabbage palms (or sabal palms, the Florida state tree). Sea oats, with large plumes that trap wind-blown sand, are important for stabilizing dunes, while coastal hammocks welcome the wiggly gumbo-limbo tree, whose red peeling bark has earned it the nickname the 'tourist tree.'

Visit the website of the Florida Native Plant Society (www.fnps.org), a nonprofit conservation organization, for updates on preservation issues and invasive species and for a nice overview of Florida's native plants and ecosystems.

Brown pelican, Fort Myers Beach (p429)

To learn about the incredible efforts to save the whooping crane, visit Operation Migration (www.operationmigration.org), a nonprofit run by Bill Lishman, whose techniques inspired the film *Fly Away Home*. Another resource is www.bringbackthecranes.org.

National, State & Regional Parks

About 26% of Florida's land lies in public hands, which breaks down to three national forests, 11 national parks, 29 national wildlife refuges (including the first, Pelican Island) and 164 state parks. Attendance is up, with more than 20 million folks visiting state parks annually, and Florida's state parks have twice been voted the nation's best.

Florida's parks are easy to explore. For more information, see the websites of the following organizations:

Florida Fish & Wildlife Commission (www.myfwc.com) Manages Florida's mostly undeveloped Wildlife Management Areas (WMA); the website is an excellent resource for wildlife-viewing, as well as boating, hunting, fishing and permits.

Florida State Parks (www.floridastateparks.org)
National Forests, Florida (www.fs.usda.gov/florida)
National Park Service (www.nps.gov)
National Wildlife Refuges, Florida (www.fws.gov/southeastl)
Recreation.gov (www.recreation.gov) National campground reservations.

Environmental Issues

Florida's environmental problems are the inevitable result of its long love affair with land development, population growth and tourism, and addressing them is especially urgent given Florida's uniquely diverse natural world. These complex, intertwined environmental impacts include erosion of wetlands, depletion of the aquifer, rampant pollution (particularly of waters), invasive species, endangered species and widespread habitat destruction. There is nary an acre of Florida that escapes concern.

JUSTIN FOULKES/LONELY PLANET IMAGES ©

Alligator, the Everglades (p153)

To its credit, Florida has enacted several significant conservation efforts. In 2000 the state passed the Florida Forever Act, a 10-year, $3-billion conservation program that in 2008 was renewed for another 10 years. It also passed the multibillion-dollar Comprehensive Everglades Restoration Plan (www.evergladesplan.org) and the associated Central Everglades Planning Project. Unfortunately, implementation of the latter plan has been delayed due to a lack of approval from federal agencies such as the Army Corps of Engineers.

Lake Okeechobee, controlled by Hoover Dike since 1928, is full of toxic sludge which gets stirred up during hurricanes and causes 'red tides' (algal blooms that kill fish). Red tides occur naturally, but they are also sparked by things such as pollution and unnatural water flows. There are talks of building a nearby reservoir system to alleviate some of the issues pressing on the lake.

More than half of Florida's lakes have elevated levels of algae, which leads to frequent toxic blooms that wipe out local wildlife.Though industrial pollution has been curtailed, pollution from residential development (sewage, fertilizer runoff) more than compensates. This is distressing Florida's freshwater springs, which can turn murky and undrinkable. Plus, as the groundwater gets pumped out to slake homeowners' thirsts, the springs are shrinking and the drying limestone honeycomb underfoot sometimes collapses, causing sinkholes that swallow cars and homes.

Residential development continues almost unabated. The Miami–Fort Lauderdale–West Palm Beach corridor (the USA's fourth-largest urban area) is, as developers say, 'built out,' so developers are targeting the Panhandle and central Florida. Projections for the next 50 years show unrelenting urban sprawl up and down both coasts and painted across

GHOST HUNTERS

Florida has more species of orchids than any other state in the US, and orchids are themselves the largest family of flowering plants in the world, with perhaps 25,000 species. On the dial of botanical fascination, orchids rank highly, and the Florida orchid that inspires the most intense devotion is the rare ghost orchid.

This bizarre epiphytic flower has no leaves and usually only one bloom, which is of course deathly white with two long thin drooping petals that curl like a handlebar mustache. The ghost orchid is pollinated in the dead of night by the giant sphinx moth, which is the only insect with a proboscis long enough to reach down the ghost orchid's 5in-long nectar spur.

The exact locations of ghost orchids are kept secret for fear of poachers, who, as Susan Orlean's book *The Orchid Thief* makes clear, are a real threat to their survival. But the flower's general whereabouts are common knowledge: South Florida's approximately 2000 ghost orchids are almost all in Big Cypress National Preserve and Fakahatchee Strand Preserve State Park. Of course, these parks are home to a great many other wild orchids, as are Everglades National Park, Myakka River State Park and Corkscrew Swamp Sanctuary.

To learn more, see Florida's Native Orchids (www.flnativeorchids.com) and Ghost Orchid Info (www.ghostorchid.info), and visit Sarasota's Marie Selby Botanical Gardens.

central Florida. It is estimated that the state's population will double between 2006 and 2060

Then there's the rising seas due to global warming. Here, the low-lying Florida Keys are a 'canary in a coalmine', being watched worldwide for impacts. In another century, some quip, South Florida's coastline could be a modern-day Atlantis, with its most expensive real estate underwater.

Survival Guide

Directory A–Z

Accommodations

Many places have certain rooms that cost above or below their standard rates, and seasonal/holiday fluctuations can see rates rise and fall dramatically, especially in Orlando and tourist beach towns. Specific advice for the best rates varies by region, and is included throughout: booking in advance for high-season tourist hot spots (eg beaches and Orlando resorts) can be essential to ensure the room you want. Note that air-conditioning is standard in all Florida accommodations (barring camping).

B&Bs

These accommodations vary from small, comfy houses with shared bathrooms (least expensive), to romantic, antique-filled historic homes and opulent mansions with private bathrooms (most expensive). Properties focusing on upscale romance may discourage children. Also, inns and B&Bs often require a minimum stay of two or three days on weekends and advance reservations. Always call ahead to confirm policies (regarding kids, pets, smoking) and bathroom arrangements: many lower end B&Bs will have shared bathrooms, although anywhere charging more than $100 per night should include private facilities. As a general rule, any property calling itself a B&B will provide a full cooked breakfast for one or two guests. Properties designating themselves as an inn may not include breakfast. If you're opting for this type of accommodation, the breakfast is often one of the best perks, so be sure to confirm what's included before your stay!

Camping & Holiday Parks

Three types of campgrounds are available: undeveloped or primitive ($12 per night), public or powered ($15 to $25) and privately owned ($25 and up). In general, Florida campgrounds are quite safe. Undeveloped campgrounds are just that (undeveloped), while most public campgrounds have toilets, showers and drinking water. Reserve state-park sites in advance (yes, you need to!) by calling ☏800-326-3521 or visiting www.reserveamerica.com.

Most privately owned campgrounds are geared to RVs (recreational vehicles; motor homes) but will also have a small section available for tent campers. Expect tons of amenities, such as swimming pools, laundry facilities, convenience stores and bars. Kampgrounds of America (www.koa.com) is a national network of private campgrounds; their Kamping Kabins have air-con and kitchens.

A growing trend is free camping (framping), where you're able to legally sleep in your car or camper, or pitch a tent on public land. Sites can be as unglamorous as casino parking lots, or as picturesque as a soft grassy knoll by a billowing brook. Note, you can't just pitch a tent wherever you want, and you can be fined by the police if

---

SLEEPING PRICE RANGES

The following price ranges refer to a standard double room at high-season rates, unless otherwise noted. Note that 'high season' can mean summer or winter depending on the region. Unless otherwise stated, rates do not include breakfast, bathrooms are private and all lodging is open year-round.

$ less than $120

$$ $120–200

$$$ more than $200

you're sleeping in the wrong place. One of the best resources for frampers is www.freecampsites.net.

Hostels

In most hostels, group dorms are segregated by sex and you'll be sharing a bathroom; occasionally alcohol is banned. About half the hostels throughout Florida are affiliated with Hostelling International USA (www.hiusa.org). You don't have to be a member to stay, but you'll pay a slightly higher rate if not; you can join HI by phone, online or at most HI hostels. From the US, you can book many HI hostels through its toll-free reservations service.

Try www.hostels.com for listings of Florida's many independent hostels. Most have comparable rates and conditions to HI hostels, and some are better.

Hotels

We have highlighted independently owned hotels in our listings, but in many towns, members of hotel chains offer the best value in terms of comfort, location and price. The calling-card of chain hotels is reliability: acceptable cleanliness, unremarkable yet inoffensive decor, a comfortable bed and a good shower. Air-conditioning, mini-refrigerator, microwave, hair dryer, safe and, increasingly, flat-screen TVs and free wi-fi are now standard amenities in midrange chains. A recent trend, most evident in Miami and beach resorts, is the emergence of funky new brands, such as aloft (www.starwoodhotels.com/alofthotels), which are owned by more recognizable hotel chains striving for a share of the boutique market.

High-end hotel chains including Four Seasons and Ritz-Carlton overwhelm guests with their high levels of luxury and service: Les Clefs d'Or concierges, valet parking, 24-hour room service, dry cleaning, health clubs and decadent day spas. These special touches are reflected in the room rates. If you're paying for these five-star properties and finding they're not delivering on any of their promises, you have every right to speak politely with the front-desk manager to have your concerns addressed – you deserve only the best.

You'll find plenty of boutique and specialty hotels in places such as Miami's South Beach and Palm Beach. While all large chain hotels have toll-free reservation numbers, you may find better savings by calling the hotel directly, or paying upfront using the hotel website or a third-party booking site.

Note that it is customary to tip in most hotels of any size or stature in the US. Anywhere between $1 and $5 is appreciated for the porter who carries your bags, the bellhop who greets you by name daily, and the driver of the 'free' airport shuttle. Some people find it a nice gesture to leave a greenback or two on the pillow for the housekeeping staff. Conversely, if you're given attitude or any sense of entitlement by any hotel staff member, do feel free to save your bucks for the bar.

Chain-owned hotels include the following:

Four Seasons (www.fourseasons.com)

Hilton (www.hilton.com)

Holiday Inn (www.holidayinn.com)

Marriott (www.marriott.com)

Radisson (www.radisson.com)

Ritz-Carlton (www.ritzcarlton.com)

Sheraton (www.starwoodhotels.com/sheraton)

Wyndham (www.wyndham.com)

Motels

Budget and midrange motels remain prevalent in Florida; these 'drive-up rooms' are often near highway exits and along a town's main road. Many are still independently owned, and thus quality varies tremendously. Some are much better inside than their exteriors suggest: ask to see a room first if you're unsure. Most strive for the same level of amenities and cleanliness as a budget-chain hotel. A motel's 'rack rates' can be more open to haggling, but not always. Demand is the final arbiter, though simply asking about any specials can sometimes inspire a discount.

The most common motel chains with a presence in Florida include the following:

Best Western (www.bestwestern.com)

Motel 6 (www.motel6.com)

Red Roof Inn (www.redroof.com)

Super 8 (www.super8.com)

Resorts

Florida resorts, much like Disney World, aim to be so all-encompassing you'll never need, or want, to leave. Included are all manner of fitness and sports facilities, pools, spas, restaurants, bars and so on. Many also have on-site babysitting services. Some resorts also tack an extra 'resort fee' onto rates, so always ask if that charge will apply.

Taxes

Taxes vary considerably between towns; in fact, hotels almost never include taxes and fees in their rate quotes, so always ask for the total

BOOK YOUR STAY ONLINE

For more accommodations reviews by Lonely Planet authors, check out http://lonelyplanet.com/hotels/. You'll find independent reviews, as well as recommendations on the best places to stay. Best of all, you can book online.

rate with tax. Florida's sales tax is 6%, and some communities tack on more. States, cities and towns also usually levy taxes on hotel rooms, which can increase the final bill by 10% to 12%.

Discount Cards

There are no Florida-specific discount cards. Florida is a *very* competitive tourist destination, so persistence, patience and thorough research often pays dividends.

Being a member of certain groups also gives access to discounts (usually about 10%) at many hotels, museums and sights. Simply carry the appropriate ID.

Seniors Generally refers to those 65 and older, but sometimes those 60 and older. Join the American Association of Retired Persons (www.aarp.org) for more travel bargains.

Students Any student ID is typically honored; international students might consider an International Student Identity Card (www.isiccard.com).

Electricity

Voltage is 110/120V, 60 cycles.

Type A
120V/60Hz

Type B
120V/60Hz

Embassies & Consulates

To find a US embassy in another country, visit www.usembassy.gov. Most foreign embassies in the US have their main consulates in Washington, DC, but some have representation in Miami, including the following nations.

Brazilian Consulate (☎305-285-6200; http://miami.itamaraty.gov.br/en-us; 3150 SW 38th Ave, 1st floor; ☺visa applications 2-3:30pm Mon-Fri)

Canadian Consulate (☎305-579-1600; www.can-am.gc.ca/miami/menu.aspx; 200 S Biscayne Blvd, Ste 1600)

French Consulate (☎305-403-4150; www.consulfrance-miami.org; 1395 Brickell Ave, Ste 1050)

German Consulate (☎305-358-0290; www.germany.info; 100 N Biscayne Blvd, Ste 2200)

Italian Consulate (☎305-374-6322; www.consmiami.esteri.it/Consolato_Miami; 4000 Ponce de Leon Blvd, Ste 590, Coral Gables; ☺9am-12:30pm Mon-Wed & Fri, plus 3-5pm Wed)

Mexican Consulate (☎786-268-4900; http://consulmex.

sre.gob.mx/miami; 1399 SW 1st Ave)

Netherlands Consulate (☎786-866-0480; www.netherlandsworldwide.nl; 701 Brickell Ave, Ste 500)

UK Consulate (☎305-400-6400; http://ukinusa.fco.gov.uk/florida; 1001 Brickell Bay Dr, Ste 2800)

Emergency & Important Numbers

Country code	☎1
International access code	☎011
Emergency	☎911
Directory assistance	☎411

Etiquette

Florida isn't terribly different from the rest of the US when it comes to etiquette. Here are some basic rules to follow.

Politics The Sunshine State is as divided as America gets when it comes to politics. While the topic may come up, it may be prudent to let others introduce it.

Greetings Florida is pretty casual when it comes to greetings. In South Florida, with its large European and Spanish-speaking populations, don't be surprised if you get a kiss on the cheek.

Bilingualism If everyone around you is speaking Spanish, try leading with *'Lo siento, no hablo español'* (I'm sorry, I don't speak Spanish).

Conversation Floridians, on average, wear their heart a little more openly on their sleeves. Don't be surprised if they broach sensitive subjects with you with little prompting.

Health

Florida (and the USA generally) has a high level of hygiene, so infectious diseases are not a significant concern for most travelers. There are no required vaccines, and tap water is safe to drink. Despite Florida's plethora of intimidating wildlife, the main concerns for travelers are sunburn and mosquito bites – as well as arriving with adequate health insurance in case of accidents.

Before You Go
HEALTH INSURANCE

The US offers some of the finest health care in the world. The problem is that it can be prohibitively expensive. Citizens from other nations should not even think about travel to the States without adequate travel insurance covering medical care. It's essential to purchase travel health insurance if your policy doesn't cover you when you're abroad. Find out in advance whether your insurance plan will make payments directly to the providers or if they will reimburse you later for any overseas health expenditures.

Accidents and unforeseen illnesses do happen and horror stories of people's vacations turning into nightmares when they're hit with hefty hospital bills for seemingly innocuous concerns are common. Hospital bills for car accidents, falls or serious medical emergencies can run into the tens of thousands of dollars. Look for an insurance policy that provides at least $1 million of medical coverage. Policies with unlimited medical coverage are also available at a higher premium, but are usually not necessary. You may be surprised at how inexpensive good insurance can be.

Bring any medications you may need in their original containers, clearly labeled. A signed, dated letter from your physician that describes all of your medical conditions and medications (including generic names) is also a good idea.

VACCINATIONS

There are no vaccination requirements for visitors to the US, and no specific vaccination needs for visiting Florida.

USEFUL WEBSITES

Consult your government's travel health website before departure, if one is available. There is a vast wealth of travel-health advice on the internet.

Two good sources:

MD Travel Health (https://redplanet.travel/mdtravelhealth) Provides complete, updated and free travel-health recommendations for every country.

World Health Organization (www.who.int/ith) The superb book *International Travel and Health* is available free online.

In Florida
AVAILABILITY & COST OF HEALTH CARE

In general, if you have a medical emergency, go to the emergency room of the nearest hospital. If the problem isn't urgent, call a nearby hospital and ask for a referral to a local physician; this is usually cheaper than a trip to the emergency room. Stand-alone, moneymaking urgent-care centers provide good service, but can be the most expensive option.

Pharmacies (called drugstores) are abundantly supplied. However, some medications that are available over the counter in other countries require a prescription in the US. If you don't have insurance to cover the cost of prescriptions, these can be shockingly expensive.

ANIMALS & SPIDER BITES

Florida's critters can be cute, but they can also bite and sting. Here are a few to watch out for:

Alligators and snakes Neither attack humans unless startled or threatened. If you encounter them, simply back away calmly. Florida has several venomous snakes, so always immediately seek treatment if bitten.

Bears and wildcats Florida is home to a small population of black bears and predatory felines such as the lynx and Florida panther: one of the rarest and most endangered species on the planet. All are generally incredibly hard to spot and live deep in wilderness areas. Should you be lucky (or unlucky) enough to encounter these critters in the wild, stay calm, do not provoke the animal and don't be afraid to make a little noise (talking, jiggling keys) to alert the animal of your presence. In the rare and unfortunate event of an attack, do your best to defend yourself and retreat to a covered position as soon as possible.

Jellyfish and stingrays Florida beaches can see both; avoid swimming when they are present (lifeguards often post warnings). Treat stings immediately; they hurt but aren't dangerous.

Spiders Florida is home to two venomous spiders – the black widow and the brown recluse. Seek immediate treatment if bitten by any spider.

INFECTIOUS DISEASES

In addition to more-common ailments, there are several infectious diseases that are unknown or uncommon outside North America. Most are acquired by mosquito or tick bites.

Giardiasis Also known as traveler's diarrhea. A parasitic infection of the small intestines, typically contracted by drinking feces-contaminated fresh water. Never drink untreated stream, lake or pond water. Easily treated with antibiotics.

HIV/AIDS HIV infection occurs in the US, as do all sexually transmitted infections: incidences of syphilis are on the rise. Use condoms for all sexual encounters.

Lyme Disease Though more common in the US northeast than in Florida, Lyme disease occurs here. It is transmitted by infected deer ticks, and is signaled by a bull's-eye rash at the bite and flulike symptoms. Treat promptly with antibiotics. Removing ticks within 36 hours can avoid infection.

Rabies Though rare, the rabies virus can be contracted from the bite of any infected animal; bats are most common, and their bites are not always obvious. If bitten by any animal, consult with a doctor, since rabies is fatal if untreated.

West Nile Virus Extremely rare in Florida, West Nile Virus is transmitted by culex mosquitoes. Most infections are mild or asymptomatic, but serious symptoms and even death can occur. There is no treatment for West Nile Virus. For the latest update on affected areas, see the US Geological Survey disease maps (http://diseasemaps.usgs.gov).

Zika This mosquito-borne virus has been linked to serious birth defects, including microcephaly, when contracted by expectant mothers during pregnancy. Although the virus was found in Miami-Dade County as recently as 2016, at the time of writing there have been no active, ongoing cases of transmission in the state.

TAP WATER

Tap water in Florida is drinkable and safe.

Insurance

Health It's expensive to get sick, crash a car or have things stolen from you in the US. Make sure you have adequate coverage before arriving.

Contents To insure yourself for items that may be stolen from your car, consult your homeowner's (or renter's) insurance policy or invest in travel insurance.

Travel Worldwide travel insurance is available at www.lonelyplanet.com/travel-insurance. You can buy, extend and claim online anytime – even if you're already on the road.

Internet Access

➡ The USA and Florida are wired. Nearly every hotel and many restaurants and businesses offer high-speed internet access. With few exceptions, most hotels and motels offer in-room wi-fi; it's generally free of charge, but do check for connection rates.

➡ Many cafes and all McDonald's offer free wi-fi and most transport hubs are wi-fi hot spots. Public libraries provide free internet terminals, though sometimes you must get a temporary nonresident library card ($10).

➡ For a list of wi-fi hot spots, check Wi-Fi Free Spot (www.wififreespot.com) or Open Wi-Fi spots (www.openwifispots.com).

Legal Matters

In everyday matters, if you are stopped by the police, note that there is no system for paying traffic tickets or other fines on the spot. The patrol officer will explain your options to you; there is usually a 30-day period to pay fines by mail.

If you're arrested, you are allowed to remain silent, though never walk away from an officer; you are entitled to have access to an attorney. The legal system presumes you're innocent until proven guilty. All persons who are arrested have the right to make one phone call. If you don't have a lawyer or family member to help you, call your embassy or consulate. The police will give you the number on request.

Drinking & Driving

To purchase alcohol, you need to present a photo ID to prove your age. Despite what you sometimes see, it is illegal to walk with an open alcoholic drink on the street outside of certain designated zones. More importantly,

don't drive with an 'open container'; any liquor in a car must be unopened or else stored in the trunk. If you're stopped while driving with an open container, police will treat you as if you were drinking and driving. A DUI (driving under the influence) conviction is a serious offense, subject to stiff fines and even imprisonment.

LGBT Travelers

Florida is not uniformly anything, and it's not uniformly embracing of gay life. The state is largely tolerant, particularly in major tourist destinations, beaches and cities, but this tolerance does not always extend into the more rural and Southern areas of northern Florida. However, where Florida does embrace gay life, it does so with a big flamboyant bear hug. Miami and South Beach are as 'out' as it's possible to be, with some massive gay festivals. Fort Lauderdale, West Palm Beach and Key West have long supported vibrant gay communities and are now regarded as some of the 'gayest' destinations in the world. Despite the tragedy of the 2016 Pulse nightclub shooting, Orlando retains a vibrant, active and strong gay community. Notable gay scenes and communities also exist in Jacksonville, Pensacola, and, to far lesser degrees, Tampa and Sarasota.

Good LGBT resources:

Damron (https://damron.com) An expert in LGBT travel offering a searchable database of LGBT-friendly and specific travel listings. Publishes popular national guidebooks, including *Women's Traveller*, *Men's Travel Guide* and *Damron Accommodations*.

Gay Cities (www.gaycities.com) Everything gay about every major city in the US and beyond.

Gay Yellow Network (www.glyp.com) City-based yellow-page listings include six Florida cities.

Out Traveler (www.outtraveler.com) Travel magazine specializing in gay travel.

Purple Roofs (www.purpleroofs.com) Lists queer accommodations, travel agencies and tours worldwide.

Media

Newspapers Florida has several major daily newspapers, including the *Miami Herald* (in Spanish, *El Nuevo Herald*), *Orlando Sentinel*, *Tampa Bay Times* and *Sun-Sentinel*.

TV Florida receives all the major US TV and cable networks.

Radio Check www.npr.org/ stations to find the local National Public Radio station.

Money
ATMs

ATMs are widely available everywhere.

Tipping

Tipping is standard practice across America.

➡ In restaurants, for satisfactory to excellent service, tipping 15% to 25% of the bill is expected.

➡ Bartenders expect $1 per drink; cafe baristas, put a little change in the jar.

➡ Taxi drivers and hairdressers expect 10% to 15%.

➡ Skycaps (airport porters) and porters at nice hotels expect $1 a bag or so. If you spend several nights in a hotel, it's polite to leave a few dollars for the cleaning staff.

Opening Hours

Standard business hours are as follows:

Banks 8:30am to 4:30pm Monday to Thursday, to 5:30pm Friday; sometimes 9am to 12:30pm Saturday.

Bars Most bars 5pm to midnight; to 2am Friday and Saturday.

Businesses 9am to 5pm Monday to Friday.

Post offices 9am to 5pm Monday to Friday; sometimes 9am to noon Saturday.

Restaurants Breakfast 7am to 10:30am Monday to Friday; brunch 9am to 2pm Saturday and Sunday; lunch 11:30am to 2:30pm Monday to Friday; dinner 5pm to 9:30pm, later Friday and Saturday.

Shops 10am to 6pm Monday to Saturday, noon to 5pm Sunday; shopping malls keep extended hours.

Post

➡ The US Postal Service (www.usps.com) is reliable and inexpensive. For exact rates, refer to http://postcalc.usps.com.

➡ You can have mail sent to you 'c/o General Delivery' at most big post offices (it's usually held for 30 days). Most hotels will also hold mail for incoming guests.

Public Holidays

On the following national public holidays, banks, schools and government offices (including post offices) are closed, and transportation, museums and other services operate on a Sunday schedule. Many stores, however, maintain regular business hours. Holidays falling on a weekend are usually observed the following Monday.

New Year's Day January 1

Martin Luther King, Jr Day Third Monday in January

Presidents Day Third Monday in February

Easter March or April

Memorial Day Last Monday in May

Independence Day July 4

Labor Day First Monday in September

Columbus Day Second Monday in October

Veterans Day November 11

Thanksgiving Fourth Thursday in November

Christmas Day December 25

Smoking

Smoking is banned in all enclosed workplaces, including restaurants and shops, but excluding 'stand-alone' bars (that don't emphasize food) and designated hotel smoking rooms.

Taxes & Refunds

➡ Florida has a state sales tax of 6%. When you add in local (ie city) taxes, the total sales tax rate can go as high as 8%.

➡ Different cities and similar local government entities may also charge hotel and resort taxes.

➡ The USA does not offer reimbursement of sales tax as European nations do with the VAT.

Telephone

➡ Always dial 1 before toll-free (☑800, ☑888 etc) and domestic long-distance numbers. Some toll-free numbers only work within the US. For local directory assistance, dial ☑411.

➡ To make international calls from the US, dial ☑011 + country code + area code + number. For international operator assistance, dial ☑0. To call the US from abroad, the international country code for the USA is ☑1.

➡ Pay phones are readily found in major cities, but are becoming rarer. Local calls cost 50¢. Private prepaid phonecards are available from convenience stores, supermarkets and drugstores.

➡ Most of the USA's cell-phone systems are incompatible with the GSM 900/1800 standard used throughout Europe and Asia. Check with your service provider about using your phone in the US. Cellular coverage is generally excellent, except in the Everglades and parts of rural northern Florida.

Time

Most of Florida is in the US Eastern Time Zone: noon in Miami equals 9am in San Francisco and 5pm in London. West of the Apalachicola River, the Panhandle is in the US Central Time Zone, one hour behind the rest of the state. During daylight saving time, clocks 'spring forward' one hour in March and 'fall back' one hour in November.

Toilets

➡ Sit-down toilets are the norm, with the exception of a few primitive camping facilities.

➡ Public restrooms can be found in some cities and are usually free, and of varying degrees of cleanliness. Visitor centers are always a good bet in this regard.

Tourist Information

Most Florida towns have some sort of tourist information center that provides local information; be aware that chambers of commerce typically only list chamber members, not all the town's hotels and businesses.

To order a packet of Florida information prior to coming, contact Visit Florida (www.visitflorida.com).

Travelers with Disabilities

Because of the high number of senior residents in Florida, most public buildings are wheelchair accessible and have appropriate restroom

facilities. Transportation services are generally accessible to all, and telephone companies provide relay operators for the hearing impaired. Many banks provide ATM instructions in braille, curb ramps are common and many busy intersections have audible crossing signals.

A number of organizations specialize in the needs of travelers with disabilities:

Flying Wheels Travel (http:// flyingwheelstravel.com) A full-service travel agency specializing in disabled travel.

Mobility International USA (www.miusa.org) Advises on mobility issues and runs an educational exchange program.

Wheelchair Travel (www.wheel chairtravel.org) An excellent website with many links.

Visas

Customs Regulations

For a complete, up-to-date list of customs regulations, visit the website of US Customs & Border Protection (www.cbp.gov). Each visitor is allowed to bring into the US duty-free 1L of liquor (if you're 21 or older), 200 cigarettes (if you're 18 or older) and up to $100 in gifts and purchases.

Visitor Visa

Nationals qualifying for the Visa Waiver Program are allowed a 90-day stay without a visa; all others need a visa.

More Information

All visitors should reconfirm entry requirements and visa guidelines before arriving. You can get visa information through www.usa.gov, but the US State Dept (www. travel.state.gov) maintains the most comprehensive visa information, with lists of consulates and downloadable application forms. US Citizenship & Immigration Services (www.uscis.gov) mainly serves immigrants, not temporary visitors.

The Visa Waiver Program allows citizens of 38 countries to enter the USA for stays of up to 90 days without first obtaining a US visa (you are not eligible if you are also a national of Iraq, Iran, Syria or Sudan). See the ESTA website (https://esta. cbp.dhs.gov) for a current list. Under this program you must have a nonrefundable return ticket and an 'e-passport' with digital chip. Passports issued/renewed before October 26, 2006, must be machine-readable.

Visitors who don't qualify for the Visa Waiver Program need a visa. Basic requirements are a valid passport, recent photo, travel details and often proof of financial stability. Students and adult males must also fill out supplemental travel documents.

The validity period for a US visitor visa depends on your home country. The length of time you'll be allowed to stay in the USA is determined by US officials at the port of entry. To stay longer than the date stamped on your passport, visit a local USCIS office (www.uscis.gov).

As of 2017, the USA has embarked on a policy of pursuing more stringent border controls. Be warned that the above information is perishable; keep an eye on the news and www.travel. state.gov.

Volunteering

Volunteering can be a great way to break up a long trip, and it provides memorable opportunities to interact with locals and the land in ways you never would when just passing through.

Volunteer Florida (www. volunteerflorida.org), the primary state-run organization, coordinates volunteer centers across the state. Though it's aimed at Floridians, casual visitors can find situations that match their time and interests.

Florida's state parks would not function without volunteers. Each park coordinates its own volunteers, and most also have the support of an all-volunteer 'friends' organization (officially called Citizen Support Organizations). Links and contact information are on the website of Florida State Parks (www.floridastateparks.org/get-involved/volunteer).

Finally, Habitat for Humanity (www.miamihabitat.org) does a ton of work in Florida, building homes and helping the homeless.

Women Travelers

Women traveling by themselves or in a group should encounter no particular problems unique to Florida.

The community resource Journeywoman (www.journeywoman.com) facilitates women exchanging travel tips, with links to resources.

These two national advocacy groups might also be helpful:

National Organization for Women (www.now.org)

Planned Parenthood (www.plannedparenthood.org)

In terms of safety issues, single women need to exhibit the same street smarts as any solo traveler, but they are sometimes more often the target of unwanted attention or harassment. Some women like to carry a whistle, mace or cayenne-pepper spray in case of assault. These sprays are legal to carry and use in Florida, but only in self-defense. Federal law prohibits them being carried on planes.

If you are assaulted, it may be better to call a rape-crisis hotline before calling the police (☎911); telephone books have listings of local organizations, or contact the 24-hour **National Sexual Assault Hotline** (☎800-656-4673), or go straight to a hospital. Police can sometimes be insensitive with assault victims, while a rape-crisis center or hospital will advocate on behalf of victims and act as a link to other services, including the police.

Work

Seasonal service jobs in tourist beach towns and theme parks are common and often easy to get, if low paying.

If you are a foreigner in the USA with a standard non-immigrant visitors visa, you are expressly forbidden to take paid work in the USA and will be deported if you're caught working illegally. In addition, employers are required to establish the bona fides of their employees or face fines. In particular, southern Florida is notorious for large numbers of foreigners working illegally, and immigration officers are vigilant.

To work legally, foreigners need to apply for a work visa before leaving home. For nonstudent jobs, temporary or permanent, you need to be sponsored by a US employer, who will arrange an H-category visa. These are not easy to obtain.

Student-exchange visitors need a J1 visa, which the following organizations will help arrange:

American Institute for Foreign Study (www.aifs.com)

BUNAC (www.bunac.org) British Universities North American Club.

Camp America (www.campamerica.aifs.com)

Council on International Educational Exchange (www.ciee.org)

InterExchange (www.Interexchange.org) Camp and au-pair programs.

Transportation

GETTING THERE & AWAY

Nearly all international travelers to Florida arrive by air, while most US travelers prefer air or car. Florida is bordered by Alabama to the west and north, and Georgia to the north. Major interstates into Florida are I-10 from the west (Alabama), and I-75 and I-95 from the north (Georgia).

Getting to Florida by bus is a distant third option, and by train an even more distant fourth. Major regional hubs in Florida include Miami, Fort Lauderdale, Orlando, Tampa and Jacksonville.

Flights, cars and tours can be booked online at www. lonelyplanet.com/bookings.

Entering the Country

A passport is required for all foreign citizens. Unless eligible under the Visa Waiver Program, foreign travelers must also have a tourist visa.

Travelers entering under the Visa Waiver Program must register with the US government's program, ESTA (https://esta.cbp.dhs.gov), at least three days before arriving; earlier is better, since if denied, travelers must get a visa.

Upon arriving in the US, foreign visitors must register with the Office of Biometric Identity Management, also known as the US-Visit program. This entails having two index fingers scanned and a digital photo taken. For information see www.dhs. gov/obim. Canadian citizens are often exempted from this requirement.

Air

Unless you live in or near Florida and have your own wheels, flying to the region and then renting a car is the most time-efficient option. Depending on your plans, you'll be missing out on lots of the best bits if you lack the freedom and convenience of a vehicle.

Airports & Airlines

Whether you're coming from within the US or from abroad, the entire state is well served by air, with a number of domestic and international airlines operating services into Florida.

Major airports:

Orlando International Airport (MCO; ☑407-825-8463; www. orlandoairports.net; 1 Jeff Fuqua Blvd) Handles more passengers than any other airport in Florida. Serves Walt Disney World®, the Space Coast and the Orlando area.

Miami International Airport (MIA; ☑305-876-7000; www. miami-airport.com; 2100 NW 42nd Ave) One of the Florida's busiest international airports. It serves metro Miami, the Everglades and the Keys, and is a hub for American, Delta and US Airways.

CLIMATE CHANGE & TRAVEL

Every form of transport that relies on carbon-based fuel generates CO_2, the main cause of human-induced climate change. Modern travel is dependent on airplanes, which might use less fuel per kilometer per person than most cars but travel much greater distances. The altitude at which aircraft emit gases (including CO_2) and particles also contributes to their climate change impact. Many websites offer 'carbon calculators' that allow people to estimate the carbon emissions generated by their journey and, for those who wish to do so, to offset the impact of the greenhouse gases emitted with contributions to portfolios of climate-friendly initiatives throughout the world. Lonely Planet offsets the carbon footprint of all staff and author travel.

Fort Lauderdale-Hollywood International Airport (FLL; ☎866-435-9355; www.broward.org/airport; 320 Terminal Dr) Serves metro Fort Lauderdale and Broward County. It's about 30 miles north of Miami: be sure to check flights into Fort Lauderdale as they are often cheaper or have availability when flights into Miami are full.

Tampa International Airport (TPA; Map p392;☎813-870-8700; www.tampaairport.com; 4100 George J Bean Pkwy) Florida's third-busiest airport is located 6 miles southwest of downtown Tampa and serves the Tampa Bay and St Petersburg metro area.

Other airports with international traffic include **Daytona Beach** (☎386-248-8030; www.flydaytonafirst.com; 700 Catalina Dr) and **Jacksonville** (JAX; ☎904-741-4902; www.flyjax.com; 2400 Yankee Clipper Dr; ☎).

Most cities have airports and offer services to other US cities; these airports include **Palm Beach** (PBI; ☎561-471-7420; www.pbia.org; 1000 James L Turnage Blvd), actually in West Palm Beach, **Sarasota** (SRQ; Map p392; ☎941-359-2770; www.srq-airport.com; 6000 Airport Circle), **Tallahassee** (Map p471; ☎850-891-7802; www.talgov.com/airport; 3300 Capital Circle SW), **Gainesville** (☎352-373-0249; www.gra-gnv.com; 3880 NE 39th Ave), **Fort Myers** (RSW; ☎239-590-4800; http://flylcpa.com; 11000 Terminal Access Rd), **Pensacola** (Map p446; ☎850-436-5000; www.flypensacola.com;

2430 Airport Blvd) and **Key West** (EYW; ☎305-809-5200; www.eyw.com; 3491 S Roosevelt Blvd).

TICKETS

It helps to know that in the US there are a number of APEX (Advance Purchase Excursion) fares of seven, 14, 21 and 28 days available, which can really save you money. It is prudent to compare flights into the state between the handful of significant airline hubs. The distance between Orlando, Fort Lauderdale and Miami, for example, is not so great, yet each city has a major airport. Rates can sometimes fluctuate widely between these destinations, depending on season and demand. If you're lucky, you could save money by flying into one airport and out of the other, or, flying into an airport a little further from your destination, and driving. The combination of Miami and Fort Lauderdale often works well in this regard.

DEPARTURE TAX

Departure tax is included in the price of a ticket.

Land

Bus

For bus trips, Greyhound (www.greyhound.com) is the main long-distance operator in the US. It serves Florida from most major cities. It also has the only scheduled statewide service.

Standard long-distance fares can be relatively high: bargain airfares can undercut buses on long-distance routes; on shorter routes, renting a car can be cheaper. Nonetheless, discounted (even half-price) long-distance bus trips are often available by purchasing tickets online seven to 14 days in advance. Then, once in Florida, you can rent a car to get around. Inquire about multiday passes.

Car & Motorcycle

Driving to Florida is easy; there are no international borders or entry issues. Incorporating Florida into a larger USA road trip is very common, and having a car while in Florida is often a necessity: there's lots of ground to cover and some of the most interesting places and state parks are only accessible by car.

Train

From the East Coast, Amtrak (www.amtrak.com) makes a comfortable, affordable option for getting to Florida. Amtrak's *Silver Service* (which includes *Silver Meteor* and *Silver Star* trains) runs between New York and Miami, with services that include Jacksonville, Orlando, Tampa, West Palm Beach and Fort Lauderdale, plus smaller Florida towns in between.

There is no direct service to Florida from Los Angeles, New Orleans, Chicago or the Midwest. Trains from these destinations connect to the *Silver Service* route, but the

---

ROAD DISTANCES

Sample distances and times from various points in the US to Miami:

CITY	DISTANCE (MILES)	DURATION (HR)
Atlanta	660	10½
Chicago	1380	23
Los Angeles	2750	44
New York City	1280	22
Washington, DC	1050	17

transfer adds a day or so to your travel time.

Amtrak's *Auto Train* takes you and your car from the Washington, DC, area to the Orlando area; this saves you gas, the drive and having to pay for a rental car. The fare for your vehicle isn't cheap, though, depending on its size and weight. The *Auto Train* leaves daily from Lorton, VA, and goes only to Sanford, FL. It takes about 18 hours, leaving in the afternoon and arriving the next morning. On the *Auto Train,* you pay for your passage, cabin and car separately. Book tickets in advance. Children, seniors and military personnel receive discounts.

Amtrak lines are subject to federal funding and regulation. Check for the latest fares and routes before you leave for your trip.

Sea

Florida is nearly completely surrounded by the ocean, and it's a major cruise-ship port. Fort Lauderdale is the largest transatlantic harbor in the US. Adventurous types can always sign up as crew members for a chance to travel the high seas.

GETTING AROUND

Air

The US airline industry is reliable, safe and serves Florida extremely well, both from the rest of the country and within Florida. Air service between Florida's four main airports – Fort Lauderdale, Miami, Orlando International and Tampa – is frequent and direct. Smaller destinations such as Key West, Fort Myers, Pensacola, Jacksonville, Tallahassee and West Palm Beach are served, but less frequently, indirectly and at higher fares.

Airlines in Florida

Domestic airlines operating in Florida:

American (www.aa.com) Has a Miami hub and service to and between major Florida cities.

Delta (www.delta.com) International carrier to main Florida cities, plus flights from Miami to Orlando and Tampa.

Frontier (www.frontierairlines. com) Serves all major Florida cities.

JetBlue (www.jetblue.com) Major low-cost airline serving major Florida cities.

Southwest (www.southwest. com) One of the US's leading low-cost carriers, offering free baggage and, at times, extremely low fares.

Spirit (www.spirit.com) Florida-based discount carrier serving Florida cities from East Coast US, the Caribbean, and Central and South America.

United (www.united.com) International flights to Orlando and Miami; domestic flights to and between key Florida cities.

Air Passes

International travelers who plan on doing a lot of flying, both in and out of the region, might consider buying an air pass. Air passes are available only to non-US citizens, and must be purchased in conjunction with an international ticket.

Conditions and cost structures can be complicated, but all include a certain number of domestic flights (from three to 10) that must be used within a set time frame, generally between 30 and 60 days. In most cases, you must plan your itinerary in advance, but dates (and even destinations) can sometimes be left open. Talk with a travel agent to determine if an air pass would save you money based on your plans.

The two main airline alliances offering air passes are Star Alliance (www.star alliance.com) and One World (www.oneworld.com).

Bicycle

Regional bicycle touring is very popular. Flat countryside and scenic coastlines make for great itineraries. However, target winter to spring; summer is unbearably hot and humid for long-distance cycling.

Some Florida cycling organizations organize bike tours. Renting a bicycle is easy throughout Florida.

Some other things to keep in mind:

Helmet laws Helmets are required for anyone aged 16 and younger. Adults are not required to wear helmets, but should for safety.

Road rules Bikes must obey auto rules; ride on the right-hand side of the road, with traffic, not on sidewalks.

Transporting your bike to Florida Bikes are considered checked luggage on airplanes, but often must be boxed and fees can be high (more than $200).

Theft Bring and use a sturdy lock (U-type is best). Theft is common, especially in Miami Beach.

For more information and assistance, a few organizations can help:

Better World Club (www.better worldclub.com) Offers a bicycle roadside-assistance program.

International Bicycle Fund (www.ibike.org) Comprehensive overview of bike regulations by airline, and lots of advice.

League of American Bicyclists (www.bikeleague.org) General advice, plus lists of local cycle clubs and repair shops.

Boat

Florida is a world center for two major types of boat transport: privately owned yachts and cruise ships.

Each coastal city has sightseeing boats that cruise harbors and coastlines. It really pays (in memories) to get out on the water. Water-taxi services along Intracoastal Waterways are a feature in Fort Lauderdale and around Sanibel and Pine Islands on the Gulf.

Cruises

Florida is a huge destination and departure point for cruises of all kinds. Miami likes to brag that it's the 'cruise capital of the world,' and Walt Disney World® runs its own Disney Cruise Line (https://disneycruise.disney.go.com), which has a number of three- to seven-night cruises throughout the Caribbean, including to Disney's own private island, Castaway Cay.

For specials on other multinight and multiday cruises, see the following:

Cruise.com (www.cruise.com)

CruisesOnly (www.cruisesonly.com)

CruiseWeb (www.cruiseweb.com)

Vacations to Go (www.vacationstogo.com)

Florida's main ports:

Port Canaveral (www.portcanaveral.com) On the Atlantic Coast near the Kennedy Space Center; gives Miami a run for its money.

Port Everglades (www.porteverglades.net; 1850 Eller Drive) Near Fort Lauderdale, and the third-busiest Florida port.

Port of Miami (☎305-347-5515; www.miamidade.gov/portmiami) At the world's largest cruise-ship port, the most common trips offered are to the Bahamas, the Caribbean, Key West and Mexico.

Port of Tampa (www.tampaport.com) On the Gulf Coast; rapidly gaining a foothold in the cruise market.

Major cruise companies:

Carnival Cruise Lines (www.carnival.com)

Norwegian Cruise Line (www.ncl.com)

Royal Caribbean (www.royalcaribbean.com)

Bus

The only statewide bus service is by Greyhound (www.greyhound.com), which connects all major and midsize Florida cities, but not always smaller towns (even some popular beach towns). Regional or city-run buses cover Greyhound's more limited areas much better; used together, these bus systems make travel by bus possible, but time-consuming. Megabus operates out of five Florida cities – Tallahassee, Jacksonville, Gainesville, Tampa and Miami.

It's always a bit cheaper to take a Greyhound bus during the week than on the weekend. Fares for children are usually about half the adult fare.

Local bus services are available in most cities; along the coasts, service typically connects downtown to at least one or two beach communities. Some cities (such as Tampa and Jacksonville) have high-frequency trolleys circling downtown, while some coastal stretches are linked by seasonal trolleys that ferry beachgoers between towns (such as between St Pete Beach and Clearwater).

Fares generally cost between $1 and $2. Exact change upon boarding is usually required, though some buses take $1 bills. Transfers – slips of paper that will allow you to change buses – range from free to 50¢. Hours of operation differ from city to city, but generally buses run from approximately 6am to 11pm.

Car & Motorcycle

Once you reach Florida, traveling by car is the best way of getting around – it allows you to reach areas not otherwise served by public transportation.

While it's quite possible to avoid using a car on single-destination trips – to Miami, to Orlando theme parks or to a self-contained beach resort – relying on public transit can be inconvenient for even limited regional touring. Even smaller, tourist-friendly towns such as Naples, Sarasota or St Augustine can be frustrating to negotiate without a car. Motorcycles are also popular in Florida, given the flat roads and warm weather (summer rain excepted).

Automobile Associations

The American Automobile Association (www.aaa.com) has reciprocal agreements with several international auto clubs (check with AAA and bring your membership card). For members, AAA offers travel insurance, tour books, diagnostic centers for used-car buyers and a greater number of regional offices, and it advocates politically for the auto industry. It also has a handy online route planner that can help you calculate the exact mileage and estimated fuel costs of your intended itinerary.

An ecofriendly alternative is the Better World Club (www.betterworldclub.com), which donates 1% of revenue to assist environmental cleanup; offers ecologically sensitive choices for services; and advocates politically for environmental causes. Better World also has a roadside-assistance program for bicycles.

In both organizations, the central member benefit is 24-hour emergency roadside assistance anywhere in the USA. Both clubs also offer trip planning and free maps, travel-agency services, car insurance and a range of discounts (car rentals, hotels etc).

Driving Licences

Foreign visitors can legally drive with their home driver's license. However, getting an International Driving Permit (IDP) is recommended; this will have more credibility with US traffic police, especially if your home license doesn't have a photo or is in a foreign language. Your automobile association at home can issue an IDP, valid for one year, for a small fee. You must carry your home license together with the IDP at all times. To drive a motorcycle, you need either a valid US state motorcycle license or an IDP specially endorsed for motorcycles.

Insurance

Don't put the key into the ignition if you don't have insurance: it's legally required, and you risk financial ruin without it if there's an accident. If you already have auto insurance (even overseas), or if you buy travel insurance, make sure that the policy has adequate liability coverage for a rental car in Florida; it probably does, but check.

Rental-car companies will provide liability insurance, but most charge extra for the privilege. Always ask. Collision-damage insurance for the vehicle is almost never included in the US. Instead, the provider will offer an optional Collision Damage Waiver (CDW) or Loss Damage Waiver (LDW), usually with an initial deductible of $100 to $500. For an extra premium, you can usually get this deductible covered as well. However, most credit cards now offer collision-damage coverage for rental cars if you rent for 15 days or less and charge the total rental to your card. This is a good way to avoid paying extra fees to the rental company, but note that if there's an accident, you sometimes must pay the rental car company first and then seek reimbursement from the credit-card company. Check your credit-card policy. Paying extra for some or all of this insurance increases the cost of a rental car by around $20 to $40 per day.

Travel insurance, either specific paid policies or free insurance provided by your credit-card company (when your travel arrangements are purchased on their credit cards), often includes cover for rental-car insurances up to the full amount of any deductible. If you plan on renting a vehicle for any significant period of time, the cost of travel insurance, which includes coverage for rental vehicles, is often way cheaper than purchasing the optional insurance from the car-rental company directly. Be prudent and do your research to avoid getting a shock when you go to sign your car-rental contract and discover all the additional charges.

Rental

CAR

Car rental is a very competitive business. Most rental companies require that you have a major credit card; that you be at least 25 years old; and that you have a valid driver's license (your home license will do). Some national companies may rent to drivers between the ages of 21 and 24 for an additional charge. Those under 21 are usually not permitted to rent at all.

Additional drivers are not usually covered under the base rate and an additional daily surcharge will be applied. If someone other than the parties authorized on the rental contract is driving the vehicle and has an accident, all paid insurances will be void: you don't want this to happen. If anyone else is likely to drive the vehicle, they need to be present at the time of collection and are required to submit their driver's license and pay the extra fee. If the additional driver is not able to be present at the time of collection, it is possible to drive into any branch of the rental company and add the additional driver on to your rental agreement at a later date. Charges may

be backdated to the day of collection.

Good independent agencies are listed by Car Rental Express (www.carrental express.com), which rates and compares independent agencies in US cities; it's particularly useful for searching out cheaper long-term rentals.

Major national car-rental companies:

Alamo (www.alamo.com)

Avis (www.avis.com)

Budget (www.budget.com)

Dollar (www.dollar.com)

Enterprise (www.enterprise. com)

Hertz (www.hertz.com)

National (www.nationalcar.com)

Rent-a-Wreck (www.rentawreck. com)

Thrifty (www.thrifty.com)

Rental cars are readily available at all airport locations and many downtown city locations. With advance reservations for a small car, the daily rate with unlimited mileage is about $35 to $55, while typical weekly rates are $200 to $400, plus a myriad of taxes and fees. If you rent from a downtown location, you can save money by avoiding the exorbitant airport fees.

An alternative is **Zipcar** (www.zipcar.com), a car-sharing service that charges hourly and daily rental fees with gas, insurance and limited mileage included; prepayment is required.

Note that one-way rentals (picking up in one city and dropping off in another) will often incur a prohibitive one-way drop fee. Experimenting with your routing, or returning the vehicle to the city from which you collected it, or one nearby, may help avoid this penalty. Also check if the location that you're collecting the car from is franchised or centrally owned: sometimes the latter will help get any one-way fees waived.

MOTORCYCLE

To straddle a Harley across Florida, contact EagleRider (www.eaglerider.com), which has offices in Daytona Beach, Fort Lauderdale, Miami, St Augustine, Jacksonville, Pensacola and Orlando. It offers a wide range of models, which start at $150 a day, plus liability insurance.

MOTORHOME (RV)

Forget hotels. Drive your own. Touring Florida by recreational vehicle (RV) can be as low-key or as over-the-top as you wish.

After settling on the vehicle's size, consider the impact of gas prices, gas mileage, additional mileage costs, insurance and refundable deposits; these can add up quickly. Typically, RVs don't come with unlimited mileage, so estimate your mileage up front to calculate the true rental cost.

Inquire about motorhome relocations: sometimes, you can get amazing deals where you're effectively being paid to move the vehicle between cities for its owner – but you'll need to be extremely flexible with your dates and routes.

Adventures On Wheels (www. wheels9.com) Office in Miami.

CruiseAmerica (www.cruise america.com) The largest national RV-rental firm has offices across South Florida.

Recreational Vehicle Rental Association (www.rvda.org) Good resource for RV information and advice, and helps find rental locations.

Road Rules

If you're new to Florida or US roads, here are some basics:

➡ The maximum speed limit on interstates is 75mph, but that drops to 65mph and 55mph in urban areas. Pay attention to the posted signs. City-street speed limits vary between 15mph and 45mph.

➡ Florida police officers are strict with speed-limit enforcement, and speeding tickets are expensive. If caught going over the speed limit by 10mph, the fine starts at $204. If you're going more than 30mph over the speed limit, that's a mandatory court appearance. Conversely, you may be fined if you're driving too slowly on an interstate.

➡ All passengers in a car must wear seat belts. All children under three must be in a child safety seat.

➡ As in the rest of the US, drive on the right-hand side of the road. On highways, pass in the left-hand lane (but anxious drivers often pass wherever space allows).

➡ Right turns on a red light are permitted after a full stop. At four-way stop signs, the car that reaches the intersection first has right of way. In a tie, the car on the right has right of way.

Hitching & Ride-Sharing

Hitchhiking is never entirely safe in any country, and we don't recommend it. Travelers who decide to hitch should understand that they are taking a small but potentially serious risk. People who do choose to hitch will be safer if they go in pairs and if they let someone know where they are planning to go. Be sure to ask the driver where they are going first, rather than telling them where you want to go.

Train

Amtrak (www.amtrak. com) trains run between a number of Florida cities. For the purpose of getting around Florida, its service is extremely limited, and yet for certain specific trips its trains can be very easy and inexpensive. In essence, daily trains run between Jacksonville, Orlando and Miami, with one line branching off to Tampa.

Walt Disney World® has a monorail and Tampa has an old-fashioned, one-line streetcar, but the only real metro systems are in and near Miami. In Miami, a driverless Metromover circles downtown and connects with Metrorail, which connects downtown north to Hialeah and south to Kendall.

Meanwhile, north of Miami, Hollywood, Fort Lauderdale and West Palm Beach (and the towns between them) are well connected by Tri-Rail's double-decker commuter trains. Tri-Rail runs all the way to Miami, but the full trip takes longer than driving.

Behind the Scenes

SEND US YOUR FEEDBACK

We love to hear from travelers – your comments keep us on our toes and help make our books better. Our well-traveled team reads every word on what you loved or loathed about this book. Although we cannot reply individually to your submissions, we always guarantee that your feedback goes straight to the appropriate authors, in time for the next edition. Each person who sends us information is thanked in the next edition – the most useful submissions are rewarded with a selection of digital PDF chapters.

Visit **lonelyplanet.com/contact** to submit your updates and suggestions or to ask for help. Our award-winning website also features inspirational travel stories, news and discussions.

Note: We may edit, reproduce and incorporate your comments in Lonely Planet products such as guidebooks, websites and digital products, so let us know if you don't want your comments reproduced or your name acknowledged. For a copy of our privacy policy visit lonelyplanet.com/privacy.

OUR READERS

Many thanks to the travelers who used the last edition and wrote to us with helpful hints, useful advice and interesting anecdotes:

Amy Lukken, David Carson, Jon Groner, Kristina Aretjäll, Michal Rudziecki, Monika Drendel, Pablo Gomez.

WRITER THANKS

Adam Karlin

Thanks: Lauren Keith and Trisha Ping, my fellow Florida authors, Matt Sheehan and Max for their hospitality, Richard Goodman and the members of the non-fiction workshop for their feedback on the dispatches, mom and dad for being them, and Rachel and Sanda, who are the best beach buddies I can ask for.

Kate Armstrong

La'Vell Brown: thank you for your magic wand, plus your passion, knowledge and insights of Disney World, and for transforming me from the Beastess into Cinderella herself. Thanks to Cory O'Born, Visit Orlando; Nathalia Romano and Ashlynn Webb, Universal Orlando; Jessica Savage, Greater Fort Lauderdale Convention & Visitors Bureau; and to Chris, for your flexibility, patience and everything (except holding my hand on the Hogwarts Express). Finally, thank you to Lauren Keith and Trisha Ping for their understanding and helping to put out a few nothing-but-Disney fireworks.

Ashley Harrell

Thanks to: editors Lauren and Trisha, and co-authors Adam, Kate and Regis, for your support. Josie, Nora and Ashley Guttuso for having me at the fort. Tiffany Grandstaff for the upgrade. Alex Pickett for existing. Trevor, Malissa and Soraya Aaronson for being my surrogate family. Tom Francis for finally coming. Alanna Bjork for dog-sitting and the cozy shack. Beanie Guez for destroying me in shuffleboard and Elodie Guez for bringing wine (and glasses). Andy Lavender for showing up in Sarasota, and in general.

Regis St Louis

Countless people helped along the way, and I'm grateful to national park guides, lodging hosts, restaurant servers, barkeeps and baristas who shared tips and insight throughout South Florida. Big thanks to Adam Karlin who did such an outstanding job on previous editions. I'd also like to thank Cassandra and our daughters, Magdalena and Genevieve, who made the Miami trip all the more worthwhile.

ACKNOWLEDGEMENTS

Climate map data adapted from Peel MC, Finlayson BL & McMahon TA (2007) 'Updated World Map of the Köppen-Geiger Climate Classification', Hydrology and Earth System Sciences, 11, 163344.

Cover photograph: Fort Lauderdale Beach, Pietro Canali/4Corners©

THIS BOOK

This 8th edition of Lonely Planet's *Florida* guidebook was researched and written by Adam Karlin, Kate Armstrong, Ashley Harrell and Regis St Louis. The 7th edition was written by Adam Karlin, Jennifer Rasin Denniston, Paula Hardy and Benedict Walker; the 6th edition was written by Jeff Campbell, Jennifer Rasin Denniston, Adam Karlin and Emily Matchar. This guidebook was produced by the following:

Destination Editors Trisha Ping, Lauren Keith

Product Editor Sandie Kestell

Senior Cartographer Alison Lyall

Book Designer Gwen Cotter

Assisting Editors Judith Bamber, Imogen Bannister, Pete Cruttenden, Melanie Dankel, Anita Isalska, Helen Koehne, Rosie Nicholson, Kristin Odijk, Sam Wheeler

Assisting Cartographer James Leversha

Cover Researcher Marika Mercer

Thanks to Heather Champion, Victoria Harrison, Genna Patterson Jessica Ryan, Angela Tinson, Tony Wheeler

Index

Map Legend

Sights

- Beach
- Bird Sanctuary
- Buddhist
- Castle/Palace
- Christian
- Confucian
- Hindu
- Islamic
- Jain
- Jewish
- Monument
- Museum/Gallery/Historic Building
- Ruin
- Shinto
- Sikh
- Taoist
- Winery/Vineyard
- Zoo/Wildlife Sanctuary
- Other Sight

Activities, Courses & Tours

- Bodysurfing
- Diving
- Canoeing/Kayaking
- Course/Tour
- Sento Hot Baths/Onsen
- Skiing
- Snorkeling
- Surfing
- Swimming/Pool
- Walking
- Windsurfing
- Other Activity

Sleeping

- Sleeping
- Camping
- Hut/Shelter

Eating

- Eating

Drinking & Nightlife

- Drinking & Nightlife
- Cafe

Entertainment

- Entertainment

Shopping

- Shopping

Information

- Bank
- Embassy/Consulate
- Hospital/Medical
- Internet
- Police
- Post Office
- Telephone
- Toilet
- Tourist Information
- Other Information

Geographic

- Beach
- Gate
- Hut/Shelter
- Lighthouse
- Lookout
- Mountain/Volcano
- Oasis
- Park
- Pass
- Picnic Area
- Waterfall

Population

- Capital (National)
- Capital (State/Province)
- City/Large Town
- Town/Village

Transport

- Airport
- BART station
- Border crossing
- Boston T station
- Bus
- Cable car/Funicular
- Cycling
- Ferry
- Metro/Muni station
- Monorail
- Parking
- Petrol station
- Subway/SkyTrain station
- Taxi
- Train station/Railway
- Tram
- Underground station
- Other Transport

Routes

- Tollway
- Freeway
- Primary
- Secondary
- Tertiary
- Lane
- Unsealed road
- Road under construction
- Plaza/Mall
- Steps
- Tunnel
- Pedestrian overpass
- Walking Tour
- Walking Tour detour
- Path/Walking Trail

Boundaries

- International
- State/Province
- Disputed
- Regional/Suburb
- Marine Park
- Cliff
- Wall

Hydrography

- River, Creek
- Intermittent River
- Canal
- Water
- Dry/Salt/Intermittent Lake
- Reef

Areas

- Airport/Runway
- Beach/Desert
- Cemetery (Christian)
- Cemetery (Other)
- Glacier
- Mudflat
- Park/Forest
- Sight (Building)
- Sportsground
- Swamp/Mangrove

Note: Not all symbols displayed above appear on the maps in this book

OUR STORY

A beat-up old car, a few dollars in the pocket and a sense of adventure. In 1972 that's all Tony and Maureen Wheeler needed for the trip of a lifetime – across Europe and Asia overland to Australia. It took several months, and at the end – broke but inspired – they sat at their kitchen table writing and stapling together their first travel guide, *Across Asia on the Cheap*. Within a week they'd sold 1500 copies. Lonely Planet was born.

Today, Lonely Planet has offices in Franklin, London, Melbourne, Oakland, Dublin, Beijing and Delhi, with more than 600 staff and writers. We share Tony's belief that 'a great guidebook should do three things: inform, educate and amuse'.

OUR WRITERS

Adam Karlin

Curator, Northeast Florida, the Panhandle Adam is a Lonely Planet author based out of wherever he happens to be. Born in Washington, DC and raised in the rural Maryland tidewater, he's been exploring the world and writing about it since he was 17. For him, it's a blessedly interesting way to live life. Also, it's good fun. He just read two good quotes, so with thanks to Italy, ancient and modern: *'Tutto il mondo e paese'* and *'Ambulare pro deus'*. If you ever meet Adam on the road, be sure to share a drink and a story. Adam also wrote the Plan Your Trip, Understand and Survival Guide sections.

Kate Armstrong

Southeast Florida, Orlando & Walt Disney World® Kate has spent much of her adult life traveling and living around the world. A full-time freelance travel journalist, she has contributed to around 40 Lonely Planet guides and trade publications and is regularly published in Australian and worldwide publications. She is the author of several books and children's educational titles. You can read more about her on www.katearmstrongtravelwriter.com and @nomaditis.

Ashley Harrell

Southwest Florida, the Space Coast After a brief stint selling day spa coupons door-to-door in South Florida, Ashley decided she'd rather be a writer. She went to journalism grad school, convinced a newspaper to hire her, and started covering wildlife, crime and tourism, sometimes all in the same story. Fueling her zest for storytelling and the unknown, she traveled widely and moved often, from a tiny NYC apartment to a vast California ranch to a jungle cabin in Costa Rica, where she started writing for Lonely Planet. From there her travels became more exotic and farther flung, and she still laughs when paychecks arrive.

Regis St Louis

Miami, Florida Keys & Key West, the Everglades Regis grew up in a small town in the American Midwest – the kind of place that fuels big dreams of travel – and he developed an early fascination with foreign dialects and world cultures. He spent his formative years learning Russian and a handful of Romance languages, which served him well on journeys across much of the globe. Regis has contributed to more than 50 Lonely Planet titles, covering destinations across six continents. His travels have taken him from the mountains of Kamchatka to remote island villages in Melanesia, and to many grand urban landscapes. When not on the road, he lives in New Orleans. Follow him on www.instagram.com/regisstlouis.

Published by Lonely Planet Global Limited
CRN 554153
8th edition – January 2018
ISBN 978 1 78657 256 1
© Lonely Planet 2018   Photographs © as indicated 2018
10 9 8 7 6 5 4 3 2 1
Printed in China